VIETNAM:

The Definitive Documentation
of Human Decisions

Volume 1

Also in this series:

The Nixon Presidential Press Conferences

The Kennedy Presidential Press Conferences

The Johnson Presidential Press Conferences
(2 volumes)

Series Editor: George W. Johnson

VIETNAM:

The Definitive Documentation of Human Decisions

Volume 1

Edited with Commentary
and Introduction by
Gareth Porter, Ph.D.

Special Introduction by
Stuart Loory

Earl M. Coleman Enterprises, Inc., Publishers
Stanfordville, New York • 1979

Library of Congress Cataloging in Publication Data

Main entry under title:

Vietnam: the definitive documentation of human
    decisions.

    Includes index.
    1. Vietnam—History—1945-1975—Sources.
2. Vietnam—History—20th century—Sources.
I. Porter, Gareth, 1942-
DS556.8.V53   959.704   79-12834
ISBN 0-930576-03-9 (v. 1)

Special Introduction

(to Viet-nam Documents Collection)

By Stuart H. Loory

In October, 1943, Henri Hoppenot, the Free French delegate to the United States, called on Adolf A. Berle, an Assistant Secretary of State, to express concern that Chinese forces might move into Indochina in the fight against the Japanese. The Frenchman explained that the Indochinese hated the Chinese so much that they would resist the supposedly anti-Japanese troop movements. French forces still in the area would also resist, Hoppenot told Berle.

That visit provoked the first known consideration within the United States government of Indochina as a foreign policy problem.

After Hoppenot left the State Department, Berle, one of Franklin D. Roosevelt's famous brain trusters, wrote a memo on the visit that said in part:

"This brings us squarely up to the problem of whether, in the Far East, we are reestablishing the Western colonial empires or whether we are letting the East liberate itself if it can do so. I feel that the matter should be discussed on a high level with the President for his decision."

Edward R. Stettinius, then Acting Secretary of State, showed the Department's complete ignorance of the area. Commenting in a memo to Roosevelt on the Hoppenot plea, Stettinius wrote:

"It is our belief that this presentation of the case involves allegations not in accord with the facts, and that the Annamites by and large, have for the Chinese a feeling of friendliness and cultural affinity."

The incident shows that from the first days of decision-making on Indochina, the United States government was mired in ignorance. The anti-Chinese fears of the Vietnamese people have been one of the basic facts of life in Southeast Asia throughout history. Chinese ruled present day North Viet-nam for a thousand years until the Vietnamese revolted in 939 A.D. The Vietnamese successfully repulsed a Kublai Khan invasion in the 13th Century and since then have been resisting Chinese attempts at domination.

One shudders to think that the U.S. State Department in 1943 had no knowledge of this history.

But then, one shudders at a whole series of American mistakes, misconceptions and miscalculations in Southeast Asia of which that Berle-Stettinius encounter was only the first.

Now 35 years old, the Indochina problem shows no signs of slipping into a quiet and uneventful middle age for this country. At this writing, American policy makers have been thrown into contortions by Vietnam's invasion of Cambodia and China's retaliatory punitive invasion of Vietnam. Three American administrations had condemned the Pol Pot regime in Cambodia for its wholesale repressions, but yet the Carter Administration felt the need to condemn the Vietnamese government for overthrowing it. That's the kind of imperiousness that led the Carter Administration last year to condemn Viet-nam for developing closer relations with the Soviet Union. The *New York Times* headline of December 6, 1978 reporting that move was unintentionally and poignantly ironic:

U.S. Warns Vietnamese
That Soviet Ties
Imperil Good Relations

The United States Government has thought since World War II, that small nations (such as Viet-nam) must sublimate their own good interests to save the capitalist system. Saving capitalism has been a principal United States mission.

That meant supporting the reentry into Indochina of the French colonialists after the war. Later, the mission broadened into one dedicated to saving the world from Communism. That meant first shoring up the French after they showed no capacity or will to fight it out themselves in Indochina and then assuming the French role after their retreat from Viet-nam.

In 1967, with the United States in torment over the Viet-nam War, David Kraslow and I (both then staff members of the *Los Angeles Times* Washington Bureau) set out to determine how sincere the United States Government was in trying to find a negotiated settlement to the war. We discovered at that time that President Lyndon B. Johnson had absolutely no interest in such a settlement because any negotiation could only mean the collapse of the Thieu-Ky government and the expulsion of the United States from Indochina. The American leadership at the time was still vain enough and blind enough to think this country could do better, that the United States military could grind down the Vietnamese enemy to the point where "a fourth rate power" would surrender and accept an imposed peace.

As we searched at the time for understanding of what had gone wrong in Viet-nam, we were told by one official:

"Never underestimate stupidity, lack of judgment and lack of coordination as factors in foreign policy. What appears to be a pattern may not be a pattern at all. Things sometimes simply happen that are not supposed to happen."

For any analyst of the United States' foreign and national security policies those are words to live by. Keep them in mind as you read Gary Porter s superbly edited collection of documents tracing from the earliest days the growth and development of this nation's involvement in Indochina.

The stupidity and lack of judgment of the American foreign policy-making apparatus jumps right off the pages.

In the World War II years, American policy-makers believe that natives of the pre-World War II colonial countries were in no way ready for self government after the war. Thus, these early policy-makers reasoned, the United States was playing the role of a Dutch Uncle to the colonized peoples of the world in helping reimpose the yokes of their imperialist masters.

The inescapable conclusion from these readings is quite the opposite, that the anti-colonial Vietnamese leadership in the early 1940s had the intellectual capacity, the organizational skills, the political acumen and the patriotic zeal necessary to organize and operate a state effectively. With the benefit of hindsight we now know that the Vietnamese Communists were much more carefully prepared for their struggle of national liberation than the United States, the French or those countries' puppet Vietnamese governments were in opposing it. Reading these documents helps you realize that all the warning signals were hoisted in the 1940s.

If only our bureaucrats had read carefully and paid attention.

An astute policy-maker would have read Ho Chi Minh's letter from abroad on June 6, 1941 (which opens this collection) and realized the correctness of

Ho's belief that Indochina then lacked independence "not because the French bandits were strong, but only because the situation was not yet ripe and our people throughout the country were not yet of one mind.

"Now, the opportunity has come for our liberation. . . . If our entire people are solidly united we can certainly get the better of the best trained armies of the French and the Japanese."

It is easy to imagine World War II policy-makers, if they ever even saw that statement, dismissing it as so much rhetoric. Similarly, the policy-makers had to ignore the detailed plan for revolution included in the "Study Document" written by Troung Chinh, secretary general of the Indochinese Communist Party at the time. Forget, for the time being the agrarian revolution, Chinh wrote, because the small landowners must be enlisted in the struggle for national liberation.

" . . . (W)e do not put forward the slogan 'Overthrow the imperialists and feudal landowners!', but must put forward 'Overthrow the Japanese and French imperialists and the traitors!" Chinh wrote.

There is a subtlety in that slogan change that is worthy of Machiavelli. The old slogan included some Vietnamese landowners whose support was now necessary for success against foreigners. The new slogan linked the French to the hated Japanese. But that's just the beginning. In subsequent statements Chinh, Ho and a former history professor named Vo Nhuyen Giap, who would become the general that would mastermind military victories from Dien Bien Phu to Saigon, laid out programs of propaganda, political agitation, terrorism, guerrilla warfare and open fighting designed to take best advantage of the situation as it developed from month to month.

Any group capable of organizing for warfare so skillfully is certainly ready to operate a civil government as well. The form may not be to everyone's liking but there can be no question that the government will work.

Arranged in counterpoint to the buildup of the Vietnamese national liberation movement is the story of the origins and growth of the American involvement from October, 1943. The documents portray President Franklin D. Roosevelt as a man resolutely in favor of self-government for the Indochinese. It had become his fate to battle against the American bureaucrats who had grown convinced that France, despite a colonial government collaborating with the Japanese, must be treated in the same manner as the staunchly anti-Axis English and Dutch, who were to be allowed back into their Asian and Western Pacific colonies after the war.

These documents show that the State Department's manipulations were from the beginning no match for the Indochinese Communists just as the military history of the war shows that our generals and admirals, backed by a long military tradition and schooled in the best of the military academies, were no match for Indochina's home grown strategists.

Porter's contrapuntal technique gives these volumes a tension and suspense worthy of a fine work of fiction. He brings the material alive with his interstitial commentary and he has produced a testament to the folly of trying to repress a nation that is dedicated to its own liberation.

As these volumes are published, the turmoil in Indochina is once again boiling over with the warfare between the Vietnamese and the Cambodians. There will be many who will comment "I told you so" on that warfare, analyzing the situation in the context of the imperialist ambitions of the Vietnamese people. It would be wiser to analyze the situation not from any doctrinaire devil theory but from the viewpoint that gives the Vietnamese leadership credit for acting as much in the best interests of its people (as it sees that interest) as our government thinks it does in our best interest.

That is the lesson of these documents. It should be heeded.

Introduction to Volume 1

VOLUME I: THE FIRST INDOCHINA WAR AND THE GENEVA AGREEMENTS
1941-1955

This volume, the first of two covering the history of the Vietnamese conflict from beginning to end, is intended to provide the most complete documentation possible in a single volume of the key decisions and the thinking behind
them. It is hoped that it will illuminate the ideology, assumptions, strategy
and tactics of the two sides, as well as the interaction between decisions made
by both sides.

The volume begins in 1941, the point at which the outbreak of World War II
in the Pacific created the opportunity for the Indochinese Communist Party to
begin planning for the eventual seizure of power in Viet-nam. The documents
trace the development of Communist strategy during World War II and then through
the August Revolution. U.S. policy toward Indochina's postwar status is
shown from Roosevelt's strong interest in Trusteeship, through the break with
that policy immediately following his death, the recognition of French sovereignty and the consequent fluctuation between strong criticism of French policy
and recognition that the U.S. had to rely on the French to accomplish its aims
in Indochina.

The origins of the Franco-Vietnamese war is treated in great detail as is
the maturation of the resistance forces through the defensive and "equilibrium
of forces" stages of the conflict. The transformation of the conflict in 1950
by extensive U.S. assistance to the French and Chinese aid to the Viet Minh, is
given extensive documentation, and the military and diplomatic events leading
to the Geneva settlement are treated from both sides. The documentation of the
policies of major parties involved in the Geneva settlement toward the implementation of the Accords during the crucial first year completes this volume.

These major themes in the volume have provided the framework for choosing
from among the totality of official documents available from all sides. Beyond
this, selection was based on the insight which the document in question offered
into the decision making of one of the parties to the conflict. It should be
noted, in this regard, that the United States is overrepresented in the volume
and France underrepresented, despite the fact that it was the French government
which was most directly involved in the first Indochina War. This is for two
reasons: first, vast quantities of documents are available from the U.S. side,
while France has neither opened its archives of the period nor published any
official compilation of documents on it. Second, because the first Indochina
War was the prologue to the second, it seems appropriate to focus primarily on
the development of U.S. policy and thinking toward the conflict, even before
the U.S. was directly involved. The documents of the State of Viet-nam, which
lasted from 1949 to 1955 are given little attention in the volume, except during and after the Geneva Conference, both because little documentation from

that source is available and it was judged much less important than the interaction of the French and U.S. decision making, given its subordinate status in
the conflict.

This compilation of documents has been made possible by the publication of
many hundreds of documents over the past eight years in the *Pentagon Papers* and
the State Department's annual *Foreign Relations of the United States* volumes
covering the period 1946 to 1951. This volume draws heavily on those sources.
In addition, I have used a number of documents found in researching the State
Department papers in the National Archives, which are now open for the period
1945-1949, and documents which have been declassified since the end of the Viet-
nam War from the period 1950-55 period, for which State Department papers in
the archives are not yet available to researchers.

On the Vietnamese side, I have made special efforts to compile and translate documents reflecting the decision making and point of view of the Vietnamese Communist leadership which were previously unavailable in English. Several
collections of original Vietnamese-language texts of documents covering the
period of the Second Indochina War, the August Revolution and the First Indochina War, which have been published by the Hanoi government, have made that task
much easier. I have also drawn liberally, of course, on the *Selected Works of
Ho Chi Minh* which have been translated by the D.R.V. Finally, I have drawn on a
previously unpublished collection of 76 documents on the events leading up to
the outbreak of the Franco-Vietnamese War in December 1946, which was transmitted to the U.S. Embassy in Bangkok by the Democratic Republic of Viet-nam in
1947. Those documents, translated by the Department of State at the time, have
remained in the State Department Central files in the archives ever since.

Unfortunately, this volume comes too early to take advantage of the declas-
sification and publication of State Department papers for the years 1951 to
1954, which is expected in 1979 or 1980. Although the *Pentagon Papers* documents include a great deal of the material on the period, particularly on 1954,
the unavailability of these documents leaves certain gaps in the history of
American decision making.

The format of these volumes has been chosen for maximum simplicity. Rather
than having extensive footnotes identifying people, places, documents, etc., in
the text, I have added no explanatory footnotes to the original. (Those few
footnotes in original texts have been kept.) In the brief introduction which I
have written for each document, I have explained only important references in
the text which might puzzle the reader. Those introductions are also intended
to place each document in historical context where necessary, suggest its significance or summarize its key contents.

Gareth Porter
Washington, D.C.

Editor's Introduction

A World-historical individual is not so unwise as to indulge a variety of wishes to divide his regards. He is devoted to the One Aim, regardless of all else. It is even
possible that such men may treat other great, even sacred
interests, inconsiderately; conduct which is indeed obnox-
ious to moral reprehension. But so mighty a form must tram-
ple down many an innocent flower - crush to pieces many an
object in its path.

Hegel, *The Philosophy of History*

Hegel's reflections on individuals in this sense is otherwise expanded to
include civilizations and States, and indeed, if his view is an accurate philosophy of history, it would appear that U.S. involvement in Southeast Asian
affairs is a painfully appropriate representative of just such conduct. Significantly, perhaps the most interesting thing which comes out of 30 years of
United States Southeast Asian foreign policy is the psychological after-shock
which has affected the psyche and political predispositions of Americans. For
slowly, most of us have come to view what has happened as tragic. But this conversion has come from afar, since we have lately been so detached from our wars.
Moreover, we have intellectualized conflict to the extent that our emotions
have become disinterested patrons of the art of war. Prepared for Vietnam by
the 50's, Americans had prejudged the motives of the Vietminh with little or no
help from those who could have provided an alternate view. There was a simple
transferrance of fear of China and the Soviet Union to a general opposition to
any country remotely acquainted with those regimes. Dispassionately, we hardly
blinked at French colonialism. To his credit, Roosevelt argued for trusteeship
in Indochina, and opposed continued French military presence there. This attitude, however, did not persevere in the Truman administration, where the President was forced to rely upon counsel which was largely pro-French in origin.
Truman does not escape blame, though, since ignorance cannot be cited as a reason for his failing to respond to personal correspondence from Ho Chi Minh.
But Truman's neglect was really nothing more than official manifestation of
what was a popular neurosis affecting the American people. For having never
been personally threatened by the ravages of war in the 20th Century, but having
been deeply involved in two massive conflicts elsewhere in the world, the U.S.
evidenced a strange dichotomy in its thinking. Although formally opposed to
Nazism and Japanese expansionism, we had a deeper and more abiding distaste for

Bolshevism and all forms of Communism. Consequently, Vietnam became a primary target for that distaste simply because of historical proximity. China had recently fallen to Mao, and Korea was initially threatened and finally partitioned. France which had been our traditional ally was, to our dismay being routinely bludgeoned in Indochina by the resistance. The scenerio seemed almost too perfect. And the United States which had and has always thought of itself as perceiving independence and self-determination with equanimity, served notice that, in fact, it would not tolerate governments which were not favorably disposed to its way of thinking. Notwithstanding French colonial aspirations, we chose to disregard factual assessment in favor of ideological predisposition, and an emotional attachment to policy formulation based on the tactics of fear. The upshot of American involvement in Indochina, therefore, was the reality of a split between theory and practice. I.e., while maintaining a strong diplomatic posture on recognition of self-determination and concern for the Vietnamese people, in fact, all that was done was to recognize as legitimate French presence in Indochina. In short, what happened was that we determined where self-determination was going to be operative. This split between what we said we meant and what did happen put all concerned on notice that America would place perceived security before the reality of national preference. Sadly, the implications of such policy were incorrectly interpreted.

George W. Johnson
Washington, 1979

Table of Contents

THE DOCUMENTS

1941-1945

(1) <u>LETTER BY HO CHI MINH FROM ABROAD</u>, JUNE 6, 1941

Source: Ho Chi Minh, *Selected Writings*, pp. 44-46.

*Following the outbreak of World War II, the Indochinese Party, recognizing that there was a new opportunity for winning independence, emphasized that national liberation was the primary task of the revolution. In May, 1941, the 8th plenum of the Central Committee met and founded the Viet Nam Independence League (*Viet Nam Doc Lap Dong Minh Hoi, *or* Viet Minh)*. After the meeting, Ho Chi Minh's letter to his countrymen was issued by the Party (Ho was then in Southern China), as an inspiration to revolt against both Japanese and French overlords in Viet-nam.*

Venerable elders!

Patriotic personalities!

Intellectuals, peasants, workers, traders and soldiers!

Dear fellow-countrymen!

Since France was defeated by Germany, its power has completely collapsed. Nevertheless, with regard to our people, the French rulers have become even more ruthless in carrying out their policy of exploitation, repression and massacre. They bleed us white and carry out a barbarous policy of all-out terrorism and massacre. In the foreign field, bowing their heads and bending their knees, they resign themselves to ceding part of our land to Siam and shamelessly surrendering our country to Japan. As a result our people are writhing under a double yoke of oppression. They serve not only as beasts of burden to the French bandits but also as slaves to the Japanese robbers. Alas! What sin have our people committed to be doomed to such a wretched fate? Plunged into such tragic suffering, are we to await death with folded arms?

No! Certainly not! The twenty-odd million descendants of the Lac and the Hong are resolved not to let themselves be kept in servitude. For nearly eighty years under the French pirates' iron heels we have unceasingly and selflessly struggled for national independence and freedom. The heroism of our predecessors, such as Phan Dinh Phung, Hoang Hoa Tham and Luong Ngoc Quyen and the glorious feats of the insurgents of Thai Nguyen, Yen Bai, Nghe An and Ha Tinh provinces will live for ever in our memory. The recent uprisings in the South and at Do Luong and Bac Son testify to the determination of our compatriots to follow the glorious example of their ancestors and to annihilate the enemy. If we were not successful, it was not because the French bandits were strong, but only because the situation was not yet ripe and our people throughout the country were not yet of one mind.

Now, the opportunity has come for our liberation. France itself is unable to help the French colonialists rule over our country. As for the Japanese, on the one hand, bogged down in China, on the other, hampered by the British and American forces, they certainly cannot use all their strength against us. If our entire people are solidly united we can certainly get the better of the best-trained armies of the French and the Japanese.

Fellow-countrymen! Rise up! Let us emulate the dauntless spirit of the Chinese people! Rise up without delay! Let us organize the Association for National Salvation to fight the French and the Japanese!

Dear fellow-countrymen! A few hundred years ago, in the reign of Tran, when our country faced the great danger of invasion by Yuan armies the elders ardently called on their sons and daughters throughout the country to stand up as one man to kill the enemy. Finally they saved their people and their glorious memory will live for ever. Let our elders and patriotic personalities follow the illustrious example set by our forefathers.

Notables, soldiers, workers, peasants, traders, civil servants, youth and women who warmly love your country! At present national liberation stands above everything. Let us unite and overthrow the Japanese, the French and their lackies in order to save our people from their present dire straits.

Dear fellow-countrymen!

National salvation is the common cause of our entire people. Every Vietnamese must take part in it. He who has money will contribute his money, he who has strength will contribute his strength, he who has talent will contribute his talent. For my part I pledge to follow in your steps and devote all my modest abilities to the service of the country and am ready for the supreme sacrifice.

Revolutionary fighters!

The hour has struck! Raise aloft the banner of insurrection and lead the people throughout the country to overthrow the Japanese and the French! The sacred call of the Fatherland is resounding in our ears; the ardent blood of our heroic predecessors is seething in our hearts! The fighting spirit of the people is mounting before our eyes! Let us unite and unify our action to overthrow the Japanese and the French.

The Vietnamese revolution will certainly triumph!

The world revolution will certainly triumph!

(2) STUDY DOCUMENT BY SECRETARY GENERAL OF THE INDOCHINESE COMMUNIST PARTY
TROUNG CHINH, SEPTEMBER 23-24, 1941 [Extracts]

Source: "The Party's New Policy" in Troung Chinh, *Cach Mang Dan Toc Chu Nhan Dan Viet-Nam: Tac Pham Chon Loc (The Vietnamese People's National Democratic Revolution: Selected Works)* (Hanoi: Su That, 1976), Vol. 1, p. 189-192, 196-199, 203-204, 206-208, 216-218. [Translation by the editor.]

Troung Chinh's essay "The Party's new Policy" was the definitive statement of the ICP's analysis and program for the new situation created by the world war. It called for the subordination of the agrarian revolution in Viet-nam to the task of winning independence, and for preparations for the armed uprising to seize political power at the proper moment. The most notable feature of the analysis is the degree to which the Vietnamese leaders saw their strategy for winning independence as being linked with international developments.

How has the situation in the world and in Indochina changed?

For the past two years, the Second World War has passed through the first phase and begun to enter into the second phase. During the first phase, the

German fascist imperialists attacked the French and British imperialists, aiming at dividing the world market. Exploiting the time gained by the imperialists attacking one another, the Soviet Union actively prepared for any unexpected development, strengthening their combat forces, striving to protect the first socialist government in the world and aiming at an opportunity to help the world's working class and the oppressed peoples turn the imperialist war into an internal revolutionary war or into a liberation war. The Soviet Union had foreseen that the fascists would sooner or later definitely attack the Soviet Union and that the war between imperialists could easily become a war between fascists and the Soviet Union or between aggressive fascism, on one hand, and the Soviet Union and other anti-fascist forces on the other.

In Indochina, the situation has also changed profoundly. The French colonialists rule Indochina, but France itself has lost its country to Germany, and become a dependency of Germany. The ranks of French imperialism have disintegrated and divided into two factions: the traitorous Petain faction, which kneels before Hitler, and the deGaulle faction which follows Britain and occupies part of the French colonies. The French ruling Indochina belong to the Petain faction. A fascist system has been established in Indochina. The Indochinese people must be slave for slaves, an extremely painful situation. After the French lost their country, the Japanese imperialists invaded Indochina. The French imperialists in Indochina, kneeling before the Japanese Emperor, offered Indochina to Japan. The Indochinese people suffered the dual yoke of the Japanese-French fascists weighing heavily on their shoulders.

The French not only surrendered to Japan but also carved a tenth of Indochina's territory for the Thai militarists, the lackies of the Japanese. The Indochinese peninsula is like a piece of meat for them to cut up as they please, like merchandise for them to exchange with each other!

The Indochinese people not only must pay taxes to make the fascist militarists fat, but must also must pay them in blood so that they can continue the war. The fascist war oppresses the lives of the Indochinese people very heavily. The fate of the Indochinese people hangs by a hair.

The Indochinese economy is declining. Dependent of the French economy, Indochina was disturbed after the French lost their country. The Japanese immediately exploited the opportunity, making themselves the masters of the Indochinese economy.

Our compatriots live in extremely bad conditions. Industry is stagnant, while agriculture is in decay. Many workers are unemployed, and peasants are being impoverished. The business of the national bourgeoisie, small landowners, and small merchants is falling off, because they lack the technical preparation, raw materials and markets, as well as having to face the competition of the Japanese economy.

War, critical economic shortage, the policy of devaluating the Indochinese piaster and speculation and hoarding are causing the prices of goods to climb. All the Indochinese people are suffering because of the cost of living, and heavy taxes, because of monopolies and subscription payments to the Japanese-French fascists.

In these circumstances, the revolutionary movement of the Vietnamese people is seething. Armed uprisings have taken place in Bac-son, in the South and in Do-luong. After the uprisings were bloodily suppressed, the movement declined somewhat, but because the situation in the world and in the Far East is changing rapidly it can leap to a high level.

The political attitude of the classes in Indochina reveal themselves rather clearly. The workers and peasants are still the most enthusiastic forces in the revolutionary struggle movement. Under the leadership of the Indochinese Communists, the rural proletariat employed agricultural workers who along with poor peasants were in the lead in the Bac Son and Southern uprisings. Confronted with the peril of bankruptcy, and their declining ability to make a living, the petty bourgeoisie is on the way to being revolutionized. The national bourgeoisie has both a national, democratic tendency and a reformist tendency, but in general it now hates the imperialists and approves and supports the revolution.

The feudal landowning class and the compradore bourgeois stratum are clearly divided. One landowner and compradore bourgeois embraces the French fascists; another would like to change masters, and follows the Japanese fascists. However, a few landowners, mostly small landowners, have lost faith in the French imperialists and also suspect the policy of Japan, so they have a sympathetically neutral attitude toward the revolution. Representatives of the landlord and reactionary compradore bourgeois strata are particularly the pro-Japanese and pro-Petain parties.

****

The big changes in the world and in the country mentioned above compel us to reexamine our entire line and policy during this period. Our party must decide on a new policy in order to mobilize all revolutionary and patriotic forces, in order to liberate the nation from the Japanese-French yoke. Naturally, the new policy of the Party must be based on a definite strategic guideline.

What is the objective of the strategic guideline? It is to aim exactly at the main enemy and concentrate the fire of the revolutionary struggle in order to destroy them; to recognize clearly the revolutionary and progressive forces in and outside the country; unite those forces in order to overthrow the common enemy; concentrate the revolutionary main force and use the reserve forces at the correct time as a guard unit, aiming at a good opportunity to attack the weakest point of the enemy. To do that we must define correctly the task of the Indochinese revolution at present in order to choose accurate slogans, determine the forms of struggle, and the method and slogans of struggle appropriate to the revolutionary movement's ups and downs. When the situation changes rapidly we must know how to use transitional forms of propaganda, organization and struggle to switch to higher forms, and swiftly take the masses to the armed uprising to win political power in the entire country.

****

With regard to the Indochinese people at present, the anti-imperialist task is more serious and urgent than the agrarian task. At present the national rights are higher than anything else. The interests of one segment must serve the interests of the entire nation. The interests of one class must stand behind the interests of all the people.

What is our main task at present? It is to complete the national liberation revolution. Because of this we must unite all classes, all strata within the people in a national united front against fascism; isolate the traitors and make them reveal their true traitorous face before the compatriots; mobilize all the popular strata, concentrate all the revolutionary forces no matter how small, to attack and overthrow the Japanese-French fascist imperialists. Liberate the nation, and then we will advance to the new tasks of the revolution. All popular strata must understand that if we want for the Indochinese revolution definitely to be victorious, the leadership of the Indochinese revolution must be in the hands of the working class (and in fact it has been in the hands of the working class for more than 10 years already). The Indochinese working class, although small is oppressed, and exploited more than all the rest. It has demonstrated a lofty spirit of courage and sacrifice, and has the strongest Indochinese party armed with Marxism-Leninism, the vanguard theory of the world revolution. Never have the interests of the Indochinese working class and the interests of the Indochinese peoples coincided with each other as they do at present. With the above conditions, the Indochinese working class is worthy of being the vanguard of the whole nation and only under the leadership of the working class can the Indochinese national liberation revolution fundamentally succeed.

****

Based on the above analysis, we see that the Indochinese revolution in the present period cannot yet resolve at the same time both tasks: the anti-imperialist task and the agrarian revolution. Why? Because the main content of the agrarian revolution is to "confiscate the land of the landowners and redistribute it to the peasants." But in the present conditions of the Indochinese revolution we cannot yet confiscate the land of the native landowners and redistribute it to the peasants (except for the land belonging to the Vietnamese traitors). Because if we do that, we cannot divide the landowning class, cannot win over or at least neutralize the small landowners, especially the intellectuals, students who are children of the landowners, and we will unintentionally deprive ourselves of our support, and increase the enemy's reserve forces.

However, the Indochinese peasants are not separated from the revolution either. We do not forget that ninety percent of the Indochinese people are peasants. If the peasant class does not participate in the revolution the national liberation revolution cannot succeed.

Therefore, we judge that we must do our utmost to win over the peasants. To do that, we must make them understand that when the national liberation revolution is victorious, it will fulfill their real interests.

****

For the above mentioned reasons, at present we do not put forward the slogan "Overthrow the imperialists and feudal landowners!", but must put forward "Overthrow the Japanese and French imperialists and the traitors!"; at present we do not say, "Confiscate the land of the landowners and redistribute it to the peasants," but only say "Confiscate the property of the Japanese and French imperialists and the traitors." Regardless of what social element they come from, all those who betray the country must be punished and their property, if any, must be confiscated. On the other hand, if anyone approves the national liberation revolution, participates in or supports the revolution by whatever means, whether they are landowners, bourgeois, officials, village chiefs, etc., they are to receive the same consideration and to be regarded as friendly allies of the revolution. We must not now put forward slogans which cause one to easily misunderstand, such as "Oppose the rulers and gougers, who harm the country," which cause the petty officials and village chiefs to fear the revolution (see the statutes of the Vietnamese Anti-imperialist National Salvation Association in Central Vietnam, May 1941) or slogans such as "Confiscate the land of religious associations," which makes it difficult for us to join hands with religious people who love independence and freedom.

In sum, we must be determined to get rid of slogans which are outdated or slogans for which the time is not yet ripe. We must determine correctly the immediate tasks of the Indochinese revolution and put forward slogans which are truly accurate and appropriate.

The Indochinese national liberation revolution at present has the following major slogans.

1. Overthrow the Japanese-French imperialists and Vietnamese traitors, and make Indochina completely independent.

2. Establish a democratic republic, in accordance with a people's democratic regime.

3. Nationalize the property of the Japanese-French imperialists and the traitors.

4. Establish eight-hour work-day law and a social insurance law.

5. Distribute the land of the Japanese-French imperialists and the traitors to poor peasants and revolutionary soldiers.

6. Carry out reduction of rents, reduction of debts, advance to the carrying out of the slogan "Land to the tiller."

7. Eliminate the present tax system and establish new equitable and appropriate taxes.

8. Establish a revolutionary army of the people.

9. Compulsory education through primary school.

10. Women and men equal in rights.

11. The peoples of Indochina are all equal and friendly and help one another advance.

12. Establish diplomatic relations between the Indochinese countries and other countries on the bases of respect for each other's independence and sovereignty, equality, and mutual interest.

13. Oppose the fascist war of aggression.

14. Support the Soviet Union's victory over international fascism.

15. Support the national liberation movement in the world.

****

Prepare for the Armed Uprising

One extremely important and urgent mission of the party right now is to prepare for the armed uprising, to prepare all the conditions necessary to insure that the armed uprising is victorious. The world situation is changing rapidly. The world revolutionary movement is more and more on the rise, in rhythm with the Soviet Union's war of national defense and the resistance war of the Chinese people. Our party must urgently organize the political and military forces of the masses in order to seize the opportune moment in time, and begin the armed uprising.

Therefore we must:

First, establish, develop, and consolidate the national United Front against Japanese-French fascism everywhere.

Second, create a broad, resolute struggle movement in order to save the country and save the people.

Third, prepare armed forces, develop and consolidate self-defense units and guerilla units; establish, develop and consolidate guerilla base areas. Propagandize soldiers of the imperialists: the red berets, green berets, French soldiers, soldiers from French colonies, and foreign legionnaires.

Fourth, arm the cadres and party members with the theory and practice of general uprising and seizing political power; research the experiences of the general uprisings in Bac Son, the South, and Do-luong; study the experience of the October Revolution and the experience of guerilla warfare of China, etc.

Fifth, consolidate and develop the party in all cities and in the countryside. We must definitely create party bases and national salvation bases in places where workers are concentrated and on strategic communications routes.

Recently due to the severe repression of the imperialists, the mass movement has declined to a degree. But because the Indochinese suffer many layers of heavy oppression and exploitation, they feel more and more that they must struggle to gain political power, so the party and the national salvation organizations not only can easily restore the organization but have conditions to develop rapidly. The world situation will change unexpectedly, creating a favorable opportunity for the Indochinese revolution. With our own subjective efforts, the conditions for the armed uprising of the Indochinese people will rapidly ripen.

(3) ARNING BY TROUNG CHINH, JANUARY 10-20, 1942 [Extract]

Source: "The Pacific War and the National Liberation Revolution in Indochina," in *The Vietnamese People's National Democratic Revolution*, Vol. I, pp. 249-255. [Translation by the Editor]

Within a month after Pearl Harbor, Troung Chinh the Secretary General and leading theoretician of the Party wrote a long analysis published by the Party's propaganda and training committee on the new situation created by the Pacific War. He predicted that the Japanese would lose and said the Indochinese people had to align themselves with the anti-fascist alliance. But he argued that the fundamental conditions for such an uprising did not yet exist in Indochina. In calling for primary emphasis on propaganda and agitation, he discusses the "uneven development" of the Indochinese revolution.

Only after assessing correctly the situation can we decide in a thorough manner on a revolutionary strategy.

The most necessary thing for the Party at this time is to produce appropriate propaganda and agitation slogans, and forms of organization and struggle in order to bring the masses up to the revolutionary front, push the broad national salvation movement and develop it rapidly. In sum we must determine new tasks raised by the Pacific war situation.

With regard to propaganda and agitation, our Party's task is to use whatever makes the masses most upset and angry in order to mobilize the masses to struggle. To do that, the Party must strive to propagandize and agitate against pillage, seizure of land, forcible conscription, forced labor, against rape, terror and killing, against increasing taxes, etc. The Party section in each province and city must prepare the printing materials to be able to go into action promptly on their own to produce small pamphlets, leaflets, and posters motivating the people to be united in resisting the robbers and killers - the Japanese-French fascists. Propaganda and agitation is particularly important right now. We must speak clearly on the outlook of the Pacific war and the prospect of the Japanese defeat, make the masses not fear the Japanese and know that the Indochinese revolution will definitely have a good opportunity to triumph. Also we must use the slogans put forward by the enemy in order to answer them. For example, take the slogans "unity" and "strength for service" of the French fascists and explain them so that the youth will unite and become Viet-nam National Salvation Youth Associations and Viet-nam National Self-Defense units, in order to have the strength to serve the Viet-nam Fatherland, drive out the Japanese-French aggressor armies, etc. In this period, armed propaganda units publicly agitate so that the broad masses can hear, using guerilla methods, and can operate *in regions having favorable conditions*. Especially at this time, Party sections must struggle against tendencies toward passivity, irresponsibility, lack of initiative, looking at past events, and failing to exploit the political, economic, cultural, physical culture and sport movements organized by the enemy, in order to steer them in a direction favorable for us, especially to influence opinion and expose the enemy's schemes. For example, the Party section in the North did not know how to take the "15 days to celebrate the empire," organized by the French invaders to extort money, to actively resist the imperialists. We must produce books and newspapers so that we can regularly take up the unmasking of the fascists and expose their crimes in every respect.

Regarding organization, the Party must reorganize self-defense groups, develop self-defense units in order to provide protection for the masses to struggle, develop guerrilla units in the mountainous region, establish guerrilla platoons in the midlands and plains and prepare to carry out sabotage and advance to the beginning of guerrilla warfare in the mountainous region, midlands and plains. We must establish National Salvation Army Associations in order to win over native soldiers and make them politically conscious. We must penetrate the mass organizations of the enemy and turn those organizations into places for the propaganda of our Party and the Viet Minh. We must consolidate the Party and develop national salvation groups aimed at the objective of preparing for the general uprising in both countryside and city. Regarding struggle, we must lead the masses to struggle against the high cost of living, to demand increase in wages, reduction in hours, reduction of rents, reduction of taxes, plundering by authorities in the market, forced conscription and forced labor, etc. We must organize demonstrations, verbal attacks on the authorities, meetings, etc. In those demonstrations, besides the basic masses, we must draw in rich peasants, national bourgeoisie and small landowners to participate, to achieve united action within the anti-fascist national front.

We must especially mobilize national salvation forces, organize struggles to support the guerrillas in Bac Son who are heroically fighting the Japanese-French aggressors and the Vietnamese traitors.

Those are, in summary, the urgent tasks of the Party at present. To fulfill those tasks means grasping the main points in order to push strongly the national salvation movement to develop and advance.

However, we must note that we are operating in circumstances of world war and not in the ordinary times. Therefore we must always be prepared to deal with any unexpected situation in order to change our strategy in time, and lead the masses through transitional forms of struggle to advance to the general uprising to gain political power in the whole country. Second, we must remember that the Indochinese revolutionary movement has characteristics to which we must pay attention to know the strong points which must be developed as well as the weak points which must be corrected.

At present, the Indochinese revolutionary movement has the following characteristics:

- In Indochina, the role of leading the revolution has been in the hands of the working class, because the Party of the working class is our party, which has really lead the movement to struggle against Japanese-French fascism. But recently, the struggle of the working class, especially industrial workers, has been weak, and not truly worthy of its role of leading the revolution.

- Because of the relation of forces between the enemy and us, the Indochinese revolution is generally developing in an uneven manner; the movement in the countryside is stronger than the movement in the cities, and the revolutionary movement in Viet-nam is stronger than the revolutionary movement in Cambodia and Laos.

- In Indochina at present, there is an absence of a national bourgeois movement and a movement of intellectuals, and students such as is usually found in colonial and semi-colonial countries.

- In Indochina at present there are not yet transitional forms of struggle to advance to the general uprising such as are usually seen in countries which have had revolutions: general political strikes, demonstrations of armed force, etc., but there have been guerrillas carrying out armed struggle against the imperialists and reactionary Vietnamese traitors.

- The Indochinese revolutionary movement is developing normally, but it is very possible that the situation in and outside the country will change rapidly and jump to a higher stage, passing over ordinary forms of struggle, and advancing to the general uprising. Therefore we must endeavor to develop national salvation self-defense units, guerrilla platoons, and make sure that local guerrilla warfare has the participation and support of the local people and is not just the separate affair of the guerrilla troops; and we must change guerrilla warfare into local general uprising.

(4) MEMORANDUM OF CONVERSATION BY THE ASSISTANT SECRETARY OF STATE, ADOLF BERLE, OCTOBER 21, 1943

Source: *U.S. Vietnam Relations, Book 7, V.B.L., pp.* 18-19.

The question of U.S. policy toward postwar Indochina arose concretely for the first time when the French Committee of National Liberation expressed concern to the State Department at reports that Chinese troops (part of the allied forces) might undertake operations in Vietnam. The Committee warned against such operations on the grounds that the Chinese and Vietnamese were hereditary enemies. In his report on the conversation, Assistant Secretary Berle saw the issue as posing the problem of U.S. policy toward Western colonial empires after the war.

M. Hoppenot came in to see me at his request. He handed me the attached memorandum, which states that the French National Committee understands that Chinese operations will presently open against the Japanese within the frontiers of Indochina. This gave great concern to the Committee of National Liberation. If Chinese troops attacked there, plainly there would not be any support from the French, since the Chinese had always claimed interest there, and it was not unlikely that the French troops would defend against a Chinese attack.

I asked whether this matter had already been brought to the attention of the Chiefs of Staff. M. Hoppenot said it had, through General Bethouart. I thanked him for the information and said that the matter presented was primarily for military consideration.

NOTE: But it is not only for military consideration. This brings us squarely up to the problem of whether, in the Far East, we are reestablishing the western colonial empires or whether we are letting the East liberate itself if it can do so. I feel that the matter should be discussed on a high level with the President for his decision. I do not know that we need to settle matters with the French Committee in Algiers. If the Chinese can do anything against the Japanese in French Indochina to the general advantage of the war, I have difficulty in seeing why we should stop them.

(5) MEMORANDUM BY THE ACTING SECRETARY OF STATE EDWARD R. STETTINIUS TO PRESIDENT FRANKLIN ROOSEVELT, NOVEMBER 8, 1943

Source: *U.S. Vietnam Relations, Book 7, V.B.L.,* p. 21.

Assured by the Far Eastern Bureau that the Vietnamese had feelings of "friendliness and cultural affinity" for the Chinese, Acting Secretary of State Edward Stettinius passed his assessment of the French Committee's position on to President Roosevelt.

M. Henri Hoppenot, the Delegate of the French Committee of National Liberation, has left with the State Department a communication, a copy of which in translation is attached hereto, giving the reasons why, in the opinion of the Committee, it would be a mistake to entrust to Chinese troops the launching of military operations against Indo-China. The main reason advanced is that the Chinese are the hereditary enemies of the Annamites and that an attack by the Chinese would therefore be resisted by the local population as well as by French troops. It is our belief that this presentation of the case involves allegations not in accord with the facts, and that the Annamites, by and large, have for the Chinese a feeling of friendliness and cultural affinity.

The problem to which these representations relates seems primarily to be a military problem for the Joint Chiefs of Staff. We understand that it has already been brought to the attention of that body by General Bethouart, Chief of the French Military Mission.

(6) MEMORANDUM BY PRESIDENT ROOSEVELT TO ACTING SECRETARY OF STATE STETTINIUS, NOVEMBER 9, 1943

Source: *U.S. Vietnam Relations, Book 7, V.B.L.* pp.21-22.

In regard to the use of Chinese troops against Annam, I agree with the State Department that the French presentation of the case is not sufficiently valid to take any action.

The whole matter should be left to the discretion of the Joint Chiefs of Staff and to the Commanding Officers in the area. This is essentially a military problem.

(7) MEMORANDUM OF CONVERSATION BETWEEN ROOSEVELT AND MARSHAL JOSEPH STALIN AT THE TEHERAN CONFERENCE, NOVEMBER 28, 1943 [Extract]

Source: *U.S. Vietnam Relations Book 7, V.B.L.* p. 24.

In a discussion of the future of Indochina at the Teheran Conference, Roosevelt agreed with Stalin that the French should not be permitted to reestablish control and raised the possibility of a trusteeship lasting 20-30 years.

MARSHAL STALIN expatiated at length on the French ruling classes and he said, in his opinion, they should not be entitled to share in any of the benefits of the peace, in view of their past record of collaboration with Germany.

THE PRESIDENT said that Mr. Churchill was of the opinion that France would be very quickly reconstructed as a strong nation, but he did not personally share this view since he felt that many years of honest labor would be necessary before France would be reestablished. He said the first necessity for the French, not only for the Government, but the people as well, was to become honest citizens.

MARSHAL STALIN agreed and went on to say that he did not propose to have the Allies shed blood to restore Indo-China, for example, to the old French colonial rule. He said that the recent events in the Lebanon made public service the first step toward the independence of people who had formerly been colonial subjects. He said that in the war against Japan, in his opinion, that in addition to military missions, it was necessary to fight the Japanese in the political sphere as well, particularly in view of the fact that the Japanese had granted the least nominal independence to certain colonial areas. He repeated that France should not get back Indo-China and that the French must pay for their criminal collaboration with Germany.

(8) MEMORANDUM BY ROOSEVELT TO SECRETARY OF STATE CORDELL HULL, JANUARY 24, 1944

Source: *U.S. Vietnam Relations, Book 7, V.B.L.* p. 30.

In response to Secretary Hull's query about his views in Indochina, Roosevelt reaffirmed his support of trusteeship for Indochina, calling the case "perfectly clear."

I saw Halifax last week and told him quite frankly that it was perfectly true that I had, for over a year, expressed the opinion that Indo-China should not go back to France but that it should be administered by an international trusteeship. France has had the country - thirty million inhabitants for nearly one hundred years, and the people are worse off than they were at the beginning.

As a matter of interest, I am wholeheartedly supported in this view by Generalissimo Chiang Kai-shek and by Marshal Stalin. I see no reason to play in with the British Foreign Office in this matter. The only reason they seem to oppose it is that they fear the effect it would have on their possessions and those of the Dutch. They never liked the idea of trusteeship because it is, in some instances, aimed at future independence. This is true in the case of Indo-China.

Each case must, of course, stand on its own feet, but the case of Indo-China is perfectly clear. France has milked it for one hundred years. The people of Indo-China are entitled to something better than that.

(9) PAMPHLET BY VO NGUYEN GIAP FOR VIET MINH CADRES, FEBRUARY 1944 [Extracts]

Source: Vo Nguyen Giap, *Dan Quan Tu Ve, Mot Luc Luong Chien Luoc (Self-Defense Militia, A Strategic Force)*, (Hanoi: Su That, 1974), pp. 11-15, excerpting chapters 5 and 10 of "Kinh Nghiem Viet Minh o Viet-bac," (Viet-minh experience in Viet-bac).[Translation by the Editor.]

Beginning in early 1943, the Viet Minh concentrated their efforts on six highland provinces in Northeastern Tonkin from the Chinese boarder down to Thai Nguyen province. Viet Minh "national salvation associations" spread quickly through whole districts, and the whole area, called the "Viet-bac" became a laboratory for political-military organization, in preparation for the "armed general uprising." A pamphlet written by Vo Nguyen Giap after one year of successful work in the Viet-bac is the best available document on Viet Minh strategy during this period before the Japanese coup of March 1945. The reference to "the organization" refers to the Indochinese Communist Party, which was never mentioned publicly as the inner core of the Viet Minh.

V. The Viet Minh experience in the Viet-bac is an experience with national salvation work of the Vietnam Independence League in Viet-bac.

The most notable characteristic of the Viet Minh in Viet-bac is its broad character, broader than ever before in the history of our country's revolution; broad in scope; each village, each canton, each ethnic minority district and each district has participated completely in the ranks of the revolution; broad with regard to its popular composition: men, women, old and young, all enthusiastically participating in national salvation activities, with the exception of a very few, who are neutral or reactionary.

The Viet Minh experience in Viet-bac is thus first of all the experience of a broad national salvation organization. That experience shows that in present conditions, when the world situation and our situation within the situation push the people throughout the country forward on the road to revolution, an extremely broad organization can be achieved, maintained, developed, and strengthened in a steady stable way. Not only that, the experience further shows that only with such a broad national salvation organization can we solve the problem of preparing the armed uprising and the problem of the armed uprising itself in a suitable way. Meanwhile, in a truly broad organization, very many problems regarding national salvation work can be put forward in a new way and can be resolved in a new way, different from the conditions of a narrow, isolated organization.

National salvation self-defense units have been organized on the bases of the national salvation associations of the masses, especially national salvation youth associations.

When first organized, national self-defense units still had few members, were incoherent, scattered and not yet active. But after undergoing a period of training and practice, the self-defense units gradually took shape, gradually became broadly organized and took on a life of their own.

Thus, training and practice is very necessary for the self-defense units. At first the number of members who agreed to go study was small, but thanks to the explanation of the organization, on one hand, and thanks to the movement to push them forward which appeared a little later, everyone went for self-defense training. At present, self-defense training is much more popular than political training. In many localities male and female self-defense units have drilled up to ten sessions, each session lasting from five or seven up to twelve days, and their work is rather accomplished, to the point that they can win praise from officers of imperialist or foreign armies. When self-defense units have trained, activities in the unit become satisfactory. The unit chief has a spirit of responsibility, and the members are prepared to be obedient.

Before too long, the needs of the masses brought forth a new problem, which was to create self-defense cadres for the localities. Those cadres were trained especially in order to return to train members of the units. Thanks to that training, recently, especially in the months when there is spare time, male and female members usually pull each other along to go for training.

In many places the organizations have organized mock battles in which 300 or 400 male and female members participate, with lectures sometimes up to two or three days and nights. The organization also organizes information assemblies for an entire canton or an entire ethnic minority district which are sometimes accomplished at night and very quickly.

In places having bandits, self-defense units have also an especially valuable function which is to guard the localities and fight the bandits. Self-defense units do this work with great care and the results are really notable, with the largest proportion of the bandits eliminated. Surveillance of the localities also helps the self-defense unit train regarding methods of night patrol, methods of standing guard, and methods of coping with the enemy: a small school for combat.

X. Recently Viet-bac entered the phase of active preparation for armed uprising. With regard to the political aspect, the organization is taking care of the formation of cadres in order to carry out the coming general uprising, by choosing good cadres and putting them on responsible committees, by giving them further training, and by continuously calling cadres' conferences to discuss problems of preparing for the armed general uprising.

With regard to association members, we must mobilize the spirit of preparing for armed general uprising; if they have money, they can contribute money; if they have strength, they can contribute strength, or by preparing to sacrifice and struggle, by calling meetings. At present each locality has at least one meeting each month, sometimes more, to discuss local affairs, to welcome the Red Wave propaganda unit, to welcome higher officials, to commemorate anniversaries of the revolution, etc. There are also meetings of each interest group to discuss the particular problems of that group.

Regarding regions not yet developed, the organizations send teams to rush in and organize, in a short time, pulling in hundreds or thousands from an entire village or canton in the association. Then another wave of cadres comes to consolidate, and only when the consolidation is completed do they set to work at actively preparing the armed general uprising.

Regarding the military aspect, the organizational activity carries out propagandizing of troops and pays attention to the formation of combat self-defense units (guerrilla cells).

Combat self-defense units include any elements in the self-defense unit which have normal strength, determination, readiness to die for the country, and which aspire to be guerrilla fighters. They must acquire some sort of weapon and have much training, most of which is especially military. They also carry out the usual self-defense unit work, but specialize in difficult or dangerous work, such as fighting bandits, doing sentry duty and protecting revolutionary organs. The problems of political officers in the self-defense units are also given special attention.

Meanwhile, the organization seeks by all means to popularize guerrilla tactics among the masses.

Regarding the aspect of provisions, the organization is consolidating concrete and appropriate plans in order to prepare. In sum, whether regarding morale or material reality, the preparing of the armed general uprising in Viet-bac has been carried out in an orderly and effective way. On many planes, the masses are excited and want to stand up in a general uprising immediately, especially when the imperialists terrorize them.

(10) MEMORANDUM BY KENNETH P. LANDON, DIVISION OF FAR EASTERN AFFAIRS, DEPARTMENT OF STATE, JULY 10, 1944

Source: *U.S. Vietnam Relations, Book 7, V.B.L.,* pp. 32-33.

The State Department's Southeast Asia specialist, Kenneth P. Landon, in a memorandum for the regional office, traced the background of Roosevelt's advocacy of trusteeship for Indochina and noted that the President opposed the use of French troops in the liberation of Indochina, in order to insure that trusteeship would follow.

On March 27, 1943 President Roosevelt, Secretary of State Hull, the Right Honorable Anthony Eden, British Ambassador Lord Halifax, Mr. Strang of the British Foreign Office, Ambassador Winant, Under Secretary Welles, and Mr. Harry Hopkins held a general conference at the White House. In the course of the discussion the President suggested that trusteeship be set up for Indochina. Mr. Eden indicated that he was favorably impressed with this proposal.

On January 3, 1944, Secretary of State Hull and the British Ambassador Lord Halifax held a conversation at the Department in which the British Ambassador remarked that information had come to him from his Foreign Office that in a conversation with the Turks, Egyptians and perhaps others during his recent trip to the Near East, the President spoke rather definitely about what purported to be his views to the effect that Indochina should be taken away from the French and put under an international trusteeship, etc. The Ambassador said that of course he had heard the President make remarks like this during the past year or more but that the question of whether the President's utterances represent final conclusions becomes important in view of the fact that it would soon get back to the French, etc. Mr. Hull said that he knew no more about the matter than the Ambassador and had only heard the President make these remarks occasionally just about as the Ambassador had heard him make them. He added that in his judgment, "the President and Mr. Churchill would find it desirable to talk this matter over fully deliberately and perhaps finally at some future stage."

In a memorandum for the President of January 14, Mr. Hull reported his conversation with the British Ambassador and asked if the President's opinion, previously expressed, that Indochina should be taken away from the French and administered by an international trusteeship, represented his final conclusions on the matter. The Secretary stated that he had informed the British Ambassador that he did not know whether the President had come to any final conclusion on the subject.

On February 17, 1944, in a memorandum for the President from the Under Secretary, on the subject of Civil Affairs problems in Indochina, the statement was made that "Subject to your approval, the State Department will proceed on the assumption that French armed forces will be employed to at least some

extent in the military operations, and that in the administration of Indochina
it will be desirable to employ French nationals who have an intimate knowledge
of the country and its problems." Across the face of the document the President in reaffirmation of his previously expressed opinion, wrote: "No French
help in Indochina ____ country on trusteeship."

On February 25, 1944, in a memorandum to Mr. Dunn, the Under Secretary mentioned the President's reception of the memorandum of February 17 above referred
to and stated that the "President expressed the view that no French troops whatever should be used in operations there [Indochina]. He feels the operations
should be Anglo-American with international trusteeship following."

(11) INSTRUCTIONS BY HO CHI MINH FOR SETTING UP OF THE ARMED PROPAGANDA BRIGADE FOR THE LIBERATION OF VIET NAM, DECEMBER, 1944

Source: Ho Chi Minh, *Selected Writings*, pp. 47-48.

*In December, 1944, in the expectation that the opportune moment for an armed
uprising was growing nearer, Ho Chi Minh gave instructions to Vo Nguyen Giap, to
form the first centrally directed military unit of what would later become the
National Army of the Democratic Republic of Vietnam.*

The name of the *Armed Propaganda Brigade for the Liberation of Viet Nam*
shows that the greater importance is attached to its political than to its military action. It is a propaganda unit. In the military field, the main principle for successful action is concentration of forces. Therefore, in accordance
with the new instructions of our organization, the most resolute and energetic
cadres and men will be picked from the ranks of the guerilla units in the provinces of Bac Can, Lang Son and Cao Bang, and an important part of the available
weapons concentrated in order to establish our main force brigade.

Ours being a national resistance by the whole people we must mobilize and
arm the whole people. While concentrating our forces to set up the brigade, we
must maintain the local armed forces which must coordinate their operations and
assist each other in all respects. For its part, the main-force brigade has the
duty to guide the cadres of the local armed units, assist them in training, and
supply them with weapons if possible, thus helping these units to develop unceasingly.

With regard to the local armed units, we must gather their cadres for training, send trained cadres to various localities, exchange experience, maintain
liaison, and coordinate military operations.

Concentrating tactics, we must apply guerilla warfare; maintain secrecy,
quickness of action and initiative (now in the east now in the west, arriving
unexpectedly and departing without leaving any traces).

The Armed Propaganda Brigade for the Liberation of Viet Nam is the first-
born unit. It is hoped that other units will soon come into being.

Its initial size is modest but it faces brilliant prospects. It is the em-
bryo of the Liberation Army and can expand from North to South throughout Viet
Nam.

(12) SPEECH BY COMRADE VAN (VO NGUYEN GIAP) AT THE CEREMONY FOUNDING THE VIET-NAM LIBERATION ARMED PROPAGANDA BRIGADE, DECEMBER 22, 1944

Source: General Vo Nguyen Giap, *Nhat Lenh, Dien Tu va Thu Dong Vien (1944-1962)
(Orders of the Day, Speeches and Mobilization Letters)*, (Hanoi: Su That, 1963),
pp. 5-10. [Translation by the Editor.]

*Former history professor Vo Nguyen Giap, as Commander of the Armed Propa-
ganda Brigade, chose 34 fighters - 31 men and 3 women - from among the best in*

14

*the Cao-Bac-Lang guerrilla zone, to join the unit. In an inspirational speech
at the unit's founding ceremony, Giap linked the fight for independence in Viet-
nam with both Vietnamese traditions of patriotic struggle and the worldwide national liberation movement which had begun to emerge during the world war.*

Comrades,

Today, December 22, 1944, in accordance with the order of the Organization,
we have gathered in this spot of green jungle and red earth, between Tran Hung
Dao canton and Hoang hoa Tham canton in Cao-Bac-Lang interzone, in order to open
the meeting founding the Viet-nam Liberation Army Propaganda unit. You comrades
certainly know that the time we are meeting here is precisely the time that the
battle between the fascist and democratic fronts is about to bring down the final
curtain in Europe: German Nazism has been thoroughly destroyed. And as for East
Asia, that battle has also entered a decisive phase with the Japanese attack on
South China and the U.S. landing in the Philippines. Then our own Vietnam could
very well be drawn into the war, and Japanese Fascism will go down to defeat.

You comrades certainly know that the time that we are meeting here is precisely the time that from East to West, the wave of new democratic revolution,
the movement of national revolution, is seethingly spreading, drawing in hundreds of millions of people in oppressed countries. From Yugoslavia to China,
countless numbers of people are struggling gloriously to win independence, freedom and happiness.

At the same time, in our country, in the context of the most extreme repression and exploitation, the contradictions between France and Japan growing
deeper every day, the Vietnamese national liberation, going along with the world
stream, is about to enter the phase of direct armed struggle. Haven't our
masses boiled up everywhere expecting the day of decisive struggle? Hasn't the
flag of armed struggle held high in Thai Nguyen?

In order to deal with the opportune moment and insure the success of the
liberation revolution, the Viet-nam Independence League has put forward a new
task: armed propaganda. And in the Cao-Bac-Lang interzone, it has entrusted
that task to us, to the Viet-nam Liberation Armed Propaganda Unit, which today
we meet to establish in a simple, rustic but solemn setting.

Comrades,

The mission which the Organization has entrusted to us in an important mission, a heavy mission. Politics is more important than military activities,
propaganda more important than combat; that mission has the characteristic of
being the mission of a transitional period; employ propaganda to appeal to
the entire people to stand up, preparing political and military bases for the
general uprising later on.

We must realize this clearly, in order to carry it out correctly and strive
to the utmost to carry it out. For the Organization to entrust this mission to
us is to put great faith and hope in us. We will carry out orders correctly
in order to avoid being ungrateful to the Organization.

Thus from this moment forward, we will advance together on the path of
armed struggle. We raise high the spirit of bravery and sacrifice, never
afraid in spite of hardship, never giving up in spite of suffering. And although our heads may fall, and blood may flow, we will still not retreat. We
are determined to advance in order to complete our mission. So great is the
anger of the nation, so many are the tragic atrocities that await a settlement
of accounts. We will reveal clearly to the whole people that the way to life
is the path of unity to prepare the armed uprising. The Liberation Army will
show that it is a military unit of the people, of the country, going in the
vanguard on the road to national liberation.

The Liberation army will be a military unit which is very respectful of
discipline, absolutely obeying each order; it will be a military unit which is

rich in the spirit of unity, sharing the bitter with the sweet. We shall be audacious and we shall be prudent, neither haughty in victory, nor discouraged in defeat. Our experience is still young, but only by doing can we gain experience, and if we do we will naturally gain experience. We have faith in our victory.

Yes, we will certainly be victorious. The Yugoslavian people have won back their fatherland with their bones and blood. The French people and the Chinese people also are exchanging their bones and blood for liberation and freedom. There is no reason why our people cannot do what the Yugoslav people, the French people and the Chinese people have done. As the nephews of Tran hung Dao and Hoang hoa Tham, we will liberate our country and will be worthy of our ancestors. And certainly, it is not a surprise that today, our propaganda unit is founded right between Tran hung Dao canton and Hoang hoa Tham canton.

Remember, Comrades: to participate in the first unit of the Liberation Army is an honor for us, and we will show that we are worthy of that honor. You have waited for the hour of armed struggle. That hour has come.

In accordance with the order of the organization, under the red flag with the five-pointed gold star, I declare the Viet-nam Liberation Army propaganda unit established and command you to advance on the road of armed struggle.

From this moment, you will follow the flag as we advance on the road of blood. We will advance, advance endlessly until the day of the liberation of the entire people.

In order to hold high the spirit of suffering and sacrifice, and in order to demonstrate our desire to recall the glorious examples of national heroes who have gone before and our determination to follow them, I suggest that tonight our unit eat together a meatless meal without vegetables and without salt, and that throughout the night, we divide into platoons to attend to the flag and to recite the oaths of honor, near the guerilla fires that we will set here in the jungle. Tonight is the first guerilla night of our propaganda unit.

Finally, on behalf of the Organization and the entire unit, I would like to express thanks for the zealous support of the masses in the interzone, especially the brothers and sisters who ignored danger to come here to lend comfort to the soldiers and participate in the founding of our unit. We will destroy the invaders and save the country in order to repay the kindness pf the masses.

I shout:
Determined to advance on the road of combat!
Long live the spirit of the Vietnam Liberation Army!
Long live the Vietnam Independence Alliance!
Long live independent Vietnam!

Comrades:

Prepare yourselves, read the ten oaths of honor, and we will have the oath-swearing ceremony under the flag:

The Ten Oaths of Honor of the Viet-nam Liberation Army

We, the Viet-nam Liberation Army propaganda unit, on our honor as fighters for national salvation, swear beneath the red flag with the five-pointed gold star:

1. Swear: to sacrifice all for the Viet-nam Fatherland, to fight to the last drop of blood to destroy the Japanese and French fascists and Vietnamese traitors, to make Viet-nam an independent and democratic country, equal to other democratic nations in the world.

2. Swear: to absolutely obey every order of commanders and whenever receiving an order, to conscientiously and with all my force, carry it out quickly and exactly.

3. Swear: To be forever determined to fight, and despite hardship and misery, never to complain, at the moment of greatest risk, nevertheless not to lose my will. When going into battle to resolve to assault, though my head may fall and blood flow, I will still not retreat.

4. Swear: At all times to be ready and alert, studying with all my force in order to forge myself as a revolutionary soldier, worthy of being a vanguard fighter for destruction of the invader and for national salvation.

5. Swear: Absolutely to keep the secrets for the army regarding internal organization, command echelons; absolutely to keep the secrets of all national salvation organizations.

6. Swear: if captured by the enemy in battle, despite the threat of execution, despite torture, always to firmly resolve to be faithful to the task of liberating the entire people, and never to make a betraying deposition.

7. Swear: To the best of my ability, to hold on to my weapon, never allowing it to be in disrepair or to fall into enemy hands.

8. Swear: To love my fellow fighters as myself, and with all my heart, to help each other ordinarily as well as in time of battle.

9. Swear: When contacting the masses, I will correctly implement the three don'ts:
- Do not take the property of the people
- Do not threaten the people
- Do not harass the people
and the three do's:
- Respect the people
- Help the people
- Protect the people
in order to create confidence and love with regard to the masses, achieve unanimity between the Army and people, destroy the invaders and save the country.

10. Swear: Always to hold high the spirit of self-criticism, to maintain an exemplary individual comportment, doing nothing to harm the reputation of the Liberation Army and the national prestige of Viet-nam.

(13) INSTRUCTIONS OF THE STANDING BUREAU OF THE CENTRAL COMMITTEE OF THE INDO-CHINESE COMMUNIST PARTY, MARCH 12, 1945

Source: *Breaking our Chains, Documents of the Vietnamese Revolutions of August 1945* (Hanoi: Foreign Languages Publishing House, 1960), pp. 7-17.

When the Japanese began their armed takeover in Indochina, on March 9, 1945, the ICP Central Committee's Standing Bureau held an enlarged meeting to assess the new situation. Three days later, the Bureau issued its instructions to the Party membership to concentrate on the Japanese as the "main, immediate and sole enemy" and to be ready to take advantage of the eventual arrival of Allied troops in Indochina. But the document indicated that the Party leadership would be prepared to launch a general insurrection before the arrival of allied troops under any one of several circumstances.

I. Analysis of the situation

1. The Japanese *coup de force*. -- At 8.25 p.m. on the March 9, 1945, the Japanese opened fire upon the French and occupied the main towns and important strategic points. The French put up but a weak resistance. They will lose in the end for three reasons:

a) Lack of fighting spirit.
b) Lack of modern weapons.
c) Lack of united action with the anti-Japanese forces of the Indochinese peoples.
2. Character and objective of the *coup de force*. -- The March 9, 1945 *coup de force* was a *coup d'etat*, that is to say one group of rulers seized power from another. Its objective was to deprive the French of all power, to occupy Indochina and to turn it into an exclusive colony of Japanese imperialism.
3. Causes of the *coup d'etat*. -- Three causes have led to this *coup d'etat*:
a) Two imperialist wolves could not share between them so rich a spoil as Indochina.
b) Facing imminent attack by the Chinese and the Americans in Indochina, the Japanese were compelled to overthrow the French to remove the danger of being stabbed in the back by the French on the landing of the Allied forces.
c) Japan had at all costs to defend the land-link with its colonies in the Indonesian region since, following the occupation of the Philippines by the Americans, its sea-lines were completely cut off.
4. Political crisis arising from the Japanese *coup d'etat*. -- We can at this very moment see the characteristic signs of an acute political crisis:
a) The two robbers are engaged in mortal combat
b) French power is disintegrating
c) Japanese power has not yet been consolidated
d) The "neutral" strata of the population are in consternation
e) The revolutionary masses are ready for action.

II. New conditions created by the new situation

1. Conditions not yet ripe for an uprising. -- The political crisis is acute but the conditions are not yet ripe for an uprising because:
a) French resistance was so weak and the Japanese *coup d'etat* was relatively easy; though the division between the French and Japanese ruling cliques has reached its climax, and the French ranks in Indochina are in extreme confusion and are disintegrating; extreme division, confusion and indecision do not yet prevail among the Japanese ruling clique.
b) The "neutral" strata of the population must necessarily go through a period of disillusionment with the disastrous results of the *coup d'etat* before they give way to the revolutionary forces and become determined to help the vanguard elements.
c) Except in localities where the natural features are favourable and where we have fighting units, in the country as a whole the vanguard, still engaged in preparations for the uprising, is not yet ready to fight nor resolved to make every sacrifice.
2. Circumstances favouring the rapid maturing of conditions for insurrection. -- Three circumstances are creating conditions for the rapid maturing of the insurrection and launching of a vast revolutionary movement:
a) The political crisis (the enemy's hands are tied, preventing them from dealing with the revolution)
b) The terrible famine (deep hatred of the people for the aggressors)
c) The war is entering the decisive phase (imminent Allied landing in Indochina to attack the Japanese).

III. Changes in the Party's tactics

1. Enemy's ranks and allied forces after the Japanese *coup de force*. -- The Japanese *coup de force* has brought about the following big changes.
a) French imperialism having lost its ruling power in Indochina is no longer our immediate enemy, although we still have to be on our guard against

the manoeuvres of the Gaullist group, who are trying to restore French rule in Indochina.

b) After the *coup de force*, the Japanese fascists have become the main, immediate, and sole enemy of the Indochinese peoples.

c) The French who are conducting a resistance to the Japanese are, for the moment, objectively allies of the Indochinese peoples.

2. Main slogans change and whole tactics change. We must energetically renounce the old slogans and old forms of struggle and pass over to new forms of propaganda, organization and struggle. Particular attention must be paid to the following points:

a) We must replace the slogan "Drive out the Japanese and French!" by "Drive out the Japanese fascists!" We must use the slogan "Establish the revolutionary power of the Indochinese peoples" in the struggle against Japanese power and the puppet government of the pro-Japanese traitors.

b) We must switch the central point of our propaganda over to two themes:

1. The Japanese bandits will not liberate our people; on the contrary, they will increase oppression and exploitation.

2. The Japanese invaders cannot consolidate their power in Indochina and will certainly be annihilated.

3. We must change to forms of propaganda, agitation, organization and struggle which are best suited to the pre-insurrectionary period, intensively mobilizing the masses for the revolutionary front and training them to march boldly forward to general insurrection.

c) A powerful anti-Japanese movement for national salvation will be launched as a pre-requisite of the general insurrection. This movement could include actions ranging from non-cooperation, strikes in workshops and markets, and sabotage, to forms of a higher degree such as armed demonstrations and guerilla activity.

d) We must be ready to switch over to general insurrection when the right conditions are obtained (e.g. on the Japanese capitulation, or when the Allied troops have established a firm position and are advancing firmly on our territory).

IV. Our attitude towards the French resistance and the setting up of an anti-Japanese front in Indochina

1. The French resistance has a relatively progressive character. -- We entirely approve the French resistance although it has no other aims than disputing imperialist interests with the Japanese; because, objectively, it is directed against our principal enemy, the Japanese fascists. Thus it has a relatively progressive character.

2. Fundamental conditions for the formation of a United Democratic Front against the Japanese in Indochina. -- The French resistants can stand by the side of the Indochinese revolutionary peoples in the United Democratic Front against the Japanese if they accept the four conditions laid down by our Party in 1943 and since amended as follows:

a) The foreigners who are fighting the Japanese in Indochina must recognize the complete and immediate independence of the Indochinese peoples.

b) The foreign anti-Japanese forces in Indochina and the Indochinese revolutionary forces must achieve united action in all fields including the military field. This united action must be based on the principle of equality and mutual assistance.

c) All Indochinese and foreign political prisoners must be released unconditionally.

d) The revolutionary governments in Indochina will ensure the protection of the lives and property of the foreigners who are fighting the Japanese fascists in Indochina and give them freedom of resistance and of trade.

3. Fight the Japanese first! -- We shall not mechanically stick to all these four conditions in all circumstances and let slip opportunities to realize united action with the French who are fighting the Japanese in Indochina. Should this united action occur, we are ready to shake hands with the French who are truly and thoroughly resolved to resist the Japanese and are fighting them arms in hand. We call on them to supply us with arms and together with us, to fight the Japanese first! This does not mean that we surrender our claims to national independence. On the contrary, we see clearly that in the end, the slogan "national independence" will be realized by the strength of the armed masses of the population, and not by the promises of the French resistants.

4. United action with the rank and file. -- But if the French resistants do not accept these four conditions and refuse to supply us with arms to fight the Japanese, our task is to strive to unite action with the rank and file of the French resistance army, to win over resolute anti-fascist elements of internationalist tendency, so that they can unite their actions with ours in the fight against the Japanese or, over the heads of selfish and irresolute higher army personnel, join our side bringing with them the weapons of the French imperialists and, together with us, set up the anti-Japanese Democratic Front of Indochina.

V. The urgent tasks

1. Propaganda
a) Slogans: "Down with the Japanese and the pro-Japanese traitors' administration!" Advance the slogan "Long live the people's revolution."
b) Forms: To switch over to bolder forms of propaganda and agitation such as: demonstrations, public speeches with displays of flags, banners and placards, and distribution of leaflets and fly-bills. To organize choruses and drills, exhibitions of books and newspapers, pictures and photographs, arms, etc...
c) Armed propaganda: To set up armed "shock units" for the wide distribution of Viet Minh proclamations of the Franco-Japanese conflict, and other revolutionary documents. Particular attention should be paid to displaying placards and familiarizing the people with the flag of the Viet Minh.
To set up armed "propaganda shock teams." To make public speeches everywhere.
2. Struggle
a) Slogans: To combine the slogans "Rice and clothing!" and "Down with requisitions of paddy and collection of taxes!", with the slogan "Revolutionary power to the people!"
b) Tactics in agitation work for the struggle: To make use of the anger aroused by the famine by agitation work among the masses, and to lead them into struggle (to organize demonstrations to demand paddy or to storm imperialist rice-stocks).
c) Forms of struggle: To switch over to higher forms: parades, demonstrations, political strikes, public meetings, strikes in schools and markets, non-cooperation with the Japanese in all fields, opposition to requisition of paddy and refusal to pay taxes.
To mobilize the self-defence groups to disarm scattered deserting or demoralized enemy soldiers.
To launch guerilla warfare where the natural features of the country are favourable.
d) To be prepared for Japanese repression:
1. If the Japanese raid a village and arrest people, we should mobilize the whole village and all the other villages in the neighbourhood to beat drums and swing rattles, blow horns, fire shots and explode fire-crackers in support of the victims to drive out the enemy. We should also lay ambushes to rescue those arrested.

2.   If the Japanese send out troops to attack our guerilla bases, our guerillas must know how to turn to good account the tactics "To scatter or to regroup forces according to circumstances", and, in co-ordination with the people
behind the enemy lines, to attack and harass the enemy in order to compel him to
withdraw.
3.   Organization
a)   To expand the Viet Minh bases:
-- To form "organizational shock teams, responsible for creating bases of
action for national salvation in places where the movement does not yet exist.
-- To make use of simple organizational forms such as Security Units,
People's Self-Defence Units, Armed Militia, Communal Committees, Committees of
Order in factories etc.., then rapidly to turn these forms into bases of action
for national salvation.
-- Particular attention should be paid to developing Self-Defence Groups for
National Salvation and a Youth League for National Salvation.
b)   Military organization:
-- To organize more guerilla units and guerilla groups
-- To set up new bases
-- To unify the resistance zones and form the "Viet Nam Liberation Army"
-- To organize the "Revolutionary Military Committee", i.e. the "Insurrection Committee" to unify the command of guerilla units in the various resistance
zones.
c)   Organization of administrative power:
-- To set up Liberation Committees in factories, mines, villages, hamlets,
streets, garrisons, schools, public and private offices, etc. The committees
will take on the character of a broad Anti-Japanese National United Front; besides, they will be something like local "pre-governments" in each factory,
village, etc.
-- To set up "People's Revolutionary Committees" and "Workers' Revolutionary
Committees" in localities where our guerillas are active.
-- To found the "Viet Nam National Liberation Committee" having the form of
a provisional revolutionary government of Viet Nam.
4.   Training
a)   We must see to it that the movement increases not only in size, but also
in quality.   Therefore, as the movement becomes organized, it will be necessary
to carry out political and military training in conformity with the "Training
Programme Worked out by the Viet Minh".
b)   All propaganda work and struggles being of a military character, cadres
at all levels and commanders of self-defence groups must receive military
training.

VI.   To hold ourselves in readiness to unite
action with the Allied troops

1.   We cannot launch the general insurrection immediately upon the arrival
of the Allied forces in Indochina to fight the Japanese.   We should not only
wait for the Allied forces to get a firm foothold, we must also wait until they
are advancing.   At the same time, we must wait until the Japanese send forces
to the front to intercept the Allied forces, thus relatively exposing their
rear, before we launch the general insurrection; only then will the situation
be favourable to us.
2.   Wherever the Allied forces land, we should mobilize the people to organize demonstrations to welcome them and at the same time arm the masses, set
up militia forces to fight the enemy side by side with the Allied forces.   In
localities where our guerillas are active, they should enter into contact with
the Allied forces and together with them fight the Japanese according to a
common plan.   But in any case, our guerillas must always keep the initiative in
the operations.

3. All over the country in the zones behind the enemy's line, we should mobilize the people to go out into the streets to welcome the Allied forces and especially to keep watch upon the least movement of the Japanese and to inform our troops and the Allied forces of any such movements. At the same time we should carry out sabotage where and when this is necessary. On the order for the launching of the general insurrection, everyone should rise up, cut off the enemy's communication lines (except where there are orders to the contrary), storm and seize the enemy's stores and garrisons, and extend guerilla warfare throughout the countryside and to the towns.

4. From now on the launching of guerilla warfare, the occupation of bases, and the maintenance and extension of guerilla activities represent the only tactics by which our people can keep the initiative in the struggle to drive the Japanese aggressors out of the country, while holding themselves in readiness to give active support to the Allied forces.

5. We cannot, however, consider the landing of the Allied forces in Indochina as the indispensable condition for our general insurrection, because such an attitude would mean total reliance upon others, and tying our hands while the general situation is developing in our favour. If the revolution breaks out and the people's revolutionary power is set up in Japan, or if Japan is occupied as was France in 1940 and the Japanese expeditionary corps is demoralized, then even if the Allied forces have not yet arrived in our country, our general insurrection can be launched all the same and win victory.

Comrades!

Raise aloft the glorious banner of our Party!

Do your utmost to overcome all difficulties and obstacles to carry out these instructions! Final victory will certainly be ours!

(14) MEMORANDUM OF CONVERSATION WITH ROOSEVELT BY CHARLES TAUSSIG, ADVISER ON CARIBBEAN AFFAIRS, MARCH 15, 1945 (EXTRACT)

Source: *Foreign Relations of the U.S., 1945*, Vol. I, p. 124.

During a conversation with his adviser on Caribbean affairs regarding trusteeship as it related to the United Nations conference, Roosevelt reaffirmed his position that France should not be permitted unconditional control over Indochina once again, although he relented on his previous insistence that Indochina be placed under United Nations trusteeship.

The Peoples of East Asia

The President said he was concerned about the brown people in the East. He said that there are 1,100,000,000 brown people. In many Eastern countries, they are ruled by a handful of whites and they resent it. Our goal must be to help them achieve independence - 1,100,000,000 potential enemies are dangerous. He said he included the 450,000,000 Chinese in that. He then added, Churchill doesn't understand this.

The President said he thought we might have some difficulties with France in the matter of colonies. I said that I thought that was quite probable and it was also probable the British would use France as a "stalking horse."

I asked the President if he had changed his ideas on French Indochina as he had expressed them to us at the luncheon with Stanley.[1] He said no he had not changed his ideas; that French Indo-China and New Caledonia should be taken from France and put under a trusteeship. The President hesitated a moment and then said - well if we can get the proper pledge from France to assume for herself the obligations of a trustee, then I would agree to France retaining these colonies with the proviso that independence was the ultimate goal. I asked the

President if he would settle for self-government. He said no. I asked him if he would settle for dominion status. He said no - it must be independence. He said that is to be the policy and you can quote me in the State Department.

[1]Col. Oliver Stanley, British Secretary of State for the Colonies, who had lunched with the President and Mr. Taussig on January 16, 1945.

(15) <u>DRAFT MEMORANDUM BY G. H. BLAKESLEE, FAR EASTERN DIVISION, DEPARTMENT OF STATE</u>, APRIL, 1945

Source: 851G.00/4-545, State Department Central files, National Archives.

While President Roosevelt was resisting pressures to assist the French military in positioning itself for the postwar reconquest of Indochina, bureaucrats in the State Department's Far Eastern Division were thinking in very different terms. In an annex to a draft memorandum on Indochina and the use of French military resources in Pacific operations, written prior to Roosevelt's death, the Division found Vietnamese unready for self-government and cited antagonism between the Vietnamese and the Khmers and Cambodians as another argument against independence. It recommended against placing any conditions on restoration of French rule or pressure on France to agree to trusteeship, in order to preserve good relations with a friendly state which was expected to join the U.S. in exercising world power. Although the exercise was apparently cut short by Roosevelt's death, it offers insight into State Department views of the Indochina problem at that time.

UNITED STATES POLICY WITH REGARD
TO THE FUTURE OF INDOCHINA

I. <u>POSSIBLE SOLUTIONS</u>

There are three possible solutions for the problem of the disposition of Indochina. It may be restored to France, with or without conditions; it may be granted independence; or it may be placed under an international trusteeship.

II. <u>RESTORATION TO FRANCE</u>

    1. <u>Considerations in favor of Restoration</u>

        a. <u>The Global Situation</u>

If France is to be denied her former position in Indochina she will be to that extent weakened as a world power. It will probably be necessary for the United States to take the lead in any move by which France will be denied her former position in Indochina. If the United States, especially in view of its many unequivocal statements favoring the restoration of the French overseas territories, is the spearhead for partial dismemberment of the French Empire, French resentment will be such as to impose a very serious strain upon our relations and thus tend to defeat basic elements underlying our policy towards France. A disgruntled, psychologically sick and sovereign-conscious France will not augur well for postwar collaboration in Europe and in the world as a whole.

If it is to be the active policy of the United States to seek and insist upon the adoption of measures by which the peoples of dependent areas are to be lifted from their present social condition and are to be given in time opportunity for full self-determination, we should consider whether that aim can best be accomplished in the case of Indochina through cooperation with the French or through denial of any role to France, and operate through an international trusteeship. In reaching that decision we must determine whether it is of more interest to us and the world as a whole to have a strong, friendly, cooperative France, or have a resentful France plus having on our hands a social and administrative problem of the first magnitude.

b. Commitments of the United States Government

"The policy of the Government of the United States has been based upon the maintenance of the integrity of France and of the French Empire and of the eventual restoration of the complete independence of all French territories." (Department of State Press Release of March 2, 1942 (no. 85) relative to situation in New Caledonia.)

"The Government of the United States recognizes the sovereign jurisdiction of the people of France over French possessions overseas. The Government of the United States fervently hopes that it may see the reestablishment of the independence of France and of the integrity of French territory." (Acting Secretary of State in note to the French Ambassador at Washington, April 13, 1942 with respect to the establishment of a consular post at Brazzaville.)

"It is thoroughly understood that French sovereignty will be reestablished as soon as possible throughout all the territory, metropolitan and colonial, over which flew the French flag in 1939." (Mr. Murphy, the Personal Representative of the President, in an unpublished letter of November 2, 1942 to General Giraud.)

"It has been agreed by all French elements concerned and the United States military authorities that French forces will aid and support the forces of the United States and their allies to expel from the soil of Africa the common enemy, to liberate France and restore integrally the French Empire." (Preamble of unpublished Clark-Darlan Agreement of November 22, 1942.)

2. Restoration Subject to Conditions Accepted by Other Colonial Powers in the Pacific and Far East.

Upon the liberation of Indochina and the termination of military operations in that area under the condition that the French Government accepts the following minimum commitments, which it is assumed will also be accepted by the other colonial powers in the Pacific and the Far East: (1) subscription to a colonial charter; (2) membership on behalf of Indochina in a regional commission; and (3) the submission of annual reports on the progress made in Indochina during the year in education, government, and social and economic conditions.

3. Restoration Subject to Additional Conditions.

The considerations which favor placing additional conditions on France are: (1) French administration of Indochina has in general been less satisfactory and less considerate of the interests of the native peoples than have been the administrations of the other leading colonial powers in the Pacific and the Far East, and (2) the French authorities cooperated with the Japanese and permitted them to enter and to effect military control of the colony.

To remedy the more outstanding weaknesses of the French administration of Indochina the United Nations in the Far Eastern area might insist that France be permitted to return to Indochina only after giving commitments to carry out the following reforms:

1. Tariff autonomy for Indochina.

2. The establishment and development of local and central representative institutions; the extension of the franchise as rapidly as possible.

3. Access on equal terms to all occupations and professions by Indo-Chinese; adequate educational and training facilities for all elements of the population.

4. Abolition of compulsory labor and effective supervision of labor contracts.

5. The development of local industries and a more balanced economy.

     The chief considerations against placing additional conditions on France are that such conditions would constitute a discrimination against France and, in view of the national sensitiveness of the French and their devotion to their colonial empire, would probably cause long-continued resentment against the United States, which might embarrass this Government in achieving all of the objectives of its global policies.

4. Restoration Subject to No Conditions.

     The French policy of commercial exclusiveness, the failure to develop representative institutions, the small use made of Indo-chinese in administration, and the failure of the French Indo-chinese Administration to resist Japanese demands, make unconditional restoration of French sovereignty over this strategic corner of Asia highly undesirable.
     A possible consideration in favor of the unconditional restoration of French administration is that if the British and the Dutch should be unwilling to make any commitments in regard to the administration of their dependencies in the Pacific and the Far East, it might appear impolitic to make discriminatory demands on France, in view of the possible unfortunate effects of such demands on United States global policies.

III. INDEPENDENCE FOR INDOCHINA

     Over 17 million of the 24 million inhabitants of Indochina are Annamites. The Annamites are one of the most highly civilized peoples in southeastern Asia, and it would seem reasonable to suppose that, after a preparatory period, they would prove to be politically not less capable than the Thai, who have successfully governed Thailand for centuries, or than the Burmese who, before the war, had achieved the substance of self-government though not the title.
     A nationalist movement of some proportions exists in Indochina. Although the French never favored the growth of an indigenous nationalism, the liberal principles of French political thought inevitably produced a desire for political liberty among educated native people. More particularly, the development of native political consciousness may be traced to grievances against the French rulers. Among these might be listed the contrast between the native standard of living and that of resident Europeans, discrimination in wage levels and in social and professional opportunities, the high cost of living which largely nullified the economic advantages produced by the French regime, inequality before the law, alleged abuses of its privileges by the Roman Catholic Church, unfilled promises of political liberties beyond the limited advisory councils in each colony, failure to train natives for progressive participation in administration, and the thwarted ambitions of the native intelligentsia.
     However, a preparatory period for independence is necessary. At the present, the elements necessary for the early establishment of an independent Indo-

china are lacking. The French policy of permitting only restricted native participation in government has allowed no opportunity for the development of a trained and experienced body of natives capable of assuming full responsibility for the direction of governmental affairs. The nationalist movement has been weakened by factional strife and by lack of solid organization, and has left the great mass of the people unaffected. The antagonism of the Annamites toward the Khmers and Laotians and toward the resident Chinese also limits the possibilities of early native unity.

IV. AN INTERNATIONAL TRUSTEESHIP

There are two considerations which might appear to favor an international trusteeship for Indochina: the interests of the natives and the interests of the United States.

The failure of France to provide adequately for the welfare of the native population might justify placing Indochina under the control of an international administration, which would follow certain prescribed standards designed to develop the basis for eventual independence and for a rising standard of living among the native population.

French administration of Indochina was not directed toward developing colonial self-government, but rather toward progressive integration of the dependency into a closely knit empire dominated by the mother country. French policy, therefore, deliberately restricted the opportunity for native participation in government. The subordinated officials in Cochin-China included a much smaller proportion of natives than would be found in a British or Dutch colony. French economic policy toward Indochina was formulated primarily in terms of the interests of the mother country, not of the colony.

The interests of the United States are opposed to imperialism and favor the progressive development, economically and politically, of dependent peoples until they are prepared for and are granted independence. The peoples in the Far East have a vigorous and emotional opposition to western imperialism and this opposition appears to have increased in strength as a result of Japanese promises and propaganda during the present war. It is to the interest of the United States to dissociate itself in every feasible way from the imperialism of the European powers in the Far East. If the United States should participate in the restoration of France in Indochina, with no conditions or provisions looking to the betterment of native conditions and the development of the people toward independence, it might well weaken the traditional confidence of Eastern peoples in the United States. If Indochina were a problem by itself the solution would appear to be the termination of French rule of an international trusteeship.

A trusteeship might be created by the projected international organization to function within the framework of the plan for international trusteeships which has been approved by the Department. Or, two or more of the leading powers might set up a trusteeship. The trustee powers would necessarily assume, in the name of the people concerned, all rights and responsibilities of sovereignty including security for the peoples, conduct of foreign relations, financial solvency of the administration, and responsibility and power for all acts of government - executive, legislative and judicial. A detailed plan for such a trusteeship has been drafted by an interdivisional committee of the Department, entitled "Draft Outline of an International Trusteeship Government for Indochina" (CAC-114 Preliminary).

The perplexing fact, however, is that France is not the only imperialist power in the Far East. Great Britain and the Netherlands also claim the return of colonies which are now under Japanese military occupation. Each of the colonial powers should give commitments to adopt measures of colonial administration, with some degree of international responsibility, which will further the development of their dependent peoples, along the path toward autonomy or independence.

The problem for the United States is whether it will be advisable, especially in view of the effect on United States global policies, to make demands on France in regard to Indochina when similar demands are not made on Great Britian and the Netherlands in regard to their Pacific and Far Eastern colonies.

(16) INSTRUCTIONS OF THE GENERAL COMMITTEE OF THE VIET MINH, APRIL 16, 1945

Source: *Breaking Our Chains*, pp. 46-51.

In large areas of the country the Viet Minh were able to seize control of the villages following the Japanese coup and set up Liberation Committees, a "pregovernment form" which carried out most of the functions of local government. Instructions sent out to local Viet Minh told how to elect the Committees and what they should do.

I. What is the Liberation Committee?

The Liberation Committee is the expression of the National United Front in the factories, villages etc...

At present imperialist power has fallen to pieces in some regions and become unstable in others.

In such circumstances the Liberation Committee is a pre-governmental form which will train the people to take revolutionary power in their hands.

II. Where may the Liberation Committees be set up?

Liberation Committees may be set up in factories, mines, plantations, schools, garrisons, public offices and private enterprises, villages and hamlets. These are primary committees. Each district, town, province, zone and "Xu" may have its Liberation Committee. The All Viet Nam Liberation Committee will in fact be the Revolutionary Provisional Government of Viet Nam.

III. What will be the tasks of the primary Liberation Committees?

A. The following are the tasks of the Liberation Committees in the factories:

1. To use every means to give a strong boost to the anti-Japanese movement of struggle for national salvation, to make contributions to the Revolution in all fields.

2. To defend the rights and interests of the workers against the oppression and exploitation of foreign employers. To reconcile the workers' rights and interests with those of Vietnamese employers with a view to gathering together all the forces for the struggle against the common enemy: Japanese imperialism.

3. To organize distribution to the workers of rice, salt, clothing, matches, soap-tickets, etc...

4. To lend help to the unemployed.

5. To organize political, military and cultural education for the workers.

6. To settle by mutual agreement disputes between workers.

7. To organize and give impetus to self-defence groups and security groups in communes, workers' quarters, "cun" or "lan" (village or hamlet in mountainous areas).

8. To prevent sabotage and to suppress traitors.

B. The Liberation Committees in the commune will assume the following tasks:

1. To use every means to give a strong fillip to the anti-Japanese strug-

gle for national salvation and to contribute their share to the Revolution in every aspect.

2.   To defend the rights and interests of the commune inhabitants against the harsh Japanese oppression and exploitation.

3.   To organize relief for the poor.

4.   To aid the people to overcome usages and customs that are antiquated and harmful.

5.   To organize the struggle against illiteracy, and to organize the political and military training of the masses.

6.   To settle matters of discord among the people.

7.   To organize and give impetus to the self-defence groups and security groups for the protection of the people's lives and property.

8.   To prevent sabotage and suppress traitors.

N.B. - The attributions of the factory and commune Liberation Committees will be the basis for determining those of the district, province or town committees, while taking into account the particular conditions pertaining to each committee. As for the tasks of the Xu Committees and National Liberation Committee they are evidently more complex and cannot be clearly defined within the framework of these instructions.

IV.   Election of Liberation Committees

1.   According to circumstances, public or clandestine meetings will be organized to elect Liberation Committees.

2.   Before the holding of a meeting, the Viet Minh local organizations must fix the number if Viet Minh candidates; they campaign with members of the national salvation organizations urging them to give their vote to these candidates.

3.   In each locality, it is necessary that each Viet Minh organization should have a representative on the Liberation Committee. Besides, it is advisable to elect to commune Liberation Committees a number of good notables or active and reliable elders. However, care should be taken to prevent opportunist elements or hooligans from penetrating the committees, otherwise their significance will be distorted.

The Liberation committees in small workshops can be composed of both employers and employees.

4.   Liberation committees can be set up even in enterprises or communes where Viet Minh primary organizations do not yet exist. In this case, the Viet Minh organizations in the nearby enterprises or communes must contribute to the election of these committees and through them lay the basis for a Viet Minh organization. But, first of all, they must help these enterprises or communes to set up an "Election Committee" to campaign for the election of the Liberation Committees.

V.   Guidance given to Liberation Committees

1.   The Viet Minh front will guide the Liberation Committees through the "Viet Minh groups". The Viet Minh representatives who are members of a Liberation Committee will form the "Viet Minh group" of the said committee. Prior to each session of the committee, the Viet Minh group must meet to adopt a common position of the various questions on the agenda.

2.   After the election of a Liberation Committee the Viet Minh Committee at the same level will remain in existence. The Viet Minh group in the Liberation Committee must be in close contact with the Viet Minh committee from which it will receive instructions.

VI. Division of tasks in the Liberation Committees

1. The Liberation Committee will appoint a chairman, a vice-chairman, a secretary and members in charge respectively of security and self-defence, social assistance, finance, propaganda and training work, etc...
2. The chairman, vice-chairman and secretary will form the Standing Bureau of the Liberation Committee (in cases where the committee has a large number of members, a few more can be added to the Standing Bureau).

VII. Sub-Committees of the Liberation Committees

1. The Liberation Committee will, according to its needs, set up sub-committees to help carry out its work:
   a) A sub-committee for the organization of shock groups.
   b) A sub-committee for propaganda and training work.
   c) A sub-committee for social assistance and finance, etc...
2. Members of these sub-committees need not necessarily be members of the Liberation Committee. But the chairmen of these sub-committees must be members of the Liberation Committee, appointed by it and responsible to it.
   N.B. Settlement of disputes, wrangles, cases of theft and assault and battery etc., will fall within the competence of a judicial sub-committee. Its decisions will be submitted for the approval of the Standing Bureau before being carried out. As for verdicts on traitors they must be examined and approved by the next higher committee.
3. For each particular action, the Liberation Committee will organize a sub-committee of struggle to mobilize the masses and lead the particular struggle.

VIII. Liberation Committee, Revolutionary Workers' Committee and Revolutionary People's Committee

1. The Liberation Committee is an organization having a pre-governmental character in the pre-insurrectionary period. Its tasks will end with the launching of the general insurrection. It will dissolve to give way, in the factories to Revolutionary Workers' Committees, and in the communes to Revolutionary People's Committees, elected by the people.
2. However, in the zones where our guerillas are active and are masters of the situation, we can immediately set up Revolutionary Workers' Committees or Revolutionary People's Committees; the foundation of Liberation Committees is no longer required in these cases.
3. The Revolutionary Workers' Committees and Revolutionary People's Committees have almost the same tasks:
   a) To arm the masses and mobilize them to join the guerillas in the struggle against the Japanese and the traitors.
   b) To use revolutionary measures to bring to the people genuine freedoms and real benefits.
   c) To consolidate the revolutionary power.

(17) <u>RESOLUTIONS OF THE REVOLUTIONARY MILITARY CONFERENCE OF NORTH VIET-NAM,</u> April 20, 1945

Source: *Breaking Our Chains*, pp. 23-24.

To step up preparations for the general insurrection, the Standing Committee of the Central Committee convened a Revolutionary Military Conference of North Viet-nam in Hiep Hoa District, Bac Giang Province, from April 15 to 20, under Truong Chinh's Chairmanship. It was the party's first major military conference and one of the important results was the nomination of a Revolutionary Military Committee of North Viet-nam which would assume the role of military high command for the whole country. The resolutions of the conference called for stepping up guerilla warfare and creating anti-Japanese resistance base areas.

The Revolutionary Military Conference of North Viet Nam opened at a time when the aggressive and anti-aggressive fronts in the world were entering a decisive phase in their struggle, while within the country the Franco-Japanese conflict was taking place. Following this conflict, the high tide of the anti-Japanese movement for National Salvation was rising, drawing huge masses of the population into the struggle against the enemy. Meanwhile, the rifle shots of the guerillas of our national salvation army touched off the armed struggle of the Vietnamese people against the Japanese aggressors.

I. International situation

Early in 1945, the international situation was full of promise for the anti-fascist front. At the Yalta Conference, the Soviet Union, the United States and Britain decided to launch a general offensive to annihilate the last resistance of Hitler Germany. The Conference also worked out a common plan for the de-nazification of Germany in all fields: military, political, economic and cultural, with the aim of destroying nazism once and for all. On the ruins of a thoroughly defeated fascist Germany, the Conference laid down a firm basis for the collective security of Europe and the future peace of mankind.

The organization of European collective security is but a starting point for international collective security. Therefore, the Soviet Union, the United States and Great Britain and China again took the initiative in convening the San Francisco Conference, gathering together 1,200 delegates from 46 big and small peace-loving states. The question of the Pacific region was placed upon the agenda, and with it, the question of the destiny and future of the oppressed nations in the Far East.

At the Hot Springs Conference, presided over by Britain, the United States, France and China, the progressive stand of the United States and China on the former French colonies was in conflict with the reticent attitude of Britain and the bad faith of France. These various conferences consolidated that anti-fascist front, and the future of humanity was thereby more secured. As Marshall Stalin said: "We shall not only have to win victory but also to turn this war into a means to ensure future world peace".

A. Situation on the European Front

On the East European front the pincers of the Red Army are closing around Berlin.

The death of President Roosevelt has not slowed down the advance of the Allied forces in Hanover. The German capital is in a hopeless position. 300,000 Soviet troops have entered Berlin. Germany is dying. Soon the war in Europe will be over with the complete collapse of fascism.

B. The East Asian Front

In East Asia the Allied offensive against the Japanese has entered its decisive phase. The Philippines battle is nearing its end. The sea-lines from Japan to its colonies in the south are completely cut off. The Burma battle is also closing with the victory of the British army. The supply line to China is wide open, and this has a great effect on the consolidation of the Chinese front and the Chinese offensive in South China.

An anti-war movement has broken out in Japan. The Koiso government has fallen. Recently, the Chinese Communist Party held a military conference in

South China. It is very likely that this event is related to the preparations for an American landing in South China.

But the most important events which have occurred in East Asia during April are the denunciation by the Soviet Union of the non-aggression pact signed with Japan, and the Soviet Union's action in placing Soviet air bases at the disposal of the Allied forces, thus enabling them to strike at the very heart of Japan. The Red Army has taken a direct part in the events that will decide the fate of the oppressed nations in East Asia. The whole of East Asia rejoices at the hopeless situation of Japan.

C. International revolutionary movement

Simultaneously with the anti-fascist war, the international revolutionary movement of liberation is growing too. In Europe, nearly all the German colonies have been liberated. "National Independence" is the first characteristic of the present revolutionary movement.

Besides, this is a "New Democratic" movement. Broad masses of workers and peasants have risen up to sweep away the shackles of the old bourgeois democratic regime. From Finland to Belgium and from Rumania to Italy, everywhere the Communists are participating in the exercise of State power. In France especially, the close alliance of the Communist and Socialist Parties has forced upon the de Gaulle government a vast economic programme and a genuinely democratic regime.

In East Asia, the Chinese resistance is going on. Under the influence of the people's movement and the progressive tendency in the world, China has become further democratized. The Kuomintang government has been partly reformed. The negotiations between the Kuomintang and the Communist Party have achieved some results.

Following the example of the Chinese people, the Korean people are intensifying their struggle for independence. The Philippines already enjoy autonomy. And in spite of the deplorable internal split between the Hindu and the Moslem sects within the National Congress, India has also been drawn into the anti-Japanese struggle.

The whole of the East, which has risen up to take part in the anti-Japanese struggle, is determined to avail itself of the opportunity to win back national independence and establish a new democratic regime.

*****

In a word, the mortal combat between the aggressive front and the anti-aggressive front is going on from Europe to Asia. The destruction of Japan, though not so imminent as that of Germany, is no longer very far off. A new world, a world of new democracy, is being built up thanks to the sacrifices of humanity fighting against fascism. This extremely favourable objective situation has boosted the Vietnamese revolutionary movement and is one of the conditions that will ensure the victory of the national liberation revolution of our people.

II. Franco-Japanese conflict in Indochina

In Indochina the Franco-Japanese conflict broke out at a time when the Japanese had been driven into a hopeless situation.

A. On March 9, 1945, the Japanese attacked and occupied the important towns and bases in Indochina. This *coup de force* was due to three causes:

First, two imperialists cannot for long share a fat spoil between them.

Second, in face of an imminent Allied landing in Indochina, the Japanese had to destroy the French to avoid the danger of being stabbed in the back.

Third, the Japanese had to consolidate their position in Indochina and cling at all cost to the continental road that links the metropolis with the colonies in the south.

B. In spite of a lot of noise made by the de Gaulle government about the French resistance in Indochina, it was in truth defeated from the very start. Except in a few localities such as Mong Cai, Lao Cay, Lai Chau and Lang Son where the resistance lasted only a few days, everywhere the great majority of the French surrendered in cowardly fashion to the Japanese, or withdrew shamefully. As a result, after a few days, the Japanese had wiped out the French forces in Indochina and the whole Indochinese administrative machinery fell into Japanese hands.

Why were the French defeated so quickly? First of all because the French troops had never had any fighting spirit. They had put all their hopes in British-American aid and not in their own strength. When they realized that the British-American forces could not land immediately to rescue them, their ranks at once disintegrated. Secondly because the French in Indochina had maintained to the last minutes an extremely reactionary and stupid attitude towards the Indochinese peoples. That was why in spite of the great efforts of the anti-Japanese organizations in Indochina such as the Communist Party and the Viet Minh Front, there could not be wide cooperation between the French and the Indochinese peoples in the anti-Japanese struggle. There were, in addition, other causes such as the numerical superiority of the Japanese forces and the superiority of their armaments. But these were of minor importance.

C. Of what importance to us is this *coup de force*?

The *coup de force* was for a certain time the nodal point of the contradictions between the two aggressors in our country. French administration has completely disintegrated and the Japanese have not yet had time to set up as effective an apparatus of repression as that of the French. Whence there has developed a political crisis particularly favourable to the development of the anti-Japanese movement. On the other hand, because the Japanese aggressors have become our only enemy and because the revolutionary people have become the only forces fighting against the Japanese, our diplomatic relations with the Allied forces can be carried out in better conditions than before.

D. After the *coup de force*

After having overthrown the French, the Japanese actively carried out a policy of deceit towards our people. They granted us a fake independence, allowed the national traitors to set up puppet governments, and did their utmost to create a pro-Japanese movement. Their intention is to make full use of manoeuvers which are meant to deceive the Vietnamese people, to use the Vietnamese against Vietnamese. But it was not long before they had to unmask themselves. Their cruelty and their policy of exploitation have stirred the awareness even of those who have until now hesitated to side with the anti-Japanese forces. The more the anti-Japanese movement grows the more acutely our enemy feels the shortage of cadres among the Vietnamese traitors. The necessity quickly to consolidate their positions in Indochina has forced them to take power into their own hands, to cling to the old feudal machinery so loathed by the people and to keep on the French functionaries. In consequence, numerous elements who were at the beginning drawn to the side of the Japanese and the traitors by promises of national liberation and independence have turned away, disappointed, to side with the anti-Japanese forces of our entire people. However, the Japanese have not as yet given up their deceitful schemes. On the contrary, they are trying all the harder to mobilize a gang of traitors from among the less implicated in the political arena, to form a puppet government. And after

the bitter failure of the Dai Viet clique and the Provisional Administrative
Committee of North Viet Nam they have set up the Tran Trong Kim cabinet. But
the people will realize that changes in pawns will not bring about any changes
in the anti-patriotic and anti-national character of the puppet government.
Therefore our task is to enlighten the Indochinese peoples as soon as possible
on this matter.

III.   The anti-Japanese movement for national
salvation of the Indochinese peoples

After the Japanese *coup de force*, having recognized the anti-patriotic character of the puppet government and the deceitful manoeuvres of the Japanese,
the Vietnamese people have risen up in a vast anti-Japanese movement for national salvation.

In North Viet Nam leaflets were distributed and placards posted in Hanoi and
in nearly all provinces exposing the Japanese schemes and calling on the people
to take part in the anti-Japanese resistance for national salvation. Meetings,
demonstrations and displays of force with banners and streamers carrying slogans
calling to resistance were held in Bac Ninh, Phuc Yen, Son Tay, Hung Yen, Ninh
Binh provinces etc. Thousands of armed demonstrators in Bac Ninh, Bac Giang,
Thai Nguyen and Ninh Binh provinces stormed the paddy stores set up by the Japanese and French reactionary planters and distributed their paddy stocks to the
poor. Our guerillas destroyed the enemy's communication lines, occupied the
district administration offices and military posts, seized enemy guns, gave
chase to traitors and ruffians and set up people's power in the provinces of Cao
Bang, Thai Nguyen, Bac Can, Bac Giang, Lang Son, Tuyen Quang etc. Political
prisoners at Nghia Lo (Yen Bay province) broke open the doors of their jails.

In central Viet Nam, the Viet Minh is particularly active at My Tho and in
the region of the Bassac (Western arm of the Mekong).

The movement of struggle against the Japanese is rising and bringing about
a powerful extension of the Viet Minh organizations. In some localities membership has increase six-fold since the *coup de force*. Liberation Committees
and People's Revolutionary Committees have been set up in various places to take
in hand local power and also to call on the people to struggle against the Japanese. Reviewing the development of the movement we find in it many good
points, but also it has many shortcomings.

Good points:

1. We have changed our tactic in accordance with the development of the
situation, concentrated our forces in good time and directed them against the
Japanese fascists.

2. The movement bears the distinct character of a powerful and armed
struggle.

3. It is in the struggle against the Japanese that there has emerged a
broad and National United Front against the common enemy.

Shortcomings:

1. In general, the movement has developed very unevenly (in some places it
has gone a bit too far and in others the impetus has been too weak).

2. We have not trained activists in each locality to lead the movement in
case the enemy resorts to terror.

3. We have not been able to set up broad basic organizations of workers,
particularly in the transport branch.

4. Not enough attention has been paid to political work in the army.

IV.   Eventual allied landing in Indochina

There are still people who hold that the Allies should take the war directly
to the territory of Japan and that once the metropolis is defeated, the Japanese
troops in the colonies would capitulate. The Conference estimates that sooner
or later Allied troops will enter Indochina. First, because of the fairly important strategic position of Indochina and because the Japanese forces stationed here are relatively big. Second, because of the conflict of interests in
Indochina between the French and British on the one hand and the Americans and
Chinese on the other. This rivalry which came to light at the Hot Springs Conference, will prompt them to rush into Indochina to defend their respective interests. Thus, toward these two groups of allies, Chinese and Americans on the
one hand and British and Gaullist French on the other, who all want to have
their share of interests in our country, our attitude must be as follows:

In the diplomatic field:
a) To profit by the antagonism between the Chinese and Americans and the
British and Gaullist French to obtain aid from the outside, sign agreements with
the Allies and bring them to recognize our national independence.
b) In addition, our diplomats must struggle for Viet Nam to be represented
at the international peace conferences.
c) To bring before world opinion documents relating to the atrocities and
reactionary deeds of the French colonialists, and the Viet Minh policy of cooperation with the French who struggled actively against the Japanese.

At home:

a) Actively to prepare our forces; not to rely on others.
b) To develop guerilla units immediately and on a large scale and keep them
ready to cooperate with the Allies.
According to our estimates, the Allied offensive could begin at various
points. In the North: the border provinces of Cao Bang, Lang Son and Ha Giang.
In the Eastern and Southern coastal areas: the Gulf of Tonkin, Cam Ranh Bay,
and Saigon. In the West: Upper Laos and Dien Bien Phu (coming from Burma).
Having foreseen this, how should we receive the Allied forces and cooperate
with them? At points where the landing takes place, we should mobilize the
people to welcome them and appoint delegates to come into contact with them.
On the other hand, local troops should be mobilized for the destruction of the
communication and supply lines of the Japanese and, together with the Allied
forces, fight the common enemy. During this time we should strive to occupy
the key positions and keep the initiative. But this does not mean that immediately after the Allied landing we should launch the general insurrection.
On the contrary, we should wait until the Japanese have thrown in all their
forces to ward off the Allied attack, until their rear lines are in disorder,
before we launch the general insurrection. There is one point we must bear in
mind: in case of abuses and extortions on the part of the landing troops (for
example on the part of Chinese troops commanded by corrupt officers) we should
use diplomacy to avoid all incidents likely to harm the common struggle against
the Japanese.

V.   Our immediate tasks

A.   In the military field

In view of the present situation, for the time being military problems have
priority over all other important and urgent tasks. We must actively intensify
guerilla warfare, set up resistance bases and prepare ourselves for the timely
launching of the general insurrection.

1. Necessity to define the limits of the resistance zones and their respective tasks:

  a) The Le Roi Resistance zone (North Viet Nam)
  b) The Hoang Hoa Tham Resistance zone (North Viet Nam)
  c) The Quang Trung Resistance zone (North Viet Nam)
  d) The Tran Hung Dao Resistance zone (North Viet Nam)
  e) The Phan Dinh Phung Resistance zone (Central Viet Nam)
  f) The Trung Trac Resistance zone (Central Viet Nam)
  g) The Nguyen Tri Phuong Resistance zone (South Viet Nam).

The Revolutionary Military Committee will reorganize the Quang Trung Resistance zone and set up the Tran Hung Dao Resistance zone. All big zones, such as the Nguyen Tri Phuong zone, can be subdivided into many sectors.

2. Necessity to establish direct liaison among the zones in the North, Centre and South of Viet Nam.

This task is entrusted to the "Vanguard Unit to Advance Southwards", which is under the direct command of the Revolutionary Military Committee.

3. Necessity urgently to create bases of Resistance for the struggle against the Japanese.

In regions having favourable conditions as to natural features, mass organizations, food supplies, and a favourable balance of forces between ourselves and the enemy, we must create bases of Resistance. For example the crescents of mountains that line the delta of North Viet Nam, the Truong Son mountain range in Central Viet Nam and the marshlands in South Viet Nam.

Within all the large bases, it is necessary to organize smaller but stronger bases which can temporarily become smaller but surer fields of operation in case of an enemy offensive. The communication and liaison lines between the bases must be safeguarded. These bases will serve as spring-boards for the general insurrection and constitute the nucleus of the future independent and free Viet Nam.

4. Necessity to unify, consolidate and develop the Liberation Army.

  a) Name. -- Viet Nam Liberation Army.
The Resistance zones can, according to their needs, organize armed propaganda groups as part of the Viet Nam Liberation Army.
  b) Composition of the Army. -- The composition of the Viet Nam Liberation Army must be in conformity with the attached table.
  c) Effective force. -- Basing itself upon the requirements of the situation, the number and quality of cadres, stocks of arms and munitions and food, the Revolutionary Military Committee must immediately re-organize the Liberation Army into a powerful force.
  d) Strengthening of the Army. -- We must stregthen our troops, select recruits, unify political and military training, carry out political work in the army, strengthen discipline, fight against the tendencies to pillage and regionalism.
  e) Development of the Liberation troops. -- We must immediately organize self-defence groups, fighting self-defence groups and regional units.

5. Unification of the military command.

  a) The Revolutionary Military Committee assumes the High Command of the whole country. It appoints Political Delegates, Regimental Commanders and Political Commissars. Junior officers are proposed or appointed by their direct chiefs, subject to approval by the Revolutionary Military Committee.
  b) Each Resistance zone has its own command and also one or several Political Delegates, representatives or envoys of the Revolutionary Military Committee.

6. Organization of special units.

-- Workers' units
-- Women's units
-- Picked units
-- Foreign combatants' units

7. Institution of a flag of honour.

We must institute a flag of honour and inscribe on it the names of units which have scored great exploits, and an order of National Salvation to reward fighters of the Liberation Army who have distinguished themselves by their heroism.

8. Armament and equipment

a) The control and distribution of arms belongs to the Revolutionary Military Committee.
b) Workshops must be set up to repair and manufacture guns, and manufacture bombs and cartridges. The Revolutionary Military Committee will work out the plan for this. By means of a circular it will request the North Viet Nam Committee and the Le Loi zone to recruit new technicians.
c) The utmost efforts must be made for the collection and purchase of weapons.
d) We must have adequate stocks of food. The communes should set up stores of paddy for the Liberation Army. In the Resistance bases, food must be stocked. The Revolutionary Military Committee will study the establishment of a system of purchase and transport of salt.

9. How we should fight against the Japanese offensive?

a) We are now in the strategic phase of "launching guerilla warfare" in preparation for the general insurrection. In consequence our tactics are to ambush and attack the enemy by surprise in small engagements when we are quite certain of success. We can thus maintain and increase our forces.
b) We will launch guerilla warfare in many resistance zones, set up new bases and be prepared for enemy encirclement.
c) In case of encirclement of a base by the enemy, our tactics will be "offence for defence". When conditions for the defence of a base no longer exist, we must withdraw without hesitation in order to keep our forces intact.
d) In case of the penetration of enemy troops into our bases we must energetically carry out the tactics of "scorched earth" and small towns must be evacuated.
e) We must perseveringly carry out active propaganda in all forms among the Japanese soldiers to destroy their morale.
f) The Resistance zones and bases must co-ordinate their actions.
g) Concerning villages situated outside our bases, if the Japanese come to concentrate the villagers and burn down houses, we must lead the masses in the struggle according to the circumstances by means of petitions, demonstrations, etc...
In case of forced concentration, our troops must help the people to organize armed struggle.

B. Extension to the whole country of the broad
anti-Japanese movement for national salvation

a) We must avail ourselves of this broad movement to widen the National United Front by actively winning over to our struggle the progressive feudal and bourgeois elements. Particular attention must be given to initiating the movement in towns, enterprises and in zones along the important communication lines.

b) We must launch guerilla warfare in the Resistance zones. This is the principal form of struggle for the promotion of the anti-Japanese movement.

c) In places where conditions are not yet suitable for waging guerilla war-fare, the main forms of struggle are meetings, political demonstrations, armed parades, displays of force, etc.

At present, the organization of self-defence groups, fighting self-defence groups and local troops is of primary importance. Agitation tactics consist in exploiting the effect of the famine and the appropriation of paddy and oil-bearing crops to fan the hatred of the people and make them understand that the Japanese have not come to liberate us. It is in this manner that we will be able to draw the people into the struggle.

d) Basing itself upon the concrete situation, the Conference estimates that at the present time we must guide the people in the organization of revolution-ary power, or transitional forms of state-power.

In the Resistance bases, we must organize Revolutionary People's Committees elected by universal suffrage or by delegates of the workers, peasants, traders, women, youth, armymen, civil servants, minority nationalities, Viet Minh cadres, etc. But these committees will not necessarily include representatives of all social strata. The power exercised by the Committees if a democratic power, that of the Anti-Japanese National United Front.

These Revolutionary People's Committees will be unified up to provincial level then to zone level.

Outside our bases, where we have not yet completely overthrown the enemy power, Liberation Committees will be set up.

In the Resistance zone, the Revolutionary People's Committees and Liberation Committees are placed under the Military Command and the Revolutionary Military Committee. These committees will divide the work among themselves in a rational way, bearing in mind the main tasks: propaganda and agitation work, suppression of traitors, economic and financial questions, social assistance, education, justice, and military questions.

The Conference proposes the convening of a National Congress composed of representatives of all social strata, political parties and personalities in the country to set up the Viet Nam National Liberation Committee and move for-ward to the founding of the Provisional Government of Viet Nam.

e) The policy to be carried out is based on the following main points:

1. General mobilization of the masses for the anti-Japanese struggle.

2. Implementation of democratic rights in the spirit of new democracy (civic rights, human rights, property rights, sex equality, national self-determination), carrying out of the Viet Minh policy while taking into account the general conditions of the struggle and the practical conditions particular to each region.

3. Improvement of the people's livelihood to stimulate them to take part in the struggle.

4. Suppression of traitors and repression of ill-doers.

f) The agrarian problem will be settled in accordance with the two follow-ing principles:

1. Implementation of the policy "land to the tiller".

2. Reconciliation of the poor peasants' interests with those of the rich peasants and landlords, in order to strengthen the National United Front.

The agrarian problem will be settled by distributing to the people land belonging to traitors or by opening up virgin land through collective work.

g) We must actively develop and unify the Viet Minh organizations; par-ticular attention should be paid to initiating the youth movement.

h) We must point out to the people how dangerous the traitors are and help them to discover and expose the manoeuvres of the pro-Japanese elements.

i) Propaganda among the enemy ranks will be carried out as follows:

With troops of Vietnamese nationality: a member of the Party's Provincial Committee will organize a provincial propaganda committee. It will arrange for reliable men to infiltrate the enemy ranks. Through their families, we will get into contact with the troops and win them over to our cause. Women will be used in propaganda work. The people should be trained for propaganda in the enemy's ranks. Appeals should be made by means of leaflets and placards.

As for the Japanese troops, leaflets and placards in Japanese and Chinese should be used.

C. Propaganda

1. At present, our propaganda must be directed to this main target: fighting the Japanese.

We must:

-- Expose their rule, their policy of oppression and deceit and point out that the puppet government has been set up to use Vietnamese to rule Vietnamese.
-- Point out why it is that resistance to the Japanese is our only way of salvation.
-- Point out that the anti-Japanese struggle, though extremely hard, will certainly be victorious (by highlighting the recent successful fights against the Japanese).
2. Forms and methods of propaganda. -- In addition to the distribution of leaflets, display of flags and use of placards and banners, we must organize meetings, speeches, and demonstrations with displays of force, and use whistles, megaphones, drums, rattles and horns to create an enthusiastic atmosphere. We must organize exhibitions and create shock propaganda units, training them to speak in public, and organize sing-songs (a handbook for speakers will be issued). We must take good care of the visitors who come to the Resistance zones and we must take photographs of these zones.
3. The paper "The Struggle Against the Japanese", issued by the Propaganda unit called "Liberation Army", will be regarded as the organ of the Viet Nam Liberation army.

Handbooks for political and military training will be prepared or reprinted.

D. Cadres

1. Political courses must be organized in the districts for the training of local cadres.
2. We must select a number of soldiers of valour in the army and train them to become commanders and political commissars.
3. A Viet Nam political and Military College for the Anti-Japanese struggle will be founded.
4. We must recruit gifted people. For the first course, X pupils will be sent to Y Resistance zone for military training.
5. All cadres must receive military training.

E. Finance

1. Establishment of a fund for the Revolutionary Military Committee: the Resistance zones must contribute 50 per cent of their receipts.
2. Issue of one million "Trust Bonds" for the use of the Liberation Army.

F.   The question of alliance with the Gaullist French
and the Chinese residents in the
anti-Japanese struggle

1.   In our alliance with the Gaullist French abroad, stress must be laid on our determination to win complete independence. As to the French who are still living in our country, we must demand that they declare their recognition of our right to independence.

2.   A sub-committee will be set up to win over the Chinese residents. Leaflets will be distributed calling on them to organize with us a Chinese - Vietnamese alliance for the anti-Japanese struggle.

G.   Setting up of the revolutionary military
committee of North Viet Nam

1.   Name. -- Revolutionary Military Committee of North Viet Nam, the Command of the Liberation Army of North Viet Nam.

2.   Organization. -- The Committee will be responsible for setting up the following organs and assigning tasks to them: a political bureau, a commissariat and finance, communications and transport, and military health ministries. It will found a Political and Military College for the anti-Japanese struggle.

3.   Responsibilities and power: The Committee assumes the political and military command of the Resistance bases in North Viet Nam and will help in the military organization of the whole country.

4.   The Committee will make an appeal to the army and the people urging them forward to fight the enemy.

H.   Self-criticism

Analysis of the anti-Japanese movement has enabled the Conference to see that in the recent period of struggle we have numerous strong points but also many shortcomings:

Strong points:

1.   We have changed our tactics in time with the development of the situation.

2.   In spite of barbarous French repression, we have maintained our clear-sighted leadership and kept our ranks firm.

3.   In propaganda work, leaflets, books and newspapers issued by the Front have made great progress in both content and form and have been particularly well received by the people.

Shortcomings:

1.   We have not as yet completely wiped out all vestiges of our old tendency to isolation.

2.   We have not made enough efforts for the training of political and military cadres.

3.   Many a time, it was found impossible to maintain communications and it follows that unified leadership could not be realized.

4.   There is still self-complacency in our ranks, those who have their heads turned by a little success.

5.   We were not vigilant enough and the control in our ranks was not as strict as it should have been so that in some places traitors were able to penetrate our bases to sabotage them.

Comrades!

We must make good these shortcomings as quickly as we can to strengthen and develop our ranks in order to meet the requirements of the movement and assume the great tasks in this pre-insurrectionary period and in the coming period of general insurrection.

(18) <u>DRAFT MEMORANDUM FOR THE PRESIDENT, DIVISION OF EUROPEAN AFFAIRS</u>,
APRIL 20, 1945.

Source: *U.S. Vietnam Relations*, Book 8, pp. 6-8.

Following Roosevelt's death on April 12, 1945, the State Department began a review of policy toward Indochina. The process was initiated by the Division of European Affairs, which recommended that the U.S. not oppose restoration of Indochina to France.

Subject: Suggested Reexamination of American Policy
with Respect to Indo-China

General Observations

1. The Japanese aggression against the French in Indo-China last month has brought about a marked increase in the number of proposals advanced by the French for the use of French forces and resources in the Pacific.

2. The consequences of these military developments make it clear that our last policy, which held that the disposition of Indo-China was a matter for post-war determination and that the United States should not become involved in military effort for its liberation, is in urgent need for reexamination and clarification. This is particularly so in order that American military and naval authorities may have guidance to enable them to take appropriate action with respect to the French proposals referred to above.

3. The United States Government has publicly taken the position that it recognizes the sovereign jurisdiction of France over French possessions overseas when those possessions are resisting the enemy and had expressed the hope that it will see the reestablishment of the integrity of French territory. In spite of this general assurance, the negative policy so far pursued by this Government with respect to Indo-China has aroused French suspicions concerning our intentions with respect to the future of that territory. This has had and continues to have a harmful effect on American relations with the French Government and people.

4. On April 3, 1945, the Secretary of State with the approval of the President issued a statement of which the following excerpt is pertinent to the present problem:

"As to territorial trusteeship, it appeared desirable that the
Governments represented at Yalta, in consultation with the Chinese
Government and the French Provisional Government, should endeavor
to formulate proposals for submission to the San Franciso Conference
for a trusteeship structure as a part of the general organization.
This trusteeship structure, it was felt, should be defined to permit
the placing under it of the territories taken from the enemy in this
war, as might be agreed upon at a later date, <u>and also such other
territories as might voluntarily be placed under trusteeship</u>."

5. General de Gaulle and his Government have made it abundantly clear that they expect a proposed Indo-Chinese federation to function within the framework of the "French Union." There is consequently not the slightest possibility at the present time or in the foreseeable future that France will volunteer to place Indo-China under an international trusteeship, or will consent to any program of international accountability which is not applied to the colonial possessions of other powers. If an effort were made to exert pressure on the French Government, such action would have to be taken by the United States alone for France could rely upon the support of other colonial powers, notably Great Britain and the Netherlands. Such action would likewise run counter to

the established American policy of aiding France to regain her strength in order that she may be better fitted to share responsibility in maintaining the peace of Europe and the world.

Recommendations

In the light of the above considerations, the following recommendations, which have been communicated to the War and Navy Departments, are submitted for your approval.

1. The Government of the United States should neither oppose the restoration of Indo-China to France, with or without a program of international accountability, nor take any action toward French overseas possessions which it is not prepared to take or suggest with regard to the colonial possessions of our other Allies.

2. The Government of the United States should continue to exert its influence with the French in the direction of having them effect a liberalization of their past policy of limited opportunities for native participation in government and administration, as well as a liberalization of restrictive French economic policies formerly pursued in Indo-China.

3. The French Provisional Government should be informed confidentially that, owing to the need of concentrating all our resources in the Pacific on operations already planned, large-scale military operations aimed directly at the liberation of Indo-China cannot be contemplated at this time.

4. French offers of military and naval assistance in the Pacific should be considered on their merits as bearing upon the objective of defeating Japan, as in the case of British and Dutch proposals. The fact that acceptance of a specific proposal might serve to strengthen French claims for the restoration of Indo-China to France should not be regarded as grounds for rejection. On the contrary, acceptance of French proposals for military assistance in the defeat of Japan should be regarded as desirable in principle, subject always to military requirements in the theater of operations.

5. While avoiding specific commitments with regard to the amount or character of any assistance which the United States may give to the French resistance forces in Indo-China, this Government should continue to afford all possible assistance provided it does not interfere with the requirements of other planned operations.

6. In addition to the aid which we are able to bring from the China theater of operations to the French forces resisting the Japanese in Indo-China, the United States should oppose no obstacle to the implementation of proposals looking toward the despatch of assistance to those forces from the southeast Asia theater of operations, provided such assistance does not constitute a diversion of resources which the Combined Chiefs of Staff consider are needed elsewhere.

(19) <u>DRAFT MEMORANDUM FOR THE PRESIDENT, DIVISION OF FAR EAST AFFAIRS,</u> APRIL 21, 1945.

Source: *U.S. Vietnam Relations, Book 8*, pp. 9-17.

The State Department's Division of Far Eastern Affairs, while agreeing with the basic recommendation of the European Division, urged that the U.S. seek assurances from France that it would extend at least a measure of self-government to Indochina - though not necessarily complete independence.

With reference to the memorandum for the President on "Suggested Reexamination of American Policy with Respect to Indochina", FE makes the following comments and suggested changes:

Paragraph 1. FE concurs.

Paragraph 2. FE believes that this paragraph should be simplified to express only the need for a determination of policy.

Paragraph 3. FE concurs with the first sentence but believes that, in amplification, reference should be made to the fact that Indochina has until recently collaborated with the enemy. It believes that the balance of the paragraph should be omitted in view of the proposed revision of paragraph 2.

Paragraphs 4 and 5. FE fully concurs, but suggests that a brief summary - which to complete the record should include President Roosevelt's views - would suffice. It also believed that the last sentence of paragraph 5 is important enough to warrant separate statement with a caveat regarding American interests in Southeast Asia.

In addition to the general observations included in the memorandum, FE believes that to present a complete picture, the memorandum should include:

A. A statement of the joint State-War-Navy decisions already made regarding Indochina.
B. Reference to the collaborationist history of the French administration in Indochina in distinction to the record of the colonies of our other Allies.
C. Statements to the increasingly profound interest of the United States in the future of Southeast Asia.
D. A statement as to the independence sentiment in Indochina.
E. Reference to the French statements on Indochina indicating some concessions to the idea of autonomy for the French administration of Indochina, but which do not indicate an intention to permit genuine Indochinese self-government; and to the apparent reasons for these concessions.
F. Reference to the effect on China of past French economic policies in Indochina, and Chinese fears for the safety of its southwest flank.
G. Reference to the danger inherent in the Thailand-Indochina boundary questions.

Recommendations 1 and 2. Recommendation 1, as drafted, refers to more than Indochina and would inject, for instance, problems involved in the Condominium Government of the New Hebrides. FE concurs in the basic policy that the United States should not seek a trusteeship for Indochina or international accountability unless similar action is to be sought from the British and the Dutch. It believes, however, that for the protection of American interests it is essential that French policies in Indochina follow a pattern more liberal than any heretofore announced. FE believes also that under present circumstances a policy of merely exerting influence to achieve such a result will not prove adequate.

Several times during the past few years the French authorities have made announcements regarding the future of Indochina which, though still inadequate to assure peace and stability in the area, indicates an intention to change their pre-war policies towards Indochina. It is the belief of FE that this change in attitude has been due, first, to a realization of the anti-French, independence sentiment among the Indochinese who must be wooed if French administration is to be successful and, second, to uncertainty as to the attitude of the United States and a feeling that United States support for restoration can be secured only by adoption of a more liberal policy. Any indication at this time that the United States will not oppose French restoration in Indochina would negate American influence in securing French policies consonant with American interest. Accordingly, FE suggests that no statement of American policy with respect to post-war Indochina should be communicated to the Provisional French Government at this time.

Because the liberation of Indochina is, in fact, dependent on American defeat of Japan; because we are sacrificing blood and treasure to assure peace and stability in the Far East, post-war maintenance of which will be largely our responsibility; because without recognition of the dynamic trends towards self-government among the peoples of Asia there can be no peace and stability in the Far East and the peoples of Southeast Asia may embrace ideologies contrary to our own or develop a pan-Asiatic movement against all western powers, FE believes that it would not be unreasonable for the United States to insist that the French give adequate assurances as to the implementing of policies in Indochina which we consider essential to assure peace and stability in the Far East.

We urge, therefore, that the policy of the United States should be not to oppose the restoration of Indochina to France, provided the French give adequate assurances as to the following:

a. Development of a national or federal government to be run for and increasingly by the Indochinese themselves with no special privileges for French or other persons who are not inhabitants and citizens of Indochina so that within the foreseeable future Indochina may be fully self-governing and autonomous along democratic lines, except in matters of imperial concern in which Indochina should be a partner in the French Union.

b. Maintenance of a policy of non-discriminatory treatment and of complete economic and commercial equality.

c. Establishment of Haiphong as a free port with tax-free transit facilities between Haiphong and China.

d. Acceptance of a frontier between Indochina and Thailand, to be determined by an impartial, international commission.

e. Acceptance of such international security arrangements, including American or international bases, as may be determined to be necessary for international security, including protection of China's southwestern flank.

Recommendation 3. FE believes that the last part of the paragraph should be modified in accordance with military plans already adopted so that the French will not vainly hope for either American military operations or American supplies for the liberation of Indochina.

Recommendation 4. FE suggests that the first sentence be clarified to specify that French offers of assistance will be considered "solely on their military merits". It believes that with this change the balance of the paragraph is unnecessary and should be omitted.

Recommendation 5. FE believes that this paragraph should be omitted. If assistance can be given the French which will aid in the defeat of Japan without interfering with American strategic considerations, the military authorities can raise any political questions involved at that time. Meanwhile, FE believes that it would be desirable politically for the United States not to lend military aid to or be associated with the reestablishment of French control over Indochina.

Recommendation 6. There are now less than a thousand French resistance forces in Indochina (the rest having crossed the border to China) and this paragraph would appear unnecessary in a statement of policy recommendations.

Attached is a suggested draft of the memorandum to the President embodying the above modifications and changes, which FE earnestly believes are of great importance for the establishment and maintenance of peace and stability in the Far East.

Subject: American Policy with Respect to Indochina

General Observations

1.   The Japanese aggression against the French in Indochina last month has brought about a marked increase in the number of proposals advanced by the French for the use of French forces and resources in the Pacific.

2.   These proposals and recent military developments make it essential that the United States reach a definitive determination regarding its policy towards Indochina rather than, as heretofore considered, the disposition of Indochina a matter of postwar determination.

3.   The joint State-War-Navy authorities have reached the decision that all American military efforts must be directed entirely to the major issue of defeating Japan in its homeland and that, for military reasons, American troops should not be used or equipment needed in American operations be utilized for the liberation of Indochina.

4.   It is established American policy to aid France to regain her strength in order that she may be better fitted to share responsibility in maintaining the peace of Europe - where her chief interests lie - and of the world.   However, in pursuing this policy, the United States must not jeopardize its own increasingly important interests in Southeast Asia.

5.   The United States Government has publicly taken the position that it recognizes the sovereign jurisdiction of France over French possessions overseas when those possessions are resisting the enemy, and has expressed the hope that it will see the reestablishment of the integrity of French territory.

6.   Until the last few weeks the French administration of Indochina has collaborated with the Japanese in marked distinction to the administrations of colonial areas belonging to our other Allies.

7.   President Roosevelt recognized the future increasing importance to the United States of Southeast Asia.   He saw the necessity of aiding the 150,000,000 people there to achieve improved social, economic and political standards.

He realized that dynamic forces leading toward self-government are growing in Asia; that the United States - as a great democracy - cannot and must not try to retard this development but rather act in harmony with it; and that social, economic or political instability in the area may threaten the peace and stability of the Far East and indeed the world.

8.   As his solution of this problem, as it relates to Indochina, President Roosevelt long favored placing Indochina under a trusteeship.   However, on April 3, 1945, the Secretary of State with the approval of the President issued a statement relative to the plans approved at Yalta which would indicate that Indochina could come under the trusteeship structure only by voluntary action of the French.   It is abundantly clear that there is no possibility at the present time or in the foreseeable future that France will volunteer to place Indochina under trusteeship, or consent to any program of international accountability which is not applied to the colonial possessions of other powers.   If an effort were made to exert pressure on the French Government, such action would have to be taken by the United States alone for France could rely upon the support of other colonial powers, notably Great Britain and the Netherlands.

9.   The prewar French administration in Indochina was the least satisfactory colonial administration in Asia, both as regards the development and interests of the native peoples and as regards economic relations with other countries. Among the Annamites there is increasing opposition to French rule.   The Chinese

are giving active support to the independence movement. France will probably encounter serious difficulty in reimposing French control in Indochina.

10. If really liberal policies towards Indochina are not adopted by the French - policies which recognize the paramount interest of the native peoples and guarantee within the foreseeable future a genuine opportunity for true, autonomous self-government - there will be substantial bloodshed and unrest for many years, threatening the economic and social progress and the peace and stability of Southeast Asia.

11. On several occasions in the past few years, French authorities have issued policy statements on the future of Indochina. These show a growing trend toward greater autonomy for the French administration of Indochina, but even the recent statement of March 24 is vague and, when examined with care, indicates little intention of permitting genuine self-rule for the Indochinese. The change in French attitude towards Indochina is believed to have been occasioned by clearer realization of the anti-French sentiment among the Annamites and a belief that American approval of French restoration can be won only by a liberalization of its policies towards Indochina.

12. China is exercised at the economic stranglehold which France formerly exercised through control of the Yunan Railroad and the port of Haiphong, and is particularly perturbed at the danger to its southwest flank first made visible by the surrender of Indochina to the Japanese.

13. It is stated American policy that the cession of territory by Indochina to Thailand in 1941 is not recognized and that this territory must be returned to Indochina. This territory, however, had in earlier years been wrested by the French from Thailand and its inhabitants are culturally akin to the Thai. Similarly, parts of Laos are Thai in character. Whatever the legalistic background may be, the entire border region between Indochina and Thailand will be a source of potential conflict unless a fair and appropriate frontier is determined by an impartial international commission. The Thai Government will accept any frontier so determined.

14. It will be an American victory over Japan which will make possible the liberation of Indochina. We are fighting to assure peace and stability in the Far East, and will, in fact, bear the major responsibility for its maintenance after the war. Encouragement of and assistance to the peoples of Southeast Asia in developing autonomous, democratic self-rule in close, willing association with major Western powers would not only be in harmony with political trends in that area, but would appear to be the one practical solution which will assure peace and stability in the Far East. If this policy is not followed, the millions who live in that area may well embrace ideologies contrary to our own - or ultimately develop a pan-Asiatic movement against the Western world. It is not unreasonable, therefore, for the United States to insist that the French give adequate assurances as to the implementing of policies in Indochina which we consider essential to assure peace and stability in the Far East.

Recommendations

In the light of the above considerations, the following recommendations, which have been communicated to the War and Navy Departments for their comment, are submitted for your approval:

1. The Government of the United States should not seek a trusteeship, international or French, over Indochina, unless it seeks similar trusteeship by the British and Dutch over Burma and the Netherlands Indies, nor should the United States seek international accountability which is not sought for the adjacent colonial areas. It should not oppose restoration of Indochina to

France, provided the French give adequate assurances that they will meet the following conditions:

a. Development of a democratic national or federal government to be run for and increasingly by the Indochinese themselves with no special privileges for French or other persons who are not inhabitants and citizens of Indochina so that within the forseeable future Indochina may be fully self-governing and autonomous, except in matters of imperial concern in which Indochina should be a partner in the French Union.

b. Maintenance of a policy of non-discriminatory treatment and of complete economic and commercial equality.

c. Establishment of Haiphong as a free port with tax-free transit facilities between Haiphong and China.

d. Acceptance of a frontier between Indochina and Thailand, to be determined by an impartial international commission.

e. Acceptance of such international security arrangements, including American or international bases, as may be determined to be necessary for international security, including protection of China's southwestern flank.

2. For the present, the policy of the United States with respect to the postwar status of Indochina should not be communicated to the Provincial French Government.

3. The French Provisional Government should be informed, confidentially, that owing to the need of concentrating all our resources in the Pacific on operations already planned, American military operations aimed directly at the liberation of Indochina cannot be contemplated until after the defeat of Japan, nor will it be possible to make any commitments for the furnishing of military equipment or supplies to resistance groups in Indochina or to French military forces in the Asiatic theatres of war.

4. French officers of military and naval assistance in the Pacific should be accepted or rejected by the military authorities solely on their military merits as bearing upon the defeat of Japan, as in the case of British and Dutch proposals.

(20) TELEGRAM FROM ACTING SECRETARY OF STATE JOSEPH GREW TO AMBASSADOR JEFFERSON CAFFERY IN FRANCE, MAY 6, 1945

Source: *Foreign Relations, 1945*, Vol. VI, p. 307.

Within days of Roosevelt's death, Secretary of State Byrnes, at the United Nations Conference on International Organization in San Francisco, discussed U.S. policy toward Indochina with French Minister for Foreign Affairs Georges Bidault. He assured Bidault that the U.S. did not question French sovereignty, thus reversing Roosevelt's policy of trusteeship for Indochina.

"The subject of Indo-China came up in a recent conversation I had with Bidault and Bonnet. The latter remarked that although the French Government interprets Mr. Welles' statement of 1942 concerning the restoration of French sovereignty over the French Empire as including Indo-China, the press continues to imply that a special status will be reserved for this colonial area. It was made quite clear to Bidault that the record is entirely innocent of any official statement of this government questioning, even by implication, French sovereignty over Indo-China. Certain elements of American public opinion, however, condemned French governmental policies and practices in Indo-China. Bidault seemed relieved and has no doubt cabled Paris that he received renewed assurances of our recognition of French sovereignty over that area."

(21) <u>RESOLUTIONS OF THE VIET MINH CONFERENCE TO ESTABLISH A "FREE ZONE"</u>, JUNE 4, 1945

Source: *Breaking Our Chains,* pp. 52-57.

By June 1945, the Viet Minh had consolidated its control over the six provinces if Cao Bang, Bac, Can, Tuyen Quang, Thai Nguyen, Lang Son, and Ha Giang, after a series of attacks on Japanese troops in the region. A conference was convened early in June to unite these provinces under a Provisional Committee to form a revolutionary base area and a single administrative organ for the "Free Zone." Particular attention was given to the organization of Viet Minh Committes at the Province level and of People's Committees at the commune, district and province levels.

I. The free zone and its provisional committee

In preparation for the forthcoming insurrection, all the areas liberated by the Liberation Army are united in a zone called the Free Zone.

The Provisional Committee in charge of the Command of the Free Zone will manage the zone in all fields: political, military, economic, cultural and social.

The Committee will organize various departments and services such as the Political Department, the Headquarters, the economic and financial service, and the cultural and social service.

The general policy of the Provisional Committee will aim at realizing these three essential points:

1. General mobilization of the people in the zone for the anti-Japanese struggle.

2. Implementation of the Viet Minh programme, taking account of the concrete conditions and requirements of the resistance. Establishment of the democratic republican regime and promulgation of universal suffrage, democratic freedoms, national self-determination and equality between the sexes.

3. Improvement of the people's living standards, abolition of head taxes and other taxes, campaigns for production, etc...

Here is the plan to turn the Free zone into a strong base of struggle against the Japanese.

II. Political tasks

A. Mobilization of the mind of the masses for the anti-Japanese struggle

a) Each district will create a propaganda committee whose members will go to every commune to distribute leaflets, post up slogans, read and comment on newspaper articles, organize meetings, theatrical performances, displays of force, etc... The propaganda committee can organize sub-committees to produce wall newspapers and documents, as well as teams of speakers amd special pioneers' and womens' groups.

b) Each commune will gather together the population twice a month for lectures and debates on various questions concerning the anti-Japanese struggle.

c) Our propaganda will bear upon the following points:
-- The barbarous and treacherous policy of the Japanese.
-- The true hideous face of the Dai Viet clique and the puppet government.
-- The anti-Japanese struggle is the only way to national salvation.
-- The anti-Japanese struggle will certainly be a hard one.
-- The certain victory of the anti-Japanese struggle.
-- The Viet Minh program .
-- What are democratic liberties?
-- How will the elections be carried out?

-- Solidarity and mutual help among our people.
-- The entire national must support the Liberation Army.
-- Living conditions in the Free zone compared with those in the occupied zones.

B. Re-organization of the Viet Minh Front

a) To unify the organizations up to provincial level within three months.
b) Particular attention will be given to the organization and development of the youth movement and the pioneers' movement

C. Re-organization of the People's Committees

a) In the first month to explain election procedures to the people.
b) In the second month (sixth lunar month) reelection of commune and district committees.
c) In the third month, election of People's Committee at provincial level.

III. Military tasks

A. Re-organization of the Viet Nam Liberation Army

-- To select recruits. To organize the units according to the "three-three system": Each group will comprise 12 men. To form, from these primary units, platoons, companies and battalions.
-- To complete within three months elementary military and political training of the new soldiers.
-- To appoint Political commisars in the army.
-- To bring the soldiers to make the "The Pledges" of the Viet Nam Liberation Army.
-- To enforce military discipline.
-- To organize Propaganda groups of the Liberation Army.

B. Re-organization of self-defence groups

-- To organize in each commune at least one self-defence group of 12 persons whose training must be completed within three months.
-- To organize in each commune at least one guerilla group of 5 persons at the least.

C. Unification of command

The Commander, Deputy-Commander and Political Commissar of each unit will make up the command of the unit.

D. Military plans

At the beginning, political work must be regarded as more important than military tasks. We must start from this principle in mapping out military plans.

E. Commissariat and intelligence service

a) Food: To organize subscriptions and set up stocks.
To confiscate food stocks belonging to traitors.
To organize a campaign for production.
b) Arms: To set up workshops for the repair and manufacture of arms. To encourage the use of firelocks, daggers and bows.
c) Management: To make an inventory of stocks and organize their management.
d) Information: To organize an intelligence service.

F. Communications

To find new routes and organize their defence by armed forces.

IV. Economic and financial tasks

a) To launch a campaign for agricultural production and cattle-breeding: to work out a plan, issue commuinques, carry out propaganda work, organize control. To give space in our newspapers to the production campaign.
b) To encourage handicrafts.
c) To organize trade. Attention should be paid to the purchase of foods for the people.
d) To organize producers' co-operatives, supply and marketing co-operatives.
e) To issue "National Salvation Bonds".
f) To encourage thrift and prevent waste.

V. Cultural and social tasks

a) To open classes for teaching reading and writing in the national language, and elementary schools for National Salvation.
b) To organize relief for victims of war and other scourges.
c) To pay particular attention to the families of soldiers of the Liberation Army and cadres.
d) To launch a campaign for hygiene.

VI. Cadres

a) To distribute the cadres in a rational way and train new ones.
b) To open schools to train military, political and administrative cadres for the communes.
c) To open a Political and Military College for the anti-Japanese struggle.

VII. Time-limit and mode of execution

This plan must be carried out within 3 months. For each task, it is necessary to map out a detailed plan.
The Province and District committees must hold meetings of cadres to discuss the above-mentioned plan and the measures necessary to ensure its thorough implementation.

---

(22) <u>TELEGRAM FROM ACTING SECRETARY GREW TO AMBASSADOR PATRICK J. HURLEY IN CHUNGKING</u>, June 7, 1945

Source: *U.S. Vietnam Relations, Book 8*, pp. 30-32.

Responding to Ambassador Hurley's need for policy guidance on Indochina, the Acting Secretary, speaking for President Truman, reported that the U.S. would not insist on trusteeship for Indochina except with the consent of the French government, even though it would seek assurances from France on "increasing measures of self-government" for Indochina.

The President thanks you for your considered telegram in regard to the problems presented by the reestablishment of French control in Indochina and the British desire to reoccupy Hongkong and fully appreciates the difficulties in which you and General Wedemeyer may be placed on account of the lack of specific directives in respect to both of these problems which have been under careful study both here and in connection with the discussions at San Francisco.
I have also received your message No. 1548 of June 6 and regret that there has been delay in replying to your earlier one owing to the study which has been required of these matters in connection with present developments at the Conference. The President has asked me to say that there has been no basic

change in the policy in respect to these two questions and that the present position is as follows:

The President assumes that you are familiar with the statement made by the Secretary of State on April 3, 1945 with the approval of President Roosevelt in which Mr. Stettinius declared that as a result of the Yalta discussions the "trusteeship structure, it was felt, should be defined to permit the placing under it of such of the territories taken from the enemy in this war, as might be agreed upon at a later date, and also such other territories as might voluntarily be placed under trusteeship". The position thus publicly announced has been confirmed by the conversations which are now taking place in San Francisco in regard to trusteeships. Throughout these discussions the American delegation has insisted upon the necessity of providing for a progressive measure of self-government for all dependent peoples looking toward their eventual independence or incorporation in some form of federation, according to circumstances and the ability of the peoples to assume those responsibilities. Such decisions would preclude the establishment of a trusteeship in Indochina except with the consent of the French Government. The latter seems unlikely. Nevertheless, it is the President's intention at some appropriate time to ask that the French Government give some positive indication of its intentions in regard to the establishment of civil liberties and increasing measures of self-government in Indochina before formulating further declarations of policy in this respect.

In the meantime the President has explained to the French Foreign Minister that whereas we welcome French participation in the war against Japan the determination of the extent that it would be practical and helpful to have French forces join with us in such operations must be left to the Commander in Chief, United States Army Forces, Pacific. The Joint Chiefs of Staff are at present engaged in a study of the possibilities of French help along the lines of the following suggestions:

(a) While avoiding so far as practicable unnecessary or long-term commitments with regard to the amount or character of any assistance which the United States may give to French resistance forces in Indochina, this Government should continue to afford such assistance as does not interfere with the requirements of other planned operations. Owing to the need for concentrating all our resources in the Pacific on operations aimed directly at the liberation of Indochina cannot, however, be contemplated at this time. American troops should not be used in Indochina except in American military operations against the Japanese.

(b) French officers of military and naval assistance in the Pacific should be considered on their military merits as bearing on the objective of defeating Japan as in the case of British and Dutch proposals. There would be no objection to furnishing of assistance to any French military or naval forces so approves, regardless of the theatre of operations from which the assistance may be sent, provided such assistance does not involve a diversion of resources which the Combined or Joint Chiefs of Staff consider are needed elsewhere.

(23) PAPER ON POSTWAR POLICY TOWARD ASIA AND THE PACIFIC PREPARED IN THE DEPARTMENT OF STATE, JUNE 22, 1945 [Extract]

Source: *Foreign Relations, 1945,* Vol. VI, pp. 557-558, 567-568.

The State Department responded to Secretary of War Henry L. Stimson's request with a paper on policy in Asia and the Pacific which foreshadowed the postwar problem of reconciling the general U.S. inclination to give independence to former colonial peoples and the desire for good relations with France. The paper noted the likelihood of a violent struggle for independence by Vietnamese nationalists, led by the Viet Minh, and the insensitivity of the French to Vietnamese demands.

AN ESTIMATE OF CONDITIONS IN ASIA AND THE PACIFIC AT THE
CLOSE OF THE WAR IN THE FAR EAST AND THE OBJECTIVES AND
POLICIES OF THE UNITED STATES

I. Introduction

Aside from the traditional American belief in the right of all peoples to
independence, the largest possible measure of political freedom for the countries of Asia consistent with their ability to assume the responsibility thereof
is probably necessary in order to achieve the chief objective of the United
States in the Far East and the Pacific: continuing peace and security.

Another condition on which peace and security depend is cooperation among
the peace-minded states of the world. One of the foremost policies of the
United States is to maintain the unity of purpose and action of all the United
Nations, especially of the leading powers. Two of these leading powers are
Great Britain and France, each of which has dependencies in the Far East in
which there is an insistent demand for a greater measure of self-government than
the parent states have yet been willing to grant.

A problem for the United States is to harmonize, so far as possible, its policies in regard to the two objectives: increased political freedom for the Far
East and the maintenance of the unity of the leading United Nations in meeting
this problem. The United States Government may properly continue to state the
political principle which it has frequently announced, that dependent peoples
should be given the opportunity, if necessary after an adequate period of preparation, to achieve an increased measure of self-government, but it should
avoid any course of action which would seriously impair the unity of the major
United Nations.

The United States, also, may utilize either the force of its example or its
influence or both. Its treatment of the Philippines has earned a rich reward
for this country in the attitude and conduct of both the Filipinos and the nationals of other Far Eastern states. The American Government influenced the
British Government to take parallel action with it in the renunciation of extra-
territoriality and other exceptional rights in China.

The solution which would best harmonize these two policies of the United
States would be a Far East progressively developing into a group of self-governing states - independent or with Dominion status - which would cooperate with
each other and with the Western powers on a basis of mutual self-respect and
friendship. The interests of the United States and of its European Allies
require that the Far East be removed as a source of colonial rivalry and conflict, not only between the Great Powers, but between the Great Powers and the
peoples of Asia.

V. French Indochina

A. Estimate of Conditions at the End of the War

1. Political

At the end of the war, political conditions in Indochina, and especially in
the north, will probably be particularly unstable. The Indo-chinese independence groups, which may have been working against the Japanese, will quite
possibly oppose the restoration of French control. Independence sentiment in
the area is believed to be increasingly strong. The Indo-chinese Independence
League, representing some ten different native political groups, is thought
to carry substantial influence with between one-quarter and one-half million
persons. The serious 1930 insurrection, in which over 100,000 peasants actively participated, and similar insurrections which took place in the fall of
1940 indicate that the supporters of independence are neither apathetic nor
supine and are willing to fight. It is believed that the French will encounter

serious difficulty in overcoming this opposition and in reestablishing French control. What effect the Japanese declarations of independence for Annam, Cambodia, and Luang Prabang will have in the period immediately following the war cannot be estimated at this time, but clearly these declarations will make the French problem more difficult.

The French government recognizes that it will have very serious difficulties in reestablishing and maintaining its control in Indochina, and its several statements regarding the future of that country show an increasing trend toward autonomy for the French administration. Even the latest statement, however, shows little intention to give the Indochinese self-government. An increased measure of self-government would seem essential if the Indochinese are to be reconciled to continued French control.

Economically, Indochina has so far suffered least of all the countries involved in the war in the Far East. Bombing and fighting before the close of the war will probably, however, have resulted in the destruction of some of its railway system, key bridges, harbor installations, and the more important industrial and power plants. This will probably intensify already existing food shortages in the north and lack of consumer goods throughout the area.

Pre-war French policies involved economic exploitation of the colony for France. Indochina had to buy dear in the high, protected market of France and sell cheap in the unprotected markets of other nations. The French realize that this economic policy, which was very detrimental to Indochina, must be changed. They have pledged tariff autonomy and equality of tariff rates for other countries. There is no indication, however, that the French intend to pursue an open-door economic policy.

B. International Relations

French policy toward Indochina will be dominated by the desire to reestablish control in order to reassert her prestige in the world as a great power. This purpose will be augmented by the potent influence of the Banque de l'Indochine and other economic interests. Many French appear to recognize that it may be necessary for them to make further concessions to Indochinese self-government and autonomy primarily to assure native support but also to avoid unfriendly United States opinion. Chief French reliance, however, will continue to be placed upon the United Kingdom, which is almost as anxious as the French to see that no pre-war colonial power suffers diminution of power or prestige. Friction between France and China over Indochina will probably continue. The Chinese government, at least tacitly, is supporting the Independence League and is thought by the French, despite the Generalissimo's disclaimer of territorial ambitions, to desire to dominate, if not annex, northern Indochina. French economic policies interfered with all nations trading with China through its access to the sea at Haiphong. China particularly will look for a complete reversal of French policy in this respect.

The Thai consider the territory acquired from Indochina in 1941 as theirs by legal and historic right, but they have indicated they will accept any border determined by an Anglo-American commission. The French consider the territory theirs and there will doubtless be border conflict unless a fair settlement is reached which eliminates causes for serious discontent.

C. United States Policy

The United States recognizes French sovereignty over Indochina. It is, however, the general policy of the United States to favor a policy which would allow colonial peoples an opportunity to prepare themselves for increased participation in their own government with eventual self-government as the goal.

(24) <u>ARTICLE BY TRUONG CHINH</u>, JUNE 28, 1945

Source: "Our Heroic Resistance War", (Co Giai phong), (Liberation Flag), Number 14, June 28, 1945, in *The Vietnamese People's National Democratic Revolution*, pp. 318-322. [Translation by the editor.]

After the Japanese coup of March 9, 1945, the Viet Minh launched a guerilla war against the Japanese occupation forces from their base area in the North. Truong Chinh, in an article in the Party press, contrasted the determination of the Vietnamese resistance to the Japanese with the failure of the French to put up a significant fight and make it clear that the Party leadership expected this resistance to be taken into account at the United Nations Conference in San Francisco.

No sooner had the gunfire of the Japanese "coup" rung out, than the gunfire of the Indochinese guerilla units resisting the Japanese and saving the country also began.

The oppressed people of Indochina have of their own accord taken up the gun in response to the Japanese scheme to seize the country. They have taken up guns in response to the Vietnamese traitors' policy of changing masters. They have taken up guns in response to the stupid enticement to surrender of Japanese army and are replying in an appropriate manner to the letter from the mindless pro-Japanese elements suggesting "cooperation".

The gunfire of guerillas broke out after March 9, 1945 had opened an heroic resistance war in the history of the national liberation revolutionary movement of the Indochinese people which is nearly a century old. It began a new period of combat of the oppressed peoples of Indochina, who are determined that this time they will win freedom and independence.

The resistance of the Indochinese people is even more heroic, because it is developing strongly and rapidly, while the weak "resistance" of the French in Indochina has quickly been defeated in a shameful manner!

It is a truth recently recorded in the history of the struggle of the anti-fascist forces that the French in Indochina, with their so many troops and weapons nevertheless cannot maintain their "resistance war". On the contrary, the Indochinese peoples, with their few rudimentary weapons, are determined <u>by themselves</u> to undertake the resistance war against the Japanese in extremely difficult circumstances.

Although allied troops have not yet poured into Indochina to join our people in fighting the Japanese, our people's resistance nevertheless does not cease to develop. Up to now, it has passed through two stages.

At the beginning, our army captured arms from worn out, defeated and fleeing French troops, not allowing them to take their guns to the Japanese ranks or to flee abroad. And at the time the French resistance forces disintegrated, our army attacked a number of posts, occupied them as necessary bases for the resistance war against Japan, while seizing a number of weapons there, rather than let them fall into the hands of the Japanese.

Have our operations obstructed the French resistance? Definitely not! On the contrary, despite the suspicions of the Gaullist French in Indochina, who are stubborn and full of ambition, and who refused to form a democratic front with us against the Japanese before the "coup", in the decisive hour we place the anti-fascist task above all and unify our actions with them in places where they are sincerely waging resistance war (such as Soc-giang, Cao-ban, Ngan-son and Bac-can). But the tardy repentence of a few lonely French resistants (who only attached themselves to the Vietnamese revolution when they had no other resource) is not enough to save the whole French resistance.

Finally, the French army in Indochina fell apart or fled across the Vietnamese-Chinese border or were captured and made prisoner.

While France was defeated, our people's resistance progressed to a new

level. Our troops continue to fight directly with the Japanese: sabotaging
the Japanese lines of communications, blocking the Japanese troops from advancing to occupy the geographical bases of the Vietnamese revolution, sweeping
Japanese forces from those geographical bases, etc... Wherever we fight, our
troops mobilize the masses of people to participate in the guerilla warfare
and establish a Revolutionary People's Committee, setting up provisional revolutionary government in the locality. Supported by the guerilla troops and
armed masses, Revolutionary People's Committees are carrying out the ardent
aspirations of the compatriots. More than a million people in the Liberated
Zone have postponed taxes, have more land, have been given democratic rights,
etc... In the process of struggle against Japan, the Viet-nam liberation army
has officially been founded, consisting of forces of the Viet-nam liberation
propaganda troops and of Vietnam national salvation troops. Military zones have
been clearly defined. A School of Military Administration to resist the Japanese has opened in the base area in order to form military cadres. Our fighters
are being forged in the school of real combat or in military and political
training courses. By seizing the invaders' weapons, our troops at the same
time fight and further arm themselves. Our troops and guerillas are developing
their strength to prepare for the expulsion of the Japanese invaders from the
country, and the establishment of a Democratic Republic of Viet-nam.
   A glorious change!
   While a group of Vietnamese traitors commends the Japanese invaders in order
to beg for a bit of dregs, a bit of leftover rice, our compatriots under the
red flag with the gold star of the Viet-minh, are sacrificing in struggle, winning back the country. Our resistance was in evidence in iron and stone showing
the world that our people are not so base as to crouch under the boot of the
Japanese, do not fight for the French rule as the De Gaulle government has
declared, and do not rely on the strength of assistance from abroad.
   At present, a terrible famine still prevails. The Japanese invaders mercilessly kill our people and directly oppress them. Never have our people been as
miserable as now, but they have never been as heroic as now. We are contributing a share of the sacrifice in bones and blood with the allied countries in
order to exterminate Japanese fascism and restore peace to mankind. We are not
deceived by the Japanese "Greater East Asia" theory. We know how to stand up and
take up arms to break the shackles,smash the yoke, and win our just living
rights. Our armed resistance to Japan must echo as far as the platform at San
Francisco. We are spilling blood in order to put before the San Francisco Conference the great demand of our people: complete independence and freedom.
   We oppose the Japanese to the end. But we are prepared to resist any power
which decides to force us to return to a life of slavery for French imperialism
or any other imperialism, after Japanese rule is overthrown. Only by taking
arms in our hands, and uniting to struggle can our people determine our own
destiny in the coming days.

(25) APPEAL OF THE NORTH VIET-NAM REVOLUTIONARY MILITATY COMMITTEE,
JULY 1, 1945

Source: *Breaking Our Chains,* pp. 58-60.

   The first message to the entire Vietnamese people by the revolutionary ad-
ministration in the "Free Zone" was an appeal from the regional Revolutionary
Military Committee which gave an account of the progress in setting up revolu-
tionary power and in the struggle against the Japanese and asserted that the
Japanese were doomed to defeat. The term "kinh" used in the text refers to the
ethnic Vietnamese majority as distinct from the ethnic minorities.

Fellow-citizens!

Combatants for national salvation!

Officers and men of the Viet Nam Liberation Army!

The struggle waged by our guerillas against the Japanese is raging. Guerilla warfare is spreading in the provinces of the High and Middle regions of North Viet Nam. Our guerillas are masters of the situation in numerous localities. Nearly the whole territory of Cao Bang, Bac Can, Tuyen Quang provinces, and a great part of Thai Nguyen, Lang Son and Ha Giang provinces are occupied by our troops. Some isolated posts in Bac Giang, Vinh Yen and Yen Bay have been attacked by surprise. Political prisoners at Nghia Lo (Yen Bay province) have risen up and broken out of their jail. Our comrades, political prisoners and tirailleurs of Quang Ngai have annihilated the Ba To post and after disarming the enemy, have withdrawn to the jungle to form guerilla units.

Following the example of the Kinh, the Muong (Hoa Binh province) and Meo (Son La province) minorities have risen up and are now fighting against the Japanese. All strata of the population, all the oppressed peoples in Indochina are closely united in the fight against the common enemy.

Regional revolutionary administration has been set up. The Revolutionary People's Committees, which have been directly elected by the people, are using revolutionary measures to bring freedom and happiness to the people.

In the Free zone, the people's property is guaranteed. The property of the enemy and the traitors is being nationalized or allotted to the poor. Fundamental democratic freedoms are being put into practice: equality and mutual aid between nationalities, equality of the sexes. Social assistance is being organized, piracy and theft suppressed, taxes abolished, land rents reduced and the working day limited. With enthusiasm boys and girls are training and are leaving for the battlefront. Rich and poor, old and young, compete with each other in production to guarantee supplies to the Army. More than one million of our compatriots have begun to enjoy the first achievements of the Revolution. The new-born Viet Nam is growing up.

But outside the Free zone, our compatriots are still suffering under the iron heel of the Japanese fascists. Driven to death's door, the aggressors ruthlessly pillage and suppress the people, systematically using all sorts of perfidious deceptive manoeuvres in an attempt to continue their criminal presence in our land. French rule in Indochina has collapsed, but the de Gaulle clique is on the watch for the opportunity to come back once more to place the yoke of French imperialism on our necks. The Allied forces will land in Indochina to fight the Japanese. Our country will become the theatre of heavy fighting.

Officers and men of the Viet Nam Liberation Army!

Comrades, men and women of Self-defence units!

Compatriots all over the country!

The danger remains. The decisive battle is but beginning. Forward! Our whole people must unit together in a single bloc to crush the enemy! Forward! Join all our efforts to break our chains, to drive the Japanese bandits out of our country! Be ready for sacrifices! Our combatants on the front-line must heroically hurl themselves at the enemy! At the same time our compatriots in the rear must increase production and organize subscriptions in order to help our valiant guerillas!

The examples of resistance set by Tran Quoc Tuan, Le Loi and Quang Trung are untarnished in our history. We have taken in our hands the National Salvation banner of Phan Dinh Phung, Hoang Hoa Tham, Doi Can and Nguyen Thai Hoc. Forward!

Our enemy is being defeated on all fronts. In South China they have scampered off like rabbits. Japan is, at present, facing invasion by the Allied forces. The Japanese troops in Indochina are more divided and more bewildered with every passing day.

We have in our hands the one and only opportunity in our history. Be united and be prepared for all sacrifices, fight resolutely and we will certainly win victory.

Annihilate all Japanese fascist aggressors!
Do away with all traitors!
Long live independent Viet Nam!

(26) TELEGRAM FROM PRESIDENT HARRY TRUMAN FOR GENERALISSIMO CHIANG KAI-SHEK, TRANSMITTED VIA AMBASSADOR HURLEY, AUGUST 1, 1945.

Source: *Foreign Relations, 1945*, Vol. II, p. 1321.

At the Potsdam Conference President Truman and British Prime Minister Clement Attlee reached an agreement which divided French Indochina at the sixteenth parallel for allied military operations. That decision gave British Admiral Mountbatten operational control over the Southern half of Vietnam and made possible the British assistance to the French which would lead to the outbreak of Vietnamese resistance there.

Top secret from the President to Ambassador Hurley.

Please deliver the following message from me to Generalissimo Chiang Kai-shek.

"1. At the Potsdam Conference the Prime Minister of Great Britain and I, in consultation with the Combined Chiefs of Staff, have had under consideration future military operations in South-East Asia.

"2. On the advice of the Combined Chiefs of Staff we have reached the conclusion that for operational purposes it is desirable to include that portion of French Indo-China lying south of 16° north latitude in the Southeast Asia Command. This arrangement would leave in the China Theater that part of Indo-China which covers the flank of projected Chinese operations in China and would at the same time enable Admiral Mountbatten to develop operations in the southern half of Indo-China.

"3. I greatly hope that the above conclusions will recommend themselves to Your Excellency and that, for the purpose of facilitating operations against the common enemy, Your Excellency will feel able to concur in the proposed arrangements.

"4. I understand that the Prime Minister of Great Britain is addressing a communication to Your Excellency in a similar sense.

(27) A GENERAL UPRISING ORDER BY VO NGUYEN GIAP, REPRESENTING THE PROVISIONAL EXECUTIVE COMMITTEE OF THE FREE ZONE, AUGUST 12, 1945.

Source: Vo Nguyen Giap; *Order the Day, Speeches and Mobilization Letters*, pp. 13-14. [Translation by the editor.]

On August 12, only one day after the Japanese asked to surrender, Vo Nguyen Giap, using the name "Van", signed the order on behalf of the Provisional Executive Committee of the Liberated Zone calling on its troops and political cadres to go into action to seize power before the landing of the allies in Indochina.

Unit chiefs, political cadres and members of Liberation Army units!
Self-defense units, peoples committees and the entire people!

On August 11, 1945, the Japanese invaders completely disintegrated and asked to surrender to Allied Forces. The Soviet, British and American conference meeting in Moscow has accepted the surrender of Japan. Thus the Pacifc war is about to end.

The hour and minute of the general uprising has arrived, the general struggle has come to a decisive time, you comrades must calmly and determinedly carry out the orders which follow:

1. Mobilize troops to strike into the cities where there are sufficient conditions for victory.
2. Deploy to attack and cut off withdrawing troops of the enemy.
3. Before acting, send an ultimatum to the Japanese army and security troops [Vietnamese troops under Japanese command, ed.] If they do not surrender, they must be annihilated.
4. With regard to Japanese forces who have surrendered, they must be treated with all kindness, a large part of them must be put into concentration camps, and one part should be propagandized, then returned to the Japanese troops in various places to exert influence.
As for Vietnamese soldiers, let them go after propagandizing them.
5. When you have fought a battle, immediately reinforce your troops with weapons captured. Unless you receive special orders, one third of the troops should stay in the locality, while two thirds should prepare to move on to another place to fight.
6. After occupying the cities, all military provisions and foodstuffs which cannot be used right away should be taken immediately to our base for storage.
7. At this present moment, liaison must be tight, troops must always stay in touch with headquarters, and must immediately notify headquarters if there is a change in the situation.
8. Peoples committees and the whole people must with all their heart do their best to coordinate with the troops. The entire army and people must be prepared for all eventualities in order to continue the struggle for complete independence for the country.
9. With regard to the French of De Gaulle, continue to follow the previous announcement, and with regard to other foreigners, there will be a separate order.
10. This is a time of military action, so discipline must be very strict.

Dear comrades!

In order to insure the success of the general uprising, you should carry out these orders quickly, determinedly, heroically, and carefully.
--Annihilate the Japanese fascists!
--Long live completely independent Viet-nam!
--Long live the Viet-nam liberation army!

(28) RESOLUTION OF THE NATIONAL CONFERENCE OF THE INDOCHINESE COMMUNIST PARTY, AUGUST 13-15, 1945 (Extract)

Source: *Breaking Our Chains*, pp. 63-67.

From August 13 to 15, the Indochinese Communist Party held a National Conference at Tan Trao to present to cadres the leadership's analysis and plan of action for seizing power. The Resolution of the Conference pointed to contradictions between the U.S. and France and between the U.S. and China as conditions which should be exploited to the advantage of the revolution. It also warned that because of conflict between the capitalist countries and the Soviet Union, the U.S. and Britain might allow the French to return to Indochina, and concluded that only the real strength of the revolution would determine the outcome.

III.   The Party's political line

1.   The very favourable opportunity for the conquest of independence will come soon.

2.   We are in an emergency. Our activities must be based on the following three principles:

a)   Concentration - To concentrate our forces upon the essential tasks.

b)   Unity - To realize unity of action and of command in the political and military field.

c)   Timeliness - To act in good time and not to let slip any opportunity.

3.   At present, the aim of our struggle is to win complete independence.

4.   The main slogans of struggle are:

Down with the aggressors!

Complete independence!

People's power!

5.   We must immediately occupy by surprise the regions where success is certain, whether they are urban centres or rural zones. People's committees must be set up where we are masters of the situation.

6.   We must carry out the following ten-point Viet Minh policy:

a)   To struggle against foreign aggression and suppress traitors. To build up a completely independent Democratic Republic of Viet Nam.

b)   To arm the people for the struggle against the Japanese, to develop the Viet Nam Liberation Army.

c)   To confiscate the property of the invaders and the traitors, nationalize it or distribute it to the poor according to the case.

d)   To abolish the iniquitous system of taxation established by the imperialists and set up an equitable and rational taxation system.

e)   To put into practice democratic freedoms and universal suffrage. To recognize equality of nationalities and of the sexes.

f)   To re-allot communal land so that the poor peasants will have land to till. To reduce land rent and interest and defer payment of loans.

g)   To put into practice the eight-hour work day, promulgate laws on social security and organize social assistance.

h)   To build up and develop national economy to encourage and help industry, agriculture and commerce. To found the National Bank.

i)   To struggle against illiteracy. To organize compulsory primary education. To train able people for various branches of activity.

j)   To maintain good relations with countries which respect the independence of Viet Nam.

7.   Attitude toward foreign residents

a)   Toward the Japanese: To disarm them, confiscate their property, suppress those who resist by force and intern the others and treat them well, winning over to our cause those who are relatively good and using them for propaganda work.

b)   Toward the Chinese residents: To ensure protection of their lives and property. To maintain good relations with them. To hand over Chinese traitors to anti-Japanese organizations of the Chinese residents to deal with them.

c)   Toward the French residents: To ensure protection of their lives and property (except for pro-Japanese elements).

d)   Toward the British and Americans: To maintain good relations with them.

8.   Attitude toward the various puppet governments: Pending the Party's concrete instruction, to carry out agitation work among the masses to bring them to oppose these governments. To put forth the slogans: "Overthrow the puppet government, set up the People's power!"

9.   Attitude toward the Allied forces landed in Indochina:

a)   Toward the Gaullist troops: Pending the Party's instructions, we must avoid all military incidents, but where they penetrate, people and their property must be evacuated; at the same time we must lead the masses to demonstrate against all attempts made by the French to re-establish their former rule in Indochina.

b) Toward the American, British and Chinese troops: Pending the Party's instructions, we should avoid collisons and maintain good relations with them.

In case they encroach upon our rights and interests, we should oppose a passive resistance by evacuating the inhabitants and their property. We should bring the masses as a whole to hold demonstrations under the slogans of complete independence for Viet Nam.

IV. Foreign policy

1. In the sphere of foreign policy, up to now and in spite of our efforts, our relations with the Chinese have not yet brought good results. Our relations with the Allies have made some progress, but the Vietnamese revolution has not as yet succeeded in winning a position on the international arena.

2. At present, in foreign policy we must fully realize the following two points:

a) We must avail ourselves of the contradictions in the Allied camp concerning the Indochina question, between the British and French on the one side, and the Americans and Chinese on the other.

b) The contradictions between Britain, the United States and France on the one side and the Soviet Union on the other, might lead the British and Americans to make concessions to the French and allow them to come back to Indochina.

3. Our policy consists in avoiding this conjuncture: to be alone in our resistance to the Allied forces (China, France, Britain and the United States) which would invade our country and force on us a French or a puppet government going counter to the aspirations of our people.

That is why we must win the Soviet Union and the United States over to our cause so that we can oppose French attempts to resume their former position in Indochina and the manoeuvres of some Chinese militarists to occupy our country.

4. However that may be, it is our own forces that will decide the success of our relations with the Allies.

5. We must set up close contact with the weak and small countries, with the Chinese and French peoples, and win their support.

(29) <u>DECISIONS OF THE PEOPLE'S CONGRESS</u>, AUGUST 16, 1945

Source: *Breaking Our Chains*, pp. 68-70.

After the Central Committee's Conference, the Viet Minh Central Committee hastily convened a National Congress to approve the policies decided on by the Party. The Congress was the authority for the establishment of the Viet Nam National Liberation Committee which would be a Provisional Government until the Viet Minh set up a central government in Hanoi.

1. In Europe, Italian and German fascism is dead and the movement of new democracy is progressing.

After having played a great part in the annihilation of fascism in Europe, the Soviet Union declared war on Japan on August 8, 1945, resolute to wage, together with the Allies, the decisive battle against the fascists in Asia.

The Japanese fascists have surrendered unconditionally. The Allied forces will soon arrive at wherever the Japanese troops are stationed.

The movement of national liberation and new democracy has grown in strength and scope all over the world.

2. In our country, Japanese power is falling to pieces. Availing itself of the opportunity, the Insurrection Committee, created by the General Committee

of the Viet Minh Front, has ordered our Liberation forces to disarm the routed Japanese troops and to widen their sphere of activity.

3. The People's Congress appeals to the whole people and revolutionary organizations to rise up, unite together in good time and struggle for the carrying out of the following ten points:

a. To seize power and build up a Democratic Republic of Viet Nam on the basis of complete independence.

b. To arm the people. To develop the Viet Nam Liberation Army.

c. To confiscate the property of the invaders and the traitors, nationalize it or distribute it to the poor according to the case.

d. To abolish the old system of taxation established by the French and the Japanese, to set up an equitable and rational one.

e. To promulgate democratic rights:
    Human rights
    Rights to property
    Civil rights: universal suffrage, democratic freedoms (freedom of conscience, thought, speech, association, and movement, equality between nationalities and the sexes).

f. To re-distribute communal land equitably, to reduce land rent and interest, defer payment of loans and organize relief.

g. To promulgate labour regulations: eight-hour-work-day, minimum wages and establishment of socal insurance.

h. To build up the national economy, develop agriculture and found the National Bank.

i. To organize national education, to fight illiteracy, popularize and make compulsory primary education. To build up a new culture.

j. To maintain good relations with the Allies and the weak and small nations with a view to winning their sympathy and support.

4. The People's Congress decided upon the setting up of the Viet Nam National Liberation Committee to lead our revolution for national liberation to victory. The Committee is tantamount to the Provisional Government of Viet Nam, pending the founding of an official government. This committee will, on behalf of the people, take in hand relations with foreign countries, and the direction of all internal affairs.

5. We are in an emergency and must act in good time. The National Liberation Committee gives the Insurrection Committee full power of command.

6. The Japanese defeat will not of itself bring independence to our country. Numerous obstacles and difficulties will crop up. We must be clear-headed and resolute. Clear-headed in avoiding all that can harm our cause and resolute to win complete independence. In the present post-war international situation, a people that is united and determined to demand its independence will certainly win it. We will be victorious.

(30) APPEAL BY HO CHI MINH FOR GENERAL INSURRECTION, AUGUST 1945

Source: Ho Chi Minh, *Selected Writings*, pp. 49-50.

After the People's Congress, Ho Chi Minh, using his familiar name, Nguyen Ai Quoc (Nguyen the Patriot), issued an appeal to all Vietnamese to join in the general uprising which was already beginning to unfold throughout the North and Center.

Dear fellow-countrymen!

Four years ago, I called on you to unite, for unity is strength and only strength will enable us to win back independence and freedom.

At present, the Japanese army has collapsed. The National Salvation Movement has spread to the whole country. The League for the Independence of

Viet Nam (Viet Minh) has millions of members from all social strata: intellectuals, peasants, workers, businessmen, soldiers, and from all nationalities in
the country: Viet, Tho, Nung, Muong, Man, and others. In its ranks our compatriots march side by side regardless of age, sex, religion and fortune.

Recently, the Viet Minh convened the Viet Nam People's National Congress
and appointed the National Liberation Committee to lead the entire people in
the resolute struggle for national independence.

This is a great advance in the history of the struggle waged for nearly a
century by our people for their liberation.

This is a source of powerful encouragement for our compatriors and great
joy for myself.

However, we cannot connect ourselves with that. Our struggle will be a
long and hard one. The Japanese defeat does not mean that we shall be liberated
overnight. We still have to make further efforts and carry on the struggle.
Only unity and struggle will bring us independence.

The Viet Minh is at present the basis for the unity and struggle of our
people. Join the Viet Minh, support it, make it even greater and stronger!

At present, the National Liberation Committee is the equivalent of a provisional government. Let us rally around it and see to it that its policies
and orders are carried out throughout the country!
This way, independence is certain to come to our people soon.

Dear fellow-countrymen!

The decisive hour has struck for the destiny of our people. Let all of us
stand up and rely on our own strength to free ourselves.

Many oppressed peoples the world over are vying with each other in wresting
back independence. We should not lag behind.

Forward! Forward! Under the banner of the Viet Minh, let us valiantly
march forward!

(31) APPEAL BY A VIET MINH REPRESENTATIVE TO A MASS MEETING IN HANOI, AUGUST 19, 1945

Source: *Breaking Our Chains*, pp. 85-87.

*On the morning of August 19, 1945, after two days of demonstrations, 1,000
Viet Minh troops entered the city. The Viet Minh led a large crowd in storming
the official residence of the imperial delegate. A crowd which the Viet Minh
estimated at 200,000 then gathered, and a Viet Minh spokesman announced the
intention of the revolutionaries to form a new government. Four days later,
the Viet Minh demanded that Bao Dai abdicate to clear the way for the formation
of the Democratic Republic of Viet-nam.*

Compatriots!
On behalf of the Viet Minh Front, we convey from this tribune our friendly
greetings (For National Salvation) to all our compatriots who have come, numerous and enthusiastic, to this meeting.

Your ardent participation is a clear evidence of your ardent love for the
country and of the great trust you have put in the Viet Minh Front. This is a
very moving encouragement to the fighters for national salvation: in these
grave hours, when armed insurrections have broken out in every corner of the
country, they feel supported in their struggle and have greater faith than ever
in the final victory of the national cause. However, their responsibilities
thus become heavier. On their behalf, we accept these responsibilities.

While the Japanese troops have, on orders from their Emperor, ceased fire
on all fronts, the French imperialists, entertaining mad ambitions to re-establish their domination in Indochina, have raised their heads and are on the

lookout for a good opportunity to act. We must assume a very clear, dignified and energetic attitude.

As for the Japanese troops, we must be very moderate and avoid all unnecessary clashes, disadvantageous to both sides. We can also use diplomacy to make them understand the situation, approve our revolution and hand their arms over to us.

With regard to the French who have the evil design of restoring their rule in Indochina, we shall resolutely oppose their manoeuvres and, if need be, fight with arms against all attempts at aggression on their part or on the part of other imperialists.

To this end, the essential thing for the time being is to set up immediately a Democratic Republic of Viet Nam, with the participation of the broad masses of the population, thus enabling the people to determine their fate themselves.

This revolutionary people's government of Viet Nam will promulgate freedoms to the whole people, set out to improve the people's living standards and mobilize the forces of the entire nation for the defence and the consolidation of our genuine independence. Only the revolutionary people's government has prestige and strength enough to realize the common earnest aspirations of the whole people: independence, freedom and happiness. Only the revolutionary people's government has prestige and strength enough to lead our nation to a bright future, worthy of the heroic past recorded in our national history.

Compatriots!

Let us be confident in ourselves, in our own strength, and show to the world the strong vitality and the stubborn fighting will of the Vietnamese people who have always striven for a free and independent life.

Let us shout together:

-- Let us crush all forces that would encroach upon the independence of Viet Nam!

-- Down with the French who want to restore their rule in Indochina!

-- Down with the Tran Trong Kim - Phan Ke Toai puppet government!

-- Let us found the Democratic Republican Government of Viet Nam!

-- Complete independence for Viet Nam!

-- Victory of the National Liberation Revolution!

(32) <u>ABDICATION STATEMENT BY HIS MAJESTY BAO DAI</u>, AUGUST 26, 1945

Source: Viet-Nam Delegation in France, Information Service, *The Democratic Republic of Viet-Nam* (Paris: 1948), pp. 5-6.

By August 22, when the strength of the Viet Minh had become apparent to him, Emperor Bao Dai had decided to ask the Viet Minh to form a new government to replace the pro-Japanese government headed by Tran Trong Kim. But before he could even act officially, Bao Dai received a message from Hanoi demanding that he abdicate and hand over power to the Democratic Republic of Viet-nam. An Indochinese Communist Party leader, Tran Huy Lieu was dispatched from Hanoi to arrange for the ceremony of abdication. On August 30, Bao Dai read his abdication statement, and then handed over the royal seal and the sword, symbolizing the passage of power from the monarchy to the Democratic Republic.

For the happiness of the Vietnamese peoples, and for the independence of Viet Nam,

We declare ourself ready to make all sacrifices, in the hope that such sacrifices will be of benefit to the Nation.

Conscious that the union of our compatriots at this moment is an absolute necessity for our Fatherland, We solemnly warned our people on August 22nd: "At this decisive moment in the nation's history, unity is life, and division death."

In view of the mighty democratic forces released in the north of our Realm, We were at first apprehensive lest conflict between the North and South should be inevitable, if We were to await the opening of a National Congress before taking a decision; and We were aware that this conflict, should it occur, would entail much suffering for our peoples besides giving a golden opportunity to the invader to despoil our territory.

We cannot escape some feeling of melancholic frustation at the thought of the achievements of our glorious ancestors who fought without respite for 400 years to extend the frontiers of our country from Thuan-hoa to Ha-tien;

Neither can We help feeling a certain regret in looking back on our 20 year-old reign, during which our position has been such that it was well-nigh impossible for Us to render any appreciable service to our Country.

Notwithstanding this, We firmly decide to abdicate our throne, and We hand over Sovereign power to the Democratic Republic of Viet Nam.

In so doing, We have but three wishes to express:

1) We request the New Government to take care of the dynastic temples and royal tombs;

2) We request the New Government to treat in a spirit of fraternity all parties and groups who have fought for the independence of the country, even though they may not have closely followed the popular movement; so that they may have the opportunity to participate in the reconstruction of the country, and proof be given that the new regime is founded upon the absolute union of the entire people;

3) We call upon all parties and groups, all classes of society as well as the Royal Family to strengthen and support unreservedly the Democratic Republic of Viet Nam, in order to consolidate our national independence.

As for Us, We have known great bitterness during the twenty years of our rule. Henceforth, we are happy to assume the status of a free citizen in an independent country. We shall allow no one to abuse our name or that of the Royal Family to sow discord among our compatriots.

Long live the independence of Viet Nam!

Long live our Democratic Republic!

(33) BROADCAST APPEAL BY DR. PHAM NGOC THACH, PROVISIONAL EXECUTIVE COMMITTEE IN SAIGON, AUGUST 28th, 1945.

Source: Saigon Radio in French, August 28, 1945, reported in British Intelligence *Fortnightly Intelligence Report* (New Delhi), no. 16, August 16-31, 1945, p. 75. In State Department Central Files, National Archives.

Exploiting its own pro-allied record during the war and its foes' collaboration with the Japanese, the Communist-led Viet Minh convened a Congress of parties and sects in Saigon on August 25 at which they announced a "Provisional Executive Committee", without direct challenge from anti-Communist groups. A key factor in the Viet Minh success was the decision of the mass-based Vanguard Youth organization, under Dr. Pham Ngoc Thach, to affiliate with the Viet Minh. Dr. Thach, not previously known to be aligned with the Viet Minh, was named Commissioner for Foreign Affairs on the Executive Committee. In the first known broadcast to the world by the Viet Minh, Dr. Thach appealed to the allies, particularly the U.S., the French people and the Soviet Union to come to the aid of the Viet-nam against the anticipated French efforts to reconquer Indochina.

The Viet Nam Democratic Front for Viet Nam independence, after fighting for four years against French and Japanese imperialism, finds itself in power from the south to the north of Indo-China by the unanimous will of the Annamite people. The Annamite people shows the world its will to live free and independent under the sign of the new democracy. We make a pressing appeal to all the Allied powers who have fought for years for the freedom of the oppressed to recognise the young Viet Nam Democractic Republic. The powerful American Republic after mobilising all her men and industrial power has seen the triumph of the democracies in the Pacific. Before the whole world she accepted the principle of the independence of the Philippines immediately after her first landings there. She has again officially declared that the entire administration would be put into the hands of the Filipinos on 1st September 1946. We are filled with respect before this noble gesture of a great democracy, a defender of the cause of world liberty. President Truman and all the people of US will no doubt defend our cause in the arena of world politics and recognise all the effort, all the courage, we have shown these last 80 years to make heard the voice of a people who want to be free and sovereign. The Republic of China, which has just been liberated forever from Japanese militarism, knows enough of foreign oppression not to permit the slavery of a neighbour. The United Kingdom has shown the world the will of its workers to work side by side with Soviet Russia for the building of a new world based on social justice and world brotherhood. We are astonished that the democratic government in France intends to maintain its sovereign rights in Indo-China. After fighting against German domination the French Provisional government proposes towards us a colonisation going against the progress of humanity. The new Indo-China statute of the de Gaulle Government is only a mask covering from the unwary the imperialism of a nation. No, the people of France, who have already given the world so much of their blood for the life of the principles of justice and liberty, the French people of 1791 and (1917) who have shown the world the rights of the people, will not fail now in their duty. As in the gravest days of her history the workers of France will know how to defend a just cause with courage. Independent Viet Nam will be thankful for this gesture, the only gesture that can erase the violent colonial history which separates our two peoples. The Annamite people therefore make a brotherly appeal to the people of France, as they know that more than once in its revolutionary progress France has brought them its material support. On the present attitude of the French people depends the future of relations between our two countries and the beginning of an era of mutual understanding between the two peoples. For the first time, through the radio, our voice will reach the great Soviet Republic. In this serious moment the Annamite people turn toward the great people of the Soviets. The Soviets, defenders of the rights of men, were the champions of the emancipation of colonised people. The great voice of the homeland of the world's proletariat will surely come to the aid of the appeal of our people, an appeal for a just cause, the cause of the workers of the world.

(34) <u>DECLARATION OF INDEPENDENCE OF THE DEMOCRATIC REPUBLIC OF VIET-NAM,</u>
SEPTEMBER 2, 1945

Source: Information Service, Viet-Nam Delegation in France, *The Democratic Republic of Viet-Nam* (Paris: Imprimerie Centrale Commerciale, 1948), pp. 3-5.

After the Viet Minh uprising had succeeded in almost all provinces, the Standing Committee of the Indochinese Communist Party met in Hanoi for the first time under Ho's Chairmanship, and decided to promulgate the Provisional Government of the Democratic Republic of Viet-nam on the same day as the Declaration of Independence. Ho drafted the entire Declaration himself during the five days preceding its public presentation by Ho at a mass meeting in Hanoi on September 2.

"We hold truths that all men are created equal, that they are endowed by their Creator with certain unalienable Rights, among these are Life, Liberty and the pursuit of Happiness."

This immortal statement is extracted from the Declaration of Independence of the United States of America in 1776. Understood in the broader sense, this means: "All peoples on the earth are born equal; every person has the right to live to be happy and free."

The Declaration of Human and Civic Rights proclaimed by the French Revolution in 1791 likewise propounds: "Every man is born equal and enjoys free and equal rights."

These are undeniable truths.

Yet, during and throughout the last eighty years, the French imperialists, abusing the principles of "Freedom, equality and fraternity," have violated the integrity of our ancestral land and oppressed our countrymen. Their deeds run counter to the ideals of humanity and justice.

In the political field, they have denied us every freedom. They have enforced upon us inhuman laws. They have set up three different political regimes in Northern, Central and Southern Viet Nam (Tonkin, Annam, and Cochinchina) in an attempt to disrupt our national, historical and ethnical unity.

They have built more prisons than schools. They have callously ill-treated our fellow-compatriots. They have drowned our revolutions in blood.

They have sought to stifle public opinion and pursued a policy of obscurantism on the largest scale; they have forced upon us alcohol and opium in order to weaken our race.

In the economic field, they have shamelessly exploited our people, driven them into the worst misery and mercilessly plundered our country.

They have ruthlessly appropriated our rice fields, mines, forests and raw materials. They have arrogated to themselves the privilege of issuing banknotes, and monopolised all our external commerce. They have imposed hundreds of unjustifiable taxes, and reduced our countrymen, especially the peasants and petty tradesmen, to extreme poverty.

They have prevented the development of native capital enterprises; they have exploited our workers in the most barbarous manner.

In the autumn of 1940, when the Japanese fascists, in order to fight the Allies, invaded Indochina and set up new bases of war, the French imperialists surrendered on bended knees and handed over our country to the invaders.

Subsequently, under the joint French and Japanese yoke, our people were literally bled white. The consequences were dire in the extreme. From Quang Tri up to the North, two millions of our countrymen died from starvation during the first months of this year.

On March 9th, 1945, the Japanese disarmed the French troops. Again the French either fled or surrendered unconditionally. Thus, in no way have they proved capable of "protecting" us; on the contrary, within five years they have twice sold our country to the Japanese.

Before March 9th, many a time did the Viet Minh League invite the French to join in the fight against the Japanese. Instead of accepting this offer, the French, on the contrary, let loose a wild reign of terror with rigour worse than ever before against Viet Minh's partisans. They even slaughtered a great number of our "*condamnes politiques*" imprisoned at Yen Bay and Cao Bang.

Despite all that, our countrymen went on maintaining, vis-a-vis the French, a humane and even indulgent attitude. After the events of March 9th, the Viet Minh League helped many French to cross the borders, rescued others from Japanese prisons and, in general, protected the lives and properties of all the French in their territory.

In fact, since the autumn of 1940, our country ceased to be a French colony and became a Japanese possession.

After the Japanese surrender, our people, as a whole, rose up and proclaimed their sovereignty and founded the Democratic Republic of Viet Nam.

The truth is that we have wrung back our independence from Japanese hands and not from the French.

The French fled, the Japanese surrendered. Emperor Bao Dai abdicated, our people smashed the yoke which pressed hard upon us for nearly one hundred years, and finally made our Viet Nam an independent country. Our people at the same time overthrew the monarchical regime established tens of centuries ago, and founded the Republic.

For these reasons, we, the members of the Provisional Government representing the entire people of Viet Nam, declare that we shall from now on have no more connections with imperialist France; we consider null and void all the treaties France has signed concerning Viet Nam, and we hereby cancel all the privileges that the French arrogated to themselves on our territory.

The Vietnamese people, animated by the same common resolve, are determined to fight to the death against all attempts at aggression by the French imperialists.

We are convinced that the Allies who have recognized the principles of equality of peoples at the Conferences of Teheran and San Francisco cannot but recognize the Independence of Viet Nam.

A people which has so stubbornly opposed the French domination for more than 80 years, a people who, during these last years, so doggedly ranged itself and fought on the Allied side against Fascism, such a people has the right to be free, such a people must be independent.

For these reasons, we, the members of the Provisional Government of the Democratic Republic of Viet Nam, solemnly declare to the world:

"Viet Nam has the right to be free and independent and, in fact, has become free and independent. The people of Viet Nam decide to mobilise all their spiritual and material forces and to sacrifice their lives and property in order to safeguard their right of Liberty and Independence."

(35) SPEECH BY VO NGUYEN GIAP, SEPTEMBER 2, 1945

Source: *Trang Su Moi (A New Page of History)*, (Hanoi: Hoi Van Hoa Cuu Quoc, 1945) Enclosure to dispatch no. 39, October 25, 1945 from Consul Philip D. Sprouse in Kunming, State Department Central Files, National Archives. [Translation by the Editor.]

In a speech to the crowd which had just heard Ho read the Declaration of the Independence, Vo Nguyen Giap made an impassioned plea to the allies not to abandon Viet-nam, which had fought on their side against the Japanese, while accurately predicting French efforts to reoccupy Indochina. In an effort to neutralize the Kuomintang Chinese, who were then entering the country to disarm the Japanese, Giap treated them as allies against imperialism, even quoting Chiang kai-shek's own anti-imperialism rhetoric.

Compatriots,

After dozens of years of fierce struggle against the aggressors, we finally found a favorable opportunity, which was the Second World War. Beginning in 1940 our people prepared to stand up and expel the French, then the Japanese, in order to win independence. Revolutionary organizations of the Viet Minh front secretly spread throughout the country; in green jungles and red mountains, guerrilla troops developed, and we advanced to form a liberated zone encompassing six mountainous and midland provinces of the North; the establishment of the Viet-nam Liberation Army began the construction of the new Viet-nam. Then the general insurrection returned political power to the hands of the people and achieved national unity from Nam-quan to Ca-mau. Only after going through countless hardships and dangers and seeing so many of our heroic fighters die for the fatherland, could we have this day. At this hour, there are hundreds of thousands of compatriots present here, as well as 20 million compatriots throughout the country, all assembled exhibited beneath the red flag with the gold star and pledging with the government to sacrifice to the last to protect the country. Today we declare to the world that we are determined to defend our people's right to live and that as a result of our people's struggle, there is a two-fold reality that no one can deny.

-- Independent Viet-nam is born.
-- The Democratic Republic of Viet-nam has been established.

That great feat has been accomplished thanks to three factors.

The first factor is the struggle of our heroic ancestors, whose heads fell and whose blood was shed for 80 years under the iron heel of the cruel aggressors, either on the execution ground or in prison or on the battlefront.

The second factor is the unity of the masses. The unity of vanguard elements in the past and of the entire people at present.

The third factor is the world wide democratic movement. The victory of the anti-fascist front had a decisive influence on the fate of our country. When Japan surrendered to the Allies, it meant that our foe had collapsed.

However, independent Viet-nam and the new Democratic Republic are still in their infancy and are still inexperienced. Therefore we must bring them rapidly to confident maturity so that no power can encroach on or shake them.

For that reason the Viet Minh front which has always been broad, has definitely become a national salvation movement of the entire people, in which all groups and all individuals having the will to serve the country stand up together and shoulder the heavy responsibility of achieving the unity of the entire people against any aggressive scheme. A Provisional Government having representatives of all elements participating has replaced the People's Revolutionary Committee elected by the National Congress convened by the Viet Minh Central Committee.

The Provisional Government embodies the will of the entire country and not the will of one political organization. From the time it was established, it has appealed to the nation to increase unity, and to make the struggle still stronger. Our people's spirit is higher every day, our people's strength is greater every day.

Center, South and North are of one mind; peasant, worker, merchant and soldiers are united in a common will. Even Buddhists and Christian clergy, even Emperor Bao Dai, have expressed their support and volunteered to fight the enemy. The Provisional Government has been formed thanks to the unity, and the fighting spirit of the people, and it makes that unity and fighting spirit deeper and broader.

To increase and strengthen that unity and fighting spirit, the Provisional Government will issue a decree tomorrow convening a National Assembly according to democratic principles. Representatives of the National Assembly are all to be elected by universal suffrage. The National Assembly will give us a constitution and a legal government.

While awaiting the National Assembly, the Provisional Government has the task of immediately carrying out urgent policies with regard to domestic affairs, foreign relations, military, economic, financial, and cultural affairs and relief. Regarding domestic affairs, the policy of the Provisional Government is unity and solidarity. There will be no more distinction among Center, North and South. Division among the peoples of Indochina will disappear. Those who have made mistakes but who know how to return to the just path will be forgiven. The property and lives of the compatriots and of foreigners will always be respected. The point worth stressing is that the people's government is determined to insure the freedom and happiness of the people.

To that end, the Government has, on one hand, begun to establish close liaison between the center and localities to carry out a single policy everywhere, so that misunderstandings or abuses can be avoided, and, on the other hand, has made plans to raise the consciousness of the masses by a campaign of propaganda and education so that the masses know how to defend and to use the democratic freedoms which they have won.

Militarily, the Liberation Army was established during the bloody days in the combat zone and recorded glorious accomplishments, is now being reorganized and broadened to become the National Army, with enough strength to protect Independence and the Government of the Democratic Republic.

The creation of military cadres to command the official army as well as guerillas and militia will be urgently organized in order to deal with the situation.

We are threatened with the French imperialists' aggressive plot, but with the unity and sacrifice of the entire people behind fearless troops, we are confident that we will win. And we will definitely break all the shackles which the invaders want to put on our people's feet once more.

Regarding economic matters, the exploitation of the French and Japanese has brought our national economy to a dangerous situation. Productive capacity has been limited by monopolies, industrial branches turned into organs for manufacturing goods useful only to the militarists, while commerce has been sharled by speculation and hoarding. There are those who think the Government must nationalize all business enterprises in order to restore the economy. But the Government will not do that. The Government will build a national economy in which everyone will have the freedom to carry on business. Moreover, the Government will encourage and assist individuals in large enterprises.

Regarding finances, we do not hesitate to declare immediately that the situation is very worrisome, and the Government will meet many difficulties. But the Government is devising means for overcoming those difficulties.

Despite difficulties which the Government had foreseen in advance, the Government will also gradually carry out policies which the people are hoping, such as eliminating head taxes and market taxes so that the living conditions of the poor will be eased.

But we must not forget that the work of construction, and particularly the building of a national army requires much money. Therefore, in order to fill the gaps in our treasury we must resort to special means such as loans, subscriptions, and income tax.

In determining to carry out such methods of resolving the problem, the Government relies primarily upon the patriotism of the compatriots. We are confident that in this critical moment, there is no one who does not recognize that if the country is lost, the individual's home must also be lost, that if independence and the Democratic Republic are shaky, then personal rights will also not be perfect. If enemy troops can return, not only the freedoms of the compatriots but also their property will be violated.

Regarding our culture, the Government will use clemency in dealing with those writers and journalists who went astray in the past. The censorship office, although temporary is expected to avoid information or propaganda which would be harmful to foreign relations or to domestic policy which is changing daily. But later, when the political situation has cleared up, freedom of opinion and freedom of expression will be immediately promulgated.

A new education is now in the organizational phase. It is certain that primary education will be compulsory, secondary education will be free, and poor students will be given scholarships. Very practical instruction will pay special attention to instilling those virtues needed for the continued existence of broad organizations and technical aptitude. In a very short time, a decree will be issued, promulgating compulsory study by Vietnamese in order to fight illiteracy. That extremely important question cannot wait until life returns to normal to be resolved. Even in the present difficult circumstances, we are determined to carry it out.

A national education system will be built immediately, beginning with the establishment of a committee of specialists to research all branches of human thought. Outmoded or depraved or reactionary customs will be fundamentally eliminated, along with filthy or vague literature which poisons the masses.

Regarding relief, the recent flood has created a major problem which could have an influence on the political situation. That is the problem of immediately feeding millions of flood victims who now have to eat and in another two months, to supply the people of those provinces lacking rice because of drought. Naturally the Government must shoulder the responsibility for insuring that the starvation which killed compatriots in past months does not return. But restaurants throughout the country must also regard relief of compatriots as a sacred responsibility, not only for the sake of humanity but also for the future of the nation.

Regarding foreign relations, opinion has paid much attention to the allied delegations which have successively arrived in Hanoi, and everybody is worried about the results of the Government's foreign relations.

First of all we hope the people will accept the situation in a calm manner in order to avoid tendencies of excessive optimism or excessive pessimism.

Our foreign policy relies on two factors: first the international setting, and second our own strength.

The international setting at present has many favorable points for the liberation of our nation. From the Pacific Charter to the Teheran, Yalta and San Franciso Agreements, the principle of national self-determination has been upheld. The great powers in the democratic front have declared that they were fighting for world peace, so there is no reason why today they would again let French imperialism bring its army here to make war against Independent Vietnam. The great powers in the democratic front have declared that they were fighting for equality among nations, so there is no reason why they would help French imperialism return to repress and exploit the Vietnamese people.

We and the whole world cannot imagine that after having, of our own volition, stood on the allied side to fight the Japanese fascists in Indochina, after having contributed bones and blood to the struggle of the allies on the Pacific front, we would be considered by the allies as having to live under the yoke of slavery of the French colonialists, who were the very ones who agreed to let Fascist Japan occupy Indochina in order to make it a base for attacking the Philippines, Malaya, Burma, South China, who surrendered to Fascist Japan and collaborated with Fascist Japan throughout the period of resistance. Right up to the time that Japan was threatened and seized all power in order to cope with the allies, the French thought about escaping or surrendering more than opposing. On the contrary, the Vietnamese masses have eagerly risen to fight Japan in the highlands and midlands of the North, and created an anti-Japanese movement, of non-collaboration with Japan throughout the country.

We must tell the allies that for three years the Viet Minh always appealed to the French in Indochina to cooperate in resisting Japan, but they not only ignored our appeal, but also repressed, arrested and killed anti-fascist fighters. Yet despite that fact every time we came across French held by the Japanese as prisoners in winning a battle, we liberated them.

Now that we have power in our own hands, with regard to French people, we still treat them with kindness. But that is not an attitude of fear or of loyalty toward them. They should be reasonable and recognize our right to complete independence. If they decide to use force to invade our country, we will shed our blood to the last drop in order to oppose them. And they will definitely suffer a grievous defeat.

That is our policy of friendship toward all countries. We have special affection for China and America. China is a country especially close to us geographically and in economic and cultural relations.

The Chinese residents here have long shared our suffering under the control of France and then Japan, have lived among us in a way no different from our compatriots, and today are all happy to see the liberation of the two peoples.

They have welcomed and supported Vietnamese independence, and the Vietnamese Government will protect their rights. They will, together with us, inherit freedom and happiness in an atmosphere of complete equality.

As for the United States, it is a democratic country, which has no territorial ambitions, but has contributed particularly to the defeat of our enemy, Japanese fascism. Therefore we regard the U.S. as a good friend.

Of our foreign problems at present, the most important is the attitude of the French Government of De Gaulle toward our independence. Its propaganda aims at creating misunderstanding among the allied countries, of the present situation in Indochina. Sometimes they say we are faithful to them, because it was they who fought Japan; sometimes they say we are the lackeys of Japan, and sometimes they accuse us of having killed French women and children. But we have enough proof to destroy those dark schemes. Politically, they have named a new Governor General and secretly incited French civil servants to plot to take back public offices. Militarily, they are preparing to bring troops back into Indochina. Generally speaking, according to information recently obtained, it is clear that they tend to reestablish their power in our country. We swear that we will defend our nation against them to the death. Our people have always desired peace, but when we must shed blood, we are also determined to do so.

Compatriots,

In the future in all fields, but especially in foreign affairs, we will meet many difficulties. We do not rely on anyone. We do not expect any such good fortune. We must take care of ourselves in order to determine our own fate. If we want an excellent domestic policy, and foreign relations victories, we must quickly create the strength by unity, forged in struggle and sacrifice, by actions supporting the government in a realistic manner.

At this time, division, doubt, and apathy are all a betrayal of the country.

At this time, the mind of each person must be directed to the struggle for independence, the concern of each person must be concern for opposing foreign aggression. Only if there is such concern can we avoid the yoke of slavery.

Beloved compatriots, nephews of Tran quoc Tuan, and of Le Loi, let us all stand up, close our ranks and await the orders of the Provisional Government.

To warn those who might decide on a repetition of plans for aggression, we repeat the words of Chiang Kai-shek on the attitude of the oppressed Asian peoples when this World War concluded: "If they are not given freedom and equality, a third World War will follow on the heels of this Second World War, just as this Second World War followed on the heels of the First World War."

The Vietnamese people must obtain independence, freedom and equality. That is not the aspiration of the Vietnamese masses alone but of all democratic countries. The masses of those countries have sacrificed in the struggle to serve the cause of justice, and not to serve oppression. Therefore the masses in those countries all earnestly hope to see the small and weak nations liberated, and they also believe with Chiang kai-shek that: "When the war ends, imperialism must also be ended, because imperialism is the cause of war."

The Vietnamese people demand independence, freedom and equality to the end. If demanding it by diplomacy and using moderate means does not work, then we must take up the sword. We are prepared for anything that might happen. We may not be as strong as the enemy but we will defeat the enemy as our ancestors in the time of the Tran dynasty.

In any case, if we are determined, and continue the struggle we will definitely maintain the victories of today. Just as Mr. Roosevelt has said, oppression and cruelty have made us know what freedom means.

Under the leadership of the Provisional Government and Chairman Ho Chi Minh, our people will give all their wealth, their bones and blood to build and beautify the fatherland, to make our beloved Vietnam bright, and wealthy and powerful after so many years of misery and exhaustion.

Following the traditions of previous generations, our generation will fight a final battle so that generations to follow will forever be able to live in independence, freedom and happiness.

(36) <u>MEMORANDA FOR SECRETARY OF STATE JAMES BYRNES FROM O.S.S. DIRECTOR WILLIAM J. DONOVAN</u>, SEPTEMBER 5 and 6, 1945.

Source: 851G.0019-545, State Department Central Files, National Archives.

Members of the U.S. Office of Strategic Services team reported on the situation in Viet-nam via Kunming. Through these reports, which were then passed on the Secretary of State, U.S. policymakers became aware almost immediately of the existence of independent Vietnamese government and the seriousness of its plans to resist the restoration of French power in Viet-nam.

The OSS representative in Hanoi, who has been instrumental in communications concerning the Japanese surrender in Indo-China, has transmitted the following information, dated 1 September, via Kunming:

The Provisional Annamese Government in Indo-China is in full control and so well organized that several attempts by French from Calcutta to parachute into the country have been frustrated. The parachutists, although not maltreated, were held as prisoners. According to the Annamese Prime Minister, should the French attempt a return, the Annamese are determined to maintain their independence even at the cost of lives. They feel they have nothing to lose and all to gain. Meanwhile, however, the Prime Minister has promised the OSS representative in Hanoi that no organized violence against Europeans will occur until the Chinese assume control in the area.

The Japanese have been destroying, selling, and otherwise disposing of stocks of rice and miscellaneous equipment in addition to arms and ammunition from their dumps. The commanding Japanese general has promised that severe disciplinary measures would be taken against violators of his orders to safeguard all property belonging to or in the possession of the Japanese Army or Japanese administration in Indo-China.

The OSS representative in Hanoi has transmitted, via Calcutta, the following information, which is a continuation of our memoranda of 21 August, 22 August, 31 August, and 5 September, concerning the Provisional Government in Indo-China:

On 2 September the head of the Provisional Annamese Government flatly refused an invitation to confer with Major Sainteny, the French representative in Indo-China. With this act, the Annamese apparently intended to close all negotiations with the French for an indefinite period. The French intend to carry on, however, and Sainteny will remain in the Governor General's palace, hoping to maintain France's prerogatives. Sainteny intends to organize an underground resistance group to work along subversive lines against the adamant Provisional Annamese Government. The Provisional Government now clearly seems to be composed of strictly left-wing elements. A strong element of the Annamese Kuomintang and certain republican factions are not represented.

The Chinese residents in Indo-China are becoming more and more politically aggressive because they believe that their Government in Chungking has prepared a puppet government with which to present the Annamese upon arrival. On the other hand, the Annamese are prepared to combat such a government openly or subversively. The French are once again becoming belligerent and are rebuking the Allies for not siding with them. Trouble seems to be brewing, and may break out after the armistice has been signed in Indo-China.

(37) LETTER BY HO CHI MINH TO THE VIETNAMESE PEOPLE TO FIGHT FAMINE, SEPTEMBER 1945

Source: Ho Chi Minh, *Selected Works*, Vol. III, pp. 40-41.

At the first meeting of the cabinet of the Provisional Government of the Democratic Republic of Viet-nam, on September 3, President Ho told his ministers that the most urgent problem facing the new government was to do everything possible to prevent starvation. The corn and yam harvest, which would help somewhat to alleviate the famine was still three or four months away, and it would take sometime to increase rice production. The only way the new government could immediately reduce starvation was to distribute the existing grain supply as equitably as possible. It did not have the administrative resources to do so by administrative fiat, however, so Ho could only appeal to the population to spare one of its meals every ten days for the poor - and to pledge to do so himself.

Dear compatriots!

From January to July this year, in the North, two million people have starved to death.

Floods adding, the famine increased, plunging the people in utter wretchedness.

How painful we are at our meals when we think of those who are dying of hunger!

Therefore I propose to you, and I will do it first:

To do without a meal every ten days, that is three meals every month, and spare this rice (one tin each meal) for the poor.

Thus these people will have something to eat while waiting for the next crop, and escape death.

I am confident that all our compatriots out of charity are eager to respond to my proposal.

Thank you on behalf of the poor.

(38) APPEAL BY HO CHI MINH TO VIETNAMESE PEOPLE, SEPTEMBER 8, 1945

Source: *Nhung Loi Keu Goi cua Ho Chu Tich* (Appeals by Chairman Ho), Vol. I, (from 1941 to 1949), 2nd edition. (Hanoi: Su That, 1958), p. 19. Translation by the editor.

Although Ho Chi Minh's government was prepared to cooperate with the Chinese in the North and the British in the South, it drew the line at French forces. This terse message to the Vietnamese people to be prepared for any eventuality indicates the strength of Ho's suspicions of French intentions.

The Vietnamese people welcome the allied troops who have come to Vietnam to disarm the Japanese army, but are determined to resist French forces entering Vietnam, because their objective is to force the Vietnamese people into slavery once more.

Compatratiots!

At present a number of French troops have landed in our country.

Be prepared and await the orders of the Government in order to fight.

(39) TELEGRAM FROM AMBASSADOR CAFFERY IN FRANCE TO SECRETARY BYRNES, SEPTEMBER 12, 1945

Source: G851G.001/9-1245, State Department Central Files, National Archives.

The French government reacted to the news of the founding of an independent Vietnamese government with confidence that the French government would be assisted by the British, Chinese and Americans in restoring the French rule to Indochina. In a conversation with the U.S. Ambassador, the Director of the French Foreign Ministry's Far Eastern Department argued that the "troubles" which were occurring were the work of the Japanese and of "Communist elements". He indicated French intentions to send troops from France to Indochina as soon as possible, again with allied assistance.

The French press has in the past several days contained a number of articles dealing with the situation in Indochina which is described as "serious" and where the press reports several cases of French nationals being massacred by natives. Baudet, Chief of Far Eastern Division of the Foreign Ministry commenting on these articles said that while the situation there was certainly most disquieting some articles which have appeared in the Paris press had given the Foreign Ministry concern because they hinted at American, Chinese and British designs on Indochina and implied that these countries might not be dissatisfied with the troubles which are occurring.

This he said did not represent the official view and added that steps are being taken to have the Information Ministry correct this erroneous impression. On the contrary he said that the Japanese who have been sponsoring a nationalist campaign and who have supplied nationalist and pro-Japanese elements with money and arms are largely responsible for the disorders and he also mentioned, "Communist elements" as a contributing factor.

He went on to say that the French had always known that when Japan was defeated there would be a difficult hiatus period in Indo-China before central authority could be restored on which nationalist elements would endeavor to capitalize. The French had hoped that this transitional period would be short. Subsequently it became apparent however that "because of the successful manner in which the Japanese had aided armed and encouraged nationalist groups this would not be the case." Accordingly the French "welcome" the idea of the temporary occupation of French IndoChina by British and Chinese military forces as the best possible means to reestablish order, particularly since "the French forces, totaling about 5,000, which escaped into China at the time the Japanese took over is not properly equipped and would not be sufficient to restore French prestige and authority. He mentioned that the trials suffered by this force in its withdrawal into China had a demoralizing effect on it.

He said that the French have no real fear of American and British, and for that matter Chinese, designs on Indo-China, but that the situation is nonetheless "serious". A telegram had just been received from Chungking reporting that "the Chinese are also worried about moving into Indochina because they fear they may meet armed resistance from native elements 'armed by the Japanese' which distrust the Chinese and fear that a Chinese occupation will result in Chinese military requisition and seizure of foodstuffs and materials." He added that the Chinese have requested the French to furnish technical and administrative personnel to assist in administration and in maintaining the public services since the Chinese Army, unlike the British and American armies, has no effective civil affairs section.

Baudet said French are also concerned by the fact that the British have informed them that they will probably not be able to undertake real occupation of southern Indochina until after the first of October and this may permit a spread of the present local disorder particularly since "fanatical nationalists and Japanese agents will be able to continue to spread disorders with no one to oppose them".

Then in conclusion he said the great French preoccupation is to see order restored by the occupational forces at the earliest possible moment and to arrange for the transport of French troops from France to Indochina as soon as possible. In the latter connection, he said, the French approached the British in London urgently (sent Dept. as 5468 rptd to Chungking as 12) several days ago to obtain a sufficient allocation of shipping for the purpose.

(40) REPORT ON O.S.S. "DEER MISSION" BY MAJOR ALLISON K. THOMAS, SEPTEMBER 17, 1945 [Extracts]

Source: *Causes, Origins, and Lessons of the Vietnam War*, Hearings before the Committee on Foreign Relations, U.S. Senate, 92nd Cong., 2nd Session, 1973, pp. 251-264.

In May 1945, the U.S. Office of strategic Services decided to send two O.S.S. teams into Tonkin to sabotage the Hanoi-Langson road and railroad. The Americans were originally to work with French and Vietnamese troops, but were informed that, contrary to French assurances, the Vietnamese would not collaborate with the French military. Since the Viet Minh were the only effective anti-Japanese guerilla organization in the region, the U.S. teams found themselves training troops and working directly with Ho Chi Minh and Vo Nguyen Giap just at the time that key decisions were being made on the August Revolution. The report by one of the team leaders, Major Allison Thomas indicates the warmth which the O.S.S. team felt toward the Viet Minh leaders and its conviction that it was a genuinely popular movement.

VI. Life in FIC from arrival of Advance Party to arrival of remainder of team.

17 July: Our camp was located on the side of a hill in a bamboo forest at the end of Kimlung Gorge about 1 kilo from the small village of Kimlung. Kimlung itself is located 27 kilos almost due east of Tuyen Quang and about 47 kilos northwest of Thai Nguyen, the provincial capital. The military coordinates on the FIC map, scale 1:100,000, are: Sheet # 26 (West), 17.5-45.5.

We were a few yards from the hut of Mr. Hoo, Viet Minh Party Chief and also a few yards from (*name omitted in original*) of AGAS. Immediately to the west of us unrolled our drop zone which consisted of a flat valley of rice paddies surrounded by forested hills.

The identity of Mr. C.M. Hoo, recognized Vietminh Party Leader, was a mystery to us. Hoo was his code name. Later, when he became President of the Provisional Government of Vietminh (Indochina) at Hanoi, he divulged his real name which is Ho Chi Minh.

Held long conference with Mr. Hoo, (Ho Chi Minh), on the subject of the French. He stated the the Vietminh Party, or League, was an amalgamation of all political parties organized for the sole purpose of ousting all foreign powers and was working for the liberty and complete independence of Indo-China. It had no political ideas beyond that as its members came from all political groups. After liberty had been achieved, then they would worry about politics. He definitely tabooed the idea that the Party was communistic. He stated that at least 85% of the people of Tonkin were members or sympathetic with its aims. It would obviously be the most ordinary observer that the peasants didn't know what the word communism or socialism meant - but they did understand liberty and independence.

Consequently, Mr. Hoo made it very clear to me that it would be impossible for Lt. Montfort, the French officer, to stay, nor would any more French be welcome. He pointed out many grievances his people had against the French and many of his people hated them worse than the Japs. In fact, everyone talked against the Jap Fascists and French Fascists with equal fervor. He said he would welcome a million American soldiers to come in but not any French even though they were soldiers and insisted that they were here to fight Japs only, because as Mr. Hoo maintained it would only be an opening wedge for them. He indicated he would gladly escort Lt. Montfort safely back to the frontier as he had done many other Frenchmen. It was agreed that I would notify my Hq on the subject and Lt. Montfort would return soonest, either by L-5 or afoot. Lt. Montfort was made aware of the situation and cabled the same information to the French at Poseh. He was most anxious to return to Kunming to explain the entire situation, inasmuch as Mr. Hoo welcomed a talk with with any high ranking French official, especially on the subject of DeGaulle's proclamation concerning FIC which contained some very vague points.

As to Sgt. LOGOS and Sgt. PHAC, Mr. Hoo consented to their staying on, however doubted if the French would release them. This turned out to be the case.

[Entries for the period July 18 to July 31 omitted]

VIII. <u>Action taken after Jap surrender 15 August</u>.

A. March to Thai Nguyen:

<u>15 Aug</u>: Decided after conference with Party leaders that in view of Jap surrender it was now the opportune time to wind up the training and hit the road in the general direction of Thai Nguyen and see what could be done in the way of "action." Troops were ordered to get ready to leave the next morning. Americans spent the day packing and getting ready to break camp. As far as the training of our troops was concerned it was not finished. What we had done had been done fast and not all subjects by any means had been covered. However, the boys picked it up fast, had been eager to learn and made up for it in spirit what they still lacked in training.

<u>16 Aug</u>: When the news was received that Jap surrender was possible I sent a wire to Poseh stating that we might be able to obtain the surrender of all Jap troops in our area, that we would follows terms of Geneva convention, and eventually turn all Jap prisoners and arms we might get over to the proper authorities, following the Allied surrender negotiations with the Japs.

The answer to this was that as far as we were concerned the war was over and under no circumstances were we to accept any Jap surrenders. This was indeed extremely disheartening to me as we all felt that we had risked our lives in coming here and now when the going was to be easy we were not allowed to get in on the gravy.

However, since there was no point any longer in staying in the deep dark mosquito bitten forests anymore we broke camp and left with the soldiers that morning at 11:30 AM. Our intention was to move at least as far as Thai Nguyen which was a fairly good size town and set up more comfortable quarters there and await developments. From this point on we received no official news on the occupation of FIC by the Allies. We learned through AGAS that probably the Chinese would occupy the Northern half of FIC and the British the Southern half.

On leaving Kimlung I had a final conference with Mr. Hoo who indicated to me he would like me to stay in FIC as long as possible. I replied that that was a question for my C.O. in Kunming, and doubted if it would be possible inasmuch as his party was not recognized nor was his country independent as yet.

Mr. Hoo had called a conference of all party leaders and delegates at Kimlung from all over Tonkin to discuss their future policy, and they were all present to see the troops off.

Arrived late last night at the village of Dong Man.

<u>17 Aug</u>: Second day of March. Stayed all night at Phuc Linh not far from Hungson. Marched on main road part of the way and we saw why the Japs had not used the road. The guerillas had torn up the bridges, dug craters, and placed large trees across the road in strategic places.

18 Aug: A section of the troops made a recce of Hungson. About 20 Japs still at the post, but Party leader, Mr. Van, decided that there was not much point in wasting a day here in trying to attack it but go for bigger game at Thai Nguyen, which was the provincial capital. The Americans and the remaining troops in the meantime headed for the village of· Thinh Dan, a few kilos south of Thai Nguyen.

19 Aug: All troops to-gether again and all moved a little closer to Thai Nguyen. The Party leaders made plans to enter the town at 4 AM in the morning, surround the post, occupy strategic spots, demand the surrender of the "Guarge Indigene" from the Provincial Governor and then issue a surrender ultimatum to the Japs in the name of the VIETMINH LEAGUE.

A group of VIETMINH party members came out from town and drew up a plan of the town showing Jap positions. They said there were about 30 to 40 Japs in the post and none in the town. The Japs had a kitchen in town but used it only in the daytime. This later proved false, and it turned out there were small detachments of Japs in four different buildings throughout the town.

We received a message from Poseh stating we were to sit tight and not go to Hanoi without orders from Hq. This again was stunning news. We could not understand this. If Hanoi was safe to enter and we being Americans we couldn't see the point but guessed that Hq. thought we would not be strictly neutral inasmuch as we worked for a few weeks with the VIETMINH. However, conversely considering everything Hq. hadn't been neutral as far as these people were concerned when we issued arms to the French. Of course, the counter argument and quite plausible one was that the French were our Allies and the VIETMINH party was a secret party working against the French whose existence was not recognized by any power. Another point we thought might have something to do with it was that since Gen'l MacArthur was in charge of surrender negotiations to OSS personnel were allowed to proceed to Hanoi.   This turned out to be erroneous because we later learned through the VIETMINH that an ALLIED mission of inquiry headed by a Capt. Patti had arrived in Hanoi. Poseh, on questioning, informed us that this was our own Capt. PATTI of OSS.

[*Entries for August 20 to 26 reporting on a battle by VIETMINH troops against Japanese troops at Thai Nguyen are omitted.*]

IX. Period of peace and rest after the battle of Thai Nguyen.

27 Aug - 9 Sept: During this period the Americans were comfortably housed in the former Provincial Governor's quarters, well-fed and cared for by the VIETMINH. The time was spent getting fat, getting sun-tan, visiting the city, and waiting for permission to go to Hanoi to get a plane for Kunming and home.

So now I can take time out here to describe somewhat our life in FIC from the mundane point of view.

Actually the country side of Tonkin is very beautiful. It is mountainous with large forests. In every valley are the rice paddies where the people eke out a meager living. Their rice diet is supplemented by a few chickens, pigs, bamboo sprouts, "jungle" team taroo (somewhat like potato.) a few forest fruits, some bananas and farther south some pineapples and grapefruit. Their diet is extremely deficient which is evident by the distended bellies of their children.

The peasants in general in Tonkin are extremely bad off. They have few clothes. What they do have consists of patched over rags and the children run around naked. But they are all hard working and honest. The people are principally of three types - Annamese, Tho and Man. They all speak different languages or dialects. The Tho are strongly VIETMINH in sentiment. The Man hill tribes are ancient peoples who live in the very remote and isolated places. Their dress is colorful. The women wear blue and always wear silver and copper coins and colorful beads. They are also VIETMINH in political sentiment.

The VIETMINH did everything to make our stay as pleasant as possible for us. They gave us their best food and we seldom went without a chicken or a duck or meat of some kind to go along with our rice. They would go for miles to obtain bananas for us. At every village we entered on our various trips the whole population would turn out to welcome us and present to us the "key to the village" as it were. The village guard would render a salute with their ancient arms. The village headman would give us a little speech of welcome and present us with gifts of bananas, eggs or flowers. Then the children in the group would sing a native song or two and then everyone would join in and sing a VIETMINH song of independence and liberty. The scenes were invariably impressive and "touching" to all the Americans as we knew they were expressing what was in their hearts and offering to us the best gifts they had.

X. Hanoi

9 Sept - 16 Sept: Our team left by foot, car, and boat and arrived at Hanoi about 4 PM. We obtained quarters through the VIETMINH party, which was authorized by the PATTI MISSION.

We spent the time from 9 Sept to 16 Sept seeing the city buying souvenirs saying good-bye to our VIETMINH friends, and making arrangements to return to Kunming. Hanoi was an extremely festive city for everyone except the French.

VIETMINH flags were flying from almost every house. Banners were stretched across the streets with various "slogans" in Annamese, English, Chinese, Russian, Indian, etc. French was noticeably absent.

Some of the slogans seen everywhere were as follows: "Welcome Allies", "Welcome Peace Commission", "Down with French Imperialism", "Let's kick out French Imperialism", "Independence of Death", "2,000,000 people died under French domination", "VIETMINH for the VIETNAMESE".

Our friend of the forest, Mr. C.M. Hoo, now Mr. Ho Chi Minh, was President of the Provisional Government and Minister of Foreign Affairs. Another friend of the forest, Mr. Van, now Vo Nguyen Giap became Minister of Interior. Party members were appointed cabinet members. The new government seems to be enthusiastically supported by the majority of the population in every province of Indochina. The new government was given strength by the resignation and abdication of Bao Dai, former puppet Emperor, who offered his services as friend and adviser.

The people know the French intend to come back but they keep saying if they come back with arms they will fight to the death.

The story of our experiences in IndoChina is melodramatic in the following sense. On July 16 we were living in the forests of Indochina with the Chief of the VIETMINH Party. Less than two months later, this same chief had become President of the new Provisional Government and was installed in the former home of the French "Resident Superior" in Hanoi.

XI. Return to Kunming.

On 16 Sept 1945 our team returned by plane to Kunming, China.

(41) LETTER FROM MAJOR GENERAL PHILIP E. GALLAGHER IN HANOI TO MAJOR GENERAL R.B. McCLURE, KUNMING, SEPTEMBER 20, 1945

Source: Original typescript in Gallagher Papers, Center for Military History, U.S. Army, Washington, D.C.

Maj. Gen. Philip E. Gallagher arrived in Hanoi following the Japanese surrender to assist the Chinese in their occupation of Northern Viet-nam. As this excerpt from his first report to the commanding General of the Chinese Combat Command in Kunming indicates, he was sympathetic to Vietnamese aspirations for independence, but was forbidden to do anything to assist the Vietnamese cause.

The letter indicates that the Vietnamese were still in the dark about U.S. intentions regarding the return of the French in Indochina.

The Annamite party, Viet Minh, led by Ho Chi Minh who is the Prime Minister, is definitely in the saddle. This Ho Chi Minh is an old revolutionist and a political prisoner many times, a product of Moscow, a communist. He called upon me and welcomed us most profusely, gave me a very beautiful banner with my name on it and some remark about the "Great American nation," etc. His political party is an amalgamation of all lesser parties. There may be some smaller bandit groups, but they are negligible, his is the dominant force. They now claim their independence, and he has told me that, regardless of the decision of the big powers regarding whether France would or would not be permitted to come back in, his party expected to fight, that they are armed, well supplied, and will resist all French efforts to take over FIC. In this regard, it is well to remember that he is a revolutionist whose motto is "Independence or Death," and since all the chips are placed down, we should not put too much stock in his statement that he is going to fight the French. He looks upon America as the saviour of all nations, and is basing all of his actions on the statement in the Atlantic Charter that the independence of the smaller nations would be assured by the major powers. Of course we know that charter was never signed. He expects us to support him in his efforts, and it will be a great shock, of course, if the French are allowed to come back, either as a protectorate or otherwise. In my discussion with him, I pointed out frankly that my job was not as a representative of the State Department, nor was I interested in the political situation, and could neither offer my sympathy nor assurance of any help, that I was merely working with Lu Han. One thing that was worrying him was that he had been given the impression that Lu Han was going to establish complete military control over the entire area for which he was responsible, and that his sole purpose therein was to disarm the Japanese and maintain peace and order, that he undoubtedly intended to use, wherever practicable existing constituted authority to run the country and to enforce peace and discipline; that Lu Han favored neither the French nor Annamites and would tolerate no violence on the part of either and would treat them as equals. I assured him that China had no territorial desires insofar as FIC was concerned. Here again I indicated to him that he must gain the confidence of Lu Han and deal with him altogether. Confidentially, I wish the Annamites could be given their independence, but, of course, we have no voice in this matter.

(42) PROCLAMATION BY GENERAL D.D. GRACEY, SAIGON, SEPTEMBER 21, 1945

Source: Great Britain, Parliament, Papers by Command, *Documents Relating to British Involvement in the Indo-China Conflict 1945-1965* (London: Her Majesty's Stationery Office, CMND 2834, 1965), pp. 52-53.

When the Supreme Allied Commander of all Allied Forces in Southeast Asia Command, Admiral Lord Louis Mountbatten, arrived in Saigon in September 1945 pursuant to the agreement at Potsdam, it was on the understanding between Britain and France that British forces would assist the French in resuming control over Indochina. But the British faced a determined Viet Minh government in Saigon. The response by the British command was to ignore the Vietnamese authorities and assert its authority in their place. The proclamation by General Gracey did so, however, on the promise of "strict impartiality" with regard to political affairs - a pledge which induced the Viet Minh officials to cooperate with the British authorities rather than openly resist.

1. With the unconditional surrender to the Allied Nations by all Japanese forces signed in the name of the Emperor of Japan at Tokyo on 2d September 1945, the Supreme Allied Commander of all Allied Forces in South-East Asia Command,

Admiral Lord Louis Mountbattan G.C.V.O., K.C.B., D.S.O., has delegated me, General D.D. Gracey C.B., C.B.E., M.C., the Command of all British, French and Japanese forces and all police forces and armed bodies in French Indo-China south of 16° latitude with orders to ensure law and order in this area.

2. Let it be known to all that it is my firm intention to ensure with strict impartiality that this period of transition from war to peace conditions is carried out peaceably with the minimum dislocation to all public and utility services, legitimate business and trade, and with the least interference with the normal peaceful activities and vocations of the people.

3. I call on all citizens in the name of the Supreme Allied Command to co-operate to the fullest extent to achieve the above object and hereby warn all wrongdoers especially looters and saboteurs of public and private property and those carrying out similar criminal activities, that they will be summarily shot.

4. The following orders will come into immediate effect.

A. No demonstrations or processions will be permitted.

B. No public meetings will take place.

C. No arms of any description, including sticks, staves, bamboo spears, etc., will carried except by British and Allied troops and such other forces and police which have been specially authorized by me.

D. The curfew already imposed on my orders by the Japanese authorities between 21.30 and 05.30 hours in Saigon and Cholon will be continued and strictly enforced.

(43) TELEGRAM FROM D.R.V. FOREIGN MINISTER HO CHI MINH TO BRITISH PRIME MINISTER CLEMENT ATTLEE, SEPTEMBER 26, 1945.

Source: Great Britain, Parliament Papers by Command, *Documents Relating to British Involvement in the Indochinese Conflict, 1945-1965*, (London: Her Majesty's Stationery Office, Cmnd. 2834), p. 53.

On September 23, French prisoners of war, with the explicit consent of Major-General Gracey, who freed them, carried out a coup d'etat *in Saigon against the Viet Minh Executive Committee. British and Indian troops participated in the fighting to secure important positions in the city, meeting considerable Vietnamese resistance. Fighting continued for several days. The D.R.V. reacted sharply to this violation of what they thought had been a policy of allied neutrality on Indochina's political future with a telegram of protest to Britain, and ordered the people in the South to resist the reoccupation by French forces throughout the South. Ho Chi Minh, in his role as Foreign Minister, protested the British assistance to the French Coup.*

Foreign Minister of Viet-Nam Republic to Premier Attlee, London.

The release of French prisoners of war with arms and ammunition leading to the French attack against Saigon and the arrests of members of the People's Committee constitutes a great violation of our national rights and is an offense to our national dignity, a non-fulfillment of the mission placed on Commander British Forces in South Indo-China by the United Nations, a failure in the carrying of the Atlantic Charter and non-observation of attitude of neutrality by the British Disarmament Forces. We therefore lodge a most emphatic protest against such smoke-screening of French aggression and express earnest hope that you would interfere on basis full respect for the independence of Viet-Nam Republic.

(44) <u>MEMORANDUM FOR THE RECORD</u>: GENERAL GALLAGHER'S MEETING WITH HO CHI MINH, SEPTEMBER 29, 1945.

Source: Gallagher Papers.

Shortly after receiving word from Kunming that the Chinese were to help the French recover power in Indochina, Gallagher met with Ho. The conversation centered on the delicate question of the allied governments' attitude toward the D.R.V. Gallagher tried to soothe Ho's fears that Vietnam was being viewed as "conquered territory," despite his knowledge that the U.S. had assured the French of its acquiescence in French reconquest.

1. Conference, Friday 28 September 1945, 1830 hours. Present were General Gallagher, Colonel Hutson, Major Patti, Lt. Ungern and Prime Minister Ho Chi Minh.

2. Mr. Ho inquired regarding the surrender proclamation issued by Lu Han, and that part in particular dealing with military control of governmental administrative functions. He was referred to Lu Han for his exact interpretation, but was informed that spirit behind policy was to use constituted authority as much as possible to continue proper administrative functions, but, at the same time have a supervisory system set up capable of controlling certain key positions is case of disorder or unrest. In this regard, and in all matters arising regarding the occupation forces or their policies, Mr. Ho was urged to formulate a close working basis with Lu Han and cooperate with him and his decisions closely. When questioned, Mr. Ho stated that there had not yet been any interference with any local authorities or controls by the Chinese.

3. Mr. Ho expressed the feeling that the Allies considered Indo China as a conquered country and that the Chinese came as conquerors. He was reassured that this was not the case, and section of surrender proclamation issued by Lu Han quoted directly as an indication of this. It was stated that the presence of the Chinese forces was hoped would have stabilizing effect and afford time for negotiation between the parties concerned. In the meantime, every effort will be made to avoid the outbreak of trouble and bloodshed.

4. Mr. Ho stated that the youth of the Viet Minh party wished to stage a large demonstration on 29 September, and asked advice as to whether he should give permission for the rally. He stated that probably anti-French posters would be displayed during the rally. He was referred in this matter to Lu Han for a decision, and urged to be honest and frank in stating the purpose of the rally and the fact that anti-French sentiment would be included.

5. Mr. Ho presented the following Associated Press dispatch from Saigon:

"The rioting Annamites killed one American officer, seriously wounded another, and beseiged U.S. headquarters one hour Wednesday in the first incident involving the U.S. forces in Indo China.

"Colonel Peter Dewey was killed by a machine gun bullet while he was attempting to pass the Annamite territory in a short automobile drive from the local airfield to his headquarters. The Annamites then attacked Colonel Dewey's headquarters and injured several more persons."

Mr. Ho expressed his profound regret at the occurance of such an incident. He assured General Gallagher that any such incident would take place in this area "only over my dead body." Mr. Ho stated that the incident might have been staged for the benefit of French propaganda by French agents, but admitted it might have been the action of unruly elements of the Annamese. He acknowledged that such incidents could in the long run only hurt the cause for which he is striving, and lessen the regard in which the Annamese people are held by the peoples of other nations. In connection with this incident, Mr. Ho stated that he would write a letter to the State Department deploring the occurance and expressing regret, and, also, explaining the situation regarding the occurence from the Annamese viewpoint, as clearly as possible. Major Patti will forward the communication.

6. Mr. Ho stated that in a conference earlier in the day with General Alessandri, the French general handed him a memorandum inviting members of the Viet Minh revolutionary movement to Chungking for conferences with high French and Chinese officials. Mr. Ho expressed concern that the invitation was not issued to the party as a governmental body, but simply as a revolutionary group. General Gallagher stated that, regardless of phraseology, the move offered an opportunity for consultation, presentation of mutual viewpoints, and the possibility of an amicable and agreeable settlement of present difficulties existing between factions; and urged that the invitation be accepted as such. In connection with the proposed visit to Chungking, Mr. Ho stated that he had consulted Lu Han and had been informed that suitable transportation would probably not be available for approximately two weeks.

7. Mr. Ho expressed concern over the fact that some French were appearing in American dress and were attempting in some instances to pass themselves off as Americans. He urged that all Americans wear positive identification.

8. Mr. Ho stated that a proclamation was being considered forbidding the French to leave the city and also forbidding their presence on the streets between 2100 and 0600 hours, and asked advice. This matter was referred to Lu Han's wishes concerning the situation.

---

(45) STATEMENT OF THE FOREIGN MINISTRY OF THE PROVISIONAL GOVERNMENT OF THE DEMOCRATIC REPUBLIC OF VIETNAM, OCTOBER 1945

Source: *Foreign Policy of the Provisional Government of the Republic of Vietnam,* (Hanoi: n.d.), enclosure no. 2 to dispatch no. 39, October 25, 1945, from Consul Philip D. Sprouse, Kunming, in diplomatic papers, U.S. Archives.

In its first official statement on foreign policy, the Provisional Government emphasized the distinction in its attitude between French and the other Allies, and made clear its need for the cooperation of Laos and Cambodia in struggling against French colonialism. The latter principle was to have far-reaching implications for the conflict when governments in both countries collaborated with the French against the Vietnamese resistance forces. The date of the declaration, and a different translation of the text, was given in Pham Van Dong's statement to the Geneva Conference, May 10, 1954.

Vietnam is now in a phase of fierce struggle. The main object of our foreign policy is to insure the victory of the nation by peaceable or forcible means, according to the attitude evinced by the foreign powers, but always in accordance with the Atlantic Charter.

a/ Therefore, towards the Allies, Vietnam will cultivate friendship and promote co-operation based upon liberty and equality, in order to build up lasting world peace. As regards China, a country united to us by many traditional links, important in every respect, geographical, historical, cultural, and economical, Vietnam wishes to bring these links even closer and stronger, so as to enable the two peoples to help each other on their way to progress.

b/ But as far as France is concerned Vietnam is at present under obligation of following a different policy. First of all, such French residents as willingly submit themselves to law and order, and respect the independence of our country, will have their lives and properties protected, according to international law. But as regards DeGaulle's Government which has expressly menaced our security, sticking to its colonial policy, we declare our determination to oppose it, if it refuses to acknowledge the full independence of Viet-Nam.

c/ As regards lesser nations, the Government of Viet-Nam Republic is prepared to engage friendly relations and co-operate with them on the principle of equality of status, in order to help mutually in the building up and maintenance of national independence.

d/ Our desire to cultivate friendship with Cambodia and Laos on the basis of self-determination of peoples is more earnest as, in the past, in the present juncture and in the future, there have been, are, and will be common features in the respective fates of the three nations. Having been under French domination, we must make common efforts to overthrow the French yoke and avoid taking any separate step which might be prejudicial to the independence of others. Mutual help is necessary to the recovery and maintenance of independence. Furthermore as Cambodia, Laos, and Viet-Nam will have many economic bounds, [sic] the three nations will assist one another to reconstruct their respective countries and advance, side by side, on the path of progress.

As the Government of Viet-Nam Republic does not make any difference between races and classes it will not make any difference between religions. Liberty of Faith will be fully respected. Therefore, regarding the Catholic as well as the other religions, the Government will show affection and respect, based on the principle of freedom of faith.

(46) TELEGRAM FROM ACTING SECRETARY OF STATE DEAN ACHESON TO CHARGE WALTER ROBERTSON IN CHINA, OCTOBER 5, 1945

Source: *U.S. Vietnam Relations, Book 8, p. 49.*

In the first U.S. official policy response to the establishment of the Democratic Republic of Viet-nam and its declaration of independence, Acting Secretary of State Dean Acheson told U.S. diplomats in India and China that the U.S. did not question French sovereignty over Indochina, while suggesting that the U.S. position would be dependent upon evidence of popular support in Viet-nam for French rule.

"US has no thought of opposing the reestablishment of French control in Indochina and no official statement by US Government has questioned even by implication French sovereignty over Indochina. However, it is not the policy of this Govt to assist the French to reestablish their control over Indochina by force and the willingness of the US to see French control reestablished assumes that French claim to have the support of the population of Indochina is borne out by future events."

(47) CONSTITUTION OF THE VIETNAM-AMERICAN FRIENDSHIP ASSOCIATION, OCTOBER 1945 [Extract]

Source: *Hoi Viet My Than Huu, Dieu Le (Vietnam-American Friendship Association, Constitution),* (Hanoi, 1945). The editor is grateful to Professor David Marr, Australian National University, who found the document at the Biblioteque Nationale in Paris and John Spragens, Jr. for bringing this translation to his attention.

The O.S.S. Mission in Hanoi, under the direction of Major Archimedes L. Patti was friendly to the Ho Chi Minh government. Officers of Patti's team, working with representatives of the D.R.V., set up a "Vietnamese-American Friendship Association" in October 1945, complete with its own Constitution, which was published in 1,000 Vietnamese copies. But the organization was to be short-lived.

CHAPTER ONE

Article one - The undersigned Vietnamese compatriots and all the Vietnamese and Americans who support the objective establishment by this constitution as approved by the administrative committee, have agreed to set up an association called VIET MY THAN HUU or VIETNAM AMERICAN FRIENDSHIP ASSOCIATION, abbreviated as V.A.F.A.

Article two - This association shall be officially established as soon as this constitution is approved and authorized by the government.

Article three - The objectives of the association are the following:

1. To seek all legitimate means to bring about a better understanding between Americans and Vietnamese so as to promote sympathetic feelings.

2. To translate publications from English into Vietnamese and vice versa, and to circulate these translated publications for a better understanding of the cultural aspects of the two nations.

3. To organize frequent lectures in English and Vietnamese.

4. To publish a monthly magazine in English and Vietnamese.

5. To hold English and Vietnamese language teaching classes for the members of the association.

Article four - There is no time limit for the existence of the association.

Article five - The head office of the association shall be at Hoang Dieu City (Hanoi translator).

CHAPTER TWO

BUDGET - MEMBERSHIP - ADMISSION - MEMBERSHIP CANCELLATION

Article six - The budget of the association shall be made up of the following monies:

1. Admission fee as determined by the administrative committee: 30$00

2. Monthly dues paid by members.

Article seven - The association shall have the following categories of members:

1. Ordinary members who pay monthly dues of 10$00 per month (50% reduction for students).

2. Supporting members who donate no less than 3000$00.

3. Life members who donate 2000$00 or who pay their monthly dues regularly for 20 years.

4. Honorary residents and honorary members shall be the Vietnamese or Americans who are invited by the association to join and help it. These are the people who have influencial power and social status that sponsor the association.

Article eight - All Vietnamese above 18 years of age, regardless of sex and social and financial status can join the association as long as they are found to be of good character and holding full citizenship rights, and have been introduced by another member of the association.

Article nine - Membership cancellation (lit. "leaving the association" and "removal of name" - translator). Any member who wants to leave the association for some personal reasons, must address his/her application to the president of the association.

Any member who, after joining the association, is found guilty of misconduct, must justify himself/herself before the administrative council. The resolution of this council shall be final.

Article ten - Any person who wants to join the association shall have to sign a standard application form to be sent to the president of the association.

(48) <u>LETTER BY HO CHI MINH TO PRESIDENT TRUMAN</u>, October 17, 1945

Source: *U.S. Vietnam Relations, Book 1, I.A.C.,* pp. 73-74.

Ho's first major diplomatic initiative was to appeal to the U.S. to support Viet-nam's independence. In a letter to President Truman, Ho relied primarily on legal arguments to convince him that Viet-nam, not France, should be represented on the United Nations Advisory Commission for the Far East. The letter, like those which followed from Ho, was never answered.

Establishment of Advisory Commission for the Far East is heartily welcomed by Vietnamese people in principle stop. Taking into consideration primo the strategical and economical importance of Vietnam secundo the earnest desire which Vietnam deeply feels and has unanimously manifested to cooperate with the other democracies in the establishment and consolidation of world peace and prosperity we wish to call the attention of the Allied nations on the following points colon:

First absence of Vietnam and presence of France in the Advisory Commission leads to the conclusion that France is to represent the Vietnamese people at the Commission stop. Such representation is groundless either *de jure* or *defacto*. stop. *De jure* no alliance exists any more between France and Vietnam colon: Baodai abolished treaties of 1884 and 1863 comma, Baodai voluntarily abdicated to hand over govern-ment to Democratic Republican Government comma, Provisional Government rectorated [sic] abolishment of treaties of 1884 and 1863 stop. *De facto* since March ninth France having handed over governing rule to Japan has broken all administrative links with Vietnam, since August 18, 1945, Provisional Government has been a *de facto* independent government in every respect, recent incidents in Saigon instigated by the French roused unanimous disapproval leading to fight for independence.

Second France is not entitled because she had ignominiously sold Indo China to Japan and betrayed the Allies. Third Vietnam is qualified by Atlantic Charter and subsequent peace agreement and by her goodwill and her unflinching stand for democracy to be represented at the Advisory Commission. Stop. We are convinced that Vietnam at Commission will be able to bring effective contribution to solution of pending problems in Far East whereas her absence would bring forth unstability [sic] and temporary character to solutions otherwise reached. Therefore we express earnest request to take part in Advisory Commission for Far East. Stop. We should be very grateful to your excellency and Premier Attlee Premier Stalin Generalissimo Tchang Kai Shek for the conveyance of our desiderata to the United Nations.

(49) HO CHI MINH'S LETTER TO BYRNES, OCTOBER 22, 1945

Source: *U.S. Vietnam Relations, Book 1, I.A.C.*, pp. 80-81.

In another letter - this time to the Secretary of State, Ho stressed the Viet Minh collaboration with the allies against the Japanese and repeatedly cited the Atlantic Charter as an anti-colonial document.

Excellency,

The situation in South Vietnam has reached its critial stage, and calls for immediate interference on the part of the United Nations. I wish by the present letter to bring your excellency some more light on the case of Vietnam which has come for the last three weeks into the international limelight.

First of all, I beg to forward to your Government a few documentary data, among which our Declaration of Independence, the Imperial Rescript [sic] of Ex-Emperor BAO DAI on the occasion of his abdication, the declaration of our Government concerning its general foreign policy and a note defining our position towards the South Vietnam incident.

As those documents will show your Excellency, The Vietnamese people has known during the last few years an evolution which naturally brings the

Vietnamese nation to its present situation. After 80 years of French oppression and unsuccessful though obstinate Vietnamese resistance, we at last saw France defeated in Europe, then her betrayal of the Allies successively on behalf of Germany and of Japan. Though the odds were at that time against the Allies, the Vietnamese, leaving aside all differences in political opinion, united in the Vietminh League and started on a ruthless fight against the Japanese. Meanwhile, the Atlantic Charter was concluded, defining the war aims of the Allies and laying the foundation of peace-work. The noble principles of international justice and equality of status laid down in that charter strongly appealed to the Vietnamese and contributed in making of the Vietminh resistance in the war zone a nation-wide anti-Japanese movement which found a powerful echo in the democratic aspirations of the people. The Atlantic Charter was looked upon as the foundation of future Vietnam. A nation-building program was drafted which was later found in keeping with San Francisco Charter and which has been fully carried out these last years: continuous fight against the Japanese bringing about the recovery of national independence on August 19th, voluntary abdication of Ex-Emperor Baodai, establishment of the Democratic Republic of Vietnam, assistance given to the Allies Nations in the disarmament of the Japanese, appointment of a provisional Government whose mission was to carry out the Atlantic and San Francisco Charters and have them carried out by other nations.

As a matter of fact, the carrying out of the Atlantic and San Francisco Charters implies the eradication of imperialism and all forms of colonial oppression. This was unfortunately contrary to the interest of some Frenchmen, and France, to whom the colonists have long concealed the truth on Indochina, instead of entering into peaceable negotiations, resorted to an aggressive invasion, with all the means at the command of a modern nation. Moreover, having persuaded the British that the Vietnamese are wishing for a return of the French rule, they obtained, first from the British command in Southeast Asia, then from London, a tacit recognition of their sovereignty and administrative responsibility as far as South Vietnam is concerned. The British gave to understand that they had agreed to this on the ground that the reestablishment of French administration and, consequently, of Franco-Vietnamese collaboration would help them to speed up the demobilization and the disarmament of the Japanese. But subsequent events will prove the fallacy of the argument. The whole Vietnamese nation rose up as one man against French aggression. The first hours of September 23rd soon developed into real and organized warfare in which losses are heavy on both sides. The bringing in of French important reinforcements on board of the most powerful of their remaining warships will extend the war zone further. As murderous fighting is still going on in Indonesia, and as savage acts on the part of Frenchmen are reported every day, we may expect the flaring up of a general conflagration in the Far-East.

As it is, the situation in South Vietnam calls for immediate interference. The establishment of the Consultative Commission for the Far-East has been enthusiastically welcomed here as the first effective step toward an equitable settlement of the pending problems. The people of Vietnam, which only asks for full independence and for the respect of truth and justice, puts before your excellency our following desiderata:

1o - the South Vietnam incident should be discussed at the first meeting of the Consultative Commission for the Far-East;

2o - Vietnamese delegates should be admitted to state the views of the Vietnamese Government;

3o - An Inquiry Commission should be sent to South Vietnam;

4o - the full independence of Vietnam should be recognized by the United Nations.

I avail myself of this opportunity to send your Excellency my best wishes.

(50) <u>LETTER BY HO CHI MINH TO BYRNES</u>, NOVEMBER 1, 1945

Source: *U.S. Vietnam Relations*, Book 1, I.A.C., p. 90.

In his continuing effort to create an opening to the U.S., Ho wrote a letter to Byrnes requesting that a large group of Vietnamese youth come to the U.S. to be trained in various fields.

Excellency,

On behalf of the Vietnamese Cultural Association, I beg to express the desire of this Association to send to the United States of America a delegation of about fifty Vietnam youths with a view to establishing friendly cultural relations with the American youth on the one hand, and carrying on further studies in Engineering, Agriculture as well as other lines of specialisation on the other.

The desire which I am conveying to your Excellency has been expressed to me by all the Vietnam Engineers, Lawyers, Professors as well as other representatives of our intelligentsia whom I have come across.

They have been all these years keenly interested in things American and earnestly desirous to get into touch with the American people whose fine stand for the noble ideals of international Justice and Humanity, and whose modern technical achievements have so strongly appealed to them.

I sincerely wish that this plan would be favored by your approbation and assistance and avail myself of this opportunity to express to your Excellency my best wishes.

(51) <u>SPEECH BY HO CHI MINH, ON THE RESISTANCE WAR IN SOUTH VIET-NAM</u>, NOVEMBER 1945.

Source: Ho Chi Minh, *Selected Works*, Vol. III, pp. 48-49.

While the D.R.V. tried to maintain good relations with the Chinese in the North in order to ward off the return of the French, it gave all-out support to the resistance war in the South. The government organized "Southward March" military units to supplement the efforts of the badly organized, ill-trained and meagerly equipped resistance forces in the South, and they were already fighting battles with the French at Cha Trang and Khanh Hoa by the end of November 1945. That same month, President Ho rallied the people throughout the country behind the resistance in the South.

Compatriots!

During the Second World War, the French colonialists twice sold out our country to the Japanese. Thus they betrayed the allied nations, and helped the Japanese to cause the latter many losses.

Meanwhile they also betrayed our people, exposing us to the destruction of bombs and bullets. In this way, the French colonialists withdrew of their own accord from the Allied ranks and tore up the treaties they had earlier compelled us to sign.

Notwithstanding the French colonialists' treachery, our people as a whole are determined to side with the Allies and oppose the invaders. When the Japanese surrendered, our entire people single-mindedly changed our country into a Democratic Republic and elected a provisional Government which is to prepare for a national congress and draw up our draft Constitution.

Not only is our act in line with the Atlantic and San Francisco Charters, etc. solemnly proclaimed by the Allies, but it entirely conforms with the glorious principles upheld by the French people, viz. Freedom, Equality and Fraternity.

It is thus clear that in the past the colonialists betrayed the Allied and our country, and surrendered to the Japanese. At present, in the shadow of the British and Indian troops, and behind the Japanese soldiers, they are attacking the South of our country.

They have sabotaged the peace that China, the United States, Britain and Russia won at the cost of scores of millions of lives. They have run counter to the promises concerning democracy and liberty that the allied powers have proclaimed. They have of their own accord sabotaged their fathers' principles of liberty and equality. In consequence, it is for a just cause, for justice of the world, and for Viet Nam's land and people that our compatriots throughout the country have risen to struggle, and are firmly determined to maintain their independence. We do not hate the French people and France. We are energetically fighting slavery, and the ruthless policy of the French colonialists. We are not invading another's country. We only safeguard our own against the French invaders. Hence we are not alone. The countries which love peace and democracy, and the weaker nations all over the world, all sympathize with us. With the unity of the whole people within the country, and having many sympathizers abroad, we are sure of victory.

The French colonialsists have behaved lawlessly in the South for almost one and a half months. Our southern compatriots have sacrificed their lives in a most valiant struggle. Public opinion in the great countries: China, the United States, Russian and Britain, has supported our just cause.

Compatriots throughout the country! Those in the South will do their utmost to resist the enemy. Those in the Centre and the North will endeavour to help their southern compatriots, and be on the alert.

The French colonialists should know that the Vietnamese people do not want bloodshed, that they love peace. But we are determined to sacrifice even millions of combatants, and fight a long-term war of resistance in order to safeguard Viet Nam's independence and free her children from slavery. We are sure that our war of resistance will be victorious!

Let the whole country be determined in the war of resistance!

Long live independent Viet Nam!

(52) TELEGRAM FROM HO CHI MINH TO FRENCH PARTY LEADERS, GEORGES BIDAULT, LEON BLUM, AND MAURICE THOREZ, NOVEMBER 13, 1945.

Source: *Appeals by Chairman Ho*, p. 55. [Translation by the editor.]

Just as the Vietnamese leaders distinguished among Frenchmen in Indochina, they also distinguished between those political forces in France which were irredeemably colonialist and those which might choose, for whatever reason, to oppose the reimposition of French power in Indochina by force. In a letter to the leaders of three political parties, Ho appealed to them to base their attitude on the traditions of the French revolution.

To:
Bidault, leader of the French Popular Movement
Blum, leader of the French Socialist Party
Thorez, leader of the French Communist Party

In the name of the Provisional government, I send sincere greetings to you. [Houses the term *ngai* - a term of special respect - translator]

Viet-nam, which was oppressed for 80 years under the French colonial system, contrary to the ideal of liberty, equality and fraternity which French put before the world from 1789, today has risen up. Viet-nam's independence and its Democratic Republic form of government was solemnly proclaimed on September 2, after Emperor Bao Dai abdicated, and the new Government was established.

The entire Vietnamese people are unanimously determined to defend their freedom and independence.

I regret that, in this situation, the French government, still wishes to encourage colonialists who, thanks to the help of the British troops, provoked bloodshed in the Southern region of Viet-nam and massacred law-abiding citizens in order to reestablish French rule.

In the name of the ideals of liberty, equality and fraternity, slogans of the French Republic, and in the name of the peace policy of the United Nations, I appeal to you gentlemen and ask you to judge those unjust actions.

I can assure you gentlemen that if France agrees to recognize the independence of Viet-nam, the Vietnamese people will be very much in accord with France. If not, the Vietnamese people are determined to bleed until the last drop of blood to protect their country.

I ask that you leaders of democratic progressive parties give your attention to the above matters, in order to direct French policy into a path in accord with the ideals of liberty, equality and fraternity, and with the mutual interests of Viet-nam and France.

I send my personal thanks and the thanks of the Vietnamese people.

(53) APPEAL BY HO CHI MINH TO YOUTH THROUGHOUT THE COUNTRY, NOVEMBER 27, 1945

Source: *Appeals by Chairman Ho*, p. 54. [Translation by the editor.]

Because of looting and other forms of misconduct by Chinese Kuomintang troops occupying the North, there was an upsurge of anti-Chinese feelings among Vietnamese, and some incidents of retaliation by overzealous youths. This was contrary to Ho's policy of cultivating friendly relations with China in the hope of preventing a Sino-French alliance against Vietnam's interest. Ho had to appeal to the youth to follow the policy of Chinese-Vietnamese friendship.

Representatives of youth!

Besides the tasks of supporting the resistance in the South, to solve the famine problem in the North and preparing for the general elections throughout the country, you also have another very important responsibility. That is to help in carrying out the policy with regard to Chinese emigrants.

We must remember that Vietnam and China are fraternal peoples, who for thousands of years have had a very intimate unity. Our Chinese brothers who make their living as merchants here have shared our happiness and suffering. Because of the Chinese troops, from the 16th parallel North, the French colonialists have not yet dared to encroach. In the South we are resisting France, and all Chinese emigrant brothers are participating in market strikes, boycotts of classes and labor strikes. That is sufficient to show that the feeling between Chinese and Vietnamese is like lips and teeth.

Thus our policy is Vietnamese-Chinese friendship. We must help the Chinese army, defend Chinese emigrants. We must completely carry out that policy. Meanwhile we must prevent any divisive scheme which hopes to create frictions between our people and Chinese, sabotaging the sympathy between the two peoples. We must find a means of creating movement for Chinese-Vietnamese friendship and cooperation. I am sure that you will fulfill that duty.

1946

(54) DECLARATION BY HO CHI MINH OF THE POLICY OF THE PROVISIONAL COALITION
GOVERNMENT, JANUARY 1, 1946

Source: Ho Chi Minh, *Selected Works*, Vol. III, pp. 51-52.

*In order to placate the Chinese, whom they feared would try to overthrow the
Viet Minh government and replace it with anti-Communist, pro-Chinese parties,
ICP leaders decided to formally dissolve the Party and to offer to reorganize
the government to include representatives of those parties in November 1945.
Right-wing parties nevertheless carried out kidnappings and violent attacks
against Viet Minh officials (see Devillers,* Historie du Vietnam du 1940 a 1952
*[Paris: Editions du Seuil, 1952], p. 197).   Ho finally negotiated with the
Chinese and the pro-Chinese parties the establishment of a "Provisional Coalition Government" in which those parties would receive five of the twelve ministerial positions. In his statement of policy on the occasion of the establishment of the coalition government, Ho noted the desire of the D.R.V. to gain
diplomatic recognition - an objective which would be frustrated until 1950.*

With a view to winning complete independence and bringing about a close
cooperation between the various political parties to further strengthen the
Government, it is now named the Provisional Coalition Government. At this
moment, if the parties unite together, the Government can overcome difficulties.
All the Vietnamese people want the Provisional Government to hold office until
the election of the National Assembly which will change it into a definite
Government. Meanwhile the Provisional Coalition Government will discuss the
following practical questions:

Home policy:
a) Political
1. Satisfactorily to carry out the general elections throughout the country.
2. To unify the various administrative organs according to democratic principles.
b) Economic
1. To endeavour to develop agriculture.
2. To encourage cultivation and stock-breeding in order to check famine.
c) Military: To unify the various armed forces under the command of the
Government. Parties are now allowed to have armies of their own.
d) Cultural: To give aid to various cultural organs. In short, in home
policy, the Government must exert itself politically to unify the country, and
intensify production in order to cope with famine and foreign invasion.

Foreign policy:
To induce other countries to recognize Viet Nam's independence. To have

friendly relations with foreign residents of Viet Nam, particularly the Chinese. With regard to the Frenchmen, we only fight the colonialists. As for those who do not seek to prejudice our independence, we will protect their lives and property.

Such is the policy of the Provisional Coalition Government of the Democratic Republic of Viet Nam, I hope that the entire people will support it to enable the Government to succeed.

Long live independent Viet Nam!

(55) ARTICLE BY HO CHI MINH ON "SELF-CRITICISM", JANUARY 1946

Source: *Appeals by Chairman Ho*, pp. 51-52. [Translation by the editor.]

After a few months in power, Ho Chi Minh published a "self-criticism" in the local press which illustrates his style of political leadership. While striking a humble tone, the content of the article was carefully calculated to build the confidence of the people in his leadership, and to focus on the problem of implementing some of his key policies.

Dear compatriots,

Because you loved and believed in me, you have entrusted the fate of the country to my care. My duty is like that of the helmsman who must steer the ship of State through the wind and waves safely to the harbor of the people's happiness.

Thanks to the force of the unity of the whole people, we won independence. But no sooner had the Government been set up than it encountered difficult circumstances.

Outside the country, although the war had ended, peace was not yet consolidated. Within the country, the South was invaded, while the North suffered famine. The old system of rule had been eliminated, but the new democratic system was not yet strong. Our people's wealth was swept clean by the colonialists, and most compatriots were in a situation of poverty.

Confronted with those difficult circumstances the compatriots did their utmost, and people shared with others, including money. As for me and the Government, we worried day and night about fulfilling our duty, so that we would not be ungrateful to the compatriots throughout the country. And only because my talent is humble and my strength is little, I have not done fully those things desired by the compatriots.

Establishing the independence of the country; leading the resistance in the South: to make every effort to appeal for increase in production and to find all means to relieve the famine in the North; organizing the first general election in our country, preparing to establish the National assembly.

Beside these things the Government which I lead has not yet done anything worth mentioning for the people.

Although it has been five months since we gained independence, no foreign governments have recognized our country.

Although our soldiers fight brilliantly, the resistance has not yet been victorious.

Although the members of the administrative committees have done well and are honest, corruption and abuses have not yet been swept away.

Although the Government has tried to reorganize, there are many places where politics is still not systematically organized.

Although the Government has always taken the position that: the two peoples of Vietnam and China are like brothers, and we must have friendly cooperation with our Chinese brothers, just as our Chinese brothers must cooperate in a friendly fashion with us; but there are places where we still have not been able to avoid frictions between Chinese emigrants and Vietnamese.

The Government has always taken the position that our people only demand independence, and are determined to oppose only the colonial system; and that, with regard to French residents peacefully making a living, we must do our best to protect their lives and property (because of humanity but also for our noble objective); nevertheless rash incidents still take place with regard to Frenchmen in some places.

One could attribute those shortcomings to the fact that the period of time has been short, or that the country is still new, or to this or that reason.

But no, I must say truly that successes are due to the compatriots efforts, but the above-mentioned shortcomings are our own fault.

People are not sacred, and no one can avoid shortcomings.

From now on, I hope the compatriots will assist me and the Government in amending these shortcomings by many methods, first of all carrying out correctly and thoroughly the orders of the Government.

The destiny of the country is in our hands. If we are of a single mind, with one heart, from top to bottom, we will definitely be victorious.

(56) <u>APPEAL BY HO CHI MINH ON THE GENERAL ELECTION</u>, JANUARY 5, 1946

Source: Ho Chi Minh, *Selected Works*, Vol. III, pp. 53-54.

Part of the agreement negotiated by Ho under pressure from the Chinese, was the postponement of elections for a National Assembly, originally scheduled for December, until January 1946, and of a guarantee of 70 seats of the total of 350 in the Assembly to the right-wing parties, which agreed in turn not to oppose the election. The January 6 elections were carried out not only in the North but in the South, where the resistance continued against the French, even in the French-occupied cities. The overwhelming vote in favor of Viet Minh candidates (97 percent in Hanoi) reflected its prestige as the Party of independence.

Tomorrow will be January 6, 1946.

It will take our people to a new path.

It will be a happy day for our compatriots, because it is the day of the general election, the first day in Vietnamese history on which our people will begin to enjoy their democratic rights.

Tomorrow our people will show to the southern fighters that while in the military field they are using weapons to oppose the enemy, in the political field, we are using our votes to consolidate our forces.

Tomorrow our compatriots will show to the world that the Vietnamese people are determined to:

-- unite closely

-- fight the colonialists

-- regain independence.

Tomorrow they will freely choose and elect worthy people to represent them in the management of State affairs.

Candidates are many and the number of deputies is limited. As a matter of course, tomorrow there will be people elected and others not elected.

Those elected must do their utmost to defend national independence and to make their compatriots happy. They must always bear in mind and put into practice the words:

Family interest should be forgotten for the sake of national interests.

Private interests should be forgotten for the sake of common interests.

We must be worthy of our compatriots and our Fatherland.

Those who are not elected should not be discouraged.

The zeal they have shown on behalf of the country and the people must always be maintained. Whether within the National Assembly or without, they will try to be useful to the country. If this time they fail, should they continue to prove their talents and virtues, then surely they will be elected by their compatriots next time.

Tomorrow all voters will not fail to go to the polls. Tomorrow everybody will enjoy the rights granted to independent and free citizens.

(57) MEMORANDUM OF CONVERSATION BY RICHARD L. SHARP, DIVISION OF SOUTHEAST ASIAN AFFAIRS, JANUARY 30, 1946.

Source: *U.S. Vietnam Relations*, Book 8, V.B.2., pp. 53-57.

General Gallagher returned from Hanoi in January 1946 and gave his assessment to the State Department officials. Gallagher did not believe the Viet Minh, who he said were not "full-fledged doctrinaire Communist", could hold out against the French militarily, nor did he think Viet-nam was ready for self-government, despite widespread demands among the Vietnamese people for independence.

Asked when, in his opinion, the Chinese would get out of Indochina, General Gallagher said that General Lu Han had told him the Chinese would move out when the job given them by the Allies was completed. General Gallagher said he thought they really intend to do this although the whole matter depends upon the removal of the Japanese. To date, shipping for this purpose has not been available but now it is understood that United States bottoms will be used. The question is, therefore, when will such ships be allocated. General Gallagher said he had recommended to General Wedemeyers that high priority should be given such allocation.

There are some 20 to 30 thousand Japanese in Haiphong and the Do Son Peninsula. No political settlement can be reached in Indochina until the Chinese move out and they cannot do that until the Japanese are repatriated. General Gallagher added that he thought US Army teams would have to be put into Indochina to concentrate and prepare the Japanese for evacuation.

General Gallagher was asked whether he knew of any arrangement whereby French forces moving into the north would overlap departing Chinese forces. He replied that in December Sainteny said that no French would enter until the Chinese left. General Gallagher thought the French were probably not getting very far in negotiating with the Chinese of problems connected with their removal. Unless in the meantime something has been arranged between the French and the Chinese, the French would probably infiltrate overland from the south rather than land in force in northern ports.

General Gallagher pointed out that little love was lost between the Chinese and the French; that the presence of the American group in Hanoi restrained anti-French Chinese action; and that he himself had influenced General Lu Han to bring Sainteny and Ho Chi Minh together and confront both with a strong directive that order must be maintained. The existence of a vacuum in the north with neither French nor Chinese troops present would be extremely dangerous, as the Annamese would react strongly against all French in the area, who would be helpless in protecting themselves. To take over successfully, the French would need a sufficient force to cover the whole north. One or two modern French divisions could, in General Gallagher's opinion, defeat the Annamese.

In response to the question whether the French could do more than take key cities, he admitted that the Annamese would take to the hills and continue guerrilla warfare. Even in Saigon, he pointed out, things are far from peaceful despite British and French claims to the contrary. Establishment of French control could be speeded up if they were able to make large-scale air drops throughout the north. The Annamese, however, are well organized and, so far as small arms go, are quite well armed, although they have no navy, shore batteries and probably little artillery.

The question was raised whether the French mission in Hanoi was in fact negotiating with Ho Chi Minh. General Gallagher replied that the Viet Minh Provisional Government was at first willing to negotiate; then in October, after de Gaulle's pronouncements on colonial policy, the Annamese refused to negotiate with the French and reacted vigorously against all French nationals in Hanoi. The Chinese may succeed in putting in a less anti-French Annamese government so that negotiation might go forward. All French efforts to stimulate a palace revolution against Ho were of no avail. Ho himself will not deal with the French. The Viet Minh is strong and, regardless of possible superficial changes in the Provisional Government, Ho will be behind any continuing Annamese movement. General Gallagher said that Sainteny had told him he expected peaceful agreement between the French and the Annamese would be reached by negotiation.

General Gallagher was asked how effective the Viet Minh administration would be with neither French nor Chinese forces present. He replied that on the whole he was impressed by the remarkably effective Annamese administration. There was an able personnel; they were all enthusiastic and young, but there were too few of them. Whatever their technical skill, they perhaps lack executive ability and experience since the technical services in Hanoi were at first very well run but gradually deteriorated. Trained people for the government and at the municipal level are lacking. In General Gallagher's opinion the Annamese are not yet ready for self-government and in full-fledged competition with other nations they would "lose their shirts". However, the demand for independence is widespread and even in the villages the peasants refer to the example of the Phillippines.

Ho is willing to cooperate with Great Britain, USSR, or the United States and would perhaps even settle for French tutelage if that were subordinated to control by the other nations. French control alone, however, will be strongly resisted. The deep-seated hatred for the French has been fanned by exceedingly clever Viet Minh propaganda.

General Gallagher was asked whether the Annamese were realistic regarding their ability to stand up against French military force. While they are too enthusiastic and too naive, he said, they probably know that they will be licked. They are strong on parades and reiterate their willingness "to fight to the last man", but they would be slaughtered and they have been told that and probably know it. The Annamese would be no match for forces with modern arms even if they themselves have some, which they may have since the Chinese found no Japanese rolling artillery and numerous Japanese anti-aircraft guns seem to have completely disappeared. United States Army representatives never did learn the extent of arms controlled by the Viet Minh. Certainly the Chinese are not turning Japanese arms over to them. Before V-J Day the Japanese undoubtedly had armed and trained many Annamese. A Japanese general claimed they had taken over on March 9 simply because the French could no longer control the Annamese, but this statement General Gallagher characterized as a lie. He had heard that under the pretext of arming Annamese gendarmes for police duty in Hanoi, the Japanese had actually armed three distinct contingents, dismissing each group when armed and bringing in a new one to be armed and trained. Furthermore, the Annamese had acquired Japanese arms from arsenals which had been opened. General Gallagher did not know whether or not Tai Li was sending arms to the Viet Minh.

General Gallagher was asked whether the presence of French hostages in the north would restrain French forces when they enter the region. He pointed out that only a few French civilians had been removed by air. All the rest, besides some five thousand disarmed French troops, were still to be removed. The Chinese cannot take them out nor would Lu Han even permit their evacuation to the Do Son Peninsula. Their presence had been a constant restraining influence on Sainteny. Asked whether the Annamese would let these French be evacuated, General Gallagher replied that they would have to if the Chinese were still there, but that these French nationals would be a real problem if the Chinese were moved out. The American Army group had to exert considerable pressure on the Chinese to get them to give any freedom at all to French civilians in Haiphong, Hue and other centers besides Hanoi. However, the Chinese and French alone had arranged for shipments of food from the south. The American group, incidentally, had to intervene to prevent the monopoly by the French of such food or of food distributed by the U.S. Army. The French nationals could be evacuated from Hongai and Tourane by the United States when the Japanese were removed if the Chinese would concentrate them at those ports. However, General Gallagher noted, that would place us in a position of working against the Annamese.

Originally, General Gallagher explained, the French expected the United States to play the same role in the north that the British were playing in the south. When they found us neutral they became more and more antagonistic and did everything possible to persuade United States personnel to favor the French position. They had no appreciation of the actual help which the American group gave to the prisoners of war and some of the civilian French in the form of food, medical aid, and so on. The Annamese, too, expected American help originally, having been thoroughly indoctrinated with the Atlantic Charter and other ideological pronouncements. In our neutral role we were thus a disappointment to both sides.

In response to a question, General Gallagher gave his opinion that Lu Han would be faithful to Thungking although as governor of Yunnan he would also be influenced to maintain as fully as possible relations between Yunnan and north Indochina which would be profitable to him.

General Gallagher said that the half dozen or so top French military officers held by the Japanese had been returned to France shortly after Sainteny reached Hanoi. He did not know what had happened to Decoux.

Asked how "communist" the Viet Minh were, General Gallagher replied that they were smart and successfully gave the impression of not being communist. Rather, they emphasized their interest in independence and their Annamese patriotism. Their excellent organization and propaganda techniques, General Gallagher pointed out, would seem to have the earmarks of some Russian influence. General Gallagher stated that the minority Cao Dai group were definitely Communist. In his opinion, however, the Viet Minh should not be labeled full-fledged doctrinaire communist.

At the present time the Hanoi radio is controlled by the Chinese so that there is communication between Hanoi and Saigon. A British military and civilian liaison team was sent to Hanoi and a Chinse counterpart to Saigon. The British in Hanoi at first made little progress with the Chinese but General Gallagher understands they have since made more headway.

The Chinese 60th Army in the south of the Chinese zone and the 93rd Army around Hanoi, both totalling some 50 thousand men, have been told to concentrate for removal to Manchuria, but whether they actually moved out or not General Gallagher does not know. By December, however, the Chinese 53rd Army had begun to come in from Yunnan and would probably provide replacements for the other two Armies.

General Gallagher noted that magnetic mines have not been entirely cleared at least from the northern ports and that the threat provided by these mines has helped and would continue to help keep the French from undertaking large-scale landing operations in that area. He felt that regular rail communications between Saigon and Hanoi might not be opened for another year.

(58) HO CHI MINH'S LETTER TO TRUMAN, FEBRUARY 16, 1946

Source: *United States-Vietnam Relations,* Book 1, I.A.C., pp. 95-97.

In his final letter addressed specifically to Truman, Ho paid tribute to the U.S. as "guardians and champions of World Justice" and called on the U.S. and the United Nations to live up to their professed ideals.

I avail myself of this opportunity to thank you and the people of United States for the interest shown by your representatives at the United Nations Organization in favour of the dependent peoples.

Our VIETNAM people, as early as 1941, stood by the Allies' side and fought against the Japanese and their associates, the French colonialists.

From 1941 to 1945 we fought bitterly, sustained by the patriotism of our fellow-countrymen and by the promises made by the Allies at YALTA, SAN FRANCISCO AND POTSDAM.

When the Japanese were defeated in August 1945, the whole Vietnam territory was united under a Provisional Republican Government which immediately set out to work. In five months, peace and order were restored, a democratic republic was established on legal bases, and adequate help was given to the Allies in the carrying out of their disarmament mission.

But the French colonialists, who had betrayed in war-time both the Allies and the Vietnamese, have come back and are waging on us a murderous and piti-less war in order to reestablish their domination. Their invasion has extended to South Vietnam and is menacing us in North Vietnam. It would take volumes to give even an abbreviated report of the crimes and assassinations they are committing every day in the fighting area.

This aggression is contrary to all principles of international law and to the pledges made by the Allies during the World War. It is a challenge to the noble attitude shown before, during and after the war by the United States Government and People. It violently contrasts with the firm stand you have taken in your twelve point declaration, and with the idealistic loftiness and generosity expressed by your delegates to the United Nations Assembly, MM BYRNES, STETTINIUS and J. F. DULLES.

The French aggression on a peace-loving people is a direct menace to world security. It implies the complicity, or at least, the connivance of the Great Democracies. The United Nations ought to keep their words. They ought to interfere to stop this unjust war, and to show that they mean to carry out in peace-time the principles for which they fought in war-time.

Our Vietnam people, after so many years of spoliation and devastation, is just beginning its building-up work. It needs security and freedom, first to achieve internal prosperity and welfare, and later to bring its small contri-bution to world-reconstruction.

These securities and freedoms can only be guaranteed by our independence from any colonial power, and our free cooperation with all other powers. It is with this firm conviction that we request of the United States as guardians and champions of World Justice to take a decisive step in support of our inde-pendence.

What we ask has been graciously granted to the Philippines. Like the Philippines our goal is full independence and full cooperation with the UNITED STATES. We will do our best to make this independence and cooperation profit-able to the whole world.

(59) PRELIMINARY FRANCO-VIETNAMESE CONVENTION, MARCH 6, 1946

Source: Enclosure to Despatch No. 366 from Bangkok, April 24, 1947, "Trans-mitting Documents relative to recent developments in Indo China, received from

Dr. Pham Ngoc Thack (sic), Vietnam Under-Secretary of State." F.W. 851.G.00/4-2447, State Department Central Files, National Archives. Translation of this and all other documents enclosed with this despatch was done by the Department of State in 1947.

After a Sino-French agreement was reached in February 1946 permitting the French to replace Chinese troops north of the 16th parallel, Vietnamese leaders were convinced that China, France, the U.S. and Britain had reached a compromise at Viet-nam's expense. They feared an attempt would be made to install a pro-Chinese government before Chinese troops left the country. So they decided to negotiate with France, to gain leverage against the Chinese and also to gain time to prepare for the ultimate fight against France. After tough negotiations in which the French refused to accept the word "independence", Ho himself proposed the phrase "a free state" as an ambiguous substitute, allowing a tenuous preliminary accord to be reached.

On the background of this agreement, see Vo Nguyen Giap, Unforgettable Months and Years, *translated by Mai van Elliott, Cornell University, Southeast Asia Program Date Paper, no. 99, p. 90. An "Agreement Supplemental" dealing with the stationing of French forces in Vietnam was signed on the same day as the published convention but apparently never published.*

Between the High Contracting Parties designated below, the Government of the French Republic, represented by MR. SAINTENY, Delegate of the French High Commissioner, regularly commissioned by Vice Admiral Georges Thierry D'ARGENLIEU, French High Commissioner, depository of the powers of the French Republic on the one hand and the Government of the Republic of Viet Nam, represented by its President, MR. HO CHI MINH and the Special Delegate of the Council of Ministers, MR. VU HONG KHANH on the other hand, it is agreed as follows:

1 - The French Government recognized the Republic of Viet Nam as a free state which has its government, its parliament, its army, and its finances, and is a part of the Indochinese Federation and of the French Union. So far as the union of the three Ky is concerned, the Government pledges itself to confirm the decisions reached by the populations consulted by means of a referendum.

2 - The Government of Viet Nam declares itself ready to receive the French Army in a peaceful manner, when it relieves Chinese troops in accordance with international agreements. A supplemental agreement attached to the present Preliminary Convention shall fix the means according to which relief operations shall take place.

3 - The stipulations formulated above shall enter into force immediately after the exchange of signatures, each of the high Contracting Parties shall take all measures necessary to bring about the cessation of hostilities immediately, to maintain the troops in their respective positions and to create the favorable atmosphere necessary for the immediate opening of friendly and frank negotiations. The negotiations shall concern particularly:

(a) diplomatic relations of Vietnam with foreign countries;
(b) the future status of Indochina;
(c) French economic and cultural interests in Viet Nam.

Hanoi, Saigon or Paris may be selected as the place for the Conference.

AGREEMENT SUPPLEMENTAL

TO THE PRELIMINARY CONVENTION ENTERED INTO BETWEEN THE GOVERNMENT OF THE FRENCH REPUBLIC AND THE GOVERNMENT OF VIET NAM:

The following is agreed upon between the High Contracting Parties designated in the Preliminary Convention;

1 - The relief forces shall be composed of:

(a) 10,000 Viet Nam soldiers with their Viet Nam Cadres who are subject to the orders of the military authorities of Viet Nam.

(b) 15,000 French forces, including the French forces in the territory of Viet Nam at the present time, north of the 16th parallel. The said forces shall be composed solely of French soldiers of metropolitan origin, with the exception of troops charged with the guarding of Japanese prisoners.

All such forces shall be placed under the French High Command, assisted by Viet Nam delegates. The progress, installation and utilization of such forces shall be defined during the course of a General Staff conference between representatives of the French and Viet Nam Commands, which shall be held when the French units land.

Mixed commissions shall be created at all levels to assure, in a spirit of friendly collaboration, liaison between the French and Viet Nam troops.

2 - The French members of the relief forces shall be divided into three categories:

(a) The units charged with the guarding of Japanese prisoners. These units shall be repatriated as soon as their mission becomes unnecessary following the evacuation of the Japanese prisoners; in any case within a maximum period of ten months;

(b) The units charged, in collaboration with the Viet Nam Army, with the maintenance of public order and the security of the Viet Nam territory. These units shall be relieved one fifth each year, by the Viet Nam Army, this relief therefore being effectively carried out within a period of five years.

(c) The units charged with the defense of naval and air bases. The duration of the mission entrusted to these units shall be defined at later conferences.

3 - At places where French and Viet Nam troops are garrisoned, clearly defined cantonment zones shall be assigned.

The French Government pledges itself not to employ Japanese prisoners for military purposes.

(60) LETTER BY HO CHI MINH TO COMPATRIOTS, FIGHTERS AT THE FRONT AND THE ADMINISTRATIVE COMMITTEE IN SOUTH VIET-NAM, MARCH 11, 1946

Source: Ho Chi Minh, *Selected Works*, Vol. III, pp. 57-58.

In an appeal for popular support for the preliminary agreement with France, Ho made it clear that it was only the beginning of the struggle for independence, and that further diplomatic gains would reflect the political military balance of forces within the country between the French and the Vietnamese resistance.

I beg to inform all compatriots and fighters that the negotiations between our Government and the French Government have achieved preliminary success, which is the suspension of hostilities in order to pave the way for the official negotiations to come. As concerns Viet Nam, this agreement is a great success: France has recognized Viet Nam as a self-governing country.

This is due to the heroic struggle of the compatriots in the whole country, particularly those of the South and the southern part of Central Viet Nam, and of all fighters during the last six months. At this hour, I respectfully pay tribute to the souls of those who have sacrificed their lives in the struggle.

This sacrifice has not been in vain, because:

1. This is the first step in the negotiation to arrive at victory.

2. These initial negotiations will create political conditions of which we must know how to take advantage in order to reach Viet Nam's complete independence.

3. Therefore the Government needs the support of the whole people. Hence, during this truce, especially when the armed forces of both parties must stop

at their present positions, preparations and the consolidation of our forces, and the respect of discipline are more necessary than ever. And in days to come, when peace has been negotiated, your combativeness will continue to be a valuable and mighty guarantee for our future national independence.

We must save each drop of our compatriots' blood to build the future of our country. In building and struggling, our compatriots' enthusiastic spirit will still have many more opportunities to develop.

In the present new stage of our country's history, our people's solidarity will score better results.

(61) APPEAL BY HO CHI MINH TO THE PEOPLE ON THE PRELIMINARY ACCORD, MARCH 16, 1946

Source: *Appeals by Chairman Ho*, pp. 79-80. Translation by the editor.

Despite disturbing signs that the French did not intend to carry out correctly the preliminary accord, Ho appealed to the population to remain calm and to maintain discipline with regard to Frenchmen, in order to provide an atmosphere in which negotiations could continue.

1. I regret that there have been a few actions by the French which are not in accord with the agreement which they signed, such as attacking our troops by surprise in the South, in Phan Rang, etc. My appeal has been supported by the people and noticed by the world.

Our Government is determined to carry out the agreement because we are sure the world and French people will support us, because we act in accord with the just causes.

2. The people's vehement patriotism is truly valuable. The brave comments of the newspapers are truly worthy of praise.

But when the two sides are about to negotiate, it is necessary to create a favorable atmosphere for talks, so I hope that the people will maintain a determined but calm mind, that newspapers will comment in an honest fashion, but words of restraint ought to be remembered.

3. Throughout the whole country there are noisy demonstrations supporting the Government and asking the Government to demand the immediate opening of negotiations as stated in the agreement. That is enough to see that our people understand that the sooner the official negotiations begin, the more our difficulties will be reduced and the more favorable will be cooperation between the two peoples.

The Government also agrees with that. But I repeat once more that our people must maintain an absolutely calm attitude, must protect the lives and property of French people as well as Chinese, in order to show that our people are an advanced and disciplined people.

4. French troops commanded by General LeClerc are coming to replace the Chinese forces. We must carry out correctly the agreement. We absolutely forbid any conflict with them, while at the same time we must create sympathy. We must show them that our people love freedom, independence, and respect peace and justice.

5. Although there will be difficulties, in the future, the Government with the support of the united people, will certainly surmount the difficulties and lead our people to complete independence.

(62) FRANCO-VIETNAMESE GENERAL STAFF AGREEMENT, APRIL 3, 1946

Source: Enclosure to Despatch No. 366, from Bangkok, April 24, 1947.

Following the preliminary convention of March 6, the military staffs of the two sides negotiated a more detailed agreement which not only imposed extraordinary restrictions on the movements and activities of French troops but created a "Mixed commission of Liaison and Control" which had ultimate authority for the application of the agreement. On paper, at least, the Vietnamese appeared to be in a strong bargaining position.

The following agreement is in effect between:

General SALAN, Military Delegate of the High Commissioner of the French Republic on the one hand,
- MR. VO NGUYEN GIAP
and MR. HONG KHANH, President and Vice President of the Superior Council of National Defense of the Republic of Viet Nam on the other hand.

Its purpose is to specify the conditions of the application from a military point of view of the Preliminary Convention of March 6, 1946 and of the agreement supplemental to the said Convention.

It shall be of a provisional nature and valid until the conclusion of general negotiations provided for in Article 3 of the Preliminary Convention.

I - RELIEF FORCES

1 - The Franco-Vietnamese relief forces shall be composed of 10,000 Viet Nam soliders and 15,000 French troops.

2 - The 10,000 Viet Nam troops and constituent units of whom 5,000 shall be armed, with their Viet Nam cadres, who are subject to the orders of the Viet Nam military authorities, shall be placed at the disposal of the French High Command, assisted by Viet Nam delegates as the requirements connected with relief arise.

They shall continue to be administered by the Viet Nam Government.

3 - The modernization of their equipment and arms, as well as matter pertaining to administration and supply in connection with which French is given, will be studied during the course of the general negotiations.

4 - The strength of French troops in the Viet Nam territory north of the 16th parallel must not exceed 15,000 men.

5 - The French forces must be composed solely of French soldiers. French soldiers of non-metropolitan origin shall be used solely for the guarding of Japanese prisoners.

II - INSTALLATION AND DISTRIBUTION OF TROOPS

1 - French Troops:
The force for the guarding of Japanese prisoners of war shall be 500 men.
The units charged with assuring, in collaboration with the Viet Nam Army, the maintenance of public order and the security of the Viet Nam territory, as well as the units charged with the defense of bases shall be stationed according to the table given as an annex (Annex No. 1). The total strength is 14,500 men.

2 - Viet Nam Troops:
The installation of Viet Nam relief troops shall be regulated according to Table Annex No. 2.

3 - The installation of relief troops may,however, be subject to revision by common agreement.

4 - Each time that installation takes place, the cantonment areas shall be selected by common agreement in the urban center. The military buildings or those of the former Indochinese guard, shall be used on a priority basis in the cantonment areas. They must be suited to the purpose envisaged. In the same way medical care shall be carried out in military hospitals or hospital infirmaries to be determined by common agreement.

The expenses for installation and operation shall be borne in proportion to the forces quartered and cared for.

5 - The bearing of arms by soldiers when not on duty shall be forbidden in principle. A regulation to that effect shall be established by common agreement for each locality.

6 - Maneuver and exercise grounds, as well as regulations for their use, shall be fixed by common agreement by the local commands.

7 - Military liaison and supply vehicles (with four armed men at the most per car) shall circulate normally and without pass between French and Viet Nam relief posts. The number of men armed on supply conveys on liaison mission shall not exceed 60. Each army shall control its own vehicles. Mixed missions shall have access at all times to control posts which shall have to submit their circulation reports. Establishment of such control posts shall be terminated by common agreement.

8 - Waterways shall be open to military traffic under the same conditions. In order to provide for certain local conditions until general security is established, the French Headquarters, however, shall consult the Viet Nam Government before setting such traffic in motion and shall consider its suggestions.

9 - Questions relating to railways and those relating to the postal, telegraph and radio services shall be the object of later agreement between the competent agencies.

III - PROGRESS OF RELIEF TROOPS

For each movement of French or Viet Nam relief troops, orders elaborated with the Viet Nam delegation at the High Command level shall be transmitted to that delegation at least 48 hours in advance. They shall fix the date, itinerary and methods of movement. The Viet Nam Government shall notify the population in order to avert incidents, in so far as possible.

In the case of frontier towns, the French troops should consider thoroughly, because of existing local difficulties, the methods recommended by the Viet Nam Government.

The movements in question should not affect in any way the plan of installation provided for in Annexes 1 and 2.

IV - USE OF TROOPS

1 - Organization of the command; - Franco-Vietnamese relief forces shall be placed under the French High Command assisted by a Viet Nam delegation permanently assigned to it and headed by a person of high rank.

The order of the High Command to the Franco-Vietnamese relief forces shall be drafted in agreement with the Viet Nam delegates. Orders concerning Viet Nam relief troops shall be countersigned and transmitted in time by the Viet Nam delegates to the Viet Nam relief troops.

2 - Order and security. French and Viet Nam relief troops under the authority of the French High Command, assisted by Viet Nam delegates, shall collaborate with the Viet Nam Army for the maintenance of order and security as follows:

(a) the guarding of certain vital points agreed upon by common accord,

(b) internal discipline in each army by its own usual methods the putting into effect of which shall be established by common agreement,

(c) contribution of pickets and patrols furnished to the local police by French and Viet Nam commanding officers at the request of Viet Nam authorities through the channel of existing permanent liaison bodies.

(d) the question of the responsibility of the French High Command in the domain of the protection of foreign life and property shall be the object of a separate protocol with the Viet Nam Government.

V. LIAISON AND SUPERVISION

1 - A mixed central commission for liaison and control shall be created. Its headquarters shall be at Hanoi. It shall be charged with supervision of the application of the clauses of the present agreement.

2 - It shall make every effort to foster friendly relations and to prevent misunderstandings and incidents between the two armies.

3 - Mixed local commissions shall be established between the Viet Nam and French relief troops according to the needs in the various installation centers.

They shall receive directives from the Commission at Hanoi.

In carrying out the directives, they shall be answerable to the French and Viet Nam local town-majors.

They shall draw up local agreements.

VI. ARMISTICE

1 - Agreement concerning the sending of an armistice commission to the southern part of Trung Bo.

2 - Reservation concerning the armistice question in Nam-Bo.[1]

ANNEX NO. I

INSTALLATION OF FRENCH TROOPS

This installation is provisional. The question of bases, that of the distribution of troops between the bases and points in the interior, as well as yearly reduction shall be studied during the course of the general negotiations.

HANOI (including 1,000 for the air base)	5,000
HAIPHONG	1,750
HONGAY	1,025
NAMDINH	825
HUE	825
HAIDUONG AND HULUONG-LAIKHE BRIDGE	650
DIEN BIEN PHU	825
TOURANE	825
FRONTIER REGIONS	2,775

REMARKS: Division of posts between French and Viet Nam troops (relief troops for the frontier region) and of forces will be defined later. These frontier posts are the following:

HONGAY LANGSON CAOBANG LAOKAY LAICHAU

[1]The question of an armistice in Ham-Bo having been brought up during the course of the conference of March 31, General SALAN replied that it was within the competence of the two Governments and could not be dealt with during the course of the conference in question. MR. VO NGUYEN CIAP insisted that

"Viet Nam delegates should leave for Saigon: and renewed his protests against the operations directed against the Viet Nam troops.

(63) <u>NOTE FROM BYRNES TO FRENCH AMBASSADOR HENRI BONNET, APRIL 12, 1946</u>

Source: *U.S.-Vietnam Relations*, Book 8, V.B.2, pp. 64-65.

Acheson's earlier caveat about popular support for the return of the French was put aside as the U.S. officially gave its approval to the reversion of all Indochina to French control in a diplomatic note from Secretary Byrnes to the French Ambassador. The note ignored the fact that France had already signed an agreement recognizing Viet-nam as a "free state".

The Secretary of State presents his compliments to His Excellency the French Ambassador and has the honor to refer to the Ambassador's note no. 167 of March 7, 1946, enclosing a copy of the Franco-Chinese Agreement with regard to the relief of Chinese forces in northern Indo-China by French forces and requesting the approval of the Combined Chiefs of Staff thereto.

The Secretary of State is pleased to inform the Ambassador that the Combined Chiefs of Staff have no objection to the relief of Chinese troops in northern French Indo-China by French forces, since they consider that such arrangements are a matter for determination by the Governments of France and China.

Since the Franco-Chinese agreement completes the reversion of all Indo-China to French control, the Combined Chiefs of Staff consider that the French military commander in Indo-China should act as a medium for the French Government for coordination with the Supreme Commander for the Allied Powers on matters relating to the repatriation of Japanese from Indo-China, and that the Chinese Supreme Commander and Admiral Mountbatten should be relieved of their duties and responsibilities for disarmament and evacuation of Japanese in Indo-China.

Current repatriation schedules envisage the completion of the evacuation of the Japanese from northern Indo-China by April 15. The Combined Chiefs of Staff consider that it is most desirable to have the French commander in Indo-China conform to present schedules.

Accordingly, Admiral Mountbatten has been directed to make the necessary arrangements with the French military commander in Indo-China regarding the transfer of his share of the above-mentioned responsibility at the earliest possible date.

The Supreme Commander for the Allied Powers and the appropriate Chinese authorities have been informed of the Combined Chiefs of Staff action on this matter.

It is understood that a memorandum has been addressed directly to the French Military Attache to the United States informing him of the above and requesting that appropriate instructions be issued to the French military commander in Indo-China.

(64) <u>TELEGRAM FROM CONSUL CHARLES S. REED IN SAIGON TO BYRNES, APRIL 27, 1946</u>

Source: *Foreign Relations*, 1946, Vol. VIII, pp. 37-38.

When talks between French and Vietnamese delegations opened at Dalat on April 17, 1946, the primary question was Cochinchina - the southern part of the country beginning north of An Loc on the Cambodian border and north of Cape St. Jacques on the South China Sea. The French position was that there could be no referendum until peace and order - under French rule - was restored. The Vietnamese insisted that Cochinchina was an integral part of Vietnam. The U.S. Consul in Saigon, in Hanoi during the Dalat talks, filed a report which was frankly pessimistic on French intentions.

Returned yesterday from Hanoi where situation tense. Called on all high French, Chinese, Vietnam officials. He [*Ho?*] dwelt largely on Cochin China issue, first, must join Vietnam, second. French must cease entering Cochin China; he also mentioned need for complete financial independence, own bank and own bank note issue. He was highly indignant action of French in arresting and dispelling [*expelling*] from Dalat Dr. Thach, Cochin Chinese delegate to Dalat conference. He expressed hope for future if French lived up to their agreements which he rather doubted but added that outside help, chiefly capital and technical aid, must be supplied.

Pessimistic views held by all French regarding success of Dalat conference which is now suspended for a few days while Vietnam demands regarding Cochin (cease hostilities, release political internees, Armistice Commission and political freedom) and French counteroffer regarding all Indochina (establish special committee to investigate Vietnam-French incidents) are being studied and that French have now adopted thesis conference merely preliminary and Paris approval must be obtained which is contrary previous understanding. French defend arrest, expelling Dr. Thach on grounds that he is notorious anti-French Cochin Chinese and that Cochin China not yet part of Vietnam.

French insistence withdrawal Chinese from north and all-over procrastination to Dalat may have ulterior motives as it is not impossible French military coup may be brought off as soon as Chinese gone. Some French civilians have spoken of this "as putting Vietnamese in their place". In any event over-all picture is not happy one and much compromise, good faith and tolerance needed to effect peaceful settlement.

(65) LETTER FROM HO CHI MINH TO COMPATRIOTS IN NAM BO, MAY 31, 1946

Source: Ho Chi Minh, *Selected Writings*, pp. 66-67.

Before leaving for France for the Fontainebleau Conference on Franco-Vietnamese relations, Ho reassured South Vietnamese that the unity of Viet-nam would be upheld in the talks in France, and urged them to be generous with fellow Vietnamese who may have opposed the resistance at first.

Dear fellow-countrymen in Nam Bo,

The news of my going to France with a delegation for official negotiation has caused concern to our people, especially in Nam Bo. What does the future hold for Nam Bo?

Please, don't worry. I pledge my word that Ho Chi Minh will never sell his country.

You in Nam Bo have been fighting self-sacrificingly for many months now to safeguard the territorial integrity of Viet Nam; for this, our entire people are grateful to you.

You in Nam Bo are citizens of Viet Nam. Rivers may dry up, mountains may erode; but this truth can never change.

I advise you to unite closely and broadly. The five fingers are of unequal length but they are united in the hand.

The millions of our fellow-countrymen are not all alike; but they are descended from the same ancestors. We must therefore be generous and broad-minded and admit the fact that the offspring of the Lac and the Hong are all more or less patriotic. With regard to those who have gone astray, we must use friendly persuasion. Only in this way can we achieve unity, and broad unity will bring us a bright future.

Through this short message written before my departure, I wish to convey my cordial greetings to all of you, dear fellow-countrymen in Nam Bo.

(66) <u>TELEGRAM FROM CAFFERY TO BYRNES, JULY 7, 1946</u>

Source: *Foreign Relations*, 1946, vol. VIII, pp. 48-49.

As the Vietnamese delegation was en route to France for the negotiations at Fontainebleau, France presented a fait accompli *on the crucial issue of Cochinchina by recognizing a "Republic of Cochinchina", which had created itself by naming a President. This move constituted the chief Vietnamese grievance against the French, as the Fontainebleau Conference opened on July 6, as the U.S. Embassy reported in its dispatch.*

Opening of Franco-Viet Nam conference at Fontainebleau yesterday brought to an apparent end pre-conference honeymoon period during which French and Indochinese officials had rivaled with each other in displays of Franco-Viet Nam friendship.

After long wait for Admiral Thierry d'Argenlieu supposed to preside over conference, unexpected announcement that "Admiral was indisposed" created uneasiness and rumors to effect Viet Nam delegates had vetoed presidency of Thierry d'Argenlieu who, in their eyes, "typified French imperialism."

Max Andre, head of French delegation, assuming Presidency at last moment, delivered innocuous speech of welcome and declared conference open. Mr. Pham Van Dong, head of Viet Nam delegation, immediately protested against this unilateral assumption of the chair of the direction of the proceedings. In a fighting speech which contrasted sharply with platitudes of Andre's address, he went immediately to the core of the worst difficulties which the conference will have to face. In sharp words, he protested against "the mutilation of the Viet Nam Motherland" through the creation of an independent state of Cochin China outside of the Viet Nam. He went on to accuse the French authorities in Indochina of having violated the accords of Dalat of March 6, 1946 and of having used these accords to penetrate peacefully in the north while military operations were being carried on in the south and in the interior.

This unexpected offensive of the Viet Nam delegation on the first day has created a sensation. Independent and impartial *Combat*, genuinely interested in colonial problems, headlines Viet Nam accusation across the entire page and recognizes French mistakes made in Indochina. Communist *Humanite* frankly sides with Viet Nam. Socialists *Populaire* gives fair and impartial account in a vein sympathetic to Viet Nam. MRP. *Aube* regrets "that French goodwill did not find a corresponding echo". In the conservative and Nationalist papers there is literally an explosion of wrath against Viet Nam delegation. Increasingly Leftist but always ultra-Nationalist *Ordre* terms Pham Van Dong's statements "shocking" and already blames Viet Nam for any future breakdown in negotiations. All these papers play up violations of Dalat agreement by the Viet Nam and underline assassinations, kidnapping and rape of Europeans as justification of continued military operations by French expeditionary corps.

On the whole conference had gotten off to bad start. Viet Nam leaders also express their regret that conference "of such considerable importance" should be held outside of Paris.

Interesting to note that yesterday afternoon conversation held between Ho Chi Minh, Viet Nam President, and Algerian deputies of friends of manifest group headed by Ferhat Abbas (my despatch 5571 of July 3) on similarity between problems facing Algeria and Viet Nam.

(67) <u>VIETNAMESE AND FRENCH PROPOSALS ON MILITARY PROBLEMS AT THE FONTAINEBLEAU CONFERENCE, JULY 17, 1946</u>

Source: Trinh Quoc Quang [Truong van Chinh] *Hoi Nghi Viet-Phap Fong-Te-No-Bo-Lo, Thang Bay 1946* [The Vietnamese-French Conference at Fontainebleau, July 1946] Vol. I (Saigon: Van Hoa, 1949), pp. 116-122. Translation by the editor.

The discussion between Vietnamese and French delegations at Fontainebleau revealed how wide the disparity was between their conceptions of Viet-nam's status as a "Free State within the French Union." On military relations, the French delegation insisted that France had ultimate authority for military plans through a combined General staff under a French Chief of Staff. The Vietnamese delegation demanded complete control over their own army in peace-time, offering only to consider French proposals for a joint command in war-time.

French Proposal

1. The Joint General Staff alongside the Chairman of the French government has the responsibility, starting immediately, to research military problems related to the entire French Union.

2. The Indochinese territories may be considered as constituting a theater of operations in liaison with the Pacific and the Indian Ocean.

The Indochinese Federation belongs to this theater of operations and to a defense system, in which the Democratic Republic of Viet-nam is found in the first rank.

3. During wartime the French commander in chief has a combined Federation general staff responsible for defense of that military zone.

4. During peacetime, there will be established a combined general staff, the chief of staff of which is French, which has complete responsibility for preparation and coordination of French forces, Vietnamese forces and the forces of other localities.

The chief of staff has no political functions.

5. Vietnamese Army has its own headquarters under the authority of a Viet-namese Minister having responsibility.

6. The combined staff researches plans for the distribution of French forces, Vietnamese forces and forces of other localities; the defense plans and preparation of defense in time of war.

Vietnamese Proposal

Introduction

Viet-nam declares that it accepts the objective and principles of the United Nations, and expresses its desire to participate in the system of collective security of that international organization.

Viet-nam, jointly responsible with France to protect all common interests of the two states, will increase its national forces, so as to be capable of carrying out its responsibility for mutual help in the French Union.

Because it has responsibilities with regard to the United Nations and to the French Union, Viet-nam will, according to its own strength and in the framework of its constitution, harmonize its military organization with the French military organization.

The above mentioned harmonization consists essentially of a clear division and coordination of responsibilities for the separate military forces based on two primary principles: national sovereignty and direct joint responsibility.

a) Only when national sovereignty is respected can an army be created which which has courage and skill in combat. If national sovereignty is to be re-spected, occupation troops must be withdrawn, all soldiers not natives of the country must be withdrawn from the cities, and important points must be neu-tralized.

b) Direct joint responsibility means only coordination within the frame-work of the French Union, without any intermediary layer, so that cooperation can be rapid and effective. If there is an intermediary organization, it is feared that it will bring a dependent relations contrary to the principle of sovereignty and the right to self-determination, causing more and more serious internal conflict, destroying unity, and causing harm to the defense system of the French Union, a primary factor for world peace and security.

(Vietnamese Draft Agreement)

1. The Vietnamese national army maintains security within the country and defends Vietnamese territory. It is under the authority of the President of the Democratic Republic of Viet-nam and is commanded only by a Vietnamese commander.

The Vietnamese national army participates directly in the collective security system established by the United Nations.

2. If Viet-nam needs training personnel and military specialists, and there are Frenchmen and foreigners with equal ability and other qualifications, the Vietnamese government will give priority to the use of Frenchmen.

3. The Vietnamese government welcomes the opinion of the French Joint General Staff. The Vietnamese general will pay heed to and study the opinions of the French Joint General Staff, especially regarding the problem of a single command authority during wartime and before a war occurs.

4. For a period of five years beginning from March 6, 1946, the Vietnamese Government agrees to the stationing of French troops - persons of French descent - in a few important locations to be decided later, in order to defend the French Union in concert with Vietnamese army.

Each year the above mentioned French troops will be reduced by one fifth (so that they are completely withdrawn by March 6, 1951) and replaced by troops in the Vietnamese national army.

A Staff Conference to be comprised half of representatives of the French Joint General Staff and representatives of the French Government and half of representatives of the Vietnamese general staff and of the Vietnamese government, will decide on the total number of non-Vietnamese troops to be stationed on Vietnamese territory or passing through Vietnamese territory, during the period of five years from March 6, 1946 to March 6, 1951. Beginning on March 6, 1951, the total number of non-Vietnamese troops stationed or passing through Vietnamese territory will be decided in a later agreement. The Staff Conference will decide the method of controlling the above-mentioned total.

5. During a limited period (to be decided later) beginning from March 6, 1946, the Vietnamese government agrees that French troops - those of French descent - shall cooperate with Vietnamese troops to equip and maintain naval and air bases (to be decided later) required for the defense of the French Union.

During a period (to be decided later) beginning from March 6, 1946, the Vietnamese government allows naval and air forces of the French Union to use these places: Gia-Lam, Hai-Phong, Da-Nang, Cam-Ranh, O Cap and Tan Son Nhat.

6. Sovereignty and ownership of Viet-nam in those places occupied by the French armed forces of course is not in any way damaged.

That portion of the Vietnamese army cooperating with French troops in the important points and military bases still belong under the authority of the Chairman of Democratic Republic of Viet-nam and are commanded by the Vietnamese command.

The Vietnamese government bears the cost of equipment and maintenance of the above mentioned military bases. The French Government bears the military expenditures for French troops stationed in those military bases.

The use of military bases and troops stationed on Vietnamese territory, to help or oppose any country, must be agreed to by the Vietnamese government in advance.

7. The Staff Conference to be comprised half of representatives of the French Joint General Staff and the French Government and half of representatives of the Vietnamese general staff and the Vietnamese Government will decide the important points and military bases mentioned in articles 4 and 5.

8. In the framework of an international security organization, Viet-nam, a country having sovereignty, is prepared to participate in a system of coordination and consultation in a zone which can include other states or territories in the French Union.

9. The Vietnamese government permits French troops stationed in or passing through Vietnamese territory the following privileges with the understanding, however, that they will respect Vietnamese sovereignty:

-- supply of goods, training, transport and information, either around the place occupied or from one point to another;

-- transport and storage of foodstuffs required for the soldiers;

-- use of a number of roads, railroads, waterways, harbors, ports, airfields, telegraph wires and wireless systems.

-- airplanes flown over Vietnamese airspace;

-- the Vietnamese government guarantees inviolable military information in accordance with international procedures.

The Staff Conference to be comprised half of representatives of the French Joint General Staff and the French Government and half of representatives of the Vietnamese General Staff and the Vietnamese government, will decide the limit on the period of the privileges which the Vietnamese government permits the French army to enjoy on Vietnamese territory.

(68) VIETNAMESE AND FRENCH PROPOSALS ON DIPLOMATIC QUESTIONS AT THE FOUNTAINE-BLEAU CONFERENCE, JULY 22, 1946

Source: [The Vietnamese-French Conference at Fontainebleau, July, 1946], pp. 56-66, 96-122. [Translation by the editor.]

In its proposal regarding diplomatic relations, Viet-nam demanded diplomatic powers appropriate to a sovereign state. The French proposal, on the other hand, made it clear that France would not permit Viet-nam to have direct diplomatic relations with other states. The "Indochinese Federation" to which the French delegation referred was never actually formed, and nothing more was heard of the idea after the French began to negotiate with Bao Dai in 1947.

Vietnamese Proposal

The Vietnamese concept of foreign relations is based on two primary principles: Vietnam's political independence, and the spirit of Vietnamese-French mutual responsibility to preserve mutual interests.

Politically independent, Viet-nam has its own separate foreign relations; however, Viet-nam accepts close cooperation with France, so Viet-nam will harmonize its own foreign policy with French foreign policy in order to protect mutual interests.

1. Viet-nam has separate representation abroad and in the United Nations.

a) Having its own separate foreign relations, Viet-nam will have its own Ambassadors in foreign countries, and has the authority to receive foreign ambassadors in Viet-nam (complete diplomatic authority, both active and passive). However, in any country where Viet-nam has not yet nominated an ambassador or consul, it will ask the French representative to protect its interests in its stead.

b) Viet-nam also has separate representation in the United Nations. The Vietnamese delegation believes that France will support Viet-nam whenever Viet-nam asks to enter the United Nations.

2. Entering into agreements with foreign countries.

The spirit of joint responsibility will be achieved by means of consultations between the two countries each time one negotiates with and enters into
agreements with foreign countries.

Viet-nam or France, whichever plans to negotiate or sign an agreement imposes an international obligation on the other country, must have the prior
agreement of the other country.

When France and Viet-nam negotiate jointly with foreign countries, each
country will only be bound by an agreement if the representative plenipoten-
tiary which it has nominated signs the agreement.

3. Participation in international conferences.

Two kinds of circumstances must be distinguished:

a) Conferences convened by the United Nations: Viet-nam as a member
country of the United Nations has separate representation.

b) Conferences not convened by the United Nations: both Viet-nam and
France participate together; or the two countries agree to nominate a common
representation; or there is a joint delegation but each country has its own
representation on the delegation; or each country has a separate delegation.

French proposal

Does Viet-nam have minimum diplomatic liberty? This is a question to which
the Vietnamese representative referred many times at Dalat, but returning to
the transcripts, I do not find the French representative responding explicitly.

I do not hesitate to answer to you that Viet-nam has been recognized as a
free state, so certainly it has a degree of diplomatic liberty. We will determine that degree, based on the mutual interests of France and Viet-nam, and
it should not be forgotten that on March 6 of this year, Viet-nam agreed to
place its freedom within two spheres: the Indochinese Federation and the
French Union.

You gentlemen can be confident that in the diplomatic field as well as in
other fields, France is prepared to recognize for Viet-nam all the freedoms
appropriate to the limitations on its sovereignty which Viet-nam itself has
freely accepted.

Thus the diplomatic freedom of Viet-nam is subject to a twofold limitation:
first by the Indochinese Federation and once more by the French Union. In
this meeting the French representative has not yet said anything about what
influence the participation in the Federation will have on the diplomatic freedom of Viet-nam. The French representative refers only to the limitations belonging to the framework of the French Union and discusses generally diplomatic
liaison of a free state in the French Union.

A basic principle in the French Union is that everyone freely accepts that
France has the role of coordination and guidance in order to protect the common
interests, pursue common ideals and carry out common policy. That responsibility is even clearer in the field of foreign relations, and all the more so,
since the French Union's foreign policy must show closed ranks to the maximum.
Moreover, only France is worthy, above all others, of serving the common
interests of all states in the French Union and the separate interests of each
state, thanks to France's past, its spiritual and real position, and its influence as a great power in the United Nations.

Thus the states within the French Union, including even the most advanced
states having the status of free states and having the most legal qualifications, have accepted that France represents the French Union in order to
achieve common policy, which is also natural.

To ease the Vietnamese representative's mind, the French representative
hastens to add that the above mentioned principle does not have an absolute or
permanent character. After a period of time, whenever the French Union has a

clear, firm foreign policy, states in the French Union having more qualifications than the rest will shoulder part of the responsibility, which will grow with time, directly with regard to foreign relations in order to carry out not only the separate foreign policy of that state, but also the common policy of the entire French Union.

1.   The French Ambassador represents the entire French Union.

In accordance with the above principle, the French delegation believes that all of the states in the French Union profit by having the French Ambassador represent them abroad. We have not yet discussed the structure of the French Union, but there are many parts which are certain, as such as the French Ambassador will represent the French President as well as the Chairman of the French Union, both those positions being held by one person.

To put it more clearly: apart from France, the "guiding state", the other states in the French Union do not have diplomatic representation directly with foreign states.

This does not mean that the member states of the French Union are completely without the right of diplomatic representation.

France hopes to acknowledge that member states in the French Union have maximum diplomatic rights compatible with the unity of the French Union. This will be advantageous both for France and for the member states. "Maximum" rights of diplomatic representation are divided by the French proposal into three contributing views on foreign policy.

In the French Union only free states can have diplomatic personnel in a few foreign countries. Diplomatic personnel of free states work in the French Embassy, under the authority of the French Ambassador but have separate personnel as well. Diplomatic personnel of free states are advisers to the French Ambassador on problems relating to their country, and are permitted to participate in negotiations related specifically to their country. Diplomatic personnel of free states are permitted, depending on their desire, to correspond with their government, but must do so through the French Ambassador. This is the separate diplomatic right "within the framework of the French Union and under the protection of France", which the French representative wishes to reserve especially for those states having the highest international legal status in the French Union.

In the area of protecting residents abroad, any state in the French Union, regardless of whether it has the legal status as a free state or not, can place its consuls anywhere the French government and the competent organ of the French Union recognizes as necessary. Consuls of member states are under the authority of the French Ambassador and correspond with their government through the French Ambassador.

Member states of the French Union also have the right to receive consuls of foreign countries. Consuls of foreign countries only have the function of protecting citizens of their own country and the property of citizens of their country. Documents recognizing foreign consuls are provided by the government of the member state, with the agreement of the commissioner of French Union representation.

2.   The French Ambassador negotiates and signs international agreements for states in the French Union.

Besides the authority to place consuls, and particular free states which can have diplomatic personnel within the French embassy, all states in the French Union are free to express their opinions within the competent organs of the French Union about problems related to foreign policy of each country separately and the common policy of the French Union.

This organ has the function of "harmonizing"; therefore, whenever a member state wishes to enter into an agreement with a foreign country, the government of that state, with the commissioner representing the French Union, plan the terms of the agreement and forward to the organ of the French Union in Paris for examination. Then, the French government sends a directive to the French Ambassador and diplomatic representative of the Chairman of the French Union. The French Ambassador will negotiate with the foreign country.

In urgent circumstances, the commissioner representing the French Union has the authority to contact the French Ambassador in a foreign country, provided that the problem is not vital, and is not related to the common policy of the French Union.

An agreement entered into under the above procedures is effective only after it is ratified by the interested member state.

However, agreements relating to the entire French Union are ratified only by the competent organ of the French Union.

3. Viet-nam's entrance into the United Nations.

There is one further question discussed fleetingly at Dalat, to which the Government of the Democratic Republic of Viet-nam paid special attention. That is the entrance of Viet-nam into the United Nations. The French government has examined this problem in a particularly benevolent spirit. Although it has not yet responded explicitly, the French delegation can also declare that France does not oppose in principle allowing states associated with it in the framework of the French Union, entering the United Nations, even though they have not yet attained complete sovereignty in regard to the international field.

However, with regard to Viet-nam, there is one caution, not with regard to whether it is permitted to participate in the United Nations or not, but regarding what form representation in international organizations takes.

Will the Vietnamese Government have its own separate, permanent representative or, because there is still the Indochinese Federation, will Viet-nam have a common representative with other states in the Federation?

The resolution of this problem must await the final definition of the statute of the Indochinese Federation, and must depend on the views of the member states of the United Nations on the request of Viet-nam and other states in the Federation to enter the United Nations.

(69) MEMORANDUM BY THE CHIEF OF THE DIVISION OF SOUTHEAST ASIAN AFFAIRS, ABBOT L. MOFFAT TO THE DIRECTOR OF THE OFFICE OF FAR EASTERN AFFAIRS, JOHN CARTER VINCENT, AUGUST 9, 1946

Source: *Foreign Relations of the U.S.*, 1946, Vol. VIII, pp. 52-54.

Relations between the French and Vietnamese delegations at Fountainebleau further deteriorated after France convened a conference at Dalat to which it invited representatives of the Royal Governments of Cambodia and Laos, as well as Cochinchina, the ethnic minorities of the highland region and even of the politically and juridically nonexistent entity called "Southern Annam". In his analysis of French policy, the Chief of the State Department's Southeast Asia Office supported the Vietnamese charges of French bad faith toward the March 6 accord.

Recent developments indicate that the French are moving to regain a large measure of their control of Indochina in violation of the spirit of the March 6 convention. The evidence, as set forth below, suggests that the French are attempting to gain their objective by manoeuvres designed to confine and weaken Viet Nam. In the event that Viet Nam decides to resist these encroachments, which is by no means unlikely, widespread hostilities may result.

The chief opposition to the reestablishment of French rule in Indochina has all along come from the Annamese, who inhabit the three east coastal provinces of Tonkin, Annam, and Cochinchina, which once comprised the Kingdom of Annam. The populations of the other two countries of Indochina - Cambodia and

Laos - are not in a high state of political development or in any condition seriously to resist French control. A *modus vivendi* between the French and the Annamese was achieved in the preliminary convention of March 6, 1946, by which the Annamese "Republic of Viet Nam" was recognized as a free state within the Indochinese Federation and the Viet Nam Government declared its readiness to receive the French Army. The convention left for future settlement two crucial problems: the status of Viet Nam in its external relations, and the geographical extent of Viet Nam. On the former point, the provisional agreement states that "each contracting party will take all necessary measures... to create the favorable atmosphere necessary for an immediate opening of amicable and free negotiations. These negotiations will bear particularly upon diplomatic relations between the Viet Nam and foreign states, the future status of Indochina, French economic and cultural interests in Viet Nam." On the latter point the agreement stated that "with respect to the bringing together of the three (provinces), the French Government pledges itself to ratify the decisions taken by the populations consulted by referendum." The crux of the present situation lies in the apparent intention of the French to settle both matters to their own advantage and without reference to Viet Nam.

The hostility of the Annamese toward the French began to mount to its present intensity when the French on June 1 announced the inauguration of the Provisional Government of the Republic of Cochinchina. Annamese leaders had long emphasized their view that the inclusion of Cochinchina in Viet Nam was a matter of life and death to their country. Cochinchina, it may be mentioned, contains the important mercantile cities of Saigon and Cholon, includes the mouths of the Mekong, and is the richest province in Indochina. Called the Southern Province by the Viet Namese, it is racially indistinct from Tonkin and Annam. Statements by the French that the referendum in Cochinchina (as pledged in the March 6 convention) would still be held failed to reassure Viet Nam leaders, who pointed out that such a referendum could not possibly be fair owing to the suppression by the French of pro-Viet Nam political parties and of all anti-French opinion. SEA's information tends to substantiate this point of view.

Tension between the French and the Annamese reached its present pitch when the French on August 1 convened a conference at Dalat (in southern Annam) to which the Royal Governments of Cambodia and Laos, the Government of the autonomous Republic of Cochinchina, and the native peoples of southern Annam and high plateau of Indochina (but *not* Viet Nam, recognized by the French as part of the Indochina Federation and French Union) to send delegates to "study the framework of the French Union". Subsequently published agenda of the conference indicated that the salient aspects of the Indochina Federation would also be deliberated. As an immediate result of this conference, the Viet Nam delegation which had been discussing the future relation between France and Viet Nam with the representatives of the French at Fountainebleau since July 6 announced that they were suspending negotiations until the French should have cleared up the "equivocal" situation which had been created. The head of the Viet Nam delegation, who had opened the conference with a violent blast against French policies, charged that the French were now trying to engineer their own statute for the Indochinese Federation and their own settlement of the status of Cochinchina and other areas claimed by Viet Nam. The view of Consul Saigon is not very different. He gave as his opinion that a front against Viet Nam was in the making, that the states participating in the Dalat Conference were at least tacitly recognized as free states by the French, and that France and these free states are now determining the status of the Indochinese federation without reference to Viet Nam. In his view it indicated double-dealing on the part of the French, and he reported that the French Commissioner for Cochinchina had forced the issue by threatening to resign unless his policy is carried out. Nothing has been said at the conference about

a referendum. Finally, Consul Saigon added that he had learned that representatives of the southern regions of the Province of Annam (which has always been
claimed by Viet Nam) will petition for inclusion of their territories in Cochin-
China. In view of the completeness of the agenda of the Dalat Conference, which
covers the essential framework of the Indochinese federation, and in view of
the deliberate exclusion of Viet Nam from the conference, the conclusion is inescapable that the French are endeavoring to whittle down Viet Nam and to settle
the future form of organization of Indochina with those who may be expected to
be amenable to French influence.

Annamese reaction to French moves has been sharp, and following the suspension of the Fontainebleau negotiations, there were pro-Viet Nam manifestations
in Saigon. The ambush of a French supply column near Hanoi by Annamese soldiers, during which the French suffered 52 casualties (one of the worst of many
incidents during the past several months), may have been related to the opening
of the Dalat Conference.

While it is to be doubted that the French will allow the Fontainebleau Conference to break down completely, Embassy Paris quotes Baudet as having stated
that French officials are in no hurry to speed up negotiations until the pacification of Indochina, and particularly of Cochinchina, has been completed.
In this connection, Consul Saigon reports that more troops are arriving in
Indochina and that the French military position has grown much stronger. Meanwhile, the Saigon press has been carrying vitriolic attacks against Viet Nam.
Since this press is completely controlled by the French, there would appear to
be no official objection to this line.

In his latest report, Consul Hanoi states that there now exists an imminent
danger of an open break between the French and Viet Nam. He adds that a rupture
of relations would probably be followed by a period of anarchy and that, although the French could quickly overrun the country, they could not - as they
themselves admit - pacify it except through a long and bitter military operation.

In conclusion, it is SEA's view that the Annamese are faced with the choice
of a costly submission to the French or of open resistance, and that the French
may be preparing to resort to force in order to secure their position throughout Indochina. It may not be advisable for this Government to take official
notice of this situation during the Peace Conference, but the Department should
be prepared, SEA believes, to express to the French, in view of our interest in
peace and orderly development of dependent peoples, our hope that they will
abide by the spirit of the March 6 convention.

(70) ORDERS OF THE DAY BY VO NGUYEN GIAP ON THE FIRST NATIONAL DAY, SEPTEMBER 2, 1946

Source: Vo Nguyen Giap, Orders of the Day, Speeches and Mobilization Letters,
pp. 15-18. Translation by the editor.

*As tension mounted in the North Vietnamese military preparations were
stepped up. On the first anniversary of Viet-nam's independence, Vo Nguyen
Giap, as Chairman of the Military Commission, reviewed the accomplishments of
the country's fledgeling armed forces, especially in the South, and ordered
them to increase their efforts. As indicated in this speech, Giap already had
plans for "regularization" of the army, bringing all the forces in North,
Central and South under a single command. The armed forces under centralized
command were called National Protection Army, after having been called the
Viet-Nam Liberation Army during the period leading up to the August Revolution.*

Generals,
Members of the National Protection Army in the Center, South and North!

Unit leaders and members of the combat self defense and self- defense militia forces in the Center, South, and North!

On the occasion of the observance of Independence, I represent the government in sending cordial greetings to all the soldiers and self-defense organizations throughout the three regions.

Last year, on this day, the first People's Provisional Government of the Democratic Republic of Viet-nam was presented to the nation, and, representing the Government, President Ho Chi Minh declared the freedom and independence of Viet-nam to the nation and the world.

Independence Day, September 2, is a glorious day in our country's history, the day on which the soldiers of the National Protection Army and self-defense organizations, together with the entire people, swore their determination to sacrifice to the end to protect the country's freedom and independence.

Independence Day is the result of a process of struggle of the people and soldiers. Every one of us still remembers the magnificent feats of arms of the National Salvation Army in Bac-Son, of the Viet-nam Liberation Army Armed Propaganda Brigade, of the Ba-to guerillas, the forerunners of the National Protection Army today. All of us still remember the tradition of heroic sacrifice, austerity and endurance, and unity between army and people, which helped those army units achieve victory.

Every one of us still especially recalls the spirit of fearless determination of those army units and self-defense organizations in the days of the August Revolution last year, when they received the general uprising order, and, coordinating with the entire people, rose up with arms to seize political power.

From Independence Day last year to the present, in order to protect the nation, all soldiers and self-defense organizations have exerted all their effort to train, accepting much sacrifice and hardship, regardless of whether they were in bases in the rear area or in the war at the frontline.

In the North, the National Protection Army has pacified scattered bandits in the Chi-linh, Dong-trieu, An-chau, Son-dong, Lang-son and Cao-bang regions, and in many other localities.

Especially in the South and South-Central regions, the National Protection Army, some of whom have marched South, and self-defense units have heroically struggled to defend the victories which the August Revolution brought to our country. Saigon, Nha-trang, and other battlefields in the South will record forever the glorious feats of arms of our army. From March 6, in circumstances in which it was necessary to fight in order to defend themselves, our troops in the South stayed closer to the people than ever before and in circumstances of extreme hardship, preserved intact the strength and honor of the National Protection Army, defending the rights of the people and the territorial integrity of the Fatherland.

Our troops have many accomplishments and, thanks to that fact, when they are in battle, the whole people warmly support the troops, especially the brother and sister workers in the factories, the brothers and sisters in specialized branches having direct contact with the troops, such as, supply, medical, etc....

Going through a period of building and fighting, our troops have become stronger with every passing day. The National Protection Army, although its history is not yet long, has traditions which are glorious. That is because we not only study the experiences of those troops who have immediately preceded us but also inherit all the precious experiences of our ancestors: the tactic of using a smaller number of troops to defeat a larger number of troops of Tran hing Dao, the spirit of the long, drawn-out resistance of Le Loi, the method of using particularly talented troops of Quang trung, the tactic of forest and mountain guerilla war of Hoang hoa Tham, the tactic of guerilla war on the plain of Nguyen thien Thuat.

Today, celebrating Independence Day, let us remember in sorrow those generals and members of units who have died for the country, holding high the example of courageous assault, our troops pledge together to make more effort.

As Chairman of the Military Commission, I hereby order:

1. To the entire National Protection Army: you must advance on the road to regularization, and at the same time, you must hold fast the virtues of a guerilla army, thoroughly obey orders, make every effort to study technique and tactics, hold high the spirit of struggle.

2. To cadres: you must advance in the command of troops, study tactics and technique, raise the level of and improve the organization of staff, political, military supply, and other agencies.

3. To the National Protection Army, self defense forces and militia in the South Central and Southern Regions: you must preserve the forces, protect the people, always be vigilant and guard against the provocative schemes of the enemy.

4. To all self-defense organizations: you must strive to heighten discipline and raise military standards; troops must try to help self-defense organizations and coordinate closely with one another.

5. To the entire National protection Army and self-defense forces: you must protect the people and achieve unity between army and people.

Our struggle and the resistance of the entire people has led the nation to Independence Day. We, along with the whole people, are defending the sovereignty and the united territory of the country. We will advance toward a regular, united, national army including Center, South and North with sufficient forces to preserve the country. Striving in that direction is the worthiest way to observe Independence.

Long live the Democratic Republic of Viet-nam!

Long live the Viet-nam National Protection Army!

Long live the heroic spirit of the self-defense forces and the militia!

Long live the spirit of people and army unity!

Long live independent Viet-nam!

Long live Chairman Ho!

(71) SPEECH BY PRESIDENT OF THE NATIONAL DEFENSE COUNCIL VO NGUYEN GIAP, HANOI, SEPTEMBER 2, 1946 (Extract)

Source: *One Year of Revolutionary Achievement, Report to the Viet Nam People at Hanoi by Vo Nguyen Giap* (Bangkok: A Vietnam News Publication, 1946), pp. 14-17.

In his speech on national day, Giap gave a detailed exposition of the serious threat of famine and financial bankruptcy which faced the new Republican government when it took office a year earlier. He claimed that extraordinary increases in food production permitted the triumph of the regime over starvation and that sacrifices by the public overcame the financial crisis.

On the economic side, after the first days of the Revolution, the situation was quite alarming. Industry and trade had come to a complete standstill. Even handicrafts had to close down. Agriculture had slumped. The area under rice cultivation had been greatly narrowed down. Mainly through Japanese economic pressure aided by French instigation, millions of hectares of former paddy-fields had been cultivated with hemp and castor oil plants. The level of water, during the flood in August 1945 in Bacbo rose to the unprecedented height of 12,60m: 700,000 hectares of paddy-fields were thus submerged and 300,000 tons of rice destroyed; inundation in Thanh-hoa and Nghe-an too damaged 100,000 tons of rice. The shortage in these areas could not be relieved by exporting rice from Nambo because of disruption of transport and communications due to the war. The situation was extremely serious: from the middle of next February to the end of May, it was anticipated that there would be a total lack of food. In addition, besides the quantity of food necessary for the population, we had to feed about 50,000 Japanese and 200,000 Chinese soldiers and our own troops as well.

However, beyond all expectations, the food shortage crisis was successfully tided over by the nation who responded to a man to the call of the Government. The slogan "INCREASE PRODUCTION" was taken up everywhere, and not only the civil population but the army as well bent all their energies to the task of increased food production. The area of paddy-fields increased by 1.5 times; the potato-fields by 3 times, their output by 5 times, the maize-fields by 5 times, their output by 4 times. The Revolution had triumphed over starvation, and in truth that triumph was one of the greatest achievements of our new Democracy.

At the same time, production and trade cooperatives were set up in many places, especially in the towns of Trungbo. The Bank of Commerce and Industry was established to help industries and crafts.

INDO-CHINA BANK REPUDIATES ITS "NOTES"

Our financial state was still more critical. When our Democratic Government was set up, the former Treasury of IndoChina was found short of 185 million piastres and the National Debts had increased to 564 million piastres. In the Central Treasury there was only a total of 1,230,000 piastres in currency including 586,000 piastres of unusuable notes. The annual period for collecting the taxes had already passed. Customs duties formerly totalling 3/4ths of the annual revenue of the whole of IndoChina had been considerably decreased due mainly to trade stoppage. Under the new regime the poll-tax was abolished, and as a consequence we lost as much as 3/4ths of the former direct general revenues. A further decrease in revenue by 60 million piastres was entailed by the total prohibition of opium and spirits. The total paper currency circulation had increased from 25 million last year to 2,500 million by 1945. The value of the IndoChina piastre had internally dropped from 500 to 10 in terms of the standard "copper sapeque." The situation was further worsened by the introduction into the country of Chinese currency notes as by the unjustifiable non-acknowledgement by the Bank of IndoChina of the 500 piastre notes issued formerly by itself. This repudiation was clearly engineered with a view to undermining our financial economy.

FINANCIAL CRISIS OVERCOME

Such were the financial difficulties which our Government had to face and overcome as a vital part of our fight for Independence. The financial crisis was tided over by recourse to the following measures:

1. Reduction of Government expenses by appealing to the spirit of personal sacrifice on the part of all Government functionaries and troops;
2. Distribution of taxation on a more equitable basis;
3. Institution of the system of "Exceptional Voluntary Contribution to National Defence" as well as of publicly organized subscriptions;
4. The issue of new currency notes.

By these different measures both the ordinary Government expenses as well as those necessitated by national defence had been met.

80,000 HONORARY TEACHERS

In the field of education, the VietNam language is replacing the French as the fundamental one, and the University is being reorganized, but the greatest work is no doubt the institution of public classes for the common people by the BDHV organization (Binh Dan Hoc Vu or Popular Educational Service). Within one year the BDHV has organized 60,000 such classes where Viet-Nam writing is taught free of charge by 80,000 honorary teachers of both sexes to 2,5 million people among whom females predominate.

OPIUM AND LIQUOR BANNED

Socially in spite of the tremendous hardships and troubles arising from the economic situation, workers' rights have been safeguarded, protection of females and children assured, and assistance to the poor in general largely extended. But most significant is the prohibition of opium and spirituous liquors. From now on, our race is preserved from the calamitous effects of these two poisons.

In the space of one year, during wartime, under all kinds of unprecedented difficulties, in spite of the heavy handicaps left us by the old regime, we have attained satisfactory results, especially in our struggle against starvation, inundation, and illiteracy. These remarkable achievements, through the democratic system, testify to the inexhaustible resources of moral and material strength latent in our people.

(72) FRANCO-VIETNAMESE *MODUS VIVENDI*, SEPTEMBER 14, 1946

Source: Enclosure to Despatch 366 from Bangkok, April 24, 1947

In protest against the Dalat Conference, the Vietnamese delegation left France, but Ho Chi Minh remained behind, hoping to reach an agreement which would gain more time for Viet-nam, which needed peace to consolidate its political, economic and military strength. The result was modus vivendi *which did not resolve the primary problem of Cochinchina but did give Viet Minh adherents in the South political freedom in return for guarantees of French cultural and economic interests.*

The Government of the French Republic and the Government of the Democratic Republic of Viet Nam have firmly decided to pursue, in a spirit of reciprocal confidence, the policy of concord and collaboration established by the Preliminary Convention of March 6 and outlined during the course of Franco-Viet Nam conferences at Dalat and Fontainebleau. Convinced that this policy alone represents the permanent interests of the two countries and the democratic traditions which they claim as theirs, the two Governments, while referring to the Convention of March 6 which continues in force, consider that the time has come to register new progress in the development of relations between France and Viet Nam, while awaiting the time when circumstances will permit the conclusion of a complete and definitive agreement. In a spirit of friendship and mutual understanding, the Government of the French Republic and the Government of the Democratic Republic of Viet Nam have signed a *Modus Vivendi* providing, within the framework of the limited agreements, provisional solutions of the main issues of immediate interest which arise between France and Viet Nam. So far as the referendum provided for in the Convention of March 6 is concerned, the two Governments reserve the right to fix later its date and form. They are convinced that all the measures contained in the *Modus Vivendi* will contribute to the establishment, in the near future, of an atmosphere of calm and confidence which will permit the carrying on of definite negotiations in the near future. They believe, therefore, that it is possible to anticipate for the resumption in January 1947 of the work which has just taken place at the Franco-Vietnamese conference in Fontainebleau.

FRANCO-VIETNAMESE *MODUS VIVENDI*

Article 1 - Viet Nam nationals in France and French nationals in Viet Nam shall enjoy the same freedom of establishment as nationals, as well as freedom of speech, freedom to teach, to trade and to circulate and in general all the democratic freedoms.

Article 2 - French property and concerns in Viet Nam shall not be subject to a stricter regime than the one reserved for Vietnamese property and concerns, particularly with respect to taxation and labor legislation. This equality of status shall be granted reciprocally to the property and enterprises of Viet Nam nationals in the territories of the French Union. The status of French property and concerns in Viet Nam may not be changed except by common agreement between the French Republic and the Republic of Viet Nam. All French property requisitioned by the Government of Viet Nam or of which persons or enterprises have been deprived by the Viet Nam authorities shall be returned to their owners and parties entitled thereto. A mixed commission shall be appointed to fix procedure for such restitution.

Article 3 - For the purpose of the resumption of the cultural relations which Viet Nam and France are equally desirous of developing, French educational institutions representing different categories shall be able to function freely in Viet Nam and they shall apply official French programs. The institutions in question shall receive, by special agreement, the buildings necessary for their functioning. They shall be open to Vietnamese students. Scientific research, the establishing and functioning of scientific institutions shall be unhindered for French nationals throughout Viet Nam territory. Viet Nam nationals shall enjoy the same privilege in France. The Pasteur Institute shall be secured in its rights and property. A mixed commission shall regulate the conditions under which the "Ecole Fracaise d'Extreme Orient" (Far Eastern French School) shall resume its activity.

Article 4 - The Government of the Republic of Viet Nam shall call, first on French nationals, whenever it needs advisers, technicians or experts. The priority granted to French nationals shall cease to be in effect only in cases where it is impossible for France to furnish the required personnel.

Article 5 - As soon as the present problem of monetary standardization is settled, one and the same currency shall have circulation in the territories under the authority of the Government of the Democratic Republic of Viet Nam and in the other territories of Indochina. The said currency shall be the Indochinese piaster.

Article 6 - Viet Nam shall form a Customs Union with the other members of the Federation. Therefore, there shall be no customs barrier within the country and the same tariffs shall be applied everywhere for entry into and departure from Indochinese territory. A coordinating customs and foreign trade committee which, moreoever, may be the same as the one dealing with currency and exchange shall study the necessary means of application and prepare the organization of the Indochinese customs service.

Article 7 - A mixed communications coordinating committee shall study the measures which will re-establish and improve communications between Viet Nam and the other countries of the Indochinese Federation and the French Union: land, sea and air transport, postal, telephone, telegraph and radio communications.

Article 8 - Until such time as the French Government and the Government of the Democratic Republic of Viet Nam conclude a definitive agreement regulating the question of the diplomatic relations of Viet Nam with foreign countries, a mixed Franco-Viet Nam Commission shall determine the arrangements to be made to ensure the consular representation of Viet Nam in neighboring countries and its relations with foreign consuls.

Article 9 - Desirous of ensuring as soon as possible, in Cochinchina and in Southern Annam, the restoration of public order as indispensable to the free development of democratic liberties as it is to the resumption of commercial transactions and aware of the fortunate effect that the cessation on the part of both of all acts of hostility or violence will have, the French Government and the Government of the Democratic Republic of Viet Nam have decided on the following measures:

(a) Acts of hostility and violence on the part of both shall cease.

(b) Agreements of the French and Viet Nam General Staff shall arrange the conditions of application and supervision of measures decided in common.

(c) It is specified that prisoners detained at the present time for political reasons shall be released with the exception of those prosecuted for crimes and offenses against the common law. The same shall apply for prisoners captured in the course of operations. Viet Nam guarantees that no prosecution shall be initiated and no act of violence tolerated against any person by reason of his attachment or loyalty to France; reciprocally, the French Government guarantees that no prosecution shall be initiated and no act of violence tolerated toward any person because of his attachment to Viet Nam:

(d) The enjoyment of the democratic freedoms defined in Article I shall be reciprocally guaranteed.

(e) Unfriendly propaganda on both sides shall be terminated.

(f) A person of note designated by the Government of the Democratic Republic of Viet Nam and approved by the French Government shall be accredited to the High Commissioner to establish the cooperation indispensable for the carrying out of the present agreements.

Article 10 - The Government of the French Republic and the Government of the Democratic Republic of Viet Nam agree to seek in common the conclusion of special agreements concerning all questions requiring them in order to stengthen friendly relations and prepare the way for a general, definitive treaty. Negotiations shall be resumed again for that purpose as soon as possible and in January 1947 at the latest.

Article 11 - All the provisions of the present *Modus Vivendi* drawn up in duplicate, shall enter into force on October 30, 1946.

(73) PROCLAMATION BY HO CHI MINH TO THE PEOPLE UPON RETURN FROM FRANCE AFTER NEGOTIATIONS, OCTOBER 23, 1946

Source: Ho Chi Minh, *Selected Works*, Vol. III, pp. 71-76.

Upon his return, Ho discussed the modus vivendi *which he had negotiated in France, emphasizing the importance of avoiding violence and reprisals and of correct behavior toward the French.*

Compatriots throughout the country,

I left for France over four months ago. Today I am back home. I am very happy to see the Fatherland and you again. I have the following statements to make:

1 - On my way to France, during my stay in France and on my way back from France, the French Government, to show its desire to cooperate with Viet Nam, received me ceremoniously. Out of sincere friendship for our people, the French people received me fraternally.

On your behalf, I have the honour to thank the French government and people.

In my absence, thanks to the clearsighted leadership of acting President Huynh, the care and help of the Assembly, the efforts of the Government, the unity and common effort of the people, many difficult questions were settled, and much progress made in constructive work.

I thank the Government, the National Assembly and all our compatriots.

I think constantly of our compatriots living abroad who have made many sacrifices in the struggle and are always faithful to their Fatherland, notwithstanding the hardships they have endured.

Thanks to the understanding of French personalities in the North and Centre of Viet Nam, most of the difficulties arising between the Vietnamese and the Frenchmen have lately been settled.

I hope that from now on cooperation between the two peoples will be closer.

My thoughts are also with the Chinese and other foreign residents who all bear in mind the sentence "Brother countries, like passengers on the same boat, must help each other."

At various places, when I met friends of Chinese and Indian nationalities, we were very happy to see each other and to show our friendliness. Now, coming back to Viet Nam, I witness the same sight.

2 - Answering the kind invitation of the French Government, I went to France with the purpose of solving the question of Viet Nam's independence and the unification of the North, Centre and South. Due to the present situation in France, these two questions have not yet been settled. We have to wait. But I dare to vouch that sooner or later Viet Nam is sure to be independent, and its three parts, the North, The Centre and the South, will be unified.

What did the Delegation and I do during the months we spent in France?

1 - We took Viet Nam's flag to France. The French Government and people and foreign residents there look on our flag with respect.

2 - We drew greater attention from the French government and people and made them understand the question of Viet Nam better than before. We also drew the attention of the world and made it understand the question of Viet Nam better than before.

3 - We caused a great many Frenchmen to become friends of the Vietnamese people and approve of Viet Nam's independence and sincere Vietnamese-French cooperation on an equal footing.

4 - We further heightened the position of the Vietnamese youth, women's and workers' organisations because respective international organisations have recognized our organizations as members.

5 - The Vietnamese-French Conference has not ended yet. It will resume next May, but the September 14 *Modus Vivendi* has firstly, permitted the Vietnamese and French to carry out their business easily. Secondly, it has paved the way for the next Conference to be conducted in a friendly manner.

*****

What have we to do from now until January?

1 - The Government and people must be single-minded in their efforts at organization, and must work for a closer unit, economic development, national reconstruction and realisation of a new mode of life in all aspects. Men or women, old or young, intellectuals or peasants, producers or traders, everyone must endeavour to work. We must show to the French government and people and to the world at large that the Vietnamese people are already in possession of all the required conditions to be independent and free, and that the recognition of our freedom and independence is a necessity.

2 - The French in France are very friendly towards us. So the Vietnamese in Viet Nam should also be friendly toward the French people.

Toward the French Army we must be correct.

Toward the French residents, we must be moderate.

Toward the Frenchmen who sincerely want to cooperate with us, we will sincerely cooperate, and that is advantageous to both parties.

All this is to show to the world that we are a civilized people, to get a greater number of Frenchmen to support us, and to further strengthen their support, so that the provokers who intend to divide us may find themselves with no pretext and our unity and independence will soon succeed.

3 - Compatriots in the South and the southern part of Central Viet Nam! The North, Centre and South are part and parcel of Viet Nam.

We have the same ancestors, we are of the same family, we are all brothers and sisters. Our country has three parts which are the North, the Centre and the South. They are just like three brothers in the same family. They are just like three regions of France: Normandy, Provence and Beauce.

No one can divide the children of the same family. No one can divide France. Likewise no one can divide Viet Nam.

During the past year, in waging the Resistance war, our compatriots have seen their property destroyed, have sacrificed their lives, or were imprisoned and exiled. But their patriotism remains unshakable.

This iron will will never be forgotten by the entire people, the Fatherland and the Government.

I respectfully bow to the memory of the martyrs, and sympathise with the compatriots who are suffering and making sacrifices.

So long as the Fatherland is not yet unified and our compatriots are still suffering, I can neither eat with an appetite, nor sleep in peace. I solemnly promise you that with your determination and that of the entire people, our beloved South will surely come back into the bosom of our Fatherland.

The French Government has acknowledged the holding of a referendum by our southern compatriots to decide on the fate of the South.

In the September 14 *Modus Vivendi*, the French Government agreed to implement the main points concerning the South as follows:

1 - To release the political prisoners and those arrested for taking part in the resistance.

2 - Our southern compatriots are to have freedom of organisation, of meeting, of the press, of movement, etc.

3 - Both parties are to stop fighting.

The French government will undoubtedly respect its signature and implement the above clauses.

Now, what must our southern compatriots have to do?

1 - The Vietnamese army like the French army must simultaneously stop fighting.

2 - Our compatriots must carry out political actions in a democratic way.

3 - Close unity must be realized with no discrimination as to political parties, social classes and creeds. Unity means strength. Division means weakness.

4 - Acts of reprisals are forbidden. Toward those who went astray, our compatriots must display a generous policy. We must let them hear the voice of reason. Everybody loves his country. It is only for petty interests that they forget the great cause. If we use the right words, they will certainly listen to us. Violent actions are absolutely forbidden. This is what you have to do at present to create a peaceful atmosphere, paving the way democratically to reach the unification of our Viet Nam.

(74) DECLARATION BY HO CHI MINH BEFORE THE NATIONAL ASSEMBLY ON THE FORMATION OF THE NEW GOVERNMENT, NOVEMBER 4, 1946

Source: Ho Chi Minh, *Selected Works*, Vol. III, pp. 77-78.

On November 4, Ho Chi Minh announced a new government before the National Assembly. It was the first government to be formed after the departure of the Chinese troops from Viet-nam, which left Ho free to choose ministers compatible with the Viet Minh program. Ho assumed the post of Foreign Minister, while

Giap became Minister of National Defense and the Ministers of Economy and Education each had Communists as Vice-Ministers.

Deputies,

According to the National Assembly's wishes, the new Government must clearly show broad solidarity with no discrimination regarding political parties. After being entrusted by the National Assembly with the formation of the Government, I have consulted many old personalities, representatives of various organisations and personalities of various sections of society.

The result is that able persons have agreed to take part in the Government. Mr. Huynh had expressed his intention to withdraw because of old age and bad health, but I wished to retain him for the sake of the great cause, and finally he agreed. Outside the Government, many personalities such as Mr. Bui Bang Doan, and the priest Pham Ba Truc, are willing to make every effort to help us. Inside or outside the Government, all have promised to make every endeavour in their work, and to be devoted to the cause of the country and people.

Thanks to everyone's zeal, I was able rapidly to form the Government. Though it is not one hundred per cent satisfactory to the National Assembly, it nearly conforms to the principles laid down by the National Assembly.

I may thus declare before the National Assembly that this Government clearly expresses the people's spirit of coalition, that it is a Government paying attention to the practical situation and that it will endeavour to win independence and national unity, and build a new Viet Nam.

This is a national Government in which all personalities from the North, the Centre and the South are taking part; especially our southern compatriots, who are not only fighting at the front to protect the country, but also enthusiastically taking part in the construction of the Fatherland.

The work undertaken by the Government will meet with many difficulties, but thanks to the support of the National Assembly and of the entire people, the Government will resolutely reach its goal.

(75) EXTRACT FROM D.R.V. REGISTER OF TELEPHONE MESSAGES ON THE HAIPHONG INCIDENT, NOVEMBER 20-22, 1946

Source: Enclosure to Despatch No. 366 from Bangkok, April 24, 1947.

Despite the Modus Vivendi, *which established a coordinating customs and foreign trade committee, control over ports and customs duties remained one of the primary sources of conflict. Before the* Modus Vivendi *was signed, the French had announced that they would unilaterally take control of all imports and exports at Haiphong on October 15, and the French proceeded to set up harbor controls despite Vietnamese protests. When Vietminh militia took some French border patrolmen prisoner in November, the French tried to free them by force, and a serious clash developed. This extract from a Vietnamese telephone message log chronicles the Vietnamese efforts to control and settle the incident.*

Dates	Hours	Senders	Addressees	Text	Station
11/20	10:30	V.M. Liaison Haiphong	Central Liaison Hanoi	Franco-Viet Nam incident, Che Sat region: We are doing all possible to settle - report follows.	Mr. Giang

Dates	Hours	Senders	Addressees	Text	Station
	11:30	id.	id.	French fire opened on Viet Nam policeman, 1 killed 2 wounded...	Mr. Giang
	2 P.M.	id.	id.	Despite our efforts for settlement, situation worsens. French armored units circulate in the street. Gun-fire from the French side. We regret behavior of certain liaison officers displaying weapons (Lt. Orsini with Thompson) for operations against which Commanding Officer Huan has protested.	Mr. Giang
	2:15	V.N. Central Liaison	French Central Liaison	Incident at Haiphong. Deployment of French armored units in various places in the city. Ultimatum issued by French Commanding Officer demanding evacuation of several V.N. posts, especially that of Blvd. formerly Henri Riviere. Request French Delegation take measures immediatly as a consequence.	Mr. Giang
	2:45	V.N. Liaison Haiphong	V.N. Central Liaison	V.N. Haiphong liaison has just handed over French detained and protests against French ultimatum.	Captain PHU
	3 P.M.	id.	id.	French troops increase firing after 2:45 P.M.	"
	3:15	id.	id.	French troops launch general offensive	"
	3:15	V.N. Central Liaison	French Central Liaison	Warns French liaison of the gravity of the situation at Haiphong and insists that the French side take adequate measures, as well as the V.N. side.	"
	5 P.M.	V.N. Liaison Haiphong	V.N. Central Liaison	Commanding Officer Huan, Chief V.N. local liaison, goes to stadium to begin parlays with French side, which sets 3 conditions: 1) to cease fire, 2) to remove the barricades and mines, 3) evacuation of Henri Riviere posts, etc...and their occupation by French troops; otherwise all artillery weapons	"

Dates	Hours	Senders	Addressees	Text	Station
				and all tanks will be put into action.	
	5:30	V.N. Central Liaison	V.N. Liaison Haiphong	Communication of the order to cease firs with instructions to the V.N. lisison for applying it in relation with French Liaison.	Mr. Phan-My
	6:30	V.N. Haiphong Liaison	V.N. Central Liaison	V.N. Liaison Haiphong has communicated the order to cease fire to the French Liaison. French Liaison states it knows nothing of this matter.	Mr. Giang
	9 P.M.	V.N. Central Liaison	French Central Liaison	1) French troops state they have also received order to cease fire. 2) call attention behavior of certain Liaison Officers re. protest Commanding Officer Huan (see communication of 2 P.M.)	Mr. Phan-My
	11 P.M.	Liaison	Liaison	Detonation of shells of 37mm " gun and sustained machine-gun firing are heard. V.N. liaison demanded explanations from French Liaison. Latter stated that it was for purpose of clearing the aviation camp of Cat-Bi in order to receive the Central Delegation which was to land there.	
11/21	4:37 A.M.	V.N. Liaison Haiphong	V.N. Central Liaison	From direction of railroad " station and thereafter, 5 or 6 bursts of fire of automatic weapons are clearly heard. Then 3 detonations of mortar shells: One at the station and 2 at the theater. V.N. Liaison lays matter before French local Liaison and invites it to go to the scene of action. Demarche without results communicates the above news to the French Liaison.	
	4:40	V.N. Central Liaison	French Central Liaison	action. Demarche without results communicates the above news to the French Liaison.	Mr. Phan-My
	8:30 A.M.	V.N. Central Liaison	id.	In spite of its efforts, V.N. local Liaison has not yet been able to get in touch with French local Liaison. As shots are still heard from time to time, and as the Central Delegation is to arrive immediately at Haiphong we request the French Central Liaison to give orders consequently to the Haiphong French Liaison to get in touch with V.N. Liaison in order to prevent any unfortunate incident.	Mr. Giang

Dates	Hours	Senders	Addressees	Text	Station
	8:45 A.M.	V.N. Liaison Haiphong	V.N. Central Liaison	Have been able to get in touch with Liaison in person of Lt. Orsini. But latter is not willing to consider the question of receiving General Delegation. French mortars continue to pound V.N. positions	Mr. Giang
	9:15	V.N. Central Liaison	French Central Liaison	Communicates above news to Captain Bonart.	Mr. Giang
11/22	6:30 A.M.	V.N. Liaison Haiphong	V.N. Central Liaison	On account of difficulty in reaching French Liaison we decided to send 2 V.N. Liaison Officers to the French Local Liaison complaining of discourteous and inhospitable attitude of Lt. Orsini who accepted it [sic] only at the insistence of Colonel Lami.	

(76) VERBAL AGREEMENT BETWEEN COLONEL LAMI AND MR. HOANG HUU NAM AT HAIPHONG, NOVEMBER 21, AND 22, 1946

Source: Dispatch No. 366, from Bangkok, April 24, 1947.

With much difficulty, local French and Vietnamese officers succeeded in restoring peace and reached agreement on a few measures to ease tension in Haiphong.

1st point - Liberation on the Viet Nam side and the French side of all the French and Vietnamese detained or arrested during the incident of November 20, 1946;

2d point - Liberation by French troops of 17 Vietnamese arrested (November 15, 16 and 17, 1946) before the incident of November 20, 1946 at Haiphong;

3d point - Provisioning of the Vietnamese who are in the former building of the Post, Telephone and Telegraph Office at Haiphong;

4th point - Establishment of a joint guard at the Haiphong railroad station for normalization of communications;

5th point - Suppression of hindrances to the Viet Nam personnel who come to repair the Haiphong-Hanoi telephone and telegraph lines.

6th point - Joint quarters for Franco-Viet Nam Haiphong Liaison and choice in the personnel of this Liaison.

(77) LETTER FROM GIAP TO MAJOR-GENERAL LOUIS MORLIERE, FRENCH COMMISSIONER IN TONKIN, NOVEMBER 21, 1946

Source: Enclosure to Despatch No. 366 from Bangkok, April 24, 1947.

While the Haiphong incident was still being settled, another incident occurred at Lang Son, in which French forces opened fire on Vietnamese military posts and seized public buildings. Minister of Defense Giap immediately sent a protest note to the French Commissioner in Tonkin.

Pursuant to my letter of today and to the communication sent to Mr. Sherer by Mr. Phan-My, I have the honor to call to your attention again the particular seriousness of the Langson incident as it has developed today. From the information which I have collected, it appears, in fact, that:

1. The French troops at Langson have until now followed a policy of systematic unfriendliness, illustrated by facts which we have had the honor to submit to you on several occasions. These last few days again, the unusual behavior of the French troops at Langson is not of a nature to reassure public opinion (reconnaissance of the terrain, regrouping of the forces at Ky-Lua, setting up of a post at Van-Vy next to a Viet Nam military cantonment, betray a very determined intention to engineer a coup.

2. The question of the disinterment of bodies has always been considered favorably by the local authorities. When it began several days ago, it caused no difficulty. But since yesterday, some French soldiers, under cover of this pious task, have been engaging in acts of military provocation: reconnaissance, taking photographs, destruction of defense works on the slope of the hill which directly overlooks the citadel, the barracks of the Viet Nam forces. Such an attitude needs no comment, and, as a matter of fact, this morning, under pretext of proceeding to search for remains, some detachments of the French army took advantage of the dangerously exposed situation of the Viet Nam posts to open sustained fire on them.

Meanwhile, some infantry formations and armored cars launched an attack unexpectedly on our public buildings in order to seize the Customhouse, the Post, Telephone and Telegraph Station, the public transportation system, and the railroad station. The execution of this plan proves positively that it had been long premeditated. And the Viet Nam forces were victims of their own good faith.

3. The Langson affair has broken out just at the time when the Haiphong affair is not yet settled. This simultaneousness becomes more disturbing when one thinks that, in both cases, the French troops aimed, with the same careful preparations and with equal ruthlessness, at our public buildings and our military points.

I have the honor to transmit to you, in the present letter, our very vigorous protests against such acts of aggression of French troops, who bear, in this case, all the responsibility for their acts. And we consider that a rapid settlement of these incidents, especially the withdrawal of the troops to their original positions, is imperative and indispensable in order to clear the present atmosphere of Franco-Viet Nam relations.

Please accept, Sir, the assurance of my very high consideration.

(78) ULTIMATUM OF COLONEL DEBES, FRENCH COMMANDER AT HAIPHONG, NOVEMBER 22, 1946

Source: Enclosure to Despatch No. 366, from Bangkok, April 24, 1947.

On November 24, Ho Chi Minh had agreed with a French delegation from Saigon to open talks in Hanoi on the operation of the mixed commission on customs and foreign trade. But the French hawks in Paris and Saigon wanted to use the Haiphong incident to gain control of the entire city. General Jean Valluy, Commander of all French troops in Indochina, went around High Commissioner for Tonkin, General Morliere, and received permission directly from Premier Bidault to unilaterally seize control of Haiphong. Thus, Colonel Debes, the local commander at Haiphong, presented the Haiphong Administrative Committee an ultimatum, which was aimed at providing the pretext for an all-out French offensive on the city. A French official later said that "no more than 6,000" Vietnamese had been killed by French naval bombardments of the Vietnamese quarters of the city on November 22. See Ellen J. Hammer, The Struggle for Indochina, 1940-1955 *(Stanford, Calif.: Stanford University Press, 1966), p. 183.*

By order of the General High Commissioner of the French Republic in Indo-China, I demand:
1. That all Viet Nam military or semi-military forces evacuate:
a) the Chinese quarter, that is, the quarter bounded on the north by the Rue de la Mission; on the west, by the Song Tam-Bac; on the south, by the Darse Bonnal; on the east, by the Blvd. Amiral Courbet;
b) the quarters to the northeast of the Avenue de Belgique (including that Avenue);
c) the villages of Lac-Vien.
2. That all the Vietnamese who were in those quarters and villages, whether or not they have their present domicile there, be disarmed and that no depot of arms or ammunition be set up there.
I demand the pure and simple acceptance of these conditions before November 23, at 9 A.M.; failing which, I reserve for myself the right to take any measure which the situation calls for.

(79) APPEAL BY HO CHI MINH TO FRENCH COMMANDER IN CHIEF IN INDOCHINA, GENERAL JEAN VALLUY ON THE FRENCH ATTACK AT HAIPHONG, NOVEMBER 23, 1946

Source: Ho Chi Minh, *Selected Works*, Vol. III, pp. 79-80.

Following the French attack on Haiphong, Ho Chi Minh appealed to General Valluy to restore peace immediately. The tone of the appeal was notably re-strained, considering the bloody consequences of the French attack.

The situation in Lang Son is not yet quietened when the situation in Hai-phong becomes serious again. Not only do the French troops not implement the clauses signed in the afternoon of November 20 by the representative of General Morliere and the representative of our Government, but this morning they have made further claims which we cannot accept. Therefore another clash has begun.
I address an appeal to General Valluy, commander-in-chief of the French army and High Commissioner, and to the French high-ranking officers in Viet Nam immediately to stop the bloodshed between the French and the Vietnamese.
I call on all my compatriots to exercise control, and on the regular army and self-defence guards to be ready to defend our national sovereignty, and the lives and property of foreign residents.
The Government is always close by your side to protect our land.
Long live independent and united Viet Nam!

(80) EXCHANGE OF LETTERS BETWEEN GENERAL MORLIERE AND GIAP, NOVEMBER 28-30, 1946

Source: Enclosure to Despatch No. 366, from Bangkok, April 24, 1947.

In response to Vo Nguyen Giap's inquiry to General Morliere about measures which might be taken to prevent the new battles from developing from relatively minor incidents, Morliere again demanded, on a non-negotiable basis, complete French military control of Haiphong, its surroundings, the roads connecting Haiphong and Hanoi and all French garrisons. Giap proposed a joint commission to discuss the issues raised, but Morliere again rejected negotiation on the French demands.

In pursuance of the communication which was sent to you yesterday through me, I have the honor to confirm to you the military conditions laid down by the French High Command for the purpose of preventing definitively the possible repetition of the serious incidents of which the Haiphong region has just been the scene:

1.   In the zone bounded on the south by the Cua Lach-Tray; on the west, by the Lach-Tray cut, the Haly cut, the Cua Cam ferry, and the Haiphong road to Nui Deo (that locality included); on the north, by the Nui Deo road to Quang-Yen; on the east, by the Cua Nam-Trieu to its mouth (all these boundaries included):

a)   Prohibition to station any Viet Nam military or semi-military formation (militia, *tu-ve*, etc.).   Safety in this zone will be assured entirely by the French troops.

b)   Transit of Viet Nam military formations or armed boats across this zone, whatever may be the method of transportation (overland or river) will be subject to French military authorization and control.

2.   There shall be free circulation of French troops on the Haiphong-Soson road.   Moreover, it is to be understood that the roads connecting various French garrisons are to be cleared of obstacles or breaks which may have been made therein.

I should appreciate a prompt reply.

Please accept, Mr. Minister, the assurance of my very high consideration.

(Signed):   Morliere

I have the honor to acknowledge receipt of your letter dated November 28, 1946.   As the French proposal is of a very important nature, I suggest to you that we agree to form a joint commission to discuss the question.

Please accept, Sir, the assurance of my very high consideration.

(Signed):   Vo Nguyen Giap

I have the honor to acknowledge receipt of your letter of today and to inform you that the measures stipulated in my letter of the morning of November 28 are the result of the very precise instructions which have been sent to me.   They are not, therefore, subject to examination by the joint commission which you contemplate, and the constitution of which I consider unnecessary, unless its sole purpose is to fix the terms and conditions of execution thereof.

Please accept, Mr. Minister, the assurance of my very high consideration.

(Signed):   Morliere

I have the honor to acknowledge receipt of your letter of the afternoon of November 28.

As the conditions of the French High Command, laid down in that letter of the morning (sic) of November 28, affect our sovereignty, I propose to you again that, in the interest of Franco-Viet Nam cooperation, you reconsider the question and that you inform the French High Command at Saigon of my suggestions.

Please accept, Sir, the assurance of my very high consideration.

(Signed):   Vo Nguyen Giap

I have the honor to acknowledge receipt of your letter of November 29, 1946.

In accordance with the desire which you expressed, I have transmitted by telegram the contents thereof to the French High Command at Saigon, which I had also kept informed of the proposal expressed in your letter of November 28, 1946.

But I confirm to you that the measures contemplated in my letter of the morning of November 28 are perfectly well-known to the French High Command at Saigon, and have received its full approval.

Moreover, I state explicitly to you, as I had already done in the course of our conversation, that these military measures in no way prejudice any Franco-Viet Nam commercial and customs agreements which are to govern the port of Haiphong later.

Please accept, Mr. Minister, the assurance of my very high consideration.

(Signed): Morliere

(81) TELEGRAM FROM ACTING SECRETARY ACHESON TO DIVISION CHIEF MOFFAT IN SAIGON, DECEMBER 5, 1946

Source: *U.S.-Vietnam Relations*, Book 8, pp. 85-86.

Despite his anxiety at French intention to reestablish control by military force, Acheson instructed State Department Chief of the Division of Southeast Asian Affairs, Abbot Low Moffat, who was visiting Hanoi, that he was to tell Ho Chi Minh that he would have to give up the D.R.V. insistence on a referendum in Cochinchina and accept a "compromise" on its status. Acheson suggested that the U.S. was interested in finding Vietnamese groups to support as an alternative to Ho's government, because of its alleged Moscow connections.

Assume you will see Ho in Hanoi and offer following summary our present thinking as guide.

Keep in mind Ho's clear record as agent international communism, absence evidence recantation Moscow affiliations, confused political situation France and support Ho receiving French Communist Party. Least desirable eventuality would be establishment Communist-dominated, Moscow-oriented state Indochina in view DEPT, which most interested INFO strength non-communist elements Vietnam. Report fully, repeating or requesting DEPT repeat Paris.

Recent occurrences Tonkin cause deep concern. Consider March 6 accord and *modus vivendi* as result peaceful negotiation provide basis settlement outstanding questions between France and Vietnam and impose responsibility both sides not prejudice future, particularly forthcoming Fontainebleau Conference, by resort force. Unsettled situation such as pertains certain to offer provocations both sides, but for this reason conciliatory patient attitude especially necessary. Intransigence either side and disposition exploit incidents can only retard economic rehabilitation Indochina and cause indefinite postponement conditions cooperation France and Vietnam which both agree essential.

If Ho takes stand non-implementation promise by French of Cochinchina referendum relieves Vietnam responsibility compliance with agreements, you might if you consider advisable raise question whether he believes referendum after such long disorder could produce worthwhile result and whether he considers compromise on status Cochinchina could possibly be reached through negotiation.

May say American people have welcomed attainments Indochinese in efforts realize praiseworthy aspiration greater autonomy in framework democratic institutions and it would be regrettable should this interest and sympathy be imperilled by any tendency Vietnam administration force issues by intransigence and violence.

May inform Ho Caffery discussing situation French similar frankness. For your INFO, Baudet in DEC 3 conversation stated 1) no question reconquest Indochina as such would be counter French public opinion and probably beyond French military resources, 2) French will continue base policy March 6 accord and *modus vivendi* and make every effort apply them through negotiation Vietnam, 3) French would resort forceful measures only on restricted scale in case flagrant violation agreements Vietnam, 4) d'Argenlieu's usefulness impaired by outspoken dislike Vietnam officials and replacement perhaps desirable, 5) French Communists embarrassed in pose as guardian French international interests by barrage telegraphic appeals from Vietnam. Caffery will express gratification this statement French policy with observation implementation such policy should go far obviate any danger that 1) Vietnamese irreconcilables and extremists might be in position make capital of situation 2) Vietnamese might be turned irrevocably against West and toward ideologies and affiliations hostile democracies which could result perpetual foment Indochina with consequences all Southeast Asia.

Avoid impression US Govt making formal intervention this juncture. Publicity any kind would be unfortunate.

Paris be guided foregoing.

(82) LETTER FROM MOFFAT IN HANOI TO THE STATE DEPARTMENT, DECEMBER 1946 (EXTRACTS)

Source: *The United States and Vietnam: 1944-1947*, Staff Study, Committee on Foreign Relations, U.S. Senate, April 3, 1972 (Washington: U.S. Government Printing Office, 1972), Appendix II, pp. 41-42.

Moffat, called on Ho Chi Minh in Hanoi at the height of the tension between the Vietnamese and the French. Ho and Deputy Foreign Minister Hoang Minh Giam did their best to get the U.S. to help Viet-nam preserve its independence, even going so far as to hold out the prospect of a U.S. naval base at Cam Ranh Bay - ironically the site of the largest U.S. base complex during the Second Indochina War. But Moffat made it clear that Viet-nam would have to have French approval for any diplomatic relationship with the U.S.

At 5:00, after a siesta, we went again to the Presidency. Giam met us in the hall and led us upstairs to Ho Chih Minh's room, where he lay in a large bed with a black muffler around his neck. Although he had no fever, he was obviously weak and his voice was often very feeble. He spoke of his friendship and admiration for the United States and the Americans he had known and worked with in the jungle, etc., and how they had treated the Annamese as equals. He spoke of his desire to build up Vietnam in collaboration with the French so that his people might be better off, and to that end they wanted independence to seek friends among other countries as well as France and to secure the capital needed to develop their country, which France was now too poor to give them. He said he knew that the United States did not like communism, but that that was not his aim. If he could secure their independence that was enough for his life time. "Perhaps fifty years from now the United States will be communist; and then the Vietnam can be also or "then they will not object if the Vietnam is also." He spoke in English, but I am not sure of his exact words. The intent, at any rate, was a smiling, and friendly "Don't worry" - which coincides with the able French views (not the popular view) that the group in charge of Vietnam are at this stage nationalists first, utilizing their party techniques and discipline to the end; that an effective nationalist state is a prerequisite to any attempt at developing a communist state - which objective must for the time being be secondary. He also stressed his desire for peace, but made it clear that he also felt that the Vietnam could not surrender to France with respect to the new order to withdraw from the environs of Haiphong. I confined my remarks to expressing a hope for a peaceful settlement and my very genuine pleasure at meeting him (as well, of course, as the reason for my trip throughout SEA).

At 5:00 Giam had an official tea for me at the Presidency. Madame Saincanny was there. Morliere, Lami and a few other French. I met some of the other Vietnamese officials, some businessmen and doctors and admired some rather lovely lacquer pictures which is a Tonkinese specialty. Giam asked if he could talk with me privately and that he had a present for me from Ho Chi

Minh and wanted to ask some questions; so I left at 6:00 and went with Jim to the Consulate where Giam joined us presently. There he presented me with an autographed photograph and a piece of "mountain brocade" inscribed to Ho. (The purpose, of course, to show that the hill people also back Ho. The Tonkinese never live above the 25 meter level, occupy the Delta, but *not* the mountains). Then he started to explain how Vietnam wanted free ports, and the right to trade freely; to get foreign capital where they would; they wanted American capital, commerce; they hoped an American airline would use Hanoi; an American shipline use Haiphong regularly, etc. In short, he kept reiterating they did not always want to be "compressed" by the French. I interrupted finally to explain that under the March 6 Agreement, their status in many respects is unsettled - "subject to future French-Vietnam negotiations" - such as foreign affairs (for which reason we do not recognize and have relations with the Vietnam Government) and finance, etc. (for which reason, until agreement is reached, we assume in such matters French laws still obtain). He demurred on this last - said the customs question was the cause of the Haiphong incident - and passed on). He then stated Vietnam had no navy and had no intention of being warlike, but would be glad to cooperate with the U.S. in developing Cam Ranh Bay as a naval base, that it was a very important location between Singapore and Hong Kong and opposite the P.I. I replied I knew nothing of the military plans of my Government, but doubted if we would be interested in such a base. (Cam Ranh Bay, as you know, is in South Annam and is presently controlled by the French). I explained that I was sure that the U.S. would want to have trade and commerce with Vietnam; mentioned the proposed route approved by CAB which includes Hanoi: but stated before there could be any direct relations, the Vietnamese and French would have to agree on the respective powers of the two governments. Giam also stated the Vietnam desire for an economic federation of Indochina; a customs union and free trade between the three states; and federal collection of customs so that the revenues could be fairly distributed to the states. But, he stated, the Vietnam was strongly opposed to any political power in the federation. I have perhaps given his remarks more coherence than they had. The impression I received was one of extreme naivety.

(83) LETTER FROM HO CHI MINH TO THE FRENCH PRESIDENT, DECEMBER 12, 1946

Source: Enclosure No. 366 from Bangkok, April 24, 1947.

The French attack on Haiphong and Morliere's demands convinced Vietnamese leaders that war could come at any time, and they began moving main forces into base areas and setting up barricades in the cities to slow down the French. In addition, the French began to move additional forces into Vietnam, in violation of the April 1946 General Staff Agreement, and Ho immediately protested to the French President.

It has been pointed out to me that, during the day of December 9, 1946, French troops, about a battalion, the majority of whom were soldiers belonging to the Africa Legion, landed at the port of Tourane without previous consent of the Viet Nam military authorities.

The Viet Nam General Staff, as well as the Ministry of National Defense of my Government, have already made a sharp protest against this landing, which violates in the most flagrant manner the Franco-Viet Nam agreements of March 6 and April 3, 1946, by the terms of which any movement in Viet Nam territory of French relief troops - which must be made up only of "Frenchmen of metropolitan origin" (Frenchmen from the mother country) - and with still greater reason, an increase of strength in excess of the total number agreed upon, must be the subject of a prior agreement of our General Staff, and the number of French relief troops stationed at Tourane was fixed at 825 men.

Moreover, before it has been possible to settle the regretable incidents of Haiphong and Langson, such military operations only strengthen in the minds of the Vietnamese the conviction that France is engaged in preparing a new attack against Viet Nam.

I wish therefore to call your enlightened attention to the exceptional seriousness of the fact, convinced that the French Government would not fail to take adequate measures as a result.

I avail myself of the occasion to renew to Your Excellency the assurance of my very high consideration.

(84) TELEGRAM FROM HO CHI MINH TO PREMIER BLUM, DECEMBER 15, 1946

Source: Enclosure to Despatch No. 366 from Bangkok, April 24, 1947.

On December 13, a Conference of Party Zonal Chiefs was convened in Ha Dong, and the Central Committee's assessment was that "French reactionaries in the colony are trying to push into war", but said the Party had to "struggle for the possibility of peace", even while "preparing urgently to carry on all-people, all-sided long-term warfare." (Quoted in Lich Su Quan Doi Nhan Viet Nam *(History of the Viet Nam People's Army), (Hanoi: Quan Doi Nhan Dan, 1974), p. 249.*

Two days later Ho sent a telegram to Blum proposing a series of steps which the two sides could take to return to the previous accords and begin "definitive negotiations". But the message was held by French authorities in Saigon until December 26 - a deliberate sabotage of any move toward negotiations by the Blum government. See Philippe Devillers, Historie du Vietnam de 1940 a 1952 *(Paris: Editions du Seuil), p. 351.*

Occasion your election Presidency French Government,

To show our confidence in you and in people France,

To show our sincere desire fraternal cooperation with French people,

To prove that our only aspiration is independence and territorial integrity of Viet Nam within French Union,

To prove our ardent desire to settle peacefully serious incidents which at present steep our country in blood,

To prove that we have always been prepared to apply loyally agreements signed by our two Governments,

To dispel atmosphere of hostility, reestablish atmosphere of confidence and friendship, and effectively prepare definitive negotiations,

I have the honor to make to you the following concrete proposals:

a) On the Viet Nam side:

1) To invite the evacuated Viet Nam population to return to the cities.

2) To take all necessary measures to assure the return to the cities of the economic life disturbed by the present state of hostility.

3) To put an end to the measures of self-protection taken by the inhabitants of the cities.

4) To assure the return to normalcy of the Hanoi-Langson thoroughfare.

b) On the French side:

1) Return of the French and Viet Nam troops to the positions held before November 20, 1946 at Haiphong and Langson, and withdrawal of the reinforcements recently sent to Tourane, contrary to the agreements.

2) To cease the so-called mopping-up operations and campaigns of repression in Cochin-China and North Annam.

c) On both sides:

1) To start working immediately the agencies contemplated for the application of the *Modus-Vivendi*, a part of the Commission at Hanoi, another at

Saigon, as the country resort of DALAT offers us no conveniences for work.

    2) To put an end to all unfriendly propaganda in French and Viet Nam radio-broadcasts and press.

    Awaiting the honor of your reply, I beg you to accept the expression of my very high consideration.

(85) <u>LETTER FROM HO CHI MINH TO MORLIERE IN HANOI, DECEMBER 18, 1946</u>

Source: Enclosure to Despatch No. 366 from Bangkok, April 24, 1947.

On December 16, the Party Central Committee's Current Affairs Committee sent a message to its Province Party organs in the South making it clear that a resistance war throughout the country would have to be fought and that the situation was "very tense". On December 17, there was a massacre of dozens of civilians by French troops in Hanoi, and troops continued unilaterally to destroy barricades. The following day the Executive Committee of the Party Central Committee began meeting in special session and decided to mobilize the population for resistance. For the next two days, fundamental problems of resistance war were discussed. On December 18, Ho sent a protest to the French Commissioner in Hanoi which was almost routine in tone, in order to avoid giving away the Party's plans.

    During our last interview, it was decided that, on both sides, we would make efforts to avoid any incident of a nature to create tension. Such a decision was made public in a press release.

    Now, I regret to state since that date incidents have multiplied, both in Hanoi and in other Viet Nam cities.

    Landing at Tourane of a battalion, with armored equipment, contrary to the agreements. No official French reply has yet been given to my letters of protest on that subject.

    In the province of Hai-Minh, for the past week, French troops stationed at Tien-Yen and Dam-ha have begun to attack the Viet Nam positions in the direction of Dien-Lap and Langson, thus causing the extension of the conflict in that sector. Our Minister of National Defense has sent a letter of protest on this subject to General Morliere; he has not yet received any French official reply.

    At Hanoi, acts of provocation and terrorism are multiplying, assuming daily a more serious nature.

    Thus, since November 21, 1946, we find 47 incidents provoked by undisciplined French military elements and causing, on the Viet Nam side, 13 deaths and 41 wounded, without mentioning material damage.

    Again yesterday, French troops destroyed the means of protection set up by the civilian population, and carried away the materials. But for the calmness of our compatriots and the discipline of our soldiers, a serious incident could have occurred, the effect of which cannot be measured.

    Moreover, on Rue des Vermicelles, the French troops fired on the civilian population, causing 80 casualties, in dead and wounded; dozens (*dizaines, tens*) of Viet Nam civilians were arrested.

    At the same time, a French soldier, on sentry-duty at the Electric Power Plant, Rue Blockhaus Nord, fired on his Viet Nam companions at the same sentry-post.

    I have just learned that the same acts of provocation were committed by French troops this very morning, causing more casualties in dead and wounded, in different parts of the city.

    You will certainly agree with me that if this state of affairs continues, Franco-Viet Nam relations will be worsened, for which condition the Government and people of Viet Nam decline all responsibility.

Consequently, I beg you to be so good as to take all necessary and adequate measures to put an end to such a situation, in the interests of our two nations.

Please accept, Mr. Commissioner, the assurance of my very high consideration.

(86) TELEGRAM FROM HO CHI MINH TO BLUM, DECEMBER 19, 1946

Source: Enclosure to Despatch No. 366 from Bangkok, April 24, 1947.

The French continued to push for a showdown with Viet-nam. On December 18, while the Vietnamese leaders were secretly discussing plans for resistance, the French occupied the Ministries of Finance and Communications in Hanoi. Ho sent another message to Blum - his fourth in five days - despite the fact that there had been no French response. He called it an "urgent appeal". It was the last communication with the French before the resistance began.

After the appeal which I sent to you, the situation, instead of improving, is growing worse.

Incidents continue to multiply.

The number of persons killed and wounded in Hanoi daily is added to the 3,000 victims of Haiphong. During the day, on December 17, 1946 alone, 49 Vietnamese men, women and children, were killed and a score were wounded by French soldiers.

The next day, our Minister of Finance saw the headquarters of his Ministry occupied by French soldiers who had come with tanks and guns.

Keeping my love for France and for the French people and the confidence which I have in you, I have requested my compatriots to remain calm in the face of these provocations. But how long must I endure seeing my fellow-countrymen killed before my eyes?

I send you this further urgent appeal. In the higher interests of our two countries. I beg you again to put an end to these provocations and this bloodshed.

Please accept, with my best regards, the assurance of my very high consideration.

(87) GIAP'S ORDER FOR NATIONWIDE RESISTANCE, DECEMBER 19, 1946

Source: *Orders of the Day, Speeches and Mobilization Letters*, pp. 19-20. [Translation by the editor.]

On the evening of December 18, General Morliere brought matters to a head by demanding the disarming of Vietnamese militia in Hanoi. That night, the Indochinese Communist Party Central Committee met and decided to begin the resistance war. At 9:00 p.m. December 19, the orders for armed struggle went over Vo Nguyen Giap's signature.

Order for Nationwide Resistance

Officers of the National Guard, Commanders of units and members of the self-defense militia and self-defense forces,

At 8 o'clock tonight, December 19, 1946, the French troops have provoked hostilities in the capital of the Democratic Republic of Viet-nam.

The Fatherland is in danger!
The hour of combat has come!

In accordance with the order of Chairman Ho and the Government, as Minister of National Defense, I order all soldiers of the National Guard and Self-defense militia in the Center, South and North to:

> Stand up in unison,
> Dash into battle,
> Destroy the invaders and save the country,

Sacrifice to the last drop of blood in the struggle for the Independence and Unification of the Fatherland.

The resistance will be long and extremely hard, but the just cause is on our side, and we will definitely be victorious.

> Annihilate the French colonialists!
> Long live independence and unified Viet-nam!
> Long live the victory of the resistance!
> Determine to fight!

(88) APPEAL BY HO CHI MINH ON NATIONWIDE RESISTANCE, DECEMBER 21, 1946

Source: Ho Chi Minh, *Selected Writings*, pp. 69-71.

In the first public statement by the Vietnamese government after the start of resistance, Ho Chi Minh explained to the Vietnamese people, the French people and the allied nations of World War II why the fighting was necessary.

We, the Vietnamese Government and people, are determined to struggle for our country's independence and reunification, but we are also ready for friendly cooperation with the French people. That is why we signed the Preliminary Agreement of March 6, 1946, and the *Modus Vivendi* of September 14, 1946.

But the French reactionary colonialists lacked sincerity and regarded those agreements as scraps of paper.

In Nam Bo they continued to arrest and massacre Vietnamese patriots and to engage in provocations. They bullied honest Frenchmen who advocated sincerity, and set up a puppet government in order to divide our people.

In southern Trung Bo they continued to terrorize our compatriots, attack the Vietnamese army, and invade our territory.

In Bac Bo, they provoked clashes to occupy Bac Ninh, Bac Giang, Lang Son and many other localities. They blockaded the port of Haiphong, thus making it impossible for Vietnamese, Chinese, other foreigners and also French residents to carry out their businesses. They tried to strangle the Vietnamese people and wreck our national sovereignty. They used tanks, aircraft, heavy artillery and warships to massacre our compatriots, and occupied the port of Haiphong and other towns along the rivers.

That was not all. They put their naval, land and air forces on the alert and sent us ultimatum upon ultimatum. They massacred old people, women and children in the capital city of Hanoi itself.

On December 19, 1946, at 8 p.m. they attacked Hanoi, the capital of Viet Nam.

The French colonialists' aim to reconquer our country is obvious and un-deniable.

The Vietnamese people are now facing these alternatives: either to fold their arms and bow their heads and fall back into slavery, or to struggle to the end for freedom and independence.

No! The Vietnamese people will never again tolerate foreign domination.

No! The Vietnamese people will never again be enslaved. They would rather die than lose their independence and freedom.

French people!

We have no grudge against each other. Only selfish interests have driven the reactionary colonialists to provoke clashes. Profits are for them, death for you, and decorations for the militarists. For you and your families, only suffering and destitution. Think the matter over. Are you going to shed your blood and lay down your lives for the reactionaries? Join us, you will be treated as friends.

Peoples of the Allied nations!

At a time when the democratic countries are striving to organize peace following the end of the World War the French reactionaires are trampling underfoot the Atlantic and San Francisco Charters. They are waging an aggressive war in Viet Nam for which they must bear full responsibility. The Vietnamese people ask you to intervene.

Fellow-countrymen!

The war of resistance will be a long and hard one. Whatever sacrifices we must endure and however long the war of resistance will last, we are determined to fight to the end, until Viet Nam is completely independent and reunified. We are 20 million against 100,000 colonialists. We are bound to win.

On behalf of the Government of the Democratic Republic of Viet Nam, I give the following orders to the Army, self-defence corps, militia and to the people of all three parts of Viet Nam:

1. If the French troops attack us, we must fight back hard with all available weapons. Let our entire people stand up to defend their Fatherland!

2. We must protect the lives and property of foreign residents and give the prisoners of war good treatment.

3. Those who collaborate with the enemy will be punished.

Those who help the resistance and participate in the defence of their country will be rewarded.

Fellow-countrymen!

The Fatherland is in danger, let all of us stand up!

Long live independent and reunified Viet Nam!

Long live the victorious war of resistance!

(89) TELEGRAM FROM HO CHI MINH TO BLUM, DECEMBER 23, 1946

Source: Enclosure to Despatch No. 366 from Bangkok, April 24, 1947.

Despite the all-out war which had begun, Ho apparently still hoped that the Socialist Blum could do something to restore the situation before the French moved in Hanoi and again expressed his willingness to return to the 1946 Franco-Vietnamese accords.

I received your telegram yesterday, December 22. Am happy to learn departure for Viet Nam of Minister Moutet, Delegate of the French Government. I have miraculously escaped bullets of the French troops attacking my resident [sic]. Our Under Secretary of State for Foreign Affairs wounded.

We deeply regret the generalization of the conflicts which began at Hanoi on December 17 by massacre. Viet Nam women, children, old people and pillage of one whole quarter, by occupation the following day of the premises of two of our Ministries, followed by ultimatum on December 19 demanding handing over of police service to French authorities and disarmament of our militia.

We sincerely desire, as do you, the maintenance of peace and loyal application of agreements signed, as I have stated in my numerous appeals addressed to you.

We hope for an order to be given to the French authorities Hanoi to take troops back to positions held before the 17th and to cease so-called mopping-up operations in order to end hostilities immediately.

(90) TELEGRAM FROM BYRNES TO CAFFERY, DECEMBER 24, 1946

Source: *Foreign Relations*, 1946, Vol. VIII, pp. 77-78.

In the first meeting between diplomats of the U.S. and France after the outbreak of armed resistance in the North and Center, the U.S. cautiously warned of the dangers of attempting a military solution to the problem, while the French disclaimed any intention of imposing a settlement by force.

The Under Secretary asked Bonnet to call yesterday afternoon to discuss the situation in Indochina. Mr. Acheson said that we are deeply concerned by the outbreak of hostilities in Tonkin and Annam and are fully aware of the unhappy situation in which the French find themselves. We had anticipated such a situation developing in November and events have confirmed our fears. While we have no wish to offer to mediate under present conditions we do want the French Govt to know that we are ready and willing to do anything which it might consider helpful in the circumstances. We have been gratified to learn of Moutet's mission and have confidence in his moderation and broad viewpoint. We believe however that the situation is highly inflammatory and if present unsettled conditions continue, there is a possibility that other powers might attempt to bring the matter up before the Security Council. If this happens, as in the case of Indonesia, the question will arise whether the matter is one of purely French internal concern or a situation likely to disturb the peace. Other powers might likewise attempt some form of intervention as has been suggested in the Chinese press. We would be opposed to such steps, but from every point of view it seems important that the question be settled as soon as possible. Mr. Acheson added that he wondered whether the French would attempt to reconquer the country through military force which was a step that the British had found unwise to attempt in Burma.

Bonnet said that he had little direct info with regard to the present situation in Indochina but referred to Leon Blum's speech in the Assembly yesterday morning. He summarized important points of the speech which he said clearly indicated that Blum's policy is to settle the question as far as possible by conciliatory means and that this was the purpose of Moutet's visit. He said that Blum had reiterated that French policy is to assure the independence (within the French empire) of Viet Nam and complete self govt. It was unfortunate that it had been impossible up to the present to implement the far reaching concessions embodied in the French agreement with Viet Nam.

He said that personally he would be surprised if the Chinese brought the question up before the Security Council at this time for he felt that the Nanking Govt was sympathetic to the French position in Indochina. He concluded by saying that he would inform his Govt of our friendly interest and of our deep concern over the situation and let us know the reaction from Paris.

(91) BROADCAST STATEMENT BY HIGH COMMISSIONER FOR INDOCHINA, ADMIRAL THIERRY D'ARGENLIEU, DECEMBER 24, 1946 (Extract)

Source: Saigon Radio in French to Overseas, December 24, 1946. Translated by Foreign Broadcast Information Service, Far Eastern Section, December 25, 1946.

In a Christmas message, the French High Commissioner, after charging Vietnam with systematic violations of the March 6 and September agreements, suggested that France was abrogating previous agreements. He went on to state the French justification for its military presence in Viet-nam, referring both to traditional French interests in the area and to the new French role in sponsoring an Indochinese federation. This document includes all of the excerpt broadcast by Saigon radio.

"The French Government has shown great patience and understanding. It would be bad policy and imprudent to test its patient any further. France cannot be bound by conventions which she alone would have to respect. France has in Indochina moral and material interests concerning which she can neither compromise nor engage in discussions.

Essential Points

"France considers as essential the preservation and free development of her cultural influence and economic interests, the protection of the ethnical minorities which have placed their trust in her for the implementation of her international obligations and the security of the strategic bases which are to serve for the common defense of the Indochinese Federation and the French Union. It is necessary to stress that France does not wish to reestablish her sovereignty in its old form over her overseas territories in Asia. She formally declared that she does not want to interfere in the administration and internal government of the Indochinese states. She wants the various states which make up French Indochina to agree to group their common interests in a federal system and to participate in the political system now in the process of elaboration.

"We cannot in the present stage of development of the peoples of Indochina grant them unconditional and total independence which would ultimately be nothing but a fiction gravely detrimental to the interests of both parties. In the statement which has annexed to the *modus vivendi* of Sept. 14 the French and Viet Nam governments expressed their conviction that the whole body of measures referred to in the *modus vivendi* would contribute to bring about in the near future an atmosphere of calm and confidence which would make it possible to engage in final negotiations. The Hanoi Government has however taken the initiative of hostilities involving bloodshed and the massacre of unarmed populations."

(92) TELEGRAM FROM CONSUL REED IN SAIGON TO BYRNES, DECEMBER 24, 1946

Source: *Foreign Relations*, 1946, Vol. VIII, pp. 78-79.

In a conversation with the U.S. Consul in Saigon, Admiral d'Argenlieu confirmed that the French would no longer deal with Ho's government and would seek to detach Annam as well as Cochinchina from Tonkin.

Unprovoked premeditated attack by Vietnam, with atrocities against innocent civilians, at time when French Govt sending representative discuss association accords and plan future French-Vietnam relations, leaves French free hand to deal with situation, especially as Vietnam Govt has fled and effectively no such govt. So said High Commissioner in conversation yesterday prior arrival Moutet. He stated French do not plan exploit situation and there is, first, no intention reconquer FIC and, second, no intention return former colonial system - enough troops will be sent restore order and assure opportunity all persons carry on peaceful pursuits. He admitted many mistakes made in past due those persons reluctant give up prewar life and policy in FIC and said mistakes will be made in future but France holds intention aid honest and meritorious aspirations native peoples (but commented difficult to treat with persons whose aim is destruction as recent events have shown to be aim of Ho and his govt) and France desired chiefly promote their economic interests. French prepared deal with any govt in which can place confidence.

He stressed federation plan is only possible solution, giving peoples of FIC measure of autonomy of which they are now capable, but not excluding possibility of larger independence when peoples are capable thereof. He felt majority natives will welcome removal Ho regime which established and maintained by terroristic methods and in no sense democratic - also felt that with fear reprisals removed, Annam would prefer be state, apart from Tonkin confederation, thus being composed of same five states as formed FIC in past. Expressed satisfaction he now had backing French Govt (with certain notable exceptions) and declared his policy vindicated especially his distrust Ho and his associates but made one remark that indicated he might not be here long. He mentioned return General Leclerc, expected here shortly, but I have reason believe High Commissioner not particularly pleased. Factually, situation in north improving and he hoped all under control within 15 days - expressed grave concern fate of French at Vinh from which no news since French surrendered.

In comment [by me?] French have one more chance impress natives their desire deal fairly with them and to give them advantages both economic and social withheld in past, and if French fail to take advantage this opportunity and institute repressive high handed measures (policy of force) of past no settlement of situation can be expected foreseeable future and period guerilla warfare will follow. [Apparent garble] however presupposes willingness Vietnam act with reasonableness and doubt whether French will treat with Ho in view of "treacherous" attack on civilians as well as military. Perhaps mediation third party only solution.

Please repeat Paris, London.

1947

(93) TELEGRAM FROM CAFFERY TO SECRETARY OF STATE GEORGE C. MARSHALL,
JANUARY 22, 1947.

Source: *Foreign Relations of the U.S., 1947, Vol. VI, p. 66.*

*The new French Prime Minister, Paul Ramadier, stated publicly that there
would be no negotiations with the Democratic Republic, as reported by Ambassador
Caffery in Paris.*

Careful reading of that portion of Ramadier's speech yesterday re Indochina discloses certain points of interest:

(1) Prime Minister was extremely firm and categoric on necessity of putting
down present disorders and restoring order and security. "We must relieve our
garrisons, re-establish essential communications and assure the security of
the peoples who have taken refuge with us".

(2) He confirmed indications that France will not negotiate with present
Vietnam Government in anticipation that new more moderate leaders will arise.

(3) At such time France will consent to inclusion of Cochinchina in Viet-
nam and will not insist on Vietnam membership in French Union being indirect
through membership in Indochinese federation. (When times comes for negotiations) "France will not fear, if the population desires it, the union of the
three Annamite countries, nor will she refuse to accept the independence of
the Vietnam in the framework of the French Union".

Department please repeat to Saigon as 2 from Paris.

(94) TELEGRAM FROM SECRETARY OF STATE MARSHALL TO CAFFERY, FEBRUARY 3, 1947

Source: *Foreign Relations, 1947, Vol. VI, pp. 67-68.*

*The first policy statement by the State Department under the new Secretary
of State, George C. Marshall, on Indochina reaffirmed recognition of French
sovereignty over Indochina but also stressed the need to satisfy Vietnamese
nationalist aspirations. While expressing the desire to restore France to its
position as a world power, it noted that colonial empires were outmoded. Significantly, it placed the blame for the outbreak of fighting on the Vietnamese
rather than on French policy, despite field reports throughout the previous
year casting doubt on the French willingness to implement the March 6 agreement.*

There is reason for increasing concern over situation as it is developing
in Indochina and for that reason I feel you might well take early occasion to
have frank talk with Ramadier or Bidault or both somewhat along lines conversations you have already had with Blum, but at this time going in fact beyond
position you took in those talks. We have only very friendliest feelings

toward France and we are anxious in every way we can to support France in her fight to regain her economic, political and military strength and to restore herself as in fact one of major powers of world. In spite any misunderstanding which might have arisen in minds French in regard to our position concerning Indochina they must appreciate that we have fully recognized France's sovereign position in that area and we do not wish to have it appear that we are in any way endeavoring undermine that position, and French should know it is our desire to be helpful and we stand ready assist any appropriate way we can find solution for Indochinese problem. At same time we cannot shut our eyes to fact that there are two sides this problem and that our reports indicate both a lack French understanding of other side (more in Saigon than in Paris) and continued resistance dangerously outmoded colonial outlook and methods in area. Furthermore, there is no escape from fact that trend of times is to effect that colonial empires in XIX Century sense are rapidly becoming thing of past. Action felt in India and Burma and Dutch in Indonesia are outstanding examples this trend, and French themselves took cognizance of it both in new Constitution and in their agreements with Vietnam. On other hand we do not lose sight fact that Ho Chi Minh has direct Communist connection and it should be obvious that we are not interested in seeing colonial empire administrations supplanted by philosophy and political organizations emanating from and controlled by Kremlin. Fact does remain, however, that a situation does exist in Indochina which can no longer be considered, if it ever was considered, to be of a local character. If that situation continues deteriorate some country in direct interest is very likely to bring matter before Security Council under Chapter 11 of Charter. We have no intention taking such action ourselves at this time, but French will surely appreciate that we do have a vital interest in political and economic well being this area. If some country should bring matter before Security Council we would find it difficult to oppose an investigation Indochinese problem unless negotiations between parties were going on. It might be added that it would not in our estimation be in France's long-range interest to use her veto position to keep matter from coming before Council. Frankly we have no solution of problem to suggest. It is basically matter for two parties to work out themselves and from your reports and those from Indochina we are led to feel that both parties have endeavored to keep door open to some sort of settlement. We appreciate fact that Vietnam started present fighting in Indochina on December 19 and that this action has made it more difficult for French to adopt a position of generosity and conciliation. Nevertheless we hope that French will find it possible to be more than generous in trying to find a solution.

(95) APPEAL BY HO CHI MINH TO THE COMPATRIOTS TO CARRY OUT DESTRUCTION, TO WAGE RESISTANCE WAR, FEBRUARY 6, 1947

Source: Ho Chi Minh, *Selected Works*, Vol. III, pp. 93-94.

One of the principles of the Viet Minh resistance war was to destroy whatever might have been of value to the French - what Truong Chinh would later call "resistance by scorched earth." The policy called for the population of towns and villages to raze all permanent structures as well as bridges and roads. That policy required even greater sacrifices of the population, and one of Ho's first concerns as the resistance began was to insure that the policy would be understood and accepted.

Compatriots who love our country,
    Why must we wage the Resistance War?
    Because if we do not wage the Resistance War, the French will occupy our country once more. They will enslave our people once more. They will force

our people to be their coolies and soldiers, and to pay them every kind of taxes. They will suppress all our democratic freedoms. They will plunder all our land and property. They will terrorize and massacre our brothers, sisters, and relatives. They will burn down or destroy our houses, pagodas, and temples. You will realize this by seeing what they have done in Hanoi and Haiphong.

Because we do not want to be buffaloes and horses to the French, because we must protect our country, we must fight the French colonialists.

To fight we must carry out destruction. If we do not do so, the French will. If our houses are solid enough to be used as bases, they will mobilize tanks and vessels to attack us, and they will burn or plunder all our property. This is why we must carry out destruction before the French can make use of our property. Suppose we want to keep sluices, roads, and houses for our own use, we can't, because the French will occupy all or destroy all.

Now we must carry out destruction to stop them, to prevent them from advancing, and from using our roads and houses.

For the sake of the Fatherland we must make sacrifices and endure hardships for a certain time. When the Resistance comes out victorious, we will pool our forces for construction and repair work and this will not be difficult at all.

On the battlefront the fighters are sacrificing their lives for the Fatherland without regret; why do we regret a section of road, a sluice, or a house which the French can use to attack our Fatherland?

You all love your country, no doubt you will have no heart to regret so.

Therefore, I earnestly call on you to exert all your efforts to carry out destruction work. We must destroy roads widely and deeply so that the French cannot use them. A pick stroke into the roads has the value of a bullet shot by our soldiers at the enemy.

I solemnly promise to you that after victory, I will endeavor to repair everything with you. We will build more beautiful roads, bridges, and sluices and better houses worthy of a free and independent nation.

Long live our victorious Resistance War!

Long live independent Viet-Nam!

* As a result of this scorched-earth appeal, all European-type dwellings and installations were destroyed in one massive wave of countrywide vandalism within all the areas under D.R.V.N. control. As a British specialist was to observe about a similar phenomenon in the Viet-Cong areas of South Viet-Nam (and including American-wrought destruction as well): "Social leveling makes the burden of the 'protracted war' a little lighter to bear. The less one has to lose the less hardship one will feel." (Dennis J. Duncanson, "How and Why the Viet Cong Hold out," Encounter, December, 1966.)

(96) TELEGRAM FROM CAFFERY TO MARSHALL, FEBRUARY 7, 1947

Source: *Foreign Relations*, 1947, Vol. Vi, p. 71.

In early February Ho offered to reopen negotiations with the French on the basis of previously signed agreements and on the principle of the political and territorial integrity of the D.R.V. within the framework of the French Union.

Baudet today confirmed to us that, as reported in press, local representatives of Vietnam yesterday transmitted unofficially to French Government another peace offer, somewhat similar in content to that received in December. He said principal points in document were substantially as follows: immediate cessation of hostilities on all front; appointment of armistice commissions to insure cease-fire is observed; withdrawal of all troops to positions previously defined by Franco-Vietnamese accords of March 6 and April 3, 1946; immediate

halt to all reinforcements for French troops in Indo-China; Government of
Ho Chi-minh to be only representative of Vietnam during negotiations; negotiations to be based on previously signed agreements between France and Viet-
nam; Moutet to proceed at early date to Indo-China to reach agreement in principle with Ho Chi-minh regarding basis for negotiations, which should be based
on recognition of political and territorial integrity of Vietnam Republic within
framework of French Union.

Baudet did not indicate what French position would be with respect to individual points of Vietnamese message but indicated French Government "might agree
to enter indo discussions with Vietnamese".

(97) APPEAL FROM HO CHI MINH TO FRENCH PRESIDENT PAUL RAMADIER AND THE FRENCH PEOPLE, FEBRUARY 20, 1947

Source: Telegram from O'Sullivan to Byrnes, February 21, 1947, in *Foreign Relations*, 1947, Vol. VI, pp. 74-75.

*In a letter whose tone was especially friendly to France, Ho again appealed
to the French for a cease-fire. French officials denied having received the
letter and then questioned the authenticity of Ho's signature.* (Foreign Relations, *1947, Vol. VI, p. 76 and p. 81.)*

[Translation:] "Once again I address an urgent appeal to the Government
and people of France.

Much French and Vietnamese blood has been shed.

Numerous Vietnamese towns and villages are destroyed and French enterprises
ruined.

Each day that this fratricidal war lasts multiplies the misery and increases
the devastation.

It is claimed that the French forces are used only to establish peace and
order. This is not true. The truth is that where there are no French troops
there is no conflict and peace and order reign. Once more we solemnly declare
that the people of Vietnam desire only their unity and independence within the
French Union, and we pledge ourselves to respect French economic and cultural
interests in Vietnam.

Can France, the champion of liberty, continue to make war on a people who
are claiming only the most legitimate rights and who wish to cooperate with
her?

France has only to give the word for hostilities to cease immediately, for
so many lives and so much property to be saved, for friendship and confidence
to reign.

If in spite of our sincere desire for peace, France insists upon continuing
the war, she will lose all without gaining anything for the war will result
only in the creation of hatred and bitterness between our two peoples.

It is true that the French troops have airplanes and tanks but we have on
our side the justice of our cause and the firm intention to resist until the
end.

We do not believe that France desires to continue this war which is the
anti-constitutional, disastrous and without glory.

We beg the French Government to be so good as to make known clearly its
policy with regard to Vietnam. We beg the French people to be so good as to
make known their opinion of this bloody and stupid conflict.

As for ourselves our position is clear: we want our unity and our independence within the French Union; we want a just peace which will do honor both
to France and to Vietnam."

(98) <u>TELEGRAM FROM CAFFERY TO MARSHALL, MARCH 27, 1947</u>

Source: *Foreign Relations*, 1947, Vol. Vi, pp. 81-82.

Even before the outbreak of open warfare, the French had suggested to news-
men and foreign diplomats that there were "moderate" (pro-French) and "extrem-
ist" (anti-French nationalist) factions within the Ho Chi Minh government.
Moves by the D.R.V. to resist extension of French military control were charac-
terized as the results of the "extremists". (See Le Monde, *December 8-9, 1946.)*
In the wake of the D.R.V. peace feeler of February 20, the French questioned
whether Ho was still in control and said they would not negotiate with him un-
less he first purged his government of "extremist" elements.

Question of authenticity of peace proposals emanating from Ho Chi Minh was
discussed with Baudet last evening. After admitting Ho's letter of February 20
had been received in Paris, Baudet stated this letter, together with other messages to French, signed Ho as well as number of orders and instructions to
Viet-Nam officials recently seized in Indo-China had been examined by number of
French handwriting experts who were unanimous and positive in their belief all
signatures were forged. Baudet confirmed recent reports in press that no one
had been found who had seen Ho Chi Minh since November [December?] 20. While
French authorities do not place much credence in reports of Ho's murder or
death they are puzzled by his complete disappearance.

Remarks attributed to Moutet, mentioned in Department's telegram under
reference, were made March 19 at Socialist National Congress which took place
during same period as Assembly debate on Indo-China. Baudet said he felt
Moutet's statement was hardly justified by information available to Government
and pointed out that following day Hoach[1] issued statement which, while cautious
in phrasing, could only be interpreted as denial of Moutet's allegations.
Baudet expressed opinion Moutet's remarks were designed to take some of edge off
Communist attacks in Assembly on his policy. Embassy is inclined to believe
Moutet was defending himself from criticism within his own party. It will be
recalled that while Socialist deputies unanimously supported Moutet and Ramadier
in Assembly, debate in party Congress on Indo-Chinese policy was bitter with
left-wing leader Boutvien leading strong opposition to Moutet.

Baudet added that instructions to new High Commissioner Bollaert had been
approved and he would presumably leave March 28 as scheduled. Baudet said,
except for administrative matters, these instructions are general rather than
detailed. Bollaert is not being told he must or must not negotiate with any
individuals or groups but his instructions provide that any conversations entered into must be with persons representing and having confidence of broad
mass of people. France cannot assist in or condone establishment of Government
of Viet-Nam which will not follow democratic principles as these are understood
in West. France feels it would be dangerous for all concerned if small minority
should be permitted to establish dictatorship over bulk of population by author-
itarian and terroristic methods such as had been practiced by Viet-Minh in
recent months. If Ho Chi Minh should emerge from his retirement and establish
contact with Bollaert he would be told, according to Baudet, that he must first
broaden base of his government and eliminate extremists. Baudet admitted reported appointment of Hoang Minh Giam as Foreign Secretary, if confirmed,[2]
would appear to be step in that direction.

Re persistent rumors of possible return of ex-Emperor Bao Dai, Baudet
again denied any negotiations with Bao were going on. He remarked that ex-
Emperor is extremely cautious person and would certainly not consider returning
to Indo-China until Viet-Minh had surrendered or been eliminated from political
picture. While instructions to Bollaert did not entirely exclude possibility

of return of Bao Dai, they make clear that any move for his return must originate with Annamite people.

Sent Department 1313; repeated to London 259, Moscow for delegation 188.

[1]Dr. Le Van Hoach, President of the Provisional Government of Cochin China.

[2]Telegram 98, March 22, 8 a.m., from Hanoi, reported Giam's confirmation on
March 17; he filled the post previously held by Ho Chi Minh concurrently. Mr.
O'Sullivan pointed out, "If French wish to deal with Vietnam, Giam is person
who could be considered as outside Vietminh Party."

(99) MESSAGE FROM D.R.V. MINISTER OF FOREIGN AFFAIRS, HOANG MINH GIAM TO THE FRENCH GOVERNMENT, APRIL 18, 1947

Source: *Foreign Relations*, 1947, Vol. VI, pp. 94-95.

*To counteract French propaganda that his government was dominated by anti-
French extremists, as well as to appeal to those French officials who wanted
a peace settlement, Ho Chi Minh continued his peace offensive. On March 1, Ho
himself addressed the French government and the French people asking for an
immediate cease-fire. And the following month, the newly nominated Foreign
Minister, Hoang Minh Giam, offered again to negotiate a peaceful settlement of
the conflict.*

"Official message to the French Government:
Vietnam is fighting for its unity and its independence. France, President
Ramadier has declared, is not opposed to this unity and independence.

The interest of the two peoples lies in collaborating fraternally within
the French Union, an association of free peoples 'who understand and love one
another'.

If the war is continued, it can only increase hatred, entail new sacrifices
in human lives, make the situation of French enterprise and the economy of
Vietnam worse, without solving the problem of Franco-Vietnamese relations.

The French Government, by the appointment of the new High Commissioner of
France in Indochina, appears to have shown its desire to direct its policy with
respect to Vietnam into a new channel, worthy of the New France.

Persuaded that the motion of the National Council of the S.F.I.O. of
March 21, 1947 'not to let an opportunity pass to enter into negotiations with
Vietnam' expresses not only the sentiments of the French Socialists but also
those of all the people of France; to prove Vietnam's sincere devotion to peace
and its friendship for the people of France; the Vietnamese Government proposes
to the French Government the immediate cessation of hostilities and the opening
of negotiations with a view to 'peaceful settlement of the conflict'."

(100) D.R.V. ACCOUNT OF HO CHI MINH-PAUL MUS MEETING OF MAY 12, 1947

Source: Translation of a Vietnamese language document distributed by the D.R.V.
in Airgram from O'Sullivan in Hanoi to the Secretary of State, June 20, 1947,
851G.00/6-2047, Diplomatic Papers, National Archives.

*In response to Hoang Minh Giam's appeal for a cease-fire and negotiations,
High Commissioner Bollaert dispatched Professor Paul Mus, a former political
adviser to General LeClerc, to present France's non-negotiable demands. This
Vietnamese account of the French position presented by Mus is confirmed by Mus
himself, although he adds two further conditions for peace: surrender of all
hostages and of all non-Vietnamese personnel serving with Viet Minh forces.
See Paul Mus, Viet-Nam:* Sociologie d'une Guerre *(Paris: Editions du Seuil,
1952), p. 315.*

"President HO and Minister of Foreign Affairs GIAM met with a representative of High Commissioner BOLLAERT in a place not far from Hanoi.

"This meeting was most cordial for the representative of the High Commissioner is an old acquaintance of President HO and Minister GIAM.

"When the discussion began on the question of the cessation of hostilities, the representative of M. BOLLAERT proposed the following conditions:

"1) The Vietnam Government will abstain from all reprisals against pro-French people upon the cessation of hostilities.

"2) The Vietnamese troops will surrender all their arms and munitions to France.

"3) The French troops have the right to circulate and occupy freely throughout the territory of Vietnam. Vietnamese troops will assemble in spots designated by the French Army.

"President HO replied to the first condition: 'After the last worldwide hostilities, if France took action against Frenchmen who delivered France to Germany, we ought to punish Vietnamese who have decided to deliver our country to a foreign nation. However, we can promise leniency toward these individuals.'

"To the other conditions, President HO replied:

"'High Commissioner BOLLAERT is a French democrat and also a patriot. I ask you if High Commissioner BOLLAERT has recognized the act by which the Petain Government delivered arms and munitions to the German Army, permitted German troops freedom of action in French territory and obliged French troops to assemble in determined positions? Is this an armistice?'

"At this point in the conversation, the representative of M. BOLLAERT said: 'In these circumstances, we have nothing more to say to you'.

"The diplomatic interview thus ended.

"President HO then asked the French representative: 'You certainly know the history of Vietnam'.

"'Yes, I have made several studies of it.'

"'In that case, you recall the feats of our ancestors. TRAN HUNG DAO who fought for five years against the Mongol armies and LE LOI who resisted for ten years against the Chinese armies. Well, at the present time, we can resist five years, ten years and more. Our compatriots are firmly decided to unite and to obey the government's orders to resist until independence and unification are obtained.'"

(101) TELEGRAM FROM MARSHALL TO CAFFERY IN PARIS, MAY 13, 1947

Source: *Foreign Relations*, 1947, Vol. VI, pp. 95-97.

The Southeast Asia Office of the State Department mustered its arguments for a more forward-looking U.S. policy which would urge the French to negotiate with the D.R.V. It succeeded in getting Secretary Marshall to sign a telegram, warning that French efforts to maintain colonial control in Viet-nam would bolster the Communists throughout Southeast Asia and jeopardize tenuous position of Western powers in the region. The telegram not only rejected the Bao Dai solution then being discussed by the French but reversed the view expressed in Marshall's previous instructions that the Vietnamese were to blame for the start of the war.

We becoming increasingly concerned by slow progress toward settlement Indochina dispute. We fully appreciate French are making effort reach satisfactory settlement and hope visit Commissioner Bollaert to Indochina will produce concrete results. The following considerations, however, are submitted for your use any conversations you may have with French authorities at appropriate time this subject. We recognize it might not be desirable make such approach to newly constituted government in first days its reorganization, but nevertheless feel early appropriate opportunity might be found inform French Gov of our concern in this matter.

Key our position is our awareness that in respect developments affecting position Western democratic powers in southern Asia, we essentially in same boat as French, also as British and Dutch. We cannot conceive setbacks to long-range interests France which would not also be setbacks our own. Conversely we should regard close association France and members French Union as not only to advantage peoples concerned, but indirectly our own.

In our view, southern Asia in critical phase its history with seven new nations in process achieving or struggling independence or autonomy. These nations include quarter inhabitants world and their future course, owing sheer weight populations, resources they command, and strategic location, will be momentous factor world stability. Following relaxation European controls, internal racial, religious, and national differences could plunge new nations into violent discord, or already apparent anti-Western Pan-Asiatic tendencies could become dominant political force, or Communists could capture control. We consider as best safeguard against these eventualities a continued close association between newly-autonomous peoples and powers which have long been responsible their welfare. In particular we recognize Vietnamese will for indefinite period require French material and technical assistance and enlightened political guidance which can be provided only by nation steeped like France in democratic tradition and confirmed in respect human liberties and worth individual.

We equally convinced, however, such association must be voluntary to be lasting and achieve results, and that protraction present situation Indochina can only destroy basis voluntary cooperation, leave legacy permanent bitterness, and irrevocably alienate Vietnamese from France and those values represented by France and other Western democracies.

While fully appreciating difficulties French position this conflict, we feel there is danger in any arrangement which might provide Vietnamese opportunity compare unfavorably their own position and that of other peoples southern Asia who have made tremendous strides toward autonomy since war.

While we are still ready and willing do anything we can which might be considered helpful, French will understand we not attempting come forward with any solution our own or intervene in situation. However, they will also understand we inescapably concerned with situation Far East generally, upon which developments Indochina likely have profound effect.

Plain fact is that Western democratic system is on defensive in almost all emergent nations southern Asia and, because identified by peoples these nations with what they have considered former denial their rights, is particularly vulnerable to attacks by demagogic leaders political movements of either ultra-nationalist or Communist nature which promise redress and revenge past so-called wrongs and inequalities. Signs development anti-Western Asiatic consciousness already multiplying, of which Inter-Asian CONF an example. Unanimity support for Vietnamese among other Asiatic countries very striking, even leading to moves Burma, India, and Malaya send volunteer forces their assistance. Vietnam cause proving rallying-cry for all anti-Western forces and playing in hands Communists all areas. We fear continuation conflict may jeopardize position all Western democratic powers in southern Asia and lead to very eventualities of which we most apprehensive.

We confident French fully aware dangers inherent in situation and therefore venture express renewed hope they will be most generous attempt find early solution which, by recognizing legitimate desires Vietnamese, will restore peace and deprive anti-democratic forces of powerful weapon.

For your INFO, evidence that French Communists are being directed accelerate their agitation French colonies even extent lose much popular support France (URTEL 1719 Apr 25) may be indication Kremlin prepared sacrifice temporary gains with 40 million French to long range colonial strategy with 600 million dependent people, which lends great urgency foregoing views. French position Indochina dispute since DEC 19, which based on Vietnam initiative attack, seems DEPT dangerously one-sided in ignoring Debes attack Haiphong NOV 23 and understandable Vietnam contention that stand had be made some point view steady French encroachments after MAR 6 on authority and territory Vietnam (e.g., establishment Cochinchinese REP, occupation southern Annam and Moi Plateau, and Dalat plan French-dominated Federation to which Vietnam would be subservient,) DEPT much concerned lest French efforts find QUOTE true representatives Vietnam UNQUOTE with whom negotiate result creation impotent puppet GOVT along lines Cochinchina regime, or that restoration Baodai may be attempted, implying democracies reduced resort monarchy as weapon against Communism. You may refer these further views if nature your conversations French appears warrant.

Saigon and Hanoi should be guided by this TEL in any conversation Bollaert.

(102) SPEECH BY HIGH COMMISSIONER EMILE BOLLAERT IN HANOI, MAY 15, 1947

Source: "The Indochinese Federation", French Press and Information Service (New York), News from France, Second Year, No. 23, (June 12, 1947), 00. 3-8.

In a speech elaborating on French policy toward Indochina for the first time since the beginning of national resistance in Viet-nam, High Commissioner Emile Bollaert, declared the "era of the imperium" over, but made it clear that France would remain in Indochina to insure its interests in the three countries. He defined the French Union as the most progressive type of association, asserting that the Vietnamese struggle against France was opposed to "progress and reason." Notably absent from the speech was any invocation of anti-Communism.

"Two months ago I had the honor of being chosen by the Government of the French Republic to represent France in Indochina. Today I want to tell you, with what may seem to be brutal frankness, my views on the Franco-Vietnamese problem and the measures which I think should be taken to solve the present difficult situation so that this land may at last be restored to calm, happiness and prosperity.

"I want to make one statement at the outset, because everything else hinges upon it: France will remain in Indochina and Indochina within the French Union. This is the first principle of our policy and it would be prejudicial to the interests of peace if the slightest doubt on this matter were allowed to arise in anyone's mind. The continued presence of France in this country is now and henceforth a fact that realists must not leave out of their considerations.

"Any man whose judgment is not warped by hatred will acknowledge that we have rights and legitimate interests in Indochina. We have sown much seed there and we are not ashamed to say that we do not wish to be cheated out of the harvest. We do not feel that we have fallen short of our responsibilities and we do not intend to give up, because France has not the right to fail.

"We shall remain. The French political parties are unanimously resolved that France shall not be dispossessed. The Constitution, adopted by the National Constituent Assembly, approved by the French people and promulgated on October 27th, 1946, makes the French Union, of which Indochina is an integral part, an institution of the Republic. The French Union thus gains a constitutional basis which precludes any notion of abandonment."

"However, the maintenance of French presence in Indochina does not mean the oppression of its people. It must not prevent this country from being happy

and free. We hope it will provide a stimulus, a ferment of new activities for
all those who wish to derive some benefit from it. We do not intend it to act
as an impediment, nor an affront to the legitimate patriotism of the Indochinese
peoples, who have a right to their place in the sun. The French Parliament, of
which I have the honor to be a member, will see to this. Indeed it considers
one of its chief tasks to be the organization of the French Union to safeguard
both the interests of France and of the member States, by ensuring the harmonious development of all in accordance with the general lines of world development.

"Surely every Vietnamese recognizes the scientific truth that becomes more
apparent every year: the tendency of all peoples to resist fragmentation and
to unite. Karl Marx discovered in the economic development of the world a law
of increasing concentration. Thus, today we see a progressive regrouping of
the peoples. In the past, the tendency was to form national States through
the union of provinces of identical structure, and through the affirmation of
their own personalities in the name of nationalism or absolute sovereignty.
Like all movements inspired by individualism, this one led to rivalries, catas-
trophes and world wars. To escape these consequences, as well as harmoniously
to develop all their potentialities, the most advanced peoples realized that
it is impossible to live in isolation or to develop their resources and raise
their standard of living without associating themselves with other peoples.
And therefore they have experimented with larger or smaller groupings such as
the British Empire, the U.S.S.R., the League of Nations and finally the United
Nations.

"Just as the right to personal property become, whether we like it or not,
more and more restricted by the higher interests of the State, so the States
have all had to sacrifice part of their rights in exchange for the benefits
of the collective system.

"Everyone knows that in the world of today, amid the complicated network
of political blocs, international agreements, economic, customs and monetary
unions, the sovereignty of the strongest States has been substantially reduced.
We have to accept the fact that the concept of independence however sentimen-
tally attached to it we may still be, has changed its meaning. We should speak
rather of interdependence, for only through it can humanity progress and a
higher social order be attained.

"That is why it does not seem logical to me that a people who passionately
desire to see their country take its place among modern nations should wish
only to live in isolation while all around them forces are being regrouped
and only great unions can make their voices heard in the concert of Powers.
Can it be that they, who are so easy a prey, hope to escape, through isolation,
from the cupidity of those who would exploit them and who have neither our
scruples nor our idealism?

"To be frank, I am afraid that the men responsible for the present tragic
state of affairs, by taking up arms against the French Union in an attempt to
secede, have set their country on a path of retrogression which runs counter
to man's inevitable progress toward a higher state of development.

"As opposed to separatism that can only weaken peoples, the formula of the
French Union embodies the most modern and most progressive type of association.
Let me repeat, there is no question of returning to the system in force in
Indochina before the war. That system was slowly elaborated and very well
adapted to a state of affairs that no longer exists. New national aspirations
have been born and merit every respect. The formula which we propose for the
French Union reconciles this magnificent patriotic ardor with the no less legitimate aspirations of France. She intends to grant the States all the freedom
that is compatible with the existence of the Union."

"The French Union is defined as a harmonious grouping of territories which
realize their interdependence and agree in their own interest to become part of

a larger family of nations which will help each of them to develop and increase its prestige in the international field. The French Union, that huge assemblage of peoples from the ends of the five continents, is infinitely better adapted than any purely regional combination, which joins only like to like, to ensure the rapid development of each of its members because of the very diversity of cultures and resources it brings together. While Indochina has nothing to gain by withdrawing into herself, while she can expect little advantage for her freedom or her trade from partnership with any Asiatic country which could only give her what she already possesses, it will always be profitable to her to team up with a France that is liberal and rich in ideas, techniques and products unknown in Asia. Nor will France have anything to lose within this Union, this chorus of many voices, she too will profit from this dialogue with Asiatic wisdom. She can draw extensively upon moral and philosophical values of the highest order, and also upon local products which she lacks, but which are difficult to dispose of on the Indochinese peninsula. Thus, the French Union, far from being the monopoly of one nation, is designed to be a means to collective enrichment and the common property of all.

"It will provide the more progressive elements whose scope is now restricted to purely local affairs with a field of action suited to their ability. The elite, who have combined the two cultures and who are no longer men with a provincial outlook, will find increasingly in the key positions of the Union ample outlets for their talents which will be more satisfying to them than to be leaders of their own miniature countries. A promise was given them in the past and it will be kept: the Indochinese will have access to all positions and types of employment within the French Union. We see, then, that it is only in appearance that the member States must renounce a part of their sovereignty since sovereignty will be exercised on the French Union level by the citizens of all the member states. They recover, on the French Union level, the rights they relinquish on the national level.

"France desires that these limitations of sovereignty, which, as we have seen, are amply compensated, be reduced to the minimum. While she intends to maintain her position on the federal level, she has no wish to have any further say in the internal administration of the States unless they ask her advice. She wishes to abstain from any interference that has not been specifically requested: the peoples will have governments of their own choosing and will settle for themselves all matters that concern them alone.

"Respect for the sovereignty of the States has far-reaching consequences. If it is the desire of populations related by race, language, traditions and feeling, France will not oppose a regrouping of certain countries. She rejects the old saying: 'Divide and rule', since the underlying philosophy of the community she is building is one of trust and unity. Nevertheless, France intends that local characteristics shall be safeguarded and that the Union shall be established without recourse to violence and totalitarian methods. For, just as the unity of the Union must not depend upon the exercise of the force of France, but on the free and confident adherence of all its members, so no Indochinese country must be compelled to adopt a system imposed upon it from the outside.

"The era of the imperium is over; the era of friendship must begin."

"This is the type of association France proposes. The Charter of the United Nations itself, with its anonymous formula of international trusteeship is more conservative. France offers the peoples who formerly composed the French Empire, an opportunity to develop side by side with her as equals within a majestic structure that enables them to forge ahead while remaining true to their own genius. Conscious of their desires, she offers the patriots of the Viet Nam enormous possibilities. She does not ask them to take up a cause which would be that of France alone. Broadening the horizon, which is still too limited perhaps for a young Asiatic nation, she offers a nobler cause that will be just as much theirs as hers. She gives them the means to play a great part in world affairs, and hopes that, eventually, each people will feel at home within this immense, common motherland that she seeks to establish for the welfare of all the smaller countries linked in a common destiny.

"It seems to me that our plan should give satisfaction to the most demanding minds and inspire enthusiasm among the least responsive. No doubt there will still be a great deal of groping and friction before the French Union can achieve satisfactory stability in Indochina. It would be Utopian not to recognize this. The men responsible for administration have their prejudices, their routine, their interests, in a word, their weaknesses. But the essential is that throughout the first period of experimentation the ideal should remain pure. It will finish by recommending itself even to men of little vision and moulding them in its own image.

"In the meantime, I want to say that we have no desire for revenge, that we know nothing great can be built upon hatred. I repeat too, that the present struggle is senseless because it goes against progress and reason. France, is still in Indochina. Other states are living and prospering on that peninsula. Contacts between them are inevitable; it would be better that they should be friendly. Sooner or later it will be necessary to cooperate with us and with the States belonging to the Indochinese Federation. Why then, put off what is inevitable, especially since every moment of delay means further ruin and bereavement? The French Union is well disposed; it anticipates the desires of the peoples; it wants to give patriots the possibility of fulfilling their aspirations in a peaceful Indochina; it concedes all the rights that are possible without compromising its own existence.

"Leaders who would prolong this tragic situation, this catastrophe which inevitably forces their country along the way to the worst retrogression, take upon their shoulders a grave responsibility. These leaders know that the country is threatened by flood and a shortage of rice; that famine will claim many victims in the coming months; more than a million people may die as a result of the scorched earth policy; epidemics stalk the populations, who are deprived of doctors and medical care. We have collected vaccines and medicines which will be distributed free through the Red Cross to the civilian population of the Viet Nam. We are making emergency shipments of rice from Cochinchina. But the peril is so grave that our effort, however great, may fall far short of the need, unless everyone cooperates with us.

"The young people of this country perhaps have a great desire for education; yet all that they are learning, all that they are doing is to fight a war already lost, intellectually, morally and materially, because it sets their country, already half ruined, without crops, without trade, without industries, back two hundred years. Tonkin will realize tomorrow that it needs its educated young men. Are you sure that it will not demand a reckoning from those who sacrificed the flower of this youth for nothing?

"Now, through the fault of a few men, one Indochinese people is suffering. When they sleep, something in them remains awake in the fearful expectation of ever new disasters. When they open their eyes to the morning light, they remember that the sunshine is only an illusion and nature only radiant on the surface; the reality is war and death. Perhaps, amid their present sufferings these people still remember the joy of living and the taste of happiness. Would they not like to come and go freely, attend to their affairs and prosper? They must envy the more fortunate towns where a man may eat his fill and where children go happily to school. They must long to see the smiling countryside again, with its sleek water buffaloes and fat hogs, where men sow the seed and replant the seedlings in the hope of a rich harvest. Surely, they must wish, after their labors in the ricefields, to come home and rest without anxiety, surrounded by a well-fed family. They must long for a golden age in which requisitions, conscription and terror will be unknown.

"Well! That golden age is within their reach. It has a name that sings in the hearts of all men of good will - peace. And the people themselves can win this peace. Let them send us representatives of all their parties - I say, 'all their parties' because France does not recognize that any one party has the exclusive right to speak in the name of the Vietnamese people. We hope that they may all work together for the reconstruction of their country in their own way and protected from totalitarian domination. Indeed, it is only in an atmosphere free from strain, distrust and restrictions, that political life, which is still disturbed, can be resumed in the Viet Nam (I hope this may be soon) and develop through the honest open functioning of liberal institutions. France, however great her desire to see calm restored to this devastated land, is firmly resolved that the democratic principles which have always guided her, shall never be betrayed.

"I am a democrat and a friend of the common people; I do not want to see them suffer any longer. I feel that I am serving not individual interests but those of all the peoples of the French Union. I know that I am the bearer of of a just and wise ideal. I would like to see the Viet Nam prosper in peace, thanks to a bold, progressive policy. I would like to see the number of schools and hospitals increased. With all my heart I desire an improvement in the conditions for the masses, through a higher standard of living and social legislation, through the equipment of the country and the ever more intensive development of its natural resources.

"I am sincere in describing our aims, but my good faith cannot be imposed upon nor tricked by shrewd maneuvers.

"These aims must be understood. Once this country, now ravaged by war, is aided and supported by the French Union with its powerful resources, it will no longer need to envy anyone. Nothing will stand in the way of its being rebuilt in comfort, patriotic zeal and liberty, until it finally recovers the peace of happy countries".

(103) AIRGRAM FROM REED TO ACHESON, JUNE 14, 1947

Source: 851G.00/6-1447, Diplomatic Papers, National Archives.

In the most complete analysis of French political policy in Indochina under High Commissioner Bollaert's regime, the Consul in Saigon gave Bollaert credit for trying to define a more liberal approach but again questioned whether his public policy was entirely sincere, noting that the terms offered Ho Chi Minh constituted a demand for "abject surrender". He noted that most Vietnamese regarded Ho Chi Minh's government as the only legitimate government of Vietnam and would look upon any French-approved alternative as a puppet regime. But he concluded that the Vietnamese were incapable of governing themselves "without Occidental check or control" and that there would have to be a compromise between Vietnamese and French interests in Indochina.

I have the honor to summarize and analyze, as of possible interest to the Department, the chronological development of the situation in Indochina from the arrival at Saigon of Mr. Emile BOLLAERT, High Commissioner of the Republic in Indochina, on April 1, 1947, to his departure for France on June 11. This period of 70 days was a particularly critical one, as Mr. Bollaert had the unenviable task of endeavoring to counteract the effect of errors of omission and commission popularly attributed to the regime of Admiral Thiery d'ARGENLIEU, former High Commissioner, and of attempting to find a solution of the complex Indochinese political problem which would be acceptable to both the French and the Annamite peoples. The extent of his success, of course, cannot be measured at this time save in relation to the state of affairs obtaining at the date of his arrival in Indochina, and only time will tell whether or not he has carried back to France a feasible plan for the restoration of peace and security and a workable recommendation for the future status of Annamite Indochina.

Prior to Mr. Bollaert's arrival the various factions in Indochina, both French and native, were actively for or against the regime of Admiral d'Argenlieu, a regime which had begun by being ostensibly liberal and open-minded but which had progressively become apparently dedicated to a policy of uncompromising firmness vis-a-vis the government of Ho Chi Minh, a policy conceding only so much as was necessary. There is no doubt but that the regime was autocratic and that many of the individual members thereof were chiefly preoccupied in maintaining the interests, power and prestige of France in Indochina. One must recognize, however, that these believed sincerely that the natives were not yet ready for the independence that they claimed. The factions that approved of the regime laid all responsibility for the deteriorating situation to the untrustworthiness of the native leaders in particular and to the incapacity of the native peoples as a whole, with great stress on the alarming possibility that those leaders were planning the eventual establishment of a communist system. The factions that disapproved of the regime, and they were inordinately articulate on the subject and virulently critical, attributed the unhappy state of affairs to a French policy, as created or interpreted by Admiral d'Argenlieu, of chicanery and double dealing, of concealed but active opposition to giving more than a semblance of independence to the Annamites, and of attempting to restore the former colonial system. The French in Indochina were a house divided, the Annamites almost united.

There was a parallelling divergence of opinion in France. While few if any advocated a return to the pre-war status, a substantial element, tacitly at least, subscribed to Admiral d'Argenlieu's methods and interpretations, holding the view that the Annamites should be given some autonomy but that France should continue to direct the destinies of this rich country and maintain as firmly as before its vast economic interests. This element insisted that there should be no further dealings with Ho Chi Minh and his party, as being responsible for the coldly calculated attack on Hanoi on December 19, 1946, and for the wave of destructive terrorism in Cochinchina. The declarations of Mr. Marius MOUTET, Minister for Overseas France, after visiting Indochina appeared to support the protagonists of this policy. But another substantial element, chiefly the communists, were for one reason or another in favor of a more liberal policy, of giving Annamite Indochina a very large measure of autonomy, even independence, and of recognizing Ho Chi Minh as the real and only representative of the Annamite peoples. This element attacked bitterly Admiral d'Argenlieu for having encroached on Annamite rights as defined in the various French-Annamite accords, for having taken unilateral decisions on questions affecting both sides, and for having followed a "divide and rule" policy as epitomized in the creation of the puppet government in Cochinchina. In France as in Indochina it was also a question of Federation or Free States within the framework of the rather nebulous French Union.

This then was Mr. Bollaert's heritage - on the French side, a people sharply divided as to the best means of dealing with the situation, as to the concessions to be made, and as to the person or persons whom France should recognize as the representatives of the Annamite peoples; on the Annamite side, a people almost universally distrustful of French intentions, convinced that the French would stop at nothing to deny the fulfilment of native aspirations, and cherishing a hatred and rancor engendered by decades of exploitation by a thoroughly selfish colonial regime. In several respects, however, he was fortunate. The situation could not have been worse - I may say with confidence that the present situation is far worse than when I arrived in February 1946. In his consideration of the thorny problem he could disregard any idea of military reconquest, as France as a whole had neither the will nor the means to embark upon such a vast undertaking, one that would be condemned by the world at large - the French

were surely aware that the hard won successes of their military in Tonkin were
more apparent than real. And he could count on the Kingdoms of Cambodia and
Laos being content to accept French guidance, inspiration and tutelage - the
Issarak movements could largely be dismissed as attempts to make dynastic
changes rather than revolts against the French position in those countries.
Moreover, the High Commissioner had the good fortune to arrive at a time when
people were tired of fighting and destruction.

Mr. Bollaert arrived on April 1 and soon made it clear that he was in Indochina to investigate all angles of and all factors in the situation. He promised no political legerdomain but only an unbiased and thorough searching out
of means of reconciling the French position with that of the native claimants
of independence. In accomplishing this he intended to visit all sections of
the country and to talk with those French and native personalities who could
assist him in his evaluation. The numerous trips in Indochina were indicative
of his attention to carrying out his first intention. He arrived on April 1;
he proceeded to Hanoi to attend on April 3 the funerals of Colonel DEBES,
Commanding Officer of the French forces in the north, and Colonel GUFFLIT,
Chief of General VALLUY's Staff; on April 16 he flew to Pnomh Penh to establish
contact with Cambodian personalities; his next trip was to Dalat on April 22
to investigate the possibilities of that city as a future capital; he returned
once more to Dalat to preside at the Economic Conference from May 5 through
May 8; almost immediately thereafter, on May 10, he went to Laos to be present
at the promulgation of the new Laotian Constitution; on May 14 he journeyed
to Hanoi, inspecting conditions in that city and in Haiphong and delivering
his first and most important speech on the political situation; his next visit
was to Hue, former capital of the former Annamite Empire, on May 25, where he
was in contact with political personalities in that region, those being chiefly
pro BAO Dai; his last extended trip was to Nhatrang and to the High Plateau
region, from June 5 through June 9; and he started his return flight to France
on June 11. Interspersed between the above more or less formal trips were
visits to Cape St. Jacques and other centers in Cochinchina. One may say that
in a relatively short time the High Commissioner saw a good part of the Indochina whose political fate and future might well lay in his hands.

In his second intention Mr. Bollaert appeared to be equally assiduous and
he established contact and exchanged views with representatives of all political
parties. Many of these interviews were kept secret and knowledge of them was
obtained only through well informed sources, such as his meeting with certain
Tonkinese at Cap St. Jacques on April 25. But in implementing this second intention the High Commissioner relied largely on various members of his Cabinet,
notably on Mr. Paul MUS of the French School of the Extreme Orient, who is an
authority on Indochina and who, above all, is intimately acquainted with Ho
Chi Minh. It was Mus who met with HOANG Minh Giam, Vietnam Minister for Foreign
Affairs, on May 7 near Hanoi, and who may have met Ho Chi Minh between May 10
and 14. Mr. Jacques ANTERIOU and Mr. Claude DE MAROLLES were also charged with
certain investigations but their services were of lesser value as neither was
well acquainted with the Far East nor versed in Oriental psychology. Onè may
note, however, that the High Commissioner was extremely chary in arranging for
conversations with long time residents of Indochina and some of these latter
were highly critical of his seeming lack of desire to hear their views. During
the latter part of his stay Mr. Bollaert did indeed get in touch with these
personalities, not all of whom, despite their long residence and manifest interests, could be classified as "colonialists". To round out this most catholic and comprehensive exchange of views, Mr. Mus proceeded to Hongkong to talk
with Bao Dai, a talk which was most unproductive or so it would appear. If
the High Commissioner did not carry away with him a definite cross section of
French and the Annamite opinion, it was not for lack of trying. The general
belief was that he had covered the ground thoroughly.

There were several notable developments from the High Commissioner's activities. As a result of his publicized desire to consult with the representatives of all political elements, reiterated in his speech at Hanoi on May 15, the local press filled columns with "programs of action", "manifestos" and "proclamations", and "open letters", those presenting all possible variations of the theme of unity and independence. The most conservative of these preached the union of the three Kys but with each having its autonomy, independence and freely chosen association with the French Union - this was the program of the "Popular Movement" of Nicholas TRAN CUU Chan and in his June 6 address, the first anniversary of the Provisional Government of the Republic of Cochinchina, President LE Van Hoach, an uninspired but honest person, virtually subscribed to this program. A second group, the "National Union Front of Vietnam", presented practically the same program but insisted that Bao Dai should be head of the government until the peoples could choose a form of government through the means of a constituent assembly - this party and its program were sharply attacked chiefly because of its leaders, NGUYEN Hai Than, NGUYEN Tuong Tam, and NGUYEN Van Sam, formerly associated with Ho Chi Minh but who had been expelled from his party, who were labelled as opportunists and in the pay of the Chinese, even in the pay of the Americans. The third and most important element was of course the one favoring Ho Chi Minh and the Viet Minh party - the official organ of that party, *Cuu Quoc*, published what may well be the last word as to that party's program: its own form of government, a national assembly, the right to emit money for internal uses, an independent customs, a national army and police for the protection of its frontiers and internal security, the right to conduct its own foreign relations and to send representatives abroad as well as receiving foreign ambassadors and consuls, each of the Kys to have autonomy in internal administrative matters but accepting a common constitution and a central government. Each of the three major political programs stressed a freely chosen association with the French Union and recognition of "legitimate" French economic and cultural interests and rights.

Noteworthy was, of course, the almost complete disappearance of the formerly proposed "Indochinese Federation", excellent as the idea may have been in the opinion of many observers. The intransigence of Ho Chi Minh towards this form of union, possibly for fear that it would evolve as a French dominated and controlled organization, was successful in forcing the French to abandon the scheme. So far as has been noted the High Commissioner never once mentioned the word Federation and emphasized solely the French Union. Mr. Bollaert's many administrative reforms in Indochina reflected this scuttling of one of Admiral d'Argenlieu's prize projects. This manoeuvre, naturally, left open the question of the overall setup in Indochina as related to Cambodia and Laos - were the former five political entities to be but three, independent of each other except in the framework of the French Union? The recommendation that Pnomh Penh be a seaport was a definite indication. Equally interesting was the increasing use of the designations "Vietnam" and "vietnamese". This was surely a sop to Annamite susceptibilities, as native aspirations harked back to their historic past. Mr. Bollaert was careful to use those designations and in his handing over of the residence of the French Commissioner in Cochinchina to President Hoach on June 1 he said that he was confiding the residence to the peoples of Vietnam, that it was to be held in trust until the true representative of those peoples had been determined. To the old colonialists this transfer was a bitter blow as they saw therein the twilight of their gods. To the followers of Ho Chi Minh the terms of the transfer were disappointing as they saw at least a partial denial of their claim that Ho Chi Minh alone was the true representative of Vietnam. To the partisans of the Provisional Government of the Republic of Cochinchina the terms of the transfer were also somewhat alarming as these indicated a possible by-passing of that Government.

Other straws in the wind, testifying to the High Commissioner's willingness to be conciliatory, were the replacement of Mr. Albert TOREL as French Commissioner in Cochinchina by Mr. Robert DEFOUR and the designation of Mr. Leon PIGNON as French Commissioner in Cambodia. Both Torel and Pignon had been the objects of repeated attacks in the clandestine and unionist press, the former for having slavishly followed in the footsteps of the very unpopular Henri CEDILE, creator of the puppet government in Cochinchina, and the latter for stubborn opposition to 100 percent acceptance of the Viet Minh desiderats. The choice of Dufour was a wise one, for although an old-timer in Indochina, he was a realist and recognized that there was no going back to the pre-war scheme of things - moreover, he was held in esteem by the Annamites of all political colorings.

From the beginning, in great contrast to the non-committal austerity of Admiral d'Argenlieu, Mr. Bollaert radiated an atmosphere of confidence and optimism, although many in his entourage were definitely pessimistic. This optimism was good psychology as it tended to impress upon people that the situation was not hopeless and that there was a solution to the complex political problem. His declaration at Dalat on May 8 that he hoped that the vacant seats at the Economic Conference would soon be filled was definitely an olive branch to the abstaining Vietnamese. His speech at Hanoi on May 15 was a presentation of the most liberal policy that the French had so far formulated. To the great majority it appeared that the High Commissioner was sincere in his endeavor to put an end to the intercine war of the past 20 months and to arrive at a mutually acceptable formula for the future. His optimism must have been shaken at times and he must have wondered whether there was any solution short of military reconquest or complete capitulation - the attack on the convoy to Mythe in which some 40 persons were killed, the ever spreading wave of terrorism in the south, and the devastation of the north, were undoubtedly causes of just concern.
One may well ask, however, whether or not Mr. Bollaert's optimism and fine speeches were entirely sincere. Thus, it is alleged that the French themselves were to blame for the failure to arrive at an armistice, as reputedly proposed by Ho Chi Minh in a letter forwarded by Mr. AESCHLIMAN of the International Red Cross to the French authorities, because the harsh terms they offered amounted to virtually a demand for the abject surrender of the Viet Minh forces. Moreover, it was well within the bounds of reason that the French hoped that Ho Chi Minh would meet with an "unfortunate" accident, which would solve the question to treat or not to treat with him. But if the French did not want to consider Ho Chi Minh as the representative of the Annamites how could they, the French, justify their dickering with Bao Dai? It is hard to believe that as sagacious a person as the High Commissioner appeared to be could believe that an obviously French created regime, around the person of Bao Dai, would succeed or that the millions of Asiatics now clamoring for independence would accept such a regime at its face value.

What plan if any the High Commissioner has taken back to France is of course not known. Logically, however, any plan likely to succeed will represent a great concession on the part of France and the unquestionable sacrifice of many of her interests. France has already jettisoned the idea of a Federation of the five entities making up the French Indochina of the past, France may well be prepared to throw overboard the Provisional Government of the Republic of Cochinchina, and France appears to be willing to accept a Vietnam Federation so long as both French and native rights are protected and not to be the spoil of an admittedly totalitarian regime. What security France can exact for such protection in the future is difficult to say. France, if Mr. Bollaert's declaration is to be given credence, will refuse to deal with any one faction. On the other hand Ho Chi Minh has always said he is not fighting the French but only the colonialists, and he has given some indication of willingness to make concessions in his acknowledgement of the right of each of the three Kys to have local autonomy. How far communist-trained Ho Chi Minh is to be trusted is problematic and his concession of local autonomy may be merely a blind. Unfortunately, the majority of natives stoutly maintain that Ho Chi Minh is the man, and the only one, who represents them and they will oppose the putting forward of any other candidate as the creation of but another pupput and the erecting of a smoke screen for France's real intentions. While the natives are tired of fighting and are apprehensive of the destruction and famine that impend for the future there is still a determined nucleous who are prepared to wage a bitter and ruthless warfare if the greater part of their claims is not met. To reconcile these differences will be difficult, but for the future of Indochina, for the stability of Southeast Asia, for the good of the whole Far East, and for the prestige of western democracy, whatever plan is adopted must be put into operation without great loss of time.

From a purely practical point of view too great concessions on the part of France might be very disastrous, if such concessions give the natives virtually a free hand. Many observers doubt whether they are capable of running an independent state and point to the fact that the Philippines after 40 odd years of benevolent tutelage, in which the advantages of education and instruction were available to all, are still not a model of good government. How much less chance would the Annamites have of making a success? The jamority of these observers opine that without Occidental check or control the result would be chaos - and in that chaos either the Soviet or the Chinese would find their opportunity. The former would be able to establish their ideology in the very heart of teeming Southeast Asia, with millions of people to indoctrinate and to prepare for the ultimate struggle with the western democracies. The latter would be able to realize their age-old desire to dominate if not to take over this part of the Far East, a desire which is even now manifest. To many observers, the Chinese danger is the greater, even if not imminent because of China's preoccupation with her own political problems. Be that as it may, something must be done to eradicate the distrust and almost contempt of the French for the natives, and to eradicate the distrust and hatred of the natives for the French; something must be done to bring home to the French the fact that times have changed and that the natives have a right to more than a semblance of independence, and to bring home to the natives that the French have a legitimate interest and place in Indochina. Mr. Bollaert must have learned that the above are imperative and that they are the stones in the foundation of peace in Indochina.

The High Commissioner has now gathered the necessary data and it is the task of the French Government to supply and apply the answer. While that Government may continue to procrastinate in the hopes of wearing down the native opposition, I believe that that Government will be led to accept a Federated Republic of Vietnam, in which each of the three Kys will have autonomy, freely associated with the French Union. And Ho Chi Minh, if he is really the nationalist and patriot that he claims to be, must accept that his totalitarian government and Tonkin cannot speak for all Annamites.

(104) TELEGRAM FROM MARSHALL TO REED, JULY 17, 1947

Source: *Foreign Relations*, 1947, Vol. VI, pp. 117-118.

By mid-1947, the U.S. State Department was taking seriously the possibility that the French would be forced to accept a unified Viet-nam under Ho's government. This telegram from Marshall reveals the Department's toying with the idea of a "national communism" in Viet-nam and the possibility that the U.S. might be able to live with it.

Request your and Hanoi's appraisal implications relation US objectives stable Southeast Asia friendly to democratic West in event French should be forced deal present Vietnam Govt and this Govt should eventually emerge as controlling power three Annamese provinces. Refer particularly the following:

1. Whether influence Communists in present coalition Govt and behind-scenes Communists like Dang Xuan Khu and Ha Ba Cang would be sufficient put Vietnam in Soviet camp.

2. Position Ho respect above. Whether your opinion evidence increasing opposition to Ho by militants tends substantiate repeated reports his abandonment Party line and to corroborate reported letter to Chiang Kai Shek in which Ho excused past Communists connection on grounds nowhere else turn, and stated only interest now independence his country. (Impression here Ho publicly attempting walk chalked line between nationalism and Communism effort retain backing both forces.)

3. Whether intellectuals backing Vietnam realize what Communism means as international political force distinct its economic aspects and whether nationalists among them feel they can cope in future with Communist leaders Vietnam.

4. Whether, with removal solidifying effect French pressure, coherent Govt likely be extended over Vietnam representing real interests Annamese and allowing reasonably free political expression or whether coalition would break in factions which would settle differences by terrorism and armed force, resulting chronic disorders or eventual police state under one-party rule.

5. Sensitivity Vietnamese to US opinion and importance this fact or future orientation Vietnam Govt. While French Communists exploit every show of US interest developments Indochina to warn of US intervention, Vietnamese apparently welcome this interest.

6. Effect on Laotians and Cambodians should Soviet-oriented Vietnam emerge. Dept fully realizes paucity solid info on which base appraisal.

(105) LETTER FROM HO CHI MINH TO COMPATRIOTS IN THE ZONES TEMPORARILY OCCUPIED BY THE ENEMY, JULY 19, 1947

Source: Ho Chi Minh, *Selected Works*, Vol. III, pp. 123-124

Although everyone in the D.R.V. was urged to evacuate any area occupied by the French troops, a significant segment of the Vietnamese population came under the control of the French, both in the cities and in the countryside. Instead of viewing that segment of the population as collaborating with the enemy, however, Ho wisely encouraged them to express patriotism in other ways and to have confidence in the resistance.

Dear compratiots,

For more than half a year the whole nation has made sacrifices and fought for unity and independence of the Fatherland. The Government and whole people always think of you as we are well aware that you are suffering.

Moral suffering - Because you are also filled with patriotism like all the other compatriots but as yet do not have the opportunity to go side by side with the whole people in fighting the enemy for national salvation.

Material suffering - Because you are all the time harassed, ill-treated, raped, oppressed in every aspect by the reactionary colonialists like fish lying on the chopping-block.

The Government and the whole people never forget you, because while everyone enjoys freedom under the power of the Democratic Republic of Viet Nam, you alone are still living in slavery.

For all these reasons, our Government, troops and people do not mind hardship and trial and are striving to fight and make sacrifice to quickly liberate you from the earthly hell.

As for you, compatriots in the French occupied zones, what should you do? You should always bear in mind that

1 - Even if the enemy could rob us of all property and ill-treat our bodies, they never could crush our patriotism and heroic determination.

2 - The enemy would certainly not have enough men to keep watch over all the streets, villages and houses. Therefore we must find every means to help our guerillas in their activity to exterminate the traitors and enemy.

3 - We should not believe in the rumours aimed at dividing us or the false news spread by the enemy and traitors.

4 - We must always keep firm our spirit, always put trust in the forces of our Government, troops and people, and be always confident that the final victory will be ours.

While writing this letter, on the one hand, I suffer very much because owing to my small talent and little virtues I cannot as yet drive out the enemy so that you should not have to endure hardships. But on the other hand, I am in very high spirit because I am certain that after going through the hard steps, we will certainly be successful as, after winter, spring is sure to come.

Compatriots, be persevering, the day of liberation will come!

The long Resistance war will win!

Unity and independence will certainly be successful.

(106) TELEGRAMS FROM VICE CONSUL JAMES L. O'SULLIVAN IN HANOI AND REED IN SAIGON TO MARSHALL, JULY 21 and 24, 1947

Source: *Foreign Relations*, 1947, Vol. VI, pp. 121-126.

In their responses to Secretary Marshall's query on the implications of a Communist-controlled Viet-nam, both O'Sullivan and Reed indicated that it would not necessarily be subservient to the Soviet Union and that the U.S. could play a role there, though O'Sullivan expressed greater hope for U.S. influence. Both predicted chaos and a "police state" in Viet-nam unless Western authority was maintained over the country.

Reference Department's telegram 66, July 17. Department's assumptions do not make clear how much French influence it expects would remain event French are forced directly with Ho Chi Minh. But assuming French will deal with Ho only in last extremity and their control would tend become negligible thereafter:

1. Influence Communists in present government would not be sufficient to put Viet Nam squarely in Soviet camp although there would be pull in that direction. Agreement with French which would satisfy nationalism of Viet Namese people would probably lead to decrease in under-cover activities of characters such as Ha Ba Cang and Dang Xuan Khu and Tongbo members who would tend to emerge from shadows. Geographic isolation Indochina from Russia and realization by Ho Chi Minh of United States power based in Philippines would be sufficient to prevent him or any government formed here from entering whole-heartedly Soviet camp.

2. Until further information available, I am very skeptical regarding apparent opposition of militants to Ho. However, Ho's very great reluctance to admit that he is Nguyen Ai Quoc or to show any connection whatsoever with Russia is indicative of his realization that he must deal with West. Ho wrote 25 years ago that national revolution must precede Communist revolution in Indochina and it is obvious his first concern is get rid of French here. He is trying to obtain aid wherever he can and will tend be oriented toward source from whence assistance comes.

3. Have impression that intellectuals backing Viet Nam do not realize what is meaning Communism as international force and that they really would not care

if it was thoroughly explained to them. They have been driven to Communism by French colonial policy here and they consider that nothing can be any worse. Hate for French blinds them to many things and makes them accept others they do not like. Intellectuals backing Viet Nam government hate French so much that any future without French is attractive.

4. Removal French pressure would unquestionably have effect of causing present government in first instance to break into factions which would then for time tend develop into more or less full-blown party movements as those understood in Indochina. There probably then would be demand use armed force to some extent as country has widely distributed arms, has held exactly one general election in last 80 years, has no democratic tradition (outside of villages) which would enable it withstand strain political differences. There unquestionably would be danger police state under one-party rule which danger would have to be combatted by whatever French influence might remain and by United States through propaganda, student exchange, etc.

5. Viet Namese people here still regard United States as promised land and earthly paradise. American flag is still best protection available. Viet Namese are exceeding sensitive to United States opinion and unquestionably would accept United States advice and/or advisers and would be more than willing to have United States intervene if such intervention were directed toward satisfaction their political and economic needs.

6. Should Soviet oriented Viet Nam emerge, Cambodia and Laos would probably be subjected to considerable pressure to overthrow present regimes there. Independent Viet Nam, whether Soviet oriented or not, and absence of protecting power such as France, could be expected to resume encroachment upon Mekong delta which was interrupted by French occupation in 1860. Viet Namese migration to southern plains has gone on for ten centuries and probably will continue.

Independent Viet Nam, not oriented toward Soviet, would probably leave Laos to its own devices.

In effect, there are dangers in French dealing with Viet Nam Government. There are dangers equally as great in French dealing with series of puppets in continuing effort to establish, despite all statements to contrary, something which strongly resembles *status quo* of before war.

Problem was and remains primarily nationalist problem in overpopulated area with illiterate populace which has no democratic traditions on national level largely because colonial power gave populace no opportunity express itself politically. With middle-class small, intellectuals who are generally ineffective, and Catholics who are split, best possibility of retaining some stability and preventing development of police state seems to be retention some degree French or international control to act as arbiter between parties.

Communist problem here results from fact French have allowed Communist group to seize and monopolize fight for felt necessity of people and Communist problem will remain without hope solution as long as this necessity is not satisfied elsewhere.

O'Sullivan

Have given considerable thought Deptel 122, July 17, and feel if French compelled treat with present Vietnam Govt their position in French Indo China will be definitely weakened, also if this Govt emerges as controlling power in three Kys gradual deterioration of ties with democratic West may be expected. Unquestionably aid from western democracies, especailly US, will be welcomed at first but query whether this Govt and in fact any native govt not subject to check or control will not develop a definitely oriental orientation and will not become a prey for non-democratic influences. Such a govt without considerable economic and moral support will not be strong enough to resist the impact of a concerted move by either the Communists or the Chinese for both of whom this part of Asia is indeed a happy hunting ground, fertile field for the inculcation of anti-western sentiment, and expansion. However, it appears improbable that solution situation can be found without treating with present Vietnam Govt but as noted above and hereafter to treat with that Govt alone is a danger but there is equal danger in treating only with puppets. If French cannot reconcile all political elements or if they try to retain any large degree control, denying independence in regard which both present Vietnam Govt and Nationalist Front elements are united, only solution may be neutral intervention to establish a Vietnam state satisfactory to majority Annamites and to exercise control to see the state is run on democratic and equitable lines. If present Vietnam Govt is honestly nationalistic, it should welcome such solution but am reasonably sure French, particularly French Communists, will view such suggestion with alarm.

Replying *ad seriatim*.

1. While tendency is toward Soviet camp as result Communist orientation Vietnam leaders, do not believe Vietnam will come out openly on side of Soviets until ground is prepared; present Soviet policy toward Vietnam appears to be one of remote control rather than open support and such policy will probably be pursued until time is ripe for avowal Soviet affiliation; in meantime Ho is straddling the fence and hopes to win support of west on platform dedicated to fulfillment nationalist aspirations.

2. As I have reported, very possible so-called militant opposition to Ho as being too moderate is only a blind; there is no proof he has renounced his Communist training but it is reasonably certain his indoctrination will be soft pedalled until independence is won and the French are out; a wily opportunist, Ho will take any aid coming his way to gain his ends without disclosing ultimate intentions.

3. Most Annamite intellectuals do not realize what communism means except that it symbolized revolution, nor do they care; as their conflict with French is basically revolutionary, they will accept communism or any other "is[m]" as a means to the end.

This part 1 - continued part 2 mytel 231, same date.

Continuing mytel 230, today: Pure nationalists among these intellectuals want independence and the future can take care of itself; average Annamite not good Communist prospect but strong leaders of aggressive minority can easily bring about evolution Communist state.

4. Removal French pressure and absence Western democracy control will result in chaos as factional fighting with accompanying terrorism will ensue; great bulk of population not prepared for self-government and destinies of country would be in hands of few, those now strongly suspected of Communist leanings; unless active steps were taken, through economic and political pressure, there would be little possibility preventing and combatting resultant police state.

5. American opinion still highly valued by all Annamites, including present Vietnam Government, and American aid is definitely desired to any other; however, if American advice and action run counter to what they think is full sum their desiderata, US might not be so popular; this difference must be noted - present Vietnam Government welcomes American aid in gaining independence, getting rid of present Vietnam Government and Communists; if firmly applied, American pressure can be the strongest influence in the country but there can be no temporizing.

6. Strong Vietnam state whether or not Soviet oriented will bring pressure on Laos and Cambodia and definite political and economic encroachments are to be expected; unless full protection given those countries, they would be forced into orbit Buddhist countries to the west and there would follow indefinite period political readjustment and dispute.

While Communist danger exists, it is future one and only when Vietnam Government is firmly established and in position disregard opinion and aid Western democracies will such government align itself with Soviet satellites - events elsewhere may make such alignment only far distant possibility. French over-stress this danger. Present dangers are (1) French terms will be such as to prevent any peaceful solution and (2) if Annamites turned loose, only way combatting resultant economic and political chaos will be totalitarian police state, with ruthless suppression opposition. Both alternatives are alarming. Also must not overlook Chinese ambitions in this area which are only inactive because of China's internal situation.

Reed

(107) TELEGRAM FROM VICE CONSUL O'SULLIVAN TO MARSHALL, AUGUST 12, 1947

Source: *Foreign Relations*, 1947, Vol. VI, pp. 131-132.

In an analysis which anticipated Bollaert's speech the following month, O'Sullivan speculated that the High Commissioner wanted to present terms obviously unacceptable to Ho in order to justify a major military campaign against the D.R.V.

Bollaert's precipitous departure, official announcement of which delayed until his plane left this morning, still not fully comprehensible. "L'Entente" states simply that he wishes to *"mettre au point"* with govt "important" speech he scheduled to make near future.

It now seems clear that night August 8 or morning August 9 he received orders from Paris, presumably Moutet and/or Ramadier, to clear text fully his "important" speech with Govt. Bollaert then decided to return, with scheduled ETA Indochina August 25.

I am inclined to believe, however, that his return due to differences of opinion between Bollaert and officials in Paris, probably along lines indicated mytel 247, August 1. Bollaert, I feel, not wanted treat with Ho and is prepared make proposition similar to Mus proposal in May with such conditions that Ho would refuse. He was then prepared to inform Paris that no agreement with Ho possible and have French military authorities launch full scale military campaign in dry fall season. It seems probable that he wishes to support this policy in Paris personally. In this connection, ranking brass now in Hanoi, possibly planning details of such autumn campaign in event negotiations fail. Prevalent French military opinion which Bollaert may have accepted, altho it has been consistently wrong in last 18 months, is that, in 3 months' fall campaign, Viet Nam Government would be crushed. In this connection see my telegram 159, May 10.

(108) MESSAGE BY HO CHI MINH TO COMPATRIOTS THROUGHOUT THE COUNTRY ON THE SECOND ANNIVERSARY OF INDEPENDENCE DAY, SEPTEMBER 2, 1947

Source: *Selected Works*, Vol. III, pp. 131-135.

After reviewing the difficulties and accomplishments of the D.R.V., Ho Chi Minh called on the Vietnamese people to be prepared to fight for however long would be required to defeat the French, citing both Vietnamese resistance wars of the past and other revolutionary wars of long duration.

On the second anniversary of Independence Day, together with our compatriots, the Government and I review the work done in order to think of the tasks to come.

I - Our difficulties

a - Economic difficulty. - The Government came into existence after our country had been oppressed and exploited for eighty years, at a time when our people were driven to poverty and our resources exhausted, and our economy in ruins.

There were, in addition, broken dikes and floods. More than two million people died of starvation.

b - Military difficulty. - Hardly had the Government been set up for a few weeks when the French aggressors occupied Nam Bo, and unleashed the war.

c - Political difficulty. - After less than one month of existence, the Government strove to save the compatriots in the North from starvation and gave help to the compatriots in the South in their struggle against the invaders, while there was a group of people who boasted to be revolutionaries but did not cooperate with the Government. They disturbed the people, sabotaged order, wishing to provoke the civil war.

In short, the Government carries the burden while there is worry at home and and danger from outside, with all kinds of difficulties.

II - Reconstruction of the country

However, with the support of the whole people and confident in the glorious destiny of the Fatherland, the Government made great efforts to overcome all difficulties and hardships and scored a few achievements.

a - In the economic field. - Together with the people, the Government repaired the dikes, increased production, abolished poll-tax, cut down taxes, saved people from starvation, and improved the people's living standard. The Government still has to build independent finance for the country.

b - In the military field. - By its own strength, the Government set up a national army, trained millions of militiamen and self-defence guards for the defence of the Fatherland against the foreign aggressors.

c - In the political field. - In spite of the reactionaries' schemes of sabotage, our Government and people completed the free general elections. It was the first time in our history that the people enjoyed democratic freedoms and rights, electing their representatives to take care of public affairs.

Besides, the National Assembly intended to issue our first Constitution.

d - In the educational field. - Owing to the encouragement of the Government, the clearsightedness of the cadres of Mass education, and the compatriots' enthusiasm, in addition to the building up of new secondary and higher education, the training of specialists and gifted people and the development of the arts, we smashed to pieces the French colonialists' policy of obscurantism.

In two years, more than four million people of both sexes were taught to read and write and there were villages and communes which had completely wiped out illiteracy. This was a glorious achievement especially at a time when we were short of everything.

Had the French colonialists not provoked the war, we would certainly have won greater achievements in these two years.

III - Resistance war for National salvation

We are peace-loving people and our Government wishes its people to live in peace and work peacefully. We want to cooperate in friendship with the French people for the benefit of both sides. That was why we signed the March 6 Agreement and the September 14 *Modus Vivendi*.

But the French reactionary colonialists broke their words, meant to occupy our country and enslave our people once more. They launced war, founded a puppet government in order to divide our people and occupy our country.

Facing that barbarous aggression, our Government, army and people have united together into a bronze wall, determined to defend the Fatherland.

Thanks to our solidarity and unbending spirit, after two years of Resistance in the South and nine months of Resistance throughout the country, the enemy forces are more exhausted with every passing day while the more we fight the stronger and more enthusiastic we become.

Experience of other countries and of our national history shows us that:

The American Revolution for national liberation was successful after eight years of struggle.

The French Revolution lasted five years, the Russian Revolution six years and the Chinese Revolution fifteen years.

Our forefathers fought against foreign aggression for five years under the Tran dynasty and ten years under the Le dynasty before winning victory.

Therefore, if France sincerely recognizes the unity and independence of our country, our Government and people are ready to cooperate with her, but if the French colonialists maintain their policy of strength and plot to divide us, we are resolved to continue the Resistance war until we win unity and independence.

On this glorious and solemn day, on behalf of the Government I call on:

All the compatriots, all the combatants,

The compatriots in the occupied zones,

Vietnamese residents abroad,

To put their trust in the glorious destiny of the Fatherland, in our solidarity and fighting spirit. We should clench our teeth to endure hardships and fight with all our strength. However long the Resistance war may be, it is worth it as it will smash the yoke of slavery of more than 80 years, and bring about freedom for thousands of years to come. The officers and men on the battlefront, the compatriots in the rear, all should unite closely and strive to put into practice the four words: Industriousness, Thriftiness, Probity and Righteousness, and our Resistance war will win.

On behalf of the Government and compatriots, I convey fraternal greetings to the Asian brother peoples, the French people and the brother peoples of the French colonies.

The whole people closely unite together!

Overthrow the French reactionary colonialists!

Long live the friendhsip between the Vietnamese and French peoples!

Long live the fraternal feelings of the Asian great family!

The Resistance war will win!

Long live united and independent Viet Nam!

(109) <u>TELEGRAM FROM REED IN SAIGON TO MARSHALL, SEPTEMBER 15, 1947</u>

Source: *Foreign Relations*, 1947, Vol. VI, p. 137-138.

Reed concluded that Bollaert's speech of September 10, 1947 was a step backward from the March 6, 1946 agreement, aimed in part at justifying what the U.S. had feared most - an attempt to destroy Ho's government by military force.

Continued study Bollaert's speech and talks with many natives (both pro-Ho and pro-Bao Dai), French and others lead to following conclusions:

French now offer less than March 6 agreement, deliberately so in order to make offer unacceptable, so army can put its plan into operation to try eliminate Ho. French putting pressure on Bao Dai to accept negotiate with them but although they probably prepared enlarged terms of offer (member High Commissariat's [admits?] poor offer as point of departure for negotiations) there is no question of independence. Accordingly French continuing divide and rule policy and show little inclination go much beyond pre-war status.

On other hand, natives are not united and even in National Front ranks there is dissension. Also so far Ho has adopted negative attitude to National Front invitation form new combined government, Ho claiming he represents people and National Front must come to him. Until natives can agree, French have some justification at this stage limiting offer to internal autonomy with supervision to see one party or another does not gain control by totalitarian methods. Moreover number of native personalities admit French offer not too bad if could be sure French would be honest in carrying out terms of offer and could be counted on to progressively accord further attributes independence. This lack of confidence in French is keynote native attitude.

Unless French prepared act honestly, sincerely, to enlarge terms of offer to place natives on equality with French in internal matters, and unless natives can sink differences and can insure internal liberty will not be signal for civil war, it does not appear there can be any immediate acceptable solution FIC situation derived through direct French-Annamite efforts. If present trouble conditions drag on, perhaps intervention (my despatch 267, July 11 [1]) may be desirable and necessary, as it is inadmissible for American prestige in this part Asia let French restore virtually pre-war *status-quo* by arms and equally bad let natives run wild, which would be signal for civil conflict and possible Communist or Chinese intervention of a kind [sic].

(110) TELEGRAM FROM O'SULLIVAN TO MARSHALL, SEPTEMBER 24, 1947

Source: *Foreign Relations*, 1947, Vol. VI, pp. 140-141.

After conversations with French military officers, O'Sullivan reported that they were confident of their ability to bring about a military solution. He conceded the French could probably reimpose their rule by force but warned in the strongest terms that it would be an irreversible blow to Western interests in Viet-nam.

ReDeptel 73, September 19. French military in both Saigon and Hanoi, when they speak campaign 3 or 4 months, seem refer campaign in middle and upper Tonkin directed against present Vietnam Government.

Believe military feels confident such campaign would result (1) seizure Lao Kay and Caobang, thereby closing Chinese frontier to in-trickle arms and supplies Vietnam Govt; (2) disruption Vietnam Government with at least some if not most leaders such as Ho and Giap killed, captured or effectively neutralized; (3) destruction of major portion regular Vietnam army and capture most its arms; (4) destruction Vietnam communications including broadcasting facilities.

Throughout summer, felt French unable with troops then here to accomplish this campaign. In light report of recent influx troops in apparently sizable numbers from south, believe it possible French have capacity at least close Chinese frontier and serious[ly] disrupt Vietnam Government.

Doubt, however, if even French military feel situation can be stabilized on their terms immediately following such campaign. They point out complete pacification Morocco took 20 years, and Tonkin took 10 or more. However, they believe after organized Vietnam Government dislocated sufficiently, armed units will tend disintegrate to piracy.

While elimination present Vietnam Government as organized armed force would seriously weaken position other Nationalists vis-a-vis French (which Bao Dai from his recent Hong Kong statement regarding urgency of opening negotiations seems to realize), it would not enable French immediately reinstall something which resembles pre-war regime. However, French administrative history Indochina such that promised concessions are eaten away by administrative practice despite sincerity in which concessions originally offered. This tendency has shown no evidence changing in past 2 years.

French ability reinstall prewar regime in coming years would depend largely on factors external to Indochina. Am inclined believe, however, in long period, given among other things a [no?] third world war or third party intervention, continued instability China and India, reasonable economic recovery France and world, French could reinstall something which minus trimmings would resemble *status quo* before war.

Such action would, of course, be catastrophic US prestige, would turn Vietnamese who distrust and hate French into violent anti-white bloc and would insure irretrievable orientation intellectuals and people toward communism and Moscow and against West.

Summary sent Saigon.

(111) STUDY ON THE VIETNAMESE RESISTANCE BY TRUONG CHINH, SEPTEMBER, 1947 (EXCERPTS)

Source: *The Resistance Will Win* (Hanoi: Foreign Languages Publishing House, 1947), Chapters X-XIII, pp. 94-101.

In these excerpts Truong Chinh discusses how Viet-nam could achieve a favorable balance of forces against a naturally stronger foe. The analysis is notable for its realistic attitude toward the difficulties the resistance might face - including possible intervention by a "third country" on the French side.

We have described our strong and weak points, and the strong and weak points of the enemy. But this exposition does not exhaust the question of victory or defeat in the war.

We should not be content with comparing the potentialities and problems, the strengths and weaknesses of the two sides, and slip into complacency because of our advantages. The attitude of groundless optimism robs us of clear vision, makes us short-sighted, passive, and without the will to make progress.

In the history of war, there have been countries which met with fewer difficulties and had fewer weaknesses than the enemy, but which failed. On the other hand, there have been countries which met with more difficulties and had more weaknesses than the enemy, but which triumphed. Why should this be so? Because the country which had the advantage of its enemy did not try hard enough, underestimated its enemy and lacked skill. On the other hand, the country whose situation was disadvantageous made strenuous efforts, "knew itself and knew the enemy", and triumphed because it had skilful leadership. The author of "Kim Van Kieu"* when he wrote: "The will of man triumphs over fate", was thinking of the talent and subjective efforts of man, which may exercise a great influence on objective conditions. Of course, if we look at this question closely, we can see that this influence is more or less powerful depending on the favourable or unfavourable objective material conditions.

When our people struggle, when our leadership is skillful we can take advantage of the favourable conditions of time and situation to turn "difficulties" into "advantages", "weaknesses" into "strengths", and there is nothing strange in this at all! Moreover, war itself is a great movement. Difficulties for the belligerents created by the war ("strengths" or "weaknesses" depending on the side), cannot remain unchanged. They change according to the development of the war. The side which is skillful and makes great efforts will be able to cause these changes to be of advantage to itself, and harmful to the enemy. On the other hand, if this side lacks vigilance, is foolish, passive, or cowardly, these changes will become advantageous to enemy and harmful to it.

Moreover, we should ask ourselves: if we have more strong points than the enemy, then why do we remain on the defensive and go on retreating? Why, looking at our situation in general, do we still remain in a passive position, and have not yet won the initiative? In our opinion, it is because most of the enemy's weaknesses are moral ones, and most of his strong points are material ones. As for us, our weaknesses are for the most part material, and our strong points moral. War is a struggle between two forces from both moral and material viewpoints. Material conditions are quite necessary to victory - even a temporary victory - in any military action, whether in war, or in an armed uprising.

That is why, to check the advance of the enemy, to defeat him, we should strive to diminish our material weaknesses, increase our moral strength, and at the same time reduce the material strong points of the enemy and aggravate his moral weaknesses.

Herein lies the question.

Because we have fewer arms than the enemy, while fighting we must on the one hand maintain and develop our arsenals, keep up and increase our flow of weapons; and on the other hand, we must destroy and capture enemy arms to a greater and greater extent. It is a pity that our firepower is still weak and that our tactics are not yet skilful: in many battles, though we have killed a considerable number of enemy soldiers, we have seized only a very small quantity of weapons. On the other hand, though we have suffered small losses in men, every time one of our fighters falls, we lose his weapon as well. While fighting we must also produce arms, both rudimentary and modern arms, and constantly improve the standard of our arms manufacture. We should overcome the tendency to overestimate modern arms and underestimate the rudimentary. Those who have these tendencies do not realise that with the technical conditions prevailing in our country, if the manufacture of rudimentary arms is not carried on, we cannot arm our guerilla forces and our entire people.

But at the same time we should overcome the tendency to attach importance only to rudimentary arms and not strive to produce the modern; if we lack modern arms, it is difficult to check the advance of the enemy's motorized troops, or to counter-attack him. On the other hand we should carry out sabotage, intercept the enemy and use guerilla warfare with a view to minimizing the effect of the enemy's modern arms. We should launch surprise attacks and blow up enemy munitions stores, set up sham targets, which are exposed and easily visible, in order to delude the enemy and inveigle him into firing, expending his ammunition to no effect.

Our troops are not as inured to war as those of the enemy; that is why, while fighting, we must learn rapidly from the experiences accumulated in every battle and study the enemy's tactics, improve our own strategy and tactics, strive to train our officers and soldiers, militia and guerilla forces. At the same time, we use strategems to deceive the enemy and drive him on to the defensive; we find out as much as possible about the enemy in order to get to know him; we keep him in the dark about our forces by depriving him of information; we should clearly foresee the enemy's plans, taking advantage of his carelessness and lack of vigilance to launch daring attacks to annihilate him, avoiding all disadvantageous "fights to the death" to conserve our forces for a long resistance, for the moment when we can switch over from a defensive to an offensive position.

At present, most of our armymen know only how to fight bravely; they do not pay attention to the study of tactics. Many officers are often concerned only with routine, knowing only the area in which they are fighting, not bothering to study and analyse matters thoroughly; or they collect experiences mechanically, and do not know how to apply them correctly to our practical situation; they limit themselves to positional warfare or to the former strategy and tactics of the colonialist army. These tendencies should be weeded out immediately.

Our level of war organisation is low; therefore we should urgently try to discover every means of improving our command, which must be unified, rapid and precise. It is necessary to simplify and militarize the various technical organs. We should give precise orders, which must reach every fighter, and strictly control the implementation of these orders. Liaison and communications must be rapid and consolidated, even in enemy-held regions. All information must be speedy and accurate. Supplies should be punctual, sufficient and regular. Militia and guerilla forces must be widely organised with a view to replenishing our reserve forces constantly, so that we can reinforce the regular army in such a way that our regular armymen receive timely relief and do not wear themselves out. At the same time, we must strive to upset the enemy's organisation by sabotage and ruses. If, to achieve the aims of the resistance war, our line and policies must be correct, and our strategy and tactics flexible and clever, organisational work, too, is very necessary, in order to ensure the implementation of lines and policies, and the correct application of strategy and tactics. We should overcome the tendency to work in an amateurish manner, according to the way we feel, without principle, in a routine fashion, without order, without planning and checking. We should at the same time struggle against the tendency to waste time and effort over trifles, not to see the question as a whole; or the tendency to do poor organisational work which is incapable of ensuring the execution of the political line.

Is our propaganda directed to foreign countries weak? We will do our utmost to explain our just cause and expose the enemy's schemes before the world.

We uphold a just cause against barbarism, employ sincerity against perfidy. Therefore, we shall certainly win the sympathy of the French people, of personalities in other countries, of small nations, particularly Asian people and the peoples of the French colonies. Furthermore, we might request the Soviet Union to raise the problem of Viet Nam before the United Nations Organisation and demand that France negotiate with Viet Nam. We should take full advantage of the contradictions between France and other countries to make propaganda against the French colonialists. That is why we must collect documents concerning French crimes against our people, against foreign residents and the adherents of various religions; and documents proving our humanitarian behaviour towards French prisoners of war, our correct policies in regard to all religious people and foreign residents. Propaganda with foreign countries must be undertaken by a responsible organ, and by a number of specialized cadres, in order to avoid negligence and a happy-go-lucky manner of working. We should also send abroad cultural delegates or National Assembly deputies to make propaganda. We should get rid of the tendency to consider propaganda with foreign countries as a completely auxiliary task and thus neglect it; or to consider it as a "panacea", or, in other words, to rely upon others without making any attempt to develop our own resources, or to make our own efforts.

Such are the things to be done to minimize our weaknesses and diminish the enemy's strong points. To develop our strong points and accentuate the enemy's weaknesses, there is no other way than to carry out the following fundamental tasks: to unite the entire people, mobilize the whole country, wage a long resistance, make skilful propaganda with the enemy and have a good foreign policy.

However, if we know how to direct our subjective efforts to turning his disadvantages against the enemy, is the enemy so stupid as not to aim our own disadvantages at our heads in return? The enemy is more perfidious and cunning than we think.

In the course of the resistance war, some disadvantages may come our way, created by efforts made by the enemy, by our own errors, or by circumstances unforeseen either by us or the enemy. For instance: natural calamities, or famine might occur, there might be intervention by a third country which would first help the French colonialists to fight us and then oust them; again, the loss of a number of our cadres and outstanding men could have a considerable effect on the leadership of the resistance; or grave errors by our officers could lead to serious losses...

Such things may happen. The duty of our leading organization** is to foresee such eventualities and take all necessary preventive measures. But when something has happened that we were unable to prevent, we should remain calm, hold out, and deal with the situation. If we stick closely to the people, we will never be defeated.

*Poem written by Nguyen Du (18th century), acknowledged as the masterpiece of Vietnamese literature.

**The leading organization here is the Indochinese Communist Party (now the Viet Nam Lao Dong Party). In this book, the author does not refer by name to the Indochinese Communist Party, the Party having proclaimed its voluntary dissolution. In fact, it continued its activities. (Editor's note).

(112) <u>TELEGRAM FROM AMBASSADOR LEIGHTON STUART IN NANKING TO MARSHALL,</u> <u>OCTOBER 18, 1947</u>

Source: *Foreign Relations*, 1947, Vol. VI, pp. 143-144.

The skepticism of the State Department toward French policy found strong support from a surprising source - the Foreign Ministry of Chiang Kai-shek's Kuomintang government, which urged a settlement with Ho Chi Minh. The KMT Vice Foreign Minister discounted the danger of a Marxist Vietnamese government to China.

In conversation with Embassy officer on subject of Indochina, Vice FONMIN George Yeh and Director of European Dept FONOFF expressed following views:

It is difficult to foresee a settlement of Indochina question under current French policy, which is making position of other powers, particularly China and US, extremely difficult. It is unlikely that a govt can successfully be formed without participation of Ho Chi Minh, as Ho and his group are the only ones having a genuinely popular following. Attempts to alienate Ho's adherents under present circumstances unlikely of success. Persistence of French in present military course carries danger of forcing entire freedom movement into hands of Extreme, Communist elements.

Ho is regarded as Communist but many Vietminh leaders are not. Vice Minister is impressed with Ho's personality and commented that Ho was an abler individual for example than Sjahrir of Indonesian Govt, both men being personally known to him. The question of possible danger to China from a Communist-influenced regime adjacent to her southern border did not appear to be of critical importance.

The National Union Front does not have a solid popular base. It consists in the main of a group of prominent figures and if these leaders were removed from the picture (the recent assassinations in Saigon and Hanoi were recalled) the movement would probably have little force left. As regards Bao-Dai "the Chinese people would not regard favorably the reestablishment of a monarchy in Indochina. Bao-Dai has not recently been in Nanking (REDEPTEL 1205, September 29) and FONOFF officials made oblique reference to a "French story" to that effect.

Embassy comment: while no direct statement was vouchsafed by FONOFF officials as to Chinese attitude toward National Union or Nguyen Hai Than, foregoing would appear to indicate FONOFF does not contemplate support of Bao-Dai who would seem to be an indispensable element in present French plans and that a dubious view, at best, is taken of National Union movement. As Dept is aware there are diverse Chinese elements interested in the Indochina situation and views given above do not purport to represent crystallized Chinese attitude. No allusion was made during interview to possible mediation by third power or powers.

(113) DIRECTIVE BY COMMANDER IN CHIEF VO NGUYEN GIAP ON GUERILLA WARFARE, NOVEMBER 14, 1947 (EXTRACT)

Source: "Activating guerilla warfare, the fundamental military task in the present phase," excerpted in Vo Nguyen Giap, *Dan Quan Tu-Ve* [Self-Defense Militia], (Hanoi: Su That, 1974), pp. 16-21. [Translation by the editor.]

In October 1947, the French launched a major operation against the Viet Minh base area, hoping to destroy the main forces of the Vietnamese government. Vo Nguyen Giap, now Commander in Chief of the National Army, responded with a directive putting renewed emphasis on guerilla warfare.

The fundamental military line for defeating the French invaders and coping with the enemy's fall-winter offensive is:

ACTIVATE GUERILLA WARFARE

This directive by the general staff has the object of making clear for Resistance Committees at all levels, and for the entire army and military, the primary work which must be done to complete the task of activating guerilla warfare.

I. There must be one firm realization: guerilla warfare is the base.

Our resistance is an all-people resistance; that is the essential assurance for its final victory.

Why do we call it an all-people resistance?

All-people resistance means: the entire people participate in the destruction of the invader and salvation of country by one means or another.

Carrying it one step further, all-people resistance also means that on the battlefield of the entire nation, there are not only regular troops but guerillas, either detached from production or not detached from production, and there are self-defense militia participating in the fighting.

Therefore, to carry out all-people resistance, we must mobilize and arm the entire people.

Therefore, guerilla warfare a form of people's war, must be considered the base in the present phase of our resistance.

II. In order to cope with the war generally, and to cope with the enemy's new tactics, activating guerilla warfare is all the more urgent.

With the enemy's fall-winter offensive, the war is expanding to our own rear area. Enemy troops will control the cities and main lines of communication; they will try to surround us from outside, forcing our troops into a position of encirclement. Thus the enemy army would have the initiative, and our army would be in a passive position.

With the enemy's tactic of parachuting into many places, the rear could very swiftly become the frontline. Enemy troops may thoroughly exploit the gaps in our deployment in order to destroy our agencies and storehouses, and to murder and pillage our people. The only way to cope with that situation is to quickly develop guerilla warfare.

If we develop guerilla warfare, it will follow that, even though the enemy comes to a place which has no troops, they will still meet resistance, will at least be harassed, gradually worn down and destroyed one small bit at a time, so that our troops will have time to deal with them.

If we develop guerilla warfare strongly, it will follow that the positions of the two sides will be reversed. Our base of an entire people armed will submerge the cities and lines of communications controlled by the enemy in our own encirclement. From a position of being surrounded, we will shift to a position of surrounding the enemy. From a passive position, we will shift to the initiative.

Therefore, if generally speaking, activating guerilla warfare is necessary, then particularly at a time when the war is widening, and the enemy parachutes into many places, activating guerilla warfare is even more necessary.

III. What have we done to activate guerilla warfare?

We have put forward the slogan of guerilla warfare for a long time. We have mobilized people to participate in it, organizing self-defense militia and guerilla militia units.

In Nam-bo, we have activated a fairly strong guerilla movement.

In many places, the regular troops have done their best to help guerillas to mature.

However, because our realization has not yet been clear, because the tactics of application are not correct, because the idea of people's war is not yet firm and arms are still lacking, guerilla warfare at present has not yet developed strongly and widely.

a) There are many localities where guerillas are still weak and where neither the protection of the localities, nor combat coordination with main forces has yet been accomplished. In some places guerilla warfare has developed but there are not yet units developed to the level of local troops.

b) There are places where guerillas have not developed, so that the tendency to regularize has grown too soon, making it impossible for guerilla warfare to develop. There are zones which have pushed guerillas into the main force too hastily, to the point of weakening guerilla bases. There are provinces in which the provincial unit has only been concerned with separate guerillas, and not paid attention to bringing up guerillas which are not separate. In wartime, there is also an inclination to attack according to regular methods, to join large battles, expending large amounts of ammunition, not regarding harassing attacks or scattered attacks which have many results, as important.

c) Combat hamlets have not yet been actively constructed everywhere. Many localities have been satisfied with a number of combat hamlets which only have a propaganda function more than an enemy-annihilating function.

d) Main force troops do not yet have a concrete and active plan to develop guerilla warfare.

IV. How do we strengthen Guerilla Warfare?

In order to strengthen guerilla warfare, we must immediately do the following things:

1) Resistance committees must pay more attention to the problem of guerilla militia and have correct lines on the problem of guerilla militia.

Each mountainous district, interdistrict and district must have a factory manufacturing grenades, mines and ammunition.

We must resolve correctly the problem of supplying arms to guerillas. Guerillas must ask the people to support and supply them and must capture arms from the enemy in order to increase equipment for themselves. That is the main strategic line. Only in this way can guerilla warfare develop to a high level, avoid being limited by the national budget's capacity for supply, and maintain guerillas in circumstances of hardship later on.

2) Any detached guerilla unit, when its activities and training have reached a certain level, can be recognized as local forces. Local forces, like main forces, belong to the army's system, and command echelons follow the same ranks as in the main forces. Local forces, depending on the needs of the locality itself, can remain in combat in the locality, so that its supply would be the responsibility of the local resistance and people's committees. Local

forces can have one part participate in the main forces once the new guerilla units have matured and have enough power to maintain guerilla warfare in the locality.

3) In the present situation, main forces have the task of activating guerilla warfare in a direct and active manner. Help guerillas with regard to cadres: of the cadres presently in the main forces, some must be moved back to the locality in order to command local guerilla units.

Help in regard to weapons: within the limits of capability, they must assist local guerillas with arms; when they capture weapons from the enemy, they must divide them up with the guerillas.

But the most realistic and effective way of helping is to deploy main forces companies as independent companies in the localities in which guerillas are still undeveloped. Besides the usual tasks, the independent company also has the task of helping the local guerillas mature. As one of its activities, the independent company must at least help a guerilla platoon become local forces.

4) Regarding establishment of combat hamlets, they must be carried out more effectively.

(114) <u>LETTER FROM KING SISAVANG VONG OF LAOS TO PRESIDENT VINCENT AURIOL OF FRANCE, NOVEMBER 25, 1947 (EXTRACT)</u>

Source: Department of External Affairs (Canberra), *Laos*, Selected Documents on International Affairs, no. 16 (April 1970), p. 6.

In March 1946, the French had reoccupied the administrative capital of Laos causing determined Laotian foes of the French, along with their Vietnamese advisers to evacuate the resistance government to Thailand. Thereafter, the situation reverted rapidly to de facto *French control over Laos. The Lao king and most of the Laotian elite were prepared to allow the French broad authority in diplomatic, military, economic and communications matters and in August 1946 a* modus vivendi *was worked out between the King and French confirming the powers which the French demanded. In this letter to the French President, King Sisavang Vong reaffirmed his government's desire to join the French Union on the terms set by the* modus vivendi.

The Constitution which was enacted by the Laotian Constituent Assembly on April 26, 1947, and which We promulgated on May 11, 1947, prescribed the inclusion of the Kingdom of Laos in the French Union as a free and associated State.

We are pleased to recall this fact at a time when the Assembly to the French Union is meeting for the first time. The Kingdom of Laos intends to appoint its representatives to this Assembly and also to the High Council. The Kingdom of Laos is indeed eager to participate, as soon as possible, in the work that will establish the form of the Charter of the French Union.

The Laotian Government, while intending to retain control over its internal affairs, recognizes the French Union's need for a single diplomacy in which its nationals will participate. It also recognizes the need to pool the means of defence of the French Union, with respect to which Laotian participation in the forces of the Union, the free circulation of forces responsible for the defence of the Union in the territory of Laos, and the installation of strategic bases are essential conditions.

In addition, the Laotian Government is most desirous of seeking to pool or coordinate Laotian and French economic interests, as well as to harmonize the means of external communications.

The Kingdom of Laos being admitted, under these conditions, on a fully equal basis with the other associated States, its Government is prepared to sign with the representatives of the French Republic all special agreements of a cultural, diplomatic, military, economic, financial and technical nature which appear necessary to define its own situation. Pursuant to Article 28 of the Constitution of the Kingdom, those agreements shall be submitted to the Laotian National Assembly for ratification.

The traditional friendship that binds Laos to France will thus be clearly affirmed for the greater benefit of our two nations...

(115) SPEECH BY VO NGUYEN GIAP, DECEMBER 23, 1947

Source: Orders of the Day, Speeches and Mobilization Letters, pp. 57-60.

The French offensive, aimed at destroying the Viet Minh, met no major resistance, but found only burned out towns and villages and Viet Minh ambushes. After heavy losses, the French had to withdraw from positions they had captured. After the operation ended, Giap, in a speech at a review of troops, acclaimed the first military victory of the resistance.

Officers of Viet-Bac,

Today, in the liberated town of Tuyen-quang, radiant with the national colors on this first anniversary of the national resistance and the third anniversary of the establishment of the liberation army, we also have the occasion to rejoice in our army's defeat of the invader army's first Autumn-Winter Offensive in Viet-Bac.

The enemy army knew that Viet-Bac is our geographical base. They knew that Viet-Bac is the symbol of our resistance, the spiritual home of our army and people.

They attacked into Viet-Bac with the aim of destroying our main forces and our leading organs, destroying the main geographical base of the resistance and causing our army and people to lose faith in final victory.

They mobilized all their navy, army and air force and deploying most of their best-trained paratroops and infantry regiments, rushed into the offensive, hoping to occupy Viet-Bac at lightning speed.

The invader's troops declared in a brazen fashion that they would come to liberate the masses of Viet-Bac. But the Viet-Bac army and people met the invaders with swords and bullets.

The invader army hoped to make the spirit of our resistance collapse, but two and a half months after their offensive, the Viet-Bac army and people and the entire country as well are fighting all the more enthusiastically, and are even firmer in their confidence.

The invader's army hoped to win a big military victory, hoping to create political influence to serve as capital for the country-selling puppets, but they stumbled into a heavy loss such as they have never experienced since the beginning of their aggressive war.

The Lo River is red with the blood of the enemy and the Bong lau pass is cluttered with the bodies of the invader. With the glorious battles at Phu Doan, Tuyen-quang, Song Gam crossroads, Cao-bang, Phu-thong, Cho Moi, on highway number 3 and West of highway number 3, the ambushes on highway number 4, the raids at Thu-cuc, Tu-vu, the battles of pursuit in the last part of November and the first part of December, etc., our army's Viet-Bac victory continues the Bach-dang and Chi-lang traditions of our ancestors.

The enemy has been defeated in the first offensive into the Viet-Bac, but they have still not given up their unjust ambitions, and are preparing another offensive, hoping to annihilate our forces on the battlefield of the whole country.

As Commander in Chief of the Viet-nam National Army and Self-Defense Militia, I command you:

1. If, when the enemy rushes in to attack, we are absolutely not pessimistic, when they withdraw in defeat, we will absolutely not be too optimistic, disdain the enemy.

2. You must study the blood and bones experience on the Viet-Bac battlefield in order to understand further and defeat the enemy army, to understand our weak points in order to remedy them in time.

3. Especially you must reorganize and train the regular forces so that they coordinate with guerilla warfare and in order to advance gradually to mobile warfare: intelligence must be fast, topography must be known thoroughly, liaison must be thorough, maneuvering must be light, command must be timely and decisive.

4. You must enthusiastically participate in the "train the army, record feats of arms", making the Viet-Bac troops a model and the Viet-Bac battlefield forever become the graveyard of enemy bodies worthy of its reputation.

Fighters of the Lo River,

70 years ago, Tuyen-quang, on the banks of the Lo River, heroically stood up and fought an invading French army when they had just come into our country.

Three years ago, Tuyen-quang province was the temporary capital of the liberated zone which had just been established.

Today, Tuyen-quang, with Phu-Doan, Binh-ca, Khe Lau, on the banks of the Lo River, have brilliantly defeated the naval ground forces of the invaders.

Today Tuyen-quang again is honored by being chosen as the place for the ceremony of reviewing troops and this citation of merit, while on the enemy's route of retreat, the gunfire of our army's pursuit has just died away.

All Viet-Bac officers,

I represent the government in respectfully presenting the merit citation to the VIET-BAC FIGHTERS [caps in original--ed.] belonging to the national guard, guerilla militia, self-defense militia, local guards and assault security units before the entire Vietnam national army and self-defense militia.

I also represent the Viet-Bac fighters in sending cordial greetings to the Viet-Bac compatriots and expressing our thanks to the compatriots who helped the combat troops; and sending our determined-to-win greetings and congratulations to the fighters all over the country who heroically destroyed the invader on all battlefronts in order to coordinate the struggle with Viet-Bac.

Officers,

The invader's army has not yet been driven completely from Viet-Bac.

Under the slogan "Sweep the enemy army from Viet-Bac" and "Prevent the invader army from returning", you officers must boldly advance!

Long live the spirit of resistance of the Viet-Bac army and people!

Long live the spirit of the Lo River fighters!

Long live the Democratic Republic of Vietnam!

Long live Chairman Ho!

1948

(116) <u>LETTER FROM HO CHI MINH TO THE CONFERENCE OF POLITICAL COMMISSARS,</u>
<u>MARCH 1948</u>

Source: Ho Chi Minh, *Selected Works*, Vol. III, pp. 140-142.

*The High Command of the Vietnamese National Army put great emphasis on the
role of the political officers or "commissars" in the army, which was not political indoctrination but insuring the high morale of the troops as well as good
relations with the population. Ho's letter to the first conference of political commissars defined their responsibilities in the resistance struggle.*

Comrades!

On the occasion of your Conference, I send you my affectionate greetings
and wish you good health. Following are some of my ideas regarding the commissars' work to help you in your discussion. The behaviour of the commissars
exerts a very important influence on the armymen. Armymen are good when their
political commissar is good. When he does not fulfil his task, his men will
behave badly. At any level, the political commissar has three main tasks with
regard to
   1 - the armymen,
   2 - the people,
   3 - the enemy.

1. With regard to the armymen:
The political commissar must constantly take care of their material life,
such as food, clothing, housing, rest, drilling, work and combative force.
In their spiritual life, he must pay attention to raising their sense of discipline, combating libertinage, developing culture and the political line in
the army. The political commissar must know clearly and report to the upper
level the effective force of his unit.
To reward the good men, and punish the bad ones is also the responsibility
of the political commissar. In the recent period, no political commissar has
proposed to reward the fighters who had achieved heroic feats, this is a serious shortcoming. With regard to the armymen, the political commissar must be
as affectionate as a sister, as just as a brother and as intimate as a friend.

2. With regard to the people:
The people are the foundation, the father and mothers of the army. The
political commissar must win their confidence, esteem and love. He must do so
that the army enjoy the people's confidence, love and esteem; to this end, he
must urge the army to help the people and to fight the enemy valiantly.

3. With regard to the enemy:
Towards the French soldiers as well as foreigners and Vietnamese serving in
the French army the political commissar must know how to make propaganda wisely

and practically in order to rouse their consciousness and win them over to our side.

The iron discipline must be in force from the upper to the lower levels, the responsibility of the military commander and of the political commissar must be defined clearly, the political commissar must set good examples in every work. These are the main points.

At present we are mobilizing the armymen to drill and achieve feats of arms, the political commissars are the important moving force in this movement. I hope that the Conference will draw up practical and clear programmes and plans so that the movement may succeed.

Lastly, I advise all armymen to make efforts, and send them my greetings, and look forward to their brilliant feats of arms.

(117) MESSAGE OF HO CHI MINH TO THE MEETING OF THE VIET MINH CENTRAL COMMITTEE, APRIL 20, 1948

Source: Ho Chi Minh, *Selected Works*, Vol. IV, pp. 148-150.

The Viet Minh Central Committee met in April 1948, three months after the Indochinese Communist Party had concluded that the war had shifted from the defensive stage to the stage of "equilibrium of forces." In his letter to the meeting Ho reviewed the "correct policies" which had guided the independence struggle. In keeping with the practice of playing down the role of the Communist leadership of the resistance, he attributed all "correct policies" not to the Party but to the Viet Minh.

Today the League holds its meeting - I am very sorry that I am too busy to attend it. I wish the delegates good health and the Congress good success. Hereunder I recall some experiences to the minds of the delegates.

If the Viet Minh had been successful it is thanks to its correct policies:

a - Since the beginning the Viet Minh's home policy has been to unite the whole people, and win independence for the Fatherland.

To reach this aim, the Viet Minh's decided to fight both the Japanese and the French. In these circumstances where there was only a group of comrades with no arms at all, and the Japanese and French joined together to repress the patriotic movement, this decision was considered as a childish one by some people. But the result showed that the Viet Minh policy was correct.

b - The foreign policy of the Viet Minh was to side with the democratic camp.

While the German, Italian and Japanese fascists ruled undisturbed and won victory upon victory, and the democratic countries were suffering bitter defeat upon defeat, such a policy was also considered as foolish by some people. But at that time the Viet Minh foresaw that the democratic Allied forces would certainly win. The result also showed that the Viet Minh's policy was correct.

c - While the Japanese and French were cooperating closely, the Viet Minh foresaw that they would betray each other, and the first would be the Japanese. Thanks to this foresight the Viet Minh had prepared a plan to turn this opportunity to advantage. The result also showed that the Viet Minh's policy was correct.

d - From the beginning, the Viet Minh was sure of the ultimate independence of the Fatherland, therefore they worked out a plan for the establishment of a free zone which would not only be used as a resistance base but also a place to train prospective military and administrative cadres. The result also showed that the Viet Minh's policy was correct.

e - When the August Revolution was victorious and succeeded in seizing power, the Viet Minh decided to organize a Government on a broad basis, including all the personalities in the country, to take in hand State affairs.

At that moment, some people thought that the prominent personalities would not gladly cooperate with the Viet Minh. But as the Viet Minh put the Fatherland's and people's interest above all, these personalities willingly joined the Government.

g - In the period when it would be necessary to further develop the unity of the whole people, the Viet Minh timely proposed and helped the organization of the Viet Nam National United Front to develop rapidly and broadly, and thus the Viet Minh was further developed and consolidated.

h - The Viet Minh's policy was to safeguard peace, but when the Resistance war broke out, the Viet Minh did its best to support the Government's policy of long Resistance. In this Resistance war, the Viet Minh foresaw that victory would certainly be ours. The past is a guarantee for the future.

In short, ever since the founding of the Viet Minh, experience has shown that all its policies were correct; these facts must be developed and highlighted.

However, the Viet Minh had a shortcoming: its rapid development did not leave time to train all cadres; that is why in many places the cadres deviated from the common policy, so much so that some cadres became debauched.

At present, on the one hand, the Viet Minh must pay attention to the training of cadres from village level upwards. On the other hand, cadres must criticize and examine themselves in order to be worthy of their hard but glorious task. And the members of the Viet Minh League must be the vanguard in every task in the Resistance and reconstruction of the country.

I hope that the Congress will work out practical plans to develop and consolidate the Viet Minh League on the lines of patriotic emulation.

(118) TELEGRAM FROM MARSHALL TO CAFFERY, JULY 3, 1948 [EXTRACT]

Source: *Foreign Relations*, 1948, Vol. VI, pp. 29-30.

On June 5, 1948, High Commissioner Bollaert signed an agreement with General Nguyen Van Xuan, head of the French-sponsored Republic of Cochinchina, who had a letter from Bao Dai as his only mandate for forming a central government, and the heads of the French-sponsored administraive committees in Tonkin and Annam. The French recognized the "independence" of Viet-nam on paper, but in fact the Xuan government had no control over government functions, which were entirely in French hands. Secretary Marshall's response to this development was to repeat earlier about the dangers of attempting a military solution and government by Vietnamese "puppets." Yet his only concrete suggestion was further French "concessions" to a French-sponsored government.

For Wallner.[1] Dept considering ways of implementing recommendations contained in final para Saigon's tel 150 Jun 30 to Dept rptd Paris as 40, and it appears desirable that with Emb, you consult informally with French officials, particularly Bollaert, as to points 1 and 2 below. Please comment on these as well as remaining points.

1) Daridan[2] has informally stated to Dept officer that in his opinion Assembly would not have to ratify Baie d'Along agreement. He pointed out, however, that definite agreement covering points mentioned in para 3 that document would assumably have to be so ratified. Dept inclined believe French Govt would have to give, however, public evidence that it backed Bollaert's signature of agreement. Pls report current French thinking this question.

2) In event Daridan's interpretation correct, Dept believes that only measure which French Govt would have to submit for approval Assembly would be question of change of status Cochinchina to allow "union 3 *kys*" to be achieved by Viets as stated Jun 5 agreement. Would such move by Schuman[3] Govt

precipitate crisis? Is there any possibility that Communists might support such a measure or at least abstain from voting against it, as their line has consistently favored "union of 3 *kys*"?

3) How can approach to French best be made? In respect Baeyens' views (Embstel 3453 Jun 30) and rptd statements of Daridan that he does not believe Schuman Govt would risk its political life to bring question before Assembly, Dept believes that if desired results to be obtained, it must be done at highest level; i.e. Schuman, Bidault and Coste-Floret in spite latter's recent statement to Assembly (Embstel 3155 Jun 15[2]) paralleled of course by high level approach to Bonnet[4] in Washington.

4) Should approach, if made, be confined for present only to change in status Cochinchina? In this connection, what is best thinking?

5) What concessions are judged necessary to give plan fair start?

Dept cognizant of fact that fighting in Indochina has now continued for almost three years; that we believe given present world political and economic conditions, French simply do not have and have no prospect of amassing sufficient strength Indochina reach mil solution; that instread of being element strength to France, Indochina since war, at present, and for foreseeable future, unless situation changes radically, will remain grievously costly enterprise weakening France economically and all west generally in its relations with Oriental peoples.

In our view, continuation of parade puppets such as French have produced over past two years will strengthen hand Ho Chi Minh and may well insure eventual emergence of state probably dominated by communists and almost certainly oriented toward Moscow. It is to avoid such eventuality that we consider it of highest importance that present so-called central government, or in fact any non-communist government, be given every chance to succeed by the granting to it of such concessions as will attract greatest possible number of non-communist elements.

[1]Woodruff Wallner, recently Associate Chief of the Division of Western European Affairs, was appointed First Secretary of the Embassy in France on July 21; he was on a visit to Paris.

[2]Counselor of the French Embassy.

[3]Robert Schuman, President of the French Council of Ministers (premier).

[4]Henri Bonnet, French Ambassador.

(119) TELEGRAM FROM MARSHALL TO THE EMBASSY IN FRANCE, JULY 14, 1948

Source: *Foreign Relations*, 1948, Vol. VI, p. 33.

In instructions to the Embassy in Paris, Marshall indicated that, if the French Assembly would approve the June 5 agreement and the change in Cochinchina's status from a French colony to an integral part of the "Provisional Government of Vietnam", the U.S. would publicly support French policy as a positive step, thus binding the U.S. more closely to the French in Viet-nam than before.

Dept approves line of action recommended last para Embtel 3621 and wishes you proceed immediately to ascertain disposition Schuman Govt toward dealing with Indochina situation before Assembly adjournment. On basis your findings you should apply such persuasion and/or pressure as is best calculated produce desired result. In applying such persuasion and/or pressure you may in your discretion convey to Schuman Govt that once Baie d'Along agreement together with change in status Cochinchina approved, Dept would be disposed consider lending its support to extent publicly approving French Govt's action as forward looking step toward settlement of troubled situation Indochina and toward realization of aspirations Vietnamese people. It appears to Dept that above stated US approval would materially assist in strengthening hands of nationalists as opposed to communists in Indochina. Keep Dept close informed. Sent Paris as 2637; rptd Saigon as 115.

(120) TELEGRAM FROM MARSHALL TO THE EMBASSY IN FRANCE, AUGUST 30, 1948

Source: *Foreign Relations*, 1948, Vol. VI, p. 40.

Repeating the same willingness to support the French publicly in ratifying the June 5 agreement, Marshall suggested that there was a "truly nationalist group" which would take support away from the Viet Minh if the French would only make enough concessions to them in future negotiations.

Dept concurs views Saigon's 188 Aug 28 similar those Deptel 136 Aug 27 Saigon (rptd Paris as agam). Dept appreciates difficulties facing any French Govt taking decisive action vis-a-vis Indochina but can only see steadily deteriorating situation unless more positive approval Baie d'Along Agreement, enactment legislation or action permitting change Cochinchina status, and immediate commencement formal negotiations envisaged that Agreement. Dept believes nothing should be left undone which will strengthen truly nationalist group Indochina and induce present supporters Viet Minh come to side that group. No such inducement possible unless that group can show concrete evidence French prepared implement promptly creation Vietnam as free state associated French Union and with all attributes free state. When you deem appropriate point out to French Govt Dept's views regarding Indochina and repeat Dept's readiness publicly approve French Govt action along above lines which will assist bringing about solution Indochina problem. In foregoing connection you might refer substance second para Deptel 3331 Aug. 26.

(121) DEPARTMENT OF STATE POLICY STATEMENT ON INDOCHINA, SEPTEMBER 27, 1948

Source: *U.S.-Vietnam Relations*, Book 8, pp. 144-148.

The State Department's first full-length policy statement on Indochina again ruled out military reconquest but also rejected French military withdrawal, on the ground that there would be "chaos and terroristic activities" - a reflection of telegrams from Hanoi and Saigon. Since the U.S. could support neither conquest nor withdrawal, it was left in an essentially passive position of accepting a French policy with which it could not agree. Despite a perfunctory expression of support for establishment of a "truly nationalist government", it admitted its "inability to suggest any practicable solution."

A. OBJECTIVES

The immediate objective of US policy in Indochina is to assist in a solution of the present impasse which will be mutually satisfactory to the French and the Vietnamese peoples, which will result in the termination of the present hostilities, and which will be within the framework of US security.

Our long-term objectives are: (1) to eliminate so far as possible Communist influence in Indochina and to see installed a self-governing nationalist state which will be friendly to the US and which, commensurate with the capacity of the peoples involved, will be patterned upon our conception of a democratic state as opposed to the totalitarian state which would evolve inevitably from Communist domination; (2) to foster the association of the peoples of Indochina with the western powers, particularly with France with whose customs, language and laws they are familiar, to the end that those peoples will prefer freely to cooperate with the western powers culturally, economically and politically; (3) to raise the standard of living so that the peoples of Indochina will be less receptive to totalitarian influences and will have an incentive to work productively and thus contribute to a better balanced world economy; and (4) to prevent undue Chinese penetration and subsequent influence in Indochina so that the peoples of Indochina will not be hampered in their natural developments by the pressure of an alien people and alien interests.

B. POLICY ISSUES

To attain our immediate objective, we should continue to press the French to accommodate the basic aspirations of the Vietnamese: (1) unity of Cochinchina, Annam, and Tonkin, (2) complete internal autonomy, and (3) the right to choose freely regarding participation in the French Union. We have recognized French sovereignty over Indochina but have maintained that such recognition does not imply any commitment on our part to assist France to exert its authority over the Indochinese peoples. Since V-J day, the majority people of the area, the Vietnamese, have stubbornly resisted the reestablishment of French authority, a struggle in which we have tried to maintain insofar as possible a position of non-support of either party.

While the nationalist movement in Vietnam (Cochinchina, Annam, and Tonkin) is strong, and though the great majority of the Vietnamese are not fundamentally Communist, the most active element in the resistance of the local peoples to the French has been a Communist group headed by Ho Chi Minh. This group has successfuly extended its influence to include practically all armed forces now fighting the French, thus in effect capturing control of the nationalist movement.

The French on two occasions during 1946 attempted to resolve the problem by negotiation with the government established and dominated by Ho Chi Minh. The general agreements reached were not, however, successfuly implemented and widescale fighting subsequently broke out. Since early in 1947, the French have employed about 115,000 troops in Indochina, with little result, since the countryside except in Laos and Cambodia remains under the firm control of the Ho Chi Minh government. A series of French-established puppet governments have tended to enhance the prestige of Ho's government and to call into question, on the part of the Vietnamese, the sincerity of French intentions to accord an independent status to Vietnam.

1. Political

We have regarded these hostilities in a colonial area as detrimental not only to our own long-term interests which require as a minimum a stable Southeast Asia but also detrimental to the interest of France, since the hatred engendered by continuing hostilities may render impossible peaceful collaboration and cooperation of the French and the Vietnamese peoples. This hatred of the Vietnamese people toward the French is keeping alive anti-western feeling among oriental peoples, to the advantage of the USSR and the detriment of the US.

We have not urged the French to negotiate with Ho Chi Minh, even though he probably is now suppported by a considerable majority of the Vietnamese people, because of his record as a Communist and the Communist background of many of the influential figures in and about his government.

Postwar French governments have never understood, or have chosen to underestimate, the strength of the nationalist movement with which they must deal in Indochina. It remains possible that the nationalist movement can be subverted from Communist control but this will require granting to a non-Communist group of nationalists at least the same concessions demanded by Ho Chi Minh. The failure of French governments to deal successfully with the Indochinese question has been due, in large measure, to the overwhelming internal issues facing France and the French Union, and to foreign policy considerations in Europe. These factors have combined with the slim parliamentary majorities of postwar governments in France to militate against the bold moves necessary to divert allegiance of the Vietnamese nationalists to non-Communist leadership.

In accord with our policy of regarding with favor the efforts of dependent peoples to attain their legitimate political aspirations, we have been anxious to see the French accord to the Vietnamese the largest possible degree of political and economic independence consistent with legitimate French interests. We have therefore declined to permit the export to the French in Indochina of arms and munitions for the prosecution of the war against the Vietnamese. This policy has been limited in its effect as we have allowed the free export of arms to France, such exports thereby being available for re-shipment to Indochina or for releasing stocks from reserves to be forwarded to Indochina.

[Sections on economic problems in Indochina and French relations with other states in the area is omitted]

D. POLICY EVALUATION

The objectives of US policy towards Indochina have not been realized. Three years after the termination of war a friendly ally, France, is fighting a desperate and apparently losing struggle in Indochina. The economic drain of this warfare on French recovery, while difficult to estimate, is unquestionably large. The Communist control in the nationalist movement has been increased during this period. US influence in Indochina and Southeast Asia has suffered as a result.

The objectives of US policy can only be attained by such French action as will satisfy the nationalist aspirations of the peoples of Indochina. We have repeatedly pointed out to the French the desirability of their giving such satisfaction and thus terminating the present open conflict. Our greatest difficulty in talking with the French and in stressing what should and what should not be done has been our inability to suggest any practicable solution of the Indochina problem, as we are all too well aware of the unpleasant fact that Communist Ho Chi Minh is the strongest and perhaps the ablest figure in Indochina and that any suggested solution which excluded him is an expedient of uncertain outcome. We are naturally hesitant to press the French too strongly or to become deeply involved so long as we are not in a position to suggest a solution or until we are prepared to accept the onus of intervention. The above considerations are further complicated by the fact that we have an immediate interest in maintaining in power a friendly French Government, to assist in the furtherance of our aims in Europe. This immediate and vital interest has in consequence taken precedence over active steps looking toward the realization of our objectives in Indochina.

We are prepared, however, to support the French in every way possible in the establishment of a truly nationalist government in Indochina which, by giving satisfaction to the aspirations of the peoples of Indochina, will serve as a rallying point for the nationalists and will weaken the Communist elements. By such support and by active participation in a peaceful and constructive solution in Indochina we stand to regain influence and prestige.

Some solution must be found which will strike a balance between the aspirations of the peoples of Indochina and the interests of the French. Solution by French military reconquest of Indochina is not desirable. Neither would the complete withdrawal of the French from Indochina effect a solution. The first alternative would delay indefinitely the attainment of our objectives, as we would share inevitably in the hatred engendered by an attempted military reconquest and the denial of aspirations for self-government. The second solution would be equally unfortunate as in all likelihood Indochina would then be taken over by the militant Communist group. At best, there might follow a transition period, marked by chaos and terroristic activities, creating a political vacuum into which the Chinese inevitably would be drawn or would push. The absence of stabilization in China will continue to have an important influence upon the objective of a permanent and peaceable solution in Indochina.

We have not been particularly successful in our information and education program in orienting the Vietnamese toward the western democracies and the US. The program has been hampered by the failure of the French to understand that such informational activities as we conduct in Indochina are not inimical to their own long-term interests and by administrative and financial considerations which have prevented the development to the maximum extent of contacts with the Vietnamese. An increased effort should be made to explain democratic institutions, especially American institutions and American policy, to the Indochinese by direct personal contact, by the distribution of information about the US, and the encouraging of educational exchange.

(122) <u>HO CHI MINH'S APPEAL ON THE SECOND ANNIVERSARY OF NATIONWIDE RESISTANCE WAR, DECEMBER 19, 1948</u>

Source: Ho Chi Minh, *Selected Works*, Vol. III, pp. 156-159.

Reviewing two years of resistance war, Ho noted the growing strength of the Vietnamese armed forces and predicted that 1949 would be more successful than either of the previous two.

Compatriots all over the country,

Fighters,

Today, the long Resistance war steps into its third year; and into its fourth year in south Viet Nam.

Let us review the situation in the past two years, in order to carry on the work in the years to come. How was the situation in these   years?

On the enemy's side:

1 - Political situation: Since the launching of the unjust war, the French government has been overthrown more than ten times.

The French government has had to change its representatives in Indo-China three times: the militarist d'Argenlieu failed, and had to go back to the seminary. Politician Bollaert also failed, and was driven out of the Senate by the French people. Now it is the turn of civil-servant Pignon, who will certainly fail.

The policy "divide and rule" and that of using Vietnamese to fight the Vietnamese people has also been defeated. Not only were the puppet traitors fiercely hated by our compatriots, but they also became a universal laughing stock.

2 - Military situation: From Generals Leclerc, Valluy and Salan to General Blaizot, the enemy had to change generals four times.

Each month, from 800 to 1,000 enemy soldiers were annihilated by us. Besides, French soldiers, French prisoners, German and Italian war prisoners, Moroccan and Senegalese soldiers were used. They also used Vietnamese youths in the temporarily occupied zone as cannon-fodder. The majority of these compatriots have been waiting for the opportunity to come back to the Fatherland.

3 - Economic situation: They had to spend millions upon millions on armaments while their economy in our country went bankrupt, and decreased by 96.97 per cent.

4 - In addition to these failures, the internal situation of France was in great confusion. In the diplomatic arena, France also met with failures, and was overruled and cheated by other imperialist countries.

On our side:

1 - While the French government was reshuffled many times, the prestige of our Resistance Government became stronger and stronger; not only did it gain the support of our National Assembly and people, its honour all over the world also constantly increased.

Our people became more closely united, the Resistance war grew in strength.

2 - In the first year of the Resistance, our army was quite young and our weapons very rudimentary. Sticks were used in south Viet Nam, and old guns in the North. However, we stayed the advance of the enemy.

At present, our army has grown up in every respect. Many times the enemy has had experience of our new arms, as in Dong Thap Muoi, at Hai Van pass, in Viet Bac, and many other battles.

We also had a big and strong force of militiamen and guerillas. Not only the sturdy guerilla units of young men, but the old people's and women's guerilla units also killed many of the enemy and scored feats of arms.

3 - Our economy, finance and culture overcome difficulties and are still on the upgrade.

Thanks to the ardent patriotism and single-minded unity of our compatriots and fighters, we obtained these glorious victories.

On this occasion on behalf of the Government, I thank and congratulate:

- All the national defence fighters, militiamen and guerillas;
- All compatriots in the free zone as well as in the temporarily occupied zone and abroad;
- Administrative and specialized cadres.

On behalf of the Government, I bow to the memory of the war martyrs and compatriots who sacrificed themselves for the Fatherland, and send my affectionate greetings of comfort to wounded and former armymen, and also to fighters' families.

According to the above-mentioned comparison, we realize that:

The enemy forces are decreasing and weakening. The enemy's situation is like the setting sun.

Our forces are increasing and strengthening. They are like streams which gather together to become an ocean.

Our Resistance war was hard *in the first year*, progressed *in the second year*; its third year will be the year for achieving the first successes.

But we must not be subjective, and underestimate the enemy. We must still go through more difficult steps than before and fight more fiercely and strongly than before, in order to reach the final victory.

Thus, all compatriots and fighters must be zealously in the vanguard in patriotic emulation.

Fighters must emulate in killing enemies, capturing guns, and scoring many feats of arms.

Compatriots must emulate in increasing production, overcoming famine, ignorance, and helping to kill the foreign invaders. Cadres must emulate in practising Industriousness, Thrift, Integrity, and Righteousness, correcting their weak points, and developing their good points. With every passing day, our unity grows closer, our army is better supplied and stronger, and thus the enemy is doomed to failure, and we are sure of our success.

The long Resistance war will win!

The struggle for independence and unity will be successful!

1949

(123) TELEGRAM FROM ACTING SECRETARY OF STATE ROBERT LOVETT TO CAFFERY, JANUARY 17, 1949

Source: *Foreign Relations, 1949, Vol. VII*, pp. 4-5.

As the French negotiations with Bao Dai on his return to head a Vietnamese government neared completion, the State Department expressed apprehension that the "truly nationalist group", meaning the opponents of the Viet Minh, would be seen as a "virtually puppet government" by the Vietnamese people once they began collaborating with the French.

Daridan[1] has expressed to Dept same view contained penultimate para urtel 107 Jan 10 qualifying his remarks however with statement that he uninformed developments past ten days which might explain optimism Overseas France officials in urtel 106 Jan 10 re negotiations with Bao Dai.

While Dept desirous French coming to terms with Bao Dai or any truly nationalist group which has reasonable chance winning over preponderance of Vietnamese, we cannot at this time irretrievably commit US to support of native govt which by failing develop appeal among Vietnamese might become virtually puppet govt, separated from people and existing only by presence French military forces. Accordingly, Emb should make no additional representations to French until and unless further instructed by Dept which does not believe it desirable go beyond position outlined Deptel 2637 July 14 its reftel 3621 Jul 9 from Paris and Embtel 5129 Sep 30.

Dept will inform Emb re possibility any common anti-Communist action Indochina (third para Embtel 107) after it has recd Brit views as Emb London reports Brit ConOff has instructed Brit Emb Wash discuss matter with Dept.

[1] Jean Daridan, Counselor of the French Embassy.

(124) TELEGRAM FROM ACHESON TO THE EMBASSY IN FRANCE, FEBRUARY 25, 1949

Source: *Foreign Relations, 1949, Vol VII*, pp. 8-9.

Reviewing the French record of the previous three years, the new Secretary of State, Dean Acheson, instructed Paris that the U.S. would not commit itself to support a Bao Dai solution until it proved successful, in terms of popular support.

Urtel 718, Feb 18. Dept despite reported progress Fr-Bao Dai negots queries whether Fr are really making such concessions as to (1) induce Bao Dai return Indochina (2) give him best opportunity succeed even if he returns there. For months, even though Commie successes China should have induced Fr make outstanding effort, negots have dragged, with Fr unable or unwilling put question status Cochinchina before Fr Assembly. Foregoing connection Dept fully realizes polit difficulties present Fr Govt putting this question before Assembly but Dept equally aware that over past three years Fr have shown no impressively sincere intention or desire make concessions which seem necessary solve Indochina question. Present formula solving status Cochinchina may have virtue but in Dept's thinking it may be but another device to obtain delay and unless proof is adduced to offset record of past three years Dept is now far from inclined give public approval any arrangements with Bao Dai. This disinclination springs from Dept's considered belief it would be unwise give public support to any arrangements for Indochina concluded by Fr unless that arrangement embodies means clearly sufficient insure its success or until it achieves substantial measure of success. Thus even though Bao Dai induced return Indochina DD Dept views failure Fr Govt take decisive action, at very least re status Cochinchina, as seriously weakening possibility ex-Emperor will obtain support any appreciable portion population. Without such support Bao Dai cannot hope, even though supported by Fr arms as he must necessarily be, wean away militant and organized followers of Ho Chi Minh.

Dept believes therefore, it should not now be committed in any way to approval Fr action vis-a-vis Bao Dai and must reserve aforementioned public expression until Fr have provided Bao Dai with means to succeed and he has demonstrated ability use successfully such means to obtain support appreciable portion Vietnamese population. This connection, Emb may recall doubts expressed in several Fr quarters re Bao Dai's capacities and abilities when negots were first undertaken with him two years ago. Accordingly Emb should make clear to FonOff that for these reasons US not prepared give public indication its approval until, in Dept's opinion, conditions noted above fulfilled.

At same time Emb may state while US remains willing reconsider its ECA Indochinese policy such reconsideration must await developments.

Sent Paris as 598. Rptd Saigon as 15.

Emb should note particulary with respect to first part para 1 that above tel was drafted before receipt embtel 771 Feb. 24, 4 p.m.

(125) THE ELYSEE AGREEMENTS: EXCHANGE OF LETTERS BETWEEN FRENCH PRESIDENT VINCENT AURIOL AND BAO DAI, MARCH 8, 1949

Source: Accords Franco-Vietnamiens du 8 Mars 1949: The Franco-Vietnamese Agreement of March 8, 1949 (Saigon: imprimerie Francaise d'Outre-Mr, 1949) in French and English, pp. 45-62.

After months of negotiations, the French concluded an agreement with Bao Dai in March 1949 which again recognized Viet-nam's "independence" within the French Union, but still gave France control over Vietnamese diplomacy and military affairs. The D.R.V. government had rejected such terms at the Fountainebleau Conference of 1946.

You kindly expressed the wish to see, with regard to the Vietnam's Unity and Independence, the principles laid down by the joint declaration issued on the 5th of June, 1948, at the Bay of Along by M. Emile Bollaert, French High-Commissioner in Indo-China, and General Nguyen-van-Xuan, President of the Central Provisional Government of Vietnam, in the presence of Your Majesty, confirmed and determined precisely.

This wish falls in with the intention of the French Government, which after discussing the matter in the Council of Ministers, requested me, in my capacity as President of the French Union, to conclude, by means of letters exchanged with your Majesty an agreement for the purpose of determining precisely for their application the principles of the 5th of June statement.

It will be incumbent on Your Majesty's Government, on the one hand, to agree with the French High Commissioner in Indo-China upon the conventions both particular or provisional which will determine the relations of the French Union with the Vietnam, account being taken of the principles expressed in the present exchange of letters and of the present state of affairs, until order and peace are restored; on the other hand, to prepare with the Representative of France and in conjunction with the Royal governments of Laos and Cambodia, the necessary regulations attendant upon the present agreements.

On this basis and under these circumstances, I confirm, in the name of the French Republic, my agreement with the following provisions:

I - UNITY OF VIETNAM

Notwithstanding former treaties of which she might have prevailed herself, France formally re-affirms her decision not to raise any *'de jure'* or *'de facto'* obstacle to the admission of Cochinchina within the framework of the Vietnam, defined as consituted by the uniting of the territories of Tonking (North Vietnam), Annam (Centre-Vietnam) and Cochinchina (South Vietnam).

But the uniting of Cochinchina to the other parts of Vietnam can be considered as legally achieved only following a free consultation of the populations concerned, or of their representatives.

The whole of the provisions of the present agreement will be valid only from the day Cochinchina is actually and legally united with the rest of the Vietnam.

To that purpose, the Government of the French Republic pledges itself to bring into play the proceedings provided for by the Constitution.

As soon as the proceedings are completed the French Government will definitely recognize the unity of Vietnam, such as it has just been defined.

The French Government renounces its right to prevail itself of the special status bestowed by Royal Order on the three cities of Hanoi, Haiphong and Tourane.

The administration of the non-Vietnamese populations whose historical home is situated on Vietnam territory, such as it has just been defined, and who have always been traditionally dependent on the Crown of Annam, will be the object of special statutes granted to the representatives of these populations by His Majesty the Emperor. These statutes will be determined in agreement with the Government of the French Republic which, in this matter, has particular duties towards these populations. They will have to guarantee the eminent rights of the Vietnam, as well as the free evolution of these populations whose traditions and customs must be respected.

II - DIPLOMATIC STATUS

The foreign policy of the French Union, within the framework of which the Vietnam exercises its rights through its delegates in the High Council and by virtue of the conduct of her diplomatic affairs, which we shall define below, will be examined and coordinated under the direction and within the responsibility of the Government of the Republic of France, at the French High Council of the Union where the Government of the Vietnam will be represented by its own chosen delegates.

For the execution of the abovementioned general directives, as far as foreign policy is concerned, H.M. the Emperor of the Vietnam will associate the activity of his diplomacy with that of the French Union.

The heads of the foreign diplomatic missions to the Vietnam will be accredited to the President of the French Union and to H.M. the Emperor of the Vietnam.

The Vietnamese heads of diplomatic missions which the Government of the Vietnam will have assigned by agreement with the Government of the Republic of France to represent it in foreign states, will receive credentials granted by the President of the French Union and initialed by H.M. the Emperor of the Vietnam.

The countries in which the Vietnam will be represented by a diplomatic mission, will be determined after an agreement with the French Government.

The unity of the international policy of the French Union in these states will be maintained both by predetermined general instructions, the High Council of the French Union being informed, transmitted by the Government of the Republic to the Government of the Vietnam, as well as by direct contacts which the French and Vietnamese diplomats will establish among themselves.

In the other states, the Vietnam will be represented by the diplomatic missions of the Government of the Republic of France which may include representatives of the Vietnam.

The Vietnam is entitled to negotiate and to sign agreements concerning its particular interests, on the express condition that, before undertaking any negotiation, it submit its projects to the Government of the Republic for strict examination by the High Council, and that these negotiations be conducted in liaison with the diplomatic missions of the Republic. Approval by the High Council will be necessary before such agreements become final.

The Government of the Republic of France is agreeable, on request of the Vietnamese Government, to intervene on its behalf for the opening of Vietnamese consulates in foreign countries where the Vietnam considers itself to have particular interests. The Vietnamese consuls will carry out their activities in states where the Vietnam has a diplomatic mission under the direction and control of the head of that mission, in liaison with the diplomatic representative of the Government of the Republic of France, in other states, under the direction and control of the head of the diplomatic mission of the Government of the Republic of France.

The Government of the Republic of France offers to put forward and to support the candidature of the Vietnam when the latter conforms with the general conditions set out by the Charter of the United Nations for admission to that organization.

III - MILITARY STATUS

The Vietnam keeps up its national army whose task it is to maintain order and internal security as well as to defend the Empire. In this latter case, it will, eventually, be backed by the forces of the French Union. The army of the Vietnam will equally participate in the defence of the frontiers of the French Union against all external forces.

The military strength of the national Vietnam army and that of the army of the French Union stationed in the Vietnam will be established by a particular agreement, so that the total of the available means may, in time of war, effectively defend the territory of the Vietnam and of the French Union.

The Vietnamese army consists of Vietnam nationals commanded by Vietnamese officers; French instructors and French technical advisers will be put at the disposition of the Vietnam.

The Vietnamese officers and N.C.O.'s will be formed in Vietnamese military schools and eventually in French schools where they will be admitted without discrimination. To facilitate cooperation in wartime, the internal composition of the Vietnamese army will approach as closely as possible that of the army of the French Union.

The Vietnam army will be dependent on the budget of the Vietnam Government. Orders for material will be forwarded by the Vietnam Government to the French Government.

In order to contribute efficiently to the defence of the French Union the army of the French Union will station bases and garrisons on the territory of the Vietnam, the nomenclature, limits and status of which will be the objects of a particular convention. In any event, this status will be such as to allow its forces to fulfill their mission while respecting the principles of Vietnamese national sovereignty. They shall be able to circulate freely, between the bases and garrisons that have been assigned to them, according to settlements to be reached at the abovementioned military convention. In accordance with the principle of total cooperation within the French Union, they will comprise Vietnam elements, the conditions under which they will be recruited being subject, also, to the abovementioned convention.

To achieve united action which will be immediately effective in time of war, a permanent military committee made up of the officers of the General Staff of both armies, will be created immediately in the period of peace, in order to prepare a common plan of defence and military cooperation between the national army and that of the French Union; the committee could, in case of need, serve as permanent organ of liaison between the two armies in peacetime. The conditions of the military committee's composition and function in peacetime will be set out in the special convention which is attached to the Franco-Vietnam treaty.

In time of war, the entire defence potential of the armies of Vietnam and the French Union armies will be pooled, the military committee forming the core of a mixed general staff under the command of a French general officer in charge of the Vietnamese theater of operations particularly affected and one of the chiefs of general Staff will be Vietnamese.

IV. - INTERNAL SOVEREIGNTY

The Vietnam government will fully exercise all the attributions and prerogatives arising from internal sovereignty. Particular or provisional conventions will be passed with the French High Commissioner in Indo-China, which conventions, account being taken of the circumstances, will determine the modalities of the transfer to the Vietnam of such powers as were formerly exercised by the French authority.

The Vietnam government will apply, in the first place, to subjects of the French Union every time it needs counsellors, technicians or experts in public services and establishments or in enterprises having a public character concerned with the defence of the French Union.

The priority granted to subjects of the French Union will only cease in case the French government is unable to supply the personnel required. The methods of application of this provision will be determined in a subsequent text.

No French citizen, no subject of the French Union will be permitted to hold a post in the Vietnamese administration unless he has previously received the agreement or approval of the French Union representative and, on the other hand, no Vietnamese will be permitted to enter a French or French Union administrative service without having previously received his Government's authorisation or approval.

V. JUDICIARY QUESTION

All civil, commercial and penal matters throughout the territory of the kingdom will come within the full and unreserved jurisdiction of Vietnam.

However, civil and commercial cases setting, on the one hand, non-Vietnamese subjects of the French Union against one another or against Vietnamese, or, on the other hand, subjects of States with which France has passed conventions involving a jurisdictional privilege, and penal action taken in the case of breaches of the law perpetrated by or impairing persons of the same categories, or gain prejudicing the French State, will be submitted to joint jurisdictions, the formation and working out of which will be the object of a judiciary convention appended to the Franco-Vietnamese treaty.

This convention, however, will take into consideration the following principles:

1° - Sentences passed will include the following executory formula: 'In the name of the French Union and the Vietnamese Nation, His Majesty the Emperor of Vietnam orders...

The execution of such sentences outside the territory of Vietnam will be the object of subsequent agreements providing for simplified proceedings with regard to foreign judgements or arbitrations awards.

2° - French law will be applied every time a Frenchman is implicated.

3° - Vietnamese law will be applied every time no Frenchman being implicated, this law will seem applicable to the solution of the conflict. Failing which, French law will be applicable.

Finally, it is specified that, in conformity with the usages of private international law, matters relating to personal status will be decided by the national law of the parties concerned. Administrative contentious matters will be settled following the same principles and on a basis of total reciprocity.

The special judiciary convention will deal with all other questions relating to the present chapter.

VI. - CULTURAL AFFAIRS

France may open freely primary and secondary public and private educational institutions in Vietnam under the one condition that territorial laws are being adhered to.

These rules and regulations should not make, directly or indirectly, any discrimination between French and Vietnamese.

The educational system requires professional and moral standards equivalent to those of France.

All of these requirements are to be applied also to the technical and professional Education system.

French institutions shall apply the curriculum in force in France, including, however, a history course of Vietnamese civilization, which will be obligatory.

Vietnamese pupils have free access to French institutions in Vietnam. These institutions shall include a course of Vietnamese language, obligatory for Vietnamese pupils. A privileged place, intermediary between the national language and foreign languages will be maintained for the French language, which is the diplomatic language of Vietnam, in Vietnamese institutions. Vietnam shall accept that a sufficiently large place is reserved in secondary schools to the French language, in order that students may be able eventually to pursue superior courses in that language. It will also strive to insure the teaching of French, to the greatest possible extent, in primary schools.

A system of equivalence between Vietnamese diplomas and French official diplomas shall be established by an agreement to be concluded to this effect as soon as the French and Vietnamese programs have been compared.

Vietnam has the right to provide freely for its higher education. It will at the same time acknowledge the right of France to continue her higher education in Vietnam, on behalf of the French Union.

However, owing to present practical difficulties, and especially in order to provide for the formation of an adequate Vietnamese teaching staff, a joint University will be created in keeping with the territorial laws and regulations.

The status of this University will be the object of a special agreement between France and Vietnam. The other Associated States in Indochina can, if they so desire, participate in this organization and enter into the necessary negotiations with France and Vietnam to achieve this goal.

The status of this University will respect the following principles:

-- The joint university will constitute an organization corresponding as closely as possible to the principles of autonomy in the higher education system applied in the majority of modern states.

It will be headed by a Rector, nominated by joint decision of the governments concerned and of France, three candidates being presented by the consultative committee of the University. The Rector will be assisted by deans for the headmastership of each superior institution and for the management of the University by a University council including, under the Rector's chairmanship, the deans, the representatives of the teaching staff, the representatives of the students and other persons interested in educational questions, as well as the directors of scientific establishments and one representative of each of the governments concerned.

Teaching will be carried out in the language chosen by the founders for foundations and special institutes.

With regard to classical education:

a) -- all branches of instruction will be taught in French,

b) -- Vietnamese will be taught according to modalities which will be fixed by the Council of University.

Diplomas granted by the joint University will be considered official by the two States. However diplomas granted in an eventual course, exclusively Vietnamese, will not automatically give access to French educational posts or to employments requiring diplomas in the French Union.

In order to facilitate, to the greatest possible extent, the expansion of higher education, entrance fees will be maintained as low as possible and will have to be approved by the governments concerned.

The joint University will reserve the number of admissions necessary to accommodate scholarship students from the Governments concerned.

The disposal of scientific establishments already existing in Vietnam will be fixed by special conventions to take place either between the French and Vietnamese States or between the Vietnamese State and the board of directors of the establishment concerned. Notwithstanding, the following principles will be compulsorily respected:

The assets of the whole of the heritage of the 'Ecole Francaise d'Extreme Orient' will be the joint property of the three Indochinese States and of France; these assets will be inalienable. The board of administrators will include representatives of the three Indochinese States and of France. The Director will be nominated by a joint decision of the four governments, on presentation of three candidates by competent sections of the French Institute.

The situation of the Pasteur Institutes already existing on the territory of Vietnam will be fixed by contracts between these organizations and the Vietnamese government.

The following principles will however be taken into consideration:

The existing establishments are the joint property of the three Indochinese states and of France, with regard to the buildings and land property in Saigon, Dalat and Nhatrang.

The buildings and land property of the Pasteur Institute in Hanoi is the property of Vietnam, which, however, pledges itself to conclude for Hanoi a contract identical to those in force with the other establishments.

The Pasteur Institute remains proprietor of the real estate received either by gift or legacy.

Scientific material remains the property of the Pasteur Institute.

The application of the present contract will continue until it expires normally, at the end of December 1949.

Archives:

Each of the governments concerned remains proprietor of its archives. The conservancy and management of these archives will be the object of modalities remaining to be fixed.

The question of Libraries, Rice Bureau, Meteorological Service, Oceanographic Institute and Museums will be the object of special agreements.

Vietnamese subjects in France or in other parts of the French Union, French subjects and subjects of the French Union in Vietnam will enjoy the same rights of establishment as nationals, within the framework of the law and of territorial regulations. They will be allowed to circulate to carry on business and, on the whole, will enjoy all democratic liberties in the territory.

Property and enterprises belonging to subjects of the French Union on the territory of Vietnam benefit by the same regime as that extended to the property and enterprises of Vietnam subjects, especially with regard to the mode of taxation and labour legislation. This equality of status will be extended on reciprocal grounds to property and enterprises of Vietnamese subjects on French Union territories.

The legal regime of enterprises and property belonging to subjects of the French Union in Vietnam can only be modified by a joint agreement between the government of the French Republic and the Government of Vietnam.

Subjects of the French Union who were dispossessed of their rights and property owing to '*de facto*' circumstances occurring in Vietnam since March 1945, will be re-established in the same. A joint committee will be appointed to fix the modalities of the restitution.

French capital can freely be invested in Vietnam, subject to the following provisions:

a) -- The Government of Vietnam will have a share, if it judges fit, in the capital of such enterprises considered as being of national interest.

b) -- The opening of enterprises concerning national defence is subordinate to the authorisation of the Government of Vietnam.

c) -- The government of Vietnam will be entitled to exercise a right of pre-emption on the assets of enterprises ceasing their activities.

A Franco-Vietnamese joint commission will determine the exact scope of the sectors as well as that of the limitations to the principles of free establishment included therein.

The aforesaid provisions do not apply to already existing properties or enterprises in Vietnam or to further developments likely to arise from their normal activities.

The Vietnam Government will administer sovereignly its finances. It will draft and administer its budget. It will dispose of all the income collected on the territory of Vietnam, with the exception of those allotted, with the agreement of the French government and that of the other associated states, to the financing of common institutions or to other uses to be determined. It will be empowered to increase both direct and indirect taxes and to create new ones. Should the latter have a particular incidence on subjects of the French Union, they will be the object of preliminary consultation of their representatives with a view to maintaining fiscal harmony between Vietnam and the other Indochinese States, as well as the normal exercise of economic activities.

Monetary union between Vietnam and the other Indochinese States will be maintained. The only currency in circulation on the territory of this monetary union will be the piastre issued by the Indochinese Bank of Issue.

The Bank of Issue can issue different notes for Vietnam, Laos and Cambodia.

The Indochinese piastre will be included in the 'franc zone'. The parity between the piastre and the franc will not, however, be immutable and might vary according to economic circumstances. But any change of parity must be the subject of consultation between the Associated States in Indochina.

The mechanism of exchanges will be fixed by the Indochinese Exchange Office.

Vietnam will form a customs union, together with the other Indochinese States. There will be no customs barrier between them. No taxes will be collected at their common borders; the same customs tariffs will be enforced with regard to both import and export duties all over the Union territory.

H.M. the Emperor of Vietnam, estimating that, in the economic and financial field, he has common interests with the Sovereigns of Cambodia and Laos, on the one hand, and with the French Union, on the other, and that it might be profitable to the Vietnamese nation that these interests be harmonized with a view to general prosperity, recognizes the advisability of creating joint organizations in order to study, harmonize and work up the aforesaid interests.

For that purpose, a conference meeting in Indochina under the auspices of the High Commissioner, at which will be represented, side by side with the Government of the French Republic and the Government of His Majesty, the Sovereigns of Cambodia and Laos, will determine the composition and the scope of these joint organizations' powers. To this effect, it seem advisable to leave the following points to the competence of the Conference:

1. -- Communications service.
2. -- Immigration control.
3. -- External commercial relations and customs.
4. -- Treasury.
5. -- Equipment Plan.

It is specified, in this connection, that the Indochinese conference, as defined above, will be called upon to give its advice on the equipment plan, at present under study.

This Conference will establish its own rules and procedure at the opening of its work.

The High Council of the French Union can eventually be referred to for advice or conciliation, if need be.

*****

Instruments will be exchanged in Saigon between Your Majesty and the French High Commissioner in Indo-China. The agreement will take effect from the date of exchange.

The joint statement of the 5th of June 1948 and the present documents as well as the complementary conventions involved, will be submitted to the French Parliament for approval as well as to Vietnamese organizations qualified to constitute the act provided for by article 61 of the Constitution of the French Republic.

The government of the Republic and myself are convinced that the speedy application by Your Majesty and the Representative of France, in a spirit of mutual confidence and willingness, of the aforementioned provisions will efficiently contribute to the re-establishment of peace in Vietnam, freely united to France in a spirit of equality and friendship.

I beg Your Majesty kindly to accept the assurance of my highest consideration.

VINCENT AURIOL

I have the honour to acknowledge receipt of today's letter worded as follows:

(Text of the President of the Republic's letter to H.M. BAO DAI, from: I - Unity of Vietnam to: the High Council of the French Union can eventually be referred to for advice or conciliation, if need be).

I have the honour to notify accord on the contents and terms of this letter. I am convinced that the working out, in a spirit of mutual confidence and comprehension, of the dispositions stated therein, will permit the speedy re-establishment of peace in Vietnam.

I am moreoever certain that the Vietnam, henceforth closely linked with France in an atmosphere of unity and equality, will efficiently contribute to the grandeur and prosperity of the French Union.

I beg you, Mr. President, kindly to accept the assurance of my highest consideration.

BAO-DAI

As agreed upon in the course of the negotiations of the Franco-Vietnamese agreement, signed at Paris this day, I have the honour to give to Your Majesty, in this letter, the additional explanations which you asked on certain particular points of the text.

I. - UNITY OF VIETNAM

1° The uniting of South Vietnam to the rest of the Empire will be accomplished according to the following procedure:

Vote by the French Parliament of the law creating the Representative Territorial Assembly of South Vietnam, provided for by article 77 of the French Constitution, and commissioned to give its opinion on the changing of the statute of the said territory;

Vote by the Representative Territorial Assembly of South Vietnam on the changing of the aforesaid statute and the integration of South Vietnam with the rest of the Empire;

Vote by the French Parliament of the law proposed in article 75 of the French Constitution, sanctioning the changing of the statute of Cochinchina.

The National Assembly will be consulted, according to the procedure of urgency, as soon as the Representative Territorial Assembly of South Vietnam has made known its point of view;

2° The agreement of the Government of the French Republic provided for with regard to particular statutes granted to the non-Vietnamese populations whose historical home is situated on the territory of Vietnam, is required at the time the aforesaid statutes are granted and also in case of further modifications.

The text of these statutes will determine the modalities of appropriation by the parties concerned. The French Government does not intend submitting the Vietnamese administration to any particular material control.

II. - DIPLOMATIC QUESTION

1° The number of delegates of the Vietnam to the High Council of the Union will be fixed subsequently by agreement with the Vietnam Government;

2° The Government of the French Republic agrees that the Vietnam be immediately represented by diplomatic missions in the following countries:

    Holy See,
    China,
    Siam.

However, if the Vietnam, owing to the incidents affecting China at the present time, deems it preferable to be allowed another post, the French Government will see no objection to China being replaced by India in the above list.

No revision or extension of the present statute can be effected without the agreement of the Government of the French Republic.

3° The Vietnamese diplomats who will be included in French diplomatic missions will be designated by the Government of Vietnam and nominated by the Government of the French Republic.

They will be commissioned especially to deal with affairs concerning the Vietnam.

They will be able to correspond with their government, under cover of the head of the French diplomatic mission, it being understood that French is the official language of the post.

4° The same dispositions will also be applied to the Vietnamese consuls in the countries where, in the absence of a Vietnamese diplomatic representative, they will carry on their activities under the direction of the head of a French diplomatic mission.

5° The 'liaison' with French diplomatic missions, when negotiations are undertaken by the Vietnam with the object of concluding and signing agreements relative to its own interests, implies not the compulsory existence of Franco-Vietnamese joint delegations, but the setting up, in each case, of a system of reciprocal information, which while leaving the Vietnam free-handed and responsible, may, if need be, permit the French Union diplomacy to support and help the Vietnamese mission through all difficulties and serious incidents which might happen in the course of the negotiations.

I beg Your Majesty kindly to accept the assurance of my highest consideration.

AURIOL

(126) TELEGRAM FROM CAFFERY TO ACHESON, MARCH 16, 1949

Source: *Foreign Relations, 1949, Vol VII*, pp. 12-14.

After the Elysee agreement was concluded between French President Auriol and Bao Dai, under which Bao Dai would return to Viet-nam as Head of State, Ambassador Caffery sent an upbeat assessment of the agreement from the viewpoint of Bao Dai's entourage. He also urged public support for the Bao Dai government from the outset, arguing that that support would be a key factor in determining its success.

We are told by influential member Bao Dai entourage who particpated recent negotiations that Bao Dai and entourage are well pleased with outcome debates on Indochina. Overwhelming vote in favor of Cochinchina assembly bill will he says be well received in Indochina and Capitant's motion of censure will be attributed to pre-election political manoeuvering in France and will soon be forgotten.

Bao Dai-Auriol agreement "while not including everything we would like to have" is considered "a very favorable point of departure launched under better circumstances than we had hoped for in view domestic French political situation" and "affords workable basis for fulfillment Vietnam aspirations."

Our source states that while elements of agreement so far made public naturally emphasize advantages to France, other side of coin is quite favorable to Vietnam and it is now up to Bao Dai's supporters to see that this aspect gets wide publicity in Vietnam. ("Very fact government hasn't dared publish agreement shows how favorable it is to us.") On economic matters there is agreement on relationship between France and Vietnam which does not infringe on latter's internal sovereignty (one example given was that Vietnam can negotiate commercial agreements with foreign countries).

Certain matters involving common services such as customs, transportation and communications will have to be regulated in conference in which Cambodians and Laotians as well as French and Vietnamese will participate. Source does not believe agreement on technical details in this regard will prove either difficult or onerous to Vietnam.

Cochinchina Territorial Assembly will be convoked about April 7 and after union with other two *ky's* approved, French National Assembly will be asked give urgent approval. Bao Dai and French both in agreement this must transpire prior to former's arrival Indochina which is scheduled for April 25. Time permitting, Bao Dai will return on French warship ceded to Vietnam flying Vietnamese flag and carrying Vietnamese crew.

Source expressed opinion work in Paris on Bao Dai solution has now been satisfactorily completed and major future developments will take place in Indochina. He stated Bao Dai and entourage place great confidence in Pignon and are satisfied he will proceed honestly in implementation of agreement.

Bao Dai's two principal tasks were described as forming government capable of really governing (which we were told is well under way) and bringing about pacification of country.

Source informed us Bao Dai hoped US would make some public statement supporting principles of agreement (which would have most important effect on Vietnamese population) that we would seriously consider some form of recognition of Vietnam and would assist in making arms available.

Source was told we could not comment on any of these points until we had received and studied text of agreement. Under no circumstances, however, could we envisage Department's approval furnishing arms directly to Vietnam. (Bao Dai is of course aware substance my talk with Chauvel[1] - Embtels 5129, September 30 and 5405, October 16, 1948.) From information so far available it appears to us that with signature agreement and Assembly vote on Cochinchina Bao Dai solution has been favorably launched from French end. Period which will elapse prior his arrival Saigon and formal ratification agreement will afford Department opportunity make serious evaluation his chances success. Upon his return Indochina, Bao Dai will be faced with primary tasks forming government including influential Vietnamese nationalist leaders who have so far remained on sidelines, of attracting maximum popular support and of reducing and eventually eliminating Viet-Minh. At present his tools are largely limited to his personal prestige, the Paris agreements and such military economic and financial assistance as he will receive in Indochina from French.

As Bao Dai represents only foreseeable opportunity for anti-Communist nationalist solution Indochina, I recommend that Department in light our declared policy preventing spread of communism in SEA and of supporting truly nationalist movements in that area, study agreement when received with view to possibility extending to Bao Dai solution as calculated risk moral and perhaps some economic support in difficult initial period following his return, support which if given will increase its possibilities success and if withheld will constitute negative rather than neutral factor.

I appreciate of course that if Bao Dai fails after receiving such support from US it will be interpreted as further blow to our own position in Asia. On other hand in view of fact that only alternative to Bao Dai solution would involve dealing with Ho Chi Minh (to whom I assume we remain unalterably opposed), I believe we should take this risk.[2]

Sent Department as 1066; repeated Saigon as 38.

[1] Jean Chauvel, Secretary-General of the French Foreign Ministry.

[2] In telegram 955, March 25, 9 p.m., to Paris, the Department stated its position in telegram 598, February 25, p. 8, "remains unchanged for the present." (851G.01/3-1849)

(127) MEMORANDUM FROM THEODORE C. ACHILLES, OFFICE OF WESTERN EUROPEAN AFFAIRS, TO JOHN D. HICKERSON, DIRECTOR, DIVISION OF EUROPEAN AFFAIRS, MARCH 25, 1949.

Source: 840.50 Recovery/3-2549, State Department Central Files, National Archives.

The State Department's Chief of Western European Affairs, anticipating a renewed French request for economic assistance for Indochina, recommended support for the Bao Dai regime as the "only solution", even while expressing little optimism about its prospects. The Chief of the European Division concurred with the recommendation.

The French have on various occasions during the past eighteen months requested us to make ECA assistance available to them for use in Indochina. On each occasion we pointed out to them that such aid could not be given at this time but that if a substantial measure of progress were made by the French Government toward finding a solution to their difficulties in FIC we would be willing to reconsider the matter. We even went so far as to tell them that "the United States had already indicated its willingness if the French Government so desired to give public indication of its approval of concrete steps by French Government to come to grips with basic political problem of Indochina". On March 8th an agreement was signed by Bao Dai and President Auriol. The prospect of favorable action by the French Assembly with regard to the status of Cochinchina and the imminence of Bao Dai's return to Indochina have led us to believe that the French may well now consider themselves in a position to request "a public indication of our approval". In view of our repeated and unsolicited offer to do so it is believed that we should go through with it unless unforeseen changes make it inadvisable to do so.

While we obviously do not wish to get ourselves involved in a repetition of the painful Chiang Kai-shek situation, we must realize that the only alternative to a Bao Dai regime is one led by the Communist Ho Chi Minh. It is therefore believed that Bao Dai, although a very weak reed, represents the only solution to France's problem in Indochina and we should give him such support as we can without getting ourselves involved with him in case he turns out to be a failure.

Should the French come to us with a request for a statement of public approval it is recommended that we issue a brief, carefully worded statement indicating our gratification over the progress being made by France and Viet Nam toward finding a solution of their difficulties. This could be done in answer to a query at a press conference.

With respect to direct ECA aid for Indochina it is recommended that when the French raise the question we inform them that we are willing to consider such a request on all its merits, and that, if a project clearly contributes to the objective of European recovery, favorable action would be considered.

(128) <u>TELEGRAM FROM ACHESON TO THE CONSULATE GENERAL IN SAIGON, MAY 10, 1949</u>

Source: *Foreign Relations, 1949, Vol. VII*, pp. 23-25.

In another turn in US policy toward the Bao Dai experiment, Acheson, while expressing a cautious attitude toward recognition of Bao Dai, introduced the idea that support by non-Communist Asain governments would help remove from the Bao Dai regime the appearance of a U.S.-French-British "gambit".

Assumption urtel 141 Dept desires success Baodai experiment entirely correct. Since appears be no other alternative to estab Commie pattern Vietnam, Dept considers no effort shld be spared by Fr, other Western powers, and non-Commie Asian nations to asure experiment best chance succeeding.

At proper time and under proper circumstances Dept will be prepared do its part by extending recognition Baodai Govt and by exploring possibility of complying with any request by such Govt for US arms and econ assistance. Must be understood however aid program this nature wld require Congressional approval. Since US cld however scarcely afford backing govt which wld have color and be likely suffer fate of puppet regime, it must first be clear Fr will offer all necessary concessions to make Baodai solution attractive to nationalists. This is step of which Fr themselves must see urgent necessity view possibly short time remaining before Commie successes Chi are felt Indochina. Moreoever, Baodai Govt must through own efforts demonstrate capacity organize and conduct affairs wisely so as to ensure maximum opportunity obtaining requisite popular support inasmuch as govt created Indochina analogous Kuomintang wld be foredoomed failure.

Assuming essential Fr concessions are forthcoming, best chance success Baodai wld appear lie in persuading Vietnamese nationalists (1) their patriotic aims may be realized promptly through Fr-Baodai agreement (2) Baodai govt will be truly representative even to extent including outstanding non-Commie leaders now supporting Ho and (3) Baodai solution probably only means safeguarding Vietnam from aggressive designs Commie Chi. While attainment these objectives depends initially upon attitude Fr and Baodai circle, Dept believes more will ultimately be required. Best hope might lie in active demonstration of interest in and support of Baodai solution by other non-Commie Asian govts. Appeal such solution to Vietnam nationalists wld presumably be far greater if it had appeared sponsored by free Asian nations animated by interest self-determination Asian peoples and their own self-preservation in face immed Commie menace rather than if it had appearance gambit engineered by Fr, US and UK as part strategy of West-East conflict.

Dept giving closest consideration to means whereby US might assist attainment these ends.

From above, you will see Dept thinking closely parallels your own. Dept agrees when time comes Baodai must certainly be fully warned of danger yielding to any temptation include Commies his govt and this connection again believes other Asian govts cld serve most useful purpose since India, Siam, Philippines, and Indonesians (both Repubs and Federalists) are fully alive growing Commie threat Asia.

Re last para urtel 141 "reliability Baodai solution" was error. Deptel 70 shld have read "viability" meaning able live.

While Dept continues believe it wld be premature and unwise for you make special point (such as trip Dalat) see Baodai, there no objection your talking informally with polit personalities close to him with whom you have doubtless already made contact in normal course carrying out your functions. In such talks you might well as suggested urtel 141 take occasion cite examples futility collaboration Commies and grave danger such course.

---

(129) MEMORANDUM OF CONVERSATION, BY CHARLTON OGBURN, JR., DIVISION OF SOUTHEAST ASIAN AFFAIRS, DEPARTMENT OF STATE, MAY 17, 1949

Source: *Foreign Relations, 1949, Vol. VII*, p. 27.

A meeting between representatives of the Western European and Southeast Asian Divisions of the Department concluded both that the Bao Dai experiment had little chance to succeed, given the terms of the March Elysee Agreement, and that the French were not going to make concessions which would give the Bao Dai government the appearance of independence.

Participants: Mr. John Davies, SP
                Mr. Douglas MacArthur, II, WE
                Mr. Elim O'Shaughnessy, WE
                Mr. G. McMurtrie Godley, WE
                Mr. Charles S. Reed, SEA
                Mr. W.S.B. Lacy, SEA
                Mr. Charlton Ogburn, Jr., SEA

The meeting was called to consider what steps, if any, we might profitably take in Indochina.

The SEA representatives noted that the agreement of March 8 between Baodai and Auriol left France in nearly full control of Vietnam's foreign relations and in substantial control of Vietnam's armed forces and hence that there seemed little chance that the agreement would appeal to Vietnamese nationalists or that the Baodai experiment would succeed.

The WE representatives explained that there was no chance whatsoever of the French making any concessions at the present time beyond those contained in the agreement, and that for us to press them to do so would only stiffen and antagonize them.

It was the consensus of the meeting that the US should not put itself in a forward position in the Indochina problem since there appeared to be nothing we could do to alter the very discouraging prospects, and we should endeavor to "collectivize" our approach to the situation.

Accordingly, it was determined that WE would instruct Embassy Paris to endeavor to obtain openly the text of the agreement between Baodai and Auriol in order that we might discuss it with the French and other governments. Embassy Paris would also be instructed to obtain copies of the documents associated with the agreement, some of which the Department has not received from any source and which are believed to include provisions for the transfer of the federal services to the Bao-dai Government.

(130) TELEGRAM FROM ACHESON TO THE CONSULATE IN SAIGON, MAY 20, 1949

Source: *Foreign Relations, 1949, Vol. VII*, pp. 28-29.

Commenting on the "Bao Dai solution," Acheson expressed the Department's view that the Vietnamese independence movement was too strong to be defeated, and that France should preserve its influence by establishing a "special relationship" with a cooperate regime based on unconditional independence. Conceding that this desired course had been rejected by France, he hoped that Vietnamese nationalists would support Bao Dai because of identification of the Viet Minh with the Chinese Communists.

Urtel 147: Dept believes extent to which Fr concessions embodies Mar 8 agreements will satisfy nationalists can be determined only by reaction nationalists themselves. Meanwhile wld appreciate your view.

While not fully informed provisions Mar 8 agreements plus associated documents, Dept fears nationalist opinion will follow line Duoc Viet editorial Apr 9 which states "although Vietnamese reassured on score their country's unification, they remain uneasy about question foreign relations and army. Vietnam sovereignty will not permit Vietnamese army be commanded by Fr general nor will requirement of sovereignty be satisfied by diplomatic representation only in China, Siam and Vatican."

As practical matter, Dept believes that when independence movement in colony too strong to be defeated, metropolitan power if it wishes preserve influence in area has no real choice but attempt establish special relationship with former colony based free acceptance terms by latter, and that assoc between metropolitan power and former colony is more likely prove fruitful and durable if based free consent of latter than if transfer of autonomous powers to latter is made conditional upon its acceptance of such important qualifications upon its independence as continued metropolitan control its for relations and command armed forces.

However, Dept persuaded Fr unlikely make further concessions this time and that any US efforts press them do so wld probably miscarry. (Paris to indicate if this not correct.) Hope is, therefore, that Fr will carry out their obligations under Mar 8 agreements with such generosity and expedition that impressively constructive atmosphere will be created and that at same time Viet nationalists will rapidly appreciate true character menace approaching from Chi and will prefer cooperate Baodai solution rather than accept alternative continued resistance and risk loss all real autonomy to Chi Commies. Presumably such outcome not impossible particularly if Fr cld let it be understood Baodai agreement does not permanently define status Vietnam but provides basis for further early evolution.

At same time, shld it appear as Dept fears that Fr are offering too little too late, Dept will not be inclined make up for Fr deficiencies by rushing into breach to support Baodai agreements at cost its own remaining prestige Asia. Dept considers US this stage shld avoid conspicuous position any kind and try reach common attitude with other interested govts, particularly UK, India and Philippines.

(131) TELEGRAM FROM ACHESON TO THE CONSULATE IN HANOI, MAY 20, 1949

Source: *Foreign Relations, 1949, Vol. VII*, pp. 29-30.

In response to some Vietnamese suspicions that the U.S. might not be opposed to participation by Viet Minh leadership in a future government, Acheson pictured Viet-nam as losing its independence either to Russia or China if the anti-Communists did not prevail, dismissing the idea of a "national communist" state as only a "theoretical possibility". He indicated the U.S. preference for an all-out effort against the Communists under the most favorable circumstances - i.e., while French troops were still in Viet-nam.

Reur informative tel 36: In talks Xuan and reps his govt you may take fol line as representing consensus informed Americans:

In light Ho's known background, no other assumption possible but that he outright Commie so long as (1) he fails unequivocally repudiate Moscow connections and Commie doctrine and (2) remains personally singled out for praise by internatl Commie press and receives its support. Moreover, US not impressed by nationalist character red flag with yellow stars. Question whether Ho as much nationalist as Commie is irrelevant. All Stalinists in colonial areas are nationalists. With achievement natl aims (i.e., independence) their objective necessarily becomes subordination state to Commie purposes and ruthless extermination not only opposition groups but all elements suspected even slightest deviation. On basis examples eastern Eur it must be assumed such wld be goal Ho and men his stamp if included Baodai Govt. To include them in order achieve reconciliation opposing polit elements and "national unity" wld merely postpone settlement issue whether Vietnam to be independent nation or Commie satellite until circumstances probably even less favorable nationalists than now. It must of course be conceded theoretical possibility exists estab National Communist state on pattern Yugoslavia in any area beyond reach Soviet army. However, US attitude cld take acct such possibility only if every other possible avenue closed to preservation area from Kremlin control. Moreover, while Vietnam out of reach Soviet army it will doubtless be by no means out of reach Chi Commie hatchet men and armed forces.

Fol is for urinfo and such reference as you deem judicious:

Dept naturally considers only Fr can through concessions to nationalist movement lay basis for solution Indochina problem. As suggested Deptel 83 to Saigon, if nationalists find concessions Mar 8 agreements inadequate, much may depend upon willingness Fr put agreements in most favorable possible context by emphasizing expectations rapid evolution Vietnam beyond status envisaged those agreements. Provided Fr display realistic and generous attitude, most important part remainder immed program - viz, winning support nationalists away

from Commie leadership - must devolve upon Baodai and Xuan group seconded by
other South Asian govts who stand in most immed danger from Commie conquest
Indochina and who by full polit and propaganda support Baodai solution might
more that anyone else be able to deprive Ho of talking-points in event he continues demand armed resistance Baodai regardless circumstances (which appears
certain in light vitriolic tone current Vietminh broadcasts on Baodai which
give no recognition any Fr concessions to nationalist demands). Even with conditions for US support Baodai realized it futile expect US be able assist effectively this initial task beyond stressing requirements situation in talks
South Asian govts and providing materials evidencing realities of Communism
through USIS for distribution as you and Congen Saigon consider desirable in
conjunction with Baodai efforts arouse compatriots to Commie menace.   Experience Chi has shown no amt US mil and econ aid can save govt, even if recognized
by all other powers and possessed full opportunity achieve natl aims, unless it
can rally support people against Commies by affording representation all important natl groups, manifesting devotion to natl as opposed to personal or Party
interests, and demonstrating real leadership.

Re Viet opinion reported Saigon's 145 that US abandonment Nationalist China
presents unfavorable augury for non-Commie regime Vietnam, there no objection
emphasizing to persons with this view that Nationalist China came to present
pass through deficiency above qualities and lack will to fight, not because US
"wrote it off".

Re Xuan query whether US wld propose Vietnam for membership UN shld Fr
renege, you sld avoid descussion this matter, at most is pressed state circumstances at moment will of course determine US action For urinfo only it unlikely
US cld even vote for Vietnam membership US if as it appears now Fr wld remain
in control Vietnam fon relations.

(132) MEMORANDUM BY THE DEPARTMENT OF STATE TO THE FRENCH FOREIGN OFFICE, JUNE 6, 1949

Source: *Foreign Relations, 1949, vol. VII*, pp. 39-45.

*Despite the conviction of U.S. officials that France would go no further in
yielding its formal position in Indochina, the State Department formulated its
views on the issue for presentation to the French government. The memorandum,
written by the Far Eastern Division, recapitulated the views which had been
expressed by Marshall and Acheson for more that two years, concluding that the
"nationalists" could only be separated from the "Communists" by giving up all
French powers which limited Viet-nam's formal sovereignty.*

The Government of the United States is most appreciative of the action of
the French Government in making available to it the text of the agreement concluded on March 8 between the President of France and the former Emperor of
Annam defining the future status of the State of Vietnam. The agreement has
been studied with the greatest interest by the Department of State.

As the French Government is aware, the United States Government has followed
with some concern the course of events in French Indochina since the end of the
war in the Pacific. This concern, it is needless to say, has been prompted by
a realization that the forces which have contributed predominantly to the character of the Vietnamese nationalist movement are manifestations of the same
forces which have worked profound changes in southern Asia generally and that
the outcome of these forces can be of considerable consequence for the world
in general.

When at the end of the war it became evident that in most of the dependent
countries of southern Asia the indigenous peoples were determined to control
their own destinies in the future, the United States Government ventured to hope

that the western nations would appreciate the strength of this resolution and willingly grant the essential demands of the nationalist movements. It was believed that in so doing, the metropolitan powers would be yielding what in any case they could expect to hold only by military force at great cost. In such event it seemed probable that the costs to the Metropolitan Government would be unrecoverable and the value of the colony and its possible contribution to world stability would be reduced by the ensuant hostilities. On the other hand it was believed that by promptly offering the necessary political concessions to the nationalist demands the metropolitan power would be adopting the course most likely to result in a continued close and mutually fruitful relationship with the former colony, in the preservation of patterns of trade and economy long intermeshed, and in a readiness on the part of the colonial people to welcome the continued technical and administrative assistance of the metropolitan power. It appeared that only on such a basis would there be any real hope that the Western powers could retain their legitimate interests in the countries so closely associated with them over such long periods, and that among the new nations of southern Asia conditions of political stability and of freedom of political and economic development could be achieved enabling them to realize their potentialities and make their full contribution to the world.

Conversely, it seemed that an intention on the part of the metropolitan power to restrain an authority which the dependent people was determined to exercise itself could result only in turning the nationalist movement into destructive channels. In these circumstances it could be expected that widespread hostilities would result and that the consequent destruction of the facilities of production in the dependent area would cause economic setbacks seriously injurious to both peoples. Furthermore, it could be anticipated that the nationalist forces would turn increasingly to an uncompromising leadership which would react against cooperation with the West and against those free institutions which European civilization has evolved through long experience in self-government.

Events in southern Asia in the past four years have caused no revision of these views; and it is in the light of this estimate that the United States Government has examined the agreement of March 8 and offers its views.

Because of its conviction that concession by France to the Nationalist movement commensurate with the strength of that movement can alone provide the basis for a resolution of the Indochinese situation and the creation of a stable, representative Vietnamese Government, the United States Government welcomes the step taken by the President of France in arriving at an agreement with ex-Emperor Bao Dai whereby the territorial unity of Vietnam, comprising Tonkin, Annam, and Cochinchina, may be realized and the Vietnamese State enjoy far reaching powers of internal autonomy. It may be stated at once that in the opinion of the United States Government the Vietnamese people would be guilty of a mistake disastrous to their future should they reject this solution and give their support not to the Vietnamese Government formed under the March 8 agreement but to the so-called Democratic Republic of Vietnam. For those in command of this Republic are men trained in the methods and doctrine of international communism, and regardless of their present espousal of the nationalist cause, it cannot be ignored that they have never disavowed their Kremlin connections or repudiated the techniques and objectives of communism, which are the cause of so much suffering in the world today. It must be assumed, therefore, that should their government succeed in its aims with the support or through the acquiescence of of the Vietnamese people, the pattern of a foreign totalitarianism will be clamped upon Vietnam under which all liberties, national and personal, will be lost. Such an outcome would not only be fatal to the welfare and hopes of the Vietnamese but would be most detrimental to the interests of all free peoples, particularly those of southern Asia who stand in most immediate danger of further Communist aggression.

However, the United States Government does not feel confident that the Vietnamese people in general will see the choice confronting them in these terms, especially in view of the isolating factors in their situation during most of the past decade. The Vietnamese nationalists who for the most part have been supporting the so-called Democratic Republic of Vietnam as the one agency which appeared to promise independence may not, it is feared, find the provisions of the March 8 agreement entirely appealing. In this connection, it should be pointed out that the United States Government is considering only this agreement since it is not familiar with the contents of any associated documents which may bear upon the matter and does not know whether the March 8 agreement is intended to define the status of Vietnam permanently or to provide a basis for the further early evolution of the Vietnamese State.

The United States Government is inclined to believe that one of the strongest motivating forces behind nationalist movements among dependent peoples is resentment of the imputation of inferiority implicit in a subordinate status. When a people has fought for the goal of independence with such tenacity as that displayed by the Vietnamese resistance forces, it appears unlikely that it will be content with a position of anything less than equality with other peoples. It is feared that the concessions granted by the French Government may be obscured in the eyes of the Vietnamese people by those terms of the agreement which are incompatible with Vietnamese national pride.

Should such feelings determine the reaction of the majority of Vietnamese to a Government formed under the March 8 agreement, then it must be supposed that the Communist-dominated "Democratic Republic of Vietnam" will continue to receive the support of these Vietnamese. Certainly as long as the Vietnamese are persuaded that the two-and-a-half-year-old war with France must be prosecuted to a conclusion if the goals for which they have fought are to be won, they will continue to regard the dominant Communist element of the Vietnamese League in the light of its effective leadership of the nationalist movement and not of its inevitible intention to subvert the nationalist cause in the end to the requirements of international Communism, with which they have little acquaintance as yet.

The United States Government would be lacking in frankness if it did not state that in its considered estimation the paramount question in Indochina now is whether the country is to be saved from communist control. Under the circumstances, all other issues must be considered as irrelevant. Much time has already been lost. The years since the end of the Pacific War have seen the Communist threat to Indochina intensified rather than otherwise. The southward progress of Chinese Communist armies toward the northern frontier of Indochina introduces a new element that transforms an already serious situation into an emergency.

As it has made clear in the past, the United States Government is of the opinion that it must prove difficult to save this situation, and to preserve Indochina from a foreign tyranny unless the French Government offers the Vietnamese the attainment of those nationalist goals which they would continue to fight for rather than forego and unless the Vietnamese can be convinced that they can, in fact, fully realize their patriotic aims through cooperation with the Government envisaged in the March 8 agreement. In its view, developments have reduced the choice in Indochina to simple alternatives: will Vietnam achieve independence through an agreement with France and with the assistance of France and maintain this independence fortified by collaboration with France, or will it achieve independence from France while at the same time falling victim to Communist totalitarianism?

The United States Government believes that the Vietnamese will willingly accept a partnership with France only if the equality of Vietnam is recognized and if, as a prior condition to the determination of the character of this relationship, the sovereignty of Vietnam is acknowledged. Observation of developments in southern Asia since the end of the war would seem to leave little doubt that a union between France and Vietnam would be far more likely of attainment and would prove more fruitful and enduring if attained were the Union conceived not as an instrument for the control of one member by the other but as an agency of cooperation in the fields of common interest, diplomatic, military, economic, and cultural, voluntarily espoused on both sides.

An approach to the future on these lines would appear to offer the greatest hope that French influence in Indochina may be preserved, which must be regarded as unquestionable the best interests of the Indochinese, and that military and naval bases in Vietnam may be retained by France and French economic rights be assured. By adopting this course the metropolitan country would appear to have little to lose and much to gain. Moreover, from a strictly practical point of view, the United States Government has been impressed by the difficulties likely to arise if in transferring autonomous powers to the government of a dependent territory the metropolitary power seeks as a condition to such transfer, to subdivide sovereignty in the area by retaining certain transcendent rights to itself. For in this case the question of the precise division of authority is prone to present itself in connection with every field of government as the process of transfer is planned. In consequence, the prestige and good will which accrue to the metropolitan power from its acceptance of a new order is likely to be dissipated in an atmosphere of discord and mistrust, as suspicion grows among the nationalists that the metropolitan power is in fact seeking to perpetuate its existing controls. In consequence the process of giving definition to the new order and establishing it in practice may be indefinitely protracted, with results which may defeat the enterprise.

A dispassionate appraisal leads the United States Government to believe, in short, that the preservation of Indochina's integrity depends, in the first place, upon the willingness of the metropolitan country to give assurances that Vietnam is to exercise control of its destinies; that its participation in the French Union will be upon terms freely accepted by representatives enjoying the confidence of the Vietnamese people when these shall have been assembled; that the powers of administration exercised by France in Vietnam will be transferred to the Vietnamese as soon as conditions permit the institution and functioning of the new regime; and that the deployment of French forces in Vietnam outside their bases to be accounted for in terms of the defense of Vietnam against the protagonists of a supranational totalitarianism who would surrender Vietnam to alien controls.

In the second place, much would appear to depend upon the readiness of the heads of the Vietnamese Government formed under the March 8 agreement to invite the participation in this Government of bonafide and truly nationalist leaders of Vietnam, including those who have heretofore supported the "Democratic Republic of Vietnam", to the end that this Government may provide dynamic leadership and obtain the confidence of the nationalist elements comprising the major part of the resistance forces.

Such an approach to the problem would best appear to lay the basis for the clear separation of nationalists from Communist elements in Vietnam; for those who persisted in resisting a Vietnamese Government through which all nationalist aims could be realized in favor of continued adherence to the "Democratic Republic of Vietnam" would in effect be acknowledging that their goals were not nationalist but Communist. The achievement of this distinction would appear to be the *sine qua non* of a solution of the Indochina problem.

Having determined its capacity to rally the nationalist majority of Vietnamese to its support, the Government formed under the March 8 agreement would - it would seem to the United States Government - have grounds for appealing for the support of all free nations. The United States Government would hope that this appeal would be generally heeded, especially by the other Governments of Southern Asia which, themselves having every reason to regard the further extension of Communist controls in the region with alarm, could fill a vitally important role by clarifying for the Vietnamese people the issues confronting them on the basis of their own experience and undoubted fidelity to the cause of self-determination by the Asian peoples.

The United States Government is, however, convinced that if the requisite concessions by the French Government to the nationalist demands are not forthcoming, the task of the Government envisaged in the March 8 agreement must prove most difficult of accomplishment and the countries adjacent to Indochina will likely be confronted by the prospect of the appearance of sizable Communist-controlled forces on their frontiers.

It goes without saying that the earnest hope of the United States Government is that the Government formed under the March 8 agreement will succeed in its crucial task. At the same time it would appear axiomatic that insofar as the probabilities of its success are related to the extent of international support it obtains, the decision of a third party in respect of the feasibility of its extending support or assistance must be governed by the extent to which the French Government has itself provided that Government with the political advantages upon which its appeal to the Vietnamese must be based. Clearly the success of this Government must rest in the first instance upon those means of accomplishing its purpose which only the French Government can provide.

In taking advantage of the relations of cordiality and mutual understanding it enjoys with the French Government by offering this frank appraisal, the United States Government has been prompted by the thought that it should not leave the direction of its thinking a matter of doubt and that an exchange of views might be advantageous considering all that is involved in the outcome of the situation in Indochina.

(133) TELEGRAM FROM CONSUL GENERAL GEORGE ABBOTT IN SAIGON TO ACHESON, JUNE 10, 1049

Source: *Foreign Relations, 1949, Vol VII*, p. 45.

After Bao Dai indicated privately his desire for U.S. assistance, the consulate in Saigon joined the Embassy in Paris in urging the Department to put aside its caution and embrace the Bao Dai Government, politically as well as economically, suggesting that the U.S. could help the ex-Emperor by "building up his prestige" through public statement of support.

Consider Bao Dai's views on hoped for aid from US (Paris telegram 2230 and 2258, June 2 and 3 [2] repeated Saigon 86 and 87) relatively modest with exception point 6 and hope Dept may feel it is possible to give them prompt consideration. In addition points brought out in Paris 2258 (with which entirely agree) feel that too long delayed indication our support new Vietnam state will deprive us of opportunity to exert influence on developments during crucial initial period when many important policy decisions will have to be taken by both French and Bao Dai.

Prolonged delay will also be interpreted by many as sign that US sees no hope for success Bao Dai and is resigned to future inclusion area in Communist sphere. Effect of this on non-Communist nationalists weighing pros and cons of throwing their lot in with Bao Dai can be imagined.

If as it is hoped the Dept is prepared to issue a favorable statement regarding the new regime, it is suggested it include friendly mention of Bao Dai in his capacity as mediator between all truly nationalist and non-Communist elements. Recent developments emphasize importance of building up prestige and authority ex-Emperor as essential cohesive element in otherwise confused political situation.

It is believed that Bao Dai's message to people planned for June 13 will contain statement of policy on democratic consultation of people re future for government agrarian and social reforms cooperation with other nations, et cetera, which might be noted in Dept's statement.

(134) TELEGRAM FROM AMBASSADOR DAVID BRUCE IN PARIS TO ACHESON, JUNE 13, 1949

Source: *Foreign Relations, 1949, Vol. VII*, p. 61-62.

Ambassador David Bruce insisted that the State Department memorandum to the Foreign Ministry not be delivered, calling it too pessimistic and repeating that France was politically incapable of going further. His recommendation was that the U.S. analysis of the problem be presented orally and that the policy conclusion be softened.

Departments's instruction 289, June 6. The following are my considered views. We are unanimous in thinking it would be a serious mistake to deliver Department's memorandum. The Secretary has read both the memorandum and my reply which follows and concurs with us that the delivery of such views expressed by the Department would at this time be inappropriate.

Embassy has attentively and exhaustively considered memorandum enclosed Department's instruction 289 and has reached conclusion that while it is an excellect summary of Department's thinking on latter day aspects of colonial problem and its relationship to both strong current of nationalism in SEA and to latter's tragic corollary of Communism, its presentation to French officials at this time would impede rather than encourage achievement by French of Department's desiderata.

Members of cabinet and other French officials concerned with formulation of Indochina policy are battered and bruised by the long struggle against prejudice, self-interest and political opportunism from which they have emerged with a partial triumph embodied in March 8 agreements and passage of Cochin-China bill. While many of them have their doubts, as has the Department, as to whether the March 8 agreements are entirely adequate or whether Bao Dai has astuteness and ability necessary for success, they are equally aware that there is no present alternative to them and that they must live with the document and with the man throughout the early phases of the experiment. In their eyes the Department's memorandum would constitute not only a discouraging document in that it unfavorably prejudges outcome of an experiment which has not yet got off to fair start and implies that US will support it only in unlikely event that it succeeds, but also an unrealistic document in that its references to further concessions suggests that March 8 agreements be renegotiated. (In this connection please see Embtel 2189, May 30 explaining why March 8 agreements cannot be renegotiated.) Under the circumstances effect produced on these officials would be opposite of constructive at time when their best efforts are required to help Bao Dai experiment succeed.

For the above reasons I strongly urge that I be authorized to give the French orally a resume of the Department's general views on problem as a whole as contained in first four and a half pages of Department's memorandum and simultaneously continue to urge the adoption of a liberal interpretation and loyal implementation of the agreements already reached and a similarly generous attitude in the negotiations still to be conducted.

At the same time I am hopeful that Department is giving sympathetic consideration to suggestions advanced in mytels 2258, June 2 and 2300, June 7.

(135) STATEMENT BY THE DEPARTMENT OF STATE ON THE ELYSEE AGREEMENTS, JUNE 21, 1949

Source: *U.S. Department of State Bulletin, XXI, (July 18, 1949)*, p. 75.

As the U.S. had promised previously to the French, the State Department issued a statement of cautious support for French policy in signing the Elysee Agreements.

The formation of the new unified state of Vietnam and the recent announce-ment by Bao Dai that the future constitution will be decided by the Vietnamese people are welcome developments which should serve to hasten the reestablishment of peace in that country and the attainment of Vietnam's rightful place in the family of nations.

The United States Government hopes that the agreements of March 8 between President Auriol and Bao Dai who is making sincere efforts to unite all truly nationalist elements within Vietnam, will form the basis for the progressive realization of the legitimate aspirations of the Vietnamese people.

(136) TELEGRAM FROM AMBASSADOR BRUCE TO ACHESON, JUNE 29, 1949

Source: *Foreign Relations, 1949, Vol. VII*, pp. 65-66.

The oral presentation by Ambassador Bruce to Foreign Minister Schuman did not criticise the French for their unwillingness or inability to go further than the limited sovereignty of the Elysee Agreement. The intention behind the State Department memorandum was thus nullified, and the U.S. advanced one step further toward supporting the government which would be based on the Elysee Agreement.

I had a long conversation with Schuman yesterday re Indochina. After giving him in detail views contained in first four and half pages of Department's memo (Depins 289, June 6), I went on to say that in case of Vietnam, US Government, without at this time offering comment on March 8 agreements, believes Vietnamese would commit serious mistake should they reject possibility of solution offered by those agreements and give their support not to government formed under them but to so-called Democratic Republic of Vietnam.

In furtherance this view US has given public welcome to formation new uni-fied Vietnamese state and has expressed hope March 8 agreements would form basis for early realization ligitimate aspirations Vietnamese people. I told Schuman US is, however, of firm opinion realization these goals would be most difficult of accomplishment in association with French Union should government-envisaged March 8 agreements fail to obtain support of truly national elements Vietnam. Our recent experience in China had given us abundant proof of fact no amount of moral and material aid can save government isolated from contact with its people and enjoying little popular support. US Government, therefore, of opinion that in absence definite schedule outlining successive steps of Vietnam's evolution towards independence, ability of new Vietnamese Government to attract popular support will, in overwhelming measure, depend on most liberal interpretation and implementation of agreements already reached and on similarly generous attitude in negotiation of various agreements remaining to be completed.

Insofar as success of government formed under March 8 agreements related to extent international support which it receives, US considers determining factor will be attitude towards new Vietnamese Government adopted by other nations SEA, many of which have, themselves, only recently emerged as independent states and who, if persuaded Vietnamese people will be given full measure self-government in near future, will be inclined not only grant new government moral status which in Asian eyes cannot be achieved by Western recognition alone, but also to enter into fruitful association with it, looking forward to solution grim common problem now facing all South Asian Governments.

I informed Schuman that in light foregoing, US feels that its future atti-tude must depend largely on those developments Vietnam which will determine pop-ular support and authority of new Vietnamese Government and on standing it achieves with neighboring governments. US of opinion attitude adopted by French Government will be major controlling factor this development and therefore urges bold and rapid implementation and interpretation March 8 agreements with view affording new Vietnamese Government maximum possibilities for realization of legitimate aspirations Vietnamese populations.

In conversation which followed I emphasized that there appeared to be two major elements essential to success Bao Dai experiment. First was internal and involved assuring new Vietnamese Government maximum opportunities obtain popular support. This was directly dependent upon liberal and enlightened French policy in rapid implementation of March 8 agreements. Second was external and depended largely on attitude which neighboring governments in SEA adopted towards new Vietnamese Government. Schuman replied that Assembly debates on Indochina and March 8 agreements marked successful realization of great step forward in evolution French policy in Indochina and assured me that French Government would implement this policy by most liberal interpretation and implementation of agreements. In this connection he remarked that for execution of its policy, France had in Pignon very able man of liberal school and moreover, General Revers had informed him - Schuman - that he had given categoric instructions to French military authorities in Indochina to give Pignon their full support and cooperation. Re neighboring countries SEA, he said he had instituted and was personally supervising program of information and interpretation. Foreign Office had already furnished text March 8 agreements to their representatives and would call them in to give them a full explanation French intentions and significance March 8 agreements.

I observed that of those countries, India seemed by far the most important and our information indicated that GOI, while so far not publicly indicating hostile attitude, was in fact most skeptical of French intentions Indochina. Schuman expressed surprise, saying that in his conversations with Indian representatives here, he had received impression GOI was favorably disposed towards Bao Dai solution. In view our information, he would personally see to it that French intentions were made clear to GOI.

(137) STATE DEPARTMENT REPORT FOR THE NATIONAL SECURITY COUNCIL, "U.S. POLICY TOWARD SOUTHEAST ASIA," (NSC 51), JULY 1, 1949

Source: Document Declassified by the National Security Council, April 7, 1973.

A comprehensive view of U.S. policy toward Southeast Asia again viewed French policy as a threat to western interests in maintaining non-Communist government in region. It accurately predicted a new conflict once French power was removed from Vietnam, in which the U.S. "working through a screen of anti-Communist Asiatics" would try to defeat the Communists.

57. The Indochinese situation is in an advanced stage of deterioration. The communists are dominant in the nationalist movement. They achieved this position by assuming the most aggressive role in resistance to French imperialism. This meant that all activist nationalist elements, including large numbers of non-communists, rallied around them to form a popular front known as the Viet Minh. The communists have maintained this dominance thanks to the constant military pressure exerted by the French, the effect of which has been to keep most nationalist elements pressed into reliance on the communists.

58. After an initial show of conciliation, French policy in Indochina was to reconquer and no nonsense. But it has simple not been in the realm of practicability for France to crush the Viet Minh by military means. The French military effort has therefore dwindled to footling punitive campaigns which have been and are a drain on the strength of France itself. As we do not contribute ERP aid directly to Indochina, the charges are passed on to us in Europe. The falseness of our position was last year made evident when, at great effort and with special Presidential sanction, we provided partial equipment for three French divisions in Germany while about 100,000 French troops with American equipment were and still are being squandered in Indochina on a mission which can be justified only in terms of Gallic mystique.

59. As the French came to comprehend that military measures were a delusion, they resorted to political maneuvers with native collaborators hoping to create a puppet regime which would, with French help, dispose of the Viet Minh and allow France to retain its paramountcy. But the French have been so niggardly in these negotiations that they have thus far failed to create an effective puppet regime capable of drawing nationalist elements away from the Viet Minh. Current negotiations with the ex-Emperor, Bao Dai, appear thus far to be of this description.

60. A constructive solution of the Indochinese impasse depends on the French yielding their claims to sovereignty to a native regime. Only if that is done will the false issue of French imperialism, which cements communists and non-communists in unity, be dissolved. A French withdrawal would permit the elementary indigenous forces in Indochina to come into full play. The basis conflict would be between nationalism and Stalinism. Nationalist elements would thereupon tend to gravitate away from the present Viet Minh popular front and coalesce in a nationalist anti-Stalinist organization. The strong anti-Chinese sentiments, now submerged by the issue of French imperialism, would likewise be released and act as a force resistant to Chinese Communist influence.

61. The French claim to sovereignty over Indochina could be yielded either to a regime composed of present collaborators of the French or to the Viet Minh. Provided that it is clear-cut and expeditious, a transfer to the former is of course preferable because the non-communist elements in Indochina would thereby be given an advantageous start. A withdrawl in favor of the Viet Minh would obviously be less desirable. It is debatable, however, whether it is more or less desirable than the Stalinist blind alley down which French policy is now blundering.

62. Whichever course were followed, civil war would sooner or later probably eventuate. With the dissolution of the present artificial situation, the new alignments would naturally be precipitated and come into conflict. Resistance to Soviet and Chinese communist influence would then for the first time possess deep and extensive roots in the Indochinese scene. But this new conflict, for foreign anti-communists, including ourselves, would be only a point of departure. It would then be necessary for us, working through a screen of anti-communist Asiatics, to ensure, however long it takes, the triumph of Indochinese nationalism over Red imperialism.

76. We should accept the fact that the crucial immediate issue in Southeast Asia - that of militant nationalism in Indonesia and Indochina - cannot be resolved by any of the following policies on our part: (1) full support of Dutch and French imperialism, (2) unlimited support of militant nationalism, or (3) evasion of the problem. Because the key to the solution of this issue lies primarily with the Netherlands and France, we should as a matter of urgent importance endeavor to induce the Dutch and French to adapt their policies to the realities of the current situation in Southeast Asia, as set forth in this paper. Our first step should be, in conjunction with the British, to set forth to the Dutch and French in candor, detail, and with great gravity our interpretation of the situation in and intentions with regard to SEA. We should make a major effort to persuade them to join us and the states mentioned in the following paragraph in a constructive overall approach to the region as a whole.

84. Because we are powerless to bring about a constructive solution of the explosive Indochinese situation through unilateral action, the determination of our future policy toward Indochina should await the outcome of the demarche recommended in paragraph 76 and the earliest feasible consultation with India and the Philippines.

(138) GENERAL CONVENTION BETWEEN FRENCH REPUBLIC AND THE KINGDOM OF LAOS, JULY 19, 1949 (Extracts)

Source: Australia, Department of External Affairs, Laos, *Select Documents on International Affairs, no. 16 (Canberra, 1970)*, p. 6.

In line with the Elysee Agreement between France and Bao Dai the French concluded an agreement with the Kingdom of Laos confirming French powers over foreign policy, military and judicial affairs, and fiscal and monetary matters.

TITLE I INDEPENDENCE - FRENCH UNION

The French Republic recognizes the Kingdom of Laos as an independent State.

The Kingdom of Laos reaffirms its adherence to the French Union as an Associated State, as expressed in the exchange of notes under date of November 25, 1947 and January 14, 1948 between the High Contracting Parties above mentioned:

Accordingly:

(a) The Kingdom of Laos undertakes to pool all its resources with the other members of the French Union to guarantee the defense of the Union as a whole. The Government of the French Republic assumes responsibility for the co-ordination of these resources and the direction of a suitable policy for preparing and ensuring such defence.

(b) The Kingdom of Laos will appoint delegates to the Assembly of the French Union within the limits and under the conditions fixed by the texts governing that organization.

(c) A special convention shall determine the representation of the Kingdom of Laos in the High Council of the French Union.

TITLE II RECIPROCAL COMMITMENTS

The French Republic undertakes:

(A) To ensure the defence of the frontiers of the Kingdom in collaboration with the Laotian National Army under the conditions to be fixed in an annexed military agreement;

(B) To make available to the Kingdom of Laos its diplomatic missions, which may include a representative of Laos as a member. Moreover, the Kingdom of Laos may be represented by its own diplomatic mission in certain countries to be determined after agreement with the French Government. . .

The unity of the foreign policy of the French Union in the State in which the Kingdom of Laos has its own diplomatic mission shall be ensured both by the general directives drawn up, after consultation with the High Council of the French Union, and transmitted by the Government of the Republic to the Government of Laos, and by direct contacts with the French and the Laotian diplomats shall maintain between themselves.

Such mission may be empowered to negotiate and sign agreements concerning Laos' own interests. Before entering any negotiation, the Royal Government undertakes to submit its proposals to the Government of the Republic for examination by the High Council; negotiations shall be conducted in liaison with the French diplomatic mission. . .

The heads of foreign diplomatic missions in Laos shall be accredited to the President of the French Union and His Majesty the King of Laos;

(C) To represent and support the candidacy of the Kingdom of Laos for membership in the United Nations when it shall have fulfilled the general conditions laid down in the United Nations Charter for admission to that organization;

(D) To provide the Royal Government with the services of technicians and experts under the conditions to be fixed by an annexed convention. . .

(E) For a specific period and under conditions to be determined, to supply Laos with financial assistance.

(F) To make temporarily available to the Royal Government, under conditions to be determined, such technical missions as it requests or undertake the performance of certain public services. . .

The Kingdom of Laos undertakes:

(A) To grant the French Union the right to have stationed and to have circulate on Laotian territory any land, sea or air forces necessary for the defence of the exterior frontiers of Laos and for the common defence of the States of Indo-China. These forces may organise on the territory of Loas such land, air and river bases as are determined in an annexed convention;

(B) To grant every facility for the recruitment of the contingents necessary to raise and maintain mixed Franco-Laotian units which form part of the troops of the French Union. . .

Justice: The Kingdom of Laos will retain full jurisdiction over all civil, commercial and criminal action throughout the territory of the Kingdom.

Nevertheless, civil and commercial action brought between French nationals or between Laotians and French nationals or nationals of the French Union other than Laotains or foreigners, and criminal proceedings instituted because of violations involving or injuring these same categories of persons or committed to the prejudice of the French State, shall be referred to courts of the French Union, which shall apply French law. . .

TITLE III ASSOCIATED STATES OF INDO-CHINA

Laos, considering the fact that it has common interests with Viet-nam and Cambodia on the one hand and with the French Union on the other . . . recognises the advisability of the creation of joint agencies for the study, harmonisation, and promotion of the said interests. To that end, Laos agrees to enter into:

(a) A monetary union with other Associated States of Indo-China. The sole currency to be legal tender in the territory of this monetary union shall be the piastre belonging to the franc area and issued by the institution of issue of Indo-China;

(b) A customs union with the Associated States of Indo-China.

Moreover, a conference, to be held in Indo-China at the instance of the High Commissioner and at which, in addition to the Government of the French Republic and the Royal Government of Laos, the Governments of Viet-Nam and Cambodia shall be represented, shall determine the composition and extent of the powers of the joint agencies in question . . .

TITLE IV

1. The exchange of notes of November 25, 1947 and January 14, 1948, the present Convention, and annexed conventions shall constitute the Act provided for in Article 61 of the French Constitution. They shall annul and supersede and previous Acts that may have been concluded between France and Laos.

2. With due regard for circumstances and for the international commitments of France, annexed conventions shall determine the methods of transfer to Laos of the powers now exercised by the French authorities . . . .

(139) LETTER BY HO CHI MINH TO THE VIETNAMESE PEOPLE, AUGUST 20, 1949

Source: Ho Chi Minh, *Selected Works, Vol. III*, pp. 175-176.

The beginning of preparations for the General Counteroffensive required a new level of mobilization of resources - both human and economic - for the battlefield in a rice economy already ravaged by war. Ho called on his people to "reward the army" for its sacrifices by each one selling ten kilograms of rice to the government.

Elders,
Prominent personalities,
Compatriots,
On the occasion of the anniversary of the National Day which will take place

on September the Second, I wish to reward our armymen who are heroically fighting to safeguard the national independence won back by our people.
    But what to reward them with?
    The sages say:
    "With sufficient food the Army is strong."
    Thus to reward them with food is the most simple and practical thing.
    But I have no rice.
    That is why I ask you to do that in my name.
    May I ask each household to sell me ten kilograms of rice under the follow-
ing conditions.
    1 kilogram of rice will be paid for with 50 dongs.
    Poor households will not sell any.
    Those who can sell a greater quantity are welcomed.
    Those who sell their rice are requested to receive due payment because I do
not want you to have too many losses.
    Delivery and payment conditions will be fixed by the village Resistance and
Administrative Committee.
    I am certain that you are ready to help me in this matter. I thank you
beforehand and I will write individual letters to thank those who sell the stated
quantity of rice in villages, districts and provinces.
    Affectionate greetings of friendship and determination to win.

(140) MEMORANDUM OF CONVERSATION BETWEEN ACHESON AND FRENCH FOREIGN MINISTER
ROBERT SCHUMAN, SEPTEMBER 15, 1949, AND AMONG ACHESON, SCHUMAN AND BRITISH
FOREIGN MINISTER ERNEST BEVIN, SEPTEMBER 17, 1949

Source: *Foreign Relations, 1949, Vol III*, pp. 86-89.

*In the first conversation between U.S. and French Foreign Ministers on the
subject of Indochina, Acheson backed away from the position taken by the Department earlier in the year on unfettered independence for Viet-nam and committed
the U.S. to help get Asian countries to recognize the Bao Dai Government.*

    Mr. Schuman outlined France's views on the Indochinese situation as follows:
    France is faced with a very serious situation in Indochina because of the
heavy financial strain it places on French budgetary equilibrium. French expenditures in Indochina would amount this year to almost 200 billion francs,
approximately one-eighth of the total French budget.
    He said that the French efforts to prevent Indochina from falling into Com-
munist hands transcended and went far beyond French national interests since
French action represented the hard core of resistance to Communists attempts to
take over Indochina with a view ultimately to take over all of Southeast Asia.
France was therefore fighting the battle of all the democratic powers and would
need assistance to hold Indochina. He realized that it was politically impossible for the United States to give military aid to Indochina but there were forms
of economic assistance which the United States could give. The assistance need
not be given directly to France but be given to the three governments (the Viet-
nam state of Bao Dai which unites the three *kys*; Laos; and Cambodia) which France
had established in Indochina. In this connection France had turned over a large
measure of independence to these governments and was sponsoring a truly nationalist movement in Indochina so that these governments could win the support of the
overwhelming majority of the inhabitants who were certainly not pro-Communist.
He said that the Bao Dai agreements of March 8 did not represent a limit to the
concessions which the French would eventually make and that France intended to
follow an enlightened course looking to greater self-government. Mr Schuman
hoped that the United States also would support these independent governments.
    In concluson Schuman said he wished to point out that a number of people
were perhaps laboring under the mistaken belief that if France got out of

Indochina the native inhabitants would have a better chance of attaining real independence. This was an erroneous viewpoint since at the present time the three infant governments were capable of succeeding also and would need French military assistance to survive the Communist efforts to take over the country and also would need French technical assistance to arrive at a point where they could cope with their own internal problems of organization. In other words the presence of the French Army and French technical advisers was indispensable to the emergence of truly nationalist and independent states in Indochina. He re-iterated that France intended to be most liberal in dealing with these govern-ments so that gradually they could attain an increasing degree of independence. He said that in a sense France had been penalized for trying to hold the line against Communist efforts in Indochina since as a result thereof Indochina had been excluded from the benefits of the Marshall Plan.

The Secretary replied that he was very glad to have had Mr. Schuman outline the French position to him and he was particularly glad to note that in many re-spects the French thinking was close to our own. The Secretary that he could not give Mr. Schuman any reply as to the question of what aid might be given to Indochina as he would have to study the matter very carefully. He said, however, that we realized that the presence of French troops and technical advisers in In-dochina was indispensable at this stage of the game and for a considerable time to come and that we had never suggested that the French withdraw and abandon In-dochina. The Secretary said that we carefully recognized the importance of In-dochina in connection with the whole Southeast Asia picture but that he did be-lieve the French could play a great role in preventing Communist domination by moving quickly wherever possible to satisfy the truly nationalist aspirations of the inhabitants.

In connection with the question of what might be done for the governments in Indochina, the Secretary said he hoped the French Parliament would ratify the March 8 Agreements rapidly but he wished to mention that at present the French position seemed somewhat anamolous in that Indochinese affairs are now being ad-ministered by the French Ministry of Overseas Areas which did not seem consistent with the French statement that the governments are to a large degree independent. The Secretary said that he also thought it was most important that the other governments of Southeast Asia, particularly India, Burma and Siam, recognize the independent status of the Bao Dai government and in this connection the French could be helpful by giving greater independence to the Indochinese governments in their foreign relations. The Secretary said that at the present time and given conditions in Indochina he realized it might be difficult to give the In-dochinese governments as much internal authority as was desirable but that in the field of foreign affairs there certainly appeared something that could be done. He said that if the United States and Great Britain rushed to recognize the Bao Dai Government it might, in a sense, be the "kiss of death" to Bao Dai since certain Asian political leaders such as Nehru, might think the United States and Great Britain were acting with imperialistic motives to insure con-tinuing full French control and domination of Indochina. On the other hand, the Secretary thought that the British might be helpful in getting the governments of India and Burma to recognize the Bao Dai Government and we would be disposed to do what we could to encourage the Governments of Southeast Asia to recognize the Indochinese nationalist government which had recently been established as a result of the March 8 Agreements.

Mr. Schuman said that he agreed with the Secretary and that he had already taken up with the French Cabinet the question of transferring responsibility for Indochina from the French Ministry of Overseas France to the French Foreign Office. While he hoped to be able to arrange for this it was difficult at the moment because of French internal considerations but that once the March 8 Agreements were ratified he thought it would be much easier and he hoped that this ratification would occur soon after the Parliament reconvened in October.

Mr. Schuman said that he also agreed with the advisability of the other Southeast Asian governments recognizing Bao Dai.

Secretary - Mr. Bevin - Mr. Schuman Conversation (September 17)

Mr. Schuman then talked about Indochina. He said the Bao Dai government was not quite complete but it was satisfactory. The government was not yet fully established but it would be and it was the only way for a permanent solution. There is no love lost between the Chinese and the Indochinese. The Indochinese are afraid of China. Some of Ho's men, if there was a threat of invasion from China, might go over to Bao Dai. If the Southeast Asian countries recognize the Bao Dai government, its prestige would be increased. Perhaps the United Kingdom and the United States could help the French with Southeast Asia. The agreement with the Bao Dai government would be ratified by the French Parliament soon. Siam perhaps could be encourage to recognize, by a word from the United States or the United Kingdom, the Bao Dai government. Bevin asked when the French Parliament would ratify the agreement. Schuman replied that Parliament meets on October 18 and should ratify it in a few weeks after that - perhaps in November. Bevin remarked that France has to ratify the agreement before anyone else can help.

The Secretary said that if the French ratify the March 8 Agreement and transfer dealings with Bao Dai to the Foreign Office, we could help with the Philippines and Siam. The Southeast Asian countries should take the first steps, otherwise recognition by the United Kingdom and the United States in advance of other countries would make the Bao Dai government look like a Western "front". Congress may take up the question of Point Four Program after the Military Assistance Pact. Perhaps we can arrange technical assistance and Export-Import Bank funds.

(141) DECREE ISSUED BY THE LAO ISSARA GOVERNMENT IN BANKOK, OCTOBER 24, 1949 (Extracts)

Source: *Laos*, pp. 6-7.

After the Franco-Lao Convention of July, 1949, the Vientiane government made a special effort to induce members of the Lao Issara exile government in Bankok to return and collaborate with the French-supported Associated State of Laos. Prince Souphanouvong, who had worked closely with the Vietnamese resistance movement as early as 1945, had quite the government in exile in March 1949 over the issue of allying Laos with the French as opposed to the Viet Minh. But the other members of the Lao Issara government chose to accept the invitation to return to Vientiane and announced the dissolution of the government in exile on October 24, 1949. After that, the only source of opposition to the French in Laos would come from those associated with the Viet Minh.

In view of the Provisional Constitution of 12 October 1945:

In view of the Royal Ordinance of 23 April 1946, confirming the powers of government and administration conferred upon the Provisional Government of Free and Independent Laos;

In view of the full powers granted the said Government by the Provisional Chamber of the representatives of the Laotian people;

In view of the decisions altering the composition of the said government;

In view of the decree of 16 May 1949 relieving Prince Souphanouvong of his functions as a member of the said Government;

In view of the general Franco-Laotian Convention of 19 July 1949 and the annexed protocol signed on the same day . . .

In view of the letters of 30 September and 6 October 1949 addressed respectively by the Prime Minister of the Royal Government of Laos and the High

Commissioner of France and Indo-China to His Highness Prince Souvanna Phouma, member of the Provisional Government of Free and Independent Laos.

In view of the minutes of the meeting of 8 October 1949 of the Council of Ministers of the Provisional Government of Free and Independent Laos;

Considering that by virtue of the aforementioned general Franco-Laotian Convention of 19 July, Laos has obtained its independence within the limits of the French Union; that the most basic and most lawful aspirations of the Laotian people are fully satisfied by this fact; that under these conditions, the original goal of the Lao-Issara Resistance Movement, namely the defence of the superior interest of the Laotian people, all personal considerations aside, has been attained; and that as a result, this Resistance Movement has lost the essence of its reason for existance . . .

DECREE:

FIRST ARTICLE - The Provisional Government of Free and Independent Laos (The Lao-Issara Government) is declared dissolved from 25 October 1949.

SECOND ARTICLE - Likewise, the Lao-Issara Resistance Movement, The Laotian Liberation and Defense Army, as well as all other organizations and all other Lao-Issara civil and military bodies responsible to the aforementioned Provisional Government of Free and Independent Laos, are dissolved from the same date . . . .

(142) TELEGRAM FROM AMBASSADOR EDWARD STANTON IN BANGKOK TO ACHESON, NOVEMBER 3, 1949

Source: 851G.00/11-349, State Department Central Files, National Archives.

After the dissolution of the Lao-Issara Government in exile in Bangkok, Prince Souphanouvong, in the name of the "Lao Liberation Committee" announced publicly in Bangkok his intention to continue the fight against French domination in Laos. Soon after that he would travel to the headquarters of the Ho Chi Minh Government in Tuyen Quang, North Viet-nam to discuss the establishment of a resistance government in Laos. In August 1950 a Resistance Congress would meet in Tuyen Quang to form a new political organization, the New Lao Issara (Free Laos Front) and a resistance government headed by Souphanouvong as Premier.

We refer to our despatch No. 392, November 1, 1949, giving a brief description of factions in Laos. As stated therein Prince SOUPHANOUVONG made it clear at a party on October 29 that the "Lao Liberation Committee" will not give up its fight against the French. The substance of his speech reported by the local press is given below:

It gives me great pleasure gratefully to thank the Thai people for their hospitality to our refugees. Our will to attain complete independence for our country has been strengthened by our contact with our Thai cousins in their free and independent country. We must enjoy further the hospitality of this country until Laos is free. That day is fast approaching, as was foreseen by Pandit NEHRU when he said "No European power can continue to hold territory in Asia."

We wish to thank all our friends and especially the press who will interpret our true intentions to the public. We restate our confidence and faith in our strength and in our people of the resistance. We are certain of victory and we are not alone on the path of righteousness. Our Indonesian, Vietnamese and Cambodian freinds are on the same road and we have the sympathy of all freedom loving people, especially those of our great neighbors, to inspire us.

(143) MEMORANDUM BY RAYMOND B. FOSDICK (CONSULTANT TO THE SECRETARY OF STATE ON FAR EASTERN POLICY), DEPARTMENT OF STATE, FOR AMBASSADOR AT LARGE PHILIP JESSUP, NOVEMBER 4, 1949

Source: Document Declassified by the Department of State, July 21, 1975.

While the State Department drifted closer to recognition of the Bao Dai regime on the grounds that there was "no alternative", opinion in the Department was not unanimous. Calling the March 8, 1949 Agreement "a kind of semi-colonialism," Raymond Fosdick called for acceptance of the Ho Chi Minh government.

In his memorandum of November 1 on Indochina, Mr. Yost argues that "a further major advance of communism will be considered as, and will in fact be, a defeat for the United States, whether or not we are directly involved". He therefore recommends, among other steps, support of the Bao Dai government (after the March 8 agreements are ratified) economic assistance to Bao Dai, etc.

It seems to me this point of view fails to take into consideration the possible, and I think the probable consequences of such a decision. In grasping one horn of the dilemma, it ignores the other. My belief is that the Bao Dai regime is doomed. The compromises which the French are so reluctantly making cannot possibly save it. The Indochinese are pressing toward complete nationalism and nothing is going to stop them. They see all too clearly that France is offering them a kind of semi-colonialism; and to think that they will be content to settle for less than Indonesia has gained from the Dutch or India from the British is to underestimate the power of the forces that are sweeping Asia today.

What kind of independence is France offering the Indochinese today in the March 8th agreements?

(1) The foreign policy of Indochina is to be under the final control of France.

(2) French military bases are to be established and the Indochinese Army in time of war is to be under French direction.

(3) France is to be in charge of the so-called General Services:
    (a) Control of immigration
    (b) Communications
    (c) Industrial development of Indochina

(4) Customs receipts are to be divided between France and Indochina in accordance with a formula to be agreed upon.

(5) Extraterritorial courts for French citizens are to be continued.

This shabby business is a mockery of all the professions we have made in the Indonesian case. It probably represents an improvement over the brutal colonialism of earlier years, but it is now too late in the history of the world to try to settle for the price of this cheap substitute. For the United States to support France in this attempt will cost us our standing and prestige in all of Southeast Asia. A lot of that prestige went down the drain with Chiang Kai-shek; the rest of it will go down with the Bao Dai regime if we support it. Ambassador Stuart calls our relationship to this regime "shameful" and I am inclined to agree with him.

Ev Case argued yeaterday that it is too late to do anything else except support Bao Dai. I disagree. It is never too late to change a mistaken policy, particularly when the policy involves the kind of damage that our adherence to the Generalissimo brought us. Why get our fingers burned twice?

Ho Chi Minh as an alternative is decidedly unpleasant, but as was pointed out at our meeting with FE yesterday, there may be unpredictable and unseen factors in this situation which in the end will be more favorable to us than now seems probable. The fundamental antipathy of the Indochinese to China is one of the factors. Faced with a dilemma like this the best possible course is to wait for the breaks. Certainly we should not play our cards in such a way that once again, as in China, we seem to be allied with reaction. Whether the French

like it or not, independence is coming to Indochina. Why, therefore, do we tie
ourselves to the tail of their battered kite?

(144) EDITORIAL BY TRUONG CHINH, NOVEMBER 15, 1949

Source: *Su That,* November 14, 1949, reprinted in *Viet-nam Trung Quoc Trong Cu
Chien Dau Chung (Vietnam and China in the Common Struggle)* Hanoi: Su That, 1961,
pp. 42-45.

As the Chinese Communists moved closer to final victory on the mainland of
China, they declared on October 30, 1949 the existence of the People's Republic
of China. The event foreshadowed a new phase of the conflict for the Vietnamese.
In the Party's newspaper, ICP First Secretary Troung Chinh assessed the significance of the Chinese Communist victory for the Vietnamese struggle and the international situation in general.

The Conference for Political Negotiations of the Chinese people concluded on
October 30, 1949 after having elected a coalition Republican Government of the
Chinese people to lead the 450 million people to complete the task of liberating
the Chinese nation from the yoke of imperialism and feudalism and bureaucratic
capitalism, building a new China which is independent, unified, democratic, free,
and prosperous.

The "Common Political Program" of the Chinese people was passed by the Conference. The foundation for the new regime in China was established. The people's democratic republican regime has just appeared in a semi-colonial, semifeudal country, in the largest country in Asia, a country whose population constitutes a fourth of mankind, a vanguard nation of the oppressed peoples.

The world working class and the oppressed peoples have just won a big round
in their fight. World peace has been further consolidated. The democratic bloc
goes all the way from Central Europe to the Cape of Camau through the Soviet
Union and China. Thus the oldest feudal system in Asia is dying and has died.
The new democratic system which steps beyond it to advance toward the socialist
system has opened for millions of people.

After the Russian October triumph of the revolution, the Chinese people's
democratic revolution is the most important development in world history.

The victory of the Chinese revolution is the worst defeat that the imperialist policy of intervention, especially that of American imperialism and its running dogs, has suffered. It is the most ignominious defeat of the puppet policy
of the aggressors, of the policy of sabotaging world peace and destroying the
democratic movement after the second great war. It is the bitterest defeat of
the capitalists, militarists and fascists of the world, especially the U.S., who
wants to encircle the Soviet Union and repress colonial and semi-colonial revolutions, who wish to prepare atomic war, a third world war, hoping to plunder
the world market, and practice genocide.

The victory of the Chinese revolution is a victory of hundreds of millions
of people who are taking up the gun to defeat the imperialists and their lackeys
a victory of the just cause and of freedom.

Like the victory of the Vietnamese national democratic revolution, the victory of the Chinese revolution is a victory of Marxism-Leninism applied to a colonial and semi-colonial country and shows the way for the achievement of socialism throughout East Asia.

Along with the establishment of the Democratic Government of East Germany,
the fact that the Soviet Union has the atomic bomb and the advances of the Vietnamese resistance, the founding the Government of the People's Republic of China
is a signal that the forces of peace and democracy are strongly advancing in the
world, and the warlike and reactionary forces are being pushed back.

In what setting has the Chinese revolution triumphed? The economy of the
imperialist countries, primarily the U.S., is being driven deeper and deeper

into crisis; the imperialist ranks are in dissention; the anti-American movement is growing stronger in countries which are the object of the Marshall Plan;
the U.S. foreign policy by atom bomb has failed, while the policy of using Tito
and his gang to provoke the Soviet Union and divide the ranks of the people's
democracies is being unmasked.

The Chinese revolution is victorious at a time when the Vietnamese resistance
is advancing in the phase of equilibrium of forces and the struggle movement of
workers in Europe and the U.S. is broadening.

Although the democratic struggle in Greece has been temporarily defeated and
the Indonesian and Malayan revolutions have met difficulties, the movement for
independence and democracy in the world generally is rising, and colonialist and
imperialist forces are declining. The capitalist world is entering a stage of
serious and continuous crisis. There cannot be a period of temporary stabilization after the Second World War. The world revolution is developing. There is
no power which can block its development. Any effort to block it will be crushed. Revolutionary movements which have been temporarily set back or are weak
will restore their strength and will develop further. Progressive movements
which are expanding will expand further. The Chinese revolution will be a motivating force for them to advance. Alongside China, the Indochinese people and
their vanguard segment, which is the Vietnamese people, will be encouraged and
helped further in the struggle to win their independence and freedom. Thanks to
strengthening themselves, and the spirit of struggle of the Indochinese people,
thanks to the help of the Soviet Union, of China and of people's democracies
throughout the world, the day of liberation of the Indochinese peoples is not
far away.

The French colonialists and the Xuan-Vinh Thuy puppets continue their tricks
and schemes, but finally, they will only be even more confused and hopeless.

(145) <u>LETTER FROM HO CHI MINH TO CATHOLICS IN PHAT DIEM, DECEMBER 9, 1949</u>
Source: Ho Chi Minh, *Selected Works*, Vol III, pp. 185-186.

*On October 16, 1949, the French dropped paratroops into the two leading Ca-
tholic strongholds of Phat Diem and Ninh Binh province and Bui Chu in Nam Dinh
province South of Hanoi. It was a unilateral move by the French to force the
Catholics to commit themselves against the Viet Minh. Ho Chi Minh's letter to
Catholics in those areas indicated that the Viet Minh would still not consider
them as the enemy, but as patriots.*

Dear Compatriots,
The French invaders and puppet paratroops have dropped in Phat Diem. They
have violated the Vietnamese holy land. This is very painful to me.

Moreover the French invaders falsely declared that they came at the invitation of the Catholics.

They did so with two wicked aims:
Firstly, to smear our Catholic compatriots and make people think that our
Catholic compatriots are betraying their Fatherland and following the colonial-
ists.

Secondly, to kindle internicine war in which we, brothers, kill each other
for their profit.

But the French invaders will fail, because for these last years, our Catholic compatriots have been enthusiastic in joining Resistance for national salvation; because for these last years, in many places the French invaders destroyed
churches, ill-treated priests, raped nuns, massacred and plundered our Catholic
compatriots as well as the non-Catholic. Therefore, though at first they sham
kindness and try to lure and buy over our Catholic compatriots, the latter are
determined not to be deceived.

The Government has sent troops to Phat Diem to fight the colonialist invaders in order to save our Catholic compatriots in this region from the shackle of these wicked satans.

Therefore you must endeavor to help our soldiers in every respect in order to smash the enemy and save yourselves and the country.

The French invaders' failure is certain, because everywhere in Viet Nam they are suffering heavier defeats with every passing day, and in France their domestic situation is becoming more and more hopeless.

I wish that you will firmly maintain your patriotic spirit and have sufficient strength to oppose the French invaders in order to fulfill your sacred duty which is:

To serve God
To serve the Fatherland.

(146) AIRGRAM FROM BRUCE IN FRANCE TO THE SECRETARY OF STATE, DECEMBER 22, 1949

Source: *Foreign Relations, 1949, Vol. VIII,* pp. 112-113.

Drawing Washington's attention to the fact that the Indochina war was jeopardizing the French economic recovery and stabilization effort, Ambassador Bruce urged that the U.S. take on part of the financial burden of the war effort, calling it a "double opportunity" for the U.S.

With reference to the Embassy's Cable No. 5197 of December 11, 1949 and to Toeca Cable No. 1435 of December 2, 1949, I have the honor here to transmit herewith a memorandum prepared in the Embassy's Combined Financial Group dealing with the burden imposed on the French public finances by military expenditures in Indochina a summary of the major lines of the attached document was contained in Toeca 1435.

The enclosed memorandum highlights the fact that Indochinese expenditures impose such a burden on the French public finances as to constitute an important obstacle to the success of the whole French recovery and stabilization effort. The 167 billion francs spent in Indochina in 1949 is not only equivalent to over two-thirds of the total direct American aid to France for 1949-50, but some ten billion francs greater than the estimated French budgetary deficit for the year; the sixty billion franc excess over budgetary estimates of actual Indochinese expenditures in 1949 more than accounts for the operating deficit of the French Treasury as of the end of 1949; and the year 1950 will probably see the Treasury saddled with at least forty billion francs more in unforeseen expenditures. It is clear that the struggle to create conditions necessary for the continued growth of a non-Communist Viet Government in Indochina, to which the French are apparently irrevocably committed, constitutes for the moment a major obstacle in the path of French financial stabilization and economic progress, with all that that implies for the European Recovery Program as a whole.

Unlike so many of the seemingly insoluable problems of the French Treasury, the Indochinese problem is one the United States can do something about. For in addition to taking the general political measures recommended in the Embassy's telegram 5197, measures designed by strengthening Bao Dai to shorten the period of necessary military activity, the United States is in a position to take direct action to relieve the French of at least a part of the financial burden of their Indochinese commitment by making use of the special fund established by the mutual Defense Act of 1949. This double opportunity to resist Communist expansion in Asia at one its most dangerous points while contributing directly to the maintenance of French economic stability, is one which in my opinion the Department should consider.

(147) TELEGRAM FROM CONSUL GENERAL ABBOTT IN SAIGON TO THE SECRETARY OF STATE, DECEMBER 27, 1949

Source: *Foreign Relations, 1949, Vol. VII*, pp. 114.

Pressure for immediate U.S. recognition of Bao Dai continued to grow as the Consulate in Saigon emphasized the cost of failing to extend recognition and cited U.S. recognition as critical to removing the taint of colonialism from the regime.

Pass Paris. Pouched to Hanoi. Assume Department is planning extend recognition Bao Dai Government simultaneously with or immediately after British (Paris telegrams 5366 and 5367, December 22, to Department). Failure to do so would be interpreted by all circles in Indochina including key fence-sitting element as further evidence that US Government indifferent and irresolute in opposing spread of Communism in SEA. Furthermore, recognition by UK alone would give Communists golden opportunity to feature Bao Dai as puppet of French-British colonialists. If we join, our record in Philippines and Indonesia sufficiently well known to people this area to take edge off such propaganda particularly in neighboring countries.

Success of Bidault in budget vote makes Schuman timetable (Paris telegram 5366) realistic January 15 would seem probable target date for recognition Bao Dai. Strongly agree with Schuman's argument that British should recognize Bao Dai before Mao Tse-tung and hope Department will urge British to delay latter. Opening of Colombo conference would seem logical excuse. British Consul General Gibbs who returned Saigon last week has telegraphed London emphasizing importance prior to recognition Bao Dai.

It seems likely that there will be an interval of relative calm on Chinese frontier. First threat from retreating Nationalist armies has been successfully avoided. Second threat from Communist armies does not seem immediate. The interval should be used to consolidate position Bao Dai and give his regime international standing as Keystone anti-Communist defense in SEA. Since period calm may well be brief urge:

(1) That decision re recognition Bao Dai should not be delayed until after Bangkok Conference.

(2) That at earliest possible moment Bao Dai be informed our plans to avoid possibility his absence on recognition date.

(3) That Embassy Paris continue press Bidault [and] Schuman expedite ratification and emphasize very real danger any further delay.

(148) TELEGRAM FROM ACHESON TO THE EMBASSY IN THAILAND, DECEMBER 29, 1949

Source: *Foreign Relations, 1949, Vol VII*, p. 113.

Although the U.S. still had not committed itself in the form and timing of diplomatic recognition of the Bao Dai government, it began to sound out non-Communist Asian governments on recognition. Acheson's telegram suggested arguments to use with Asian governments.

Fr Govt has informed Emb, Paris, it intends submit Mar 8 Agreements for ratification Fr Assembly together with similar agreements concerning Laos and Cambodia before end Dec.

On assumption such ratification will take place in near future, pls report what action re recognition Bao Dai regime Govt to which you accredited is likely to take.

In formulating your estimate you may, in your discretion, approach informally appropriate governmental officials. Shld you make any such approach, you should emphasize fol:

Determined to safeguard their national independence from the French colonialists the Vietnamese people and army are fighting heroically and are nearing
final victory. Throughout these years of resistance, Viet Nam has won the sympathy and support of the people of the world. The Government of the Democratic
Republic of Viet Nam declares to the Governments of the countries of the world
that it is the only lawful Government of the entire Vietnamese people. On the
basis of common interests, it is ready to establish diplomatic relations with
the Governments of all countries which respect the equality, territorial
sovereignty and national independence of Viet Nam in order to contribute to
safeguarding peace and building world democracy.

(153) EXCHANGE OF TELEGRAMS BETWEEN ACHESON AND STANTON, JANUARY 17 and 19, 1950

SOURCE: *Foreign Relations, 1950, Vol. VI*, p. 697

*The refusal of Thailand and other Asian states to follow the U.S. and
British lead on Bao Dai's government raised Acheson's ire at the "indifference"
of the Asians toward Communism. That brought a response from Ambassador
Stanton defending the Thai preoccupation with Western colonialism rather than
with Communism. The exchange defined the essential positions which would later
divide the U.S. from Asian "neutralism."*

Dept concerned by apparent lack of understanding on part of Thai Fon Min
that Ho Chi Minh is not patriotic nationalist but Commie Party member with all
the sinister implications involved in the relationship (urtel 23, Jan 12).
This apparent indifference to the possible success of one of the strongest Commie leaders in Southeast Asia raises doubts in the Dept of the desirability of
strengthening the Thai against Commie aggression if the Thai are actually unaware or indifferent to the approaching menace. On a suitable occasion you
shld emphasize the foregoing strongly.
For ur info. Apparently this point of view is common among South Asian
nations including India, Burma, Indonesia, and the Philippines, as shown in
replies similar to yours from posts in those countries. This general indifference or lack of understanding may prove to be disastrous for those nations
as Communism relentlessly advances. It is impossible for the United States to
help them resist Communism if they are not prepared to help themselves. All
for such action as in circumstances and in your discretion you deem advisable.

I believe Department under misapprehension re basic reason for reluctance
Thailand and probably other Southeast Asian countries extend recognition Bao
Dai. Basic reason is detestation by these countries of colonialism and their
repugnance voluntarily to recognize any regime which in their minds represents
perpetuation of colonial rule. It is my belief if French forthwith granted
Bao Dai real independence as Dutch have to Indos, there would be much less
reluctance to extend recognition. In my opinion this feeling is so strong in
their minds that it completely outweighs danger Ho Chi Minh establishing Communist Government Indo-China. I believe veiled threats from US withhold assistance these Asian countries would have little influence on their thinking or
the position they have adopted on this matter.
Sent Department 43, pouched Rangoon, Manila, Jakarta, New Delhi, Saigon.
Department please repeat London, and Paris.

(154) TELEGRAM FROM AMBASSADOR LOY HENDERSON IN INDIA TO THE SECRETARY OF
STATE, JANUARY 7, 1950

SOURCE: *Foreign Relations, 1950, Vol. VI*, pp. 692-693

The U. S. and Britain had been working hard to convince Indian Prime Minister Nehru that Ho Chi Minh was a Communist and not a nationalist, in the belief that it would incline him to support French efforts to defeat the Viet Minh. U.S. Ambassador Loy Henderson reported these arguments had failed to sway Indian Prime Minister Jawaharlal Nehru from his sympathy for the Democratic Republic of Vietnam and the Viet Minh resistance movement.

I believe that decision of Department outlined in telegram January 5, 2 a.m. re Vietnam is most constructive that could be taken in circumstances. I believe Nehru will not be pleased for UK and US to go ahead in this matter without regard to line adopted by India, nevertheless, I am convinced time has come for US to follow policies in Asia which are in accord with our concept of world situation regardless of GOI attitudes. Our approach towards international situation for considerable period is certain to be quite different from that of India and for us to make no move without protracted attempts at coordination would result in vacillation and would give impression of lack of convictions.

Although according to this morning's press Nehru stated during press conference yesterday there was no present intention of officially recognizing any government in Indochina, his sympathies for present at least are clearly with Ho Chi-minh. Although from this vantage point it would seem that Bao Dai in view of many factors operating against him has slim chance of survival unless forces opposed to further extension communism in Asia display more decisiveness than in past, nevertheless, our recognition particularly if accompanied by greater display of interest in fate of Vietnam should improve Bao Dai's chances and increas respect for us here even among those who disapprove our policy.

(155) TELEGRAM FROM ACHESON TO THE EMBASSY IN THE UNITED KINGDOM, JANUARY 30, 1950

SOURCE: *Foreign Relations, 1950, Vol. VI*, pp. 703-704

In announcing the Department's decision to recognize the Bao Dai government de jure, Acheson conceded that it would give up leverage on France to yield control over diplomacy and armed forces. Gullion's argument based on assumed short-term political benefit to Bao Dai of de jure recognition had prevailed.

Re Lond's 479, rptd Paris 137, Jan 27. Fol comments on recognition Viet Nam shld be passed to Brit:

As Dept understands it the purpose of according recognition to Bao Dai is to give him stature in the eyes of non-communist nationalist elements in Viet Nam and thus increase his following. This being the case recognition, if accorded by U.K. or ourselves, wld appear most effective if given without any strings attached, i.e. the *de facto* step contemplated by Brit as a bargaining point with the Fr in order obtain further concessions. Dept has come to view that the Fr have for the moment gone as far as they can in according independence. This does not mean of course that either we, the Brit or the Fr shld not continue to view the Mar 8 Agreements as an evolutionary step in the independence of Viet Nam.

We are of course aware of fact that the UK does not have unanimous support of the commonwealth re recognition and that no formula re Viet Nam cld be found at Colombo acceptable to all participants. We nevertheless believe that a straightforward recognition without the qualification of *de facto*, or for that matter *de jure*, wld best serve our and UK interests and this viewpoint shld be pressed upon the commonwealth govts. In this connection, it shld be borne in mind that simultaneous recognition will have to be accorded to Laos and Cambodia, whose govts fulfill the requirements for the *"de jure"* status.

The Mao Tse Tung govt on the other hand appears indeed to be a *"de facto"* form of govt altho it was simply "recognized" without qualifications.

Along the lines above Dept is of opinion that merely to give the UK ConGen in Saigon the "courtesy of rank of minister" is a skittish and timorous approach to problem of according diplomatic recognition to Viet Nam which wld tend in large measure to negate the benefits of such recognition. Dept considering making ConGen Saigon a diplomatic agent accredited to all 3 govts with personal rank of minister if this appears indicated.

(156) STATEMENT BY ACHESON ON SOVIET RECOGNITION OF DEMOCRATIC REPUBLIC OF VIET-NAM, FEBRUARY 1, 1950

SOURCE: *U. S. Department of State Bulletin, XXII (February 13, 1950),* p. 244

Acheson's statement in response to the Soviet Union's recognition of the D.R.V. did not attack the Soviets but attacked the D.R.V. - referred to only as "Ho Chi Minh's Communist movement in Indochina" - because it now had acknowledged ties with Moscow.

The recognition by the Kremlin of Ho Chi Minh's Communist movement in Indochina comes as a surprise. The Soviet acknowledgement of this movement should remove any illusions as to the "nationalist" nature of Ho Chi Minh's aims and reveals Ho in his true colors as the mortal enemy of native independence in Indochina.

Although timed in an effort to cloud the transfer of sovereignty by France to the legal Governments of Laos, Cambodia, and Viet Nam, we have every reason to believe that those legal governments will proceed in their development toward stable governments representing the true nationalist sentiments of more than 20 million peoples of Indochina.

French action in transferring sovereignty to Viet Nam, Laos, and Cambodia has been in process for some time. Following French ratification, which is expected within a few days, the way will be open for recognition of these legal governments by the countries of the world whose policies support the development of genuine national independence in former colonial areas.

Ambassador Jessup has already expressed to Emperor Bao Dai our best wishes for prosperity and stability in Viet Nam and the hope that closer relationship will be established between Viet Nam and the United States.

(157) PAPER ON MILITARY AID FOR INDOCHINA BY A WORKING GROUP IN THE DEPARTMENT OF STATE, FEBRUARY 1, 1950

SOURCE: *Foreign Relations, 1950, Vol. VI,* pp. 711-715

In January, a working group had been formed consisting of representatives of the Office of Western European Affairs, the Office of Philippine and Southeast Asian Affairs, and the Mutual Defense Assistance Program, to prepare a paper on possible U.S. military aid to the French for Indochina. The paper reflected the atmosphere of crisis and confrontation with Communism then prevailing in Washington; it failed to examine the dangers of involvement in the Indochina War along with the perceived dangers of the defeat of the French there; it gives the French version - long since discredited by U.S. officials on the scene - of the beginning of the war. Also notable are the beginning of the use of the term "legal government" to refer to Bao Dai's State of Viet-Nam and the extreme optimism about French military success, in stark contrast to the internal assessment of mid-1949 before the decision on recognition had been made.

I. THE PROBLEM

Should the United States provide military aid in Indochina and, if so, how much and in what way.

II. ASSUMPTION

A. There will not be an effective split between the USSR and Communist China within the next three years.

B. The USSR will not declare war on any Southeast Asian country within the next three years.

C. Communist China will not declare war on any Southeast Asian country within the next three years.

D. The USSR will endeavor to bring about the fall of Southeast Asian governments which are opposed to Communism by using all devices short of war, making use of Communist China and indigenous communists in this endeavor.

III. FACTS BEARING ON THE PROBLEM

1. When the Mutual Defense Assistance Act of 1949 was being written, the question of providing military aid to Southeast Asia was examined and it was decided not to include specific countries in that area, other than the Republic of the Philippines.

2. The attitude of the Congress toward the provision of military and economic aid to foreign countries recently has stiffened due to both economy and to policy considerations.

3. At the same time, the Congress has shown considerable dissatisfaction with policies which are alleged to have contributed to the Communist success in China and which are involved in the current United States' approach toward the question of Formosa.

4. Section 303 of the Mutual Defense Assistance Act of 1949 makes available to the President the sum of $75 million for use, at the President's discretion, in the general area of China to advance the purposes and policies of the United Nations.

5. Section 303 funds are unrestricted in their use.

6. The British Commonwealth Conference recently held at Colombo recognized that no SEA regional military pact now exists due to divergent interest and that such an arrangement was now unlikely.

7. Communism has made important advances in the Far East during the past year.

8. Opposition to Communism in Indochina is actively being carried on by the three legally-constituted governments of Vietnam, Cambodia and Laos.

9. Communist-oriented forces in Indochina are being aided by Red China and the USSR.

IV. DISCUSSION

1. Indochina has common border with China and Burma, thus making it subject to invasion by Red China.

2. Its population is some 27 million concentrated in the delta regions of the Mekong and Red Rivers. Of the total population, Chinese account for between 600,000 and a million, concentrated largely in the cities.

3. Indochina has an agricultural economy based principally on rice of which it is an exporter. World War II and its aftermath seriously disrupted the national economy. The country presently has an annual trade deficit of about $85 million.

4. There are three subdivisions of Indochina: Vietnam, Laos, and Cambodia. An agreement was signed March 8, 1949, between France and Vietnam which provides for the latter to become an Associated State within the French Union. Ratification of the Agreement, followed by the recognition of the Vietnam by the West, is expected in the near future. French policy aims at making Laos and Cambodia Associated States within the French Union at the same time.

5. Governmental stability is poor in Indochina. In Vietnam, less than

one-third of the country is controlled by the legal government with the French in control of the major cities; in Cambodia and Laos, the French maintain order but unrest is endemic. Before World War II Indochina was made up of four French Protectorates (Tonkin, Annam, Laos and Cambodia) and the colony of Cochinchina. It was occupied after the war by Chinese troops in the north (Tonkin) of the French upon promises of independence within the French Union. French negotiations with Ho were broken off following the massacre of many foreigners in Tonkin and Cochinchina in December 1946 by Ho's forces. Hostilities have continued to date.

6. The French are irrevocably committed in Indochina and have sponsored Bao Dai as a move aimed at achieving non-Communist political stability. It was a case of backing Bao Dai or accepting the Communist government of Ho Chi Minh. This latter alternative was impossible not only because it would obviously make their position in Indochina untenable but would also open the door to complete Communist domination of Southeast Asia. Such a communist advance would have severe repercussions in the non-communist world.

7. Military operations in Indochina represented a franc drain on the French Treasury of the equivalent of approximately $475 million in 1949. This constitutes nearly half of the current French Military Budget.

8. Ho Chi Minh, a Moscow-trained Communist, controls the Viet Minh movement which is in conflict with the government of Bao Dai for control of Vietnam. Ho actually exercises control of varying degree over more than two-thirds of Vietnam territory and his "government" maintains agents in Thailand, Burma and India. This communist "government" has been recognized by Communist China and the USSR.

9. Most Indochinese, both the supporters of Bao Dai and those of Ho Chi Minh, regard independence from the French as their primary objective. Protection from Chinese Communist imperialism has been considered, up to now, a secondary issue.

10. Unavoidably, the United States is, together with France, committed in Indochina. That is, failure of the French Bao Dai "experiment" would mean the communization of Indochina. It is Bao Dai (or a similar anti-communist successor); there is no other alternative. The choice confronting the United States is to support the French in Indochina or face the extension of Communism over the remainder of the continental area of Southeast Asia and, possibly, farther westward. We then would be obliged to make staggering inverstments in those areas and in that part of Southeast Asia remaining outside Communist domination or withdraw to a much-contracted Pacific line. It would seem a case of "Penny wise, Pound foolish" to deny support to the French in Indochina.

11. The US plans on extending recognition to the newly-created states of Vietnam, Laos and Cambodia, following French legislative action which is expected in early February 1950.

12. Another approach to the problem is to apply the practical test of probability of success. In the present case we know from the complex circumstances involved that the French are going to make literally every possible effort to prevent the victory of Communism in Indochina. Briefly, then, we would be backing a determined protagonist in this venture. Added to this is the fact that French military leaders such as General Cherriere are soberly confident that, in the absence of an invasion in mass from Red China, they (the French) can be successful in their support of the anti-Communist governments in Indochina.

13. Still another approach to the problem is to recall that the United States has undertaken to provide substantial aid to France in Europe. Failure to support French policy in Indochina would have the effect of contributing toward the defeat of our aims in Europe.

V. CONCLUSIONS

A. Significant developments have taken place in Indochina since the Mutual Defense Assistance Act of 1949 was drawn up, these changes warranting a reexamination of the question of military aid.

B. The whole of Southeast Asia is in danger of falling under Communist domination.

C. The countries and areas of Southeast Asia are not at present in a position to form a regional organization for self-defense nor are they capable of defending themselves against militarily aggressive Communism, without the aid of great powers. Despite their lack of military strength, however, there is a will on the part of the legal governments of Indochina toward nationalism and a will to resist whatever aims at destroying that nationalism.

D. The French native and colonial troops presently in Indochina are engaged in military operations aimed at denying the expansion southward of Communism from Red China and of destroying its power in Indochina.

E. In the critical areas of Indochina France needs aid in its support of the legally-constituted andi-Communist states.

VI. RECOMMENDATIONS

1. The United States should furnish military aid in support of the anti-Communist nationalist governments of Indochina, this aid to be tailored to meet deficiencies toward which the United States can make a unique contribution, not including United States troops.

2. This aid should be financed out of funds made available by Section 303 of the Mutual Defense Assistance Act of 1949.

(158) MEMORANDUM BY ACHESON TO TRUMAN, FEBRUARY 2, 1950

SOURCE: *Foreign Relations, 1950, Vol. VI,* pp. 716-717.

In recommending to Truman that the U.S. recognize the three Indochinese governments which had reached accommodations with France, Acheson made it clear that the U.S. would be recognizing states which were not sovereign but were still subordinate to France. Truman approved U.S. recognition at a Cabinet meeting the following day.

1. The French Assembly (Lower House) ratified on 29 January by a large majority (396-193) the bill which, in effect, established Vietnam, Laos and Cambodia as autonomous states within the French Union. The opposition consisted of 181 Communist votes with only 12 joining in from other parties. The Council of the Republic (Senate) is expected to pass the bills by the same approximate majority on or about February 3. President Auriol's signature is expected to follow shortly thereafter.

2. The French legislative and political steps thus taken will transform areas which were formerly governed as Protectorates or Colonies into states within the French Union, with considerably more freedom than they enjoyed under their prior status. The French Government has indicated that it hopes to grant greater degrees of independence to the three states as the security position in Indochina allows, and as the newly formed governments become more able to administer the areas following withdrawal of the French.

3. Within Laos and Cambodia there are no powerful movements directed against the governments, which are relatively stable. However, Vietnam has been the battleground since the end of World War II of conflicting political parties and military forces. Ho Chi Minh, who under various aliases, has been a communist agent in various parts of the world since 1925 and was able to take over the anti-French nationalist movement in 1945. After failing to reach

agreement with the French regarding the establishment of an autonomous state of Vietnam, he withdrew his forces to the jungle and hill areas of Vietnam and has harassed the French ever since. His followers who are estimated at approximately 75,000 armed men, with probably the same number unarmed. His headquarters are unknown.

The French counter efforts have included, on the military side, the deployment of approximately 130,000 troops, of whom the approximately 50,000 are local natives serving voluntarily. African colonials, and a hardcore made up of French troops and Foreign Legion units. Ho Chi Minh's guerrilla tactics have been aimed at denying the French control of Vietnam. On March 8, 1949 the French President signed an agreement with Bao Dai as the Head of State, granting independence within the French Union to the Government of Vietnam. Similar agreements were signed with the King of Laos and the King of Cambodia.

Recent developments have included Chinese Communist victories bringing theose troops to the Indochina border; recognition of Ho Chi Minh as the head of the legal Government of Vietnam by Communist China (18 January) and by Soviet Russia (30 January).

4. Recognition by the United States of the three legally constituted governments of Vietnam, Laos and Cambodia appears desirable and in accordance with United States foreign policy for several reasons. Among them are: encouragement to national aspirations under non-Communist leadership for peoples of colonial areas in Southeast Asia; the establishment of stable non-Communist governments in area adjacent to Communist China; support to a friendly country which is also a signatory to the North Atlantic Treaty; and as a demonstration of displeasure with Communist tactics which are obviously aimed at eventual domination of Asia, working under the guise of indigenous nationalism.

Subject to your approval, the Department of State recommends that the United States of America extend recognition to Vietnam, Laos and Cambodia, following ratification by the French Government.

(159) LETTER FROM TRUMAN TO BAO DAI, FEBRUARY 4, 1950

SOURCE: *Foreign Relations, 1950, Vol. VI*, p. 720

In informing Bao Dai of U.S. diplomatic recognition of his government, Acheson officially credited Viet-Nam with being an "independent State" within the French Union, in contrast to internal documents which pointed out that the Associated States were not yet independent. Indicative of the confusion about Bao Dai's government was Acheson's use of the title "Republic of Vietnam" rather than "State of Vietnam" which was actually adopted by Bao Dai and the French. Similar letters were delivered to King Sis-Vang Vong of Laos and King Narodom Sihanouk of Cambodia.

"His Imperial Majesty Bao Dai, Head of State of the Republic of Vietnam. YOUR IMPERIAL MAJESTY: I have Your Majesty's letter in which I am informed of the signing of the agreements of March 8, 1949 between Your Majesty, on behalf of Vietnam, and the President of the French Republic, on behalf of France. My Government has also been informed of the ratification of February 2, 1950 by the French Government of the agreements of March 8, 1949.

Since these acts establish the Republic of Vietnam as an independent State within the French Union, I take this opportunity to congratulate Your Majesty and the people of Vietnam on this happy occasion.

The Government of the United States of America is pleased to welcome the Republic of Vietnam into the community of peace-loving nations of the world and to extend diplomatic recognition to the Government of the Republic of Vietnam. I look forward to an early exchange of diplomatic representatives between our two countries.

I take this opportunity to extend my personal greetings to Your Majesty with my best wishes for the prosperity and stability of Vietnam."

(160) STATEMENT BY THE DEPARTMENT OF STATE ON RECOGNITION OF VIET-NAM, LAOS AND CAMBODIA, FEBRUARY 7, 1950

SOURCE: *Department of State Bulletin, February 20, 1950*, pp. 291-292

In announcing its recognition of the Associated States of Indochina, the State Department asserted that the accords reached by France with the three states established their independence. Instead of expressing hope for further evolution toward independence, therefore, it referred only to hopes for stability and democratic institutions.

The Government of the United States has accorded diplomatic recognition to the Governments of the State of Viet Nam, the Kingdom of Laos, and the Kingdom of Cambodia.

The President, therefore, has instructed the American consul general at Saigon to inform the heads of Government of the State of Viet Nam, the Kingdom of Laos, and the Kingdom of Cambodia that we extend diplomatic recognition to their Governments and look forward to an exchange of diplomatic representatives between the United States and these countries.

Our diplomatic recognition of these Governments is based on the formal establishment of the State of Viet Nam, the Kingdom of Laos, and the Kingdom of Cambodia as independent states within the French Union; this recognition is consistent with our fundamental policy of giving support to the peaceful and democratic evolution of dependent peoples toward self-government and independence.

In June of last year, this Government expressed its gratification at the signing of the France-Viet Namese agreements of March 8, which provided the basis for the evolution of Viet Namese independence within the French Union. These agreements, together with similar accords between France and the Kingdoms of Laos and Cambodia, have now been ratified by the French National Assembly and signed by the President of the French Republic. This ratification has established the independence of Viet Nam, Laos, and Cambodia as associated states within the French Union.

It is anticipated that the full implementation of these basic agreements and of supplementary accords which have been negotiated and are awaiting ratification will promote political stability and the growth of effective democratic institutions in Indochina. This Government is considering what steps it may take at this time to further these objectives and to assure, in collaboration with other like-minded nations, that this development shall not be hindered by internal dissension fostered from abroad.

The status of the American consulate general in Saigon will be raised to that of a legation, and the Minister who will be accredited to all three states will be appointed by the President.

(161) TELEGRAM FROM BRUCE TO ACHESON, FEBRUARY 6, 1950

SOURCE: *Foreign Relations, 1950, Vol. VI*, pp. 721-722.

In response to U.S. and British urging of a statement on the future evolution of the Indochinese states, the French Foreign Ministry indicated that it had no intention of stirring "unrealistic nationalistic appetites."

Parodi received Gullion this morning and in reviewing international situation in Indochina on eve recognition three new states by US and principal Commonwealth powers spoke in following terms:

"US and UK asked two things of us in connection your recognition New Indochina states. First was evolutionary statement. We have not made this statement. Because of situation both in France and Indochina we cannot call our shots. We cannot tell French Parliament that agreements they have just, after much soul searching, ratified are of merely passing value; on eve highly delicate inter-state conference during which allocation of principal economic controls (currency, customs, immigration, etc.) as between France and three states and as between three states themselves is to be made, we cannot afford to kindle unrealistic nationalist appetites whose necessary disappointment by us would have retrograde rather than progressive effects out there at a time when cohesive effort is more than ever necessary. Our intentions are evolutionary as results will show. For instance, we have already told Vietnamese they can establish diplomatic Missions in Washington and London, which constitutes important extension of March 8 agreements. Similar extensions will inevitably follow as justified. Secondly you asked that control of Indochina affairs be transferred from Overseas France Ministry to Quai D'Orsay. This is well on its way to realization and there is agreement in principle that undersecretaryship for the three associate states under Foreign Office will be established. This is of course political and not administrative question. I am hopeful that occasion offered by reshuffling of Bidault Cabinet which is now occurring will not be missed. Events in Indochina have taken a dramatic turn which poses very serious problems for us and for principal non-Communist powers. As I have told your Ambassador, we intend, after profound and thoughtful consideration among ourselves of all elements of situation, to request your views and those of British. Just what form this consultation will take, whether through diplomatic channels or by proposal by us for three way talks, has not been decided."

Sent Department 585 repeated London 193 Department pass Saigon 47.

(162) <u>PAMPHLET BY VO NGUYEN GIAP ON SHIFTING TO THE GENERAL COUNTEROFFENSIVE</u>,
<u>FEBRUARY 1950 (Extracted)</u>

SOURCE: Vo Nguyen Giap, *Nhiem Vu Quan Su Truoc Mat Chuyen Sang Tong Phan Cong* (Immediate Military Tasks for Switching to the General Counteroffensive). Ha Dong: Resistance and Administrative Committee of Ha Dong Province, 1950. Original document in Vietnamese language collection, South Asia Section, Library of Congress. [Translation by the Editor].

On February 2, 1950, the ICP's Third National Conference, which had begun twelve days earlier, concluded that the time had come to "complete preparations to switch over to the stage of general counteroffensive." 1950 was seen as the year of transition to the final stage of the war. The analysis of the third stage of the war, written by General Giap after this conference, is the most detailed and comprehensive account of his strategic thinking available from the first Indochina War. It is a remarkably careful and prescient analysis which predicts the expanded role of the U.S. in the war and the possibility of the third stage being prolonged and comprising several periods. The document also reveals that Giap's primary worries were weakness of his army's material base and the French ability to exploit the Indochina-wide scope of the war. It should be noted that this analysis, revealing the top Communist strategists thinking on all major issues, was written specifically for study by troops and cadres of the army - not simply for discussion among party and government leaders.

Part Three
The General Line of the Third Phase

1950 is a year of a strategic change of direction, when our revolutionary war shifts to the third phase, the phase of the General counteroffensive.

What is the strategy, and what are the concrete strategic objectives of the third phase? What is the general line of the third phase? Those are the problems we must understand clearly in order to guide the war to victory.

Counteroffensive Strategy

Our strategy during the third phase is a Counteroffensive strategy, while the strategy of the enemy is a strategy of withdrawal. We counterattack until complete victory, until we have swept the enemy's troops from Indochina soil, and reconquered the whole territory.

Looking generally at the counteroffensive throughout the entire phase of counterattack until final victory, we call the third phase the phase of General counteroffensive. The General counteroffensive means just this, and not that our counteroffensive will be carried out everywhere on battlefields from South to North, from Vietnam to Laos and Cambodia. Furthermore, it does not mean that the counteroffensive will occur in one swift moment everywhere, or will succeed easily at once like the August general uprising. On the contrary, because of objective and subjective conditions, our general counteroffensive may be prolonged and may be carried out in waves, prevailing on each battlefield until the enemy has finally lost, and we have won complete victory.

Our strategic objectives during the third phase are:
1) Annihilate the enemy's manpower.
2) Reconquer the entire territory.
3) Destroy the will of the French colonialists to resist.

The objective of annihilating the enemy's manpower is correct from a strategic standpoint. In the first phase, we wore the enemy's troops down gradually, and in the second phase, we continued to wear their troops down gradually. All combat, whether war of attrition or war of annihilation throughout the three phases, is aimed at one final objective: the anihilation of all the enemy's manpower.

With regard to territory, our strategic objective is to reconquer the entire territory of Indochina, the territory of all three countries, Vietnam, Cambodia and Laos, from the Nam quan gate to the ca mau cape, from Dong hai shore to banks of the Mekong and the Dangrek mountain range.

We must also destroy the invaders' will to resist, because that is the objective of the whole war. Moreover, France is far from Indochina, but the Indochina War for France is a colonial war, taking only one part of French forces; we cannot attack the colonialists right in the heart of their own country; if their will to resist is not yet destroyed, the war could still continue.

The above three objectives are closely related to each other. But the main objective is to annihilate the enemy's manpower.

Characteristics of the General Counteroffensive Phase

The war of the Indochinese peoples against France is a revolutionary war of weak peoples who are growing strong, against imperialism which is weakening. That war is taking place in Southeast Asia, a very important region economically as well as strategically; and it is also taking place after the second world war, when democratic forces have grown strong, and imperialist forces are weak.

All those characteristics of the revolutionary war have an influence on the General counteroffensive phase.

1) The General counteroffensive phase begins in conditions of our absolute superiority in morals, which we will continue to maintain.

Our army and people have an intense faith in final victory and dispose of a very high spitit of sacrifice and struggle, and compared with previous years of resistance war, that faith and spirit of sacrifice has multiplied.

As for the enemy, the majority of the people as well as soldiers not only do not want to continue to fight but believe that the French war of aggression will definitely be defeated.

Our superiority in morale is very important; our strategic and tactical conduct of the war must aim at developing that superiority to the utmost and must exploit it thoroughly so that the enemy's morale is further reduced.

2) The General counteroffensive phase begins under the condition that our material power, although improved, is still generally inferior to the enemy's. The counteroffensive phase will continue in conditions in which we will still meet many difficulties in maintaining and increasing our material power.

Our backward agricultural economy, which was previously a favorable factor in mobilizing guerilla warfare, now becomes an obstacle in the work of building national defense industry and resolving the problem of equipping an army advancing to regularization, and an obstacle in the work of building the rear area required for a regular army.

Our war strategy, generally speaking, must always aim at the objective of remedying the above deficiencies; strategic and tactical guidance must also be appropriate to conditions in which our material power is still weak, and exploit all our strong points and the enemy's weak points in order to remedy those deficiencies.

3) The counteroffensive phase begins under the conditions that international influence becomes very important to us as well as to the enemy. During the entire counteroffensive phase international influence will become increasingly more direct and more important.

Previously, international influence had a large effect on the Indochina war situation, but before this, that effect was more favorable to the enemy than to us.(1) From the time the Chinese revolution was victorious international conditions changed, becoming fundamentally favorable to us.

Because the territory of new China, which is also the territory of the new democratic world, from west to east, is contiguous to Indochina, Indochina has become an advanced position of the democratic world in Southeast Asia.

Because of the intervention of the U. S. and Britain, of international reactionaries, from another standpoint, their plan is to turn Indochina into a bastion in their "anti-Communist" defense line.

Our strategy generally must develop to the utmost our capabilities and not disregard our difficuties on the international plane. Strategic and tactical conduct must follow closely those favorable and difficult conditions.

4) The General counteroffensive phase begins and continues in conditions in which our guidance is steadier with every passing day, while the enemy's is more and more deficient.

Our guidance of the war, both strategic and tactical, has been forged in years of resistance, and today we also have the conditions to combined experiences from the Indochina war with the extremely rich experiences of armed struggle of people's democracies. That conduct will definitely improve and become more clearsighted and steady.

On the contrary, the enemy's guidance of the war, both strategic and tactical, encounters many contradictions: contradictions between U.S. interests and Franch interests, between reactionary colonialists and the French people, between the intentions of the command and the anti-war spirit of the soldiers. It will encounter many unexpected factors; the extraordinary maturation of our army, the high tide of resistance of the people in the heart of the enemy, the uprising of battlefields which were peaceful before, the assistance to us from democratic countries, etc.... So while even before this they were hesitant, subjective, and shortsighted, now more than ever they have no design, and are more and more subjective, shortsighted and hesitant. We must exploit all the weak points in the enemy's conduct of the war and strengthen our own conduct.

All of the above characteristics determine the path of development of the third phase, determine the strategic and tactical policy of the third phase, and determined that the third phase will conclude in victory for us and defeat for the enemy.

Mobile Warefare is Primary, Guerrilla Warfare is Secondary, Positional Warfare is Auxiliary

During the third phase, in order to achieve the strategic objectives mentioned above, based on the characteristics we have analyzed, what forms of combat tactics will we apply?

Our fundamental line regarding this aspect is:

Mobile warfare is primary;

Guerilla warfare is secondary;

War of position is auxiliary.

Mobile warfare is the primary tactic, first of all because mobile warfare can exploit to utmost the spiritual element to defeat the invader, and because in the general counteroffensive phase, our army must advance to besiege and destroy the enemy's power.

Based on the change in the form of the war on the battlefield, mobile warfare will have a greater and greater content every day. Confronted with the progress of our force generally, in regard to the degree of concentration, the technical level, combat effectiveness, and the enemy's deployment and manner of using his troops will change. The enemy will reinforce his positions, reinforce his intervention units and his reserve units. In the mission of defending positions, intervention units at the subsector and sector level will become more important. In the mission of defending the whole battlefied, the enemy advances to the use of large mobile troops and strong reserve forces. Therefore the tactics of destroying the enemy's positions must be linked with the tactic of destroying his intervention units; and, if we want mobile warfare to progress, our troops must be built up to take care of positions, advance to big battles of encirclement, while at the same time advancing to encircling and destroying strong mobile troop units in order take care of interventionary units.

Mobile warfare, on the Indochina battlefield, will still emphasize the guerrilla element during a rather long period, because of conditions of equipment, supply, and because of conditions of concentration; and soon there will be a positionaal war element, because of the enemy's manner of defensive deployment. Mobile warfare will usually be carried within a narrow framework, because of the conditions of the battlefield, because of the way in which the enemy uses his troops, and because of our conditions of equipment and concentration.

Guerrilla warfare is secondary, but still has a very important position. That is because guerrilla warfare is a form of combat which employs high combat morale and is appropriate to the conditions of inferior equipment and technology.

While the main forces carry out mobile warfare, the missions of guerrilla warfare are to wear down and hold back the enemy's forces, coordinate combat with the main forces, expand combat results and destroy the enemy at the local level. In order to obstruct the enemy's plan to concentrate or maneuver his forces, guerrilla warfare also has the mission of destroying all roads and attacking all the enemy's means of communications and transportation. In the important strategic zones, guerrilla bases must be developed and consolidated in order to coordinate with main force combat.

On every battlefield, guerrilla warfare must be developed to a high level, in order to coordinate with mobile warfare and to help the development of mobile warfare, until the time when, because of proper coordination between mobile warfare and guerrilla warfare, we have won on that battlefield, the enemy's manpower has been annihilated, and the locality liberated, so that local guerrilla warfare no longer exists. That means until it goes out of existence in a particular locality or battlefield, guerrilla warfare in that locality or battlefield must develop to a high level. After we have won on the battlefields, one after another, the scope of guerrilla warfare gradually narrows, at the same time that the main forces grow rapidly stronger, and guerrilla warfare generally speaking gradually takes on a secondary position. Therefore, we should not misunderstand the line "guerrilla warfare is auxiliary" to mean that we do not need to pay attention to its development while the battle is still going on. To understand it in this way is incorrect and very harmful.

Positional warfare will appear on battlefields during the final phase; at first elements of positional warfare will appear only on scattered occasions in combat. Because the combat morale of the enemy is poor, because we have armed bases right in the enemy's heart, many battles will end in the disintegration of the enemy, after big victorious battles by our army. For that reason, the possibility of positional battles is also reduced.

We must accelerate the wearing down and annihilation of very much of the enemy's manpower when they are still dispersing their forces and maneuvering, in order to prevent the enemy from reconcentrating their forces, in order to reduce positional warfare, or in order to create conditions for defeating the enemy army once we have to carry out positional warfare. Positional warfare demands a very high level of equipment and technology, in which our army is inferior, so our strategic and tacticl guidance must make every effort to reduce positional warfare. The more we can reduce it, the more successful we will be.

How Will The General Counteroffensive Phase Evolve?

How will the third phase begin and how will it evolve?

Does the third phase begin with a fundamental battle, a decisive battle or not?

Not necessarily.

It is possible that the third phase will open with a fundamental battle which will unbalance the relation of forces, just as the second phase began with the Viet-Bac battle.

But it is also possible that the second phase will pass into the third phase through a very long period, during which there are a number of big battles; a number of campaigns accumulate, creating a change in the relation of forces. In those circumstances, the third phase will also begin with a big battle, but that big battle itself will not necessarily have a fundamental character. The reason this may be is the characteristic of the war between France and us and the French method of dispersed deployment, because strategic geographical position is not only an important point on the Indochinese battlefield, and because of the combat conditions of our army.

Will the third phase be drawn out or will it be cut short?

Due to the above mentioned characteristics, due to the favorable conditions and unfavorable conditions, the third phase of the Indochinese revolutionary war could be cut short and on the contrary, could be prolonged.

It could be cut short because of our absolute superiority in morale. Due to that superiority, on our side there could be unprecedented advances, unprecedented advances by our army, unprecendented sacrifices of the entire people, resistance high tide and uprisings in the occupied zone; our forces and the general mobilization of manpower, material means and the possible international help could increase very rapidly. Also due to the above-mentioned superiority, major disintegration could take place in the ranks of the enemy's troops, or anti-war actions by French soldiers; the situation in France could also encounter many disorders due to defeat in Indochina, and the anti-war movement; or due to campaigns for independence by the colonies. The French strategic conduct of the war could also commit major errors.

But the third phase could also be prolonged:

a) Because our material power is weak, many periods are required to overcome that weakpoint;

b) Because the enemy can exploit the Indochinese terrain to prolong the war, continuing the fight in the South after he is defeated in the North;

c) Because the U.S., and Britain will intervene actively, to give assistance to France.

In the circumstances that the third phase is prolonged, our struggle will become fierce. In regard to the form of combat, the war will gradually lose the character of ordinary colonial wars; with one side having very strong military forces and one side very weak. The regular form of combat will develop very highly, and perhaps there will be mobile warfare on a rather large scale, and the possibility of positional warfare will increase. Our army will need to become modern in order to dominate the battlefield and destroy completely the enemy's power.

In the event that the third phase is prolonged, the Southern battlefield will meet many new difficulties. Therefore, in our strategic conduct of the war, we must pay special attention to the strategic geographical conditions of the Indochinese theater, overcome the disadvantages that those conditions create for us, and prevent the enemy from exploiting advantages they create for him. When aiming at a battlefield to make the main battlefield, the increase of forces on other battlefields should not be forgotten. When concentrating forces to destroy the enemy in the North, do not let them have time to consolidate their bases and prepare to prolong the war in the South.

In reality whether the third phase will be cut short or prolonged will be determined by our conduct and efforts. That guidance must be clearsighted, flexible, realistic, exploiting all possibilities, strong, bold and timely. That effort must be extraordinary and continuous, not only when switching over to the General Counteroffensive but throughout the entire Counteroffensive phase until complete victory.

* * * *

Based on experiences and shortcomings on the battlefield and based on the strongpoints and weakpoints of the enemy and ourselves, in our combat plan we must pay attention to the following principles:

1) Concentrate forces to a high degree, and achieve superiority in campaigns and in combat, in order to annihilate the enemy's manpower. At the same time prevent the enemy from concentrating his forces, force the enemy to maintain the present situation of dispersal, destroy the enemy part by part, while he is still dispersed.

2) Destroy positions at the same time as his intervention units; concentrate the attack on ordinary positions, then big positions, advancing to attacks on cities; concentrate the attack on small intervention units, advancing to attacks on big mobile units.

3) We must have secrecy, and must have a big decoy plan to mislead the enemy with regard to major campaigns, attack audaciously in order to achieve surprise, and exploit thoroughly the morale factor.

4) Because the enemy's weakest point is the weak morale of his soldiers, especially the morale of puppet troops, we must coordinate propaganda among enemy troops with combat in the campaigns, concentrating the attack on places where the enemy's morale is shaken.

5) Main forces must have one part attacking while one part rests, in order to maintain continuity in campaigns. Prepare forces in order to reinforce and expand main forces in a timely manner.

6) Develop guerrilla warfare to a high level, emphasizing the technique attacking and destroying transporation, communications routes and setting fire to storage sites, because that is a big weakpoint of the enemy; develop combat hamlets in order to protect villages, to struggle with violent sweeps about

to take place; beseige and sabotage the enemy's economy; protect our economic base.

7) Determinedly remedy existing weakpoints, develop guerrilla bases in strategically important regions, accelerate the organization of secret military units in the cities in order to achieve coordination of combat with main forces.

8) Overcome disadvantageous conditions, narrow terrain, interrupted lines of communication, determined to move forces from one battlefield to another when necessary, in order to achieve a high level of concentration. Make every effort to strengthen weak battlefields, in order to coordinate combat more effectively and exploit the enemy's gaps.

9) Coordinate the entire Indochina theater.

10) Have a general plan and disseminate rapidly new experiences, make efforts to study technology.

Grasping firmly the above principles, we must carry out to the utmost the mission of annihilating an important part of the enemy's manpower, in order to reinforce our forces and help build our forces, to achieve military superiority.

* * * *

(1) Britain helped France in the South, and the Kuomintang Chinese helped France in the North, right after the war ended. Later, the U.S. and Britain continued to help France financially and with weapons.

(163) MEMORANDUM OF CONVERSATION BY ACHESON, FEBRUARY 16, 1950

SOURCE: *Foreign Relations, 1950, Vol. VI*, pp. 730-733

In a conversation with Acheson and an aide-memoire French Ambassador Bonnet indicated for the first time the French desire for a united front with Britain and the U.S., and U.S. military assistance for Indochina on the basis that it was now a primary confrontation between the West and the Soviet Union. This memorandum was drafted for Acheson by Acting Assistant Secretary of State for Far Eastern Affaires, Livingston T. Merchant.

The French Ambassador called on me this afternoon at his request, indicating that the subject which he wished to discuss was Indochina and that it was a matter of some urgency.

Before recapitualating the contents of the attached *aide-memoire* which the Ambassador left with me, he stated that he wished to review the attitude of the French Cabinet in the light of recent developments in Indochina. The Ambassador pointed out that the French Government had been engaged for an extended period in a serious and expensive military effort in French Indochina. The Ambassador went on to point out that the recognition of Ho Chi Minh by the Peking and Moscow Governments seemed clearly to indicate that it was in this area that the two communist powers proposed to take aggressive action. The second development, to which the Ambassador referred, was the ratification by the French Government of the March 8 Agreements, followed by recognition on the part of the United States and Great Britain. He went on to say that the French proposed loyally to carry out the terms of those Agreements and to foster the development of democratic institutions and processes in the three Kingdoms.

At this point the Ambassador made a slightly obscure statement to the effect that the French Government at some point must reach a decision with regard to the recognition of Peking. He said that this decision had not yet been made but he was anxious for me to know that at some point it would be made. I asked him at this juncture what bearing the recognition of Ho Chi Minh by Peking might have on their consideration of recognition of the Chinese

Communists. The Ambassador admitted that it obviously was an important factor which would have to be taken into account and asked me if I had some message in this connection for him to transmit to his Government. I made clear that I was making no suggestion but merely attempting to ascertain the present thoughts of the French Cabinet on this point. The conclusion I drew from this side discussion was that the French are not contemplating for the immediate future recognizing Peking but that they do not by any means exclude such action, despite Peking's recognition of Ho Chi Minh.

I then reverted to the Ambassador's statement that the French proposed to foster the development of democratic institutions in Vietnam, Laos and Cambodia and asked him whether or not the French Government had in mind at this time the desirability of making a public statement to the effect that the March 8 Agreements represented only a step in an evolutionary process. I pointed out that the reluctance of certain Asiatic countries such as Thailand, India, the Philippines and Burma to recognize Bao Dai and the Kings of Laos and Cambodia rested apparently on their belief that these three States did not in fact enjoy independence. I said that in our case we had brushed aside this question in making our decision to recognize but that I was extremely fearful, in the absence of some expression of intent or further action on the part of the French, the reluctance of the Asiatic powers to come forward, a development so important for the future of the three States, would persist. The Ambassador replied that France had every intention of fostering the further development of these States along democratic lines, but that he felt quite certain that the Cabinet did not feel that it could make any statement of possible future actions having legal force. He added that it would be unfortunate if suspicion were permitted to grow in the minds of the Vietnamese as well as other Asiatic countries that they had not achieved, in fact, a very high degree of independence within the framework of the French Union. He intimated that a statement along the lines that I had suggested may arouse rather than allay such suspicion. I stated that I thought it might be useful if we could sit down with the French and examine this question further in view of the importance of doing everything possible to assure the future success of these new States. The Ambassador promised to convey the views I had just expressed to Paris.

The ambassador then briefly summarized the three points of his *aide-memoire*. He expressed the hope that it would be possible for the United States to make a declaration of solidarity with France in this crucial area of Communist aggression an assessment which he felt would be strengthened by the adherence of the British. I questioned him at this point to ascertain whether the French Government was thinking in terms of a statement such as we had made in connection with Hong Kong, to the effect that armed aggression from outside would be a grave matter and call into play the machinery of the United Nations, or whether Paris was thinking in terms of a commitment on our part in advance to provide U.S. military forces in such an event. The Ambassador indicated that the thought was closer to the former and pointed out that the French Army was in French Indochina and France must expect to continue to bear the brunt of the operation.

The Ambassador went on to his second point, which was military aid, pointing out the hope of the French Government that with Section 303 funds the immediate needs of the French military and Indochina could be supplied. At the same time he stated that his instructions from his Government contained the hope that staff talks could be initiated and that American officers could proceed to Indochina for a joint study with the French military of the supply requirements and the military situation on the ground.

Lastly, the Ambassador stated that the French Government trusted that the United States Government would find it possible to render economic assistance and lighten the heavy burdens of the States of Laos and Cambodia, and above all, Vietnam.

I asked the Ambassador if Ambassador Bruce in Paris had received a copy of this communication. Ambassador Bonnet was not clear on this point though he felt certain our Embassy had been kept currently informed of the development of the thoughts of the French Government on this subject. I thanked the Ambassador for his call and assured him that these proposals would receive our immediate attention.

(164) REPORT BY THE BUREAU OF FAR EASTERN AFFAIRS, DEPARTMENT OF STATE, ON MILITARY ASSISTANCE FOR INDOCHINA, FEBRUARY 16, 1950

SOURCE: *Foreign Relations, 1950, Vol. VI*, pp. 735-738

Even before the French request for military assistance, the State Department's Far Eastern Bureau had recommended that military assistance be extended to the French military effort in Indochina. This report, written for the Mutual Defense Assistance Program Director, marked the first time that the term "Communist aggression" appeared in official documents on Indochina.

Military Assistance Program for Indochina for Fiscal Year 1951

A. *U. S. political and economic objectives in Indochina.*
The principal U.S. political objective toward Indochina is to insure the existence of governments in the three newly formed states of Vietnam, Laos and Cambodia which represent the legitimate nationalist aspirations of those Indochinese people who do not desire to see Communist-oriented governments in Indochina.

The U.S. has made strong representation to the French Government to extend liberal terms to the three newly formed states to indicate not only to the Indochinese people but to the neighboring Asian countries and to the world that France is the friend and supporter of legitimate nationalism and recognizes that the era of pre-war colonialism is ended. At the same time, the U.S. recognizes that the inherent weakness within the new states does not permit, for reasons both of extenal and internal security, that French military forces could be withdrawn from Indochina at the present time.

U.S. economic objectives in Indochina are directed toward the support of a program of aid and technical advice which will permit the three newly formed states to establish economic stability and to thereby lessen the danger of communism in the area. At the same time, economic stability in Indochina will assist in the rehabilitation of metropolitan France and therefore contribute directly toward a lessening of U.S. aid to metropolitan France.

1. Both the politial and economic objectives in Indochina are extremely important to not only the U.S. position of lessening Communist expansion but urgently necessary towards that end.

2. Special problems of internal security.
a. A political solution is required since it has been demonstrated during five years of French military effort that a military solution alone cannot succeed. The political effort must, however, be backed up by a continuing police-type military action with will enable non-communist oriented governments to maintain themselves in power. Economic problems of rehabilitation must be dealt with concurrently in order to wean away from communist leanings the peoples of Indochina.
b. The Governments of the three new states are willing to work toward the solution outlined in *"a."* above, but without outside support are unable, due to lack of trained administrative personnel, lack of experience and lack of military strength, to withstand communist aggression, backed up by Chinese Communist or by Soviet assistance.

3. The special problems of maintaining external security rests strongly on the Army of the French Union which has the responsibility in time of emergency or war of maintaining the area against external aggression.

a. Since the Army of the French Union now in Indochina, which includes upwards of 50,000 Indochinese, has been unable during the past five years to effectively stabilize the area against internal communist guerrillas under the direction of Ho Chi Minh, it is obvious that the same forces are unable to protect Indochina from either an invasion by mass of Chinese communist armies or by an increased indigenous communist army which is supplied from outside sources. The solution, therefore, to protect Indochina from either of these threats must rest with military and economic aid from the non-communist oriented countries of the world.

b. The Governments of the three new states appear to be willing to contribute toward non-communist defense of the area but are unable to contribute more, in a general way, than they now supply.

4. Because of the internal weaknesses of Indochina, none of the three new states is in a position to assist other countries in the area which are friendly to the United States, to maintain security.

B. In order to achieve U.S. political and economic objectives, it is recommended that both military and economic aid be given to the Governments of Vietnam, Laos and Cambodia, plus assistance to the Army of the French Union, which will remain the responsible agency for defense.

1. Assistance furnished to the armies of Vietnam, Laos and Cambodia would, it is planned, contribute toward combating communism both within Indochina and against an aggressor. Since the over-all control of military measures would rest with the Army of the French Union, it may be assumed that military aid would be used to achieve U.S. objectives.

2. A military solution would effectively contribute toward appropriate political and economic solutions although U.S. or foreign military and economic assistance would be played up by the communist propaganda agency as a demonstration that U.S. aid was being used to further French colonialism. Therefore, as much aid as possible should be given directly to each of the three new states in order to overcome this propaganda.

3. The three new states cannot improve their military strength without injury to their economies except that additional manpower (without equipment) could be supplied.

4. On the assumption that the anti-communist efforts will be successful in this area, then security needs from their own resources might be supplied to a certain extent by the three new Governments but would probably continue to require for some time direction by local French authorities and probably small amounts of assistance from France.

C. The general nature and extent of proposed military assistance is now being studied by French and Indochinese military authorities, and will be supplied to the U.S. through channels already established.

1. The nature and purpose of U.S. military assistance to Indochina would be psychological, to estabilsh U.S. abhorrence to further communist expansion in Southeast Asia; political, by strengthening the non-communist governments of the three states; and practicable in that both the politacal and psychological effects are in full accord with U.S. policy for Southeast Asia.

2. While the extent of assistance is as yet unknown, it is expected that it will be more than token and would include material aid and other assistance available only from U.S. sources.

3. Timing.

a. It is essential that military aid begun in 1950 through the French be continued during fiscal year 1951 in order to continue to contain communist aggression in Southeast Asia which has already begun.

b. If aid were not supplied during fiscal year 1951, it appears that communist aggression would successfully swallow up not only Indochina but threaten the remainder of Southeast Asia.

4.   The probable duration of proposed military aid is uncertain because of the unknown factors concerning communist plans for the area.   However, it is obvious that the more quickly aid can be given the more quickly the threat can be stopped.   The slower the aid is in arriving, the more prolonged the effort must be.

D.   1.   U.S. political involvement in Indochinese affairs would be expected to be concerned only with advice to France as well as to the three new states and to continuing efforts to orient the neighboring Asian countries towards a non-communist solution for the area.

2.   Economic involvement would depend on the successes of both political effort and military aid but should not be expected at this time to include long-term economic assistance.

3.   The consequence of withdrawal of military aid before a planned termination date would allow communist domination of Indochina and Southeast Asia.

E.   1.   The recipient Governments will welcome U.S. military aid.

2.   Adjacent countries will welcome U.S. military aid if it is combined with French assurances that such aid is supplied and utilized for the purposes of maintaining countries whose Governments represent the legitimate nationalist aspirations of the peoples of Indochina and not to reimpose French colonialism control.   U.S. military aid should be expected to have a violent reaction from the USSR and satellite countries.   However, there does not appear to be any political Asiatic consolidation of opposition against the recipient countries and to the United States except from Communist China and from North Korea whose positions are already quite clear.

(165)   ARTICLE BY TRUONG CHINH ON THE DIPLOMATIC RECOGNITION OF THE DRV, FEBRUARY 18, 1950

SOURCE: Su That, February 18, 1950, reprinted in *Cach Mang Dan Toc Dan Chu Nhan Dan Viet-nam, Tac Pham Chon Loc*.   (The Vietnamese People's Democratic Revolution.)   Selected Works (Hanoi: Su Than, 1975), Vol. II, pp. 238-242.   [Translation by the Editor]

The diplomatic recognition of the DRV by the Soviet Union and its allies opened a new phase of the Vietnamese revolution.   In this article, written immediately after the Party's Third National Conference, presented for the first time, the new international line of the Vietnamese revolution.   A major feature of the Party's foreign policy was to present itself as being the "advance post" in the struggle against imperialism - the mirror image of the one used by the Bao Dai regime to emphasize its importance to the U.S.

The fact that the Soviet Union and People's Democratic have just officially recognized the Ho Chi Minh Government has stirred up world opinon as well as opinion in the country.

It is an important political victory for the Democratic Republic of Viet-nam, for the Vietnamese people who are waging resistance war, and at the same time a big defeat for the French colonialist aggressors.

The Soviet Union and people's democracies recognized the Ho Chi Minh Government before the U.S.-British imperialists and their camp recognized the puppet Bao Dai, showing that, with regard to democratic world, the Ho Chi Minh Government is the sole legal government, the true representative of the Vietnamese people.   The Bao Dai puppets are a gang of lackeys, for the French colonialists and U.S. imperialists.   The French policy of setting up and supporting the puppet government is not only regarded by the Vietnamese people with contempt but severely condemned by the democratic and progressive forces in the world.

For more than four years, the Vietnamese nation has struggled to gain freedom, independence for itself, while protecting world peace.   The French colonialists invade Vietnam and destroy world peace. At the present time, the right of the Vietnamese nation to exist and the interest of world peace are closely related to each other.

The resistance of the Vietnamese people is supported by the forces of peace and democracy in the world. The fact that the Soviet Union, China and other people's democracies have recognized the Government of the Democratic Republic of Viet-nam cannot be isolates; the Vietnamese people have many friends, have big friends such as the Soviet people, the Chinese people, etc. The Democratic Republic of Viet-nam is part of the democratic and socialist system stretching from Central Europe to Southeast Asia. Viet-nam naturally stands on the side of democracy and against imperialism. As the advance post on the line of defense against imperialism in Southeast Asia, Viet-nam now is the focal point of conflict between the democratic and anti-democratic forces in the world. The Vietnamese-French was not only reveals the highest degree of contradiction between the Vietnamese people and Franch colonialism. It is one part of the struggle between the two camps: the domocratic anti-imperialist camp and the anti-democratic imperialist camp after the second world war.

The fact that the Soviet Union and the people's democracies recognize the Government of the Democratic Republic of Viet-nam shows clearly that the Vietnamese problem is an international problem. While the world imperialists recognize the puppet Bao Dai, provide further money and arms to French colonialism and Bao Dai to attack the Vietnamese people, the Soviet Union and the people's democracies officially recognize and establish diplomatic relations with the Government of the Democratic Republic of Vietnam. The forces of peace and democracy in the world wanted to gain time to support and assist the resistance of the Vietnamese people before U.S. imperialism intervenes directly in the Vietnamese problem, turning Viet-nam and Indochina into a colony and strategic base of the U.S.

The great diplomatic victory which the Government of the Democratic Republic of Viet-nam has just achieved is the result of more than four years of sacrifice and heroic struggle of the army and people of Viet-nam, the result of the correct line and policy of the Government of the Democratic Republic of Viet-nam lead by Chairman Ho. It strengthens the position of the Democratic Republic of Viet-nam in the international arena, increasing the influence of the Vietnamese people. Thanks to this diplomatic victory, the friendship between the Vietnamese people and the people of socialist and democratic countries in the world is warmer, and the assistance of friendly countries for the Vietnamese people's resistance and national construction is increased. The Vietnamese people will have further favorable conditions to study the experiences of the people of friendly countries.

At the same time, the recent diplomatic victory also places on the shoulders of the Vietnamese people further heavy responsibilities. The Vietnamese army and people must understand that they have the responsibility to liberate completely their own Fatherland from the yoke of imperialism, but also have the responsibility to contribute their efforts to breaking up the plan of war preparations of world imperialism, lead by the U.S.

(166) REPORT TO THE NATIONAL SECURITY COUNCIL BY THE DEPARTMENT OF STATE, FEBRUARY 27, 1950

SOURCE: *Foreign Relations, 1950, Vol. VI.*, pp. 744-747.

In a report which portrayed a gloomy picture of the prospects for France and the Bao Dai government, the State Department recommended plans for preventing the fall of Indochina to the Communists. The report's brief sketch of the background to the conflict continued the drift away from historical reality which had begun in 1949. (Ho is portrayed as having failed to obtain French

recognition for the D.R.V.) It was approved by the National Security Council
on April 18 and by President Truman on April 24.

NOTE BY THE EXECUTIVE SECRETARY TO THE NATIONAL SECURITY COUNCIL ON THE POSITION OF THE UNITED STATES WITH RESPECT TO INDOCHINA

The enclosed report by the Department of State on the subject is submitted herewith for urgent consideration by the National Security Council and the Secretary of the Treasury.

It is recommended that, if the Council and the Secretary of the Treasury adopt the enclosed report, it be submitted to the President for his considera-tion with the recommendation that he approve the Conclusions contained therein and direct their implementation by all appropriate executive departments and agencies of the U.S. Government under the coordination of the Secretary of State.

James S. Lay, Jr.

THE POSITION OF THE UNITED STATES WITH RESPECT TO INDOCHINA

The Problem

1. To undertake a determination of all practicable United States measures to protect its security in Indochina and to prevent the expansion of communist aggression in that area.

Analysis

2. It is recognized that the threat of communist aggression against Indo-china is only one phase of anticipated communist plans to seize all of South-east Asia. It is understood that Burma is weak internally and could be invaded without strong opposition or even that the Government of Burma could be sub-verted. However, Indochina is the area most immediately threatened. It is also the only area adjacent to communist China which contains a large European army, which along with native troops is now in armed conflict with the forces of communist aggression. A decision to contain communist expansion at the border of Indochina must be considered as a part of a wider study to prevent communist aggression into other parts of Southeast Asia.

3. A large segment of the Indochinese nationalist movement was seized in 1954 by Ho Chi Minh, a Vietnamese who under various aliases has served as a communist agent for thirty years. He has attracted non-communist as well as communist elements to his support. In 1946, he attempted, but failed to secure French agreement to his recognition as the head of a government of Vietnam. Since then he has directed a guerrilla army in raids against French installa-tions and lines of communication. French forces which have been attempting to restore law and order found themselves pitted against a determined adversary who manufactures effective arms locally, who received supplies of arms from outside sources, who maintained no capital or permanent headquarters and who was, and is able, to disrupt and harass almost any area within Vietnam (Tonkin, Annam and Cochinchina) at will.

4. The United States has, since the Japanese surrender, pointed out to the French Government that the legitimate nationalist aspirations of the people of Indochina must be satisfied, and that a return to the prewar colonial rule is not possible. The Department of State has pointed out to the French Government that it was and is necessary to establish and support governments in Indochina particularly in Vietnam, under leaders who are capable of attrating to their causes the non-communist nationalist followers who had drifted to the Ho Chi Minh communist movement in the absence of any non-communist nationalist move-ment around which to plan their aspirations.

5. In an effort to establish stability by political means, where military measures had been unsuccessful, i.e., by attracting non-communist nationalists,

no followers of Ho Chi Minh, to the support of anti-communist nationalist leaders, the French Government entered into agreements with the governments of the
Kingdoms of Laos and Cambodia to elevate their status from protectorates to
that of independent states within the French Union. The State of Vietnam was
formed, with similar status, out of the former French protectorates of Tonkin,
Annam and the former French Colony of Cochinchina. Each state received an increased degree of automony and sovereignty. Further steps towards independence
were indicated by the French. The agreements were ratified by the French Government on 2 February 1950.

6. The Governments of Vietnam, Laos and Cambodia were officially recognized
by the United States and the United Kingdom on February 7, 1950. Other Western
powers have, or are committed to do likewise. The United States has consistently brought to the attention of non-communist Asian countries the danger of
communist aggression which threatens them if communist expansion in Indochina
is unchecked. As this danger becomes more evident it is expected to overcome
the reluctance that they have had to recognize and support the three new states.
We are therefore continuing to press those countries to recognize the new
states. On January 18, 1950, the Chinese Communist Government announced its
recognition of the Ho Chi Minh movement as the legal Government of Vietnam,
while on January 30, 1950, the Soviet Government, while maintaining diplomatic
relations with France, similarly announced its recognition.

7. The newly formed States of Vietnam, Laos and Cambodia do not as yet
have sufficient political stability nor military power to prevent the infiltration into their areas of Ho Chi Minh's forces. The French Armed Forces, while
apparently effectively utilized at the present time, can do little more than
to maintain the *status quo*. Their strength of some 140,000 does, however,
represent an army in being and the only military bulwark in that area against
the further expansion of communist aggression from either internal or external
forces.

8. The presence of Chinese Communist troops along the border of Indochina
makes it possible for arms, material and troops to move freely from Communist
China to the northern Tonkin area now controlled by Ho Chi Minh. There is
already evidence of movement of arms.

9. In the present state of affairs, it is doubtful that the combined native Indochinese and French troops can successfully contain Ho's forces should
they be strengthened by either Chinese Communist troops crossing the border, or
Communist-supplied arms and material in quantity from outside Indochina strengthening Ho's forces.

Conclusions

10. It is important to United States security interests that all practicable
measures be taken to prevent further communist expansion in Southeast Asia.
Indochina is a key area of Southeast Asia and is under immediate threat.

11. The neighboring countries of Thailand and Burma could be expected to
fall under Communist domination if Indochina were controlled by a Communist-
dominated government. The balance of Southeast Asia would then be in grave
hazard.

12. Accordingly, the Departments of State and Defense should prepare as a
matter of priority a program of all practicable measures designed to protect
United States security interests in Indochina.

(167) <u>TELEGRAM FROM ACHESON TO BRUCE IN FRANCE, MARCH 4, 1950</u>

SOURCE: *Foreign Relations 1950, Vol. VI.*, p. 749.

*Aware that channelling military assistance to France would be another sym-
bol of Vietnam's lack of independence, Acheson sought to find a formula which*

would permit Bao Dai to be the "publicized" recipient while in fact, giving the aid to France. The Embassy in France agreed to the Acheson suggestion two days later.

In connection with possible military assistance to be given to Indochina Dept is interested in knowing your views on Fr plans regarding the manner and extent of participation by Bao Dai in this aid. Bao Dai's extravagant requests as presented in his memo to Jessup (which we are assuming has not been seen by the Fr) indicate that he may soon raise the question. The granting of arms to Bao Dai raises question about Fr supervision. In order to build up his political position in Vietnam the Dept considers it important that some formula be found to make Bao Dai appear to be the overt recipient of such aid. This may, of course, involve more of a concession than the Fr are prepared to make at this time, but may, from US viewpoint, be necessary. Dept may wish to ask you to discuss with Fr an approach by us to Bao Dai along the fol lines:

1) That his ideas for equipping Vietnamese army, militia, air force and navy, as set forth in his memo to Jessup seem beyond the realm of practical possibility.

2) That for long time to come he will have to look primarily to Fr for supplies of arms, training and military assistance in general.

3) It is up to him as much as it is to Fr to establish a *modus vivendi* re this question which will enable him to receive from them adequate support to pacify the country without jeopardizing his own position as the chief of an independent Viet Nam.

4) We are considering making a contribution to the joint Fr-Vietnamese war effort in the area. However, in view of urgency of their joint need for assistance it will, for purely practical reasons, be necessary to extend material assistance to them thru the Fr., but preserving Bao Dai as publicized recipient.

5) Since the appearance of it being a joint Franco-Vietnamese operation is of great importance politically we are likewise suggesting to the Fr that they associate him in their request for an arms program for Indochina.

Emb's comments urgently requested. No action should be taken with Fr on above without further instructions.

Rptd Saigon as 122 for info only.

(168) MEMORANDUM BY FRENCH PREMIER BIDAULT ON U.S. ECONOMIC AID TO INDOCHINA, MARCH 14, 1950

SOURCE: *Foreign Relations, 1950, Vol. VI.,* p. 762

French Premier Bidault gave the U.S. Embassy a memorandum during Ambassador Phillip Jessup's visit which insisted that France be a party to all U.S. economic aid agreements with Indochina and determine its distribution as well, sharply contradicting U.S. plans for its aid programs there.

(1) In view of the relationships which exist between France on the one hand and the Associated States on the other in the framework of the French Union, the French Government considers it desirable that the agreements relative to economic aid should be signed by the 3 Associated States and countersigned by France. It considers it preferable that the agreements be embodied in documents which are common to the 3 states rather than instruments particular to each one of them.

(2) It appears essential that the local French authorities should be closely associated in the management and distribution of American aid. To this end it contemplates the establishment of a joint quadripartite service wherein France and each of the associated states would be represented. The contemplated

procedure appears necessary in order to insure the most efficient use of the aid and its distribution under conditions conforming closely to the interests of the three states. This procedure is moreover in harmony with the spirit of the agreement between France and the Associated States and in which each one of the latter has recognized that it has common interests in the economic and financial fields with each of the two others and with the French Union.

(3) In the light of the experience gained in the implementation of the economic assistance program to France, the French Government believes that the import operations to be effected from the assistance funds should be handled through private trade channels.

(169) TELEGRAM FROM ACHESON TO BRUCE, MARCH 29, 1950

SOURCE: *Foreign Relations, 1950, Vol. VI*, pp. 768-771

New instructions to the Paris Embassy oral presentation to the French Foreign Ministry, marked a retreat from the previous position of pressure for an "evolutionary statement." Acheson now pressed only for a statement by France on how far it had already gone in making concessions to nationalism in Indochina, in order to improve the international image of the French effort.

Dept has predicated its course of action in Indochina since Feb 2 this year on assumption that fundamental objectives of US and France in Indochina are in substantial coincidence. Dept assumes:

1. That French are determined to protect IC from further Commie encroachments by polit, econ as well as mil measures.

2. That French understand that success of mil operation, i.e. containment of northern border against Commie penetration as well as reductions of Ho's forces elsewhere IC, depends, in the end on overcoming opposition of indigenous population.

3. Therefore France proposes in support of this policy to strengthen Bao Dai and the Kings of Laos and Cambodia in every practical way to end that non-Commie nationalists abandon Ho, support Bao Dai and Kings and can thus reduce guerrilla activity.

It is evident from reaction asian states to US and Fr effort to secure their recognition Bao Dai, from attitude Scandinavian powers and from reactions US press that large segment public opinion both East and West continues to regard Bao Dai and two Kings as French puppets not enjoying nor likely to enjoy degree of autonomy within Fr Union accorded thm under Mar 8 agreements, analogous to that accorded Indo by Neth.

US Govt has used its polit resources and is now engaged in measures to accelerate its econ and financial assistance to IC states. As you know Dept has requested Joint Chiefs of Staff to "assess the strategic aspects of the situation and consider, from the mil point of view, how the United States can best contribute to the prevention of further Communist encroachment in that area." You are of course familiar with position Jessup has taken re SEA during his recent tour. Dept accordingly considers that its position is clear and that the character of its past actions and proposed undertakings justifies its suggesting to Fr a course of action which it believes requisite to success of operation Indochina.

As said foregoing it appears to Dept that true character Fr concessions to IC nationalism under Mar 8 agreements and ultimate intentions in that area are clear to Dept but not clear to other interested parties. Dept believes that Indochinese natl movement, interested Asiatic states and large segment public opinion Western world unsympathetic and apathetic to this great issue because Fr have not made these elements sufficiently clear. You will surely understand that Dept does not believe that present situation IC call for further substantive concessions from Fr at this time involving parliamentary action to Bao Dai or two Kings. Obviously Bao Dai and company barely able to discharge responsibilities they are now facing. No part of representations which Dept suggests you make to Fr shld be construed as arguing for increase in concessions at this time. This connection, Dept strongly of view that transfer of Palace to Bao Dai most important single propaganda move possible now; Abbot emphasizes this, suggesting suitable attendant ceremonies. It must be clear to you and through you to Fr that Dept's concern at present is only that Fr make its present position and future intentions clear to non-Commie neutral world.

Dept had previously considered asking that you transmit in appropriate form to Fr FonOff note quoted below. Upon reflection in the course of which views Jessup and Butterworth recd, Dept believes you shld make strong oral representations Fr FonOff using fol lines as basic guidance in such manner as wld in your judgment best serve the achievement objectives identified foregoing. Your advice as to manner and timing of such approach awaited by Dept.

"The US Govt has expressed its gratification at the ratification by the Fr Govt of the agreements with the Govts of Vietnam, Laos and Cambodia. The real and continuing interest of the US in the strengthening and stabilization of anti-Commie natl regimes in Indochina is well known to the Govt of France as is the full confidence of the US in the intentions of the Fr Govt to adopt all measures requisite to providing the three states with the strength, polit and mil, without which they will be unable to defeat Ho Chi Minh and his foreign Commie allies.

The Govts of France and the US have long considered that the recognition of the govts of the three states by Asian states was a matter of prime importance in order that the anti-Commie natl movements in Indochina be accorded, in the eyes of the world, their true character as genuine natl movements and not, as world communism alleges, the creatures of 'Western imperialism'. The US Govt has, during the past several weeks, approached the several Asian govts most immed concern with the state of affairs in Indochina, impressing upon them the desirability of their immed recognizing the govts of the three new states. The Thai Govt recognized the Indochinese states on Feb 28. Unfortunately, the US reps accredited to the remaining Asian countries have been informed by the officials of those countries that they regard the govts of the three states as Fr puppets and that, more important, they are not convinced of the genuine character of Fr intentions ultimately to accord the states of Vietnam, Laos and Cambodia the full measures of independence and sovereignty which have recently been transferred by the Neth to Ind. The responsible ministers of the Asian powers concerned have stated in substance that were the Republic of France to announce publicly that the present agreements were the first steps in an orderly evolutionary process, the end and purpose of which is to accord the three states of Indochina complete independence, sovereignty and administration of their own affairs (within the Fr Union), those Asiatic states wld be prepared favorably to consider recognition of the three states in Indochina even before such additional transfers of sovereignty wld have actually been made. Therefore, while Dept obviously unable guarantee recognition and support fol such statement, Dept believes that in absence such statement further acts of recognition by Asian states not forthcoming. Dept keenly aware of self-evident fact that Indos cannot administer complexities Indochinese affairs without Fr assistance. Dept determined as matter of general policy to emphasize interdependence France and Indochina as was successfully done in case Neth and Indonesians. Dept believes that independence and autonomy of three IC states must clearly be understood to lie within Fr Union.

The Govt of the US is aware of the concessions granted by the Republic of France in negotiating and ratifying the Agreements. The US Govt has indicated to the Govt of France its desire to be of assistance to the three states and to the Fr admin in Indochina in enabling them successfully to contain and liquidate communism in Indochina. The US Govt is aware of the fact that the Govt of France shares its concern that communism be excluded not only from Indochina but from the entire SEA region. The execution of this policy requires, above all things, a unanimity of support on the part of the nations of SEA of the anti-Commie Indochinese nationalist govts of Indochina.

With full consciousness of the difficulties involved, the US Govt requests the Govt of France seriously to consider the issuance at the earliest possible moment of a public statement of the character identified in the foregoing. While it is not for the Dept to suggest the particularities of the text of such a statement, the Dept believes that the Fr Govt shld make clear therin the concessions to Indochinese nationalism which it made in the Mar 8 agreements and the supplementary accords, lest both Fr accomplishments and intentions in this great matter be tragically misunderstood not only in Asia but in the Western world as well."

(170) TELEGRAM FROM ACHESON TO THE LEGATION AT SAIGON, MARCH 29, 1950

Source: *Foreign Relations, 1950, Vol. VI*, pp. 771-772.

176. Reurtels 204,205 and 207, for urinfo Dept informed Fr High Commissioner IC believes Vietnam Govt may refuse attend interstate conference or agree become member of a quadripartite group which wld either submit individual state requirements for both econ and mil aid, or a single document embodying requests from three states plus separate Fr. needs. In either case it was Fr proposal that Fr authority countersign.

Pignon apparently believes this new attitude of Vets is due their misapprehension that perhaps as result Griffin mission and other expressions US friendship it will be necessary for Viets deal with other states or Fr in drawing up and submitting list mutually agreed requirements.

Dept desires such misapprehension be dispelled as in rapid and dipl a manner as possible.

US, having recognized status of States under Mar 8 and similar agreements has no intention allowing its position to be interpreted in such manner as to free Fr or IC states from performance under agreements.

While we will continue push Fr to interpret liberally terms their agreements with the states we also expect the three states, and particularly Bao Dai, to discharge their undertakings under the agreements. A specific case in point is their tendency overlook the responsibility provided by the Mar 8 agreements to Fr in matters affecting defense of the three states.

Dept continues feel problem of mechanics of aid is one which requires first the mutually agreed desire of three states and France and secondly acceptable US policy, resources and public opinion. If either interstate or quadripartite talks are made impossible by Viet intransigence it is obvious no mutual program can be formed for submission to US. Equally obvious wld be strong US public reaction against attempting deal with new states and Fr when they are unable in view urgency situation as pointed out by both sides, to agree among themselves.

The tendency which the Viets are showing to play us off against the Fr where mil and econ aid are concerned is one which might well jeopardize our plans in this respect. It should be made plain to them the early creation of a quadripartite organization to which econ and mil aid can be directed is of the greatest importance to this government in determining extent such aid.

Example urgency solution is fact that may be possible find 37mm ammunition available for shipment within short time. However funds cannot be allocated until title of recipient determined.

Dept continues desire and assumes Fr accept desirabIlity making three States publicized recipients mil as well econ aid, while actually utilizing channels most appropriate. Dept does not desire disturb any way Fr mil authority upon whom not only problems distribution falls but major share end use mil aid. Required therefore is mutually acceptable procedure applicable all types mil aid regardless end use. This decision need not any way prejudice quadripartite distribution committee allocations after arrival aid.

As an interim measure to apply to emergency items such as C-54's and 37mm ammunition Dept is considering practicability vesting title and resting consignment in Commander-in-Chief Combined French Indochinese Forces. Do you believe similar formula desirable for all subsequent military aid? Cld title be vested in quadripartite personality and consignment made in the case of military assistance to Cmdr-inChief?

(171) LETTER FROM SECRETARY OF DEFENSE LOUIS JOHNSON TO ACHESON, APRIL 14, 1950

Source: *Foreign Relations, 1950, Vol VI*, pp. 780-783.

The Joint Chiefs of Staff began for the first time to play a central role in formulating U.S. policy toward Southeast Asia when they offered the military view of Indochina and the region as a whole. The Joint Chiefs, with Secretary Johnson's concurrence, declared a non-Communist Indochina "critical" to U.S. security in the world, suggesting for the first time that the U.S. had to control the mainland of Southeast Asia to stem the tide of Communism in the Far East. The recommendations for action also foreshadowed a more aggressive policy aimed at roll-back of Communism in China.

MY DEAR MR. SECRETARY: In March I asked the Joint Chefs of Staff for their views and recommendations regarding:

"a. The strategic importance, from the military point of view, of Southeast Asia;

b. NSC 64, a report by the Department of State on the position of the United States with respect to Indochina, which is now before the National Security Council for Consideration;

c. The measures that, from the military point of view, might be taken to prevent Communist expansion into Southeast Asia;

d. The order of magnitude and means of implementation of such measures; and

e. A French *aide-memoire* on the subject of aid for Indochina, dated 16 February 1950."

These views and recommendations have now been received, and I am forwarding them in this letter to you for your information and action. Although there are some points that may require joint discussions by our respective Departments, in particular paragraphs 10 and 18 below, I generally concur in these views and recommendations. I wish to point out that the Joint Chiefs of Staff, in paragraph 15 below, have stated their belief "in the possibility of success of a prompt coordinated United States program of military, political and economic aid to Southeast Asia and feel that such a success might well lead to the gaining of the initiative in the struggle in that general area." Therefore, I strongly recommend that we proceed along the lines hereinafter set forth, with the details being worked out by our staffs.

"1. In the light of U.S. strategic concepts, the integrity of the offshore island chain from Japan to Indonesia is of critical strategic importance to the United States.

2. The mainland states of Southeast Asia also are at present of critical strategic importance to the United States because:

a. They are the major sources of certain strategic materials required for the completion of United States stock pile projects;

b. The area is a crossroad of communications;

c.   Southeast Asia is a vital segment in the line of containment of communism stretching from Japan southward and around to the Indian Peninsula. The security of the three major non-communist base areas in this quarter of the world - Japan, India, and Australia - depends in a large measure on the denial of Southeast Asia to the Communists. If Southeast Asia is lost, these three base areas will tend to be isolated from one another.

d.   The fall of Indochina would undoubtedly lead to the fall of the other mainland states of Southeast Asia. Their fall would:

(1)   Require changing the Philippines and Indonesia from supporting positions in the Asian offshore island chain to front-line bases for the defense of the Western Hemisphere. It would also call for a review of the strategic deployment of United States Forces in the Far East; and

(2)   Bring about almost immediately a dangerous condition with respect to the internal security of the Philippines, Malaya, and Indonesia, and would contribute to their probable eventual fall to the Communists.

e.   The fall of Southeast Asia would result in the virtually complete denial to the United States of the Pacific littoral of Asia. Southeast Asian mainland areas are important in the conduct of operations to contain Communist expansion;

f.   Communist control of this area would alleviate considerably the food problem of China and would make available to the USSR important strategic materials. In this connection, Soviet control of all major components of Asia's war potential might become a decisive factor affecting the balance of power between the United States and the USSR. 'A Soviet position of dominance over Asia, Western Europe, or both, would constitute a major threat to United States security'; and

g.   A Soviet position of dominance over the Far East would also threaten the United States position in Japan since that country could thereby be denied its Asian markets, sources of food and other raw materials. The feasibility of retention by the United States of its Asian offshore island bases could thus be jeopardized.

3.   In the light of the foregoing strategic considerations pertaining to the area of Southeast Asia, the Joint Chiefs of Staff, from the military point of view, concur in the conclusions in NSC 64.

4.   Military forces of both France and the United Kingdom are now actively opposing communism in Southeast Asia. Small indigenous forces are allied with them. In addition, the generally inadequate indigenous forces of the independent states are actively engaged in attempting to maintain internal security in the face of Communist aggression tactics.

5.   It appears obvious from intelligence estimates that the situation in Southeast Asia has deteriorated and, without United States assistance, this deterioration will be accelerated. In general, the basic conditions of political and economic stability in this area, as well as the military and internal security conditions, are unsatisfactory. These factors are closely interrelated and it is probable that, from the longterm point of view, political and economic stability is the controlling factor. On the other hand, the military situation in some areas, particularly Indochina, is of pressing urgency.

6.   With respect to the measures which, from the United States military point of view, might be taken to prevent Communist expansion in Southeast Asia, the Joint Chiefs of Staff recommend early implementation of military aid programs for Indochina, Indonesia, Thailand, the Philippines, and Burma. Malaya might also be included provided the British by their actions in the areas in Asia where they have primary interest evince a determined effort to resist the expansion of communism and present sufficient military justification for aid.

The effectiveness of these military aid programs would be greatly increased by appropriate public statements of United States policy in Southeast Asia.

7. The Joint Chiefs of Staff recommend that the military aid from funds already allocated by the President for the states of Southeast Asia be delivered at the earliest practicable date. They further recommend that the presently unallocated portion of the President's emergency fund under Section 303 of Public Law 329 (81st Congress, 1st Session); be planned and programmed as a matter of urgency.

8. Precise determination of the amounts required for military aid, special covert operations, and concomitant economic and psychological programs in Southeast Asia cannot be made at this time since the financial requirements will, to a large extent, depend on the success of aid and other programs now in the process of implementation. In the light of the world situation, however, it would appear that military aid programs and other measures will be necessary in Southeast Asia at least during the next fiscal year and in at least the same general over-all order of magnitude. The Joint Chiefs of Staff, therefore, strongly recommend that appropriations for over-all use in the general area of Asia be sought for the next fiscal year in terms similar to those under Section 303 of Public Law 329 (81st Congress, 1st Session). It is believed that approximately $100,000,000 will be required for the military portion of this program.

9. In view of the history of military aid in China, the Joint Chiefs of Staff urge that these aid programs be subject, in any event, to the following conditions;

   a. That United States military aid not be granted unconditionally; rather, that it be carefully controlled and that the aid program be integrated with political and economic programs; and

   b. That requests for military equipment be screened first by an officer designated by the Department of Defense and on duty in the recipient state. These requests should be subject to his determination as to the feasibility and satisfactory coordination of specific military operations. It should be understood that military aid will only be considered in connection with such coordinated operational plans as are approved by the representative of the Department of Defense on duty in the recipient country. Further, in conformity with current procedures, the final approval of all programs for military materiel will be subject to the concurrence of the Joint Chiefs of Staff.

10. The Joint Chiefs of Staff recommend that a Southeast Asia Aid Committee be appointed with State, Defense and ECA representation which will be responsible for the development and implementation of the program for the general area of Southeast Asia. Requests for aid should be screened by the field representatives of the committee in consultation with the local authorities in the countries concerned.

11. Present arrangements for military aid to Indonesia through the military attaches and to the Philippines through the Joint Unites States Military Aid Group appear to be satisfactory and should be continued.

12. A small military aid group should be established in Thailand to operate in conformity with the requirements in paragraph 9 above. Arrangements for military aid should be made directly with the Thai Government.

13. In view of the very unsettled conditions in Burma, the program for military aid to that country should, for the time being at least, be modest. The arrangements should be made after consultation with the British, and could well be handled by the United States Armed Forces attaches to that country. Arrangements for military aid to Malaya, if and when authorized, should be handled similarly except that request should, in the first instance, originate with British authorities.

14. The Joint Chiefs of Staff recognize to political implications involved in military aid to Indochina. It must be appreciated, however, that French armed forces of approximately 140,000 men are in the field and that if these

were to be withdrawn this year because of political considerations, the Bao Dai regime probably would not survive even with United States aid. If the United States were now to insist upon independence for Vietnam and a phased French withdrawal from that country, this might improve the political situation. The French could be expected to interpose objections to, and certainly delays in, such a program. Conditions in Indochina, however, are unstable and the situation is apparently deteriorating rapidly so that the urgent need for at least an initial increment on military and economic aid is psychologically overriding. The Joint Chiefs of Staff, therefore, recommend the provision of military aid to Indochina at the earliest practicable date under a program to implement the President's action approving the allocation of 15 million dollars for Indochina and that corresponding increments of political and economic aid be programmed on an interim basis without prejudice to the pattern of the policy for additional military, political and economic aid that may be developed later.

15. In view of the considerations set forth in paragraph 14 above, the Joint Chiefs of Staff recommend the immediate establishment of a small United States military aid group in Indochina, to operate in conformity with the requirements in paragraph 9 above. The Joint Chiefs of Staff would expect the senior member of this group to sit in consultation with military representatives of France and Vietnam and possibly of Laos and Cambodia. In addition to screening requests for materiel, he would be expected to insure full coordination of military plans and efforts between the French and Vietnamese forces and to supervise the allocation of materiel. The Joint Chiefs of Staff believe in the possibility of success of a prompt coordinated United States program of military, political and economic aid to Southeast Asia and feel that such a success might well lead to the gaining of the initiative in the struggle in that general area.

16. China is the vital strategic area in Asia. The Joint Chiefs of Staff are firmly of the opinion that attainment of United States objectives in Asia can only be achieved by ultimate success in China. Resolution of the situation facing Southeast Asia would therefore be facilitated if prompt and continuing measures were undertaken to reduce the pressure from Communist China. In this connection, the Joint Chiefs of Staff have noted the evidences of renewed vitality and apparent increased effectiveness of the Chinese Nationalist forces.

17. The Joint Chiefs of Staff suggest the following measures with military implications:

a. An increased number of courtesy or 'show the flag' visits to Southeast Asian states;

b. Recognition of the 'port closure' of Communist China seaports by the Nationalist as a *de facto* blockade so long as it is effective. Such action should remove some of the pressure, direct and indirect, upon Southeast Asia; should be of assistance to the anti-Communist forces engaged in interference with the lines of communication to China; and should aggravate the economic problems and general unrest in Communist China;

c. A program of special covert operations designed to interfere with Communist activities in Southeast Asia; and

d. Long-term measures to provide for Japan and the other offshore islands a secure source of food and other strategic materials from non-Communist held areas in the Far East.

18. Comments on the French *aide-memoire* of 16 February 1950, are contained in the substance of this memorandum. The Joint Chiefs of Staff do not concur in the French suggestion for conversations between the 'French and American General Staffs' on the subject of Indochina since the desired ends will best be served through conferences in Indochina among the United States military aid group and military representatives of France, Vietnam, Laos, and Cambodia. The Joint Chiefs of Staff are not unmindful of the need for collaboration and consultation with the British and French Governments on Southeast Asia matters

and recommend, therefore, that military representatives participate in the forthcoming tripartite discussions on Southeast Asia to be held at the forthcoming meeting of the Foreign Ministers."[1]

I am forwarding that portion of this letter containing the views of the Joint Chiefs of Staff to the National Security Council for consideration in connection with NSC 64. If you desire to discuss this matter, General Burns or I will be pleased to do so at the earliest mutual convenience.

[1] Documentation on the meeting of the Foreign Ministers of the United States, the United Kingdom, and France in London, May 11-13, 1950, is scheduled for publication in volume III [of the *Foreign Relations of the U.S.*]. Regarding Conference consideration of Southeast Asia, see also memorandum by Lacy to Rusk, May 22, p. 94 [of the *Foreign Relations of the U.S.*].

(172) GRIFFIN MISSION REPORT ON NEED FOR U.S. ECONOMIC AND TECHNICAL AID IN INDOCHINA, MAY, 1950 (EXTRACTS)

Source: Report No. 1 of the U.S. Economic Survey Mission to Southeast Asia. Available from State Department Historical Office.

In its report on the need for economic assistance to the Associated States of Indochina, the Griffin Mission emphasized the importance of succeeding in establishing a "new pattern of cooperation" between the West and ex-colonial countries, in order to preserve Western prestige and influence in the region. It further made explicit the implicit acceptance during 1949 and 1950 that a "political solution" was only an adjunct to the military suppression of revolutionary nationalist opposition to the Bao Dai regime.

II. Economic and Political Significance of Indochina

A. Economic

Indochina is normally one of the three major rice-exporting countries (with Thailand and Burma) of Southeast Asia "rice bowl." Its great exports, reaching 1,762,000 metric tons of rice and paddy in 1936, have normally gone to feed the rice-eating areas of the world under French control, for its rice has cost too much to compete readily in free markets, at least before the war.

These rice exports were important to the consuming areas: they were important to France, which might otherwise have had to find sterling or dollars (as at present) to purchase the needed rice; and they might be of great importance to the food-deficit areas of China - a fact that can hardly be ignored in the light of China's desperate need for food today, and in the expansionist, imperialist nature of the communism that has already engulfed China.

Before the war, Indochina also produced much corn, which went primarily to France for fodder (exports reached 557,000 metric tons in 1936). It produced coal (1,725,000 metric tons exported in 1936). It produced rubber (57,900 metric tons exported in 1938). And it exported some tin, iron, salt, zinc, cement, tea, and dried fish.

Although not a major earner of foreign exchange before the war, Indochina was helpful to France in producing substantial quantities of goods for which France would otherwise have had to expend foreign exchange. Its economic revival as a saver or as an earner of foreign exchange would contribute substantially to that better balance in world trade which ERP and other U.S. and international economic programs are intended to help achieve.

B. Political

Indochina is politically important in several ways. First, it is a former colonial area in which a new pattern of cooperation between East and West is being attempted. The success of this effort will markedly affect Western prestige and Western influence in the whole of Southeast Asia. In the Philippines, in Indonesia, in Burma, less Western economic or political control remains than is envisioned by the March 8 agreements in Indochina. If these agreements can be implemented in cooperation with a united people in each of the three Indochinese countries, much mutual advantage can be gained by both parties, and the possibilities of increasing world cooperation in voluntary association of both Eastern and Western countries will be enhanced. On the other hand, if French influence is increasingly opposed and if the result of attempts to compromise is a widespread revulsion against the West, Vietnam, Cambodia, and Laos may draw away from association with Western countries and may seek the will-o'-the-wisp of "neutral" isolation, or may be drawn into a power bloc that intentionally sabotages genuine international cooperation.

Second, Indochina provides a natural invasion route into the ricebowl of Southeast Asia, if the Communists in China adopt this form of external aggression. In centuries past, invasions have come down the coast from China. Cochinchina itself is one of the great food-surplus producing areas, and control of its surpluses might appeal mightily to the famine-stricken Chinese. Moreover a Communist-controlled Indochina would have a potent impact on the development of Communist influence and power in Thailand, Burma, Malaya, and perhaps in Indonesia, even if no overt invasion of those areas occurred.

Political developments in Indochina, therefore, may help or hinder greatly the eventual development of a truly United Nations organization, and they will certainly affect the future orientation of the other States of Southeast Asia.

III. Dominant Political and Economic Problems

A. Political Problems

The over-riding political problem of the day, and the problem that must be solved before any substantial economic recovery or development can take place, is the conflict raging in Vietnam and touching Cambodia and Laos as well.

1. The Bases of the Conflict. Indochina faces a world in turmoil, has a powerful and potentially unfriendly neighbor, and yet is fettered by its legacy from the past.

Vietnam, Cambodia, and Laos look far back in history to their independently developed cultures and traditions and want again to live lives independent of each other, despite the advantages that would derive from common or at least coordinated economic and financial policies, and probably also from coordinated political policies.

The French in Indochina look back to a history of colonial administration in which they take great pride, and during which the economic resources of the area were substantially developed, public health was greatly improved, education of an "elite" was encouraged, and the three countries drew real benefits from economic and political integration. There is a natural desire on the part of the French not to see these advances wiped out by an extremist, unrealistic nationalism and by hastily conceived economic and political policies.

The Vietnamese, Cambodians, and Laotians look back on French control with a jaundiced eye, understating its contributions and magnifying its political and economic restrictions. Fired by an intense nationalism that so far is primarily negative, a reaction against control, they naturally tend to give less than enough attention to planning and carrying out positive, constructive policies.

Finally, the fairly recent past has also narrowed the possibilities of mutual adjustment, for the virulent disease of communism has infected some of the most effective and popular leaders in Indochina, a country where there are too few leaders who are either effective or popular.

The French have a large stake in prestige, in investments, and in their responsibility to the peoples with whom they have long worked. They are understandably reluctant to pull out until the three governments are going concerns, able to carry their full burden both domestically and internationally. The Vietnamese want the French to leave as soon as possible, and feel that everywhere, including the military field, responsibility is being transferred much too slowly. The Communist-led rebels (who include many non-Communists) take the same view but much more violently and uncompromisingly. Besides their extreme and impetuous nationalism, of course, the rebels are more and more committed to the inflexible Communist line.

Among all three groups, deeply felt emotions have been so exacerbated that reason and mutual accommodation have been unable to play anything like their proper part. These fetters from the past, made up of old ideals and dreams and now heavily encrusted with emotion, greatly hinder the working out by all non-Communist groups of what, to an outside observer, might be a thoroughly fair and reasonable solution.

2. The Solution Being Attempted in Vietnam. (Because Vietnam is by far the largest of the three States and because the three elements that must be reconciled are most irreconcilable in Vietnam, the following discussion pertains only to that country.)

French policy has been to find and support those responsible and respected leaders among the Vietnamese whose nationalism (ardent among all) was not so unreasoning as to make impossible an evolutionary adjustment to "independence within the French Union." The French sincerely believe that Vietnam will derive important advantages from its association with the other countries within the French Union and that the strength of the whole Union will thereby also be enhanced.

Bao Dai, formerly Emperor of Annam (one of the three parts of modern Vietnam), and now called "Chief of State of Vietnam" believes that the status negotiated with the French and spelled out in the March 8 agreements will be beneficial to Vietnam. He is supported by a number of respected and able Vietnamese leaders and by a substantial part of the population.

He is not, however, a French "puppet," although he is regarded as such by many Vietnamese and other Asiatics since his vigorous protests to the French have never been made publicly, and since he has failed to elicit from the French firm promises of future concessions. Where French aid and cooperation will help Vietnam, Bao Dai seeks it. Where he believes that the French are not acting in the best interests of Vietnam or are not acting fast enough to turn over the reins of agreed authority, he is quick to protest vigorously. The continuous popular pressure resulting from the more extreme nationalist demands of the Viet Minh, the widespread antagonism to and suspicion of the French, and the continuing need to win over the fence-sitters by evidence that he is able to forward Vietnam's independence and interests, combine to push Bao Dai and his government into continual efforts to wring more and faster concessions from the French. That complete freedom of action is not achieved by him does not at all mean that he is subservient to French demands. Quite the contrary, he is making continual demands of the French.

On the other hand, Bao Dai sees in Ho Chi Minh a rival leader, who has been and still is personally immensely popular and yet who is Moscow-trained, apparently a devoted Communist, relying on a clique of avowed Communists, and heading a "government" that has been recognized by Moscow and by Communist China as the "legitimate" Government of Vietnam.

The possibility of compromising with such a group, without losing effective control to them, is very small; and their control of the country would mean a foreign domination, and a vicious unremitting kind of domination, that would be worse than any of which the French were ever accused and certainly far worse than any of the French controls envisioned under the March 8 agreement. Some of the "fence-sitters" have stated that the reason they do not commit themselves to Bao Dai is that they wish Vietnam to receive a status comparable to that of India, Pakistan, and Indonesia; others are still waiting it out, not because they want Ho Chi Minh to win, but because they are afraid of having been against him if he does win. They also fear immediate reprisal and even assassination from Viet Minh agents who they believe are everywhere. It is no wonder that Bao Dai welcomes French military aid in quelling the rebellion of such a group.

The Viet Minh is strong, well led, well organized, well armed. It receives aid from China and from sympathizers all over Indochina. It receives indirect aid by virtue of the very fact that many personally unsympathetic Vietnamese are afraid to commit themselves to support of Bao Dai, for fear of what may happen to them either now or after a possible Viet Minh victory.

Bao Dai's military police forces are growing. They are being armed and trained by the French, and are being given more and more responsibility both for policing and for front-line action. They are not yet strong enough, however, to stand up to the Viet Minh alone. It is only honest to say that, today, however general would be Bao Dai's support in a fair and secret election, his government could not last long if French troops withdrew from the country.

Besides nationalism and Moscow communism, there is another force influencing the situation in Indochina. This is Chinese communism.

According to previous estimates there are between 600,000 amd 1,000,000 Chinese in Indochina. They are hardworking, aggressive, competent and shrewd. They dominate much of the business in the country. Some 200,000 to 300,000 of them live in Cholon, the twin city of Saigon.

Although they live and work in Indochina, few of the Chinese minority feel any deep loyalty to the country. They owe allegiance to friends, family, and business associates, many of whom are in China. Unlike similar groups in Thailand and Malaya, they have never been active in the political life of the country. Moreover, communist doctrine and practices are presumably a threat to their business interests. Nevertheless, pressures may be exerted on them from Communist China and through Communist organizers to make them a potential subversive force. It would be very surprising if the Chinese minority now supported the government of Bao Dai.

There is always present, moreover, the unlikely possibility of outright invasion from the north. Long-standing antipathy exists between Chinese and Vietnamese and the Vietnamese hold bitter memories of the looting by Chinese Nationalist troops in 1945 when they occupied all of Tonkin and parts of Laos and Annam down to the sixteenth parallel, after the Japanese surrender. Such an invasion would undoubtedly go far toward uniting the people of Vietnam in opposition to any group that was allied with the invader. On the other hand, inasmuch as the Chinese Communists are probably well aware of the antipathy that exists towards China and the fear of Chinese imperialism, they may well maintain an officially correct attitude and hold out prospects of friendly relations as an additional drawing card for Ho. This policy would not prevent the Chinese Communists from continuing to supply Ho with material and some technical assistance.

In the meantime, however, the presence of a strong, modern French Army near the northern border gives many Vietnamese a feeling of security against at least one danger. This is clearly recognized by Bao Dai and by the other leaders who support his policy of working for Vietnam with, not against, the French.

The situation boils down to this:

a) The French are gradually turning over much responsibility to Bao Dai and his Government, but retain certain powers as French Union powers. Prominant among these powers is military defense of the area against internal and external aggression;

b) The Viet Minh wants the French out completely, wants no part of the French Union, and wants to control the country for communism (and probably calculates correctly that only the French are now strong enough to deny Ho Chi Minh this control);

c) Bao Dai wants as much authority for a Vietnamese Government as possible, but knows the country would be lost to Communist control if the French Union now withdrew its military support. He supports the March 8 agreements, but will undoubtedly continue to press for an evolutionary interpretation of those agreements, as fast as he believes the Vietnamese can themselves maintain law and order in the country and administer its affairs.

In this situation, the balance can only be shifted and a solution achieved by

a) Military suppression of the Viet Minh, by the Vietnamese so far as possible, and backed up by the French so far as militarily necessary. This is apparently feasible in the accessible areas that contain the majority of the population, food production, and industry; or

b) Convincing enough fence-sitters and enough of the non-Communist nationalists in the Viet Minh that Bao Dai can and will promote Vietnamese national interests, as fast and as far as is feasible, given Vietnamese military and political effectiveness. This "political solution" if the one for which both Bao Dai and the top-level French are striving.

[*Sections IV, V, VI, and VII are omitted*]

VIII. Special Considerations Affecting the Provision of Aid to Indochina

To have the maximum effect on the internal political situation in Vietnam, American aid should arrive quickly, should be distributed through the Vietnamese themselves, and should be widely and effectively publicized as aid made possible by direct U.S.-Vietnam arrangements. On the other hand, continual attention must be given to retaining the benefit of French experience and competence in a mutually beneficial cooperative endeavor.

A. *The Need for Prompt Action*

So much interest has been stimulated by U.S. recognition of Vietnam, Cambodia and Laos, by the visit of the U.S. Navy, and by the discussions with the U.S. Economic Survey Mission, that failure to follow through promptly with concrete action, even if minor, would bring about a great let-down. An issue has already been made by the Vietnamese, Cambodians, and Laotians of their capacity and intention to state their own needs for economic aid, without French intervention. If their statements of needs and assertions of independence are not quickly given substance, there will have been a considerable tempest about nothing, with loss of potential influence both for the local governments and for the United States.

B. *The Case for Direct Aid*

There are two very important aims to be served by direct U.S.-Vietnam relationships on economic aid. In the first place, it would make possible the avoidance of any control, or even appearance of control, by the French. In the second place, it would build up the prestige and authority of Bao Dai - not simply as an independent agent working directly with the United States (although this would be significant) but also as head of an effective Government interested in the welfare of the people themselves, and able and ready to take actions to help them.

C. *Letting the People Know*

It is not Bao Dai's Government that needs to be impressed by the fact of United States economic aid, or by the directness of such aid. The Government is composed of men who are already committed. It is among the fence-sitters and the great unconvinced portion of people that new strength must be sought, by demonstrating the genuine interest of the United States in the economic and political development of the three countries. Economic aid will therefore have relatively little impact on the political situation unless it is widely and effectively publicized. This may mean opening up new channels of communication, such as village radios, where inadequate channels now exist. It may mean adapting audio-visual techniques to the special needs of Indochina. And it may mean a substantial increase in the total cost of United States aid. It is, however, a *sine qua non* of any economic program that is intended to have both an economic and a political effect.

D. *French Responsibilities in Connection with Economic Aid*

France has been for some time, and is at present, pouring large sums of money into Indochina, to support the large-scale military effort there, to cover the budget deficits of the three local governments, to cover the balance of payments deficit of the area, and to pay for those central administrative functions (other than military) that remain the responsibility of the High Commissioner. Quite apart from the military operation, French financial support has been absolutely necessary to keep the three local governments afloat.

In the last analysis, of course, the French financial contribution to the area has been made possible by ECA aid to France, and the balance-ofpayments deficit of the area has been made into account in calculating France's need for ECA aid. The United States is therefore already indirectly aiding Indochina. On the other hand, so long as Indochina remains a part of the franc area (its piaster is already supported by France at an unrealistically high rate vis-a-vis the franc)so long as the three countries use a common currency and continue their customs union, and so long as French contributes heavily to the costs of government in the area, there will be financial questions of common interest to all three countries that cannot be settled without French participation nor, in fact, without French leadership. Direct or indirect, as United States aid may be, France will have to continue to aid, and will therefore have a right and a duty to participate in discussions of problems affecting the need for her contribution. Carrying out these French responsibilities will continue to require a central commissariat with administrative authority in Indochina.

Moreover, certain economic activities are of such immediate importance to all three countries, and also to France, that they are administered by a quadripartite organization (for example, the rice board). There are other fields in which the economies of the three countries are interdependent, such as transportation and meat supply, from Cambodia and Laos to Vietnam, but where no quadripartite planning or administration now goes on.

Finally there are fields, such as power, where future development may require joint planning if not administration.

This is recognized in the March 8 agreements, section Vii of which reads in part as follows;

> H.M. the Emperor of Vietnam, believing that, in the economic and financial field, he has common interests with the sovereigns of Cambodia and Laos, on the one hand, and with the French Union, on the other, and that it might be profitable to the Vietnamese nation that these interests be harmonized with a view to the prosperity of all, recognizes that joint organizations might well be formed for the purpose of studying and harmonizing these interests, and getting action under way.

In order to reach agreement on the composition, scope, and powers of such joint organizations, it is intended shortly to call a quadripartite conference, to be concerned particularly with the communications services, immigration control, customs and external commercial relations, treasury, and plans for reconstruction and modernizing of agricultural and industrial equipment.

The French consider that the need for unified direction in these several areas, based on the requirements of administrative efficiency, or on the countries' financial or economic interdependence, argues strongly for central direction and control over the economies of the three countries. They therefore propose that additional quadripartite entities be created to carry out this function. The three local governments minimize the importance of quadripartite action, and wish to aviod it wherever possible. Not only is there suspicion of and antipathy towards the French, but there is also considerable mutual suspicion among the three countries. The resolution of this question will significantly affect the amount and kind of American technical and economic aid requested, the manner of distribution of economic aid, and the status and functions of technical experts provided.

(173) MEMORANDUM OF CONVERSATION WITH FRENCH HIGH COMMISSIONER FOR INDOCHINA LEON PIGNON, BY MINISTER CHARLES BOHLEN IN PARIS, MAY 5, 1950

Source: *Foreign Relations, 1950, Vol. VI*, pp. 798-801.

French High Commissioner Pignon, in Paris to help prepare for a meeting of U.S. British and French Foreign Ministers, indicated to Bohlen that France wanted to reach agreement with the U.S. on a "political program" for relations between France and the Associated States which would give the French a stronger bargaining position with the Bao Dai government.

The following are the points in regard to Southeast Asia and Indochina at the forthcoming London conference and U.S.-French bilateral relations thereto made by M. Pignon, French High Commissioner for Indochina.

1. *General Southeast Asia Area*

M. Pignon said that in Indochina and he believed in other areas of Southeast Asia the tripartite conference in London has aroused great expectation among the people of that area. At the present time he felt the dominant feeling of the masses of people in Southeast Asia was one of fear and a sensation of the absence of protection against the communist advance in Asia which they tend to regard as an expression of Chinese and Soviet imperialism. The people in that area see the relentless and coordinated Soviet-communist advance in progress, but on the side of the west they see good intentions but indecision and vacillation. He felt therefore it was of cardinal importance that out of this tripartite meeting should emerge a clear indication of the intention and determination of the three Western Powers to concert their policies and efforts in order to prevent Southeast Asia from falling into the communist network. A vague declaration in generalities would not be enough; there must be some indication that the West would be prepared to counter the Soviet-communist thrust with effective action. He thought personally it would be wise if at the meeting in London in addition to a declaration of policy of that nature it could be announced that there would be staff talks at some place in Southeast Asia such as Singapore. He was aware of the views held in some quarters than any such declaration by white nations might be coolly received by the native populations, but in his considered opinion this was secondary to the local feeling of fear and lack of protection against the communist menace. He emphasized very strongly that if nothing of this nature came out of the London meetings, he felt the psychological effect in Southeast Asia and particularly Indochina would be very bad.

2. *The Situation in Indochina.*

Pignon stated that the military situation in Indochina was quite satisfactory but the terrorism and fifth column activities had shown a sharp increase and he was convinced that this was a prelude to large-scale action on the part of Vietminh forces based upon increased assistance from the Chinese communists when the dry seas began in October. According to French information, it is doubtful if Mao would use Chinese troops, but a large increase of military supplies with possibly some planes piloted by Chinese or even Russians is definitely to be expected. He said that he genuinely felt that the masses of people on the whole were not favorable to the Vietminh position; that they wanted above all peace and tranquility and therefore they were not unfavorable to the French but he admitted that the elite were still vacillating and sitting on the fence. He said that there had been a marked shift in Vietminh propaganda from a nationalist to a strongly Cominform-Stalinist basis.

3. *The forthcoming Schuman-Acheson Meeting in Paris.*

Turning to the question of U.S.-French discussions and American assistance to Indochina, Pignon very strongly emphasized his belief that the French Government must and he believed would produce for Mr. Acheson a political program indicating with complete frankness and sincerity how the French Government viewed the progressive development of their relations with the associated states in Indochina, what France was prepared to do immediately, and what France was prepared to do progressively as the situation permitted. He felt that this was absolutely essential if American assistance was to be effective in the area and the only way he could see of avoiding the danger of having the Vietnamese attempting to play off the United States against France. He said that if the French Government produced such a political program and it received general U.S. approval, it could then form a basis to guide the actions of both the French officials in Indochina and the American representatives there. Without some such agreed perspective as to future political developments and programs to be followed, M. Pignon seemed to be convinced that the Vietnamese would succeed in keeping the French and the Americans in Indochina divided and working against each other.

On the economic side, M. Pignon expressed himself as very pleased and satisfied with the agreement on economic assistance reached in the talks with Mr. Blum here in Paris and the manner of its handling. He felt that this formula for assistance would be workable and would help maintain a common position in this field of activity in Indochina. He emphasized that although the amount of economic aid was small, it represented not only psychologically but also on the spot economically a very important factor, particularly in regard to any counterpart funds which might result from American assistance which in his opinion should be used by the associated states to pay the Vietnam forces which otherwise could constitute a severe drain on the resources of these states and of France.

The London Discussions.

M. Pignon said that he did not feel that the difficulties which had been encountered in London over the draft estimate of the situation were too serious. They related, he understood, only to paragraph 7 and particularly paragraph 8 of the draft. It was felt by the French here that in view of the gravity and importance of the situation as set forth in the first six paragraphs, paragraph 8 dealing with U.S. attitude was "feeble." He was confident, however, that this question which he regarded more as wording would be straightened out.

Military.

M. Pignon did not go into any military details of requirements but stated that the formula which had been worked out for the reception of arms between him and Gullion (concerning whom he spoke very highly) was a satisfactory formula. He said he thought it was a mistake to dwell upon aid being direct or indirect since those terms could be misleading. The important thing was to handle it on the spot so as to accomplish the maximum psychological and military results. He mentioned in this connection his intention to have the arms for the Vietnam battalions turned right over to the units at shoreside on arrival and that the Vietnam commanding officer would become directly responsible for this materiel. He said what he and General Carpentier did not wish to happen was to have the military equipment turned over on any generalized vague basis to the Vietnam administration.

In general, Pignon appeared to attach maximum importance to the following points.

1. A strong declaration of intention which he felt should come from the three powers with indications of future action for the psychological effect throughout the area.

2. The cardinal importance of a French political program which would be communicated to the U.S. in order to insure harmony of approach in this field in Indochina.

3. Military preparation for a Vietminh offensive backed by the Chinese communists this fall.

He seemed quite optimistic that if action on the above lines could be taken this spring the chances were good in Indochina.

(174) <u>TELEGRAM FROM CHARGE EDMUND GULLION IN SAIGON TO ACHESON</u>, May 6, 1950 (Extract)

Source: *Foreign Relations, 1950, Vol. VI,* pp. 802-809.

In his first major analysis of the situation and recommendations for policy, Charge Edmund Gullion called for a new element in U.S. aid programs in Vietnam: sending psychological warfare experts to use U.S. "advertising techniques" to promote the Bao Dai government and "black" political warfare - propaganda disguished as the work of Communists - to confuse and divide the Viet Minh.

****

4. *Propaganda and political warfare.* We should suggest not push transfer of HC balance to Bao Dai. We should attach American public relations expert to Bao Dai under cover. Book unmasking Communist Viet Minh should be published written by American under Vietnam cover. Plans for giving Viet administration "new look", e.g. native uniforms, postage stamps, government forms, street signs, bank notes, seals etc. should be pushed. Efforts to insure sympathy youth, labor, religious groups systematically energetically promoted exchange of persons increased. American know-how drive advertising techniques should put to use of French.

Psychological warfare committees should be organized informally Saigon with with ourselves and British as silent partners.

"Black" political warfare should be aggressively pushed - playing on dispersed character Viet Minh promoting discord, defeatism, confusion using all media borrowed or bought - radio pamphlets, press agents word of mouth with all shades of allegiance tailored to fit all target groups. Sponsoring friends of Vietnam should be organized immediately as well as league for Viet Minh. American experts for these purposes should be assigned Saigon immediately closely geared to military operations.

****

(175) TELEGRAM FROM CHARGE JAMES C. H. BONBRIGHT IN FRANCE TO ACHESON, May 11, 1950

Source: *Foreign Relations, 1950, Vol. VI,* pp. 813-815.

Following the discussion between Acheson and Schuman in Paris, E.C.A. official Robert Blum and two other U.S. officials met with Pignon and Foreign Ministry officials in Paris to work out an understanding on U.S. assistance to the French and Associated States. Key elements of the compromise were U.S. agreement that France have a role in coordinating aid programs for the three countries and that the U.S. would maintain constant contact with Pignon on aid questions.

1. After receiving Ecato 495,[1] we informed French proposed *aide-memoire* unacceptable and showed them draft letter notification to states approved final paragraphs Ecato 495. Did not have full discussion as meeting with Pignon not possible until today.

2. Meanwhile, we concerted among ourselves in order to make fresh approach to formalities for initiating economic aid based on principles emerging from Ecato 495 and conversations between Secretary and Schuman on May 8. It was apparent we and French had been talking not only at cross-purposes but of different things. French concern about psychological impact of US economic aid on relations between them and associated states had before May 8 conversations led them to attempt to enlist our support in their negotiations with states for formation of quadripartite organization. This was not only unacceptable to us since it involved us in Franco-Vietnamese relations, but it also seemed unnecessary in light of May 8 conversations, which clearly established principle that US aid was in support of joint Franco-Vietnamese effort and question of substitution was excluded. It, therefore, seemed possible both to disengage ourselves from involvement in Franco-Vietnamese relations on matters of concern to forthcoming conference and to give French reassurance they were pressing for on psychological, if not actual, effect of substitution which presence of American mission with technicians might have in minds of Vietnamese.

3. Accordingly, when Blum, Wallner, and Koren[2] met with Pignon, Du Gardier, and Ledoux today they presented them with draft containing following principles:

a. Mission members will be guided by following principles emerging from May 8 talk: (*a*) Defense IC essential to that SEA which in turn closely connected with that of West. (*b*) Restoration security IC responsibility France and Associated states. (*c*) US aid complementary without intention substitution. (*d*) US conceives aid as reinforcing joint effort France and states.
b. Aid goes to states on basis bilateral agreements with such approval by France as required by existing agreements.
c. Desirable that France and three governments agree on coordination of aid programs to extent problems are common.
d. Mission will have contact with states, French, and coordinating body if established.
e. Mission members subject authority mission chief and will not become part administration Associated states. It was made clear this text had not been approved by Washington, and it was suggested that if informal agreement could be reached on principles contained therein, we could proceed to question of formalization.

4. French almost immediately accepted our text as meeting their principal concerns. Pignon asked that one additional thought be added, to the effect that US officials should remain at all times in contact with him on questions concerning aid to Associated states. Although this idea was already implied in point d, because Pignon attached such importance to it as evidenced in both this and previous meetings, we felt it wise to accept in principle.

5. We then raised question of whether and how principles contained in tentatively agreed text should be communicated to Associated states. French said they had no objection to document in its entirety being incorporated into letter of notification, point out, however, that we would no doubt prefer to modify point a in order to remove bilateral Franco-American implications. We observed that point to be added at Pignon's suggestion could hardly appear in document to be handed to states. It was agreed at end of meeting that we would seek clearance from our governments of understanding reached up to this stage.

6. We feel that satisfactory agreement is to be found in proposed letter of notification to states and France that embodies agreed points mentioned above. Letter might be made public. Suggested text based on our discussions today and no doubt acceptable to French appears in immediately preceding cable. We feel this text overcomes objections to earlier proposal while being satisfactory to French and recommend its approval.

7. In order meet Pignon's point, it would be necessary send additional (and unpublished) letter to French referring to first and stating it was understood that US officials would maintain constant contact with French authorities Saigon on matters relating to aid to states.

8. Please furnish comments soonest. Pignon leaving for Saigon early next week.

[1]May 6, p. 809.

[2]William A. Koren, Jr., Second Secretary and Consul in the Embassy in France.

---

(176) <u>LETTER FROM BRUCE TO THE PRESIDENT OF THE FRENCH UNION</u>, May 24, 1950

Source: *Foreign Relations, 1950, Vol. VI,* 817-181.

Based on the understandings reached in Paris on the principles to guide the handling of U.S. assistance to Indochina, the U.S. handed an official letter of intent to the governments of France and the three Associated States. As previously agreed with Pignon, the U.S. did not mention the secret assurance that France would be consulted at all times on any question involving aid to any of the three states.

I have the honor to inform you that the Govt of the United States has decided to initiate a program of economic aid to the States of Cambodia, Laos, and Vietnam. My Government has reached this decision in order to assist Cambodia, Laos, and Vietnam to restore stability and pursue their peaceful and democratic development.

With these purposes in mind, the United States Government is establishing, with headquarters in Saigon and associated with the US Legation, a special economic mission to Cambodia, Laos, and Vietnam. This mission will have the responsibility of working with the Governments of Cambodia, Laos, and Vietnam and with the French High Commissioner in developing and carrying out a coordinated program of economic aid designed to assist the three countries in restoring their normal economic life. The members of the American economic mission will at times be subject to the authority of the Government of the United States and will not become a part of the administrations of the Associated States.

The Government of the United States recognizes that this American assistance will be complementary to the effort made by the three Associated States and France, without any intention of substitution. American aid is designed to reinforce the joint effort of France and the governments and peoples of Cambodia, Laos, and Vietnam, on whom rests the primary responsibility for the restoration of security and stability.

United States economic aid will be granted in accordance with separate bilateral agreements between each of the Associated States and the United States of America. The approval of these agreements will be subject to legal conventions existing between the Associated States and France. Initial economic aid operations, however, may begin prior to the conclusion of these agreements.

The United States Government is of the opinion that it would be desirable for the three governments and the French High Commissioner to reach agreement among themselves for the coordination of those matters relating to the aid program that are of common interest. The American economic mission will maintain contact with the three Associated States, with the French High Commission in Indochina and, if desired, with any body which may be set up by the Associated States and France in connection with the aid program.

Mr. Robert Blum has been appointed Chief of the U.S. special economic mission to Cambodia, Laos, and Vietnam.

Identical letters are being addressed today to the governments of Cambodia, Laos, Vietnam and the President of the French Union.

(177) LETTER FROM BRUCE TO HIGH COMMISSIONER PIGNON, May 24, 1950

Source: *Foreign Relations, 1950, Vol. VI, p. 819.*

A confidential letter to Pignon delivered as the letters to France and the three Associated States were made public, confirmed the U.S. pledge of consultation with him on aid matters.

"Confidential Dear Mr. High Commissioner: In connection with the identical letters dated May 22, 1950, addressed by the American Charge d'Affaires at Saigon to the Chiefs of State of Cambodia, Laos and Vietnam, and by myself to the President of the French Union, informing them of [the intent of] my government to initiate a program of economic aid for the three associated states. I am glad to confirm understanding reached during your recent visit in Paris that members American economic mission to Cambodia, Laos and Vietnam, will, at all times, remain in contact with you on matters relating to aid to the associated states."

(178) TESTIMONY OF ASSISTANT SECRETARY RUSK, June 8, 1950

Source: *Executive Sessions of the Senate Foreign Relations Committee (Historical Series), Vol. II, 81st Cong., 1st and 2nd Sessions, 1949-1950.* (U.S. Government Printing Office, 1975), pp. 454-455.

When the State Department began persuading Congress and public opinion to support its policy in Vietnam, it had to deal publicly for the first time with some delicate political issues relating to Indochina. In this exchange between Dean Rusk, then Assistant Secretary for Far East, and members of the Senate Foreign Relations Committee, Rusk gave the Department's public line on the nature of and prospects for the Bao Dai regime.

Mr. RUSK. We are hopeful that we can get a lot of these fence sitters to swing over to the side of Bao Dai.

THE CHAIRMAN. Wouldn't Bao Dai have to get rid of that title of his, "Emperor," to get very far?

Mr. RUSK. That title seems to carry more weight in Indochina than it would here. It seems to be the feeling that that title is an asset, because of the traditional attitude of the people.

I think, Senator Green, your problem can be dealt with over a period of some time, not immediately, because the French must be in there in the short run.

Senator GREEN. The same thing was true of the Dutch in Indonesia, but they made a satisfactory arrangement with the natives. Is there any likelihood of the French making further concessions to satisfy the natives?

Mr. RUSK. We do not have at the present time any commitment by the French that that will be the case, but I think it is fair to say that the pressure and force of events will almost certainly force them to recognize the legitimate aspirations of the Indochinese people.

Senator GREEN. Then I go back to my first question. Until they do, there is no likelihood of the civil war being ended, is there?

Mr. RUSK. I do not believe, sir, that it is necessary for the French to go all the way in order to swing preponderant influence and power in Indochina over to Bao Dai or non-Communist nationalism.

Senator GREEN. Do you think they will have to go as far as the Dutch did in Indonesia?

Mr. RUSK. I think a development of that sort would greatly strengthen Bao Dai. It would be difficult to expect the French to turn to that immediately as their program.

Senator KNOWLAND. That is no cure-all in any event, is it, Mr. Rusk, because the British went pretty much whole hog in Burma, but they haven't brought peace by doing so. So too rapid withdrawal can mean just as much disorder as too slow withdrawal.

Mr. RUSK. I think you will find that not only do many of the nationalists in Indochina hope that the French will stay even at the moment that they are asking for the independence, but that many people in the rest of Asia, particularly in Southeast Asia, hope that the French will stay long enough to leave behind them a going non-Communist concern, and of course that complicates the problem a great deal. If the French pulled out right away, the situation there is such that it is probable that Ho Chi Minh would take over.

Senator GREEN. I understand that. But the answer to the question is, it is quite indefinite, it is in the indefinite future, when the French will make enough concessions to avoid continuance of civil war, and then that is the excuse for keeping French armies there and that is the excuse for not sending them back to Europe.

U.S. SUPPORT FOR THE FRENCH ARMIES

Mr. RUSK. I do not believe, sir, that the presence of the French armies is the cause of the civil war.

Senator GREEN. I don't think it is either. It is a result of it.

Mr. RUSK. If there is a Communist plan to move in on Southeast Asia, that plan would be prosecuted whether the French Army were there or not, and we would face the same problem without having the help that you have got in that part of Asia in those French troops there.

Senator GREEN. So far as you understand it, is it U.S. policy to help the French keep their armies there until the civil war is ended?

A CIVIL WAR CAPTURED BY THE POLITBURO

MR. RUSK. If this were an ordinary civil war, against colonialism, Senator, that would not be our policy. I think the record of the United States over the last few years and its influence in such situations as India and Burma and Indonesia, and our action in the Philippines, shows clearly what our attitude is toward that sort of situation. But this is not that kind of civil war. This is a civil war which has been in effect captured by the Politburo and, beside, has been turned into a tool of the Politburo, so it isn't a civil war in the usual sense. It is a part of an international war, and on that one I don't think we can look at it in simple terms of liberal democratic revolution. We have to look at it in terms of which side we are on in this particular kind of struggle, and because of that and because Ho Chi Minh is tied in with the Politburo our policy is to support Bao Dai and the French in Indochina until we have time to help them establish a going concern, based on agreement between the French and Indochina as to their mutual relationship.

OUTLOOK FOR A SETTLEMENT

Senator GREEN. And there is no prospect of that, really, is there, at present?

Mr. RUSK. I am not at all sure, sir, that we are faced with a long-term period here of this disorder. I cannot tell you now when it is going to come to an end, but we are not pessimistic about the possibility of seeing something brought out of this. We were making considerable strides there for a while when Bao Dai first came in. Then there were some political problems of transferring the tokens of sovereignty which slowed things down there, and for a while there has been a sort of balance. About as many defections were going in one direction as were coming in the other. Now we feel a little bit more of an increase in the movement toward Bao Dai. At what point that will become real security or real stability is something that it is very difficult to anticipate.

[Discussion was continued off the record.]

Senator GREEN. Do the rebels control most of the country outside of the big cities?

Mr. RUSK. No, sir. The French and Vietnamese forces control the big delta areas in which most of the population lives. As a matter of fact, in the most crucial area, the delta area of Tonkin and north, not only do the French Forces control it but the attitude of the local peasants is, from our point of view, very helpful, because they have had recent experiences with Ho Chi Minh. He took them up into the hill country and they were uncared for. Their abilities were destroyed; their dikes were ruined. Now they have come back in behind French Forces as a result of recent military operations. They find their abilities destroyed; their fields need mechanical help in plowing because the sun has baked them up so hard, and their feeling is bitterly anti-Ho Chi Minh, and there is a considerable element of strength in there on which you can build in the north and in Indochina in the south, in the French area, then you will be able to deliver that vast impossible area lying in between on that coastal strip.

Senator GREEN. Do you think the nature of the rebellion in Indochina is very different from what it was in China?

Mr. RUSK. I think sir, that there was from the very beginning a much stronger nationalist impact behind the rebellion in Indochina, because there was quite a colonial power at which it was directed. I don't think there is any question that the leadership of both revolutions fell into the hands of the Politburo, and they are closely tied in, and we should operate on that assumption. The presence of the French made some difference there.

ASIAN ATTITUDES TOWARD THE STRUGGLE

Senator SMITH of New Jersey. Mr. Rusk, do you feel that because we are lined up with the French there the prejudice is against us as being allied with Western colonialism? I have heard that comment made.

Mr. RUSK. There is always that danger, Senator, and one of the difficulties is that you can't bank any good will on that kind of point. We should have considerable good will in Asia on the basis of Mr. Roosevelt's efforts on behalf of India, and the traditional attitude of this country for many years toward India, our own action in the Philippines, and our own vigorous action in the case of Indonesia. However, it is possible that a good many Asiatics will look with considerable suspicion on us until this issue is resolved. However, I think the predominant Asiatic view is that of watchful waiting to see who wins. The Indian Government has not recognized Ho Chi Minh. They say neither Ho Chi Minh nor Bao Dai represents the country.

(179) TELEGRAM FROM RUSK TO BRUCE, June 22, 1950

Source: *Foreign Relations, 1950, Vol. VI*, pp. 827-829.

In June 1950, a "Conference of the Associated States" opened at Pau, France, in which France negotiated with the three governments of Indochina whose "independence" it had recognized on the powers of the various states in immigration, foreign currency control, navigation on the Mekong and other matters. The State Department's attitude toward the conference was expressed by Assistant Secretary Rusk, who explicitly limited the U.S. interest in the conference to urging France to seize the opportunity to convince the world of French generosity toward the Indochinese countries.

2953. For Bruce from Rusk. Dept aware of Fr desire to maintain Pau conf on a technical level and to keep it a "family affair." These and the other points brought out in Embtel 2896, June 15 and Saigon's 478, June 19,[1] have been noted and Dept agrees with Paris and Saigon views in this matter.

However, in ur discretion, and if you believe that it wld serve a useful purpose, you may wish to bring to Schuman's attn Dept's thinking with regard to the possility of using occasion of the Pau conf to counteract certain of the wide-spread misunderstandings which exist concerning the relationship of France and the Govts of Cambodia, Laos, and Viet Nam and the nature of their independent status within the Fr Union.

The holding of the conf might provide a useful opportunity to publicize extent and nature of Fr concessions to the IC states and progress made since the declaration of the Baie d'Along.[2] Also the purpose for which the interstate conf was called, the nature of its agenda and its accomplishments in formalizing the independence of the three states within the Fr Union may offer opportunities for favorable publicity.

During the course of th mtgs or immed fol them an opportunity might be found to make a public declaration re the conf and Fr intentions by a high ranking official (perhaps Pres Auriol as Pres of the Fr Union) which cld usefully be publicized. Bao Dai, of course, might be encouraged to make a similar declaration at the same time.

Pls assure Mr. Schuman that in presuming to make suggestions to him concerning what the US Govt recognizes is a family affair between Fr and the member of the Fr Union we are giving the most sympathetic consideration to the weight of France's obligations as having primary responsibility for the area of Indochina and seek only to reduce the burden of such responsibilities by suggesting that full use be made of a unique opportunity to make the extent and true nature of the concession made by Fr to the Associated States known.

It is not necessary to remind the Fon Min that in the US, as in other countries, there is a growing uneasiness in sections of the press and public opinion - a tendency to misinterpret present and future Fr intentions in Indochina and to regard Emperor Bao Dai as a "Fr puppet". This same press and public opinion is often unaware of the heavy sacrifices in lives and money made by the mother country in establishing and helping to maintain the integrity of the new Independent States within the Fr Union. Similar misunderstandings are encountered to a much greater degree in Asiatic countries. To use the circumstance of the Interstate Conference as a means of helping to dispel such impressions through the power of the printed word, public statements and other publicity is in Dept's opinion a course which can only lighten the burden of Fr and her allies with respect to Indochina.

Believe we shld limit our efforts with the Fr now to securing the points outlined above rather than striving to influence the agenda of a family discussion. If you think it feasible we can consider further steps to strive to influence the course of the conference itself.

[1]Neither printed.

[2]For documentation of the French-Vietnamese negotiations leading to the Ha Long Bay (Baie d'Along) Agreement of June 5, 1948, see *Foreign Relations*, 1948, vol. VI. pp. 19 ff. For the text of the agreement, see France, *Journal Officiel de la Republique Francaise, Lois et Decrets* (March 14, 1953), p. 2409. An English translation appears in Cameron, p. 117.

(180) <u>ARTICLE BY TRUONG CHINH ON THE GENERAL COUNTEROFFENSIVE</u>, July 1950

Source: "Hoan Thanh Nhiem Vu Chuan Bi, Chuyen Manh Sang Tong Phan Cong," ("Complete the Task of Preparation, Switch Strongly to the General Counteroffensive,"), *Tap chi Cong san (Communist Journal)*, no 1, July, 1950, in Truong Chinh, *The Vietnamese People's National Democratic Revolution*, Vol. II, pp. 250-265 (Translation by the editor).

During the spring and summer of 1950, Party leaders were troubled by signs that both over-optimism and doubts were appearing in the ranks of the people and the Party itself. In an article aimed at correcting these "deviationist" tendencies, Truong Chinh warned that there was still much to be done before the final phase of the war could begin, and that the final phase might be prolonged. He gave particular attention to the problem of U.S.-British assistance which allowed the French to nullify much of the military success of the resistance war.

The Democratic Republic of Viet-Nam has been recognized by the Soviet Union and the people's democracies. The anti-war movement in France is on the rise. We have fought several big battles. Cambodian and Lao people's guerrilla warfare is developing. Right in a number of big cities temporarily occupied big demonstrations and important acts of sabotage have occurred. These events make our people and cadres over optimistic, thinking that French colonialism is already finished, so whenever the Party and Government order the general counteroffensive, we have only to carry our kits into Hanoi.

On the other hand, the French colonialists recently attacked all across the Northern plain, the U.S. imperialists pushed their intervention in Indochina; the cost of living rose, a few places experienced famine, etc. . . . . That situation caused many other people to go bad and to doubt the Party's slogan, "complete the task of preparation, switch strongly to the general counteroffensive." Among those doubters are popular masses and cadres, people outside the party and party members. They raise many questions. Their concerns are not without reason.

This article aims at criticising groundlessly optimistic thinking and pessimistic thinking, explaining misunderstandings around the problem of completing the task of preparation and switching strongly to the general counteroffensive, with a view to making our comrades judge correctly and act correctly.

What About the General Counteroffensive?

In the political report and military report at the Third National Conference, the Central Committee explained about the general counteroffensive. Here I only summarize the Central Committee's judgment and emphasize points which have been wrongly understood and must be corrected.

From the standpoint of space, the general counteroffensive is a strong counteroffensive on the main battlefield while on other battlefields we hold back the enemy. Holding back here means counterattacking to a certain degree with the objective of annihilating and wearing down the enemy in order to disperse the enemy's forces and holding on to the enemy. We concentrate our forces to master the main battlefield, then gradually master the other battlefields, until the enemy's forces have been swept from Indochina. There could also be times when there are sufficient conditions to master two or three battlefields at once, but the main thing is to dominate the primary battlefield.

From the standpoint of time, the general counteroffensive is a counteroffensive throughout an entire strategic phase; that phase may be divided into many periods; in each period, we open one or several big or small campaigns, aimed at achieving the final objective of the resistance war, which is to drive the enemy army from the country.

Thus, in the circumstances of the present relation of forces between the enemy and us the general counteroffensive is not a counteroffensive on all battlefields at once, nor is it fighting a single, swift battle to decide victory or defeat, which is over in five or ten days. The counteroffensive is a process of fierce and decisive struggle; victories and defeats may follow one another, but defeat is the smaller part, and victory is the primary one; defeat is temporary, but victory is decisive.

The general counteroffensive in the present resistance war is the completion of the task of liberating the nation which the August General Uprising (1945) began. The general counteroffensive and the General Counteroffensive are closely linked with each other. But we should not compare the general counter offensive with the General Uprising of August and conclude that the general counteroffensive is easy like the General Uprising of August was. We should not understand them in a mechanical matter because of the word "General." Historical phenomena never fit together in the same manner. The conditions are different each time. The situation of the French colonialists now is different from that of the Japanese before. In August 1945, we attacked the Japanese little, but we scored a big victory because Japan had been defeated by the whole democratic front which had the Soviet Union leading it, while Japan's allies, Nazi Germany and Italy had been overthrown. Therefore we acknowledge having seized the government in a relatively easy manner. On the contrary, today we must shoulder the responsibility for defeating French colonialism in our country, while it is aided by U.S. imperialism, but is not (or not yet) having to cope with many battlefields outside Indochina.

At present French colonialism is being actively aided by American and British imperialism, so we must still contend with the enemy and in the future, our counteroffensive phase may be prolonged. Every time the French colonialists exhaust their strength, U.S. imperialism inject them with another dose of medicine to restore it, making them healthy again for a period of time until they lose their strength once more. Of course, the illness is critical and difficult to treat, so the medicine can only put off the hour of death and not save the patient's life. But we must make the enemy lose more than they can replace (remembering that the amount replaced is comprised of the efforts of the French colonialism in part and of U.S.-British assistance to France in part). To put it another way, we must fight until the enemy cannot increase assistance and cannot re-place losses in time, for only then will they be prepared to surrender at last.

We have friendly socialist countries and People's democracies supporting and helping us. But to be victorious, above all else, we must make our own ef-forts. Our efforts are primary, while help from abroad is very important, but only adds further to those efforts. Therefore, we cannot depend on the aid from abroad. We must use that assistance well and turn it into our own material strength. Remember that friendly countries do not bring troops to fight in place of us, and those countries are not the "omnipotent" talisman of a sorcerer.

The anti-war movement of the French people and political change which could take place in France will have a big influence on our resistance war. But we must correctly assess the struggle of the French people for nation, democracy, and peace, and absolutely have no illusions. Depending on the character of political change in France we assess what influence it will have on us. If there is a change in a progressive direction, bringing the pro-peace faction into power, obviously it will be favorable for us. But if it is a change in the reactionary direction, then obviously, it will not only not be favorable but will be harmful. There could also be a time when a change having a reac-tionary character pushes the French people to rise up and oppose it, and at that time, we must consider how the French people react to decide. However we ought not and cannot expect a complete disintegration of French expeditionary force as happened to the Japanese army in August 1945. The disintegration of the French army, if it occurs, will have to be caused by the victory of the Vietnamese resistance war and nothing else.

To Carry Out the General Counteroffensive,
We Must Complete the Task of Preparing for the General Counteroffensive

At present we are in the period of completing the task of preparation for switching strongly over to the general counteroffensive.

Many people only pay attention to the end of the slogan, "switch strongly over to the general counteroffensive," and forget the beginning, "complete the task of preparation." For that reason, they think that the general counterof-fensive has arrived already. If switching over to the general counteroffensive is not yet the general counteroffensive, then completing the task of preparing to switch over to the general counteroffensive is even more clearly not yet the general counteroffensive, nor is it having already switched over to the general counteroffensive.

[Nine paragraphs elaborating on this point are omitted.]

We must exert all our efforts to push strongly the following principal preparation tasks.

a) General mobilization of manpower, material resources and financial re-sources for the resistance war. Only thus can we rapdily increase our military strength, increase the supply of manpower and economic resources for the front-line to carry out the general counteroffensive. To carry out the general mobil-ization well, we must follow the mass line, and make the masses to understand and volunteer on their own: those who have money contribute money, those who have paddy contribute paddy, those who have strength contribute strength, those who have sagacity contribute sagacity, in accord with the slogan, "Everything for the frontline, everything for victory." But cadres at all echelons, and branches of the government must absolutely not exploit the general mobilization to coerce people, or appropriate their property, or make the people suffer. On the contrary, we must exert ourselves to mobilize the people to emulate one an-other to increase production; while carrying out policies on land and taxes and other democratic policies to nourish the strength of the people, and develop the democratic rights of the people.

b) Push strongly the building of the people's armed forces; including: main force troops, local troops, guerrilla militia and "hidden military units" in the regions controlled by the enemy, including all the cities. We must realize clearly that guerrilla militia are the inexhastible source of replacements for the local troops; local troops are the inexhaustible source of replacements for the main force troops. Speaking generally of the whole country, guerrilla militia must be larger than main force troops. Concentrating guerrilla militia and raising them to the local troops, as well as concentrating local troops and raising them to be main force troops must be done at the correct time, neither too soon nor too late. If it is too soon, people's armed forces will have a large head and a small behind; too late and strategic mobile forces will not be sufficient to open big campaigns aimed at annihilating the enemy's power.

In order to develop the people's armed forces in a regular manner, we must do everything possible to take care of creating and rearing cadres, to take care of rear work to insure the supply of food, weapons, ammunition and military equipment used by the troops to fight the invader.

c) Annihilate the enemy's manpower further, penetrate more deeply the strategic contradictions of the enemy. If we want the relation of forces between the enemy and us to change favorably for us, and create conditions for us to switch to the general counteroffensive, the people's armed forces must fight hard to annihilate still more of the enemy's strength. Thus we must develop guerrilla war, while developing regular warfare. On the basis of developing guerrilla warfare broadly, main force troops open big or little campaigns, attack the concentrated forces, annihilate most of the enemy's manpower, and make the enemy's forces decline, reduce their numbers and make the morale of their soldiers fall apart.

At present, the big contradiction of the enemy's forces is the desire to concentrate strategic mobile forces in order to cope with big, medium and small attacks by our army on many different battlefields; if they want to occupy land, herd the people, use war to feed war, they must disperse their forces, spread their forces thinly; to concentrate their main force to launch big military operations, they have to give up land and people. Thus, we must fight hard to penetrate deeply those contradictions of the enemy, and push the enemy into a passive position and even bigger defeat.

d) Make efforts to consolidate our rear area. In order to switch strongly over to the general counteroffensive, one more important matter is to make efforts to consolidate our rear area, and to harass the enemy's rear area.

Only if our rear area is consolidated can we be in a stable position to advance to the general counteroffensive. To consolidate the rear area, we must do the following necessary things: 1) develop the resistance economy, push production strongly make the people in the free zone have enough of the basic necessitites of life; 2) consolidate the National United Front relying on the worker-peasant alliance: 3) consolidate the people's democratic government; 4) make every effort to prevent spy activities, punish spies and oppose the enemy's espionage war.

To harass the enemy's rear area, we must develop guerrilla warfare in the enemy's rear and increase all forms of sabotage right in the zone controlled by the enemy, including breaking up the puppet lackey government of the enemy.

To carry out the above tasks, our position and strength must increase, and the position and strength of the enemy must weaken, and at that time, we will have enough counteroffensive strength to annihilate much of the power of the enemy, and drive the enemy army out of the country.

[Four pages summarizing the problem of the timing of the general counteroffensive, and discussing the problems of over optimism and pessimism, are omitted.]

Judging correctly what is completing the task of preparation, and switching strongly to the general counteroffensive, we will lead the popular masses to be prepared to advance to a new stage in a firm, certain manner, without wandering or wavering.

Speak truthfully to the masses about the advantages and the difficulties of the resistance but always make the masses confident in the Party and in themselves; correct shortcomings and weak points in order to advance - that is the obligation of all of us communists at present.

(181) <u>MEMORANDUM OF CONVERSATION BETWEEN AMBASSADOR HENRI BONNET AND RUSK</u>, July 31, 1950

Source: *Foreign Relations, 1950, Vol. VI*, pp. 839-840.

Pushing for a common policy among the three Western powers in Southeast Asia, the French Ambassador suggested for the first time that France wanted U.S. air support in the event of a Chinese Communist attack on the Tonkin border.

Ambassador Bonnet called this afternoon at his request. He began by mentioning the contradictory intelligence reports his Government was receiving regarding movements of troops within China, mentioning that some reports stated troops were being withdrawn from the Canton area toward Hankow, while other reports indicated Communist troops were moving toward the Indochina border. He also said that there were reports on the building of roads in Yunnan and particularly Kwangsi. He pointed out that these roads might be used to move up tanks for an attack upon the Tonkin border.

Ambassador Bonnet then suggested that the time has arrived for the establishment of a common Western policy with regard to Southeast Asia. Within this framework the Ambassador thought that it was necessary to establish a common military policy, possibly by establishing a theater of Southeast Asia in which each country interested would have a specific field of responsibility. He pointed out that the British were already committed in Malaya and Hong Kong, and that the French should, of course, bear the major responsibility in Indochina, where they had 150,000 troops at the present moment. He averted to the conversations in Saigon between the French and General Erskine of the Melby Mission, and said that the French were particularly concerned, should the Chinese Communists launch an attack on the Tonkin border, as to who would provide the tactical air support for the French defenders. He said that the French had insufficient aircraft to provide such support themselves.

In reply to a question, Mr. Bonnet said that he did not believe an attack by the Chinese on the Tonkin border would cause further mobilization in France.

He said that the French had, however, already appropriated an additional 80,000,000,000 francs for military expenditures and were stretched very thin.

In reply to a question, he indicated that the French were not certain that the Chinese Communist attack on the Tonkin border would be coordinated with an attack inside Indochina launched by Ho Chi Minh, but that they assumed liaison between Ho and the Chinese Communists was very close.

Mr. Rusk said that he would consult with his colleagues and that he felt a reply to the French proposal would take a considerable amount of study.

(182) <u>VO NGUYEN GIAP'S APPEAL ON THE ANNIVERSARY OF THE FOUNDING OF THE CHINESE PEOPLE'S LIBERATION ARMY</u>, August 1, 1950

Source: Giap, *Orders of the day, Speeches and Mobilization Letters*, pp. 98-100.

In the months that followed the triumph of the Chinese communists, the Vietnamese and Chinese liberation armies began to work on plans to get military supplies from China into North Vietnam. Despite French efforts to block communications routes from China to the Viet Minh base areas, by mid-1950, substantial supplies were beginning to arrive from China. By the time of the Chinese People's Liberation Army's anniversary on August 1, relations between the two armies had grown extremely close, as indicated by Giap's appeal on that occasion.

All officers of the National Protection Army, local troops and militia throughout the country,

Today, August 1, 1950, is the 23rd anniversary of the founding of the Chinese People's Liberation Army. Under the clearsighted leadership of the Chinese Communist Party and Chairman Mao Tse-tung, passing through so many years of hard struggle against imperialists, feudalists and bureaucratic capitalists, the liberation army played a major role in the revolution of the Chinese people.

In the autumn and winter of 1949, the liberation army swept away the army of the Chiang Kai-Shek reactionary clique, which was being aided by the U.S. imperialism and liberated the entire Chinese territory, establishing the People's Republic of China. The success of the Chinese Revolution marked a big victorious phase for the people of the oppressed nations of the world. After the great Russian October Revolution, the Chinese Revolution is the greatest revolution.

The Chinese People's Liberation Army is one of the strongest armies of the new democratic countries at present.

The liberation army attacked to the death the forces of imperialists, led by the U.S. The liberation army not only liberated the Chinese people but has also contributed greatly to the struggle for peace and democracy in the world.

The victory of the Chinese people and the Chinese liberation army has a big influence on our resistance. For that reason, August 1 has an important significance for us. Because the Vietnamese and Chinese nations are brothers, the two armies are brothers, and the feeling of being of one family is more and more intimate all the time.

Comrades!

On the occasion of this anniversary of the founding of the Chinese People's Liberation Army, I appeal to you to:

- Actively study the spirit of serving the people, the concept of people's war, the mass concept of the Chinese liberation army, make every effort to increase your political work and build strategic and tactical theory of our army.

- Make every effort to tighten the solidarity between the Vietnamese and Chinese armies, follow the example of heroic struggle and victorious tradition of the Chinese liberation army in order to fulfill the mission of destroying the French colonialists and the American interventionists, win independence and unify the Fatherland.

Long live the spirit of solidarity between the Vietnamese army and the Chinese liberation army!

Annihilate the French colonialist invaders and the U.S. interventionists!

Long live world peace and democracy!

Long live Chairman Ho.

Long live Chairman Mao.

(183) <u>TELEGRAM FROM CHAIRMAN OF THE JOINT SURVEY MISSION JOHN F. MELBY TO RUSK</u>, August 7, 1950

Source: *Foreign Relations, 1950, Vol. VI, pp. 845-848.*

In a pessimistic report to the Far Eastern Division of the State Department Melby reverted to the U.S. view of the 1945-48 period - that a military solution to the problem of Indochina was probably impossible and that the only answer was a French promise of complete independence some years in the future, as the U.S. had done in the Philippines.

171. Tomap. No distribution. For Rusk and Lacy from Melby. In appraising Indochina situation certain facts stand out which highlight important facets of

Indochina problem and may be suggestive of helpful course of action. This telegram is based on collected observations by all survey mission members, as well as conversations with wide variety of individuals. Erskine concurs with it.

1. Indochina is keystone of SEA defense arch. Failure here will inevitably precipitate balance of SEA mainland into Communist orbit with excellent prospect of similar eventuality in Indonesia and Philippines, barring American occupation of latter. Within Indochina complex, Vietnam is the crisis point whose resolution will largely determine outcome in Laos and Cambodia.

2. French are dedicated, at least officially, to proposition problem can be solved by military means and that this is only hopeful course. Pignon has agreed that political and economic measures should accompany or follow but his agreement lacks ring of conviction. Unfortunately his departure for Paris has denied opportunity for genuinely frank and confidential discussions with him. On other hand some other French in private talks, notably Carpentier, have revealed a conviction that although there is no reason why proper application of force cannot break military back of Viet Minh, such course will not solve basic Vietnam problem which will only re-emerge later in same or other form. Carpentier insists French are incapable of applying requisite complementary political action. Vietnamese state, and many French reluctantly agree, that hatred and distrust of French so deeprooted that no basis for long-range cooperation exists or can exist on present basis.

3. French military effort despite some successes in Red River Delta, has so far failed to break Viet Minh military strength. High local French commanders even state basic Viet Minh military strength actually increasing rather than decreasing. French entranced with analogy of tapping on a jar which later suddenly shatters. This doubtless had nineteenth century validity and might even today if Vietnam could be totally isolated; but given what we know of Communist hydra-headed policy of force, terror, propaganda, penetration, and cynical exploitation of any opportunity this concept would appear fatuous, even dangerous. French strategy largely one of static defense accompanied by disturbing amount of apathy. Division of opinion now centers around whether postrainy season operations should concentrate on expansion of Tonkin pacified area for Chinese reasons or on cleaning up Mekong Delta area for economic reasons. Defensive attitude only encouraged by woeful lack of materiel. French also fail make proper use Vietnamese troops apparently on hypothesis, as Commanding Officer Langson put it, if more use made then greater concessions to Vietnam would also be required. Obvious French also fear armed Vietnamese might turn on them - surely a confession of something and perhaps not wholly without warrant under present conditions. Our evidence is that Vietnamese troops properly trained and equipped could make major contribution. Growth Viet Minh military strength is a demonstration native troops can be rapidly and effectively organized for combat.

4. Erskine convinced Chinese border could be made impregnable and coastline sealed off from external aid to Viet Minh. Present forces on border insufficient to prevent increasing arms traffic or stop any major invasion effort. It has been suggested locally that Japanese troops experienced in warfare in this kind of terrain might be used. Once border sealed Viet Minh problem would be immeasurably simpler with proper combination of military and political activities.

5. Illustrative of difficulties confronting French militarily is Red River Delta situation. To French pacification seemingly means control of certain strongpoints, absence of important enemy armed action, and ability of peasants to cultivate their fields by day unmolested. Balance of picture as we saw it in Tonkin in an area French cleaned out one year ago was our inability to move anywhere without armed guards, failure to restore and maintain minimum adequate road system, endless series of assassinations even in Hanoi, continuing and increasing volume of Communist propaganda without corresponding and effective counter-effort. French state Viet Minh are everywhere. I agree what has been

done represents improvement but it is neither sufficient nor decisive especially considering lapse of time involved. I have no evidence anyone knows what
Viet Minh does by night in Delta area. In absence of evidence to contrary and
in light our Chinese experience, evidence recent Huk expansion in Cagayan Valley, and general knowledge of Communist methods, I believe we must assume Viet
Minh actively engaged in organizing and disciplining peasant lowest common de-
nominator for opportune use. In this connection recall December 19, 1946.[1]
Only ally French armed force has had in this nocturnal warfare appears to be
Viet Minh excesses. I also partially discount muchly touted Tonkinese dislike
of Chinese, especially in contrast to attitude toward French. Rude noises were
once made that Chinese dislike of Russians would prove stronger than ideological pull.

6. As for Vietnamese attitudes and aspirations, Governor Tri, a truly impressive person, gave the best synthesis of statements by other responsible
Vietnamese. He and others protest that total French withdrawal at this time
would be disastrous and result only in Communist victory, due in major part to
French failure to assist in establishment of Vietnam armed force adequate to its
internal responsibilities. French can never genuinely pacify Viet Minh areas,
and as noted above some French agree. Only Vietnam can do this. (One Mission
member who participated in Vietnam night raid on a Viet Minh village was shocked
and impressed by thoroughness and savagery with which patrol was carried out.)
French should assume responsibility for protection against external threat or
aid to Viet Minh and proceed rapidly to enable Vietnam to handle internal situation. There must also be some assurances concerning what future thereafter
would hold. Primary Vietnam concern is eventual independence. Vietnam will
have it regardless of anything else and will seek allies wherever it may be
necessary. Other problems can be handled after that. Most Vietnamese secretly
admire the Viet Minh for having fought the French to standstill and by the same
token are not wholly displeased with North Korean successes. (Carpentier has
expressed his and Pignon's fears that under certain circumstances Vietnam will
reach some agreement with Viet Minh.) No French guarantee can ever be acceptable, since post-war developments have made it abundantly clear that France intends to re-establish itself in Indochina as far as possible. Any guarantee
must be countersigned by someone in whom Vietnam has confidence. (Having a
dirty mind, one presumes this means US.)

7. Line of reasoning in paragraph 6 has certain obvious gaps and deficiencies. I also assume a certain percentage of it is designed for our benefit.
Still, the Vietnam attitude is a political reality which can hardly be ignored.
Inevitably the confidence with which they speak of their own abilities leads to
the naughty suspicion that they are overestimating themselves. This however is
no reason we should underestimate them. If the border were effectively closed,
it might matter relatively little what happened inside, except to the French
who might rather understandably take a dim view of having to shut up on top of
all they have already put up.

In summary then there is good reason to believe that proper application of
sufficient military force, plus goading the French into a more offensive spirit,
can hold the lid on the Indochinese kettle for the predictable, if relatively
limited, future. It will not however solve the long-range problem. Neither
can the French do it on their present promises or without a radical change of
heart and approach. If American interests can be served by the short-range approach then the rest need not concern us. This must be determined with relationship to over-all world situation, prospects, and time factors. If however
the longer alley is important, then Franco-Vietnamese behavior in that alley,
to borrow from the Churchillian analogy of the gorilla in the jungle, is a
matter of the gravest concern.

If the latter be the case and the foregoing analysis valid, a satisfactory
solution can only be found when the French have been persuaded to sweeter

reasonableness and the Vietnamese firmly led by the hand through the growing pains of adolescence. Recent Korean precedent may be suggestive. I could propose consideration of following: French undertaking for Vietnam independence within specified period of 5, 10, 20, or 30 years with certain special compensations for French such as are found in Philippines-American arrangements.[2]

French would undertake to guarantee inviolability Indochina border. Vietnam national army would be rapidly created to assure responsibility internal situation and as this progressed French forces would withdraw to border areas or where unnecessary depart. Civil administration would increasingly be Vietnam responsibility. All such agreements would have UN public guarantee and such supervision as necessary. Assumably [*sic*] US would as usual pay most of bills. If US can bring its Korean responsibilities within UN framework, there is little solid reason why French cannot do same for Indochina.

Ever recognizing that this form is hardly likely to provoke dancing in the streets of Paris, it may well be that this or something similar is only real prospect for salvaging anything and French must be coerced into realizing it and behaving accordingly. If Vietnam has determined on complete independence as all evidence suggests, it probably cannot get it for a long time in face of French opposition, but it can create the kind of uproar which will constitute a continuing drain on French strength and in end benefit only Communists. Coincidentally, American identification with French in such eventuality will further weaken American influence in Asia. Historically no ruling group has ever remained more or less indefinitely in power in face of active or even passive resistance from the governed, or without ruining itself in the process. There is no convincing evidence Nationalism in Indochina proposes to be an exception.

[1]For reports on the outbreak of hostilities in Tonkin on December 19, 1946, see *Foreign Relations*, 1946, vol. VIII, pp. 15 ff.

[2]For documentation on United States relations with the Philippines, see pp. 1399 ff.

(184) TELEGRAM FROM MINISTER DONALD R. HEATH IN SAIGON TO ACHESON, August 9, 1950

Source: *Foreign Relations, 1950, Vol. VI*, pp. 849-851.

In a counterpoint to Melby's pessimism, Heath cited French official claims of military success and the beginning of U.S. military aid as a critical factor, without, however, mentioning the increase in Viet Minh military supplies from China.

183. Tomap. We believe survey Mission's recommendations for increased scale of assistance to French forces as presented in Legtel 170, August 7, are very sound and Legation desires add its emphasis of importance urgent implementation. We will comment on specific recommendations after study of group's final report. While we agree with these conclusions, we have following comments and reservations to make on several aspects of introductory argumentation in Legtel 170.

1. Re stalemate after five years of warfare. In Legation and Attaches opinion this ignores progress French have made and are continuing to make in expanding their areas of control and penning Viet Minh organized units (as opposed to individual Viet Minh terrorists) into increasingly well-defined enclaves. Moreover, it is not realistic to date beginning of fighting here from 1945 when French force was nonexistent. The real base line date should be December 19, 1946, when Ho attacked by surprise and brought to end all efforts to negotiate with him.

First French efforts with limited forces were in the nature of raid and punitive expeditions. It was only relatively late in campaigning season of 1949 that policy of clearing deltas began to be applied, largely as result of local initiative on part of General Alessandri and Pignon as opposed to the cautious counsels of Paris. Furthermore, the campaigning part of each year during which major deployments are undertaken is only from October to June. (It is possible, however, that with specialized equipment, more could be undertaken during rainy season. Unless one has campaigned in this country it is probably difficult to be certain on this point.) In any event test of capabilities will come when fall offensive opened, and any assumption of failure is considered premature.

2. Re statement that French forces appear to have lost considerable amount offensive spirit. We naturally would defer to General Erskine's appraisal of any matter subject to professional military judgment. Our first hand observations of several months leads us to believe that morale among junior commanders and troops is high. As regards High Command we doubt whether sufficient weight has been given in report to factor of pitifully small and obsolescent supplies hitherto available to French general staff, to difficulties if not impossibility of replacing casualties, to need of husbanding men and material against Chinese Communist threat which French until most recent past could only contemplate having to meet alone. There are only 21 batteries of field artillery in the country and not 1 90 mm anti-aircraft piece. There are no tanks.

We do not deny that a certain "command caution" has been apparent at the high echelons. Pignon has at times told us that the thought Carpentier was too attentive to the War Ministry which is said to take cautious view of overextension in a conflict as far from Paris as Korea from parts of the US. This command caution is possible responsible for limited number of night patrols. Yet General Alessandri called his shot on delta campaign and beat his own estimates by two months. He now says he could end effective Viet Minh resistance here in 18 months. So far as spirit of troops is concerned it must be recalled to hand, kill or be killed combats by individual GI's for three and half years of murderous jungle war. Problem in future will be of course transition from relative command caution in period of straitened supplies to vigorous offense when adequate logistic support available. We think French areas eager as ourselves to destroy Viet Minh.

3. Re political concessions by French and US or UN backed "definite plans for eventual independence". We agree, of course, that no military solution is possible in political and economic vacuum. We believe that it would be at least premature to write off our present policy or to recommend at this time the political *demarche* of the kind envisaged in survey mission's preliminary reports (see Legtel 171, August 7).

4. It might be noted that interim report contained in reftel makes no reference to amounts and kind equipment for native troops. French initial requests were for equipment of twelve Cambodian, Laotian and Vietnamese battalions which will actually arrive within few days. Yet during mission's stay Viets asked for equipment for 20 battalions plus certain additional supplies and other states had occasion to present statements more recent than those on which original French requests based.

Nor does reftel go into amount and ratio of distribution of arms among home guard, various stateguards and other auxiliaries. These are questions with which Legation and MAAG will be continually concerned.

Above comments based on initial scrutiny of survey group report[1] received just prior group's departure.

Sent Department 183, repeated info Paris 85, Singapore for survey mission unnumbered.

[1]For the covering letter of the report, August 6, see p. 840.

(185) TELEGRAM FROM MINISTER HEATH TO ACHESON, August 23, 1950

Source: *Foreign Relations, 1950, Vol. VI*, pp. 864-867.

In its first major assessment after the Melby-Erskine survey mission, the U.S. legation in Saigon came down clearly on the side of optimism, looking to the creation of a Vietnamese National Army as a key to success in Indochina. Heath's telegram called for using the commitment of major new assistance as a bargaining chip to force France and the Bao Dai government to agree to an acceptable program of action, including significantly increased U.S. influence over the conduct of the war.

265. Personal for Secretary Rusk and Lacy. No distribution. Paris 864. August 17 to Department. Pleven's important decision press for information of Vietnam national army has coincided with Legation's preliminary survey of conditions for American aid to IC following the Korean war. Our conclusion on broad lines are as follows:

1. Since the Korean war began it has become increasingly evident that economic and military aid to IC will and should be on a larger scale than originally programmed. The threat to Vietnam is assuming sharper outline with the concentration of Viet Minh troops in China. The MDAP joint survey mission has not made its final recommendations but it clearly envisions expanded military aid. Plans for French rearmament in Europe must involve at least a compensation increase in the number of Viets under arms in IC as French units are redeployed. US aid will be invoked to finance and equip the new units.

2. American assistance on the scale now in sight will modify the concept that our aid merely "supplements" but does not "supplant" the French especially if it is accompanied by redistribution of French troops to Europe. Our experiences in Nationalist China and the Philippines suggest that we should not commit ourselves to any substantial expenditures without being satisfied that French and Viets (and Cambodian and Laotian) operations, administration and policies will effectively serve the common aims of rapid extinction of Communist civil war within IC and building up of prosperous progressive and stable Indochinese governments. We should make no substantial new commitment until there is agreement between them and ourselves and unless we are assured of the means of making our advice continuously effective. The French must continue to bear the greater burden in financing the Indochinese states and military operations and will of course have here the greatest voice in any control measures but our influence must also be felt not only through the gravitational pull of our aid program but in actual participation in certain controls and in accelerating certain French concessions. Such participation will be welcomed by the Vietnamese and other IC states.

3. For example with reference to the creation of a Vietnam national army, which has already been linked with US aid by Pleven, Legation believes we must ascertain French intentions and express our views before aid is increased or any commitments given. Our advice on war plans should be sought and heeded. We should give our views on organization and training of army and advancement of senior Viet officers. US aid has such repercussions on Indochinese Government financing that we should participate officially or unofficially in fiscal planning. There should be an immediate sharing and synchronization of intelligence arrangements. We should advise on propaganda and political warfare and should improve Bao Dai's public relations.

4. As to concessions by the French we agree that the most fruitful and immediate should be creation of the Viet national army. Pleven's decision to accelerate its formation is a most welcome one even though he contemplates at the same time some withdrawal of French forces here. This decision, quickly exploited and publicized, could effect a very real improvement in the internal political-military situation in IC. Properly developed it would point way out of dangerous situation of political impasse and inconclusive military progress. It might also help convince the doubters of the honesty of French intentions to grant them full independence. The increase in Viet troops should be very much larger and more rapid than the reduction in French forces and with proper training and control of the former the obstacle to Communist invasion of IC might shortly be a more imposing one than now exists. It was evident to Melby mission as it has been increasingly to us that the Viet Minh revolt cannot be extinguished without a very considerable increase in police and troops. The French cannot now increase their forces here. The increase must come from native forces.

5. It may be remarked here that the Melby-Erskine report and recommendations must be substantially restudied, revised and extended. Although recognizing need for getting more Viets under arms, the military aid recommended by the report make practically no provision of an expansion in Viet forces beyond level envisaged pre-Korea nor is any concrete recommendation made with respect to Viet army.

6. The French must make very clear that it is true Viet army they are forming which after a specified training period, say three to four years, will be under independent Viet command. During the training period the high and intermediate command of course must be French. (In this connection it would be appreciated if Paris could specify just what Pleven has proposed and if possible what Bao Dai now has in mind.)

7. An accelerated recruiting of Viet forces will require an increased financial contribution which presumably France and certainly the IC states are not at present able to make nor has our military aid program contemplated for IC such direct cash assistance. We should grant such direct assistance for a period of two years or longer if we want real results in IC. If within that period French and enlarged native forces could really stamp out the rebellion in the lower Mekong region, the Viets and Cambodians might thereafter be able to meet the pay of augmented forces from their own increased revenues. The bulk of the normally great IC export surplus comes from this region.

8. Although the creation of a national army appears to be most important immediately feasible French concession, we believe that there are many secondary political measures which can and should be taken and which should constitute not departure from but implementation of the March 8 accords. As we see it in order to be politically effective here, announcement of an increase in Viet national forces and related action should be accompanied by a number of those implementing measures which should be convincingly publicized as "new deal for Vietnam". Another French concession now fully due would be to turn over the High Commissioner's palace to Bao Dai. Now may also be time for French to bring forward candidacy of Vietnam, Cambodia, and Laos for UN.

9. These concessions may require changes in personnel. We have reservations whether General Carpentier would be the man to put through a policy of rapid formation of a Viet Army. His distrust of the Viets as soldiers and officials is in contrast with the attitude of General Alessandri, commander in the north who is rather liked and respected by Viets and who has advocated increasing Viet militia forces in his region.

10. As regards Viet concession, these should begin with Bao Dai emerging from Oriental seclusion and publicly interesting himself in the welfare of his subjects and the administration of his state. It is also high time or shortly will be, to make some kind of start towards setting up Viet legislative bodies.

It is however apparent that such bodies could not at this time be nationally representative nor could initial selection be on basis of unrestricted suffrages. Bao Dai should also not object to some Franco-American control over the dilatory fiscal collections of Vietnam.

11. The policies and programs of the nations chiefly interested in IC were framed prior to the Korean invasion. All of them seem to be undergoing some reassessment of which Pleven's new approach is an important illustration. The discussions at Pau and the conversations which the French are holding with Bao Dai and Viet leaders will also affect the IC future.

12. We believe the time has now come for a review of IC affairs, appropriately at next Foreign Ministers conference if one to be held at an early date. We should go fully into Franco-Viet policies and give our ideas for a program. US dollar aid alone may not give US all that leverage on Franco-Viet affairs which the situation requires. It now seems to us more than ever indispensable that there should be early strategic US-UK-French conversation on SEA at the highest levels supplemented by frequent theater conferences.

(186) <u>TELEGRAM FROM ACHESON TO THE LEGATION IN SAIGON</u>, September 1, 1950

Source: *Foreign Relations, 1950, Vol. VI,* pp. 868-870.

Acheson responded to the political and military deterioration of the French Union position not by raising fundamental questions of the course the U.S. was following but by calling for a major new propaganda move by the French and Bao Dai: announcement of a Vietnamese national army under Bao Dai's command, which would then be put under French command for the duration of the war.

238. Dept has viewed growing signs of polit and mil deterioration in Indochina with increasing concern. The failure of the Vietnam Govt and its leaders to inspire support, the slow pace of the Pau Conf and inability or disinclination of Bao Dai to assume leadership as exemplified by his prolonged stay in Fr are among disturbing polit factors. Of even greater immediate import are mil considerations - the increasing indications of Chi Commie - Viet Minh military collaboration and ever present threat of Chi invasion.

Whatever prompt action we can take ourselves or recommend to Fr to stem unfavorable tide must bear fol objectives in mind:

1) Have sufficient dramatic impact to stir all factions of Vietnamese polit thought, preferably to extent of swaying fence sitters;

2) Serve to repudiate claim that Fr ar not sincere in implementing Mar 8th Accords and are using "independence within Fr Union" as a cloak for colonialism;

3) Have sufficient psychological attraction to nationalists to appease, at least temporarily, their hunger for further evidences of autonomy;

4) Will not in any way jeopardize the already inadequate Fr and allied mil potential in Indochina;

5) Attract other potential non-Commie combatant units (Cao Daists, Hoa Hoa, Catholics) to side of Fr Union troops;

6) Cause no further depletion of West Eur mil potential and even improve it by releasing Fr troops from service in IC.

Dept concurs fully with Paris and Saigon that formation of natl army, at least in Vietnam and possibly to lesser extent in Laos and Cambodia, is action which approaches closest to these requirements while still remaining within realm of possibility.

We are, nevertheless, conscious of complexity of technical and other problems involved in accomplishing task and aware that it might be matter of years before armies actually exist in usual sense. We, therefore, are seeking means whereby psychological benefits of action may begin to be harvested immed even though full realization must, in fact, be delayed. The fol plan is therefore submitted for your study, comment and discussion with appropriate Fr authorities and possibly Bao Dai.

1) At earliest moment it be solemnly (and simultaneously) declared by Fr (Auriol?) and Bao Dai that in keeping with provisions of March 8 Accords, Vietnam Natl Army under command of Emperor will become fact and that all indigenous troops then serving in Fr Union forces are incorporated into new Natl Army.

2) That pursuant to Art 3 of Mar 8 Accords it is declared that a state of natl emergency exists and that His Majesty as Commander in Chief has therefore placed natl forces under command of Fr High Command in the face of threat of fon invasion.

3) That fol emergency Natl Army will be released from service under Fr command to resume fundamental task of assuring internal order, etc., and that in meanwhile offer and NCO training program will proceed.

These are bare outlines which if found feasible may later be enlarged to include invitation to other partisan forces to join colors, provide for Viet staff officers on Fr staff, devise program for replacement Fr officers by Viets, etc.

In suggesting such a plan Dept does not seek to oversimplify problem or overlook drawbacks. It is realized that for the time being this will only be a paper transfer which will be subj to customary Viet criticism of another meaningless gesture. However, it wld legally establish a Viet Army presumably with distinctive *insigne* and to this extent represent a step forward. We believe need for action so great we must give consideration every possible action within practical limitations.

Nor does Dept intend ignore obvious corollary Alphand Pleven request 200 billion francs two year period for establishment Natl Army. Paris may inform French this question receiving active consideration and comment thereon will be forthcoming soonest.

For ur conf info matter of formation Natl Armies will be brought up in conjunction our discussion IC at FonMinConf preliminaries of which commence today. Ur and Paris recent reporting this related subjs of which ur 265 Aug 23 outstanding have been very helpful.

(187) TELEGRAM FROM ACTING SECRETARY OF STATE WEBB TO THE LEGATION IN SAIGON, September 16, 1950

Source: *Foreign Relations, 1950, Vol. VI,* pp. 880-881.

Acheson, Bevan and Schuman met in New York on September 14, and Acheson agreed to support the Vietnamese national army financially and to start high level military conversations with Britain and France on Southeast Asia, but not to provide tactical air power against a Chinese intervention. There was apparently no discussion of political questions regarding Indochina.

278. Infotel Sept 14. Fol is summary of results informal conversations IC between US and Fr staff NY and tripartite conversations canvassing history of Fr effort IC since Sept 1946. Turning to suggestion of Nat Armies Schuman described his Govt as particularly eager that this project advance in spite of occasional apparent indifferences of some Fr functionaries in IC. Obstacles to successful development Nat armies: (1) Shortage of officers, many of whom do not wish to leave Armies Fr Union (2) Lack money which France hopes US will provide. (3) Uncertain prospect of Chi invasion against which contingency Schuman made formal request for direct US tactical air assistance should inva-

sion eventuate. Schuman then emphasized importance of earliest possible tripartite military conversations on high level. He concluded by saying that he realized that the volume and timing of US assistance in IC depended upon the military situation elsewhere at any given time; that he also realized that it was impossible for the US to make any firm commitment of US forces at this moment.

Mr. Bevin said he had nothing to add.

Acheson said that the US considered the development of military power in IC both native and Fr, as of high importance; that the US had accorded its assistance programs to IC high priority; that US proposed to increase its military assistance program; that US needed further details of the Fr program for the development of National Armies upon which details his staff and that of Mr. Schuman's were now working. (*Note:* Dept officers and Wallner preparing list of questions answers to which will be necessary to final high level decision in Wash as to extent and character US final participation in National Armies project. Info supplied by Fr delegation at NY inadequate.) Acheson said it was US desire to contribute to National Armies project through provision of end-use items; that we did not wish to contribute money for local use.

Acheson said US cld not promise tactical air support in event Chi invasion.

Acheson said US wished to commence tripartite high level military conversations on IC soonest; that these shld take place Far East where lessons of Korean campaign shld be taken into account.

Schuman expressed thanks, said Secy's remarks strengthened their hopes and bolstered their potential position. Expressed hope that improvement Korean situation wld result increased US assistance IC. (Mr. Bevin made no comment.)

(188) <u>VO NGUYEN GIAP'S APPEAL AT THE BEGINNING OF THE FRONTIER CAMPAIGN</u>, September 16, 1950

Source: Giap, *Orders of the Day, Speeches and Mobilization Letters*, pp. 101-103 [Translation by editor.]

In June 1950, the ICP Central Committee decided on a major campaign to attack French forces in the Chinese border region, to open communications with China further and broaden the Viet-Bac base area. At the end of July, it was decided to broaden the purpose of the campaign to include the liberation of a section of the border from Cao Bang to That Khe. The preparations for the offensive were extensive, involving the shifting of one-third to one-half of all local cadres to civilian labor tasks. On the day the campaign began, Giap explained its significance and exhorted his troops.

All command echelons and fighters of the National Protection Army, local troops, and guerrilla-militia!

In accordance with the order of Chairman Ho, the Cao-Lang campaign has begun.

This campaign is our first major campaign.

If we win this battle, we will not only destroy the enemy's power, open communications routes and broaden our base areas, but also make the enemy's morale decline, break up by their Autumn-Winter plan, influence directly the Northwest and the midlands, create conditions to open a new situation in the North, and create further confidence and encouragement for the people and army in the entire country.

If we win this battle, it will mean winning a big battle at a time when our army is switching from guerrilla attacks to mobile warfare attacks and attacks against defense construction, accumulating many rich experiences, creating fine traditions, and establishing good bases for the development of our strength later on.

In order to carry out Chairman Ho's order to your utmost ability, in order to win complete victory in the campaign,

All command echelons must realize clearly their great and glorious mission, understand the enemy, understand ourselves; preparations must be complete, plans must be meticulous: you must resolutely guide the troops, advancing to win victory.

All fighters, including infantry, artillery and engineers, must thoroughly obey each order, fearlessly struggle, kill many enemies, capture prisoners, capture weapons, overcome every difficulty and hardship, complete in recording accomplishments, to earn the title of combat hero of Cao-Lang, and of model unit of Cao-Lang.

All staff personnel must follow closely the enemy situation, understand clearly our forces, increase military intelligence, espionage, pay attention to information liaison, help lower command echelons to be resolute and to determine their plans.

All personnel in political work must make every effort to mobilize the spirit of struggle of their troops, ensure that all cadres and fighters observe discipline carry out policy, and fulfill your mission.

All supply personnel must realize clearly that the supply mission is very important in a big campaign, ensure in a timely manner the transport of foodstuffs and ammunition to the frontline. Brother medical corpsmen must increase their work right on the frontline, swiftly binding up and caring for wounded fighters.

On the coordinated battlefields, command echelons and all fighters must actively struggle, attack strongly, kill many of the enemy and ensure victory for the primary campaign, seize the common victory to broaden the combat results.

The campaign is a campaign concentrating large forces. Thus command must unify the concentration, unity of coordination must be close and of one mind.

Battlefield discipline must be raised, war booty must be rewarded, the property of the people must be respected, prisoners of war and surrendered troops must be treated with kindness.

If we wish to win a big victory this time, we must launch several battles continuously, so everyone from cadres to each unit member must make his utmost effort, not minding difficulty or weariness, and fully prepare our spirits for continuous struggle.

We must:

Resolutely annihilate the enemy's manpower.

Assault cadres, set an example of completing your mission, raise the spirit of unity, coordinate the common effort to destroy the enemy's army. All cadres and fighters must thoroughly obey orders, struggle heroically, assault fearlessly, strive to complete in the recording of accomplishments, and win total victory for the campaign.

On the Cao-Lang battlefield, our army is concentrating its forces, will be fully equipped, the level of its tactics and technology are improved, the spirit of killing the invader is very ardent, and we are supported by the entire people and the immense masses in the rear areas with all their hearts.

Chairman Ho has appealed to us to compete in killing the invader and recording accomplishments.

In order to respond to Chairman Ho's appeal and continue the tradition of Bac-son, Cao-bang, and of the Cao-Bac-Lang combat zone, all command echelons and fighters, fearlessly advance!

We will definitely win!

We are determined to defeat the enemy!

(189) <u>DRAFT STATEMENT OF U.S. POLICY ON INDOCHINA FOR NATIONAL SECURITY COUNCIL CONSIDERATION</u>, October 11, 1950

Source: *Foreign Relations, 1950, Vol. VI*, pp. 888-890.

The National Security Council had a draft policy statement prepared which called for the U.S. to insist on an agreed military plan for Indochina as well as coordination of any military response to an invasion from outside, although it was unclear that this was to be a condition for increased military assistance.

    1. Firm non-Communist control of Indochina is of critical, strategic importance to U.S. national interests. The loss of Indochina to Communist forces would undoubtedly lead to the loss of Southeast Asia as stated in NSC 64. In this respect, the National Security Council accepts the strategic assessment of Southeast Asia which the Joint Chiefs of Staff made on 10 April 1950 (Annex No. 1).

    2. Regardless of current U.S. commitments for provision of certain military assistance to Indochina, the U.S. will not commit any of its armed forces to the defense of Indochina against overt, foreign aggression, under present circumstances. In case of overt aggression, the department of Defense will immediately re-assess the situation, in the light of the then existing circumstances.

    3. To strengthen the security of Indochina against external aggression and augmented internal Communist offensives, the Joint Chiefs of Staff are authorized to conduct military talks with U.K. and French military commanders in the Far East. Such talks would seek, first, an agreed military plan for the internal defense of Indochina and, second, the coordination of operations in Southeast Asia in the event of invasion. Such talks should clearly indicate to French authorities that increases in U.S. military aid will be provided in accordance with operational plans which are acceptable to the U.S. and are compatible with U.S. capabilities in the light of other U.S. commitments.

    4. The U.S. should secure plans from the French and the Associated States for, and assist the French and the Associated States in the prompt acceleration of the formation of new national armies of the three Associated States (Annex No. 3 contains descriptive information on the magnitude of such plans). The employment of such armies would be for the purpose of maintaining internal security with a view to releasing the bulk of the French forces in Indochina for other duties, in accordance with the strategic plan for the defense of Indochina. In due course, as these national armies are able to assume responsibility for the functions of national defense, the U.S. will favor the phased withdrawal from Indochina of French forces in order to strengthen the defense of Metropolitan France under the NATO arrangements. U.S. and French support for the formation of national armies in Indochina should be given wide and vigorous publicity. Since it is a policy of the United States (NSC 48/2) to use its influence in Asia toward resolving the colonial-nationalist conflict in such a way as to satisfy the fundamental demands of the Nationalist movement, while at the same time minimizing the strain on the colonial powers who are our Western allies, the U.S. should, for the time being, continue to press the French to carry out, in letter and spirit, the agreements of March 8, 1949 and the conventions of December 30, 1949 providing for self-government within the French Union.

    5. Since the security of the Associated States of Indochina will be affected, to some extent, by the capabilities of neighboring or nearby countries to resist Communist encroachments, the U.S. should use its influence, wherever appropriate, to promote close relations and firm understandings, in political, military and economic fields, among the Associated States and Thailand, Burma and the Philippines. In particular, the U.S. should seek to envelop full diplomatic relations between the Associated States and other countries in Southeast

Asia, collaboration among military staff officers of these countries on the security of neighboring or adjacent frontiers, and effective agreements on the control of arms smuggling and the movement of subversive agents. The U.S. continues to favor the entry of the three Associated States into the United Nations. As a culmination of these efforts the U.S. should encourage the Associated States, in due course, to participate in such arrangements for regional security under Articles 51 and 52 of the United Nations' Charter, as will effectively contribute to the common defense of the area.

6. The U.S. will have to devote substantial resources if the policies stated above are to be carried out effectively enough to assist in strengthening the security of Indochina. It is impossible at this time to set the exact cost in dollars to the United States of the formation of the national armies. When the details of the U.S. contribution have been determined, after discussions with representatives of France and the Associated States, the U.S. plan for assisting in the formation of the National Armies of Indochina will be submitted to the National Security Council for approval.

(190) <u>TELEGRAM FROM HEATH TO ACHESON</u>, October 13, 1950

Source: *Foreign Relations, 1950, Vol. VI*, pp. 890-893.

Heath, who had earlier expressed the view that the U.S. should increase its influence over the policies of France and the Associated States, recommended that a U.S. advisory role over military, economic and political policies in Indochina be institutionalized, with the Chief of MAAG becoming military advisor to French High Command and General Staff as well as the Ministers of Defense and military commanders of the Associated States.

546. In my view, US should have some voice not only with respect to French "military operations" but with respect political and financial policy which are, of course, inextricably entwined with military considerations.

Secondly, with due regard to local sensibilities and the need for making our participation unobtrusive as well as effective, we must have an advisory if real influence over the military, political and fiscal policies of the three Associate States, in particular over those of the Vietnamese Government. Cambodia and Laos present much smaller problem.

Thirdly, it is not sufficient to have high-level general agreement between the Defense and Foreign Affairs Departments of our two governments. The French should be given to understand at this stage that we expect the Legation to be advised and to some extent advisory on local French planning and operations. Paris sets policy for IC but when put into operation here such policy frequently has quite different aspect than when it left Paris.

I do not propose that we take over managerial responsibilities or a veto role out here, even if we could. The Legation with MAAG does not have the special experience nor ability to fill such a role even if possible or desirable.

On the military side, it would not be desirable or practicable to have US military participation by US officers on the operational staff. I contemplate that the Chief of MAAG, General Brink,[1] should act solely in an advisory capacity to French High Command and General Staff in IC and occupy similar capacity in relation to Ministries of National Defense of three Associate States and the commanders of the Associate State's armed forces. On French side, the French Command would be expected to keep MAAG Chief thoroughly informed of current operations including performance of US equipment and to consult with him during planning phase.

Obviously General Brink could not fulfill this function, purely advisory and consultative as it would be, without some increase in MAAG. His curbstone estimate is that he would require 15 officers. These would keep in touch at top-level with both the French and Associate States' military staffs attached to the three Ministries of National Defense, the heads of French Army, Navy and Air Forces top field GHQ for North Vietnam, Vietnamese Army headquarters and training centers and heads of Associate States' Armies. It would probably not be necessary to increase MAAG by this number since some of the officers already assigned could be utilized.

It would seem unnecessary in preliminary talks with French in Washington to discuss the small augmentation in MAAG which General Brink would require to fulfill his advisory functions. It would suffice to say that General Brink and MAAG should have continuing access to and general consultation with levels indicated above.

It is to be expected that Paris probably and the local High French Command would register objections to even advisory participation in military decisions and policy, particularly in view of absence, to date of any staff talks and arrangements, with the French and of a unified strategic concept. However, French complacency has been rudely shaken by the Caobang affair; and in Washington they are requesting further aid about equal in amount to their military expenditures in IC.

I believe the close and continuing practical advice is immediately needed here in IC and unless systematized arrangements for it are made at once, success of our entire program will be jeopardized. Lack of joint or unified strategic concept for this area should not be overriding impediment for advisory participation we are recommending in this localized theatre.

Although our personal relations with General Carpentier, French Commander in Chief, are good, he is very sensitive to any slight hint of American intervention in his command. For example, Legation has rarely been told by his staff of completed operations such as Caobang until well after press has been informed. We have learned and reported developments only by our own devices. And there are the factors of vestigial colonial mentality and French fears that American participation would be a derogation from French prestige in eyes of Associate States. Our advisory participation should be subtle and unadvertised. It should not be such as to undermine the French nor should it give grounds to Vietnamese for the belief we are irrevocably committed to support French aims and policy. I am confident General Brink would carry out activities outlined above with great tact and discretion. He is an old friend of General Alessandri for whom he has high professional respect. The proper degree of US participation here can best be arranged between Washington and Paris with Paris issuing appropriate instructions to HICOM and General Carpentier. Both would be inclined to yield readily enough to direct orders from Paris.

We, of course, could not ask or expect to obtain any definite engagement from the Chiefs of the IC states or the heads of their government to consult with us or accept our advice. No such arrangements or engagements would in fact be necessary. If our military and economic aid is administered on a specific project or short-term basis and its continuance or expansion subject to previous project performance, we should have all the influence and leverage required.

As to US grant of funds directly to states, Legation believes this legal under accords. (President Huu has expressed this view to me.) We believe French would, reluctantly, accept it. They would point out, what is perfectly true, that native states presently imcompetent to present proper estimates, budgets or justifications and that French help would be required all along line. If such grants are feasible under US laws and procedure, and if lack of local funds is limiting factor on useful increase of native forces, idea should be seriously entertained. We fully aware difficulties of undertaking, in view loose procedures and undependability local authorities. We should have to consult with French, and we should require from all authorities a much more exact accounting of receipts and expenditures than any so far available in order to be sure that our aid would be a net contribution and not merely substituted for normal expenditures of local governments.

If substantial direct dollar assistance is given toward support national armies, Legation urges that one condition which should be insisted upon by US is that French Government through their foreign exchange authorities in Paris and Saigon or as otherwise appropriate should formally undertake to ensure that foreign exchange additional to IC's current requirements will be made available finance necessary imports in an amount equivalent to piastre value dollar aid. If this is not done, the additional piastre purchasing power which US dollar support of national armies will generate will simply increase already dangerous inflationary pressures in IC and thereby make it even more difficult than at present for IC's exports to compete in world markets. It makes little difference whether additional foreign exchange be granted in dollars, francs, or other currencies since from US viewpoint dollars spent in IC will eventually be used through Metropolitan French gold and dollar pool arrangements either to finance additional dollar imports from US or other services including retirement debt or for building up France's dollar reserve. Actually last might be preferable US interests as it would defer drain on US resources with latter's contributory effect on inflationary situation in US.

Sent Department 546; repeated info Paris 261. Department pass Paris.

[1]Brig. Gen. Francis G. Brink.

(191) <u>TELEGRAM FROM HEATH FOR RUSK AND JESSUP</u>, October 15, 1950

Source: *Foreign Relations, 1950, Vol. VI*, pp. 894-896.

After the Viet Minh had successfully attacked Cao Bang and forced the French to abandon key posts in the frontier region, Heath described the setback in grave terms, noting consistent French underestimation of the Viet Minh combat potential, and the tardiness of U.S. military assistance, he called for more urgent provision of aid and joint U.S.-French military planning.

A. Military and political situation in Indochina demands highest level consideration US Government with respect to what immediate steps may be taken here to prevent loss of Indochina and with it, all of SEA.

1. Consequences French defeats in Northern Tonkin are far graver than indicated by loss of 9 battalions with 7,000 men and key positions along Chinese frontier. We believe:

(*a*) Loss of entire mountainous frontier region from Lao Kay to Mon Cay is now almost inevitable. Highly problematic if French can withdraw or link up garrisons, and losses might involve as much as 20 percent all French union forces (exclusive of Viets) in Indochina. At this writing several additional posts surrounded and preparations for withdrawal from Langson bastion are almost certainly underway.

(*b*) French offensive plans scheduled for north next month cannot now be implemented in view elimination strategic reserves and loss of pivotal positions.

(*c*) In these circumstances and while build-up of new model VM army in southern China continues, control of all Tonkin delta including Hanoi and Haiphong and of northern Indochina including Laos can no longer be assured.

2. Prime source of danger is snow-balling effect produced by impacts of defeats on already deteriorating political situation. We fear continuation of defeats may set up chain reactions in rear areas where fence-sitting Viets will be tempted to seek an accommodation with Ho Chi Minh.

3. Successes so far obtained by VM who have only committed about third of elements trained in China doubtless have exceeded even Chinese and VM expectations. Chinese participation will surely take ample forms. We look for much-increased flow of Viet recruits to China training camps and before long their new forces may well be able to hurl tank-led plane-covered assault against delta which French have no means to resist.

4. If French reveal no better military form than in past 10 days, then we must also add deficient French generalship and military intelligence to debit side of ledger for which we seek balancing factors. In spite of our constant warnings, they do not up to present time appear to have grasped full implication of practical disappearance of Chinese border as line of demarcation between Red China and Ho Chi Minh. Moreover, they have shown continuing squeamishness about taking any action which would provoke Chinese Communists, even including necessary high level aerial frontier reconnaissance.

5. Although French knew and informed Legation months ago that attack on RC 4 line possibly impending, they neither withdrew nor reinforced their positions. Apparently no one wished to take responsibility for hauling down flag. French insisted that fall of Dongkhe was an isolated action and failed to admit connection between gathering threat in north and increasing terrorist preparations in large cities and around airports. They woefully underestimated the enhancement of Viet combat efficiency due to addition automatic weapons and an adequate field artillery. Although France's great hope is to induce US to undertake eventual air intervention, they have neglected to inform us currently and completely of recent actions in time for our government to make estimate of situation which would be required to move carriers or air into position if indeed such were our intention. We now fear that the situation may be gradually sliding into one of all-out Sino-Viet general offensive without French recognizing it as such and sending up in time the necessary danger signals to the world.

B. In this situation most measures now being applied by US are little and late. Our small program of economic aid is just beginning to take hold. Military aid is too little and is so far based on what we in Saigon believe to be an inadequate appreciation of dangers of present situation in Indochina and importance of Indochina to eventual defense of US. Although we understand Indochina in "highest priority" for MDAP assistance, measure of urgency secured by such priority is fact that vitally needed fighter aircraft demanded in February are arriving only in November.
We have lately placed much hope in rapid formation of Viet national army. This cannot happen in time to affect present situation nor can it have the same appeal as it would have had before recent defeats.

C. In view of these inadequacies, we therefore propose following for earliest high level consideration:

1. Although formation of Viet army promises less than formerly, nevertheless decision and declaration for formation of such an army might put spirit in Viets provided that such an army has its own commander, nucleus of its own staff and supply services, and that it will cooperate with french as an ally and associate rather than as tutelar. Also that its numbers will constitute a set increase in forces under arms in Indochina. These conditions do not appear to be adequately met under present French plans. As we have indicated in previous telegrams, we believe that US will be called on for some direct financing of this force.

2. Scale of urgency for delivery of US aid must be completely transformed. With all respect, we suggest that most urgently needed items should be moved to this theater with same rapidity as they would be moved under directions of JCS

to a US force engaged in Pacific area. Although this may be outside the framework of MDAP procedures, I have directed MAAG to prepare with the French topmost priority list needed today, to meet a massive VM thrust. French understand this not in pursuance of instructions US Government.

3. Newpapers report that Indochina is on agenda of meeting in mid-Pacific. We do not know whether or not this be the case. Legation has long urged, and at Foreign Minister's conference it was decided to hold, earliest strategic conversations in this area. It would have been better had these been held before present difficulties but they now all the more necessary. Respectfully suggest that both in US and, at conclusion of mid-Pacific meeting, statements to effect that US line of defense runs through chain of islands off shore from Asia should be avoided. Each time this thesis has been stated in last year, we have had perturbed reaction [and] would be critical blow to Western Power interests.

4. Also believe time has come, as Legation has recently urged; for need French-US consultation in military planning in this area.

5. We hope some way can be found to apply some of resources of UN to this theater. Arbitration or good offices now seem out of question, not only because Soviet bloc interference but because proposal of cease fire and conciliation would now seem be impossible for French to accept or for US to propose. Moreover, such interposition would confer cloak of legality on Ho Chi Minh and weaken world-wide front against Communists. Furthermore, any engagements taken as result such intervention would not be respected by Communists.

We assume, however, Department considering possibility of UN border commission operating under Assembly mandate with terms of reference restricted to establishing responsibility for border violations and actively abetting aggression on a neighboring state. We realize, of course, that Soviet bloc is, in its view, holding commerce with legally recognized Ho Government.

Fact is that Russia-China is invading Indochina using VM forces they are rapidly training and equipping as an invasion force. We must now reckon with possiblity that it may be only question of weeks or even days before China overtly participates in this aggression.

Department pass Paris; sent Department 556, repeated information Paris 266.

(192) <u>TELEGRAM FROM HEATH TO ACHESON</u>, October 23, 1950

Source: *Foreign Relations, 1950, Vol. VI*, pp. 902-905.

Delivering an oral message to Bao Dai prepared by the State Department, which urged him to exercise more aggressive leadership, Heath found the ex-Emperor deeply cynical about French intentions and pessimistic about the value of new initiatives which the U.S. put so much hope in. Bao Dai explained his own inactivity as a form of passive resistance to his own government's subordinate status.

635. Reference Deptel 384, October 18. Presented credentials Sunday morning[1] at Dalat. In afternoon saw Bao Dai alone, delivering substance of message contained reftel. I had French translation of message with me to which I referred occasionally during conversation to mark that this was communication made under instructions my government.

I delivered message without essential change up through the 5th paragraph of reftel. I necessarily used different approach for the 6th and 7th paragraphs since Bao Dai, in replying my remarks accompanying presentation credentials had stated "he had personally assigned himself the mission of taking into his hands the formation of Vietnamese National Army" and at the beginning of private conversation had informed me that he intended to proceed immediately Tonkin via

Hue and would also make public appearance Saigon. He further stated he intended to personally take over reigns of government "with his collaborators" and
expressed full understanding of necessity of greatest government activity during this grave menace confronting his country. Accordingly, I paraphrased 6th
paragraph but saying that news of Bao Dai's intentions as above stated would
be very reassuring to my government which considered such activity on part of
himself and his government urgently necessary.

As regards paragraph 7, I inquired whether he intended to take up his residence in Saigon stating I had heard from Pignon the High Commissioner's Palace
had been offered him. Bao Dai, in replying, said that in fact Letourneau and
Pignon had called on him last summer but had only "vaguely mentioned" his taking over the Palace. He denied there was firm offer. I said I thought his
establishing himself in Saigon would have an excellent effect both within his
country and abroad and intimated that he might now take up the matter again
with the French. Bao Dai demurred that he should take any initiative. It was
up to the French freely to offer him the Palace and the Vietnamese Government
would then take upon itself the provision of proper substitute residence for the
High Commissioner. In any case, Bao Dai said the effect of such a move now
would not be great; it was four years too late. I expressed the opinion it was
not too late.

I did not in view of Bao Dai's assurances as above reported consider advisable to warn him as directed in paragraph 7 of reftel that procrastination in
facing realities or prolonged periods of seclusion would raise question of wisdom of continuing support Vietnamese Government which proved itself incapable
exercise autonomy acquired. Please instruct whether Department wished me to
issue this warning on occasion of next interview.

Bao Dai insisted that he had no feeling against the French and that he saw
advantages for Vietnam to remain within the French Union. The French, however,
must allow him to form National Army, must give him the means to accomplish
this mission and they must make it possible for him to rule. The delay in formation of the National Army was due to French fears that a Vietnamese force
would turn against them. If the Vietnamese Army were formed and commanded by
himself, Bao Dai, there was no danger for the French. The French have wanted
to maintain direct command and put French officers and non-coms in the new
Vietnamese battalions. That simply would not work. The French were quite
right in entertaining doubts as to the loyalty of such battalions as were now
under French command. At the time the Japs struck on March 9, 1945 French commander [*commanded*] Vietnamese troops had outnumbered the Japanese but certain
units refused to obey orders of their French officers to resist the Japanese.[2]
That was understandable. If they had been Bao Dai's troops and Vietnamese commanded, they would have resisted. French had agreed in the accords of March 8
to form Vietnamese Army but there was always great difference between agreements in principle and their execution due to French distrust and the influence
of the old Colonial functionaries. Of course, the French would have to train
the new troops and he had selected French officers to command during the period
of training but these officers must be responsibile directly to him and not to
the French High Command. He saw the status of Vietnamese Army under his command as somewhat similar to that of American forces in World War I which had
their own commanders but were under the High Command of Marshal Foch. I inquired when he would have definite plan for formation of the National Army, he
replied it would be ready within a month. I replied I hoped the main lines of
Vietnamese Army project would be ready before that date since time was of the
essence in this grave situation in which our aid had been solicited. He replied that the army plan must be solid and realistic one that would stand up.
In addition there were many local complications such he intimated as the presence of the armed religious groups, Catholic, Cao Daists, Hoa Hoas, etc. (In
the morning he said that during his trip to Rome he had told the Pope that

Vietnamese Catholics were indulging too much in politics instead of confining themselves to religious activities. The Pope showed great understanding of threat to Vietnam and had explained that he planned to give Vatican recognition to Vietnam but by "etapes". Bao Dai did not elaborate on the "etapes".) Bao Dai said he had no illusions that modern complete Vietnamese Army could be set up within six months or year. Returning to the question of the failure of French to implement their agreements, he cited the case of the officers school in Dalat. The French had not furnished the requisite equipment and had delayed furnishing the proper instructors. Terminated this chapter of his remarks by approving the recent interview given by Huu to the journal *De L'Extreme Orient* (Legtel 592, October 18).[3]

He then qualified his undertaking to visit the North and make public appearances by saying that he would have to hear what Letourneau and General Juin had decided before going to Hanoi. He assumed, however, they would call on him but he had, as yet, no request for an audience. He said that Letourneau and Juin must not make unilateral decision to abandon any part of the country. The Vietnamese Government [would?] never abandon Tonkin and it would find forces to protect it against Ho Chi Minh. I remarked that I understood it was not question of abandoning Tonkin but merely certain frontier posts which because of their isolation, the lack of communications and sufficient troops to support them represented danger to French-Vietnamese military operations in the North. Bao Dai said he could understand that but his point was that no decision of this kind should be made without consulting him.

Our talk was most friendly one and Bao Dai expressed himself with every appearance of sincerity of his appreciation of American help and intentions. In view of his declaration of intention to take over the government and make public appearance in the country, I was extremely careful and tactful in referring to the bad impression his prolonged absence abroad created. He was, however, quite aware of the implied criticism and at the end of the interview said that, while he could understand his action was not understood abroad, the reasons for his actions were perfectly understood and approved of by Vietnamese people. I saw nothing to be gained on this occasion arguing this statement. Very probably his advisors have given him that idea and he believes it because he wants to believe it. I personally think his prolonged absence was not understood by the Vietnamese people and that it has done harm to his prestige. Bao Dai expressed the desire to have fairly frequent, private talks with me in the future.

Sent Department 635, repeated info Paris 306.

[1]October 22.

[2]On March 9, 1945, Japanese occupation forces disarmed French troops in Indochina and evicted the French administration. For documentation on this event, see *Foreign Relations*, 1945, vol. VI, pp. 293 ff.

[3]Not printed.

(193) TELEGRAM FROM ACHESON TO HEATH, October 30, 1950

Source: *Foreign Relations, 1950, Vol. VII*, pp. 913-914.

In response to Heath's report on his conversation with Bao Dai, Acheson, the Secretary, instructed Heath that the U.S. was not wedded to support of Bao Dai personally, and that it might support alternative leadership if they sought to replace him.

462. Reurtel 635 Oct 23. In including Para 7 in msg to be delivered to Bao Dai (Depts 384 Oct 18) Dept did not seek to accentuate the point that he move his residence from Dalat to Saigon altho such a move wld be welcome. Pri-

marily, we wish to impress on Bao Dai our urgent hope that he will see fit to abandon his aloof attitude toward Vietnamese governmental affairs in favor of a more active participation in day to day problems. A change of residence to Saigon wld be a step forward but of little consequence unless, concurrently, the Chief of State discarded his present system of dealing with matters of state only after prolonged delay, from afar, and through the intermediary of a palace clique. We wld seek to have Bao Dai devote himself to more productive efforts in dealing with the multitudinous problems now facing Vietnam and use the influence which only he can command with his compatriots toward constructive ends.

Moreover, it was the Depts purpose in Para 7 of msg to give Bao Dai first official implication that US Govt does not regard him as indispensible to contd existence and growth in stability of legal Govt of Vietnam. It is not inconceivable that if Bao Dai's ineffectiveness continues another non commie Viet Nationalist leader might seek to replace him as Chief of State and that the Dept might view such a development as not obstructing the objectives we now seek in carrying out the present policy of furnishing econ and mil aid to Vietnam.

It is therefore urged that you deliver the contents of Para 7 during the course of ur next interview with Bao Dai placing less emphasis on the ques of residence in Saigon and more on other aspects. The Dept shld not like to think that Bao Dai uses the controversial question of the palace in Saigon as an excuse to stay in Dalat where he can remain aloof from tiresome problems and pursue his pleasures without being in the public eye.

We are encouraged by his statements concerning the formation of Natl army, his own intention to assume command and plans to visit central and north Vietnam in the near future. Pls continue to push these points with him at every opportunity.

(194) TELEGRAM FROM BRIG. GEN. F. B. BRINK, CHIEF OF MILITARY ASSISTANCE ADVISORY GROUP TO ACHESON, November 4, 1950

Source: *U.S.-Vietnam Relations, Book 8,* pp. 405-410.

After extensive consultation with the French High Command on the military situation following the successful Viet Minh offensive on the northern frontier, the chief of the U.S. Military Assistance Advisory Group (MAAG) reported that the French who were withdrawing to a new defense line in Northern Tonkin had been shocked by the defeat in the North and unable to undertake any counter-offensive actions.

French are gradually withdrawing from northern frontier and plan to hold general line Moncay-Loakay in Tonkin; in order protect Hanoi-Haiphong area and coal mining area north of Haiphong. Perimeter of these areas is to be organized as main line of resistance. Pacification measures throughout rest of Indochina will continue in effect. Northern portion of new defensive area is mountainous with corridors running generally, but not invariably so, toward the Haiphong-Hanoi Delta area. No natural barriers lie between the new line and the Delta area. Haiphong and Hanoi are both surrounded by open Delta paddy country with numerous winding tributaries of the Red River. Railroads lead from Hanoi to Langson and Haipong. The latter, along with the highway, are the main supply routes to the operational area. The presence of Viet Minh troops prevents land communications between Saigon and Hanoi requiring movements by water and air only. Average time for movements of troops and materiel from Saigon to Haiphong or Hanoi by water and rail varies from 3 to 4 weeks. Airlift between the same places is 36 hours.

Weather during November, December and January in Tonkin area generally excellent with intermittent thunderstorms; in central coastal area poor with average of 20 days per month heavy rain and low ceilings. In southern area generally excellent with intermittent thunderstorms. In the Tonkin Delta area February weather is extremely poor with heavy fog and mist. In central coastal area February weather conditions remain unchanged until June. Weather, therefore, favors general offensive operations in next 3 months by the Viet Minh which has not yet materialized.

Army: The Army combat strength equals the combat strength of the Viet Minh. Army superiority in artillery, engineer services, weapons, transportation signal equipment and level of supply. It is inferior to Viet Minh in mobility. The Army Needs:

(A) Minimum 9 additional battalions in North Tonkin area to make a limited offensive possible. These battalions are not available in Indochina and must come from France or its possessions.

(B) Weapons and equipment to supplement materiel now in use and to replace unserviceable materiel. Adequate spare parts must be furnished.

Navy: Navy has complete Naval superiority and can operate freely along the coast; and inland waterways provided formations of armored craft are used. Navy mission is:

(A) To support ground forces in shore operations by providing shipping convoys for the transportation of personnel and equipment;

(B) To furnish gunfire support and maintain control of off shore areas to prevent Viet Minh smuggling and possible amphibious assault. The Navy has moved additional amphibious craft and commando units to Tonkin

(a) To reinforce the line Haiphong-Moncay,
(b) To prevent possible flanking by sea and
(c) To conduct operations with ground force along inland waterways.
The flexibility and ability to move concentrations rapidly as needed, made possible by employment of amphibious units, should prove a powerful advantage in Delta fighting. At present the line of defense is still to far inland to allow much Naval participation in active combat.

Air: Viet Minh air strength reported as 40 aircraft which can be successfully engaged by French Air Reserve. Viet Minh anti aircraft artillery is negligible at this time (a few 20mm guns have recently made their first appearance). French have a small and highly coordinated efficient air transport organization for routine and emergency supply and troop movements which has been operating for 3 years from Hanoi Bay. It is capable of ready expansion. Military Air Transport can be supplemented by commercial airlines. There is a specific need for light bombers, fighter bombers, air transport craft and low level reconnaissance planes for photography. The potential of the French Army, Navy and Air supported by their greater resources of all kinds is greater than Viet Minh potential. But as present closer coordination of the action of these forces is needed.

The French state that they now comtemplate changing their troop dispositions from a "pacification pattern" of widely scattered small units in North Tonkin intended to gain the good will of the natives and keep down local incidents, to an "operational pattern". This will require a political decision.

The present problem in Indochina under current plans is:

(A) To regroup companies and smaller units now in Tonkin area into combat fighting battalions or regiments with cross-country ability in order to maintain a flexible line of resistance,

(B) To achieve the proper coordinated action of these forces in local area action,

(C) To at least maintain the pacification status quo throughout remainder of Indochina.

A withdrawal to the Hanoi-Haiphong Delta area will permit a stronger coordinated defense in which Combined French Army, Navy, and Air Forces can begin dual support and be employed to their utmost capabilities, when their action is properly coordinated. There are excellent fields of fire for Infantry and Artillery. Air will not be forced to operate in restricted mountainous areas and targets will be better defined and more accessible. Numerous waterways in the Delta area will greatly hamper Viet Minh movements because of the necessity to move on foot. Viet Minh routes of advance will be canalized and opportunity for rendezvous made more difficult. French troops will have greater ground, water and air transportation facilities which will afford greater opportunity for quick concentration of larger French troops against the Viet Minh forces. The withdrawal will also permit a regrouping of troops for local offensive action or a general offensive. French supply lines will be shortened and Viet Minh lines lengthened forcing them to establish sub-arsenals and sub-depots south of the frontier where they will be subject to French air attack and ground penetration. The withdrawal, however will permit the Viet Minh to consolidate the area from which these units are withdrawn giving them airstrips, better bases in Indochina and permit political organization and their conscription of the population and may produce an unfavorable chain reaction among the population of Indochina. It is possible that relatively few weapons and possibly aircraft will be given by the Chinese Communists as token gift to the Viet Minh. Chinese Communists may be loath to spare many of these weapons because of their commitments in Manchuria, Changhai-Amoy area, Kowloon, Canton and Tibet.

It must be assumed that, in general, French are fighting in unfriendly territory in all their military efforts in Vietnam. Their military operations may be jeopardized by transfer of loyalty to the Viet Minh throughout Vietnam unless further politically effective concessions are made by France to Vietnam and the formation of Vietnamese Army is initiated.

Weakness of present French military organization appears to be:

(A) An excessively static organization of defensive area with no provisions for mutual support. Detachments from general reserves are sent to the areas as needed and pass to control of area commander,

(B) There are not yet combat organizations greater than battalion size and this does not provide adequate striking forces for strong military effort,

(C) Lack of proper coordination of forces. Few air-ground liaison teams exist.

Conclusions:

(1) There has been unduly exaggerated military importance attached to Cao Bang incident; political effect has been serious,

(2) French military forces have been greatly shocked by this incident and better reorganization of their fighting forces can be expected,

(3) Contemplated withdrawal will involve series of difficult operations and further French losses must be expected,

(4) If adequate military aid arrives within next two months and French forces in Tonkin receive an additional 9 battalions and are reorganized and

properly trained as the French plan, serious penetrations by Viet Minh of Hanoi-Haiphong Delta area and coal mines north of Haiphong can be prevented,

(5) Moncay-Laokay line is over-extended and can be easily penetrated by Viet Minh forces. Laokay itself offers little military advantage except as bar to Viet Minh advance down Red River but can be by-passed or captured by Viet Minh. Possession of Moncay denies Viet Minh port on the gulf. This port and the port immediately south, if held, can be used as bases from which to launch French counter-offensive,

(6) French at present are in no position initiate counter-offensive to drive Viet Minh to northern border, nor will they be in predictable future in view of increasing Viet Minh strength, unless additional trained troops are brought in from France or its possessions,

(7) Viet Minh activities Cambodia and Laos as well as Vietnam are increasing and no troops can be spared from these areas or operations in Tonkin,

(8) Formation of Vietnamese Army is still under discussion, and not likely to become consolidated force within a year, and will not have any appreciable military value before 1952 except possibly as police force in pacification areas. Conclusions are based on assumption that Chinese Communists will not openly participate in Viet Minh operations and immediate military aid requested in Legtel 566, October 16 will arrive by 1 January 1951.

Extremely fast-moving political situation in Indochina presents many complications for French Military Command. Current plans of French military here are at present still dependent on controversial negotiations and political decisions which must be made quickly, and the military is being delayed in implementing their current plans. Three main questions at this time are:

(A) Decision which must yet be made as to changing the mission of military in Tonkin entirely from pacification to direct operational,

(B) Manner and speed with which Vietnamese Army will be activated,

(C) Speed with which military air will be delivered. Current French plans will be successful only if these questions are resolved successfully without delay.

Participated in conference with Juin and have discussed situation and plans with Carpentier here, Allessandri in Hanoi, and chiefs of major forces. General Valluy, Juin assistant, has remained here with him and I have had similar discussion with him.

(195) TELEGRAM FROM ACHESON TO BRUCE, November 11, 1950

Source: *Foreign Relations, 1950, Vol. VI*, pp. 920-921.

The British Ambassador in Paris suggested a demarche urging on the French government a pledge to give up all controls over the Associated States. Acheson made it clear that the U.S. was still concerned about the impact of such a statement on the morale of French troops in Indochina, without whom the war would be lost to the Viet Minh. Pressure on the French to make such a statement, Acheson told Bruce, should only come after the political and military situation was more favorable.

2558. Dept has followed developments concerning suggestion that UK Amb Paris inform Fr Govt that "they make formal statement of intention release control Indochina without, however, mentioning time limit" with interest (Lond's tel 2234, Oct 18).

We had agreed fully with reasoning behind Harveys request that he use discretion as to timing approach to Schuman and that it be delayed at least until end Pau Conference. As matter has and will, undoubtedly, continue to be discussed with Fr by Malcolm McDonald Dept now considering suggestion to Brit Govt that their *demarche* to Fr through McDonald or Harvey be coordinated not joined with similar one on our part. Do not believe joint *demarche* advisable as traditional Fr suspicion UK FR might lead them resent Brit action. Joining Brit might thus reduce effectiveness our approach.

In forming approach to Fr we do not wish to overlook consideration that morale of troops fighting in Indochina is of prime importance and that, therefore, Fr Govt should not be urged to make any statement concerning further relinquishment Fr controls except under most favorable conditions. Dept would include among factors which might constitute "favorable conditions" (re: Embtel 2436, Nov 3): (1) demonstration renewed Fr mil potential in form absence further deterioration, (2) visible proof of formation National Armies beyond present paper steps which are excellent beginning, (3) further evidence Bao Dai's intention and ability assume active leadership his govt, still waited.

Moreover, Dept agrees that considerations morale troops Indochina and public opinion Fr in face expenditures lives and money will make it necessary that statement be not so extreme as to remove whatever stake for Fr in Indochina is sufficient to assure their continued acceptance of "primary responsibility" to extent of proceeding with present program. Dept eager in this matter, as in others relating to Indochina, to strengthen ties Fr Union and maximize protection Fr economic interests Indochina.

Nevertheless Dept is increasingly of conviction that further evolutionary statement is required to consolidate gains which development National Armies, support Franco-Vietnamese mil potential and enhancement Bao Dai Govt's authority either as result decisions Pau Conference or, possibly, as we hope, through his own revitalization. We are also obviously concerned to see that every means to increase effectiveness of use our own considerable financial and military aid be brought to bear. This would include as a minimum, official declaration by Fr at highest level (Auriol or Schuman) on present and future intentions regarding Indochina, as they have been stated to us by various high officials including Schuman, Moch and Letourneau, on several recent occasions.

Points outlined in Embtel 2436, Nov 3, Para two, are those which we consider should be included. Without attempting suggest actual form we would view something along lines of Letourneau's statements at Saigon press conference (Saigon 657, Oct 24) and Embassys suggestions in reftel as basic text to build on.

Todays Paris press despatches report McDonald will continue discussions re Indochina with Fr officials during coming week. We would welcome invitation Emb officer participate but as approach shld not be joint realize this might be impossible. Emb shld continue exchange views with McDonald and Fr separately, informing former of our thoughts on concurrent Anglo-U.S. approach to Fr and latter of our agreement with Brit views as expressed to Bruce by McDonald.

London note and, after consultation Paris, inform ForOff our views and general concurrence theirs as expressed McDonald; sound out possibilities similar approach Fr.

(196) <u>HO CHI MINH'S INSTRUCTIONS AT THE CONFERENCE REVIEWING THE SECOND LE HONG PHONG MILITARY CAMPAIGN</u>, November, 1950

Source: *Ho Chi Minh on Revolution*, pp. 201-205.

Following the successful campaign to gain control of the Sino-Vietnamese border area, which was the most important military victory scored by the Viet

*Minh up to that time, the army held a review conference in which both positive
and negative aspects of the campaign were studied. In remarks to the Conference, Ho repeated themes which he and other Vietnamese leaders had often
stressed: the correctness of the Party's line, the "subjectivity" of the
French, and the heroism of the Vietnamese people.*

About this review conference, I have some opinions:

At this conference, there are officers who directly took part in the campaign and are back here to review both their achievements and shortcomings.
There are also cadres and officers from the various interzones, army units, and
public services who did not take part in the campaign but who are here to learn
experiences. To make criticism and self-criticism, to review our work, and to
learn from our experiences are very good things which should be developed into
a style of work in the army, administration, and mass organizations. In this
review, I want to draw your attention to some points.

1. *Heighten discipline.* Discipline must be observed at all levels. Critical reviews must be made at all levels, from lower levels upward and from
higher levels downward. We must help all the men and officers of the army to
understand thoroughly the necessity for this work. Only then can we achieve
success.

2. *Strictly carry out orders from higher levels.* Orders from higher levels
must be unconditionally and strictly carried out. There is a Chinese proverb
saying that "military orders are as firm as mountains," that is, whenever an
order from a higher level is issued, it must be carried out at any cost. Don't
misunderstand democracy. When no decision is yet taken, we are free to discuss. But when a decision is taken, we should not discuss any longer. Any
discussion then could be only discussion on the ways and means to carry out the
decision quickly and not to propose that it should not be carried out. We must
prohibit any such act of unruly freedom.

3. *Love the soldiers.* The officers must love the men under their command.
As regards sick armymen or invalids, the officers must look after them and in-
quire into their helath. The commanders and political commissars must be the
brothers, sisters, and friends of the soldiers. So long as they are not so,
they have not yet fulfilled their tasks. Only when officers are close to soldiers, like the limbs of the same body, can the soldiers love the officers like
their kith and kin. Only so can the instructions, orders, and plans from higher ranks be actively and strictly implemented by the armymen. We must congratulate and reward all armymen who have achieved meritorious services, promote
all progressive officers and men, especially those who have a long service in
the army.

4. *Respect the people.* We must respect the people. There are many ways
of showing respect to the people. It is not sufficient to greet people in a
polite manner. We must not waste the manpower and property of the people.
When mobilizing the people, we must see to it that their contributions do not
exceed the requirements in order to avoid waste. We must avoid anything which
is prejudicial to the people's life. To know how to assist the people is also
to respect them. Help them to harvest crops and organize literary classes for
local militia and armymen.

5. *Take good care of public property and war booty.* Public property is
the fruit of the collective labor of the people. The army must preserve and
take good care of it and must not waste it. Put an end to such acts as selling
the rice contributed by the people, damaging tools, and wasting ammunition.
War booty is also public property. It belongs to the nation, not to the
enemy. Munitions, medicine, equipment, and food are the sweat and blood of our
people. Our soldiers had to shed blood to recover them. We must prize and

take good care of them, and not waste them or make them our personal property. When looking after them, we must arrange them neatly and protect them carefully against rain and sun.

6. *Sincerely make criticism and self-criticism.* In your reports to the conference, you must pay attention to this point. When making criticism and self-criticism, we must sincerely expose our shortcomings. If we make mistakes but don't want to expose them, that is like a patient who refuses to tell his disease to the doctor. When we do a lot of work it is difficult for us to avoid making mistakes. So we use the method of criticism and self-criticism to help one another in correcting our errors; we are determined to correct them in order to make progress together. Besides exposing our shortcomings, we must also report our achievements in order to develop them. In order to achieve good results in criticism and self-criticism, cadres at all levels, especially high-ranking cadres, must *be exemplary before anyone else.*

Many experiences, good and bad alike, may be drawn from this campaign. We must review them, popularize them and learn from them. They may be summed up in the following main points:

1. The leadership of the Central Committee is clearsighted. The leading committees at all levels have also adopted correct lines of leadership. The various organs of the army, mass organizations, and administration have united, closely coordinated their actions, and adopted a unified plan of work.

2. Our soldiers are very zealous and heroic. This has been amply proved by the examples of the man who had his broken arm chopped off to facilitate his movement in the assault, of another man who rushed into an enemy stronghold with a charge of dynamite in his hands, or of many others who did not eat anything for three or four days but continued to fight with all their ardor and heroism, and other examples.

3. Our people are very good. Never before have such big contingents of women of the Kinh, Man, Tho, Nung, and other nationalities volunteered to carry supplies to the front as in the recent campaign. Hardship, privation, and danger could not lessen their ardor, cheerfulness, and heroism. That is really admirable. This is partly thanks to Comrade Tran Dang Ninh and other cadres of the Viet Bac interzone who have correctly implemented the policies of the Party and the Government and partly to the ardent patriotism and self-sacrificing spirit of our compatriots.

These are major experiences which must be pointed out in the reviewing report.

I also draw your attention to the following points:

1. *Concerning propaganda work.* In practice, the enemy has been making much more propaganda for us than we have ourselves. We have not concentrated all means and mobilized all our abilities for propaganda. That is why our information is still very slow and does not reach broad masses. The campaign closed on October 15, yet until October 30, the people and cadres in many localities did not yet know anything or only knew very little of it. Or if they had heard about it, they did not know how to popularize the news. Our propaganda among the prisoners of war and enemy troops, as well as abroad, is still very weak. We did not know how to make excerpts from enemy newspapers which expressed anger at the colonialist military commanders, politicians, and administrative authorities who only cared for having a good time and disputed about personal interests while their soldiers died on the battlefields "without a wreath being laid or a tear being shed for them." We have failed to capitalize on this material to write leaflets for agitation among the enemy's ranks, give explanations to the prisoners of war, and make propaganda among the population in enemy-held areas.

2. *Let us not indulge in subjectivism and underestimate the enemy.* Do not indulge in naive subjectivism and think that from now on victory will always be ours and there will be no more difficulties or failure. This victory is only a preliminary success. We still have to make great efforts and win many more victories like this or even greater ones before we can switch over to a general counteroffensive. From now to the day of complete victory, we shall meet with many difficulties and perhaps shall go through many failures. In a war, to win a victory or suffer a defeat are common things. The essential is that we must win final victory. We must help all officers and men and the people to bear that firmly in mind so that they will not be self-complacent when winning and disappointed when losing, but instead will always make utmost efforts to over-come difficulties and hardships and advance toward final victory.

Do not underestimate the enemy. The enemy is pulling himself in, not to lie still, but actually to leap forward again. He is striving to win time and prepare to hit back. In the meantime, they will seek to bomb and strafe the areas under our control with the aim of intimidating us, as was the case in Ha Giang, Tuyen Quang, and Bac Giang recently.

3. *We must win time.* We too must win time in order to make preparations. That is a condition for defeating the opponent. In military affairs, time is of prime importance. Time ranges first among the three factors for victory, before the terrain conditions and the people's support. Only by winning time can we secure the factors for defeating the enemy. It is precisely to win time that this conference should be a short one. The reports must be concise and raise the main and necessary problems. Don't be wordy. This would only waste time and bring no result at all.

4. *Lastly, we must keep absolute secrecy.* Secrecy is a very important thing. Everybody must keep secrecy. We must seek every means to keep secret all activities and in all circumstances: in an inn, in our talks, and in our work, we must observe secrecy. It is not sufficient for the army and public offices alone to keep secrecy. We must teach the people to keep secrecy if we want to keep our work in complete secrecy. If we succeed in keeping secrecy, that is already one step toward our success.

From all the questions I raise above, this conference should try to solve some. After the conference, if you decide to solve the remaining ones, we will surely succeed in our future battles.

The Party, Government, and people call upon all officers and men to carry out these recommendations.

(197) <u>MEMORANDUM BY THE DEPUTY DIRECTOR OF THE MUTUAL DEFENSE ASSISTANCE PRO-GRAM JOHN OHLY TO ACHESON</u>, November 20, 1950 (Extracts)

Source: *Foreign Relations, 1950, Vol. VI,* pp. 925-930.

As the pressures on the U.S. to become full partners in the Indochina War mounted rapidly, the director of the military assistance program asked Acheson to name a special task force under the National Security Channel to reassess U.S. policy in Indochina before plunging further into the conflict. Noting the reports from military observers which cast grave doubts on the ability of the French Union forces to defeat the Viet Minh, he emphasized that the U.S. could not afford to supply the sums required to support the anti-Communist forces in Indochina and at the same time meet its other global defense commitments.

I. This memorandum is designed to stress the urgent necessity for an imme-diate, thorough and realistic re-examination of our policy with respect to Indo-china. From the standpoint of the Mutual Defense Assistance Program, such a re-examination is imperative, because the continuance of the present policy of substantial aid may, without achieving its intended purpose, make impossible the fulfillment of mutual defense objectives elsewhere in the world. Such a re-examination may well lead to a reaffirmation of this policy without significant change, but in my opinion, and in the light of the considerations set forth below, it would be the height of folly to pursue such policy further in the absence of a far more searching analysis than has heretofore been made of its possibilities of success and its global consequences. Even if the need for such an approach was not urgent before (and I believe it was), it has certainly been made so by the direct Chinese Communist intervention in Korea which (1) places large additional operating demands upon the limited materiel resources available for both U.S. requirements and *all* foreign military assistance programs and (2) indicates that the Kremlin may be prepared to accept the risks inherent in the actual commitment of Chinese troops to assist Ho Chi Minh, a step which would, as subsequently indicated, completely transform the character of the military problem in Indochina.

****

(3) Assuming that enough equipment and effective manpower can be provided, will there be the will, the morale and the kind of leadership necessary effectively to handle the military situation? The military observers who have been to Indochina, including General Erskine and members of his group, have uniformly commented on the lack of offensive spirit among the French forces, the faultiness of French tactics, the poor use made of certain weapons (particularly artillery), and the poor generalship. These observers have similarly stated that unless some or all of these weakness can be removed, the chances of success in Indochina are not particularly good. While the morale of the French Union forces has held up surprisingly well in the face of 5 years of little tangible progress in defeating the Viet Minh and in the face of severe setbacks in Tonkin, the question is naturally presented as to how long this can continue to be the case, particularly if more of the Red River Delta area goes. There is the further question of the ability of the French and Bao Dai, within the political frameworks now existing or likely to be developed in the near future, to obtain the kind of morale and will to fight which is needed to make the nascent national armies effective combat units in warfare against the Viet Minh. What little evidence is available on this particular score is somewhat encouraging.

(4) Will it be possible to prevent a political deterioration that will nullify accomplishments in the military field? The answer to this question depends on a series of factors which can better be developed by other offices of the State Department. It would appear, however, that at least three important subsidiary points must be considered:

(*a*) the rapidity and extensiveness of further Viet Minh successes and their impact on native attitudes and on key individuals whose loyalties may be wavering;

(*b*) the capacity of Bao Dai and those around him to assert and exercise effective leadership, utilizing the authority and power in those fields where they already possess them; and

(*c*) the willingness of the French, both in letter and in spirit, to make those concessions which appear to be necessary if the new native governments are to receive the popular support upon which their continuance depends.

As indicated earlier, this paper does not attempt to provide answers to the foregoing crucial questions, but I would like to call attention to the grave doubts which have repeatedly been expressed in the intelligence evaluations of all of the principal intelligence agencies of the government. . . .

****

C. *What will be the costs and consequences elsewhere of attempting to attain the objective of firm non-Communist control of Indochina?*

We will consider this question solely in relation to the internal security objective, since there appears to be little that can be done, short of outright U.S. intervention, to repel a Chinese Communist invasion if attempted. This does not mean, of course, that we must not weigh these costs and these consequences with a view to the possibility that such an invasion may occur and create a situation in which the costs have been incurred and suffered, to no avail. These costs fall principally into two categories:

(1) military equipment, largely from U.S. sources, and
(2) manpower otherwise available for French forces in Western Europe.

As to the former, we have already indicated our belief that immediate foreseeable requirements will be in the neighborhood of $500,000,000 and that these requirements will substantially increase. The Joint Chiefs of Staff have indicated that these requirements cannot be met without a substantial impact on the military assistance program for Western Europe. This will be true to an even greater extent in the case of military assistance programs for Greece, Turkey and Iran, which have a lower priority than the programs of North Atlantic Treaty countries. Moreover, as and to the extent that Korean operations consume increasing quantities of available American equipment, the effect in Europe and elsewhere of doing what is needed in Indochina will materially increase. In other words, the development of effective forces in Western Europe which must, for the time being, rely almost exclusively on American equipment, will be substantially delayed; the effort to place Greek forces in a position to resist Bulgarian and/or Albanian invasion may have to be postponed indefinitely; and it will not be possible to carry through measures which are urgently required to make the Turkish army a really effective combat force. While it is true that a time will come, perhaps 12 or 18 months hence, when the mobilization of American industry, as a result of orders now being placed, will eliminate a situation of equipment scarcity and make it possible to catch up, we must accept as a fact, that the mounting of the Indochina program will seriously affect other MDAP programs in the interim.

It is impossible to assess the impact of materially reduced MDAP delivery schedules on the augmentation of forces in the North Atlantic Treaty area and on the North Atlantic Treaty itself. It is clear, however, that apart from any effect on the actual development of combat-ready divisions, there will be an effect, deriving from the lack of training equipment, on the speed of forming units and raising forces. This same problem is affected by the other important cost of pursuing the present policy in Indochina, namely the cost in French manpower. We are counting on the ability of the French to provide 10 divisions by the end of 1951 and some 27 divisions by the beginning of 1954. Apart from equipment, the great bottleneck in meeting these commitments will be the provision of enough qualified and fully trained commissioned and non-commissioned officers to form the cadres for, and to train, these large forces. Every officer and non-commissioned officer diverted to Indochina materially reduces the prospect that the French can even approximate the present objective, since the period of training for technicians, non-com's, and commissioned officers is measured in years and not in months and, unfortunately, one of the crucial requirements in Indochina is for this same general category of personnel. In addition, of course, the diversion of enlisted personnel to another theater reduces the amount of manpower available for the rank and file for the kind of French army needed in Western Europe just as quickly as it can be formed. In this connection, it should be noted that French casualties in Indochina since 1945, without taking into account the recent debacles, have exceeded 50,000, and that French officers are being lost in this campaign at a faster rate than they are being graduated from officer schools in France.

The present tight equipment situation, and therefore the impact which meeting Indochinese requirements may have, can perhaps best be understood by reference to the Joint Chiefs of Staff estimates concerning the time when equipment might be made available for German units. Short of tapping the Austrian stockpile, the Joint Chiefs of Staff estimate that it will be impossible to provide full TO and E equipment for the first 4 German infantry divisions until at least September 1952, or almost two years hence, and that even training equipment for an additional 11 divisions could not be provided until June of 1952. Moreover, short of full industrial mobilization, and a sufficiently high priority for the allocation of equipment to German units, it will be impossible to equip them with heavy equipment, such as tanks and heavy artillery, until the early part of 1954.

The impacts on other programs may well be such that the Indochina program will have to drop far below a No. I priority, and if this proves to be the case, then of course it affects the answer to A above.[1]

D. *Does our present policy in Indochina make sense when considered in the light of its possibility of success and in terms of its consequences to the accomplishment of U.S. objectives in other areas of strategic importance?*

The answer to this question will largely depend upon the answers to A, B,[2] and C above, plus an appraisal of the relative importance of achieving our objective in Indochina and our objective in Indochina and our objectives elsewhere in the world. Without carefully thought out answers to A, B, and C above, and without making a thorough assessment of the strategic importance of Indochina vis-a-vis the strategic importance of areas whose security will be adversely affected by our present policy in Indochina, the issue posed in this paragraph cannot be intelligently discussed. However, it is believed that the problem involved can be illustrated by the following *purely* hypothetical questions, each to be considered in relation to two alternative assumptions - first, that our policy in Indochina has a reasonable prospect of success, and second, that the prospects of its success are not very good:

(1) Is it worth a delay of 6 months in the date when North Atlantic Treaty forces will be adequate to resist Soviet aggression, or, put another way, to meet the force and equipment requirements of the Medium Term Plan?

(2) Is it worth a delay of 6 months in the formation, training, and equipping of German units?

(3) Is it worth a delay of 6 months in the time when Greek forces would be capable of withstanding Bulgarian and/or Albanian invasion?

(4) Is it worth a delay of 6 months in the time when Turkish forces can be placed in a position to offer maximum resistance to Russian forces or, alternatively, in the event of a global war, to tie down the maximum amount of Soviet forces?

IV. *Recommendations*

I strongly recommend that before any further substantial commitments of equipment, prestige or forces are made in Indochina, the kind of assessment suggested in the preceding pages be undertaken. I suggest that this be done by a special task force under the auspices of the National Security Council, because it is so urgent that it cannot and should not be pursued through slower channels. We have reached a point where the United States, because of limitations in resources, can no longer simultaneously pursue all of its objectives in all parts of the world and must realistically face the fact that certain objectives, even though they may be extremely valuable and important ones, may have to be abandoned if others of even greater value and importance are to be attained. The situation is not unlike that which faced the United States in the early days of the last war, when a choice had to be made between pursuing the offensive in either the West or the East and not in both places at once.

As an after thought, and by way of additional caveat , I would like to point out that the demands on the U.S. for Indochina are increasing almost daily and that, sometimes imperceptibly, by one step after another, we are gradually increasing our stake in the outcome of the struggle there. We are, moreover, slowly (and not too slowly) getting ourselves into a position where our responsibilities tend to supplant rather than complement those of the French, and where failures are attributed to us as though we were the primary party at fault and in interest. We may be on the road to being a scapegoat, and we are certainly dangerously close to the point of being so deeply committed that we may find ourselves completely committed even to direct intervention. These situations, unfortunately, have a way of snowballing.

(198) TELEGRAM FROM BRUCE TO ACHESON, NOVEMBER 24, 1950

Source: *Foreign Relations, 1950, Vol. VI.,* pp. 936-937.

Reviewing the debate on Indochina in the French National Assembly, Bruce expressed his satisfaction with the French government's statements of policy and urged that the Bao Dai Government be pressed to concentrate on concrete tasks.

Embassy believes that Letourneau statement to National Assembly re French policy IC can be described as satisfactory. He has emphasized "independence" of Associated States within framework of French Union. He has expressed government's intention to proceed as rapidly as possible with creation of national armies in IC. He has in effect characterized evolutionary nature of March 8 accords by pointing out that French Government will carry out not only letter of accords, but also spirit. He has stated that French functionaries in IC after January 1 with exception certain categories, will be limited to those placed at disposition three states. He has pointed to French government intentions not to give up struggle in IC, but to increase its effort. Although belated, such statements should be beneficial under present circumstances.

Pleven's speech to National Assembly also strikes helpful note, particularly with reference to recognition necessity creation Vietnam national army, recognition IC problem cannot be solved by force, quotation from Auriol letter July 1949 to Bao Dai indicating Vietnamese freedom chose regime, political institutions and government and French Government's intention increase its own military effort IC. Significant portions these two speeches included Pleven's statement French Government would take troops from France if necessary and Letourneau's statement France would not appeal to UN unless Tonkin border crossed by Chinese Communist troops.

While French Government knowledge US government's views re French policy IC plays important part in these statements by Letourneau and Pleven, it is believed MacDonald's influence exerted during his recent visit to Paris also had an effect - perhaps a more immediate one.

Socialist Party's position during national Assembly's debate on IC completes almost full circle in reversal its position in earlier years. It has swung from favoring negotiations with Ho-Chi-Minh to seeking UN solution and during debates Socialists present position as presented by Pineau is that appeal to UN would have no positive results as international solutions can become outdated; what was possible before Chinese Communist arrival at Tonkin border having now become impossible. Pineau indicated that while no UN solution desirable, US and UK must take increased interest and closer cooperation must be established by France and her allies. This same note struck very pointedly by Pleven in his reference to need for concerting with France's allies necessary steps to be taken in event Chinese Communists crossed Tonkin border.

Pleven Government has weathered this crisis, probably very much as was to be expected. It has not been expected that IC problem in itself would endanger Pleven Government, but if further reverses IC do occur after government has been granted authority and powers it seeks, what has been described as National Assembly's feeling of uneasiness, even though it voted approval of *ordre du jour* may in future express itself in much stronger terms.

Reaction as shown in debate gives some indication of how far National Assembly has come in its thinking on IC problem, which naturally is influenced by strong desire find some solution this problem. Letoureau's emphasis on "independence" Associated States within French Union, reference to March 8 accords, transfer internal administrative authority to Associated States and withdrawal most French functionaries IC passed almost unnoticed and both his and Pleven's statements re creation national armies IC were accepted without any real dissent.

It seems to Embassy that French Government statements of its policy IC now provide opportunity for Bao Dai and Vietnam Government to buckle down to tasks facing them and Embassy suggests Legation might take opportunity offered by these statements of French Government intentions again to draw attention Vietnamese to those things which are essential to improvement in situation and which they alone can do.

(199) STATEMENT BY RUSK AT PRESS CONFERENCE, NOVEMBER 27, 1950

Source: Department of State Press Release No. 1187, November 27, 1950, reprinted in *U.S. Vietnam Relations, Book 8.*

The State Department chose to embrace the new expression of French policy as fulfilling the political requirement which had been viewed for so long as a crucial factor in success. As Rusk's public statement suggests, however, the political significance of the French declaration was far from clear.

The United States Government welcomes the definition of the policy of France in Indochina as described in the statement of Monsieur Letourneau, the Minister of Associated States, as confirmed by the Prime Minister, Monsieur Pleven, and by the resolution of the National Assembly which approved that policy. It will be particularly reassuring to nations of the free world to know that the independence of the Associated States of Indochina within the framework of the French Union is now assured and that the military and economic resources of the French Republic and of the Associated States of Indochina will be directed with boldness and renewed resolution to the defense of Indochina against communist colonialism.

To the end that the armies of the Associated States of Indochina and the French Union accomplish their mission and in order that the new states in Indochina attain stability and offer their people a better life, the United States is extending to them military and economic assistance.

The United States Government hopes that the other free nations will make every contribution within their power to enable the Associated States and their partners in the French Union to accomplish their mission of freedom.

(200) NSC 64/1: MEMORANDUM BY THE JOINT CHIEFS OF STAFF TO SECRETARY OF DEFENSE GEORGE C. MARSHALL, NOVEMBER 28, 1950

Source: *Foreign Relations, 1950, Vol. VI.,* pp. 945-948.

Based of the Joint Strategic Survey Committee analysis and the report of Brig. Gen Brink, the Joint Chiefs of Staff offered their recommendations for U.S. policy on Indochina. Their analysis attributed the deteriorating military situation to the lack of popular support for the anti-communist effort in Indochina and called for a program for "eventual self-government" and the formation of national armies to strengthen the political position of the French Union forces. The memorandum was accepted by the National Security Council as NSC 64/1.

In accordance with the request contained in your memorandum, dated 13 October 1950, the Joint Chiefs of Staff have studied the "Proposed Statement of U.S. Policy on Indochina for NSC Consideration", which you enclosed, in the light of the message enclosed herewith (Enclosure "A" [*Subenclosure "A"*]) from Brigadier General F.G. Brink (USA), Chief, Military Assistance Advisory Group, Indochina. You will recall that the Joint Chiefs of Staff withheld final comment on the subject draft policy statement until the Brink report was received.

The Joint Chiefs of Staff consider that the statement of United States policy proposed by the Southeast Asia Aid Policy Committee conforms generally to their previously expressed views, including those contained in their memorandum to you on Indochina dated 27 October 1950. They are of the opinion, however, that the draft statement of United States policy on Indochina proposed by the Southeast Asia Aid Policy Committee should be recast so as to meet more effectively the immediate and critical situation in that country. Accordingly, the Joint Chiefs of Staff have formulated the following statement of short-term and long-term policies which they recommend be substituted for those included in the paper prepared by the Southeast Asia Aid Policy Committee.

The Joint Chiefs of Staff recognize that the military problems of Indochina are closely interrelated with the political problems of the area. Accordingly, many of the policies recommended herein lie largely in the political field. The Joint Chiefs of Staff consider, however, that the fundamental causes of the deterioration in the Indochinese security situation lie in the lack of will and determination on the part of the indigenous people of Indochina to join wholeheartedly with the French in resisting communism. The Joint Chiefs of Staff consider that, without popular support of the Indochinese people, the French will never achieve a favorable long-range military settlement of the security problem of Indochina.

The Joint Chiefs of Staff recommend the following short-term objectives for Indochina:

Short-Term Objectives

a. The United States should take action, as a matter of urgency, by all means practicable short of the actual employment of United States military forces, to deny Indochina to communism.

b. As long as the present situation exists, the United States should continue to insure that the primary responsibility for the restoration of peace and security in Indochina rests with the French.

c. The United States should seek to develop its military assistance program for Indochina based on an over-all military plan prepared by the French, concurred in by the Associated States of Indochina and acceptable to the United States.

(1) Both the plan and the program should be developed and implemented as a matter of urgency. It should be clearly understood, however, that United States acceptance of the plan is limited to the logistical support which the United States may agree to furnish. The aid provided under the program should be furnished to the French in Indochina and to the Associated States. The allocation of United States military assistance as between the French and the national armies of Indochina should be approved by the French and the United States authorities in Indochina.

(2) Popular support of the Government by the Indochinese people is essential to a favorable settlement of the security problem of Indochina. Therefore, as a condition to the provision of those further increases in military assistance to Indochina necessary for the implementation of an agreed over-all military plan, the United States Government should obtain assurances from the French Government that:

   (a) A program providing for the eventual self-government of Indochina either within or outside of the French Union will be developed, made public, and implementation initiated at once in order to strengthen the national spirit of the Indochinese in opposition to communism.
   (b) National armies of the Associated States of Indochina will be organized as a matter of urgency. While it is doubtful that the build-up of these armies can be accomplished in time to contribute significantly to the present military situation, the direct political and psychological benefits to be derived from this course would be great and would thus result in immediate, although indirect, military benefits.
   (c) Pending the formation and training of Indochinese national armies as effective units, and as an interim emergency measure, France will dispatch sufficient additional armed forces to Indochina to insure that the restoration of peace and internal security in that country will be accomplished in accordance with the timetable of the over-all military plan for Indochina.
   (d) France will change its political and military concepts in Indochina to:

   i. Eliminate its policy of "colonialism".
   ii. Provide proper tutelage to the Associated States.
   iii. Insure that a suitable military command structure, unhampered by political interference, is established to conduct effective and appropriate military operations. The effective implementation of these changes will require competent and efficient political and military leaders who will be able to cope with the conditions in that country.

(3) At an appropriate time the United States should institute checks to satisfy itself that the conditions set forth in subparagraph *c* - (2) above are being fulfilled.

   d. The United States should exert all practicable political and diplomatic measures required to obtain the recognition of the Associated States by the other non-communist states of Southeast and South Asia.
   e. In the event of overt attack by organized Chinese Communist forces against Indochina, the United States should not permit itself to become engaged in a general war with Communist China but should, in concert with the United Kingdom, support France and the Associated States by all means short of the actual employment of United States military forces. This support should include appropriate expansion of the present military assistance program and

endeavors to induce States in the neighborhood of Indochina to commit armed forces to resist the aggression.

f. The United States should immediately reconsider its policy toward Indochina whenever it appears that the French Government may abandon its military position in that country or plans to refer the problem of Indochina to the United Nations. Unless the situation throughout the world generally, and Indochina specifically, changes materially, the United States should seek to dissuade the French from referring the Indochina question to the United Nations.

g. Inasmuch as the United States-sponsored resolution, "Uniting for Peace", has been adopted by the General Assembly of the United Nations, and should a situation develop in Indochina in a manner similar to that in Korea in which United Nations forces were required, the United States would then probably be morally obliged to contribute its armed forces designated for service on behalf of the United Nations. It is, therefore, in the interests of the United States to take such action in Indochina as would forestall the need for the General Assembly to invoke the provisions of the resolution, "Uniting for Peace".

The Joint Chiefs of Staff recommend the following long-term objectives for Indochina:

Long-Term Objectives

a. United States security interests demand that this government by all means short of the actual employment of United States military forces, seek to prevent the further spread of communism in Southeast Asia generally, and in particular, in French Indochina.

b. The United States should seek to insure the establishment of such conditions in Indochina that no foreign armed forces will be required for the maintenance of internal security.

c. The United States should continue to press the French to carry out in letter and in spirit the program referred to in paragraph 4-c (2) - (a) above, providing for the eventual self-government of Indochina either within or outside of the French Union.

d. The United States should continue to favor the entry of the three Associated States of Indochina into the United Nations.

e. The United States should encourage the establishment of an appropriate form of regional security arrangement embracing Indochina and the other countries of Southeast Asia under Article 51 and 52 of the United Nations Charter.

6. There is enclosed (Enclosure "B" [*Subenclosure "B"*] for possible use by the National Security Council Staff the Analysis which was prepared for the Joint Chiefs of Staff in connection with the study of the problem. This Analysis, however, has not received their detailed approval.

---

(201) MEMORANDUM BY MR. ROBERT HOEY OF THE OFFICE OF PHILIPPINE AND SOUTHEAST ASIAN AFFAIRS TO JESSUP, DECEMBER 27, 1950 [Extract]

Source: *Foreign Relations, 1950, Vol. VI.*, pp. 955-958

Commenting on the Joint Chiefs of Staff memorandum, the Office of Philippine and Southeast Asian Affairs projected it as too concerned with popular attitudes in Vietnam. This memorandum put forward for the first time in the discussion of Indochina policy that Viet Minh rebellion could be defeated despite the political sympathies of the majority of the population. The issue of Vietnamese independence was viewed as no longer relevant.

Paragraph 1. PSA considered in November that the policy statement proposed by the Southeast Asia Aid Policy Committee had been overtaken by events. It would therefore appear that any discussion of that policy paper would be academic.

Paragraph 3. PSA agrees that a long range or a short range favorable settlement of the security problem in Indochina requires an increased awareness by the people of the dangers of Communism and an increased effort to combat it. Neither the French Union army nor the Vietnam State army has had in the past difficulty in securing volunteers. Therefore the size of an anti-Communist force is presently limited by the fiscal and technical ability of France and the United States to supply training and equipment not available from Indochinese resources. The national army project agreed to on December 8 establish the legal basis for a large national army, transferred certain unites (7 infantry battalions) from the French Union forces to the Vietnam state army and set forth a working arrangement by which metropolitan France would contribute approximately 1.5 billion piastres toward the pay and maintenance of an increased Vietnam state army. The Vietnam Government would contribute approximately 750 million piastres. The equipment for some 30 infantry battalions was requested of the United States on 18 December in a list prepared by the French military, the Vietnam Government and approved by the US MAAG. This step is the legal and factual basis for the future development of a Vietnamese National Army whose eventual size would be approximately 45 battalions plus irregulars. If and when achieved this would be larger than the army of Burma. Similar steps were taken with regard to national armies in Laos and Cambodia. PSA, however, does not agree with the third sentence in paragraph 3 regarding the fundamental causes of deterioration in the Indochinese security situation. The deterioration has been caused by the increased capability of the indigenous Communist movement under Ho Chi Minh realized by extensive Chinese Communist assistance in both materiel and personnel. We believe that this is important and should be included in any study of the area.

Paragraph 4. Short-term objectives, paragraphs *a,b,c* and *c* (1) have long been a part of Departmental policy. Paragraph *c* (2) (a), (b), (c), (d), (3), *d,* and *e:* These points are raised more or less verbatim from previous Departmental papers. We consider that they have been already accomplished or are in a satisfactory state of development. Paragraph *f* The reconsideration of U.S. policy toward Indochina demonstrated herein was a part of NSC 64, prepared by PSA in March 1950. The Department is aware of the necessity for recasting political policy in the event of successful Chinese Communist aggression in Southeast Asia but is not aware of any plans of the Department of Defense in such a contingency. The U.S. has advised, not "dissuaded" the French from referring the Indochina question to the UN. In September 1950 having been approached by the French in this regard we advised them that in our opinion the political attitudes of the Asian states in the UN was such that the result of a reference of the Indochina matter to the UN would probably be unsatisfactory. At the same time, however, we made clear to the French that the Department was not advising France or any other country in danger of Communist invasion that such an act should not be reported to the UN. Paragraph *g* agreed.

Long-Term Objectives

b. While PSA recognizes the desirability of such a happy condition in Indochina as well as in the Philippines, Burma and Malaya the achievement of peaceful conditions or at least those conditions which would permit indigenous forces without outside help to maintain internal security cannot be realized so long as Communist aggression follows its present militant course.

c. We believe that this has already been satisfactorily achieved.

d. Agreed.

e. PSA while recognizing the desirability of regional security arrangements believes that the US encouragement of such a body would be the "kiss of death". Department policy, however, supports such an arrangement under Asian sponsorship. This now seems beyond the capability of any Southeast Asian leader.

Conclusion

Since the paper which gave rise to this effort on the part of the Joint Chiefs was prepared in September and was overtaken by November, we presume that it is not a "recasting" of that paper which is required so much as a new NSC paper. From our preceeding comments, however, it is obvious that NSC 64/1 not be adopted, or; *(b)* that it be revised by a joint State-Defense effort, or; *(C)* that in view of the near satisfaction of our political efforts that the Department of Defense be directed by the NSC to prepare without delay (1) a strategic estimate of Southeast Asia in which there be embodied studies of the capabilities of the present anti-Communist forces; those forces augmented by the maximum US materiel assistance; the capability and intentions of world Communism toward Southeast Asia leading to a conclusion which would for the first time identify the possible results anticipated from the Chinese Communist invasion of Southeast Asia which now appears so imminent. The Department of Defense should at the same time be directed by the NSC to participate in the millitary conversations agreed upon in September by the three Foreign Ministers.

(202) CENTRAL INTELLIGENCE AGENCY, NATIONAL INTELLIGENCE ESTIMATE (NIE-5), DECEMBER 29, 1950

Source: *Foreign Relations, 1950, Vol. VI.*, pp. 959-963.

The President's Intelligence Advisory Committee, which included representatives from all elements of the Intelligence community, commissioned a series of National Intelligence Estimates beginning in the Fall of 1950 on critical situations around the world. They represented the work of interdepartmental working groups coordinated by the CIA's Office of National Estimates, as revised and finally approved by the Intelligence Advisory Committee. NIE-5 was the first such estimate on the situation in Indochina. The conclusion, reprinted here held out no hope that the Viet Minh could be defeated and forecast the probable defeat of the French in Tonkin within 6 to 9 months.

The French position in Indochina is critically endangered by the Viet Minh, a communist movement that has exploited native nationalism. The Chinese Communist regime is already furnishing the Viet Minh materiel, training and technical assistance. Official French sources report that Chinese Communist troops are already present in Tonkin in some strength. If this aid continues and French strength and military resources are not substantially increased above those presently programmed, the Viet Minh probably can drive the French out of North Viet Nam (Tonkin) within six to nine months. French loss of Tonkin, even assuming the evacuation of French forces in substantial numbers, would jeopardize the French position in the remainder of Viet Nam, Laos, and Cambodia.

2. Under these circumstances there is only a slight chance that the French can maintain their military position long enough to build up an independent Vietnamese government and an effective national army which might win the support of non-Communist nationalists, and, in conjunction with French forces, contain the Viet Minh. For these and other reasons there are grounds for questioning the French will to remain in Indochina.

3. The intervention of Chinese Communist troops in force in support of the Viet Minh would render the military position of the French untenable. At present there are about 185,000 Chinese Communist troops in the Tonkin border area, and approximately half of these could be committed to operations in Indochina. Even a relatively small number of Chinese Communist troops (25,000 - 50,000) would enable the Communist forces to drive the French out of Tonkin in a relatively short time.

4. Direct intervention by Chinese Communist troops may occur at any time. It may have already begun (see para.1). It is almost certain to occur in strength

whenever there is danger either that the Viet Minh will fail to attain its military objective of driving the French out of Indochina, or that the Bao Dai Government is succeeding in undermining the support of the Viet Minh. The scale of Chinese Communist intervention, however, would be limited mainly by anti-communist activities in China and by Chinese military commitments elsewhere.

5. The expulsion of the French by the Viet Minh with or without Chinese Communist intervention, would almost certainly lead to the transformation of Indochina into a Communist satellite.

6. We believe that control of Indochina by the Viet Minh would eventually entail Communist control of all mainland Southeast Asia in the absence of effective Western assistance to other countries of the area.

DISCUSSION

1. The French position in Indochina is precarious. Confronted with rebellion by a strong Communist movement that has exploited native nationalism (the Viêt Minh led by Ho Chi Minh), the French have tried to weaken it by winning over non-Communist nationalists to support a semi-autonomous, pro French Government under native leadership (the Viet Nam Government under Bao Dai). Concessions to nationalist sentiment, leading toward full sovereignty for the Bao Dai Government, have been forthcoming so slowly and with such seeming reluctance on the part of the French that the Bao Dai Government has not in fact won a strong nationalist following in any quarter. As a result, the French so far have been unable to undermine the political strength of the Viet Minh.

2. At the conclusion of the Pau Conference in late November 1950, the French made a new intensive effort to convince the Vietnamese that the powers of government would be turned over to them as rapidly as possible. The French agreed to establish an independent Army of Viet Nam with Bao Dai, in "supreme command," responsible only to the French High Command in Indochina. According to this plan, French officers and cadres would be employed by the Viet Nam Government, wear Vietnamese uniforms, and be subject to Bao Dai's command. It is too early to judge what the effect of this new French bid for native support will be. Even though Vietnamese suspicions of French good faith should be overcome, and Bao Dai should develop qualities of leadership hitherto unrevealed, it would be well over a year before an effective Vietnamese army could be organized, trained and equipped and before broad political support for Bao Dai could be consolidated.

3. The armed forces of the Viet Minh (approximately 225,000 troops of which 93,000 are well-armed regulars) have for some time been successfully contesting French military control in many regions of Indochina and recently have captured key French outposts and inflicted heavy losses on French forces in the norther border area adjoining China. In the critical area, Tonkin, where the French now hold mainly the Red River Delta area and a narrow strip along the coast, 55,000 French regular Army troops are opposing 62,000 Viet Minh regulars. The magnitude of the French military effort currently required in the whole of Indochina can be inferred from the following facts: (a) the French have 147,000 army regulars deployed throughout Indochina, and in addition maintain 200,000 native forces engaged in security tasks, para-military duties, and local defense; (b) the regular army of Indochina comprises 49% of France's career enlisted personnel, 20% of its regular army officers, and 28% of its career NCO's; (c) French officer losses in Indochina currently equal the annual output of graduates from St Cyr; and (d) 37% of the 1949 French militart budget was spent on the Indochina operation.

4. The Chinese Communists have been training and equipping large numbers of Viet Minh troops in China and are supplying the Viet Minh considerable amounts of materiel. A small number of Chinese Communist advisory personnel wearing Viet Minh uniforms probably are already serving with the Viet Minh forces. In

fact, official French sources report that Chinese Communist troops are already in Tonkin in some strength. Although the ability of the Chinese to furnish military equipment is limited, they should be able to make available to the Viet Minh enough small arms and artillery to give the Viet Minh a distinct superiority over present French forces. Viet Minh capabilities continue to be enlarged faster than the French have expanded their own. Unless French strength and military resources are substantially increased above those presently programmed, there is only a slight chance that the French can maintain their military position in the face of steadily increasing Viet Minh pressure during the period of about a year that would be required to strengthen Bao Dai's Government politically and to organize an effective Vietnamese army. For these and other reasons, there are grounds for questioning the French will to remain in Indochina.

5. The French position is further jeopardized by the fact that Viet Minh Strength can be increased by successive increments of Chinese Communist troops (as well as materiel) as a counter to any increase in French capabilities. In particular, if the Viet Minh shows signs of failing to attain its military objective of driving the French out of Indochina or if the Bao Dai government begins to show considerable promise of winning nationalist supporters away from the Viet Minh, we believe that the Chinese Communists will resort to direct substantial military intervention in Indochina by committing "volunteer" troops for service with the Viet Minh unless other considerations intervene. Similarly, if US or other non-Communist military forces intervened directly in support of the French, the Chinese Communists almost certainly would intervene.

6. The Chinese Communists may well believe that they can intervene in force in Indochina without too great a risk of causing either US or UN military intervention or of precipitating a general war. From the Soviet point of view, there might be substantial advantages in involving the US in a full-scale war with the Chinese Communists. US strength would be further dissipated in a Far Eastern military operation, and the US might lose or alienate some of its allies and potential allies. There are considerations, however, that would tend to deter the Chinese Communists from direct intervention in the war. Chinese Communist intervention (a) might bring certain Asian countries into opposition to Communist China; (b) might antagonize nationalist elements in Indochina and thereby weaken Ho Chi Minh's control of his own party and his prospects of support for the rest of the country; (c) would involve the use of Chinese troops in a situation already developing favorable from the Communist point of view simply as a result of supply equipment and training for Viet Minh troops.

7. The intervention of Chinese Communist troops in force in support of the Viet Minh would render the military position of the French untenable. At present there are about 185,000 Chinese Communist troops in the Tonkin border area, and approximately half of these could be committed to operations in Indochina. Even a relatively small number of Chinese Communist troops (25,000-50,000) would enable the Communist forces in substantial numbers, would jeopardize the French position in the remainder of Viet Nam, Laos, and Cambodia. The scale of Chinese Communist intervention, however, would be limited by anti-Communist activities in China and by Chinese Communist military commitments elsewhere.

8. In addition to a report from French official sources that Chinese Communist troops are already in Tonkin in some strength, there are at present many other indications of impending intervention in Indochina by the Chinese Communists. These include numerous reports of the recent movement of Chinese Communist armies to the Kwangsi-Tonkin border and of the concentration of armor in South China, the closing of French consulates in China under Chinese Communist pressure, Peiping charges of French border violations, Viet Minh and Chinese Communist accusations of persecution of the Chinese minority in Indochina, and the general Chinese Communist propaganda line that names Indochina, together with Korea, Japan and Formosa, as a base for "imperialist aggression" against China.

9.   There is little doubt that a Viet Minh victory would lead to the transformation of Indochina into a Communist satellite. Ho Chi Minh is a Moscow-
trained professional revolutionary and there have always been Communists in his
government. At the present time, the Viet Minh regime is openly Communist in
ideology and pro-Soviet in statements on foreign affairs. The recognition of
the Ho regime by various international Communist groups as a full-fledged "people's
democracy," formal recognition of the regime by Communist China and the Soviet
bloc, and the failure of the Viet Minh to acknowledge the recognition tendered
by Yugoslavia, all offer reasonable clear indications of the alignment of the
Viet Minh leadership with the USSR, with Communist China, and the international
Communist movement.

10.   The strong probability is that the loss of Indochina to Communist control would mean the eventual loss of all mainland Southeast Asia, in the absence
of Western assistance to the other countries of the area. Without such assistance, the proximity of well-trained Viet Minh forces would place nearly irresistible pressure on Thailand, increasing the proclivity of Thai officialdom to
accomodate itself to the winning side. If Thailand were under Communist control,
the Communist rebels in Malaya could be furnished military assistance that would
be very likely to cause the British to lose control of the area. The Burmese
government, already plagued by internal Communist problems, would find it difficult to resist diplomatic pressures backup by both Chinese and Indochinese
Communist forces on the borders of Burma. In addition, in Indonesia and the
Philippines, the principal effect of Communist control of Indochina would be to
strengthen indigenous Communist movements. Moreover, there might be a trend
in Indonesia toward accomodation with the Communist bloc in Asia. As each successive country came under Communist influence, the non-Communist resistance in
the remaining countries would be weakened.

1951

(203) <u>TELEGRAM FROM HEATH TO ACHESON</u>, JANUARY 1, 1951

Source: *Foreign Relations*, 1951, Vol. VI, pp. 332-338.

*In a New Year's assessment of the situation in Indochina, Heath pro-
jected the possible loss of Hanoi, even without Chinese intervention, but
urged the assumption that Chinese units would invade Vietnam. He expressed
satisfaction with concessions made by the French at the Pau Conference of
France and the Associated States, but noted that Vietnamese were less impressed by French good will. The legation recommended that direct financial
aid to the Associated States to underwrite their national armies be seriously considered, and that the U.S. launch a major program to "sell" Bao
Dai's government to its own people.*

With reference to Deptel 813, December 29.[1] Battle for Indochina and
possibly all SEA being fought in Tonkin at this moment. Assumption unavoidable that sooner or later and probably soon Chinese Communist will
invade IC with organized units. In this situation there are additional
steps which we can and must take immediately and within next six months if
IC is to be held. Of measures recommended in part 2 Legation would attach
highest priority to: (1) Acceleration and increase of existing programs of
military aid; (2) Pressure on Bao Dai[2] to form and lead government of national union which can take effective action and, (3) Immediate organization
by French and IC states of counter-guerrilla and resistance forces to carry
war to enemy-held territory.

Part 1 gives our present views on the political and military situation
and part 2 lists new and additional measures which should be given immediate
consideration.

1(A). At end of 1950 IC military situation characterized by following
salient factors:

1. Entire north, except shrinking Hanoi-Haiphong beachhead, must be
written off for time being with additional possibility Hanoi itself will
be lost or abandoned, all without mass intervention by Chinese Communists;

2. Policy must be based on assumption of invasion by Chinese as
organized units from now on. Chinese Communist units plus VM could within
six months liquidate Haiphong, obtain control of IC south at least to
Vinh. Concurrently VM activities and terrorism may increase in south
sufficiently to contain French and Viet forces there. Combined VM forces
would then be in position directly to assault south Vietnam, or turn against
Laos, Cambodia, Burma and Thailand for forced or negotiated surrenders.[3]
Situation would not be lost at this point but with VM installed in Hanoi,
one of historic Asian capitals and city which typifies Viet nationalism to
much greater degree than Saigon, with Chinese and VM troops supreme in
north, and with Chinese and Soviet representatives installed in capital of
government they recognize, weight of manpower, logistics and morale would
then be in Sino-VM favor and defense of IC and SEA would enter final phase,
in truth, last ditch affair.

(B) Most important policy aspects IC political situation at end 1950 were:

1. Organic relationship between Associated States (AS) and France, while not yet contending Viet nationals had more satisfactory and viable framework than at any previous time since end last war. Transfer substantial economic sovereignty to AS at Pau,[4] decision to activate true national armies, assurance drastic reduction number French officials in IC, cession all local revenues to AS have established new high water mark IC progress toward independence. Good will which might normally have attached to French as result this body of concessions is, however, marred by Viet suspicions that VM strength, menace of Chinese Communists, imperative of French position in Europe contributed preponderantly to grants of last two months. Volatile Viets who only recently complained French would never leave now have begun to doubt French intent to see war in IC through. Had French willingly made two years ago 1950 concessions and had Bao Dai and his government had two years experience under new formula, there would have been radically different IC situation. Basic political question today is whether there is time enough to utilize new political framework to mobilize mass allegiance behind Bao Dai.

2. Viet Government has thus far failed to display any real dynamism and has not yet won confidence of public in its ability to provide security or welfare. The Chief of State has yet to exhibit sustained energy or the know-how of leadership, its cabinet lacks stature, color, and broad representativeness; its administrators are generally inexperienced and frequently venal. There have, however, been occasional flashes of energy; in Huu,[5] Giao,[6] and Tri,[7] Bao Dai has a second level of recognized leaders; the government senses some of its inadequacies and is turning increasingly to US for advice and assistance; and, very importantly, the Viet military forces, armed religious groups and ethnic minorities have stood firm with Bao Dai and display will to fight.

3. Lack of unity among IC's neighbors within SEA and divergencies in Far East policy of great powers are further weaknesses in IC situation. These in turn make UN position re Chinese aggression in IC equivocal. This general lack of cohesion and clarity in west is today one of the Communists' greatest advantages in its SEA march.

(C) Economic situation at end 1950 as measured by traditional indices no worse than for past 18 months. However, attention called reported pressure on exchange authorities convert piasters into francs, slackening rate imports particularly in north, and near-panic conditions latter area with French trying dispose of stocks in real estate in anticipation VM victory. Military success warranting belief French and Bao Dai regimes could remain Tonkin might reverse them negative trends. Basically mass IC are relatively better off re food, shelter and clothing than many other Asiatic peoples. Only breakdown in transportation such as occurred 1946 in Tonkin could bring about famine conditions. On other hand economy for decades has been underdeveloped with chronic state of semi-unemployment in north and lack full employment in south, while for last 4 years its balance of international payments has been balanced only by massive imports financed directly or indirectly by French payments for military costs, for other budget deficits, etc. To attack either of latter two problems, however, is long-term project requiring provision capital, improvement agricultural practices, etc.

Only important immediate emergency economic problems would appear to be: (1) Handling of growing influx of refugees, particularly in north and (2) financing additional military burdens are expected to incur, while building up their national armies early 1951. Hitherto burden military expenses almost entirely French, but with signing Pau and December 18[8] military convention,[8] states are given all public revenues from IC sources and in turn expected by French carry appreciable cost of national armies. Out of total resources of about 2.1 billion piasters for instance, Viet expected by French to earmark about 500 million and secure another 500 from reduction other expenditures, increasing tax yields, and levying additional taxes. These conditions might cripple VN government at start to say nothing of drastically limiting necessary social and economic reform progress whose absence hitherto one of Bao Dai's greatest weaknesses.

Accumulating evidence also indicates at least some Viet business and political "leaders" looking forward assumption formerly French economic apparatus of dirigisme in order line own pockets and that whole transfer governmental and economic powers may create serious problem for new governments due lack trained personnel and reluctance continuance rely on French advisers. Another Philippine situation clearly possible.[9]

II(A). Military.

1. Immediate shipment all items requested by French in emergency list recommended Legtel 566 and later request for equipment of Viet army, Legtel 1077 of December 16 pouched Paris plus greatest expedition of possible shipment remaining fiscal year 1950 and fiscal year 1951 MDAP items.[10]

2. French must be convinced prepare or at least consent to preparation of counter-guerrilla and resistance organization for operation within and behind enemy lines, and for communications network in upper Tonkin. Correlation of such activities with systematic aid to Chinese Nationalists guerrillas in southern China provinces should be established. So far counter-guerrilla war and implantation of resistance organization have been slighted by French; nor is there any sure indication that De Lattre[11] will move at an early date to remedy this deficiency.

3. Area military conference of at least US-UK-France to be held earliest possible date to explore possibilities unified strategic concept. Almost year has passed since Legation recommended joint staff talks and systematic intelligence exchanges within area and from time to time suggestion has received various endorsements. View deepening IC crisis conference should be no longer be delayed.

4. Legation believes projected MDAP allocations for Title III countries[12] 1952 should be rescanned determined whether IC which must meet primary threat and where fate all other SEA countries will in large measure be determined could receive increased supplies.

5. If financial aid for national armies necessary under conditions posited part I Legation recommends serious consideration to grant direct financial aid.

6. If Chinese Communists intervene in open aggression Legation assumes UN and US must assist French and AS. Form of this assistance in primary stages would be air units and carrier strikes. In meantime Legation would urge review decision no US carrier now available for transfer to French in IC and immediate earmarking carrier units for eventual US operations against Sino-VM. Readiness these units and ability for them become operational in IC immediately on Chinese invasion would be incalculable benefit.

7. Legation recommends acceptance principle direct equipment local urban police and provincial guard units under MDAP and with MAAG observation.

8. On assumption imminent Chinese invasion US should promptly recommended to French air reconnaissance Chinese border area including Hainan. French now operate under strict orders confine flights eight kilometers this side northern frontier.

9. US should make available air and surface facilities to assist in evacuating large number important Tonkinese officials and private citizens some of whom could constitute useful resistance leaders.

10. MATS route through Saigon approved by competent officials more than month ago should be promptly instituted to provide east-west air lift critical supplies.

(B) Political.

1. In view new attributes sovereignty conferred on AS at Pau, French should promptly sponsor UN membership for AS, Cambodia, Laos and Vietnam. While applications may not prosper it should be made clear that only Soviet world is opposed.

2. Immediate consideration should be given to ways of utilizing new UN facilities such as observation committees in IC situation. While access to VM territory doubtless would be denied, air observation of border movements could be undertaken.

3. Renewed efforts should be made by US and UK diplomacy to obtain recognition AS by Burma, Indonesia, Philippines, India, Pakistan. With Chinese aggression in Korea and Tiber.[13] Communists need for resources of SEA, and militant revolutionary expansionism of Peking, IC's neighbors should be asked to recognize threat to area and to each of them Communist success in IC would represent. At same time, transfer of economic powers including 100% revenues to AS plus formation national armies should dispel much of their earlier objections to French Union formula.

4. Renewed attempt should be made align US-UK-French policy in FE. If this not practicable, clear understanding should be reached on IC. Legation is particularly disturbed lest lack of understanding should facilitate French or UK-French negotiations with Chinese Communists. Legation not convinced that preliminary explorations this possibility were insignificant (London's 3613, December 28)[14]. . .[It has been] stated to Legation officer informally. . .that British are pressing French to negotiate. Rumors same effect are beginning circulate locally. Whole matter may be Cominform propaganda but it serves emphasize need for urgent tripartite consultations on IC. This mission uninformed re Truman-Attlee conversations on IC.[15]

National:

5. Renewed effort should be made to animate Bao Dai to sustained and vigorous effort of leadership. Whatever excuse may have existed in past to effect that Bao Dai could not link his future to government not truly sovereign no longer exist today after Pau transfers and in face Chinese menace.

6. US will exert pressure for constitution broadened national unity government which would forthwith announce plans and proceed to implementation liberal program social educational, and economic betterment (with present and if necessary increased ECA funds) and would set in motion machinery for institution representative organs.

7. US will indicate availability under approved circumstances forms of assistance to facilitate defections from VM. Legation suggests this must be activity another agency.

(C) Economic.

View nature AS economic problems sketched part I, present STEM program, in character if not in quantity or rate, regarded as reasonably satisfactory. Though its importance should greatly increase in 1951 as organization and planning period of 1950 is translated into major deliveries of current fiscal year, every effort should continue be made speed procurement and shipment programmed items. In next six months military effort must be given priority, although in long run economic assistance through capital development and improved technology necessary put AS on truly sound economic base.

Emergency economic needs are: (1) US may have to finance anticipated AS budgetary deficits 1951 as explained part I, if French unwilling or unable to do so, (2) preparations for assisting in handling northern refugees if large numbers make way south, and (3) settling soonest with French issue of US being able in spite March 8 accord furnish advisers AS governments to supplement, not supplant French, in order assist more efficient and honest administration, lack of which may contribute discourage the whole-hearted support for Bao Dai's government which is so badly needed.

(D) Informational.

This activity should approach if not parallel importance our military and economic programs. The executive staff of USIS now consists of two junior officers. The focus should shift from "sell America" to "hit the enemy." We must expand our use of all media, employing materials collected and edited locally. The program outlined by Goodfriend mission should be backed with funds and personnel. Efforts to insure sympathy of youth, labor and religious groups should be energetically promoted. Viets must be coached by American technicians in giving Viet government "new look"; uniforms, stamps, seals, government forms, street signs, money, etc. As long as Bao Dai is our candidate he must be ingeniously "sold"--an American advisor should be stationed with him. Bao Dai should issue now first of series of "last calls" to erring VM nationalists--he should announce, in his name, projects for building, "two year plans" and the like.

Political warfare should be aggressively pushed--playing on dispersed nature Viet Minh, promoting discord, defeatism, confusion, using all media borrowed or bought--radio, pamphlets, press, agents, word-of-mouth--with all shades of allegiance and experts for these activities should not be further delayed. Legation should inaugurate cooperation with projected Franco-British joint committee for psychological warfare Saigon.

Certain of foregoing recommendations will involve expenditures for which appropriations may not now be earmarked for IC. Legation final recommendation is for all interested US agencies survey current funds to determine if special deficiency appropriations will be needed for defense of IC in next six months. If they may be, we recommend promptest submittal necessary bills.

[1] In telegram 813 to Saigon, December 29, 1950, the Department requested the Legation's suggestions on additional steps which the United States might take in the immediate future to strengthen Indochina. The Legation was also asked for its general analysis of the situation. For text of telegram 813, see Foreign Relations, 1950, vol. vi. p. 958.

[2] Chief of State of Viet-Nam; former Emperor of Annam.

[3] For additional documentation on U.S. concern regarding the Communist threat to Southeast Asia, see pp. 1 ff.

[4] The interstate conference at Pau, France, attended by representatives of France and the Associated States of Indochina, ended on November 27, 1950, after almost five months of negotiations. For texts of ten quadripartite agreements concluded at the conference and signed on December 16, 1950, see France, Direction de la Documentation, Notes et Etudes Documentaires, No. 1425 (January 24, 1951), pp. 1-38.

[5] Tran Van Huu, Prime Minister of Viet-Nam.

6

    Phan Van Giao, Governor of Central Viet-Nam.

7

    Nguyen Huu Tri, Governor of Tonkin.

8

    A French-Vietnamese military convention signed on December 8, 1950, established a Vietnamese national army by effecting the transfer of certain units from French to Vietnamese control.

9

    For documentation on U.S. relations with the Philippines, see pp. 1491 ff.

10

    Telegrams 566, October 16, 1950 and 1077, December 16, 1950, from Saigon, are not printed. For other documentation on French requests for military assistance, see Foreign Relations, 1950, vol VI., pp. 690ff.

11

    General d'Armee Jean de Lattre de Tassigny, French High Commissioner in Indochina; Commander of French Union forces in Indochina.

12

    Reference is to the Mutual Defense Assistance Act of 1949 (Public Law 329, 81st Cong.; 63 Stat. 714) as amended in 1950 (Public Law 621, 81st Cong.; 64 Stat. 373) under which military assistance was being programmed. Title III, Section 303, authorized aid to countries in the "general area" of China.

13

    Documentation on the Korean War is scheduled for publication to volume vii; see also Foreign Relations, 1950, volume vii. For documentation on the Chinese invasion of Tibet, October 7, 1950, see ibid., vol. vi, pp. 256 ff.

14

    Not printed.

15

    President Truman and Clement R. Attlee, Prime Minister of the United Kingdom, met in Washington from December 4 to December 8, 1950, to discuss the situation arising from Chinese Communist intervention in Korea. Indochina did not receive extensive consideration. The record of the first meeting, December 4, does attribute the following to Secretary of State Acheson, however: "If the Communists are successful in Korea, this may so weaken the French in Indochina that they will pull out. He doubted if any one of the President's advisers would urge him to intervene in that situation." For the record of the first meeting and other documentation on the Truman-Attlee conversations, see Foreign Relations, 1950, vol. III, pp. 1789 ff. For additional documentation on the conference, see ibid., vol. VII, pp. 1237 ff.

(204) TELEGRAM FROM BRUCE TO ACHESON, JANUARY 8, 1951

Source: *Foreign Relations, 1951, Vol. VI, pp. 343-344.*

Bruce responded to the Saigon legation's recommendations with warnings about violating the principle of primary French responsibility, which, he argued ruled out any significant direct U.S. financial aid to the Vietnamese national army or to the budgetary deficits of the Associated States.

Embassy in general agreement with Saigon comments and recommendations but believes that two basic factors in Indochina situation should be kept in mind in considering Legation's recommendations:

(1) Principle of primary French responsibility in Indochina was accepted during conversations with French Government at Paris in May 1950 and Embassy believes that no action should be taken by US Government, in view its present and probable future commitments in other areas of world, which would tend to vitiate this principle. Some of Legation's recommendations, as for example with respect to direct financial aid for national army, underwriting Associated States budgetary deficits and US assistance in handling refugees from north, would appear, if adopted in toto, represent a trend toward breakdown of principle of primary French responsibility. Embassy's comment is directed not against specific recommendations of Legation but toward action which would have over-all effect of weakening principle of primary French responsibility in absence of any fresh decision on this point.
(2) Although Legation does not so indicate, Embassy assumes that discussion with French Government prior to action is envisaged on various of its recommendations where there would be very definite French concern rather than merely matter of US action. This would seem to be particularly necessary in matters such as constitution broadened national government in Vietnam, question problem of facilitating defections from Viet Minh, question of US advisers and informational activities.

Embassy strongly supports Legation's recommendation regarding desirability preparing counter guerrilla and resistance organizations for operations within and behind enemy lines.
Embassy considers important that joint US-UK French military staff talks be held at earliest possible date. In this connection, Foreign Office official informs us that British have expressed to French Government agreement on urgent necessity such talks and that Schuman[1] is taking matter up direct with Pleven[2] with view to pushing matter.
If decisions have already been reached with respect to US Government course of action in event Chinese Communist aggression against Indochina, it would be helpful for Embassy to be informed of these decisions. It is inevitable that among questions French Government would raise in joint staff discussions Indochina situation would be that of action to be taken in event Chinese Communist overt crossing border into Tonkin, either through use of "volunteers" or with openly organized units of regular Chinese Communist armies, as well as whether US Government was prepared to assist with air and naval forces, or even ground forces. Pertinent to the foregoing would also be question whether problem would require immediate discussion in and action by UN and whether US Government prepared to act with or without UN sanction.

[1]Robert Schuman, French Foreign Minister.

(205) MEMORANDUM BY THE JOINT CHIEFS OF STAFF TO MARSHALL, JANUARY, 10, 1951

Source: *Foreign Relations*, 1951, Vol. VI, pp. 347-348.

Asked by Secretary Marshall for their view on the French proposal for tripartite military talks on Indochina, the Joint Chiefs reiterated their previous view that the U.S. should stay out of Indochina militarily, even in the event of a Chinese Communist invasion. They expressed their reluctance to enter into formal military talks with the French and the British.

Subject: Proposed Military Talks Regarding Defense of Indochina.

1. This memorandum is in response to your memorandum of 21 December 1950 dealing with the matter of proposed military talks regarding defense

of Indochina.

2. In view of the present United States military position in the Far East, the Joint Chiefs of Staff believe the following to be basic:

a. The United States should not permit its military forces to become engaged in French Indochina at this time, and

b. In the event of a communist invasion of Indochina, therefore, the United States should under current circumstances limit its support of the French there to an acceleration and expansion of the present military assistance program, together with taking other appropriate action to deny Indochina to communism, short of the actual employment of military forces.

In light of the above, and in view of the considerations expressed in their memorandum to you of 8 December 1950, the Joint Chiefs of Staff feel, from the strictly military point of view, that no additional military staff talks are desirable at this time.

3. On the other hand, the Joint Chiefs of Staff recognize that the political considerations raised in your memorandum of 21 December 1950 may be regarded as overriding. Under such circumstances, the Joint Chiefs of Staff would not interpose further objection to the holding of additional tripartite military staff talks at this time. Any such talks, however, would be restricted in scope by the Joint Chiefs of Staff and would not be permitted to deal with matters of strategy affecting United States global policies and plans.

4. In the event of a global war, the major United States measures in support of the French in Indochina would of necessity also be limited to the acceleration and expansion of the present military assistance program as feasible, and, operationally, to matters connected with convoy, routing, and protection of shipping. If the decision is made to hold the proposed additional military talks involving military operational commanders, it would be appropriate, therefore, that the chief United States military representative should be an officer designated by the Commander in Chief, Pacific (CINCPAC), and that he should be assisted by General Brink.

(206) AIRGRAM FROM ACHESON TO CERTAIN DIPLOMATIC OFFICES, JANUARY 19, 1951

Source: *Foreign Relations*, 1951, Vol. VI, pp. 349-350.

Citing the turning over of governmental functions to the Associated States at the Pau Conference, Acheson called on U.S. diplomats in non-Communist Asian states to try once more to persuade those states to extend diplomatic relations to the State of Vietnam, Laos and Cambodia. Acheson also urged U.S. diplomats to point to the alleged danger of Chinese military intervention in Indochina to impress upon non-Communist Asia the need for cooperation with the anti-Communist forces in Asia.

Subject: Discussion of Indochina political situation with neighboring Asian governments.

The Department wishes to draw your attention again to the continuing need that you bring your influence to bear on the governments to which you are accredited concerning their policy toward the Associated States in Indochina.

Assistant Secretary Rusk's press release of November 27th[1] and other recent public declarations, including most recently the Tillman Durdin article published in the New York Times on January 15 (14), 1951,[2] have served to publicize in the United States the facts concerning the autonomy recently acquired by the Associated States from France as a result of the decisions reached at Pau. Yet there has been little if any notice of the fact outside France, particularly in the Asian nations where it is most essential that the facts be known. We cannot allow the Asians to overlook the significance of recent developments because of a failure of their own and French information services to publicize them. It is our hope that, in encouraging the other Asian Governments to restudy the matter, they may even be inclined to take a realistic view and arrive at the inescapable conclusion that the Associated States are in fact autonomous even while retaining membership in a commonwealth of nations, not an unprecedented action.

If the hesitation of Asian nations, excepting Thailand, to grant recognition to the Governments of the Associated States is actually based, as has been stated, on doubts concerning the extent of sovereignty they enjoy, recent developments have entirely changed these considerations and the matter should be reviewed. As you know, for all practical purposes the last functions being administered by the French in Indochina were turned over to the local governments on January 1, 1951.

Any consideration of Indochina policy on the part of neighboring Asian States cannot be disassociated from the circumstance of the present threat of Chinese intervention and Communist domination of the Indochinese peninsula. The Department considers that recognition by other and similarly concerned, if for the moment less seriously threatened Asian nations, of the established governments of the Associated States would be a considerable stimulus to the anti-Communist forces there and a serious blow to the Viet Minh. The time is particularly propitious now coinciding as it would with other lesser encouragements including an increase in overall military potential, the January 1 political developments, progress in the enlargement of National Armies and the energetic, effective and benevolent administration of General de Lattre, Commander in Chief of the Franco-Vietnamese Union forces.

You are therefore instructed to seek an early opportunity to discuss this matter again with the governments to which you are accredited along lines to be developed at your discretion. You should attempt to assist the government in acknowledging the facts in the matter without giving an impression that this is a subject the United States is pursuing solely for its own interests or that we are attempting to over-influence other friendly governments in their acknowledged right to decide this and other questions on their own initiative and in their own interests which, incidentally, we believe the decision we hope will emerge from their considerations would be.

[1]See circular telegram 187, November 27, 1950, which contains the text of the press conference statement by Dean Rusk, Assistant Secretary of State for Far Eastern Affairs, Printed in Foreign Relations, 1950, Vol. VI, p. 938 ff.

[2]The New York Times, January 14, 1951, p. 11, col. 1.

(207) TELEGRAM FROM HEATH TO ACHESON, JANUARY 21, 1951

Source: Foreign Relations, 1950, Vol. VI., pp. 352-353.

General Jean De Lattre de Tassigny's mission when he arrived in Indochina in late 1950 was to stiffen the morale of the French Union troops and prevent the loss of Tonkin to the Viet Minh. After a visit with De Lattre, Heath reported that the military situation in Tonkin had improved, although De Lattre could not yet foresee a counter-offensive against the Viet Minh.

With General Brink I visited General De Lattre in Tonkin January 18 and 19. First day De Lattre flew us over the "redoubt" he is constructing around Hanoi which has circumference of about 50 miles. He is constructing some 300 cement block houses where he will place machine and anti-tank guns and 2 reserve airfields. Work is being pushed rapidly but it will not be entirely completed before June. This "redoubt", De Lattre insists, is not for defense against VM but against possible Chinese invasion which he still believes to be at least several months off. Following day flew and jeeped over recent battle area of Vinh Yen and Phuoc Yen. Very obviously French Union troops had fought with supreme gallantry but it was their superiority in aviation and artillery that threw back VM. According French accounts, VM attacked in this area with 21 battalions French defenders only numbering 6 or 7 battalions. French losses were extremely high. In case of a mobile reserve unit of 3 battalions totalling around 2,000 men, there were 540 casualties.

A *suppletif* battalion made up of Muongs Thais from the tiger hunting country fought with great success and minimum losses. VM losses were undoubtedly much heavier and the estimate of at least thousand VM killed is probably not excessive. Several hundred prisoners were taken and total wounded is doubtless still higher. Use of napalm furnished by MDAP was one decisive factor in French holding. French Union troops and officers I saw looked battle weary but apparently morale was high. De Lattre told me his first public declarations that French Union forces would not yield an inch of terrain and his action in stopping evacuation of Hanoi was to strengthen morale; he had not then been sure the French forces could hold against VM. Now he insists that he is certain of being able withstand VM attacks but he must receive promptly necessary reinforcements from French. Contrary his statement few days ago that he would ask only for few battalions, he now insists that having observed the fanatic fighting spirit and seeing the excellent tactical direction of VM troops, he will need at least division and half. If French Government will not furnish them then he would resign his command. These reinforcements would only be temporary. Within a year he would expect to have built up Viets national army to point where certain Viet units at least could take place of French troops.

De Lattre said he had no plans for counter-offensive at this time. For the moment he could only hope repel VM attacks. Furthermore, it would be great mistake for him to talk about counter-offensive measures such as the retaking of Langson. The French Parliament would refuse him any reinforcements if they thought he was indulging in what they regarded as risky counter-offensive. There was opposition to the war in Indochina in France. Moreover, he did not want to do anything that would give Chinese pretext of invasion. For that reason he was against use of American training units. The moment, however, a Chinese battalion was identified as being on Viets soil, he would ask for American instructors and troops too if he could get them.

According his intelligence, VM had withdrawn all their battalions to north for 10 day period of regrouping. They were extremely surprised and disheartened over their failure break the French lines. VM had been confident their last attack would be successful. His post commanders told me that the initial assault waves of VM were composed of recruits armed with grenades and machine pistols. They attacked in relatively close order and were followed by first class battalions of VM forces.

Governor Tri expressed the prevailing local estimate when he said to me "thanks to De Lattre it seems probable VM will be be able drive French from Tonkin. Had there been no change in command, VM would probably have been successful".

(208) <u>TELEGRAM FROM ACHESON TO THE LEGATION IN SAIGON</u>, JANUARY 30, 1951

Source: *Foreign Relations*, 1951, Vol. VI., pp. 368-369.

In a summary of the Pleven-Truman talks in Washington on January 30, Acheson reported Pleven as wary on DeLattre's request for reinforcement and needing assurances of sufficient U.S. financial assistance for the creation of national armies in order to justify further French commitments. Pleven was also reported as raising the possibility of negotiations with the D.R.V. for the first time since the start of the war.

The fol is rough summary of Truman-Pleven discussions of yesterday as they pertain to IC:

Pleven presented his position as fols:

1) Events in the Far East make it necessary for the Western Powers to coordinate economically, militarily and politically and procedure for permanent consultation between US, Brit and Fr shld be established. It might include the establishment of a permanent tripartite body for this purpose.

2) As far as IC is concerned three hypotheses shld be considered:

a. The present situation of fighting an internal rebellion which FR is and has faced for the last five years. With a reinforced VM Fr can only foresee heavier and heavier losses. The only possible daylight in matter lies in the planned development of Viet natl army. Immed question to be faced is whether Gen de Lattre's demands for reinforcements shld be met or declined in the realization that similar demands may be expected regularly hereafter and cannot be met. The fact that Fr present effort entailed a comparable drain on her contribution to the defense of Western Europe is also pertinent. Amt of US aid to be anticipated is dominant consideration in arriving at decision in matter. Formation of four Vietnamese divisions during 1951 under study. Wld involve a cost of 58 billion francs, 25 billion of which cannot be covered in the contemplated contributions from both Fr and Vietnamese budgets. Particular mention was made of the furnishing of an aircraft carrier. Recommended that this and other technical questions shld be studied by Fr-US mil experts.

b. The second possibility is that which wld be created by an overt Chi Commie attack. Before the Fr can make any decision of action to be taken in this eventuality they must ask for further clarification of the US position vis-a-vis aid in both men and material. Fr Govt wld also appreciate info concerning anticipated US aid in the event of a forced evacuation.

The Fr invite us to consider the effect of the loss of Tonkin or of all IC on the rest of SEA (polit, econ and mil). A study of this matter might be considered by the group suggested in para one.

c. The third possibility is that which wld be created if peace negotiations were undertaken. While Fr observe that it is impossible to calculate if such possibility exists they believe consideration must be given to it "especially in the light of the recent reverses suffered by the VM."

Although detailed minutes are not available fol is a brief summary of our replies to various questions:

Although we are not prepared to consider question of tripartite SEA command as suggested by FR we are prepared under certain specific and limiting conditions to adhere to our agreement to take part in high level tripartite mil conversations as agreed at the Sep FonMin Conf. We are prepared to appoint man from Admiral Radford's[1] staff to represent us.

We assured Fr that our aid program to IC will be carried out as present-ly planned, barring unforeseen developments. We are prepared to give the Fr more detailed info on the way our aid program works and specific con-sideration being given to IC in overall picture. We have told the Fr we are not prepared to commit ground forces but wld, dependent on circumstances applicable at time, supply logistic support in the event of a forced evacu-ation.

Re the 25 billion franc deficit in sum required for natl armies (Fr state only 33 billion of 58 required can be covered by Fr and Viet budgets combined). The Fr made us a formal request for additional aid of 70 million dollars. We have given them no assurance in that regard and are now en-gaged in detailed studies at specialists level concerning matter. For your info it is very unlikely that this Govt will engage itself to finance the budgetary deficit of another govt but we hope to devise some other method to assure that necessary funds for the development of the natl armies be forthcoming.

Although we did not accede to the Fr request for another air-craft carrier, Gen Marshall[2] informed Pleven that the present restrictions on the use of the Langley wld be removed, thus apparently making Langley available to Fr for use in Far Eastern waters if they so choose. We assured the Fr that the effect of the loss of Tonkin or of all of IC to rest of SEA is constantly under study by this govt.

We had no comment concerning third hypothesis.

The 58 billion franc figure for the formation of the natl armies is based on armies of 41 battalions. Of this sum it is estimated that the Fr budget cld only make a 15 1/2 billion franc contribution and the Viet one of 17 billion as a maximum (40% of estimated total receipts). The deficit is thus 25 1/2 billion francs or roughly $70 million. Of this sum approximately 2/3 wld be required for payroll and 1/3 for equipment and goods payable in francs and piasters. Eventually natl armies wld consist of four Vietnamese divisions of 34 battalions plus five Cambodian and two Laotian battalions. Fr have stated it will be impossible for them to furnish any equipment for battalions still to be formed and they count on the US for that.

[1]Adm. Arthur W. Radford, Commander in Chief, Pacific.

[2] General of the Army George of the Army George C. Marshall, Secretary of Defense.

(209) MEMORANDUM BY RUSK TO DEPUTY UNDER SECRETARY FREEMAN MATTHEWS, JANUARY 31, 1951 (extracts)

Source: *Foreign Relations*, 1951, Vol. VI, pp. 16-18, 20-22.

Viewing Indochina as the "keystone" of U.S. policy in Southeast Asia and buoyed by the belief that Southeast Asian states would tend to align themselves with the U.S., Rusk supported the U.S. doing whatever was necessary to insure the success of the U.S. "investment" in Indochina. Rusk's statements that Bao Dai had achieved a degree of independence which Ho Chi Minh had failed to obtain was fundamentally inaccurate, since the D.R.V. had refused to accept arrangements similar to the March 1949 agree-ment as incompatible with Vietnamese independence.

Problem:
To determine the extent of the United States military assistance pro-gram in Southeast Asia, and the priority to be assigned to it, in view of

current favorable political developments in the area and, at the same time, the imminence of a communist invasion of that area. The area comprises the following countries: Burma, Thailand, Indochina, Malaya, Indonesia, and The Philippines.

Discussion:

It has become increasingly apparent during the last several months that, in spite of their unwillingness to accept United States view of the proper solution of the Korean problem, the countries comprising the area known as Southeast Asia are disposed to move in the direction of the United States and of the political and economic systems of which it is the principal protagonist. This tendency is due in some part to the effectiveness of American diplomacy, in some part to Southeast Asian fears of Chinese imperialsim and, in any case, the belief that the United States can and will defend the Southeast Asian neutrals against Chinese and Russian aggression. Although certain Southeast Asian states (Indonesia and Burma) have adopted an attitude of neutrality in the present Sino-U.S.-USSR conflict in the hope of avoiding general conflict in the Far East, it seems likely to the Bureau of Far Eastern Affairs that, if the Communists succeed in Korea, Southeast Asian fears of Chinese imperialism will increase and that these fears alone will probably serve to accelerate the tendency of Southeast Asia to align itself with the United States through the adoption of benevolent neutrality or in some cases, outright alliance.

While this development in Southeast Asia may be regarded as a source of gratification to the United States, it also confronts the United States Government with a problem of the most serious character: If our diplomacy succeeds in Southeast Asia in the United States must decide how much it is prepared to pay in the way of military assistance to validate that success. If, upon careful consideration of all the factors involved, the United States Government decides that it can afford to supply to the countries of Southeast Asia military assistance requisite to their making a stand on their own and our behalf, well and good. If, on the other hand, it is our carefully considered conclusion that, due to the demands for military assistance from other areas of strategic importance to the United States we can not follow through on the military program which our political program foreshadows, then we must trim our sails accordingly. In a word, the United States has in Southeast Asia reached the point where we must decide whether we shall put up or shut up.

Meanwhile, the threat of Chinese Communist invasion of Southeast Asia (Indochina and Burma in particular) increases. While intelligence estimates do not indicate an increase in the intention of the Chinese to invade the area, all intelligence reports testify to an increase in their ability to do so. Indirect Chinese Communist involvement in Ho Chi Minh's military operations is at the same time increasing daily.

The strategic, political and economic importance of the region known as Southeast Asia has long been recognized by both the military and the political authorities of this Government (see NSC 64, Tab (A); Joint Chiefs estimates, Tabs (B) and (C); letter from General Marshall, Tab (D).[1]

In full recognition of the strategic importance of the area, the United States Government has embarked upon programs for the extension of military and economic assistance to the several countries comprising the area described below. It should be borne in mind at all times that the Governments of the area as well as the Governments of France, the United Kingdom and the Netherlands are predicating their policy on the supposition that those programs will be executed by this Government.

The United States Government has pursued its policy in Southeast Asia with the expenditure of relatively little in the way of money and materiel.

The following lists (in thousands of U.S. dollars) the amount the United States is spending for military assistance, economic and technical assistance programs in the countries of Southeast Asia during 1950-51:

Country	Mutual defense assistance	Economic and technical assistance programs
Burma	$3,500	$4,350
Thailand	10,001	4,190
Indochina	164,000	7,650
Malaya*		
Indonesia	3,000	6,273
The Philippines	11,247	130
Total	$191,748	$22,593

Burma

The Union of Burma is a country of considerable strategic importance because of its geographic location between India and China and because of its ability to produce, even under present unsettled conditions, an export surplus of more than 1,000,000 tons of rice per annum. During the early period of its independence (1948-1949) the country was on the ideological borderline, and the question of possible military assistance was held in abeyance pending a clarification of the attitude of Burma toward international Communism. Its potential value to us was lessened by the widespread disorder that prevailed in the country during that period.

During the past year, however, our efforts to win over Burma to the side of the democratic nations have met with remarkable success, partly as a result of the measures that we have taken and partly as land were to go Communist it would simplify Viet Minh or Chinese Communist action in flanking any resistance in either Indochina or Burma. Thailand furthermore is voluntarily channeling its rubber and tin to the Western powers and is generally cooperating economically.

Such support from Thailand has cost the United States little except careful diplomatic handling. It has received no large loans nor any extensive aid programs. A $20,000,000 surplus property credit was granted after World War II of which Thailand used less than $7,000,000. A $10,000,000 military aid program for 1950 has been approved in order to equip the Thai Army against possible internal Communist efforts but of this amount only a fraction has actually been shipped. It is believed, however, that in view of Communist successes in Korea and in Tonkin that military aid for Thailand should be substantially increased in quantity and in priority in order that this nation might continue to stand against Communist aggression.

Indochina

It is generally acknowledged that if Indochina were to fall under control of the Communists, Burma and Thailand would follow suit almost immediately. Thereafter, it would be difficult if not impossible for Indonesia, India and the others to remain outside the Soviet-dominated Asian bloc. Therefore, the Department's policy in Indochina takes on particular importance for, in a sense, it is the keystone of our policy in the rest of Southeast Asia.

Even before the Japanese Army of Occupation had been evacuated from Indochina it became evident that there was a nationalist movement brewing there which would have to be dealt with promptly in one way or another. A military solution was impossible and the French decided, either for that reason or in acknowledgement of the fact that some sort of alteration in the prewar type of colonial administration of overseas territories would eventually be required, chose the only practical course open to them at that time--to negotiate with Ho Chi Minh. The Fontainebleau Pact which followed proved to be a miserable failure. Its principal purpose in the end, ironically enough, was to serve as a precedent for the series of agreements which the French were later to conclude with Ho Chi Minh's greatest rival, Bao Dai, and which were to result in a degree of independence for the Associated States which Ho Chi Minh had never been able to obtain, either by political or military means.

By the time Ho had gone underground in December 1946 certain essential facts were becoming evident to us as they were to the French. They included the realization that Ho was not the benevolent nationalist patriot he claimed to be but rather a clever and devoted disciple of the Kremlin. A solution to the Indochina problem could not be achieved through him if Western interests were to be served. Until an alternate could be found there was no course but to oppose Ho by force of arms. The alternate was and is, Bao Dai, the only man in Indochina capable of commanding a following comparable to that of Ho and serviceable as a framework within which a non-Communist government could be formed.

The Department's policy at this time, late 1948-early 1949, had gelled. It was, in simplest terms, to prevent Ho and his Kremlin allies from gaining control of Indochina by every means possible and to bring a friendly influence to bear on the French to make whatever concessions to the Indochinese were required to bring about the restoration of internal security and the establishment of a stable non-Communist nationalist government capable of maintaining it. The course we have and are pursuing is an outgrowth of these two basic objectives.

In the short period of time since the present mold was set by the Baie d'Along Agreement of June 1948, remarkable progress has been made in "Operation Eggshell". There is no need to dwell on the series of developments culminating recently in the decision of the French Government to grant the Associated States a full measure of independence within the French Union as exemplified by the agreements reached at the Pau Conference.

However satisfactory progress may have been, we are now in a crucial period. Aside from the ever present threat of Chinese intervention, which would of course change everything, we are now in a stage where our participation in the over-all operation must be greater than ever before. French cooperation in the form of political concessions and assurances of continued military and financial aid has been received. We can expect little, if anything, more from the French side.

It is, moreover, doubtful if the French concessions would ever have been made if our assurances of financial and military aid to them and to the Associated States had not been forthcoming at the same time. It is certain that without our military and financial aid the attainment of the ultimate goals we have been aiming at during the long difficult operation of the last five years will be impossible. Unless we carry out our present program, it is questionable whether the French can be counted on to carry out their program. At best it will be a period of years before the Associated States are able to fully assume the responsibility they have so recently acquired. They will need constant aid. They must turn to us for it if they are not to turn elsewhere.

Above all, we cannot afford to jeopardize the considerable measure of success our policy has already had in Indochina by neglecting to provide the proper maintenance for our investment. French cooperation will be required at all times and can only be assured if we, ourselves continue to give constant evidence of our determination to see the matter through. In sum, to neglect to pursue our present course to the upmost of our ability would be disastrous to our interests in Indochina and, consequently, in the rest of Southeast Asia.

(210) REPORT BY HO CHI MINH TO THE SECOND NATIONAL CONGRESS OF THE VIETNAM WORKER'S PARTY, FEBRUARY 11-19, 1951 [Extract]

Source: Ho Chi Minh, *Selected Writings*, (Hanoi: Foreign Languages Publishing House, 1977), pp. 101-129.

As early as January 1948, the Central Committee of the Indochinese Communist Party determined that it should "advance toward the convening of a National congress" of the Party for the purpose of "revising its platform and line regarding the revolutionary movement in the country," to "assemble experiences and unify theory and action" in the Party. But for reasons which are not clear, it was not until February 1951 that the Second Party Congress was held - the first since 1935. By that time, the leadership had decided that the Party was needed to lead the resistance publicly rather that from the background. At the same time, the revolutionary movements in Laos and Cambodia had reached the stage where they needed their own Communist Parties. So the Second Party Congress coincided with the emergence of the Party into the public light and its change of name from the Indochinese Communist Party to the Viet-nam Worker's Party (Dang Lao Dong Viet-nam). In its political report to the Congress, Ho Chi Minh reviewed the history of the Party and Government and addressed himself particularly to the problem of the counteroffensive stage, repeating previous warnings against impatience already made by Giap and Troung Chinh.

VIII. THE PROTRACTED WAR OF RESISTANCE

The enemy schemed for a *lightening war*. They wanted to attack swiftly and win swiftly. For our part our Party and Government set forth the motto: *Protracted war of resistance*. The enemy plotted to sow dissensions among us, so our watchword was: *Unity of the entire people*.

Thus right from the start, our strategy prevailed over the enemy's.

To wage a protracted war of resistance, there must be an adequate supply of arms and munitions to the army, of food and clothing to the troops and the people. Our country is poor and and our technical level low. Cities and towns with some industry are all occupied by the enemy. We must seek to offset our material deficiencies by the enthusiasm of our entire people. So the Party and the Government have promoted *patriotic emulation*. Emulation covers all fields but it is aimed at three main objectives: to get rid of famine, liquidate illiteracy and annihilate the foreign invaders.

Our workers have emulated one another in manufacturing weapons for our troops, who have trained hard and scored good results. Our recent victories in battle are proof of this. Our people have ardently emulated one another and recorded satisfactory results. Although our country is economically backward, we have been waging the war of resistance for nearly 5 years and can keep fighting without suffering too many privations. This is a fact. The majority of our population have been freed from illiteracy. This is a brilliant achievement admired by the world. I suggest that our Congress send cordial thanks and praise to our troops and fellow-countrymen.

However, concerning the work of organization and supervision and the exchange and summing up of experiences we are still weak. These are shortcomings. From now on we should strive to overcome them; then the emulation movement will certainly reap more and better results.

Military activity is the keystone in the war of resistance.

When the war of resistance began *our army* was still in its infancy. Though full of heroism, it lacked weapons, experience, officers, everything.

The enemy army was well-known in the world. It had land, naval, and air forces. Moreover, it was supported by the British and American imperialists, especially the latter.

The discrepency between our forces and the enemy's was so great that at the time some people likened our war of resistance to a fight between " a grasshopper and an elephant."

And such a fight it would be if things were looked at with a narrow mind, solely from the angle of material strength and in their present state. Indeed against the enemy's airplanes and artillery we had only bamboo sticks. But our Party is a Marxist-Leninist one. We look not only at the present but also to the future and have firm confidence in the spirit and strength of the masses, of the nation. Therefore we resolutely told those wavering and pessimistic people:

Yes, it's now grasshopper versus elephant,

But tomorrow the elephant will collapse.

Facts have shown that the colonialist "elephant" is getting out of breath while our army has grown up into a powerful tiger.

Although at the beginning, the enemy was so strong and we still so weak, we none the less fought with the greatest energy, scored many successes, and kept firm confidence in our final victory. This is because our cause is just, our troops courageous, our people united and undaunted, and because we are supported by the French people and the world democratic camp. This is also because our strategy is correct.

Our Party and Government have estimated that our war of resistance includes three stages:

- *In the first stage,* which went from September 22, 1945 to the end of the Viet Bac campaign in autumn-winter 1947, our efforts were aimed at preserving and increasing our main forces.

- *In the second stage,* from the end of the Viet Bac campaign in 1947 up to now, we have actively contended with the enemy and prepared for the general counter-offensive.

- *The third stage* is to be that of the general counter-offensive.

On this last point, because they did not grasp the policy of the Party and the Government, a number of comrades got wrong ideas. Some thought that the slogan of "preparation for general counter-offensive" was premature. Others wanted to know the day and hour of the general counter-offensive. Still others believed that the general counter-offensive would certainly be launched in 1950 etc.

These wrong conceptions were harmful to our work. We must first of all keep in mind that *the war of resistance will be long and hard, but will certainly end in victory.*

The war of resistance must be a protracted one because our population and territory are small and our country poor. Long and all-around preparations have to be made by our entire people. We must always bear in mind that in relation to us the French invaders are quite strong, and, in addition, they are assisted by the British and Americans.

They are like a "tangerine with a thick rind" and so we must have time to "sharpen our finger-nails" in order to peel it.

We must also understand that each stage is linked up with others: it succeeds the one that precedes it and produces seeds for the one that follows.

Many changes occur in the course of the passage from one stage to another. Each stage also contains changes of its own.

It is impossible to determine major stages on the basis of the general situation but it is not possible to separate one stage completely from the other, like slicing cake. The length of each stage depends upon the situation at home and in the world, and on the changes in the enemy's forces and in ours.

We must understand that protracted resistance is closely connected with preparations for a general counter-offensive. As the war of resistance is a long one, long preparations are also needed for a general counter-offensive. Whether the general counter-offensive will come early or late depends on changes in the enemy's forces and in ours, and also on changes in the international situation.

In all circumstances, the more careful and complete the preparations, the more steadily and favourably the general counter-offensive will proceed.

The slogan *"To prepare for a vigorous switch to the general counter-offensive"* was set forth early in 1950.

Did we make preparations during that year?

Yes, we did. The Government issued the general mobilization order and launched the movement for patriotic emulation. As is well-known, our troops and our people have made active preparations and have obtained good results.

Did we make the move in 1950?

Yes, we did and are still doing it. The great diplomatic successes scored early in 1950 and the great military victories won towards the end of that year were proof of this.

Have we launched the general counter-offensive?

We have been preparing to switch over vigorously to the general counter-offensive, but have not yet actually launched it. We must fully grasp the meaning of the words, "To prepare for a vigorous switch to . . . "

Once *the preparations are fully completed* we will launch the general counter-offensive. The more complete, the more fully complete, the preparations, the sooner the general counter-offensive will come and the more favourable the conditions for its success.

We should avoid precipitation, rashness and impatience.

The troops, the people, the cadres, everybody and every branch must *strive to make fully complete preparations*. When our preparations are completed we will launch the general counter-offensive and then it will certainly be successful.

IX. CORRECTION OF SHORTCOMINGS
AND MISTAKES

Our Party has recorded many achievements but has also committed *not a few mistakes*. We must sincerely engage in self-criticism in order to correct them. Efforts must be made to correct our mistakes so as to progress.

Before speaking of our shortcomings we must recognize that our Party has cadres - especially those in the zones still temporarily under enemy control - who are very heroic and devoted, who, in spite of all hardships and dangers, always keep close to the people, stick to their work without fear or complaint, and are ready to sacrifice even their lives.

They are model fighters of the nation, meritorious sons and daughters of the Party.

It can be said that since the founding of the Party, *its policies on the whole have been correct*. If they were not, how could we have recorded such tremendous achievements? But we have also shown major shortcomings and weaknesses:

Doctrinal studies are still inadequate, many Party cadres and members are not yet mature ideologically and their theoretical level is still low. As a result, in the carrying out of the policies of the Party and the Government there have occurred erroneous tendencies, either "leftist", or rightist (as in problems relating to land, the Front, the national minorities, religion, the administration, etc.).

Our organizational work is also still weak, and often cannot ensure correct implementation of the policies of the Party and the Government.

Therefore, *to study our doctrine, sharpen our ideology, raise our theoretical level and perfect our organization* are urgent tasks for the Party.

Besides, in leading organs at all levels there still exist fairly prevalent and grave mistakes in the style of work, measures adopted and manner of guiding. These are *subjectiveness, bureaucracy, commandism, narrow-mindedness* and *arrogance.*

Subjectiveness manifests itself in the belief that the long-term war of resistance can turn out to be a short-term war.

Bureaucracy is evidenced by red tape, divorce from the masses and by failure to conduct investigations and surveys, to engage in control and supervision, and learn from the experiences of the masses.

Commandism reveals itself in reliance on administrative compulsion to get things done, and failure to conduct propaganda and explanatory work to make the people work on their own.

Narrow-mindedness is apparent in judging non-Party people with undue severity, or slighting them and refusing to discuss with them or ask for their opinion.

As for *arrogance,* it is revealed in the following:

- To boast of one's past acheivements, extol oneself and consider oneself the "saviour" of the people and the "meritorious servant" of the Party. To ask for position and honour. Unable to fulfil major tasks, one is unwilling to accept minor ones. Arrogance is very harmful to solidarity both within and without the Party.

- To rely on one's position as Party member to make light of discipline and hierarchy in mass organizations or government organs.

The comrades affected by this disease do not understand that each Party member must be a model of discipline, not only Party discipline but also that of mass organizations and organs of revolutionary power.

The Central Committee is partly responsible for that disease and others which affect Party members, because it has not paid adequate attention to *control work.* Ideological training has not been given to all, nor in sufficient amount. Inner Party democracy has not been broadly practiced. Criticism and self-criticism have not yet become a regular habit.

However, these defects are being corrected to a certain extent. The recent critical reviews and the movement for criticism and self-criticism have yielded good results in spite of a few deviations.

Stalin said that a revolutionary party needs criticism and self-criticism just as a human being needs air. He also said that close control can help avoid many grave mistakes.

From now on the Party must try to dispense doctrinal education in order to raise the political standards of its members. *A collective style of work* must be promoted. *Relations between the Party and the masses* must be strengthened. *Observance of discipline, respect of principles and Party spirit* must be heightened in every Party member. The Party must widen the movement for criticism and self-criticism within the Party, the State organs, the mass organizations, in the press and among the people. Criticism and self-criticism must be conducted regularly, in a practical and democratic way, from top to bottom and from the bottom upwards. Lastly there must be close control by the Party.

By so doing, we shall commit fewer errors and make quicker progress.

X. NEW SITUATION AND NEW TASKS

A. New situation:

As is well-known the world is at present divided into two distinct camps:

- *The democratic camp* headed by the Soviet Union and comprising the socialist countries and the new democracies in Europe and in Asia. It also embraces the oppressed nations which are struggling against aggressive imperialism and the democratic organizations and personalities in the capitalist countries.

The democratic camp is a powerful camp which is growing in strength. The following few points are sufficient evidence of this:

Let us look at a map of the world: From Eastern Europe to Eastern Asia the USSR and the new democracies form an immense bloc of 800 million people. In this bloc the nations are united, pursue the same goal and are not divided by any antagonisms. It is the symbol of progress and of the bright future of mankind. It is an extremely powerful force.

At the Second Congress of the Peace Front held in the Polish capital in November 1950, the representatives of 500 million peace fighters in 81 countries pledged their determination to safeguard world peace and to oppose imperialist wars. This is the *United Front* of the peaceful and democratic world. This is a very powerful force whose strength is growing with every passing day.

- *The anti-democratic camp* is headed by the US. Immediately after the end of World War Two, the US became the ringleader of world imperialism and reaction. Britain and France are its right- and left-hand men and the reactionary governments in the East and the West its henchmen.

Aspiring to world hegemony, the US holds out dollars in one hand to entice people and brandishes the atomic bomb in the other to meance the world. The Truman Doctrine, Marshall Plan, NATO Pact, and Programme for Southeast Asia are all US manoeuvres aimed at preparing for a third world war.

But the US ambitions have run into a tremendous obstacle: the immense force of the Soviet Union, the movement for democracy and peace, and the movement for national liberation seething all over the world.

At present, the US policy is as follows:

- In Asia, to assist the reactionaries such as Chiang Kai-shek, Syngman Rhee, Bao Dai, etc. ; to help the British imperialists repress the resistance forces in Malaya and the French colonialists crush the Resistance in Viet Nam, while the US itself is waging an aggressive war against Korea and is occupying Taiwan in an attempt to undermine the Chinese revolution.

- In Europe the US has, through the Marshall Plan and NATO, seized control over the Western countries in the military, political and economic fields, and at the same time has been striving to arm them and compel them to supply cannon-fodder, as in the plan for setting up 70 divisions in Western Europe under an American commander-in-chief.

However, the US camp has a great many weaknesses:
Besides the strength of the democratic camp, the US camp faces another threat: economic crisis.

There are many contradictions in the US camp. For example: The US wants Western Germany to set up an army of ten divisions but this has been opposed by the French people. Britain conversly opposes the US because the two are contending for oil in the Near-East and for influence in the Far-East.

The people, especially the toiling sections in countries "aided" by the US, hate it for encroaching upon their economic interests and the independence of their countries.

The US is too greedy. It schemes to set up bases all over the world. It helps every reactionary group and every reactionary government. Its front extends beyond measure, consequently its forces are spread thin. Clear proof of this is supplied in Korea, where the United States together with 40 of its vassals are suffering defeats at the hands of the country they have invaded. The US helped the reactionary clique in China, the Kuomintang headed by Chian Kaishek, but Chiang was defeated. The US helps the French colonialists in Viet Nam, yet the Vietnamese Resistance is winning.

In short, we can foretell that the reactionary imperialist camp will certainly be defeated and the camp of peace and democracy will certainly be victorious.

Viet Nam is a part of the world democratic camp. It is at present a bastion against imperialism, against the anti-democratic camp headed by the US.

Since the beginning of our war of resistance, Britain and the US have helped the French colonialists. And since 1950, the US has openly intervened in our country.

At the end of 1950, Britain and France prepared to set up a "united" front to join forces against the resistance in Malaya and in Viet Nam.

Thus, the international situation is closely related to our country. Every success of the democratic camp is also ours, and every success won by us is also one for the democratic camp. Therefore, at present our main slogan is: *"To crush the French colonialists and defeat the US interventionists in order to regain unity and complete independence and safeguard world peace."*

B. New tasks:

The comrades of the Central Committee will report on such important questions as the Party's political programme and constitution, the military question, the administration, the National United Front, the economy, etc. This report will only emphasize some main tasks among our new ones:

1. *To bring the war of resistance to complete victory.*
2. *To organize the Viet Nam Workers' Party.*

1. Efforts must be made to develop the strength of the troops and the people in order to win success after success and advance towards the general counter-offensive.

This task aims at these main points:

- *In the building and development of the army,* all-out efforts must be made towards the organization and consolidation of *political and military* work among our troops. Their political consciousness, tactics and techniques, and *self-imposed discipline* must be heightened. Our army must become a genuine *people's* army.

Simultaneously, the *militia and guerilla units* must be developed and consolidated in organization, training, leadership and combat strength. They must make up a vast and solid steel net spread all over the country so that wherever the enemy goes he will get enmeshed.

- *To enhance patriotism* - Our people are inspired by ardent patriotism. This is an invaluable tradition of ours. At all times, whenever the Fatherland is invaded, this patriotism forms an immensely powerful wave sweeping away all dangers and difficulties and drowning all traitors and aggressors.

Many great wars of resistance in our history are proofs of our people's patriotism. We can be proud of the glorious pages of history written by our people in the days of the Trung Sisters, Lady Trieu, Tran Hung Dao, Le Loi, Quang Trung, etc. We must engrave in our minds the achievements of our national heroes because they are the symbols of a heroic nation.

Our fellow-countrymen today are worthy of their forefathers. White-haired folk, children, people residing abroad, people living in the areas still under enemy control, in the plains, in the highlands - all are imbues with ardent love for the country and hatred for the aggressor. Fighters at the front go hungry for days on end in order to remain in contact with the enemy and annihilate him. Government employees in the rear go hungry for the sake of the troops. Women urge their husbands to enlist in the army while they themselves help to transport supplies. Combatants' mothers take care of the troops as they would their own children. Workers and peasants of both sexes emulate one another to increase production, shrinking from no hardships in order to contribute their part to the Resistance. Landowners offer their lands to the Government. These lofty gestures are all different; yet they are similar for they stem from the same ardent patriotism. Patriotism is like valuable objects. Sometimes these are exhibited in a glass or a crystal vase and are thus clearly visible. But at other times they may be discreetly hidden in a trunk or a suitcase. Our duty is to bring all these hidden valuables into full view. That is, every effort must be made in explanation, propaganda organization and leadership so that the patriotism of all may find expression in work benefiting the country and the Resistance.

Genuine patriotism is altogether different from the chauvinism of the reactionary imperialists. It is part and parcel of internationalism. It was thanks to their patriotism that the army and the people of the Soviet Union crushed the German and Japanese fascists and safeguarded their socialist Fatherland, thereby helping the working class and the oppressed peoples of the world. It was thanks to their patriotism that the Chinese Liberation Army and the Chinese people destroyed the traitorous Chiang Kai-shek clique and drove out the American imperialists. It is thanks to their patriotism that the Korean troops and people, together with the Chinese volunteers, are routing the American imperialists and their henchmen. It is also thanks to their patriotism that our troops and people have for long years endured untold sufferings and hardships, determined to smash the colonialist aggressors and the Vietnamese traitors, and to build an independent, re-unified, democratic free, and prosperous Viet Nam, a new democratic Viet Nam.

- *To step up patriotic emulation.* First, let the troops emulate one another to exterminate the enemy and score feats of arms; second, let the people emulate one another to *increase production.* We must devote ourselves heart and soul to these two tasks.

- In the great work of carrying on the war of resistance and engaging in national construction, *the Lien Viet-Viet Minh* Front, the trade-unions, the peasants' associations and other mass organizations exert great influence. We must help them develop, strengthen and work vigorously.

- *Concerning the land policy,* in the free zones, we must strictly implement the reduction of land rent and interest rates, confiscate lands belonging to the French and the Vietnamese traitors and temporarily distribute them to the poor peasants and the families of armymen, with a view to improving the livelihood of the peasants, heightening their spirit, and fostering their forces for the Resistance.

- *Concerning the economy and finance,* we must safeguard and develop our economic bases and fight the enemy in the economic field. There must be an equitable and rational tax system. A balance must be achieved in receipts and expenditures in order to ensure supplies for the army and the people.

- *Cultural work* must be speeded up to form the new man and train new cadres for the Resistance and for national construction. All vestiges of colonialism and the enslaving influence of imperialist culture must be systematically rooted out. Simultaneously, we must develop the fine traditions of our national culture and assimilate the new in world progressive culture in order to build a Vietnamese culture with a national, scientific and popular character.

Following our victories, the *areas still under temporary enemy control* will be liberated one after another. Therefore, preparations must be made to consolidate the newly-liberated areas in all respects.

- The life and property of *foreign residents* who abide by the Vietnamese law will be protected. *Chinese residents* should be encouraged to take part in the Resistance. If they volunteer to do so they will enjoy every right and fulfil every duty of a Vietnamese citizen.

We are waging our war of resistance, the brother Cambodian and Lao nations are also waging theirs. The French colonialists and the American interventionists are the common enemy of our three nations. Consequently, we must strive to help our Cambodian and Lao brothers and their wars of resistance, and proceed to set up a Viet Nam-Cambodian-Lao Front.

- Our successes in the Resistance are partly due to the sympathy of the *friendly countries* and of the people of the world. Therefore, we must strengthen the friendship between our country and the friendly countries, and that between our people and the people of the other countries in the world.

2. To carry these points into effect, we must have a legal party organized in a way consistent with the situation in the world and at home in order to lead our people's struggle to victory. This party is named the *Viet Nam Worker's Party.*

As regards its *composition,* the Viet Nam Workers' Party will admit the most enthusiastic and most enlightened workers, peasants, and intellectuals.

As regards its *doctrine,* it adheres to Marxism-Leninism.

As regards its *organization,* it adopts the system of democratic centralism.

As regards *discipline,* it has an iron discipline which is at the same time a self-imposed one.

As regards its law of *development,* it makes use of criticism and self-criticism to educate its members and the masses.

As regards its *immediate goal,* the Viet Nam Workers' Party unites and leads the entire people to wage the war of resistance, take it to complete victory and win back national unity and complete independence; it leads the entire people to realize new democracy and create conditions for the advance to socialism.

The Viet Nam Workers' Party must be a great party - powerful, firm, pure and thoroughly revolutionary.

The Viet Nam Workers' Party must be the clear-sighted, determined, and loyal leader of the working class and toiling people, of the Vietnamese people, whose aim is to unite and lead the people in the resistance until complete victory, and to realize new democracy.

In the present stage, the interests of the working class and toiling people and those of the nation are at one. It is precisely because it is the party of the working class and toiling people that the Viet Nam Workers' Party must be the Party of the Vietnamese people.

The first task, the most urgent task of our Party today, is to *lead the war of resistance to victory.* The other tasks must be subordinated to it.

Our task is immense, our future glorious. But we shall have to experience many more difficulties. The war has its difficulties; victory has its own for example:

- Ideologically, our cadres, Party members and people are not yet mature enough to cope with all developments at home and abroad.

- The American imperialists may give the French aggressors even greater assistance, causing the latter to act even more rashly.

- We are facing more and more work, but we have not enough cadres and those we have lack ability and experience.

- We must solve economic and financial problems in the most rational way, one that is the most beneficial to the people, etc.

We do not fear difficulties. But we must foresee them, clearly realize them, and be prepared to overcome them.

With solidarity and unity of mind, the determination and dauntless spirit of our Party, Government and entire people, we will certainly surmount all difficulties and gain complete victory.

The October Revolution triumphed. The building of socialism in the Soviet Union has been successful. The Chinese Revolution was victorious. These great successes have opened the way to success for the revolution in our country and many other countries in the world.

We have a great, powerful Party. Its greatness and strength is due to Marxism-Leninism, to the constant efforts of all our Party members, and to the love confidence and support of our entire army and people.

That is why I am convinced that we will fulfil our heavy but glorious tasks, which are:

- To build the Viet Nam Workers' Party into a most powerful one;
- To bring the Resistance to complete victory;
- To build a new democratic Viet Nam; and
- To contribute to the defence of democracy in the world and a lasting peace.

(211) REPORT BY TRUONG CHINH TO THE SECOND NATIONAL PARTY CONGRESS, February 11-19, 1951 (Extract)

Source: Truong Chinh, *The Vietnamese Peoples' National Democratic Revolution,* pp. 167-170 [Translation by the editor]

By mid-1950, the Party Central Committee had informed its members that the name of the Party would be changed to the Viet-nam Workers' Party. The change was officially ratified at the Party Congress, but only after Truong Chinh had explained the change of name and responded to some of the doubts which had been raised. The words "Dang Lao Dong" can be translated either as "Labor Party" or "Workers' Party," and while D.R.V. publications have usually translated it as "Workers' Party," Truong Chinh made explicit reference to the British Labor Party and indicated that there was some sensitivity to having the same name as a Party which was seen as reactionary.

Beloved comrades,

The line and policy of the Vietnamese revolution has been presented above. To lead the working class and the Vietnamese people in carrying out that line and that policy, we must have a vanguard party. In our Viet-nam, that party is our Party, which the Central Executive Committee proposes to this Congress take the name of *Viet-nam Workers' Party.*

Where does the Viet-nam Workers' Party come from? It comes from the *Indochinese Communist Party.* According to the above proposal, the Vietnamese section of the Indochinese Communist Party would be detached to become a party specifically in Viet-nam taking the name *Viet-nam Workers' Party.*

Why must we found a Viet-nam Workers' Party? The announcement of the Central Committee of July 1950 explained it clearly. Here I only present the main reason:

Establishing the Viet-nam Workers' Party is aimed primarily at strengthening the leading role of the working class, consolidating the worker-peasant alliance, linking the working class with other popular laboring strata, unifying the national democratic forces under the Party's leadership, defeating the imperialists and their lackies, completing the national liberation, developing the people's democratic regime, protecting world peace and democracy, and preparing to advance to socialism.

Taking the name Viet-nam Workers' Party is not only advantageous to the unification of the entire people to defeat the invading army, but also advantageous to the anti-imperialist united front of Viet-nam, Cambodia, and Laos against French-U.S. imperialism, and the winning of complete national independence.

A number of our comrades do not yet understand the naming of our Party as the Viet-nam Workers' Party. There are comrades who are worried because of sentiment, thinking that so many comrades have sacrificed themselves for the

Indochinese Communist Party, and now suddenly must suddenly say goodbye to that beloved name that it will be too painful! Or they think that the name "Labor Party" has not been liked by the masses in Britain, so why should we bother to be connected with that name.

Naturally, leaving behind the name Indochinese Communist Party is a sacrifice. Any sacrifice is painful. But a sacrifice in the interest of the revolution is a necessary sacrifice. We should not judge the problem of the Party's name from a standpoint of narrow sentiment; judging it the standpoint of the interest of the revolution is more correct.

Our Party is not alone in using the workers' party name. Revolutionary parties of the working class in countries such as Albania and Korea have also taken that name. Revolution in those countries not only has not been weakened but has advanced rapidly. The British Labor Party is a reformist party, but the term worker is still beautiful.

We should remember that in 1919, Lenin insisted that true revolutionary parties of the working class take the name Communist party and have all the other qualifications before being admitted to the Communist International, primarily in order to distinguish vanguard parties of the revolutionary working class from reformist social democratic parties.

Today, the situation has changed. The Soviet Union has triumphed over fascism and marches at the head of the worker movement for peace and democracy. The Soviet Union is the first country to successfully establish socialism. In many countries, the communist and workers' parties have become true Marxist-Leninist parties, powerful mass parties, and the sole leading force or have gained political power. Many people's democracies have been established and are building people's democratic regimes or have begun to construct socialism. The imperialists are in terrible crisis and are preparing a new world war. The right-wing social democrats have lost faith in the popular masses. Many intermediary strata in various countries respect and love the Soviet Union and communist parties, and like the people's democratic regime and admire socialism. In those circumstances, our Party is not convinced that we must take the name communist party, but believe we can take another name, provided that our Party still follows Marxism-Leninism, that the final objective of the Party is still communism, and that the change of name is advantageous for the revolutionary movement, for the development of the Party into a powerful mass party, the consolidation of the Party's leading role, and the strengthening of relations between the Party and masses.

(212) PLATFORM OF THE VIET-NAM WORKERS' PARTY, February 19, 1951

Source: Vietnam News Agency, in English Morse to Southeast Asia, March 12, 1951.

At the end of its National Congress, the Vietnam Workers' Party adopted a new platfrom which defined the tasks of the Vietnamese revolution as including the development of a People's Democracy and laying the foundations of socialism. This D.R.V. English translation is the only D.R.V. English translation available and no Vietnamese language text is available. It should be noted, however, that a different translation was published in a supplement to People's China, *III, No. 9 (May 1, 1951) [Vol. I. pp. 164-175]. It is reprinted in Allen W. Cameron (ed.)* Viet-Nam Crisis, A Documentary History, *Supplement, pp. 4-9. An important difference between the two translations is in Chapter Three, point 12. The* People's China *translation refers to "long-term cooperation with a view to bringing about an independent, free, strong and prosperous federation of the states of Viet-Nam, Laos and Cambodia, if the three peoples so desire." The V.N.A. version refers to "single-mindedness between the three peoples." The disparity can only be accounted for by a fear on the part of D.R.V. leaders that the federation idea would be the target of propaganda by the French. The Indochinese federation idea, supported by the Indochinese Communist Party from its foundings was dropped by the Lao Dong Party after 1954.*

"North Vietnam - Here is the full text of the platform adopted by the Vietnam Lao Dong Party, which was founded at an 8-day national congress held in North Vietnam from Feb. 11-19, 1950:
"Platform of the Vietnam Lao Dong Party:

"Chapter one
'The World and Vietnam:'

"1 - After the Second World War German, Italian, and the Japanese fascism collapsed, capitalism entered a grave crisis; the Soviet Union became more prosperous and powerful with each passing day; the democratic movement daily gained momentum. The world split into two camps: the antiimperialist democratic camp led by the Soviet Union and the antidemocratic imperialist camp headed by the United States.
"The democratic camp became stronger, while the imperialist camp weakened day after day. With the Chinese people's revolution gaining victory and with the founding of the German Democratic Republic, the balance of strength tipped on the side of the democratic camp.
"At present the American imperialists and their accomplices are making frenzied preparations for a (third) World War and are attempting to expand their aggressive wars. The menace of a new World War is obvious. The central task of the working class and peoples of the world is, therefore, to struggle for the maintenance of peace. Under the leadership of the Soviet Union and the world camp of peace is strongly opposing the imperialist warmongers. The peace movement has become stronger and more widespread than ever before in history. For the imperialists to start a third World War would be tantamount to committing suicide.

"2 - After the Second World War socialism got the upper hand of fascism; the people's democratic revolution spread out and met with success in many countries of Eastern Europe and the Far East. Many people's republics were set up and broke away from the imperialist system. The people's democratic regime became more consolidated day after day and is paving the way for socialism. People's democracy under the present historic conditions of the world is a stepping stone to world socialism for many countries.

"3 - A striking feature of the world after the Second World War is the widespread national liberation movement which gains in strength day after day and which is rocking the whole imperialist system. It has become an integral part of the world-wide movement for peace and democracy and against the imperialist warmongers.

Continuing Suppression

"The British, French, Dutch, and other imperialists are using (tricks) to suppress colonial peoples, granting them faked independence, bribing the reactionary feaudal landlords and bourgeois compradors, and splitting the ranks of the peoples in an attempt to maintain their rule over these countries. For their part the American imperialists are using all possible means to turn the colonies of other countries into markets for their own goods and military bases for aggression.
"However, colonial and semicolonial peoples are more and more convinced that the only path to national liberation is that of national unity, close alliance with other peoples in the world, and relentless, persistent armed

struggle under the leadership of the working class. Experience shows that any oppressed people that takes to this path is sure to win victory.

"4 - Vietnam is an outpost of the democratic camp in Southeast Asia. The Vietnam revolution is a part of the world-wide movement for national liberation and for the defense of peace and democracy. By fighting for their own independence and freedom, the Vietnam people contribute to the maintenance of peace in the world and to the development of the people's democratic regime in Southeast Asia.

"Thanks to the efforts of the entire Vietnam people and the progress of the democratic camp, especially the gigantic victory of the Chinese people, the Vietnam people's revolution will surely meet with success.

"Chapter two
'The Vietnam society and the Vietnam revolution'

"1 - Prior to the French imperialist conquest, the Vietnam society was a feudal society. After the establishment of French domination, Vietnam became a monopolized market, a source of raw materials and manpower, a place of usury, and a military base of the French colonialists.

"After the First World War the French mining industry and smaller industries started operating in Vietnam. The Vietnam feudal regime was shaken up. The working class of Vietnam took shape and quickly became mature. Vietnam capitalism came into being but was unable to develop owing to the oppression by French capitalism.

"The French colonial policy made Vietnam completely dependent on France. It hampered the development of production forces in Vietnam. It combined the forms of capitalist oppression and exploitation with those of feudal oppression and exploitation, driving the Vietnam people, especially the workers and peasants, into the darkest misery. For this reason the Vietnam people never ceased to struggle for independence and democracy. In 1930 the Communist Party of Indochina was founded. Since then the leadership of the revolution has remained in the hands of the Vietnam working class.

"During the Second World War, the Japanese invaded Vietnam. Under the French-Japanese fascist yoke the Vietnam people suffered a great deal. Many uprisings broke out. Guerrilla bases were set up and developed. After the Japanese putsch of Mar. 9, 1945, the people's rule was set up in the liberated area of the uplands of North Vietnam. As a whole the Vietnam society then was still a colonial and semifeudal society.

"But the French imperialists invaded Vietnam once again in the hope of imposing their old colonial rule. The Nation-wide total and long-standing resistance of the Vietnam people began.

"2 - People's democracy is what the Vietnam people have been longing for. In contrast, the colonial system has been a scourge for them. Vestiges of feudalism and semifeudalism hinder the progress of the new Vietnam and weigh heavily upon the bulk of the Vietnam people, especially the peasants. The entire Vietnam people need independence and freedom and resolutely do not want to be enslaved once again. The bulk of the Vietnam people, the peasants, need land.

"The primordial task of the Vietnam revolution, therefore, is to drive out the imperialist aggressors to gain complete independence and unity for the people, to wipe out the colonial system in the enemy-occupied areas and root up the vestiges of feudalism and semifeudalism so that there is land for those who till it, to develop the People's Democratic Regime, and to lay foundations for socialism.

"The driving forces of the Vietnam revolution are now the Vietnam people, comprising workers, peasants, petty bourgeois, and national bourgeois, as well as patriotic and progressive personages and landlords. The basis of the people is composed of the workers, peasants, and intellectual workers--intellectual workers belong to various strata of the people, mostly to the petty bourgeoisie. The leading class in the Vietnam revolution is the working class.

"Judging from the basic tasks it aims to fulfill and from the fact that its driving forces are the people led by the working class, the Vietnam revolution is a national people's democratic revolution. This national people's democratic revolution will lead the Vietnam people toward socialism on a road of long-term struggle passing through several stages.

The Aims of Revolution

" In the present stage one Vietnam revolution is spearheaded against the imperialist aggressors. It aims to rally all the forces of the people to con- solidate the National United Front to fight persistently against the imperialist aggressors and their lackeys. At the same time it seeks to improve the living conditions of the people, especially the working masses, so that they can take part more actively in the resistance. The main task in the present stage is to fight against imperialist aggression. The other tasks must aim to serve this task.

"Chapter 3
'Policy of the Vietnam Laodong Party'

" - The Vietnam Laodong Party is determined to complete the liberation of the Vietnam people to curb the influence of feudalism, to advance toward the eradi- cation of feudal and semifeudal vestiges, to develop people's democracy, to build an independent, unified, democratic, prosperous, and powerful Vietnam, and to lead it toward socialism.

"During and immediately after the liberation war, the Vietnam Laodong Party plans to carry out the following policy aimed at bringing an early and complete victory to the resistance and at laying the basis for the building up of a prosperous and powerful state:

"1 - Fighting until complete victory - The entire Vietnam people are re- solved to fight to the end in order to wipe out the French colonialists, defeat the American interventionists, punish the traitors, and gain complete indepen- dence and unity for the Fatherland.

"The liberation war of the Vietnam people is a people's war, a Nation-wide, total, and long-drawn-out war. It must pass through three stages: a defensive stage, and attrition stage, and a counteroffensive.

"The central task of the Vietnam people from now until the final victory of their resistance is to complete preparations for a general counteroffensive and launch a victorious general counteroffensive. In order to win complete victory, they must at the same time mobilize their manpower, their material and finan- cial resources for the liberation war in accordance with the slogan, 'All for the front, all for victory,' and continually recoup their fighting power. They must bear in the mind the following strategic principles of the resistance:

Basic Principles of Resistance

"All political, economic, and cultural works must aim to insure military victories and the military struggle must be coordinated with the political, economic, and cultural struggle. Frontal fighting against the enemy must be closely coordinated with guerrilla fighting and sabotage work in the enemy's rear. The liberation war of the Vietnam people must be closely coordinated with the armed resistance of the people of Laos and Cambodia and with the world-wide struggle for peace and democracy.

"2 - Consolidating the people's rule - the political power in our country is a democratic power of the people, that is, of the workers, peasants, petty bourgeois, national bourgeois, and patriotic and progressive personage and landlords. The form of this regime is the People's Democratic Republic. Its essence is the people's democratic dictatorship - democratic toward the people, dictatorial toward the imperialist aggressors and the reactionaries.

"The people's rule relies on the National United Front on the basis of the alliance between the workers, peasants, and intellectual workers under the leadership of the working class.

(Editor's Note: The following is a continuation of a VIETNAM NEWS AGENCY transmission carried on Page FFF5 of the Mar. 14 DAILY REPORT)

"The principle of orgnization of the people's rule is democratic centralism. The strength of our people's rule is due to the active participation and support of the peoples, the . . . of the working class, and the assistance rendered by the Soviet Union, China, and other People's Democracies. Thus in order to consolidate our peoples rule we must continually strengthen the relations between the State power and the popular masses; increase the participation of workers, peasants, and women in the Government organizations, particularly in the People's Councils; put into use a genuine people's democratic constitution; enhance the Party's leadership in Government organizations of all levels; and strengthen the relations between Vietnam, the Soviet Union, China, and other People's Democracies.

"3 - Consolidating the National United Front - The National United Front of Vietnam united all political parties, people's organizations, and patriots, irrespective of class, nationality, religion and sex, in the common struggle for liberation and national construction. The National United Front is one of the pillars of the people's power. It has the task to mobilize, organize and to inform the Government about the wishes and initiative of the people.

"The Vietnam Laodong Party cooperates closely with all the political parties, people's organizations, and personages in the National United Front according to the following principles: Sincere Union and friendly mutual criticism with a view to speeding up their common progress, cooperation, and negotiation in view of struggling for a common program and for long-term cooperation during and after the long-standing resistance.

"In order to strengthen the National United Front we must complete the merger of the Viet Minh and Lien Viet Leagues; enhance the alliance between the workers, peasants, and intellectual workers as a solid basis for the front; mobilize the bourgeois and landlords to participate actively in the Lien Viet League; develop the organization of the Front in the enemy-occupied areas, in the areas inhabited by religious people, and those inhabited by national minorities; consolidate the Party's leadership of the front.

"4 - Building up and developing the People's Army - The Vietnam Army is a People's army organized by the people, entertained and assisted by the people, and fighting for the people. It has a national, popular, and democratic character. Its discipline is a very strict and self-convinced discipline.

"While fighting, it carries on widespread political work, strengthening the single-mindedness between the rank and file and between the Army and the people and strives to carry out propaganda work among the enemy with a view to shattering their morale.

"In order to build up and develop the People's Army we must develop the local people's forces, militia, and guerrillas in the villages and select the draftees captured by us or who crossed over to our side, so as continually to recoup our regular Army. Also, we must capture the enemy's arms, munitions, and food supplies, so as partly to solve the equipment and supply problems.

"5 - Developing the economy - Our economic policy is now to increase production, so as to meet the demands of the liberation war and to raise the living standard of the people, benefiting both the Government and the private individuals, both labor and capital. Attention must be paid at present to the development of agriculture, industry, handicrafts, and home trade and the establishment of trade relations with other countries to lay a basis for State economy and for the development of a cooperative economy.

"With regard to the national bourgeoisie our Party seeks to encourage, assist and guide it in its enterprise.

"In the financial field we urge the raising of income through production increases, reduction of expenses and economy, and the implementation of democratic contributions. In regard to the enemy economy we urge planned sabotage and blockade in a way beneficial to the liberation war and the people, confiscation of the properties of the imperialist aggressors and traitors to be put at the disposal of the people's power.

"6 - Carrying out agrarian reform - Our agrarian policy mainly aims at present in carrying out the reduction of land rent and interest, as well as other reforms such as the following: Regulation of the leasehold system; provisional allocation of the land formerly owned by the imperialists and traitors to the poorer peasants and families of disabled former Army men and war dead; redistribution of communal land; rational use of land belonging to absentee landlords and of waste land; and so forth.

Peasant Movement

"These reforms must be thoroughly carried out so as to improve the living conditions of the peasants and to increase the participation of the bulk of the Nation, mostly the peasants, in the armed resistance to raise production and insure supplies. In order to carry out these reforms systematically, our party must organize and awaken the peasant masses and steadily lead the peasant movement. We must carry out this agrarian policy step by step upwards according to local conditions.

"In South Vietnam, where land is more concentrated than in North and Central Vietnam, this policy must be carried out at greater speed. We must prepare conditions so as gradually to give each farmer his own plot.

"7 - Developing culture and education - In order to train new men and new cadres and to push up the liberation war and the national construction, it is necessary to wipe out the vestiges of colonialist and feudal culture and education and develop a national, scientific, and popular culture and education.

"Thus the task of Vietnam culture and education at the present stage is to develop the people's hatred against the imperialist aggressors, their patriotism, and spirit of internationalism; to develop the essence of the people's culture and at the same time to learn the progressive culture of the world, especially that of the Soviet Union and China; to develop the culture of the national minorities; to develop the People's science technique and arts; to mobilize the people to observe a new way of life; and to liquidate illiteracy, reform the education system, and develop vocational schools.

"8 - The Party's stand toward religion - The Vietnam Laodong Party respects and guarantees the freedom of religious belief of the people and opposes the French imperialists' policy of abusing religion to hoodwink the people and to split up the National United Front of Vietnam.

"9 - The Party's policy toward the nationalities - All the peoples living on Vietnam territory are equal in rights and duties; they must unite (well) and help one another in order to carry out the armed resistance and the national construction. Our Party resolutely opposes narrow-minded nationalism and is determined to smash the plots of the imperialists and traitors to sow hatred among them and divide the people. It seeks to raise the living standard of the national minorities, help them to make progress in all spheres of activity, and insure their participation in the people's power. Each national minority will learn in its own native language.

"10 - The Party's policy concerning the enemy-occupied areas and the newly liberated areas - We attach the same importance to the work in enemy-occupied areas as to that in the liberated areas. The work in enemy-occupied areas consists in bringing about a broad unity between all strata of the people, stepping up guerrilla warfare, building up and consolidating the people's power, destroying the puppets' administrations and shattering the draftees' ranks, mobilizing the people to struggle against the enemy's oppression and exploitation, and coordinating action between the enemy-occupied areas and the liberated areas.

"With regard to the lackeys of the enemy, we recommend punishment against the unrepentant leading traitors and clemency toward stray people who seek to make up for their mistakes and return to the side of the Fatherland.

"With regard to the newly liberated areas, we recommend unity among the population, the maintenance of security vigilance against and the wiping out of the traitors, and the rehabilitation of the economy.

Foreign Relations

"11 - External policy - Vietnam's external policy must be based on the principles of mutual respect of national independence and territorial integrity, equality of rights, and defense of world peace and democracy. Our Party recommends the strengthening of friendly relations between Vietnam, the Soviet Union, China, and other People's Democracies' semicolonial countries, and establishment of diplomatic relations with all countries that are willing to respect Vietnam's national sovereignty on the (basis) of freedom, equality, and mutual benefit. We recommend the broadening of people's diplomacy and the protection of Vietnam nationals in foreign countries.

"12 - Our policy toward Laos and Cambodia - The Vietnam people must unite closely with the peoples of Laos and Cambodia and give them an (sic) all-out assistance in the common struggle against imperialist aggression for the complete liberation of Indochina and for the preservation of world peace. On the basis of serving the common interests of the three peoples, the Vietnam people are willing to cooperate on long (sic) terms with the peoples of Laos and Cambodia and will strive to bring about single-mindedness between the three peoples.

"13 - Our policy toward foreign nationals - The lives and properties of all foreign nationals who respect Vietnam law are protected. They have the right to reside and carry out business on Vietnam's territory. Foreign nationals belonging to the People's Democracies, especially Overseas Chinese in Vietnam, are allowed to enjoy the same rights and perform the same duties as Vietnam citizens. If they so desire and if they have the approval of the governments of their own countries and the Vietnam People's Government.

"14 - Struggling for world peace and democracy - To struggle for the defense of world peace and democracy is an international task of the Vietnam people. To fight against the imperialist aggressors is the most active means for our people to fulfill this task. We recommend that the Vietnam people coordinate their liberation war with the struggles of other peoples of the world, especially the peoples of France and the French colonies.

"15 - Patriotic emulation - The patriotic-emulation campaign is a Nation-wide movement reaching into all branches of activity and aiming mainly to defeat three enemies - illiteracy, famine, and foreign aggression. The Army, the rural areas, the State-owned enterprises, the schools, and the Government organizations are the main places where the emulation campaign is carried out.

"We recommend that homage be paid to emulation heroes and labor combatants, so as to mobilize the entire people to take part in the liberation war and the national construction."

VIET MINH PUBLICATIONS - The Vietnamese Workers Party has started publishing a paper entitled NHAN DAN - THE PEOPLE. The task of the Party's paper is to respect faithfully the aspirations of the people and the facts of the resistance and to lay down the policy and the viewpoint of the Party. The Vietnamese Workers Party invites the whole people to contribute actively to that paper in order that it may become the voice of the Vietnamese resistance in the free zone, as well as in the temporarily occupied zone. (Voice of Vietnam/ Ho Government/, Mar. 16, 1951 -S) The Vietnam Laodong Party, which was founded at an 8-day national congress held in North Vietnam in February 1951, will publish a weekly to be named PEOPLE. This journal will faithfully reflect the wishes of the people, the realities of the liberation war, and present the Party's policy and plan. It will also serve as a place for the exchange of views and opinions and mutual criticism between the Party and the people. The Vietnam Laodong Party has called on the Vietnam people to contribute actively to the paper so as to make it the voice of freedom-seeking Vietnam, both in the enemy-occupied and liberated areas.

(213) REPORT BY ACHESON TO THE NSC ON CONVERSATIONS BETWEEN PRESIDENT TRUMAN AND FRENCH PRIME MINISTER RENE PLEVEN, February 23, 1951 (Extract)

Source: *Foreign Relations, 1951, Vol. VI,* p. 367.

During two days of meetings with President Truman in Washington, January 29-30, 1951, French Prime Minister Rene Pleven lobbied unsuccessfully for more formal coordination of policies among the three Western powers in the Far East and for U.S. financial support to cover the budgetary deficits of the Associated States. The substance of the discussion, as reported by Acheson, suggested a common feeling that Indochina might have to be abandoned in the event of Chinese intervention, and an American fear of becoming militarily overcommitted there. The passages in quotation marks were taken from the published final communique of January 30.

"Far East

4. *a.* 'The President and the Prime Minister found themselves in complete agreement as to the necessity of resisting aggression and assisting the free nations of the Far East in their efforts to maintain their security and assure their independence.' The U.S. and France should not over-commit themselves militarily in the Far East and thereby endanger the situation in Europe.

b. 'The President and the Prime Minister agreed that continuous contact should be maintained between the interested nations on these problems.' The Prime Minister's suggestion to create a U.S., U.K. French consultative body to coordinate the three governments' Asiatic policies was not accepted by the President, who preferred to rely on existing mechanisms.

c. 'The situation in Korea was discussed and they concurred that every effort must be exerted to bring about an honorable solution there. Until that end can be accomplished, resistance by United Nations forces to aggression must continue. Both France and the United States will support action directed toward deterring aggression and toward preventing the spread of hostilities beyond Korea.'

d. With regard to Indochina, 'the Prime Minister declared that France was determined to do its utmost to continue' its efforts to resist 'the Communist onslaught in order to maintain the security and independence of the Associated States, Viet Nam, Cambodia, and Laos.'

e. It was desirable to build up the native Indochinese forces as rapidly as possible. We held out no hope for the provision of U.S. budgetary assistance for the National Army in Indochina. We cannot become directly involved in local budgetary deficits of other countries.

f. 'The President informed the Prime Minister that United States aid for the French Union forces and for the National Armies of the Associated States will continue, and that the increased quantities of material to be delivered under the program authorized for the current fiscal year will be expedited.' Additional measures for U.S. aid to Indochina included: (1) an indication of our willingness to relax the original restrictions placed on the use by the French of the U.S. aircraft carrier *Langley* in the Mediterranean in view of our inability to provide another U.S. carrier for service in Indochina; and (2) an agreement to study the possibility of reallocating funds now available in an effort to provide equipment for four Vietnamese divisions.

g. The President said that the United States was agreeable to U.S., U.K., French military consultations on Indochinese matters.

h. In the event of a Chinese Communist attack on Indochina, the U.S. desires to assist in the evacuation of French forces if such action becomes necessary. The extent of the aid would be limited by other demands on our forces, such as Korea, which exist at the time any request for assistance is made."

(214) SPEECH BY TRUONG CHINH AT THE CONGRESS FOR UNIFICATION OF THE VIET MINH AND LIEN VIET, March 3, 1951 (Extracts)

Source: Truong Ching, "The Party's National United Front Policy," *The Viet-namese People's National Democratic Revolution, Selected Works, Vol. II,* pp. 266-276 (Translation by the editor).

The Viet Minh had come into existence as a broad coalition of nationalist groups in which Communists maintained a low profile, even while providing its political leadership. With the reemergence of an overt Communist Party in Viet-nam, the Party leadership wanted to create a new front organization in which the class nature of the front, its political functions and the leadership of the Workers' Party would be explicitly understood by all. At the Conference on March 3, 1951 in which the Viet Minh merged into the Lien Viet, or National United Front, Truong Chinh explained in detail the purposes and structure of the new front.

Mr. Chairman,
Representatives.
First of all, we sincerely thank the Central Executive Committee of the Lien Viet Front for having warmly welcomed our Party's joining the Front. As a member of the Front, we have the responsibility to present to you our Party's Front policy.

To rule the people of their country and of the colonies, the imperialists usually use schemes of repression, deception and division.

To win victory in the people's national democratic revolution, that is, our present revolution, what must our people do? In our view, they must strengthen the following victorious factors:

- A strong vanguard party, having a correct political line.
- An anti-imperialist national united front.
- A people's liberation armed forces.
- International solidarity.
etc., etc. . . . .

But the most important factor is the vanguard party and the correct political line of the Party. If the line is correct, the people will follow. If the people follow, there will be a Front and a people's armed forces (because those forces come from the people and are nourished by the people). If there are people's armed forces, they can capture the weapons from the enemy to attack the enemy. If the line is correct, we can gain foreign assistance and have many friends abroad help us. If the line is correct, it must be raised and firmly grasped by a vanguard party. That party leads the masses of people forward in accord with the correct line in order to achieve the revolutionary objective.

The French colonialists invaded our country, and want to put the colonial yoke on our necks of our people again. The entire people are determined to resist them. For that reason, the national united front is set up to concentrate the forces of the whole people for resistance war, national construction and to win final victory.

Our front is a national front, not a popular front. Our national united front is a unity bloc among four classes within the people: the working class, the peasant class, the petty bourgeois class, and the national bourgeois class, and a certain number of patriotic landowners, relying on the basis of the worker-peasant alliance, and led by the working class. At the same time, the front is a broad organization with a view to achieving unity of action, coordination and mutual assistance among parties, organizations and democratic and patriotic personalities opposing the common enemy of the nation which is the invading French colonialists, and the U.S. interventionist, along with their gang of lackeys, to win complete independence and freedom, construct a people's democratic Viet-nam, a new democracy.

The history of the Vietnamese revolution over the past twenty years confirms the leading revolutionary role of the Vietnamese working class. Those viewpoints which hold that in Viet-nam today the working class and the petty bourgeois intellectual stratum cooperate to lead the revolution or that the Front leads the revolution are incorrect.

But that does not mean that the Front is not important. The Front is one of the pillars of the government. In people's democracies in Eastern Europe, there are people who say: The people's democratic state has three pillars: the United Front, People's Councils and the state economic sector. In our country, all three of those exist, but our state economic sector is still very small, while people's councils are common. On the other hand, we have a very firm pillar in the Lien Viet Front; we have a very strong force, which is the People's Army.

We agree very much with the opinion of the representative of the Viet-nam Democratic Party who said: "The Front supports the government." The Front is a pillar of the State, and supports the government. Those two things are not in contradiction with each other. But if one says, "The Front leads the government," it is incorrect, because the role of leading the Vietnamese revolution generally, as well as leading the people's government specifically belongs to the most revolutionary class in Viet-nam, which is the Vietnamese working class. The Vietnamese working class relies on its party, which is the Viet-nam Workers' Party, to lead the revolution. As for the statement, "The Front is the master of the government," that is also not really correct. Because the masters of the government are the people. The front is an organization unifying the people supporting the government. The front belongs to the people and the government is also the property of the people. In our peoples democratic system, each of those organizations has a definite function.

Front policy relies on the principle: Unite sincerely, make concessions to one another, cooperate for the long-term, help one another progress together. There are friends who ask: "What about the Communists' theory of class struggle? If you have class struggle, how can you also unify the classes within the people?"

True. We advocate class struggle. Society is still divided into classes, and therefore there must still be class struggle. But when facing the aggressor enemy, which is the French imperialism and U.S. interventionists, facing the peril of cruel war which threatens humanity, face to face with the common enemy, our people's strata, revolutionary classes in our country cannot fail to reasaonably compose their interests in order to concentrate their forces to oppose the common enemy; cannot fail to reasonably resolve class contradictions within the country in order to join all their efforts to defeat the foreign enemy who has come to seize their country. As far as we are concerned, this resistance war is high form of national struggle and class struggle. A resistance war of the entire nation led by the working class against foreign imperialists invaders and Vietnamese traitors, puppets, representatives of the feudal landers and pro-French compradore bourgeoisie, has the character of a struggle to liberate the nation, and at the same time is also a class struggle whose primary point is aimed abroad.

If we want to defeat the aggressor army, the people's strata, the revolutionary classes in the country must unite. To unite, they must make concessions to each other. But making concessions must be guided by a principle, which is to take the interest of the revolution, the interest of the people as the criterion. Making concessions aims at raising the revolutionary consciousness of the masses of people, making the vast majority of the people eagerly and actively participate in the resistance and construction of the country.

We wage long-term resistance. Our revolutionary struggle is a long-term struggle. After the resistance war, we will still have to oppose reactionary forces in the world and in the country. Therefore we advocate long-term cooperation. We cooperate in the resistance war and after the resistance war, cooperate to resist and to build the country. Our objective is to achieve an independent, unified, democratic, free and prosperous Viet-nam, a people's democratic Viet-nam, a new democracy, so long-term cooperation among us necessary.

[Two pages of the original text are omitted.]

The immediate tasks of the Front, in our view, are:

First, Unite the whole people in order to wage resistance war, build the country and struggle to protect peace and democracy in the world. If we want to unite the entire people, we must compose interests among the people's strata, and create favorable conditions in order to unite the people's strata in the Front.

Second, Disseminate the the policy of the Front of the Government among the people, making the people understand clearly and actively carry out that policy.

Third, Bring the opinions and aspirations of the people up to government organs at various levels; bring initiatives suggested by the people to the government, or convey the judgments and criticisms of the people to the government.

Fourth, Propagandize and educate the people, making them understand their interests and duties, exert efforts in resistance and building the country, support the troops, and support the people's government.

Fifth, Mobilize the masses of people to participate in the resistance and building the country, in accord with the slogan: Those who have money, contribute money, those who have talent, contribute talent; everyone fulfill actively fulfill their duty to defeat the aggressor army and build a new Viet-nam.

[The last two pages of the text are omitted.]

(215) <u>TELEGRAM FROM HEATH TO ACHESON</u>, March 11, 1951

Source: *Foreign Relations, 1951, Vol. VI*, pp. 392-394.

In the most frank discussion by a French official about relations with the U.S. over Indochina, De Lattre told Heath that France still suffered from an "inferiority complex" which the U.S. would have to take into account in Indochina. He expressed a fear of unnamed sources in the U.S. who wanted to harm "French prestige" in Indochina.

1605. At noon yesterday De Lattre gave luncheon in honor of Sarraut, Governor of IC 40 years ago. Before the lunch, De Lattre approached me and said that he had just received my letter and though he could reconcile the ECA irrigation project at Sontay with his military plans and in general thought there need be no conflict between us regarding America's aims to extend American influence in IC. I interrupted to say that was not our aim and I thought we should have a very frank talk as soon as possible. He fixed the hour at 7 p.m.

For more than two hours he discussed the military and political situation in Viet Minh [Nam]. (See preceding Legtels numbers 1603 and 1604 dated March 11, repeated Paris 693 and 694.) I had the impression he wished to avoid a discussion of the conflict of American and French aims in IC which he had alleged in his last talks with me and with Blum.

Finally I interrupted to say that I had been disturbed over the insinuations in our last talk that American policy and operations were pursuing a course inimical to legitimate French policy in Indochina.

We had come into the area with a supplementary program of arms and economic aid, and had recognized Bao Dai on the request of the French Government and on assurances of the sincerity of French policy for revolutionary development of the independence of the Associated States within the framework of the French Union. This continued to be American policy and there was determination in Washington and the Legation that we would carry out this policy locally. If he had any criticism of our carrying out our policy, I hoped he would voice it frankly and immediately to me. If his criticism were founded, I would take prompt action to correct the American persons or operations concerned.

De Lattre replied: "I am a soldier, not a diplomat, and am accustomed to speak frankly without any detours." I interrupted him saying that I was a diplomat accustomed to speak clearly and with the frankness that must characterize the diplomacy of any really great nation.

But De Lattre did not, as might have been expected from his initial statement, launch into a frank bill of complaints. Instead he delivered a long, and I though an excellent analysis of the state of French spirit as a result of the last war and French economic losses and inferiority. France would revive but meanwhile he and we as the dominant nation must reckon with the inferiority complex and feeling of the humiliation in the French Government and among their people and particularly among the French officials and the French colony in Indochina.

I said I had made it my endeavor to see that the Legation staff should recognize the legitimate position France should enjoy in Indochina as a result of her sacrifices of blood and treasure, and asked for any particulars wherein we had failed of such recognition.

The only specific complaint that De Lattre then brought forth was that at Hanoi annual "Kermesse" or charity festival, last winter, the USIS exhibit had the most impressive and [apparent omission] exhibit putting French exhibits in shade. As result he had not attended the Kermesse.

I remarked that the size had been awarded by the Vietnamese authorities and that I, and doubtless he, had observed that the Viets fairly frequently yielded to the very human temptation of showing undue attention to Americans with idea of promoting rivalry and conflict between French and Americans. He agreed with a smile to this statement and said that such actions were to be expected from Vietnamese and were not to be taken too seriously. He appreciated that I had acted loyally and only asked that in our operations we used attitude and moderation that took into account French susceptibilities and interests. I replied we would of course keep that in mind.

In spite our declared policy of cooperation there were, De Lattre alleged, forces in the US that were pushing American policy in IC to actions injurious to French prestige but he accepted my assurance that our official policy remained firm in the lines of cooperation laid down year ago. I could count on his complete frankness, which he had just displayed, in his exposition of the Viets military and political situation.

He would not have thought that such a pitch of confidence and frankness would have been reached in our relations in mere matter of three months.

Comments: I doubt that as a result of our talk De Lattre is entirely cured of his suspicions of American activities which are constantly fanned and refomented by certain members of his entourage. I believe however our talk did a good deal to put him straight and I hope our relations will henceforth be good. They are bound to be sometimes marred by the unpredictable squalls of De Lattre's susceptibilities and temperament.

I would appreciate Department's comments or instructions with respect to conversation reported in this telegram and mytel 1567, March 7.[1]

Sent Department 1605, repeated info Paris 695, Hanoi unnumbered.

[1]For text of telegram 4820 to Paris (repeated to Saigon as telegram 1188), March 15, which contains a comment by the Department of State, see footnote 1, p. 402 [*Foreign Relations, 1951, Vol. VI*].

(216) NSC 48/4, "STATEMENT OF POLICY ON ASIA," May 17, 1951 (Extracts)

Source: *U.S.-Vietnam Relations, Book 8,* pp. 435-436.

A major new statement of policy toward Asia noted that the Viet Minh were capable of defeating the French in Indochina and reaffirmed the basic U.S. policy of support for the French Union forces without committing U.S. armed forces. The document recognized explicitly that in Southeast Asia, U.S. programs were aimed at gaining time to "build up the defense of the off-shore island chain," while the U.S. sought ways to weaken and ultimately overthrow the People's Republic of China.

****

14. With respect to Southeast Asia, the United States should:

a. Continue its present support programs to strengthen the will and ability to resist communist encroachment, to render communist military operations as costly as possible, and thus to gain time for the United States and its allies to build up the defense of the off-shore chain.

b. Continue programs of information and educational exchange in the countries of Southeast Asia.

c. Encourage the countries of Southeast Asia to restore and expand their commerce with each other and the rest of the free world, stimulate the flow of the raw material resources of the area to the free world, and assist in establishing small arms production in appropriate locations in Southeast Asia under suitable controls.

d. In Indochina:

(1) Continue to increase the military effectiveness of French units and the size and equipment of indigenous units by providing timely and suitable military assistance without relieving the French authorities of their basic military responsibilities or committing United States armed forces.

(2) Continue to encourage internal autonomy and progressive social and economic reforms.

(3) Continue to promote international support for the three Associated States.

e. In Indonesia, the United States should seek to strengthen the non-communist political orientiation of the government, promote the economic development of Indonesia, and influence Indonesia toward greater participation in measures with support the security of the area and Indonesian solidarity with the free world.

(217) <u>NATIONAL INTELLIGENCE ESTIMATE</u> (NIE-20), March 20, 1951

Source: *Foreign Relations, 1951, Vol. VI, pp. 27-31.*

Assessing the likely consequences of a Communist victory in Vietnam, the intelligence community concluded that a Viet Minh victory without direct Chinese intervention would not immediately threaten Vietnam's neighbors, but would increase likelihood of an eventual overthrow of the existing governments. A Chinese military move into Southeast Asia, was judged irresistible by the governments.

THE PROBLEM

To assess the will and ability of Thailand, Burma, and Malaya to resist Communist political and military pressures or outright invasion in the event of a Communist victory in Indochina in 1951.

CONCLUSIONS

1. A Viet Minh victory in Indochina in 1951, if accomplished without the intervention of Chinese Communist forces, would result in increased intimidation and subversive activity directed against Thailand and Burma, but it would not necessarily lead to the early establishment of Communist or Communist-dominated governments in these two countries.

2. A Viet Minh victory in Indochina in 1951, if accomplished through Chinese Communist military intervention, would increase the susceptibility of Thailand and Burma to Communist pressures and we believe that, in the absence of effective internal countermeasures and outside support, these two countries would be obliged to seek an accommodation with the Communist powers.

3. Communist domination of Thailand and Burma, as well as Indochina, would greatly increase British security problems in Malya. We believe that the British under these circumstances would not be able to maintain even their present degree of control in Malaya without a very considerable increase in their military and economic commitments.

4. It is most unlike that the Viet Minh, without Chinese Communist participation, would attempt to conquer Thailand and Burma in 1951.

5. If the Chinese Communists, after establishing control over Indochina, continued their military advance into Burma and Thailand, we believe that both those countries would rapidly fall to the Communists, unless the UN or the Western Powers interposed their own forces. A Chinese Communist invasion of Malaya would be more difficult, but would probably succeed unless Malaya were greatly reinforced.

6. It is most improbable that a regional defense of Southeast Asia could be organized in time to stop the Chinese Communists if they followed up the conquest of Indochina in 1951 with a military advance into other countries of the area.

DISCUSSION

7. In the event that the Viet Minh should succeed in conquering Indochina during 1951 without large-scale intervention by Chinese Communist forces, the prestige of Ho Chi Minh would be greatly enhanced throughout Southeast Asia. Furthermore, the defeat of the French Union forces despite US support would intensify the feeling of insecurity in the neighboring countries and facilitate the spread of Communism in the area.

   a. Initially, if the Viet Minh did not demonstrate the intention, either alone or in collusion with the Chinese Communists, to embark on further military aggression, the governments of Burma and Thailand would continue to oppose Communism internally and would not align themselves with the Communist powers. Burma would probably recognize the Viet Minh Government and attempt to cultivate friendly relations with it. The Government of Thailand, although it also might recognize the Viet Minh Government, would attempt to build up its own defenses against Communist forces and undoubtedly would request increased US aid.

   b. A Viet Minh victory, nevertheless, would expose Burma and Thailand to increased subversion and intimidation which, in the absence of effective internal countermeasures (which they might not be capable of taking) and outside aid, might well lead to the eventual overthrow of the present non-Communist governments. Under such circumstances, the British security problem in Malaya would be greatly magnified.

8. Large-scale participation of Chinese Communist military forces in a Viet Minh victory would cause far greater repercussions in Southeast Asia than a victory by the Viet Minh alone. It would be interpreted as a success for Chinese arms rather than a victory for Indochinese nationalism. Throughout Southeast Asia, where there is already a strong antipathy for the Chinese, it would intensify fears of Chinese invasion and domination. In view of the general weakness of the countries in the area, however, Chinese Communist military intervention in Indochina would undermine the will of Thailand and Burma to resist and would increase the probability that they would accommodate with the Communist powers.

9. In Malaya, the British, with some 39,000 regular troops and 100,000 regular and auxiliary police, have not succeded in suppressing about 5,000 local Communist guerrillas. The Malays, although forming the bulk of the present police force and generally supporting the British out of fear of the Chinese, would continue to contribute little to the British military effort if opposition were increased. The aggressive and economically powerful Chinese element has generally failed to cooperate with the British in suppressing the guerrillas, and a considerable number of them could be expected to turn against the British if Malaya were seriously threatened by Communist China. Furthermore, Communist control over Indochina, Thailand, and Burma would facilitate transborder aid to the Malayan rebels and deprive Malaya of its essential rice supply. In these circumstances, the opposition to the British would not be able to maintain even their present degree of control in Malaya without a very considerable increase in their military and economic commitment.

10. We believe that an attempt to conquer Thailand or Burma by the Viet Minh without Chinese Communist participation is most improbable in 1951, although border incursions of northeast Thailand cannot be excluded.

11. If the Chinese Communists, after a victory in Indochina, continued a military advance into Burma and Thailand and if the UN or the Western Powers did not interpose their own forces, we believe that both these countries would rapidly fall to the Communists because they do not possess the military strength to resist such an invasion. Thailand, perhaps after a token resistance, would

soon install a government acceptable to the Communists in the hope of retaining at least a semblance of autonomy. Burma, if directly attacked, would probably fight but would soon be defeated. A Chinese Communist invasion of Malaya would be more difficult because of the terrain and the presence of British military forces, but it would probably succeed unless Malaya were greatly reinforced.

12. Present or planned outside military aid to Burma and Thailand, although it will eventually strengthen these countries, will not in the predictable future enable either of them to defend itself successfully against a Chinese Communist attack. Military aid to Burma - which has been chiefly British - has been of limited effectiveness owing to lack of Burmese cooperation, and because it has been largely expended in the Burmese internal conflict. The US aid planned for Thailand, when completed, would help Thailand to maintain internal security, but would not enable it to do more than fight a delaying action against a Chinese Communist invasion. The Thai, however, would probably not fight even a delaying action unless previously assured of support by outside military forces.

13. In view of the limited capabilities of the countries of Southeast Asia and their wide divergencies of interest, it is most improbable that a regional defense of Southeast Asia could be organized in time to stop the Chinese Communists, if they followed up the conquest of Indochina in 1951 with a military advance into other countries of the area.

(218) NSC STAFF STUDY ON OBJECTIVES, POLICIES AND COURSES OF ACTION IN ASIA, (ANNEX TO NSC 48/4), May 17, 1951 [Extract]

Source: *U.S.-Vietnam Relations, Book 8*, pp. 438-445.

The NSC staff analysis underlines the point that the U.S. was not free to devote maximum resources to its policy objectives in Asia, but had to constantly weigh them against the requirements of its European commitments.

PROBLEM

1. To determine United States national objectives, policies, and courses of action with respect to Asia.

UNITED STATES LONG-RANGE NATIONAL OBJECTIVES IN ASIA

2. The long-range national security objectives of the United States with respect to Asia are:

a. Development by the nations and peoples of Asia, through self-help and mutual aid, of stable and self-sustaining non-communist governments, oriented toward the United States, acting in accordance with the purposes and principles of the United Nations Charter, and having the will and ability to maintain internal security and prevent communist aggression.

b. Elimination of the preponderant power and influence of the USSR in Asia or its reduction to such a degree that the Soviet Union will not be capable of threatening from that area the security of the United States or its friends, or the peace, national independence and stability of the Asiatic nations.

c. Development of power relationships in Asia which will make it impossible for any nation or alliance to threaten the security of the United States from that area.

d. In so far as practicable, securing for the United States and the rest of the free world, and denying to the communist world, the availability through mutually advantageous arrangements, of the material resources of the Asian area.

ANALYSIS OF THE SITUATION

3. United States objectives, policies, and courses of action in Asia should be designed to contribute toward the global objectives of strengthening the free world vis-a-vis the Soviet orbit, and should be determined with due regard to the relation of United States capabilities and commitments throughout the world. However, in view of the communist resort to armed force in Asia, United States action in that area must be based on the recognition that the most immediate threats to United States security are currently presented in that area.

4. Current Soviet tactics appear to concentrate on bringing the mainland of Eastern Asia and eventually Japan and the other principal off-shore islands in the Western Pacific under Soviet control, primarily through Soviet exploitation of the resources of communist China. The attainment of this objective on the mainland of Eastern Asia would substantially enhance the global position of the USSR at the expense of the United States, by securing the eastern flank of the USSR and permitting the USSR to concentrate its offensive power in other areas, particularly in Europe. Soviet control of the off-shore islands in the Western Pacific, including Japan, would present an unacceptable threat to the security of the United States.

5. Asia is of strategic importance to the United States.

   <u>a</u>. The strategic significance of Asia arises from its resources, geography, and the political and military force which it could generate. The population of the area is about 1,250,000,000. The demonstrated military capacity of the North Korean and Chinese armies requires a re-evaluation of the threat to the free world which the masses of Asia would constitute if they fell under Soviet Communist domination.

   <u>b</u>. The resources of Asia contribute greatly to United States security by helping to meet its need for critical materials and they would be of great assistance in time of war if they remained available. At least until stockpiling levels are met, this phase of the area's importance to the United States will continue. Further, the development of events which might lead to the exhaustion of such stockpiles would magnify the importance of this source of supply. The area produces practically all the world's natural rubber, nearly 5% of the oil, 60% of the tin, the major part of various important tropical products, and strategic materials such as manganese, jute, and atomic materials. Japan's potential in heavy industry is roughly equal to 50% of the Soviet Union's present production. Therefore, it is important to U.S. security interests that U.S. military and economic assistance programs be developed in such a manner as to maximize that availability of the material resources of the Asian area to the United States and the free world.

   <u>c</u>. Control by an enemy of the Asiatic mainland would deny to us the use of the most direct sea and air routes between Australia and the Middle East and between the United States and India. Such control would produce disastrous moral and psychological effects in border areas such as the Middle East and a critical effect in Western Europe.

6. The fact of Soviet power and communist aggression in Asia establishes the context within which the policies of the United States must operate.

   <u>a</u>. The problem of China is the central problem which faces the United States in Asia. A solution to this problem, through a change in the regime in control of mainland China, would facilitate the achievement of United States objectives throughout Asia. Therefore, United States policies and course of action in Asia should be determined in the light of their effect upon the solution of the central problem, that of China.

b. The communist attack in Korea has transformed the Far East into a theater of combat. Whether the Kremlin or Peiping intends that hostilities be extended into other areas of Asia or aggression committed in another part of the world is as yet unknown. The United States must expect either eventuality. In any case, the United States should use the resources which can be disposed, without unacceptably jeopardizing our objectives elsewhere, to prevent the communists from achieving a victory in Korea and to build resistance to communist encroachments in Asia.

c. Our ability to achieve national objectives in Asia will be conditioned by the capabilities and global commitments of the United States and by the weight of the effort the enemy is willing and able to make. Consequently, there is required a constant and careful scrutiny of policies and actions on the basis of which decisions can be made which will advance us toward our ultimate objectives without sacrificing immediate security interests.

7. The guiding principle of U.S. foreign policy as it relates to meeting the threat of Soviet aggression is the promotion of the establishment of a system of collective security based on the principles of the UN Charter. The United States is consequently forced inevitably to weigh elements of policy toward Asia against their effect upon the free world coalition, a coalition fundamental to our world-wide struggle for security against Soviet aggression.

8. The principal obstacles to the execution of United States policy in pursuit of its objectives in the Far East are as follows:

a. The policy and action of the Soviet Union.

(1) The Soviet Communists have historically considered Asia as one of their principal objectives; Bolshevik ideology devotes a prominent place to the capture of the "colonial and semi-colonial" areas of the world, by which is meant principally Asia. Soviet policy in Asia has been aided by the fact that communists have been successful to a large degree in subverting indigenous nationalist movements; the capture of these movements has been a goal of Kremlin policy.

(2) The Kremlin has not yet resorted to the large-scale and open employment of Soviet armed forces, although the aggression by both North Koreans and Chinese Communist indicates that the Kremlin is willing to undertake greater risks than in the past.

(3) The Kremlin, besides supplying and directing leadership of communist parties in Asia, and building centers of subversion, infiltration, and revolution, is providing military assistance to communist forces in Asia, both in materiel and in technical personnel.

(4) The fact that the Soviet threat is world-wide in character has prevented the concentration of free world effort against the various forms of communist aggression in Asia. The combination of political, military, technical and propaganda support given by the Soviet Government to the communist assault in Asia confronts the United States and its principal allies with a major challenge which vitally affects world power positions.

b. The policy and action of Communist China.

(1) Communist China is already involved in a major military aggression in Korea, is publicly committed to an attempt to seize Formosa, may attack Hong Kong, and may increase its support to Ho Chih [sic.] Minh to include the use of Chinese forces in Indochina. Communist success in these efforts would expose the remainder of Southeast Asia to attack and would sharply increase the threat to Japan and the remainder of the off-shore island chain. Such prospects lend greater effective-

ness to the ordinary communist techniques of penetration and subversion and cause many Asians to remain on the side lines during the present phase of the struggle.

Strengthening of Southeast Asia

41. It is important to the United States that the mainland states of Southeast Asia remain under non-communist control and continue to improve their internal conditions. These states are valuable to the free world because of their strategic position, abundant natural resources, including strategic materials in short supply in the United States, and their large population. Moreover, these states, if adequately developed and organized, could serve to protect and contribute to the economic progress and military defense of the Pacific off-shore islands from Japan to New Zealand. Communist control of both China and Southeast Asia would place Japan in a dangerously vulnerable position and therefore seriously affect the entire security position of the United States in the Pacific. The fall of the mainland states would result in changing the status of the off-shore island chain from supporting bases to front line positions. Further, it would tend to isolate these base areas from each other, requiring a review of our entire strategic deployment of forces. Communist domination of the area would alleviate considerably the food problem of China and make available to the USSR considerable quantities of strategically important materials.

42. In the absence of overt Chinese Communist aggression in Southeast Asia, the general problems facing the United States in this area are: the real threat of Chinese Communist invasion and subversion, the political instability and weak leadership of the non-communist governments, the low standards of living and underdeveloped resources of the peoples of the area, the prevailing prejudice against colonialism and Western "interference" and the insensitivity to the danger of communist imperialism. Further acts of communist aggression in Southeast Asia can be expected to stimulate resistance on the part of countries which have thus far failed to take a positive stand.

43. Therefore, the general objectives of the United States in Southeast Asia are: (a) to contribute to the will and ability of all countries in the region to resist communism from within and without, and (b) to aid in the political, economic and social advancement of the area. For this purpose, the United States has developed support programs to strengthen the governments' administrative and military capabilities, to improve living standards, to encourage pro-Western alignments, and to stave off communist intervention.

44. Chinese Communist conquest of Indochina, Thailand and Burma, by military force and internal subversion, would seriously threaten the critical security interests of the United States. However, in the event of overt Chinese aggression, it is not now in the over-all security interests of the United States to commit any United States armed forces to the defense of the mainland states of Southeast Asia. Therefore, the United States cannot guarantee the denial of Southeast Asia to communism. The United States should continue its present support programs to strengthen the will and ability to resist the Chinese Communists, to render Communist military operations as costly as posposible, and to gain time for the United States and its allies to build up the defenses of the off-shore chain and weaken communist power at its source.

45. The United States should develop its support programs in such form and in such manner in each country as will effectively stimulate the use of its resources to the advantage of the free world, contribute to the development of sound economies and adequate military establishments, and take into account the ability of each country to absorb and its willingness to put to effective use American aid. In any instance where a government friendly to the United States

is conducting actual resistance to internal subversive force or overt aggression, the United States should favorably consider contributions to the ability of such a government to continue resistance.

46. The general security problems of Southeast Asia are the subject of military staff conversations among the United States, the United Kingdom and France.

47. Programs of information and educational exchange should be continued in the countries of Southeast Asia and should be designed to develop on the part of the governments and peoples of the area, realization, and action in accordance therewith, of the vital objectives which they share with the United States and of the ways in which the achievement of these objectives are threatened by the aggressive purposes of Soviet Communism.

48. At the present time, the United States faces the following major problems in Southeast Asia:

a. <u>Defense of Indochina</u>. The loss of Indochina to communist control would greatly increase the threat to the other mainland states of Southeast Asia and to Indonesia. The Viet Minh with the aid of strong Chinese Communist military intervention can conquer Indochina. Therefore, the forces opposing the Viet Minh must rapidly increase their military strength. Increased anti-communist manpower must come from the Associated States, principally Vietnam.

b. <u>Chinese Imperialism</u>. The United States should expand and intensify the psychological warfare effort to increase an awareness in the area of the threat which Soviet and Chinese imperialism poses to the national independence, economic betterment and traditional ideals of each country in the region. The United States should seek to reduce the ties between the Chinese communities in Southeast Asia and the Peiping regime, to neutralize the pro-communist support among these communities, and to endeavor to direct the political power and economic wealth of the Chinese communities toward the support of the countries which they are resident.

c. <u>The Role of Singapore and Malaya in the Defense of Southeast Asia</u>. The location of the Malayan Peninsula makes it of great importance to Indonesia and Australia and New Zealand in the even Indochina and Thailand fall to the communists. Although the defense and internal security of Singapore and Malaya are British responsibilities, the Peninsula cannot be defended against an invasion from the north without outside support. Accordingly, the United States should coordinate its operational planning with the United Kingdom with respect to Malaya and adjacent areas.

d. <u>The Alignment of Indonesia</u>. Indonesia's strategic position, economic wealth including oil reserves, and political importance as an independent, non-communist nation are assets to the security of the United States in the Pacific. Consequently, the policies and actions of the United States must be directed to strengthening and maintaining the non-communist political orientation of the government and to promoting economic health and development. At present the Indonesian Government is pursuing a policy of political neutrality. The United States must endeavor to influence Indonesia toward greater participation in measures which promote the security of the area and toward solidarity with the free world. Among the factors which affect United States aid to Indonesia are (1) the results to be achieved in terms of United States national interests, (2) the attitude of the Indonesian government, (3) the needs of Indonesia, and (4) the ability to use aid profitably. The United States should give particular attention to the problem of technical assistance, in view of the serious lack of leadership and trained personnel in the country.

49. With respect to Southeast Asia, the United States should:

a. Continue its present support programs to strengthen the will and ability to resist communist encroachment, to render communist military operations as costly as possible, and to gain time for the United States and its allies to build up the defense of the off-shore chain.

b. Continue programs of information and educational exchange in the countries of Southeast Asia.

c. Encourage the countries of Southeast Asia to restore and expand their commerce with each other and the rest of the free world, stimulate the flow of the raw material resources of the area to the free world, and assist in establishing small arms production in appropriate locations in Southeast Asia under suitable controls.

d. In Indochina:

(1) Continue to increase the military effectiveness of French units and the size and equipment of indigenous units by providing timely and suitable military assistance without relieving the French authorities of their basic military responsibilities or committing United States armed forces.

(2) Continue to encourage internal autonomy and progressive social and economic reforms.

(3) Continue to promote international support for the three Associated States.

e. In Indonesia, the United States should seek to strengthen the non-communist political orientation of the government, promote the economic development of Indonesia, and influence Indonesia toward greater participation in measures which support the security of the area and Indonesia solidarity with the free world.

(219) <u>TELEGRAM FROM HEATH TO ACHESON</u>, June 29, 1951

Source: *Foreign Relations, 1951, Vol. VI,* pp. 432-439.

In the face of obvious French hostility to any U.S. actions which hinted at a lack of support for a long-term French role as protector of Indochina, Heath recommended renewed efforts to reassure the French of such U.S. support. He called for a stance in Indochina which would eliminate any distinction between French and U.S. views on French relations with the Associated States.

2355. Attention which has recently been focussed on De Lattre, on his mil qualities which border genius, on his personal irascibilities and psychological motivations, on his political prejudices shld not obscure the urgently important issues of political and economic substance which lie behind the complex personality of this present-day Lyautey. These issues are vital to the attainment of our foreign policy ends in SEA.

I believe time has come for Dept to review its policy toward IC. I believe certain decisions must now be taken and instructions given.

In epitome, the directive I was given when I left for this post a year ago, was that it was policy of US "to supplement but not to supplant" Fr in IC. This policy had not only economic implications - that France wld continue to carry major share of IC burden - but political connotations as well - that US wld not seek to replace or to oust France from IC or Assoc States from Fr Union. I understood Dept believed in and accepted assurances of Fr Govt that its policy was evolutionary and designed to perfect independence of the three Assoc States within the framework of the Fr Union. With those assurances and in face of Communist aggression we inaugurated programs of mil and economic aid to the Assoc States as independent govts within the framework of the Fr Union. If our policy toward those states cld be summarized in briefest and collateral form, it was "to support but not to subvert". We wld support them as we cld, we wld assist in strengthening their nascent political and admin structures, we wld help to shelter them while they acquired civic maturity and mil experience, we wld not attempt to turn their loyalties from the Fr Union.

I believed this was a workable policy for mid-1950 and I believe that it is workable today. Moreover, in my opinion successive events have strengthened the necessity for strict and unswerving adherence to its fundamentals.

In 1950 we were troubled by three orders of doubt concerning IC. The first was our apprehension that the Fr were moving too slowly and too grudgingly in granting evolutionary concessions toward the independence of the three IC states. We became very rightly concerned that there were unused political and economic competencies within the Assoc States' govts which were not being mobilized for the common struggle. These doubts largely disappeared with the substantial concessions made by France in the Pau accords signed in Dec 1950.

The second was our even greater apprehension re mil situation. Whatever Gen Carpentier's virtues, he evidently did not have the full ability to cope with the IC mil problem or the prestige necessary to obtain from the Fr Defense Min needed reinforcements and supplies. With the arrival of Gen De Lattre and the equally timely delivery of US MDAP supplies, the mil situation and the morale and efficiency of the Fr Union forces changed, almost overnight, for the better. IC wld henceforward be no easy prey for the Communists.

Our third uncertainty in 1950 concerned the Vietnamese themselves, the ability of their govt to enlist popular enthusiasm, the willingness of their people to make the sacrifices of their present and future liberties wld require. The events of 1950 and early 1951 in this regard have been the most disappointing. Yet progress even here has not been negligible. If the cabinet reorganization of last Feb, following perhaps too close upon the Fr Union Tonkin defeats of Nov and Dec, was not productive of a broad-gauged govt of natl unity, the famed Vietnamese fence-sitters did not yet choose to make their personal commitment to the fortunes of the Franco-Vietnamese alliance, if narrower interests of faction and sectional rivalries proved obdurate before this test of the common good, one contrary and beneficent fact of enormous import was also demonstrated. The people stood firm. In the face of an unrelieved series of Fr Union mil reverses there was little panic, no bandwagon onrush to come to terms with the Commies, no mass defection to the Viet Minh.

The second Huu Govt was formed, has survived, is continuing to make slow, painful progress toward the acquisition of governmental exercise and authority. Resentment honestly felt by many Viets during Cabinet crisis over De Lattre's brusque insistence that he be consulted re Def Fin and Interior portfolios has abated as De Lattre has acquired greater finesse in treating with Viet Govt and as justice of his position during present emergency has come into better perspective. De Lattre is primarily a soldier but he is by no means insensible to political considerations; indeed his role in the 1951 Cabinet crisis was managed with rather more skill than Pignon's in the 1950 change. He has succeeded in convincing both Bao Dai and Huu of the sincerity of his interpretation of the Fr position and of his respect for Vietnamese aspirations. As he comes into wider contacts with Vietnamese circles and particularly as he meets with Bao Dai more regularly, the influence of his personal dedication to the Viet cause will spread. The natl army project upon which any ultimate hope for solution in IC must rest is proceeding more slowly than cld perhaps be desired, but it is proceeding and Fr caution that the new native officer corps shall first of all be loyal to Fr Union concept is the one that we can challenge only at the peril of repetition of the China aid program.

These developments are assets. They in no wise relieve the continuing gravity of the IC situation. The frontier between Red China and upper Laos-Northern Tonkin has ceased to exist as a barrier to the shipment of Commie arms and the transfer of Commie reinforcements. 150,000 VM regulars with 150,000 coolies are emplaced in Tonkin; the former are professional soldiers in every sense of the term. They possess to their rear "a privileged sanctuary" for training, rest and re-equipment; they hold in the field at least tactical and even strategic initiative. The decisive battle for IC is yet to be fought. Pressures for this larger IC battle can be expected steadily to mount; if hostilities in Korea are brought to a halt they may come to a head by this fall. Within the time periods within which we must work only Fr arms and Fr resources can hold IC, can check the Communist advance thru SEA, can guarantee the conditions for the integrity of Vietnam. No other means are at hand. Free and independent Vietnam in the jargon of Viet intellectuals cld not survive for six weeks. Present-day Vietnam returned to peace by an international agency and given a coalition govt as a result of some form of internationally-observed free election wld fall to the Commies no less surely, no less slowly, and perhaps rather more cheaply than did the East Eur states of the immed post war period. Only Fr willingness to spend $850 million annually in IC and only the Fr will to persevere in casualty rates of 30,000 men annually can hold this critical pass against Commie domination and exploitation. The Fr ask only that while they defend the country and continue to move steadily away from colonialism they be supported loyally and that nothing be done to encourage or assist separatism or subversion in their rear. These are claims we cannot lightly disregard.

That there are increasing indications that the Fr believe the operation of our econ aid program is contrary to US policy followed in almost all other aspects of our relations with IC is not I believe to be denied. They feel that our insistence on a bilateral approach not only in negs for the form of an aid agreement but in our day to day relations with each of the three Associated States conflicts with the Fr Union idea and the triangular nature of any econ relations between an Associated State Fr and any third power. They find our direct transactional negots with Associated States officials, which they often learn of only from those officials themselves after the event offensive to the spririt of Franco-American cooperation. Above all they regard the publicity which in the local press and elsewhere has attended ECA operations as disproportionate to the US contribution, as invidious to the much greater econ and mil sacrifices made by France in IC, and as suspect in motive and objective since it has almost never been discussed in advance with the High Commissariat.

The Fr know well that part of this publicity is due sly Viet delight in playing up the US as against Fr. They have long appreciated what might be called Viets "ambivalence". They realize fully both that many Viets in and out of govt take advantage their contacts with members Leg and US missions to voice distrust and criticism of the Fr - sometimes justified - and that Viets separatism and division feed on Amer assents which may often be only careless courtesy or on silences indicative in most cases not of assent but only of an unwillingness or an incapacity to debate these complex matters.

(I feel I shld observe that so far as my own relations with De Lattre are concerned the Gen sincerely believes that I personally in my contacts have argued against improper criticism of the Fr. I do not believe he is wrong in thinking that such has not always been case in all contacts of the 200 officers and clerks in Leg STEM, MAAG and USIE. Of some significance was his remark to me in Hanoi that he had entire confidence in sincerity of my cooperative intentions but realized that time wld be necessary before I cld overcome certain difficulties, which he did not specify, in giving him full effect.)

It may well be pointed out that this Fr sensitivity is (a) irrational or excessive, (b) that it represents undue concern with face, and (c) that it shld not be permitted interfere with content or admin of our econ aid program. I cld agree as to a and b, and to c, but am convinced that unless prompt remedial action is taken c will almost certainly result. Advantages of the bilateral approach are ably argued in Saigon Toeca 721 June 19.[1] I believe these advantages can be preserved with a more consultative approach in the admin of STEM and in preparation its publicity. I must rpt here as I did in mytel 2218 June 14 that these observations are in no sense criticism of efficient and tactful direction of STEM by Robert Blum. He has in all respects faithfully executed instrs Wash has given him. What seems required is reassessment, in the light of basic US policy toward IC, of the development of STEM procedures here. Our common concern is that STEM be in position make it maximum contribution to Amer policy in IC. I would like therefore at an early date be able say to De Lattre of Dept instrs fol:

(1) He take steps to stop anti-Amer and false reports of his entourage and secret police re Amer aims and operations in IC.

(2) ECA will discuss in gen way in advance both their projects and their publicity with any members his staff he may designate. We will by no means promise invariably accept all Fr suggestions but they will be welcome, they will be sought in advance, and there will be unremittant and sympathetic understanding of Fr position. (To extent that this approach is at present being followed it will represent no change; to extent that it is not, change is required.)

(3) Although for the moment I believe I can assure De Lattre that there are no other Amer Govt operations in progress in IC beyond those he is informed of, such operations undertaken in IC without his full advance knowledge and consent. I do not consider, of course, as "operations" the individual and entirely legitimate activities of members of this Leg, the atts, etc in receiving info and intel from any source available. (I wld observe at this point that these further assurances involve no real sacrifice on our part since our whole experience here indicates impossiblity conducting such operations without their discovery by Fr and Viets auths.)

(4) The officer and clerical staffs all US missions here are being personally briefed by me to insure that they fully understand extent and value to the gen cause of freedom of the Fr effort here and the validity of the Fr desire that the Assoc States remain in Fr Union.

I will make it clear that they must not listen or give encouragement to improper criticism of Fr sacrifices and intentions and that violation this rule will be regarded as insubordination. (Re this point Brit Min here tells me his instrs are make very clear to Viets that while UK sympathizes with Assoc States gaining their independence, that independence shld be within the association of Fr Union. He tells me his instrs are categoric at this point and I have reports his staff are taking his categoric line in their contacts with Viets.)

(5) Within terms our mutual cooperation and to assist us in discharge of responsibilities we have undertaken not only in IC but elsewhere in SEA, we expect greater and fuller frankness on all matters capable of affecting types and quantities our aid. We believe specific instrs necessary to certain key officials on his staff to enter into more forthcoming relationship with designated polit and econ officers of the Leg. While our mil liaison is much improved since his arrival, we are particularly concerned re info concerning Commie dispositions and intentions both strategic and polit and measures contemplated to counter these enemy plans.

I have not chosen in this cable to discuss operation of the other agencies in IC.

I believe instrs I am requesting are fully consonant with the line of our policy in IC. I believe they are necessary.

It is unquestionably true nonetheless that this approach will seem to some of our officials now in IC either a departure from previous practice or a freezing of policy in an undesirable direction. They argue, as do certain of our Amer publicists, that central facts IC problem are the rising tides of Asian nationalism and embittered hatred of Viets people for Fr; they maintain that all sections of opinion unite on proposition Fr must go and differ only as to means of their expulsion.

They hold that Fr can never make the massive contribution necessary win war in IC and that attempts sustain the conflict at the present level constitute only an abscess for the Western world. They seem feel moreover there is something shameful in the Fr concept of the still undefined Fr union; they point to the absence of parliamentary institutions, to the censorship, to the secret police, to the lack of true polit party or trade union activity, to the econ monopoly the Fr continue or continued until recently to enjoy, to the corruption tolerated and the gambling profits shared, to the opium trade, and to the ominpresence of Fr officials, names and culture as manifestations of the most sordid and restrictive colonialism. And they say the US shld withdraw from this pestilence or shld perhaps stay and attempt covert y to undercut the Fr and assure Viets that the US also desires the elimination of Fr from the FE and shares the blithe conviction that all social ills will depart with the Fr, while an aroused citizenry metes out to the Commie armies the fate they so richly deserve.

The determination of the merits of these several propositions and of this gen view point will very largely be function of history. Number of assumptions are obviously highly debatable. Number of them have certain weight and it is this weight that makes the definition and application of policy in IC supremely difficult. But even if far more validity attached to these views than can in all justice be granted them, even if results of withdrawals of other colonizing powers in Asia were far more impressive than they have been to date, it is childish think of ousting the Fr from IC and stemming Communism in SEA with the means now at hand. Militarily, I take it no other non-Commie power or combination of powers is today prepared take over from the Fr expeditionary corps. Politically, whatever might have been situation 2 years ago, no party, no newspaper, no group no individual in Vietnam today publicly espouses the elimination of Fr execpt the VM. There is literally no place behind which such Amer influence cld be exerted, and none is likely be permitted arise. Nor cld such a party or such a pro-Amer movement be built overnight out of mil and econ aid programs of the size available for IC. Economically, present ECA and MAAG budgets are minor compared with Fr expenditures. They are sufficient if wrongly applied to embitter Franco-Amer relations; they are not enough replace the Fr contribution.

Present IC phase is a holding operation and it is idle to seek or expect an IC solution out of the context of durable Far Eastern settlement. All the evidence now at hand suggests that settlement will not precede but be an integral part of the world-wide resolution of Stalinist aggression. In this holding phase, differences will doubtless arise in the future as they have in the past between the Fr and the Amer concepts of practicable IC evolution. Our counsel has been helpful in past and will continue be if we operate within framework of loyal and trusted cooperation. If we squander our influence and our energies on projects of uncertain aim and intent we will accomplish nothing and lose opportunities we have for discreet but continual pressure.

There is of course one final factor which suggests our loyal cooperation with the Fr. Our common interests neither begin nor end in IC. Our mutual endeavors demand give and take and spirit of adjustment. The interests of the partnership require in IC our loyal, ungrudging but not uncritical support of the Fr. Their objectives here and ours are not so very different in the present period as to make that cooperation any sacrifice of any part our vital interests.

I shld be grateful for earliest expression of the Dept's views and if it concurs, for instrs I have requested. This cable has been shown Mr. Blum, chief of IC STEM.

Sent Dept 2355, rptd info Paris 944.

[1]Telegram Toeca 721 was transmitted by RobertBlum, Chief of the Special Technical and Economic Mission at Saigon, to William C. Foster, Economic Cooperation Administrator, and R. Allen Griffin, Director of the Far Eastern Program, ECA. It referred to telegram 2218 from Saigon, June 14 (p. 42) and read in part as follows:

It is clear, therefore, that entire subject discussed in reftel goes to heart of ECA's activity in IC. ECA was asked by State Dept to undertake program wld strengthen young and fragile political and administrative institutions of Assoc States, cementing the loyalties of masses of people to anti-Communist govts, wld provide peoples of these countries with demonstration of interest in their independence and welfare of US with its liberty-loving and anti-colonial tradition, and wld contribute toward revival of economic activity. Altho it is difficult to judge how far we have succeeded, our efforts have been principal ones extended toward achievement of these goals. I believe that if we are to continue to serve same purposes our program must be carried on along same lines as heretofore. That there are possible points of friction between this policy and that of Fr was recognized from beginning but did not deter us a year ago. We shld try to eliminate these if we can but we shld change our policy only if you feel situation has altered since last year so as to require it or if you decide that earlier policy was wrong." (ECA Cable File: FRC Acc. N. 53A278)

(220) TELEGRAM FROM ACHESON TO HEATH, July 7, 1951

Source: *Foreign Relations, 1951, Vol. VI*, p. 439, fn. 3.

Acheson gave his approval for the steps recommended in Heath's telegram, except for the assurance to De Lattre that there were no U.S. "operations in Indochina of which he had not been informed.

"Legs excellent analysis present sit IC fully appreciated. Dept believes you shld proceed at appropriate time with representations proposed Legtel 2355 Jun 29, incorporating therein such modifications in tone as Paris 77 Jul5 [*post*, p. 442] suggests, except for #3 see immed fol para. Dept assumes however that you agree that no *such* representations shld be made until present difficulties surrounding consumation of ECA bilateral agreement have been resolved.

"As for proposed numbered 3 section 3 urtel, you will receive special instr soonest. Meanwhile you shld not volunteer representation on this pt.

"Dept, for its part, proposes to engage in full and frank discussion US policy and objectives IC with Amb Bonnet and Min Daridan soonest after resolution of bilateral difficulty."

(221) TELEGRAM FROM HEATH TO ACHESON, July 11, 1951 (Extract)

Source: *Foreign Relations, 1951, Vol. VI*, pp. 445-447.

In a conversation with Heath, Bao Dai revealed that his conception of a Vietnamese national army was that its loyalty would have to be to him rather than to the fatherland, which he asserted would be impractical because the idea was "too new." His statement throws additional light on the contrasting ideas of political legitimacy of the Bao Dai and Ho Chi Minh governments.

96. Bao Dai arrived Saigon yesterday afternoon for brief visit and I saw him at noon today by appointment.

While Bao Dai insisted that he remained firmly optimistic that in long run VM wld be suppressed and Vietnam wld finally emerge as truly independent state, with stable govt and economy, he said he was very worried over effect in Fr of conclusion of what he calls "compromise" between UN forces and Chi-North Korean forces. There had always been strong element in Fr Parliament and Govt in favor "compromise" with Ho Chi Minh which wld allow Fr withdraw their forces with semblance of honor and with great saving blood and treasure (see Legtel 1340, Jan 30; 1363, Feb 2; and 1537, Mar 2). Peaceful arrangement Korean question might well strengthen this movement. He said that De Lattre wld never consent such arrangement since he was now entirely committed to victory over VM. De Lattre, Bao Dai insisted, wld resign before he wld consent be made instrument any arrangement which wld mean the rapid take over all IC by the international Commies.

Bao Dai then inquired whether actually there was any important element in Amer legis or exec branch which wld favor compromise with the Commie Viet Minh. I answered very firmly that while there were probably few in Congress who were not informed of true nature VM, I felt my govt was fully informed and aware dangers of any appeasement which wld allow Ho Chi Minh and his Commie directors of VM to share govt or territory of IC. What had happened in Czechoslovakia, Poland and other satellite states was clearly present in Wash's mind. Bao Dai then asked me inform my govt that the elite of Viets Nationalists were now entirely anti-Commie and aware impossibility any compromise with Ho Chi Minh.

Full nationalist strength against Ho Chi Minh cld not be mobilized however until there was true Viets natl army entirely Viets commanded. For moment there were merely scattered battalions of indifferent morale and spirit because they were Fr commanded. Fr command was necessity at this transition stage but transition shld be brief as possible. Furthermore, it must be an army, he asserted, loyal to himself as chief of state. Idea of forming army with loyalty to Vietnam "the patrie" was entirely impractical at present moment. Idea of the "patrie" was too new. Vietnam's "independence" was too recent. Strength of Bao Daists, Hoa Haos and other sectarian mil forces was their loyalty to a person, agent or chief of the cult.

****

(222) TELEGRAM FROM ACHESON TO THE LEGATION IN SAIGON, July 25, 1951

Source: *Foreign Relations, 1951, Vo. VI*, pp. 461-462

The French Ambassador pressed Acheson for steps leading to a joint U.S.-British-French plan for defense of Indochina against China, on which Acheson appears to have been noncommittal.

127. Fr Amb called on Secy July 23 to discuss defense of IC with particular reference to possible effects on defense IC and SEA of truce in Korea. Amb stated his Govt eager to determine, as far in advance as possible what steps cld be taken in event of large-scale Chi intervention by US, UK and Fr in concert successfully defend IC. He suggested on behalf his Govt two courses of action either or both of which might provide a basis for satisfactorily anticipating requisite action and forestalling Chi intervention:

(*a*) A convocation of reps of US, UK, Fr FonOffs to discuss implementation of recommendations made at mil conf Singapore. In this connection Fr Amb remarked on evidence Chi build-up on Tonkin was key to defense of SEA.

(b) Discussion by "interested parties" of guarantees against Chi aggression against parts of Asia other than Korea; Amb said his Govt understood such matters cld not be incorporated in present mil truce discussions and thought they shld take place fol conclusion of truce. In reply to Secy's question Amb replied that it was inevitable that such discussions wld include Chi Commies, as such undertaking on such broad matters by North Koreans alone wld be useless. Further efforts on part Secy to determine when and between whom such discussions shld take place proved unavailing. Secy took this opportunity to suggest desirability Schuman's personally participating Jap Treaty ceremony San Francisco fol which Secy impled he wld discuss this matter with Schuman. Fr Amb at first agreed desirability Schuman attending San Francisco ceremony but later pointed out that he thought latter wld be unable to attend if the Assoc States IC were excluded from list of signatories. He engaged however to pass suggestion on to Schuman at appropriate time.

Secy assured Fr Amb that Dept seriously considering manner in which Singapore recommendations shld be carried out and had given most earnest consideration to manner in which security of Asian countries other than Korea, particularly IC might be assured in connection with, or in consequence of Korean truce. He told Fr Amb that we were doing our best to find some formula which wld satisfactorily deal with problem inclusion Assoc States as signatories Jap Treaty in face of opposition other Asian states. Bonnet suggested possibly announcing at commencement Treaty ceremonies that signature to Treaty did not imply change in relations between signatories, i.e., India by signing together with Assoc States does not imply recognition latter by former (this had previously been suggested to Fr Amb by Mr. Dulles as possibility for consideration).

Fr Amb stated his Govt realized proposal (a) difficult to pursue; hoped proposal (b) might be dealt with relatively soon.

Sent to AmLegation Saigon 127; rptd info AmEmbassy Parts by pouch, AmEmbassy London by pouch.

---

(223) NIE-35, "POSSIBLE DEVELOPMENTS IN INDOCHINA DURING THE REMAINDER OF 1951," August 7, 1971

Source: *Foreign Relations, 1951,* pp. 469-475.

The intelligence community projected a stalemate in the military situation through 1951, with increased Chinese assistance to the Viet Minh matching the step-up in the French effort and U.S. assistance. The estimate noted a lack of political support for the Bao Dai government as a continuing program.

THE PROBLEM

To estimate the current situation and probable developments in Indochina during the remainder of 1951.

CONCLUSIONS

1. The current military stalemate in Indochina appears likely to continue at least through the end of 1951, unless the Chinese Communists directly intervene with forces over and above the estimated 30,000 "volunteers" which they can introduce as individuals or in small units in probable continuation of present assistance to the Viet Minh.

2. If the Chinese Communists directly intervene with large forces over and above those introduced as individuals or in small units, the French would probably be driven back to a beachhead around Haiphong. The French should be able

to hold this beachhead for some time, unless the Chinese Communists achieve air superiority.

3. Direct Chinese Communist intervention is not likely as long as the Chinese Communists are extensively committed in Korea.

4. If hostilities in Korea end, or the Communist commitment there can be substantially reduced, there will be an increased likelihood of direct Chinese Communist intervention in Indochina. On balance, however, we consider such intervention unlikely during the period under review.

DISCUSSION

The Current Situation

5. The present military situation in Indochina is one of stalemate. In the period since General de Lattre Tassigny assumed command, the Franco-Vietnamese forces have repulsed the Viet Minh drive to conquer Tonkin, and firmly hold the key Red River delta around Hanoi and Haiphong (see map). French successes apparently resulted from: (a) the energetic leadership of General de Lattre, who revived flagging French morale; (b) MDAP aid; (c) the arrival of French reinforcements; (d) the inexperience at large-scale warfare of the Viet Minh guerrillas; and (e) the limitations of Chinese Communist support. The inadequate staff work and lack of supporting arms of the Viet Minh forces placed them at a serious disadvantage in pitched battles with the French, who were strengthened by the timely arrival of US military aid, including aircraft, napalm bombs, patrol and landing craft, and ground combat materiel. The Chinese Communists, upon whom the Viet Minh forces are dependent for logistical support, have been supplying them with ammunition, light weapons, and some artillery. Some 10,000 Chinese personnel have been infiltered into the Viet Minh in cadre, technical, and advisory capacities. This number is believed to be increasing. However, the Chinese Communists, while apparently maintaining roughly the same level of material assistance as of last December, have not intervene directly or with substantial "volunteer" forces or noticeably stepped up arms aid. Under these circumstances General de Lattre, drawing reinforcements from other areas of Indochina and skillfully using mobile reserve forces, was able to hold the Franco-Vietnamese position intact and to inflict heavy losses on the Viet Minh.

6. Political developments, however, have been less favorable. Despite the gradual French transfer of certain responsibilities, the Vietnamese government has been slow to develop and has continued to suffer from a lack of strong leadership. It has had to contend with: (a) French reluctance to relinquish ultimate control of political and economic affairs; (b) lingering Vietnamese suspicion of any French-supported regime, combined with the apathetic and "fence-sitting" attitude of the bulk of the people, which has deprived the government of broad-based popular support; (c) the difficulty common to all new and inexperienced governments, of training the necessary personnel and building an efficient administration; and (d) the failure of factional and sectional groups to unite in a concerted national effort.

7. In January 1951 the opportunity arose of forming a borad-based cabinet representing most non-Communist group[s] in Vietnam; in stead Premier Huu formed a cabinet composed primarily of members of his own pro-French faction. Although Huu has displayed some administrative skill and his government has gained slowly in effectiveness, the weakness of the Huu cabinet and its alleged "French puppet" status have limited its appeal to Vietnamese nationalism and have alienated strong nationalist groups, including the powerful Dai Viet group in Tonkin. Communist control of much of the country and Viet Minh infiltration of large areas under nominal French control have also discouraged many people from openly allying themselves with the government.

Chinese Communist Capabilities and Intentions

12. It is a basic Chinese Communist and Soviet policy to promote Communist control over Southeast Asia, and Peiping and Moscow recognize Indochina as a key to this region because of its strategic location and because of the advanced revolutionary situation already existing there. Peiping has already supported the Viet Minh regime by recognizing Ho Chi Minh's regime and by providing it with technical and material aid. There are numerous indications of Chinese preparations for greater military support of the Viet Minh, possibly including direct intervention with Chinese Communist forces.

13. The Chinese Communists are capable of substantially increasing their present type of aid to the Viet Minh, particularly by the integration of sizeable numbers of personnel as individuals or cadres into the Viet Minh Army. We believe that the reinforced Franco-Vietnamese forces could hold the bulk of their Tonkin perimeter against the Viet Minh even if the Viet Minh were supported by as many as 30,000 infiltrated personnel, although with such additional support the Viet Minh might win some local victories. Continued Chinese Communist infiltration on a large scale, however, would gradually make the French position increasingly precarious.

14. Turning to Chinese Communist capabilities for large scale intervention with their own forces, we estimate that roughly 100,000 Chinese Communist field force troops could now be made available and logistically supported for an invasion of Indochina. The poor transport net and forbidding terrain of the border region limit the forces which could presently be employed to that number. They could be logistically supported only for short offensive operations of about one week at a time, passing to the defensive during the intervals for replenishment of supplies. However, the Chinese Communists are slowly increasing their capabilities for stockpiling supplies by improving road and rail supply routes into Tonkin and are improving airfields in the border region. Consequently Chinese Communist logistical capabilities for offensive operations are gradually increasing.

15. In addition the Chinese Communists have the capability of mounting intense air attacks of short duration against the French, whose aircraft are concentrated on three vulnerable airfields in Tonkin. Successful Chinese Communist air attacks of this sort would materially enhance Communist capabilities for large-scale ground operations. Communist air superiority in the Tonkin area would also materially hamper French surveillance and naval blockade of the Tonkin Gulf, and consequently permit increased over-water aid to the Viet Minh.

16. If the Chinese Communists intervene before the end of 1951 with 100,000 troops, they could probably eventually drive the French into a beachhead at Haiphong. The French, however, should be able to hold this beachhead for some time, unless the Chinese Communists achieve air superiority.

17. The Chinese Communists will undoubtedly be influenced in deciding whether or not to intervene directly in Indochina by the future development of the situation in Korea. So long as the Chinese Communists remain heavily in Korea, we consider it unlikely that they will intervene directly in Indochina. Although the Chinese Communists might drive the French from Tonkin, such a major victory is not assured. An indecisive and protracted campaign would place additional severe strains on total Chinese Communist resources.

18. If the Korean fighting is stopped under conditions which appear to remove the threat of renewed UN attacks, transportation difficulties in the border region would continue to limit the ground forces which could be supported in Tonkin, but the possible diversion of resources from the Korean-Manchuria area would permit early intervention with greater assurance of the continued arrival of supplies and replacements for the operation. We estimate that by

two months after a Korean armistice, Chinese Communist capabilities for invading Indochina could be significantly increased, while air capabilities could be greatly increased. The Chinese Communists and the USSR might then consider that Indochina offers more favorable opportunities for a quick and decisive victory with less risk of US and UN intervention than did Korea. They might calculate that the US and UN would be unwilling to undertake another operation of the Korean type and that some UN members would be unwilling to defend what they regard as French colonialism in Indochina. Thus in the even of a cessation of hostilities in Korea, the likelihood of early Chinese Communist intervention in Indochina, particularly after the rainy season ends in October, would increase.

19. On the other hand, the Chinese Communists would probably hesitate to intervene openly in Indochina while they were negotiating for an over-all Korean settlement, including the withdrawal of UN forces, and these negotiations would doubtless take considerable time. Moreover, if Communist acceptance of a cease-fire in Korea indicated a desire to seek a temporary "relaxation" of world tensions, early intervention in Indochina would be unlikely. We also believe that the continuing inadequacies of its line of communications, the strengthening of the French forces, and the risk of foreign intervention, would probably lead Peiping to conclude that it still could not count with certainty on achieving a quick and decisive conquest of all Tonkin, but might become involved in another protracted and costly campaign in which the risk of foreign intervention might increase. Finally, the Communists might expect that through increased cadre, material and technical aid to the Viet Minh they could still wear down the French and achieve successes without the necessity of early large-scale intervention.

20. On balance, therefore, we believe that the increased Chinese preparations in the Tonkin border region probably reflect an intent to facilitate the flow of "volunteers" and material aid to the Viet Minh forces, which preparing for possible large-scale intervention, rather than an intent to intervene during 1951.

21. Consequently, the probable outlook through the end of 1951 in Indochina is one of continued military stalement, if the Chinese Communists do not directly intervene. The tightening of Viet Minh political control, the further development of the Viet Minh forces, and increased Chinese Communist aid will probably be balanced by the arrival of French reinforcements, more MDAP assistance, and progress toward creating a Vietnam Army. Some territory may change hands but we do not foresee any major victories on either side, at least through the end of 1951.

(224) MEMORANDUM BY HEATH ON NIE-35, August 1951

Source: *Foreign Relations, 1951, Vol. VI*, pp. 485-486.

In a memorandum written in Paris and undated, but completed during his visit in Paris in August, Heath differed sharply with the political assessments in NIE-35 on relations between France and the State of Viet-nam and the revolutionary side's political support. He asserted that there had been a "very considerable decline in the popularity of the Viet Minh."

I agree with the conclusions of the reference paper and particularly with the final estimate that direct Chinese Communist intervention in Indochina is unlikely to occur during the remainder of 1951. The possibility of early intervention, however, while unlikely during the next few months, should not be entirely ruled out.

Par. 5 of paper. I question the statement that French successes during the period since General de Lattre assumed command are in part due to "(c) the arrival of French reinforcements" or "(d) the inexperience at large scale warfare of the Viet Minh guerrillas during the past ten months failed because of their inexperience in large-scale warfare. The Viet Minh attacks were shrewdly planned and energetically executed. De Lattre is of the opinion that the operation against Vinh-Yen was planned by European officers.

I believe that the estimate that 10,000 Chinese personnel have been infiltrated into the Viet Minh is somewhat excessive. The French have no exact intelligence on this point but at a French staff briefing in June the number was placed as "in excess of 5,000."

Par. 6. The statement that the slowness of development of the Vietnamese Government is in part due to "(a) French reluctance to relinquish ultimate control of political and economic affairs" in Viet Nam, is not true today. Under de Lattre, intervention in internal political affairs has been limited, and the French cannot be said to be exercising ultimate control of economic affairs beyond the fact that they are heavily subsidizing the maintenance and equipment of the new Viet Nam national army, and supporting the exchange rate of the piaster.

Par. 8. Present plans call for the expansion of the Viet Nam army to 120,000 men, not to 100,000.

While in the past there have been differences of opinion between the Vietnamese Government and the French over control of the Viet Nam army, there is no such conflict at the present time.

Par. 9. The statement: "we are unable to determine whether the Viet Minh is actually losing any of its popular appeal" is surprising. I do not believe that any informed observer would deny that in the past twelve months there has been a very considerable decline in the popularity of the Viet Minh.

Par. 14. With regard to the estimate that 100,000 Chinese Communist troops could now be made available and logistically supported for invasion of Indochina, I believe that General de Lattre's estimate is that a maximum of 150,000 Chinese troops could be employed in the Tonkin area.

---

(225) <u>ECONOMIC COOPERATION AGREEMENT BETWEEN THE GOVERNMENT OF THE U.S.A. AND THE GOVERNMENT OF VIETNAM</u>, September 7, 1951.

Source: *U.S. Vietnam Relations, Book 8,* pp. 449-451.

After weeks of delay by the French Government, which was exercising its authority under the Elysee Agreement to concur in all treaties negotiated by the State of Viet-nam, the latter was permitted to sign its first bilateral treaty with the U.S. on September 7, 1951. Similar agreements were also signed with Cambodia and Laos at that time.

The Government of the United States of America and the Government of Vietnam:

Recognizing that individual liberty, free institutions, and independence depend largely upon sound economic conditions and stable international economic relationships;

Considering that the Congress of the United States of America has enacted legislation enabling the United States to furnish assistance to the Government of Vietnam and the measures which the two Governments will take individually and together in furtherance of the above objectives: with due regard to accords and agreements previously entered into by the High Contracting Parties;

Have agreed as follows:

ARTICLE I

The Government of the United States of America will, subject to the terms and conditions prescribed by law and to arrangements provided for in this Agreement, furnish the Government of Vietnam such economic and technical assistance as may be requested by it and agreed to by the Government of the United States of America. The Government of Vietnam will cooperate with the Government of the United States of America to assure that procurement will be at reasonable prices and on reasonable terms. Commodities or services furnished under the present Agreement may be distributed within Vietnam on terms and conditions agreed upon between the two Governments.

ARTICLE II

In order to assure maximum benefits to the people of Vietnam from the assistance to be furnished under the present Agreement by the United States of America, the Government of Vietnam will use its best endeavors:

A. To assure efficient and practical use of all resources available and to assure that the commodities and services obtained under this Agreement are used for purposes consistent therewith and with the general objectives indicated in the aid program presented by the Government of Vietnam and agreed to by the Government of the United States of America.

B. To promote the economic development of Vietnam on a sound basis and to achieve such economic objectives as may be agreed upon.

C. To assure the stability of its currency and the validity of its rate of exchange, and generally to assure confidence in its financial stability.

D. To cooperate with other countries to reduce barriers to international trade, and to take appropriate measures singly and in cooperation with other countries to eliminate public or private restrictive practices hindering domestic or international trade.

ARTICLE III

The Governments will, upon request of either of them, consult regarding any matter relating to the application of the Agreement or operations thereunder. The Government of Vietnam will provide detailed information necessary to carrying out the provisions of this Agreement including a quarterly statement on the use of funds, commodities, and services received under the present Agreement and to evaluate the effectiveness of assistance furnished or contemplated.

ARTICLE IV

The Government of Vietnam agrees to receive a special Technical and Economic Mission which will discharge the responsibilities of the Government of the United States of America under the present Agreement and upon appropriate notification from the Government of the United States of America will consider this Special Mission and its personnel as part of the Diplomatic Mission of the United States of America in Vietnam for the purpose of enjoying the privileges and immunities accorded to that Diplomatic Mission and its personnel of comparable rank. The Government of Vietnam will further give full cooperation to the Special Mission, including the provision of facilities necessary for observation and review of the carrying out of this Agreement including the use of assistance furnished under it.

ARTICLE V

1. This Agreement shall take effect upon notification by the Government of Vietnam to the Government of the United States of America that all necessary legal requirements in connection with the conclusion of this Agreement by the Government of Vietnam have been fulfilled.[1] This Agreement shall continue in force until the date agreed upon by the two Governments or may be terminated three months after a written notification has been given by either of the two Governments.

2. The Annex to this Agreement forms an integral part thereof.

3. This Agreement shall be registered with the Secretary General of the United Nations.

IN WITNESS WHEREOF, the undersigned, duly authorized for the purpose, have signed the present Agreement.

DONE AT SAIGON this Seventh day of September, 1951 in duplicate, in each of the English, French, and Vietnamese languages, all texts authentic except that in the case of divergencies, the English and French texts shall govern.

[1]Sept. 7, 1951.

(226) .MINUTES OF MEETING BETWEEN ACHESON AND SCHUMAN, WASHINGTON, September 1, 1951.

Source: *Foreign Relations, 1951, Vol. VI*, p. 492.

During the meeting of the Foreign Minister of the U.S.; Britain and France in Washington September 10-14, 1951, Schuman told Acheson that France could not continue the effort in Indochina and meet its obligations to NATO without massive U.S. financial help.

Indochina

1. M. SCHUMAN said that his Government was preparing a note on Indochina dealing with the present troop strength and causualties and containing a projection of plans and problems for 1952.[1] Without going into details it was clear that it would be impossible for France to carry out the proposed effort in Indochina and to fulfill its obligations with respect to the defense of Europe. France planned to spend a billion francs a day in Indochina alone and faced many problems in obtaining a maximum effort there as it was engaged to do. As to the financial problem the Finance Ministers would be discussing it further. In brief, after July 1, 1952, the French would be unable to continue their effort at the present rate and would face a 150 billion franc deficit for the year. This deficit incidentally was included in the French estimate on the dollar gap. It was not suggested that the U.S. finance French policy directly but it was hoped that the U.S. could assist by arms and other troop supplies, especially in establishing the national armies of the Associated States. In this connection General de Lattre hoped to expand the present strength of 25 battalions to 50 battalions.

2. MR. ACHESON said that M. Mayer; French Finance Minister, had discussed this matter with General Marshall and had made a deep impression upon him. The need for a solution was generally recognized. There was general agreement on the principle as discussed during the talks with M. Pleven, that France should continue to be primarily responsible for Indochina, that U.S. troops should not be used, and that first priority in military aid should go to Indochina. This difficult problem needed careful study, since funds directly avalable for Indochina under the present aid program were not sufficient. Both General Marshall and Mr. Foster of ECA were examining all possible ways to find other routes to reach the common goal. All that could be said now was that the importance of this problem was fully understood, that the question would be given urgent attention, and that the U.S. had the will - even if it were not sure as to the means - to assist in solving this problem. Perhaps General de Lattre would be able to make some helpful suggestions.

3. M. SCHUMAN said that Mr. Acheson's reply was cause for hope in the future. He recalled the first promise in May 1950 for aid to Indochina which has been effective and well used. General de Lattre would develop more information on the long-term problem and relate it to the Singapore Conference.

When he presented General de Lattre to Mr. Acheson personnally on September 14 it might be possible to explore this problem further.

[1]The note under reference was presented to Acheson by Schuman on September 12. For its substance, see telegram to Paris, September 15, p. 505 [*Foreign Relations, 1951, Vol. VI.*].

(227) MEMORANDUM OF CONVERSATION: MEETING OF ACHESON, SCHUMAN AND DE LATTRE DE TASSIGNY, September 14, 1951

Source: *Foreign Relations, 1951, Vol. VI*, pp. 502-504.

De Lattre indicated to Acheson and other U.S. officials during his Washington visit that his plan envisioned the elimination of the "Viet Minh" as a fighting force within two years, and that his only serious worry was a Chinese invasion. He portrayed Vietnamese youth as having no particular political predisposition and therefore just as useful to either side.

General de Lattre opened the conversation with the remark that he was particularly pleased to see the Secretary today for he had not expected to see him until after the Ottawa talks. That he should meet him on his first day in the United States and on the same day he had met the President was especially gratifying. He spoke of the cordial and "encouraging" interview he had had at noon with the President. He believed that the President had a thorough understanding of the Indochina problem and had been very reassured by his statement to the effect that *"we would not let Indochina fall into enemy hands"*.

After the formalities had been completed, Mr. Schuman made a particular point of stating to the Secretary that he was glad to be able to present General de Lattre himself and to state that General de Lattre *would be speaking on behalf of the French Government during his visit to the United States*. The Secretary acknowledged this fact and remarked that General Marshall, Mr. Lovett and our own officials in the Department were all looking foward to discussing the details of the Indohcina problem with the General.

During the main body of the conversation General de Lattre reviewed the Indochina scene in a general sense. There was little stated that added to what Saigon and Paris had already reported.

The General spoke of the improvement in the overall French military potential since he had taken command and MDAP goods began to arrive. He spoke of the victories in Tonkin of last season as having marked the turning of the tide. He stated that if it were made possible to carry out his present military plans and there were no Chinese military intervention the Viet Minh could be eliminated as a fighting force in a period of between one and two years. The General did not seek to minimize the danger of Chinese intervention, stating that there were 120,000 men or an estimated six to eight well-trained and armed Chinese divisions at the frontier who could intervene at any time. Their intervention would be disastrous. The General did not think that any Chinese invasion would be immediately fatal for the sings of a Chinese aggression would be evident in advance; the French could presumably fight a delaying action, if nothing else.

The General spoke in some detail on the subject of the national armies. In his estimation the young Vietnamese make excellent soldiers. He spoke of the two Vietnamese parachutist battalions now in service which have become able and effective units after only a few weeks of training. He observed that it was essential that the loyalist side train the youth for active service for if we did not Ho Chi Minh would (and does). The General termed the youth of Vietnam as being as numerous as the rice shoots - as ready for plucking and as useful. He described the Vietnamese as being very flexible politically. The same man who has been made into Grade A parachutist in the governmental forces would make a fanatical communist guerrilla if Ho Chi Minh had reached him first. He spoke of the problem of filling the officer cadres in the national army and remarked that Bao Dai and President Huu had given him considerable support in this regard but the problem was very far from being solved. He hoped more progress would be made after his return from the United States with news that the Americans had promised to support the Franco-Vietnamese program on the basis that in Vietnam, as in the rest of the Orient, nothing succeeds like success.

The National Army of Vietnam, as contemplated, will have 120,000 men and 4,000 officers. The ofers must *all* be Vietnamese; a single French officer would handicap the effecitveness of any unit.

The General referred to Bao Dai as the ablest statesman in Vietnam. At this comment Mr. Schuman interjected that he was perhaps the only one. De Lattre spoke with enthusiasm of the Emperor and his authority. He recounted several recent instances when Bao Dai showed the proper cooperative spirit and, in some cases, even initative.

The Secretary stated that the nature of the war in Indochina was not entirely clear to him. Did, for instance, the General have to face a continuous front or was it a broken one. The General replied that although in the past there had been no front in the Western sense, the recent Viet Minh offensives in Tonkin had been done on a frontal basis with a set line of combat. The front is never stable, however, for the moment a line is established the enemy soldiers one has been facing slip through one's feet and a few hours later on are at one's back. The General stated that the only method to combat the Viet Minh was by using their own tactics of surprise enveloping movements, the success of which depended entirely on the ability of keeping the plan of attack secret in advance. Mr. Schuman interjected at this point that one of the functions the French hoped to improve with the formation of the national armies was intelligence. De Lattre agreed with the comment that intelligence was only effective by using natives to deal with natives.

At this point General de Lattre referred again to his hope that he would return to Vietnam with news of a successful American trip. The Secretary stated, referring to the Department's responsibilities in the matter, "we shall support you very strongly".

De Lattre referred to the prospect of peace in Korea and his hope that, if successful, it would result in the diversion of military materiel from Korea to Indochina. The Secretary answered that he didn't think the prospects of a cease fire in Korea were particularly bright at this moment. The General expressed his theory that the Korean and Indocina wars were "one war" and that in order to be effective there must be "one peace".

Toward the end, the General referred with considerable emphasis to the danger of allowing the Vietnamese to slip behind the Asiatic iron curtain. He stated that there was no country so potentially useful to the communists as the Associated States. Their youth, he said, was very clever and learned very quickly but were very unstable. The General felt that once a Vietnamese became a communist he was a communist forever and an exceedingly fanatical one. If the French were not in Vietnam, the communists would most certainly be.

Finally, Mr. Schuman spoke of the excellent impression the Associated States delegations had made at San Francisco. The Secretary agreed with this observation.

The interview closed with the General's comment that "we must save these countries from the fate of communism"; the Secretary reaffirmed this conviction and the Department's intention to cooperate fully with the General in the course of his presentation to the United States authorities.

(228) <u>RECORD OF MEETING WITH JEAN DE LATTRE DE TASSIGNY AT THE PENTAGON,</u> September 20, 1951 (Extract)

Source: *Foreign Relations, 1951, Vol. VI*, pp. 517-519.

De Lattre reiterated the theme that the U.S. had to give him the necessary military means for the Indochina War if it wanted to keep the entire region out of Communist hands and threatened to recommend publicly that France not continue the war if the U.S. failed to do so, and to blame the loss on the U.S. Deputy Secretary of Defense Lovett made it clear, however, that the U.S. could not give the same priority to Indochina as did to Korea, because there would be a strong Congressional reaction.

Mr. Lovett welcomed General de Lattre and invited him to open the conversation.

General de Lattre spoke at length about the importance of the war in Indochina. He said that every day he asks those whom he meets in the United States if Indochina and Korea are not one war. The answer is always "Yes". He said that General Collins had agreed with him that "if you lose Korea, Asia is not lost; but if I lose Indochina, Asia is lost." Tonkin is the key to Southeast Asia, if Southeast Asia is lost. India will "burn like a match" and there will be no barrier to the advance of Communism before Suez and Africa. If the Moslem world were thus engulfed, the Moslems in North Africa would soon fall in line and Europe itself would be outflanked.

General de Lattre recalled that at Fort Benning, the previous day, he had spoken of the paramount importance of infantry in the war of today and the war of tomorrow. He recalled that at the end of World War II, the Soviet Marshall Zhukov had told him that Russia would need fifteen years to replace the calamitous losses among her youth before she could fight another war. This is the importance of Asia to the Russians, as illustrated in Korea - to fill their need for young manpower for the infantry to fight their wars. The United States must decide if it is necessary to hold Asia. If the answer is yes, then it must give him the material he needs for the defense of Indochina.

Mr. Lovett recalled that last Friday he had expressed to General de Lattre the hope that he would regard the Pentagon "comme chez vous". General de Lattre did not need any further expression of our understanding of his problem. However, Mr. Lovett wished to clear up something that may confuse the General, as it confuses many American citizens. He explained that an appropriated of funds for FY 1951 means that these funds are to be obligated in FY 1951, but does not necessarily mean that the actual production of materiel will take place in that year. The American fiscal year begins on July 1st. Mr Lovett said that in order to meet General de Lattre's problem, which we so well understand, we must take account of what we are able to do. He pointed out that Congress has not yet approved the Military Aid funds for 1952. Beginning about March 1952, we will get more industrial production than we are getting now.

Mr. Lovett said that General de Lattre had made a very persuasive presentation of the needs of his theater. Although, in one sense, your theater of war is the same as ours, we must recognize that the United States has a primary obligation in other theaters, whereas your primarly obligation is in your own theater. Mr. Lovett said that he would ask General Collins to respond specifically to the requests which General De Lattre had made this morning.

General de Lattre interrupted to remark that he had seen in the paper yesterday evening that the Department of State had made a statement exactly contrary to what he was aiming to achieve.

Mr. Lovett said that he would like to explain how this had come about. There had been a report from the French press agency that the United States would place Indochina on the same or higher priority than Korea, where the United States has had 89,000 casualties. There was an immediate Congressional reaction that such a decision would be wrong. The Department of State had responded to the rumor by stating the facts, i.e., that such a decision had not been made. The purpose of this statement had nothing to do with General de

Lattre's visit. Mr. Lovett said he thought General de Lattre would find encouragement in the information which General Collins was about to give him.

General de Lattre referred to the battles of last May and June in Indochina.
Earlier, the Vietminh had been able to support their troops in battle for only
a day or a few days at a time. With each succeeding month, they were able to
sustain their forces in longer operations. This resulted in an ever-increasing
rate of wear and consumption of material by the French and Vietnamese forces.
In June, there had been less than 6,000 shells in all Indochina. General Brink
had told him that additional supplies of ammunition were expected momentarily.
Then it was learned that the ship carrying them had been diverted to Korea.
Consequently, during eight days the French forces were "in a most dramatic situation". Owing to the lack of reserve ammunition, it was impossible to counter-
attack. When no counter-attack was ordered, his men were asking if the General
had lost his energy because of the death of his son, but he could not tell them
the real state of affairs. The General said that he no longer felt personal
ambition. His future is nothing. He is only trying to do his duty to his
country and the whole free world. Nevertheless, he would not volunteer for
disaster. If the means to continue the war were not made available to him, he
could not recommend to his country that it continue to sacrifice the flower of
its youth without hope of victory, and he would explain to his country and to
the United States why it was impossible to carry on.

Mr. Lovett expressed his understanding. The U.S. wants to do whatever is
possible, but it would be misleading to let General de Lattre think that everything is possible.

(229) <u>TELEGRAM FROM ACHESON TO THE LEGATION IN SAIGON</u>, September 26, 1951

Source: *Foreign Relations, 1951, Vol. VI*, pp. 524-525.

*Acheson reported to Saigon that De Lattre's visit would certainly result in
the acceleration of military aid, and that the State Department would support
his request for a reexamination of the supply program. He confirmed that there
were no longer any differences between the U.S. and France over political
issues in Indochina.*

442. Gen de Lattre departed Wash 24th for West Pt, thence to New York
where he was guest of honor at dinner given by Luce of *Time-Life* on 24th. Departed for Paris by air evening 25th.

In addition visits service installations and official entertainment Gen had
conversations high officials Defense and Dept including four hour session Sept
17 in Dept attencded by reps White House, Defense and ECA, as well as Dept officials concerned IC and Fr affairs. Gen's principle thesis was that Korea and
IC are one war and therefore illogical for US grant higher priority to Korea.
His exposition delivered with candor and considerable vigor. All questions put
to him disposed of satisfactorily. After Gen's effective presentation and general discussion Acting Asst Secy Merchant stated in conclusion that Dept not
competent to change existing priority for IC mil Aid Program and that, furthermore, it was our opinion that Gen was ill advised to press for change of priority as extremely unlikely this cld be accomplished for reasons which Gen as
soldier and patriot wld understand. Merchant advised on behalf of Dept that
Gen rather devote his efforts to making up detailed list of materiel required,
noting reasons and dates, and have it submitted by members of his staff (Allard
and Cogny) to U.S. officers charged with implementation aid program and, finally, that Gen himself take up question in detail with Service Secys, Gen Collins
and Secy Lovett.

De Lattre called on Gen Collins 20th, Secy Lovett same day and Naval and Air Secys and Chiefs of Staff subsequently. Notes these conversations where available will be pouched.

In general Dept informed that Secy Lovett and each Service Secy promised de Lattre to look again into possibility of expediting delivery of supplies under 1951 program which is being delivered far behind de Lattre's current requirements. Similarly they assured Gen they wld attempt to expedite 1952 program. Among others, specific promise was given in instance of 1951 ground program that all of 4,500 wheeled vehicles wld be delivered by Jan 1952. This will involve certain agreed substitutions of types. Army promised to investigate FECOM stockpiles in effort locate available materiel and find additional supplies requested by him under the '52 program.

At conclusion Lovett interview Secy Defense said we regarded Gen de Lattre as comrade in arms and will do everything wihtin our capabilities to meet U.S. share of requirements for his theatre.

De Lattre did not, to our knowledge, discuss the question of a fiscal grant for general purposes including the maintenance of National armies. This subj touched upon in Schuman note (already transmitted) will probably be brought up against during and fol Oct NATO talks which will include further examination Fr Budgetary position. Nor did he raise question of SEA Theatre Command.

De Lattre's forceful personality has, without question, advanced awareness in Dept and Defense as well as U.S. public opinion of extreme importance of IC urgency of sit there. Dept of Defense re-examination of aid program will undoubtedly result in an accelerated flow of materiel.

Dept assured de Lattre that his political program was in complete consonance with Dept's estimate of what the actual situation required and we would continue to impress upon the Dept of Defense the desirability of re-examining the status of the supply program in keeping with our conviction that the defense of IC is essential to the defense of the balance of SEA.

Sent to AmLegation Saigon 442; repeat to AmEmbassy London for info 1696, AmEmbassy Paris for info 1818 (pass MacArthur).

(230) <u>TELEGRAM FROM BRUCE TO ACHESON</u>, October 10, 1951

Source: *Foreign Relations, 1951, Vol. VI*, pp. 528-530.

The financial burden of the Indochina war had serious implications not only for budgetary politics in France but for NATO politics as well. The diversion of resources to Indochina inevitably meant a smaller contribution to NATO, with adverse consequences for the acceptance of German rearmament in France. Discussing these ramifications of the War, Bruce warned that France might not be able to provide sufficient budgetary support to maintain the effort in Indochina.

2118. Toisa. Ref Deptel 2008, October 5.

1. Decision of Fr cab before departure of Mayer to Washington was to limit mil budget for Indochina to 350 billion francs in cal 1952. During past few years Fr Govt has repeatedly tried to use this ceiling device to compress Indochinese expenditures without much success. In each year the initial budgeting has been purposely optimistic and a deficiency appropriation has been obtained later in year when it is inevitably proved that active mil operations could not be compressed within ceiling. Our info is that Fr budget officials recognized that ceiling cab hoped to impose for '52 was not realistic.

Estimate of 430 billion francs presented in Washington in Schuman's note is that used by De Lattre's advisers. Since his return to Paris De Lattre has succeeded in reopening question of level of '52 mil budget for Indochina. He is strongly supported by Letourneau. Final decision by cab should be somewhere between 350 billion and 430 billion francs but it is not likely that such an agreement will be reached until first of next week when cab members will have returned from electioneering tasks.

2. Our understanding is that Fr still intend to seek supplementary aid through devices suggested by Guindey in September 13 meeting in Washington. Final details of presentation and components of aid to be requested also require further consideration at cab level. We have been promised additional info by end of this week.

3. Suggest you may wish to reply to sec II (C) of Fr note immediately by indicating that US is prepared to consider statment of assistance for Indochina in more specific terms during talks now scheduled for end of October. We believe it would be helpful for you to send interim reply to Fr note on balance of payments dated September 1, 1951 and forwarded in Embtel 1402. Our suggestion assumes you have made final decision to proceed with Oct talks here and that ISAC exercise to prepare answer to letter from Pres Truman will develop adequate estimates and instructions to permit us to negotiate usefully with Fr. We should at least be in position to promise some assistance on interim basis to try to avoid adverse repercussions on mil prog and polit situation which may arise from developing balance of payments difficulties. Some interim arrangement will probably be most desirable manner of proceeding because US should be able to take a firmer position on amount and nature of French mil effort for 52 after TCC has completed its exercise.

4. Emb and missions would like to see substantial part of any assistance to France earmarked as offset for support of Indochina mil operations or substantial assistance direct to Indochina. Ever-increasing Indochina burden is having effect not only of diminishing possible extent Fr effort in support her Eur def obligations but also affects Fr position on size of Ger contribution to Eur def and on occupation costs in Ger. A contribution in forces and finances from France to Eur def at least equal and preferably superior to that of Ger is in their view a polit necessity for agreement on Ger rearmament even within Eur army framework.

Prob becomes more difficult if Fr must now assume occupation costs for Fr troops in Ger and if Ger does not have naval forces. Fr finance officials do not fin complete answer in keeping Ger financial contribution small although this is their present position. They also want Ger to carry an equitable burden of def thereby avoiding a deterioration for France in French-Ger payments relations. Accordingly, they are seeking means to have Ger make financial contribution outside its contribution to Eur def either by continuing occupation costs, by a special payment for infrastructure, by a "burden-sharing" contribution, or by giving other Eur countries a credit for forces in being.

Personal view of most Fr officials in EDF conf is that France cannot receive occupation payments once EDF treaty is in force. They are, however, so anxious to see desired balancing of Fr and Ger contributions in EDF framework that they have even considered advisibility of having Ger continue to pay occupation costs to US and UK alone as offsetting margin outside EDF. Such an arrangement would of course by very difficult to have accepted in France.

Obviously French position would be better if Fr could reduce obligations outside Eur def. We must keep in mind, therefore possibility that with Fr realization of growing Ger def contribution in relation to their own polit and mil situation plus continued weakening of Fr franc Fr Govt may fail to continue furnishing sufficiently large mil budget for IC to enable it, even with our presently scheduled assistance, to maintain successfully IC mil operations. Result would be progressive deterioration Fr position, giving rise to renewed and perhaps increased pressures here for some kind of negotiated settlement with Ho Chi-minh.

Sent Dept prity 2118 reptd info London 522 Frankfort 240 Paris for OSR.

(231) <u>TELEGRAM FROM GULLION TO ACHESON</u>, October 15, 1951

Source: *Foreign Relations, 1951, Vol. VI*, pp. 532-534.

   *One of De Lattre's major public themes was that there could no longer be
any question of profit motivating French policy. In response to that claim,
Gullion documented the French control over the economic resources of Indochina
and termed French economic relations with Indochina a "transfer from French
taxpayers to other Frenchmen."*

   837. As reported in London tel 11, October 9 sent Dept 1744 Paris 674
[*673*][1] De Lattre once again indicated that, since Fr investment in IC totalled
only 2 billion dollars and since Fr was spending for IC war about 1 billion
annually obviously no profit motive in Fr determination remain in IC. HICOM
has made several similar public statements recently. Leg assumes these must
be for fon, particularly US, consumption. For excluding fract Fr mil expenditures IC 1951 more nearly 80 million than one million (Legdes 42, July 23)[2]
and that De Lattre presumably referring only private commercial and industrial
investments, fol factors prejudice simplicity this line reasoning.
   1. The 800 million dollars now being spent IC wld be spent on mil purposes
irrespective of whether there were or were not war IC, i.e., for defense western Eur rather than for defense IC. Fr taxpayers, provided Fr were to continue devote maximum possible of gross natl income to mil ends, wld not be required IC.
   2. Fr interests are not surrendering their econ positions in IC. They
still own: (*a*) All of Fr-IC and all of cabotage, shipping, (*b*) all important
public utilities, (*c*) all rubber plantations, (*d*) all banks except for two Brit
ones (*e*) all important import-export houses, (*f*) most of the coffee and tea
plantations, (*g*) concessions on almost all known mineral resources. (SCAP cannot assist Jap in exploiting new salt drying bed in Vietnam without entering
into arrangement with private Fr concessionaries, (*h*) all large-scale enterprises - textiles, breweries and distilleries, cement and glass works.
   3. Through Pau conventions Fr retained veto power over key econ fields of
fin policy and fon trade. This necessary as long as piaster tied to francs,
but no provision made for automatic removal this veto when IC economy again becomes self-sufficient. Almost all informed AS business and governmental circles
aware this situation and that of 2 above. Often refer obliquely but approvingly
to Iran's action re Brit oil interests.
   At same time IC economy is transferring piasters into francs on same basis
at annual rate $187 million. Latter payments include profits, dividends,
soldier and family remittances, insurance payments and other "fin operations".
Both figures exclude "commercial operations". It is true that this flow payments metropole tends shift inflationary pressures from IC to Fr, but at same
time it benefits private interests. Income mostly Fr because Fr control most
of IC's liquid wealth. It constitutes in large part transfer from Fr taxpayers
to other Frenchmen (legdes 598 March 30).
   Above comments are submitted with hope that, shld other data available to
Dept require correction in them, Leg may be instructed. They concern themselves
of course entirely with Gen's specific statement re Fr's econ position re war
in IC and make no attempt assess heavy and irreplaceable losses human life.
   Sent Dept 837, rptd info Paris 338, London unnumbered.

[1]Telegram 1744, October 9, reported on the visit of General de Lattre de
Tassigny to London, October 4-7, during which he expressed views on Indochina
similar to those he had delivered in Washington in September (751G.55./10-951).

(232) <u>ADDRESS BY RUSK, SEATTLE</u>, November 6, 1951 (Extract)

Source: *U.S.-Vietnam Relations, Book 9*, p. 459

Reflecting the absence of serious differences between the U.S. and France over the issue of French domination in Indochina, Rusk declared the issue of colonialism "well on its way to solution."

****

In Indo-China, the United States has taken a friendly interest in the efforts made to resolve points of difference between France and the Associated States and has vigorously supported the determination of France and of the Associated States to restore security and order in the country. Many Americans have been troubled in the past about the issue of colonialism in Indo-China. We believe that that question is well on the way to solution, that the peoples of the Associated States are free to assume the extensive responsibility for their own affairs that has been accorded them by treaties with France. It is not surprising that doubts remain in this point in Indo-China, among other countries of Asia, and among some heritage of bitterness and suspicion, those who have recently passed through a colonial experience are sensitive and distrustful of western influence, and the slowness with which the Associated States have been able to assume the responsibility which is awaiting them has not demonstrated the extent to which the issue of colonialism has been resolved. The real issue in Indo-China is whether the peoples of that land will be permitted to work out their future as they see fit or whether they will be subjected to a Communist reign of terror and be absorbed by force into the new colonialism of a Soviet Communist empire. In this situation, it is generally agreed in the United States that we should support and assist the armies of France and of the Associated States in meeting the armed threat in Indo-China and should furnish economic and technical assistance to the Associated States as they shoulder the heavy burdens of independence.

****

(233) <u>TELEGRAM FROM SPECIAL FAR EAST REPRESENTATIVE E.C.A., R. ALLEN GRIFFIN TO RICHARD M. BISSELL JR., ACTING ADMINISTRATOR, E.C.A.</u>, NOVEMBER, 1951

Source: *Foreign Relations, 1951, Vol. VI*, pp. 548-550.

After a visit to Indochina, R. Allen Griffin, who had been the Chief of the first official U.S. Mission to Southeast Asia on economic assistance, presented a radically different view of the Vietnam conflict. The primary weakness of the Huu government, he argued, was that it had no program for, and no interest in, improving the lives of the poverty-stricken peasant population. In the sharpest language used by any U.S. offficial about the government the U.S. was supporting, he called the Saigon regime "a relic of the past as much as French colonialism."

613. Dept pass ECA. To Bissell from Griffin.

1. US econ aid program Viet basically on right track for US objectives and should be contd as orig conceived. Those objectives remain sound and practical if new govt is to be supported in policies necessary to build loyalty and appreciation among population. However, I believe it is necessary for US clearly to realize the greatest impediment to success of US program and attainment objectives is nature of present Huu Govt, its lack of vitality and public leadership, its lack of enthusiasm for progressive progress that wld improve the gen welfare of peasants.

2. We are dealing with able land owners - mandarin type - functionaire govt. Its weakness is not that it is subordinate in many ways to Fr but that it is in no sense the servant of the people. It has no grass roots. It therefore has no appeal whatsoever to the masses. It evokes no popular support because nature of its leaders tends to an attitude that this wld be a "concession". This govt might reluctantly try to mollify public opinion, but it does not consist of men who wld lead public opinion. Therefore though France-Vietnam Armed Forces may cont to win small engagements for ltd objectives, no real progress is being made in winning war, which depends equally on polit solution.

3. It has been perhaps error in judgment in believing essential struggle has been between the constricting polit influence and pressure of Fr - which undoubtedly still exists and patriotic effort of Viets to win increasing degree of independence. Perhaps the essential struggle is one not undertaken - which is to get grass roots ability, conviction and patriotism on behalf of people of Viet into govt. So-call independence Huu Govt represents means nothing to masses. It simply means a change of functionaires, not a change of social direction, not a drive to advance lot of the people. Revolution will continue and Ho Chi-minh will remain popular hero, so long as "independence" leaders with Fr support are simply native mandarins who are succeeding foreign mandarins. The period of mandarin and functionaire govt in Asia is over. The present type of govt in Viet is a relic of the past as much as Fr colonialism.

4. I believe this predicament is now fully realized by Fr. There is little doubt of fact they know they are fighting war that cannot be won without a polit solution, and the polit solution depends at least as much upon the relationship of Govt of Viet with masses of people of Viet as upon the relationship with Fr on subj of independence. The issue in Viet, in my mind, is more than nationalism and Francophobia. It is old Asian issue that destroyed the Kuomintang in Chi, Communist opportunity to exploit insecurity, and hunger and wretchedness of masses of people to whom their govt has failed to make an effective appeal. The Huu Govt makes no such appeal. Its heart is not in that kind of appeal. If it talked land reform it wld never be believed. It is my opinion that Fr are now fully awake to this predicament. They realize that their interests are not being served by a Viet Govt that not only has no appeal to masses but that has no program and perhaps only doubtful sympathy for masses. Such condition will not help the Fr to extricate themselves from the milit burden. Nor will it help US to lessen the load of increasing costs the Fr require us to share. It is my opinion that we shld consider this problem jointly with the Fr, to the end that a govt with some grass roots instincts, intentions and social purpose may result.

5. It may be pointed out that US is now engaged in massive milit assistance in Indochina and an econ program of great potential social and polit impact. Fr are insisting on an even greater Amer participation in Fr costs of defending this semi-independent state. US has paid for right to exercise stronger voice in determination of policies. Fr failure to achieve satis polit results out of compliant, obedient landowners nonreform Cabinet may now make possible a practical and farsighted program for improving polit situation, which in itself awaits improvement of social outlook Viet Govt, a condition now obvious to Fr. I believe Fr are ready for that. If we fail to secure their collaboration for setting up a govt fitted for its job by something better than obedience to Fr, then one day we will discover that the Fr in disgust and discouragement will abandon their attempt to defend this flank of sea.

6. I have discussed this outlook with Heath but did not have time to draft cable before leaving Saigon.

Dept pass Saigon, Paris. Sent Dept 613, rptd info Saigon 20 for Heath (Saigon ECA for Wilkinson [*Williamson*]), Paris 3 Paris OSR for Porter).

(234) <u>TELEGRAM FROM HEATH TO ACHESON</u>, December 9, 1951.

Source: *Foreign Relations, 1951, Vol VI*, pp. 558-559.

In response to Griffin's analysis of the Saigon government, Heath noted that there were no leaders with popular support who would be willing to serve the French-sponsored regime.

1156. Re Singapore tels 618 and 621, Nov 30.

1. As Dept aware, I have for some time been concerned re inadequacies Huu Govt and I welcome Griffin corroborations. I am also pleased register my concurrence with his finding that present STEM programs fundamentally sound in this trying situation.

2. I am not sure, however, when Griffin speaks of govt with grass roots he means Cabinet nominated by present methods but including agrarian and popular leaders or whether he has in mind govt clothed with some popular mandate based on development forms of popular consultation. As to former, I doubt that much can be done at this time outside possible Catholic participation and acceptance of post by Tri, even this wld be limited advance since Catholics are minority sometimes suspected of too much western orientation and Tri, in entering govt, wld have to swallow disgrace and suppression his Dai Viet backers, who altho in sense "grass roots" have Asiatic fascistic, exotic, secret society aspects.

3. Fact is that no leaders with "grass roots" support presently known who wld join govt constituted on basis existing Franco-Viet relations and if there were such persons, doubtful if Fr wld accept them or that they wld be proof against Asiatic neutralism or Viet Minh infiltration. Fr know this which accounts for their quandary about replacement for Huu.

4, If by new govt Griffin means Cabinet emerging from some kind of popular suffrage, this difficult so long as polit life circumscribed by polit emergency. Time may be approaching for emergence parliamentary forms but it wld have been premature to force this development before beginning Natl Army, before armature govt machinery created at Pau, and before Fr adequately conditioned to idea they fighting in IC for something more than Fr supremacy. Process cannot be accelerated at cost threatening line of communications or weakening efficacy Fr forces. For example of process by which polit institutions may now be developed, I may cite interrelation of pacification, census, mobilization and elections: In pacified areas new census brings govt and people together in noncontroversial relationship; helps accustom masses to central govt hegemony; prepares mind for mobilization; conscription (in very limited form) further develops relationship; its admin establishes which are as amenable to govt auth, develops local govt machinery, helps provide security within which elections can eventually take place.

5. I believe it at least incomplete to imply that Fr appreciate predicament of govt as crisis of popular support which they never expected. Their criticisms govt have been directed almost exclusively to Huu, his misuse funds, concentration of Ministries, and alleged intriguing in France against De Lattre and Mar 8 framework.

6. Huu Govt has some solid accomplishments to its credit in addition to deficiencies accurately observed by Griffin. It has created beginnings Viet public admin, has improved security and public order, has survived first mobilization in country's history, and has made various plans for econ and social reforms. With respect to land reform, reftels do not credit efforts already

made by Huu Govt (see Legdesps 691 and 123 June 7 and Aug 31, 1951). Govt de-
crees now fol policy of letting displaced persons and squatters remain on liberated land, holds out hope of compensation landlords. Problem here not land redistribution so much as agrarian credit for acquisition land, financing crop,
shaking off usurer. Govt has plans which like all else here depend on increasing revenues. US econ aid might help rebuild farm credit institutions.

7. I entirely agree our aid entitles us to special role in IC and govt
performance can be improved by our representations to Viets and Fr. We can
ask or require Viets to produce budget, increase govt revenues, curb graft,
fol through on land reform, and display more energy. Our approach can be coordinated with Fr on all these matters. We may also wish ask Fr for measures
to curb IC disinvestment, to admit Viets to greater measure ownership their
cops, to increase area polit liberties, and to accelerate native command staff-
ing natl armies. Entire process must be worked out among three of us with
patience and forbearance.

8. Re De Lattre's alleged anti-Americanism, Dept and Leg aware Gen's
irascibilities which spring perhaps in part from his immense concern for Amer
opinion and support. Infinite tolerance required and justified in view of contributions De Lattre has made and can still make. Leg has not and will not refrain from demanding proper treatment for Amers and recognition our position in
IC. His trip to Washington has resulted in De Lattre's better understanding
our programs and intentions. I believe we now have measure Gen's fears and
misapprehensions and that we need not be too worried about them.

Sent Dept 1156, rptd info Bangkok for Griffin 46, Paris unn.

---

(235) MEMORANDUM BY ACTING ASSISTANT SECRETARY OF STATE FOR FAR EASTERN
AFFAIRS, JOHN M. ALLISON TO ACHESON, December 19, 1951

Source: *Foreign Relations, 1951, Vol. 1*, pp. 562-3.

*While heavy fighting continued in Tonkin, the concern of the U.S. govern-
ment was still focused on China. The Acting Assistant Secretary noted indications of an imminent invasion of Viet-nam by Chinese troops, even pinpointing
December 28 as the approximate date of the invasion. He urged an immediate
staff study on what the U.S. might do in the event of such an invasion. Such a
study was ordered by the N.S.C. that same day, but the invasion never occurred,
nor is there any evidence that one was ever contemplated by the P.R.C.*

In view of the ominous character of intelligence reports concerning a
Chinese preparation for massive intervention in Indochina, it is suggested you
may wish to make some brief reference to the Indochina situation at the meeting
of the National Security Council on December 19.

In this connection you might say that intelligence reports emanating from
Taipei, Hong Kong, Bangkok, Hanoi and Saigon would indicate that the Chinese
Communist capability of effecting a massive intervention in Indochina and perhaps Burma has increased significantly. It is reported that there are at present some 200,000 Chinese Communist troops in Kwansi province prepared to move
on Indochina as "volunteers"; that the volume of materiel assistance from Red
China to the Vietminh has increased; and that rail and road communications between Kwansi province and Tonkin have been put in good working order. The
consensus of intelligence reporting would indicate that action on a large scale
against French Union and Vietnam forces in Tonkin may be expected on or about
the 28th of December. Embassy Paris, meanwhile, reports that Messrs. Pleven
and Monnet have expressed to our Ambassador grave doubts as to the ability of
the French to continue the war in Indochina unless further assistance from the
United States is immediately forthcoming. We have asked Embassy Paris's opin-

ion as to the unpleasant possibility, which we have long feared, that the French may be preparing to withdraw from Indochina.

It is therefore suggested that the NSC direct, as a matter of urgency, that a staff study be prepared with a view to determining what action this government can take in the event of Chinese Communist support on a large scale of the Vietminh forces either overtly or by means of "volunteers".[1]

[1]Action 597, taken by the National Security Council at its 110th Meeting, December 19, indicates that the Council discussed the situation in Indochina in light of possible Chinese Communist intervention, and, at the suggestion of the Secretary of State, directed its Senior Staff to expedite preparation of a report on U.S. policy toward Southeast Asia, with particular reference to possible courses of action regarding Indochina (S/S Files: Lot 62D1).

(236) TELEGRAM FROM BRUCE TO ACHESON, December 22, 1951

Source: *Foreign Relations, 1951, Vol. VI*, pp. 571-572.

Citing intelligence data on the likelihood of Chinese direct intervention in Vietnam, French Prime Minister Pleven, in a note to Acheson, again pressed for tripartite talks to discuss common action. Acheson brought Pleven's note to the personal attention of President Truman one week later.

3765. Personal attention Secretary. Ref my immediately preceding cable. Informal translation Pleven note follows:

"Prime Minister French Govt calls attention of US Govt to fact that possibility of Chi intervention in Indochina appears to be becoming more definite.

Analysis of entirety intelligence reports concerning South China and assistance given Viet Minh by Mao Tse-Tung Govt gives fol results:

Effectives of Chi forces stationed southern provinces bordering on Tonkin have increased in last six months from 170, 000 to 290,000 men.

South China communications network and particularly roads leading to Tonkin border being constantly reconditioned and already much improved in correlation this improvement of South China rail and road system, highways in Viet Minh area of North Tonkin are being reconditioned. For instance Kunming-Yen Bay road now open to traffic.

Lastly, Chi materiel aid to Viet Minh has vastly increased over last three months. During recent operations French has ascertained that great part captured equipment was of US origin and have seized arms dated 1950 which apparently are part war booty Chi troops in Korea.

Furthermore, analysis of Chi press over last few weeks shows that emphasis once more place on struggle of Viet Minh against French Union forces Indochina.

Quite clear that while Franco-Viet forces are successfully standing up to Viet Minh activities, nonetheless true that former do not possess strategic reserves ("masse de manoeuvre") necessary to oppose Chi attack.

Consequently French Govt considers it of utmost importance that conversations which were to take place between US, UK and French following recommendations of Singapore conference commence immediately. It desires that this wish be brought to personal attention of President Truman."

Dept pass Saigon, sent Dept 3765, rptd info London 1005, Saigon 215.

(237) TELEGRAM FROM BRUCE TO ACHESON, December 26, 1951

Source: *Foreign Relations, 1951, Vol. VI*, pp. 573-578.

Bruce warned that French policy in Indochina was rapidly reaching the point where a fundamental reexamination would be unavoidable, and that the U.S. might be asked both to step up its assistance dramatically and make certain defense commitments with regard to Indochina. The alternative, he said, would probably be overwhelming sentiment in France for withdrawal.

3796. Deptel 3563, Dec. 18.

1. In light of domestic official and public opinion Fr policy in regard to Indochina war is rapidly moving toward a crisis. Two years ago no Fr govt wld have survived a proposal that Indochina be voluntarily abandoned. Today Emb feeling is that while such a decision wld be generally greeted by Fr public with a sense of emotional relief, yet we do not believe that Fr govt for variety of reasons wld propose such a course of action in the near future. Majority of Fr wld probably agree that France cannot continue this burden even at present tempo for more than another few months. Increasing awareness of expenditure and mil casualty figures is everywhere apparent. There is almost universal recognition that the metropole's security is adversely affected in an increasing degree by this distant adventure in an area which will never again be an asset to France.

2. Among considerations which wld cause Fr Govt to avoid for as long as possible any proposal much less decision to withdraw voluntarily from Indochina except under circumstances of forced mil evacuation are:

a. Admission of failure of policy which has cost so much in men and money;
b. Humiliation of natl pride and loss of prestige abroad;
c. Logistical problem of evacuating under mil and guerrrilla pressure Fr Union troops, Fr civilians and such loyal Vietnmaese as practical to include in such evacuation;
d. Almost certain massacre or oppression of incalculable number of Fr Union nationals left behind;
e. Voluntary nature of act which wld strike at very roots of Fr Union concept and particularly constitutional commitment (Art 62) to defend union, with inevitable repercussions of gravest sort in rest of union, particularly Fr North Africa;
f. Terrific impetus to Commie prestige and propaganda both in France and Fr overseas territories. Parliamentary reactions to balancing above considerations against those in favor of withdrawal are so unpredictable as to cause grave crisis whether govt emerged intact or not. (In this connection, as well as for gen background purposes, Dept may care to review Embets 4633 Dec 1, 1949, 620 Feb 7, 746 Feb 16, 837 Feb. 23 [22], 840 Feb 22, and 860, Feb. 23, 1950).

3. Gaullists would certainly at this time reject abandonment thesis. Rank and file of Socialist Party wld probably prefer some internatl disposition of problem, but Socialist leaders have thus far generally supported present govt position altho many individual Socialists have always favored withdrawal. Mendes-France (Radical-Socialist) for some time represented voice in wilderness, but his thesis of complete abandonment is obviously one that has gained increasing number of adherents. Monnet says that Fr cannot make her proper contribution to defense in the west while supporting any major mil establishment in Indochina. Under existing circumstance she favors complete withdrawal regardless of consequence. Devinat (influential Radical-Scoialist and former min) has told us in effect: "We cannot continue in IC as at present. Mendes-France is absolutely right and there is no escaping his logic. The only question is how and when the change be made to one of the three fol courses of action: *(a)* problem to be internationalized; *(b)* France to receive massive additional financial aid and US equipment and troops; *(c)* France to pull out". Raymond Aron

is also pessimistic about continuance effort there that he has refrained from publishing his views.

4. Difficulties of prob confronting Fr in its effort to rearm in Eur while maintaining Fr Union forces in Indochina are causing increasing uneasiness, which is reflected in many ways. Editorial and other newspaper comment on this subject is widespread (Newspaper comment embodied in a fol tel). One consideration which plays part in present thinking is possibility successful conclusion Korean armistice negots which Fr believe might unleash Chi Commie troops for use against Indochina.

5. While campaign of press comment re Indochina may in some cases spring from special inspirations, it nonetheless both reflects and encourages popular reaction and govt uneasiness North African and metropolitan forces have been depleted to meet Fr needs in Indochina. Govt has frequently pointed out that Fr officers and non-commissioned officers presently in Indochina are sufficient to form cadre for ten divisions in Eur. Budgetary aspects of problem in terms of Fr expenditures in Indochina have previously been reported in detail in Embtels and will be discussed further in separate cable.

6. As indicated in increasing volume of press comment, and in conversations we have had with various govts, polit and newspaper personalities, Fr public has come to point where it considers, as has long been govt's position repeatedly presented to Wash, that Fr effort in Indochina represents no longer purely natl interest and responsibility, but rather interests of all free nations. While realizing importance of present US assistance in Indochina, they think that question shld be squarely faced by all whether Indochina operations shld not be considered part of western effort rather than primarily Fr responsibility.

7. Fr govt also apparently sees no end in sight to hostilities in Indochina. Perhaps particularly for that reason we have statement such as Pleven made to Natl Assembly Nov 16 re possibility contacts with China, and ref in communique issued at conclusion High Council Fr Union Nov 30 re possibility internatl conf for purpose ending fon intervention SEA.

8. It is quite obvious that the nature of the struggle in Indochina has radically altered during the past two years. The Fr effort immed after the liberation was designed purely to protect France's empire, and public and private interests in Indochina. With the overthrow of Chiang Kai-shek and the increasing assistance with which the Chi have been furnishing the VM in both training and materials, the war has taken on the aspects of a struggle against the expansion of Commie imperialism. The VM has been converted from a largely nationalistic group to a completely Commie dominated mil and terroristic organization of growing resources and possibilities.

9. Altho, thanks largely to Fr initiative, some progress has been made, the polit sitn in Vietnam continues unsatisfactory. Fr has granted the Assoc States a very considerable measure of autonomy - probably more than they are able to handle. A beginning has been made in the creation of a Natl Viet Army. Yet it seems quite clear that there has not yet been created an anti-Commie nationalist native force which is able alone to meet the VM successfully, even in local engagements. A withdrawal of the Fr Union forces either now or within the next two years wld produce a definitive collapse of the present Assoc States polit organization and its replacement by a Commie state. Very large numbers of influential natives are on the fence. There is, on our side of the fence, a minimum of native politico-mil dynamism.

10. Altho Gen De Lattre has stated that in the absence of an invasion by large forces of Chinese volunteers or regulars he can clean sitn up in 12 to 18

months. I believe this is whistling in the wind. As long as the Viet-Minh continue to be trained, reformed, supplied and able to seek sanctuary in China, no annihilation of VM forces seems possible.

11. The Fr Union army has already lost 35,000 killed, of whom 800 deaths, as of July 4, 1951, represented St Cyr graudates. About two-thirds of their most competent non-coms and perhaps one-half of their officers are stationed there, as well as the cream in quality and the preponderance in quantity of their professional troops.

12. Altho Fr have complained bitterly of delays in materiel shipments to Indochina, De Lattre has recognized that had it not been for US contributions of those and items which have been delivered, Fr cld not have contained some of VM attacks in 1951. If Chi shld enter conflict only with jets they cld sweep Fr Air Force as now equipped from the skies. Fr ascribe much of their success this year to unchallenged air operations.

13. The Fr and the Brit are urging us to hold staff conversations on the stin in SEA. Pleven's note (Embtel 3765, Dec 22) last Saturday again raised this issue. We will be hearing from Churchill on same subj next month. There is no doubt that the most satisfactory result of these conversations from the Fr point of view wld be the recognition of the internatl character of the Indochina war and the resultant decision that the burden being borne by France shld be shared by others to a greater degree than at present. While a commitment of Amer armed forces under present conditions has never yet been officially requested by the Fr, they have already urged us to make greater contributions in money and materials.

14. We may soon be presented with a definite either/or situation: Either we increase our present aid to Indochina to a very considerable extent and make certain definite commitments as to what we will do in the event of a Chi invasion, or the Fr will be compelled to re-examine their entire policy in the area.

15. The issue is not entirely or even primarily whether the Fr will continue their effort at the now existing level. The present level will not be high enough if, even without an actual invasion, the Chi further step up their assistance to the VM. The Fr are becoming increasingly sensitive to the possibility of a sitn in which the Fr govt might be confronted either with the necessity for rapid withdrawal or a military disaster. In the circumstances we must decide whether we wish to go much further than we have heretofore in the direction of a multilateral approach to the problem.

16. If we agree in principle to a multilateral approach, it wld seem that we must immed engage in tripartite conversations, not only at the mil but also at the polit level. Amongst other considerations, we might, for instance, wish to reach a tripartite decision as to the accuracy of present Fr estimates of the mil and polit sitn, and the wisdom of existing plans to deal with them.

17. To conclude, I believe that the snowball has started to form, and public sentiment for withdrawal, in the absence of adoption of some course of action envisaging either internationalization of Indochina problem or Fr receipt of massive additional aid, will gain steadily and perhaps at accelerated rate. It wld be incorrect to assume that Fr Govt is trying merely to horse trade or bargain with US. It is responding slowly and unwillingly to pressures far stronger than party positions. Consequently, Emb recommends that US reexamine problem in the light of these changing circumstances prior to a final precipitation of these mixed elements in order avoid risk of a sitn threatening

the security of all SEA and entailing grave polit and mil repercussions elsewhere.

Dept pass Saigon; sent Dept 3796, rptd info Saigon 220, London unnumbered.

[1]In telegram 3606, December 17, Ambassador Bruce reported on discussions
with Premier Pleven concerning the French military budget. Pleven had said
that he could not see how France could satisfy its obligations under the North
Atlantic Treaty Organization and its commitments in Indochina within the budgetary resources available to it. Bruce further reported that Pleven "felt
that despite his many efforts and those of other French visitors to US to explain magnitude of problems involved in Indochinese war that they had been
unsuccessful in convincing our officials of tragic situation, financially and
other-wise, in which France found itself because of this operation. Indeed,
the situation was becoming even more serious. In one day last week French
Union Forces had lost 1000 men and had expended six weeks' ammunition in an
engagement that had lasted only three days. Very same Viet Minh regiments
which had been badly mauled a few months ago had again appeared, brought up to
full strength, completely equipped, well-officered, and in good fighting spirit.
Undoubtedly this indicated a replenishment of troops, possibly including Chinese, and certainly furnishing by Chinese Communists of full equipment replacements. Current intelligence reports from Indochina indicate that Chinese Commies are preparing for greater and more active participation in thar area."
Moreover, Pleven had stated that Jean Monnet, Commissioner General of the
French National Planning Commission and a leading proponent of Western European
cooperation, had become convinced that the drain imposed on France by the war
in Indochina precluded an adequate defense posture in Europe. (740.5/12-1751)
The Full text of telegram 3606 is scheduled for publication in volume IV
[*Foreign Relations, 1951*].
In telegram 3563, December 18, the Department of State requested the Em-
bassy's evaluation of this apparent growing movement within the French Government to consider withdrawal from Indochina (740.5/12-1751).

[2]The French National Assembly debated the Indochina question on December 28
and 29 in the course of consideration of military credits for the Associated
States. Premier Pleven and Minister for the Associated States Letourneau delivered statements defending the position of the government. However, former
Premier Edouard Daladier urged that the issue of the war be placed before the
United Nations with a view to obtaining a cease-fire and an internationally
supervised plebiscite. The National Assembly endorsed exisitng government
policy on December 29 by approving the military credits by a vote of 510 to
109. Only the Communist members were in opposition. For the record of these
deliberations, see France, *Journal Officiel, Assemblee Nationale, 1951, Debats,*
10048-10116, *passim.*

(238) <u>NOTE FROM HEATH TO PREMIER TRAN VAN HUU</u>, December 27, 1951

Source: *Foreign Relations, 1951, Vol. VI*, pp. 578-579.

*In an extraordinary intervention in the internal affairs of the State of
Viet-nam, Heath handed a note to the Premier which urged him to prepare a budget and name a full-time Defense Minister.*

"I have the honor to refer to our conversation of Nov 9, 1951, at which
time I expressed to you the concern of the US Govt at the lack of a budget for
the state of Vietnam. Under instrs from the US Govt I now wish to confirm
these views. In the absence of a budget, it is very difficult for the US Govt
adequately to assess the amt of econ and milit aid which it ought to supply, to

know to which fields its efforts ought to be addressed, or to measure the efficacy of its assistance. In the near future the US exec depts will be required to present their plans for regular and supplementary econ and milt aid programs for Vietnam to the reviewing agencies and to the US Cong. Without a budget the task of justifying these aid programs to the office of the Pres (Bureau of the Budget) and to the Cong is rendered much more difficult

"Altho the US Govt and the Leg are well aware of the many heavy and peculiar difficulties confronting the Viets Govt, partly growing out of the recent transfer of powers and wartime conditions, it nevertheless hopes that the Viet Govt will find it possible to complete its budget preparation and to publish a budget in due form in the near future.

"You will also recall that you have from time to time been good enough to discuss with me your efforts to constitute the Ministry of Def as effectively and as soon as possible. The US Govt shares your concern, especially since its contemplated aid programs are increasingly directed to the equipping of the Viets Natl Army. I have had many occasions to appreciate your own great contributions to the creation of the army and to the planning for its admin, and I have wondered that you have been able to do so much while carrying on your other heavy duties. It is my understanding, however, that for some time the possibility of designating an outstanding full-time Min of Def to carry on with the work inaugurated by you has been under consideration. My govt ventures to hop that in the interest of more effective use of US milit aid such an appointment can soon be made.

"I look forward to receiving your views on these subjs and I shall be pleased to communicate them to my govt.

"I shld like to take this opportunity to express my pleasure at your return to your high post after the important first mtg of the High Council of the Fr Union. I shld like also to congratulate you upon the valorous conduct of the Natl Army of Vietnam in its inital trials and to renew my wishes for its continued success and that of the Govt of His Majesty Bao Dai.

"Pls accept. etc.

1952

(239) <u>TELEGRAM FROM ACHESON TO THE LEGATION IN SAIGON</u>, January 15, 1952

Source: *U.S.-Vietnam Relations, Book 8*, pp. 465-467.

The Tripartite military discussions on Southeast Asia requested by the French were held in Washington January 11, 1952. The U.S. and Britain both resisted French urging for a commitment of military intervention in the event of a Chinese invasion but agreed to recommend to their governments communication to China of a threat of retaliation "not necessarily limited to the area of aggression."

Tripartite MIL conversations held Washington JAN 11 concerning defense SFA were convened through direct NEGOTS between three Chiefs of Staff. Only at last moment were single REPS of each FONOFF permitted to be present as observers. DEPT had no opportunity contribute to agenda nor formally participate in discussions. Nevertheless LEG TELS concerning this SUBJ were and are most helpful.

Part one of agenda entitled "Exchange of Views with Respect to Southeast Asia" consists of two PTS.

1. Problems of SEA in light of world wide implications of situation, and
2. Defense SEA including action in event of deterioration of situation.

Part two concerned recommendations of Singapore Conference.

Summary of discussions covering both Parts has been given to BARTLETT for transmittal to LEG. He is expected to arrive Saigon APPROX JAN 26.

FOL is brief summary of discussions on Part one.

1. GEN Bradley advised GEN Juin that he was unable to commit his GOVT at this time as to extent and character of US MIL assistance in event of massive CHI intervention. This SUBJ being considered at highest official level as matter of urgency. Field Marshal Slim concurred. Juin appealed for US and UK dispatch of air and naval support if not ground forces. Air cover necessary to allow his forces to retire on Haiphong.

2. Juin stated, under INSTPS from his GOVT, that FOL massive CHI intervention FR Union forces WLD retire to Haiphong and fight to last man. Air cover needed for this operation while naval assistance needed in evacuating 50,000 FR and Indochinese civilians. Juin stated that if Haiphong held, invasion of IC difficult or impossible.

3. Three Chiefs agreed to recommend to their GOVTS the transmittal of a declaration to Red China that aggression against SEA WLD bring certain retaliation from the three powers, not necessarily limited to the area of aggression. An AD HOC COMITE of REPS of the three powers plus AUSTRAL and NZ

was appointed to study and report urgently on the measures the five GOVTS might take singly or jointly in event Red China failed heed warning. Above two steps resulted from mutual recognition that present problems consist of (1) discouragement against aggression and (2) retaliation.

4. All agreed that CHI aggression against SEA might well mean war with China.

5. Neither the recommendation as to proposed declaration nor the report of AD HOC COMITE have been recd by DEPT.

6. It SHLD be noted that the language of proposed declaration must still be approved by each of the five GOVTS concerned as well as joint agreement reached concerning method and timing of transmittal to Red China. Likewise, the recommendations of AD HOC COMITE which WLD presumably be of very broad nature WLD necessarily influence course of action of the five GOVTS with respect to transmittal proposed declaration.

Bartlett has been fully briefed and LEG will be informed of developments as they occur.

(240) NSC STAFF STUDY, "U.S. OBJECTIVES AND COURSES OF ACTION WITH RESPECT TO COMMUNIST AGGRESSION IN SOUTHEAST ASIA," February 13, 1952

Source: Document declassified by NSC, March 3, 1976.

A senior staff study annexed to NSC 124 rejected any negotiated settlement by the French with the Communists which would involve withdrawal of French forces, given the weakness of the French-sponsored governments and the "dubious attitudes of the population even in areas under French control." It recommended that the U.S. oppose any French move to withdraw and consider measures which it could take, along with other nations, to prevent Communist victory, without specifying what measures would be recommended. In the event of a Chinese intervention, either overt or covert, it called for "appropriate military actions against Communist China" under UN auspices if possible, but as part of a collective international action in any case.

THE PROBLEM

1. To determine the policy of the United States toward the countries of Southeast Asia, and in particular, the courses of action which may be taken by the United States to strengthen and coordinate resistance to communism on the part of the governments and peoples of the area, to prevent Chinese Communist aggression, and to meet such aggression should it occur.

ANALYSIS

I. CONSEQUENCES TO THE UNITED STATES OF COMMUNIST DOMINATION OF SOUTHEAST ASIA

2. Communist domination of Southeast Asia, whether by means of overt invasion, subversion, or accommodation on the part of the indigenous governments, would be critical to United States security interests. Communist success in this area would spread doubt and fear among other threatened non-communist countries as to the ability of the United States and the United Nations to halt communist aggression elsewhere. It would strengthen the claim that the advance of communism is inexorable and encourage countries vulnerable to Soviet pressure to adopt policies of neutralism or accommodation. Successful overt Chinese Communist aggression in this area, especially if achieved without encountering more than token resistance on the part of the United

States of the United Nations, would have critical psychological and political consequences which would probably include the relatively swift alignment of the rest of Asia and thereafter or the Middle East to communism, thereby endangering the stability and security of Europe. Such a communist success might nullify the psychological advantages accruing to the free world by reason of its response to the aggression in Korea.

3. The fall of Southeast Asia would underline the apparent economic advantages to Japan of association with the communist-dominated Asian sphere. Exclusion of Japan from trade with Southeast Asia would seriously affect the Japanese economy, and increase Japan's dependence on United States aid. In the long run the loss of Southeast Asia, especially Malaya and Indonesia, could result in such economic and political pressures in Japan as to make it extremely difficult to prevent Japan's eventual accommodation to the Soviet Bloc.

4. Southeast Asia, especially Malaya and Indonesia, is the principal world source of natural rubber and tin. Access to these materials by the Western Powers and their denial to the Soviet Bloc is important at all times and particularly in the event of global war. Communist control over the rice surpluses of the Southeast Asian mainland would provide the USSR with a powerful economic weapon in its relations with other countries of the Far East. Indonesia is a secondary source of petroleum whose importance would be enhanced by the denial to the Western Powers of petroleum sources in the Middle East. Malaya is the largest net dollar earner for the United Kingdom, and its loss would seriously aggravate the economic problems facing the UK.

5. Communist control of all of Southeast Asia would render the United States position in the Pacific offshore island chain precarious and would seriously jeopardize fundamental United States security interests in the Far East. The extension of communist power via Burma would augment the communist threat to India and Pakistan and strengthen the groups within those countries which favor accommodation. However, such an event would probably result in a stiffer attitude toward communism on the part of the Indian government.

6. Communist domination of mainland Southeast Asia would place unfriendly forces astride the most direct and best-developed sea and air routes between the Western Pacific and India and the Near East. In the event of global war, the development of Soviet submarine and air bases in mainland Southeast Asia might compel the detour of U.S. and allied shipping and air transportation in the Southeast Asia region via considerably longer alternate routes to the south. This extension of friendly lines of communication would hamper U.S. strategic movements in this region and tend to isolate the major non-communist bases in the Far East - the offshore island chain and Australia - from existing bases in East Africa and the Near and Middle East, as well as from potential bases on the Indian sub-continent.

7. Besides disrupting established lines of communication in the area, the denial of actual military facilities in mainland Southeast Asia - in particular, the loss of the major naval operating bases at Singapore - would compel the utilization of less desirable peripheral bases. Soviet exploitation of the naval and air bases in mainland Southeast Asia probably would be limited by the difficulties of logistic support but would, nevertheless, increase the threat to existing lines of communication.

II. REGIONAL STRATEGY

8. The continued integrity of the individual countries of Southeast Asia is to a large extent dependent upon a successful coordination of political and military measures for the entire area. The development of practical mea-

sures aimed at preventing the absorption of these countries into the Soviet orbit must therefore recognize this interdependence and must, in general, seek
course of action for the area as a whole.

9. However, it must be recognized that the governments and peoples of
Southeast Asia have little in common other than their geographic proximity and
their newly awakened nationalism and anti-colonialism. For the most part,
their economies are competitive rather than complementary. The countries are
divided internally and from each other by language and ethnic differences. The
several nationalities and tribal groups are the heirs of centuries of warfare,
jealousy, and mutual distrust. In addition, their present governments are
sharply divided in their attitudes toward the current East-West struggle. The
governments of the three Associated States of Indochina are not recognized by
any other Asian states except Nationalist China and Thailand.

10. In the strategic sense, the defense of Tonkin is important to the
defense of mainland Southeast Asia. If Communist forces should succeed in
driving the French Union forces from Tonkin, military action in the remainder
of Indochina might have to be limited to delaying action and the perimeter defense of certain coastal areas pending reinforcement or evacuation. With the
appearance of communist success, native support would probably swing increasingly to the Viet Minh.

11. Thailand has no common border with China and no strong internal
communist element. It adjoins areas of Indochina now controlled by the Viet
Minh, but the border areas are remote and difficult. Hence, communist seizure
of Thailand is improbable except as a result of the prior loss of either Burma
or Indochina.

12. Communist control of either Indochina or Burma would expose Thailand
to infiltration and severe political pressures, as well as to the threat of direct attack. Unless substantial outside aid were forthcoming, it is possible
that in such a case, political pressure alone would be sufficient to bring
about the accommodation of Thailand to international communism within a year.
However, substantial aid, together with assurance of support by the United
States and the UN might be sufficient to preserve a non-communist government in
Thailand in spite of any form of pressure short of overt attack.

13. Thailand would be difficult to defend against an overt attack from
the east by way of the traditional invasion route through Cambodia. Thailand
is more defensible against attack from Burma owing to the moutainous terrain
and poor communications of the Thai-Burmese border. In either case it might be
possible to defend an area in southern Thailand centering on Bangkok. Since
any attack on Thailand would necessarily be preceded by communist encroachment
on Indochina or Burma, the defense of Thailand would probably be part of a
broader pattern of hostilities.

14. If the loss of Thailand followed the loss of Burma, the defense of
Indochina would be out-flanked; and any substantial communist forces based on
Thailand would render the position of the French Union Forces in Indochina untenable in the long run. If the collapse of Thailand followed the loss of Indochina, the psychological and political consequences would accelerate the deterioration of Burma. However, the military consequences in such a case would
be less immediate, owing to the difficult terrain of the Thai-Burmese border
country.

15. Communist control of Thailand would aggravate the already serious
security problem presented by the Thai-Malayan border and greatly increase the
difficulties of the British security forces in Malaya. However, assuming control of the sea by the Western Powers, Malaya offers a defensible position
against even a full-scale land attack. The Kra Isthmus of the Malayan Penin-

sula would afford the best secondary line of defense against total communist domination of Southeast Asia and the East Indies. Such a defense would effectively protect Indonesia against external communist pressure. By thus defending Malaya and Indonesia, the anti-communist forces would continue to hold the most important strategic material resources of the area, as well as strategic air and naval bases and lines of communication.

16. The strategic interdependence of the countries in Southeast Asia, and the cumulative effect of a successful communist penetration in any one area, point to the importance of action designed to forestall any aggression by the Chinese Communists. The most effective possible deterrent would be a joint warning by the United States and certain other governments regarding the grave consequences of Chinese aggression against Southeast Asia, and implying the threat of retaliation against Communist China itself. Such a warning should be issued in conjunction with other nations, including at least the United Kingdom, France, Australia and New Zealand. Participation in such a warning involves all the risks and disadvantages of a precommitment to take action in future and unknown circumstances. However, these disadvantages must be weighed against the alternative of a costly effort to repel Chinese invasion after it has actually occurred. A second, but probably less effective, means of attempting to deter such an invasion would be to focus world attention on the continuing threat of Chinese Communist aggression against Southeast Asia and to make clear to the Soviet and Chinese Communist Governments the fact that the United States views the situation in Southeast Asia with great concern. In fact, statements along these lines have already been made. Such means might also include a Peace Observation Commission, if desired and requested by the countries concerned, public addresses by U.S. officials, and "show the flag" visits by naval and air units.

17. The Chinese Nationalist forces represent considerable reserve upon which to draw in the event of military action against Communist China. The deficiency in equipment and training seriously limits the possible employment of these forces at present, however, continuation of our training and supply efforts should serve to alleviate these deficiencies. The manner of employment of these forces is beset not only with military but also with political difficulties. Hence the decision as to the best use of these forces cannot be made at this time. Nevertheless, we should be prepared to make the best practicable use of this military augmentation in light of the circumstances existing at the time.

III. <u>INDOCHINA</u>

18. In the long run, the security of Indochina against communism will depend upon the development of native governments able to command the support of the masses of the people and national armed forces capable of relieving the French of the major burden of maintaining internal security. Some progress is being made in the formation and development of national armies. However, the Vietnamese Government has been slow to assume its responsibilities and has continued to suffer from a lack of strong leadership. It has had to contend with: (a) lingering Vietnamese suspicion of any French-supported regime, combined with the apathetic and "fence sitting" attitude of the bulk of the people; (b) the difficulty, common to all new and inexperienced governments, of training the necessary personnel and building an efficient administration; and (c) the failure of factional and sectional groups to unite in a concerted national effort.

19. The U.S. economic aid program for Indochina has as its objectives to increase production and thereby offset the military drain on the economy of the Associated States; to increase popular support for the Government by improving the effectiveness of Government services; to make the Government and the

people aware of America's interest in their independence and welfare; and to use economic aid as a means of supporting the military effort. Because of their strained budgetary situation, the Associated States cannot meet the local currency costs of the projects; about 60 percent of the program funds is, therefore, devoted to importing needed commodities which are sold to generate counterpart.

20. The military situation in Indochina continues to be one of stalemate. Increased U.S. aid to the Franco-Vietnamese forces has been an essential factor in enabling them to withstand recent communist attacks. However, Chinese aid to the Viet Minh in the form of logistic support, training, and technical advisors is increasing at least at a comparable rate. The prospect is for a continuation of the present stalemate in the absence of intervention by important forces other than those presently engaged.

21. While it is unlikely under the present circumstances that the French will suffer a military defeat in Indochina, there is a distinct possibility that the French Government will soon conclude that France cannot continue indefinitely to carry the burden of her total military commitments. From the French point of view, the possible means of lessening the present burden include: (1) a settlement with the communists in Indochina; (2) an agreement to internationalize the action in Indochina; (3) reduction of the NATO obligations of France.

22. A settlement based on a military armistice would be more complicated in Indochina than in the case of Korea. Much of Indochina is not firmly under the control of either side, but subject to occasional forays from both. Areas controlled by the opposing sides are interspersed, and lines of contact are fluid. Because of the weakness of the native governments, the dubious attitudes of the population even in areas under French control, and the certainty of continued communist pressure, it is highly probable that any settlement based on a withdrawal of French forces would be tantamount to handing over Indochina to communism. The United States should therefore continue to oppose any negotiated settlement with the Viet Minh.

23. In the event that information and circumstances point to the conclusion that France is no longer prepared to carry the burden in Indochina, or if France presses for a sharing of the responsibility for Indochina, whether in the UN or directly with the U.S. Government, the United States should oppose a French withdrawal and consult with the French and British concerning further measures to be taken to safeguard the area from communist domination. In anticipation of these possiblities, the United States should urgently re-examine the situation with a view to determining:

a. Whether U.S. participation in an international undertaking would be warranted.
b. The general nature of the contributions which the United States, with other friendly governments, might be prepared to make.

24. A cessation of hostilities in Korea would greatly increase the logistical capability of the Chinese Communists to support military operations in Indochina. A Korean peace would have an even more decisive effect in increasing Chinese air capabilities in that area. Recent intelligence reports indicate increased Chinese Communist military activity in the Indochinese border area. If the Chinese Communists directly intervene with large forces over and above those introduced as individuals or in small units, the French would probably be driven back to a beachhead around Haiphong. The French should be able to hold this beachhead for only a limited time at best in the absence of timely and substantial outside support.

25. In view of the world-wide reaction to overt aggression in Korea, Communist China may prefer to repeat in Indochina the method of "volunteer" intervention. Inasmuch as the French do not control the border between China and Indochina nor large areas north of Hanoi, it may be difficult to detect the extent of preparation for such intervention. It is important to U.S. security interests to maintain the closest possible consultation with the French Government on the buildup of Chinese Communist intervention in Indochina. The Government of France has agreed to consult with the United States before it requests UN or other international action to oppose Chinese Communist aggression in Indochina in order that the two countries may jointly evaluate the extent of Chinese Communist intervention.

26. If it is thus determined that Chinese Communist forces (including volunteers) have overtly intervened in the conflict in Indochina, or are covertly participating to such an extent as to jeopardize retention of the Tonkin Delta by the French forces, the United States should support the French to the greatest extent possible, preferably under the auspices of the UN. It is by no means certain that an appropriate UN resolution could be obtained. Favorable action in the UN would depend upon a change in the attitude of those governments which view the present regime in Indochina as a continuation of French colonialism. A new communist aggression might bring about a reassessment of the situation on the part of these governments and an increased recognition of the danger. Accordingly, it is believed that a UN resolution to oppose the aggression could be passed in the General Assembly by a small margin.

27. Even if it is not possible to obtain a UN resolution in such a case, the United States should seek the maximum possible international support for and participation in any international collective action in support of France and the Associated States. The United States should take appropriate military action against Communist China as part of a UN collective action or in conjunction with France and the United Kingdom and other friendly governments. However, in the absence of such support, it is highly unlikely that the United States would act unilaterally. It is probable however, that the United States would find some support and token participation at least from the United Kingdom and other Commonwealth countries.

28. The U.S. forces which would be committed, and the manner of their employment, as well as the military equipment which could be furnished to bolster the French Union forces, would be dependent upon certain factors which cannot now be predicted with accuracy. These include the extent of progress in U.S. rearmament, whether or not hostilities in Korea were continuing, and strategic developments in other parts of the world. It would be desirable to avoid the use of major U.S. ground forces in Indochina. Other effective means of opposing the aggression would include naval, air and logistical support of the French Union forces, naval blockade of Communist China, and attacks by land and carrier-based aircraft on military targets in Communist China. The latter could be effective against the long, tenuous, and vulnerable supply lines by which Chinese operations in Indochina would have to be supported. In the event of a forced evacuation, U.S. forces might provide cover and assistance. United Kingdom participation in these measures might well result in the seizure of Hong Kong by the Chinese Communists.

29. It is recognized that the commitment of U.S. military forces against Communist China would: (a) increase the risk of general hostilities in the Far East, including Soviet participation under cover of the existing Sino-Soviet agreements; (b) involve U.S. military forces in another Asiatic peripheral action, thus detracting from U.S. capabilities to conduct a global war in the near future; (c) arouse public opposition to "another Korea"; and (d) imply willingness to use U.S. military forces in other critical areas subject to com-

munist aggression. Nevertheless, by failing to take action, the United States would permit the communists to obtain, at little or no cost, a victory of major world consequence.

30. Informed public opinion might support use of U.S. forces in Indochina regardless of sentiment against "another Korea" on the basis that: (a) Indochina is of far greater strategic importance than Korea: (b) the confirmation of UN willingness to oppose aggression with force, demonstrated at such a high cost in Korea, might be nullified by the failure to commit UN forces in Indochina; and (c) a second instance of aggression by the Chinese Communists would justify measures not subject to the limitations imposed upon the UN action in Korea.

31. The military action contemplated herein would constitute, in effect, a war against Communist China which would be limited only as to its objectives, but would not be subject to any geographic limitations. Employment of U.S. forces in a de facto war with a formal declaration would raise questions which would make it desirable to consult with key members of both parties in Congress in order to obtain their prior concurrence in the courses of action contemplated.

[Sections on other Southeast Asian countries are omitted.]

(241) ORDERS OF THE DAY BY GENERAL GIAP ON THE OCCASION OF THE HOA-BINH VICTORY, February 27, 1952.

Source: Vo Nguyen Giap, *Orders of the Day, Speeches and Mobilization Letters,* pp. 148-153.

In November 1951 De Lattre launched an offensive aimed at occupying Hoabinh Province, south of Hanoi, cutting the Liberation Army's lines of communications and supply, and disrupting any plans for an offensive by the Vietnamese. But Giap took advantage of the French attack to launch a major campaign and regained the initiative. After four months of fighting, in which main force attacks aimed at putting the maximum number of French forces out of action were coordinated with guerrilla and political actions in the rear area of the French, French forces were forced to withdraw from Hoa-binh. Two million people were liberated from the French, according to the Vietnamese high command. Giap celebrated the victory in Hoa-binh town and recounted the history of the campaign.

All cadres and fighters of main forces, local forces, and guerrilla militia throughout the country!

Today, in the middle of liberated Hoa-binh, next to the imposing Ba-vi mountain, by the side of the Da River still smelling of the blood of the invader, before the representatives of the victorious units on all fronts of the Northern battlefield, representatives of government organs and local organizations, before representatives of Muong compatriots just escaped from the clutches of the enemy, we have heard the instructions of Chairman Ho, read the congratulations and directive of the Central Committee of the Viet-nam Workers' Party, of the National Assembly, of the National Lien-Viet Committe, and together rejoice in the glorious victory of the campaign to liberate Hoa-binh.

I send happy greetings and respectfully compliment the units who have triumphed on fronts throughout the country and especially compliment the units which are fighting on the frontline as well as in the enemy's rear. I express my concern over the health of the brother wounded soldiers and wish you a speedy recovery. Representing the army, I send thanks to all compatriots in the free zone as well as in the temporarily-occupied zone who have helped the troops with all their heart during the period of the recent battle.

As soon as the invader advanced on Hoa-binh, we annihilated an important part of his manpower at Cho Ben and at Thu-cuc - Lai dong. After that we launched three successive offensive waves.

In the first wave, we annihilated the enemy at Tu-vu, attacked Phat-diem town, beseiged the enemy's Da River defense line and contained them in their rear area.

In the second wave, we annihilated the enemy at the Da River, at Ba-vi, and broke the enemy's defense line at the Da River. At the same time we destroyed many positions in the Southern part of the Bac-ninh, liberated the zone south of the Duong River, and destroyed many positions in Hoa-dong, and raided Nam Dinh city.

In the third wave, we attacked and surrounded Hoa-binh city, cutting highway No. 6. Meanwhile, we raided Bac-giang town, raided Bac-ninh town, destroyed their position at Thuan-thanh interdistrict town, controlled highway No. 5 and the Haiphong-Hanoi railroad. In the third Interzone, we raided Phu-ly town, crossed the Hong River, attacked the left bank, razed many camps and annihilated military supply units of the enemy in Thai-binh.

A guerrilla warfare high tide developed strongly in the midlands and plains, pushing the enemy even further into a very difficult situation.

Attacked strongly in the North as well as in the Center and South, damaged heavily on the frontlines as well as in his rear, on February 23, the enemy had to risk opening a path of blood in order to withdraw their defeated troops in Hoa-binh. In this insecure withdrawal, the enemy was pursued by us, suffered the annihilation of his manpower, and had to leave behind many stockpiles, vehicles, wounded and dead.

Cadres and fighters!

In the campaign to liberate Hoa-binh, the entire North is a battlefield having very close coordination of the Central and Southern battlefields. We continuously attacked and continuously defeated the enemy during three months. From the standpoint of space and time, this campaign was the biggest campaign thus far. On the whole Northern battlefield and on each front we coordinated both inner and outer fronts very closely, and coordinated the regular battlefield with the guerrilla battlefield on a broad scale.

The result of the campaign is that we annihilated 22,000 of the enemy's forces, captured and forced to surrender 6,867, liberated Hoa-binh and the Da River region, Ba-vi, opened communications routes between the Viet-bac and the fourth interzone, developed guerrilla warfare to a high level, widened many guerrilla base areas, broke up piece by piece the puppet army, and government, won back broad fertile lands, liberated millions of compatriots, and helped unify the various popular strata. Our army has improved rapidly regarding the idea of actively annihilating the enemy's manpower, and continuous fighting, have improved and studied further many experiences in the techniques of riverine fighting, artillery fighting, and mechanized fighting, and methods of attacking fortified positions, mobilizing in the region in the enemy's rear, and in the tactics of attacking important bases which are newly occupied, and of surrounding a town and attacking the enemy as he retreats. Local troops and guerrilla militia have also improved greatly in destroying puppet village committees, punishing traitors, destroying enemy troops and mobilizing the people's armed struggle.

The people in the region in the enemy's rear are very enthusiastic, hate the invader army more and more every day, understand more and more clearly the policy of great national unity of Chairman Ho and the Government, and have risen up in great numbers, actively participating in the resistance. The great influence of the campaign has contributed a large share to the task of economic struggle with the enemy, completing the collection of agricultural taxes, pushing forward the people's movement to increase production and economize.

The victory of this campaign is a military victory, a political victory and an economic victory. It defeats Tassigny's scheme of trying to win back the initiative. It defeats the scheme of occupying the strategic position of Hoa-binh in order to cut communications lines between the Viet-bac and interzone four, while oppressing and exploiting our Muong compatriots. It destroys one important part of the enemy's strategic plan in the Northern plain aimed at "pacifying" his rear area, using Vietnamese to fight Vietnamese, and using the war to nourish war.

The victory of this campaign is a precious gift of our army and people to greet the Viet-nam Workers' Party, the Lien-Viet Front and the Vietnamese-Cambodian-Laotian Alliance on the occasion of the approaching March 3 anniversary. It raises high the spirit of solidarity in struggle between our people and the French people and the people of the French colonies struggling against French colonialism and American interventionists. At the same time, it is a contribution of the Vietnamese nation to the movement to preserve world peace.

We must always remember that we have triumphed gloriously thanks to the clear sighted leadership of the Viet-nam Workers' Party, the Government and Chairman Ho, thanks to the heroic struggle spirit and the improvements of the army in the recent period of ideological retraining, and thanks to the compatriots' boundless spirit of self-sacrifice, active service to the frontlines and assistance to the troops.

Cadres, and fighters,

The enemy has lost heavily and is now in confusion. But the American reactionaries are trying to breathe life into them. They are actively carrying out a plan to urgently reinforce the defeated troops at Hoa-binh - highway No. 6 in order to sweep and consolidate the enemy's rear area, trying to kill, rape and plunder our people.

But our forces in the enemy's rear area have grown stronger, while the enemy forces have diminished. In the longterm and difficult struggle in the enemy's rear, we will definitely inflict a painful defeat on the enemy and make his situation more and more serious every day.

In order to finish the task mentioned above, as Commander in Chief of the Vietnamese National Army and Militia, I command all cadres and fighters:

1. You must realize clearly the significance of the important victory of the campaign to liberate Hoa-binh, while seeing clearly the new plan of the enemy in the rear area and be determined to smash that poisonous scheme. You must propagandize widely among the people, making them also determined to struggle.
2. Main force troops, local troops and guerrilla militia must coordinate closely with the people, unite with the people to form a bloc, especially in the enemy's rear, consolidate and broaden guerrilla bases, be prepared to fight the enemy's attacks or sweeps.
3. You must exert efforts to study the rich experiences of the campaign to liberate Hoa-binh, study and develop those experiences immediately in combat, in order to consolidate the present victories and win bigger victories. "Do not be proud because of victory, nor subjectively underestimate the enemy," as Chairman Ho has taught. We must all endeavor to push strongly the emulation movement to kill the invaders and record feats of arms.

Long live independent and unified Viet-nam!
Long live Chairman Ho!

(242) <u>CENTRAL INTELLIGENCE AGENCY SPECIAL ESTIMATE ON "CONSEQUENCES OF CERTAIN POSSIBLE U.S. COURSES OF ACTION WITH RESPECT TO INDOCHINA, BURMA, OR THAILAND,"</u> February 29, 1952

Source: *U.S.-Vietnam Relations, Book 8,* pp. 477-484.

The proposal that the U.S., Britain, France, Australia and New Zealand join together in threatening military retaliation against China if it intervened in Southeast Asia was the subject of a special estimate by the intelligence community. It concluded that if the Chinese initiated an intervention in spite of such a warning, it would mean that they were prepared for "general hostilities" in the Far East.

THE PROBLEM

To estimate the consequences of certain possible US courses of action with respect to an identifiable Chinese Communist military intervention[1] in Indochina, Burma, or Thailand.

ASSUMPTION

The United Kingdom, France, Australia, and New Zealand will join the United States in warning Communist China that the five powers will meet Chinese Communist military intervention in Southeast Asia with military counteraction. Whether or not the four other powers will join the US in such a warning is beyond the scope of this estimate. We are also unable to assess which of various conceivable methods of transmitting a warning would have the greatest deterrent effect.

ESTIMATE

I. THE EFFECT OF A JOINT WARNING AGAINST CHINESE COMMUNIST MILITARY INTERVENTION IN SOUTHEAST ASIA.

On Communist Intentions

1. We do not believe that a joint warning against an "identifiable military intervention" by the Chinese Communists in Southeast Asia would tend to provoke such intervention. If, however, the Chinese Communists contemplate an early "identifiable military intervention" in Southeast Asia, or if in the future they should contemplate such an intervention, a joint warning by the five powers would tend to deter them.[2]

2. Even in the absence of a joint formal warning, the Chinese Communists probably estimate that "identifiable military intervention" in Southeast Asia would entail substanial risk of joint military conteraction, and that such a risk is unwarranted in view of the prospects for further Communist gains in Southeast Asia without such intervention. They may, however, discount this risk, estimating that there are differences in policy among the five powers and that these powers may not be able or willing to take timely[3] and effective military counteraction.

3. The effectiveness of a joint warning as a deterrent would depend in large measure on Communist conviction that:

    a. The five powers were not bluffing, and were united among themselves as to the military counteraction to be taken.

    b. The five powers were actually capable of timely and effective military counteraction.[3]

    c. The counteraction would be directed against Communist China itself as well as toward repelling the Chinese Communist intervention.

4. If the Communists were convinced on the foregoing points they would have to recognize that intervention in Southeast Asia would bring military counteraction, the probable consequences of which would be general hostilities between Communist China and the five powers, if not global war. It is improbable.

Therefore, that they would initiate an "identifiable military intervention" in Indochina, Burma, or Thailand in the face of a joint warning by the five powers unless, on the basis of global considerations, they were willing to accept global war or at least general hostilities in the Far East. So far both Communist China and the USSR have shown a desire to localize the hostilities in Korea, Indochina, Burma, and Malaya. Furthermore, the favorable prospects for the success of present Communist tactics in Southeast Asia make probable a continuation of these tactics, unless, because of global considerations, the USSR and the Chinese Communists decide to accept grave risk of global war.

5. It is unlikely that additional signatories would increase the effectiveness of a joint warning. India would almost certainly refuse to participate in such a warning. It is improbable that Japan would take such a provocative step at this time and uncertain whether Thailand would do so. Few, if any, additional governments would join in a formal warning. Even if the Philippines, Japan, and Thailand did participate, the Communists would discount their adherence because of the military weakness of these countries and their existing ties with the West. The Communists would assume Chinese Nationalist support of the warning, whether or not explicitly expressed.

Other Effects

6. A public joint warning would considerably improve the morale of the Thai and Vietnamese governments. In Burma any encouragement derived from the warning would probably be offset by fear of involvement in a conflict between the great powers and by general suspicion of Western "imperialist" motives.

7. Elsewhere in East and South Asia the effect would be mixed. There would be a tendency, notably in Japan and the Philippines, to applaud this new manifestation of Western determination to check Communist aggression. On the other hand, the feeling would be widespread, especially in India and Indonesia, that the warning represented another instance of Western meddling in Asian affairs in pursuit of colonial objectives.

8. The effect of a warning on other countries probably would not be of major importance. A warning might well revive the fears in the smaller NATO powers regarding the dangers of general war or of an overextension of Western strength in the Far East, but it is unlikely that the basic attitudes of these countries would be changed.

9. The inclusion in the warning of a threat to use atomic weapons would produce a widespread and serious adverse reaction throughout the non-Communist world.

II. INITIATION OF ACTION IN THE UN AND PROBABLE UN REACTIONS THERETO

10. If identifiable Chinese Communist military intervention in Southeast Asia actually took place, the UN could probably be led to adopt countermeasures similar to those taken regarding Korea if the US, UK, and France advocated these measures. Action by the Security Council would certainly be blocked by a Soviet veto, but the matter could then be taken to the General Assembly within twenty-four hours under the "Uniting for Peace" resolution. The General Assembly would probably begin by calling for a cease-fire. Were this action to be ignored (as it presumably would be), a two-thirds majority could probably be mustered for resolutions condemning Communist China as an aggressor, recommending military counteraction to repel the aggression, and setting up a unified military command (though not necessarily under the US) to that end. Most UN members, however, because of their fears of a general war, would probably not be willing to give specific authorization for military counteraction against Communist China itself.

11. The willingness of the UN to adopt a stand against Communist intervention in Southeast Asia would be affected by the readiness of the victim to appeal to the UN, Indochina and Thailand would almost certainly be prompt in

seeking UN assistance against Chinese Communist military intervention, but Burma might fail to make a timely appeal or fail to support an appeal by another member.

12. The degree of UN support for action against Chinese Communist aggression would hinge on various other factors. A large number of Arab and Asian countries probably would abstain if Indochina, which they regard as a French puppet, were invaded. The Arab-Asian reaction might be more favorable if the victim were Burma, which has followed a policy of non-involvement. If the five powers took any countermeasures without UN authorization, support of their action would be considerably lessened.

III. PROBABLE EFFECTS OF THE EXECUTION OF JOINT MILITARY COUNTERMEASURES

Reaction of the Chinese Communist and Soviet Governments[4]

13. If the Chinese Communists undertook an identifiable military intervention in Southeast Asia despite a joint warning against such a move, Chinese Communist planning unquestionably would have considered the likelihood of Western counteraction and would have been coordinated with the USSR. It is possible that such an intervention might be undertaken in the belief that the warning was a bluff, or at least that the countermeasures would be confined to the area of the aggression. In this case the execution of forceful military countermeasures might induce the Communists to seek a settlement. It appears far more likely, however, that such an intervention would be undertaken in full recognition of the risks involved. Under these circumstances, the immediate reaction to such military counteraction would probably be an attempt to accelerate Chinese Communist military operations. The Chinese Communists would probably attempt to extend their operations to other parts of Southeast Asia and, having already accepted the danger of expanded hostilities, they might well intensify operations in Korea and seize Hong Kong and Macao. Highest priority would be given, however, to the defense of Communist China.

14. Chinese Communist defiance of a joint warning would almost certainly involve the prior consent of the USSR. The degree of Soviet aid to Communist China would depend upon (a) the nature, scope, and degree of success of the Western counteraction, and (b) the degree to which the existence of the Peiping regime seemed to be jeopardized.

[1]The term "identifiable Chinese Communist military intervention" is intended to cover either an open and acknowledged military intervention or an unacknowledged military intervention of such a scale and nature that its existence could be demonstrated.

[2]The Special Assistant, Intelligence, Department of State, would add the following sentence: "On the other hand, if the Communist leaders conclude from Western actions and statements that the West intends to attack Communist China regardless of Communist actions in Southeast Asia, the deterrent effect of a warning would be nullified."

[3]The Special Assistant, Intelligence, Department of State holds the view that the Communists might be seriously concerned over the prospect of <u>delayed</u> military counteraction, even though they believed that <u>timely</u> counteraction need not be feared. He therefore believes that the words "timely and" should be omitted.

[4]SE-20: "The Probable Consequences of Certain Possible US Courses of Action with Respect to Communist China and Korea" treats most of the material discussed in this section in more detail.

(243) MEMORANDUM BY THE JOINT CHIEFS OF STAFF FOR THE SECRETARY OF DEFENSE, March 3, 1952

Source: *U.S.-Vietnam Relations, Book 8*, pp. 486-499.

The Joint Chiefs, responding to NCA 124's recommendation that the U.S. be prepared to go to war with China if it sent troops into Indochina, Thailand or Burma, noted that it would increase U.S. commitments and would require an increase in assistance to Southeast Asia and Formosa as well as an increase in U.S. forces and defense production. But it concurred in the recommendation, despite the admittedly increased risk of global war.

1. In accordance with the request contained in your memorandum, dated 16 February 1952, the Joint Chiefs of Staff have studied NSC 124, a draft statement of United States policy on the above subject, and a staff study relating thereto, both prepared by the National Security Council Staff. The views of the Joint Chiefs of Staff regarding the proposed policies enunciated therein are set forth below.

2. NSC 124 recommends United States courses of action in the several areas of Southeast Asia. Taken either separately or together, acceptance of most of these courses of action and hence of NSC 124, involves the making of a single basic decision. The basic decision is whether or not the United States, in support of the objective of NSC 124 stated as "to prevent the countries of Southeast Asia from passing into the Communist orbit," would be WILLING to take military action which would, in effect, constitute war against Communist China. An affirmation at this time within the National Security Council of such a willingness does not necessarily involve making a decision now whether or not to go to war in advance of the nature and extent of the aggression becoming apparent. On the other hand, affirmation of this willingness should be made with a clear understanding of the implications which the adoption of these courses of action would entail. In addition, such affirmation of this willingness is essential in order to provide the basis for determining:

    a. The cost of these courses of action, in terms of men, money, and materiel;
    b. The impact of these courses of action upon the economy of the United States;
    c. The impact of these courses of action upon United States military assistance programs with particular reference to the inevitable reduction in the United States contribution to the North Atlantic Treaty Organization (NATO) effort; and
    d. The firmness of support of our principal allies for our global policies generally and these courses of action in particular.

3. The military action, as proposed in NSC 124, would be limited as to its objectives, but it would not be subject to any geographic restrictions with respect to Communist China. In this connection, the Joint Chiefs of Staff believe that any new communist aggression in Asia undoubtedly would stem from a deliberate design, in the formulation of which the possiblity of counteraction by the United States against the source of aggression would, in all probability, have been considered.

4. The making of such a decision now or in the eventuality of overt aggression by Communist China against a country of Southeast Asia is complicated by, among other things, the following:

    a. Whether or not the United Nations would be willing to call upon its members to engage in hostilities with Communist China;

b. Whether or not the member nations of the United Nations would be willing to engage in military action against aggression by Communist China in Southeast Asia;

c. Whether or not the United Kingdom and France would be willing to engage directly in military action against Communist China itself, other than action limited to the area of and/or the approaches to the land battle with the aggressor forces;

d. The ability and the willingness of the United States to take the military actions involved including unilateral action against Communist China itself, in event of Communist Chinese military aggression in the countries of Southeast Asia. Such actions would call for considerable increase over current military production rates with a corresponding curtailment of the production of goods for the civilian economy; until increased U.S. production is achieved, these actions would reduce the military assistance programs to other nations, especially those in high priority.

e. The possible effect upon United States alliances in Europe and upon the United Nations organization itself if the United States Government should consider it necessary, in its own interests, to take military action unilaterally against Communist China; and

f. The implications and the political effects of a probable refusal by the United States to provide ground forces for collective United Nations action or for combined military operations in support of France and the United Kingdom in Southeast Asia.

5. The basic decision, in light of the factors set forth in paragraph 3 above, those developed in NSC 124, and the military considerations set forth herein, is essentially political in nature. Its resolution will have direct bearing upon future United States global strategy. Accordingly, the Joint Chiefs of Staff believe that consideration by the members of the National Security Council itself of these factors and military considerations is necessary prior to any final decision regarding the policy statement in NSC 124.

6. The Joint Chiefs of Staff wish to report that, during the course of their preliminary discussions with representatives of the Chiefs of Staffs of the United Kingdom and France on the matter of possible courses of action to meet Chinese Communist aggression against Southeast Asia, the British and French military position opposed even the concept of action against Communist China other than that limited to the area of, or approaches to, the land battle in opposition to the aggressor forces. The Joint Chiefs of Staff believe that the British and French would, at least initially, oppose taking military action against Communist China as a nation, even in the face of aggression.

7. The British and French appear to think almost exclusively in terms of defense, at least as far as Europe and Southeast Asia are concerned. Their unwillingness to take even those measures for the defense of Southeast Asia which are within their capability, indicates that they may not recognize the actual long-term danger to themselves involved in the possible loss of Southeast Asia.

8. Piecemeal actions by Soviet satellites, such as the overrunning of Southeast Asia, can eventually lead to attainment by the USSR of its objective, among others, of dominating the continent of Asia and possibly the continent of Europe. It is emphasized that each Communist gain directly involves a loss to the Western World.

9. The Joint Chiefs of Staff recognize that there would be grave danger to United States security interests if Southeast Asia should pass into the Communist orbit.

10. The military problems which would arise as a result of any overt Chinese Communist aggression against Southeast Asia are different in character and

in scope from those of Korea. The Joint Chiefs of Staff are of the opinion that any restrictions which would limit the military action taken in French Indochina, Thailand, and/or Burma to the area of, or the approaches to, the land battle in opposition to the aggressor forces would result in such military action becoming wholly defensive in character. Such action would, in their opinion, at best be indecisive and would probably extend over an indefinite period.

11. The Joint Chiefs of Staff consider that military measures taken to prevent the Chinese Communists from gaining control of Southeast Asia by military aggression should, from the outset, be planned so as to offer a reasonable chance of ultimate success. After consideration of the military factors involved, the Joint Chiefs of Staff are of the opinion that in order to offer such chance of success, military operations in defense against Chinese Communist invasion of French Indochina, Thailand, and/or Burma must be accompanied by military action against the sources of that aggression, namely, Communist China itself. Accordingly, and in view of the foregoing, the Joint Chiefs of Staff would recommend, SOLELY FROM THE POINT OF VIEW OF MILITARY OPERATIONS, that a strong defense be maintained against such Chinese Communist aggression and that concurrent offensive operations be undertaken against the nation of Communist China. They would point out, however, that this course of action, while offering promise of ultimate success, might result in a long war, and an expensive one at least materiel-wise.

12. The Joint Chiefs of Staff, from the military point of view, must, in any event, oppose acceptance of all of the military commitments devolving from NSC 124 without a clear understanding that the United States must be accorded freedom of action and, if possible, support in the undertaking of appropriate military action to include action against Communist China itself. Failing such freedom of action, the United States should accept the possibility of loss of at least Indochina, Thailand, and Burma. Such acceptance would call for a United States policy which would limit United States military commitments in Southeast Asia to those necessary to cover and assist possible forced evacuations of the French and/or the British from their positions. The Joint Chiefs of Staff reaffirm their position that United States ground forces should not be committed in French Indochina, Thailand, or Burma and for the defense of those countries. Further, they strongly oppose the United States joining a combined military command for the defense of those countries.

13. Military action by the United States against Communist China would inevitably involve the acceptance of increased risks. Such risks, however, should not necessarily be an overriding deterrent to United States action. As NSC 48/5 points out, the risk of global war "should not preclude undertaking calculated risks against specific areas in the over-all interests of the United States."

14. If Communist China commits overt major acts of aggression against French Indochina, Thailand, or Burma and if in the face of such aggression the British and/or French refuse to offer either military or political support to possible United States action against Communist China itself, the effect of United States unilateral action upon our military alliances and positions in Europe as well as in Asia should be appraised and the risk calculated. Further, in such an eventuality, the validity of our alliances might well be re-examined.

15. In the light of all of the foregoing and, to meet the contingencies:

a. That Chinese Communist aggression in Southeast Asia poses a threat unacceptable at that time to the position of the United States, both in the Far East and world-wide, and

b.   That the United Kingdom and/or France decline to support action against the nation of Communist China,

the Joint Chiefs of Staff, form the military point of view, strongly recommend the inclusion in any National Security Council policy statement with respect to Southeast Asia stipulation that the United States Government will consider taking military action, unilaterally, if necessary, against the nation of Communist China.

16. Acceptance of the policies proposed in NSC 124 would serve to increase the commitments of the United States. The Joint Chiefs of Staff consider that such increase should be accompanied by a substantial upward revision of our economic and military assistance programs for Southeast Asia and for Formosa and by some (possibly substantial) increase in our forces in being. In this connection, current slippages in the military production programs have already reduced planned United States and allied military readiness. There should be no increase in the risk resulting from such shortages in military production. Accordingly, the increases in our assistance programs and our ready forces, required by acceptance of the proposed policies, would call for a substantial and immediate increase in the scale of United States production, and pending that increase, would reduce the military assistance programs to other nations, especially those in high priority.

17. The Joint Chiefs of Staff concur in paragraph 67 of the study in the Annex to NSC 124, which is quoted below for ready reference:

"In order to pursue the military courses of action envisaged in this paper to a definite favorable conclusion within a reasonable period, it will be necessary to divert military strength from other areas thus reducing our military capabilities in those areas, with the recognized increased risks involved therein, or to increase our military forces in being, or both. The magnitude of the United States military requirements to carry out these courses of action and the manner in which they could best be met can be determined only after study by the Joint Chiefs of Staff."

Such determination will follow completion of the military studies called for in subparagraph 6c (3) of the draft policy statement in NSC 124 dealing with the military measures called for in subparagraphs 6d, 7f, 8c, 9b, and 10c thereof. In this connection, an armistice in Korea will not of itself permit major redeployment or redisposition of ground forces in the Far East in the near future except at the risk of losing Korea and endangering Japan in the event hostilities in that area are resumed.

18. In connection with the foregoing, the Joint Chiefs of Staff contemplate no employment of United States ground force units in French Indochina, Thailand, or Burma; rather the Joint Chiefs of Staff anticipate that the major increase in United States forces required for contemplated operations against aggression in that area would be naval and air force units. It should be noted that the creation of any new units would, in general, strengthen the United States military position for the eventuality of global war and that such forces would be capable of rapid redeployment in that eventuality.

19. The Joint Chiefs of Staff, from the United States military point of view, do not wish to join in a combined military command at this time or under present circumstances for the defense of Southeast Asia against Chinese Communist aggression. In this connection, the Joint Chiefs of Staff believe that the United States should not at this time contemplate relieving the French of their responsibility in Indochina if present United States global strategy, including France's role therein, is to be continued. Further, they feel that, while French Indochina, Thailand, and/or Burma are being defended by other friendly nations, the role of the United States in support of such defense

should be primarily military action against Communist China itself. This latter action should, of course, involve military support from the British and French as well as from other friendly nations, but should remain under the control of the United States.

20. It will be noted that the foregoing comments are in general limited to United States courses of action relative to Indochina, Thailand, and Burma. The Joint Chiefs of Staff consider it premature for the National Security Council to attempt to decide now as to the military courses of action which would be taken with respect to Malaya, Indonesia, or in the Southwest Pacific in the event the integrity of any of these is directly threatened by foreign aggression which could only follow aggression in Indochina and/or Burma. Accordingly, in the event that the Chinese Communists threaten Malaya or Indonesia, the United States should then, in the light of the world situation generally and the situation in the Far East specifically at that time, consider the military measures it might take as a part of a United Nations collective action or in conjunction with the United Kingdom and any other friendly governments.

21. In the light of all the foregoing, the Joint Chiefs of Staff recommend that the National Security Council consider:

a. Whether the United States, unilaterally, if necessary, would be willing to extend the war to the forces and territory of Communist China in event of Communist Chinese military aggression in Southeast Asia;

b. Whether the United States should insist that French Indochina, Thailand, and/or Burma be defended by other friendly nations and that the role of the United States in support of such defense be primarily military action against Communist China itself; and

c. Failing freedom of action against Communist China itself, United States policy should limit United States military operations to those necessary to cover and assist possible forced evacuation of the French and/or the British from their positions.

22. The Joint Chiefs of Staff have a number of substantive and specific comments with respect to the statements of policy in NSC 124. These comments are contained in the Enclosure attached. The Joint Chiefs of Staff recommend that the Enclosure and their views herein be furnished to the National Security Council prior to its action on this paper. The military studies referred to in the Annex to NSC 124 and in paragraph 17 of this memorandum will be furnished in due course to the Representative of the Joint Chiefs of Staff on the National Security Council Staff, if such action is indicated following National Security Council action.

ENCLOSURE
DRAFT

MEMORANDUM FOR THE NATIONAL SECURITY COUNCIL SENIOR STAFF

Subject: United States Objectives and Courses of Action with Respect to
Communist Aggression in Southeast Asia.

1. The following specific comments by the Joint Chiefs of Staff on NSC 124 are submitted in order that these may be reflected as appropriate in the revision of that document.

2. Change subparagraph 2 c to read (changes indicated in the usual manner):

"Communist control of all of Southeast Asia ~~would render the U.S. position in the Pacific offshore island chain precarious~~ would seriously jeopardize fundamental U.S. security interests in the Far East."

REASON: In the interests of conciseness and accuracy. In the light of the discussion in the analysis, the original wording overstates the immediate military threat to the U.S. position in the Pacific offshore island chain in the event of the fall of Southeast Asia.

3. Revise the present last sentence of subparagraph 5 d in such a manner as to refer to every paragraph in the paper (in addition to subparagraphs 6 d, 7 f, and 8 c) which involves military measures against Communist China.

4. Add the following sentence at the end of subparagraph 5 d:

"In this connection, it should be made clear to the other nations that United States ground forces will not be committed to the defense of French Indochina, Thailand, or Burma."

REASON: For consistency and accuracy and in order to preclude misunderstanding.

5. Change subparagraph 5 h to read as follows (changes indicated in the usual manner);

"Take ~~whatever~~ such measures other than military as may be practicable to promote the coordinated defense of the area, and encourage and support the spirit of resistance among the peoples of Southeast Asia to Chinese Communist aggression and to the encroachments of local communists."

REASON: For preciseness and to preclude any implication that the Unites will join in a combined military command for the defense of the area.

6. Change subparagraph 6 c (3) to read as follows (changes indicated in the usual manner):

"In view of the immediate urgency of the situation, involving possible large-scale Chinese Communist intervention, and in order that the United States may be prepared to take whatever action may be appropriate in such circumstances, ~~make-the-plans~~ determine now the measures necessary to carry out the courses of action indicated in subparagraph d below."

REASON: This subparagraph as presently written directs the Department of Defense and other agencies to engage in certain formal planning which, in the case of the Department of Defense, would involve the formulation of specific war plans. In addition, formal military planning would have to be initiated with the French, with the British, with the Chinese Nationalist Goverment, with the Government of Burma, and possibly with other friendly governments, including States Members of the United Nations. The Joint Chiefs of Staff question the feasibility and desirability of such action and, in any event, from the military point of view, they would find it impracticable to formulate war plans for all of the contingencies suggested in the basic paper beyond United States military courses of action and force bases thereof. On the other hand, the Joint Chiefs of Staff support the desirability of undertaking unilaterally appropriate studies of the problem involved.

7. Change subparagraph 6 c (4) to read as follows (changes indicated in the usual manner):

"~~In-the-event-that-information-and-circumstances-point-to-the-conclusion-that-France-is-no-longer-prepared-to-carry-the-burden-in-Indochina,-or if-France-presses-for-a-sharing-of-the-responsibility-for-Indochina,-whether-in-the-UN-or-directly-with-the-U.S.-Government;~~ Oppose a French withdrawal ~~and-consult-with-the-French-and-British-concerning-further-measures to-be-taken-to-safeguard-the-area-from-communist-domination~~ from Indochina."

REASON: The United States should not at this time contemplate relieving the French of their responsibility in Indochina if present United States global strategy, including France's role therein, is to be continued. There would, however, be no objection to a discussion of this contingency appearing in the analysis to the basic paper.

8. Change subparagraph 6 d (3) to read as follows (changes indicated in the usual manner):

"Consistent with world-wide U.S. commitments take appropriate military action against the forces and territory of Communist China as part of a UN collective action or in conjunction with French and the United Kingdom and any other friendly government."

REASON: To emphasize that any military action against Communist China must be without geographic limitations.

9. Insert the following new subparagraph immediately following subparagraphs 6 d, 7 f, and 8 c and any others referring to possible military measures against Communist China, renumbering subsequent paragraphs accordingly:

"In the event that the United States, in the face of Chinese Communist aggression into Southeast Asia, overt or volunteer, deems it advisable to take military action against Communist China itself, and if the United Kingdom and/or France refuse to support such action, the Unied States will consider in the light of the world situation at the time, and in the light of the possible consequences upon the role of the United Kingdom and France in United States world strategy, whether United States security interests require taking such military action unilaterally."

REASON: In the opinion of the Joint Chiefs of Staff this reservation is vital to the security of the United States.

10. Change the first sentence of subparagraph 7 b to read as follows (changes indicated in the usual manner);

"Arrange to conduct a full and frank exchange of views with the British Government with the object of reexamining policy toward Burma and seeking any joint or coordinated action other than military which might contribute toward an improvement in the situation in Burma."

REASON: For preciseness and to preclude any implication that the United States will join in a combined military command for the defense of the area.

11. Change the first sentence of subparagraph 7 d to read as follows (changes indicated in the usual manner):

"Encourage the British to develop united action and cooperation among indigenous, anticommunist groups in Burma to resist communist encroachments."

REASON: Burma is an area of British responsibility.

12. Change subparagraph 7 f (2) to read as follows (changes indicated in the usual manner):

"Consistent with world-wide U.S. commitments take appropriate military action against the forces and territory of Communist China as part of a UN collective action or in conjunction with France and the United Kingdom and any other friendly governments."

REASON: To emphasize any military action against Communist China must be without geographic limitations.

13. Change subparagraph 8 b (2) as follows (changes indicated in the usual manner):

"Immediately put into effect whatever measures other than military may be determined as feasible to forestall an invasion of Thailand or a seizure of power by local Thai communists."

REASON: Military operations by the United States in Thailand would, in all probability, be infeasible in the premises.

14. Change subparagraph 8 c (2) to read as follows (changes indicated in the usual manner):

"Consistent with world-wide U.S. commitments take appropriate military action against the forces and territory of Communist China as part of a UN collective action or in conjunction with France and the United Kingdom and any other friendly governments."

REASON: To emphasize that any military action against Communist China must be without geographic limitations.

(244) SPEECH BY HO CHI MINH OPENING THE CENTRAL COMMITTEE'S FIRST IDEOLOGICAL REMOLDING COURSE, May 11, 1952

Source: Ho Chi Minh, *Selected Works, Vol. III*, pp. 356-358.

Throughout the resistance war, the Party leadership was concerned with the ideological level of its cadres, which it saw as a key factor in determining the level of morale and performance of the Party, military forces and the population generally. Given the urgency of other tasks, however, cadres had not received adequate political training, resulting in ideological and personal deviations for the Party's standards. The Central Committee convened an ideological remolding course for higher-level cadres, who were then expected to carry out a similar course in the ranks of the Party and army.

Dear comrades,
On behalf of the Central Committee I welcome you to this first ideological remoulding course which paves the way for the ideological remoulding of the whole Party.
Why have we to carry out the ideological remoulding of the Party?
Our Party has led our class and people successfully to carry out the August Revolution and has liberated our people from colonial rule and monarchical regime to set up people's power.
At present, our Party's task is to unite and lead our class together with the people to wage the Resistance War and build the country. This is a heavy, and glorious task which can be performed only by our Party - the Party of the working class and of the toiling people.
Our Party possesses Marxism-Leninism which is the most revolutionary and most scientific ideology. Its line and policies are correct. Its bases exist all over the country. Its cadres and members are unconditionally devoted and tested through heroic struggles.
But owing to difficult conditions, a great number of our cadres and members have not yet received adequate training. That is why they have a low ideological and political level and many deviations. This is obvious in such mistakes as unclarity on the policy of long-term resistance war and self-sufficiency, no clear cut discrimination between enemies and friends; arrogance, bureaucracy, grave corruption and libertinage, etc.
As a leading Party, our Party must be strong, pure and exemplary.
The whole Party must be united in mind and deed to be able to fulfil the tasks entrusted to it.

The aim of the ideological remoulding of the Party is to raise the ideological and political level of the Party cadres and members to enable them to act in full keeping with the proletarian viewpoint and standpoint.

If the Party ideological remoulding campaign is successfully carried out, it will develop our success in the military, political and economic fields, etc.

It is through this campaign that the Party tempers, readjusts and strengthens its ranks to keep up the long Resistance War until victory. This is the significance of the ideological remoulding of the Party.

The campaign must have a focus: ideological re-adjustment before re-adjustment of organisation. The ideological remoulding course must be organised for Party cadres first.

Therefore, the task of the comrades attending this first ideological remoulding course is to devote themselves to study, to be frank in making self-criticism and criticism, to gain more experiences and revolutionary virtues. When this course is over you must emulate with one another to help the Central Committee carry out the ideological remoulding of the whole Party and the whole army and improve mass-work.

The cadres decide everything. You are all high-ranking cadres and are assuming important responsibilities. The success or failure of the work depends for the most part on your ideology, virtues, attitude and style of work.

The Central Committee earnestly hopes that during this course, you will strive to emulate with one another in studying and tempering yourselves to become model cadres, worthy of the expectation and trust of the Party, the Government, the army and the people, to become most able fighters in building the Party and helping it bring the Resistance War and national construction to success.

We are revolutionaries. We have determination; moreover we receive assistance from the brother parties, so however great may be the difficulties, we are resolute to fulfil our task. I hope that you will make every effort and will attain success.

(245) STATEMENT BY ACHESON TO THE PRESS, June 18, 1952

Source: Department of State Press Release No. 473, in *U.S.-Vietnam Relations, Book 8,* pp. 518-519.

In June 1952, Jean Letourneau, Minister of Associated States and High Commissioner for Indochina visited Washington. Acheson took advantage of Letourneau's visit to portray the Associated States as assuming the main burden of defense and as far more independent than in their public image.

As you are aware, M. Jean Letourneau, Minister of the Associated States for the French Government, has been spending the last few days in Washington exchanging views with representatives of various agencies of this Government. The Ambassadors of Cambodia and Vietnam have also participated in conversations with Mr. Letourneau and with our own representatives.

A communique covering the substance of the talks will be issued later today and I will therefore not go into details now. Yet I would like to share with you the feeling of encouragement and confidence which M. Letourneau inspires. His thorough grasp of the situation and his constructive approach to the problems involved - military, political and economic - have impressed us all.

As you know, the Communist aggression in Indochina has been going on for six years. It has been greatly stepped up because of assistance received from Communist China during the past two years. Yet, under French leadership, the threat to this part of the free world has been met with great courage and admirable resourcefulness. The military situation appears to be developing favorably. It has been good to hear from M. Letourneau of the part played in achieving this result by the considerable quantities of American arms and materiel which the magnificent fighting qualities of the French Union forces, including those of the Associated States, have justified us in devoting to this area of the struggle against Communist aggression. The effort to make of Vietnam, Laos and Cambodia secure and prosperous members of the free world community has made great progress.

I have been particularly impressed by what M. Letourneau has told me of what is being done to enable the people of the three Associated States to play the constantly greater role in their own defense to which they rightly aspire. Much has been accomplished toward the creation, training and equipping of the national armies. Units of these armies have distinguished themselves in battle and are performing vital security functions in many parts of the country. They look forward with confidence and determination to assuming an increasing share of the burden of carrying on the struggle. Their effectiveness fully justifies the program of expansion to which the governments concerned are committed and underlines, I believe, the soundness of our own decision, subject of course to the availability of Congressional appropriations, to render increasing assistance in building these armies. M. Letourneau described these programs in the course of his address before the Overseas Writers yesterday.

Favorable developments have not been confined to the fighting fronts and to the national armies. There are increasing evidences of the growing vitality of the Associated States in handling their political, financial and economic affairs. M. Letourneau's account of the manner in which these new member States of the French Union are envisaging and meeting their responsibilities was heartening. I do not think it is generally realized to what extent these new states in fact control their own affairs. Only a limited number of services related to the necessities of the war remain temporarily in French hands.

We in the United States are aware of the vital importance of the struggle in Indochina to the cause of the free world. We have earmarked for Indochina economic and materiel aid to a considerable abount during the past two years. We are doing our best to activate deliveries: as you are aware the 150th ship bearing American arms and munitions to Indochina arrived in Saigon within the last few weeks. We are now bearing a considerable portion of the total burden of the war in Indochina expressed in financial terms, although of course the entire combat burden is being carried by the French Union and the Associated States with the latter assuming a constantly increasing share.

The Communists have made a most determined effort in Indochina. Their aggression has been checked and recent indications warrant the view that the tide is now moving in our favor. Once again the policy of meeting aggression with force is paying off and we can I believe be confident that as we carry out the plans upon which we have agreed we can anticipate continued favorable developments in the maintenance and consolidation of the free world bulwark in Indochina.

(246) JOINT COMMUNIQUE REGARDING DISCUSSIONS BETWEEN REPRESENTATIVES OF THE UNITED STATES, FRANCE, VIET-NAM AND CAMBODIA, June 18, 1952.

Source: Department of State Bulletin, June 30, 1952, p. 1010

After discussion between Letourneau and various U.S. officials, with the participation of Cambodian and Vietnamese Ambassadors in Washington, a joint communique was issued reaffirming the "primary role" of France in Indochina, a phrase which had been used by the U.S. in Franco-U.S. negotiations to mean that the U.S. could give no defense commitments relating to Indochina under any circumstances.

M. Jean Letourneau, Minister in the French Cabinet for the Associated States in Indochina, has just concluded a series of conversations with U.S. Government officials from the Department of State, Department of Defense, the Office of Director for Mutual Security, the Mutual Security Agency, and Department of the Treasury. The Ambassadors of Cambodia and Viet-Nam have also participated in these talks.

The principle which governed this frank and detailed exchange of views and information was the common recognition that the struggle in which the forces of the French Union and the Associated States are engaged against the forces of Communist aggression in Indochina is an integral part of the world-wide resistance by the Free Nations to Communist attempts at conquest and subversion. There was unanimous satisfaction over the vigorous and successful course of military operations, in spite of the continuous comfort and aid received by the Communist forces of the Viet-Minh from Communist China. The excellent performance of the Associated States' forces in battle was found to be a source of particular encouragement. Special tribute was paid to the 52,000 officers and men of the French Union and Associated States' armies who have been lost in this six years' struggle for freedom in Southeast Asia and to the 75,000 other casualties.

In this common struggle, however, history, strategic factors, as well as local and general resources require that the free countries concerned each assume primary responsibility for resistance in the specific areas where Communism has resorted to force of arms. Thus the United States assumes a large share of the burden in Korea while France has the primary role in Indochina. The partners, however, recognize the obligation to help each other in their areas of primary responsibility to the extent of their capabilities and within the limitations imposed by their global obligations as well as by the requirements in their own areas of special responsibility. It was agreed that success in this continuing struggle would entail an increase in the common effort and that the United States for its part will, therefore, within the limitations set by Congress, take steps to expand its aid to the French Union. It was further agreed that this increased assistance over and above present U.S. aid for Indochina, which now approximates one third of the total cost of Indochina operations, would be especially devoted to assisting France in the building of the national armies of the Associated States.

Mr. Letourneau reviewed the facts which amply demonstrate the determination of the Associated States to pursue with increased energy the strengthening of their authority and integrity both against internal subversion and against external aggression.

In this connection Mr. Letourneau reminded the participants that the accords of 1949, which established the independence within the French Union of Cambodia, Laos and Viet-Nam, have been liberally interpreted and supplemented by other agreements, thus consolidating this independence. Mr. Letourneau pointed out that the governments of the Associated States now exercise full authority except that a strictly limited number of services related to the necessities of the war now in progress remain temporarily in French hands. In the course of the examination of the Far Eastern economic and trade situation, it was noted that the Governments of the Associated States are free to negotiate trade treaties and agreements of all kinds with their neighbors subject only to whatever special arrangements may be agreed between members of the French Union.

It was noted that these states have been recognized by thirty-three foreign governments.

The conversations reaffirmed the common determination of the participants to prosecute the defense of Indochina and their confidence in a free, peaceful and prosperous future for Cambodia, Loas, and Viet-Nam.

Mr. Letourneau was received by the President, Mr. Acheson, and Mr. Foster, as Acting Secretary of Defense. Mr. John Allison, Assistant Secretary of State for Far Eastern Affairs, acted as Chairman of the U.S. Delegation participating in the conversations.

(247) SPEECH BY HO CHI MINH AT THE MEETING OF OFFICERS PREPARING FOR THE NORTHWEST MILITARY CAMPAIGN, September 9, 1952.

Source: Ho Chi Minh, *Selected Works, Vol. III*, pp. 364-370.

As early as April 1952, the Party Central Committee decided to shift the direction of their offensive from the plains to the mountainous Northwest. It was a strategic area for the French, both to menace the revolutionary Viet-Bac base area and to protect Southern Laos. The campaign, aimed at destroying the manpower of the French Union forces and capturing territory and population, would involve three divisions of the Vietnamese Army, and would last until the end of the year. After months of preparation, a conference of officers was convened to go over the battle plan in detail. Ho Chi Minh's remarks were general and inspirational, but he noted the significant fact that most of the enemy troops were Vietnamese rather than European and African and urged that agitation among them be considered a major aspect of the offensive.

Yesterday it rained heavily and all the streams were flooded. Arriving at a brook with a strong current and seeing a group of compatriots sitting on the other side waiting for the water to subside, I said to myself, "shouldn't I cross the stream at once so as not to keep you waiting." So a few other comrades and I took off our clothes and groping our way with sticks we succeeded in wading across the brook. On seeing my success, the group of compatriots also made up their mind to cross the stream. This is an experience for you, comrades. Whatever we do - big or small - if we are determined we shall be successful and shall imbue other people with the same determination.

Now I speak of the military campaign:

The Party Central Committee and the Party General Committee of the Army have carefully weighed the advantages and difficulties of the coming campaign and are determined that this campaign must be carried out successfully. It is not enough that only the Central Committee has determination. You must weigh and clearly see for yourselves the advantages and difficulties in order to be imbued with this determination. It is not enough that the Central Committee and you are determined, we must act in such a way that this determination permeates every soldier. This determination from the Central Committee must reach the rank and file through you. It must become a monolithic bloc from higher to lower ranks and from lower to higher ranks. To have determination does not mean to speak glibly of it but to have deep confidence. When meeting with advantages we must be determined to develop them and when encountering difficulties we must be determined to overcome them. Everyone in the army must be deeply imbued with determination.

In this meeting, the Party General Committee of the Army has disseminated in detail the Central Committee's resolutions and you have debated them. The significance and objective of the military campaign are:

- to annihilate the enemy's manpower,
- to win over the people,
- to liberate territory,

but the main task is *to annihilate the enemy's manpower*.

You have discussed the advantages and difficulties. When meeting with an advantage if we are not determined to develop it, it may likely turn into difficulty. When meeting with a difficulty, if we are determined to overcome it, it will become an advantage. In truth, nothing is easy and nothing is difficult. For example, it is easy to break off a branch. But if we are not determined and do it half heartedly we may not be able to break it off. It is difficult to carry out the revolution and to wage the Resistance War but with our determination we will be successful.

Determination does not lie in the meeting-place and in words but in work and deeds. We must have determination to promote a valiant fighting style. We must have determination to oppose all negative, wavering and selfish acts, and false reports.

We must be determined to fight, to endure hardships, difficulties and to overcome them, and determined to implement the policies of the Central Committee and the Government. In other words, in our behaviour, mind, deeds and fighting, in everything - big or small - we must be determined to win success.

The army is strong when it is well fed. The comrades in the commissariat must have determination to supply the troops with adequate food and weapons.

On their side, the troops must be determined:

- to light-heartedly endure privations,
- to strive to give a hand to the commissariat if necessary.

Food and weapons are sweat and tears of our compatriots, blood and bones of our troops, so we must value, spare, preserve and properly use them.

War-booty is not a gift from the enemy. It is thanks to the sweat and tears of our compatriots and the blood and bones of our troops that we can capture it. Prior to its capture, it belongs to the enemy, after it, it is ours. Therefore concerning war-booty we distribute to our compatriots what ought to be distributed, hand over to the Government what should be, and what should be used as reward for the troops must be given in an equitable and rational way. Corruption and waste must be absolutely avoided.

The Government has issued policies concerning the national minorities, you and the troops must implement them correctly. This is a measure to win over the people, frustrating the enemy's scheme of "using Vietnamese to harm Vietnamese". We must so do that each fighter becomes a propagandist. You must behave in such a way that the people welcome you on your arrival and give you willing aid during your stay and miss you on your departure. This would be a great success.

You must be aware that only a small part of enemy troops are Europeans and Africans while the majority are puppet troops. A great number of the latter are press-ganged into the army by the French. If you cleverly carry out the work of agitation among the puppet troops this would be a way to annihilate enemy manpower.

Our units are helped by civilians moving with them. You must educate and take good care of the volunteer workers, explain our policies to them and encourage them to work light-heartedly. A close friendship and solidarity must prevail between the troops and the volunteer workers, so that the latter are unwilling to go home, and like to stay on and help the troops. This is one of the factors for victory. If you fail to do so we shall meet with many difficulties.

It is thanks to good education, correct policies and strict discipline that the troops are strong. That is why *discipline must be strict.* There are two points in discipline that call for attention:

- Punishment
- and reward

Up to now, punishment and reward have been insufficient and that is a big mistake. There must be units mentioned in dispatches and awarded with medals. After you have proposed someone for a medal the proposal has immediately to be made public. The Government, the High Command and I are ready to reward those who score achievements. On the other hand those who have wrongly carried out the orders or made false reports must be punished severely.

The units must emulate with each other and the cadres between themselves to promote the movement for valiant fighting.

We must bear in mind that the revolutionary troops, first of all, the Party members, do not shun difficulties but must overcome them. We must learn the spirit of the Soviet Red Army and of the Chinese Liberation Army: when carrying out some difficult task, the unit which is entrusted with it prides itself on this honour, whereas those which are not appointed, feel quite unhappy to find that they have not yet the capacity required.

You can learn from this attitude. I am convinced that thanks to the leadership of the Party and the Government you will be able to take it up.

Divisional commanders down to groupleaders must share joy and hardships with the soldiers, take care, help and treat each other like blood brothers. This is a tradition of the Soviet Red Army and of the Chinese Liberation Army that our soldiers must learn as well. To succeed in so doing is tantamount to partially triumphing over the enemy before fighting him.

The units must emulate with each other to do as I advise you.

Are you determined to emulate with each other? (the meeting place resounded with 'Yes, we are!)

You are determined, so you must by all means score successes in your fighting. I am waiting for news of victory from you. I promise a reward to the troops in the period from September 2nd to December 19th. It is a small reward but of great value because I have made it myself.

There are other rewards beside this one for the units that are the first to perform feats of arms.

Are heroes not only the troops who exterminate the enemy and perform feats of arms but also the supply men who strive to serve the troops. In each of you exists heroism in the bud, you must develop it.

If you fulfil your task I shall always be cheerful and in good health.

As is known to some of you, on the setting up of our army, our men were equipped with only a few commodities and the few rifles they got were bought in contraband. We obtained great achievements notwithstanding, and the August Revolution was victorious.

Now that we have numerous troops, good generals and everyone has determination, we will certainly be successful.

(248) NSC 124/2: STATEMENT OF POLICY BY THE NATIONAL SECURITY COUNCIL ON STATES OBJECTIVES AND COURSES OF ACTION WITH RESPECT TO SOUTHEAST ASIA, June 25, 1952

Source: *U.S.-Vietnam Relations, Book 8*, pp. 522-534.

An NSC policy statement initially considered at the NSC meeting of March 5, 1952, was reconsidered in June 1952. It reaffirmed the U.S. determination to oppose any French withdrawal but again failed to specify what the U.S. would do beyond consulting with Britain and France. The text of NSC 124/2 represents only a slight change from the earlier draft, 124/1. In paragraph 5, for example, 124/1 had used "important" rather than "critical."

OBJECTIVE

1. To prevent the countries of Southeast Asia from passing into the communist orbit, and to assist them to develop the will and ability to resist communism from within and without and to contribute to the strengthening of the free world.

GENERAL CONSIDERATIONS

2. Communist domination, by whatever means, of all Southeast Asia would seriously endanger in the short term, and critically endanger in the longer term, United States security interests.

a. The loss of any of the countries of Southeast Asia to communist control as a consequence of overt or covert Chinese Communist aggression would have critical psychological, political and economic consequences. In the absence of effective and timely counteraction, the loss of any single country would probably lead to relatively swift submission to or an alignment with communism by the remaining countries of this group. Furthermore, an alignment with communism of the rest of Southeast Asia and India, and in the longer term, of the Middle East (with the probable exceptions of at least Pakistan and Turkey) would in all probability progressively follow. Such widespread alignment would endanger the stability and security of Europe.

b. Communist control of all of Southeast Asia would render the U.S. position in the Pacific offshore island chain precarious and would seriously jeopardize fundamental U.S. security interests in the Far East.

c. Southeast Asia, especially Malaya and Indonesia, is the principal world source of natural rubber and tin, and a producer of petroleum and other strategically important commodities. The rice exports of Burma and Thailand are critically important to Malaya, Ceylon and Hong Kong and are of considerable significance to Japan and India, all important areas of free Asia.

d. The loss of Southeast Asia, especially of Malaya and Indonesia, could result in such economic and political pressures in Japan as to make it extremely difficult to prevent Japan's eventual accommodation to communism.

3. It is therefore imperative that an overt attack on Southeast Asia by the Chinese Communists be vigorously opposed. In order to pursue the military courses of action envisaged in this paper to a favorable conclusion within a reasonable period, it will be necessary to divert military strength from other areas thus reducing our military capability in those areas, with the recognized risks involved therein, or to increase our military forces in being, or both.

4. The danger of an overt military attack against Southeast Asia is inherent in the existence of a hostile and aggressive Communist China, but such an attack is less probable than continued communist efforts to achieve domination through subversion. The primary threat to Southeast Asia accordingly arises from the possibility that the situation in Indochina may deteriorate as a result of the weakening of the resolve of, or as a result of the inability of the governments of France and of the Associated States to continue to oppose the Viet Minh rebellion, the military strength of which is being steadily increased by virtue of aid furnished by the Chinese Communist regime and its allies.

5. The successful defense of Tonkin is critical to the retention in non-Communist hands of mainland Southeast Asia. However, should Burma come under communist domination, a communist military advance through Thailand might make Indochina, including Tonkin, militarily indefensible. The execution of the following U.S. courses of action with respect to individual countries of the area may vary depending upon the route of communist advance in Southeast Asia.

6. Actions designed to achieve our objectives in Southeast Asia require sensitive selection and application, on the one hand to assure the optimum efficiency through coordination of measures for the general area, and on the other, to accommodate to the greatest practicable extent to the individual sen-

sibilities of the several governments, social classes and minorities of the area.

COURSES OF ACTION

Southeast Asia

7. With respect to Southeast Asia, the United States should:

a. Strengthen propaganda and cultural activities, as appropriate, in relation to the area to foster increased alignment of the people with the free world.

b. Continue, as appropriate, programs of economic and technical assistance designed to strengthen the indigenous non-communist governments of the area.

c. Encourage the countries of Southeast Asia to restore and expand their commerce with each other and with the rest of the free world, and stimulate the flow of the raw material resources of the area to the free world.

d. Seek agreement with other nations, including at least France, the UK, Australia and New Zealand, for a joint warning to Communist China regarding the grave consequences of Chinese aggression against Southeast Asia, the issuance of such a warning to be contingent upon the prior agreement of France and the UK to participate in the courses of action set forth in paragraphs 10 c, 12, 14 f (1) and (2), and 15 c (1) and (2), and such others as are determined as a result of prior trilateral consultation, in the event such a warning is ignored.

e. Seek UK and French agreement in principle that a naval blockade of Communist China should be included in the minimum courses of action set forth in paragraph 10 c below.

f. Continue to encourage and support closer cooperation among the countries of Southeast Asia, and between those countries and the United States, Great Britain, France, the Philippines, Australia, New Zealand, South Asia and Japan.

g. Strengthen, as appropriate, covert operations designed to assist in the achievement of U.S. objectives in Southeast Asia.

h. Continue activities and operations designed to encourage the overseas Chinese communities in Southeast Asia to organize and activate anti-communist groups and activities within their own communities, to resist the effects of parallel pro-communist groups and activities and, generally, to increase their orientation toward the free world.

i. Take measures to promote the coordinated defense of the area, and encourage and support the spirit of resistance among the peoples of Southeast Asia to Chinese Communist aggression and to the encroachments of local communists.

j. Make clear to the American people the importance of Southeast Asia to the security of the United States so that they may be prepared for any of the courses of action proposed herein.

Indochina

8. With respect to Indochina the United States should:

a. Continue to promote international support for the three Associated States.

b. Continue to assure the French that the U.S. regards the French effort in Indochina as one of great strategic importance in the general international interest rather than in the purely French interest, and as essential to the security of the free world, not only in the Far East but in the Middle East and Europe as well.

c. Continue to assure the French that we are cognizant of the sacrifices entailed for France in carrying out her effort in Indochina and that,
without overlooking the principle that France has the primary responsibility in Indochina, we will recommend to the Congress appropriate military,
economic and financial aid to France and the Associated States.

d. Continue to cultivate friendly and increasingly cooperative relations with the Governments of France and the Associated States at all levels with a view to maintaining and, if possible, increasing the degree of
influence the U.S. can bring to bear on the policies and actions of the
French and Indochinese authorities to the end of directing the course of
events toward the objectives we seek. Our influence with the French and
Associated States should be designed to further those constructive political, economic and social measures which will tend to increase the stability
of the Associated States and thus make it possible for the French to reduce
the degree of their participation in the military, economic and political
affairs of the Associated States.

e. Specifically we should use our influence with France and the Associated States to promote positive political, military, economic and social
policies, among which the following are considered essential elements:

(1) Continued recognition and carrying out by France of its primary
responsibility for the defense of Indochina.

(2) Further steps by France and the Associated States toward the
evolutionary development of the Associated States.

(3) Such reorganization of French administration and representation
in Indochina as will be conducive to an increased feeling of responsibility on the part of the Associated States.

(4) Intensive efforts to develop the armies of the Associated
States, including independent logistical and administrative services.

(5) The development of more effective and stable Governments in the
Associated States.

(6) Land reform, agrarian and industrial credit, sound rice marketing systems, labor development, foreign trade and capital formation.

(7) An aggressive military, political, and psychological program to
defeat or seriously reduce the Viet Minh forces.

(8) U.S.-French cooperation in publicizing progressive developments
in the foregoing policies in Indochina.

9. In the absence of large scale Chinese Communist intervention in Indochina, the United States should:

a. Provide increased aid on a high priority basis for the French Union
forces without relieving French authorities of their basic military responsibility for the defense of the Associated States in order to:

(1) Assist in developing indigenous armed forces which will eventually be capable of maintaining internal security without assistance
from French units.

(2) Assist the French Union forces to maintain progress in the restoration of internal security against the Viet Minh.

(3) Assist the forces of France and the Associated States to defend
Indochina against Chinese Communist aggression.

b. In view of the immediate urgency of the situation, involving possible large-scale Chinese Communist intervention, and in order that the
United States may be prepared to take whatever action may be appropriate in
such circumstances, make the plans necessary to carry out the courses of
action indicated in paragraph 10 below.

c. In the event that information and circumstances point to the conclusion that France is no longer prepared to carry the burden in Indochina,

or if France presses for an increased sharing of the responsibility for Indochina, whether in the UN or directly with the U.S. Government, oppose a French withdrawal and consult with the French and British concerning further measures to be taken to safeguard the area from communist domination.

10. In the event that it is determined, in consultation with France, that Chinese Communist forces (including volunteers) have overtly intervened in the conflict in Indochina, or are covertly participating to such an extent as to jeopardize retention of the Tonkin Delta area by French Union forces, the United States should take the following measures to assist these forces in preventing the loss of Indochina, to repel the aggression and to restore peace and security in Indochina.

    a. Support a request by France or the Associated States for immediate action by the United Nations which would include a UN resolution declaring that Communist China has committed an aggression, recommending that member states take whatever action may be necessary, without geographic limitation, to assist France and the Associated States in meeting the aggression.

    b. Whether or not UN action is immediately forthcoming, seek the maximum possible international support for, and participation in, the minimum courses of military action agreed upon by the parties to the joint warning. These minimum courses of action are set forth in sub-paragraph c immediately below.

    c. Carry out the following minimum courses of military action, either under the auspices of the UN or in conjunction with France and the United Kingdom and any other friendly governments:

    (1) A resolute defense of Indochina itself to which the United States would provide such air and naval assistance as might be practicable.

    (2) Interdiction of Chinese Communist communication lines including those in China.

    (3) The United States would expect to provide the major forces for task (2) above; but would expect the UK and France to provide at least token forces therefore and to render such other assistance as is normal between allies, and France to carry the burden of providing, in conjunction with the Associated States, the ground forces for the defense of Indochina.

11. In addition to the courses of action set forth in paragraph 10 above, the United States should take the following military actions as appropriate to the situation:

    a. If agreement is reached pursuant to paragraph 7-e, establishment in conjunction with the UK and France of a naval blockade of Communist China.

    b. Intensification of covert operations to aid anti-communist guerrilla forces operating against China and to interfere with and disrupt Chinese Communist lines of communication and military supply areas.

    c. Utilization, as desirable and feasible, of anti-communist Chinese forces, including Chinese Nationalist forces in military operations in Southeast Asia, Korea, or China proper.

    d. Assistance to the British to cover an evacuation from Hong Kong, if required.

    e. Evacuation of French Union civil and military personnel from the Tonkin delta, if required.

12. If, subsequent to aggression against Indochina and execution of the minimum necessary courses of action listed in paragraph 10-c above, the United States determines jointly with the UK and France that expanded military action against Communist China is rendered necessary by the situation, the United

States should take air and naval action in conjunction with at least France and
the UK against all suitable military targets in China, avoiding insofar as
practicable those targets in areas near the boundaries of the USSR in order not
to increase the risk of direct Soviet involvement.

13. In the event the concurrence of the United Kingdom and France to expanded military action against Communist China is not obtained, the United
States should consider taking unilateral action.

(249) TELEGRAM FROM HEATH TO ACHESON, December 5, 1952

Source: *U.S.-Vietnam Relations, Book 8*, pp. 538-539.

*The offensive by resistance force in the Northwest not only forced the
French to abandon strategic positions in the region but threatened the major
French base at Na San. This military pressure forced the French to request
150 U.S. Air Force mechanics to help with the urgent airlift required to hold
Na San. On December 22, Acheson notified Saigon of the Department's concurrence in the sending of 25 to 30 U.S. Air Force mechanics to Viet-nam on a temporary basis.*

The French have not (rpt not) asked for additional aircraft. What they do
request and General Trapnell is urgently recommending is that the 30 F-8's already programmed be expedited to arrive here not (rpt not) later than January
and that delivery of the 8 B-26's scheduled to arrive at rate of one a month
during calendar year 1953 be accelerated.

The French yesterday made, however, urgent request on which in Trapnell's
and my opinion immediately favorable action in some form or other should be
taken. The request is that 150 American Air Force mechanics be detailed immediately to Nhatrang Air Base for one month to give 50-hour checks to 18 C-47's
and 100 hour checks on another 18 C-47's. Nhatrang was chosen presumably because presence mechanics would be less conspicuous than if detailed to at Tonkin base or to Saigon. The French have made the same imperative request of
the French Air Ministry, but according local information, French Metropolitan
Air Force has only a few if any surplus mechanics for immediate despatch. The
French request is entirely legitimate. When Salan asked for and was granted
the 50 additional C-47's late last summer (21 were provided by US), sufficient
crews were available for normal maintenance. It was expected these would be
used for tactical drops of parachute troops. No (rpt no) sustained air lift
operation was or could have been forseen at that time. With loss of Nghialo
and the ensuing necessary decision of French command to attempt hold Na San to
prevent overrunning that country and Laos, an air lift had to be instituted.
As a result, the C-47's are operating at several times the normal rate, entailing urgent increased maintenance.

As an alternative to sending American mechanics, Trapnell and I have suggested possibility of the 36 planes being sent for repairs and checks to Clark
Field. Trip to Manila would add extra flying time to the planes, but that
might be the more practical operation. I can see no (rpt no) policy objection
either to despatching American maintenance crews for a few weeks stay here or
providing maintenance at Clark Field. On several occasions we have provided
mechanical specialists for brief periods for instruction and repair of certain
American equipment. This emergency maintenance is vital to holding of Na San
and for meeting any other emergency air-borne operations.

General Chassin, CINC French Air Force Fe, arrives today from Tonkin to
consult with Trapnell.

(250) LETTER FROM BRIGADIER GENERAL T. J. H. TRAPNELL, CHIEF, MILITARY ASSIS-
TANCE ADVISORY GROUP, INDOCHINA, TO GEN. COLLINS, December 20, 1952

Source: *U.S.-Vietnam Relations, Book 9*, pp. 2-3.

*The chief of the U.S. military mission in Saigon reported that the French
had been taken by surprise by the start of the "Viet Minh" winter offensive in
the Northwest on October 15. He noted the major problems in the military situation: a defensive posture, a ceiling on French Air Force personnel in Indochina, and insufficient numbers of troops - a problem the French were trying to
remedy by an expansion of the Vietnamese National Army by 40 battalions.*

It became increasingly evident after my arrival in Indo China and seeing
the terrain, visiting the troops, and knowing the type of combat, that the
most important and immediate need to the successful conclusion of the war in
Indo China was more troops. During the past year, the Vietnamese Army has been
organized as scheduled. However, most of these units have been activated by
merely transferring and renaming units in the Vietnamese Army which were already in being in the French Colonial Army. I am convinced that additional
Vietnamese battalions, over and above the units approved for support by the
Joint Chiefs of Staff, should be activated.

In an informal conversation, the matter was discussed with General Salan
who agreed to the need but felt that the cost of many additional battalions and
the cadre requirements were beyond the capacity of France to support, but that
a realistic number should be set up to be supported and trained. In order to
have a clear picture of the requirements, a study was made on the basis of an
additional forty (40) battalions.

In a short conference with General Alessandri, Military Advisor to His Majesty Bao Dai, he stated that he recognized the immediate need for additional
Vietnamese troops, and he explained to me his concept for the organization of
additional battalions. These troops would be armed only with shoulder weapons,
light machine guns, and 60-MM mortars and would be trained in maneuvers over
mountainous terrain, capable of finding and destroying the enemy in his own
territory. Each battalion would be cadred with a minimum of seven (7) French
officers and thirty (30) French non-commissioned officers. French cadres would
be furnished as far as possible from the Vietnamese battalions already in being,
but which are at present being employed on a static guard-duty basis. Military
schools would be expanded in order to permit the battalions to be ready for a
combat assignment in December 1953.

This is an ambitious program, but one which (if implemented) will most
surely bring this war to a quicker end. There is no problem as to manpower
availability. The equipment required can be met by substitution of items already scheduled for programming in the FY 1954 MDA Program; however, the big
problem is the money necessary for the pay, rations, and individual equipment.
The French state that this is beyond the financial capacity of the Vietnamese
government or France. Their estimate for these additional forty (40) battalions is twelve (12) billion francs for equipment and seventy (70) billion
francs a year for maintenance. This figure is high in comparison with our estimate, because it includes the construction cost for schools and barracks, as
well as pay, rations, ammunition, POL, and clothing. The French staff is now
drawing up plans for this proposed expansion.

The French Air Force in Indo China has been hampered by (1) a late delivery
of MDAP programmed items and (2) a personnel ceiling imposed by Metropolitan
France, which is well below that required to do an efficient job. The types
and number of aircraft assigned are, in general, satisfactory for support of
ground actions. In the case of airborne operations involving considerable number of troops, additional airlift and personnel must be brought in for temporary periods. Since greater emphasis has been placed upon this theatre and a

high supply priority established, the supply picture has improved considerably in the past three (3) months and shows every indication of being completely re-lieved in another three to six months. The personnel shortage, however, will remain and will continue to adversely affect operations. The French have placed an arbitrary ceiling of 10,000 air-force personnel for FIC and we be-lieve this figure is about 5,000 short of that needed for efficient operations of the total number of aircraft currently assigned and employed. A conserva-tive estimate indicates that the French Air Force could double its sortie rate with even a 33% increase in personnel.

In addition to the military problem there are political, economic, and so-cial considerations which must be solved. An extensive psychological warfare program can and must be implemented. Also the French must change their tacti-cal thinking from defensive action to one of vigorous offense.

The Viet Minh launched their winter offensive in Tonkin on 15 October 1952, taking the French by surprise not only as to time (three weeks earlier than anticipated), but also as to the direction and objective. The enemy has conse-quently retained the initiative ever since. However, operation LORRAINE (com-bined airborne-ground maneuver), initiated by the French-Vietnamese forces on 10 November, successfully cut off the Viet Minh divisions from their Chinese supply routes and overran substantial forward supply dumps. On 26 November, the French withdrew their forces back into the perimeter in order to release several Groups Mobile for action to counteract Viet Minh infiltration in the southern part of the Delta. Am convinced if the French could have remained in the PHU DOAN area and extended their operation to YEN BAY, the Viet Minh reac-tion would of necessity have been to reverse the direction of their operations, engage the French in that area to clear their supply routes, with the result that a decisive action would have resulted under conditions favorable to the French-Vietnamese forces.

General de Linares is still hoping to make a trip to Korea, but both he and General Salan feel that he should not leave at this time.

1953

(251) REPORT BY HO CHI MINH TO THE FOURTH CONFERENCE OF THE PARTY CENTRAL
COMMITTEE, January 25-30, 1953 (extract)

Source: Committee to Research Army History, Political Directorate, Viet-nam
People's Army, *Lich Su Quan Doi Nhan Dan Viet Nam (History of the Viet-nam
People's Army)* (Hanoi: Quan Doi Nhan Dan, 1974), pp. 511-513 (Translation by
the editor).

*The Central Committee's Fourth Conference concentrated on two major prob-
lems: putting an effective rent reduction program into effect to lay the
groundwork for land reform, and setting the military line for 1953. Ho Chi
Minh presented a report to the Conference reviewing the course of the war in
1952 and the situation in 1953. He warned that the war would become even harder and more complex, because the U.S. and France would step up their efforts,
hoping to "occupy our country and make it a military base to attack China."
Regarding military policy, he presented ten principles to guide the strategy of
the resistance.*

1. Avoid strong points and attack weak points in order to disperse the
enemy's forces and destroy the enemy's manpower and widen the free zone.
That is our strategic line at present.

2. Main force troops on the North battlefield must use fluid mobile warfare, in order to annihilate the enemy's manpower bit by bit and weaken the
enemy and must coordinate it with attacks on fortified positions, one by one
in order to take important points and small towns where the enemy has gaps or
is weak. We do this in order to achieve the objectives of fighting where we
are sure of victory, and of broadening the free zone. At the same time, we may
use positional warfare to draw the enemy's forces to us in order to attack them,
disperse the enemy's forces, confuse the enemy's plans and create conditions
for mobile warfare.

3. The battlefield in the enemy's rear must broaden guerrilla warfare in
order to annihilate and wear down small parts of the enemy; in order to resist
enemy sweeps, protect the lives and property of the people, harass, sabotage,
and dominate the enemy; propagandize and educate the masses in those zones, reduce the pool of recruitment for puppet troops, widen our guerrilla zones and
guerrilla base areas, and establish and strengthen resistance bases in the enemy's rear.

4. Besides increasing main force troops and building local troops, the
free zone and rather large guerrilla bases, we must build guerrilla militia organizations not detached from production. Those guerrilla militia organizations not only can take responsibility for repression of counterrevolutionaries,
maintain security in the villages, protect the interests of the masses and

struggle with the enemy and coordinate combat with main force troops, but also can be used for replacements for main force troops.

5. Regarding the military guidance we must combine the forms of struggle mentioned above in a flexible, shrewd manner. That would be profitable, on one hand, for the main force troops who can find many opportunities to annihilate the enemy; and on the other hand, it can help guerrillas operate and help our guerrilla bases in the enemy's rear develop and be consolidated.

6. In the guidance of the forms of struggle mentioned above, we must realize clearly the long-term character of resistance war. Therefore, we must pay much attention to maintaining the certain combat strength of the army, not causing it to be worn down or too tired. At the same time we must ask the troops to accept difficulty and hardship, to be resolute and fearless and to emulate in killing the enemy and recording feats of arms. Those two things are not in conflict but are united with each other.

7. We must strengthen political work always raising the political level and class consciousness of our troops; we must insure the implementation of the policy of the Party and Government; we must thoroughly maintain self-conscious discipline regarding the military and political aspect. Thus we must strengthen the leadership of the Party in the army and must achieve democracy in the army.

8. We must strengthen military work, first of all always regarding training troops as important. We must strive to bring up cadres, forge their thinking, and raise the level of political consciousness as well as the tactical and technical level of the cadres. That is the most important point in various kinds of work.
We must strengthen the work of the General Staff and of the Supply Directorate. Only if the work of the General Staff is strengthened can we raise the tactics and technique of the troops. Only if the work of the Supply Directorate is strengthened can we insure sufficient supplies to the war and raise the combat strength of the troops.
But we must resolutely resist the erroneous tendency for agencies to become swollen.

9. We must have a common plan for the building and reinforcement of the army. Besides mobilizing youth in the free zone to join the army, we must pay much attention to winning over and reforming puppet troops who have surrendered to us in order to reinforce our troops. In organizing new troops, we must use completely new cadres and new officers, but must use the method of taking old troops and making them the foundation for broadening new troops. At the same time, we must not clean out guerrilla troops in order to provide replacements for main force troops.

10. We must strengthen and improve gradually the equipment of our troops, especially the construction of artillery.

(252) RESOLUTION ON THE STRATEGIC MILITARY LINE ADOPTED BY THE FOURTH CENTRAL COMMITTEE CONFERENCE OF THE VIETNAM WORKERS' PARTY, January 25-30, 1953 (Extract)

Source: "Contribution to the History of Dienbienphu" *Vietnamese Studies (Hanoi) No. 3*, March 1965, pp. 37-39.

After hearing Ho's report the Central Committee adopted a resolution on the general military line of the Party which reflected Ho Chi Minh's ten points. The main elements of the strategy were attacking the enemy's weakest points, fighting only where victory was certain, and then piecemeal destruction of the enemy's forces.

Text:

. . . At its meeting from January 23 to 27, 1953, the Central Committee of the Workers' Party had already defined the great lines of the strategy to be adopted.

In the North, we had important regular forces, whereas in the Centre and the South, our troops were not yet in a position to constitute a great threat to enemy positions. That was why the enemy had concentrated two-thirds of their forces in the northern theatre of operations, leaving unprotected several fronts in Central and South Vietnam, and in Laos and Cambodia as well. The Northern delta was thus a "tough spot" to avoid, whereas the other fronts were "soft" ones where we could launch offensives.

"Our strategic orientation is to exert our efforts in the direction of 'soft' spots, attacking the enemy wherever he is weak, compelling him to scatter his forces. We shall thus create conditions for the liberation of the Northern delta. To give our efforts such an orientation does not mean to remain inactive in the North. On the contrary, we must intensify the war in the North, intensify guerilla warfare in the enemy's rear, in the plains, so as to narrow down the enemy-occupied zones gradually. If conditions are favourable, we shall concentrate regular forces to liberate the smaller towns, in such a way as to be able, when the situation allows us to do so, to entirely liberate the Northern delta. (. . .)

The leading principle of our patriotic war is to think of it as a protracted war which is to be carried out by relying essentially on our own forces; that is why we must avoid subjectivism, which incites us to underestimate the enemy, as well as to impatience and adventurism. We must strike only when success is certain and advance cautiously. If we are sure of victory, we shall fight to the end; if not, we shall resolutely avoid battle.

The theatre of operations in our country is but small; we have few troops; on the whole, we have only the right to win; we cannot afford to suffer defeats. . . . We must enlarge our bases, intensify guerilla warfare, extend our guerilla bases in the enemy's rear, and prevent him from encircling and smothering us.

So, from the point of view of strategy, our regular forces must essentially engage in mobile warfare, a very flexible kind of mobile warfare. The point is to annihilate enemy forces, not in a single sweep, but piecemeal. We must ensure for our forces such supremacy as to wipe out whole enemy units at a time, not engage in battle of attrition, not content ourselves with merely putting enemy troops to flight.

However, part of our troops must be able to capture enemy fortified positions; otherwise, we shall not be able to liberate whole regions and expand our bases. In the course of mobile warfare, we must seek opportunities to capture fortified positions and this positional warfare will in turn create favourable conditions for mobile warfare. The enemy front may be likened to a chain, of which we must seek out the weakest link, concentrate our forces to break it and thus dislocate the whole chain. (. . .)

To wipe out enemy forces is the main task; at the same time one must strive to free areas of strategic importance where the enemy is relatively weak. . . . In the Centre and the South, in the enemy's rear, guerilla warfare remains the principal form of fighting."

(253) <u>VO NGUYEN GIAP'S TET LETTER</u>, January 1953 (extract)

Source: Vo Nguyen Giap, *Orders of the Day, Speeches and Mobilization Letters,* pp. 177-180 (Translation by editor).

The Northwest Campaign succeeded in liberating some 28,000 square miles of territory in the Northwest formerly under French control, including the Dien Bien Phu Valley, and some 250,000 people, while inflicting heavy losses on French troops. In his Tet letter, Giap discussed the victories of the previous year and looked ahead to the strategic requirements for 1953. The main emphasis in his analysis was on the necessity for land reform, which had just been decided by the Party Central Committee at its Fourth Conference.

Today, the first day of Tet, while we are all welcoming the new year together with the people, welcoming our new task and happily reading the Tet greetings from Chairman Ho, we review the great victories during the past year: the Spring victory at Hoa-binh, the fall-winter victory in the Northwest, and the victory thoughout the year in the enemy's rear area in the Northern plain. In the enter and South, the guerrilla warfare held firm and on the An-khe front we are winning a big victory.

In one year of struggle, we have annihilated 65,000 of the enemy's manpower. That is a big accomplishment compared with the year before.

Those victories show the clearsighted leadership of the Party, the Government and Chairman Ho.

Those victories show the big results of the political retraining and the progress of our army on all aspects: ideology, strategic guidance, and tactics technology.

These victories show the spirit of heroic sacrifice, the determination to struggle to complete our army's mission and our people's spirit of determination to serve the frontlines, particularly the brother and sister civilian laborers on all battlefields.

Those victories show the firm faith of our army and people in the leadership of the Party, Government and Chairman Ho, and their confidence that the longterm and difficult resistance war will definitely win.

Those victories have caused the enemy to meet many difficulties and forced them to disperse their main forces in order to cope with us, made them even more passive than they were before, and further our consolidated posture of holding the initiative on the Northern battlefields.

The glorious victories of our army and people mentioned above mesh with the victories of the Korean People's Army and the Chinese volunteer army struggling to annihilate the American imperialist aggressors and their gang of lackies, with the victories of the Asian and Pacific Peace Conference, of the Conference of World's People struggling to protect peace in Vienna and increases further the forces of the front of world peace and democracy lead by the Soviet Union.

In the new year, we are happy to receive these new tasks:

1. We must continue our political retraining, and strengthen political retraining in the military.

2. We must raise our determination, establish a style of energetically annihilating the enemy, heroically struggle, and annihilate still more of the enemy's manpower.

3. We must actively execute the policy of the Party and Government, and especially participate in the approaching great mobilization of the peasants. This year, the Party Central Committee, the Government and Chairman Ho have decided to launch the mobilization of peasants to thoroughly reduce rents, carry out reduction of debts, and distribute communal land and the land of French colonialists and Vietnamese traitors to the peasants. The main thing is to reduce rents, aiming at satisfying initially the just demand of the peasants for land and winning political preeminence for the peasants.

The Central Committee of the Party, the Government and Chairman Ho have decided on this because the peasants are the main force of the revolution and the resistance, and because serving their real interests and gaining political pre-eminence for the peasants in the countryside means strengthening the primary forces of the people, and increasing the power of the resistance.

As cadres and fighters of the People's Army, an army whose composition includes an absolute majority of peasants, we must recognize clearly the importance and the great function of mobilizing the peasants. We must actively participate in the task of mobilizing the peasants, not only to take back the rights for the people in the rear area but to take back rights for ourselves as well. We must actively study and carry out the policy of the Party and Government, and endeavor to forge further the class standpoint, the mass concept and the sense of serving the people.

Going to the frontlines, you heroically kill the invader; returning to the rear area, you actively participate in and support the struggle of the peasants --that is the task and honor of each cadre and fighter in the army.

In the new year, our task is very heavy but also very glorious. Under the leadership of the Party, Government and Chairman Ho, having confidence in the strong forces of the laboring people and in the support of the front of world peace and democracy lead by the Soviet Union, we will definitely succeed in political retraining, fight heroically, annihilate a great part of the enemy's manpower, win back and protect the people, develop guerrilla warfare strongly, and take the resistance war to complete victory.

(254) MEMORANDUM FROM THE JOINT CHIEFS OF STAFF FOR SECRETARY OF DEFENSE CHARLES WILSON, March 13, 1953

Source: *U.S.-Vietnam Relations, Book 9*, pp. 11-14

Joint Chiefs of Staff were requested to reassess U.S. assistance to the French effort in Indochina soon after the Eisenhower Administration took office. Their recommendations included additional aid for expanding the Vietnamese forces, the lifting by France of the ceiling on its Air Force personnel in Indochina, improvement of port and air facilitation and giving the Vietnamese military forces more autonomy.

1. The Joint Chiefs of Staff have re-examined the problems of United States participation in the Indochina operation as requested by your memorandum dated 19 January 1953, subject as above, and submit herewith their comments and recommendations.

2. The Joint Chiefs of Staff have considered broadening U.S. participation in the Indochina operation both from within and without the framework of the Mutual Defense Assistance Program (MDAP) with a view toward speeding and improving the development of indigenous combat forces and supporting logistical and operating facilities. Special consideration has been given, as requested by your office, to the training of indigenous forces and maintenance of U.S. supplied equipment by U.S. personnel.

3. NSC 124/2 with regard to Indochina states in part that " . . . we should use our influence with France and Associated States to promote positive political, military, economic and social policies," and "Continued recognition and carrying out by France of its primary responsibility for the defense of Indochina." NSC 124/2 also states that . . . "Our influence with the French and Associated States should be designed to further those constructive political, economic and social measures which will tend to increase the stability of the Associated States and thus make it possible for the French to reduce the degree of their participation in the military, economic and political affairs of the Associated States." In keeping with the foregoing policy, the Joint Chiefs of Staff consider that actions to broaden U.S. participation in Indo-

china would require sensitive selection and application to avoid any semblance of usurpation of French responsibilities and prerogatives. It is anticipated that any attempt by the United States to intrude in the French military responsibilities in Indochina would be strongly resisted, but the U.S. should seek to impress upon the French the necessity and desirability of granting the Associated States ever-increasing responsibilities with respect to expansion of their economic, political and military potentialities.

4. The U.S. Ambassador to Indochina has reported that the French and Vietnamese are in general agreement on the necessity of expanding the Vietnamese Army by some 57 light battalions involving approximately 40,000 troops. The details on financing and the degree of autonomy and military responsibility to be allowed the Vietnamese Army have yet to be decided. It is envisaged that these additional battalions will provide the Franco-Vietnamese forces with sufficient strength to undertake effective offensive action in Vietminh-held territory. It is the opinion of the Joint Chiefs of Staff that this augmentation of the Vietnamese Army is one of the most important and feasible actions that can be taken to improve the situation in Indochina and that United States support of the program should be undertaken as necessary upon receipt of definite planning data from the French.

5. The addition of another squadron of transport aircraft would materially aid offensive operations by providing increased troop-carrier and supply support capabilities.

6. The report of the ad hoc committee, formed in accordance with your memorandum for the Joint Secretaries dated 19 January 1953 and which considered the foregoing projects has a final conclusion:

> "The final determination of the feasibility of implementation of the augmentation of Vietnamese forces cannot be accomplished until receipt of a concrete proposal from the French Government."

The Joint Chiefs of Staff consider that the French should be encouraged to expedite the submission of such proposals in order that the United States may take steps to provide such aid as may be deemed appropriate. In this connection the Joint Chiefs of Staff indicated in a memorandum for you, dated 11 February 1953, that plans now under consideration to expand the Republic of Korea Army may introduce some competing requirements, primarily in non-critical items. However, certain ammunition requirements could be both critical and competing.

7. The Joint Chiefs of Staff consider that the augmentation mentioned above should be energetically prosecuted and financially supported in order that the Franco-Vietnamese forces will be able to undertake offensive operations during the 1953-54 dry season.

8. In view of their experience and the language difficulties involved, it is considered that the French are better qualified to conduct the training of the indigenous forces than United States personnel would be. However, it is believed that the French might profit by applying some of the methods the United States forces in Korea are using in training Republic of Korea troops and officers. In this connection the Commander in Chief Far East (CINCFE), and General Juin have agreed to exchange French and Vietnam officers from Indochina to Korea, and Korean Military Advisory Group (KMAG) personnel to Indochina. Accordingly, there appears to be no need for further United States participation in the training of the Vietnamese forces unless specifically invited.

9. The formation of effective Vietnamese forces is handicapped by deficient Vietnamese incentive and lack of qualified indigenous military leadership. Consequently the French should be given encouragement to grant Vietnamese

forces more military autonomy and to train indigenous officers to assume more responsibility for control of local forces.

10. Although the U.S. Air Force has recently assigned some aircraft maintenance crews, on a temporary basis, to help the French overcome a critical period in their aircraft operations, it is considered that the French have the ability and can provide the personnel which would permit maximum utilization of their aircraft. Current practice provides for Military Assistance Advisory Group (MAAG) to obtain the aid of special technical groups from the U.S. Services whenever there is a need to instruct the French in the maintenance and operation of United States supplied equipment. This type of assistance is deemed adequate to meet current maintenance requirements.

11. The studying possible courses of action to be taken in the defense of Indochina, the inadequate port facilities at Haiphong and air facilities in the Hanoi area have been pointed up as major items in restricting the support of military operations. The Chief, MAAG, Indochina, has mentioned that the movement of supplies into the delta could be speeded by two or three months if Haiphong were able to receive and unload deep-draft vessels. The air depot at Bien Hoa is in particular need of expansion in order to accelerate air shipments. The improvement of the port and air facilities would not only provide impetus to military operations, but would benefit the economic status of Vietnam. Such improvement could be made with U.S. monetary and material aid, but in order to avoid possible Chinese reaction, significant numbers of U.S. personnel should not be utilized.

12. In a letter to the Chief of Staff, U.S. Army, dated 20 December 1952, the Chief, MAAG, Indochina stated that the shortage of French Air Force personnel has had considerable adverse effect on operations. He mentioned that, as a conservative estimate, the sortie rate could be doubled if the personnel strength were increased by one-third. The U.S. Ambassador to Indochina and the U.S. Consul, Hanoi, have both reported that French officials in Indochina will press for an increase in the air force personnel ceiling for Indochina. It is believed the French should be encouraged through diplomatic channels to increase the Indochina air force ceiling.

13. Active combat participation by the United States in the Indochina operation is not favored in view of the capability of France and the Associated States to provide adequate forces thereof, and present United States worldwide military commitments.

14. However, in order to provide impetus and support to the military operations in Indochina, it is recommended that:

a.   The French Government be encouraged to take early action to augment the Vietnamese forces and increase their air force personnel strength in Indochina.

b.   Steps be taken to improve the port and air facilities in the Tonkin Delta area as early as practicable.

c.   The United States furnish material and financial support to assist in accomplishment of a and b above upon receipt of a definite program from French.

d.   The United States give serious consideration to utilizing this increased support to impress upon the French the necessity and desirability for granting the Associated States more responsibility with respect to expansion of their economic and political potentials, and to granting more autonomy to Vietnamese military forces.

(255) TELEGRAM FROM SECRETARY OF STATE JOHN FOSTER DULLES TO AMBASSADOR C. DOUGLAS DILLON IN PARIS, March 19, 1953.

Source: *U.S.-Vietnam   Relations, Book 9*, pp. 15-16.

The new Secretary of State, John Foster Dulles, instructed his Ambassador in Paris, C. Douglas Dillon, to inform the French government that the U.S. believed a plan for destroying the "principal regular enemy forces" within approximately two years was "essential." He indicated that the U.S. would have to be able to assure Congress that French plans were sound in order to obtain the necessary financial support for them. Thus the U.S. was about to enter a new phase of involvement in the strategic conduct of the war.

Recent Paris working-level discussions added substantially to our factual background on Indochina. Please express to Foreign Minister my appreciation for cooperation all concerned. Also take early opportunity discuss informally on my behalf with Mayer or Bidault forthcoming conversations along following general lines:

QTE Secretary Acheson in December 1952 and I last month have discussed with our French colleagues the Indochina situation. On both occasions we received indications French Government was planning to request US GOVT to increase already considerable share of financial burden of the struggle which it is now bearing. I assume that when Mayer, Bidault and Letourneau come to Washington they will furnish further particulars regarding French Government's plans and resulting requirements. It may be helpful to them in formulating their position to express to them informally some of considerations involved not only in matter of additional aid but also in continuation American assistance at present substantial level. Considerations are:

First, Government and people of US are fully aware of importance to free world of war being waged in Indochina by armies of France and Associated States. They appreciate sacrifices which have been and are being made and degree to which Communist plans have been thwarted by magnificent defense carried out in Indochina against Communist aggression.

Second, we envisage Indochina situation with real sense of urgency. We believe continued military stalemate will produce most undesirable political consequences in Indochina, France and U.S. Therefore, we heartily agree that considerable increased effort having as its aim liquidation principal regular enemy forces within period of, say, twenty-four months is essential. We obviously do not wish share Franco-Vietnamese responsibility for conduct operations. However, if interested Departments this Government are to urge Congress to make necessary appropriations for Indochina for FY 54, those Departments must be convinced that necessarily top secret strategic plans for Indochina are sound and can be and will be aggressively and energetically prosecuted.

Third, I share concern frequently expressed in French circles regarding adequacy of the financial contribution to prosecution of war derived from residents of the Associated States including French businessmen. While I welcome increased Vietnamese Government contribution recently made, I believe there is ground for thoroughgoing re-examination this problem into which balance of payment and rate of exchange considerations enter and which of course is of interest to us in its bearing upon the need for U.S. aid.

Fourth, I look forward to opportunity talking with my French colleagues on question of free world policy in Far East as whole and particularly the policies which we should adopt in order to discourage further Chinese Communist aggression. I hope to reach agreement that speedy defeat of Viet Minh forces in Indochina would deter rather than provoke Chinese Communist aggression in Tonkin since it would be a clear indication of our joint determination to meet force with effective force.

Fifth, I should appreciate receiving any views which my French friends may care to convey regarding relations between the U.S. and the Associated States of Indochina and particularly regarding participation by latter in discussions of military and economic policy and in reception of U.S. aid. END QUOTE

Please handle on strictly oral basis and let me have reaction. The specified points are designed to be exploratory; I would welcome any ideas French may wish to convey on these or other topics prior to our conversation.

(256) TELEGRAM FROM SECRETARY OF STATE DULLES TO AMBASSADOR DILLON, March 26, 1953 (Extract)

Source: *U.S.-Vietnam Relations, Book 9*, pp. 17-18.

In disucssions with French Premier Meyer and Minister Letourneau, President Eisenhower emphasized the need to convince both Americans and the people of the Associated States that the latter were fighting for their own independence. Mayer assured him that Franco-Vietnamese plans were aimed at reducing the revolutionary forces to a "negligible factor" within two years.

Re EDC President stressed major importance attached thereto both by American people and himself. EDC vital not only because it provides best means obtain German contribution without which no real defense of Europe can be undertaken but also because it provides means for eventual European viability, also impossible keep Germany much longer under occupation status.

President declared that EDC so important in American eyes that American people would not support aid to France if they were given impression that France resorting to dilatory tactics in order to postpone ratification this vital development. Therefore, when setting forth any conditions precedent to ratification, French must be very careful to point out why these conditions are in fact vital to France and not inconsequential details or obstructionist moves.

Concerning Indochina President expressed full American sympathy for valiant French struggle as part of over-all fight against Communist aggression.

He recognized this struggle not just another colonial war but advised French to make this very clear as many Americans still under misapprehension. President expressed great American interest in French program leading to solution of Indochina problem making clear that he was not talking in terms of a complete victory. However requests for further American assistance could not be considered without full knowledge of French political and military plans permitting US Government to see why its assistance was required and how it would be used. President expressed great interest in measures being taken by French to obtain greatest possible support by local populations through convincing them they were fighting their own war for their own independence.

. . . .

Re Indochina Mayer started by referring to NAC Resolution December 1952 re QTE continuing aid UNQTE from NATO Governments. He said French political and military plans would be communicated to us later during the talks. Meanwhile he stressed his full agreement with President that the task was two-fold: militarily, Associated States Armies had to be developed for victory and for internal pacification. Politically it was necessary to develop popular basis for national government to protect them from eventual take-over by Vietminh forces. While expressing the greatest interest in Gen Clark's report following visit to Indochina Mayer was careful to point out differences between Korea and Indochina.

Le Tourneau said that details of recent Dalat agreements would be given to us later but that in meanwhile he can say that these will permit presentation of a Franco-Vietnamese plan which should lead within two years to reduction of

Vietminh to a negligible factor in Indochina if no material increase in Chinese or Soviet aid in meanwhile. LeTourneau expressed confidence that popular support for local governments was increasing day by day, pointing to success of January elections in Vietnam, to fact that much more officer material is now available for National Armies and that all enlisted men needed under present financial limitations were available on volunteer basis. Finally he expressed confidence that local populations supported local governments more vigorously now that Vietminh was clearly recognized as the agent not only of Communism but also of traditional Chinese enemy.

(257) TELEGRAM FROM DULLES TO DILLON, March 27, 1953

Source: *U.S-Vietnam Relations, Book 9*, pp. 19-20.

Mayer and Letourneau expressed their concern that a Korean armistice would increase the danger of a Chinese intervention in Indochina. But Dulles disagreed, citing the threat of U.S. air and sea attack as an adequate deterrent to Chinese attack. Again Letourneau stressed the French belief that they could break the back of their adversaries in 24 months.

French delegation met with Secretary, Secretary of Treasury, Director Mutual Security (Defense represented by Assistant Secretary Nash) for three hours yesterday afternoon. Ambassadors Cambodia and Vietnam attended initial portion session devoted general expose to Indochina situation. Following their departure further discussion Indochina problem took place and Secretary also replied to points made by Mayer to President during morning but which latter had not repeat not had time answer. . . .

Mayer in introducing Letourneau made it clear Vietnam and Cambodia independent states and their peoples fighting maintain their freedom. Letourneau stressed French interest in creating strong free states Indochina that would later not repeat not lose through political weakness what they had gained militarily. He also highlighted importance recent "Dalat decisions" providing increased Vietnamese financial effort and creation 54 new Vietnamese battalions comprising 40,000 men. . . . While he could not repeat not promise complete victory he believed implementation this plan which is reasonable and practical would result in breaking back Vietminh in 24 months. Finally he stated his conviction true Vietnamese nationalism resided Bao Bai and his government and supporters and not repeat not Vietminh who were Soviet-controlled.

Cambodian and Vietnamese Ambassadors made brief remarks. Secretary concluded this portion meeting reiterating our realization this was common war which while now restricted Korea and Indochina, might break out anywhere. He expressed hope for program commensurate with peril which we realized might call for additional assistance our part. He concluded such assistance depended on many factors most important was whether plan France and Associated States was practical.

After departure Associated States Ambassadors Secretary stated we understood French feeling tiredness in Indochina after seven years warfare but expressed conviction feeling would evaporate in face of positive constructive program and concluded we must not repeat not be immobilized by fear.

Mayer and Letourneau posed questions what we would do event Chinese Communist offensive Indochina and if we didn't think Korean armistice might cause considerable risk Chinese attack Indochina. Secretary said he thought Chinese Communist attack unlikely because they realize would start chain disasters far outweighing any possible gains and while there no repeat no question land invasion of China, vista of trouble through sea and air attack would be strong deterrent to them. Nash stated recent talks on five-power cooperation Southeast Asia had made considerable progress and mentioned forthcoming meeting Honolulu where five-power talks would continue on invitation Admiral Radford. Secretary agreed might be necessary for military reasons talks about what he would do in event evacuation but concluded firmly he convinced there would be no re- peat no evacuation. He also noted, in unlikely event Korean armistice, that if Chinese obviously simply concluded such arrangement order transport troops attack Indochina, armistice would have automatically failed purpose. Finally he referred to integral connection two wars as contained President's State Union Message.

(258) SPEECH BY FRENCH PREMIER RENE MEYER, Washington, D.C., March 27, 1953 (Extract)

Source: Press release text, Ambassade de France, Service de Presse et d'in- formation, pp. 7-11.

In a renewed bid for U.S. public support, French Premier Meyer suggested that the "Viet Minh" offensive had actually been aimed at preparing a thrust at Thailand and Burma - an allegation contradicted both by Communist documents as well as subsequent developments. Meyer also claimed that Ho Chi Minh had once promised that he would be in Hanoi by Christmas 1950. In fact, all Communist documents emphasized the long-term nature of the struggle, and warned against expectations of ending the war by any particular date.

. . . For France, an effective organization of European defense is an or- ganization that puts France in position to fulfill her duty toward the free world, not only in Europe, but also in the rest of the world, and especially in Indo-China.

In that part of the world, France is deeply convinced that the future will vindicate the unremitting devotion of its efforts. To realize how much the Communist enemy has been slowed down you have only to recall that Ho Chi Minh, the leader of Viet Minh, solemnly promised that he would be in Hanoi by Christ- mas 1950. The decline of the Viet Minh is shown on the economic front by the collapse of its currency and on the political front by the extent of popular support that has rallied to the cause we are defending. Nevertheless, the struggle continues; and, since it is understood between us that I am speaking here in perfect candor, let me point out to you that, while I pay my respects to the objectivity and the wisdom of your commentaries, the character of our struggle in Indo-China is not yet, so far as I can tell, fully understood in all its aspects.

There has been talk in connection with Indo-China even in the French press about the "dirty war", the "colonial war", the "forgotten war". More recently, it has been described as the "seven-year war", and, alas, I cannot repudiate that particular epithet. But I myself should now like to propose to you a new name: the "misunderstood war". I am not addressing these remarks to you en- lightened gentlemen before me: but how many Americans know that in Indo-China, in each of the two camps, there are today more than 400,000 combatants? I know that in Korea even greater masses of men are involved; but the Indo-Chinese war is, nevertheless, a truly important war, a "major war".

How many Americans - even, if I may say so, how many even of you gentlemen - are aware that the French High Command has positive proof that the target of the last offensive of the Viet Minh was not the Tonkin Delta but the Mekong River? The strategic maneuver of the Viet Minh, which we have been able to frustrate, was, and continues to be, to split our forces by thrusting toward the Gulf of Siam. Its goal obviously is to bring within the reach of interna- tional Communism the countries of Thailand and Burma, the first bastions on the road to India. Our suspicion of this plan is confirmed by the fact that the Communist regime in Peking has recently created a so-called "Autonomous Govern- ment of the Thai Nationalities of Yunnan". This new political monstrosity is obviously intended by the Chinese Communists to become a magnetic pole to attract Laotians, Siamese, and the Thai tribes of China and Indo-China into one group. It is apparent, therefore, that in Indo-China the major objective of the Viet Minh at this moment is not simply the Gulf of Tonkin but also the Gulf of Siam and the approaches to India. The battles being waged by French and Vietnamese troops in the rice paddies and on the plateaus are serving not merely to protect Indo-China against subversion but to protect the whole of Southeast Asia.

There is one final point I should make to you, but I shall have to choose my words with great care, because on so grave a matter there must be no misunderstanding. I refer to the analogy between the war in Korea and the war in Indo-China. I have said already that the soldiers of your country and mine, who are fighting and dying in Korea and in Indo-China, are engaged at the two extremeties of the same battle front, struggling and sacrificing for the same cause. In this connection, the recent meeting in the Far East between those two great veterans of the Italian campaign, General Mark Clark and Marshal Juin, appears symbolic to all of us. But in truth, the Indo-Chinese war is not really comparable to any other war today. The Vietnamese Government and our own must maintain a continuous front in Tonkin, the most northern sector of Indo-China. In vast areas behind the main battle lines they must cope with guerilla warfare. Finally, and above all, they must rally to their side the timid and the hesitant, which means that they have to assure the safety of extensive regions in which the established power must still expect sporadic outbreaks of terrorism. It stands to reason that such problems as these cannot be solved by methods which in other places and in other circumstances have succeeded in Korea. However, in both Korea and in Indo-China, the essential problem is to enlist the aid of local populations organized in their own national armies. We are convinced that we can pool the experience gained in Korea and in Indo-China by our respective military staffs to the common advantage of us all. The French Government calls earnestly for a close co-ordination of our strategy and our methods in the Far East. . . .

(259) <u>JOINT U.S.-FRENCH COMMUNIQUE</u>, March 28, 1953 (Extract)

Source: Department of State *Bulletin*, April 6, 1953, pp. 491-492.

After two days of talks, French and U.S. officials issued a joint communique warning China that if it took advantage of a Korean ceasefire to attack anywhere else in the Far East, it would face the "most serious consequences."

1. Representatives of the United States and France, meeting in Washington, today concluded a detailed review of a wide range of problems which face both governments in Europe, the Far East and the Near East. Peace will always remain the basic policy of the United States and France. The discussions, therefore, centered on measures for obtaining peace where there is fighting and for consolidating peace where threats exist.

2. It was agreed, in the absence of any tangible proof to the contrary, that recent developments in the Soviet Union had not changed the basic nature of the threat confronting the free world. The representatives of both countries were in full agreement on the necessity of concerting their efforts so as to defeat Communist aggression in the Far East and to strengthen the defenses of the free countries in the West. They remain convinced that true peace can be achieved and maintained only by constructive efforts of all free nations.

3. It was recognized that Communist aggressive moves in the Far East obviously are parts of the same pattern. Therefore, while the full burden of the fighting in Indochina falls on the forces of the French Union including those

of the Associated States, and similarly the United States bears the heaviest burden in Korea, the prosecution of these operations cannot be successfully carried out without full recognition of their interdependence. This in turn requires the continuation of frequent diplomatic and military consultation between the two Governments.

The French Government reasserted its resolve to do its utmost to increase the effectiveness of the French and Associated States forces in Indochina, with a view to destroying the organized Communist forces and to bringing peace and prosperity to her free associates within the French Union, Cambodia, Laos and Viet-Nam. The Ambassadors of Viet-Nam and Cambodia were present and participated in this phase of the discussions.

Advantage was taken of this meeting to continue discussion of plans prepared by the High Command in Indochina for military action there. These plans are being developed with a view to achieving success in Indochina and are being given intensive study so as to determine how and to what extent the United States may be able to contribute materiel and financial support to their achievement.

Obviously any armistice which might be concluded in Korea by the United Nations would be entered into in the hope that it would be a step toward peace. It was the view of both Governments, however, that should the Chinese Communist regime take advantage of such an armistice to pursue aggressive war elsewhere in the Far East, such action would have the most serious consequences for the efforts to bring about peace in the world and would conflict directly with the understanding on which any armistice in Korea would rest. . . .

(260) EDITORIAL IN *NHAM DAN:* "THE LIBERATION OF SAM-NUA," April 16-20, 1953 (Extract)

Source: *Cuoc Khang Chien Than Thanh cua Nhan Dan Viet-Name (The Sacred Resistance of the Vietnamese People)* (Hanoi: Su That, 1960), Vol. IV, pp. 42-45.

The founding of the Viet-nam-Laos-Cambodia front in 1951 and the success of the Northwestern campaign paved the way for the Vietnamese to send troops, in the form of "volunteers," to Laos. In April 1953, Vietnamese troops and the Laotian Liberation Army, which the Vietnamese had trained, advised and supplied for several years, seized all of Sam-nua Province. The official newspaper of the Workers' Party explained the significance of the victory in Laos.

The Lao Liberation Army and Vietnamese volunteer troops have entered Sam-nua and destroyed large parts of three enemy battalions retreating on the Sam-nua-Xieng-khoang road.

According to official information from the Pathet Lao Resistance Government, the Lao Liberation Army and our volunteers have entered Sam-nua town and liberated it on April 13. Threatened enemy troops fled during the night of April 12-13 during a big rainstorm, leaving nearly all the storehouses, ammunition and medicine, which they could not destroy in time. The Lao Liberation Army and our volunteers immediately pursued them on their route of withdrawal from Sam-nua to Xieng-khoang stretching over 200 kilometers. Many fights took place along the way, at Muong-ham 16 kilometers from Sam-nua, at Na-noong 35 kilometers away, at Hua-muong near Muong-lap 100 kilometers away. The greater part of 3 battalions withdrawing was annihilated, including one major killed, 2 majors and 7 captains who were also "Province Chiefs" and Deputy Province Chiefs" and the entire puppet government apparatus captured. Small enemy positions in the Sam-nua sector were also cleaned out. The entire province of Sam-nua was liberated. Meanwhile, Non-het, an important position on Road No. 7, which the enemy used as a base for attacking the rear of our Ngee-an Province, was also annihilated.

Sam-nua is a collection of 11 important bases. They were the biggest military positions of the enemy in Laos with regard to ground troops and fortifications (The Tran-ninh position near there had just been reinforced). Sam-nua was the enemy's base for threatening and attacking our free zone, a screen protecting lower Laos, and an important point in the Lai-chau - Na-san - Sam-nua - Tran-ninh defense line. Sam-nua is a province having large manpower and material resources. The liberation of Sam-nua is a big victory of the Lao resistance. For us, the liberation of Sam-nua reduces greatly the enemy's threat to the Moc-chau, Hoa-binh and Thanh-hoa free zones. As for the enemy, losing Sam-nua means that their Western defense line has had one piece broken, thus isolating Na-san, a position more than 300 kilometers from Hanoi and Xieng-khoang and making the enemy's plan of attacking the Northwest from Na-san even more difficult to achieve. Therefore, the liberation of Sam-nua is a heavy defeat for the enemy, the biggest defeat for them since the Northwest Campaign.

Our country and Laos are two fraternal countries, closely related to each other militarily, politically, and economically: the poisonous scheme of the French invaders is to divide the Vietnamese and Lao people, using the Lao operational zone to attack Vietnam, and using the Vietnamese operational zone to attack Laos, hoping to put the two countries under their barbaric rule. . . .

(261) MEMORANDUM FROM THE JOINT CHIEFS OF STAFF TO SECRETARY OF DEFENSE CHARLES E. WILSON, April 23, 1953

Source: *U.S.-Vietnam Relations, Book 9*, pp. 24-26.

The Joint Chiefs, after reviewing Letourneau's presentation, expressed some reservations about various aspects of the plan, primarily its lack of aggressiveness. They nevertheless pronounced it "workable," although their recommendation for U.S. support of the plan was subject to several conditions relating to other U.S. defense requirements and to budgetary procedures.

1. With reference to your memorandum, dated 2 April 1953, subject as above, the Joint Chiefs of Staff have considered the proposed French plan for concluding the war in Indochina and submit herewith their comments (Appendix) and recommendations. The Joint Chiefs of Staff point out that the French plan was not presented in writing. The present knowledge of this plan is limited to that obtained through the minutes of oral presentations by M. Letourneau and General Allard, supplemented by questions related thereto during subsequent discussions.

2. While the French plan as presented was lacking in detail, certain weaknesses are indicated which are summarized briefly as follows:

   a. It does not appear to be sufficiently aggressive.
   b. Excessive effort appears to be devoted to cleaning up Viet Minh pockets without sufficient consideration being given to cutting the enemy's supply lines, particularly in Northern Indochina.
   c. It appears that insufficient emphasis is given to placing of responsibility in the hands of the Vietnamese and the training of leaders thereof.
   d. The plan appears to rely extensively on small-unit operations.

While the Joint Chiefs of Staff consider that the French plan could be improved in light of the foregoing comments, they feel that the plan is workable. Further, the Joint Chiefs of Staff agree that augmentation of Vietnamese forces will be necessary in order to bring the conflict in Indochina to a successful conclusion.

3. In connection with the foregoing and the comments set forth in para-
traphs 8 and 9 of the Appendix hereto, attention is invited to the following
pertinent documents which are attached as Annexes hereto:

a. A Dispatch received from the Chief, Military Assistance Advisory
Group (Indochina) (DA IN 257701) (Annex "A");

b. Dispatches requesting General Clark's views on the strategic situation in Indochina (DA 934687) (Annex "B"): his initial views (DA IN 251110)
(Annex "C"); his modified views (DA IN 253811 (Annex "D"); and his final
recommendations (DA IN 258870 (Annex "E").

c. A dispatch received from Admiral Radford expressing his views on
the strategic situation in Indochina (260315Z) (Annex"F").

It will be noted that General Clark's views are somewhat more optimistic than
those expressed in this memorandum. This may be due in part to the fact that
General Clark's views are probably based almost entirely on information acquired during his brief visit to Indochina.

4. While reserving further opinion as to the merits of the French plan,
the Joint Chiefs of Staff recommend that the proposed augmentation of forces in
Indochina be supported subject to the following:

a. There will be no compensating reduction in over-all U.S. armed
forces because of fiscal limitations.

b. The specific requests for U.S. support will be processed through
normal channels for screening of force requirements and scale and type of
equipment.

c. France and the Associated States will contribute to the maximum extent of their capabilities.

d. The additional financial support beyond that for MDAP requirements
necessary to assure the successful execution of the plan will be made
available by the United States from other than U.S. military or MDAP funds.

e. No financial commitment will be made to France until:

(1) The cost of the program can be considered in relation to all
other MDA needs; and

(2) A decision has been made to authorize adding new requirements
generated by the French plan to the regular MDAP for FY 1954 (as presented by the military departments to the Office of the Secretary of
Defense and the Bureau of the Budget in the FY 1954 Special Budget Review), and to MDA Programs subsequent to FY 1954.

5. The Joint Chiefs of Staff feel that as much pressure as is feasible
should be placed on the French from a political point of view to obtain a clear-
cut commitment to:

a. Modernize training methods;

b. Prosecute the proposed plan with redoubled determination and vigor;

c. Expedite the transfer of responsibility to the Government of the
Associated States and accelerate the rate of training of indigenous forces
with emphasis on leadership training;

d. Intensify efforts to cut enemy supply lines;

e. Wrest the initiative from the Viet Minh and take more effective
steps to insure that recaptured areas are retained under Vietnamese control;
and

f. Utilize more extensively, where appropriate, units larger than battalions.

In connection with the requirement for improvement in training methods, the
United States would be willing to furnish such specialized assistance as may be
desired by the French.

(262) TELEGRAM FROM UNDERSECRETARY OF STATE WALTER BEDELL SMITH TO THE EMBASSY
IN PARIS, April 24, 1953

Source: *U.S.-Vietnam Relations, Book 9*, p. 31.

*The Joint Chiefs of Staff indicated informally to State Department officials
that their reservations about the French military plan were serious, and that
they would not recommend U.S. support unless a series of changes were made in
the direction of more offensive operations, including the nomination of a more
aggressive French military commander.*

At State-JCS meeting April 24 JCA in informal discussion made it clear they
attach great weight to reservations they have made as to feasibility and prospects of success of military plan for Indo-China presented by French in Washington. It is apparent Chiefs feel that plan might be "workable" but only if
French pursue course of action which would in effect remove basis for JCS reservations. JCS described this course of action as including such things as appointment bold and aggressive French military leader to Indo-China Command,
revision French strategy in direction more immediate and telling offensive action, use Vietnamese forces in large rather than small units etc.

JCS informally stated belief it was imperative US should forcefully present
such ideas to French and that unless French would follow such advice it was
possible US aid to French for Indo-China would in fact be wasted.

JCS felt US Government position could only be developed after Secretary's
return from NATO meeting and that promptly thereafter it might be wise have
joint military and political discussions with French in Paris.

Above JCS views suggest caution in indicating to French now that US approves French military plan.

(263) TELEGRAM FROM DILLON TO DULLES, April 26, 1953

Source: *U.S.-Vietnam Relations, Book 9*, pp. 34-36.

*In a memorandum on U.S. assistance to France, the U.S. offered to recommend
to Congress up to $460 million in military aid for Indochina for Fiscal Year
1954 - 40 percent of the projected annual French war expenditures. Further
assistance was promised on the basis of detailed agreement on increasing the
Franco-Vietnamese military effort.*

1. The U.S. Delegation has given further study to the question of aid to
Fr from the MSP, and related matters.

It is understood that the Fr govt will present its financial plans to the
Fr Parliament in May of this year. It is understood from the Fr govt that
these financial plans as prepared by the Fr govt will include certain reductions in the current 1953 budget, which may entail certain unavoidable reductions in defense expenditures; certain tax reforms designed to bring in some
additional revenue; and arrangements for internal financing adequate for the
remainder of 1953. It is understood that there is also a need for additional
dollar resources to be made available at an early date.

2. In light of the extension of the war in Indo-China by the new aggression in Laos, the US is now prepared to make this one immediate unconditioned
commitment to make available to Fr the sum of $60 million as a grant from the
MSP as an advance payment in relation to US FY 1954 aid to Fr. This $60 mil-
lion, or such portion as may be required, may be used as a special resource to
pay any balances needed in the EPU settlements.

3. Subject to substantial achievement of the financial program contemplated by the Fr govt and described in para 1 above, the US will give favorable

consideration to a proposal for an Ex-Im Bank loan in the amount of one-half ($100 million) of the existing $200 million of offshore procurement contracts, to be repaid by means of one-half of the receipts as they are earned under the contracts, and will give favorable consideration to a request for the use of the franc counterpart of the $60 million after June 30, 1953, at any time during US FY 1954 and as a part of the US FY 1954 aid program for France.

4.   The further FY 1954 MSP is dependent upon:

(a) Congressional action:
(b) A Fr defense contribution from their own resources in CY 1954 in line with NATO discussions as to France's political-economic capabilities; and (3) a Fr mil program for CYs 1953 and 1954 for its NATO forces in line with NATO recommendations, it being understood that the 1954 goals at this time are provisional only and that, as the Fr Min of Def reported to NATO, the air goals would need to be adjusted especially.

5.   Subject to the conditions set forth in paras 3 and 4 above, the US will recommend to Congress a FY 1954 MSP for Fr as follows:

(a) The US to provide the funds for a special Fr artillery, automatic weapons, and munitions payment program for Fr metropolitan forces assigned to SACEUR, in the amount of $100 million.
(b) The US to provide funds up to a maximum of $460 million, which is estimated to be approximately 40 percent of the current rate of expenditure on the Indo-Chinese war, of which $60 million will be advanced under para 2 hereof.
(c) Subject further to the adoption by the Fr govt of a satisfactory military program which in all its aspects holds the promise of success in I-C, the US is prepared to provide a portion of a mutually agreed additional Fr effort in I-C, involving especially additional trained forces of the Assoc States. This portion would be of a moderate amount of dollars and subject to specific subsequent agreement before it is to be considered a commitment.

6.   The US makes these substantial proposals with confidence in the fundamental strength of the Fr economy, and with the belief that if the Fr govt takes the necessary and desirable decisions, Fr will have both economic and military success in these matters.

7.   These proposals are apart from the anticipated delivery of certain military end-items and the probable award on a competitve basis of certain offshore procurement contracts, both of which will proceed under normal procedures and conditions.

(264) MEMORANDUM BY ASSISTANT SECRETARY OF STATE FOR CONGRESSIONAL RELATIONS DOUGLAS MACARTHUR II, April 27, 1953

Source: *U.S.-Vietnam Relations, Book 9,* p. 38.

Dulles reported to Eisenhower that the French desperately needed C-119 transport planes to cope with the new military threat posed by the loss of Sam-nua Province. The French wanted U.S. Air Force personnel to fly them, but Dulles suggested that civilian pilots in Formosa be used to fly them instead. The reference was to personnel of Civil Air Transport, a company which had been acquired by the Central Intelligence Agency to carry out air operations in the Far East. The loan of six planes was approved by the Joint Chiefs, and they were flown by CIA-controlled CAT pilots.

At a meeting with the President at the White House this afternoon for the purpose of briefing the President on the recent NATO Paris meeting and bilateral talks with the British and the French, the President asked Secretary Dulles what the French views were on the situation in Laos.

The Secretary replied that the French were very gravely concerned about the situation there. He said that when he had met with Prime Minister Rene Mayer last evening just prior to departure from Paris, M. Mayer had stated that the French needed more urgently the loan of some C-119 aircraft to help them get tanks and heavy equipment into Laos to assist in its defense. Having such equipment might mean the difference between holding and losing Laos. M. Mayer had envisaged U.S. Air Force personnel operating the aircraft during the period of the loan.

The Secretary said to the President that such a procedure would mean the sending of U.S. personnel on combat missions in Indochina. This, obviously, was a decision which would have repercussions and would raise many problems. However, there was an alternative, which would be to loan the French the C-119's, which he understood the Department of Defense was willing to do, and have civilian pilots fly them. Following his return to Washington this morning, the Secretary had made inquiry and had ascertained that there were pilots in Formosa who were not members of the U.S. armed forces and who might well be able to carry out these missions. This possibility was being explored on an urgent basis to see whether it would not be possible to have the aircraft loaned and the above-mentioned personnel in Formosa operate them.

(265) ROYAL LAOTIAN GOVERNMENT NOTE ON THE "RESISTANCE GOVERNMENT" IN LAOS, May 5, 1953 (Extracts)

Source: *Laos*, p. 11.

Following the successful Vietnamese-Lao offensive in Sam-nua Province, the Provisional Government headed by Prince Souphanouvong declared itself the "legal government of Pathet Lao." This drew an immediate response from the Royal Lao Government, which dismissed the resistance government as an instrument of the "Viet Minh." The reference to Souphanouvong and "armed groups from the Sino-Burmese border" apparently recalls Souphanouvong's proposal several years earlier that the Lao Issara government in Bangkok use tribal groups to help them fight the French. (See Paul F. Langer and Joseph Zasloff, *North Vietnam and the Pathet Lao* [Cambridge, Massachusetts: Harvard University Press, 1970], p. 40.) *There is no evidence that Souphanouvong lived in Communist China as asserted by this note.*

The fact that there are no Laotians among the invading troops can be easily verified. As far as the 'Free State of Laos', of which Prince Souphanouvong is President, is concerned, the following points are relevant:

(1) Tiao Souphanouvong, who has not lived in Laos for more than 20 years, was a member of the Lao Issara or 'Free Lao' in 1946;
(2) He was excluded from this Movement on 16 May 1949 because of his communist leanings, his total dependence in this regard on the Viet Minh and, more precisely, because he agreed that armed groups from the Sino-Burmese border should enter Laotian territory;
(3) The Lao Issara, established in October 1946, was dissolved in October 1949 after the signing of the Franco-Lao Convention, all members having rallied to the Royal Government after returning to Laos. Out of the seven Ministers now in the Royal Government, four, including the Prime Minister himself, were members of the Lao Issara;
(4) Tiao Souphanouvong, since his exclusion from the Lao Issara, has been entirely devoted to the Viet Minh under whose auspices he has lived in Communist China;

(5) Tiao Souphanouvong . . . has no popular mandate . . . to represent the aspirations of the Lao people and they have no interest in him.

(266) <u>TELEGRAM FROM SMITH TO DILLON</u>, May 18, 1953

Source: *U.S.-Vietnam Relations, Book 9*, pp. 40-41.

The U.S. took another step toward deeper involvement in the war when the State Department informed the Embassy in Paris that the U.S. wished to serᵈ a high-level military mission to Indochina to participate in drafting the military plan discussed in Washington.

You will recall that at the final meeting with Mayer at White House on March 28, President made certain general comments regarding Letourneau plan for bringing hostilities in Indochina to successful conclusion. In reply Mayer in name of French GOVT said that he would welcome our sending US military officers to Indochina in order to pursue evaluation of plan, and President expressed willingness to arrange it. Defense has now completed its study of material furnished by Letourneau and Allard and wishes to take advantage of Mayer's suggestion to send high level military mission to Indochina in order to study situation with General Navarre and explore ways and means through which American assistance can best be fitted into workable plans for aggressive pursuit of hostilities under present circumstances. A principal objective of mission will be to ascertain what military plans and capabilities PAREN manpower, equipment and particularly air force END PAREN will be required so that there will be firm prospect of reversing current military trend by beginning of next fighting season, i.e., OCT 1953. Proposed agenda will of course be submitted in due course.

Please inform Mayer of the above as soon as possible requesting him to indicate (a) his continued readiness to have such a mission visit Indochina and (b) approximate date at which mission could proceed to Indochina.

Department understands General Navarre arrives Saigon about May 19; he will obviously wish to become familiar with the details of the situation before receiving proposed American mission. We have in mind for the arrival of the latter a date such as June 10. The mission would probably stay in Indochina for not more than a month. It will probably include a State Department representative in an observer-advisory capacity although the leadership and objectives will be military.

Department believes this mission can represent important forward step so far as Indochina situation is concerned and hopes that Mayer and Navarre will agree. For your information such military evaluation would presumably lead later to talks at political level and to determination of additional American aid for Indochina.

(267) <u>NATIONAL INTELLIGENCE ESTIMATE</u>, NIE-91, June 4, 1953

Source: *U.S. Vietnam Relations, Book 9*, pp. 45-55.

Following the successful Vietnamese thrust into Laos, the intelligence Community issued a grim assessment of the prospects for the French Union effort. It predicted further deterioration in the military situation, with the possibility of "very rapid" deterioration later in the year. A Chinese direct intervention, which had seemed imminent in late 1952, was viewed as unlikely.

THE PROBLEM

To estimate French Union and Communist capabilities and probable courses of action with respect to Indochina and the internal situation throughout Indochina through mid-1954.

ASSUMPTION

There is no major expansion of the Korean war.

CONCLUSIONS

1. Unless there is a marked improvement in the French Union military position in Indochina, political stability in the Associated States and popular support of the French Union effort against the Viet Minh will decline. We believe that such marked improvement in the military situation is not likely, though a moderate improvement is possible. The over-all French Union position in Indochina therefore will probably deteriorate during the period of this estimate.

2. The lack of French Union military successes, continuing Indochinese distrust of ultimate French political intentions, and popular apathy will probably continue to prevent a significant increase in Indochinese will and ability to resist the Viet Minh.

3. We cannot estimate the impact of the new French military leadership. However, we believe that the Viet Minh will retain the military initiative and will continue to attack territory in the Tonkin delta and to make incursions into areas outside the delta. The Viet Minh will attempt to consolidate Communist control in "Free Laos" and will build up supplies in northern Laos to support further penetrations and consolidation in that country. The Viet Minh will almost certainly intensify political warfare, including guerrilla activities, in Cambodia.

4. Viet Minh prestige has been increased by the military successes of the past year, and the organizational and administrative effectiveness of the regime will probably continue to grow.

5. The French Government will remain under strong and increasing domestic pressure to reduce the French military commitment in Indochina, and the possibility cannot be excluded that this pressure will be successful. However, we believe that the French will continue without enthusiasm to maintain their present levels of troop strength through mid-1954 and will support the planned development of the national armies of the Associated States.

6. We believe that the Chinese Communists will continue and possibly increase their present support of the Viet Minh. However, we believe that whether or not hostilities are concluded in Korea, the Chinese Communists will not invade Indochina during this period.[1] The Chinese Communists will almost certainly retain the capability to intervene so forcefully in Indochina as to overrun most of the Tonkin delta area before effective assistance could be brought to bear.

7. We believe that the Communist objective to secure control of all Indochina will not be altered by an armistice in Korea or by Communist "peace" tactics. However, the Communists may decide that "peace" manuevers in Indochina would contribute to the attainment of Communist global objectives, and to the objective of the Viet Minh.

8. If present trends in the Indochinese situation continue through mid-1954, the French Union political and military position may subsequently deteriorate very rapidly.

DISCUSSION

THE CURRENT SITUATION

9. *Military Situation.*[2] The Viet Minh occupation of the mountainous Thai country of Northwest Tonkin in late 1952 and the follow-up thrust into northern Laos in Paril 1953 demonstrate that the Viet Minh have retained the military initiative in Indochina. Although the Viet Minh did not defeat any large French Union forces in these operations, they did force the French to withdraw the bulk of their offensive striking power from the Tonkin delta and disperse it in isolated strong points, dependent on air transport for logistic support. At the same time, strong Viet Minh guerrilla elements plus two regular Viet Minh divisions sufficed to contain the 114,000 regular French Union forces remaining in the Tonkin delta. The Viet Minh now appear to have withdrawn the bulk of their regular forces from Laos. They probably have left behind political cadres, some regular forces, and well-supplied guerrilla units in the areas which they overran in order to consolidate Communist political and military control, to prepare bases for future operations, and to pin down French Union garrisons.

10. The invasion of Laos may have been undertaken as part of a long-range Communist design to develop unrest in Thailand and ultimately gain control of all Southeast Asia. Viewed solely in terms of the Viet Minh objective to win all of Indochina, however, the Viet Minh offensive in Laos is an extension of the 1952 winter's offensive in northwestern Tonkin, and represents a shift in Viet Minh military tactics. This shift in tactics is probably largely explained by the inability to defeat the main French Union forces in the Tonkin delta by direct assault. Faced with this position of strength, the Viet Minh began during 1952 to turn the bulk of their regular forces toward the conquest of northwestern Tonkin and northern Laos, areas lightly held by isolated French Union garrisons.

11. In this manner, the Viet Minh probably hope to retain the military and political initiative and, by dispersing French Union forces, to prevent either a clean-up by the French Union in the Tonkin delta or offensive operations by the French Union against Viet Minh troop concentrations and supply installations outside the delta. The Viet Minh may well believe that by gradually extending their base areas in lightly defended regions of Laos, Cambodia, and central Vietnam they can keep French Union forces dispersed and pinned down indefinitely. In time, they probably expect to sap the morale of the Vietnamese and the French and finally so alter the balance of power as to make possible successful Viet Minh attacks against the key areas of Tonkin and South Vietnam.

12. The deployment of four divisions into Laos by the Viet Minh and the fact that the French did not attack their long and exposed lines of communication typify the over-all situation in Indochina. French Union forces still outweigh the Viet Minh in numbers, firepower, and materiel. French ability to air lift troops and equipment, although strained at the present time, provides the French Union with the tactical flexibility in planning defensive and offensive operations. The Viet Minh, however, by their skill in guerrilla war, their ability to move rapidly and to infiltrate and control areas under nominal French occupation, have caused the French to commit large forces throughout Indochina to static defense, thus seriously reducing French ability to take the offensive.

13. Viet Minh regular forces in northern Indochina have continued their gradual evolution from lightly armed guerrilla bands to a regularly organized military force. They have made noticeable advances in the development of field communications, and unit firepower has increased although they still possess only limited amounts of artillery. Viet Minh combat effectiveness is still limited by

a lack of medical supplies and an inability to sustain major military operations.

14. Military aid from the US has enabled the French Union to equip adequately their regular ground forces. The French air forces, with US logistical support, and with no air opposition, have maintained a fair degree of effectiveness in paratroop operations, supply by air drops, and daylight attacks on enemy supply dumps. French naval forces have improved in combat effectiveness and have maintained control of the seacoasts and inland waterways. However, the Viet Minh have the continuing capability to threaten control of the inland waterways by a mining campaign. Some Vietnamese National Army units have performed creditably in combat, but desertion and "missing in action" figures remain high. For the most part, Vietnamese National Guard and other local security forces lack the firepower, discipline, and leadership to hold positions alone against regular Viet Minh units which infiltrate the Tonkin delta.

15. Although French Union military capabilities have improved slightly, the French Union military effort has been inhibited by considerations of domestic French politics, French security in Europe, and fear of involvement in a war with Communist China. These considerations have caused French commanders in Indochina to forego aggressive military operations that would entail heavy casualties and have prevented them from obtaining reinforcements on a scale that might make possible the defeat of the Viet Minh.

16. The development of the Vietnamese National Army, promised by the French in 1949, has been retarded by a shortage of officers and non-commissioned officers, by French lack of faith in the Vietnamese and by French fiscal problems. There has also been an unwillingness among many Vietnamese leaders, not including Premier Tam, to undertake a major mobilization effort until the French grant further political concessions and until the Vietnamese character of the new army is fully guaranteed.

17. *Political.* Some political progress has been made in Vietnam during the past year. Premier Tam's administration has enlisted the cooperation of the strongly nationalist Dai Viet leader Nguyen Huu Tri, and nationalist concern over Tam's francophilia has to some extent dissipated. Tam has also added to the political vitality of Vietnam by holding local elections in secure areas of Vietnam. Another Vietnamese program, undertaken with US economic assistance, which involves the relocation of scattered villages in the delta into centralized and defensible sites may be an important step toward the eventual "pacification" of heavily infiltrated areas. The decisions of March 1953 to increase the size of the Vietnamese National Army while expanding the area of Vietnamese strategic and operational responsibility, could also be of major political significance.

18. Despite these advances, Vietnam still lacks the degree of political strength essential for the mobilization of the country's resources. Tam's "action" program remains more shadow than substance Elected local councils have no real power, promised land reform and other social and economic reforms which might generate popular support have not left the planning stage, and the Vietnamese government is handicapped by incompetent cabinet ministers and the lack of competent administrators. While Bao Dai refuses to assume active direction of the affairs of state, he remains hostile toward new leadership and democratic activities.

19. Of more basic importance in the failure of Vietnamese to rally to the Vietnamese government following the French grant of independence within the French Union in 1949 have been the following:

    a. Many Vietnamese doubt the ability of French Union forces to defeat the Viet Minh and prefer to remain apart from the struggle.

b. The French Government has not dared to promise complete national independence at some future date, as demanded by the Vietnamese, because of the fear that the French national assembly would then refuse to support a war in a "lost" portion of the French Union.

c. The Vietnamese, despite many evolutionary steps toward complete independence since 1949, are generally inclined to believe that the French intend to retain effective control over the affairs of Vietnam.

d. The nationalist appeal and military prestige of the Viet Minh remains strong among significant numbers of the Vietnamese.

20. In Cambodia, internal political strife has weakened the government, dissident nationalist elements have continued to sap popular loyalty to the throne, and the King is demanding greater independence from the French in order to strengthen his political position at home. Meanwhile, the 9,000 Viet Minh combatants in Cambodia, while under fairly constant attack by French and Cambodian forces, are capable of exploiting disorders which may develop.

21. Laotian stability has been upset by the recent Viet Minh incursion. The Laotians are generally hostile to the Viet Minh but are unable to contribute a great deal to the defense of their homeland. A small group of pro-Communist Laotians returned to Laos with the Viet Minh during the recent incursion. It is led by a disaffected Laotian nobleman, Prince Souphanouvong, and calls itself the "Free Government of Pathet Lao" (Laos).

22. Meanwhile, the Viet Minh leadership, with Chinese Communist material and advisory assistance since 1949, has demonstrated the necessary zeal, ruthlessness, and tenacity to exploit to the maximum the limited resources at their command. The Viet Minh have expanded the area under their complete control and their prestige has probably increased throughout Indochina as a result of military successes in northwest Tonkin and Laos.

23. In the areas of Viet Minh occupation, Viet Minh control is believed to be effective, and minimum food requirements are being met. The Viet Minh have taken on increasingly the conventional characteristics of a "Peoples Republic" and are now engaged in programs to confiscate and redistribute land to eliminate "traitors" and "reactionaries." Although this departure from national front tactics has increased realization that the Viet Minh are under complete Communist domination, the Viet Minh control many villages within areas of nominal French Union occupation through terror, compulsion, and their continued nationalist appeal.

24. The Viet Minh and the Chinese Communists continue to maintain close relations. It is estimated that there are less than a thousand Chinese Communist advisers and technicians with the Viet Minh in Indochina. The Chinese Communists are providing the Viet Minh with military supplies at an estimated average level of 400 to 500 tons per month, and some Viet Minh troops are sent to Communist China for training. Small Chinese Communist units reportedly have entered the mountainous northwest section of Tonkin on several occasions to assist the Viet Minh against French-supported native guerrillas, but no Chinese Communist troops have been identified in forward areas. There was some evidence during the past year that Viet Minh policy statements may be "cleared," if not written, in Peiping. Close Viet Minh relations with Communist China are complemented, superficially at least, by equally warm relations with the Soviet Union, but we are unable to determine whether Peiping or Moscow has ultimate responsibility for Viet Minh policy.

PROBABLE TRENDS IN FRENCH UNION CAPABILITIES AND COURSES OF ACTION

25. French plans for dealing with the war in Indochina now revolve around the development of national armies in the Associated States, particularly in Viet-

nam. In March 1953, the Franco-Vietnamese High Military Council approved a new program calling for an increase in Vietnamese strength during the current year of 40,000 men, organized in 54 "commando" battalions.[3] A further expansion of 57,000 men has been proposed for 1954 and will probably be undertaken if the initial reinforcement is successful and if equipment is made available by the US. With these additional Vietnamese forces, the French hope to undertake widespread clearing operations and subsequently to organize sufficient mobile groups to being by early 1955 the destruction of the Viet Minh regular forces in Tonkin.

26. Progress has been made in carrying out the troop reinforcement program thus far, and the Vietnamese may have close to 40,000 reinforcements recruited, trained, and available for combat by early 1954. However, the Viet Minh invasion of Laos and the threat of similar operations will probably keep French mobile reserves deployed outside the Tonkin delta in isolated strong points. The addition of 40,000 untested and lightly armed Vietnamese will not offset the absence of these regular French forces, and effective clearing or offensive operations cannot be undertaken until French Union forces are regrouped. Moreover, the French military leadership has been so dominated by concepts of static defense as to be unable to conduct the planned operations with the vigor necessary for their success. How the new military leadership may alter this we cannot estimate. Finally, unless the French Union forces prove strong enough to provide security for the Vietnamese population, it will not be possible to sweep the guerrillas out of the areas as planned. Not only will the populace fail generally to provide the intelligence required to rout the guerrillas but, as in the past, they will frequently give warning of the presence of the French Union forces, thus permitting the guerrillas to take cover and later to emerge when the danger is past.

27. The French are fearful that they cannot achieve a military decision in Indochina. Unless the French Union military plans achieve great success during the period of this estimate, the conviction will grow in France that the Indochina problem can only be solved through some over-all East-West settlement in the Far East. The difficulties of the French financial position impel the French to seek relief from the mounting costs of the Indochina war, and French apprehensions concerning eventual German rearmament not only make them reluctant to increase the military establishment in Indochina but impel them to seek the early return of French troops to Europe. The French Government will therefore remain under strong and increasing domestic pressure to reduce its military commitment in Indochina. On the other hand, the French Government is under strong pressure to maintain its position in Indochina. There is still considerable sentiment against abandoning the heavy investment wich France has poured into Indochina. More important, there is great reluctance to accept the adverse effects on the cohesion of the French Union and on French prestige as a world power which would accompany the loss of France's position in Indochina. In these circumstances, we believe that the French will continue without enthusiasm to maintain their present levels of troop strength through mid-1954 and will support the planned development of the National Armies of the Associated States. At the same time, France will probably continue to seek maximum financial and material assistance for the French Union effort while resisting any measures which would impair French pre-eminence among the Associated States, including the making of any commitments concerning the eventual political status of the Associated States.

28. Political strength in Vietnam may grow slightly during 1953 as progress is made toward a stronger national army, as the Vietnamese assume increasing governmental responsibilities, and as Premier Tam's social and political programs serve to decrease distrust of French intentions. There will probably also be a growing understanding, and fear, of the true Communist nature and purpose of

the Viet Minh. However, these developments will not bring about a significant increase in Vietnamese will and ability to resist the Viet Minh during the period of this estimate because the Vietnam leadership cannot in this brief period overcome popular apathy and mobilize the energy and resources of the people. Moreover, if events should persuade Vietnam leaders that no progress toward national independence is possible under the French or that French Union forces cannot defeat the Viet Minh, it is probable that the political strength of Vietnam would decline rapidly. Substantial Viet Minh military victories in the Tonkin delta or elsewhere in Indochina would also produce such a decline.

29. In Cambodia, political stability is likely to decline as the result of tension between the monarchy, the politically divided people, and the French colonial administration. Even if French concessions to the King insure his adherence to the French Union, unrest in Cambodia or a Viet Minh penetration into southern Laos might force the deployment of strong French forces to Cambodia.

30. In Laos, political attitudes will be determined almost entirely by military developments. The Laotians will probably remain loyal to the French Union if they are defended aggressively. They will not, however, offer effective resistance to Communist efforts to consolidate political control if French Union forces retreat from the country or if the French Union forces defend only a few strong points.

PROBABLE TRENDS IN VIET MINH AND CHINESE COMMUNIST CAPABILITIES AND COURSES OF ACTION

31. *Viet Minh Capabilities and Probable Courses of Action*. Barring serious Viet Minh military reverses, which could occur if Viet Minh forces should overextend themselves or make frontal attacks on French Union strong points, the Viet Minh regime will probably increase its total strength slightly during the period of this estimate. Viet Minh prestige will be increased by their recent gains in Laos. The organizational and administrative effectiveness of the regime will probably continue to increase with experience and Chinese Communist guidance. The program of expropriation and distribution of lands to tenants now being carried out probably weakens the Viet Minh appeal among some classes, but will probably strengthen Viet Minh controls at the village level and thus facilitate the collection of rice.

32. Militarily, the Viet Minh are unlikely to expand greatly their armed forces because they are already experiencing manpower difficulties. Their combat efficiency probably will increase, however, as the result of a modest augmentation of their unit firepower and a steady improvement in staff planning and coordination of forces. The Viet Minh probably will continue to receive a steady flow of material assistance from the Chinese Communists, and the amount may increase at any time. The Viet Minh do not have, and probably cannot develop within the period of this estimate, the capability to make such effective use of heavy equipment - artillery, armor, and aircraft - from the Chinese Communists as to permit successful attacks against strong concentrations of regular French forces. Over a longer period, however, a great increase in Viet Minh capabilities, including the development of an air force, is possible.

33. We believe that during the period of this estimate the Communists in Indochina will probably attempt to avoid combat except where they can achieve surprise or great superiority in numbers. They will attempt to consolidate Communist controls in "Free Laos" and will build up supplies in northern Laos to support further penetrations and consolidation in that country. If they reach the Thai border, they probably will attempt to organize guerrilla forces among the Vietnamese in northeastern Thailand, but we do not believe they will have the capability to provide much material assistance to such forces through mid-1954. The Viet Minh forces in Laos may hope to receive assistance from the

Vietnamese population in Thailand. The Viet Minh will almost certainly intensify political warfare, including guerrilla activities in Cambodia.

34. We believe that neither the French Union nor the Viet Minh will be able to
win a final military decision in Indochina through mid-1954. The Viet Minh,
with their principal striking forces operating from the Tonkin base area, will
probably retain the initiative during the period of this estimate by maintaining attacks against lightly defended French Union territory. The French Union
can hold key positions in Laos and may attempt by attacks against Viet Minh
lines of communication, to prevent the Viet Minh from moving southward in force
towards southern Laos and Cambodia. We believe, however, that Viet Minh guerrillas in southern Laos will develop sufficient strength to control much of the
countryside and that guerrilla activities in Cambodia will be intensified. The
French Union probably will reduce, but not eliminate, Viet Minh strength in
south Vietnam. Viet Minh infiltration of the Tonkin delta will probably be
maintained at a high level and the Viet Minh may undertake major attacks against
the delta if they can weaken French defenses by drawing French strength elsewhere.

35. Unless there is a marked improvement in the French Union military position
in Indochina, political stability in the Associated States and popular support
of the French Union effort against the Viet Minh will decline. We believe that
such marked improvement in the military situation is not likely, though a moderate improvement is possible. The over-all French Union position in Indochina
therefore will probably deteriorate during the period of this estimate.

36. *Chinese Communist Capabilities and Probable Courses of Action.* The Chinese
Communists will have the capability during the period of this estimate to improve airfields in south China, to train Viet Minh pilots, to continue improvement of transportation facilities, and to increase their present level of logistic support for the Viet Minh. The Chinese Communists will probably retain
their present capability to commit and support logistically 150,000 Chinese
Communist troops for an invasion of Indochina. The combat efficiency of this
potential invasion force could probably be increased considerably by the use of
combat-seasoned troops who have been rotated from Korea in the past year. The
ability of Chinese Communist forces to sustain offensive operation in Indochina
would probably be increased should logistic requirements in Korea remain at low
levels for a prolonged period.

37. A Chinese Communist force of 150,000, added to Viet Minh forces, would
probably be able to overrun the Tonkin delta area before effective assistance
could be brought to bear. The Chinese Communists now have, and will probably
continue to have during the period of this estimate, sufficient jet and piston
aircraft, independent of operations in Korea, for small-scale but damaging attacks against French Union installations in Tonkin. With surprise, they probably could neutralize the French Air Forces in Tonkin. The Chinese Communist
air forces do not appear, however, to possess the capability at present of conducting sustained air operations in Indochina because of a lack of improved
airfields in south China and stockpiles of supplies. Such preparations would
take several months.

38. We believe that whether or not hostilities are concluded in Korea, the
Chinese Communists will not invade Indochina during the period of this estimate.[4] Although they possess the capability, the following considerations militate against intervention by regular Chinese Communist forces or by large numbers of Chinese Communist "volunteers":

    a. The Communists probably consider that their present strategy in Indo-
china promises success in a prolonged struggle and produces certain immediate
advantages. It diverts badly needed French and US resources from Europe at

relatively small cost to the Communists. It provides opportunities to advance international Communist interests while preserving the fiction of "autonomous" national liberation movements, and it provides an instrument, the Viet Minh, with which Communist China and the USSR can indirectly exert military and psychological pressures on the peoples and governments of Laos, Cambodia, and Thailand.

    b. Communist leadership is aware that the West, and in particular the US, would probably retaliate against Communist China if Chinese Communist forces should invade Indochina. We believe that fear of such retaliation and of the major war which might result are important deterrents to open Chinese Communist intervention in Indochina.

39. We believe that the Communist objective to secure control of all Indochina will not be altered by an armistice in Korea or by Communist "peace" tactics. However, the Communists may decide that "peace" maneuvers in Indochina would contribute to the attainment of Communist global objectives, and to the objective of the Viet Minh.

  [1]The Deputy Director for Intelligence, The Joint Staff, believes that the intelligence available is insufficient to permit a conclusion at this time that the Chinese Communists will or will not invade Indochina prior to mid-1954.

  [2]See Annex A for Estimated French Union Strengths and Dispositions;
See Annex B for Estimated Viet Minh Strengths and Dispositions;
See Annex C for French Far Eastern Air Force Strengths and Dispositions; and
See Annex D for French Far Eastern Naval Strengths and Dispositions.

  [3]The 40,000 are to be recruited and will represent a net increase in French Union strength. Planned transfers of native units from the French Army to the Vietnamese Army will also strengthen the Vietnamese Army but will not represent any net increase in French Union strength.

  [4]The Deputy Director for Intelligence, The Joint Staff, believes that the intelligence available is insufficient to permit a conclusion at this time that the Chinese Communists will or will not invade Indochina prior to mid-1954.

(268) TERMS OF REFERENCE FOR THE CHIEF OF THE U.S. MILITARY MISSION TO INDO-CHINA, June 10, 1953

Source: *U.S.-Vietnam Relations, Book 9,* pp. 60-67.

The Joint Chiefs of Staff, in collaboration with the State Department, prepared guidelines for Lieutenant General John W. O'Daniel, who was appointed Chief of the U.S. Military Mission to Indochina. The document made it clear that the mission would assess French war plans, influence the final plan and encourage more U.S. involvement in day-to-day military planning and operations.

    1. As Chief of a U.S. Joint Military Mission to Indochina, Lt. Gen. John W. O'Daniel will discuss with General Navarre, Commander in Chief, French Armed Forces, Far East, requirements for and utilization of U.S. military aid in relation to French plans for successfully concluding the war in Indochina.

    2. Discussions will, as a point of departure, take up U.S. evaluation of the Letourneau-Allard concept for successfully concluding the war in Indochina, particularly in light of developments since subject concept was formulated, and with a view toward:

a. Gaining sufficient information concerning the development of indigenous forces and strengthening of the French Expeditionary forces in Indochina to equate the expenditure of U.S. military aid with net return, both current and planned.

b. Gaining sufficient detailed knowledge of French military plans to acquaint U.S. leaders thoroughly with the plan of future conduct of the war in Indochina, the chances for ultimate victory and its timing, and the adequacy of coordination of programmed aid with military planning.

c. Thorough discussion with the French in order to influence them to:

(1) Expedite revision and aggressive implementation of French military plans for successfully concluding the war in Indochina, including the early initiation of aggressive guerrilla warfare, aimed at knocking the enemy of balance, disrupting enemy supply lines, and gaining the initiative for anticommunist forces.

(2) Expand training methods with a view to more rapid development of loyal, aggressive, and capable indigenous forces.

(3) Expedite the transfer of leadership responsibility to the Associated States and accelerate indigenous military leadership training.

d. Devise ways and means of promoting closer and continuing French-U.S. Military Assistance Advisory Group (MAAG) contact on the plans and operations level without, of course, impinging upon the responsibilities of France and the Associated States for conduct of the war in Indochina.

3. In the course of discussions the Chief of Mission will be guided by the following:

a. The approved U.S. National Policy as contained in NSC 124/2.

b. The appropriate military views regarding Indochina previously expressed by the Joint Chiefs of Staff.

c. Approved Mutual Defense Assistance Programs (MDAP) for Indochina.

d. Views and instructions of CINCPAC.

e. NIE 91 - Probable events in Indochina through mid-1954.

4. Although the invitation upon which the mission is based was conveyed by the French Prime Minister acting unilaterally for France, it is essential that the military authorities of Vietnam, Laos, and Cambodia be given a maximum sense of participation consistent with security requirements. The Chief of Mission will wish to take a very early opportunity of discussing this aspect of his task with General Navarre.

5. The Chief of Mission will be supported by a carefully selected group of military personnel representing all three Services and with special knowledge of the problems associated with Indochina. The delicate nature of the mission and the difficulty of accommodating a large group in a war area dictates that the party be kept as small as possible consistent with this requirement. The mission will comprise approximately the following personnel, to be designated by their respective Services: Army - Chief of Mission plus two officers; Air Force - two officers; Navy - two officers; State Department - one representative. It is essential that all members of the mission be aware that this is a highly important military mission concerned with reexamination of U.S military policy toward this area of critical significance to U.S.security.

6. Prior to his departure from Washington, D.C., the Chief of Mission will be briefed by both military and political officers with respect to the U.S. position regarding the situation in Indochina. Enroute to Indochina the Chief of Mission will obtain the views of the Commander in Chief, Pacific.

7. Coordination of the Mission's activities will also be effected with Chief, MAAG, Indochina. Close collaboration with General Trapnell and his participation in the work of the Mission are essential.

8. Because of the unescapable and highly significant political aspects which cannot be divorced from military operations in Indochina, the mission will include a Department of State representative conversant with problems associated with Indochina who will be available for consultation on political matters. In addition, the U.S. Ambassador in Saigon and his staff will be available to the Chief of Mission. With respect to over-all political considerations closely associated with subject mission, the Chief of Mission may present the following as the general views of the U.S. Government.

a. The achievement of an anti-Communist military victory in Indochina is largely dependent upon the availability of adequate military forces, to be obtained, at least in part, through the development of the National Armies of the Associated States. If the enemy continues to set the pace as he has done during the past six-month dry season, it is not realistic to think that the Vietnamese Government will be able to raise, train and direct necessary reliable native levies at the same time that the Viet Minh Army has the initiative and is straining the resources of the French Union Army. Consequently, early aggressive military action against the Viet Minh is essential in order to develop an atmosphere of military control and progress under which the Vietnamese Government will be able to produce maximum numbers of reliable troops.

b. Assuming that French aims in Indochina are compatible with, or capable of compromise with, aspirations of the Associated States, the anti-Communist effort in Indochina would gain immeasurably by a clear and well advertised enunciation, at the appropriate time, of the future position of the French in that Country. This must of necessity be accompanied by sufficient fundamental detail to explain satisfactorily to the people of the Associated States how that position is being accomplished.

c. Concessions in the military field to give a greater degree of local leadership involving, of course, appointment of more high ranking indigenous military leaders would be of significant psychological value in the political field, provided local leadership were exercised under successful conditions.

9. Target date for completion of the mission is approximately thirty days after arrival in Indochina. Prior to departure, the Chief of Mission should consider the desirability of one or two members of the mission remaining in Indochina to witness early operations of the coming dry season and should make recommendations to the Joint Chiefs of Staff accordingly.

Indochina, the Chief of Mission will submit a written report to the Joint Chiefs of Staff via CINCPAC containing comments and recommendations concerning:

a. The adequacy of present U.S.-French and Associated States efforts and plans to win the war in Indochina including the effectiveness with which the French utilize U.S. military assistance. This will cover changes, if any, in the French strategic concept resulting from the current change in military command in Indochina.

b. The extent to which French military conduct of the war has been and is being hampered by political directives and considerations.

c. The adequacy and scope of U.S. end-use supervision of U.S. military assistance.

d. The desirability of direct United States participation in advising, training and/or planning for the operation of the National Armies of the Associated States.

<u>e</u>. Whether or not the indigenous military potential, including man-power and leaders, is being effectively and sufficiently developed for National Armies of the Associated States.

<u>f</u>. Whether Korean military training lessons may be utilized advanta-geously by the forces in Indochina.

<u>g</u>. Whether or not the scheduled build-up of Associated States forces during 1953 and 1954 will take place as planned and, together with existing French forces will be sufficient to accomplish a decisive defeat of the Viet Minh by 1955. This will include, in particular, views concerning any deficit of force.

<u>h</u>. Prospects for the French wresting the initiative from the Viet Minh in the near future and retaining the initiative thereafter.

<u>i</u>. What measures should be taken to improve utilization of air poten-tial, particularly air transport potential.

<u>j</u>. What additional measures, if any, should be taken by the French and the Vietnamese in order properly to administer and protect liberated areas.

11. Chief, MAAG, Indochina will be directed to furnish necessary steno-graphic assistance to the Mission during its stay in Indochina.

(269) <u>DECLARATION BY THE FRENCH GOVERNMENT</u>, July 3, 1953

Source: Release by the Press and Information Service of the French Embassy, New York, July 1953.

As part of an overall program to improve its sagging military position in Indochina, the government of Premier Joseph Laniel declared that it would "com-plete the independence and sovereignty of the Associated States," by the trans-ferring of remaining powers to each of the native governments. It invited the governments to negotiate on such transfers as it desired, while reaffirming the structure of the French Union, which implied some limitations on their sovereignty.

The Government of the French Republic, meeting in Council of Ministers, has reviewed the relations of France with the Associated States of Indochina.

It considers that the time has come to adapt the agreements concluded by them with France to the position which they have succeeded in acquiring, with her full support, in the community of free peoples.

Respectful of national traditions and human freedoms, France, in the course of nearly a century of cooperation, has led Cambodia, Laos and Vietnam to the full expression of their personality and has maintained their national unity.

By the Agreements of 1949, she recognized their independence and they agreed to associate themselves with her within the French Union.

The Government of the Republic wishes today to make a solemn declaration.

In the four years which have elapsed since the signing of the agreements, the brotherhood of arms between the armies of the French Union and the national armies of the Associated States has been further strengthened thanks to the development of the latter, which are taking a daily increasing part in the struggle against the common enemy.

In the same period, the civil institutions of the three nations have put themselves in a position to assume all the powers incumbent upon modern States, while the voice of their Governments has been heard by the majority of coun-tries constituting the United Nations Organization.

France considers that, under these conditions, there is every reason to complete the independence and sovereignty of the Associated States of Indochina by ensuring, in agreement with each of the three interested Governments, the transfer of the powers that she had still retained in the interests of the States themselves, because of the perilous circumstances resulting from the state of war.

The French Government has decided to invite each of the three Governments to agree with it on the settlement of questions which each of them may deem necessary to raise in the economic, financial, judicial, military and political fields, in respect of and safeguarding the legitimate interests of each of the contracting parties.

The Government of the Republic expresses the wish that agreement on these various points may strengthen the friendship which unites France and the Associated States within the French Union.

(270) REPORT BY LT. GEN. JOHN W. O'DANIEL TO JOINT CHIEFS OF STAFF [Extracts] ON U.S. JOINT MILITARY MISSION TO INDOCHINA, July 14, 1953

Source: *U.S.-Vietnam Relations, Book 9,* pp 69-79, 85-86.

General O'Daniel's report on the U.S. military mission shows that what has become known as the "Navarre Plan" owed more to O'Daniel's ideas than to those of the French command in Indochina. O'Daniel got the French to organize three new divisions from northern Indochina as an offensive striking force to wrest the initiative from the "Viet Minh" immediately. He believed the French Union forces would "accomplish the decisive defeat of the Viet Minh" by 1955, given the reorganization which he proposed.

1. The attached Report of the U.S. Joint Military Mission to Indochina is submitted as directed by paragraph 10 of the "Terms of Reference for the Chief of the U.S. Military Mission to Indochina".

2. In summarizing the subject report I wish to emphasize the following:

a. General Navarre, Commander-in-Chief, French Forces, Far East, submitted to me in writing a new aggressive concept for the conduct of operations in Indochina which, in brief, calls for (a) taking the initiative immediately with local offensives, emphasizing guerrilla warfare, (b) initiating an offensive (utilizing the equivalent of three (3) divisions) in Tonkin by 15 September 1953, (c) recovering a maximum number of units from areas not directly involved in the war, (d) reorganizing battalions into regiments and regiments into divisions, with necessary support units and (e) developing the Armies of the Associated States and giving them greater leadership responsibility in the conduct of operations.

b. General Gambiez, Chief of Staff to General Navarre, presented a discussion of operations to take place during the balance of the current rainy season. These operations include four (4) offensive operations outside the Tonkin perimeter aimed at destroying enemy personnel and existent enemy supply dumps, a clearing operation in North Annam, and an offensive operation in South Annam aimed at linking the Phan Thiet beachhead with Plateau forces and thus permanently severing the principal enemy supply line to Cochin China. These operations are to be followed by a large-scale offensive in Tonkin on or about 15 September 1953.

c. General Navarre agreed to establish a French MAAG organization to supervise all training of the military forces of the Associated States and to include three (3) U.S. officers. This will provide an excellent opportunity for indirect U.S. participation in the training of indigenous forces and for exercising follow up action on matters already agreed upon with the French and the Associated States.

d. General Navarre agreed to cooperate wholeheartedly in (1) providing the U.S. with increased intelligence and (2) the stationing of one or two military attaches in Hanoi for this purpose.

e. General Navarre agreed to keep the Chief, MAAG, Indochina informed of French plans and stated that he will invite MAAG officers to attend all operations.

f. General Lauzin, Commander-in-Chief, French Air Force, Indochina agreed to (1) the removal of the six (6) C-119's from Indochina, (2) request C-119's in the future on a temporary basis only, (3 or 4 days) to support airborne operations requiring the simultaneous drop of forces in excess of two battalions, (3) step-up pilot and mechanic training and (4) organize a Vietnamese National Air Force.

g. Admiral Auboyneau agreed to a reorganization of French Naval forces to include a Joint Amphibious Command for the purpose of (1) attaining increased amphibious effectiveness and (2) delegating increased responsibility to Vietnamese leaders and units.

h. Once the French became convinced of the soundness of our initial proposals they became increasingly receptive to our subsequent recommendations.

i. As evidence of French sincerity in carrying out actions designed to improve the status of anti-communist military forces in Indochina, General Navarre and other French officers repeatedly invited me to return in a few months "to witness the progress we will have made".

3. I recommend that the Joint Chiefs of Staff:

a. Note the contents of the attached report and take appropriate action where required.

b. Propose to the Secretary of Defense that he recommend to the Secretary of State the sending of a small group of qualified experts to Indochina to study the desirability of the U.S. assisting in the development of Associated States small industry capable of producing certain military items or military-support items such as small arms, batteries or recap tires.

c. Approve an increase in artillery units in the force basis for Indochina if MAAG and Department of the Army screening indicates such increase is necessary for a balance of forces in the new divisional organization.

d. Approve my return to Indochina in 3 or 4 months for a follow-up of the mission's activities, and

e. Insure that the Chief, MAAG, Indochina, receives copies of the approved report for his guidance and that he be instructed to take follow-up action where appropriate.

4. I recommend that the Chiefs of the individual Services approve necessary personnel augmentations of the MAAG, Indochina to allow for three (3) U.S. officers (one from each Service) for attachment to the French Training Command, and that the Chief of Staff, U.S. Army assign two (2) additional U.S. Assistant Army Attaches to be used for collecting combat intelligence in conjunction with the French G-2 in the Hanoi area.

(271) REPORT TO THE NATION BY DULLES AND ROBERTSON, July 17, 1953 (Extracts)

Source: *U.S.-Vietnam Relations, Book 9*, pp. 105-106.

After discussions with British and French Foreign Ministers Dulles and Robertson hailed the French intention to negotiate with the Associated States to "complete" their independence as removing the basis for legitimate criticism of the French and making it "easier to stop Communist aggression" in Indochina.

. . . Last Tuesday night we finished a five-day meeting of the Foreign Ministers of Britain, France, and the United States. . . .

.　.　.　.　.　.　.　.　.　.　.　.　.　.　.

In the past, there has been some criticism of the French Republic for failing to promise liberty and independence to the three Associated States of Indochina, - Vietnam, Laos and Cambodia. It was felt that the peoples of these countries needed something of their own for which to fight. The basis for that criticism should now be removed. The French Government has given assurance that it stands ready to grant complete sovereignty and independence to the three Associated States. Negotiations on this matter will start in the near future.

Last Monday, Mr. Bidault, the French Foreign Minister, and I invited the representatives of these three States to meet with us. We found that they looked forward eagerly to working out arrangements with the French Government to complete their sovereignty and independence. It seemed that they do not want to be wholly divorced from France. They have, with France, strong bonds of a cultural, economic and military nature. These can be preserved, consistent with full independence, within the French Union, which, like the British Commonwealth, offers a possibility of free association of wholly independent and sovereign nations.

This action of the French Government makes clear the distinction between those who would grant independence and those who would destroy it. It should make it easier to stop Communist aggression in that part of the world.

We discussed plans for military operations in Indochina. These are being developed by the French General Navarre who has recently gone there. Our Government sent General O'Daniel to confer with him. We believe that the new French plans are vigorous and deserve to be implemented in that spirit. The United States has a large interest in the matters because our position in the Western Pacific could be put in jeopardy if Communists were allowed to overrun the Southeast Asian peninsula of which Indochina forms a major part. We are already helping there with material aid. This involves the second largest cost item of our Mutual Security Program, participation in the NATO Army being first. I believe we should help effective resistance to Communist aggressors everywhere, and in Indochina it may save us from having to spend much more money to protect our vital interests in the Pacific.

.　.　.　.　.　.　.　.　.　.　.　.　.　.　.

We also agreed that an armistice in Korea must not result in jeopardizing the restoration of peace in other parts of Asia. In this connection we thought particularly of Indochina.

As President Eisenhower said in his April 16 address, an armistice in Korea that merely released aggressive armies to attack elsewhere would be a fraud. We are on our guard against that.

.　.　.　.　.　.　.　.　.　.　.　.　.　.　.

2. Our program for Europe and Asia is a program for peace and for the liberty and justice which are necessary if peace is to be durable. Repression can give the illusion of peace, but it is only illusion. For sooner or later the repression becomes unbearable and human emotions explode with violence. . . . That is why we seek peace in Indochina on the basis of freedom and independence which the French Government now promises the peoples.

(272) TELEGRAM FROM DILLON TO DULLES, July 29, 1953 (Extract)

Source: *U.S.-Vietnam Relations, Book 9,* pp. 107-108.

French Premier Joseph Laniel informed Dillon that the Navarre Plan would require an additional 150 billion francs, which would have to come from the U.S. if France was to balance its budget. Having been informed in Washington that it was impossible for the U.S. to get additional funds, Laniel said it would mean eventual withdrawal.

.　.　.　.　.　.　.　.　.　.　.　.　.　.

It is also the policy of his government to win the war in Indochina. To do this, they are prepared to adopt the general principles of the Navarre plan, including sending approximately nine battalions of additional troops to Indochina. However, the cost of sending and maintaining these additional troops in Indochina, plus the cost of arming, training, and equipping the necessary additional battalions of Vietnam troops, will be approximately 100 billion francs for the French calendar year 1954. Therefore, the Laniel government, in order to carry out its overall plan of winning the war in Indochina and balancing the French budget, needs an additional 150 billion francs for Indochina in calendar 1954. Laniel said that the 100 billion franc figure for the extra cost in Indochina in 1954 was a maximum figure, and that he had instructed General Navarre to do his best to reduce it somewhat.

Laniel said that Bidault had reported, after his Washington trip, that the Secretary of State and Mr. Stassen had told him that there was no hope of getting any additional funds whatsoever from the US for Indochina, and that Bidault was very discouraged to have to make this report. Laniel added that there was no point in sending any additional French forces from France to Indochina unless the funds were also available to build up the Vietnam army for its eventual assumption of responsibility. He pointed out that it would be impossible for him to make the economies which he plans to make in the civil areas of the budget unless he can make similar economies in the military side of the budget, including Indochina. If funds are not available to carry on in Indochina, the only alternative is eventual withdrawal, the only question being the exact method and date on which the withdrawal will take place. He has instructed General Navarre to prepare a new plan on the assumption that no funds will become available, and this plan will be ready shortly and will be available for our information.

Thus, in conclusion, Laniel pointed out that not only the whole question of Indochina, but also the whole problem of balancing the French budget and putting France back into a position where she could make a strong contribution to the European and Atlantic communities, depended on whether or not approximately 150 billion francs additional could be made available for Indochina in calendar 1954.

(273) REPORT BY THE DEPARTMENT OF STATE TO THE NATIONAL SECURITY COUNCIL ON FURTHER U.S. SUPPORT FOR FRANCE AND THE ASSOCIATED STATES, August 5, 1953 [Extract]

Source: *U.S.-Vietnam Relations, Book 9,* pp. 126-133.

In a report to be considered by the National Security Council at its August 6 meeting, the State Department presented the Laniel Government's three-part "package" solution to its political, military and fiscal problems, which would require an estimated $400 million in Fiscal Year 1954 - about 61 percent of the annual cost of the war. The report recommended support for the Laniel policy arguing that his government would be the last one that would be willing to continue the war in Indochina.

The winding up of the Indochina war is a necessary condition to enable France to check both these trends and reassume a more confident and positive role on the continent.

4. The lack of success so far in Indochina is traceable largely to French failure:

a. by timely grants of sovereignty and impressive military success, to win a sufficient native support to permit more rapid development of larger and more effective native armies, and to frustrate nationalist appeal of the Viet Minh.

b. to plan and execute aggressive military operations.

5. The present French government is the first in seven years which seems prepared to do what needs to be done to wind up the war in Indochina. Its plans offer the United States at last an opportunity to attack the major Indochinese and Metropolitan French problems as a whole. The French Premier has assured our representatives that his government is anxious to continue the struggle and to press on to win, but he can carry through his program against political opposition only if he offers a "package" solution, not only of Indochina but of the related French weakness in Europe and at home. For this purpose the new government has developed the following program:

a. Military Initiative. A new commander, General Navarre, has taken over in Indochina and is determined to assume the offensive. The initial operations under his command testify to this resolve. He has revised the plan originally presented in outline to us by M. Letourneau in March 1953 for breaking the back of Viet Minh resistance during the campaign season of 1954-55. His plans include an increase in the native armies by approximately the following figures: 59,600 in 1953; 76,000 in 1954, and 20,000 in 1955 for a total of 331,650 by January 1956. At his request, the French government is prepared, despite popular opposition, to send nine more regular infantry battalions plus ancillary units from France, if the rest of the program is agreed on. The Navarre operational plans drawn up on Indochina were approved by Lt. Gen. O'Daniel, USA, in his report on his recent mission.

b. Political Program. Pursuant to the French declaration of July 3, M. Laniel has assured U.S. representatives of his determination to grant genuine independence to the Associated States without the strings which have marked the previous grants of "independence". He apparently envisages something very much like Dominion status, retaining only such French authority and privileges as may be agreed.

c. Fiscal Rehabilitation. Laniel conceives his project for Indochina as an integral part of a new and supreme effort by France to "put its house in order". He plans to approach a balanced budget during CY 1954. This will involve a cut in French military as well as civil expense for that year. At the same time he contemplates a greater effort in Indochina. To do this he asks the U.S. for additional assistance amounting to about $400 million for FY 1954.

6. a. Attached are two tables showing (1) the financing of the Indochina war in CY 1953 and as proposed for CY 1954; and (2) U.S. aid for France and Indochina under 1953 program and 1954 appropriations. They contain tentative figures for 1954.

b. As the first table makes clear, under the proposed program, the United States would assume about 50 per cent of the 1954 budgetary expenditures ($829 million out of $1,676 million) and, if end-item aid is included, would be carrying about 61 per cent of the total financing. This would represent about two and one-third times the amount of U.S. aid for CY 1953.

c. As shown by the second table, this program would entail an increase of $403 million over the assistance now planned for France $1,286 million). Of the total French military budget for both Indochina and NATO, the presently planned U.S. aid, including end items, would be 26 per cent; if the aid were increased as requested, such U.S. assistance, including end items, would be 34 per cent of the total.

d. Finally, as the first table indicates, under the program, the total expenditures for Indochina for 1954, including end items, would be $2,160 million as compared with $1,700 for CY 1953.

7. The program presents substantial risks. Under it, the French build-up in Europe would be slowed down in some degree, both by the limited troop diversion and the cut in the French military budget. Moreover, in the best of circumstances, the Indo-Chinese war cannot be successfully closed out before the 1954-55 fighting season. Consequently, in addition to any supplemental aid furnished now, we would have to contemplate a comparable further contribution a year from now to assure a satisfactory conclusion. Furthermore, there is the risk that the French Union forces in Indo-China might suffer reverses before the projected additional effort can be brought to bear.

8. Despite these risks and uncertainties it is believed that the U.S. should agree, in its own security interests, to furnish the additional $400 million of aid to France. Various factors lead to this conclusion:

a. The Laniel government is almost certainly the last French government which would undertake to continue the war in Indo-China. If it fails, it will almost certainly be succeeded by a government committed to seek a settlement on terms dangerous to the security of the U.S. and the Free World. The negotiation of a truce in Korea, added to the frustrations and weariness of the seven years' war, has markedly increased the sentiment in France for some kind of negotiated peace in Indo-China. In the recent protracted French governmental crisis, every leading candidate bid for popular support with some kind of promise to reduce the Indo-China commitment in some way. For the first time in seven years, latent defeatist impulses emerged into real efforts by political and parliamentary leaders to "pull out".

b. Under present conditions any negotiated settlement would mean the eventual loss to Communism not only of Indo-China but of the whole of Southeast Asia.

c. The loss of Indo-China would be critical to the security of the U.S. Communist control of Indo-China would endanger vital raw material sources; it would weaken the confidence of other Southeast Asian states in Western leadership; it would make more difficult and more expensive the defense of Japan, Formosa and the Philippines; and complicate the creation of viable Japanese economy. If the French actually decided to withdraw, the U.S. would have to consider most seriously whether to take over in this area.

d. On the other hand, if the proposed program does succeed, and the French are able to achieve victory in Indo-China within two years, the effect will be to strengthen the Free World and our coalition in Europe as well as Southeast Asia. France will be enabled to adopt in Europe the active role which her weakness has undermined in the preceding period.

Recommendation

9. Accordingly it is recommended that the National Security Council agree to an increase in aid to France in the current fiscal year by an amount not exceeding $400 million above that already committed, provided only that (a) the Joint Chiefs of Staff inform the National Security Council that in their view the French plan holds the promise of military success; and (b) the Director of the Foreign Operations Administration ascertain the available sources within

currently appropriated funds and, the extent to which a special supplementary appropriation will be necessary when Congress reconvenes in January 1954.

TAB A

FINANCING THE WAR IN INDOCHINA
(millions of dollars)

	1953	1954
Present estimate of requirements		
French Expeditionary Corps	866	866
Reinforcements under Navarre plan	0	54
French Air Force and Navy	137	137
Total French forces	1003	1057
Associated States forces		
Regular Armies	335	400
Light battalions and support troops	43	196
Air and naval forces	9	23
Total	387	619
Total budgetary requirement	1390	1676
Financing of requirements		
French budget or equivalent		
French fiscal resources	975	690
U.S. financial assistance		
Presently available	258	426
Requirement yet to be financed	0	403
Total	258	829
Total French budget or equivalent		
including U.S. financial assistance	1233	1519
Associated States fiscal resources	157	157
Total budgetary resources	1390	1676
Total U.S. aid for Indochina		
Financial assistance (as above)	258	829
Miltary end-item program	255	429
Common-use program	30	30
Economic aid to Associated States	25	25
Total	568	1313
Total financing by France, Associated States and the U.S.		
Budgetary	1390	1676
Other	310	484
Total	1700	2160
Total U.S. financing as percent of total program	33%	61%

NOTE: U.S. Fiscal year 1954 aid program is related
         to French calendar year 1954 budget program.

TAB B

U.S. AID TO FRANCE AND INDOCHINA
(millions of dollars)

	Program 1953	Proposed 1954	Appropriated 1954
I. Aid related to April memorandum*			
Mutual defense financing			
Attributed French NATO budget	169	100	85
Attributed Indochina budget	48	400	400
Total	217	500	485
Defense support assistance			
Attributed French NATO budget	158	0	0
Attributed Indochina budget	210[a]	0	0
Total	368	0	0
"Kitty" to cover partial costs of expansion Indochina forces	0	100	26[b]
Total aid related to April memorandum	585	600	511
II. Laniel request for aid to finance proposed Indochina program			829
Total U.S. aid now available for Indochina in relation to April memorandum			426
Requirement yet to be financed.			403
III. U.S. aid in addition to April memorandum			
Military end-item program: France	0[d]	364	291[c]
Military end-item program: Indochina	255	429	429
Common-use program for Indochina	30	30	30
Economic aid to Associated States	25	25	25
Total	310	848	775
IV. Total U.S. aid for France and Indochina			
Presently available funds	895	1448	1286
Requirement yet to be financed			403
Total			1689

TAB B (Cont'd)

	Program 1953	Proposed 1954	Appropriated 1954
V. Total military program of France and the Associated States, including U.S. assistance in all forms French military budget			
NATO and other areas	2730		2444
Indochina			
Present French budget plan	1233		1090
Additional U.S. financing requested	0		429
Total	1233		1519
Total French budget with U.S. support	3963		3963
Associated States military budgets	157		157
U.S. aid outside April memorandum	310		775
Total program with U.S. aid	4430		4895
VI. Total U.S. aid as percent total programs finananced by U.S., France and Associated States			
Presently available funds	20%		26%
Including requirement yet to be financed			34%

*Memorandum on aid prepared by U.S. delegation to the North Atlantic Council meeting in Paris and handed to the French Government by the U.S. delegation on April 26, 1953.

NOTES:

U.S. fiscal 154 aid program is related to French calendar 1954 budget program.

a. Figure arbitrary since attribution has not yet taken place: figure based upon 1952 experience, and also includes counterpart of $60 million provided out of fiscal 1953 appropriation, under April memorandum.

b. Available from unprogrammed portion of carry-over into fiscal 1954 of unobligated fiscal 1953 appropriations for Far East military aid.

c. Arbitrarily reduced 20 percent to reflect proportionate reduction in European military aid appropriation below figures proposed to Congress.

d. This figure shown as zero because of reprogramming which took place in course of the year, because of over-programming for France for the period FY 1950-1953; in effect, no net additional funds were therefore necessary for the French end-item program out of the 1953 appropriations.

(274) <u>EDITORIAL IN *NHAN DAN* ON THE JULY 3 FRENCH DECLARATION</u>, August 6-10, 1953

Source: *The Vietnamese People's Sacred Resistance War, Vol. IV*, pp. 75-78.

The Vietnamese Workers' Party newspaper analyzed the new French plan to negotiate with the Associated States to "complete" their independence as a trick to continue the war in the face of the resistance war's success. A second theme of the editorial, was that the July 3 declaration was a reflection of the growing influence of the U.S. in Indochina.

On July 3, 1953, the French government transmitted to the puppet governments a declaration promising to "complete the independence of the associated states" Viet-nam, Cambodia and Laos, meaning that the puppets would be given broader powers. The declaration further indicated that the French government had decided to open "negotiations" with the puppets primarily to make the "convention" signed between France and the puppets in 1949 appropriate to the new situation.

A.F.P. Radio from France further declared on July 5, 1953 that France has decided to discharge 2,865 French civil servants in Indochina in order to turn over a further share of ruling authority to the puppets. Meanwhile French and puppet Tam's radios have blown up the news that the French command is turning over command authority in Phan-rang sector in Southern Central Viet-nam to the Vietnamese puppet government.

The whole thing is a deceitful farce, a farce in which there is nothing new.

The July 3, 1953 declaration is a completely deceitful scheme by the French colonialism. What did the puppets agree to with France in 1949? Country-selling articles which recognized the ruling authority of France, promised to supply men and materiel for the French war of aggression. And on top of all those articles was a *false independence and unity* with which they hoped to dupe our compatriots. Now French colonialism again declares that it will review those articles with its puppets in order to "complete the independence of the associated states."

Patriotic Vietnamese - Cambodian - Lao people are determined not to be duped by the invaders. The puppets embrace the French colonialists and resort to U.S. imperialism to maintain their selfish interests. Only by resistance war to the end, destroying French colonialism, defeating American intervention and destroying the puppet government and army can the Vietnamese - Cambodian - Lao peoples be truly independent. There is no other path to independence.

But the puppets responded swiftly to the French declaration of July 3. Accepting that declaration, puppet Tam hastily commended it. He said, "In order to respond to the complete independence which France is bestowing, Viet-nam still institutes a general mobilization of its strength," and will find a new reason to "tighten the deep relationship between Viet-nam and France." Truly shameless! French colonialism uses the deceitful slogan "complete the independence of the Associated States" hoping to make their puppets more attractive and use them to further plunder the human and material resources in order to continue the war of aggression. The French invaders must use a trick more cunning than before because the Vietnamese - Cambodian - Lao resistance war, which is stronger every day, is forcing them to use up much manpower and materiel; they are meeting very many difficulties, and have to use the slogan "complete independence" implement of the policy of using war to nourish war, using Vietnamese to fight Vietnamese. . . .

Now the Laniel government has been established. One of its first acts was to issue the declaration of July 3, 1953. We remember that before that French radio had mentioned that the U.S. government encouraged the French government to broaden the authority of the puppets so that the U.S. would assist more effectively. Therefore in the French colonialist scheme, we see the hand of U.S.

imperialism. At a time when France was encountering difficulties in every aspect, they pushed the French to make further little concessions to the puppets so that they could get hold of the puppets more easily, have further opportunity to encroach on the French more strongly and intervene more deeply in the Indochinese situation.

The Vietnamese - Cambodian - Lao people must remember that: The French colonialists are seizing our country by force, and they want to *complete the annexation* of Viet-nam - Cambodia - Laos, and not to "complete the independence" at all. U.S. imperialism are not demanding the French make concessions to the puppets for our people, but only because they want to attract the puppets away from the French and get direct control of them to use them to contest French interests.

Annihilate French aggression and U.S. intervention!

Annihilate the country-selling puppets!

Vietnamese - Cambodian - Lao people are united in resistance until complete, genuine independence!

Independence and freedom must be won by hard struggle; it cannot be asked for, nor can it be bargained for with the imperialists!

Let all patriotic Vietnamese - Cambodian - Lao people spit on the deceitful July 3 declaration of the French colonialists and realize the bad intentions of the French-U.S. imperialists and the puppets in this matter.

(275) MEMORANDUM FROM THE JOINT CHIEFS OF STAFF TO THE SECRETARY OF DEFENSE, August 28, 1953

Source: *U.S.-Vietnam Relations, Book 9*, pp. 140-141.

The Joint Chiefs gave general agreement to U.S. financial support for the Navarre Plan, but noted signs that the French were not following through on the points to which they had agreed with O'Daniel. They recommended that the U.S. insist on French implementation of jointly-agreed plans and continued willingness to "receive and act upon U.S. military advice" as conditions for additional U.S. financial support.

1. In a memorandum for you, dated 21 April 1953, subject: "Proposed French Strategic Plan for the Successful Conclusion of the War in Indochina," the Joint Chiefs of Staff pointed out certain weaknesses in the LeTourneau-Allard plan, but felt that it was workable. During the visit of the U.S. Joint Military Mission to Indochina, Lieutenant General O'Daniel, Chief of the Mission, a paper entitled "Principles for the Conduct of the War in Indochina" appended hereto, which appears to correct these weaknesses and which presents a marked improvement in French military thinking concerning operations in Indochina.

2. In his report Lieutenant General O'Daniel stated that, in his opinion, the new French command in Indochina will accomplish under the Navarre concept the decisive defeat of the Viet Minh by 1955 and that the addition of two or more French divisions from outside of Indochina would expedite this defeat. Additions other than in divisional organization would be in error since it is the divisional team, with its combat proven effectiveness, which is sorely needed in Indochina. Lieutenant General O'Daniel further reported that French military leaders were most cooperative with the mission, that several agreements were accomplished to improve the effectiveness of the proposed military operations, and that repeated invitations were extended to the U.S. mission to return in a few months to witness the progress the French will have made.

3. Based on past performances by the French, the Joint Chiefs of Staff have reservations in predicting actual results which can be expected pending

additional proof by demonstration of continued French support and by further French performance in Indochina. The Joint Chiefs of Staff are of the opinion that a basic requirement for military success in Indochina is one of creating a political climate in that country which will provide the incentive for natives to support the French and supply them with adequate intelligence which is vital to the successful conduct of operations in Indochina. If this is accomplished and if the Navarre concept is vigorously pursued militarily in Indochina and given wholehearted political support in France, it does offer a promise of military success sufficient to warrant appropriate additional U.S. aid required to assist. U.S. support of the Navarre concept should be based on needs of the French Union Forces in Indochina for additional equipment necessary to implement the organization of the "Battle Corps" envisaged by the Navarre concept and necessary support of the planned expansion of indigenous forces, such needs to be screened by the Military Assistance Advisory Group in Indochina. In addition, to improve the chances of success, this support should include continued close liaison and coordination with French military authorities together with friendly but firm encouragement and advice where indicated.

4. In furtherance of the O'Daniel Mission the Joint Chiefs of Staff are receiving Progress Reports from Indochina. Information received from Indochina indicates the French are not pursuing agreements reached between General O'Daniel and General Navarre (including the Navarre concept) as vigorously as expected by General O'Daniel and as contemplated by him in his report. Progress reports state that (a) the French have "no plans for a general fall offensive beyond limited objective operations designed to keep the enemy off balance", (b) reorganization into regiments and division-size units "is still in the planning stages", (c) there is "no sense of urgency in the training of senior Vietnamese commanders and staff officers", (d) the organization of a training command is awaiting the solution of "political problems" and (e) the "organization of the amphibious plan has not gone beyond the planning stages".

5. In light of the apparent slowness of the French in following up the Navarre concept and other agreements reached between General Navarre and General O'Daniel, the Joint Chiefs of Staff believe that additional U.S. support should be conditioned upon continued implementation of French support, demonstration of French intent by actual performance in Indochina, and continued French willingness to receive and act upon U.S. military advice. Further, the French should be urged at all levels to support and vigorously prosecute the Navarre concept to the maximum extent of their capabilities.

(276) APPEAL BY HO CHI MINH ON AUGUST REVOLUTION DAY AND NATIONAL DAY, September 2, 1953

Source: Ho Chi Minh, *Selected Works, Vol. III*, pp. 392-399.

While viewing the Korean Armistice as a victory for the "world camp of peace and democracy," Ho's annual September 2 message was marked by a cautious tone with regard to popular hopes for peace, as well as fear of the Americans and forthcoming Vietnamese hardship. His remarks suggested that the Party leadership was already thinking in terms of a period of fighting and negotiating.

Compatriots,
Fighters and officers,
Today, we are jubiliantly commemorating our August Revolution and Independence Day.
This independence was won as a result of 80 years of heroic struggle by our people.

This independence has been maintained as a result of 8 years of valiant resistance of our nation.

Throughout nearly a century, the imperialists and feudalists kept our people in the hell of slavery. They thought they had stamped out our people's patriotism. But they were grossly mistaken. Internally, thanks to the close solidarity and valiant struggle of our people; internationally, thanks to the victory of the Soviet Union over Japanese imperialism, our August Revolution was victorious, our country has been unified and has become independent.

But the aggressive imperialists and the die-hard Vietnamese traitors have provoked war in an attempt to reimpose their domination upon our country. In the face of this aggressive action, our Party and Government are determined to lead and unite the people to fight to the end, thereby continuing the glorious cause of the August Revolution and maintaining the unity and independence of our Fatherland.

****

Reviewing the past years of resistance we clearly see that: *Our position is growing stronger and stronger, the enemy's position grows weaker and weaker.*

Concerning us: at the beginning of the resistance, our people's morale was high, but materially we lacked many things. The enemy attacked us violently. We had to stay in a defensive position. Although we fought under very hard conditions, our Party and Government far-sightedly put forward the slogan: *The Resistance will certainly be victorious, but it must be long, hard and self-reliant.*

Facts have proved that the policy of our Party and Government is correct: The more trials we endure, the higher the morale of our army and people, and the stronger our material strength. Since the end of 1950, we have driven the enemy away from the Viet Nam-China border, made deep thrusts into its rear, and won many glorious battles. Everywhere, our local army units, militia and guerillas have developed and displayed great activity.

These are successes in the *military* field. In the *economic, financial, administrative, cultural, social* and other branches, we have also made continuous progress. For example: thanks to the correct policy of our Party and Government and the enthusiastic emulation in production by our compatriots, we have built up a democratic *economy and finance*. Under the difficult conditions of the resistance, our government has reduced the agricultural tax on the peasants, and at the same time taken a step in improving the life of the armymen, workers and cadres. These are obvious advances of our economy and finance.

The good results of the *ideological remoulding courses in the Party, the army and the various administrative organs* constitute a very great *political* success for us.

The mobilization of the masses to carry out the agrarian policy, in a planned and orderly way, step by step, and with leadership, will improve the peasants' life, gradually free millions of peasants from the feudal yoke of the landlords, help develop the national economy, broaden the National United Front, consolidate the people's democratic power, strengthen the people's army and push forward the resistance to complete victory.

At the beginning of the resistance, the national liberation movement of Cambodia and Laos was still weak. Today, the resistance of Cambodia and Laos has recorded many successes. The solidarity between the three brother nations of Viet Nam, Cambodia and Laos has become stronger and stronger.

At the beginning of our resistance, the Soviet Union and the new democracies in East Europe had to heal the serious wounds caused by the Second World War; the Chinese revolution was meeting with difficulties; the world peace movement was not yet organized. Today, the Soviet Union is powerfully advancing towards communism, the East European democracies are actively building socialism, China has brought her revolution to victory and is actively building a new democracy. Today, the world peace movement is developing mightily, the Korean resistance has been victorious. The successes of our brothers are also our own successes.

Concerning the enemy, when the resistance began, the truculent French invaders thought they were going to swallow us alive. They boasted that they would re-occupy our country in 5 or 6 weeks' time. They have brought more than one-fourth of France's officers, nearly half of her non-commissioned officers, and hundreds of thousands of soldiers to invade our country. But every year, they lost tens of thousands of men, thousands of millions of francs, and the result is that they suffered defeat after defeat.

The war in Viet Nam has aggravated France's economic recession, exhausted her finances, caused taxes to become ever heavier, her people to be more and more unhappy, her political situation to be more and more troubled, and her military position to become weaker and weaker. The war in Viet Nam has impoverished the French people, exhausted France's resources, and made her more and more dependent on U.S. imperialism.

Today, even reactionary Frech newspapers and polticians have to admit that never before has the French army in Viet Nam, Cambodia and Laos been in such a dangerous position as at present, suffering defeat after defeat, and having to pull back on more than 500 kilometres, from the Viet Nam-China border to the Plain of Jars (in Laos). The have to admit that the war in Viet Nam has exhausted France's vital forces. Not only has France no hope to win, but she even cannot avoid defeat.

In the imperialist camp headed by the United States, economic crisis has been sharpening, and contradictions among imperialist countries have become more and more acute. They have met heavy failure in China and Korea, the working people in their countries are struggling ever stronger against their war-seeking policy. More and more colonial and dependent nations have risen up against them. In spite of the ever stronger interference of the United States in the aggressive war in Viet Nam, Cambodia and Laos, they certainly cannot avoid failure.

In short, the enemy's position is growing weaker and weaker, the French-U.S. imperialist camp is also growing weaker and weaker.

****

The cease-fire in Korea is a great victory for the Korean and Chinese peoples, a great victory of the world camp of peace and democracy, and at the same time a victory for our people.

This victory was won because of the close unity of the Korean army and people; because of the valiant fight of the Korean Liberation Army and the Chinese People's Volunteers; because of the support of the world peace movement. This victory was won by a hard fight and tremendous sacrifice.

The U.S. imperialists and the U.S. side had to agree to the ceasefire, because they had failed bitterly, and could not carry on the fight. However, from ceasefire to peace, there remain many difficulties, because U.S. imperialism may resort to sabotage. Therefore, the Chinese and Korean armies and peoples and the world camp of peace and democracy as a whole must struggle and be vigilant against sabotaging schemes of the imperialists and their lackeys.

Korea's victory has convinced our army and people that our camp is very mighty, to see more more clearly that the imperialists' position is growing weaker and weaker, and to realize more clearly that only through a tremendously hard fight can we win glorious victory.

The ceasefire in Korea has inspired the French people to push forward their movement against the aggressive war in Viet Nam, it has shaken the morale of French troops and caused greater bewilderment in the puppet army and administration. That is why the French colonialists, the U.S. interventionists and their stooges are, on the one hand, lavishing propaganda stunts about fake peace and independence and deceitful reforms in an attempt to stem our people's determination to fight. On the other hand, they are hurriedly mustering and reinforcing troops and weapons to step up the war. Our army and people must therefore constantly remain cool-headed and be prepared to smash their schemes, and must dismiss any fear of the Americans, of hardship, and any illusion about peace.

We always stand for peace. But we know that only when our long and hard resistance will be victorious can we win peace. Only with real unity and independence can we have peace.

****

On the occasion of National Day, on behalf of our people, army and Government, I express thanks for the support of the people of friendly countries, of the French people and people all over the world who are struggling for peace.

I bow respectfully before the memories of the martyrs who have sacrificed themselves for the Fatherland.

I convey my heartfelt consolations to disabled and sick armymen and families of martyrs.

Congratulations to all fighters of the National Defence Army, local armies, militia, guerilla and public security forces,

War servicemen and women,

Model workers and farmers,

Cadres of the army, people's organizations, administration and Party,

Elderly people, my nephews and nieces, the youth and children,

Compatriots living in temporarily-occupied zones and abroad.

On this occasion, I call on those who have strayed from the right path by following the enemy to think over their error and return to the Fatherland. Our Government and people are always lenient towards those who have returned to the right path.

Though we have won many great successes, we absolutely must not be complacent and underestimate the enemy. To win real independence and unity, our resistance must still be long and hard, our army and people must be determined to overcome all difficulties, and to carry out the following tasks:

- The army must strive in political and military training, heighten its fighting spirit, annihilate more enemy forces and smash all enemy attempts at offensive.

- The people must emulate with each other in increasing production and practising economy and taking part in the resistance.

- The people living in the enemy's rear must strive to support the resistance, struggle against enemy raids, pressganging and destruction of production, and defend their lives and property.

- Let everybody actively take part in and support the mobilisation of the masses to carry out the agrarian policy.

- Our cadres must strive in political study, develop their qualities and correctly carry out the Party and Government's policies, and correctly follow the mass line.

To fulfil these tasks, our army, people and cadres must:

- Strengthen their conviction that our resistance must be long and self-reliant, clearly realize who are ourselves, who are our friends and who are our enemies; always remain coolheaded and strive to smash all deceitful and offensive attempts of the enemy, and smash the policy of "using Vietnamese to fight Vietnamese, using war to feed war."

Let the entire people unite, overcome all difficulties, fulfil their tasks, push forward the resistance and firmly maintain our independence.

Our long resistance will certainly be victorious!

Independence and unity will certainly be achieved!

Greetings of affection and determination to win
1953

(277) ADDRESS BY DULLES, ST. LOUIS, September 2, 1953 (extract)

Source: Department of State *Bulletin,* September 14, 1953, pp. 341-342.

*At the end of remarks in which he had repeated his warning to China against
any invasion of Indochina, Dulles suggested for the first time that the U.S.
would agree to have peace settlement in Indochina discussed at the political
conference on Korea, if the Chinese were willing.*

****

The War in Indochina

We do not make the mistake of treating Korea as an isolated affair. The
Korean war forms one part of the world-wide effort of Communism to conquer
freedom. More immediately it is part of that effort in Asia.

A single Chinese Communist aggressive front extends from Korea on the north
to Indochina in the south. The armistice in Korea, even if it leads to a political settlement in Korea, does not end United States concern in the Western
Pacific area. As President Eisenhower said in his April 16th speech, a Korean
armistice would be a fraud if it merely releases Communist forces for attack
elsewhere.

In Indochina a desperate struggle is in its eighth year. The outcome affects our own vital interests in the Western Pacific, and we are already contributing largely in material and money to the combined efforts of the French
and of Vietnam, Laos and Cambodia.

We Americans have too little appreciated the magnitude of the effort and
sacrifices which France has made in defense of an area which is no longer a
French colony but where complete independence is now in the making. This independence program is along lines which the United States has encouraged and justifies increased United States aid, provided that will assure an effort there
that is vigorous and decisive.

Communist China has been and now is training, equipping and supplying the
Communist forces in Indochina. There is the risk that, as in Korea, Red China
might send its own army into Indochina. The Chinese Communist regime should
realize that such a second aggression could not occur without grave consequences
which might not be confined to Indochina. I say this soberly in the interest
of peace and in the hope of preventing another aggressor miscalculation.

We want peace in Indochina, as well as in Korea. The political conference
about to be held relates in the first instance to Korea. But growing out of
that conference could come, if Red China wants it, an end of aggression and
restoration of peace in Indochina. The United States would welcome such a development.

(278) PRESS CONFERENCE STATEMENT BY DULLES, September 3, 1953

Source: Department of State *Bulletin,* September 14, 1953, pp. 342-343.

*Asked at his press conference on September 3 whether his St. Louis speech
was subject to conflicting interpretation as to whether the United States was
willing to include the question of a possible restoration of peace in Indochina
at the Korea political conference, Secretary Dulles made the following reply:*

I do not think that I ever said that these political talks would necessarily be limited exclusively to Korea. We have said that the conference as originally set up, in our opinion, should be limited to Korea. But also I think I
have made clear that, if matters at that conference go well and the Chinese
Communists show a disposition to settle in a reasonable way such a question as
Indochina, we would not just on technical grounds say, "No, we won't talk about
that."

Of course, any discussions which dealt with Indochina would have to have a different participation than the conference which dealt with Korea. For example, the Republic of Korea is an indispensable party to a conference such as is projected about Korea. But Korea would not be an indispensable party to discussions about Indochina. So that in effect it would not be the same conference. Certainly in any discussion about Indochina, for example, the three Associated States of Viet-Nam, Laos, and Cambodia would be necessary parties. They are not parties to the Korean conference. What we mean is that if the atmosphere, insofar as it may be contributed to by Communist China, seemed to be conducive for the settlement of the Indochina war, we would not be opposed to that.

(279) BRIEFING PAPER FOR NATIONAL SECURITY COUNCIL MEETINGS, September 8, 1953

Source: *U.S.-Vietnam Relations, Book 9*, pp. 144-149.

A paper prepared for consideration at the NSC meeting on September 9 quoted Eisenhower as saying at the August 6 NSC meeting that the U.S. should support the Laniel proposal only if the French would agree publicly to a "program which will insure the support and cooperation of the native Indochinese" - a tougher position on French relations with the Associated States than any U.S. administration had taken in four years.

SUMMARY AND COMMENTS

1. This very important and complex matter is being rushed to such an extent that there remain a number of questions which are not completely answered at this time. However, a successful termination to the Indochina problem is so desirable with respect to all our Far Eastern policies, and the pressure of time so great due to the approaching end of the rainy season there (about October 1 - after which major operations by the Viet Minh may recommence), that action in principle if felt to be essential by the Secretary of State is warranted at this time. The State Department asserts that if this French government which proposes reinforcing Indochina with our aid, is not supported by us at this time, it may be the last such government prepared to make a real effort to win in Indochina. (This may be somewhat over-pessimistic.)

2. This brief is written without having available the final papers upon which the NSC will be asked to act. These are still (7 September) in process of being drafted by the State Department. However, we are aware generally of their probable content.

3. As you remember, General Bedell Smith presented to the NSC on 6 August the proposals of the Laniel government to finish up the Indochina situation. This involved a request for about $400 million additional U.S. aid (now $385 million), and Laniel's statement that his program for Indochina would have to be paralleled by a program to balance the French budget or it would not be politically acceptable to the French Assembly. The NSC (see Tab "A", Action No. 874) agreed at this time that State, FCA and the JCS should proceed promptly with further exploration with the French and that if these agencies felt the French program held promise of success, they should submit detailed recommendations to the NSC. This has now been done and the recommendations will be considered at Wednesday's meeting.

4. At the 6 August NSC meeting, the President commented on the Laniel proposals, saying he thought we should support the French proposals only under the following conditions (see Tab "B", Brief of NSC Meeting, 6 August.):

a. We must get the French to commit themselves publicly to a program which will insure the support and cooperation of the native Indochinese. The later increments of our increased aid should be provided only if the French have made real progress in giving the natives greater independence.

b. If we are to give greatly increased support, the French must invite our close military advice in the conduct of the war in Indochina.

c. The French should give us renewed assurances regarding passage of the EDC.

d. He, the President, would not propose to call Congress back for an extra session to vote any additional funds for Indochina.

e. We might invite Laniel to visit the United States and be prepared to make a conditional commitment regarding further support for Indochina operations.

5. Action on this matter was somewhat delayed by the general strikes in France, but on 1 September the State Department received further, more detailed information from the French (paragraph 7 below), and the Joint Chiefs of Staff have reviewed the French program, which is based on the "Navarre Plan" described to General O'Daniel when he visited Indochina some months ago. The JCS state (see Tab "C"), Memorandum for the Secretary of Defense, 28 August 1953).

a. " . . . a basic requirement for military success in Indochina is one of creating a political climate in that country which will provide the incentive for natives to support the French and supply them with adequate intelligence which is vital to the successful conduct of operations. . . . If this is accomplished and the Navarre concept is vigorously pursued militarily in Indochina and given wholehearted political support in France, it does offer a promise of military success sufficient to warrant appropriate additional U.S. aid required to assist."

b. That information from Indochina indicates the French are not pursuing agreements reached between General O'Daniel and General Navarre as vigorously as expected. (Even more recent information from Saigon indicates some slight improvement, however.)

c. In light of the French slowness in following up the Navarre concept, additional U.S. support "should be conditioned upon continued implementation of French support, demonstration of French intent by actual performance in Indochina, and continued French willingness to receive and act upon U.S. military advice."

6. On Friday, 4 September, at the joint State - JCS meeting, the JCS further stated they believed the necessary financial support should be granted, conditioned upon the French assurance of expanded effort. They felt this financial support should not be doled out in a bargaining fashion but should be made available, with such savings as possible, for the stated purposes. We should leave the French no loophole in this regard to consider that we were showing lack of intent to support the Indochina operation and hence give them an excuse for insufficient action.

7. On 1 September, the French presented to the United States a memorandum, in answer to the U.S. questionnaires, which gave fairly detailed information on their programs. This memorandum states that even if France's financial situationa requires a reduction of her military budget, the French government nevertheless intends to carry out General Navarre's recommendations, and implementation has already begun. Complete execution remains subject, however, to U.S. aid amounting to $385 million up to the end of 1954. It goes on to say: "In the event this aid could not be granted, a complete reconsideration of the plan of operations in Indochina would be unavoidable." The memo then gives further information on plans and requirements. The French have indicated 9 additional infantry battalions of French Union forces can be in Indochina by 1 November,

that they are increasing the build-up of the native forces, that they are offering independence to the Associated States and that they will remove "colonial-minded" French officials.

8. The FOA has considered the legality of providing the funds required to meet the French program. They state that by use of the President's powers to transfer funds within "Titles" of the MSP Act, plus money already appropriated for additional support for Indochina, the requirements can be met. However, this may require a transfer of up to $285 million from "Title I", the NATO area, and we have not yet fully worked out what the impact of this transfer would be on NATO programs and on "offshore procurement" in the NATO area.

9. Mr. Dulles, at the NATO Council meeting in April of this year told the NATO countries he expected offshore procurement contracts in Europe during our fiscal year 1954 to amount to $1.5 billion, subject to appropriations by Congress. This was important for helping meet the European balance of payments. Congress seriously cut appropriations, and the transfer to Indochina of an additional $285 million from available funds will further reduce opportunities for offshore procurement in Europe (although some of the Indochina funds may be expended in France for OSP). However, the military services have been reviewing world-wide overall MDAP end-item programs during the past month against the foreign military units, in being or clearly to be created, which would receive the end-items. This review is scheduled to be complete in about a week, but very rough preliminary indications seem to show up lessened requirements to meet priority programs due to slowness in the creation of foreign military units. Therefore, in a very tentative way, it seems that the transfer of $285 million from NATO requirements to Indochina will not have a disastrously bad impact on NATO. It would be highly desirable to complete this review before acting finally on the Indochina proposal, in order to permit a better understanding of the impact on NATO and how to deal with it, but delay is not essential if the urgency of acting in Indochina is great enough in the eyes of the Secretary of State.

10. FOA points out the high desirability of consulting with Congressional leaders concerning the Executive's intention to provide additional aid to Indochina. The hearings on this year's MSA programs brought out Congressional worries over the degree of U.S. involvement in financial support for Indochina. Such consultation, which we hear may be undertaken by the President himself, will require some time and may thus permit the better evaluation of the impact of the proposals on NATO and offshore procurement (per paragraph 9 above).

11. It is not yet known precisely what the State Department will recommend to the NSC for consideration. (Mr. Dulles is taking this matter up with the President and is not expected back in Washington until late on Monday, September 7.) However, they may recommend NSC approval in principle for the provision of aid required to meet the French request, subject to:

a. French agreement to the following conditions:

(1) French to make every effort to achieve the elimination of the regular enemy forces.
(2) French to promptly increase native and French Union forces in Indochina, and agree to carry on the campaign under the Navarre concept.
(3) French to continue to pursue policy of generously and freely negotiating with the Associated States re their independence.
(4) French to welcome continuing exchange of information and views with U.S. military, especially re intelligence and training.
(5) The Indochina program will not entail any basic or permanent alteration of France's NATO plans and programs .
(6) End-item assistance required will be agreed upon in Saigon.

(7) Not to exceed $385 million will be all the U.S. will provide for "mutual defense financing" up to 1 January 1955, realizing that additional funds may be needed thereafter. (Source of the $385 million need not be disclosed to French but it may be desirable to make certain savings in FY 54 end-item programs for France and Indo-China.)

(8) Any savings accruing from more detailed planning and screening will reduce the U.S. aid required.

(Note that the President's suggestion re EDC is left out of the above. This is because opponents of either program may join forces in the French Assembly to defeat the Indo-China program. However, it should be made clear to French that failure to include ratification of EDC as a condition of aid does not indicate that our <u>assumption</u> that she will ratify has changed in any respect.)

<u>b</u>. Consultation with Congressional leaders.
<u>c</u>. Aid agreement with French will be reduced to clear written detail in a classified Note or Aide Memoire to avoid the frequent and divisive controversies surrounding this subject in the past.

<u>RECOMMENDATIONS</u>:

12. It is recommended that you:

<u>a</u>. Ask for full discussion of the impact of the transfer of funds from aid to NATO on NATO force levels and offshore procurement, and the likely political results on the other NATO government. (Mr. Dulles, Mr. Stassen and Admiral Radford may comment thereon.)

<u>b</u>. Ask if the Secretary of State believes it essential for the NSC to act in principle at this meeting:

If the Secretary of State replies that the NSC should act at once, then we recommend you approve the proposal in principle to be followed by the immediate conduct of thorough discussions with appropriate Congressional leaders and subject to French acceptance of the conditions listed in paragraph 11 <u>a</u>, above.

If the Secretary of State believes it is possible to delay action until a later meeting, we recommend you suggest this be done so that you may give the NSC a better evaluation of the impact of the proposal on NATO and offshore procurement before the NSC takes final action.

<u>c</u>. That you agree with the Statement Department in not conditioning U.S. support for this Indochina program with French ratification of the EDC.

(280) <u>TELEGRAM FROM DULLES TO DILLON</u>, September 9, 1953

Source: *U.S.-Vietnam Relations, Book 9*, pp. 150-152.

Dulles instructed Dillon to advise the French government that the U.S. had approved additional aid for Indochina, provided that France give a series of assurances on its political and military policies. Dillon was to begin working on language for a French note embodying the assurances.

1. Subject to our receiving necessary assurances from French, FSC today approved additional aid proposed for Indochina based on substance DEPTEL 827, with Presidential approval expected tomorrow. Comments URTELS 939, 940, 941 fully taken into account in presentation to NSC.

2. On most confidential basis you should therefore now informally advise Laniel and Bidault above action and indicate assurances desired are to effect that French Government is determined:

a. put promptly into effect program of action set forth its memorandum Sept 1;

b. carry this program forward vigorously with object of eliminating regular enemy forces in Indochina;

c. continue pursue policy of perfecting independence of Associated States in conformity with July 3 declaration;

d. facilitate exchange information with American military authorities and take into account their views in developing and carrying out French military plans Indochina;

e. assure that no basic or permanent alteration of plans and programs for NATO forces will be made as result of additional effort Indochina;

f. provide appropriate info to US Govt of amount of expenditures for military program set forth in memo of Sept 1.

3. We would expect these assurances be embodied in note which US in reply would acknowledge. US reply would go on to make clear that:

a. appropriately established financial requirements for military program as indicated in Sept 1 memo from French Govt, not rpt not to exceed $385 million or its equivalent in Calendar Year 1954, will be met by US Govt (see para 8 below);

b. amount of $385 million or its equivalent in francs or piasters is deemed to satisfy in full request made by French memo of Sept 1;

c. no further financial assistance may be expected for Calendar Year 1954;

d. US Govt retains right to terminate this additional assistance should for any reason French Govt plan as outlined in memo of Sept 1 prove incapable of execution or should other unforeseen circumstances arise which negate the understandings arrived at between the two govts.

4. You should immediately begin informally to work out language with French covering paragraph 2 above. (We will cable soonest new draft of US reply.) It should be made crystal clear to French that final US Govt agreement will be given only when satisfactory language for exchange notes has been obtained.

5. During time you are working out exchange with French, Administration will inform interested leaders both houses Congress since new program involves important change in orientation foreign aid program as enacted by Congress. We have begun and will continue work on this phase of matter with greatest urgency and hope have it completed by time you wind up negotiations with French. Please impress on your French colleagues overriding necessity maintain complete secrecy on all aspects this matter until Congressional leaders informed and negotiations actually completed and notes exchanged between two govts.

6. It was agreed by FSC there should also be assurances from French Govt re intention move ahead on EDC, but that for various reasons such assurances need not necessarily be contained in formal notes exchanged between govts. Would like your current views on how most satisfactory assurances can best be obtained.

7. While procedures whereby payments to French or Associated States will be made will have to be worked out, it is important that French understand clearly our basic approach to this additional aid - US is agreeing to finance a specific action program up to an agreed dollar figure. Consequently, we will pay or reimburse French or Associated States on basis of agreed franc and/or piaster expenditures as they occur at rates of exchange then current. US should receive benefit any reduced costs resulting from screening, devaluation, or other causes. Appropriate safeguards will be included in US note. FOA will forward details of suggested procedures shortly.

8. We have very serious problem finding $385 million and unless there are compelling reasons to contrary we would plan to release counterpart accruing Calendar Year 1954 (now estimated $70-80 million) to help meet total. Realize French may be counting on this counterpart for other purposes but trust you will be able reach agreement along these lines. This connection, would like to know lines French thinking on how they would present US aid figures to parliament, whether as separate amount outside regular French budget for 1954 or as item only on resources side as shown heretofore.

9. Will expect you keep us currently informed regarding negotiations on language of note.

10. Copy memo submitted NSC being pouched FYI. Copy NSC action paper will follow soonest. Will inform Heath separately of developments. FYI, current planning envisages following NSP sources for $385 million:

> 1. $70-80 million NSA counterpart accruing in Calendar Year 1954;
> 2. Rescreening of Fiscal Year 1954 French MDAP program;
> 3. Rescreening of Fiscal Year 1954 Indochina MDAP program;
> 4. Transfer of Title I and possibly II MDAP funds from defense to FOA

(thereby possibly producing amount of regular OSP that NATO countries including France could otherwise have received).

(281) ADDRESS BY DULLES, ST. LOUIS, September 24, 1953 (Extract)

Source: Department of State *Bulletin*, October 5, 1953

Citing the French declaration of July 3, and its implementation, Dulles asserted that it "transformed" the war, and made possible U.S. assistance "in good conscience" to the French Union forces.

In Indochina another war goes on. There has been danger that resistance to Communist aggression might collapse, with resultant jeopardy to our vital interests in the West Pacific. Many of the people of Indochina had been persuaded that their choice between two forms of subjection never gives rise to much enthusiasm or much willingness to sacrifice and die.

Now, the French, by declaration of July 3, have made clear their intention to grant full independence to the Associated States of Indochina as these States desire it. They are in the process of implementing that declaration, and there is every evidence that they are doing so in complete good faith. Thus, the character of the war becomes transformed. The United States can, in good conscience, contribute substantially, in money and materiel, to the successful conclusion of this war. It has become genuinely a "war for independence," and the aggressive character of the Communist warfare now stands exposed.

****

(282) MILITARY REPORT BY GIAP TO THE POLITICAL BUREAU OF THE CENTRAL COMMITTEE
Late September 1953

Source: "Contribution to the History of Dien Bien Phu," p. 39.

Commander in Chief Giap presented two alternative strategic orientations for the Winter-Spring combat plan to the Political Bureau at a meeting at the end of September. After hearing the report the Political Bureau, following Ho's advice, reaffirmed its previous strategic orientation and chose the second alternative, (See History of the Vietnam People's Army, *p. 531).*

Either to concentrate the major part of our regular forces to counter enemy attacks on the Northern delta and threats on our liberated areas; after ensuring the protection of our free zones and wiping out part of the enemy troops, to leave our regulars in the delta or to move them elsewhere, according to circumstances.

Or to avoid engaging the enemy in the delta where fighting conditions are favourable to him and where we can only gain small victories while running the risk of wearing out our forces. To send our troops where the enemy is exposed, to wipe out his troops under conditions favourable to us, to oblige him to scatter his forces to parry our blows, while intensifying guerilla warfare on all fronts. If the enemy attacks in the direction of our free zones, he will scatter his forces even further, and if our regulars win victories where the enemy is exposed, he will be forced to withdraw his troops from our free areas.

(283) U.S.-FRENCH SUPPLEMENTARY AID AGREEMENT ON INDOCHINA: LETTERS EXCHANGED BY DILLON AND FOREIGN MINISTER BIDAULT, September 29, 1953

Source: Document Declassified by the State Department, August 25, 1975.

The supplementary aid agreement on Indochina between the U.S. and France consisted of six letters exchanged between Dillon and Bidault on September 29, 1953. Of these letters, the two primary documents, in which the French government gave the assurances demanded by the U.S. and the U.S. specified the amount, terms and conditions of supplementary aid, are published here.

My dear Mr. Ambassador:

With reference to the exchange of views which has taken place during recent weeks between the Government of the United States and the Government of the French Republic concerning the additional aid necessary for the financing of the military operations in Indochina, I have the honor to confirm to your Excellency the information contained in the memorandum of September 3, 1953 of the French Government which indicated the plans, programs and policies of the French Government for the intensified prosecution of the war against the Vietminh by the forces of France, Cambodia, Laos and Vietnam.

At the moment when the Government of the United States is considering the possibility of such additional aid, I consider it equally useful to state briefly the intentions of the French Government as follows:

1. France is firmly resolved to apply fully its declaration of July 3, 1953, by which it announced its intention of perfecting the independence of the three Associated States of Indo-China.

2. In the view of the French Government, the purpose of the additional aid in question is to enable it to put into effect the strategic and tactical principles of a military action program in Indo-China, the terms and timing of which are set forth in Annex No. 4 of the memorandum of September 3. As outlined in the aforementioned document, the strategic plan of the French Command consists essentially of retaking the offensive with a view to breaking up and destroying the regular enemy forces. Convinced that the military problem in Indo-China can be settled only in conformity with such a plan, the French Government confirms that it intends to carry forward vigorously and promptly the execution thereof. In accordance with the basic strategic concepts of the Navarre Plan, the French Government has already commenced to build up the Associated States forces and is proceeding to despatch French reinforcements to General Navarre.

3. The French Government will continue to facilitate exchanges of information and views on a continuing basis between French and United States military

authorities and will take into consideration the views expressed by the latter with respect to the development and carrying out of the French strategic plans without in any way, of course, detracting from exclusive French responsibility for adoption and execution thereof.

4. The French Government is prepared to provide to the United States Government all appropriate information regarding the type and amount of expenditures necessitated by the military program.

5. The French Government considers that the increased effort which it intends to make in Indo-China under the conditions set forth in the memorandum of September 3 will not entail any basic or permanent alternation of its plans and programs concerning those of its forces which are placed under the command of the North Atlantic Treaty Organization.

I avail myself of this occasion to renew, my dear Ambassador, the assurances of my highest consideration.

(s) Bidault

Excellency:

I have the honor to refer to Your Excellency's letter of September 29, 1953, to my reply thereto of the same date, and to the memorandum of the French Government of September 3, 1953. This memorandum, together with its annexes, outlines the plans, programs and policies of the French Government for the intensified prosecution of the war against the Viet Minh by the forces of France, Cambodia, Laos, and Vietnam.

I. In accordance with the request of the French Government, the United States Government has carefully considered these documents with a view to determining the contribution which it could make in support of the additional military effort, with a view to helping to bring the hostilities in Indo-China to a satisfactory conclusion within the foreseeable future. In consequence of this consideration and in light of the request of the French Government and of the understandings set forth in our exchange of letters under reference, as well as in the following paragraphs of this letter, the United States Government will make available, prior to December 31, 1954, additional financial resources not to exceed $385 million, or its equivalent in French francs, in support of the additional military effort of the French Union in Indo-China. This amount is additional to: (1) the $460 million in aid described in the memorandum handed to the French Government by representatives of the United States Government in Paris on April 26, 1953; (2) the economic aid program to the Associated States; (3) the item of $85 million appropriated by Congress for the United States fiscal year 1953/54 for artillery, ammunition and semi-automatic weapons for the French forces under the command of the North Atlantic Treaty Organization; (4) any dollar funds that may be made available to France from United States fiscal year 1953/54 appropriations for basic materials development, overseas territories development, and technical assistance; and (5) it is likewise additional to the end-item assistance to the French Government and the Associated States out of past or currently available United States appropriations, after the adjustments required by Congressional action and by the present augmentation of financial aid to France have been made. The end-item assistance to be made available for Indo-China operations and referred to above has been discussed and will be determined by the United States Government in the near future.

II. This commitment of the United States Government is made upon the understandings derived from the above-mentioned exchange of letters, dated September 29, 1953, and from the memorandum of September 3, 1953.

III.   It is understood that the total amount of United States assistance described in paragraph I of this letter is the full extent of assistance which the United States Government will be able to make available to the French Government and to the Associated States for the calendar year 1954 from the United States fiscal year 1953/54 appropriations.   It is further understood that there will be counted as a part of the additional United States assistance described in this letter ($385 million or its equivalent in French francs) releases of counterpart (except for the counterpart of any of the types of special assistance described in paragraph I (4) above) accruing during the calendar year 1954 in the Special Account of the Credit National from dollar aid allotments to France from United States fiscal year 1952/53 and prior appropriations, to the extent that such releases increase the total of counter-value receipts in support of the French military budgets for the calendar years 1953 and 1954 above a franc amount equivalent, at the rate of exchange current at the time described below in this paragraph which has been or is to be made available in support of the French military budgets for the calendar years 1953 and 1954 from United States fiscal year 1952/53 and 1953/54 appropriations.   The amount of this aid is $1,070 million, made up as follows:

(a) $485 million of assistance from United States fiscal year 1953/54 appropriations, composed of $400 million for Indo-China and $85 million for French forces under the command of the North Atlantic Treaty Organization;

(b) $217.5 million of budget-supporting offshore procurement already effected from United States fiscal year 1952/53 appropriations;

(c) $367.5 million of defense support aid from United States fiscal year 1952/53 appropriations.   The franc resources to be realized from this latter amount of aid will, of course, be net of the 10 percent counterpart set aside for the use of the United States Government.   This net amount is calculated at $330.75 million.   Thus when counterpart withdrawals for military purposes from the Special Account of the Credit National in the two calendar years 1953 and 1954 taken together exceed the franc equivalent of $330.75 million computed at the rate of exchange at which the counterpart is deposited, additional accruals during the calendar year 1954 will be counted as a part of the amount of 135 billion francs of additional assistance described in this letter.

IV.   In its memorandum of September 3, the French Government has estimated that during the calendar year 1954 the plans outlines in the aforementioned memorandum for increasing the forces of the Associated States will cost a total of 195 billion francs, of which it is planned that the Governments of the Associated States will finance 60 billion francs (the equivalent of 6 billion piasters at the present rate of exchange).   On these assumptions the sum of $385 million referred to above, or its equivalent in French francs, is considered by the United States Government to represent the full amount of 135 billion francs requested in the memorandum of September 3, which stated that the complete execution of the recommendations of General Navarre was subject to the grant of this additional aid.   It is of course understood that in the review in detail of the cost of financing the various components of these plans, savings might be developed which would be applied first to reimburse the French Government for any expenditures it may have to make in order to meet any shortfall in the proposed contribution by the Associated States of the equivalent of 60 billion francs, and thereafter to reduce the ceiling figure of $385 million in additional aid described in this letter.

V.   The United States Government concurs in the proposal made by the French representatives that the process of refining the estimate of costs, together with the development of procedures for determining the requirements for funds and for making the additional aid available, should be worked out in detail between representatives of the Governments concerned, and should be carried on continuously throught the calendar year 1954. It is understood that the procedures to be worked out will be based upon the principle that the United States Government will provide the financing for agreed franc and/or piaster expenditures (outside the 60 billion francs referred to in paragraph IV above) relating to the National Armies of the Associated States, as such expenditures actually arise, up to the aforementioned maximum of $385 million computed at the rates of exchange current at the time when the expenditures are made. Any changes in costs which may result from any adjustments in the rates of exchange will of course be taken into account in determining the amount of United States financing to be made available, provided, however, that the total amount of the addition United States assistance described in this letter will in no case exceed $385 million.

VI. Should, for any reason, the French Government's plan, as outlined in the memorandum of September 3 and Your Excellency's letter of September 29 referred to above, prove incapable of execution or should other unforeseen circumstances arise which negate the above assumptions or understandings, the United States Government would not consider itself, insofar as the additional aid referred to above is concerned, committed beyond the amounts it had theretofore made available to the French Government, and it would desire to consult urgently with the French Government as to the future course of action.

VII. The United States Government has reached its decision to increase its assistance for Indo-China in the conviction that the heroic efforts and sacrifices of France and the Associated States to prevent the engulfment of Southeast Asia by the forces of international Communism, and to permit thereby the emergence of the free and independent states of Cambodia, Laos and Vietnam, are in the interest of the entire free world. It is also confident of the ability of France, with the ever-increasing assistance of the Associated States, to bring this long struggle to an early and victorious conclusion.

I avail myself of this occasion to renew to Your Excellency the assurances of my highest consideration.

Douglas Dillon

(284) TELEGRAM FROM DULLES TO HEATH, October 21, 1953

Source: *U.S.-Vietnam Relations, Book 9*, pp. 169-170

From October 15 to 17, 1953, an unofficial gathering political figures connected with neither the Bao Dai regime nor the D.R.V., calling itself the National Congress of the State of Viet-nam, met in Saigon and passed resolutions calling for abrogation of all treaties and conventions between France and Viet-nam. Dulles deplored the anti-French sentiments and "demagoguery" at the Congress and urged the Embassy to emphasize Viet-nam's continuing need for French help. For the full text of the Resolutions of the Congress, see Cameron (ed.) Viet-Nam Crisis, *pp. 207-209.*

Department continues much concerned at repercussions in France and elsewhere of ill-considered action Vietnamese National Congress Oct. 16. Although Department hopes and believes that statesmanlike action and utterances of Bao Dai, Tam on one hand and Laniel, Bidault on other will prevent damage from becoming irreparable. Department believes essential find ways revitalize concept mutuality of interest between France and Vietnam. Your continuing views and comments would be appreciated.

Department deplores atmosphere prevailing at National Congress, utterances and resolutions of which have jeopardized war effort upon successful outcome of which lives and property most members of Congress in effect depend. Failure of

Congress to express appreciation of efforts and sacrifices of 300,000 Vietnamese fighting Viet Minh appears even more extraordinary than failure to express similar sentiments regarding essential French sacrifices and effort. Bao Dai statements have helped but insufficiently.

Mutuality of interest in outcome of struggle is major present factor which needs emphasis and Department confident everything possible being done Saigon and Paris.

In addition however there is problem of reconstruction which will arise when war is won PAREN if it is lost, neither French nor we will have any such problem ENDPAREN. That problem will include necessity for providing reconstruction of country devastated by eight years of war, restoration of communications and reintegration into national life of several hundred thousand soldiers. Vietnam will need French help for this purpose and France will perhaps continue to need our assistance. PAREN There is obviously no commitment which can be made on our behalf at this time. ENDPAREN. Department wonders however whether establishment of high level planning authority for purpose of laying foundations of reconstruction-rehabilitation effort might not be useful. Perhaps this authority should spring from Vietnamese initiative with French invited to participate. Prospect of fruitful cooperation in constructive work after war is won might have sobering effect on political dreamers and doctrinaires. It might divert attention from constitutional verbiage and empty demagoguery and start people thinking of and perhaps developing vested interest in the practical problems which will face the new Vietnam made possible by curren expenditure of Franco-Vietnamese blood and US-French-Vietnamese treasure.

Department advances above purely tentatively and would appreciate your comment and comments derived your continuing discussion with French and Vietnamese contacts.

(285) <u>TREATY OF AMITY AND ASSOCIATION BETWEEN THE FRENCH REPUBLIC AND THE KINGDOM OF LAOS, SIGNED IN PARIS,</u> October 22, 1953

Source: Release by the Press and Information Service of the French Embassy, New York, February 1954.

The first agreement to be negotiated by France with one of the Associated States following the declaration of July 3 was a treaty which recognized Laos as a "fully independent and sovereign State." The Kingdom of Laos in turn reaffirmed its membership in the French Union. The end of the French control over various governmental powers was still to be negotiated.

M. Vincent Auriol, President of the French Republic, President of the French Union,

and

His Majesty Sisavang Vong, King of Laos,

Noting that France has entirely fulfilled the commitments she had made for the purpose of ensuring to Laos the exercise of full sovereignty and independence, confirmed by the declaration of July 3, 1953,

Both equally desirous to maintain and strengthen the bonds of traditional friendship which unite the two countries and which were previously confirmed and strengthened when the Kingdom of Laos joined the French Union,

Have agreed to the following:

Article First

The French Republic recognizes and declares that the Kingdom of Laos is a fully independent and sovereign State. Consequently, the latter shall replace the French Republic in the exercise of all rights and the fulfillment of all obligations resulting from any international treaty or special convention contracted by France on behalf of the Kingdom of Laos or of French Indochina, prior to the present convention.

Article 2

The Kingdom of Laos freely reaffirms its membership in the French Union, an association of independent and sovereign peoples, with freedom and equality of rights and duties, in which all the associates place in common their resources in order to guarantee the defense of the Union as a whole.

It reaffirms its decision to sit in the High Council, which, under the chairmanship of the President of the French Union, ensures the coordination of these resources and the general conduct of the affairs of the Union.

Article 3

France pledges herself to support and uphold the sovereignty and independence of Laos before all international bodies.

Article 4

France and Laos pledge themselves to participate jointly in any eventual negotiation designed to modify the conventions currently binding the Associated States.

Article 5

Each of the High Contracting Parties pledges itself, on its own territory, to guarantee to the nationals of the other the same treatment as reserved to its own nationals.

Article 6

Should the agreements currently governing their economic relations come to be modified, the two High Contracting Parties mutually pledge themselves to grant to each other certain privileges, especially in the form of preferential tariffs.

Article 7

Special Conventions shall define the modalities of the association between the French Republic and the Kingdom of Laos. The Treaty and the Special Conventions shall cancel and replace all similar acts previously concluded between the two States.

Article 8

The present Treaty and the Special Conventions - unless other stipulations are made concerning the latter - shall go into effect on the date of their signature. The instruments of ratification of the present Treaty shall be exchanged as soon as the Treaty is approved by the French and Laotian constitutional bodies.

Done at Paris, the twenty-second of October 1953.

(286) SPEECH BY FRENCH PREMIER JOSEPH LANIEL BEFORE THE NATIONAL ASSEMBLY, October 27, 1953 (Extract)

Source: Press Release, Press and Information Service, French Embassy, October 28, 1953.

Presenting the French Union military position as growing stronger, Laniel suggested that the Ho Chi Minh government might wish to negotiate because of a realization that it could not win the war. He pledged to consult with the Associated States on any peace proposal from the D.R.V. Referring to a resolu-

tion of the Vietnam National Congress that independent Viet-nam would be "un-able to participate in the French Union in its present form," Laniel indicated that France would interpret its "coordinating" role in the French Union in such a way as to meet Vietnamese aspirations.

" . . . France will not abandon her friends, but she would have no reason whatsoever to continue her sacrifices if the meaning of these sacrifices were misunderstood or betrayed by the very people for whom she had agreed to make them.

"When we say that the genuine sentiments of the Vietnam National Congress in Saigon were misrepresented by a motion which resulted from lack of experience, we are not making use of a diplomatic formula in order to conceal an unpleasant truth. That is actually what happened.

"Our country bases its judgments less on words than on actions and, in the face of Vietnam's increased participation in the common struggle, in the face of the demonstrations of friendship made at the close of, or following, the congress itself, we shall certainly not lose faith in the friendship of a young nation whose victory and independence we desire. A blunder led to uneasiness. And this uneasiness, in turn, gave rise to a reaction. We should like to hope that all that will be left of the tomorrow will be the pursuit, by common agreement, of our policy of liberation and peace.

"We have given the Commander in Chief in Indochina increased fighting power because we want it made completely clear to our opponent that he will have no chance of precipitating the departure of the French Union troops from Indochina by force.

"That is the primary condition of an honorable peace, that is, of a peace that will guarantee the life and property of the French, Eurasians, and Vietnamese who are fighting side by side with us and want their country to be free to choose its own system of government. Our military potential there is increasing in both men and materiel, while the time when the Vietminh was at the peak of its power now seems to have passed.

"The French Union is founded upon a vital notion: the necessity of placing in common the appropriate resources for the defense of the member States, from which proceeds the necessity of recognizing France's coordinating role in the use of these resources.

"Let us make it clear that the question here is one of coordination in the execution of plans and not of unilateral authority, since decisions concerning utilization of these resources have to be reached in common and on a footing of equality.

"Armed with the approval of the French Parliament, the Government would not be opposed to an interpretation sufficiently flexible to take into account the legitimate aspirations of the peoples and the force of the great upsurge of ideas that inspires them. Thus agreements might be reached which, far from being incompatible with the spirit of the Constitution would serve as a fitting complement to it.

"The time is past when the Vietminh could gamble on a difference of opinion among the Western powers with regard to our Indochina policy. . . . What could be a better answer to these insinuations than the recent statement of the head of the State Department, recognizing and formally encouraging the flexible and amicable structure which the French Union constitutes between the Associated States and ourselves.

"Which of us would object to the idea of negotiations on the international plane for the reestablishment of peace in Indochina?

"Unfortunately there are some who do not seem to agree. I mean Ho Chi Minh. I mean the Vietminh general staff. I mean the little group of leaders of a movement which can no longer compromise. . . . My Government now stands ready to avail itself of every opportunity to make peace, whether it is to be found

in Indochina or on the international level. But, although the Government
agrees to study any constructive proposal, it obviously could not do this except
in full agreement with the Associated States which it has recognized, helped,
supported and for whom it has won the recognition of thirty-three free nations.
    "We are not conducting a crusade or a war of extermination. If one day Ho
Chi Minh and his team - realizing that they cannot possibly win and that the
struggle is utterly senseless - should consider giving up the attempt; if they
should show themselves disposed to make certain proposals, then it would be up
to the French Goverment and to the other interested Governments, especially the
Governments of the Associated States, to consult together, to examine these
proposals, to take stock of their value and to follow them up as would seem, by
common consent, to be required.
    "We are fighting so that tomorrow Vietnam, a member of the French Union,
should not be subjected to a tyranny which would make of the the independence
we have given it only a vain word.
    "Do you think that we would keep our African possessions for long if all
Asia should become hostile to us? There are choices that are illusory. Such
choices must not be made.
    "It is true that the war in Indochina is unpopular. But there is one thing
that is even more unpopular in France, that is to betray one's friends and fail
in one's duty. Peace is our only objective. But it has to be admitted that up
until the present time, all the appeals that we have made to reason have remained unanswered. We shall make every effort to bring this war that was imposed on France to a just and honorable conclusion, in other words a solution
arrived at in agreement with those who are fighting in Indochina, side by side,
without own soldiers. . . ."

(287) RESOLUTION ON INDOCHINA ADOPTED BY THE FRENCH NATIONAL ASSEMBLY, October
28, 1953

Source: Press Release, Press and Information Service, French Embassy, October
28, 1953.

    On October 28, 1953, the French National Assembly passed, by a vote of ___
to 260, the following resolution on Indochina which was supported by the government:

    The National Assembly,
    "Sends it confident greetings to and expresses its admiration of the [*unclear*]
ant troops of the French Union which are defending liberty and civilization in
Southeast Asia.
    "Urges the Government to define and apply a policy which will

    1) Develop the armed forces of the Associated States to the point
        where they will gradually be able to replace the French troops,
    2) Do everything possible to achieve a general peace in Asia by nego-
        tiation,
    3) Assure, from the international viewpoint, a fair balance in the
        efforts and sacrificies made by the free nations in different
        parts of the world, and finally, insist that the defense and inde-
        pendence of the Associated States be realized within the French
        Union."

(288) REPLIES BY HO CHI MINH TO THE SWEDISH NEWSPAPER *EXPRESSEN*, November 26,
1953

Source: Ho Chi Minh, *Selected Writings*, pp. 153-154.

In an interview with a Swedish newsman, Ho Chi Minh indicated a Vietnamese readiness to negotiate an armistice with France, provided that France showed "sincere respect for the genuine independence of Viet Nam." Ho's answer also reflected the Vietnamese conclusion that contradictions between U.S. and French interests had grown acute and were an important factor in French politics and policy. The interview represented the opening of a new "diplomatic front" in the Indochina struggle.

QUESTION: *The debate in the French National Assembly has shown that a great number of French politicians are for a peaceful settlement of the conflict in Viet Nam through direct negotiations with the Vietnamese Government. This is spreading among the French people. Is it welcomed by yourself and your Government?*

ANSWER: The war in Viet Nam was launched by the French Government. The Vietnamese people were obliged to take up arms and have heroically struggled for nearly eight years now against the aggressors, to safeguard their independence and their right to live in freedom and peace. If the French colonialists continue their aggressive war, the Vietnamese people are determined to carry on their patriotic resistance until final victory. However, if the French Government have drawn a lesson from the war they have been waging these last few years and want to negotiate an armistice in Viet Nam and solve the Viet Nam problem by peaceful means, the people and Government of the Democratic Republic of Viet Nam are ready to meet this desire.

QUESTION: *Will a ceasefire or an armistice by possible?*

ANSWER: An armistice can take place in Viet Nam, provided that the French Government ends its war of aggression in Viet Nam. The basis for such an armistice is that the French Government should show sincere respect for the genuine independence of Viet Nam.

QUESTION: *Would you agree to mediation by a neutral country for a meeting between you and representatives of the High Command of the other side? May Sweden offer such a mediation?*

ANSWER: If some neutral countries try to help bring a speedy end to the hostilities in Viet Nam by means of negotiations, such an effort will be welcomed. However, the negotiation for an armistice essentially concerns the Government of the Democratic Republic of Viet Nam and the French Government.

QUESTION: *In your opinion, is there any other way to end the hostilities?*

ANSWER: The war in Viet Nam has brought havoc to the Vietnamese people and at the same time has caused much suffering to the French people. That is why the French people have been struggling for an end to this war.

I have constantly shown my sympathy and esteem for the French people and the French peace fighters. At present not only is the independence of Viet Nam seriously encroached upon but the independence of France itself is also gravely threatened. On the one hand, the US imperialists are pressing the French colonialists to continue and expand the aggressive war in Viet Nam, hoping thus to weaken France more and more and eventually replacing it in Indochina; on the other, they oblige France to ratify the European defence treaty, which means the revival of German militarism.

Therefore, the struggle of the French people for independence, democracy and peace and for an end to the war in Viet Nam, constitutes one of the important factors of a peaceful settlement of the Viet Nam question.

(289) <u>CLOSING REPORT BY GIAP TO THE CONFERENCE OF SENIOR ARMY CADRES</u>, November 23, 1953 (Extract)

Source: "Contribution to the History of Dienbienphu," pp. 44-46.

During a Senior Cadre Conference of the Vietnam People's Army called to dis-
cuss the Winter-Spring Campaign, Giap received the news that Navarre had para-
chuted significant forces into the French base at Dienbienphu. In his closing
report, he explained how the V.P.A. would respond to possible French moves and
presented the broad outlines of the campaign.

****

We are not yet precisely informed on what places were occupied by the enemy
and for how long, but we have none the less foreseen this operation: if the
Northwest is threatened, the enemy will bring reinforcements there. Thus,
faced with our initiative, the enemy has been reduced to the defensive and compelled to scatter part of his mobile forces, by bringing troops to Dien Bien
Phu to protect the Northwest and Upper Laos and to check our offensive.
What will he do in the days to come?
He may try to keep both Laichau and Dien Bien Phu, with Dien Bien Phu as
the main position and Laichau as the secondary one. If our threat becomes more
serious, he may fall back on one single position and bring reinforcements there;
we don't know yet what his choice will be, but it will probably be Dien Bien
Phu. If he is pressed, he may reinforce this position considerably and turn it
into an entrenched camp, but he may also withdraw.
At present, we cannot judge whether the enemy will entrench himself or will
withdraw, whether he will occupy one or two positions, and for how long, how
many reinforcements he will bring, etc., because precise information is still
lacking and also because the enemy is meeting with many difficulties. If he
withdraws his troops, he will lose territory; if he reinforces his positions,
he will scatter his mobile forces.   It may well be that he has not yet taken
any decision, or that having taken a decision, he has changed his mind on account of our action.
At any rate, whatever changes may happen inside the enemy camp, the dropping of his troops on Dien Bien Phu has created a situation in the main favourable to us. It lays bare the contradiction in which the enemy finds himself
entagled, viz, that between the occupation of territories and the regrouping
forces, between the occupation of mountain regions and the reinforcement of the
delta fronts."

[General Giap then disclosed the operational plans for the Winter-Spring
campaign.]

a) The Northwest is the main front. Our task consists in wiping out enemy
forces, intensifying political work among the population and liberating the
Laichau region so as to consolidate and widen our resistance base in the Northwest and threaten Upper Laos, which will scatter the enemy forces even further
and creat favourable conditions for future campaigns.
Forces to be employed: 2 to 3 divisions.
Part of our troops must move rapidly there so as to prevent the enemy from
withdrawing from or bringing reinforcements to Laichau, and to annihilate part
of his forces should he try to withdraw them. The main body of our troops will
follow suit. If the enemy seeks to reinforce himself, we must be ready to
bring to this front 3 divisions or even more if necessary. (. . .)

c) The delta is a co-ordination front. In the theatre of operations of
the North, one must wipe out part of the enemy forces attacking in the direction
of the north and intensify guerilla activities in the enemy's rear so as to
consolidate and extend our guerilla bases and zones, thus acting in coordination with other fronts.
If the enemy attacks in the direction of the Southern Sector, one must seek
to wear him out and annihilate part of his forces. If he launches attacks out-

side the occupied zones, in the northern or southern direction, one must take advantage of the opportunity to infiltrate forces into his rear.

(290) <u>REPORT BY HO CHI MINH TO THE NATIONAL ASSEMBLY</u>, December 1, 1953

Source: Ho Chi Minh, *Selected Writings, Vol. III*, pp 158-170.

In December 1953, the National Assembly of the D.R.V. met for the first time since the resistance war began, primarily to pass land reform legislation. Land reform was most important and most difficult political decision regarding domestic matters which the Communist leadership had made. To undertake an agrarian revolution, with the social upheaval which that implied, in the midst of the resistance war, was a gamble that the renewed enthusiasm of the poor and landless peasant majority for the resistance would more than compensate for the time and energy spent by cadres, and the conflict, not only in the villages but within the ranks of army and government, which were staffed to a great extent by relatives of landowners. As Ho's presentation to the National Assembly made clear, land reform had become a top priority equal to and closely related with the resistance war.

> *Deputies to the National Assembly,*
On behalf of the Government, I am happy to welcome you to this special session of the National Assembly.
I send my cordial greetings to the deputies who cannot attend it on account of their resistance work.
On behalf of the Government, I pay respectful homage to those members of the National Assembly who have heroically laid down their lives for the Resistance, for the Fatherland.
On behalf of the Government, I also welcome the delegates of the Front coming to greet the National Assembly.
> *Deputies,*
For the last eight years, our entire people have been carrying out the greatest task of all: the resistance.
We must push forward the war of resistance to ensure success for land reform.
We must strive to implement land reform in order to secure complete victory for the war of resistance.
At this special session, the National Assembly will hear a report on the resistance during the last few years, discuss the land reform policy and approve the land reform law.
Our country is a part of the world. The situation in our country has an effect on the world and the situation in the world also exerts an influence on our country. For this reason, before reporting on the resistance and the land reform policy, I shall report briefly on the situation in the world and in our country.

THE WORLD SITUATION

We can say right away that our camp is growing stronger with every passing day while the enemy camp is become weaker and weaker.
The *Soviet Union*, the bulwark of peace and democracy in the world, is vigorously advancing from socialism to communism. Mankind's dream of happiness for so many centuries is being gradually realized on one-sixth of the globe.
To safeguard world peace, the Soviet Union also possesses A bombs and H bombs, but it has time and again proposed the banning of these weapons.
With the wholehearted assistance of the Soviet Union, the *East-European people's democracies* are devoting all their effort to building socialism.

China has gained great successes in the fight against the US imperialists to help Korea, and has repeatedly recorded great achievements in the first year of the Five-Year Plan and in all construction work.

The great electoral successes of the Italian Communist Party and the French Communist Party, the mammoth strikes (August and September 1953) in these two countries, the struggle waged by the toiling class in various countries, and the national-liberation movement in Malaya, the Philippines, North Africa, Central Africa, Guiana, etc., have proved that the struggle waged by the people throughout the world is developing.

The Conference for Peace in Asia and the Pacific (held in October 1952) and the World Conference for the Defence of Peace (held in November 1952) have shown the tremendous strength of the world camp of peace and democracy.

During the recent period, the greatest success gained by the world camp of peace and democracy was the cessation of hostilities in Korea. In their most heroic struggle, the Korean army and people, hand in hand with the Chinese volunteers, have annihilated more than one million soldiers of the USA and its camp. For their part, the forces of democracy and peace in the world are extremely powerful. Like a pair of pincers, these two forces have forced the USA and its camp to accept an armistice in Korea.

Last October, the Third World Congress of Trade Unions, on behalf of more than 88 million workers in 79 countries, took the resolution that the 19th of December this year will be "the Day of Solidarity with the Heroic Vietnamese People and of Struggle for the Cessation of the Aggressvie War in Viet Nam". This is an expression of warm internationalism, of positive class feelings; it inspires our people with more enthusiasm to carry on the war of resistance, and more confidence in final victory.

That is a summary of the situation in our camp.

What about the imperialist camp headed by the USA? *The USA and sixteen countries of its camp* (including Great Britain and France) have suffered an ignominious defeat in Korea. Ever since the late 19th century, the USA has repeatedly relied on war to enrich itself and become a chieftain. This is the first time (but it will not be the last) it has suffered a great failure, losing not only men (more than 390,500 American soldiers dead and wounded), and money (more than 20,000 million dollars), but also its face before the other countries. The position of the USA in the United Nations is growing weaker, its camp is becoming more and more divided and its economy is plunged into an ever more acute crisis.

The Capitalist countries dependent on the USA, such as Great Britain and France, are facing ever greater economic and political difficulties due to their arms race policy, the people's movement at home and the movement of national liberation in their colonies.

The present US scheme is to kindle war in the hope of gaining world hegemony.

In Asia it sabotages the convening of the political conference, seeking to rekindle war in Korea; rearms Japan; prevents China from joining the United Nations; and interferes more actively in the war in Viet Nam, Cambodia and Laos.

In Europe, it frustrates the unification of Germany, and rearms West Germany with a view to turning it into the mainstay of the "European Army".

****

Our camp is becoming ever stronger and more united in front of democracy and peace headed by the Soviet Union.

Our present *main goal* is to relax international tension; we advocate that all international disputes be solved by means of negotiations.

The present task of the world's people is to consolidate their achievements, maintain vigilance and guard against US schemes, and strongly push forward the world peace movement.

The world situation is favourable to us. We support the world peace movement. But we must not harbour the illusion that peace can be realized easily. It can be gained only through hard struggle. As the French colonialists and American interventionists are persisting in their aggressive war in our country, we must overcome all difficulties, rely essentially on our own forces and strongly push forward the war of resistance until complete victory is won.

THE DOMESTIC SITUATION

A. On the enemy's side:

In the military field: The enemy has suffered great losses (about 320,000 men by November 1953). There is growing shortage of European and African manpower. On the main battlefields, the enemy's passive posture has worsened. Recently, he has tried to launch a few thrusts into the free area in the Third Interzone and into some coastal localities in the Fourth Interzone, but he is basically passive.

However, at present the enemy still has strong forces. We must not underestimate him.

Political situation. Contradictions are becoming ever more acute between the Americans and the French, between the French and the puppets, and between the pro-French puppets and the pro-American puppets.

In the areas still temporarily occupied by the enemy, his policies of deception and exploitation are resolutely opposed by our people.

In France, the anti-war movement is spreading.

Economy and finance. The enemy has incurred ever greater expenditures (from 1946 up to now, he has spent more than 3,000 billion francs).

But he can still get rubber and coal, export a certain quantity of rice, collect taxes and plunder the people's property in areas still under his temporary control. In addition he is given "assistance" by the Americans.

On the other hand, he is doing his utmost to destroy our production and communications in the free areas, guerilla bases and guerilla zones.

In the cultural and social fields. In the areas still under his temporary occupation, the enemy strives to disseminate a depraved culture and hooliganism in order to poison our people, especially our youth. He seeks to use religions to divide our people.

His main scheme is to *"use Vietnamese to fight Vietnamese and feed war with war."*

****

What is the enemy doing at present and what are his intentions?

The Americans are interfering more and more in the war in Viet Nam, Cambodia and Laos, and giving the French and the puppets ever more money and weapons. They buy over the Vietnamese, Cambodian and Lao puppets and speed up the organization of puppet armed forces. They force the French to make concessions to the puppets, that is, to them. They have a plan to replace the French step by step, but continue to use the latter as stooges for the implementation of their war policy.

Apart from their economic exploitation and plundering, the French and American imperialists practise such deceitful policies in the political field as:

- Declaring sham "independence" and "democracy", holding fraudulent elections.

- Pretending to carry out "land reform" to deceive the peasants in areas still under their temporary occupation.

- Setting up "yellow" trade-unions to mislead the workers.

- Advancing a peace fable to hide the truth from the French people and the world, and to deceive our people.

Meanwhile, General Navarre feverishly mustered his mobile forces to attack us, disturb our rear areas, expand commando activities and intensify intelligence activities.

In short, the French and the Americans are striving to implement their scheme, which is to extend the war by "using Vietnamese to fight Vietnamese and feeding war with war".

We must not be subjective and underestimate the enemy. We must always be vigilant and ready to frustrate his schemes. But we can say that his activities betray weakness, not strength. He is afraid of our policy of protracted resistance. He is afraid of the world peace movement.

In order to foil the enemy's schemes, we must push ahead with our war of resistance. To this end, we must carry out land reform.

B. On our side.

In the military field. From the autumn-winter of 1950 up to now, we have gained great victories in seven military campaigns and held the initiative on the main fronts. We have liberated the greater part of the vast Northwest area. The guerilla movement has developed strongly everywhere.

The ideological remoulding and technical training drives in the army have brought good results. Our army has grown up rapidly in both number and quality.

Many regular, regional and guerilla units have recorded heroic and glorious military feats.

Political situation. The ideological remoulding courses for cadres within and without the Party have had good results (nearly 18000 cadres from central to village levels have attended these courses).

The Lien Viet (National United Front) has been consolidated and enlarged.

The alliance between Viet Nam, Cambodia and Laos has grown closer.

The diplomatic activities of our Government and people have expanded and have won the sympathy and support of the people of the world, especially the people of the friendly countries and of France.

Economy and finance. Our people have overcome many difficulties, emulated one another in production, and contributed greatly in manpower and wealth to the war of resistance. Our finances have gradually stabilized. We have established commercial relations with China, which is very advantageous to our people.

In the cultural and social fields. An ever greater number of toiling people are now engaged in study. The number of general education schools and that of students have increased many times. The training of specialists has been gradually reorganized and expanded.

On the whole, the position of the enemy is weakening with every passing day while ours is growing ever stronger.

The above is a summary of the major achievements of our people, Government and Party, but our work has also shown shortcomings: in the previous stage of our land policy we were too much concerned about achieving unity with the landlords for the sake of the Resistance and did not attach due importance to the peasant question and the agrarian question.

Recently, our Government and Party have corrected this shortcoming, and much progress has been made. But in some localities the policy of the Central Committee has not been strictly implemented. A number of cadres think and act contrary to the policy of the Government and Party; they lack the sense of organization and discipline. Other cadres attach importance only to fighting feudalism and neglect the struggle against imperialism.

We must set right these shortcomings and prevent both "leftist" and rightist deviations.

LAND REFORM

Concerning this problem, I only wish to stress the following points:
The significance of land reform:

Our revolution is a people's democratic national revolution against aggressive imperialism and its prop, feudalism.

Our slogan during the war of resistance is "All for the front, all for victory!" The more the war of resistance develops, the more manpower and wealth it requires. Our peasants have contributed the greatest part of this manpower and wealth to the resistance. We must liberate them from the feudal yoke and foster their strength in order fully to mobilize this huge force for the resistance and win victory.

The key to victory for the resistance lies in consolidating and enlarging the National United Front, consolidating the worker-peasant alliance and the people's power, strengthening and developing the Army, consolidating the Party and strengthening its leadership in all respects. Only by mobilizing the masses for land reform can we carry out these tasks in favourable conditions.

The enemy actively seeks to use Vietnamese to fight Vietnamese and to feed war with war. They are doing their utmost to deceive, divide and exploit our people. Land reform will exert an influence on our peasant compatriots in the enemy's rear areas and will encourage them to struggle even more vigorously against him in order to liberate themselves, and to give even more enthusiastic support to the democratic Government of the Resistance; at the same time it will have an impact on the puppet armed forces and cause their disintegration because the absolute majority of the puppet soldiers are peasants in enemy-occupied areas.

The overwhelming majority of our people are peasants.

Over these last years, it is thanks to their forces that the war of resistance has been going on successfully. It is also thanks to the peasant forces that it will gain complete victory and our country will be successfully rebuilt.

Our peasants account for almost 90 per cent of the population but they own only 30 per cent of the arable land; they have to work hard all the year round and suffer poverty all their lives.

The feudal landlord class accounts for less than 5 per cent of the population but they and the colonialists occupy about 70 per cent of the arable land and live in clover. This situation is most unjust. Because of it our country has been invaded and our people are backward and poor. During the years of resistance, the Government has decreed the reduction of land rent, the refunding of excess land rent and the temporary distribution of land belonging to the French and the Vietnamese traitors and that of communal land to the peasants in the free areas. But the key problem remains unsolved: the peasant masses have no land or lack land. This affects the forces of the resistance and the production work of the peasants.

Only by carrying out land reform, giving land to the tillers, liberating the productive forces in the countryside from the yoke of the feudal landlord class can we do away with poverty and backwardness and strongly mobilize the huge forces of the peasants in order to develop production and push the war of resistance forward to complete victory.

The goal set for land reform is to wipe out the feudal system of land ownership, distribute land to the tillers, liberate the productive forces in the countryside, develop production and push forward the war of resistance.

The general line and policy is to rely entirely on the landless and poor peasants, closely unite with the middle peasants, enter into alliance with the rich peasants, wipe out feudal exploitation step by step and with discrimination, develop production, and push forward the war of resistance.

To meet the requirements of the resistance and the National United Front, which consist in satisfying the land demands of the peasants while consolidat-

ing and developing the National United Front in the interests of the resistance
and production, in the course of land reform we must apply different kinds of
treatment to the landlords according to their individual political attitudes.
This means that depending on individual cases we shall order confiscation or
requisition with or without compensation, but not wholesale confiscation or
wholesale requisition without compensation.

The *guiding principle for land reform* is boldly to mobilize the peasants,
rely on the masses, correctly follow the mass line, organize, educate and lead
the peasants to struggle according to plan, step by step, with good discipline
and under close leadership.

The dispersion of land by landlords after the promulgation of the land rent
reduction decree (July 14, 1949) is illegal (except for particular cases mentioned in the circular issued by the Prime Minister's Office on June 1, 1953).

The land confiscated or requisitioned with or without compensation is to be
definitively allotted to the peasants who have no or not enough land. These
peasants will have the right of ownership over the land thus distributed.

The *guiding principle for land distribution* is to take the village as unit,
to allot land in priority to those who have been tilling it, to take into consideration the area, quality and location of the land, so as to give a fair
share to everyone; especial consideration must be given to the peasants who
have previously tilled the land to be distributed. As for the diehard elements
bent on sabotaging land reform, the traitors, reactionaries, and local despots,
those among them who are sentenced to 5 years' imprisonment and more will not
receive any land.

****

The mass mobilization launched this year gives experience in preparation
for the land reform drive to be carried out next year. From this experience we
have drawn a number of lessons. In general, in those localities where the
Party and Government policies have been firmly grasped and the mass line correctly followed (in spite of mistakes and deviations by some cadres in some
places), satisfactory results have been recorded.

But failures have happened wherever the movement has been launched hurriedly by hot-headed local cadres before the decision had been taken by the central
authorities.

Land reform is a policy to be applied throughout the country, but it must
be carried out step by step, in accordance with local conditions.

After the land reform law has been approved by the National Assembly, the
Government will, next year, fix the dates and the places in the free zone for
land reform to be carried out.

The Government will later on take decisions concerning the regions inhabited
by national minorities, the Fifth Interzone, Nam Bo, and the guerilla bases.
In guerilla and enemy-occupied areas, land reform will be carried out after
their liberation.

In those localities where mass mobilization has not yet been launched for
radical land rent reduction, the latter must be completed before land reform is
undertaken. This is in order to organize the peasants, raise their political
consciousness, build up their political supremacy in the villages and at the
same time to train cadres, adjust organization and prepare the political conditions for land reform.

No locality is allowed to start mass mobilization for land reform without
authorization by the Government. Land reform is a peasant revolution, a class
struggle in the countryside; it is a large-scale, hard and complex struggle,
which requires careful preparations, clearly mapped-out plans, close leadership,
judicious choice of places, strict time-table and correct implementation.
These are conditions for success.

The experience gained in other countries shows that a successful land reform will help overcome many difficulties and solve many problems.

In the *military field,* our peasant compatriots will joint the resistance even more enthusiastically, hence it will be easier to build up the army and recruit voluntary civilian manpower. Our soldiers, with their minds at peace about their families, will fight even more resolutely.

In the *political field,* political and economic power in the countryside will be in the hands of the peasants, the people's democratic dictatorship will be truly carried into effect, the worker-peasant alliance will be consolidated, the National United Front will include more than 90 per cent of the people in the countryside and will become prodigiously great and strong.

In the *economic field,* liberated from feudal landlordism, the peasants will enthusiastically carry out production and practise thrift, their purchasing power will increase, industry and commerce will develop and the national economy as a whole will expand.

Thanks to the development of production, the livelihood of the peasants, workers, soldiers and cadres will be improved more rapidly.

In the *cultural and social field,* the large majority of the people, now having enough food and clothing, will study even harder, in accordance with the saying: "One must have enough to eat before one could practise the good doctrine." Good customs and habits will develop. The experience drawn from localities where mass mobilization has been launched shows that our compatriots are very fond of study and that there are good opportunities for the intellectuals to serve the people.

As said above, land reform is an immense, complex and hard class struggle. It is all the more complex and all the harder because we are conducting a war of resistance. But it is precisely because we want to push the resistance forward to victory that we must be determined to make land reform a success.

Because it is a complex and hard struggle, a number of cadres, whether they are Party members or not, might commit mistakes and deviations in their thoughts and deeds while implementing it. To prevent and set right these shortcomings and mistakes, we must firmly grasp the policies of the Party and the Government, completely rely on the masses and correctly follow the mass line.

The Government and the Party call on all cadres and Party members to abide by the policies of the Government and the Party, keep discipline, side entirely with the peasants, lead them in struggle. Whenever their own private interests or those of their families run counter to the interests of the resistance and those of the peasant masses, they must sacrifice the former to the latter.

We must mobilize the entire Party, the entire Army and the entire people to ensure the implementation of the land reform, to fulfil this great task.

For the Party members and the cadres, for the democratic parties and the patriotic personalities, this is a tremendous trial. All of us must win this trial, just as we are winning this other immense trial: the war of resistance against aggressive imperialism.

So our two central tasks in the next year will be: to fight the enemy and to carry out land reform.

We must fight the enemy on all fronts, annihilate as much of his force as possible, and smash his new military schemes.

We must mobilize the masses to carry out land reform in the regions fixed by the Government.

To carry out land reform is aimed at securing victory for the war of resistance.

To fight the enemy and to annihilate his forces is aimed at securing success for land reform.

All other undertakings must be focused on those two central tasks and serve them. In 1954, we must pay particular attention to three great tasks, combining them with land reform:

To strengthen the armed forces (the regular army, the regional forces, the militia and guerilla unites) in all respects: organization, training, raising of their political consciousness, technical level and combat strength.

To train cadres and raise their ideological level, promote them to appropriate posts, reorganize the Party bases in the countryside.

To develop agricultural production; to meet the requirements of the resistance and supply food to the people; to push forward the national economy.

The full implementation of these two central undertakings and three tasks will create more favourable conditions for the carrying out of other duties: firmly to maintain and develop the struggle in the enemy's rear areas, to consolidate the people's democratic power in the villages, to reorganize the security service, to develop and consolidate the National United Front, to collect agricultural taxes, to develop our economy and finances, to intensify propaganda and education and to promote work in the cultural and social fields.

****

Our strength lies in the tens of millions of our peasant compatriots who are ready to organize themselves under the leadership of the Government and the Party and to rise up and smash the feudal and colonial yoke. With skillful ganization and leadership, these forces will shake heaven and earth and sweep away all colonialists and feudalists. We can conclude that under the firm and correct leadership of the Government and the Party and with the whole-hearted assistance of the National Assembly and the Front, the successful completion of land reform will take us a long way towards victory for the resistance and success for national construction.

(291) EDITORIAL IN *NHAN DAN* ON HO CHI MINH'S REPLY TO *EXPRESSEN,* December 6-10, 1953

Source: *The Vietnamese People's Sacred Resistance War, Vol. IV,* pp. 150-152.

The day after Ho's interview with Expressen, *the Party Central Executive Committee issued a circular expalining the interview by saying that the "flag of peace" had to be in the D.R.V.'s hands, but warning against the "illusion that peace will come quickly or easily." Some days later* Nhan Dan *carried an editorial which followed closely the lines of the circular. It again signalled the D.R.V.'s readiness to begin the process of peace negotiations, while continuing the military struggle, asserting that Viet-nam would be negotiating from a position of strength rather than weakness as claimed by the French.*

The answers of Chairman Ho responding to a Swedish newspaperman have had a very big echo around the world. Journalists in various countries have reported those answers. Many in the French Government and other governments, French politicians and people, the world's people are discussing Chairman Ho's words excitedly.

The French people and peace loving people of the world are very encouraged. The French reactionaries and reactionaries around the world are bewildered, because they don't know how to deal with it.

The Vietnamese traitors and puppets are worried and confused. They are bewildered and worried because of the Voice of Chairman Ho is the voice of justice, the strong and sincere voice of heroic people determined to protect their independence and freedom to live in peace. They follow each other in distorting the truth, trying to misrepresent the meaning of Chairman Ho's answers in order to deceive the Vietnamese people, the French people and the people of the world.

They fabricate the story that they want peace but we don't want peace. The truth is our people and government always advocate peace in order to construct a truly independent Viet-nam. This was true before, now and will be true in the future. The truth is that French colonialists provoked atrocious war on our soil seven or eight years ago, and it is precisely for independence and peace that our army and people are determined to wage resistance war. If the French Government now sincerely respects our country's right to true independence and wishes to negotiate with us in order to end the war, we are prepared to talk. That is clear.

They brazenly say that we seek peace because we are in a weak position. In truth the more we fight the stronger we become. The enemy suffers more and more loss everyday. France spends more money, materiel and blood everyday. For that reason the movement of the French people against the war is constantly rising. Today not only the French workers oppose the war but other strata, including one section of the French bourgeoisie. At the end of 1948, in the French National Assembly, besides the Communist representatives, there were only 5 representatives of other parties, who opposed the war in Viet-nam. At the end of this year, besides the Communist representatives, more than 150 representatives of other parties oppose the war in Viet-nam.

Our nation holds high the banner of independence and peace, because we have the strength of justice, the strength of an entire people with one thought, the strength of the enormous support of the French people and the peace loving people of the world. The resistance war of seven or eight years shows our people's colossal strength which no weapon can defeat. The truth had been clear.

If the French colonialists blindly refuse to see that truth, are still stubborn and follow the orders of U.S. imperialism to continue their war of aggression in Viet-nam, the Vietnamese people, under the leadership of Chairman Ho and the Democratic Republic of Viet-nam are determined to resist until complete victory. The patriotic war of the Vietnamese people has the sympathy of the French people and the people of the world, and though it must be long-term and hard, it will definitely win.

The Vietnamese people know from their own experience that independence and peace are a protracted, hard struggle.

The Vietnamese people resolutely refuse to have any illusion that peace is easy. The previous experience of the Korean people demonstrates that.

Independence, unification have not yet been completely achieved; the Vietnamese people are always vigilant, determined to resist, and ready to smash every military and political scheme of the enemy.

1954

(292) REPORT BY GIAP TO SENIOR FIELD COMMANDERS ON THE DIENBIENPHU CAMPAIGN, January 14, 1954 (Extract)

Source: "Contribution to the History of Dien Bien Phu," pp. 50-52.

In December 1953, the Political Bureau decided to launch the biggest campaign of the war to annihilate the French garrison at Dienbienphu. In his presentation to the field commanders for the campaign in January Giap surveyed VPA victories on other fronts and explained how they had forced Navarre to disperse his mobile forces - a major strategic objective of the resistance. Then he discussed the objective and significance of the Dienbienphu campaign.

Two main objectives:

1. To annihilate an important part of enemy forces.
2. To liberate the whole of the Northwest.

This campaign has a great significance:

a) It will be the greatest positional battle in the annals of our army. Hitherto, we have attacked fortified positions only with forces numbering up to one or two regiments; now we are throwing into action several divisions; we have never before co-ordinated infantry and artillery action on a large scale; we have succeeded only in capturing positions defended by one or two companies, one battalion at most. This time we shall have to coordinate the action of several branches of the army on a large scale and to annihilate an entrenched camp defended by 13 battalions.

Our victory will mark a big leap forward in the growth of our army, which will have an enormous influence on the future military situation.

b) By annihilating such an important part of enemy forces, by liberating such a wide area, we shall foil the Navarre plan, which is the French and American imperialists' plan for the extension of the war, and shall create conditions for destroying enemy forces on all fronts.

What does this mean, to foil the Navarre plan?

The enemy is seeking to concentrate mobile forces in the delta: we compel him to scatter them in mountain regions where they will be destroyed piecemeal.

He is seeking to increase the size of the puppet army and to bring reinforcements from France: we shall annihilate an important part of his forces to aggravate his manpower crisis beyond retrieve.

He is seeking to pacify the Northern plans and various theatres of operations in the South: our victory at Dien Bien Phu will make it possible for our forces to intensify their action on those various fronts thus creating conditions for the annihilation of important enemy forces and foiling his plans for pacification.

The enemy is seeking to wrest back the initiative; our victory will drive him further to the defensive and will consolidate our offensive situation.

c) From the political point of view, this battle will have a very great influence. On the internal plane, it will consolidate our rear, and *ensure the success of the land reform.* By winning a victory, the People's Army, which is fighting imperialism by force of arms, will make an effective and glorious complement to the mighty battle being waged in the rear by millions of peasants against feudalism.

This battle is taking place at a time when French imperialism is meeting with numerous difficulties in Vietnam, Laos and Cambodia, when the French people's struggle for an end to the war is increasing and when the struggle of the world's peoples for the defence of peace and an end to the war in Vietnam has reached unequalled designs and will be *an important contribution of our army to the defence of world peace.*

(293) REPORT BY GIAP TO A CONFERENCE OF CADRES, February 7, 1954 (Extracts)

Source: "Contribution to the History of Dien Bien Phu," pp. 54-55.

While active preparations were underway for the Dienbienphu campaign, Giap reviewed the results of the strategic orientation adopted for the Winter-Spring combat plan: the French forces had become increasingly immobile and dispersed. In a portion of the report not included in the document as published by Hanoi, he reported that the Navarre plan had already been frustrated on all of its key objectives: concentration of mobile forces, pacification of the Tonkin delta in the South and offensive against the D.R.V. "free zone."

In short, in two months of activities, we have:

- annihilated 20,000 enemy troops, among them the major part of 4 battalions of Europeans and Africans, one puppet paratroop battalion and one puppet infantry battalion;
- liberated vast areas in the Northwest and the Taynguyen (High Plateaux in Central Vietnam);
- intensified guerilla warfare and expanded our guerilla bases in the Northern delta, firmly kept up our guerilla activities in Binh Tri Thien (Central Vietnam) and intensified guerilla warfare in the South.

Besides, the Pathet Lao has expanded its resistance bases in Upper, Middle and Lower Laos.

On the whole, the general aspect of the fronts are characterized by two essential features:

First, enemy mobile forces hitherto concentrated in the Northern delta have been scattered and are now immobilized in a series of important positions.

Those scattered and immobilized forces include 14 battalions at Dien Bien Phu, 18 in the Northern delta, 22 in Middle and Upper Laos, 8 in Pleiku, 13 at Tuy Hoa. Navarre has had the Seventh Regiment transferred from the Northern delta to Luang Prabang, and if the threat against this town becomes more serious, he will be compelled to reinforce its garrison still further, and will thus further scatter his forces.

Second, our forces are most active and have reaped victories on all theatres of operations.

****

Dien Bien Phu remains the most important "head-on" front, for the most important part of the enemy forces have been immobilized there. The will of the Central Committee remains unchanged: to wipe out all the enemy forces in that base.

We have previously favoured swift attacks with a view to quick victory. However, in the course of the period of preparation, the situation in the enemy camp has changed, and the Central Military Committee has decided to modify our operational plans and principles and the artillery emplacement. (. . .)

Our new operational principle is as follows: steady attack, steady advance. Which does not exclude a quick victory through swift attacks should favourable circumstances prevail.

(294) <u>SPEECH BY PREMIER LANIEL BEFORE THE NATIONAL ASSEMBLY</u>, March 5, 1954 (Extracts)

Source: Press Release, Press and Information Service, French Embassy Speeches and Press Conferences, No. 19, March, 1954.

Presenting his government's policy on the Geneva negotiations to the Assembly, Laniel indicated that France would demand regroupment zones for "Viet Minh" troops outside the populated areas in the North and Center and the disarmament or evacuation of "Viet Minh" in the South. He said nothing about a political settlement, but suggested that a cease-fire with military controls would have to be put in effect before any political talks could be held. The text below consists of the portions of the speech translated and distributed by the French Press and Information Service.

The Geneva Conference Should Prepare the Way for Peace in Asia

"In setting us the goal of seeking a general peace in Asia, has not the Assembly itself invited us, in preference, to take advantage of opportunities for proceedings, looking towards a settlement, that would be conducted in common with all the interested powers? . . . Does not China - without whose proximity, the war in Indochina would have been brought to an end long ago - need peace for internal consolidation? May she not fear lest a prolongation of the conflict should result in her involvement? Can she not count on obtaining concrete advantages from a meeting with the Western powers in return for the aid she might give in the reestablishment of peace in Indochina? Does not the search for agreement with the Western Powers on peace in Asia meet the wishes of Russia to the extent that Moscow would like to see American forces withdrawn from Korea and perhaps also fears any autonomous initiative of China in the Far East, especially in Southeast Asia? As for the great democracies, which up until the present time have furnished us with considerable aid for the war in Indochina, their presence at these negotiations would be not only valuable, but essential, as it would greatly increase the chances of accomplishing something. . . .

"At Berlin our most important objective was attained, under the best possible conditions - in other words in complete agreement with our Allies - thanks to the highly effective action of the Minister of Foreign Affairs. A few weeks ago there seemed to be hopeless opposition between M. Molotov's thesis - which placed no limits on the competence of an eventual five-power conference - and that of Mr. Foster Dulles - who rejected the very idea of such a conference. Both admitted that the settlement of the Indochinese conflict could and should be the object of an international meeting which would bring together, along with the other interested States, the United States, France, Great Britain, the Soviet Union and China. . . .

The Military Conditions for a Cease-Fire

"The Geneva Conference will meet about fifty days hence. Even if the conference were nearer still, we would not have the right to neglect any opportunity that might arise in the interim of putting an end to the hostilities in an honorable and effective manner. Just because a war has been going on for more than seven years, we do not therefore have the right to neglect a chance of bringing it to an end a day sooner. Many noble spirits have thought as we do. Quite recently Pandit Nehru publicly formulated the wish of seeing an immediate cease-fire in Indochina. I pay homage to the nobility of a thought which has the same inspiration as the unanimous wishes of France."

[M. Laniel then read the declaration of the Prime Minister of India. He continued]: "In its form, this speech cannot be considered as an offer of mediation. But, fundamentally, it raised a question - which had already been raised in the public mind - as to whether France could immediately adopt the following very simple formula: 'Cease fire first. Negotiate afterwards.' We have given due attention to the study of this question. Our answer is dictated by a single overriding consideration, the security of our expeditionary corps, composed of Frenchmen and of friends of France, during the period - perhaps a long one - which would elapse between the preliminary cease-fire and the final agreement. . . .

"What sort of peace do you want? What sort of agreement do you consider acceptable? What sort of agreement would you reject as unacceptable? My answer to these questions is that we consider unacceptable any project which, under color of an immediate cease-fire, would begin by endangering our soldiers and our friends, without our having obtained sufficient guarantees to assure the development of normal negotiations and the chance of a durable peace.

"Those who favor a truce as a prelude to negotiations evidently have the Korean precedent in mind. In Korea, guarantees could be obtained relatively easily, in fact, owing to the existence of a continuous front clearly separating two zones, each of which was completely and permanently controlled by one of the adversaries. In Indochina the situation is quite different.

"First of all there is the case of Laos. . . . Nothing in the attitude of the Government of Laos could have furnished a pretext for the Vietminh invasion. We do not wish to anticipate here the terms of an eventual agreement, which furthermore should be negotiated with the interested parties, but it is immediately evident that the first condition for laying down our arms would be the complete evacuation of Laos by the infiltrating troops. In Cambodia, although the military situation is completely different, similar precautions would be necessary.

"In Vietnam, the war presents a great variety of forms and intensity depending upon the region involved. No uniform system seems conceivable. Undoubtedly different solutions would have to be found for each main theatre of operations. The delta, however, constitutes geographically a well definded area. A sort of no man's land could be created around the periphery of the delta and the Vietminh units which had infiltrated at different points would have to evacuate these zones. This evacuation would have to be strictly controlled, a task all the more delicate where the structure of the Vietminh units is more fluid.

"In Central Vietnam, the Vietminh units would return to zones of encampment markout in such a manner as to guarantee the security of our troops and of the people. In South Vietnam, where the Vietminh forces are less concentrated than in the North or Center, the enemy forces should be disarmed or evacuated. . . .

"To all these guarantees would have to be added other measures of security or control intended to ensure that our adversaries would not be able to take advantage of a truce in order to do certain construction work, bring up reinforcements or regroup their forces as was the case in Korea during the long period of negotiations.

The Political Conditions for Agreement With the Vietminh

"Extreme precautions would be indispensable for the security of our troops and of the Armies of the Associated States. They would be all the more imperative in view of our past experience of the manner in which the Vietminh has kept its promises heretofore. We cannot forget that they took advantage of the modus vivendi of 1946, especially in Cochinchina, to terrorize the members of the Vietminh who had shown themselves favorable to cooperation with France. . . .

"A truce could thus only the result of carefully conducted negotiations, for which we will be ready very soon, once we have proceeded to the necessary studies with the Associated States; the best possible conditions for such negotiations can be found at Geneva, thanks to the efforts of our diplomacy. If we should happen to receive a concrete proposal before Geneva, it would be examined in the spirit that I have just described to you. . . .

The Conflict Should Be Settled Through Negotiation

"Up until 1953, there were two opposed tendencies in French public opinion. Some sought the end of the conflict through negotiation. The others believed that France could triumph by force of arms. . . . Now we are indeed unanimous in desiring a settlement through negotiation. That is agreed; there is no longer need for anyone to argue in favor of this point of view.

"But let us consider the conditions under which we should prepare for the forthcoming conversations and under which they should take place. During this period it goes without saying that our military effort must not be relaxed. It remains basic, because it is thanks to this effort that we have compelled the enemy to change his tune, if not his conduct, and because it is thanks to it that we are keeping him in a position where he cannot hope to win by force. . . .

"Put an end to the war, of course! But let us watch out. . . . Negotiations as delicate as those that are about to begin cannot be satisfactorily conducted without concerted preparation carried out with the necessary discretion. This secrecy, always necessary in diplomacy, is particularly important when one has to deal with people who received their training in totalitarian schools.

"A peace negotiated with due respect for the national honor, for the freedom of the individual, and for the security of our expeditionary corps - that is our goal. This is the hour of hope. In the name of France, I salute all the fighting men of the Associated States and of the French Army who, by their sacrifices of yesterday and of tomorrow, make this hope."

(295) APPEAL BY VO NGUYEN GIAP TO ALL CADRES AND FIGHTERS, UNITS AND SERVICES, ON BEGINNING THE DIENBIENPHU CAMPAIGN, March 1954

Source: Vo Nguyen Giap, *Orders of the Day, Speeches and Mobilization Letters*, pp. 202-204 (Translation by the editor).

After three months of preparation, during which the Party leadership suspended work on land reform in order to concentrate all human resources on material support for the campaign, Giap was ready to begin the attack on Dienbienphu. In a message to those who would be participating in the campaign, Giap said it would deal a death blow to the Navarre plan and contribute to the pressure on France to negotiate a peace settlement.

All cadres and fighters!

The Dienbienphu campaign is about to begin.

This is the largest scale positional campaign in the history of our Army up to the present.

During the past three months, from the time the enemy forces parachuted into Diebienphu, our army has surrounded and confined their main force in there, creating conditions for continuously defeating the enemy on all battlefields in the entire country.

Today Lai-chau was liberated, the Nam-hu River defense line of the invaders was broken, and there is no shadow of an invader in Phong Saly. Dienbeinphu has become a collection of important points completely isolated, standing alone in the middle of our broad rear area.

Today, the time has come for our main forces to bring the attack on Dienbienphu.

If we are victorious at Dienbienphu, we will annihilate a very important part of the invaders' manpower, liberate the entire Northwest territory, widen and consolidate the broad rear area of our resistance war, and help to insure that the land reform achieves success.

If we are victorious at Dienbienphu, our heroic People's Army will take a stride forward, and our resistance war will achieve a very important victory.

If we are victorious at Dienbienphu, we will smash the Navarre plan, which has already been heavily defeated. The victorious Dienbienphu campaign will have a resounding influence both within and outside the country; it will be a worthy contribution to the world peace movement demanding an end to the war in Vietnam - Cambodia - Laos, especially at a time when the French Government is being defeated continuously and has begun to have to talk of negotiating in order to peacefully resolve the problem of the war in Indochina.

In accordance with the order of the Party Central Committee, the Government and Chairman Ho,

While our troops are exerting efforts to kill the invaders on battlefields throughout the country in coordination with us,

I appeal to all cadres and fighters, all units and all services on the Dienbienphu front:

You must realize clearly the honor of participating in this historic campaign,

You must have very high determination to kill the invaders,

You must grasp firmly the line "Attack strongly, advance firmly,"

You must surmount all hardship,

Overcome all difficulties,

Coordinate closely,

Fight continuously,

Annihilate the entire enemy army at Dienbienphu, win a big victory for the campaign.

The hour to go to battle has come!

Let all cadres and fighters, all units, all services fearlessly advance, emulate in recording feats of arms, and hoist the "Determined to fight, determined to win" flag of Chairman Ho.

(296) MEMORANDUM BY THE JOINT CHIEFS OF STAFF FOR WILSON, March 12, 1954

Source: *U.S.-Vietnam Relations, Book 9,* pp. 266-270.

Confronting directly for the first time the likelihood that any negotiated settlement in Indochina would involve a coalition government, partition, or elections, the Joint Chiefs recommended that the U.S. disassociate itself from any settlement which would not insure the "future political and territorial integrity of Indochina." For the first time, they urged the U.S. maintain "freedom of action" to continue the war without the French.

1. This memorandum is in response to your memorandum dated 5 March 1954, subject as above.

2. In their consideration of this problem, the Joint Chiefs of Staff have reviewed UNITED STATES OBJECTIVES AND COURSES OF ACTION WITH RESPECT TO SOUTHEAST ASIA (NSC 5405), in the light of developments since that policy was approved on 16 January 1954, and they are of the opinion that, from the military point of view, the statement of policy set forth therein remains entirely valid. The Joint Chiefs of Staff reaffirm their views concerning the strategic impor-

tance of Indochina to the security interests of the United States and the Free World in general, as reflected in NSC 5405. They are firmly of the belief that the loss of Indochina to the Communists would constitute a political and military setback of the most serious consequences.

3. With respect to the possible course of action enumerated in paragraph 2 of your memorandum, the Joint Chiefs of Staff submit the following views:

a. Maintenance of the status quo. In the absence of a very substantial improvement in the French Union military situation, which could best be accomplished by the aggressive prosecution of military operations, it is highly improbable that Communist agreement could be obtained to a negotiated settlement which would be consistent with basic United States objectives in Southeast Asia. Therefore, continuation of the fighting with the objective of seeking a military victory appears as the only alternative to acceptance of a compromise settlement based upon one or more of the possible other courses of action upon which the views of the Joint Chiefs of Staff have been specifically requested in your memorandum.

b. Imposition of a cease-fire. The acceptance of a cease-fire in advance of a satisfactory settlement would, in all probability, lead to a political stalemate attended by a concurrent and irretrievable deterioration of the Franco-Vietnamese military position. (See paragraph 27 of NSC 5405.)

c. Establishment of a coalition government. The acceptance of a settlement based upon the establishment of a coalition government in one or more of the Associated States would open the way for the ultimate seizure of control by the Communists under conditions which might preclude timely and effective external assistance in the prevention of such seizure. (See subparagraph 26b of NSC 5405.)

d. Partition of the country. The acceptance of a partitioning of one or more of the Associated States would represent at least a partial victory for the Viet Minh, and would constitute recognition of a Communist territorial expansion achieved through force of arms. Any partition acceptable to the Communists would in all likelihood include the Tonkin Delta area which is acknowledged to be the keystone of the defense of mainland Southeast Asia, since in friendly hands it cuts off the most favorable routes for any massive southward advance towards central and southern Indochina and Thailand. (See paragraph 4 of NSC 5405.) A partitioning involving Vietnam and Laos in the vicinity of the 16th Parallel, as has been suggested (See State cable from London, No. 3802, dated 4 March 1954), would cede to Communist control approximately half of Indochina, its people and its resources, for exploitation in the interests of further Communist aggression; specifically, it would extend the Communist dominated area to the borders of Thailand, thereby enhancing the opportunities for Communist infiltration and eventual subversion of that country. Any cession of Indochinese territory to the Communists would constitute a retrogressive step in the Containment Policy, and would invite similar Communist tactics against other countries of Southeast Asia.

e. Self-determination through free elections. Such factors as the prevalence of illiteracy, the lack of suitable educational media, and the absence of adequate communications in the outlying areas would render the holding of a truly representative plebiscite of doubtful feasibility. The Communists, by virtue of their superior capability in the field of propaganda, could readily pervert the issue as being a choice between national independence and French Colonial rule. Furthermore, it would be militarily infeasible to prevent widespread intimidation of voters by Communist partisans. While it is obviously impossible to make a dependable forecast as to the outcome of a free election, current intelligence leads the Joint

Chiefs of Staff to the belief that a settlement based upon free elections would be attended by almost certain loss of the Associated States to Communist control.

4. The Joint Chiefs of Staff are of the opinion that any negotiated settlement which would involve substantial concessions to the Communists on the part of the Governments of France and the Associated States, such as in c and d above, would be generally regarded by Asian peoples as a Communist victory, and would cast widespread doubt on the ability of anti-Communist forces ultimately to stem the tide of Communist control in the Far East. Any such settlement would, in all probability, lead to the loss of Indochina to the Communists and deal a damaging blow to the national will of other countries of the Far East to oppose Communism.

5. Should Indochina be lost to the Communists, and in the absence of immediate and effective counteraction on the part of the Western Powers which would of necessity be on a much greater scale than that which could be decisive in Indochina, the conquest of the remainder of Southeast Asia would inevitably follow. Thereafter, longer term results involving the gravest threats to fundamental United States security interests in the Far East and even to the stability and security of Europe could be expected to ensue. (See paragraph 1 of NSC 5405.)

6. Orientation of Japan toward the West is the keystone of United States policy in the Far East. In the judgment of the Joint Chiefs of Staff, the loss of Southeast Asia to Communism would, through economic and political pressures, drive Japan into an accommodation with the Communist Bloc. The communization of Japan would be the probable ultimate result.

7. The rice, tin, rubber, and oil of Southeast Asia and the industrial capacity of Japan are the essential elements which Red China needs to build a monolithic military structure far more formidable than that of Japan prior to World War II. If this complex of military power is permitted to develop to its full potential, it would ultimately control the entire Western and Southwestern Pacific region and would threaten South Asia and the Middle East.

8. Both the United States and France have invested heavily of their resources toward the winning of the struggle in Indochina. Since 1950 the United States has contributed in excess of 1.6 billion dollars in providing logistic support. France is reported to have expended, during the period 1946-1953, the equivalent of some 4.2 billion dollars. This investment, in addition to the heavy casualties sustained by the French and Vietnamese, will have been fruitless for the anti-Communist cause, and indeed may rebound in part to the immediate benefit of the enemy, if control of a portion of Indochina should now be ceded to the Communists. While the additional commitment of resources required to achieve decisive results in Indochina might be considerable, nevertheless this additional effort would be far less than that which would be required to stem the tide of Communist advance once it had gained momentum in its progress into Southeast Asia.

9. If, despite all United States efforts to the contrary, the French Government elects to accept a negotiated settlement which, in the opinion of the United States, would fail to provide reasonably adequate assurance of the future political and territorial integrity of Indochina, it is considered that the United States should decline to associate itself with such a settlement, thereby preserving freedom of action to pursue directly with the governments of the Associated States and with other allies (notably the United Kingdom) ways and means of continuing the struggle against the Viet Minh in Indochina without participation fo the French. The advantages of so doing would, from

the military point of view, outweigh the advantage of maintaining political unity of action with the French in regard to Indochina.

10. It is recommended that the foregoing views be conveyed to the Department of State for consideration in connection with the formulation of a United States position on the Indochina problem for the forthcoming Conference and for any conversation with the governments of the United Kingdom, France, and, if deemed advisable, with the governments of the Associated States preliminary to the conference. In this connection, attention is particularly requested to paragraphs 25 and 26 of NSC 5405; it is considered to be of the utmost importance that the French Government be urged not to abandon the aggressive prosecution of military operations until a satisfactory settlement has been achieved.

11. It is further recommended that, in order to be prepared for possible contingencies which might arise incident to the Geneva Conference, the National Security Council considers now the extent to which the United States would be willing to commit its resources in support of the Associated States in the effor to prevent the loss of Indochina to the Communists either:

> a. In concert with the French; or
> b. In the event the French elect to withdraw, in concert with other allies or, if necessary, unilaterally.

12. In order to assure ample opportunity for the Joint Chiefs of Staff to present their views on these matters, it is requested that the Military Services be represented on the Department of Defense working team which, in coordination with the Department of State, will consider all U.S. position papers pertaining to the Geneva discussions on Indochina.

(297) MEMORANDUM BY GENERAL G. B. ERSKINE TO THE PRESIDENT'S SPECIAL COMMITTEE ON INDOCHINA, March 17, 1954

Source: *U.S.-Vietnam Relations, Book 9,* pp. 271-275.

The President's Special Committee on Indochina produced a report on the question of U.S. policy toward a possible peace settlement at Geneva. Representing the views of the Department of Defense and the Joint Chiefs, with the State Department reserving its position, it concluded that "no solution to the Indochina problem short of victory is acceptable." It recommended that the U.S. try to get Britain and France to reject any conceivable peace settlement before the Geneva Conference and actively oppose any effort to achieve such a settlement, and it mentioned possible pressure against the French in North Africa as well as in NATO in order to force acceptance of the U.S. position.

SUBJECT: Military Implications of the U.S. Position on Indochina in Geneva

1. The attached analysis and recommendations concerning the U.S. position in Geneva have been developed by a Subcommittee consisting of representatives of the Department of Defense, JCS, State, and CIA.

2. This paper reflects the conclusions of the Department of Defense and the JCS and has been collaborated with the State Department representatives who have reserved their position thereon.

3. In brief, this paper concludes that from the point of view of the U.S. strategic position in Asia, and indeed throughout the world, no solution to the Indochina problem short of victory is acceptable. It recommends that this be the basis for the U.S. negotiating position prior to and at the Geneva Conference.

4. It also notes that, aside from the improvement of the present military situation in Indochina, none of the courses of action considered provide a satisfactory solution to the Indochina war.

5. The paper notes that the implications of this position are such as to merit consideration by the NSC and the President.

6. I recommend that the Special Committee note and approve this report and forward it with the official Department of State views to the NSC.

Military Implication of U.S. Negotiations on Indochina at Geneva

I. PROBLEM

To develop a U.S. position with reference to the Geneva Conference as it relates to Indochina, encompassing the military implications of certain alternatives which might arise in connection with that conference.

II. MAJOR CONSIDERATIONS

A. The Department of Defense and the JCS have reviewed NSC 5405 in the light of developments since that policy was approved from a military point of view and in the light of certain possible courses of action as they affect the Geneva Conference. These are:

1. Maintenance of the status quo in Indochina.
2. Imposition of a cease-fire in Indochina.
3. Establishment of a coalition government.
4. Partition of the country.
5. Self-determination through free elections.

B. The Department of Defense and the JCS have also considered the impact of the possible future status of Indochina on the remainder of Southeast Asia and Japan and have considered the effect which any substantial concessions to the Communists on the part of France and the Associated States would have with respect to Asian peoples as a whole and U.S. objectives in Europe.

C. Indochina is the area in which the Communist and non-Communist worlds confront one another actively on the field of battle. The loss of this battle by whatever means would have the most serious repercussions on U.S. and free world interests, not only in Asia but in Europe and elsewhere.

D. French withdrawal or defeat in Indochina would have most serious consequences on the French position in the world; the free world position in Asia; and in the U.S. on the domestic attitude vis-a-vis the French. It would, furthermore, constitute a de facto failure on the part of France to abide by its commitment in U.N. to repel aggression.

E. Unless the free world maintains its position in Indochina, the Communists will be in a position to exploit what will be widely regarded in Asia as a Communist victory. Should Indochina be lost to the Communists, and in the absence of immediate and effective counteraction by the free world (which would of necessity be on a much greater scale than that required to be decisive in Indochina), the conquest of the remainder of Southeast Asia would inevitably follow. Thereafter, longer term results, probably forcing Japan into an accommodation with the Communist bloc, and threatening the stability and security of Europe, could be expected to ensue.

F. As a measure of U.S. participation in the Indochinese war it is noted that the U.S. has since 1950 programmed in excess of $2.4 billion dollars in support of the French-Associated States operations in Indochina. France is estimated to have expended during the period 1946-1953 the equivalent of some $5.4 billion. This investment, in addition to the heavy casualties sustained by the French and Vietnamese, to say nothing of the great moral and political involvement of the U.S. and French, will have been fruitless for the anti-Communist cause if control of all or a portion of Indochina should now be ceded to the Communists.

III. FACTS BEARING ON THE PROBLEM

A. NSC 5405, approved January 16, 1954, states U.S. policy with respect to Indochina.

B. The French desire for peace in Indochina almost at any cost represents our greatest vulnerability in the Geneva talks.

IV. DISCUSSION

For the views of the JSC see Tab A.

V. CONCLUSIONS

A. Loss of Indochina to the Communists would constitute a political and military setback of the most serious consequences and would almost certainly lead to the ultimate Communist domination of all of Southeast Asia.

B. The U.S. policy and objectives with respect to Southeast Asia as reflected in NSC 5405 remain entirely valid in the light of developments since that policy was approved.

C. With respect to possible alternative courses of action enumerated in paragraph IIA above, the Department of Defense has reached the following conclusions:

1. Maintenance of status quo in Indochina. It is highly improbable that a Communist agreement could be obtained to any negotiated settlement which would be consistent with basic U.S. objectives in Southeast Asia in the absence of a very substantial improvement in the French Union military situation. This could best be accomplished by the aggressive prosecution of military operations.

2. Imposition of a cease-fire. The acceptance of a cease-fire in advance of a satisfactory settlement would in all probability lead to a political stalemate attended by a concurrent and irretrievable deterioration of the Franco-Vietnamese military position.

3. Establishment of a coalition government. The acceptance of a settlement based upon this course of action would open the way for the ultimate seizure of control by the Communists under conditions which would almost certainly preclude timely and effective external assistance designed to prevent such seizure.

4. Partition of the country. The acceptance of this course of action would represent at the least a partial victory for the Viet Minh and would constitute a retrogressive step in the attainment of U.S. policy and would compromise the achievement of that policy in Southeast Asia.

5. Self-determination through free elections. Many factors render the holding of a truly representative plebiscite infeasible and such a course of action would, in any case, lead to the loss of the Associated States to Communist control.

VI. RECOMMENDATIONS

A. That the U.S. and U.K. and France reach an agreement with respect to Indochina which rejects all of the courses enumerated above (except No. 1 on the assumption that the status quo can be altered to result in a military victory) prior to the initiation of discussions on Indochina at Geneva. Failing this, the U.S. should actively oppose each of these solutions, should not entertain discussion of Indochina at Geneva, or having entertained it, should ensure that no agreements are reached.

B.   If, despite all U.S. efforts to the contrary, the French Government elects to accept a negotiated settlement which fails to provide reasonably adequate assurance of the future political and territorial integrity of Indochina, the U.S. should decline to associate itself with such a settlement and should pursue, directly with the governments of the Associated States and with other Allies (notably the U.K.), ways and means of continuing the struggle against the Viet Minh in Indochina without participation of the French.

C.   The Special Committee has reviewed the findings and recommendations of the Department of Defense and considers that the implications of this position are such as to warrant their review at the highest levels and by the National Security Council, after which they should become the basis of the U.S. position with respect to Indochina at Geneva.   The Special Committee recognizes moreover that certain supplementary and alternative courses of action designed to ensure a favorable resolution of the situation in Indochina merit consideration by the NSC.   These, and the Special Committee recommendations with respect thereto, are:

1.   The political steps to be taken to ensure an agreed U.S.-U.K.-French position concerning Indochina at Geneva.   That the NSC review the proposed political action designed to achieve this objective with particular attention to possible pressure against the French position in North Africa, and in NATO, and to the fact that discussions concerning implementation of course 2 and 3 hereunder will be contingent upon the success or failure of this course of action.

2.   Overt U.S. involvement in Indochina.   That the NSC determine the extent of U.S. willingness, over and above the contingencies listed in NSC 5405, to commit U.S. air, naval and ultimately ground forces to the direct resolution of the war in Indochina with or without French support and in the event of failure in course 1 above.   That in this connection the NSC take cognizance of present domestic and international climate of opinion with respect to U.S. involvement and consider the initiation of such steps as may be necessary to ensure world-wide recognition of the significance of such steps in Indochina as a part of the struggle against communist aggression.

3.   The development of a substitute base of operations.   That the NSC consider whether this course of action is acceptable as a substitute for 1 and 2 above and recognizing that the hope of implementation thereof would be one of major expenditure and long-term potential only.

(298) PRESS CONFERENCE STATEMENT BY DULLES, March 23, 1954

Source: Department of State *Bulletin,* April 5, 1954, pp. 512-513

With Dienbienphu under seige and the possibility of a major Communist military victory looming, Dulles spoke publicly in reassuring terms about the military situation.   But he strongly impled that the U.S. would rule out a negotiated peace as long as China supported the Vietnamese resistance war.

I do not expect that there is going to be a Communist victory in Indochina. By that I don't mean that there may not be local affairs where one side or another will win victories, but in terms of a Communist domination of Indochina, I do not accept that as a probability.

There is a very gallant and brave struggle being carried on at Dien-Bien-Phu by the French and Associated States Forces.   It is an outpost.   It has already inflicted very heavy damage upon the enemy.   The French and Associated States Forces at Dien-Bien-Phu are writing, in my opinion, a notable chapter in military history. Dien-Bien-Phu is, as I say, an outpost position where only a very

small percentage of the French Union forces is engaged and where a very considerable percentage of the forces of the Viet Minh is engaged.

Broadly speaking, the United States has, under it previously known policy,
been extending aid in the form of money and materiel to the French Union Forces
in Indochina. As their requests for materiel become known and their need for
that becomes evident, we respond to it as rapidly as we can. Those requests
have assumed various forms at various times. But I think that we have responded in a very prompt and effective manner to those requests.

If there are further requests of that kind that are made, I have no doubt
that our military or defense people will attempt to meet them.

As soon as this press conference is over, I am meeting with Admiral Radford.
But so far I have not met General Ely, and I do not know what requests he has
made, if any, in that respect because that would be primarily a matter for the
Defense people in any case. The policy has already been established so far as
the political aspects of it are concerned.

We have seen no reason to abandon the so-called Navarre plan, which was,
broadly speaking, a 2-year plan which anticipated, if not complete victory, at
least decisive military results during the fighting season which would follow
the present fighting season, which is roughly a year from now.

As you recall, that plan contemplated a very substantial buildup of the
local forces and their training and equipment. It was believed that under that
program, assuming there were no serious military reversals during the present
fighting season, the upper hand could definitely be achieved in the area by the
end of the next fighting season. There have been no such military reverses,
and, as far as we can see, none are in prospect which would be of a character
which would upset the broad timetable and strategy of the Navarre plan.

*Asked whether that ruled out any possibility of a negotiated peace at
Geneva, Mr. Dulles replied:*

At any time if the Chinese Communists are willing to cut off military assistance and thereby demonstrate that they are not still aggressors in spirit,
that would, of course, advance greatly the possibility of achieving peace and
tranquility in the area. That is a result which we would like to see.

To date, however, I have no evidence that they have changed their mood.
One is always hopeful in those respects, but so far the evidence seems to indicate that the Chinese Communists are still in an aggressive, militaristic, and
expansionist mood.

(299) RECORD OF ACTIONS BY THE NATIONAL SECURITY COUNCIL AT ITS 190th MEETING,
March 25, 1954 [Extract]

Source: Document Declassified by NSC, September 30, 1977.

*With the President presiding, the National Security Council decided on
further study of the question of direct U.S. participation in the war.*

ACTION
NUMBER

1074. U. S. POLICIES WITH RESPECT TO CERTAIN CONTINGENCIES IN INDOCHINA

    a. Directed the NSC Planning Board to consider and make recommen-
       dations, prior to the Geneva Conference, as to the extent to
       which and the circumstances and conditions under which the
       United States would be willing to commit its resources in sup-
       port of the Associated States in the effort to prevent the loss
       of Indochina to the Communists, in concert with the French or
       in concert with others or, if necessary, unilaterally.

(300) <u>EDITORIAL IN NHAN DAN ON U.S. INTERVENTION</u>, March 26-31, 1954

Source: *The Vietnamese People's Sacred Resistance War, Vol. IV,* pp 261-264
(Translated by the editor).

*The Vietnamese Communist leadership was watching anxiously for signs of
U.S. inclination to become involved directly in the conflict. In an editorial
in the party newspaper published in the last week in March, they charged that
the U.S. was looking for ways to prevent any diplomatic settlement of the war
by the French and was considering U.S. military intervention in Indochina.*

French opinion now sees more clearly than ever that it must end the aggressive war in Indochina. Even many individuals who previously appealed for
war, have had to admit that the Indochina war is hopeless for France. Discussion in the French National Assembly recently demonstrated that. The only ones
who want to continue the war are the American imperialists and their slave who
leads the French government, Laniel. *Combat,* a French capitalist newspaper, on
February 21 wrote in a despondent tone, "France no longer is the master of its
own affairs in Europe and Asia. Washington forces us to do two things at once:
continue the Indochina War and pass the European Defense Community agreement."

Under American orders, Laniel still hasn't changed his attitude, intending
to continue the war, but hundred of American planes, thousands of tons of U.S.
weapons, and hundreds of U.S. pilots recently sent to Indochina still cannot
save the French colonialists. They are still losing and losing more heavily.
After the big defeats at Cat-bi, Gia-lam, Highway 5, Dienbienphu, French capitalists' newspapers all express the opinion that the Navarre plan had been defeated, and also cried for an end to the war more strongly. A number of American Congresspeople are also worried. John Stennis, (Democratic Senator) after
hearing the news of the destruction of 78 planes at Gia-lam and Cat-bi airfields
sent a telegram immediately to U.S. Defense Secretary Wilson, requesting that
he "withdraw immediately American planes." Smith (U.S. Republican Senator)
also was worried: "If we aren't directly making war in Indochina, we are very
close to making war, which is very dangerous."

Faced with this situation, the U.S. imperialists have further increased
the level of their intervention. On one hand, they push the French colonialists, and on the other hand, they infringe further on the authority of the
French colonialists. The U.S. Ambassador in France, Dillon, met Bidault three
times to discuss Dienbienphu. He warned Laniel that the U.S. would not accept
negotiations on Indochina, because the U.S. had absorbed more than 75 percent
of the cost of the French war in Indochina, and if the French Government sought
a peaceful solution, it would mean surrender. Under U.S. orders, on March 17,
the Laniel government had to meet urgently for two and half hours to discuss
how to cope with the Dienbienphu situation, while the French Chief of Staff
went to Washington to receive orders from the U.S. U.S. radio broadcast the
news that U.S. Secretary of State Dulles and French Foreign Minister Bidault
would meet in April to discuss the problem of U.S. military training personnel
in Indochina. Meanwhile, the U.S. urgently sent more arms to Indochina. According to U.S news, on March 16, in order to avoid delay due to a strike by
workers at 3 ports, the U.S. government ordered the hiring of porters in New
York to urgently load 11 ships carrying arms to Indochina. O'Daniel, chief of
the U.S. military mission was also ordered immediately to Indochina to carry out
the establishment of the puppet army according to U.S. plan.

Confronted with the serious situation in Indochina, U.S. President
Eisenhower was increasingly unable to hide his warmongering face. According to
the U.S. Constitution, the authority to declare war or participate in war belongs to Congress. But the fact that the U.S. participated in the Korean War,
and now directly intervenes in the aggressive war in Vietnam, Cambodia and Laos
is due to the American militarists who are certain arms merchants. On March 17,

replying to a number of legislators and journalists reminding him of U.S. law, Eisenhower declared that the problem worrying him was that "American technicians could be attacked, and in that circumstance, I cannot generalize, but while naturally the Constitution must be respected, the essential thing is that we must guarantee the protection of the U.S."(!) He sends people to kill the people of another country but wants them to be secure. "Protecting the U.S." by means of participating in an aggressive war in countries tens of thousands of kilometers from the U.S.! Eisenhower's words smell of warmongering. Eisenhower and Wilson also summoned MacArthur, an American executioner in Korea up to now, to a meeting to discuss the situation in the Far East and Indochina. What did they discuss? Nothing other than further plans for sabotaging the Geneva Conference and aggression in Indochina and Asian countries.

The war in Indochina is the only big war still continuing in the world. The American imperialists live by war, so they don't want the Indochina War to end. The above actions and plots show all the more clearly that the American imperialists are trying to obstruct the restoration of peace in Indochina, and trying to exploit the opportunity to take control of the war.

****

The bellicose French and American imperialists are blind to an obvious truth of history. The Vietnamese, Cambodian and Lao people love peace very much, but are very determined to win their true independence and unity; the Chinese people, the people of Asia and the people of the whole world are determined to maintain long-term peace. The American people have also raised their voices to denounce the U.S. plot to sabotage peace. *Worker's World,* the organ of the Communist Party of the U.S. on March 5 called on the American people. "not to let a single ship carry American youth to war in Indochina. The American people must demand that the U.S. government end the policy of sabotaging a ceasefire in Indochina." Recently the fact that thousands of Americans in New York held a meeting to oppose the U.S. using the "anti-Communist" title to intervene in the internal affairs of Guatemala (a small country in Central America) shows even more clearly that the American people recognize the danger of the U.S. "anti-Communist policy."

If the U.S. imperialists still refuse to recognize that truth, they will be isolated, and both French and American aggressors will defnitely find themselves on a deadend road, a road of ignominious defeat.

The Vietnamese people clearly recognize the enemy's plot and always remain wide awake and determined to destroy the aggressors, no matter where they come from.

(301) MEMORANDUM BY THE CHAIRMAN OF THE JOINT CHIEFS OF STAFF, ADMIRAL ARTHUR RADFORD, FOR THE PRESIDENT'S SPECIAL COMMITTEE ON INDOCHINA, March 29, 1954

Source: *U.S.-Vietnam Relations, Book 8,* pp. 277-285.

Admiral Radford's report on conversations with French General Ely revealed that the crisis gathering around Dienbienphu was not bringing the two allies any closer together. Radford pressed unsuccessfully for Ely's acceptance of a direct U.S. role in training Vietnamese troops and expressed grave fears that the French would not be able to hold Indochina. Ely openly expressed French unhappiness at Americans who appeared to want to "control and operate everything of importance." Radford concluded with a plea for U.S. readiness to intervene in force in Indochina. Radford did not mention, however, his own suggestion to Ely that the U.S. carry out bombing raids at Dienbienphu from bases in Manila. See Philippe Devillers and Jean Lacouture, End of a War, *(New York: Praeger, 1969), pp. 74-75, and interview with Admiral Radford, cited in Melvin Gurtov,*

1. During the period 20-24 March I conducted a series of discussions with General Ely, Chairman of the French Chiefs of Staff, on the situation in Indo-china. I am setting forth herein a summary report of these discussions with particular relation to those items which were included in Phase A report submitted by the Special Committee.

2. General Ely requested urgent action for the United States to effect early delivery of various items of material that had previously been requested through the MAAG-Indo-China. These requests were all met to the satisfaction of General Ely with exception of:

    a. 14 C-47 aircraft which are in critical supply and were not in the urgent category.

    b. 20 helicopters and 80 additional U.S. maintenance personnel. An alternative solution is now being worked out through routine channels.

3. In connection with the foregoing is the solution that was evolved to meet the French request for 25 additional B-26 aircraft for a third squadron. There is no doubt that French capabilities for maintenance and aircraft utilization fall far short of acceptable standards and that the supply of additional aircraft alone is not the remedy to inadequate air power in Indo-China. However, in view of the importance of the morale factor at the present time in relation to the struggle for Dien Bien Phu, it was agreed, and the President has approved, to lend the French these aircraft. Certain conditions were imposed which General Ely accepted:

    a. A special inspection team headed by an Air Force General Officer would proceed to Indo-China immediately to examine French maintenance, supply problems, and utilization of U.S. aircraft furnished the French. A report will be made to the Secretary of Defense with a copy being given to General Navarre.

    b. The aircraft will be returned to the U.S. Air Force at the end of the current fighting season about the end of May, or earlier if required for service in Korea. Decision as to permanent acceptance and support of the third B-26 squadron will be made after the report of the special examination (para 3 a above) has been analyzed.

4. General Ely informed me that steps had been taken by the French Air Force to supply additional aviation mechanics to Indo-China and to replace our 200 U.S. Air Force mechanics along the following lines:

    a. The tour of duty of 200 French mechanics due for early return to France is being extended two months. This will permit the operation of the 25 additional B-26s without need for more U.S. personnel. 15 Air crews now in training in France and North Africa are being sent by air to Indo-China.

    b. Fifty mechanics are being sent from France within the next month and beginning 1 June, one hundred additional per month will be sent to a total of 450.

    c. The 200 U.S. Air Force mechanics can be released "within 8 days of 15 June".

5. General Ely raised the question of obtaining authorization to use the C-119 transports to drop napalm at Dien Bien Phu. Although the U.S. does not expect spectacular results, this was approved on condition:

    a. No U.S. crews were involved.

    b. The French high command requested the diversion of this air lift capability to meet the emergency situation at Dien Bien Phu.

6. I presented to General Ely our views in regard to expanding the MAAG to assist the French in training the Vietnamese, indicating to him the importance which we attach to this action, first, to obtain better results, secondly to release French officers for combat service. General Ely was most unsympathetic to any encroachment on French responsibilities or significant expansion of the MAAG. The reasons given related to French "prestige", possible lack of confidence in French leadership by the Vietnamese, "the political situation in France" etc. The only commitments I was able to get from General Ely were:

a. He would urge General Navarre to be most sympathetic to the advice given by the officers recently assigned to MAAG (such as Colonel Rosson).
b. He would request General Navarre to discuss the utilization of U.S. staff officers with General O'Daniel "on the spot in a broad, understanding and comprehensive manner". I would make a similar request of General O'Daniel.
c. He would make some informal soundings in Paris on the subject of increased U.S. participation in training and would communicate further with me - informally - through General Valluy.

I conclude that the French are disposed firmly to resist any delegation of training responsibilities to the U.S. MAAG.

7. Much the same attitude was manifested by General Ely in regard to U.S. operations in the fields of psychological, clandestine and guerrilla warfare. No commitment was obtained except that General Ely would discuss the matter with Mr. Allen Dulles (which he did).

8. General Ely submitted a request in writing, copy attached as Enclosure "A", as to what action the U.S. would take if aircraft based in China intervened in Indo-China. I exchanged the following agreed minute with him on this matter:

"In respect to General Ely's memorandum of 23 March 1954, it was decided that it was advisable that military authorities push their planning work as far as possible so that there would be no time wasted when and if our governments decided to oppose enemy air intervention over Indo-China if it took place; and to check all planning arrangements already made under previous agreements between CINCPAC and the CINC Indo-China and send instructions to those authorities to this effect."

9. The particular situation at Dien Bien Phu was discussed in detail. General Ely indicated that the chance for success was, in his estimate, "50-50" He discounted any possibility of sending forces overland to relieve the French Garrison. He recognized the great political and psychological importance of the outcome both in Indo-China and in France but considered that Dien Bien Phu, even if lost, would be a <u>military</u> victory for the French because of the cost to the Viet Minh and the relatively greater loss to the Viet Minh combat forces. Politically and psychologically the loss of Dien Bien Phu would be a very serious setback to the French Union cause, and might cause unpredictable repercussions both in France and Indo-China.

10. In regard to the general situation in Indo-China General Ely's views were essentially as follows. The loss of Indo-China would open up all of South East Asia to ultimate Communist domination. Victory in Indo-China is as much a political as a military matter. The French hope to get agreement with the Viet Nam in current discussions in Paris which will implement the July 3rd declaration and lead to more enthusiastic cooperation and participation in the war by the Vietnamese. They hope also to get more positive leadership from Bao Dai who, at this time, is the only potential native leader. From the more optimistic point of view, assuming that Dien Bien Phu was held and native support assured, he expected that military successes but not total military victory would be achieved in 1954-1955, following the broad concept of the Navarre Plan and

within presently programmed resources. Ultimate victory will require the creation of a strong indigenous army, extending operations to the north and west,
manning and defending the Chinese frontier and the commitment of resources
greatly in excess of those which France alone can supply. He envisages some
sort of a coalition or regional security arrangement by the nations of South
East Asia.

11. I raised with General Ely the question of promoting General Navarre in
order that General O'Daniel might retain his rank of Lt. General without embar-
rassment to Navarre. General Ely made no commitment, pointing out that rank in
the French Army resulted from a Cabinet action depending upon seniority. He
indicated that the Cabinet might possibly consider a promotion for General
Navarre if Dien Bien Phu was held.

12. General Ely made quite a point of explaining in "great frankness" actions on the part of the United States which were causes of friction. Those
mentioned specifically were:

> a. Americans acted as if the United States sought to control and oper-
> ate everything of importance; that this was particularly true at lower
> levels and in connection with FCA operations.
> b. The United States appears to have an invading nature as they under-
> take everything in such great numbers of people.
> c. French think that McCarthyism is prevalent in the U.S. and actually
> is akin to Hitlerism.
> d. Americans do not appreciate the difficulties under which the French
> must operate as a result of two devastating wars.
> e. Many Americans appear to favor Germany over France.
> f. U.S. administrative procedures are enormously wasteful, irritating
> and paper heavy.
> g. In Germany the U.S. forces have the benefit of better weapons and
> most modern techniques, whereas the French forces do not.
> h. In connection with offshore procurement, the U.S. appeared to lack
> confidence in the French in the manufacture of most modern weapons and
> equipment.

I endeavored to set the record straight on each of these particulars and
stressed the fact that Americans were growing very impatient with France over
its lack of action on the EDC and German rearmament and French tendencies to
overemphasize their prestige and sensitivities.

13. General Ely indicated that the leaders of the present French Government
were fully aware of the importance of denying Indo-China to the Communists and
the prevention of Communist domination of South East Asia. He stated that they
would take a strong position at the Geneva Conference but, inasmuch as France
could make no concessions to Communist China, they looked to the United States
for assistance as the United States could contribute action that the Communist
Chinese sought, i.e., recognition and relaxation of trade controls.

14. During the course of the discussions General Ely stressed that, from
the military standpoint, one of the major deficiencies in Indo-China was offensive air power. I took this opportunity to pose the proposition of incorporating an air component within the framework of the Foreign Legion or alternatively forming an International Volunteer Air Group for operations in Indo-China.
General Ely manifested casual interest but made no commitment to do more than
consider the matter further on his return to Paris.

15. As I stated in a brief memorandum to the President, copy attached as
Enclosure "B", I am gravely fearful that the measures being undertaken by the
French will prove to be inadequate and initiated too late to prevent a progres-
sive deterioration of the situation in Indo-China. If Dien Bien Phu is lost,

this deterioration may occur very rapidly due to the loss of morale among the mass of the native population. In such a situation only prompt and forceful intervention by the United States could avert the loss of all of South East Asia to Communist domination. I am convinced that the United States must be prepared to take such action.

(302) <u>ADDRESS BY DULLES, NEW YORK CITY</u>, March 29, 1954

Source: Department of State *Bulletin*, April 12, 1954, pp. 539-540.

Radford's suggestion for U.S. air intervention at Dienbienphu was being seriously considered by the Eisenhower Administration during the last days of March, (see Devillers and Lacouture, End of a War, *pp. 77-80). But it was clear that such an intervention would require Congressional approval and therefore acceptance by the U.S. public. Dulles used the occasion of a speech at the Overseas Press Club in New York to indicate that the situation might require U.S. military intervention, regardless of whether Chinese troops intervened in the conflict. The phrase he used, "united action," suggested that the U.S. wanted other nations to join in action to save Indochina.*

This provides a timely occasion for outlining the administration's thinking about two related matters - Indochina and the Chinese Communist regime.

Indochina is important for many reasons. First, and always first, are the human values. About 30 million people are seeking for themselves the dignity of self-government. Until a few years ago, they formed merely a French dependency. Now, their three political units - Viet-Nam, Laos, and Cambodia - are exercising a considerable measure of independent political authority within the French Union. Each of the three is now recognized by the United States and by more than 30 other nations. They signed the Japanese peace treaty with us. Their independence is not yet complete. But the French Government last July declared its intention to complete that independence, and negotiations to consummate that pledge are actively under way.

The United States is watching this development with close attention and great sympathy. We do not forget that we were a colony that won its freedom. We have sponsored in the Philippines a conspicuously successful development of political independence. We feel a sense of kinship with those everywhere who yearn for freedom.

The Communists are attempting to prevent the orderly development of independence and to confuse the issue before the world. The Communists have, in these matters, a regular line which Stalin laid down in 1924.

The scheme is to whip up the spirit of nationalism so that it becomes violent. That is done by professional agitators. Then the violence is enlarged by Communist military and technical leadership and the provision of military supplies. In these ways, international communism gets a stranglehold on the people and it uses that power to "amalgamate" the peoples into the Soviet orbit.

"Amalgamation" is Lenin's and Stalin's word to describe their process.

Communist Imperialism in Indochina

"Amalgamation" is now being attempted in Indochina under the ostensible leadership of Ho Chi Minh. He was indoctrinated in Moscow. He became an associate of the Russian, Borodin, when the latter was organizing the Chinese Communist Party which was to bring China into the Soviet orbit. Then Ho transferred his activities to Indochina.

Those fighting under the banner of Ho Chi Minh have largely been trained and equipped in Communist China. They are supplied with artillery and ammunition through the Soviet-Chinese Communist bloc. Captured materiel shows that much of it was fabricated by the Skoda Munition Works in Czechoslovakia and transported across Russia and Siberia and then sent through China into Viet-Nam. Military supplies for the Communist armies have been pouring into Viet-Nam at a steadily increasing rate.

Military and technical guidance is supplied by an estimated 2,000 Communist Chinese. They function with the forces of Ho Chi Minh in key positions - in staff sections of the High Command, at the division level, and in specialized units such as signal, engineer, artillery, and transportation.

In the present stage, the Communists in Indochina use nationalistic anti-French slogans to win local support. But if they achieved military or political success, it is certain that they would subject the people to a cruel Communist dictatorship taking its orders from Peiping and Moscow.

The Scope of the Danger

The tragedy would not stop there. If the Communist forces won uncontested control over Indochina or any substantial part thereof, they would surely resume the same pattern of aggression against other free peoples in the area.

The propagandists of Red China and Russia make it apparent that the purpose is to dominate all of Southeast Asia.

Southeast Asia is the so-called "rice bowl" which helps to feed the densely populated region that extends from India to Japan. It is rich in many raw materials, such as tin, oil, rubber, and iron ore. It offers industrial Japan potentially important markets and sources of raw materials.

The area has great strategic value. Southeast Asia is astride the most direct and best-developed sea and air routes between the Pacific and South Asia. It has major naval and air bases. Communist control of Southeast Asia would carry a grave threat to the Philippines, Australia, and New Zealand, with whom we have treaties of mutual assistance. The entire Western Pacific area, including the so-called "offshore island chain," would be strategically endangered.

President Eisenhower appraised the situation last Wednesday [March 24] when he said that the area is of "transcendent importance."

The United States Position

The United States has shown in many ways its sympathy for the gallant struggle being waged in Indochina by French forces and those of the Associated States. Congress has enabled us to provide material aid to the established governments and their peoples. Also, our diplomacy has sought to deter Communist China from open aggression in that area.

President Eisenhower, in his address of April 16, 1953,[1] explained that a Korean armistice would be a fraud if it merely released aggressive armies for attack elsewhere. I said last September[2] that if Red China sent its own army into Indochina, that would result in grave consequences which might not be confined to Indochina.

Recent statements have been designed to impress upon potential aggressors that aggression might lead to action at places and by means of free-world choosing, so that aggression would cost more than it could gain.

The Chinese Communists have, in fact, avoided the direct use of their own Red armies in open aggression against Indochina. They have, however, largely stepped up their support of the aggression in that area. Indeed, they promote that aggression by all means short of open invasion.

Under all circumstances it seems desirable to clarify further the United States position.

Under the conditions of today, the imposition of Southeast Asia of the political system of Communist Russia and its Chinese Communist ally, by whatever means, would be a grave threat to the whole free community. The United States feels that that possibility should not be passively accepted but should be met united action. This might involve serious risks. But these risks are far less than those that will face us a few years from now if we dare not be resolute today.

The free nations want peace. However, peace is not had merely by wanting it. Peace has to be worked for and planned for. Sometimes it is necessary to take risks to win peace just as it is necessary in war to take risks to win victory. The chances for peace are usually bettered by letting a potential aggressor know in advance where his aggression could lead him.

I hope that these statements which I make here tonight will serve the cause of peace.

****

[1]BULLETIN of Apr. 27, 1953, p. 599.

[2]*Ibid.*, Sept. 14, 1953, p. 339.

(303) TELEGRAM FROM DULLES TO THE EMBASSY IN LONDON, April 1, 1954

Source: *U.S.-Vietnam Relations, Book 9*, pp. 291-292.

Dulles indicated that the U.S. was already acting on the basis of "active opposition" to any settlement which would lead eventually to loss of Indochina to the Communists. He expressed irritation with British Foreign Minister Anthony Eden's failure to join in U.S. pressure against a peace settlement and instructed Ambassador Aldrich to press for British support of the U.S. position.

FYI We were disturbed at Berlin by Eden's position on Indochina which was in effect that this was problem between US and France, with the UK standing on the sidelines as an uninterested party, situation which actually encouraged French seek negotiated settlement. This was not only unhelpful but unrealistic, since if Indochina goes, Malaya, Australia, and New Zealand will be directly threatened (areas where UK has definite responsibilities), as will be Burma, Thailand, the Philippines, Indonesia, and over period of time Japan and whole off-shore island chain.

It seems to us one of best ways keep French from taking any steps which might prove disastrous re Indochina is for US and UK have solid alignment and let French know we will not only not be party to but will actively oppose any solution of any kind which directly or indirectly in near future or over period of time could lead to loss Indochina to Communists. To bring UK to greater recognition its own responsibilities, we are talking very frankly to Australians and New Zealanders here regarding problem (which involves their vital security) in hope they will press British stand firmly with us on above fundamental principles. Secretary also is calling in Makins (who is absent from town) April 2 and will impress upon him forcefully our views. End FYI

With above in mind and following Secretary's talk with Makins which will be reported to you, you should see Eden and reiterate to him our position along following lines:

1. We clearly understood from Bidault at Berlin that our agreement to discuss Indochina at Geneva was on condition France would not agree to any arrangement which would directly or indirectly result turnover area to Communists. We presume British because of vital security interests in area as well as their role in free world would solidly support this position.

2. Our views on any special position for Communist China at Geneva have already been made clear (DEPTEL 4982 repeated Paris as 3340).

3. Our basic position on Communist China is contained in Secretary's March 29 speech of which you should give copy to Eden if you have not already, particularly emphasizing eighth paragraph from end in which is contained following

sentence: "We shall not however be disposed to give Communist China what it wants from us merely to buy its promises of future good behavior."

4. Insofar as development US position is concerned, our preliminary views on substance and procedure contained numbered paragraphs 1 and 2 DEPTEL 3401 to Paris (repeated London 5067, Saigon 1814) and these views should also be conveyed Eden.

5. We believe it essential at this time have understanding above basic points on which we would hope for strong British support with French.

6. Re foregoing DEPTEL 3353 to Paris repeated London as 5079 also provides further guidance.

(304) TELEGRAM FROM DILLON TO DULLES, April 4, 1954

Source: *U.S.-Vietnam Relations, Book 9,* pp. 296-297.

Laniel and Bidault, bolstered by Radford's support for U.S. bombing strikes around Dienbienphu made an official request to Dillon for carrier aircraft support late in the evening of April 4. They argued that this U.S. effort could save it from defeat, and presented new evidence of Chinese military personnel in Tonkin.

URGENT. I was called at 11 o'clock Sunday night and asked to come immediately to Matignon where a restricted Cabinet meeting was in progress.

On arrival Bidault received me in Laniel's office and was joined in a few minutes by Laniel. They said that immediate armed intervention of US carrier aircraft at Dien Bien Phu is now necessary to save the situation.

Navarre reports situation there now in state of precarious equilibrium and that both sides are doing best to reinforce - Viet Minh are bringing up last available reinforcements which will way outnumber any reinforcing French can do by parachute drops. Renewal of assault by reinforced Viet Minh probable by middle or end of week. Without help by then fate of Dien Bien Phu will probably be sealed.

Ely brought back report from Washington that Radford gave him his personal (repeat personal) assurance that if situation at Dien Bien Phu required US naval air support he would do his best to obtain such help from US Government. Because of this information from Radford as reported by Ely, French Government now asking for US carrier aircraft support at Dien Bien Phu. Navarre feels that a relatively minor US effort could turn the tide but naturally hopes for as much help as possible.

French report Chinese intervention in Indochina already fully established as follows:

First. Fourteen technical advisors at Giap headquarters plus numerous others at division level. All under command of Chinese Communist General Ly Chen-hou who is stationed at Giap headquarters.

Second. Special telephone lines installed maintained and operated by Chinese personnel.

Third. Forty 37 mm. anti-aircraft guns radar-controlled at Dien Bien Phu. These guns operated by Chinese and evidently are from Korea. These AA guns are now shooting through clouds to bring down French aircraft.

Fourth. One thousand supply trucks of which 500 have arrived since 1 March, all driven by Chinese army personnel.

Fifth. Substantial material help in guns, shells, etc., as is well known.

Bidault said that French Chief of Air Staff wished US be informed that US air intervention at Dien Bien Phu could lead to Chinese Communist air attack on delta airfields. Nevertheless, government was making request for aid.

Bidault closed by saying that for good or evil the fate of Southeast Asia now rested on Dien Bien Phu. He said that Geneva would be won or lost depending on outcome at Dien Bien Phu. This was reason for French request for this very serious action on our part.

He then emphasized necessity for speed in view of renewed attack which is expected before end of week. He thanked US for prompt action on airlift for French paratroops. He then said that he had received Dulles' proposal for Southeast Asian coalition, and that he would answer as soon as possible later in week as restricted Cabinet session not competent to make this decision.

New Subject. I passed on Norstad's concern that news of airlift (DEPTEL 3470, April 3) might leak as planes assembled, Pleven was called into room. He expressed extreme concern as any leak would lead to earlier Viet Minh attack. He said at all costs operation must be camouflaged as training exercise until troops have arrived. He is preparing them as rapidly as possible and they will be ready to leave in a week. Bidault and Laniel pressed him to hurry up departure date of troops and he said he would do his utmost.

(305) TELEGRAM FROM DULLES TO DILLON, April 5, 1954

Source: *U.S.-Vietnam Relations, Book 9,* pp. 359.

At a meeting at the White House on April 3 Congressional leaders informed Dulles that they could not approve of U.S. airstrikes at Dienbienphu unless there was a coalition of nations behind the intervention, and unless the French accelerated process of granting independence to the Associated States and promised to continue the war with their own ground troops. The following day, Eisenhower, in a meeting with Dulles and Radford, decided that the U.S. would intervene only if those three conditions were met. Dulles instructed Dillon to inform the French of the decision.

As I personally explained to Ely in presence of Radford, it is not (rpt not) possible for US to commit belligerent acts in Indochina without full political understanding with France and the other countries. In addition, Congressional action would be required. After conference at highest level, I must confirm this position. US is doing everything possible as indicated my 5175 to prepare public, Congressional and Constitutional basis for united action in Indochina. However, such action is impossible except on coalition basis with active British Commonwealth participation. Meanwhile US prepared, as has been demonstrated, to do everything short of belligerency.

FYI US cannot and will not be put in position of alone salvaging British Commonwealth interests in Malaya, Australia and New Zealand. This matter now under discussion with UK at highest level.

(306) NSC PLANNING BOARD REPORT ON NSC ACTION NO. 1074-a, April 5, 1954

Source: *U.S.-Vietnam Relations, Book 9,* pp. 298-305.

The first substantive discussion of U.S. military intervention in Indochina presented three possible scenarios: 1) intervention by the U.S. with French cooperation; 2) by the U.S. and regional grouping with French cooperation; 3) without the French. The report conceded that, despite U.S. statements to the contrary, the French effort was viewed by many as "essentially colonial or imperialist in character" and said the U.S. should try to modify that view, if intervention in conjunction with the French was comtemplated.

Problem

1. To analyze the extent to which, and the circumstances and conditions under which, the United States would be willing to commit its resources in sup-

port of the effort to prevent the loss of Indochina to the Communists, in concert with the French or in concert with others or, if necessary, unilaterally.

Issues Involved

2. The answer to this problem involves four issues:

    a. Will Indochina be lost to the Communists unless the United States commits combat resources in some form?
    b. What are the risks, requirements and consequences of alternative forms of U. S. military intervention?
    c. Should the United States adopt one of these forms of intervention rather than allow Indochina to be lost to the Communists and if so which alternative should it choose?
    d. When and under what circumstances should this decision be taken and carried into effect?

Prospect of Loss of Indochina

3. The first issue turns on whether the French Union can and will prevent the loss of Indochina and what further actions, if any, the United States can take to bolster or assist the French effort. Some of these questions were covered by the Report of the Special Committee of March 17, 1954. Others are matters of continuous intelligence estimates. At the present time there is clearly a possibility that a trend in the direction of the loss of Indochina to Communist control may become irreversible over the next year in the absence of greater U.S. participation. There is not, however, any certainty that the French have as yet reached the point of being willing to accept a settlement which is unacceptable to U.S. interests or to cease their military efforts. Moreover, regardless of the outcome of the fight at Dienbienphu, there is no indication that a military decision in Indochina is imminent. It is clear that the United States should undertake a maximum diplomatic effort to cause the French and Associated States to continue the fight to a successful conclusion.

Risks, Requirements, and Consequences of U.S. Intervention

4. The attached Annex addresses itself to the second issue: The risks, requirements and consequences of certain alternative forms of U.S. military intervention. In order to permit analysis of military requirements and allied and hostile reactions, this annex assumes that there will be either: (1) a French and Associated States invitation to the United States to participate militarily; or (2) an Associated States invitation to the United States after a French decision to withdraw, and French willingness to cooperate in phasing out French forces as U.S. forces are phased in. If neither of these assumptions proved valid the feasibility of U.S. intervention would be vitiated. If the French, having decided on withdrawal and a negotiated settlement, should oppose U.S. intervention and should carry the Associated States with them in such opposition, U.S. intervention in Indochina would in effect be precluded. If, after a French decision to withdraw, the Associated States should appeal for U.S. military assistance but the French decided not to cooperate in the phasing in of U.S. forces, a successful U.S. intervention would be very difficult.

Desirability and Form of U.S. Intervention

5. The third issue is whether the United States should intervene with combat forces rather than allow Indochina to be lost to the Communists, and which alternative it should select?

    a. U.S. commitment of combat forces would involve strain on the basic western coalition, increased risk of war with China and of general war, high costs in U.S. manpower and money, and possible adverse domestic political repercussions. Moreover, the United States would be undertaking a com-

516

mitment which it would have to carry through to victory. In whatever form it might intervene, the U.S. would have to take steps at the outset to guard against the risks inherent in intervention. On the other hand, under the principles laid down in NSC 5405, it is essential to U.S. security that Indochina should not fall under Communist control.

b. Of the alternative courses of action described in the Annex, Course A or B has these advantages over Course C. Neither Course A or B depends on the initial use of U.S. ground forces. For this reason alone, they obviously would be much more acceptable to the American public. For the same reason, they would initially create a less serious drain on existing U.S. military forces. But either Course A or B may turn out to be ineffective without the eventual commitment of U.S. ground forces.

c. A political obstacle to Course A or Course B lies in the fact that the present French effort is considered by many in Southeast Asia and other parts of the world as essentially colonial or imperialist in character. If the United States joined its combat forces in the Indochina conflict, it would be most important to attempt to counteract or modify the present view of this struggle. This would also be essential in order to mobilize maximum support for the war within Indochina.

d. An advantage of Course B over Course A lies in the association of the Asian States in the enterprise which would help to counteract the tendency to view Indochina as a colonial action. There would be advantages in Course B also in that U.S. opinion would be more favorable if the other free nations and the Asian nations were also taking part and bearing their fair share of the burden.

e. As between UN and regional support it appears that regional grouping would be preferable to UN action, on the ground that UN support would be far more difficult to get and less likely to remain solid until the desired objective was reached.

6. In order to make feasible any regional grouping, it will be essential for the United States to define more clearly its own objectives with respect to any such action. In particular, it would be important to make perfectly clear that this action is not intended as a first step of action to destroy or overthrow Communist China. If the other members of a potential regional grouping thought that we had such a broad objective, they would doubtless be hesitant to join in it. The Western powers would not want to increase the risks of general war which would, in their opinion, flow from any such broad purpose. The Asian countries would be equally reluctant to engage in any such broad activity. Both groups would doubtless want to make very clear that we object essentially to the expansionist tendencies of Communist China and that, if those ceased, we would not go further in attempting to carry on military activities in the Far East. Furthermore, to attract the participation of Asian States in a regional grouping, the United States would undoubtedly have to undertake lasting commitments for their defense.

Timing and Circumstances of Decision to Intervene with U.S. Combat Forces

7. The timing of the disclosure or implementation of any U.S. decision to intervene in Indochina would be of particular importance.

a. In the absence of serious military deterioration in Indochina, it is unlikely that France will agree to the arrangements envisaged in Alternatives A, B, or C in light of the hopes widely held in France and elsewhere that an acceptable settlement can be achieved.

b. On the other hand, inaction until after exhaustive discussions at Geneva, without any indication of U.S. intentions, would tend to increase the French government and people settling, or accepting the inevitability of settling, on unacceptable terms. Hints of possible U.S. participation would tend to fortify French firmness, but might also tend to induce the Communists to put forward more acceptable terms.

c. On balance, it appears that the United States should now reach a decision whether or not to intervene with combat forces, if that is necessary to save Indochina from Communist control, and, tentatively, the form and conditions of any such intervention. The timing for communication to the French of such decision, or for its implementation, should be decided in the light of future developments.

8. If the United States should now decide to intervene at some stage, the United States should now take these steps:

a. Obtain Congressional approval of intervention.
b. Initiate planning of the military and mobilization measures to enable intervention.
c. Make publicized U.S. military moves designed to make the necessary U.S. air and naval forces readily available for use on short notice.
d. Make maximum diplomatic efforts to make it clear, as rapidly as possible, that no acceptable settlement can be reached in the absence of far greater Communist concessions than are now envisaged.
e. Explore with major U.S. allies - notably the UK, Australia, and New Zealand, and with as many Asian nations as possible, such as Thailand and the Philippines, and possibly Nationalist China, the Republic of Korea, and Burma - the formation of a regional grouping.
f. Exert maximum diplomatic efforts with France and the Associated States designed to (1) bring about full agreement between them, if possible prior to Geneva, on the future status of the Associated States; (2) prepare them to invite U.S. and if possible group participation in Indochina, if necessary.

ANNEX

I. GENERAL

Scene of This Annex

1. This Annex seeks to assess the risks, requirements, and consequences of alternative forms of U.S. military intervention in Indochina.

Objective of U.S. Intervention in Indochina

2. The immediate objective of U.S. military intervention in any form would be the destruction of organized Viet-minh forces by military action limited to the area of Indochina, in the absence of overt Chinese Communist intervention. However, whether or not the action can be limited to Indochina once U.S. forces and prestige have been committed, disengagement will not be possible short of victory.

Risk of Expanding the War

3. The increased risk of such Chinese Communist intervention is assessed under each alternative form of U.S. military intervention. U.S. action in the event that the Chinese Communists overtly intervene in Indochina is covered by existing policy (NSC 5405).

4. The implication of U.S. intervention go far beyond the commitment and support of the military requirements identified below under the several alternative courses. To meet the increased risk of Chinese Communist intervention and possibly of general war, measures must be taken inside the United States and in areas other than Indochina to improve the defense posture of the United States. Military measures would include the increased readiness of the existing forces and the re-positioning of U.S. forces outside the United States.

Domestic measures would include those outlined below under "Mobilization Implications." A reexamination and possibly complete revision of U.S. budgetary and fiscal policies would be required.

Availability of Military Forces

5. The military forces required to implement the various courses of action described in this paper are presently assigned missions in support of other U.S. objectives. A decision to implement any of these courses would necessitate a diversion of forces from present missions. It would also require the mobilization of additional forces to assume the functions of the diverted forces and to meet the increased risk of general war. The foregoing is particularly true with respect to U.S. ground forces.

Mobilization Implications

6. All the domestic consequences of U.S. intervention cannot be forecast, being dependent on such factors as the degree of opposition encountered, the duration of the conflict and the extent to which other countries may participate, but in varying degree some or all of the following steps may become necessary:

> a. Increase in force levels and draft quotas.
> b. Increase and acceleration of military production.
> c. Acceleration of stockpile programs.
> d. Reimposition of materials and stablization controls.
> e. Speed-up of readiness measures for all continental defense programs.

Whether or not general mobilization should be initiated, either at the outset or in the course of U.S. intervention, is a major question for determination.

Use of Nuclear Weapons

7. Nuclear weapons will be available for use as required by the tactical situation and as approved by the President. The estimated forces initially to be supplied by the United States under the alternatives in this paper are based on the assumption of availability. If such weapons are not available, the force requirements may have to be modified. The political factors involved in the use of nuclear weapons are assessed under the various alternatives.[1]

Political Conditions

8. U.S. military intervention in concert with the French should be conditioned upon satisfactory political cooperation from the French and French agreement to grant independence to the Associated States in a Form that will contribute to their maximum participation in the war. The Associated States undoubtedly would not invite U.S. or allied intervention without lasting guarantees of territorial integrity, U.S. contribution to a full-scale reconstruction and development program in Indochina must also be anticipated.

(No paragraphs 9 and 10)

II. ALTERNATIVE FORMS OF COMMITMENT OF U.S. COMBAT FORCES FOR OPERATION IN INDOCHINA

A. In Concert with the French

Assumptions

11. The Associated States and France invite the military participation of the United States.

12. It is impracticable to organize a UN or regional military effort.

13. The military situation in Indochina is approximately as at present, i.e., stalemate with elements of deterioration.

14. France and the Associated States will carry forward the scale of military effort envisaged in the Laniel-Navarre Plan.

Military Requirements

15. Estimated forces to be supplied by U.S. initially.

    a. Ground forces - (None, provided French Union forces afford adequate security for local defense of U.S. forces in Indochina.)
    b. Naval forces - (Total personnel strength of 35,000).

        (1) 1 carrier task group plus additional units consisting of:

            Amphibious lift for 1 RCT
            Minecraft
            Underway replenishment group
            VMPRON's

    c. Air Force forces - (Total personnel strength of 8,600).

        (1) 1 fighter wing (3 sqdns with integral air defense capability)
        (2) 1 light bomber wing
        (3) 1 troop carrier wing
        (4) 1 tactical control sqdn.
        (5) 1 tactical recon. sqdn.

16. Command Arrangements: Theater Command

    a. This should be U.S., since this command must be a combined as well as a joint command and U.S. commanders have had considerably more experience in commanding combined and joint commands. Further, should it become necessary to introduce U.S. ground forces, it would be much better to have a U.S. commander already operating as theater commander rather than effect a change at the time U.S. ground forces become involved. All services of the United States, France, and the Associated States will have representatives at the combined headquarters. Similar representation will be necessary at the Joint Operations Center (JOC) to be established.
    b. Political considerations and the preponderance of French Union forces may dictate the assignment of theater command to the French, at least during the early phase of the participation.

17. Logistic Requirements: This course of action can be logistically supported with the following effects:

    a. No delay to NATO deliveries.
    b. No drain on Army logistic reserves, negligible drain on Air Force logistic reserves, a partial drain on certain logistic reserves of the Navy, particularly aircraft and ammunition.
    c. Some Navy production schedule increases in aircraft and ammunition (depending on extent of operations), some increases in Air Force production schedule with emphasis on ammunition, no effect on Army production schedules.
    d. No additional facilities at bases in Indochina required.

18. The training of indigenous forces is crucial to the success of the operation. The United States should therefore insist on an understanding with the French which will insure the effective training of the necessary indigenous

forces required including commanders and staff personnel at all levels. The United States must be prepared to make contributions of funds, materials, instructors and training devices as agreed with the French. A United States program for the development of indigenous forces would stress the organization of divisional size units. The battalion organization does not particularly well fit the approved concept for operations formulated by General Navarre, nor does it represent the best return in striking power for the manpower investment made. A reasonable, attainable goal in Associated States forces which the United States might develop and train is on the order of 330,000 (an increase of 100,000 over the present forces.) This would be accomplished by a reorganization of the presently formed battalions into divisions followed by further training stressing regimental and divisional exercises. New units would be developed as necessary to complete the program.

Political Aspects

19. Political Aspects: The French would expect U.S. military participation in Indochina:

> a. To relieve them from the prospect of defeat or failure in Indochina and to this extent they would welcome U.S. intervention.
> b. To highlight the inability of the French to handle the situation alone, with resultant weakening of the general international position of France.
> c. To lead to a strengthening of the position of the Associated States as against the French, and a weakening of the French Union concept.
> d. To tend to result in channeling U.S. support for the Indochina war directly to the theater of operations, thus reducing the financial benefits to metropolitan France.
> e. To increase the risk of Chinese Communist intervention and, through a series of actions and counteractions, to increase the risk of general war with the USSR.

On balance, the French would prefer to find a solution of the Indochina problem which did not involve U.S. military participation, although such solution might in our opinion risk the ultimate loss of Indochina. In the event of U.S. military participation the French could be expected to attempt progressively to shift the military burden of the war to the United States, either by withdrawing their forces or failing to make good attrition.

20. Associated States Reaction: The Associated States would not be interested in US. intervention unless they were satisfied (1) such intervention would be on a scale which seemed adequate to assure defeat of the Vietminh organized military forces and to deter Chinese Communist aggression, and (2) the United States would assume lasting responsibility for their political independence and territorial integrity. On these terms non-Communist Indochinese leaders would welcome U.S. intervention, and would be unlikely to succumb to Communist peace proposals. The war-weary Indochinese people, however, might be less favorable, particularly if U.S. intervention came at a time when an end to the fighting seemed otherwise in sight. The Associated States would expect to profit from U.S. intervention in terms of increased independence from the French, and would constantly seek to enlist U.S. influence in bolstering their position vis-a-vis France. The Indochinese, however, would be worried over the possibility that U.S. intervention might invite Chinese Communist reaction and make Indochina a battleground of destruction on the Korean scale. Accordingly, they would be expected to oppose the use of nuclear weapons in Indochina.

21. Free World Reaction: The U.K., apprehensive of the possibility of war

with Communist China, would approve a U.S. intervention in Indochina only if convinced that it was necessary for the prevention of further expansion of Communist power in Asia. Australia and New Zealand would fully support such a U.S. action, and Canada to a lesser extent. Nationalist China and the Republic of Korea would welcome U.S. intervention in Indochina, since both would hope that this would lead to general war between the United States and Communist China. Present Rhee, in particular, might be tempted to believe that his chance of involving the United States in a renewal of Korean hostilities were greatly enhanced. Thailand, if assured of U.S. guarantees of adequate perman-ence would probably permit the use of Thai territory and facilities. The Philippines would support U.S. intervention. Japan would lend unenthusiastic diplomatic support. India and Indonesia strongly, and Ceylon and Burma to a lesser extent, would disapprove U.S. intervention. Other members of the Arab-Asian bloc would be unsympathetic especially because of seeming U.S. support for French colonialism. The NATO countries, other than those mentioned above, would generally support U.S. military action, but their support would be tempered by fear of expansion of the hostilities and the effect on the NATO build-up. The attitude of most of the Latin American countries would tend to be non-committal.

22. Free World Reaction in the Event of U.S. Tactical Use of Nuclear Weapons: U.S. allies would almost certainly consider that use by the U.S. of nuclear weapons in Indochina (a) would remove the last hope that these weapons would not be used again in war, and (b) would substantially increase the risk of general war. Our allies would, therefore, doubt the wisdom of the use of nuclear weapons in Indochina and this doubt would develop into strong disap-proval if nuclear weapons were used without their being consulted or against their wishes. On the other hand, France and, if consulted, the UK, Australia, New Zealand, and possibly the Netherlands, might support such action but only if convinced by the U.S. that such action was essential to keep Southeast Asia from falling under Communist control and to preserve the principle of collec-tive security. Other NATO governments, if similarly consulted would probably not public disapprove of such U.S. action, if they were persuaded during con-sultation that such action was essential to prevent collapse of the collective security system. Nationalist China and the Republic of Korea would probably approve such action in the hope that this would result in general war between the U.S. and Communist China. Japan would almost certainly publicly disapprove. Most Asian states and those of the Arab Bloc would probably object strongly to such U.S. action. Certain of these nations led by India, would almost certain-ly seek to have the UN censure the U.S.

23. Soviet Bloc Reaction:

a. The Communist Bloc would almost certainly seek to create differences between the United States and the French, and for this purpose would prob-ably put forward "plausible" peace offers to the greatest extent possible in light of the Geneva Conference. It is unlikely, in the first instance, that the USSR would take any direct military action in response to U.S. participation in the Indochina war. The Soviet Union would, however, con-tinue to furnish to the Chinese Communists military assistance for Vietminh utilization in Indochina.

b. The Chinese Communists probably would not immediately intervene openly, either with regular or "volunteer" forces, but would substantially increase all other kinds of support. However, if confronted by impending Vietminh defeat, Communist China would tend toward intervention because of the prospect that Communist prestige throughout the world would suffer a severe blow, and that the area of U.S. military influence would be brought to the southern border of China. On the other hand, Communist China's desire to concentrate on domestic problems, plus fear of what must appear to Peiping as the virtual certainty of U.S. counteraction against Communist China itself, would tend to deter overt intervention. The chances are about even that in this situation Communist China would decide upon overt intervention rather than accept the defeat of the Vietminh.[2]

c. <u>Soviet Bloc Reaction in the Event of U.S. Tactical Use of Nuclear Weapons</u>. Initial Communist military reactions would probably be substantially the same as in the case of no nuclear weapons. Politically, the Communists would intensify their world-wide campaign to brand the U.S. as an aggressor, with the expectation that considerable political capital could be realized out of the adverse world reactions to U.S. use of nuclear weapons. If U.S. use of nuclear weapons should lead to impending Vietminh defeat, there is a split of opinion within the Intelligence Advisory Committee as to whether the Chinese Communists would accept the risk involved and intervene overtly to save the Communist position in Indo China: three members believe the chances they would not openly intervene are greater than assessed in par. 23-<u>b</u> above; three members believe the chances are better than even they would openly intervene.

24. <u>Foreign Aid Considerations</u>: Military assistance to finance the French and Associated States military effort and to supply military hardware would continue at approximately current rates (FY 1954 = $800 million; Fy 1955 = $1130 million). Expenditures for economic assistance in Indochina would be substantially increased over the present rate of expenditure ($25 million). These figures do not take into account the cost of U.S. military participation or the possible cost of post-war rehabilitation in Indochina.

B. In Concert with the French and Others

Assumptions

25. The Associated States and France invite the military participation of the United States and other nations.

26. It is practicable to organize a UN or regional military effort.

27. The military situation in Indochina is approximately as at present, i.e., stalemate with elements of deterioration.

28. France and the Associated States will carry forward the scale of military effort envisaged in the Laniel-Navarre Plan.

Military Requirements

29. Same as II-A (pars. 15-18 above). Ground forces contributed by other nations will supplement French Union ground forces, air or naval forces contributed by other nations might substitute for U.S. air and naval forces.

Political Aspects

30. <u>a</u>. <u>UN Action</u>. An appeal to the UN for assistance against Communist aggression, in order to secure the requisite two-thirds majority in the General Assembly, would necessarily have to come from the Associated States, acting as independent states, and be supported by the French. A request for assistance by France alone would probably fail of passage as being merely a request for assistance in a colonial war. Even with an appeal from the Associated States, it is probable that, though a two-thirds majority might be secured, there would be not more than 36 affirmative votes, and many abstentions. During the course of the debate, there would be major

efforts to incorporate in the resolution a call for a cease-fire and negotiated settlement, or provisions for limiting the conflict to Indochina.
U.S. control of the character of the resolution would be extremely difficult, although not necessarily impossible. In sum, it might be possible
to secure UN action for armed assistance to the Associated States, but the
difficulties in staving off UN pressure for a negotiated settlement or UN
mediation would be considerable. The majority for a satisfactory UN resolution would, at best, be slim and conceivably might take more time to achieve
than is available. Failure to obtain UN action, if attempted, would seriously prejudice the prospects of any effective intervention.

　　b. Regional Grouping. Any regional grouping should enlist maximum
Asian participation. It would be possible to develop a regional grouping
which would lend moral and some military support to a U.S. intervention in
Indochina if it were clear that the United States had decided (1) to undertake the commitment of U.S. forces to the Indochina area, and (2) to assume
commitments of a lasting character for the defense of the Associated States,
Thailand and Malaya. Australia and New Zealand, while concerned about the
effect on the ANZUS organization, would probably be willing to participate
in a broader organization for the defense of mainland Southeast Asia. The
U.K., already disturbed at its exclusion from ANZUS, and in general ready
to support U.S. intervention in Indochina, would be prepared to enter a
South East Asian regional grouping which carried with it U.S. guarantees
for Malaya. Thailand, if given lasting U.S. defense commitments, would
also participate in such an organization and would probably provide bases
and facilities for support of military operations in Indochina and possibly
modest military forces. The Philippines would also support a regional organization and might provide modest military forces. The Nationalist Government of China and the ROK would seek inclusion in any regional organization which sponsored military action in Indochina, in the hope of an extension of hostilities to Communist China. For this reason, their inclusion
would probably be opposed by at least the UK and French governments. Such
a regional grouping would almost certainly be less inclined than the UN to
respond to plausible Communist peace offers, and more likely to persevere
to an acceptable solution in Indochina.

31. French Reaction: The French would prefer a regional grouping to UN
sponsored assistance. They might consider such a grouping as less desirable
than U.S. intervention alone. The French would probably feel, however, that
they would have to go along with the formation of such a regional grouping if
they could see no other way out of their difficulties in Indochina. After active multilateral armed intervention in Indochina, France would probably seek
progressively to reduce its share of the military burden.

32. Associated States Reaction: The Associated States would probably prefer UN sponsored military assistance to any other form of outside intervention.
They would, however, be more than willing to accept such assistance from a regional grouping, and would be eager to participate in such a grouping if it
included effective U.S. military participation.

33. Free World Reaction:

　　a. In general. The reaction to U.S. military intervention in Indochina under the aegis of a regional grouping would be somewhat more favorable than the reaction to U.S. military intervention alone. UN sponsorship
of U.S. military participation would materially decrease the hostility of
the Arab-Asian bloc to U.S. intervention, and might also strengthen somewhat the support for such action in Latin America and Western Europe.

b. To U.S. Tactical Use of Nuclear Weapons. Reactions of other nations, including the participating nations, would be substantially the same as in par. 22 above.

34. Soviet Bloc Reaction: The fact that the United States was initially only one of a group would probably not appreciably reduce Peiping's apprehension at the presence of U.S. power on the southern borders of China. Peiping might well believe that in the end, as in the case of Korea, the situation would evolve into a continuing and largely U.S. unilateral commitment. Thus, the chances of overt Chinese Communist intervention would remain substantial.

35. Soviet Bloc Reaction in the Event of U.S. Tactical Use of Nuclear Weapons: Whether or not the other participating powers concurred in U.S. use of nuclear weapons, the chances of Chinese Communist overt intervention would be the same as stated in paragraph 23-c above.

36. Foreign Aid Considerations: In addition to the increased program under A above (par. 24) the United States would probably have to provide additional expenditures for provision of military equipment and supplies to the forces of some of the participating states.

C. In the Event of a Proposed French Withdrawal, the United States Acting in Concert with Others or Alone

Assumptions

37. France refuses to continue participation in the war in Indochina.

38. The Associated States invite the military participation of the United States with others or alone.

39. There has been no serious deterioration in the French Union military situation prior to U.S. take-over.

40. The French will so phase their withdrawal as to permit orderly replacement of their forces.

41. The Associated States will cooperate fully with the United States in developing indigenous forces.

42. It may be practicable to organize a UN or regional military effort.

Military Requirements

43. a. Ground forces. (Total personnel strength of 605,000)

    (1) Indigenous forces of 330,000.
    (2) U.S. or allied forces of six infantry and one airborne division (each the equivalent of a U.S. division in strength and composition) plus necessary support personnel totaling 275,000.

b. Air Force forces. (Total personnel strength of 12,000)

    1 air defense fighter wing
    1 light bomb wing
    1 troop carrier wing
    2 tactical recon. sqdns.
    1 fighter bomber wing
    1 tactical control sqdn.

c. <u>Naval forces</u>. (Total personnel strength of 35,000)

    1 Carrier Task Group plus additional units consisting of:

        Minecraft
        VPRONS
        Amphibious lift for 1 RCT
        Underway replenishment group

d. <u>Training forces</u>. (included in above)

e. <u>Logistic implications</u>. This course of action can be logistically supported with the following effects:

    (1) Effect on NATO deliveries:

<u>Army and Navy</u>	- No adverse impact.
<u>Air Force</u>	- No effect until second quarter of FY 1955, when certain units scheduled for withdrawal from INCFE are retained in that area, due to the Indochina commitment and are not available to fulfill the NATO commitment.

    (2) Drain on logistic reserves:

<u>Army</u>	- Negligible on all items that are in production, assuming necessary adjustments in production schedules (par. 43-<u>e</u>(3) below).
<u>Navy</u>	- Partial drain on certain logistic reserves, principally aircraft.
<u>Air Force</u>	- Negligible in all instances.

    (3) Effect on production schedules:

<u>Army</u>	- Require revision of ammunition schedules for 105 mm howitzers and for 4.2, 60mm and 81mm mortars which are currently being cut bac.
<u>Navy</u>	- Increased production schedules for aircraft and ammunition may be required, depending upon the extent of operations.
<u>Air Force</u>	- Some increases in certain production schedules with emphasis on ammunition depending on the extent of oeprations.

    (4) Additional facilities required at bases in Indochina

<u>Army</u>	- A logistic support base similar to but on a smaller scale to that established at Pusan, Korea.
<u>Navy</u>	- Base requirements can be met with existing mobile logistic support units now in FECOM and by expansion of bases in the Philipppines.
<u>Air Force</u>	- Light and fighter bomber and interceptor wings will operate from existing facilities in Indochina. This operation may require two wings to operate from one airbase. POL can be supplied. The majority of FEAF's airlift capability must be made available to insure effective operation if units are required to move in on short notice.

f. <u>Materiel Requirements</u>: The major share of the burden for provision of replacement equipment, ammunition and over-all logistic support for all forces involved will have to be undertaken by the United States. The equipment and materials relinquished by the French forces should assist in meeting the initial materiel requirements.

g. Impact on U.S. Military Programs: This course would undoubtedly have the following effects: an increased calculated risk of war with Communist China or of general war, adversely affecting war plans; alterations in fiscal and budgetary policies and programs dependent on the scale and duration of operations; and a reversal of policy planning to reduce the size of the U.S. armed forces.

Political Aspects

44. U.N. Action: French disassociation would largely remove Asian suspicions that the actions of the United States and the West were directed toward perpetuating French colonialism in the area and thereby enhance support for UN action. However, there might be increased pressure for a negotiated settlement and UN mediation, and equally strong pressure for limiting any hostilities to Indochina.

45. Regional Action: It would be feasible to secure support of a regional grouping for U.S. replacement of French forces in Indochina. In the contingency of French withdrawal Thailand, in particular, and the other states in general, would wish to assure themselves that the United States was really committed to fully replacing French strength in the area. If they were convinced this was the case, and if the nature of French withdrawal made replacement by U.S. troops practicable, they would support a U.S. effort.

46. Effect on France: A French decision actually to withdraw would signal a major change in the French position in the world. France might be expected to lose interest in the Far East, to resign itself to a diminution of U.S. assistance and support, and to an abrupt loss of its role as a major power. The French political position in North Africa would be seriously prejudiced. The effect on French policy toward NATO and EDC or in Europe has not been estimated.

47. Associated States Reaction: The Associated States would be concerned by a French withdrawal largely by reason of the practical obstacles which they would believe would have to be overcome in any replacement of French forces. If convinced, however, that these obstacles could be overcome, they would continue to fight in support of U.S., regional, or UN military efforts in Indochina; but the war-weary Indochinese people would be less willing to fight, particularly if intervention comes at a time when the end of the fighting is otherwise in prospect.

48. Free World Reaction:

a. In general. Free world reaction would vary. If the French withdraw the rest of the free world would probably prefer UN action to U.S. intervention alone. But, if convinced that the only alternative to Communist domination was unilateral U.S. action, most of the free world would support such action. The NATO countries would be concerned with U.S. diversion of resources to the Far East and the increased risk of general war.

b. To U.S. Use of Nuclear Weapons. Reactions of other nations, including any participating nations, would be substantially the same as in par. 22.

49. <u>Soviet Bloc Reaction</u>: (Same as in paragraph 23 above.)

50. <u>Soviet Bloc Reaction in the Event of U.S. Use of Tactical Nuclear Weapons</u>. (Same as in paragraph 23-<u>c</u> above.)

Foreign Aid Considerations

51. In addition to the increased economic aid set forth in previous contingencies (pars. 24 and 36 above), the United States would be required to replace key French advisors to governments of the Associated States with U.S. personnel and greatly increase expenditures for relief and rehabilitation. In addition, the requirement for military aid for indigenous forces would be at least as great as under present plans. The savings in the U.S. contribution for the support of French forces in Indochina would partly serve to offset the greatly increased costs of U.S. forces taking their place.

[1] State considers the military effect of use or non-use of nuclear weapons should be made clear in the estimates of military requirements to assist in making a decision.

[2] For fuller discussion of the split of opinion within the IAC on this question, see SE-53, "Probable Communist Reactions to Certain Possible U.S. Courses of Action in Indochina through 1954" (published December 18, 1953).

(307) DRAFT REPORT BY THE PRESIDENT'S SPECIAL COMMITTEE; SOUTHEAST ASIA - PART II, April 5, 1954

Source: *U.S.-Vietnam Relations, Book 9,* pp. 346-358.

Reaffirming the position taken in previous policy papers that the U.S. should accept "nothing short of a military victory" in Indochina, the President's Special Committee urged "all possible political and economic pressure on France" to insure that the French continued the war. It also listed a series of radical new steps the U.S. should take in the region, including sponsorship of a mutual defense treaty between the Associated States and Thailand, creation of "volunteer" military units for Indochina as well as other countries, and covert operations to promote certain individual political figures and groups in Southeast Asia.

I. THE PROBLEM

To set forth recommendations concerning longer range policy and courses of action for possible future contingencies in Southeast Asia not covered by NSC 5405.

II. MAJOR CONSIDERATIONS

A. The Special Committee has reviewed NSC 5405, "U.S. Objectives and Courses of Action with Respect to Southeast Asia", dated 16 January 1954, and considers that this statement of policy remains valid and should be continued in effect insofar as it concerns the specific contingencies enumerated therein.

B. NSC 5405 covers the contingency of possible Chinese Communist intervention in Indo-China and along with Part I of the Special Committee Report establishes U.S. courses of action designed to secure the military defeat of Communist forces in Indo-China in the absence of Chinese Communist intervention.

  C. There are, however, at least two additional factors not covered by NSC 5405 which merit additional policy consideration of the U.S. Government. These are:

    (1) The fact that the Communist threat to Southeast Asia will continue to be a major obstacle to U.S. policy and objectives in Southeast Asia even though a solution to the Indo-Chinese war which is satisfactory to the U.S. may be obtained.
    (2) The fact that the threat of Communist domination in Southeast Asia will be infinitely increased in the event that Indo-China should fall under Communist domination despite the present efforts of the U.S. to the contrary.

III. FACTS BEARING ON THE PROBLEM

  A. Southeast Asia comprises some 170 million people in an area just emerging from the colonial era. Standards of living and of literacy are very low. With the exception of Viet Nam, military forces are inconsiderable. The number and quality of leaders, administrators, and technicians is far below minimum requirements. The prospects of political or economic stability during this generation are dim, except in the Philippines and perhaps in Thailand.

  B. The peoples of Southeast Asia are accustomed to the rule of the many by the very few at the level of their central government. Their principal national political vitality expresses itself as "anti-colonialism" and the termination of all foreign domination rather than in a desire for political democracy or for the political liberties upon which the Western concept of the world ideological struggle is based.

  C. Southeast Asia is a part of and ethnically associated with the Asian continent, principally China. China today is the base of international Communism in the Far East. With the exception of Australia, to which Southeast Asian states are not ideologically oriented, anti-Communist bases are very distant. Certain of them are associated with colonialism in the minds of the people of Southeast Asia. Western influence, both in Southeast Asia and in Korea, has not been effective in preventing the spread of Communism. This results in increased vulnerability of some Southeast Asian countries to Communist influences.

  D. Nationalism that expresses itself in Asia as anti-colonialism, if properly guided, is also a potential weapon against Communist imperialism. At the present time, however, some Asians tend to regard "Western colonialism" as more evil and pressing than the possible future threat of Communist imperialism.

  E. Economically, the countries of Southeast Asia vary in their products and markets. Many major export products of the area (rubber, tin, copra, etc.) are absorbed by the West. However, rice production is a matter of pan-Asian concern as is oil production.

  F. Southeast Asia as a region is less homogeneous than the Atlantic Community or the American Republics in the factors making for real regional consistency and strength. There are major ethnic and religious differences as well as traditional emnities. There is no sense of a common danger as regards Communist imperialism.

  G. Current developments, including military operations in the Associated States and the forthcoming Geneva Conference, will have a major influence on future U.S. policy throughout Southeast Asia.

H. U.S. position and policy in the area are most effectively represented in the Philippines and in Thailand, from which countries - outside of Indo-China - any expanded program of Western influence may best be launched.

IV. CONCLUSIONS

A. The Special Committee considers that these factors reinforce the necessity of assuring that Indo-China remain in the non-Communist bloc, and believes that defeat of the Viet Minh in Indo-China is essential if the spread of Communist influence in Southeast Asia is to be halted.

B. Regardless of the outcome of military operations in Indo-China and without compromising in any way the overwhelming strategic importance of the Associated States to the Western position in the area, the U.S. should take all affirmative and practical steps, with or without its European allies, to provide tangible evidence of Western strength and determination to defeat Communism; to demonstrate that ultimate victory will be won by the free world; and to secure the affirmative association of Southeast Asian states with these purposes.

C. That for these purposes the Western position in Indo-China must be maintained and improved by a military victory.

D. That without compromise to C, above, the U.S. should in all prudence reinforce the remainder of Southeast Asia, including the land areas of Malaya, Burma, Thailand, Indonesia, and the Philippines.

V. RECOMMENDED COURSES OF ACTION*

A. The Special Committee wishes to reaffirm the following recommendations which are made in NSC 5405, the Special Committee Report concerning military operations in Indo-China, and the position paper of the Special Committee, concurred in by the Department of Defense, concerning U.S. courses of action and policies with respect to the Geneva Conference:

(1) It be U.S. policy to accept nothing short of a military victory in Indo-China.

(2) It be the U.S. position to obtain French support of this position; and that failing this, the U.S. actively oppose any negotiated settlement in Indo-China at Geneva.

(3) It be the U.S. position in event of failure of (2) above to initiate immediate steps with the governments of the Associated States aimed toward the continuation of the war in Indo-China, to include active U.S. participation and without French support should that be necessary.

(4) Regardless of whether or not the U.S. is successful in obtaining French support for the active U.S. participation called for in (3) above, every effort should be made to undertake this active participation in concert with other interested nations.

B. The Special Committee also considers that all possible political and economic pressure on France must be exerted as the obvious initial course of action to reinforce the French will to continue operations in Indo-China. The Special Committee recognizes that this course of action will jeopardize the existing French Cabinet, may be unpopular among the French public, and may be considered as endangering present U.S. policy with respect to EDC. The Committee nevertheless considers that the free world strategic position, not only in Southeast Asia but in Europe and the Middle East as well, is such as to require the most extraordinary efforts to prevent Communist domination of Southeast Asia. The Committee considers that firm and resolute action now in this regard may well be the key to a solution of the entire problem posed by France in the free world community of nations.

C. In order to make the maximum contribution to free world strength in Southeast Asia, and regardless of the outcome of military operations currently in progress in Indo-China, the U.S. should, in all prudence, take the following courses of action in addition to those set forth in NSC 5405 and in Part I of the Special Committee report:

Political and Military:

(1) Ensure that there be initiated no cease-fire in Indo-China prior to victory whether that be by successful military action or clear concession of defeat by the Communists.
Action: State, CIA

(2) Extraordinary and unilateral, as well as multi-national efforts should be undertaken to give vitality in Southeast Asia to the concept that Communist imperialism is a transcending threat to each of the Southeast Asian states. These efforts should be so undertaken as to appear through local initiative rather than as a result of U.S. or UK, or French instigation.
Action: USIA, State, CIA

(3) It should be U.S. policy to develop within the UN charter a Far Eastern regional arrangement subscribed and underwritten by the major European powers with interests in the Pacific.

a. Full accomplishment of such an arrangement can only be developed in the long term and should therefore be preceded by the development, through indigenous sources, of regional economic and cultural agreements between the several Southeast Asian countries and later with Japan. Such agreements might take a form similar to that of the OEEC in Europe.
Action: State, CIA, FOA

b. Upon the basis of such agreements, the U.S. should actively but unobtrusively seek their expansion into mutual defense agreements and should for this purpose be prepared to underwrite such agreements with military and economic aid and should be willing to become a signatory to such agreements upon invitation, as in Korea, Japan, the Philippines, and Formosa.
Action: State, Defense, CIA

c. As an immediate move in this direction, the U.S. - working through indigenous channels - should sponsor the negotiation of a mutual defense treaty directed against Communist aggression between the several states of Indo-China and Thailand, and particularly between Cambodia and Thailand.
Action: CIA, Defense, State

(4) The U.S. should undertake the immediate organization within the several states of Southeast Asia of an increased number of military units, including guerrilla and para-military organizations, as well as anti-subversion police forces. In particular, this should be accomplished in Thailand and if possible in Indonesia and Burma. This should include the establishment of U.S. military missions through the assignment of U.S. officers who might, where necessary, serve on a contract basis with local military forces. In addition, the U.S. should stand ready to offer such assistance in Malaya as the UK my require.
Action: State, Defense, CIA

(5) The U.S. should take the initiative in establishing an International Volunteer Air Group to be used in Indo-China and elsewhere as required. In addition, the U.S. should consider the advisability of establishing an International Volunteer Corps of ground forces for use in Southeast Asia. So long as the French retain the major responsibil-

ity for military operations, such forces should only be utilized with French consent.
Action: Defense, CIA
(6) The U.S. should support when appropriate any Asian-inspired development of regional or area orgnizations, conferences, and agreements and should seek unbtrusively to promote such inter-Asian rapport.
Action: State, USIA, CIA, FOA, Defense
(7) With respect to Malaya, Burma, and Thailand, the U.S. should seek UK agreement to measures designed to ensure the retention of these areas in the free world. A statement that any change in the present security status of these areas would be considered a fundamental threat to US-UK interests in the area might be appropriate.
Action: Defense, State, CIA, USIA
(8) The U.S. should, largely through covert means, take steps:

a. To promote and support, energetic, able and honest indigenous anti-Communist leaders in Southeast Asia in order to provide more effective government in the area.
b. To exploit opportunities to strengthen western-oriented anti-Communist political parties and other influential indigenous groups in Southeast Asia.
Action: CIA

Economic

(1) The U.S. should be prepared, as in Korea, to underwrite the ecconomic potential of the Associated States in the event of a satisfactory solution in that area. A statement to this effect at the present time might have a favorable effect on the Geneva Conference.
Action: State, FOA
(2) The U.S. should affirmatively attack the economic problems that grow out of the instability of demand for primary products (such as rice, tin, oil, etc.) in the area, and should give major attention to the development of mutually desirable economic programs and assistance as between the U.S. and Southeast Asia.
Action: FOA, State, Commerce
(3) Technical programs, particularly those designed to achieve improvement in agricultural skilled and semi-skilled labor, should be stepped up. Leadership programs, however useful, cannot alone overcome the deficiencies in these areas.
Action: State, FOA
(4) Capital investment associated with indigenous interests in the area should be encouraged. This includes the establishment of:

a. A climate of opinion in the countries concerned favorable to foreign investment.
b. The establishment by treaty of the rights and obligations of U.S. investors in the countries.
c. The creation in the U.S. through a system of guarantees of adequate and attractive investment opportunities.
Action: State, Commerce, FOA, Treasury

(5) The Export-Import Bank and the International Bank should be encouraged to extend loans to Southeast Asia for economic development.
Action: State, FOA
(6) The U.S. should discreetly promote reasonable reparations settlements between Japan and Southeast Asian countries.
Action: State

D. The courses of action outlined above are considered as mandatory regardless of the outcome of military operations in Indo-China.

(1) If Indo-China is held they are needed to build up strength and resistance to Communism in the entire area.

(2) If Indo-China is lost they are essential as partial steps:

<u>a</u>. To delay as long as possible the extension of Communist domination throughout the Far East, or

<u>b</u>. In conjunction with offensive operations to retake Indo-China from the Communists.

(3) Should Indo-China be lost, it is clear to the Special Committee that the involvement of U.S. resources either in an attempt to stop the further spread of Communism in the Far East, (which is bound, except in terms of the most extensive military and political effort, to be futile) or to initiate offensive operations to retake and reorient Indo-China, (which would involve a major military campaign), will greatly exceed those needed to hold Indo-China before it falls.

(4) Furthermore, either of these undertakings (in the light of the major setback to U.S. national policy involved in the loss of Indo-China) would entail as an urgent prerequisite the restoration of Asian morale and confidence in U.S. policy which will have reached an unprecedentedly low level in the area.

(5) Each of these courses of action would involve greater risk of war with Communist China, and possibly the Soviet Union, than timely preventive action taken under more favorable circumstances before Indo-China is lost.

Proposed Implementing Procedures for the Establishment of a Southeast Asian Regional Concept

1. In considering various methods by which a project to develop a reasonable understanding in Southeast Asia might be undertaken, it appears that, in any case, considerable time may elapse before an effective organization may be developed. However, it does appear that a preliminary survey should be made by the individual appointed by the President for the development of this project. For initiation of the preliminary phase it is believed that the procedure outlined in the following paragraphs should be undertaken.

2. The President should appoint an individual of international standing as a special and personal representative of the President. Such an appointment, during the preliminary phase, should not be limited to any specific assignment. This individual should not be classified as a "roving Ambassador" but he should have ambassadoral rank.

3. Having appointed this individual, the President should immediately and publicly request this special representative to undertake a survey of Southeast Asia for the purpose of making a detailed report on conditions and problems directly to the President. This report to form the basis for further development of the regional arrangement among Southeast Asian States.

4. The special representative should have no other official assignment and should be relieved of any duties which would tend to restrict his interests to any one country or particular area.

5. The President's special representative should be empowered to enter into discussions with all U.S. military and civilian officials in the area and with the chiefs of state of the several Southeast Asian countries. He should go to Formosa, the Philippines, Thailand, the Associated States, Malaya, and Indonesia. Thereafter, he should probably also go to Korea and Japan. It is

not thought that the special representative should go to Burma except upon receipt of a specific invitation from the Burmese government.

6. The special representative should enter into any discussions with the governments of Southeast Asia through the respective Ambassadors and any arrangement made with those governments should be consumated by the Ambassadors or by the government itself.

7. It should be the publicly announced mission of the special representative to undertake a fact-finding mission. He should not himself publicly interfere or intercede in the continuing relations by the U.S. and the Southeast Asian countries or among the several Southeast Asian states themselves.

8. On the contrary, the special representative should act only as a catalytic agent and should offer to assist in the solution of problem areas by appropriate intercession in the U.S. For this purpose, the special representative should initially be based in the U.S. although for his initial survey he may wish to establish an advance headquarters with a small staff in some appropriate Southeast Asian country.

9. It should also be the mission of the special representative to seek an expansion of bilateral and multilateral agreements between the several Southeast Asian states such as those already established between Cambodia and Laos and between Thailand and Viet Nam.

10. Initial agreements may probably best be obtained in the field of economic or cultural agreements; defense arrangements should initially be secondary.

11. The special representative should, of course, report through the Department of State but should specifically have access to all departments of government for the purpose of expediting the solution of any problems in which the U.S. may contribute to the achievement of better regional understanding and association among the Southeast Asian countries.

12. Upon the completion of his inital survey, the special representative should return to the U.S. for the purpose of making recommendations to the President and to secure the implementation of recommendations developed during the survey.

[1]The Department of State representative recommends the deletion of paragraphs A and B hereunder as being redundant and included in other documents.

(308) <u>TELEGRAM FROM DULLES TO EMBASSIES IN CANBERRA AND WELLINGTON</u>, April 6, 1954

Source: *U.S.-Vietnam Relations, Book 9,* pp. 367-369.

Talking with Ambassadors of Australia and New Zealand, Dulles indicated that he expected the United Kingdom, Australia and New Zealand to pledge to contribute troops, if necessary, as part of a coalition of states to save Indochina.

The following are main points made by Secretary in conversation with Ambassadors Spender and Munro April 4.

(1) Situation in France is deteriorating and there is very real possibility that unless new element interjected into Indo-China situation French will seek settlement at Geneva which will amount to a sell-out.

(2) We see no prospect of negotiated settlement at Geneva which does not boil down to one of following alternatives: (a) a disguised surrender of the French or (b) a disguised retreat of the Communists. We have carefully

studied other possiblities including division of Indo-China and consider them impracticable.

(3) In our view required new element in situation should be creation before Geneva of an ad hoc coalition of states directly interested in area who had pledged themselves to work together and, if necessary, to contribute forces. Nations we have in mind are US, France, Associated States, United Kingdom, Australia, New Zealand, Thailand, Philippines. Proposal presupposes continuation of French military effort in Indo-China. US is prepared to contribute and play its full part in such a common effort.

(4) Secretary stressed attitude of UK, Australia, and New Zealand, particularly former, was key to problem. With passage of time danger would increase and capacity for united action would be reduced. It would be difficult to hold unity of free world if we waited until danger was at our very doorstep. If danger not recognized by United Kingdom and Commonwealth, which is much closer to it than we are, we cannot move.

(5) Matter would at some time be laid before UN with view to broadening support as much as possible. However, coalition we had in mind was indispensable and we could not count on UN for effective action.

(6) We believe action by coalition would not lead to Chinese intervention. However, if this happened we would all consult.

Spender referred to Australian election May 29 and obviously feared interjection of issue in campaign. However, he personally felt action should be taken if we believed French situation would deteriorate irretrievably in next two months.

Munro referred to New Zealand commitments in Middle East which would need to be changed and said attitude of United Kingdom would be of greatest significance to his government.

In reply to inquiry concerning expected Australian and New Zealand contribution Admiral Radford indicated Australian carrier and New Zealand naval effort comparable to what it had contributed in Korea would be satisfactory.

Ambassadors indicated they would consult their governments immediately.

For Peaslee: As Spender raised Australian election as possible difficulty, Merchant at Secretary's direction today had supplemental talk with Spender suggesting matter might be manageable politically if Australians took initiative and thereby gained credit as they had on creation of Anzus. You may have opportunity plant same seed with Manzies or Casey.

For Peaslee and Scotten: Please follow up urgently with Australian and New Zealand governments at highest levels with view to early favorable response.

(309) ARMY POSITION ON NSC ACTION NO. 1074-A, April 1954

Source: *U.S.-Vietnam Relations, Book 9*, p. 346-358.

The U.S. Army, in an unsigned paper on the NSC Staff analysis of scenarios under which the U.S. might intervene militarily, pointed out several military facts omitted from the analysis: that air and naval forces alone would not assure victory, and that the equivalent of 12 U.S. divisions would be required if the French were to withdraw and the Chinese intervened.

1. There are important military disadvantages to intervention in Indochina under the assumptions set forth in NSC Action No. 1074-a.

2. A military victory in Indochina cannot be assured by U.S. intervention with air and naval forces alone.

3. The use of atomic weapons in Indochina would not reduce the number of ground forces required to achieve a military victory in Indochina.

4. It is estimated that seven U.S. divisions or their equivalent, with appropriate naval and air support, would be required to win a victory in Indochina if the French withdraw and the Chinese Communists do not intervene. However, U.S. military intervention must take into consideration the capability of the Chinese Communists to intervene.

5. It is estimated that the equivalent of 12 U.S. divisions would be required to win a victory in Indochina if the French remain and the Chinese Communists intervene.

6. The equivalent of 7 U.S. divisions would be required to win a victory in Indochina if the French remain and the Chinese Communists intervene.

7. Requirements for air and naval support for gound force operations are:

    a. Five hundred fighter-bomber sorties per day exclusive of interdiction and counter-air operations.
    b. An airlift capability of a one division drop.
    c. A division amphibious lift.

8. One U.S. airborne regimental combat team can be placed in Indochina in 5 days, one additional division in 24 days, and the remaining divisions in the following 120 days. This could be accomplished partially by reducing U.S. ground strength in the Far East with the remaining units coming from the general reserve in the United States. Consequently, the U.S. ability to meet its NATO commitment would be seriously affected for a considerable period. The time required to place a total of 12 divisions in Indochina would depend upon the industrial and personnel mobilization measures taken by the government.

(310) JOINT STATEMENT BY DULLES AND FOREIGN SECRETARY ANTHONY EDEN, April 13, 1954

Source: Department of State *Bulletin*, April 26, 1954, p. 622.

The Dulles proposal for "united action" disturbed the British and French Governments, which were concerned that moves toward internationalizing the war would jeopardize the Geneva Conference. The French response suggested that the proposed coalition should come only if no agreement was possible at Geneva, and the British was similar to that. (See Devillers and Lacoutre, End of a War, pp. 84-85.) The wide gulf separating the three allies suggested the need for immediate consultations among them, so Dulles went to London on April 11 for two days of talks. The joint statement reflected the British refusal to go along with the immediate formation of an ad hoc coalition to intervene in Indochina, committing Britain only to examine the "possibility" of a collective defense agreement in Southeast Asia.

At the conclusion of their meetings in London on April 12 and 13, during which they discussed a number of matters of common concern, Mr. John Foster Dulles and Mr. Anthony Eden issued the following statement:

We have had a full exchange of views with reference to Southeast Asia. We deplore the fact that on the eve of the Geneva Conference the Communist forces in Indochina are increasingly developing their activities into a large-scale war against the forces of the French Union. They seek to overthrow the lawful and friendly Government of Viet-Nam which we recognize; and they have invaded Laos and Cambodia. We realize that these activities not only threaten those now directly involved, but also endanger the peace and security of the entire area of Southeast Asia and the Western Pacific, where our two nations and other friendly and allied nations have vital interests.

Accordingly we are ready to take part, with the other countries principally concerned, in an examination of the possibility of establishing a collective defense, within the framework of the Charter of the United Nations, to assure the peace, security and freedom of Southeast Asia and the Western Pacific.

It is our hope that the Geneva Conference will lead to the restoration of peace in Indochina. We believe that the prospect of establishing a unity of defensive purpose throughout Southeast Asia and the Western Pacific will contribute to an honorable peace in Indochina.

[One paragraph on atomic energy matters is omitted.]

(311) JOINT STATEMENT BY DULLES AND BIDAULT, April 14, 1954

Source: Department of State *Bulletin*, April 26, 1954, pp. 622-623.

Talks with French Foreign Minister Bidault on April 14, Dulles pressed for a commitment by France to the internationalization of the war. Bidault explained the necessity for France to appear sincere in its negotiations at Geneva, which ruled out any such move unless the conference failed. The joint statement therefore closely followed the Dulles-Eden statement, promising nothing more than examination of the "possibility" of a Southeast Asia pact.

Following their conversations in Paris on April 14th, the United States Secretary of State, Mr. John Foster Dulles and the French Minister of Foreign Affairs, M. Bidault, issued the following statement:

For nearly two centuries it has been the practice for representatives of our two nations to meet together to discuss the grave issues which from time to time have confronted us.

In pursuance of this custom, which we hope to continue to the benefit of ourselves and others, we have had an exchange of views on Indochina and Southeast Asia.

Mr. Dulles expressed admiration for the gallant fight of the French Union forces, who continue with unshakeable courage and determination to repel Communist aggression.

We deplore the fact that on the eve of the Geneva Conference this aggression has reached a new climax in Viet-Nam particularly at Dien-Bien-Phu and has been renewed in Laos and extended to Cambodia.

The independence of the three Associated States within the French Union, which new agreements are to complete, is at stake in these battles.

We recognize that the prolongation of the war in Indochina, which endangers the security of the countries immediately affected, also threatens the Pacific. In close association with other interested nations, we will examine the possibility of establishing, within the framework of the United Nations Charter, a collective defense to assure the peace, security and freedom of this area.

We recognize that our basic objective at the Geneva Conference will be to seek the re-establishment of a peace in Indochina which will safeguard the freedom of its people and the independence of the Associated States. We are convinced that the possibility of obtaining this objective depends upon our solidarity.

(312) MEMORANDUM FROM WILSON TO THE SERVICE SECRETARIES AND THE JOINT CHIEFS OF STAFF, April 15, 1954

Source: *U.S.-Vietnam Relations, Book 9,* pp. 382-383.

At the National Security Council meeting of April 6, Eisenhower expressed the view that, if a regional grouping could be organized, Congressional authorization for U.S. military intervention should be sought. In the meantime, it was agreed that contingency planning for intervention in Indochina should start.

Wilson directed the Joint Chiefs and Armed Services to prepare the necessary plans.

1. At its meeting on 6 April 1954, the National Security Council agreed on the following, which has been subsequently approved by the President (NSC Action No. 1086-a, b and c):

a. Noted and discussed the reference report and postponed decision on the recommendation in paragraph 7-c thereof, but agreed that military and mobilization planning to be prepared for this contingency should be promptly initiated.

b. Agreed that the United States should direct its efforts prior to the Geneva Conference toward:

(1) Organizing a regional grouping, including initially the U.S., the U.K., France the Associated States, Australia, New Zealand, Thailand, and the Philippines, for the defense of Southeast Asia against Communist efforts by any means to gain control of the countries in this area.
(2) Gaining British support for U.S. objectives in the Far East, in order to strengthen U.S. policies in the area.
(3) Pressing the French to accelerate the program for the independence of the Associated States.

c. Noted the President's view that, if agreement for the organization of the above-mentioned regional grouping could be achieved, Congressional authorization for U.S. participation therein should then be requested.

2. The action set forth in paragraph 1-a above has been referred to the Secretary of Defense and the Director, Office of Defense Mobilization for appropriate implementation and was discussed at the Armed Forces Policy Council on 15 April 1954. The action in paragraph 1-b was referred to the Secretary of State.

3. It is requested that the Joint Chiefs of Staff promptly prepare the military plans involved under paragraph 1-a above. It is further requested that the Joint Chiefs of Staff, in close collaboration, under existing arrangements, with the Secretaries of the Military Departments and the Assistant Secretaries of Defense (Supply and Logistics), (Manpower and Personnel) and (Comptroller), promptly develop the supply, manpower and other requirements arising from these military plans which might affect production, manpower and budgetary planning by the Department of Defense and the Office of Defense Mobilization. This military planning and the development of requirements should cover not only specific intervention in Indochina, but also any augmentations in forces or supplies required to permit the United States to maintain at present levels its present defense commitments and to be prudently prepared to face possible increased risks of (1) Chinese Communist intervention and (2) general war.

4. It is further requested that the Joint Chiefs of Staff report to my office on the above by 10 May 1954. If it has not been possible to complete the planning by that date, a progress report on 10 May 1954 is requested.

5. The Assistant Secretaries of Defense (Supply and Logistics) and (Manpower and Personnel) will collaborate with the Office of Defense Mobilization, as appropriate, in the preparation of production and manpower plans based upon and required to implement the military plans.

6. Because of the security senstivity of this planning, appropriate security precautions will be taken by all concerned.

(313) DRAFT POSITION PAPER ON THE GENEVA CONFERENCE, SUBMITTED BY THE OFFICE SECRETARY OF DEFENSE FOR INTERNATIONAL SECURITY AFFAIRS, April 15, 1954

Source: *U.S.-Vietnam Relations, Book 9*, pp. 385-387.

Expressing concern that the U.S. did not yet have an official position on the Geneva Conference, despite extensive discussions in the Indochina Working Group, Vice Admiral A. C. Davis sent a draft paper to the Coordinator of the U.S. delegation to Geneva, U. Alexis Johnson. The paper reiterated the positions previously taken by the N.S.C. and Defense that the U.S. should inform France that it would disassociate itself from any settlement which would involve possible Communist victory in Indochina. It further recommended putting diplomatic pressure on France by implicitly threatening to end its status as one of the "Big Three" and U.S. support for the French position in North Africa.

Assumptions

1. NSC 5405, approved 16 January 1954, continues to be the policy of the United States with respect to Southeast Asia.

2. It is highly improbable that Communist agreement could be obtained to a negotiated settlement which would be consistent with basic United States objectives in Southeast Asia. (JCS memorandum, 12 March 1954).

3. At Geneva, the French Government under continued domestic pressure will favor a negotiated settlement of the fighting in Indochina at almost any price.

Discussion

The French Government has been under considerable domestic pressure to terminate the hostilities in Indochina. In order to forestall a showdown prior to Geneva, M. Laniel, in a public statement, proposed six points as conditions for a cease-fire in Indochina. These six points would unquestionably be unacceptable to the Communists, particularly if reinforced by additional conditions to assure enforcement of the armistice terms. However, domestic pressure on the French Government to terminate hostilities is expected to increase during the course of the Geneva Conference, rather than decrease. In view of this, it would be extremely difficult for the French Government not to accept an agreement which would be less than the conditions of the Laniel proposal. It should be noted that although the above factors make it almost certain that the French Government will seek agreement at Geneva at practically any price, there has been no indication that this "price" has been considered realistically by the French Government or public.

Communist tactics at Geneva are likely to follow closely those tactics employed by Communist negotiators at Panmunjom. Communist intransigence and other tactics, short of actually breaking off negotiations, led to prolonged discussions which worked to the disadvantage of our side. As a result, the Korean Agreement in its final form produced an armistice bringing about a cease-fire but with which it has been impossible to assure Communist compliance. On the other hand, in Korea the United Nations Command is required to live up faithfully to the terms of the armistice. It should be noted that this problem would be considerably more complex and disadvantageous to the French in Indochina.

The Department of Defense has considered the military implications of terminating the fighting in Indochina under conditions less than a military defeat of organized Viet Minh forces. It was the conclusion of the Department of Defense, as indicated in Assumption No. 2 above, that inasmuch as it is highly improbable that Communist agreement could be obtained to a negotiated settlement which would be consistent with basic United States objectives in Southeast Asia, a continuation of fighting with the objective of seeking a military victory appears as the only alternative in Indochina. (JCS memorandum, TAB A).

Conclusions

If the Communists follow the same tactics they employed at Panmunjom, they will be prepared for a long and difficult negotiation. The French will find it almost impossible to withstand pressures for a weakening of their position (the Laniel proposal) and will most likely give way under these pressures. Further, the French, once engaged in a negotiation, will of necessity be required to seek every possible means of settlement.

The United States should not join with the French in any Indochina negotiations at Geneva unless there is prior French commitment not to accept terms leading directly or indirectly to the loss of Indochina. This commitment should be positive and definite, for it would be difficult, if not impossible, for the United States to disassociate itself from the negotiations once they had begun. Thus, if the negotiations result in a settlement leading to the ultimate loss of Indochina, the United States would have participated in this loss.

Recommendations

It is recommended that:

a. The United States adopt the position that it is highly improbable that the Communist agreement could be obtained to a negotiated settlement at Geneva which would be consistent with basic United States objectives in Southeast Asia;

b. The United States position for Geneva be positive and definite that we will agree to no settlement which would in any way compromise our objectives with respect to Southeast Asia;

c. The French Government be informed of the United States position (a and b above) at the earliest possible date;

(1) If France through one means or another countenances a Communist takeover in Indochina, it will mean far more than the end of France's position in the Far East. Rather it will be a public exhibition of France's inability to carry on any longer as an equal member with the United States and the United Kingdom of the Big Three;

(2) The effect of abandonment would be so severe in North Africa as to have serious repercussions not only on the French position there, but also on the nature of the relationship between France and the United States in that area.

(3) If the Indochina war ends on terms considered unsatisfactory by the United States, our dollar aid to France would, of course, automatically cease.

(4) Beyond these points, conclusion of negotiations by France resulting in Communist domination of Indochina, an area of extreme strategic interest to the free world, would result in consequences in Europe as well as elsewhere whose seriousness would have no apparent limitation.

e. If the French Government refuses to agree to the United States position, the United States Government should not participate in the Indochina discussions at Geneva;

f. The United States immediately determine whether in the event of (e) above, we should approach the Governments of the Associated States and our allies with a view to continuing the struggle in Indochina either jointly with the French, in concert with our allies, or, if necessary, unilaterally.

(314) <u>STATEMENT BY DULLES</u>, April 19, 1954

Source: Department of State *Bulletin*, May 3, 1954, pp. 668-669.

Upon his return to Washington, Dulles invited Britain and France to attend "Preparatory talks" in Washington beginning April 20. But on April 18, the British Ambassador, Sir Roger Makins, informed him that the British government would not attend, because it did not want any such talks to take place before the Geneva negotiations had been given a chance. (See End of a War, *pp 88-89.) At that point, the U.S. plan for a military coalition to save Vietnam was dead. But the following day, Dulles issued a statement in which he gave the impression that progress was being made in the direction of establishing such a coalition.*

I have reported to President Eisenhower on my recent trip to London and Paris, where I discussed the position in Indochina.

I found in both Capitals recognition that the armed Communist threat endangered vital free world interest and made it appropriate that the free nations most immediately concerned should explore the possibility of establishing a collective defense. This same recognition had already been expressed by other nations of the Southeast Asian area.

The Communists in Viet-Nam, spurred on by Red China, have acted on the assumption that a quick, easy victory at Dien-Bien-Phu would open the door to a rapid Communist advance to domination of the entire Southeast Asian area. They concluded they were justified in recklessly squandering the lives of their subjects to conquer this strongpoint so as to confront the Geneva Conference with what could be portrayed as both a military and political victory for communism.

The gallant defenders of Dien-Bien-Phu have done their part to assure a frustration of the Communist strategy. They have taken a toll such that, from a military standpoint, the attackers already lost more than they could win. From a political standpoint, the defenders of Dien-Bien-Phu have dramatized the struggle for freedom so that the free world sees more clearly than ever before the issues that are at stake and once again is drawing closer together in unity of purpose.

The Communist rulers are learning again that the will of the free is not broken by violence or intimidation.

The brutal Soviet conquest of Czechoslovakia did not disintegrate the will of the West. It led to the formation of the North Atlantic Treaty alliance.

The violent conquest of the China mainland followed by the Korean aggression did not paralyze the will of the free nations. It led to a series of Pacific mutual security pacts and to the creation under the North Atlantic Treaty of a powerful defensive force-in-being.

The violent battles now being waged in Viet-Nam and the armed aggressions against Laos and Cambodia are not creating any spirit of defeatism. On the contrary, they are rousing the free nations to measures which we hope will be sufficiently timely and vigorous to preserve these vital areas from Communist domination.

In this course lies the best hope of achieving at Geneva the restoration of peace with freedom and justice.

In addition to discussing with the President the situation in Indochina, I reported to him with reference to the Korean phase of the forthcoming Geneva Conference which opens on April 26.

At Berlin the Soviet Union agreed that "the establishment, by peaceful means, of a united and independent Korea would be an important factor in reducing international tension and in restoring peace in other parts of Asia."[1] To achieve that goal is the purpose of the conference which will be held between the representatives of the Soviet Union and of the Chinese and North Korean Communist regimes, and the representative of 16 nations which participated, under the United Nations Command, in the defense of the Republic of Korea.

The United States, working in close consultation with the Republic of Korea and the representatives of the other allied nations, will adhere steadfastly to this purpose of establishing by peaceful means a united and independent Korea.

I also discussed with President Eisenhower the prospective meeting of the NATO ministerial council to be held in Paris on April 23. Since the military program for NATO has now been established on a stable and durable basis, this particular ministerial meeting will be confined to an exchange of views between the foreign ministers with reference to the worldwide political situation as affecting the NATO members.

In preparation for this meeting I reviewed with President Eisenhower the United States estimate of the world situation and the persistence in varying forms of the menace of Soviet communism which makes it imperative that there be collective measures to meet that menace.

The President expressed his great personal satisfaction that NATO, as it completes its fifth year, has already made a large contribution to peace and faces the future with a prospect of growing strength and unity.

I leave for Geneva confident that the Western Allies are closer than ever before to a unity of purpose with respect to world problems, not only of the West, but of the East.

[1]*Bulletin* of Mar. 1, 1954, p. 317.

(315) TELEGRAM FROM DULLES IN GENEVA TO THE STATE DEPARTMENT, April 25, 1954

Source: *U.S.-Vietnam Relations, Book 9*, pp. 388-389.

Eden informed Dulles that the British would oppose intervention by air at Dienbienphu and would support the French in reaching a diplomatic settlement. Only if the Conference failed, he said, would Britain consider military action.

I met with Eden this evening at 10:15 p.m., following his arrival from London. He had consulted Churchill, the Cabinet and British chiefs. He said that the United Kingdom is strongly opposed to any intervention at Dien Bien Phu because it does not think it will have decisive effect and will not be understood by United Kingdom or free world opinion. He indicated that the views of the British chiefs differ with ours and that British chiefs look forward to a discussion and estimate with Radford in London. In summary the British position is as follows: (1) The United Kingdom is prepared now to join with the United States in a secret study of measures which might be taken to defend Thailand and the rest of Southeast Asia if the French capitulate.

Eden saw Bidault at Orly tonight on his way through Paris (where he stopped to pick up Mrs. Eden) and outlined to him the British position as follows: (1) The United Kingdom will give the French all possible diplomatic support in Geneva to reach a satisfactory settlement on Indochina. (2) If such a settlement is reached the United Kingdom will be willing to join with United States and others in guaranteeing that settlement. (3) If Geneva fails the United Kingdom will be prepared to join the others to examine the situation urgently to see what should be done.

I said to Eden that while I had reservations myself about air intervention at Dien Bien Phu at this moment without an adequate political basis for such action, his reply was most discouraging in that it seemed to leave the French nothing to fall back on. If French are to stand loss of Dien Bien Phu they must be strengthened and a declaration of common intent would do this. In essence the United Kingdom was asking the French to negotiate and at the same time telling them that if the negotiation failed that they would be glad to examine what could be done. Given the present French situation with which Eden is fully familiar, I said to Eden that I doubted that there would be French will to stand up to their adversaries at Geneva.

Eden made quite clear that the United Kingdom is opposed to air intervention at Dien Bien Phu and also opposed to becoming directly involved in any way
with the Indochinese war.

Referring to the rest of Southeast Asia, he said the British were confident
that they had the situation in Malaya in hand and mentioned the they had 22
battalions there and 100,000 native police. He said that there was no parallel
between Indochina and Malaya.

Eden also showed me a map of Indochina prepared by Alexander and the British
chiefs. The map indicates that virtually all of Vietnam, Laos, and Cambodia is
under or subject to imminent control by the Viet Minh. The British believe
that the only way to cope with the situation is to commit a strong force to the
Hanoi delta and generally work outward concentrically consolidating their position as they go with loyal natives. This they believe is a "tremendous project
involving lots of time and considerable forces."

I said to Eden I felt the position which his Government had taken would
have so little in it in way of comfort to the French that the prospect of the
latter standing firm here was very slight. It would be a tragedy not to take
steps now which would prevent Indochina from being written off.

Eden said that there was obviously a difference in the United States and
the United Kingdom estimates and thinking but the United Kingdom proposals
which he had outlined above were as far as the British Government could go.

(316) <u>COMMUNIQUE BY THE STATE OF VIET-NAM</u>, April 25, 1954

Source: *Documents Relating to British Involvement in the Indo-China Conflict*
1945-1965, p. 87.

Anticipating a compromise agreement involving the partition of Viet-nam,
Bao Dai's Cabinet released a statement warning that it would not be bound by
any such agreement.

With regard to Viet-Namese unity, it is known that various plans have been
drawn up which would entail a partition of Viet-Nam. Such solutions may offer
certain specious advantages of a diplomatic nature, but their adoption would
present extremely grave disadvantages and dangers for the future. . . . Viet-
Nam would never be prepared to consider the possibility of negotiations in
which France, violating the basic principles of the French Union from which her
authority is derived, were to negotiate with those who are in rebellion against
the Viet-Namese nation or with hostile Powers, thereby disregarding or sacrificing her partner.

Whatever may happen, neither the Head of the State nor the Viet-Namese
Government will consider themselves bound by decisions which by running counter
to national independence and unity would violate the rights of peoples and reward aggression, contrary to the principles of the United Nations Charter and
to democratic ideals.

(317) <u>TELEGRAM FROM DULLES IN GENEVA TO AMBASSADOR WINTHROP ALDRICH AND DILLON</u>,
April 26.

Source: *U.S.-Vietnam Relations, Book 9*, pp. 390-391.

After discussion with Bidault and Eden, Dulles expressed his view that Eden
had arrived with instructions to "actively encourage" the French to agree to a
ceasefire on almost any terms, because of fear of a U.S. war with China. Dulles
reported that he advised Bidault to fight on rather than withdraw under the
"most difficult conditions" - apparently referring back to his argument that

the native populations would rise up against and massacre the French in the event of a ceasefire.

I met for about an hour this afternoon with Eden and Bidault at latter's villa. Meeting was called at latter's request with no (repeat no) indication its purpose.

After some discussion procedural problems Indochina conference (reported separately) discussion turned to Bao Dai's declaration in Paris and current attitude. Bidault told us that he understands Bao Dai named as his personal representative and observer a former member Ho Chi Minh's cabinet but that Bidault has not (repeat not) been able to confirm observer's arrival at his station in Evian.

Bidault then launched into rather confused discussion of problem his government faces with regard to establishing position for Indochina negotiation which he said was extremely difficult during progress of Dien Bien Phu battle. He touched lightly on whole range of possibilities including collective defense, cease-fire and partition. He mentioned further deterioration in political situation in Associated States.

Eden picked up the question of cease-fire and encouraged further discussion by Bidault this subject with cryptic remark that a month ago British had felt cease-fire due to general infiltration was dangerous but that now without having any clear view they were not (repeat not) so sure. I pointed out that cease-fire at Dien Bien Phu locally would be in fact surrender and that cease-fire generally would involve serious risk of native peoples' rising with resultant massacre of French. Side conversations later made it clear French believe with support of their military authorities in Indochina that general cease-fire lacking any control or safeguards would make it impossible for French Union forces to resume fighting once cease-fire established. Bidault said that the French Government had queried French High Command in Indochina and had received a reply that there would either have to be a final cease-fire or further reenforcements would have to be sent to Indochina during the conference.

As indicative of Bidault's continuing courage, he said that when he saw Molotov tomorrow he intended to stand on Laniel's statement of March 5 and attempt to draw Molotov out without ceding ground himself and without getting involved in detailed discussions of substance on an Indochina settlement.

In my judgment, Eden has arrived with instructions actively to encourage French into almost any settlement which will result in cessation hostilities in Indochina. My guess is that behind this lies British fear that if fighting continues, we will in one way or another become involved, thereby enhancing risk Chinese intervention and possibility further expansion of war. This estimate of mine is confirmed by fact that Chauvel told MacArthur that French believe Eden's instructions are to press actively for a cease-fire.

I made clear to Bidault privately that we would have no (repeat no) part in settlement at Geneva of Indochina war which constituted surrender of Indochina to Communists, and that France has better chance by fighting on rather than by attempted withdrawal which would be under most difficult conditions. I intend to see Eden alone tomorrow morning to talk with extreme bluntness to him expressing my dismay that British are apparently encouraging French in direction surrender which is in conflict not (repeat not) only with our interest but what I conceive theirs to be.

(318) <u>TELEGRAM FROM DULLES TO THE STATE DEPARTMENT</u>, April 29, 1954

Source: *U.S.-Vietnam Relations, Book 9,* pp. 397-398.

Reviewing his talks over the previous days, Dulles portrayed the French government as drifting and probably temporary, and suggested that the only hope

*for keeping France in the war was an anti-Communist concert of nations backing
a French effort centered on defensible enclaves. Britain's negative attitude
toward intervention led him to reemphasize the importance of the U.S. making
decisions based on its own judgment on the West's interests.*

Developments have been so rapid and almost every hour so filled with high-
level talks that evaluation has been difficult. My present estimates follow:

(1) Indochina: Delay in fall of Dien Bien Phu has resulted in some French
discounting of this development. Nevertheless, it must be assumed the French
will not continue in any long-range operation unless it will definitely relieve
the strain on French manpower in Indochina. Present French Government holding
on because their Parliament in recess and probably no one eager to take over
at this jucture. Bidault given considerable discretion because present Cabinet
cannot make up its mind on any course. Therefore, we do not have anyone on
French side with whom we can make any dependable agreements. After deputies
return and Dien Bien Phu falls, there may well be a change of government,
probably to the left, committed to liquidate Indochina. However, this is more
easily said than done and it is possible that as this fact develops a French
Government might be prepared to sit down with us seriously and consider some
joint program which is something that so far they have evaded.

I do not know whether from military standpoint it would be deemed possible
to end the scattering and exposure of military forces for local political reasons and withdraw present forces to defensible enclaves in deltas where they
would have US sea and air protection meanwhile retain enough territory and
enough prestige to develop really effective indigenous army along lines suggested by O'Daniel. This might, I suppose, take two years and would require in
large part taking over training responsibility by US. Also full independence
and increased economic aid would probably be required to help maintain friendly
governments in areas chosen for recruitment.

I do not have any idea as to whether this is militarily feasible and Admiral
Davis inclines to view that it is not. However, from political standpoint this
type of program appears to offer best hope of France staying in war. If France
and US agree on such a plan, there would be fair chance of Australia and New
Zealand coming along. However, this estimate can be improved in next day or
two after I have conferred further with Foreign Minister Casey and Prime Minister Webb. It is unlikely that the UK would initially participate and would
probably use its influence to prevent participation by Australia and New
Zealand. The UK situation would be difficult internally and externally, and
there would probably be undesirable repercussions upon other NATO partners.
Thailand could be expected to cooperate if we act promptly. Foreign Minister
Wan gave further assurance today and urges quick military conversations.

The attitude here of Molotov and Chou En-lai's statement yesterday lead me
to rate more highly than heretofore the probability that any open US intervention would be answered by open Chinese intervention with consequence of general
war in Asia.

(2) UK attitude is one of increasing weakness. British seem to feel that
we are disposed to accept present risks of a Chinese war and this, coupled also
with their fear that we could start using atomic weapons, has badly frighted
them. I have just received a note from Eden referring to my paper placed before
NATO restricted council where Eden again urges necessity of consultation before
any use. He says,"You show our strongly-held views on the need for consultation before any decision is taken."

(3) General: The decline of France, the great weakness of Italy, and the
considerable weakness in England create a situation where I think that if we
ourselves are clear as to what should be done, we must be prepared to take the
leadership in what we think is the right course, having regard to long-range US

interest which includes importance of Allies. I believe that our Allies will be inclined to follow, if not immediately, then ultimately, strong and sound leadership. In saying this, I do not underestimate the immense difficulty of our finding the right course in this troubled situation. Nor do I mean to imply that I think that this is the moment for a bold or war-like course. I lack here the US political and NSC judgments needed for overall evaluation.

(319) <u>NATIONAL INTELLIGENCE ESTIMATE, NIE 63-54</u>, April 30, 1954 (Extract)

Source: *U.S.-Vietnam Relations, Book 9*, pp. 400-402.

The intelligence community predicted that if Dienbienphu fell to the "Viet Minh," it would accelerate the deterioration of the French Union position in Indochina, which could lead to collapse before the end of 1954 if not checked.

THE PROBLEM

To estimate the probable consequences within Indochina during the next two or three months of the fall of Dien Bien Phu within the near future.

SCOPE

The consequences of the fall of Dien Bien Phu on the political situation in France, and the repercussions of Major decisions in France or Geneva on the situation in Indochina, are excluded from the scope of this estimate.

CONCLUSIONS

1. The fall of Dien Bien Phu would have far-reaching and adverse repercussions, but it would not signal the immediate collapse of the French Union political and military situation in Indochina. As a consequence of the fall of Dien Bien Phu, the morale of French Union forces would receive a severe blow. A crucial factor in the military sitution thereafter would be the reliability of native units, particularly the Vietnamese. There would almost certainly be increased desertions, and the possiblity cannot be excluded that the native components of French Union forces might disintegrate. However, we believe that such disintegration would be unlikely during the ensuing two or three months, and that for at least this period the major part of the native troops would probably remain loyal.

2. Assuming no such disintegration, the fall of Dien Bien Phu would not in itself substantially alter the relative military capabilities of French Union and Viet Minh forces in Indochina during the next two or three months. The French stand at Dien Bien Phu has produced certain compensatory military results. It has prevented an overruning of Laos and has resulted in the inflicting of casualties upon the Viet Minh comparable in number to the total French force committed at Dien Bien Phu. The bulk of Viet Minh forces released by the fall of Dien Bien Phu would probably not be able to move, regroup, and re-equip in time to be employed in new major operations during the next two or three months, although some lightly equipped infantry battalions might be made available more rapidly for operations in the Delta region.

3. Although the Viet Minh have a substantial capability to organize demonstrations and carry out sabotage and terrorist activities in the major cities of Indochina, we believe that French Union forces could maintain control in those cities.

4. The political consequences in Indochina of the fall of Dien Bien Phu would be considerably more adverse than the strictly military consequences and would increase the tempo of deterioration in the over-all French Union position in Indochina, particularly in Vietnam. There would probably be a serious decline

in the Vietnamese will to continue the war and to support the Vietnamese military programs. However, we believe that general collapse of French and native governmental authority during the next two or three months would be prevented by the continued existence of organized French Union forces and the hope among Indochinese that the US might intervene in Indochina.

5. We believe that although the fall of Dien Bien Phu would not immediately lead to collapse of the French Union position in Indochina, it would accelerate the deterioration already evident in the French Union military and political position there. If this trend were not checked, it could bring about a collapse of the French Union position during the latter half of 1954. It should be emphasized that this estimate does not consider the repercussion of major decisions in France or Geneva and elsewhere, which could have a decisive effect on the situation in Indochina.

****

(320) <u>NEWS CONFERENCE STATEMENT BY PRESIDENT DWIGHT EISENHOWER</u>, May 5, 1954 (Extract)

Source: Department of State *Bulletin*, May 17, 1954, p. 740.

Despite Eden's rebuff to Dulles in Geneva, Eisenhower issued a statement which again conveyed the impression that the Western allies and certain Asian countries were progressing toward a collective defense organization which could intervene in Indochina.

****

The Indochina phase of the Conference is in process of being organized and the issues have not yet been clarified. In this matter a large measure of initiative rests with the Governments of France, Viet-Nam, Laos, and Cambodia, which are the countries most directly concerned.

Meanwhile plans are proceeding for the realization of a Southeast Asia security arrangement. This was publicly suggested by Secretary Dulles in his address of March 29. Of course, our principal allies were advised in advance. This proposal of the Secretary of State was not a new one; it was merely reaffirmation of the principles that have consistently guided our postwar foreign policy and a reminder to interested Asian friends that the United States was prepared to join with others in the application of these principles to the threatened area. Most of the free nations of the area and others directly concerned have shown affirmative interest, and conversations are actively proceding.

Obviously, it was never expected that this collective security arrangement would spring into existence overnight. There are too many important problems to be resolved. But there is a general sense of urgency. The fact that such an organization is in process of formation could have an important bearing upon what happens at Geneva during the Indochina phase of the Conference.

The countries of the area are now thinking in constructive terms, which include the indispensable concept of collective security. Progress in this matter has been considerable and I am convinced that further progress will continue to be made.

(321) <u>TELEGRAM FROM SMITH IN GENEVA TO DULLES</u>, May 5, 1954

Source: *U.S.-Vietnam Relations*, Book 9, pp. 423-424.

Undersecretary Smith reported that Bidault had asked his government to support a hardline negotiating position at Geneva along the lines of the March 5

Laniel speech: a ceasefire with international controls, regular troops re-grouped into delimited areas, followed by discussion of political issues.

Following is outline given this morning by Chauvel to Dennis, Allen and Achilles of proposal which Bidault last night sent to French Cabinet for authorization to make when substantive discussion of Indochina starts:

1. Vietnam problem is purely Vietnamese with no question of partition, only military struggle for control of government.

2. Situation different in Laos and Cambodia which are victims of external aggression.

3. Under Berlin agreement, purpose of Geneva conference is to establish peace in all three countries. To this end there should be a cease-fire guaranteed by adequate military and administrative controls under supervision. Cease-fire would take effect only when such guarantees had been embodied in armistice conventions, which might be different for each three states, and when control machinery had been established and was in place. Controls would be based upon Laniel's March 5 conditions. When cease-fire occurred, regular troops would be regrouped into delimited areas and all other forces disarmed. The control machinery would be "international" and would require considerable body of personnel.

4. After peace had been re-established by the cease-fire, political and economic problems could be examined.

In discussing this draft proposal Chauvel said French assumed Russians would propose immediate cease-fire followed by political settlement based on coalition and immediate elections, which would force West into position of opposing cease-fire. French public desire for cease-fire was emotional and French Government could defend its proposal, even though it would in effect delay any cease-fire for long time if not indefinitely, on grounds that conditions demanded were essential for safety of troops themselves. The continued resistance at Bien (sic.) Bien Phu long after public opinion had discounted its fall had conditioned French opinion to believe its loss would not mean loss of war. He did not exclude possibility of conference calling on opposing forces not to undertake new military operations during negotiations. He assumed very lengthy negotiations would be necessary to reach any armistice agreement and felt that during this period Communist uncertainty as to united action of US intervention might be increased.

Allen inquired whether at some stage in proceedings working out of armistice details might be left to combattants themselves as suggested in Colombo communique. Chauvel did not like this idea but said it might be considered. In response to question as to whether he envisaged conference turning into indefinite Panumjom Chauvel said it might turn armistice negotiations over to working group and adjourn to reconvene when warranted.

In response to Achilles inquiry as to whether "international" meant "UN" supervision, Chauvel stated French had no firm position on this but subsequent discussion indicated French continue to oppose use of UN machinery as establishing precedent which would be used against them in North Africa and elsewhere and that British definitely share their point of view. Allen suggested something like peace observation commission would be preferable to UN auspices. Achilles stressed importance of insisting on UN auspices.

Chauvel said studies by French military had confirmed their impression that withdrawal of French Union Forces from Cambodia and Laos except for two bases in latter would be of definite military advantage rather than disadvantage.

(322) <u>TELEGRAM FROM DULLES TO THE AMERICAN CONSUL IN GENEVA</u>, May 6, 1954

Source: *U.S.-Vietnam Relations, Book 9*, pp. 426-429.

In a meeting with members of Congress, Dulles reviewed the events of the previous weeks, emphasizing the urgent French request for intervention, the British opposition to it, and finally, the French inability to fulfill the prerequisites. Dulles conceded that Viet-nam would "probably" not be able to join a collective defense organization in Southeast Asia, because of the outcome of the war, but said he still expected to have Laos and Cambodia as members.

Secretary held hour and half briefing of 25 leading members Congress yesterday. Generally friendly, constructive atmosphere, no direct criticism, although considerable discussion on future plans and weakness of British and French.

Secretary described set-up of Conference and briefly went over Korean developments. Explained difficulty with Allies on all-Korean elections and trouble finding someone to speak up in defense of US against Communist vilification. Congressmen showed interest in this and asked about positions our various Allies.

Turning to Indochina, Secretary traced developments in our thinking and plans since inception massive aid program last fall. Three prerequisites demanded from French had then seemed to be met: understanding A.S. become independent, effective program for rapid training of natives, aggressive military plan. Prerequisites would lead to our desired objectives. Navarre Plan still sound, but French will for offensive action and even ability govern themselves disintegrated. Following development united action concept and as French military situation deteriorated, we began think of US military intervention. In April 3 meeting with Congressmen agreed objectives of earlier prerequisites must be met to increased degree and other interested nations must join in before such intervention could be authorized. Secretary described London-Paris trip and Eden's reneging on communique. Some adverse Congressional comment on latter and Secretary said thought Nehru had pressured British.

Secretary described two informal French requests for US air intervention on April 4 and 22 and his replies thereto. Described French mood of extreme urgency said British Cabinet confirmation of reversal of agreement in communique of April 13. British terrified by H-bomb, pressured by Nehru, contrasted their giving up India with French call for help to keep Indochina, and gave higher rating to risk of Chinese intervention and global war if West intervened. Secretary read from memo of conversation in which he had chastised Eden for British stand. Number adverse Congressional comments on British position, especially Judd.

Secretary said had reached three conclusions. US should not intervene militarily until and unless rerequisites agreed on at April 4 [3?] meeting were fulfilled. Conditions must exist for successful conclusion of war and such was not now case. Participation other allies academic since French had not fulfilled prerequisites. Considerable opposition to internationalization of war in France anyway. This was Administration position on intervention. No Congressional comments on this.

Secondly, US must push rapidly for development of SEA community, probably without Vietnam but hopefully with Laos and Cambodia. British might come in and they might want Burma and India too. We were agreeable to Burma. This community might offer fair chance quote insulate unquote rest SEA against possible loss of Vietnam.

Third conclusion was we should not write off British and French in spite of their weakness in Asia. Lack of 100 per cent cooperation one of welcome disadvantages of democratic system.

DULTE 51 then received and Secretary read pertinent parts. Considerable discussion ensued on Eden's idea of quote five white powers unquote consultation and conclusions 2 and 3 above. Judd strongly against Eden quote plan unquote, wanted Asians in even without UK and France. Knowland agreed on im-

portance of Asians, as did several others. Knowland said we should have commitments from UK, Australia, New Zealand and others to help us if needed in
Korea or Japan, et cetera, if we were to have collective security pact with
them for SEA, which he personally favored. Secretary said Burma, Thailand,
Philippines plus A.S. would help and that he told Eden he wanted Formosa in if
British brought in India. McCormack and Smith supported Secretary on conclusion three and several others did too.

Secretary described effect of Indochina developments on French government
and EDC. Russell paid fine tribute to Secretary for briefings and cooperation
with Congress and others expressed appreciation.

(323) MINUTES OF MEETING BETWEEN PRESIDENT EISENHOWER, DULLES AND ROBERT
CUTLER, SPECIAL ASSISTANT TO THE PRESIDENT, May 7, 1954

Source: *U.S.-Vietnam Relations, Book 9,* pp. 436-438.

*Informed of the position of the military members of the NSC Planning Board
that the U.S. should not support the Bidault proposal for a ceasefire but should
propose to France an "internationalization" of the war, in which the U.S. would
become an equal partner in the war. Eisenhower indicated he would want the
conditions of such "internationalization" to include a regional coalition and
an invitation from the indigenous governments.*

At a meeting in the Prsident's office this morning with Dulles, three
topics were discussed:

1. Whether the President should approve paragraph 1b of the tentative
Record of Action of the 5/6/54 NSC Meeting, which covers the proposed answer to
the Eden proposal. The Secretary of State thought the text was correct. Wilson and Radford preferred the draft message to Smith for Eden prepared yesterday by MacArthur and Captain Anderson, and cleared by the JCA, which included
in the Five Power Staff Agency Thailand and the Philippines. Radford thinks
that the Agency (which has hitherto been not disclosed in SEA) has really completed its military planning; that if it is enlarged by top level personnel,
its actions will be necessarily open to the world; that therefore some Southeast Asian countries should be included in it, and he fears Eden's proposal as
an intended delaying action.

The President approved the text of paragraph 1b, but suggested that Smith's
reply to Eden's proposal should make clear the following:

1. Five Power Staff Agency, alone or with other nations, is not to the
United States a satisfactory substitute for a broad political coalition
which will include the Southeast Asian countries which are to be defended.

2. Five Power Staff Agency examination is acceptable to see how these
nations can give military aid to the Southeast Asian countries in their
cooperative defense effort.

3. The United States will not agree to a "white man's party" to determine the problems of the Southeast Asian nations.

I was instructed to advise Wilson and Radford of the above, and have done so.

2. The President went over the draft of the speech which Dulles is going
to make tonight, making quite a few suggestions and changes in text. He
thought additionally the speech should include some easy to understand slogans,
such as "The US will never start a war," "The US will not go to war without
Congressional authority," "The US, as always, is trying to organize cooperative
efforts to sustain the peace."

3. With reference to the cease-fire proposal transmitted by Bidault to the French Cabinet, I read the following, as views principally of military members of the Planning Board, expressed in their yesterday afternoon meeting:

1. US should not support the Bidault proposal.
2. Reasons for this position:

    <u>a</u>. The mere proposal of the cease-fire at the Geneva Conference would destroy the will to fight of French forces and make fence-sitters jump to Vietminh side.
    <u>b</u>. The Communists would evade covertly cease-fire controls.

3. The US should (as a last act to save IndoChina) propose to France that if the following 5 conditions are met, the US will go to Congress for authority to intervene with combat forces:

    <u>a</u>. grant of genuine freedom for Associated States
    <u>b</u>. US take major responsibility for training indigenous forces
    <u>c</u>. US share responsibility for military planning
    <u>d</u>. French forces to stay in the fight and no requirement of replacement by US forces.
    (<u>e</u>. Action under UN auspices?)

This offer to be made known simultaneously to the other members of the proposed regional grouping (UK, Australia, NZ, Thailand, Associated States, Philippines) in order to enlist their participation.

I then summarized possible objections to making the above proposal to the French:

    <u>a</u>. No French Government is now competent to act in a lasting way.
    <u>b</u>. There is no indication France wants to "internationalize" the conflict.
    <u>c</u>. The US proposal would be made without the prior assurance of a regional grouping of SEA States, a precondition of Congress; although this point might be added as another condition to the proposal.
    <u>d</u>. US would be "bailing out colonial France" in the eyes of the world.
    <u>e</u>. US cannot undertake <u>alone</u> to save every situation of trouble.

I concluded that some PB members felt that it had never been made clear to the French that the US was willing to ask for Congressional authority, if certain fundamental preconditions were met; that these matters had only been hinted at, and that the record of history should be clear as to the US position. Dulles was interested to know the President's views, because he is talking with Ambassador Bonnet this afternoon. He indicated that he would mention these matters to Bonnet, perhaps making a more broad hint than heretofore. He would not circulate any formal paper to Bonnet, or to anyone else.

The President referred to the proposition advanced by Governor Stassen at the April 29 Council Meeting as not having been thoroughly thought out. He said that he had been trying to get France to "internationalize" matters for a long time, and they are not willing to do so. If it were though advisable at this time to point out to the French the essential preconditions to the US asking for Congressional authority to intervene, then it should also be made clear to the French as an additional precondition that the US would never intervene alone, that there must be an invitation by the indigenous people, and that there must be some kind of regional and collective action.

I understand that Dulles will decide the extent to which he cares to follow this line with Ambassador Bonnet. This discussion may afford Dulles guidance in replying to Smith's request about a US alternative to support the Bidault proposal, but there really was no decision as to the US attitude toward the cease-fire proposal itself.

(324) <u>ADDRESS TO THE NATION BY DULLES</u>, May 7, 1954 (Extract)

Source: Department of State *Bulletin*, May 17, 1954, pp. 739-744.

As the Geneva Conference opened and immediately following the fall of Dien-bienphu to the Viet-nam People's Army, Dulles emphasized that the period of primary French responsibility for Indochina was over, and that the only solution was an internationalization of the war under the auspices of a collective defense organization. He suggested that the "present conditions" did not provide a "suitable basis" for U.S. military intervention but that the U.S. would seek to organize a coalition of nations to take primary responsibility for protecting the Associated States of Indochina in case of either an unfavorable settlement or the continuation of the war.

I welcome this opportunity to talk with you about the Conference now going on in Geneva and the related aspects of our foreign policy.

First of all, I join with you in paying tribute to the gallant defenders of Dien-Bien-Phu. May it be given us to play a worthy part to defend the values for which they gave their lives.

This week I returned from the Geneva Conference. My return was not connected with any developments at the Conference. As long ago as last February when the Conference was called, I said I would attend only the opening sessions, and then have my place taken by the Under Secretary of State, General Bedell Smith. He is highly qualified to head our delegation at Geneva.

Since the Conference may last for some weeks, I did not feel able to stay with it that long. I have been out of the United States during much of the last 6 months to attend the Bermuda Conference, the Berlin Conference, the Caracas Conference, and two NATO Council meetings in Paris. These meetings strengthen the links with our allies and enable us to present the position of the United States to others. But the Secretary of State must also keep in close touch with our own people and with the Congress. In order to exercise our full influence in foreign affairs, the Government must have the understanding and support of the American people for its policies.

The Geneva Conference has two tasks. The first is to try to find a way to unify Korea. The second task is to discuss the possibility of restoring peace in Indochina.

The Soviet delegation, however, has sought to use the Conference for other purposes. By various devices, it has tried to create the false impression that this meeting accepted Red China as one of "five great powers" or conferred on it a new international status.

Both of these issues had been fought out in connection with calling the Conference and the Soviets had then conceded that the Conference would not be a five-power affair nor involve any recognition for Red China. We and our allies stood firmly and solidly on that position and the Soviets ended by accepting it.

****

Let me turn now to the problem of Southeast Asia. In that great peninsula and the islands to the south live nearly 200 million people in 7 states - Burma; the three states of Indochina - Laos, Cambodia, and Viet-Nam; Thailand; Malaya; and Indonesia. Communist conquest of this area would seriously imperil the free world position in the Western Pacific. It would, among other things, endanger the Philippines, Australia, and New Zealand, with all of which the United States has mutual-security treaties. It would deprive Japan of important foreign markets and sources of food and raw materials.

In Viet-Nam, one of the three Indochinese states, war has been going on since 1946. When it began, Indochina was a French colony just liberated from Japanese occupation. The war started primarily as a war for independence. What started as a civil war has now been taken over by international communism for its own purposes. Ho Chi-Minh, the Communist leader in Viet-Nam, was trained in Moscow and got his first revolutionary experience in China.

In the name of nationalism, the Communists aim to deprive the people of Viet-Nam of their independence by subjecting them to the new imperialism of the Soviet bloc.

What is going on in Indochina is a perfect example of the Soviet Communist strategy for colonial and dependent areas which was laid down by Lenin and Stalin many years ago and which the Communists have practiced to take over much of Asia.

The Indochina area was vulnerable. The Governments of Viet-Nam, Laos, and Cambodia had not yet received full political independence. Their peoples were not adequately organized to fight against the Communist-led rebels, and they did not feel that they had a stake in the struggle which justified great sacrifice.

President Eisenhower became familiar with the problem when he was the Supreme Commander of NATO in Europe. He had seen the strain and the drain which the Indochina war put upon France. He was aware of the growing discontent in France resulting form the long war where the French were assuming the principal burden of the fight and where human and material costs were mounting.

I recall in December 1952 when General Eisenhower, as President-elect, was returning from his Korean trip on the cruiser *Helena*, we discussed gravely the problem of Indochina.

We realized that if Viet-Nam fell into hostile hands, and if the neighboring countries remained weak and divided, then the Communists could move on into all of Southeast Asia. For these reasons, the Eisenhower administration from the outset gave particular attention to the problem of Southeast Asia.

Our efforts took two complementary lines. We sought to strengthen the resistance to communism in Indochina. We sought also to build in Southeast Asia a broader community of defense.

Indochina Measures

In Indochina itself, the following steps seemed to us important:

1. The French should give greater reality to their intention to grant full independence to Viet-Nam, Laos, and Cambodia. This would take away from the Communists their false claim to be leading the fight for independence.

2. There should be greater reliance upon the national armies who would be fighting in their own homeland. This, we believed, could be done if the peoples felt that they had a good cause for which to fight and if better facilities for training and equipment were provided for them.

3. There should be greater free-world assistance. France was carrying on a struggle which was overburdening her economic resources.

Much progress was made in each of these respects. The French declaration of July 3, 1953, pledged full independence to Viet-Nam, Laos, and Cambodia. Already, a treaty of independence has been concluded with Laos, and Emperor Bao Dai told me, in Paris, 2 weeks ago, that he felt that Viet-Nam was assured of its independence.

On the military side, a 2-year plan was worked out by General Navarre. It was designed to speed the training of native forces.

The cost of this operation would be considerable. The United States, which was already paying part of the cost of the war, agreed to bear the greater part of the total cost. We are now paying at the rate of about $800 million a year, plus a very large provision of military equipment.

Despite the gains on these fronts, there has been a growing belief by the French people that France was overextended, in view of its responsibilities in Asia, in Africa, and in Europe. As a result, when I met in Berlin last January and February with the Foreign Ministers of France, Great Britain, and the

Soviet Union, the French Government asked that the projected conference on Korea be expanded to discuss also the problem of peace in Indochina.

Shortly after the Berlin Conference adjourned, the Communists, as was to be expected from them, began to expend their military assets, human and material, in a desperate effort to win some victory which they would exploit for political purposes. They concentrated on a mass assault against one of the French outposts - that of Dien-Bien-Phu. That assault was pushed with a callous disregard of human life.

Now, Dien-Bien-Phu has fallen. Its defense, of 57 days and nights, will go down in history as one of the most heroic of all time. The defenders, composed of French and native forces, inflicted staggering losses on the enemy. The French soldiers showed that they have not lost either the will or the skill to fight even under the most adverse conditions. It shows that Viet-Nam produces soldiers who have the qualities to enable them to defend their country.

An epic battle has ended. But great causes have, before now, been won out of lost battles.

The Chinese Communists have been supplying the forces of Viet Minh rebels with munitions, trucks, anti-aircraft guns, radar, and technical equipment and technical advisers. They have, however, stopped short of open intervention. In this respect, they may have been deterred by the warnings which the United States has given that such intervention would lead to grave consequences which might not be confined to Indochina.

Collective Defense

Throughout this period the United States has also followed the second course of trying to develop strength in Southeast Asia through collective measures.

Back in 1951, I negotiated treaties with the Philippines, Australia, and New Zealand. These recognized that this area was one of vital importance to the United States. These treaties also recognized that they were only initial steps toward the development of a more comprehensive system of collective security in the area.

This we have constantly sought. However, it has proved difficult to achieve this result. There were differences of race and culture and differences in the development of national self-government. The countries which had won or were winning their independence from Western colonialism and Japanese imperialism were often more concerned with past dangers from which they were extricating themselves than with the threat of new peril. The memories of the past blinded them to the present perils of Communist imperialism. They were not disposed to make the sacrifices inherent in any collective security system.

However, this situation began to change and by the spring of this year it seemed that there could be a broader program of collective defense.

On March 29, 1954, after consultations with Congressional leaders of both parties, and after having advised our principal allies, I stated: "The imposition on Southeast Asia of the political system of Communist Russia and its Chinese Communist ally, by whatever means, would be a grave threat to the whole free community. The United States feels that that possibility should not be passively accepted but should be met by united action."

This declaration was nothing new, although the circumstances of the moment gave the words a new significance.

President Eisenhower speaking almost a year earlier, in his address of April 16, 1953, had said that "aggression in Korea and in Southeast Asia are threats to the whole free community to be met by united action."

After having explained our purposes to the American people, we promptly conferred with the representatives of nine free nations having immediate interest in the area, namely, Viet-Nam, Laos, Cambodia, Thailand, the Philippines, Australia and New Zealand, France, and the United Kingdom. We informed others whose interests could be affected.

The Governments of the United Kingdom and of France asked me to visit their capitals to develop further our concept. After conferences at London on April 12 and 13 with Sir Winston Churchill and Mr. Eden, we issued a joint U.S.-U.K. communique which, after reciting the danger to the entire area of Southeast Asia and the Western Pacific caused by Communist warfare in Indochina, concluded: "Accordingly we are ready to take part, with the other countries principally concerned, in an examination of the possibility of establishing a collective defense, within the framework of the Charter of the United Nations, to assure the peace, security and freedom of Southeast Asia and the Western Pacific."

A similar agreement was reached in Paris with Prime Minister Laniel and Foreign Minister Bidault.

The progress thus made was that which the United States had sought. We had never sought any sudden spectacular act such as an ultimatum to Red China. Our goal was to develop a basic unity of constructive purpose. We advanced toward that goal. I feel confident that unity of purpose persists, and that such a tragic event as the fall of Dien-Bien-Phu will harden, not weaken, our purpose to stay united.

The United States and other countries immediately concerned are giving careful consideration to the establishment of a collective defense. Conversations are taking place among them. We must agree as to who will take part in the united defense effort, and what their commitments will be.

It must be recognized that difficulties have been encountered, but this was expected. The complexity of the problem is great. As I have pointed out, the complications were such that it was not possible even to get started until recent months. Under all the circumstances, I believe that good progress is being made. I feel confident that the outcome will be such that Communist aggression will not be able to gain in Southeast Asia the results it seeks.

This may involve serious commitments by us all. But free peoples will never remain free unless they are willing to fight for their vital interests. Furthermore, vital interests can no longer be protected merely by local defense. The key to successful defense and to the deterring of attack is association for mutual defense. That is what the United States seeks in Southeast Asia.

Current Hostilities in Viet-Nam

The question remains as to what we should do about the current hostilities in Viet-Nam.

In Korea we showed that we were prepared under proper conditions to resort to military action, if necessary, to protect our vital interests and the principles upon which stable peace must rest.

In Korea, we, along with others, joined in the defense of an independent government, which was already resisting an armed assault. We did so at the request of the Republic of Korea and under a United Nations mandate. The Korean people were inspired by a deep sense of patriotism and eager to develop a power of their own. The issues were clarified before the world by decisions of the United Nations. Under these circumstances, we and our allies fought until the enemy sued for an armistice.

In Indochina, the situation is far more complex. The present conditions there do not provide a suitable basis for the United States to participate with its armed forces.

The situation may perhaps be clarified as a result of the Geneva Conference. The French have stated their desire for an armistice on honorable terms and under proper safeguards. If they can conclude a settlement on terms which do not endanger the freedom of the peoples of Viet-Nam, this would be a real contribution to the cause of peace in Southeast Asia. But we would be gravely concerned if an armistice or a cease-fire were reached at Geneva which would provide a road to a Communist takeover and further aggression. If this occurs, or if hostilities continue, then the need will be even more urgent to create the conditions for united action in defense of the area.

In making commitments which might involve the use of armed force, the Congress is a full partner. Only the Congress can declare war. President Eisenhower has repeatedly emphasized that he would not take military action in Indochina without the support of Congress. Furthermore, he has made clear that he would not seek that unless, in his opinion, there would be an adequate collective effort based on genuine mutuality of purpose in defending vital interests.

A great effort is being made by Communist propaganda to protray it as something evil if Asia joins with the nations of the Americas and Europe to get assistance which will help the peoples of Asia to secure their liberty. These Communist nations have, in this connection, adopted the slogan "Asia for the Asians."

The Japanese war lords adopted a similar slogan when they sought to subject Asia to their despotic rule. The similar theme of "Europe for the Europeans" was adopted by Mr. Molotov at the Berlin Conference when he proposed that the Europeans should seek security by arrangements which would send the United States back home.

Great despotic powers have always known that they could impose their will and gain their conquests if the free nations stand apart and none helps the other.

It should be observed that the Soviet Communist aggression in Europe took place only against countries which had no collective security arrangements. Since the organization of the North Atlantic Treaty, there has been no successful aggression in Europe.

Of course, it is of the utmost importance that the United States participation in creating collective security in Asia should be on a basis which recognizes fully the aspirations and cultures of the Asian peoples. We have a material and industrial strength which they lack and which is an essential ingredient of security. Also they have cultural and spiritual values of their own which make them our equals by every moral standard.

The United States, as the first colony of modern history to win independence for itself, instinctively shares the aspirations for liberty of all dependent and colonial peoples. We want to help, not hinder, the spread of liberty.

We do not seek to perpetuate Western colonialism and we find even more intolerable the new imperialist colonialism of communism.

That is the spirit that animates us. If we remain true to that spirit, we can face the future with confidence that we shall be in harmony with those moral forces which ultimately prevail.

(325) SPEECH BY FOREIGN MINISTER BIDAULT, TO THE GENEVA CONFERENCE, May 8, 1954

Source: Great Britain Parliament, Papers by Command, *Documents Relating to the Discussion of Korea and Indo-China at the Geneva Conference, April 27-June 1954* (London: Her Majesty's Stationery Office, Cmd. 9186, 1954), pp. 107-111.

The French proposal for peace in Indochina, as presented by Foreign Minister Bidault, called for concentration of all forces in certain areas, with international supervision, and provided for no political settlement in conjunction with a ceasefire.

Mr. Chairman, at the outset of this Conference I should like to describe its dramatic prelude and the most cruel battle in a fight that has been carried on for seven years. This broke loose after Berlin on February 18. The Conference of Four Ministers of Foreign Affairs had adopted a resolution which brought about the first light of hope for the restoration of peace in Indo-China. The decisive assault of a deplorably unequal fight, which lasted for fifty-five days, took place on the very eve of the date which had been earmarked for this meeting in Geneva, and the prospect for which alone should normally muzzle the guns. Thus, that bloody event takes place betwen two meetings both of which are to be placed under the sign of the relaxation of tension. We have already had an experience of sudden slaughter immediately after such peaceful negotiations - an experience that actions can so cruelly disprove words. And it is not on our side that was wanted, when the peace was spoken about, a hardening of the fight, going so far as preventing the wounded being evacuated contrary to the laws of war and to the principles of the civilised world. The outcome of the Battle of Dien Bien Phu had been announced yesterday by the Commander-in-Chief in these words: "The garrison of Dien Bien Phu has fulfilled its task which has been given to it by the command." The French Delegation cannot conceal here its deep emotion and its pride in the face of the heroism of the soldiers and the troops of France, of the Viet Nam, and of all of the French Union who have resisted beyond human endurance.

Such events dictate imperiously to the French Delegation its line of behaviour and conduct in the negotiations which are about to start. These negotiations are pre-conditioned by two terms of equal firmness: To insure the restoration of Indo-China to peace, which would be both lasting and fair; and to accompany this peace with the necessary guarantees so that peace could not be threatened afresh.

The responsibilities that we have assumed, the part we take in the conflict which had been imposed upon us in Indo-China, the close ties by which we are united with the peoples and the independent Governments of Viet Nam, Cambodia, and Laos, those are our titles to open this debate, which is of such paramount importance to peace, and from which we hope an acceptable solution will stem, and a solution acceptable to all. We have met here in order to try to obtain results that will be both practicable and concrete, and also in order to put an end to hostilities. No effort will be spared on our part in order to obtain solutions that would be based on reason and equity which are to be found if one genuinely and really wishes, as issued in the Berlin communique, the restoration of peace.

If we wish to discover the elements and the prospects of such settlement it is necessary, in the first place, that we should consider the over-all problems. Once those have been delineated I shall say how the French Delegation considers that we should work, if this Conference wishes to obtain results that would be speedy; that we all wish, so that bloodshed should stop at long last.

We have heard repeated about Asia in the course of the general debate on Korea. I may say that the way in which certain delegations consider this problem appears to me unilateral in its nature. We have heard statements here to the effect that Asia - a scene of upheavals, the scope and magnitude of which can be noted by all - had now been engaged on the path upon which it had been thrown by the Revolution of 1917 in Russia. If I understand it correctly, this means that inevitably the peoples of Asia will be led to establishing regimes similar to that of the Soviet Union. If this point of view is really that which is being held by some of my colleagues, it seems to me that such a view would be rather bold, or, to repeat, expressions that we have already heard, one which is contrary to facts - the facts show, in fact, that the peoples of Asia, who enjoy independence, have been able to accede to it with the agreement and in accordance with the decision of Powers which are being paradoxically described as imperialists. On the contrary, everywhere where so-called "popular regime" had been installed it can be established only as a conseuqence of several wars, or as a consequence of occupation by foreign armies. I believe that this ought to be recalled rather than distort history. It is highly desirable, in fact, that this Conference should avoid engaging in too ideological discussions, which would merely serve as a prevention to the ob-

taining of possible solutions and would merely strengthen and harden the specific
positions. If, indeed, we refer to agreement and at the same time accept only
unilateral solution; if, in order to obatin the triumph of that solution and of
that solution alone, the war is being pursued which has no independence as its
goal, since independence has already been completed, but it is rather for the
purpose of domination and opppression; if, finally, at the very time when the
hope of a pacific and peaceful negotiation appears, the fight is being intensified with the support of more considerable armament from a well-known source,
obstacles are being accumulated on the road towards justice, freedom and peace.

In order to solve this problem correctly, I believe it is necessary that I
should recall certain facts and certain circumstances. On the eve of the
Second World War the States and the countries of Indo-China had been in all respects in the processes of development. The population had risen gradually
from 16 to 26 million inhabitants in the course of the last 30 years. The
efforts that have been made in order to develop the country have brought about
an increase in the production of the main goods through the construction of a
network of communications, hydro-electric plants, processing industries, &c.
Two million hectares of fallow land have thus been turned into fertile fields
in Cochin-China. The production of rice exceeded six million tons. Considerable had been done in order to save the population from natural scourges and
from a period of epidemics. Indo-China thus stood on the way toward modern
civilisation which called, within necessary solidarities, for full sovereignty
and independence.

The world war slowed down that development and the Japanese coup in 1945
stopped it altogether. As war came to an end and on the departure of those
troops which had been called upon to disarm the Japanese, we could have hoped
that peace would be rapidly restored and that progress should be renewed. But
a plot took place.

In the beginning of August, 1945, in North Viet Nam and under the chairmanship of Ho Chi-Minh, a committee of 10 members had been set up, all of them belonging to the Communist Party and which a few days later had set up in Hanoi
a provisional government through the adjunction to minor positions of certain
foreign people who were not members of that party.

France, desirous of favouring the return of peace, had in the course of
1946 negotiated with the Vietminh in the spirit of complete and constant good
faith. However, by the end of 1946 the break which would have been wanted by
the Vietminh, first of all, resulted in slaughter and then in fight. The war
had started in Indo-China. That war, the Vietminh had alleged, had started
under the guise of independence. However, France had asserted as early as 1945
its will that the people of the peninsula should succeed to independence and to
freedom. Without the war Cambodia and Laos have been able to develop normally
and under the very best conditions. As early as 1946 both of these countries
have been able to adopt democratic constitutions. They passed general elections.
Their independence has been consecrated by treaties which have been signed with
France.

In Viet Nam, and in spite of the war, France has been able to keep its promises and full independence has been recognised and has become effective.
Thirty-five free countries, by recognising those three States, and a number of
interational organisations by accepting them in their midst, have consecrated
that independence. The national Government of Viet Nam has been able to set up
an administration to organise its finance, to develop its economy, to establish
diplomatic relations with the main free countries. It built up an army. All
those elements mean sovereignty.

However, the war that Vietminh had stated it leads for the independence of
Viet Nam is continuing. It has now spread to the neighbouring States. Cambodia
and Laos, who were living peacefully under the authority of Governments that

their population had freely elected, have been already for one year the subject of characterised aggression on the part of the foreign troops of Vietminh.

On April 2 last, that is on the very eve of this meeting of the Conference at Geneva, the new aggression committed against Cambodia took place. The increasing assistance given by the Communist countries to the Vietminh army has allowed for developing without ceasing their spirit of domination.

The true nature of the war in Indo-China no longer appears as clearly as before. The independence of those States is not at stake. The attempt at present is made to grab the resources and to rule the peoples of Asia. The free nations cannot be deceived. They know that the free States of Indo-China and France are fighting for the cause of liberty. On our side, we are thinking in terms of defence and not of a crusade. And that is why the will of peace of France and of the Associated States has not waited for the meeting of a Conference in Berlin in order to manifest itself. Long before that date, and for the last time as soon as the prospects of an Armistice in Korea had become likelihood, the French Government had expressed a desire to see to it that that peace should spread through contagion and that it should not be concentrated in one particular point in Asia. It was necessary, however, to wait still for many months; it was necessary that great efforts and patient efforts had to take place before decisions be made and that a Conference be convened which would be entrusted with, not in order to examine all the problems of the world as it was proposed but rather to bring a real positive contribution to peace through trying to find a solution to the problem of Korea and putting an end to the hostilities in Indo-China.

The French Government is thus confident that it has done everything in its power to put an end to the conflict. Not only has it removed all reason for this conflict to exist by recognising fully and unreservedly the independence of Viet Nam, Laos and Cambodia but furthermore, the French Government has manifested for a long time its readiness and its desire of obtaining a reasonable settlement which would allow for the hostilities to be brought to an end. This is the main and primary task assigned to this Conference.

As to the political problems, the Governments of the three States competent in this regard will have to tell us how they visualise the solution of the problems where they arise once the war has been terminated.

In order to get out of the present war situation, the French Delegation, sure that it is responding to the profoundly felt feelings of the peoples cruelly tried, and by all peace-loving countries, believes that it is our duty to suggest the following method which seems to us the most appropriate with a view to bringing about a rapid agreement along the lines desired.

We propose that the Conference should, first of all, declare that it adopt the principle of a general cessation of hostilities in Indo-China based upon the necessary guarantees of security, these terms of the principles thus enunciated being inseparable in our mind and in our resolution.

The necessary guarantees are required to preserve the security of the troops of the parties involved and for the protection of the civil populations from abusive exploitation of the suspension of hostilities. The measures of implementation will have to be established once this principle has been adopted. It will immediately be seen that the situation does not present itself in exactly the same way to the States concerned. And it will be wise, therefore, to take account of these differences. In two of these States, Laos and Cambodia, the problem is clear. There , there is no civil war but an invasion, without motive and without a declaration of war, an invasion which furthermore threatens the neighbouring countries.

The solution consists therefore in agreeing upon the withdrawal of the invading forces and the restoration of the territorial integrity of those States. In order that the implementation of this agreement may be uncontested and in order that the applicationof it may go forward without hindrance, a system of

International Supervision is called for. On such bases, the Conference can in a very short time ensure, on conditions in conformity with equity, the restoration of peace in Laos and Cambodia.

In Viet Nam the situation is very different and more complex. There, there is a civil war in reality. For France, there is a Viet Nam State of which the unity, territorial integrity and independence must be respected. With the presence at this Conference of a party which, in order to fight against this State, has organised armed forces, has been admitted as a necessity with a view to bringing about a cessation of hostilities, this presence must not be interpreted as implying on our side any kind of recognition. The situation thus defined makes it necessary to provide for a transitional phase in the course of which, hostilities having ceased, political problems may be progressively resolved. The elements of this solution depend, first and foremost, in our opinion, upon the opinion which will be expressed by the Government of Viet Nam. I shall confine myself here to indicating that the most just solution of the political problem can be found and finally assured only when the population is in a position to express in complete freedom its sovereign will by means of free elections. For the present moment, I repeat, the problem is that of bringing about a cessation of hositilities and the guaranteeing of that cessation. These guarantees, in our opinion, must be of two kinds.

These guarantees, as I say, in our view should be of two kinds. On the one hand, while the other armed forces are disarmed the regular forces of the two parties would be brought together in clearly demarcated regrouping zones. On the other hand, the implementation of the agreement should be placed under the supervision of International Commissions. As long ago as March 5, last the head of the French Government stated his views regarding the implementation of such a decision. These points and many others, too, will, of course, have to be cleared up between us. The essential thing is to know whether these principles are recognised by all the participants as being the principles which must govern the settlement which the Geneva Conference is called upon to bring about.

It is desirable, and indeed normal, that the agreement that it is our duty to obtain here both as to the settlement at Laos and as to the settlement at Cambodia and as regards Viet Nam should be guaranteed in appropriate conditions by the States participating in the present Conference. That, in its main lines, is the method which is proposed by the Delegation of France. Our conception of the problem and of the solution is inspired by the desire to bring about a settlement which can be counted upon to last. Experience teaches us that without solid guarantees, agreements of this kind are essentially fragile. Instead of consolidating peace they represent only brief interludes, or ill-respected armistices.

In the case now under consideration, the consequences of a breach would be unpredictable. We have not the right to run such a risk.

I have thus defined the conception of the French Government with regards the cessation of hostilities. The imperious duty of the French Government, of attending to the security of the forces which are in Indo-China under French command, will always reamin present in our thoughts in the course of the negotiations. But the French Delegation will also be guided, while giving necessary attention to all legitimate interests, by the desire to put an end as rapidly as possible to the sufferings and sacrifices that are going on and to put an end to a conflict, the length and aggravation of which constitute a danger for the peace of the world.

It is in this spirit that the French Delegation has the honour to submit to you, Mr. President, a series of proposals inspired by the considerations which I have just stated. The French proposal is as follows:

I. *Viet Nam*

    1. All regular units to be assembled in assembly areas to be defined by the Conference on the basis of proposals by the Commanders-in-Chief.

    2. All elements not belonging either to the army or to the policy forces to be disarmed.

    3. All prisoners of war and civil internees to be released immediately.

    4. Execution of the above provisions to be supervised by international commissions.

    5. Hostilities to cease as soon as the agreement is signed.

The assembly of troops and disarmament of forces as above provided to begin no later than x days (the number to be fixed by the Conference) after the signature of the agreement.

II. - *Cambodia and Laos*

    1. All regular and irregular Vietminh forces which have entered the country to be evacuated.

    2. All elements which do not belong either to the army or to the police forces to be disarmed.

    3. All prisoners of war and civil internees to be released immediately.

    4. Execution of the above provisions to be supervised by international commissions.

III. These agreements shall be guaranteed by the States participating in the Geneva Conference. In the event of any violation thereof there shall be an immediate consultation between the guarantor States for the purpose of taking appropriate measures either individually or collectively.

This, Mr. President, is the proposal submitted to the Conference on the responsibility of the French Delegation and by that Delegation. Thank you, Sir.

(326) SPEECH BY HEAD OF THE CAMBODIAN DELEGATION, SAM SARY, TO THE GENEVA CONFERENCE, May 8, 1954

Source: *Documents on the Discussion of Korea and Indochina*, pp. 114-115.

The representative of Royal Cambodian Government called the Cambodians fighting with the Viet Minh "foreigners," and without referring to the Vietnamese by name, suggested that any association with Vietnamese was harmful to Cambodia.

If there is a Free Government of Free Khmer, we do not know of that government, and I would submit that it has been created for a particular purpose. The representative of the Democratic Republic of Viet Nam has said that the peoples of Free Khmer have liberated vast territories and improved the standard of life of the populations inhabiting those territories. I would like to say, Mr. President, that I do not know anything about these various territories. There have been territories occupied for a few days by these forces previous to the arrival of the regular troops of Cambodia. When these troops arrived, the occupying forces took flight and took refuge in the mountains.

But what is the position with regard to the so-called Free Khmer Government? In the first place, it has no territory. I showed in the first part of my statement that such territory as it can be said to have is very small, is elastic, varying in size, and doubtful with regard to its future. In other words, it is not clearly demarcated territory of a state. Secondly, as regards regular troops, I have already said that the troops of the Free Khmer movement are not regular troops at all. They are more in the nature of bandits, partly under the control of Vietminh. They are engaged in pillage and they are not regular troops at all. Thirdly, as regards the regularity of the government, as I said in the first part of my statement, there is no government here. If there is anything that can be called a government at all it existed only since April 3, and it consists of only two or three persons; in other words, a body invented and created by our enemy. Those are the conditions which are required if a state is to exist, and which are not fulfilled in the present case.

What is it that the so-called Free Khmer represent? They represent only themselves. Thre are only a very few of them and they represent only themselves. Three times there have been general elections in Cambodia and these people have never been elected to office. They, therefore, do not represent any department or locality in Cambodia.

Finally, these Free Khmers are foreigners who are being manipulated by a foreign *bloc*, a foreign *bloc*, incidentally, which has always worked to the harm of our country. The real Free Khmers are the real nationalists who love peace, who have already rallied to the Government of Cambodia. These acts of submission and support took place recently in connexion with Chantarangsei and Savang Vong.

What is left is not a body of Free Khmers at all but a few slaves. And these are the people that you want to invite to this Conference.

Finally, Mr. President, the delegation of Cambodia would appeal to the members of this Conference to reject the proposal made by the delegation of the Democratic Republic of Viet Nam. Or if the question must be studied, we would ask for the adjournment of the meeting so that the four Inviting Powers can study it.

(327) SPEECH BY SOVIET FOREIGN MINISTER VYACHESLAV MOLOTOV TO THE GENEVA CON-FERENCE, May 8, 1954 (Extract)

Source: *Documents on the Discussion of Korea and Indochina,* p. 114.

The Soviet Foreign Minister argued that all the parties concerned should take part in the discussion, including the Khmer and Pathet Lao resistance governments.

Mr. Chairman and Gentlemen: This Conference is proceeding to discuss the problem of the re-establishment of peace in Indo-China. From the weighing of this agenda item, it follows that the Conference must discuss the problem of re-establishing peace in all the three States of Indo-China, in Viet Nam, Khmer and Pathet Lao. It is quite obvious that in order to make the work of our Conference successful, all the parties concerned must take part in it.

With respect to Viet Nam, this has already been recognised by the participants of the Conference, with the result that we have among us the representatives of the Democratic Republic of Viet Nam. It is known, however, that a war of national liberation is being waged, not merely in Viet Nam, but also in Pathet Lao and Khmer. The peoples of these countries, like those of Viet Nam, are fighting for their national independence, national unity and freedom.

In the course of this struggle, there have been formed in Khmer and Pathet Lao, democratic governments which heeded the struggle for national liberation for peoples of these countries. Considerable areas of Pathet Lao and Khmer are now under the control of these democratic governments.

The delegates of the governments of Khmer and Pathet Lao which are collaborating with the French authorities have already been invited to this Conference. This being so, there is no ground whatsoever for denying to the delegates of the governments of Pathet Lao and Khmer, which head the national liberation struggle of the people of these countries, the right to take part in the Conference.

(328) SPEECH BY SMITH TO THE GENEVA CONFERENCE, May 8, 1954

Source: *Documents on the Discussion of Korea and Indochina,* pp. 113-114.

The U.S. delegation rejected the D.R.V. proposal to invite the resistance governments in Laos and Cambodia, calling them "non-existent, so-called governments.

The United States delegation takes this opportunity to recall that at Berlin, the United States joined with France, the United Kingdom, and the Soviet Union in agreeing to organise a Conference at Geneva to consider the problems of Korea and Indo-China. Subsequently, the same four Powers reached agreement as to the composition as to the Indo-China phase of the Conference. That agreement reflected, in the presence here to-day of the nine delegations in this hall, as in the case of the Korean phase, that there are only four Inviting Powers: the United Kingdom, France, the Soviet Union and the United States. Therefore, if, as has been stated in the press, the invitation issued to the so-called Democratic Republic of Viet Nam appears in the name of both the Soviet Union and the Communist Chinese regime, that invitation is in its form at variance with the clear understanding of the Foreign Ministers present at Berlin last February.

Assuming the press reports to be accurate, the United States delegation can only regret that the Indo-China phase of this Conference should be initiated by a procedural evasion of previously-reached agreements.

At Berlin, we also agreed that the problem of restoring peace in Indo-China would be discussed at this Conference, to which representatives of the United States, France, the United Kingdom, the Union of Soviet Socialist Republics, the Chinese People's Republic and other interested states will be invited.

At Geneva, the four Inviting Powers have agreed that in addition to the participation specified at Berlin, there should be representatives at this Conference of the Governments of Laos, Cambodia and the Viet Nam. The United States cannot agree to the suggestion which has just been made that non-existent, so-called governments or states, such as the so-called Pathet Lao of Free Cambodians, can in any way be considered as qualified for invitations to this Conference under the Berlin Agreement.

The United States proposes that any idea of inviting these non-existent, so-called governments by rejected. If there is opposition to this United States proposal, the United States suggests that this meeting be adjourned after the delegate who has just been speaking has completed his presentation, in order to allow for further discussion on this point between the four Inviting Powers.

(329) SPEECH BY THE HEAD OF THE LAOTIAN DELEGATION PHOUI SANANIKONE, TO THE GENEVA CONFERENCE, May 8, 1954

Source: *Documents on the Discussion of Korea and Indochina,* pp. 115-116.

Opposing any invitation to the Pathet Lao to participate in the conference, the Lao delegation cited the dissolution of the Lao Issarak government in October 1949 and Prince Souphanouvong's expulsion from it to buttress the legal argument that his resistance government had no standing.

Mr. President, with regard to the proposal of the Democratic People's Republic of Viet Nam that we should invite Khmer and Pathet Lao to take part in the Conference, I must say, surprised me very much. If I may I would like briefly to say what Pathet Lao is. The transformation of the Kingdom of Laos into an independent democratic state has been completed and it was completed with the participation of all the citizens of Laos. The movement Lao Issarak in Pathet Lao existed until 1949. The members of that movement desired to await certain guarantees before giving their approval to the reorganisation, the conversion of the Kingdom into the new state. These guarantees were given in 1949 and they satisfied the members of the Lao Issarak movement. The movement, therefore, dissolved itself voluntarily and its participants returned to the free territory of Laos at the time when, with the French Government, the agreement was signed setting up the free Laos. The representatives of Laos Issarak were consulted and they were present at this time of the setting up of the free state.

The members of the Laos Issarak movement returned to the territory and participated in the life of the country, co-operating in the government. Two Ministers of the Royal Government, including the President of the Council of Ministers, belonged formerly to the movement. And I repeat that the movement dissolved itself voluntarily on October 24, 1949. Its dissolution was complete and final and the majority of the members of the movement returned to the territory and took part in the national life.

Thus, Mr. President, in the Kingdom of Laos there is complete unanimity. When in April, 1953, there was invasion of Laos by these foreign regular forces, the Government and people of Laos learned with great surprise of this so-called government of Pathet Lao under the leadership of Prince Souphanugvong. That Prince left Laos when he was only of school age, and he took part in the Laos Issarak movement in 1946. He was excluded from it in May, 1949, because of his complete dependence upon foreign elements and powers.

As I have already said, the movement was dissolved in 1949, and its members returned to Laos and rallied to the Government. Prince Souphanugvong, however, remained abroad where he formed links with Vietminh. He is not entitled in any way to say he represents Free Laos. He has no mandate from Laos, who simply do not know him.

Where is he? Where has he his administration? Where is his government, if there is such a thing? He may indeed have found a few of the population in certain frontier zones, but these dupes will return to Laos as soon as the Prince goes abroad again, across the frontier.

This so-called Pathet Lao represents absolutely nothing. It would be almost comic to recognise him as representing anybody. If that were done, all local leaders and party leaders and leaders of movements in all countries would consider they had the right to form governments and represent states.

Finally, let me say the delegation of Laos will oppose the invitation of the so-called Pathet Lao.

(330) SPEECH BY D.R.V. PREMIER PHAM VAN DONG TO THE GENEVA CONFERENCE, May 8, 1954

Source: *Documents Relating to the Discussion of Korea and Indochina,* pp. 112-113.

In his first speech to the Conference Pham Van Dong offered a resolution inviting representatives of the resistance governments in Cambodia and Laos to participate in the discussions.

Mr. President and Gentlemen: The task of the Conference is to examine the problems, and to put an end to the hostilities and to restore peace in Indo-China. This task is an extremely important one. Upon it depends the destiny of the peoples of Indo-China and the peace and security of the people of South-Eastern Asia and the peace of the world as a whole.

The peoples of Indo-China desire a cessation of hostilities and the restoration of peace in Indo-China. They are prepared, by negotiation, to assert their national rights. The peoples of France and nearly all the political circles in France call for the restoration of peace in Indo-China. The peoples in Indo-China and of France desire the restoration of friendly relations between France and the peoples of Indo-China. The people of South-East Asia and Asia want to put an end to the war and to re-establish peace in Indo-China, since the war in Indo-China constitutes a threat to the peace and security of South-East Asia and Asia.

At present, this threat has become more serious and pressing because of those who intend to prolong and extend the war in Indo-China. That is why the peoples of South-East Asia and Asia demand ever more energetically, the cessation of hostilities and the re-establishment of peace in Indo-China.

The people of the whole world want to put an end to the war and to re-establish peace in Indo-China, in order to reduce international tension and to consolidate peace in the whole world.

Enjoying the approval and support of the people of the whole world, this Conference is under favourable conditions to achieve the successful settlement of this problem of the re-establishment of peace in Indo-China. We welcome everything that helps us to realise this task. And one should not miss this opportunity under any pretext whatever.

In the same spirit, expressing the sentiment of the three peoples of Viet Nam, Khmer, and Pathet Lao, the delegation of the Democratic Republic of Viet Nam proposes to the Conference that it invite the official representatives of the Government of resistance of Khmer and of the Government of resistance of Pathet Lao to take part in its work. We submit this proposal having in mind the following: -

The peoples of Indo-China, the people of Viet Nam as well as the people of Khmer and Pathet Lao are greatly concerned about the question of the cessation of hostilities and the re-establishment of peace in Indo-China. For a long time, the people of Khmer and Pathet Lao, closely tied with the people of Viet Nam, fought for peace, independence and democracy. In the course of this struggle, the peoples of Khmer and Lao established the Government of resistance of Khmer and that of Lao. Under the leadership of these Governments of resistance of the peoples of Khmer and Pathet Lao, the peoples of Khmer and Pathet Lao have liberated vast areas of their national territory. The Governments of resistance have exerted all their efforts in creating a democratic Power and in raising the living standard of the population in liberated areas. That is why the Government of resistance of Khmer, as well as that of Pathet Lao enjoy the support and warm affection of the population in liberated areas, and they enjoy great prestige and influence among the population of both countries.

These Governments represent the great majority of the people of Khmer and Laos, the aspirations of whom they symbolise. Therefore, the presence of the official representatives of the Governments is necessary at this Conference, the task of which is the settlement of the problem of cessation of hostilities and of the re-establishment of peace in Indo-China. The peoples of the governments of resistance of Khmer and Pathet Lao, as well as the people and the government of the Democratic Republic of Viet Nam are bent upon using negotiations in order to put an end to the war and to re-establish peace in Indo-China, and at the same time to achieve their national rights which are independnence, unity, and democracy.

In the second part of March of this year, the Ministers for Foreign Affairs of the governments of resistance of Khmer and Pathet Lao declared that they support the resolution of the Berlin Conference regarding the Geneva Conference. In conformity with the aforesaid, the delegation of the Democratic Republic of Viet Nam is convinced the the presence of the official representatives of the governments of resistance of Khmer and Pathet Lao, who will bring to the attention of the Conference the aspirations and proposals of the peoples they represent, instead of being an obstacle, on the contrary will be a guarantee of the success of our Conference. Such is the will not only of the Indo-China peoples, but also of the peoples of the whole world, as well as all the peace-loving peoples who are really anxious to settle the problem of the cessation of war and that of the re-establishment of peace in Indo-China.

Alas, the delegation of the Democratic Republic of Viet Nam proposes to the Conference that it adopt the following resolution: -

"In view of the present situation of the countries of Indo-China and in the interests of the thorough and objective examination of the question of the cessation of hostilities and the re-establishment of peace in Indo-China, the Conference recognises the necessity to invite the representatives of the governments of resistance of Khmer and Pathet Lao to take part in the work of the Conference in regard to the question of the re-establishment of peace in Indo-China."

Having submitted this proposal to the Conference, I would ask the President of this meeting to authorise me to continue my stated when the Conference has discussed the proposal that I have submitted.

(331) <u>PROPOSAL BY THE CAMBODIAN DELEGATION TO THE GENEVA CONFERENCE</u>, May 10, 1954

Source: *Documents on the Discussion of Korea and Indochina*, p. 121.

The Royal Government demanded the surrender of its foes and the withdrawal of Vietnamese troops under International supervision.

1. All regular and irregular Vietminh forces which have invaded the country since April 2, 1954, or which penetrated into it before that date to be completely evacuated.
2. All elements which do not belong either to the army or to the policy forces to be disarmed.
3. All prisoners of war and civilian internees to be released or exchanged.

These three operations to begin immediately after the conclusion of the general agreement on the cessation of hostilities and to be completed within two months at the latest after the date of the signing of such agreement.

4. Execution of the above provisions to be supervised by International Commissions, the members of which shall be proposed by the Conference and chosen as far as possible from States which have not taken part in the fighting in Indo-China.

Other measures will be proposed in due course by Cambodia according to the solution to be adopted for Viet Nam, its immediate neighbour, with which it has lived a life in common for almost a century and whose destiny is bound to affect the Khmer country.

(332) <u>PROPOSAL BY THE D.R.V. DELEGATION TO THE GENEVA CONFERENCE</u>, May 10, 1954

Source: *Documents on the Discussion of Korea and Indochina*, pp. 116-117.

The D.R.V. peace proposal also called for regroupment zones but provided for free elections in each country and recognition of zones administered by the anti-French resistance organizations pending the elections.

1. The sovereignty and independence of Viet Nam over the whole territory of Viet Nam to be recognised by France as well as the sovereignty and independence of Khmer and Pathet Lao.

2. An agreement for the withdrawal of all foreign troops from the territories of Viet Nam, Khmer and Pathet Lao to be concluded within a period to be fixed by agreement between the belligerent parties. Before the withdrawal of such troops, agreement must be reached on the question of assembly areas for the French troops in Viet Nam, and special attention must be given in this connexion to reducing the number of these assembly areas to the minimum. It is understood that the French troops shall refrain from interfering in the affairs of the local authorities in the districts where they are stationed.

(333) SUPPLEMENT BY D.R.V. DELEGATION CHIEF PHAM VAN DONG TO THE GENEVA CONFERENCE, May 10, 1954 (Extract)

Source: *New Times* (Moscow), May 15, 1954, Supplement, pp. 7-13.

The D.R.V. delegation, after blaming the pressure of the U.S. for the continuation of the war and charging the U.S. with trying to draw other countries into the war, proposed a ceasefire, the immediate regroupment of French forces (referred to as "dislocation" in the translation) in Viet-nam withdrawal of all foreign forces from all three countries within an agreed period, and free elections in all three countries to be supervised by local commissions. The reference to "all foreign troops" in the proposal was meant to include Vietnamese troops serving in Laos and Cambodia. The Vietnamese proposal also specified the reprisal against those engaged on either side during the war would be prohibited something which the French proposal had not mentioned.

Towards the close of 1947, the French colonialists launched a major offensive in Viet Bac, in the hope that its success would bring the war to a close. But the offensive failed; the Vietnamese scored a resounding victory and demonstrated their strength.

This ushered in a new period in the war. The fighting became more intensive and violent on all fronts, and the situation steadily developed in favour of Viet-Nam.

It was at this juncture that the American imperialists began their intervention in the Indo-China war.

AMERICAN INTERVENTION.
AMERICAN RESPONSIBILITY FOR THE PROLONGATION AND
EXTENSION OF THE WAR

The American imperialist policy of intervening in the Indo-China war is a component part of the policy of strength which the U.S.A. has pursued ever since the second world war with the object of establishing its world domination.

The weakening of France as a result of the Indo-China war and her need of American assistance to continue that war, created the necessary pretext and conditions for U.S. intervention.

The purpose of that intervention is gradually to oust the French from Indo-China and convert the latter into a U.S. colony, seize its economy and natural resources, suppress the national-liberation and democratic movement of its peoples and turn the country into a springboard for the conquest of Southeast Asia, into an American war base. But American imperialism has another object too in intensifying its intervention in the Indo-China war and prolonging and extending it. It is endeavouring to save the American economy from the grave threat of crisis which has become especially pronounced since the Korean armistice.

The record of U.S. intervention clearly reveals these aims, and the methods employed at various stages to attain them.

In August 1947, an American diplomat visited Hong Kong and had talks with Bao Dai. Later, in September 1947, he conferred with the French authorities in Indo-China and then went to France for negotiations with the French government. In December 1947, he insisted on American intervention in Indo-China, stating that "Bao Dai ought to be recognized and helped to build up an army." He categorically told the French: "If France rejects this course, America will have to take the matter into her own hands."

A new phase in American imperialist intervention in the Indo-China war began in 1950, when the Chinese People's Liberation Army defeated the Chiang Kai-shek forces and completed the liberation of the vast China mainland.

In the early part of 1950, the Jessup mission to Indo-China decided that American military and economic teams should be sent to Indo-China. Jessup also promised the French colonialists military assistance in exchange for an undertaking to set up at an early date a so-called national government that would have an army of its own and enjoy broad powers in matters of foreign relations. The Jessup mission was followed by official American promises of intervention in Indo-China.

The heavy defeat it sustained at the close of 1950, greatly worsened the position of the French Expeditionary Corps, which now had to contend with increasingly powerful attacks of the Vietnamese people's army. The American interventionists took advantage of this to intensify their interference in the war.

The conclusion of the Korean armistice in 1953 prompted the American imperialists to devote more attention to Indo-China. U.S. ruling circles emphasized the "importance" of Indo-China and the necessity of helping the French colonialists. Last year witnessed new victories for the peoples of Viet-Nam, Khmer and Pathet Lao on all the battle fronts. In France, too, the popular struggle against the war in Indo-China scored new successes in 1953, spreading to the broadest sections of the population and to all segments of public opinion. The fact that the French colonialists had reached a dead end, that their position was desperate, was a convenient pretext for increasing American imperialist intervention. It took the form of larger military credits, and also of direct American imperialist participation in the strategic direction of the war, notably in the preparation and execution of the Navarre plan.

Yet, despite this steadily increasing American intervention, the French forces have sustained one defeat after another, while the peoples of Viet-Nam, Khmer and Pathet Lao continue to score victory after victory. In the latter part of 1953 and in the opening months of this year, the armed forces of Viet-Nam, Khmer and Pathet Lao intensified their activity on all the fronts and scored further substantial victories. The Navarre plan, far from improving the enemy's strategic position, made it still worse. The American imperialists took advantage of this fact, too, to increase their intervention: the 1954 military aid program was considerably increased, more aircraft and personnel were dispatched for direct participation in the attempt to annihilate the peoples of Viet-Nam, Khmer and Pathet Lao. In exchange for all this, the Americans demand a share in the training of the so-called "national" army.

The imposing victories scored by the peoples of Indo-China in these past months, the progress of the peace movement in France and the prospects for restoring peace offered by the present Geneva Conference, are causing the American interventionists much uneasiness. They are now working out new schemes ("united action," "collective security" . . .) in an effort to drag out and extend the war with the aid of the French "war to a finish" advocates. This policy of coercion and war has aroused protests from the peoples and governments of various Southeast Asian countries.

The American interventionists are trying to justify that policy on the plea of defending the United States, defending Southeast Asia, defending liberty.

Defence of the United States? In other words, we, the peoples of Indo-China, represent a menace to the United States! No sane-minded person can even for a moment believe that absurdity.

Defence of Southeast Asia? The peace and security of Southeast Asia, and of Asia generally, are indeed imperilled, but not by the peoples of Indo-China or of any other Asian country. They are imperilled by the American imperialists.

Defence of liberty? But it is we, the oppressed peoples of Indo-China, the oppressed nations of the world, who are the staunchest and most consistent defenders of liberty, liberty for us and for all peoples to choose their own form of government and to resist all threats of imperialist enslavement.

The following facts are indicative of the evolution of American intervention in the Indo-China war:

The American imperialists are converting France into a weapon of their policy and, at the same time, are preparing to oust her from Indo-China. But the "relentless war" advocates in France, in their reactionary blindness, insist on continuing the war. To do that, they must have American assistance and, consequently, surrender themselves to the mercy of the American interventionists, who, at the opportune moment, will undertake the burden of "replacing" the impotent or intransigent French. On the other hand, in compelling the French to continue the war, the American imperialists want to weaken France in order the more conveniently to bring her under their sway in Europe too.

That is one aspect of American intervention.

Another is the attempt to set up a so-called national regime which France is expected to grant complete "independence." The formation of a so-called national government, and the formation of a "national" army independent of the French Expeditionary Corps, are the conditions which the American imperialists are imposing on the French colonialists as the price of military aid. This would enable them to bring under their direct control the so-called national governments and armies, complete the process of ousting the French, give full scope to their policy of "using Indo-Chinese against Indo-Chinese," and lastly, intensify armed action and extend the area of the war.

Every conceivable pressure is being exerted on France by the rulers of America to enlarge the area of the war in Indo-China. They demand the dispatch of more French contingents, Legionaires and mercenaires of every description, including German nazis, and African troops. The U.S. and French imperialists want to continue the war in furtherance of their own interests, but at the cost of the blood of others.

They even count on involving other countries in the war. And all for the purpose of prolonging and extending it with the object of turning Indo-China and its neighbours into American colonies. Such are the plans of the sworn enemies of peace in Indo-China. But they are being foiled by the heroic resistance of Indo-China's peoples. And that resistance is growing ever more powerful and effective. The enemy's strategic position is now more difficult than ever, particularly after the big victory scored by the D.R.V. Liberation Army at Dien Bien Phu on the eve of our conference. The significance of that victory is clear to all. Confident in their rights, and strong in their unity, the peoples of Indo-China are fully determined to frustrate all the plans of the American interventionists.

And so, the American interventionists and the French "war to a finish" advocates are today the chief obstacle to a cessation of hostilities and the restoration of peace in Indo-China.

In their attempts to continue and extend the Indo-China war, the American interventionists are demanding the participation of a number of countries in that war, thereby creating a new menace to peace in Asia and the world generally.

This aggressive policy and these incitements to war run counter to the interests of the peoples of Viet-Nma, Khmer and Pathet Lao, run counter also to the interests of the French and American peoples. The peoples of Viet-Nam, Khmer and Pathet Lao want peace, independence, unity and democracy; they want friendly relations with all the nations of the world. And their aspirations coincide with the interests of all the nations. The cause of the peoples of Viet-Nam, Khmer and Pathet Lao is the cause of peace, and is therefore bound to triumph.

SUCCESSES IN RESISTANCE AND CONSTRUCTION

The peoples of Viet-Nam, Khmer and Pathet Lao are fighting a heroic battle against the imperialist invaders.

In the course of their resistance, the people and army of the Democratic Republic of Viet-Nam have fostered and strengthened their forces of resistance militarily, politically, economically and culturally. At present the democratic republican regime has, under the guidance of the government, been firmly established on more than three quarters of the entire territory of the country. And throughout this area the government's program is being successfully implemented. It calls for comprehensive national unity irrespective of class, race, or political and religious beliefs; guaranteed democratic freedoms, notably freedom of belief and religious worship; an economic and financial policy designed to increase production, reduce taxation, curb inflation, stabilize prices and currency and develop home and foreign trade; gradual implementation of a just and fair agrarian policy; elimination of illiteracy and promotion of education.

These achievements have won the government of the Democratic Republic a high prestige and influence in all the areas temporarily occupied by the enemy. That fact has long since been acknowledged by political leaders who have closely studied the situation in Indo-China and by journalists who have visited our country. This prestige and influence are due to the fact that the Democratic Republic expresses the desire of the entire Vietnamese people for peace, national independence, territorial integrity and democratic freedoms.

With regard to foreign policy, the government of the D.R.V. announced, on January 14, 1950, that it was "prepared to establish diplomatic relations with countries which respect Viet-Nam's right to equality, territorial integrity and national sovereignty, with a view to jointly safeguarding world peace and promoting democracy throughout the world."

The Democratic Republic of Viet-Nam has been recognized by countries with an aggregate population of over 800 million, and it enjoys the cordial sympathy of the vast majority of the population of all other countries.

The outstanding achievements of the D.R.V. government in the resistance war and in constructive development are due to the correctness of its policy of "waging prolonged resistance by our own efforts." The Vietnamese have unswerving faith in their boundless potentialities, and are bending every effort to mobilize, develop and organize these potentialities to crush the imperialist invader and to build up their country.

The people and the strength of the people are an invaluable asset unavailable to imperialist aggressors in spite of all their moved to deceive, corrupt and suppress the people. The imperialists prate about liberty, independence and democracy, when it is they who are the malignant foes of liberty, independence and democracy. What they call liberty, independence and democracy is nothing but deceit, a camouflage for their policy of conquest and subjugation. In the areas they control, they have launched total war, reducing villages to ashes and vast rice fields to barren wastes. Theirs is a systematic policy of pauperization, of corrupting the masses in order to make it the easier to use Indo-Chinese against Indo-Chinese.

As for the government set up in the temporarily occupied territory, all the world, even our enemies, know and admit that it represents only itself and those who appoint and dissolve it, that it has no support among the people and that its sole function is to conduct a policy of imperialist war under the guise of independence and democracy.

Following the victory of the August revolution in Viet-Nam, the people of Pathet Law rose in revolt and wrested the power from the Japanese fascists. On October 12, 1945, a Provisional Government of Pathet Law was established and the independence of the country proclaimed. King Sasavang Vong abdicated.

Ever since the French reinvaded the country the government of Pathet Lao has given leadership to the people's resistance. Towards the close of 1950, a conference of representatives from all parts of Pathet Lao appointed a new government and drew up a politcal program for the country, a program of armed resistance and national construction. The Pathet Lao resistance movement has scored many successes, especially since 1953, having destroyed a large part of the enemy's forces and liberated over half of the country. The Pathet Lao Resistance Government has carried out democratic reforms in the liberated areas, taking all the necessary measures to raise the people's living standards and enhance their strength in the struggle.

In Khmer, the French colonialists, when they set out to reconquer the country in October 1945, encountered the resistance of a people determined to fight for liberation from colonial bondage and monarchism.

A national conference of people's representatives held in April 1950 and attended by delegates from every class of society, appointed a National Liberation Committee and proclaimed the independence of Khmer. The first action of the National Liberation Committee was to proclaim the democratic freedoms. Subsequently, that Committee was reorganized into a Provisional Government, and under its guidance the people of Khmer have scored many a victory in their struggle against the French colonialists, the American interventionists and the monarchy. Democratic government has been set up in the liberated areas, and living standards raised. This has heightened the prestige of the government, which enjoys support also in the districts temporarily held by the enemy.

In their struggle against imperialist aggression, the peoples of Viet-Nam, Khmer and Pathet Lao have the sympathy and ardent support of the freedom-loving nations of the world, because theirs is a righteous struggle and also because the aggressive war which the imperialists have unleashed in Indo-China and which they are trying to prolong and extend constitutes a serious menace to peace in Asia and the world generally.

The nations of the world, and specifically the nations of Asia and Southeast Asia and the great People's Republic of China, the great Indian people, the peoples of Indonesia, Burma, etc., have demonstrated their staunch solidarity with the Indo-Chinese. In Asia and Southeast Asia, as everywhere else in the world, public opinion was outraged by the recent American imperialist moves for so-called "united action and collective security" which, in actual fact, represent a threat to extend the war and endanger the peace of Asia and the whole world.

THE WAY TO RE-ESTABLISH PEACE

The facts I have give clearly show:

1. That the most profound desire and legitimate right of the peoples of Viet-Nam, Khmer and Pathet Lao, is peace, independence, unity and democracy. They are the sacred right of every nation. And when foreign aggressors trampled upon this aspiration and right, the three peoples were forced to take to arms in defence of the very existence of their countries.

2. That ever since its inception, the Democratic Republic of Viet-Nam has unswervingly pursued a policy of peace and friendship with France. Its government negotiated with the government of France on three occasions, and concluded with it the preliminary agreement of March 6, 1946, and the modus vivendi agreement of September 14, 1946. But the French colonialists have persistently

sought to torpedo all negotiations, and have violated the agreements in an endeavour to reimpose their colonial rule by means of war. Now the American interventionists and the war advocates in France are exerting every effort to extend the Indo-China war. They represent the chief obstacle to cessation of hotilities and restoration of peace.

3. That the people and government of the Democratic Republic of Viet-Nam have always striven for peace and are "determined to support the policy of settling all international conflicts by negotiation, securing relaxation of international tension and establishing and maintaining friendly relations between all the nations of the world" (Report of the D.R.V. Government to the Third Session of the National Assembly, December 1, 1953). President Ho Chi Minh, replying to questions put by a correspondent of the *Expressen* in the closing days of November 1953, stated that the people and government of the Democratic Republic were prepared to negotiate with a view to the restoration of peace in Indo-China.

This is the position held in common by the people and government of the Democratic Republic of Viet-Nam, the people and Resistance Government of Khmer, and the people and Resistance Government of Pathet Lao.

The Foreign Ministers of the respective three countries endorsed the decision taken in Berlin to hold a conference in Geneva to discuss the restoration of peace in Indo-China.

Proceeding from these facts, our delegation declares, on behalf of the government of the Democratic Republic of Viet-Nam:

"The people and government of the Democratic Republic of Viet-Nam, and the peoples and Resistance Governments of Khmer and Pathet Lao are prepared to negotiate the restoration of peace in Indo-China on the basis of recognition of the national rights of the Indo-China peoples: national unity and independence and the democratic freedoms, thereby creating the conditions for a resumption of friendly relations between the peoples of Indo-China and France, based on equality and respect for one another's interests. That is the way to re-establish a just, honourable, stable and lasting peace in Indo-China, the only way of effectively safeguarding peace and security in Southeast Asia and Asia, and one that would effectively contribute to a lessening of international tension and to the maintenance and promotion of peace throughout the world."

The American interventionists fear peace. They are working in every way to mobilize the most reactionary and bellicose elements to frustrate every effort towards restoration of peace in Indo-China. The governments and peoples of the Democratic Republic of Viet-Nam, Khmer and Pathet Lao are prepared to unite their efforts with those of the people of France and of men of goodwill everywhere in order to ensure that the Geneva Conference leads to a satisfactory peace settlement in Indo-China.

The delegation of the Democratic Republic of Viet-Nam is prepared to work with other delegations at this conference to ensure its success.

In conformity with the aforesaid, the delegation of the Democratic Republic of Viet-Nam submits to the conference the following proposals for the restoration of peace in Indo-China:

RESTORATION OF PEACE IN INDO-CHINA

1. Recognition by France of the sovereignty and independence of Viet-Nam over the entire territory of the country, and recognition of the sovereignty and independence of Khmer and Pathet Lao.

2. Agreement to withdraw all foreign troops from Viet-Nam, Khmer and Pathet Lao within time limits to be agreed upon by the belligerents. Pending withdrawal of the foreign forces, agreement shall be reached as to the dislocation of French forces in Viet-Nam, particular attention being paid to limiting

the number of dislocation areas to a minimum. It shall be provided that the French forces may not interfere in the affairs of the local administration in the areas of their dislocation.

3. The holding of free general elections in Viet-Nam, Khmer and Pathet Lao. The convening of consultative conferences of representatives of the governments of the two sides in Viet-Nam, Khmer and Pathet Lao respectively, for the purpose of preparing and conducting, with guarantees of freedom of activity for patriotic parties, groups and public organizations, the free general elections with a view to establishing a single government in each country. All outside interference shall be precluded. Local commissions shall be set up to supervise the preparation and conduct of the elections.

Pending the establishment of a single government in each of the aforementioned countries, the governments of the two sides shall respectively administer the areas which are under their control after the settlement prescribed by the armistice agreement.

4. Declaration by the delegation of the Democratic Republic of Viet-Nam that the government of the D.R.V. is prepared to examine the question of entering the French Union on a voluntary basis, and the conditions of such entry. Similar declarations to be made by the governments of Khmer and Pathet Lao.

5. Recognition by the Democratic Republic of Viet-Nam, and by Khmer and Pathet Lao, that France has cultural and economic interests in these countries.

Following the formation of single governments in Viet-Nam, Khmer and Pathet Lao, the economic and cultural relations of these countries with France shall be subject to settlement in accordance with the principle of equality and respect for reciprocal interests. Pending the formation of single governments in the three countries, Indo-China's economic and cultural relations with France shall temporarily remain as at present. However, in areas where communication and commercial relations have been disrupted, they may be re-established by mutual agreement.

The citizens of each side shall enjoy privileged status, to be determined later, in respect of domicile, movement and business activity in the territory of the other side.

6. Each side undertakes not to persecute persons who collaborated with the other side during the war.

7. Mutual exchange of war prisoners.

8. Implementation of the measures enumerated in points 1-7 shall be preceded by a cease-fire in Indo-China in accordance with agreements concluded between France and each of the three countries, which shall contain the following provisions.

a) A complete and simultaneous cease-fire throughout the territory of Indo-China by all the armed forces of the belligerents--land, naval and air. With a view to consolidating the armistice, the two sides shall, in each of the three Indo-Chinese countries, delimit the areas under their control, and shall not hinder the passage of troops of the other side through their territory in the course of this delimitation.

b) No new land, naval or air units or personnel, or weapons and ammunition of any description, shall be dispatched to Indo-China.

c) Supervision of the armistice agreement and the appointment for this purpose of mixed commissions of representatives of the two side in each of the three countries.

****

The delegation of the Democratic Republic of Viet-Nam is confident that its proposals will meet with the support of the Resistance Governments and peoples of Khmer and Pathet Lao.

It should be perfectly clear that restoration of peace in Indo-China requires that the shipment of American weapons and ammunition to Indo-China be stopped, that American military missions, advisers and instructors be recalled, and American interference in the affairs of Indo-China, in whatever shape or form, be abandoned.

The proposals of our delegation provide for the establishment of economic and cultural relations between France and the Democratic Republic of Viet-Nam. This means that the D.R.V. is prepared to establish close economic relations with France, develop trade with her and, if necessary, use her mercantile marine and, on certain conditions, retain French cultural institutions in Viet-Nam.

The purpose of our proposals is threefold:

1) Cessation of the war and establishment of peace;
2) Restoration of peace to be based on recognition of the national rights of the Indo-China peoples;
3) Friendly relations between the countries of Indo-China and France.

It should be emphasized that a fundamental stipulation of our proposal is restoration of peace based on recognition of the national rights of the peoples of Viet-Nam, Khmer and Pathet Lao.

Solution of that fundamental question, as of the question of Indo-China's relations with France, will lead to the establishment of a just, honourable, stable and lasting peace.

Another thing to be emphasized is that our proposal calls for restoration of peace throughout the whole of Indo- China. History has shown that in matters both of war and peace, the territory of Indo-China is indivisible. From this it follows that cessation of hostilities and restoration of peace must be simultaneous in the three countries--Viet-Nam, Khmer and Pathet Lao, and must follow identical principles, methods and procedures, with due account for the national sovereignty and the specific conditions of each of the countries.

Thus, settlement of all the questions involved in restoration of peace in Indo-China requires the participation of all the parties concerned, without exception.

We feel sure that our proposals are in keeping with the requirements of the present-day situation: both restoration of peace based on recognition of the national rights of the peoples of Indo-China, and establishment of friendly relations between Indo-China and France.

We feel sure that every citizen of Viet-Nam, Khmer and Pathet Lao who loves his country and wants to see national independence, unity, the democratic freedoms and peace established in his land, will wholeheartedly support our proposal.

We feel sure that the mass of the French people, and the different political and public circles in France who want to see the war brought to a close and friendship established between their country and the countries of Indo-China, will agree with us.

We feel sure that the peoples of Southeast Asia, and with them all the peoples of Asia, who are faced with the threat of an extension of the Indo-China war, and the peoples of the whole world, who, after the cease-fire in Korea, are insisting on the termination of the war in Indo-China, will side with us.

And it is precisely for that reason that we submit our proposal to this conference, in the firm belief that it provides a fruitful basis for settling the Indo-China issue.

That concludes my statement. But I should like to say a few words regarding the statement of the French delegation.

1) Insofar as that statement deals with developments in Indo-China in the recent or distant past, my statement provides material for a more objective and

fair appreciation of those developments, especially concerning relations between the Indo-China countries and France.

No one can in good faith deny that nearly a century has passed since the French conquest of, and the establishment of French colonial rule in, the China countries; that during World War II the French authorities in Indo-China surrendered to Japan; that after Japan's capitulation the Vietnamese rose in revolt, took power into their own hands and founded the Democratic Republic of Viet-Nam; that France concluded agreements with the Democratic Republic of Viet-Nam, later violated by the colonialists, who were bent on reconquering our country by force of arms; that the resistance offered by the peoples of Viet-Nam, Khmer and Pathet Lao is becoming more and more victorious; that the continuation of the war in these past several years is due to American imperialist intervention, and that the advocates of the war, in conjunction with the American interventionists, are using every conceivable means to prolong and extend it.

2) In connection with the proposal of the French delegation, the following preliminary remark must be made:

Inasmuch as the proposal fails to reckon with the facts of the military situation in the Indo-China states, it cannot serve as a serious basis for a satisfactory solution of the cease-fire question and for the restoration of peace throughout Indo-China, for such a solution must embrace both the military and political issues.

It proceeds, furthermore, from the obsolete imperialist and colonialist conception which is out of all keeping with the present situation in Indo-China and the world generally.

In contrast to this, the proposal advanced by the Democratic Republic of Viet-Nam pays due account to the situation that has arisen in the three Indo-China countries and furnishes a broad basis for a positive settlement and for restoration of peace in Indo-China; it is a contribution to a satisfactory solution of this problem, that is, to the establishment of a stable, lasting, just and honourable peace.

(334) SPEECH BY FOREIGN MINISTER MOLOTOV TO THE GENEVA CONFERENCE, May 14, 1954 (Extract)

Source: *Documents on the Discussion of Korea and Indochina,* pp. 127-131.

Calling attention to the danger of American military intervention in Indochina, Molotov called on the conference to stop the fighting in Indochina as soon as possible with an agreement satisfying the legitimate claims of the Indochinese peoples. He again criticized the French proposal for its failure to deal with political problems.

There is a growing danger of an extension of the war in Indo-China.

The more insistently the peoples' demand that an end be put to the war in Indo-China, the more frequent are the statements made by influential circles in the United States of America on the necessity of open-armed intervention by the United States of America in the war in Indo-China. Strenuous efforts are now being made to find at least the appearance of a pretext of any kind for such intervention. Particular care is being taken that the United States of America should not find itself absolutely isolated in carrying out the relevant new plans for aggression in Asia.

Of late we have witnessed persistent attempts to form for these purposes a certain *bloc* with the participation of the United States of America, France, Great Britain and some other States. As the time for the Geneva Conference drew nearer, these attempts became more persistent than ever. No less a Conference began strenuously to advocate extending United States intervention in the

Indo-China war. This time there was talk of creating another "defence community" although here again it was, of course, not at all concerned with the defence of the United States of America , France, Great Britain or any other State, but with forming a new military *bloc* for combating the national liberation movement of the peoples of Indo-China and South-East Asia.

It is obvious that the creation of the new aggressive *bloc* also serves definite military strategic aims. It means the establishment of new American bases in this area, which cannot be viewed with indifference by those states whose safety is affected in connexion with the plans for the creation of the aforesaid *bloc* and the extension of American intervention in Indo-China.

It is said that the planned new *bloc*, as well as American intervention in Indo-China, was necessary in order to protect the peoples of South-East Asia against some sort of danger from outside. Leaving aside the question as to where the real threat to the people and independence of these countries comes from, it is legitimate to ask--is it proper to proclaim oneself the protector of the peoples of these countries, which, as is well known, have not requested the United States to do so? Is it not at least immodest to take upon oneself the role of self-styled protector of the peoples of South-East Asia, when these peoples want only one thing--peace, national independence and freedom.

At present, as you are aware, work is going on behind the scenes on the formation of this new aggressive *bloc*. The purpose of this *bloc* is to unite States interested in maintaining colonial regimes and prepared for this reason to extend the war in Asia.

The Geneva Conference is taking place at the very moment when efforts are being made to extend the war in South-East Asia instead of restoring peace in Indo-China. That will be the outcome of the new aggressive plans now being worked out by influential circles in the United States of America, about which so much has been said and written of late.

In recent years, the United States of America has intervened increasingly in events in Indo-China, following here also a policy of supporting the colonial system. It will suffice to quote the figures relating to the financial aid given by the United States to France and the Indo-Chinese Governments associated with France over the past few years. The relevant figures for the past few years are as follows: in 1952-53 - 314 million dollars, in 1953-54 - more than one thousand million dollars, which amounts approximately to four-fifths of the total expenditure on the war in Indo-China. For the 1954-55 financial year, the estimate for these appropriations is 1,133 million dollars. And, as we know, he who pays the piper calls the tune.

These ever larger appropriations made by the United States of America were, devoted mainly to financing the colonial war being waged in Indo-China. At the present time, one can already speak of direct American intervention in the Indo-Chinese colonial war.

American intervention in Indo-China is now increasing steadily, taking the form of the supply of arms and war materials, and the dispatch of military advisers, instructors, technicians, &c. This constitutes the main obstacle to the restoration of peace in Indo-China. Moreover, the result of this intervention is to extend the scale of military operations in Indo-China with all the attendant consequences.

The intervention, further, shows the desire of the United States of America to establish its domination in Indo-China as a matter of fact. There, much has already been done to replace the colonial domination of one country by the colonial domination of another.

The intervention of the United States of America in Indo-Chinese affairs is, in addition, evidence of its desire to bring about a conflict between the peoples of Indo-China fighting for their freedom and independence, and other peoples of Asia; and to exploit the conflicts between the peoples of Asia for its own ends.

All this testifies to the fact that, in the East as well, intensified preparations are being made for a new world war.

Explaining the significance of these American plans in the Far East, the
United States Secretary of State, on January 13 this year made the following
statement: -

"The interest of the United States in that part of the area is, from
a strategic standpoint, very closely tied in to what is commonly called
the offshore island chain. The offshore island chain has, in essence,
two land bases: At the north, the Korean mainland; and in the south,
we would hope in Indo-china. Then in between are the islands themselves - Japan, the Ryukyus, embracing Okinawa, Formosa, the Philippines,
Australia and New Zealand. The United States has a security tie, of one
sort or another, with each of these areas, not formalized in some cases,
in the form of a treaty, but nevertheless very real and very actual."

It is clear from this statement by the United States Secretary of State that
the rights and destinies of the peoples of Indo-China or of the other peoples
of this area are of no concern whatever to the persons engaged in working out
the strategic plans of the United States of America. On the other hand, it is
evident that these American strategic plans, which are preparing to extend the
war in this area, constitute a serious threat to the peaceful development of the
peoples of the whole of this extensive region. It is not yet certain whether
the United States will succeed in building up a military *bloc* with the participation of various states in order to carry out their plans; but these plans are
obviously calculated to support colonial regimes in Asia by all and any means.

A great responsibility is incumbent on the Geneva Conference as to whether
it willfulfillits obligation to oppose these aggressive plans for extending the
war in South-East Asia. Only decisive counteraction to these plans will fulfill
the purpose of the Geneva Conference, the aim of which was and continued to be
to restore peace in Indo-China.

What is meant by helping to restore peace in Indo-China? The Geneva Conference cannot interpret this task as meaning that the cessation of military
operations in Indo-China should become, as it were, a cunningly devised respite
for one of the parties, intent on exploiting this breathing-space for preparing
to extend the war into Indo-China. The task of the Geneva Conference should be
understood as meaning that it must bring about a cessation of fighting in Indo-
China as soon as possible, and at the same time reach such an agreement as would
enable the legitimate claims of the Indo-Chinese peoples to be satisfied in regard to securing their national independence and democratic rights.

The Head of the delegation of the Democratic Republic of Viet Nam has at
this Conference made proposals which provide a basis for the settlement of the
Indo-Chinese question, and a possibility of securing the restoration of peace
in Indo-China. So far, we have heard here neither any justified criticism of
these proposals nor any willingness to accept any particular points in them.

In the opinion of the Soviet delegation, the gist of these proposals, if
we select the most important points, is as follows: -

1. France shall insure recognition of the sovereignty and independence of
Viet Nam, and also of Khmer and Pathet-Lao.

At the same time, there shall be an agreement for the withdrawal of all
foreign troops from the territory of Viet Nam, Khmer and Pathet-Lao within a
period to be fixed by agreement between the two parties.

2. Free general elections shall be in Viet Nam, Khmer and Pathet-Lao, and
a single democratic government shall be set up in each of these states as the
result of these elections.

Prior to these elections, advisory conferences of the representatives of
both parties shall be held in Viet Nam, Khmer and Pathet-Lao, and freedom of

activity for the patriotic parties, groups and social organizations shall be ensured.

3. The Government of the Democratic Republic of Viet Nam, and also the governments of Khmer and Pathet-Lao, shall declare their readiness to examine the question of these States entering the French Union in accordance with the principles of free consent.

In addition to the Governments of Viet Nam, Khmer and Pathet-Lao shall recognize the fact that France has economic and cultural interests in these states, and the relevant questions shall be regulated in accordance with the principles of equality and mutual interest.

4. The implementation of the above measures and the execution of the other measures mentioned in the draft of the Democratic Republic of Viet Nam must be preceded by the cessation of military operations in Indo-China and the conclusion of appropriate agreements completely stopping the movement to Indo-China, from outside, of any fresh troops, arms and military supplies of any kind.

In addition to the points I have enumerated, agreement will also have to be reached on a number of other questions: exchange of prisoners of war; undertaking to refrain from action against persons who have collaborated with the opposing party during the war, &c. It is also essential that the four points mentioned above should take due account of the legitimate desires of both parties in reaching agreement on both political and military questions.

These aims are fully attainable provided both parties show a real desire to establish a genuinely stable and lasting peace in Indo-China.

The aims of the proposals made by the Democratic Republic of Viet Nam is to reach an agreement with France. These proposals are founded on the expediency of mutual recognition and of the principles of justice and honour, on the basis of which it is perfectly possible to establish new friendly relations between the peoples of Indo-China and France. These proposals may perhaps not satisfy the advocates of the colonial policy, with their clinging to old, obsolete ideas. These persons, by rejecting the possibility of reaching an agreement on the Indo-Chinese question, are furthering not national interests but the interests of those foreign aggressive circles who are anxious to extend the war instead of to restore peace in Indo-China.

At our first meeting, the French delegation put forward its proposals for the settlement of the Indo-Chinese question. In the meantime, we have had an opportunity to make a close study both of the French plan and of the proposals submitted by other delegations.

A defect of the French proposals is that they do not deal at all with political problems. But everybody realises that the cessation of the protracted war in Indo-China cannot be divorced from the solution of some at least of the problems of that nature.

The French draft reveals an under-estimation of the struggle for national liberation that has widely developed in Laos and Cambodia. Yet the question of the situation in Indo-China cannot be narrowed down simply to events in Viet Nam.

Moreover, the French draft also refers to guarantees for the agreements reached at this conference. The draft reads: -

"These agreements shall be guaranteed by the States participating in the Geneva Conference. In the event of any violation thereof there shall be an immediate consultation between the guarantor States for the purpose of taking appropriate measures either individually or collectively."

The Soviet Union delegation cannot entirely agree with this proposal. It recognises, however, the acceptibility in principle, of the French proposal that the agreements reached at this Conference should be guaranteed by the States participating in the Geneva Conference, and that in the event of any violation of the agreements there should be consultations between the guarantor States. The object of these consultations should be the adoption of collective measures to implement the agreements. It would be desirable for the other participants at this Conference to make known their attitude with regard to this important proposal of the French delegation.

It also pointed out that the draft of the Democratic Republic of Viet Nam provides for the establishment of supervisory machinery to ensure implementation of the provisions of the agreement on the cessation of hostilities only by joint committees of representatives of the belligerent parties in each of the three countries. In this connection it is emphasized that the draft does not provide for supervision by international bodies of any kind.

In view of the great importance of reaching agreement on this matter, the Soviet Union delegation suggests an addition to these proposals. It would be possible to come to an agreement that supervision of implementation of the provisions of the agreement on the cessation of hostilities should be entrusted to commissions composed of representatives of neutral countries. No insuperable difficulties should be encountered in determining the composition of these commissions.

The Soviet Union delegation accordingly submits the following addition to the above mentioned draft proposals. *(See Document No. 16.)*

In connexion with the Geneva Conference, France is faced with the important problem of deciding what course to adopt in Indo-China, which involves extending the war on behalf of foreign aggressive plans and bodes no good for the satisfaction of French national interests. The other alternative is negotiations, first of all with the Viet Namese people, and further steps of a similar nature to bring the war to an end and establish peace in Indo-China as speedily as possible. Adoption of the latter alternative would make it possible to establish mutual understanding and friendly relations between France and the peoples of Indo-China.

The Geneva Conference must do everything in its power to promote this peaceful settlement of the Indo-Chinese question.

The Soviet Union delegation will, of course, make known its attitude with regard to all the questions asked by the United Kingdom representative at the last meeting. It must be stated even at this stage, however, that it would be inappropriate to narrow the matter down to these questions and to by-pass those problems of a military and political character that have already been raised by events in Indo-China.

The Soviet Union delegation, like the delegation of the Chinese People's Republic, attaches great importance to the proposals and hopes that they will receive all due attention. At the same time, the Soviet Union delegation expresses its confidence that the Geneva Conference will also examine any other proposals that will really help to establish peace in Indo-China.

The Soviet Government believes that a settlement of the Indo-Chinese question, due regard being paid to the national interests of the peoples of Indo-China, would constitute an important contribution not only to the cause of strengthening peace in Asia, but to that of strengthening peace throughout the world.

(335) SPEECH BY SMITH TO THE GENEVA CONFERENCE, MAY 10, 1954

Source: *Department of State Bulletin,* May 24, 1954, pp. 733-734.

The U.S. delegation supported the French proposal as a basis for discussion but pointedly refrained from any commitment to guarantee the final settlement.

The U.S. delegation warmly welcomes the proposals made and accepted this afternoon for the evacuation of the long-suffering wounded of Dien-Bien-Phu and hopes sincerely that this evacuation will be effected without delay.

Regrettably, for the subsequent two hours of our session we listened to a remarkable distortion of the events of the past few years in Indochina. The Viet Minh spokesman is well trained in the Communist technique of distorting history and calling black white. The world has learned to evaluate such spurious allegations. The charges made against the United States by the Viet Minh representative are substantially identical with those made by other Communist representatives during the opening phase of the Korean discussion. They have been already amply and adequately refuted, and I see no reason to divert this Conference from its important task by according them further attention at this time. I cannot refrain, however, from commenting on this remarkable effrontery in describing the brutal Viet Minh aggression against Cambodia and Laos as a movement of "liberation." At present I will merely say that after his statement, it is extremely difficult to believe that the Viet Minh representative has come to this Conference with any intention of negotiating a just and durable peace.

The United States has come here with sincere hopes that the work of this Conference at Geneva will result in the restoration of peace in Indochina and in the opportunity for Cambodia, Laos, and Viet-Nam to enjoy their independence under conditions of a real and lasting peace.

The United States has watched with sympathy the development of the peoples of Indochina toward independence. The United States and many other countries have recognized the three States of Cambodia, Laos, and Viet-Nam. We have followed with great interest the negotiations which have been undertaken by France and the Associated States to perfect the independence of the Associated States.

The United States has shown in many ways its sympathy for the effort of the Associated States to safeguard their independence. We have provided material aid to France and the Associated States to assist them in this effort and have given them support to enable them to resist open and covert invasion from without their borders. We will continue to do so, for the simple reason that it is the wish of the American people to assist any nation that is determined to defend its liberty and independence.

The United States maintains that the first principle of any settlement in Indochina must be to assure the independence and freedom of the States of Cambodia, Laos, and Viet-Nam.

The United States also maintains that any settlement in Indochina must give assurance of real and lasting peace. To this end, the United States believes that any settlement must be preceded by an armistice agreement which incorporates effective and adequate safeguards.

The United States maintains that such an armistice agreement can be effective only under international supervision. The United States, therefore, believes that any settlement must include provisions for effective international supervision and assurance of powers and privileges on the part of the international supervising authority equal to enable it to carry out its various responsibilities.

The United States welcomes the French initiative and believes the French representative has made a helpful contribution toward the restoration of peace in Indochina. The French proposals are consistent with the general principles to which any satisfactory settlement must conform. In our opinion, they should be accompanied by a program for the resolution of political problems. We look forward to hearing the views of the Government of Viet-Nam on such a program.

The United States notes the French proposal that "agreements shall be guaranteed by the States participating in the Geneva Conference." The United States has already demonstrated its devotion to the principle of collective security and its willingness to help in the development of collective security arrangements in Southeast Asia, as elsewhere. Until it is possible to see more clearly the exact nature of the agreements to be guaranteed and to determine the obligations of the guarantors, we will, of course, not be able to express any judgment on this section of the proposal.

The U.S. delegation suggests that the Conference adopt the French proposal as a basis of discussion and hopes that we will move forward constructively and rapidly in bringing about a restoration of peace in Indochina.

The U.S. delegation has listened with sympathy to the factual recital of the representatives of Cambodia and Laos and will study with interest their proposals for the restoration of peace in Cambodia and Laos.

(336) PROPOSAL BY THE DELEGATION OF THE STATE OF VIET-NAM TO THE GENEVA CONFERENCE, MAY 12, 1954

Source: *Documents on the Discussion of Korea and Indochina*, p. 118.

The delegation of the Bao Dai government demanded that the settlement recognize it as the sole legal government of Viet-nam and rules out even de facto *partition of Viet-nam into two administrative zones.*

The Berlin Conference recommended the restoration of peace in Indo-China. Such restoration implies: --

(A) a military settlement, to put an end to hostilities, and
(B) a political settlement, to establish peace on real and lasting foundations.

A.--Military settlement

1. The Delegation of the State of Viet Nam declares itself ready to consider any working document submitted for this purpose to the Conference, provided such document represents a serious, positive effort, made in good faith and is calculated to lead to a satisfactory military settlement.

2. It must include adequate guarantees for the ensurance of a real and lasting peace and the prevention of any possibility of further aggression.

3. It must not involve any division, whether direct or indirect, definitive or temporary, *de facto* or *de jure*, of the national territory.

4. It must provide for International Supervision of the cease-fire terms.

B.--Political settlement

As regards relations between the State of Viet Nam and France:
Such relations must be regulated on the basis of the joint Franco-Viet Nam Declaration of April 28, 1954, which provides for the signature of two fundamental treaties: the first of these treaties recognises the complete independence of the State of Viet Nam and its full and entire sovereignty; the second establishes a Franco-Viet Nam association within the French Union based on equality.

As regard the internal political settlement of Viet Nam:
1. By reason of the political and territorial unit of Viet Nam, recognition must be accorded to the principles that the only State entitled to represent Viet Nam legally is the State of which His Majesty Bao-Dai, Head of State, is the embodiment. In this State alone are vested the powers deriving from the internal and exteral sovereignty of Viet Nam.

2. Recognition must be accorded to the principles of a single army for the whole territory. That army is the national army under the control and responsibility of the State of Viet Nam.

The status of the soldiers of Vietminh within the framework of the legal army of the State of Viet Nam shall be regulated in conformity with the above-mentioned principle and in accordance with methods to be determined.

Application of the aforesaid regulation shall be carried out under International Supervision.

3. Within the framework and under the authority of the State of Viet Nam, free elections shall be held throughout the territory, as soon as the Security Council determines that the authority of the State is established throughout the territory and that the conditions of freedom are fulfilled. International Supervision must be exercised under the auspices of the United Nations so as to ensure the freedom and genuineness of the elections.

4. A representative Government shall be formed under the aegis of His Majesty Bao-Dai, Head of the State of Viet Nam, after the elections and in accordance with their results.

5. The State of Viet Nam shall undertake to refrain from any prosecution of persons who collaborated with Vietminh during the hostilities.

6. The political and territorial integrity of the State of Viet Nam shall be guaranteed internationally.

7. Assistance shall be furnished by the United Nations towards the development of the national resources of Viet Nam and raising the standard of living in the country.

(337) PRESS CONFERENCE STATEMENTS BY DULLES, MAY 11, 1954

Source: *Department of State Bulletin*, May 24, 1954, pp. 781-782

Responding to questions on Indochina and an Asian collective security agreement, Dulles conceded for the first time the possibility that the U.S. might have to accept a Communist victory in Viet-nam, Laos and Cambodia.

At his news conference on May 11, Secretary Dulles was asked whether he considered that he or the United States suffered a diplomatic defeat at Geneva. Mr. Dulles made the following reply:

I have read about that in the press - foreign, domestic, Communist, and non-Communist. I don't know what it is talking about. It is true that at Geneva we have so far not achieved the unification of Korea, nor does it seem likely that we will achieve the unification of Indochina under conditions of freedom and peace. We never thought that there was a good chance of accomplishing those results. In all of these conferences, we go into them realizing that the Communists have a pattern of their own, which they have applied in Germany, which they have applied in Korea, which they are applying now in Indochina. This means that they will hold on to what they have got and try to get us to accept a scheme whereby they can get some more. We keep on trying. But I do not call it a diplomatic defeat that we are not able to lead the Communists to give up, as long as they don't lead us to make any costly concession, which we do not intend to make.

Asked whether the armistice proposal put forward at Geneva by the Viet Minh Communists was acceptable to the United States, Mr. Dulles made the following reply:

I think very little of it because it is the same pattern that has been applied in the past in Germany, Austria, and Korea; namely, to compel a withdrawal of the forces which sustain a free society and to set up a system under which the Communists can grab the whole area.

It is certainly unacceptable in its totality. Whether there is any particular word or phrase in it that is acceptable I would not want to say without further study. But it is not acceptable in its totality.

Asked whether the French proposal was acceptable to the United States, Mr. Dulles replied:

The French proposal I regard as acceptable. Of course a great deal of detail would have to be worked out. But the general concept of an internationally controlled armistice seems to me to be one that is acceptable.

Secretary Dulles was asked whether there were not insuperable difficulties in the creation of a genuinely effective Asiatic-Pacific defense alliance. He replied:

There are certainly great difficulties, as I pointed out in the speech which I made a few days ago. The concept of collective security in the area is nothing new. It is in the treaties which I negotiated in 1950 and in 1951 with Australia, New Zealand, and the Philippines, and also with Japan, wherein we talked of the development of a more comprehensive system of security in the area. The difficulties in the way have been very great. I wrote an article, I remember, in *Foreign Affairs*, I think in January of 1952, on the problem of trying to develop an enlarged Asian or Pacific-South Asian or Pacific security pact. Now the difficulties are very great because of the difference between the different nations, their different degrees of independence or lack of independence, differences of race and religion, and a lack of common traditions. It is an extremely difficult area in which to operate, and it is inevitable that progress should be slow, and in many of these situations the willingness to cooperate has a certain relationship to the measure of fear which is entertained by the peoples concerned. I do not say the difficulties are insuperable. If I felt that, I wouldn't have put my shoulder to the task of trying to create it.

Asked what would be required to constitute an effective commitment in any such agreement, Secretary Dulles replied:

I believe that the commitments should be of such a character that if they were openly challenged we would be prepared to fight, just as our similar commitments carry that implication in relation to the other mutual-security arrangements we have made - the North Atlantic Treaty, the ANZUS Treaty, Philippine Treaty, the Rio Treaties, and so forth.

Asked what would bring such an agreement into operation, he said:

If the states of Viet-Nam, Laos, and Cambodia are comprehended in this collective security pact, I would feel then it would be appropriate to use force to put down attacks such as are now going on there.

Asked if such a pact would include the Associated States, he replied:

That depends a good deal upon the views of other countries and ourselves. It depends upon the views of the Governments of Viet-Nam, Laos, and Cambodia, on the views of the French, on the views of some of the other participants. I can't forecast that at the present time because the situation is very much in a state of flux.

Asked if such a concept was designed specifically to meet the situation in Indochina or the broader area, he replied:

The situation in that area, as we found it, was that it was subject to the so-called "domino theory." You mean that if one went, another would go? We are trying to change it so that would not be the case. That is the whole theory of collective security. You generally have a whole series of countries which can be picked up one by one. That is the whole theory of the North Atlantic Treaty. As the nations come together, then the "domino theory," so-called, ceases to apply. And what we are trying to do is create a situation in Southeast Asia where the domino situation will not apply.

And while I see it has been said that I felt that Southeast Asia could be secured even without perhaps Viet-Nam, Laos, and Cambodia, I do not want for a minute to underestimate the importance of those countries nor do I want for a minute to give the impression that we believe that they are going to be lost or that we have given up trying to prevent their being lost. On the contrary, we recognize that they are extremely important and that the problem of saving Southeast Asia is far more difficult if they are lost. But I do not want to give the impression either that if events that we could not control and which we do not anticipate should lead to their being lost, that we would consider the whole situation hopeless, and we would give up in despair. We do not give up in despair. Also, we do not give up Viet-Nam, Laos, or Cambodia.

(338) SPEECH BY PREMIER CHOU EN-LAI TO THE GENEVA CONFERENCE, MAY 12, 1954 [Extract]

Source: *Documents on the Discussion of Korea and Vietnam*, pp. 124-126.

Chou En-lai repeated Pham Van Dong's criticism of the Bidault proposal as ignoring the existence of the D.R.V. and as putting forward "unilateral terms" for peace.

Mr. Chairman and Fellow Delegates, the Chinese people have maintained for a long time a profound friendship with the Indo-Chinese peoples. In the last hundred years, subjected similarly to colonial aggression, the Chinese people and the Indo-Chinese peoples have sympathised with each other in their respective movements for national liberation. This is only natural.

After the founding of the People's Republic of China, the Democratic Republic of Viet Nam established formal diplomatic relations with the People's Republic of China. The Governments of the two countries have also established normal economic and cultural relations under the principles of equality and mutual benefit. Such friendly relations are developing the common desire of the Governments of the People's Republic of China and the Democratic Republic of Viet Nam as mutual respect for each other's independence and sovereignty and non-interference in each other's internal affairs, and the safeguarding of peace in Asia and the world.

For the sake of safeguarding peace in Asia and the world, the Chinese people honestly hope that the war can be stopped and peaceful life restored in Indo-China at an early date. Not only the Chinese people but other Asian peoples as well are in favour of a peaceful settlement of the Indo-China question. The demand for the termination of war in Indo-China has been continuously voiced in India, Indonesia, Burma, Pakistan, and other countries.

The recent conference held in Colombo by the Prime Ministers of five Asian States has also expressed its concern about the restoration of peace in Indo-China. The peoples of Europe and other continents are no less desirous of ending the fighting in Indo-China than are the peoples of Asia. Moreover, even among the American statesmen, not every one of them is in favour of embarking upon military ventures in Indo-China or South-East Asia.

In this connexion, special reference should be made to the peace policy of the Union of Soviet Socialist Republics. The Government of the Soviet Union and the Soviet people have insisted all along on a peaceful settlement of the Indo-China question, and have consistently stood for the national rights of the Indo-China peoples at various international conferences.

Mr. Chairman, the Indo-China peoples have fought for nearly a century for the sacred cause of national liberation. In order to enable this Conference to have a better understanding of the aspirations of the people of Viet Nam and other peoples of Indo-China, I would like to suggest that we read the Declaration of Independence issued by the Democratic Republic of Viet Nam on September 2, 1945.

It may surprise some gentlemen that the Declaration of Independence of the Democratic Republic of Viet Nam begins with the following sentences which paraphrase the Declaration of Independence of the United States of America, of 1776:--

"All men are born equal. They are endowed by nature with certain inalienable rights, among which are life, liberty and the pursuit of happiness."

The Declaration of Independence of the Democratic Republic of Viet Nam then quotes the French Declaration of the Rights of Man, of 1789: -

"Men are born and remain free and equal in rights."

The Declaration of Independence of the Democratic Republic of Viet Nam then states: -

"A people who have courageously opposed the French domination for more than eighty years, a people who have courageously fought on the side of the Allies against fascism during the past several years, this people should be free, this people should be independent."

Gentlemen, can it be said that these demands of the Indo-Chinese people are excessive? I think that the Governments of those countries which had issued the two great Declarations, of 1776 and 1789, should recognise that the people of Indo-China, like the peoples of the United States of America and France, must be fully entitled to the rights of independence, liberty and equality.

The Delegation of the People's Republic of China hopes that this Conference will consider in a most serious manner the statement and proposals made on behalf of the Viet Namese people by Mr. Pham Van Dong, head of the Delegation of the Democratic Republic of Viet Nam, with respect to the restoration of peace in Indo-China and the achievement of national independence, national unity, and democratic liberties for Viet Nam, Khmer and Pathet Lao.

We are of the opinion that the statement and proposals of the Delegation of the Democratic Republic of Viet Nam truly expresses the will of the Indo-Chinese peoples to fight for peace, independence, unity and democracy as well as their legitimate demands. These proposals, in the view of the Chinese Delegation, have already opened the way for the peaceful settlement of the Indo-Chinese question.

However, M. George Bidault, chief of the French Delegation, in his statement of May 8, still maintained the attitude of a colonial ruler. He continued to ignore the existence of the Democratic Republic of Viet Nam which the French Government had recognised, and the fact that the Government of the Democratic Republic of Viet Nam enjoys the support of the broad masses of the people of Viet Nam. He refused participation by the representatives of the resistance governments of Khmer and Pathet Lao at this Conference. He let aside the political basis for the restoration of peace in Indo-China, and acted like a victor laying down unilateral terms for cessation of hostilities and demanding their acceptance by the peoples of Indo-China.

This line of action is unrealistic, unreasonable and inconsistent with the principles of negotiating with equal rights.

Mr. Chairman, now that we are assembled here to examine and study the ways of restoring peace in Indo-China, it is essential, in accordance with the existing situations in Indo-China and in Asia, and on the basis of recognising the national rights of Indo-China peoples, to seek terms that will be considered honourable, fair and reasonable by the two sides concerned, and to take effective measures so as to achieve at an early date an armistice in Indo-China and restore peace there. If all the delegates to this Conference are genuinely desirous of restoring peace in Indo-China, I believe that there exists the possibility of reaching agreement in this Conference.

The Delegation of the People's Republic of China expresses its full support for the statement and proposals made by Mr. Pham Van Dong, head of the

Delegation of the Democratic Republic of Viet Nam, and feels that these proposals can serve as the basis for this Conference to discuss the termination of war and the restoration of peace in Indo-China, and to adopt appropriate resolutions thereupon.

These proposals, in our view, are consistent with the wishes of the Indo-Chinese peoples for peace, independence, unity, and democracy, and are in the interests of peace for the French people and the peoples of other nations of the world.

(339) TELEGRAM FROM DULLES TO SMITH, MAY 12, 1954

Source: *U.S.-Vietnam Relations*, Book 9, pp. 457-459

Conveying instruction approved by the President, Dulles informed Smith that the U.S. would not associate itself with any agreement which gave any recognition or territory to the D.R.V. or the resistance forces in Laos and Cambodia.

The following basic instructions, which have been approved by the President, and which are in confirmation of those already given you orally, will guide you, as head of the United States Delegation, in your participation in the Indochina phase of the Geneva Conference.

1. The presence of a United States representative during the discussion at the Geneva Conference of "the problem of restoring peace in Indochina" rests on the Berlin Agreement of February 18, 1954. Under that agreement the US, UK, France, and USSR agreed that the four of them plus other interested states should be invited to a conference at Geneva on April 26 "for the purpose of reaching a peaceful settlement of the Korean question" and agreed further, that "the problem of restoring peace in Indochina" would also be discussed at Geneva by the four powers represented at Berlin, and Communist China and other interested states.

2. You will not deal with the delegates of the Chinese Communist regime, or any other regime not now diplomatically recognized.

(340) SPEECH BY BIDAULT TO THE GENEVA CONFERENCE, MAY 14, 1954 [Extract]

Source: *Documents on the Discussion of Korea and Indochina*, pp. 132-136.

In the first substantial comments by the French on the D.R.V. proposal, Bidault insisted that a political settlement would have to follow a ceasefire rather than precede it. He also supported the claim of the State of Viet-nam to be the only legal government of Viet-nam.

Mr. Chairman,

The French delegation has studied with close attention the statement made here on the 10th of this month by Mr. Pham Van Dong. It has done so in the spirit of the final communique of the Berlin Conference, which states that the problem of restoring peace in Indo-China will be discussed at the Geneva Conference. No flights of eloquence can further our common concern, no polemics can help us to accomplish our task. The general discussion which is now going on is valuable only to the extent that it enables delegations to express their views clearly and to expound the conclusions they have reached. So long as it is conducted in this spirit, it provides the necessary groundwork for the negotiations proper, which must bear on specific points.

For these reasons I shall not reply to the whole of Mr. Pham Van Dong's statement. I have already told you what I thought about a particular way of writing - or rewriting - history, and there is no need whatever for me to revert to the subject. Of this statement, then, I will comment only on the first sentence and the proposals with which the statement concludes.

Mr. Pham Van Dong tells us that Vietminh's fundamental position is: peace, independence, unity and democracy. All of us here, I think, can subscribe to these words, and the French delegation has no hesitation in doing so. Peace, as I recently recalled, has been, ever since Berlin, the very purpose of our Conference. Independence is the final goal of a process of development which began immediately after the Second World War and which has already been achieved, a fact proclaimed in this very place and in the most precise and detailed manner by the representatives of the three states. Unity, in the case of Viet Nam, is not open to question: the French delegation, at any rate, considers that the territorial unity of Viet Nam, and the inviolability of its frontiers, must be respected in any future settlement. Lastly, democracy is a principle which is common to all the nations of the free world. To our mind it must find expression in the normal exercise of civic rights and human freedoms. If all the delegations here present accept these four terms in their authentic connotation, our task will be greatly simplified.

The French delegation feels that the proposals made by Mr. Pham Van Dong at the end of his statement call for more substantial comment.

These proposals are striking, first, for their monumental character. Their amplitude is due to the fact that they include everything, all mixed up together. They deal with Laos, with Cambodia, with Pathet Lao and the Khmer Issaraks, with cultural and economic relations between France and Viet Nam, with the French Union, and finally with means of restoring peace in Indo-China. I suppose it was Mr. Pham Van Dong's desire to paint a broad picture of the problems concerning the three countries of Indo-China. I am also of the opinion that a number of these problems are outside the competence of our Conference. I shall say first which and for what reasons.

I have already expressed our astonishment at the insistence with which Vietminh constitutes itself the spokesman of Laos and Cambodia, or more particularly of Pathet Lao and the Khmer Issarak movement. On these two groups I can add nothing of value to the very pertinent remarks already made by the delegations of Laos and Cambodia. On Vietminh's competence to speak for the three movements, I shall say only that I see in it an unexpected survival of a distant past. I recollect the insistence with which Mr. Ho Chi Minh, in 1946 and even later, rejected federation for Indo-China. Does he perhaps now want to restore it for the benefit of Vietminh?

I hasten to add that if ever the three States one day wished to re-establish in any form this Indo-Chinese community whose disappearance they desired, the decision would rest with them and with them alone. The French Government, at any rate, has taken their wishes into account. It has recognised the independence of Laos and Cambodia. In the exercise of this independence, both States have adopted constitutional democratic institutions, and have consequently proceeded to free elections. Both Governments have negotiated agreements regulating relations between their countries and France, on a bilateral basis, and in complete equality. These negotiations are complete in the case of Laos, and will shortly be completed in the case of Cambodia. It seems, therefore, that the problems referred to in paragraphs 1, 3, 4 and 5 of the Vietminh proposals are disposed of in the case of Laos and Cambodia, and that there is absolutely no reason why our Conference should discuss them further. In the case of Laos, and in the case of Cambodia, the only question to be dealt with is that of the invasion of their territories by foreign forces, and the foreign forces are those of Vietminh. Now I note that Mr. Pham Van Dong's proposal evades this fundamental problem, unless there is an implied reference in paragraph 2, which provides for an agreement on the withdrawal of all foreign troops from the territories of what are called "Khmer" and "Pathet Lao."

As has been clearly stated here by the delegations of Laos and Cambodia, the Laotian problem and the Cambodian problem consist in first obtaining, and then supervising, the withdrawal of the Vietminh forces. This withdrawal and this supervision imply specific measures of the kind referred to in paragraphs 2, 6, 7 and 8 of the Vietminh proposals. These measures, however, must not be confused with those required in the infinitely more complex question of settling the present situation in Viet Nam, precisely because the problem of Laos and the problem of Cambodia, which are distinct from the other, must also not be confused with the problem of Viet Nam, which is quite different: the arrangements for disposing of them must be considered separately. That is why in the French delegation's basic proposals, while Viet Nam is dealt with in Chapter 1, the special provisions relating to Laos and Cambodia are brought together in Chapter 2, and the provisions of Chapter 3 apply to all the settlements to be reached.

The French Government stands by these proposals. It will gladly supplement them in the sense advocated by the delegations of Laos and Cambodia. Finally, even though it hardly seems to it that French troops in countries associated with France can be considered as "foreign" in the usual sense of the term, the French Government is ready, subject to the opinion of the governments concerned, to withdraw its own troops if the invading forces are themselves withdrawn. On this particular point it accepts in advance the views of the Governments of Laos and Cambodia.

From the foregoing observations it follows that the questions relating to these two States are simple, that they are independent of the question of Viet Nam and that they can be disposed of without delay. The French Government hopes that they will be disposed of at once. It depends on the goodwill of Vietminh whether so desirable a development is possible. All that is needed is for Vietminh to recognise the facts for what they are.

I now come to what in my view is the essential part of the statement by Vietminh, namely, the problem of peace in Viet Nam.

Here again, I must make a preliminary observation. The Vietminh proposals pay scant regard to facts and events. I would remind you first of all that there does exist a Government of the State of Viet Nam. That Government is the government of His Majesty, Bao Dai, which is recognised by thirty-five states, is a member of various international organisations, and which is represented here in the eyes of all those who have recognised it. This Government is fully and solely competent to commit Viet Nam. With it the French Government has conducted a series of negotiations which, as I mentioned at the beginning of this statement, led to the joint declaration and to the conclusion of two treaties which the delegation of Viet Nam read to the Conference on the 12th of this month. The sovereignty and independence of Viet Nam are therefore recognised by France over the whole territory of Viet Nam, a fact which demonstrates the superfluity of paragraph 1 of the Vietminh proposals. The association of Viet Nam with the French Union on the basis of free consent, and the conditions for such association, are therefore already determined. Paragraph 4 of the Vietminh proposals is accordingly pointless.

With regard to paragraph 2, I must point out that movements of French troops in Viet Nam territory are governed by the conduct of the war, and will continue to be until peace is restored. Once peace is restored the French Government has no intention of keeping any forces in Viet Nam against the will of that country's legal government. It is therefore for that government to say whether it considers it advisable, in the light of its own security requirements, to maintain or to modify the agreements on this subject. The French Government, at any rate, does not intend to make the re-establishment of peace in Indo-China conditional on any undertakings whatever on that point.

The recognition by Viet Nam of the fact that France has economic and cultural interest in that State, referred to in paragraph 5 of the Vietminh proposals, is already the subject of agreements or of negotiations still in progress with the Government of the State of Viet Nam. I may add that, here again, the French Government has never thought of making the cessation of hostilities in Indo-China conditional on the conclusion of these negotiations.

Paragraph 3 of the Vietminh proposals is in a different category. It deals with the conditions for the establishment of democratic institutions to ensure Viet Nam's political unity.

For a long time now the French Government has been devoting considerable thought to this problem as it affects Viet Nam, in the same way as in relation to Korea and other countries. It is convinced that only by applying these two principles of democratic institutions and political unity will it be possible to efface the political consequences of the war, and consolidate the re-establishment of peace. But the lesson of experience is that, without the indispensable measures of supervision, so-called free elections can spell the death of freedom. The plan proposed by the Vietminh delegation is so similar to plans we have heard elsewhere and are still discussing, that at first glance its purpose seems obvious. The sole purpose of the method proposed is to ensure, even before the elections are held, that Viet Nam shall be completely dominated by Vietminh. That is not the way to find a real solution to the problem before us. Arrangements must be made for safeguards and inspection. We know from Mr. Nguyen Quoc Dinh's statement that it is also the Viet Nam Government's desire that freedom of choice for the electors at the general elections should be ensured by the provision of a suitable system of inspection.

The Plan it has already submitted constitutes a useful basis for discussion in that connexion. Since it would be impossible in practice to provide the indispensable safeguards and to carry out an election in motion before the cessation of hostilities has had time to exercise a pacifying effect, the French delegation does not think that an agreement on the political settlement ought to precede, and thus delay, the application of a military settlement. While not unmindful that the two are connected, it feels that the former should be not a precondition of but should follow from the latter.

There is nothing in paragraphs 6 and 7 of the Vietminh proposals to which the French delegation can object, since the first goes without saying and the second is partly taken from our own proposals. While agreeing on the principle, the French delegation reserves the right to examine the methods of application. As regards prisoners of war and civil internees, it has, as everyone knows, proposed that they should be set free immediately hostilities cease.

Paragraph 8 is obviously essential, since it deals with the cessation of hostilities in Indo-China.

The first sub-paragraph of this paragraph is ambiguous. Does it mean that an agreement on the measures listed in paragraph 1 to 7 must *precede* the cessation of hostilities? Or does the Vietminh delegation agree that the political aspects of the general settlement it is proposing if they have not been dealt with already, can be dealt with after the cessation of hostilities? The French delegation is convinced that, if concrete results are to be speedily achieved, solution of the political problem cannot be a condition of the end of hostilities.

The French delegation notes that the Vietminh proposals envisage, to secure the restoration of peace, a settlement for each country. As I have already said, that is also the view of the French Government. But in the case of Laos and Cambodia, there can hardly be a Franco-Laotian and a Franco-Cambodian settlement because France, as we all know, is not at war with either of those States. The Viet Nam settlement, on the other hand, should be reached by means of an agreement between the opposing Commands in accordance with terms decided upon by this Conference.

Sub-paragraph (a) provides for a complete and simultaneous cease-fire throughout Indo-Chinese territory. While it has no objection of principle to this procedure the French delegation does not, however, think it necessary to bind itself to what looks like a rigid and precise formula but is in fact a very vague one: for in the first place a cessation of hostilities can undoubtedly be much more easily achieved in Laos and Cambodia than in Viet Nam, and can therefore take place earlier on Laotian and Cambodian territory than on Viet Nam territory, and secondly, for Viet Nam proper a gradual region to region method has been suggested. The French delegation sees no reason why the two Commands should be prevented from examining this suggestion.

The French delegation listed, in section I of the basic proposals it submitted to the Conference on the 8th of this month, the safeguards which would have to be provided in any agreement concluded before the cessation of hostilities.

It observes that the Vietminh proposals take up the idea of assembly areas and of a readjustment of those areas contained in paragraph 1 of section I of the French proposals, that is, the part of those proposals which relates to Viet Nam. It considers that the method by which these operations are to be carried out should be carefully and clearly defined; that the troop movements involved in the assembling should be regulated by agreement between the Commands. The French delegation feels that sub-paragraph (b) of paragraph 8 of the Vietminh proposals requires more detailed explanation of a number of points.

It notes that the Vietminh proposals do not provide for the disarmament of elements not belonging either to the army or to the police forces. On this point it confirm the proposal contained in paragraph 2 of section I of its text of May 8.

Lastly, the French delegation observes that the provision concerning supervisory machinery is taken up in sub-paragraph (c) of paragraph 8 of the Vietminh proposals. The nature of this machinery is, however, different from what was proposed in its text of May 8, which mentioned International Commissions. The Vietminh text of May 10 merely refers to joint committees. The French delegation considers the establishment of international supervisory machinery to be an indispensable guarantee for the proper implementation of the agreements.

It also points out that, according to section III of the French proposals of May 8, the agreements would be guaranteed by the States participating in this Conference, and notes that the delegations of the United Kingdom, the United States of America, and of Viet Nam, Laos and Cambodia have already given their consent to the principle of international supervision and guarantee of the agreements.

And now, having concluded this comparison of the texts of the French and Vietminh proposals, the French Delegation wishes to reply to the very pertinent questions put by the Head of the United Kingdom Delegation on the 12th of this month: -

Question 1. - France considers that in Viet Nam the troops on both sides should be concentrated in determined areas.

Question 2. - France has proposed that the Laotian and Cambodian problems should be dealt with separately, and proposes that the Vietminh forces should be withdrawn from the territories of those countries.

Question 3. - As regards Viet Nam, France considers that it is for the Conference to work out the areas of concentration, on the understanding that the respective Commanders-in-Chief would be consulted by both sides. The Commanders-in-Chief would be responsible for the details of the concentration.

Question 4. - France has proposed the disarmament of irregular forces. In Viet Nam the procedure for this disarmament will have to be decided in the light of the arrangements for the concentration of regular troops.

Question 5. - France has proposed international supervision. She is prepared to consider any proposals that may be made regarding the composition of the Commissions and the method of supervision. If the principle of international supervision is accepted, then in Viet Nam joint bodies might be employed, the terms to be settled by mutual agreement, to work under the International Commissions and assist them in their task.

The French Delegation puts these views before the Conference in the belief that it will thereby be helping in the task to which we must all devote our energies. It hopes they will be studied in the same objective and constructive spirit as that in which they are made. Its primary concern, I repeat, is to prepare the way for concrete negotiations, which it hopes will not be long delayed. It is accordingly prepared to consider any methods of procedure calculated to expedite our work.

(341) TELEGRAM FROM DILLON TO DULLES, MAY 14, 1954

Source: *U.S. Vietnam Relations, Book 9,* pp. 462-464.

Laniel and Schumann indicated to Dillon their eagerness to negotiate with the U.S. an agreement for U.S. military intervention in Indochina. They raised objection, however, to the U.S. demand that the Associated States have the option of withdrawal from the French Union, which they said French public opinion would not understand.

I saw Laniel and Schumann this evening regarding DEPTEL 4023. Before discussion started on REFTEL, Laniel made a number of observations and asked two additional questions. He said that he was sending General Ely to Indochina immediately. He will leave on Saturday or Sunday and will stay in Indochina only two to four days. Purpose of his visit is to check up on military situation on the spot and on physical and mental condition of General Navarre. Because of Ely's prospective absence from Paris, Laniel suggested that General Trapnell or whoever else we plan to send to Paris in answer to Laniel's request for American military advice, arrive approximately Thursday of next week. General Ely will undertake such regrouping of French forces and shortening of lines as may be necessary. This will probably include withdrawal of portion, and maybe large portion, of the French forces now in Laos. Final decisions, however, will only be taken upon return of General Ely to Paris.

Laniel then posed following two questions: One, could the United States find a way to guarantee the borders and the independence of Laos and Cambodia. If such a guarantee could be made, he felt it would be of great help after the French forces had been withdrawn. Laniel's second question dealt with action United States will take in the case of intervention by MIG 15's aircraft. He said that for his own protection here he would like definite assurance, written if possible, that U.S. aviation would come instantly to the help of French forces in Delta if they were attacked by MIG's. He said that he would have no defense before parliament or French public opinion if he was not able to obtain some such assurance as there were no adequate anti-aircraft defenses in the Delta.

Finally, Maurice Schumann transmitted a request of Bidault's that U.S. do everything possible in the next days to accelerate delivery of planes and equipment in the event that a cease fire should be negotiated at Geneva which would naturally bring to a halt such deliveries.

I then referred to question of location of negotiations and expressed Dept's views in favor of Paris. Schumann and Laniel agreed that Paris would be preferable to Washington and accordingly it can be accepted as agreed that negotiations along lines of REFTEL will continue to take place in Paris.

I then outlined requirements listed in paragraphs 2 and 3 of REFTEL. Laniel and Schumann listened very quietly and seriously and on the whole appeared well pleased with this clarification of U.S. position. They said that naturally they did not have any info regarding the views of other countries in the area and they would appreciate being kept informed by U.S. of progress toward fulfilling condition indicated in paragraph 2(B) which was beyond their control. They were particularly impressed and pleased by indication in that paragraph that actual participation by U.K. was no longer a prerequisite to U.S. action.

Laniel and Schumann had one serious objection to U.S. conditions. This, as expected, was to the condition that France publicly accord to associated states right of withdrawal from French Union at any time. When I explained U.S. reasons for this position as outlined in DEPTEL 4064, they said they could see how such a statement might be of some help with Nehru but that French public opinion would never understand why it was necessary to make such a statement when it had never been requested by any of the three associated states. They then pointed out the fact that the Viet Minh armistice proposals, dishonest though they were, nevertheless looked toward the possibility of the Vietminh joining the French Union. (Comment: I am certain that unless we can find some way to get around this requirement, French will never ask for outside assistance.) After hearing strong statement on the subject by both Laniel and Schumann, I said that I hoped we could continue conversations on this subject in order to find a formula that would satisfy U.S. requirements and at the same time could be accepted by the French parliament. Laniel and Schumann agreed that we should talk further on this subject.

Laniel and Schumann had one other question referring to subparagraph 2(E) which states that forces from U.S. would be principally air and sea "and others". They asked me to find out what was meant by other forces. Laniel indicated that it would be very important to have artillery forces as well as some ground forces. In this connection, they mentioned the possibility of the use of marines. (Comment: I feel that while French govt would not look forward in present circumstances to the necessity of any substantial involvement by U.S. ground forces, they nevertheless feel that it is very important that we provide at least some token ground forces so that our participation is not limited strictly to naval and air forces.)

Both Laniel and Schumann accepted without question as being wholly justified U.S. requirement that conditions be accepted by French Cabinet and endorsed by National Assembly. They then said that they would probably want to speak to me over the weekend after they had had time to think further regarding U.S. conditions. I made it clear that conditions as outlined represented present high level thinking in Washington and did not represent as yet any commitment on the part of U.S. govt. Schumann then said that negotiations should be pursued in the greatest secrecy until such time as full agreement had been reached. He said that premature press leaks could make things most difficult and he referred to an AP press story today from Washington. Laniel and Schumann then said that they hoped that negotiations could continue rapidly and that when and if full agreement had been reached, we would be in a position to make public declaration of a sort which would influence Communist negotiations at Geneva.

(342) <u>MEMORANDUM BY ADMIRAL RADFORD FOR WILSON</u>, MAY 20, 1954

Source: *U.S.-Vietnam Relations, Book 9*, pp. 477-479.

Radford gave Wilson the position of the Joint Chiefs of Staff on issues to be negotiated with France in regard to U.S. participation in the fighting. He indicated that the Joint Chiefs assumed the use of atomic weapons "whenever it is to our military advantage" and would urge bombing of supply lines in China.

1. In recent discussions between the French and the Department of State relating to U.S. military intervention in Indo-china, the U.S. Government specified certain conditions which would have to obtain if U.S. military intervention were to be undertaken. Among these conditions were:

    <u>a</u>. That France would undertake not to withdraw its forces from Indochina during period of united action so that forces from U.S. principally air and sea and others would be supplementary and not in substitution;

    <u>b</u>. That agreement would have to be reached on training of native troops and on command structure for united action.

2. On the assumption that United States armed forces intervene in the conflict in Indochina, the Joint Chiefs of Staff have agreed that a Department of Defense position should be formulated as to the size and composition of U.S. force contributions to be made and the command structure to be established. In formulating these views the Joint Chiefs of Staff have been guided by several factors, among which are:

    <u>a</u>. The limited availability of U.S. forces for military action in Indochina.

    <u>b</u>. The current numerical advantage of the French Union forces over the enemy, i.e., approximately 5 to 3.

    <u>c</u>. The undesirability of basing large numbers of U.S. forces in Indochina.

    <u>d</u>. The primary need of an expanded and intensified training program as being the current greatest need.

    <u>e</u>. The lack of required facilities for superimposing U.S. Air Force forces on existing facilities in Indochina.

    <u>f</u>. The implications of a reaction by the Chinese Communists in the event of U.S. participation.

    <u>g</u>. Atomic weapons will be used whenever it is to our military advantage.

3. The Joint Chiefs of Staff consider that the basic principle underlying any command structure for operations in Indochina which is acceptable to the United States must enable the U.S. to influence future strategy in Indochina. In addition, they believe that some new means to furnish the military guidance which heretofore has come from Paris must be found. A possible solution for over-all strategic guidance is a Military Representatives Committee with membership from those nations contributing the principal forces of the coalition with a steering or standing group along the lines of NATO. This group would be served by a staff organized along the lines of the U.S. Joint Staff composed primarily of U.S. and French officers.

4. Although the Allied Commander in Chief in Indochina should be French, there must be a U.S. Deputy with sufficient staff assistance to provide liaison

with the French and coordinate U.S. activities with the over-all operations. CINCPAC would exercise command over all U.S. forces based in Indochina and other forces assigned to him for operations in Indochina. In addition, a U.S. Air Advisor would be provided the French Commander in Chief for the purpose of advising him concerning the air effort.

5. The Joint Chiefs of Staff believe that the best military course for eventual victory in Indochina is the development of effective native armed forces. Thus far the French have been unsuccessful in their efforts to develop such forces. A firm commitment by the French and firm requests from the respective government of the Associated States for the training and development of native forces by the United States should be a prerequisite of U.S. participation. It is estimated that an augmentation of MAAG Indochina on the order of 2250, with an appropriate logistic support force, would be required to initiate this program. The size of this force and security arrangements therefore will be determined in light of recommendations requested from CINCPAC and Chief, MAAG Indochina.

6. The Joint Chiefs of Staff recommend that U.S. participation be limited primarily to Naval and Air Forces. The composition of these forces should be on the order of the following:

    a. <u>Naval Forces</u>. A fast carrier Task Force and supporting forces as necessary in accordance with developments in the situation.

    b. <u>Air Forces</u>. U.S. Air Force units operating from present bases outside Indochina as may be required. The order of magnitude of this effort cannot now be estimated since it will depend on developments in the situation.

7. The Joint Chiefs of Staff note that the principal sources of Viet Minh military supply lie outside Indochina. The destruction or neutralization of those outside sources supporting the Viet Minh would materially reduce the French military problems in Indochina.

8. The Joint Chiefs of Staff believe that committing to the Indochina conflict Naval forces in excess of the above or basing substantial air forces therein will involve maldeployment of forces and reduced readiness to meet probable Chinese Communist reaction elsewhere in the Far East. From the point of view of the United States, with reference to the Far East as a whole, Indochina is devoid of decisive military objectives and the allocation of more than token U.S. armed forces to that area would be a serious diversion of limited U.S. capabilities.

(343) <u>PRESS CONFERENCE STATEMENTS BY DULLES</u>, MAY 25, 1954

Source: *Department of State Bulletin*, June 7, 1954, pp. 862-64.

Dulles declared in a press conference that France may have gone as far as it should legally go in giving independence to the Associated States, but conceded that the people themselves did not yet feel that they had real independence. In another answer, he stated, inaccurately, that the French had not requested U.S. military intervention in Indochina.

At his news conference on May 25, a correspondent recalled to Secretary Dulles his report to the Nation following his return from Geneva in which he set forth the conditions under which the United States intervened in Korea. Mr. Dulles was asked to relate those conditions to the Indochina situation. Mr. Dulles made the following reply:

I pointed out, I think, the existence of certain conditions in the case of Korea, and I went on to say that the situation in Indochina was different and more complex.

I think that broadly speaking the attitude of the United States toward this situation has been made clear by statements which the President has made and which I have made. I think it is fair to say that the United States attitude in this matter has been one of the few stable aspects in an otherwise changing and fluid situation.

The position of the United States toward collective security in Southeast Asia has been known basically for quite a long while. In fact, it really goes back to the time when I went out to the Far East in, I think, January of 1951 on a mission to try to create a collective security pact in that area. That effort failed at that time in the sense that we were not able to put together a collective security arrangement of any large proportions, and we ended with a series of separate pacts - one with Japan, one with Australia and New Zealand, and another with the Philippines. But there was not a regional security pact created at that time.

Then I think I pointed out that, in his great address of April 16 of last year, President Eisenhower made a statement which did not attract at the time the attention it deserved perhaps because of other aspects of his speech where he referred to Korea and Southeast Asia and said there should be united action for the defense of Southeast Asia.

I repeated that statement in my March 29 speech after having previously discussed it with congressional leaders and with our principal allies.

The general conditions under which the United States is prepared to participate in collective defense there or elsewhere, for that matter, are quite well known. We are willing to participate in collective defense basically upon the terms that are laid down by the Vandenberg Resolution of June 1948, which laid down basic conditions under which the United States would be prepared to participate on the basis of mutuality and in accordance with the principles of the United Nations.

We are not prepared to go in for a defense of colonialism. We are only going to go in for defense of liberty and independence and freedom.

We don't go in alone; we go in where the other nations which have an important stake in the area recognize the peril as we do.

We go in where the United Nations gives moral sanction to our action.

All of those conditions are known. They have been known. They are a basic part of American foreign policy, and they are, as the President said in one of his press conferences, a "stable" element in the situation.

Mr. Dulles was then asked what was initiated by this Government in the period between March or April of 1953 and May of this year to bring about a Southeast Asian pact. He replied:

We did have conversations, particularly with the French and the representatives of the Associated States who under conditions then existing were apt to form the core of any defensive action in that area.

A correspondent recalled that one of the conditions laid down by Mr. Dulles in his speech of May 7 was to give independence to the Associated States. The correspondent said that France and Viet-Nam had initialed proposed treaties of independence and association. He asked Mr. Dulles how far those treaties go toward meeting this point. Mr. Dulles made the following reply:

I think what France is doing will, from what you might call a juridical standpoint, be a very large step in fulfillment of their pledge of July 3 of last year of complete independence to the Associated States. The main difficulty, I would say, at the present moment is not so much juridical as it is the translation of legal documents into a sense on the part of the peoples of Viet-Nam, Laos, and Cambodia that they really have an independence for which it is worthwhile for them to fight and, if need be, to die.

It takes time to translate papers that are signed in Paris into the living spirit; and it also takes time to overcome a certain feeling on the part of many of the Asian nations that France is not really sincere in its promises. I believe the French are going a long way down that path - perhaps from a legal standpoint as far as it is either wise or necessary to go at the present time. But it is one thing to have the letter and another thing to have the spirit, and I would say at the moment the principal deficiency is a translation of the spirit of liberty into the area and in the conduct of the French people in relation to the native peoples. There is quite a bit to be done, I think, in that practical respect.

A reporter cited as one of the general conditions for participation a place where the United Nations gives moral sanction. He asked if the United States had any plans for seeking that kind of sanction from the United Nations. Mr. Dulles answered:

There have been discussions off and on, I am sorry to say more off than on, over the past year or more with reference to bringing the United Nations into this situation. At the moment the prospects look somewhat better than they have recently, but in the past we have been very close to the United Nations action without its being actually taken. So I don't want to forecast at the present time.

Asked if we would support any appeal to the United Nations for a peace mission or observation mission to be sent into the Southeast Asian area, he replied:

I believe if such an appeal were made, the United States would support it.

Mr. Dulles was asked if the United States had before it any request from the French Government for intervention in Indochina. He replied:

No, the French Government has made no such request of the United States. They have had some conversations to explore the conditions under which that might be possible, and in that respect the French have been told much the same thing that has been publicly said by the President and me as to the conditions, which as I say have been stable and unchanging over a considerable period of time, under which such intervention would be considered possible. Of course, let me make clear that one of the conditions which we have always stood on is that there must be congressional sanction to any such action.

(344) TELEGRAM DULLES TO DILLON, MAY 26, 1954

Source: *U.S.-Vietnam Relations, Book 9*, pp. 484-486.

Only one day after his press conference remarks on the independence of the Associated States, Dulles outlined a series of steps for Dillon to discuss with the French to have an "immediate and convincing impact" on opinion in Vietnam as well as the rest of the world. He wanted France to sign the treaty of independence then being negotiated with the state of Viet-nam as soon as possible and to declare that the French Union was composed of equal and sovereign states.

We have given consideration (Embtel 4514, repeated Geneva 287, Saigon 542) to question of further clarification of independence of Associated States and following views should guide your discussions with French:

1. While fully aware of importance of juridical and constitutional factors in establishment of permanent and complete independence of Vietnam, it seems to me what is primarily needed now is something which will have immediate and convincing impact on world opinion and above all on Vietnamese themselves. We cannot wait for abolition of all deep-rooted abuses and extra-territorial privileges in times like these. We can, however, attempt have it made unmistakably clear that the Treaty of Independence between France and Vietnam represents full and unqualified commitment on part of France which will be carried out in practice.

2. Our present thinking is that in order achieve this, certain declaraties and measures are required in immediate future, both by France and by other countries associated in regional grouping for collective defense. United States in addition to such appropriate statements as might be made by President at time of his going to Congress for authority to intervene, might join with other countries concerned in a formal pledge of fulfillment of full independence and sovereignty provided by Article I of Treaty of Independence. This statement, couched in form of a common declaration of purpose, would have to be simple and explicit so there would be no room for doubt as to validity of pledge or as to intentions of countries participating in it.

3. Following represents certain minimum measures which we believe French should take now, and which we feel will not (repeat not) place government in more difficult position that it is already:

   a. France and Vietnam should sign draft treaties promptly.

   b. At moment of signature, President of Republic, in his capacity as President of French Union, should make statement to effect that Union is composed of equal and sovereign states.

   c. A declaration that French will withdraw their expeditionary force from Indochinese states at earliest practicable date after end of hostilities, consistent with France's obligations to Associated States, unless invited by respective governments of Associated States to maintain their forces. (Comment: We consider this to be at heart of any action French could take to convince world opinion they are in earnest. We feel such declaration should be made at actual time of igning or at least immediately after. Would appreciate your view as how and by whom this could be most effectively made.) This provision would not (repeat not) prejudice any base agreements which might be reached with Associated States. If United States or any other forces have been committed, we and any other countries would join in or make similar declaration.

4. Unless above are followed promptly by concrete actions which bear out professed intentions of good faith, hoped-for favorable reaction will not (repeat not) take place, and disappointment will set in correspondingly quickly. We suggest therefore that following measures be taken simultaneously, or as soon as practical:

   a. Participation of Associated States in programming all aid and direct receipt of military materiel aid. (This might require eventual renegotiation of pentapartite military agreement, but should not (repeat not) delay implementation.)

   b. French should promptly find specific ways of giving Associated States, and particularly Vietnamese Ministry of Defense and Vietnam national army greater sense of participation in measures required for defense of their territory. We conceive such participation as being progressive in character.

5. Fundamental to problem is establishment at earliest date possible of representative and authentic nationalist governments. We would hope insofar as Vietnam concerned that French would join with us in impressing Bao Dai with necessity adopting prompt and effective measures to this end.

6. Furthermore, we believe series of measures could be taken locally, even in advance of full implementation Treaties, which should have favorable public effect in Associated States. These could take form of liberalization existing Franco-Associated States accords in such manner as to attain some of objectives toward which we are working. Owing to rapid military and political developments in Associated States, we are unable specify at this time exactly what these measures may be, but believe Embassy Saigon and Commissariat General in consultation may be able make appropriate recommendations to Department and Paris.

(345) LETTER FROM CHARLES A. SULLIVAN, U.S. DELEGATION TO THE GENEVA CONFERENCE TO ADMIRAL A. C. DAVIS, DEPARTMENT OF DEFENSE, MAY 28, 1954.

Source: *U.S.-Vietnam Relations, Book 9*, pp. 498-499.

A member of the U.S. delegation representing the Department of Defense reported that U.S. delegation chief Bedell Smith accepted the probability of partition of Viet-nam, and believed there was little the U.S. could do to influence the French position. He reported general agreement in the U.S. delegation that any settlement which left Communist forces intact would result in the loss of the area to the Communists.

Developments over the past few days very clearly indicate that we are approaching a stage in the conference where it is evident that the French are going to settle on terms which the U.S. could not, under present NSC directives, associate itself with. The British have long favored an Indochina settlement on the basis of partition. The Viet Minh in their proposals submitted at the restricted session on May 25 (TOSEC 302) made a proposal which would in effect be partition. The Russians and Chinese have, of course, supported the Viet Minh proposal. In the face of this, the French have no firm position, nor has there been an indication that they have a minimum position. As a result, I feel that we are moving toward the probability that there will be a settlement which will, directly or indirectly, result in the partition of Indochina.

I have discussed the foregoing points at considerable length with Herman Phleger and Alex Johnson. They both recognize the dangers of partition and the impossibility of supervising an armistice in Indochina. There appears to be a feeling of hopelessness inasmuch as the U.S. is not in a position to control the situation. The U.S. position is not at all clear. Someone indicated before the conference we should be flexible - I would say we are now fluid. At the morning staff conferences, during the past two days, there have been discussions of U.S. tactics, and General Smith has indicated that the U.S. should remain firm. He has indicated, however, that we should be realistic, and face the probability that there will be some sort of a negotiated settlement which will result in a loss of at least part of Indochina, and will result in some type of partition. There has been no mention of the point at which the U.S. will disassociate itself from the negotiations. On the contrary, there have been indications that the U.S. will probably have to go along with a settlement even though it is unsatisfactory to the U.S.

Yesterday I attended a meeting with General Smith, Alex Johnson and Ambassador Heath in which we met with Eden and Bidault. The subject of discussion was Eden's proposal which he put forth in the sixth restricted session. Bidault had thoughts of his own on the subject taking a slightly different approach as you will note from the enclosed copy of his proposal. The thing I noted most in the discussion was the all-out effort that the various conferees are making to develop a position to which they feel the Communists will agree. Both Eden and Bidault referred to international supervision of the cessation of hostilities. However, it was quite clear from the discussion that neither is aware of the many difficult problems which will be involved in enforcing an armistice in Indochina. The question was raised by one of Eden's staff regarding the number of troops required to enforce the cessation of hostilities in Indochina. Various estimates were discussed. However, it was generally agreed that the number of troops required would be in excess of two divisions.

Since it is obvious that the conference is headed toward partition, I feel it significant to bring the foregoing information to your attention. There is very little that the Defense Department can do to influence the negotiations, since a political decision has been made that the U.S. will continue to participate even though we know that partition of Indochina, whatever form it may take, will ultimately result in its loss to the Communists. The view seems to prevail in the U.S. Delegation that there is very little the U.S. can do to influence the French and no useful purpose would be served in dissociating ourselves from the negotiations. I have little to offer in the way of recommendations. I have continued to point out the views of the Secretary of Defense and the Joint Chiefs of Staff that from a military viewpoint a settlement in Indochina which results in leaving the Communists military forces intact will ultimately result in the loss of the area to Communist control. Also there should be little doubt that there is no form of international supervision that will effectively stop further Communist infiltration and their eventual control of Indochina. Although there seems to be general agreement with the U.S. Delegation on these points there is a feeling that we cannot disassociate ourselves from the negotiations.

In outlining this gloomy situation I would like to mention one bright spot. As a result of your recommendations to General Smith I have been given every consideration and there has been complete cooperation. Due to the small number of U.S. representatives who can attend the restricted sessions on Indochina, I have not been to all of them. However, I have been included in all important discussions. Though there is obviously a difference in view between the Defense and State Department representatives here on Indochina, it is a frank, honest and friendly difference. I fully appreciate the State Department's difficulties, and though they share our view on what will ultimately result from partition, they feel compelled not to break with our allies.

I shall keep you informed of further developments.

(346) COMMUNIQUE BY THE GENEVA CONFERENCE, MAY 29, 1954

Source: *Documents on the Discussion of Korea and Indochina,* pp. 136-137.

In order to facilitate the early and simultaneous cessation of hostilities, it is proposed that:

(a) Representative of the two commands should meet immediately in Geneva and contacts should also be established on the spot.

(b) They should study the dispositions of forces to be made upon the cessation of hostilities, beginning with the question of regrouping areas in Vietnam.

(c) They should report their findings and recommendations to the Conference as soon as possible.

(347) <u>TREATY OF INDEPENDENCE OF THE STATE OF VIET-NAM</u>, JUNE 4, 1954

Source: France, *Direction de la Documentation, Articles et Documents, No. 067* (June 15, 1954), *"Textes du Jour,"* p. 1. [Translation by Gail Theisen].

The treaty by which France was to have given Viet-nam its final and complete independence was signed by the Premiers of the two states in the midst of the Geneva Conference. Under the treaty of Viet-nam was responsible for international obligations undertaken by France on its behalf - including, of course, the Geneva Agreement. However, the agreement was only initialed and not signed, nor was it ever ratified by either government. As a result, France remained legally responsible for the implementation of the agreement, despite the fact that the State of Viet-nam was treated as a fully independent state.

ARTICLE I:

France recognizes Vietnam as a fully independent and sovereign state and invested of all powers recognized by international law.

ARTICLE II:

Vietnam is substituted for France in all laws and obligations resulting from international treaties of conventions contracted by France on behalf of or in the name of the State of Vietnam or all other treaties or conventions concluded by France in the name of French Indochina to the measure in which these acts concerned Vietnam.

ARTICLE III:

France pledges to transfer to the Vietnamese government the powers and public services still guaranteed by (France) on Vietnamese territory.

ARTICLE IV:

The present treaty, which will enter into force on the date of its signing, abrogates (all) previous acts and provisions contrary to it. The instruments of ratification of the present treaty will be exchanged as of its approval by qualified representatives of France and Vietnam.

(348) <u>TELEGRAM FROM DULLES TO SMITH</u>, JUNE 7, 1954

Source: *U.S. Vietnam Relations*, pp. 533-534.

Dulles declared to his delegation chief that he did not believe the French really wanted to "internationalize" war but were merely using it to strengthen their bargaining position at Geneva.

I have your Dulte 157. I share the views there expressed, emphasizing however, your remark that we should seek to avoid formal identification with open partition or the creation of two states where one now exists.

Referring to your SECTO 389 I feel that Heath has somewhat overstated the case, perhaps deliberately for morale reasons. Our military authorities do in fact take a rather gloomy view of military situation and the QTE explorations UNQTE designed to strengthen military and political position are pretty much at a standstill not by our election but because the French themselves have never yet really decided on whether they want the war to be QTE internationalized UNQTE on the conditions which long ago we laid down at Paris. Therefore Dupont's advice to us to make up our mind QUT quickly UNQTE is rather irrelevant. We made up our mind some time ago with the qualification however that we receive the right to review the situation if by the time the French acted the situation had deteriorated beyond salvage. The latter seems to be happening.

I have long felt and still feel that the French are not treating our proposal seriously but toying with it just enough to use it as a talking point at Geneva.

(349) SPEECH BY BIDAULT TO THE GENEVA CONFERENCE, JUNE 8, 1954

Source: *Documents on the Discussion of Korea and Indochina,* pp. 137-142.

Bidault outlined the progress achieved by the Conference, primarily in beginning the process of negotiating an agreement on regroupment areas in Vietnam, and the major issues on which agreement in principle had not yet been achieved, notably the question of an all-Indochina ceasefire and the character of international supervision.

After six weeks' Conference and a month's debate on Indochina, the French Delegation feels that the time has come to see how far our discussions have got, to define the points of agreement, to recall the problems still pending and, finally, to bring out the important questions on which it has been impossible so far to reconcile the opposing views.

To go back to the beginning, I would remind you that it took two weeks to establish the list of members of the Conference. As a result of exchanges of views between the French Delegation and the Soviet Delegation, the list was finally settled with the agreement of the nine participants, subject to the reservation included in the Berlin communique that "neither the invitation to, nor the holding of, the above-mentioned Confernece shall be deemed to imply diplomatic recognition in any case where it has not already been accorded."

At the very first meeting of the Conference, on May 8 last, the French delegation set out its views, in a plan which has been communicated to you all, on the conditions and method of application of a cessation of hostilities in Indo-China. Four public meetings enabled the other delegations to explain their position in turn and some of them to submit, like my delegation, proposals on several points. Bearing in mind these first indications on May 14 I made a second general statement in which on two important points - machinery of supervision and withdrawal of French forces from the three countries of Indo-China - I was at pains not to reject but even to meet halfway the stated terms of the opposing party.

Once this first phase was concluded, the Conference decided to hold restricted meetings, which it did from May 17 onwards. An immediate decision was taken, at the request of the French Delegation, to begin with a study of the military aspects of the cessation of hostilities. So long as blood is being shed in Indo-China, these aspects take priority, the final political settlement obviously depending upon what can be done to end the fighting. That proposal was accepted by all. It has enabled us to make some progress, which is far from negligible.

This procedural point having been settled, the French Delegation would have liked the Conference to deal first of all with the case of Laos and that of Cambodia.

In this connexion it pointed out that these two cases were both different in nature from that of Viet Nam, and more easily settled. It was not a question, as in Viet Nam, of civil strife but of an invasion of two States by foreign forces. To put an end to hostilities in those two territories, all that was necessary was to secure the evacuation of those forces. Such a decision could be taken rapidly and peace thereby restored over vast areas. In order to facilitate such a desirable result, my Government was prepared, subject to its contractural engagements and to the opinion of the Governments concerned, to withdraw its own troops.

This proposal, which was supported by five delegations, and first and foremost by the representatives of Laos and Cambodia, was not accepted. The reply to our argument was that peace is indivisible since the war is indivisible. It was maintained that the three countries constituted a single theatre of operations and that a cessation of hostilities was impracticable unless it applied to all parts of that theatre. It was argued that the same principles applied to all places, although it was agreed that their application might differ in each of the three States. It was agreed, moreover, to proceed in the first instance with an examination of the conditions peculiar to Viet Nam, considered, in the words of Mr. Pham Van Dong on May 24, as "the most important theatre of operations."

Purposely overlooking the fact that this statement contradicted the argument about the war's indivisibility, the French delegation accepted that procedure. It holds that it is our duty to restore peace wherever possible and as soon as possible. That is why we preferred not to delay, by arguing the question of simultaneous operations, the study of the conditions for the restoration of peace throughout the whole of the territories in question. I am obliged, however, to note that, while the study of general principles has led to some appreciable progress, and while further progress, likewise not without value, has been realised in connexion with Viet Nam, the cases of Laos and Cambodia have so far been discussed only intermittently. Indeed on those two cases practically everything remains to be said.

With regard to Viet Nam then, on May 24 the French delegation put before the Conference a concrete proposal, a seven-point plan of work. This plan was not incompatible with the five-point plan submitted at the same time by M. Molotov. The two together have served as a basis for the discussions which have been going on since. In order to avoid any confusion, I shall, if you permit, go over what is common to both as well as what is peculiar to each, and shall consider with you the stage we have now reached in our work.

On May 8 the French delegation asked the Conference to adopt the principle of a general cessation of hostilities in Indo-China. Of this all members of the Conference have now acknowledged the necessity. The Soviet, Chinese and Vietminh delegations have also insisted that the cease-fire should be simultaneous in the three countries. On this question other delegations have expressed the same reservations as the French delegation, but all have stated uneqivocally that in fact they agreed to a simultaneous cease-fire. This common viewpoint, resulting from the conciliatory spirit shown by the majority of the Conference, has made unanimous agreement on the first general principle possible.

Six of the nine delegations have pointed out that this problem only arose in Viet Nam, since in Cambodia and Laos all that is needed is to obtain the withdrawal of the Vietminh forces.

In the case of Viet Nam, the French plan of May 8, as amplified and clarified on May 14, proposed that the two parties' regular units should be regrouped in areas the limits of which would be fixed by the Conference after consultations with the High Commands. In the course of his substantial statement on May 12, the Viet Nam representative endorsed these principles. Mr. Pham Van Dong, too, on May 10, proposed a readjustment of the areas. The clarification of his views furnished by his statement on May 25 was particularly interesting in that it provides evidence of a clear evolution in Vietminh thinking during recent days.

In these circumstances the Conference felt that it was fruitless to continue further with the general debate and that the representatives of the High Commands should be invited to meet in Geneva to study the assembly areas in Viet Nam, as I proposed on May 14. In the course of a procedural debate on May 27, 28 and 29, various draft resolutions, including a French draft were examined; the text proposed by Mr. Eden on May 29 was finally adopted. Before its adoption the various delegations expressed both their support and their reservations. As far as the French delegation is concerned its comments, as my colleagues will recall, were two-fold: the problem of regrouping only arises in the case of Viet Nam and the principle of the unity of Viet Nam is not open to question. The French delegation is happy to recall that the Chairman of the Conference, on that day M. Molotov, clearly proclaimed this principle on behalf of his colleagues, at the meeting on May 29.

The agreement reached in this way is a positive achievement, since it has enabled the representatives of the High Commands to meet in Geneva since Wednesday, June 2. Their work must go on in the strictest secrecy, and I shall therefore make no comment on it. I should only like to express the French delegation's hope and desire that the military discussions will progress so that the Conference may soon be in a position to examine specific recommendations including the assembly areas marked on the map. That is a prerequisite for further examination of the cessation of hostilities in Viet Nam and, more especially, of the subsequent measures linked with the establishment of the assembly areas, such as administration of the areas, economic and financial provisions, irregulars, practical arrangements for supervision, &c. Finally, the resolution of May 29 provides for meetings on the spot between representatives of the High Commands; the purpose of these meetings, for which arrangements are now being made, is to enable the necessary further studies and the concessions decided on at Geneva to be carried out.

We note with satisfaction the progress achieved with the second item of the agenda. But, let us not disguise the fact, the problem of assembly areas is a complex one and will require a good deal of unremitting effort.

The delegations of Viet Nam and France have stressed the importance of this problem on several occasions. More than a third of the Vietminh forces belong to the category of what are called irregulars. It would be remarkable if the decisions of the Conference whose task it is to restore peace in Indo-China left a substantial part of one of the adversaries' forces entire freedom of action in the territory in which they happen to be. The prospects of restoring peace would be jeopardized. The Conference will have to consider this question carefully once we have made sufficient progress with the assembly areas. Certain of Mr. Pham Van Dong's words on May 25 do not exclude possibilities of agreement in this field.

An armistice, we have been told time and again, must contain an undertaking by each of the parties not to increase its total military strength.

It is obvious, although it has not always been stated, that such a clause is only conceivable as applying equally to the two parties.

I repeat that it should also cover war supplies manufactured locally. It implies strict supervision of the land and sea frontiers of Viet Nam, without which the undertaking would be illusory and the guarantee fraudulent. Most delegations have not had time to give their views on the problem. I shall merely note that agreement on the principle of such an undertaking in Viet Nam does seem possible.

There has been no objection to the release of prisoners of war and civil internees immediately after the cessation of hostilities. Agreement between members of the Conference appears to be complete.

All those who hate war can only welcome this with a feeling of satisfaction for the present and hope for the future.

The last three restricted meetings of the Conference have been devoted to supervision and, to a lesser extent, guarantees. Our discussions on these subjects have, up to the present, been very thorny, even disappointing.

The problem is three-fold. To begin with, there is one principle that must be clearly established right at the start - the principle of neutral international supervision covering all the clauses of the armistice. In Indo-China, men have been fighting for eight years. Whatever the value of the agreements we reach they will be difficult to carry out and there is danger of clashes.

Unless neutral and impartial supervisors, umpires or observers are empowered to deal with the differences and disputes likely to arise between parties which have been at war for so long, violations and perhaps serious incidents are to be feared. Without neutral supervision, there is a danger of the agreements losing all real force, and any chances of peace killed by perpetuating the atmosphere of mistrust.

As long ago as May 8, the French delegation proclaimed the principle of international supervision. Five delegations have expressed the same conviction. At the three restricted meetings devoted to supervision, I three times stated the position of the French delegation. On June 2, I circulated the written text of our observations to the members of the Conference. On June 4, I submitted a specific plan containing a detailed study of the duties and structure of the International Supervisory Commission and of the joint bodies to be attached to it as working instruments. That is the second element of the problem.

Under this plan, the International Commission will supervise the execution of the clauses of the agreements. It will install throughout the country, on its own responsibility, a complete supervisory system, party fixed and party mobile, and equipped with modern transport, communications and observation facilities. It will not be a Commission of just a few members scattered here and there over an immense territory, but a solid organization, numerous and flexible enough to meet changing needs. Finally, the International Commission will have at its disposal, for specified duties, a number of joint commissions, composed of representatives of the two commands acting under its authority and in accordance with its instructions. In the event of any violation, directly it is is clear that the parties cannot reach agreement and that consequently the joint commissions are powerless , the International Commission will deal with the dispute and enforce its decisions. Decisions of the Commission will in all cases be taken by a majority vote.

On May 10, Mr. Pham Van Dong submitted a counter-proposal. Supervision should, in his view, be ensured by a joint Commission composed of representatives of the two parties. The experience of 1946 has taught us what to think of this kind of arrangement which, against all commonsense, is based on the principle that the same person is both judge and party.

Following M. Molotov's speech of May 14, his position was slightly modified. Provision for a neutral commission was added to the original Vietminh proposals. The main duty of this neutral commission would be to supervise the entry of foreign supplies into Indo-China. On this point, we entirely agree with Mr. Dong. But as regards the other clauses of the armistice, in the most cases, those where the two parties come face to face in the course of movements of regular troops on either side of the dividing line between the assembly areas &c. Mr. Dong wishes to entrust the primary responsibility for supervision to the joint Commission. The French delegation has not yet been able to fathom in what circumstances that Commission would have to intervene. Under our plan, the joint commissions would be working instruments, subordinate to the International Commission. Mr. Dong and the Union of Soviet Socialist Republics and Chinese delegates after him, expressed his opposition to this system. There is a serious divergence here which will have to be bridged.

The third element of the problem is the membership of the International Commissions. In the French view the qualification for selection are simple: objectivity, impartiality and efficiency. Any country possessing these qualifications is acceptable. As Mr. Eden very rightly remarked, if the International Commission is the political counterpart of the joint commissions it will be paralysed in the same way. The proposal put forward by M. Molotov would have precisely this effect: four neutral powers, selected two by two for their particular sympathies, would be reduced to impotence. A supervisory body composed on this basis would be no guarantee for anyone. All that we, for our part, are trying to secure is the certainty that firm decisions will be taken whenever necessary.

Finally, there is the problem of the authority to which the International Control Commission is to be responsible. Unless the Commission has proper backing there is a danger of its decisions remaining a dead letter for lack of a court appeal. Some body must be set up or selected to which the International Commission can appeal if circumstances so require. This body in turn would appeal to the guarantors. In our view, the guarantors should be the members of the Geneva Conference, that is the signatories of the future agreements. The problem of guarantees has not yet been seriously studies by the Conference. Only the principle has been accepted. All I need say to-day is that it must be impossible for the guarantees to be paralysed by any right of veto.

To end now a statement which I would have liked to have been shorter, we have to record that the Conference has already achieved appreciable results. It has chosen an appropriate working method in agreeing, as the French delegation requested, to devote its present efforts to the military aspects of the problem of the cessation of hostilities. It has accepted the principle of a complete cessation of hostilities to apply, if possible, simultaneously throughout the whole of Indo-China.

In Viet Nam, it has adopted the principle of regrouping in assembly areas and entrusted the study of it to the competent persons. In the field of supervision, it has agreed to international commissions. We have already advanced several stages along the road that leads to peace.

I will not go so far, however, as to say with M. Molotov that the principals put forward in the Chinese proposal have met with the unanimous agreement of the Conference. Unfortunately, as I have already shown, serious differences of opinion have come to light during our debates on essential points. And, whatever spirit of conciliation we may show, there are limits beyond which we cannot go without infringing on essential principles. In each case, the French delegation has endeavored to be conciliatory; this has been particularly evident in the field of supervision.

I will merely recall, that on three, either we have not yet completed our examination or have not yet reached our conclusions.

The cases of Laos and of Cambodia have still to be discussed. We have explained in what they consist. In the circumstances I have described, it has not been possible for us to embark on a thorough discussion of them. It is clear, and it is precisely the argument of the Soviet, Chinese and Vietminh delegations, that we cannot restore peace in Viet Nam and leave Vietminh forces operating on its flank beyond its frontiers.

The military experts are getting on too slowly with their work which should lead to the establishment of the assembly areas. They have, however, to deal with concrete facts, and are not concerned with the political aspects. We hope that the geographical definition of the military agreement will be speeded up.

Finally and especially, it is an imperative necessity for all of us to reach agreement of the methods of application and supervision. I will not repeat what I have said on this subject. There are some problems of structure which are very important. There is the question of which countries should be chosen to carry out the supervision and that choice is crucial. Without effective supervision, I see no way out. Without the power of rapid decision, there would be disorder and all the risks attending the unforeseen.

Difficulties await us and we must not close our eyes to the fact that they are still extensive. I trust we may overcome them quickly. Efforts have been made and some progress has been achieved. The results obtained point the way to future agreements. We must neglect nothing in an endeavor to complete our work. The ediface that has only been started must be completed. It is on the completion of our work and not just on its beginning that depends the accomplishments of our task, which is the restoration of peace.

(350) <u>PROPOSAL BY THE CAMBODIAN DELEGATION TO THE GENEVA CONFERENCE,</u>
JUNE 8, 1954

Source: *Documents on the Discussion of Korea and Indochina,* p. 142.

The Cambodia delegation submitted a proposal which called for the withdrawal of all "Vietminh" forces, regular and irregular, to Vietnamese territory. The term "Vietminh" was meant to cover all Cambodian forces fighting against the Royal Government of Cambodia alongside the Viet Minh.

1. A cessation of hostilities shall be proclaimed in Cambodia, if possible at the same time as a cessation of hostilities in Laos and Viet Nam. In case of an agreement on a simultaneous cessation of hostilities, the three plans for Cambodia. Laos and Viet Nam respectively shall be put into effect simultaneously.

2. - (a) All regular and irregular Vietminh forces shall, on the date of the cessation of hostilities, be evacuated from Cambodian territory and regrouped, in Vietminh territory, in the assembly areas assigned to the Vietminh command by agreement between the French, Viet Nam and Vietminh commands.
For this purpose, the Cambodian and Vietminh commands shall meet on the spot to fix the method of execution of the evacuation.
(b) All armed elements belonging neither to the army nor to the police forces shall, on the date of the cessation of hostilities, be disarmed and dispersed. Foreign non-national elements shall be returned to their country of origin.

3. Prisoners of war and civil internees shall be released or exchanged after agreement between the Cambodian and Vietminh commands.

4. A system of international supervision by neutral countries or a system of supervision by the United Nations shall be established to supervise the execution of the above agreements. The system of international supervision must be installed and ready to operate on the date of the cessation of hostilities.

(351) <u>TELEGRAM FROM DULLES TO SMITH</u>, JUNE 8, 1954

Source: *U.S. Vietnam Relations, Book 9,* pp. 540-541.

Dulles indicated that the U.S. would not try to commit other states to united action until the French had fulfilled all the conditions and requested international action. Furthermore, he insisted that the U.S. had to reserve judgement on going ahead with intervention even if all the conditions were fulfilled, based on the circumstances then existing.

Numbered paragraph 1 Reftel. We would be interested any specific ideas Bidault might propose with view simplifying request to other nations, so long they meet basic condition that US will not (repeat not) intervene alone. Until we have full agreement, at least in principle, with French on conditions US military participation there would be no actual negotiations with other interested nations. So far we have kept them generally informed concerning current discussions in Paris and have obtained their tentative views. We would seek firm views once French authority tell us they want to internationalize the Indochina war. Meanwhile, UK views are well known and soundings indicate almost certainly New Zealand and probably Australia would not (repeat not) participate without UK. Our soundings indicate Thailand and Philippines would most likely come along.
Numbered paragraph 3. We agree undesirable President should make formal pledge unilaterally and refer you paragraph 2 Deptel 4272, repeated Geneva TOSEG (?) 269, which stressed joint character any such pledge. President would

necessarily deal with independence question in any request to Congress for authorization use US forces for combat in Indochina.

Numbered paragraph 4. While we would agree substitution words Quote after re-establishment for rest sentence definitely preferable to that proposed by Bidault. His text carries overtone France retaining right decide timing first and then getting Vietnamese Government to agree after, which precisely type implication we consider it necessary avoid if independence of Viet Nam to be crystal clear.

Numbered paragraph 5. We feel Bidault's proposed text for paragraph 2 of Deptel 4286, repeated TEDUL 133, conflicts with assurance sought by our test. While Bidault's language might be helpful for EDC debate it provides loopholes for abusive interpretation justifying later claims right withdrawal on one or other of courts listed. When occasion offers suggest you point out to Bidault that we could not (repeat not) commit forces and US prestige in situation when there would be any question concerning premature French withdrawal their forces.

Numbered paragraph 6. After full agreement reached on all conditions and French Government has reached decision it wishes request US intervention, US must have opportunity at that time make its own decision whether prevailing circumstance warrant implementation of formal steps leading to US military participation. We cannot grant French indefinite option on us without regard to intervening deterioration. Only after these decision taken would we expect Laniel submit agreement and request for internationalization to Parliament for endorsement and ratification; also he must not (repeat not) prejudice our liberty of decision by approaching Parliament in such way that we would appear be morally committed intervene prior to our decision.

(352) <u>NEWS CONFERENCE STATEMENTS BY DULLES</u>, JUNE 9, 1954

Source: *Department of State Bulletin*, June 21, 1954, pp. 947-949.

Commenting on the Geneva talks, Dulles charged the Communists with deliberately "dragging out" the talks and referred once again to the U.S. "united action" proposal, but he volunteered the point that such action was becoming far less practical because of the deterioration of the situation in Indochina.

Text:

In reply to a question of his assessment of the Geneva talks concerning Indochina to date, Mr. Dulles said:

The primary responsibility in those negotiations is being carried, of course, by the French delegation in association with the delegations of the three Associated States of Indochina, Viet-Nam, Laos, and Cambodia.

The United States is playing primarily the role of a friend which gives advice when it is asked for, and of course we have a very deep hope that the result will be one which will maintain the genuine independence of the entire area and bring about a cessation of the fighting.

Whether that result is obtainable or not is of course problemmatic. It seems that the Communist forces in Indochina are intensifying their activities. They have done so ever since the proposal for peace in Indochina, which was taken at the Berlin Conference. There has been, I think, a deliberate dragging out of the negotiations at Geneva while the Communist military effort has been stepped up in Indochina itself. The fact that under these circumstances the Communists are dragging their feet on peace and intensifying their efforts for war is a commentary upon the general attitude of the Communists and gives a lie, I think, to their greatly professed love for peace.

Asked what, in his view, was the best way to meet a situaion where the Communists were intensifying war and dragging their feet on peace, Mr. Dulles said:

The United States has made a number of suggestions which all fit into a common and consistent pattern.

The first suggestion of that order was, as I have recalled to you, the proposal that the President made over a year ago in his April 16 address when he proposed that there should be united action in relation to Indochina. That suggestion was not adopted, although, as I mentioned here, I think, in my last press conferences, it was followed up in private negotiations by the United States Government.

I renewed the same suggestion in my March 29, 1954, speech, and the position of the United States with respect to that matter still stands, subject of course, to the possibility that a time may come when that particular suggestion is no longer a practical one. But it has been a practical one ever since President Eisenhower first made it, and I believe it is still a practical one.

Asked whether the alternative, should the plan for united action not become practical, might imply the United States' dealing with this situation single-handedly or unilaterally, Mr. Dulles replied:

No. The United States has no intention of dealing with the Indochina situation unilaterally, certainly not unless the whole nature of the aggression should change.

"What change?" Mr. Dulles was asked. He replied:

Well, if there should be a resumption by Communist China of open armed aggression in that area or in any other area of the Far East that might create a new situation.

Asked how long he felt the United States and other free nations should continue to sit at Geneva in a sincere effort to negotiate while Communists dragged their feet at Geneva and intensified the war in Indochina, Mr. Dulles said:

As I pointed out earlier, the primary responsibility in that respect has to be assumed by the countries that are carrying the principle burden of the fighting in the area, which on our side are France and Viet-Nam. They are recognized by us as having a primacy in this matter. It would be their decision in this respect which would be controlling. I would not want to attempt to establish what I thought should be their policy in this matter.

Mr. Dulles was asked what the objectives of united action would be - would it mean intervention, the holding of a special line in Indochina, or some other objective? The Secretary replied:

It would obviously have an objective. The objective would be to retain in friendly hands as much as possible of the Southeast Asian peninsula and island area. Now the practicability varies from time to time. What was practical a year ago is less practical today. The situation has, I am afraid, been deteriorating.

Mr. Dulles was asked what progress had been made toward general acceptance of the united action idea. He replied:

I would say that progress has been made only in this sense, that two of the conditions precedent have been advanced. Namely, considerable further progress, I think, has been made in clarifying the prospective status of the states of Viet-Nam, Laos, and Cambodia as regards their complete independence. And, also, the fact that on the application of Thailand the Security Council voted 10 to 1 to put that on its agenda, and to begin to get into the matter. That, again, is a movement on one of the fronts which we have felt to be indispensable in relation to united action. In those two respects some progress has been made.

The Secretary was asked about the progress of the Washington military staff talks and about parallel talks with Asian countries. He replied:

We have had a series of talks the first of which I think took place here in Washington with the representative of the Government of Thailand with reference to their military position and steps which might be taken to strengthen it. Then Secretary Wilson, when he was in Manila a few days ago, had a series of talks, himself and his military advisers, with the representatives of the Philippine General Staff.

The talks that are going on here in Washington with the United Kingdom, France, Australia, and New Zealand are the same type of talks designed to gather together military information, to assess military possibilities so that if and when it is necessary to take political decisions there will be available at hand the military elements of the problem. I expect a further visit to this country of the Philippine Chief of Staff and possibly a similar visit from Thailand. We are trying to keep in as close touch as we can with the military position, as I say, because that has to be taken into account in reaching political decisions.

Asked about reports that the Administration might ask Congress to adopt some sort of resolution on the Indochina situation, Mr. Dulles replied:

There is no present plan for going to Congress for any authority in this matter. As is well know, the general scheme which the United States has had for this area and which I have already described here, would, if it were implemented, probably require congressional action. But there has so far not been a sufficiently general acceptance of the program to make it, as a matter of practical politics. a question of going to Congress.

(353) <u>STATEMENT BY SMITH AT THE GENEVA CONFERENCE</u>, JUNE 9, 1954 (Extract)

Source: *Department of State Bulletin,* June 21, 1954, p. 944.

Addressing three issues on which the two sides were still far apart, Smith supported the separation of Laos and Cambodia from Viet-nam in terms of a cease-fire agreement, binding authority for the international supervisory commission over the joint Vietnamese truce commission and an international commission without a Communist veto.

At this moment we are still confronted with three important issues which have been debated at length at a number of meetings and without result. The first of these is, as I and others of my colleagues said yesterday afternoon, the special nature of the problem existing in Laos and Cambodia.

I believe that both Mr. Eden and Mr. Bidault unanswerably demonstrated the necessity of separate treatment for those two countries where peace would automatically be restored by the withdrawal of the invading Viet Minh force.

The second issue is that of the powers of the international supervisory commission for Viet-Nam. This commission must obviously have the authority and facilites to settle any problems or differences which cannot be adjusted by the joint commissions of the belligerents, and logically, therefore, its decisions must be binding on those joint commissions.

The third vital issue is the composition of the international supervisory commission. As I and others of us said before, a commission containing states unable to meet the test of impartiality - that is, a commission the counterpart of that set up in Korea, on when Communist state members have been able by veto to prevent effective supervision - is obviously an unsatisfactory and an unacceptable proposal. Yesterday the representative of the United Kingdom proposed the Colombo powers. I welcomed that proposal. This afternoon the representative of Viet-Nam proposed the U.N. That would be acceptable.

Both are reasonable proposals. The proposal of the Soviet Union, from my point of view, and I think from that of the majority of my colleagues, is not reasonable.

I am obliged to state that the Soviet, the Chinese Communist, and the Viet Minh delegations have, so far, shown no signs of willingness to resolve these issues on any reasonble basis which could be acceptable to this conference, or which would inspire and insure the return of peace to Indochina. I hope that I am wrong, but the negative results of our last meeting seem to support this conclusion.

(354) TELEGRAM FROM DULLES TO SMITH, JUNE 9, 1954

Source: *U.S. Vietnam Relations,* Book 9, pp. 550-551.

Dulles repeated to Bonnet the U.S. position that it could not give a "blank check" to Paris to be used regardless of circumstances, even if the original conditions were fulfilled.

Ambassador bonnet (sic) came to see Secretary Dulles Wednesday afternoon and raised question of participation of US Marines Indochina. He said he had received telegram from Maurice Schumann expressing excitement and dismay at information from Valluy that Radford had said there was no rpt no question of utilization Marines Indochina. Ambassador said this conflicted with what French Govt had hitherto understood to be intentions US Government this respect. He further stated suggestion made by Radford to Valluy that three Korean divisions might be used in Indochina was unacceptable.

Secretary said US position had been clear from start and that we were not rpt not willing to make commitment ahead of time which French could use for internal political maneuvering or negotiating at Geneva and which would represent a kind of permanent option on US intervention if it suited their purpose. A month ago, French had been explicitly informed conditions which must be met and fulfilled by them before President took decision whether to go to Congress and ask for authority use American armed forces in relation Indochina. Among these conditions was need for French and Associated States to request US and certain other interested countries to come in. We were still in dark as to what French intentions really were. Secretary said he felt French desire obtain firm commitment from us on which they could draw was understandable, but equally understandable in circumstances is our determination not rpt not to give them such blank check. Secretary confirmed US position as stated by Dillon (4766 from Paris) that use of Marines would not rpt not be concluded provided an agreed operational plan required their presence. He said it was useless and illusory to attempt to obtain from us at this time a commitment more specific on this point than that which we had already given.

With regard to what we would do in event act of open aggression by Chinese, Secretary read relevant extracts (last four paragraphs of section __ Roman four) from his Los Angeles speech which is being separately transmitted.

Bonnet expressed surprise that we considered that French Govt had not rpt not made up its mind with regard to internationalization of Indochina war and said he considered request had already been made by French. Secretary pointed out that our offer on basis certain specific conditions had been made a month ago in context of situation at that time, which confirmed and made precise much earlier representation. Since then things had changed rapidly and would doubtless continue to change. For this reason delay was regrettable and further delay would not rpt not improve situation with regard to any role we might consider playing.

(355) TELEGRAM FROM ACTING SECRETARY OF STATE ROBERT MURPHY TO SMITH AND DILLON, JUNE 10, 1954

Source: *U.S. Vietnam Relations*, Book 9, pp. 553-554.

In another step back from intervention in Indochina, the State Department refused General Ely's request for military talks on possible U.S. military intervention and refused to consider sending a military training mission to Viet-nam, due to the deterioration of the military situation.

Following translation text message from Ely to Radford received evening June 9:

QUOTE: I have not yet made a survey of the military situation, especially in Tonkin. However, it seems to me that the decision I will have to take regarding the operations will rest on the US intentions, in the present situation, as well as those they anticipate in the future.

QUOTE: Therefore, I would very much like to have, either in Paris, where I expect to be probably on the 19th June, or here in Saigon, as soon as possible an exchange of views with a qualified representative of Admiral Radford, in order to know which I can expect on the part of the U.S.A. UNQUOTE.

Prior to French decision to request internationalization, we consider undesirable to start yet another series conversations which would inevitably provoke on French side all kinds hopes and interpretations with regard basic issue US intervention which would only cause further confusion. In other words, it is our feeling that we should not be eased into a series of piecemeal commitments resulting from collateral military conversations in the absence of an understanding with the French Government based on our general proposal described in TEDUL 54. Radford has accordingly informed General Valluy orally that US position was given to Ambassador Bonnet by Secretary June 9 and that he is not (repeat not) in position at this time to respond to Ely's request for conversations on subject raised his message.

With regard to US training Vietnamese troops, we feel that situation Viet Nam has deteriorated to point where any commitment at this time to send over US instructors in near future might expose us to being faced with situation in which it would be contrary to our interests to have to fulfill such commitment. Our position accordingly is that we do not (repeat not) wish to consider US training mission or program separately from over-all operational plan on assumption conditions fulfilled for US participation war Indochina.

(356) TELEGRAM FROM DULLES TO DILLON, June 14, 1954

Source: *U.S. Vietnam Relations*, Book 9, pp. 559-560

Dulles confirmed that the deterioration in Indochina was such as to make military intervention unlikely and blaming it on French and British indecision.

It is true that there is less disposition now than two months or one month ago to intervene in Indochina militarily. This is the inevitable result of the steady deterioration in Indochina which makes the problem of intervention and pacification more and more difficult. When united defense was first broached, the strength and morale of French and Vietnam forces were such that it seemed that the situation could be held without any great pouring-in of U.S. ground forces. Now all the evidence is that the morale of the Vietnamese Government, armed forces and civilians has deteriorated gravely; the French are forced to contemplate a fall-back which would leave virtually the entire Tonkin Delta population in hostile hands and the Saigon area is faced with political disintegration.

What has happened has been what was forecast as for example by my Embassy Paris 4117 TEDUL 78 of May 17. I there pointed out that probably the French did not really want intervention but wanted to have the possibility as a card to play at Geneva. I pointed out that the Geneva game would doubtless be a long game and that it could not be assumed that at the end the present U.S. position regarding intervention would necessarily exist after the Communists had succeeded in dragging out Geneva by winning military successes in Indochina. This telegram of mine will bear rereading. That point of view has been frequently repeated in subsequent cables.

I deeply regret any sense of bitterness on Bidault's part, but I do not see that he is justified in considering unreasonable the adaptation of U.S. views to events and the consequences of prolonged French and U.K. indecision.

I do not yet wholly exclude possibility U.S. intervention on terms outlined PARIS 402 TEDUL 54. UK it seems is now more disposed to see movement in this direction but apparently the French are less than ever disposed to internationalizing the war.

(357) TELEGRAM FROM DULLES TO SMITH, JUNE 14, 1954

Source: *U.S. Vietnam Relations, Book 9,* pp. 561-562.

Dulles asserted that final adjournment of the Geneva Conference was desirable, provided it would not appear to the French an abandonment by the U.S. and Britain.

1. It is our view that final adjournment of Conference is in our best interest provided this can be done without creating an impression in France at this critical moment that France has been deserted by US and UK and therefore has no choice but capitulation on Indochina to Communists at Geneva and possibly accomodation with the Soviets in Europe. Because of this, if the French want to keep the Conference at least nominally alive, we would go along with the idea of recess and the maintenance of the small observation group as you propose in Geneva. We trust that the developments at Geneva will have been such as to satisfy the British insistence that they did not want to discuss collective action until either Geneva was over or at least the results of Geneva were known. I would assume that the departure of Eden would be evidence that there were no adequate reasons for further delaying collective talks on SEA defense.

2. Re paragraph 1 above we assume any recess would only relate to the Indochina phase of Conference and the Korean phase would be closed out as indicated last para DULTE 179 and SECTO 435.

3. We believe that you should leave Geneva no (repeat no) later than Eden.

4. Assume that you will as soon as appropriate opportunity offers talk with Bidault as well as Eden about these matters.

(358) TELEGRAM FROM SMITH TO DULLES, JUNE 16, 1954

Source: *U.S. Vietnam Relations, Book 9,* pp. 572-573.

Smith reported that the private military talks were leading to a partition of the country. He emphasized to the French delegation the importance of avoiding complete partition by holding a French enclave in the North.

Chauvel informed me this morning that in Franco-Viet Minh "underground military talks" (conducted by Colonel de Brebission on French side) Viet Minh had demanded all of Tonkin and entire delta area including Hanoi (to become Headquarters Viet Minh Army) and Haiphong be turned over to Viet Minh. French without agreeing had implied that if anything like this settlement were made, French would demand free hand in south, indicating area south of line starting approximately 18 parallel on Laotian border and running southeast approximately to Badon (this line marked somewhat indefinitely on map in Chauvel's office) French had also indicated necessity for enclave and port in delta area, implying temporary tenure for troop withdrawal. Chauvel indicated Ely felt he could not defend delta area and better have French forces therein by negotiations than lose them in battle. French raised question evacuation their troops, French citizens, and Vietnam Catholics from Tonkin area but had received no reply from Viet Minh. Chauvel also stated French had made clear that Laos and Cambodia were not involved in this proposed settlement. No mention was made regrouping Viet Minh forces south this line. Last conversation three days ago and nothing has developed since. Chauvel continued that Vietnamese had no knowledge this proposal and if acceptable to French it would be most difficult to sell it to them, which might be necessary within next few days. He implied that Ambassador Heath might be of real service this connection.

I informed Chauvel of Zhukov-Kingsbury Smith conversation (SECTO 423 repeated Paris 418) emphasizing advisability French retaining foothold in north preferably Haiphong-Hanoi area, but at least Haiphong. This, with possibly, small compensating enclave for Viet Minh south of line, would avoid appearance of outright partition. Chauvel was somewhat dubious whether this would be possible but thought that maybe foothold on delta coast at Hon Gay, where there are important French coal interests, might be retained. I told Chauvel that we did not wish be suddenly placed in position where these secret negotiations might have result of our being abruptly confronted with agreement or proposed settlement which we would not feel able to accept and from which we might have to disassociate ourselves, and stressed need our being informed on continuing basis of conversations. Suggested Colonel Dwan be liaison officer this respect. Chauvel agreed.

(359) <u>TELEGRAM FROM DULLES TO SMITH</u>, June 16, 1954

Source: *U.S. Vietnam Relations, Book 9*, pp. 570-571.

Responding to a message from Bidault which concluded that the U.S. was no longer willing to intervene on the basis of the May 11 policy statement, Dulles refused to rule out intervention in the event of a request from a French Government with a hard-line policy toward a negotiatied settlement.

Bonnet has just left after reading a long message from Bidault, the substance of which was that the French no longer felt that US was committed to intervention on the conditions stated in our May 11 basic cable to Paris and that this left them in a very difficult negotiating position at Geneva.

I said that it was quite true that the French could not have a continuing option to call US into war at some future undetermined date and under conditions which could not now be foreseen. On the other hand if and when there was a French Government which had the confidence of the Assembly and if it should then decide that it could not conclude an honorable armistice and that it was thus necessary to continue the struggle, the US would be prepared promptly to respond and that response would probably be along the lines of our May 11 telegram unless in the meantime the situation had further deteriorated to a point where the making of a stand in Indochina had become impracticable or so burdensome as to be out of proportion to the results obtainable.

I said that I regretted not being able to make a response that would be more satisfactory to Bidault but that I could not conceive that it would be expected that the US would give a third power the option to put it into war at times and under conditions wholly of the other's choosing.

I suggest that Under Secretary or Ambassador paren whoever sees Bidault first end paren should summarize foregoing to Bidault as am not confident that Bonnet who was in highly emotional state will adequately report.

(360) TELEGRAM FROM SMITH TO DULLES, JUNE 17, 1954

Source: *U.S. Vietnam Relations, Book 9,* pp. 574-575.

In conversation with Eden, Chou En-lai indicated that regroupment areas would have to be established in Laos, but not in Cambodia, and that the Vietnamese would withdraw their volunteers from the two countries as part of a general withdrawal of foreign forces. Chou's proposal was ultimately accepted as the basis for the settlement in both countries.

Dennis Allen (UK) gave Johnson this morning additional details on conversation with Chou En-lai. Chou stated that in case Cambodia resistance forces were small and all that was necessary was a political settlement by the present royal government with them "which could easily be obtained." In case of Laos, resistance forces were larger, and it would be necessary recognize this fact by formation of regrouping areas along the border with Vietnam and China. The task of both States was twofold: The removal of foreign forces and dealing with the problem of domestic resistance movements. The military staff should get down to this task.

In reply to Eden's query as to whether it would not (repeat not) be difficult obtain Viet Minh admission Viet Minh forces were in Laos and Cambodia, Chou stated it would "not (repeat not) be difficult" to get Viet Minh to agree to withdrawal all foreign forces. Chou made no (repeat no) direct reply to Eden's refrence to French-Laotian treaty on French bases in Laos. Eden expressed personal view that Chou wants settlement, but has some doubt with regard to degree of control he exercises over Viet Minh.

In long talk with Bidault this morning (first direct contact with Chinese and French) Chou substantially repeated what he told Eden yesterday (in conversation with Bidault, Chou referred to Viet Minh forces in Cambodia and Laos as "volunteers"). Bidault had also seen Molotov this morning and reported that both Molotov and Chou are obviously greatly concerned over any break-up Indochina conference in pattern of Korean conference as well as of lowering level conference below level of Foreign Ministers. Bidault said they clearly want to keep the conference going. Bidault and I agree (Eden did not (repeat not) comment) that it was very important we do nothing dispel Chou's worries over US bases in Laos and Cambodia.

I also expressed personal opinion that important Laos and Cambodia move ahead as quickly as and as vigorously as possible with appeal to UN. Eden and Bidault agreed, Eden adding that important Vietnam not (repeat not) get mixed up with Laos and Cambodia cases UN.

Chauvel showed me handwritten note from Ely, in his political capacity, urging against attempting hold any enclave in delta and recommending straight partition formula. I could not (repeat not) resist expressing contempt for such an easy "selling-out" of last remaining foothold in north and said we could under no (repeat no) circumstances publicly associate ourselves with such a solution.

(361) STATEMENT BY FRENCH PREMIER PIERRE MENDES-FRANCE TO THE NATIONAL ASSEMBLY, JUNE 17, 1954 [Extract]

Source: French Press and Information Service, *French Affairs*, No. 10 (June 21, 1954), pp. 1-3.

Pierre Mendes-France, a long-time opponent of the French War in Indochina, addressed the National Assembly after being asked to form a government. He had been informed by high French military officials that the Expeditionary Corps faced possible catastrophe during the weeks prior to the rainy season. So he was determined to obtain a settlement that would avert such a catastrophe. In this speech delivered one day before his investiture as Premier, he made clear his commitment to a compromise settlement at Geneva and gave his government four weeks to reach an agreement, promising to resign if he failed. He hinted at tougher measures which would be taken by France in that event.

I come before, entrusted by the President of the Republic with the same mission as a year ago, almost to the day.

At that time I proposed a policy of recovery and national renovation, and I told you that this policy constituted a single unit of which you could not accept a part and reject the rest without making the entire program ineffective. Three hundred and one among you approved the program as a whole, but 205 abstained, thus indicating, I think, that although they agreed with me on a great many points, they could not, however, give me their wholehearted support on others.

If I did not get their votes, it was not because of the strictness of my economic program, which set great goals for the nation to attain without concealing the difficulties that stood in their way; it was not because they were reluctant to choose a difficult course, but rather because we were then divided on one problem: the problem of Indochina.

I speak to those who abstained a year ago. The events that have occurred since then must have brought our views closer together. And we can now be united, it seems to me, by a common desire for peace, which corresponds to the aspiration of the entire country.

We are also engaged together in negotiations now under way. It is my duty to tell you in what state of mind I shall take these negotiations, if you entrust me with that task.

For some years now I have felt that a peace through compromise, a peace negotiated with the enemy, was warranted by the facts, and that on such a peace depended the rehabilitation of our finances, and the recovery and expansion of our economy, for that war laid upon our country a burden too heavy for it to bear.

And now a new and fearful danger has emerged: if the conflict in Indochina is not settled - and settled very soon - it is the risk of war, of an international and perhaps atomic war, that we must face.

It is because I wanted a better peace that I wanted it sooner, when we held more trump cards in our hand, but there are concessions and sacrifices which even the present situation does not call for. France need not accept, and will not accept, a settlement under conditions which would be incompatible with her most vital interests. France will maintain her presence in the Far East. Neither our Allies nor our enemies should harbor the slightest doubt as to the significance of our determination.

We have entered into negotiations at Geneva in liaison with our Allies and with the Associated States. The Government I shall form, if you so decide, will pursue these negotiations, prompted by a constant will to peace, but equally resolved - in order to safeguard our interest and reach an honorable settlement - to play for all they are worth the trump cards still held by France: the concentration of our material and spiritual forces in wide areas;

the interest and support of our Allies; and, last, the valor and heroism of our soldiers - the essential factor on which France relies above all else. I say this emphatically and pay them a solemn homage, by recalling the painful glory of Dienbienphu and so many sacrifices made in unknown as well as famous battles.

That is why the security of the Expeditionary Corps and the maintenance of its strength are imperative duties in which neither the Government nor the Parliament will falter.

That is why no measure will be neglected that might prove necessary for this purpose.

And that is why, finally, he who stands before you - and whose feelings on the Indochinese problem have never changed - now makes his appeal for support to a majority made up of men who have never, directly or indirectly, espoused the cause of those who are fighting against us, men, therefore, who can demand the confidence of our soldiers and negotiate in complete independence with the enemy.

I have studied the record closely and at length. I have consulted with the most qualified military and diplomatic experts. They have confirmed my conviction that a peaceful settlement of the conflict be possible.

We must, therefore, have a rapid cease-fire. The Government I shall form will give itself - and our adversaries - a period of four weeks to bring it about. Today is June 17. I shall come before you before July 20 and report on the results. If no satisfactory solution can be reached by that date, you will be released from the contract which binds us and my Government will hand its resignation to the President of the Republic.

It goes without saying that, in the meantime - I mean beginning tomorrow - all the necessary military measures will be taken to fulfill the most immediate needs as well as to put the Government that would succeed mine in a position to continue the fight, if it should unfortunately have to do so. If certain of these measures require a parliamentary decision, they will be proposed to you.

(362) TELEGRAM FROM SMITH TO DULLES, JUNE 18, 1954

Source: *U.S.-Vietnam Relations, Book 9*, pp. 578-579.

The U.S. delegation informed the French at Geneva that the surrender of all enclaves in the North would force the U.S. to disassociate itself publicly from the settlement, but pledged support to the French effort to get the best settlement possible. The French defended the partition solution as more enforceable then the "leopard spot" alternative.

PARIS EYES ONLY AMBASSADOR; SAIGON EYES ONLY AMBASSADOR

Johnson saw Chauvel this morning and discussed with him conference situation in light TEDUL 211. Johnson stated seemed to us that such fundamental questions as composition, voting procedures and authority or international control commission would be dealt with in conference rather than by committee. If conference reached decision on fundamental principles, working out of details could be done by committee of experts of principally interested parties in same pattern as present Franco-Viet Minh military conversations.

Chauvel said this would be agreeable except that question of authority, which he termed "relationship between international commission and joint committees" could be dealt with by technical committee, thus implying France not (repeat not) prepared to maintain principle of subordination joint committees to international commission. As French have already circulated proposal contained SECTO 460 through secretariat, it was agreed we would make suggestion along foregoing lines at today's restricted meeting. Chauvel said they did not (repeat not) yet have any further indication as to what attitude

Chinese would take on French proposal entirely clear from conversation with Chauvel that his main interest is in keeping some conference activity of nine going and that if regardless of level representation we prepared continue some conference meetings would probably meet French point of view. Appears French proposal made on assumption that there would be complete recess of conference with departure of Smith and Eden.

Chauvel made reference to his conversation with Smith yesterday (DULTE 193 - last paragraph), making inquiry as to exactly what we had in mind. Johnson in reply read to him paragraphs 5, 6 and 7 basic instructions (TOSEC 138) stating that French willingness surrender even minimum enclave in north of Haiphong would so clearly contravene the principles which the US considered essential as to require our public dissociation with such a solution. In reply to Chauvel's questions, Johnson made it clear we were speaking only of public disassociation from such a settlement. The US had in the past and of course would continue working with and supporting France in every possible way and wherever we could. Chauvel indicated full understanding our position. He said they had come to conclusion that what he termed any "leopard spot" solution was entirely impracticable and unenforceable. From standpoint of future it would be much better to retain a reasonably defensible line in Vietnam behind which there would be no (repeat no) enclaves of Viet Minh and do all possible behind that line to build up effective Vietnamese Government and defense. They had no (repeat no) intention of "any immediate surrender of Haiphong" which in any event must remain under their control for a considerable period for purely military reasons to effect evacuation of French Union Forces from the north. However, if, as appeared likely, choice was giving Viet Minh an enclave in south in exchange for French enclave in Haiphong, they thought it preferable to give up Haiphong. He said no (repeat no) French parliament would approve conditions which the US had laid down for its intervention, and French had no (repeat no) choice but made the best deal they could, obtaining as strong position as possible in south. Chauvel understood fully we would probably not (repeat not) be able to publicly associate ourselves with such a solution, but he hoped that when it came time to put it to the Vietnamese the US would consider it possible very discreetly to let the Vietnamese know that we considered it best that could be obtained under the circumstances and our public disassociation would not (repeat not) operate so as to encourage Vietnamese opposition. Johnson replied he did not (repeat not) see how it would be possible for us to do this, and in any event he would of course have to see what the solution was. Chauvel said that such a solution as partition should come as no (repeat no) surprise to the Vietnamese as Buu Loc had sometime ago indicated to Dejean. There had been conversations between Vietnamese and Viet Minh in which Viet Minh had made it clear that only two alternatives were coalition government or partition. Chauvel said Ngo Dinh and Diem are very unrealistic, unreasonable, and would probably prove to be "difficulte".

Chauvel said the line French had in mind had been made available to US defense representatives at some five-power talks, but was vague about time and place. He referred to it as "line of the chalk cliffs", which he said was defensible position running from the sea across Vietnam and Laos to the Mekong. Understand this is a line roughly 19 parallel running from vicinity of Dong Hoi to Thakhek. Replying to query, Chauvel said French Union Forces removed from the north would be deployed along that line.

Chauvel said all indications were Mendes-France would succeed in forming government next day or two and would probably himself assume Foreign Minister post. Said he had been in touch with Mendes-France and had sent emissary to Paris this morning to brief him on situation in Geneva. Chauvel said was anxious to show complete continuity of French effort here in Geneva and hoped there could be another restricted meeting tomorrow. Chauvel said, "Underground military talks" last night had been completely unproductive, Viet Minh obviously taking strong line in view of French Government situation.

(363) <u>TELEGRAM FROM SMITH TO DULLES</u>, JUNE 19, 1954

Source: *U.S.-Vietnam Relations, Book 9*, pp. 580-588.

Molotov confirmed to Smith the willingness of the Vietnamese to withdraw forces from Laos and Cambodia and the Communist insistence on a substantial zone of control in Laos, though not in Cambodia. Smith expressed doubt as to the willingness of the D.R.V. to withdraw from those countries, and suggested that the Vietnamese were demanding too much of North Vietnam. Smith concluded that the Communists now discounted U.S. intervention and were raising their demands accordingly.

I saw Molotov at his villa yesterday evening at my request to inform him of my departure, and because I felt time had come to sound a note of warning. Talk lasted more than hour and a half. Molotov asked what I thought would be best thing to do with Conference, to adjourn it temporarily or to keep it going. I replied as far as we concerned should be kept going while there was hope of reaching resonable settlement, but that there was no use referring to "committees" matters of major policy which must be decided by the Conference as a whole. Before my departure I felt it would be desirable to exchange views, in order that mistakes of the past should not be repeated as the result of misunderstanding of our respective positions. With regard to Korean phase, I had only to say that in reserving our position re final Chinese proposal had not implied to exclude Communist China from future discussions on Korean question. As matter of fact, China was belligerent there against UN and for practical reasons would have to be party to settlement.

Regarding Indochinese phase Molotov said he had impression US avoided reaching solution and cited in this regard Robertson objection in yesterday's restricted session to acceptance Chou's proposal on Laos and Cambodia. I said that while proposal might be satisfactory in some respects it made no mention of Vietminh withdrawal or of adequate supervision. So long as regular Vietminh forces remained in Laos and Cambodia we could not help but view situation in very serious light. Molotov cited Pham Van Dong's remarks regarding withdrawal Vietminh "volunteers" and emphasized importance of beginning direct negotiations regarding Laos and Cambodia of type now taking place regarding Vietnam. I regretted that I was not at all convinced that Pham Van Dong really meant what he said. His statements sounded well enough, but his written proposals did not bear them out.

I said I wanted to make our position on Laos and Cambodia entirely clear. In addition to regular Vietminh forces in these countries, which I enumerated, there were some dissident elements in Laos and a much smaller number in Cambodia. If regular Vietminh forces were withdrawn, elections could be held, with guarantees that individuals would be discriminated against as regards their electoral rights for having supported either side. Dissidents would be able to vote for any candidates they chose, Communists included. However, while Vietminh forces remained in these countries, there could be no peace nor could free elections be held.

In private conversations with Mr. Eden and others, Communist delegates, in particular Chou En-lai, had taken an apparently reasonable view on Laos and Cambodia, but that here again, when we came to the point of trying to get open agreement on specific points we were unable to do so. I specifically mentioned Chou En-lai's statements to Eden in which he said that China would have no objections to recognizing the kingdoms of Laos and Cambodia or to these States having forces and arms sufficient to maintain security, or their remaining in

French Union so long as they were not used as military based by the United States. We could not disagree with any of this, although if we kept out the Chinese would have to keep out, and these small states would have to be allowed to join with their neighbors in whatever regional security arrangements would best protect their integrity without constituting a threat to any one else. Chou En-lai might be anxious about possibility of US bases in Laos and Cambodia. We wanted on our part to be sure that these countries were not handed over to the Chinese. Molotov said that while he did not know about what attitude Chinese might have on other questions in future, he could assure me that Chinese attitude on this particular questions was not at all unreasonable, and that there was nothing in it which would give rise to conflicts. He added, however, that if we continued to take a one-sided view and insist on one-sided solutions, he must "in all frankness say that this would not succeed." There were, he said, some differences of views between us on Laos and Cambodia, especially in regard to our refusal to recognize resistance movements; point he wanted to make, however, was that basis for reaching agreement was present and that agreement could be reached so long as neither side "adopted one-sided views or put forward extreme pretensions." This, he said, could only lead to other side's doing same.

Resistance movements existed, in Laos and Cambodia, Molotov asserted. About 50% of the territory of Laos was not under the control of official government. It was true that much smaller resistance movement existed in Cambodia. He said that in fact conditions in all three Indochinese countries were different - large resistance movement controlling three-quarters of territory in Viet Nam, substantial movement in Laos controlling, as he had indicated, about half territory, and much smaller movement in Cambodia. I said, with regard to two latter countries solution was simple. Withdraw invading Vietminh forces and let dissident elements elect communist representatives to general assemblies if they wished. But the elections must be actually "free". Regarding Viet Nam, I said we recognized relative strength of the Vietminh but they were demanding too much. It seems Vietminh demanded all Delta, including both Hanoi and Haiphong. The French were our allies, and we took grave view of this extreme pressure. Molotov said that if French were to have something in South and something in North, and probably in center as well, this would add up to three-quarters of country or better, which was wholly unreasonable. He said there was old Russian proverb that if you try to chase two rabbits at once you are apt to miss both of them, and added that in this case wanting something in North and in South was like chasing two rabbits. If French were to give way to Vietminh in North, they would gain territory probably greater in extent in South in recompense. I said appearance of "partition" was repugnant to US, and that as far as proverb about rabbits went I felt that Vietminh were chasing two rabbits in wanting both Hanoi and Haiphong. Vietminh demands for all the Delta, or efforts take it all by force prior to reaching political solution through elections, was serious matter in view of my Government. Molotov disagreed, stating that present French position in area was due only to Vietminh restraint, and that two cities did not even have normal communications between each other. In regard to US aversion to partition, he said that this problem could easily be solved by holding elections at once, which would decide "one way or the other." He repeated that important thing in reaching agreement on any of these questions relating Indochina was to be realistic about actual facts, and to avoid putting out one-sided views or extreme pretensions. If French were encouraged to disregard actual situation and to ask for too much, he said, one could only expect conflict to continue. (He made it clear that he considered US as party likely to do the encouraging.) I replied that US was not one of principals to Indochinese dispute and did not cast deciding vote to which Molotov remarked "maybe so, but you have veto, that word I hear you use so often," and went on to say that among other delegations present at

Conference there seemed to be real willingness to reach agreement. Agreement had in fact, he added, very nearly been reached, although he hoped I would realize this was not information for publication. (This remark, obviously, referred to private French-Vietminh military conversations which I have mentioned.) I said I must emphasize my Government held serious views on issues involved in Indochina situation, more serious, perhaps, than did some of other governments represented at Conference. I hope he would give consideration to this, and assist in overcoming some of the deep-rooted suspicions of Asiatic participants, which became apparent every time we tried to reconcile formal proposals.

COMMENT:

Throughout conversation Molotov maintained friendly and mild tone evident in all informal conversations. He is completely sure of himself and of his position. What he had to say regarding Delta, Laos and Cambodia confirms Communist intentions to play all the cards they hold. His avoidance of endorsing Chou's remarks to Eden concerning Laos and Cambodia indicated that simple withdrawal of Vietminh forces from these countries was not acceptable and that some form of *de facto* partition was intended in Laos, at least. His remarks seemed to indicate that Communists have eye on as much as half of country. This conversation, together with the inflexible position which Molotov took during his last conversation with me regarding the composition of a Neutral Nations Supervisory Commission for Indochina, as well as his speech on Tuesday, June 8, and all subsequent speeches on the Communist side, which took firm positions on points the Communists know to be unacceptable to Eden, Bidault and me, are highly significant. The recent emphasis by all three Communist spokesmen that France should carry on direct political as well as direct military negotiations with Vietminh show their interest in having a convenient way of holding out for greater gains in their direct negotiations with the French as well as within the framework of the Conference.

Molotov in effect told France in his June 8 speech that her position and that of the Government she was supporting in Indochina were hopeless and that she had best face up to facts and capitulate in direct negotiations with the Vietminh. His speech, of course, was in large part intended to assist in the destruction of the French Government for the implications that that would have on the European as well as the Asiatic scene. Nevertheless, his harsh and even insulting language seemed to reflect the confident, nearly triumphant mood in which he has been lately. It would be misleading to ascribe the harder line which Molotov brought back with him from Moscow entirely to Soviet tactical considerations in regard to the French Government crisis. While the Soviets may think that the blocking of EDC through the destruction of the French Government would reduce future threats to them in Europe, the fact remains that the Indochina conflict potentially involves a much more immediate threat of general war.

It is probable that initial Soviet tactics were to forestall US intervention in the Delta by some kind of a compromise formula involving Hanoi and Haiphong if it appeared that such intervention were imminent. The recent raising of the ante in the negotiations here by the Communist side probably reflects an estimate on their part that our intervention is improbable and that they are safe to go ahead there, keeping, of course, a sharp eye out for indications of change in our attitude.

While the Communist position on Laos and Cambodia remains more flexible than their position in regard to the Delta, they will get all they can in Laos now. In the whole area the determining factor for the Communists will continue to be their estimate of the likelihood of US or joint intervention and nothing short of a conviction on their part that this intervention will take place

will stop them from going ahead with their plans for taking all of it eventually, through military conquest, French capitulation, or infiltration.

Realize much of above is repetitious, but it will serve as final summary.

(364) TELEGRAM FROM DILLON TO DULLES, JUNE 24, 1954

Source: *U.S.-Vietnam Relations, Book 9*, pp. 589-591.

*In a conversation with the new French Premier, Mendes-France, Chou agreed
with the French position that a political settlement could be reached after
the military settlement in direct negotiations between the two Vietnamese
governments. Nor did he object to Mendes' comment that there could not be
early elections to reunify the country. Both positions were rejected, however,
by the D.R.V. delegation.*

Since Mendes was tied up in National Assembly today, he asked me to see
Parodi and Chauvel regarding his talk with Chou. Chauvel did all the talking
and described the meeting as follows:

He said that Mendes opened the meeting telling Chou that he had been glad
to agree to Chou's idea of a meeting and that he was interested to hear anything Chou had to say. Chou then spoke very fully and most of the time at
the meeting, which lasted a little over two hours, was taken up by Chou's
statements and the necessary translations.

Chou in general followed the same line as he previously had taken with
Eden and Bidault, with certain important exceptions, which Chauvel considered
to represent a considerable advance over Chou's previous position.

Chou started by talking about Laos and Cambodia. He said that the immediate problem was to obtain the withdrawal of all foreign forces including
Viet Minh from the entire territory of both countries. He said that then the
governments of the two countries should arrange political settlements within
their own countries based on the will of the majority of the people. Chou said
that while there should be no persecution of minorities, he had no objection
to the two countries retaining their monarchical form of government if they so
desired. The one thing upon which he insisted was that there should be no
(repeat no) US bases in either Laos and Cambodia. He stated that he saw no
objection to Laos and Cambodia remaining within the French Union, provided they
so desired.

The talk then turned to Vietnam where Chauvel considered important advances
in Chou's position were revealed. Chou said that he recognized that there were
now two governments in the territory of Vietnam, the Viet Minh Government and
the Vietnamese Government. According to Chauvel, this was the first time that
Chou had recognized the valid existence of the Vietnamese Government.

Chou then said that the settlement in Vietnam should be reached in two
stages. First, an armistice which should be reached as soon as possible,
and second, peace, which would obviously take longer to achieve. Chauvel said
that Chou clearly accepted, and for the first time, the French thesis that
there should be two phases; first military and second political to the eventual
settlement of Vietnam. Regarding military settlement, Chou said that there
should be regroupment of troops in large zones in order to stop the fighting.
Chou said that he was ready to discuss the division of zones if Mendes so
desired. Mendes answered that he was not yet prepared for such a detailed discussion and said he preferred that it be handled by the delegations at Geneva.
Therefore, there was no discussion in detail regarding the make-up of the
eventual zones.

Regarding the final political settlement, Chou said this should be reached
by direct negotiations between the two governments in Vietnam, i.e., the Vietnamese Government and the Viet Minh Government. Chou further said that France

might be able to help in these negotiations. He added that he saw no reason why the eventually united state of Vietnam should not remain within the French Union.

Mendes at this point said that since the war had been going on for 8 years and passions were high, it would take a long time before elections could be held as the people must be given a full opportunity to cool off and calm down. Chou made no objection to this statement by Mendes and did not press for early elections.

Mendes then told Chou that negotiations with the Viet Minh for reasons not very clear to the French had been at a practical standstill for the past week or ten days and he suggested that a word from Chou to the leader of the Viet Minh delegation might be helpful in speeding things up which seemed to be Chou's desire as well as Mendes'. Chou agreed to intervene with the Viet Minh and ask them to speed up negotiations.

The conversation never touched on any subject other than Indochina. According to Chauvel, no other item of Far Eastern policy was touched upon, nor was Europe nor the UN or possible recognition of China by France ever mentioned.

Chauvel is returning to Geneva tonight and will see the head of the Viet Minh delegation tomorrow in an attempt to get the military talks under way again.

(365) <u>TELEGRAM FROM SMITH TO DULLES</u>, JULY 3, 1954

Source: *U.S.-Vietnam Relations, Book 9*, pp. 600-602.

In an effort to persuade Pham Van Dong that the D.R.V. should give up its demand for administration of three provinces in South Central Vietnam long under revolutionary control, the head of the French delegation, Chauvel, raised the possibility of an "extension" of the war if the French proposal was refused.

PARIS EYES ONLY AMBASSADOR

SAIGON EYES ONLY CHARGE

In Johnson's absence, Chauvel this afternoon, informed Bonsal regarding his talk with Kuznetsov last night and with Dong this morning.

Chauvel raised with Kuznetsov pending questions on control. He found Kuznetsov adamant on necessity of inclusion Communist power and rejection thesis Communists can not (repeat not) be neutral. Kuznetsov added that Colombo powers are after all sworn to influence of London which in turn is influenced by Washington. Upshot of talk on this point was that matter of composition might be set aside for present and left for Ministers to settle when they return. Concerning acceptance by parties of decisions or recommendations of international commission, Chauvel stressed importance of establishing "rule of law" accepted beforehand by both sides. Chauvel had impression Kuznetsov not (repeat not) unmoved by his arguments this point, although he gave no (repeat no) indication of change in Soviet position.

On military questions, Chauvel made clear to Kuznetsov that these are held up because Viet Minh have made unacceptable proposal of demarcation line along thirteenth parallel (about Tuy Hoa). On other hand, Chauvel stated French have proposed line acceptable not (repeat not) only to French, but one which French have reason to believe would be acceptable to conference as a whole, and thus would avert risk of internationalization of conflict. Kuznetsov replied that difficulty arises from fact that three provinces south of Faifo have been held for many years by Viet Minh (area in question would appear to run from just south of Faifo and include provinces of Quang Ngai, Quang Nhon and perhaps all or part of Song Cau; Department will recall in this connection, recent violent Viet Minh attack against French forces withdrawing from Ankhe which is in this general area). Kuznetsov suggested French and Viet Minh might examine area between fourteenth and eighteenth parallel and exchange views as to specific areas of particular interest to each party. Chauvel stated this could not (repeat not) be considered and repeated position regarding line French have already offered.

Chauvel's talk with Dong took place this morning at residence of Chinese Communist delegation. There was an exchange of views about control and particularly regarding prior agreement to accept decisions or recommendations of international commission. Dong stated that he would consider this further. He is aware that French, British and Soviet delegations are working on specific proposals (SECTO 553).

Chauvel reports that he spoke most firmly to Dong regarding military discussions. He said French have accepted Viet Minh proposal that Viet Minh receive Tonkin area, including Capital, but that further Viet Minh proposal for demarcation line is unacceptable. Chauvel reiterated in strongest terms fact that French proposal for demarcation line just north of Dong Hoi would be acceptable to conference and would thus eliminate danger of extension of war. (Chauvel stated to Bonsal that of course French would have to hold Haiphong and adjacent zones for considerable period.)

Dong raised question of Viet Minh troops and sympathizers in area south of Faifo. Chauvel stated he assumed regular troops would be evacuated and others would return to their villages. He said that presumably there would be no (repeat no) objection to any persons desiring to do so removing to Viet Minh controlled territory. (Bonsal expressed interest and emphasized United States view this subject as set forth paragraphs of aide memoire contained Department telegram 4853.)

Dong endeavored to raise question of eventual political settlement but Chauvel stated that in present discussions must be limited to military matters and reaching of armistice. He stressed purpose of present conversation is to make arrangements for removal from Tonkin of 300,000 Franco-Vietnamese troops. He said that French have no (repeat no) aggressive military intentions, although obviously it is essential for French to reinforce their position both by regrouping their forces in delta and by measures agreed on in Paris in order to insure so far as possible, security of their troops. (He told Bonsal he did not (repeat not) believe either French or Viet Minh would take aggressive military action under present circumstances.)

Alluding to political matters, Chauvel took occasion to point out to Dong that elections have not (repeat not) yet been held in Communist China and that Dong would probably agree on need for considerable period of pacification and reconstruction before elections would be held. Dong made no (repeat no) comment.

Chauvel read Bonsal passages from letter he had received from Mendes-France indicating that French negotiators should avoid appearance of overeagerness to reach settlement. Deadline date of July 20 which Mendes-France has set himself is not (repeat not) so pressing as to induce French to accept Viet Minh proposal of thirteenth parallel.

In view Department telegram 9, Bonsal drew Chauvel's attention to presence here of new Vietnamese representative Tran Van Do and to latter's interest in seeing Chauvel. (Chauvel apparently not (repeat not) fully informed by his subordinates on this score.)

(366) <u>TELEGRAM FROM DULLES TO DILLON</u>, JULY 3, 1954

Source: *U.S.-Vietnam Relations, Book 9*, pp. 603-605.

Still fearful that the French would negotiate an agreement which would lead to Communist control of Indochina, to which the U.S. would be expected to adhere, Dulles expressed concern that a public disassociation by the U.S. might endanger the settlement and create antagonism in France.

We are considering here what position we should take as regards the French negotiations in Indochina. These negotiations appear to have gone underground and we have little reliable knowledge of what is really in the minds of the French Government or what is likely to emerge. We have ourselves agreed with the British on the 7 points previously communicated to you. However, we have the distinct impression that the British look upon this merely as an optimum solution and that they would not encourage the French to hold out for a solution as good as this. Indeed, during the talks here the British wanted to express these 7 points merely as a "hope" without any indication of firmness [of each?].The word "respect" was agreed on as a compromise. The fact is however, that the U.S. would not want to be associated in any way with a settlement which fell materially short of the 7 point memorandum.

We fear the French may in fact without prior consultation with us or more that perfunctory character agree to a settlement which though superficially resembling the 7 points will in fact contain such political clauses and restrictions that Laos, Cambodia, and Southern Vietnam will almost surely fall in a few months under Communist control. No doubt such a solution would be accepted with satisfaction by the French people and parliament who would rejoice in the ending of the fighting and close their eyes to the possible future implications of the settlement. At this point the US may be asked as one of the powers which convoked and participated in the Indochina phase of the Geneva Conference to sing or otherwise adhere to the settlement. Also the Communists may insist upon this and take the position that if we do not do so that would be a violation of the understanding upon which the armistice was negotiated and they might even threaten to withdraw their armistice terms if the US did not adhere to them. The Communist tactic would well serve their purpose of creating animosity between France and the US at a time when the defeat of EDC is a major Soviet objective.

We are giving consideration to various possibilites such as the withdrawal of the remnants of our delegation from Geneva or clarification of our position as regards the French position. This latter matter would not (rpt not) serve the desired purpose unless it were public and if it were public it might be looked upon as a threat which would create the French antagonistic reaction which we want to avoid.

Possibly you could find out whether or not there is the danger which [I?] apprehended and whether or not the French are negotiating on the assumption that we not be a party to the settlement. If the French are operating on this basis and if they know that the Communists also accept this premise, the situation is not dangerous. If either or both French and Communists are operating on assumption we will adhere to any settlement they agree to, then we may be headed for serious trouble. I would like your personal thoughts on this matter.

(367) TELEGRAM FROM DILLON TO DULLES, JULY 6, 1954

Source: *U.S. Vietnam Relations, Book 9*, p. 608.

The French Foreign Ministry pointed out an apparent inconsistency between the U.S. insistence on the possibility of peaceful reunification and its rejection of any political provisions which would risk loss of the retained area to Communist control."

Parodi this morning gave me French reaction to US-UK terms for Indochina settlement. He said the terms generally parallel present French position and

are welcomed by French Government. However, they have one important reservation in that they consider that paragraphs 4 and 5 may be mutually contradictory.

French feel that eventual agreement will have to contain provisions for
elections which would comply with paragraph 5 of US-UK agreement. However,
if elections should go wrong way, this would seem to contradict paragraph 4
of US-UK agreement, which says there should be no (repeat no) political provisions which would risk loss of the retained area. Accordingly, they request
clarification from us as to US and UK position regarding elections.

In addition Parodi said that French do not (repeat not) fully understand
what we mean when we say we would be willing to "respect" agreement. Parodi
said that the word "respect" seemed weak and unclear and French would like
clarification if at all possible.

(368) <u>TELEGRAM FROM DULLES TO DILLON</u>, JULY 7, 1954

Source: *U.S. Vietnam Relations, Book 9*, pp. 616-617.

*Dulles answered the French query by urging that the elections be put off as
long as possible and that the terms provide for international supervision, so
as to give the anti-Communist side the best possible chance.*

We see no real conflict between paragraphs 4 and 5 US-UK terms. We realize
of course that even agreement which appears to meet all seven points cannot
constitute guarantee that Indochina will not one day pass into Communist hands.
Seven points are intended provide best chance that this shall not happen. This
will require observance of criteria not merely in the latter but in the spirit.
Thus since undoubtedly true that elections might eventually mean unification
Vietnam under Ho Chi Minh this makes it all the more important that they should
be only held as long after cease-fire agreement as possible and in conditions
free from intimidation to give democratic elements best chance. We believe
important that no date should be set now and especially that no conditions
should be accepted by French which would have direct or indirect effect of
preventing effective international supervision of agreement ensuring political
as well as military guarantees. Also note paragraph 3 of President and Prime
Minister joint declaration of June 29 regarding QTE unity through free elections
supervised by the UN UNQTE.

Our interpretation of unwillingness QTE respect UNQTE agreement which might
be reached is that we would not (repeat not) oppose a settlement which conform-
ed to seven points contained Deptel 4853. It does not (repeat not) of course
mean we would guarantee such settlement or that we would necessarily support
it publicly. We consider QTE respect UNQTE as strong a word as we can possibly
employ in the circumstances to indicate our position with respect to such arrangements as French may evolve along lines points contained DEPTEL 4853. QTE
respect UNQTE would also mean that we would not seek directly or indirectly
to upset settlement by force.

You may convey substance above to French.

(369) <u>SPEECH BY PREMIER MENDES-FRANCE TO THE NATIONAL ASSEMBLY</u>, JULY 7, 1954

Source: French Embassy, Press and Information Service, *Speeches and Press
Conferences, No. 25*, July 1954.

*In a speech to the Assembly before his departure for the critical phase of
peace talks, Mendes-France explained that the failure to obtain peace by July
20 would force the French Government to send conscripts to Vietnam. By implication, he was also warning that his successor would take a tougher line on a
peace settlement than he.*

"I am leaving for Geneva shortly to conduct to the very end - which I hope will be a happy one - the negotiations for a cease-fire in Indochina.

"You know in what spirit I have followed these negotiations. My Government has set as its first goal to put an end to the bloodshed that has lasted for so many years in a land which France once brought peace. It is my determination to reestablish that peace and to fulfill the mandate with which you entrusted me for this very purpose. Since the debate which took place at the time of my investiture, I have bent all my efforts to this end; and soon, at Geneva, I shall devote my whole strength to it.

"It is evidently impossible for me, at this time, to predict the outcome of the negotiations. They go through periods of progress and times of deadlock. Nothing can be inferred from oscillations that are common in such cases. I have already said that reasons to hope for a favorable and honorable solution are not lacking. That is still my opinion today.

"Yet, between hope - however well-founded it may be - and certainty, there is a gap that we cannot bridge without being guilty of unforgivable laxity. It is the duty of all of us to foresee everything in time so as to be able to meet any eventuality, even the worst. It is our duty, first of all, to the Expeditionary Corps, for any lack of foresight on our part would jeopardize its material resources and even affect its morale at a time when its strength, like its courage and its heroism, more than ever constitute a decisive trump card.

"Must I say again that in being prepared for the worst, we are strengthening the position of our negotiators in order that they may obtain the best.

"That is why I must consider with you, although I do not want to believe it, the possibility of failure in our attempt to obtain peace within the prescribed time.

"Undoubtedly the question will not come up before the July 20 deadline. Experience has proved that it is in the last hours of international negotiations that the most delicate questions are settled.

"If the negotiations should fail, however, on July 20, we would have to face the situation, in military terms, that is ensure the safety of the Expeditionary Corps and maintain sufficiently powerful military equipment on the spot to convince the enemy that he cannot hope to reach a decision by continuing hostilities, but that, on the contrary, it would be to his advantage to resume talks with - be it said in passing - a new French Government.

"In my statement of policy, I told you that my Government would take, before July 20, all the military measures necessary to meet the immediate needs of the Expeditionary Corps. This it has done and is continuing to do day after day. I said further that I would also take all measures necessary to put the Government that would succeed mine in a position to continue the fight if it should unfortunately have to do so.

"It is on this assumption that I speak to you today; it is on this assumption that I have acted in the last few days when I undertook, with the Minister of National Defense and the Chief of Staff of the Armed Forces, a detailed study of the military resources and eventual needs of the Expeditionary Corps in the event the cease-fire negotiations were broken off.

"We tried, first of all, to determine whether it was possible to form new units by transferring professional soldiers from the existing forces in Metropolitan France and North Africa. This is the way in which we have been constantly relieving the Expeditionary Corps. But considerable forces are now needed merely to relieve the Corps, because of losses suffered in so many costly engagements. I have only to recall the tragic drama of Dienbienphu, which alone deprived us of 15,000 elite troops, of which it has been said, and rightly so, that they constituted the spearhead of our forces.

"Moreover, the necessity of substantially expanding the strength of the Expeditionary Corps during the last year has entailed an increase in the number of troops periodically needed as replacements.

"Consequently, assuming as I must - although I refuse to believe it possible - that the war should be continued, we would not be able, by using professional soldiers and volunteers along, to furnish the Expeditionary Corps with the immediate and substantial reinforcements needed to face the new dangers to which it would be exposed, and to ensure the safety of the fighting men already exposed to difficulties which I need not describe.

"The only possible method of solving the problem today consists, therefore, in sending to the Far East troops from the general reserve, which the preceding Government had decided to set up and begun to constitute for this purpose. These units are made up of soldiers finishing their legal term of military service. In other words, it means sending conscripts.

"You cannot doubt the feeling prompting the man who now stands before you, when for years he has been constantly putting you on your guard, warning you of the inevitable consequences of the Indochina war, telling you that a day would come when, if that war were not brought to an end in due time, we would have to take the painful decision which it is my duty to call to your attention.

"I say my duty - for the safety of the Expeditionary Corps is at stake.

"This decision requires measures to be taken both by the Government and by the Parliament. It is up to the Government to work out a plan for the transportation of additional units; to make the necessary preparations concerning health, clothing and equipment. All this has been done or is in the process of being done. Furthermore, the day before yesterday, we obtained the agreement of the Supreme Command of NATO on all the dispositions for which its approval is necessary, in view of our international engagements. In a word, everything has been done so that we should be ready to reinforce the Expeditionary Corps if necessary. In a word, the necessary precautions have already been taken to enable us to send reinforcements immediately should the current negotiations fail.

"However, Ladies and Gentlemen, when I told you that my Government felt it was its duty to take such precautions, I added that certain measures would require a parliamentary decision.

"Among these is the authorization to send the conscripts to Indochina temporarily.

I shall not ask you for this authorization today, and that for a number of reaons. On the one hand, as I have just told you, the preparatory measures are already under way and no time is being lost. On the other hand, I have been assured, along with the Minister of National Defense, that if the authorization is voted immediately following the July 20 deadline, the Expeditionary Corps would not have to suffer from any delay in the departure of the conscripts, since the necessary provisions would have been made.

"Finally and above all, I feel that at the present time when my Government is playing the card of peace, it is not appropriate to take a measure of this character as long as we are not forced to do so.

"If it had been necessary - if my discussions with the Minister of National Defense and our military chiefs had made its necessity evident - I would have chosen to ask for an immediate vote; and it is perhaps this determination that I was known to have which gave rise to inaccurate rumors that I was going to ask you for a decision today, for which I hope I shall never have to ask and for which, in any case, it would have been out of place to ask you before it was evident that the negotiations had failed.

"It has been understood between us that in this case, the Government would resign. This pledge on my part still holds. But the last act of the Government, if it is to live up to all its promises, would be, after the eventual failure of the talks at Geneva, to submit to the Assembly without delay, the necessary text and to seek an immediate vote. The possibility of a prolonged ministerial crisis cannot be excluded; the national interest thus demands that the vote be already obtained when I hand in my resignation. My mission is to prepare, to place in readiness and, in any case, to leave in the hands of the future Government such means of action as might be necessary.

"Thus I will remain faithful to the desire that I have expressed of leaving my successor with a better situation than I myself inherited.

"I am well aware that to send young soldiers finishing their compulsory military service to a distant theatre of operations is an act which it will cost us all a great deal to decide upon. But no one could misunderstand the significance of our decision. For Frenchmen it would be a case of going to the aid of other Frenchmen in danger. It would be a case of bringing help to comrades upon whom the combat would be imposed, not by our will but by that of the adversary - and this would have been clearly proved.

(370) LETTER FROM DULLES TO MENDES-FRANCE, JULY 10, 1954

Source: *U.S. Vietnam Relations, Book 9,* pp. 625-630.

Dulles wrote to Premier Mendes-France that the U.S. feared France would accept a settlement that fell short of the minimum regarded as acceptable, and that the U.S. could not endorse such a settlement. This was the reason, he explained, that Dulles and Bedell Smith were staying away from the Conference.

My dear Mr. President:

President Eisenhower (who has been kept closely informed) and I have been greatly moved by your earnest request that I or General Bedell Smith should return next week to Geneva for what may be the conclusion of the Indochina phase of the Conference. I can assure you that our attitude in this respect is dictated by a desire to find the course which will best preserve the traditional friendship and cooperation of our countries and which will promote the goals of justice and human welfare and dignity to which our two nations have been traditionally dedicated. We also attach great value to preserving the united front of France, Great Britain and the United States which has during this postwar period so importantly served all three of us in our dealings with the Communists.

What now concerns us is that we are very doubtful as to whether there is a united front in relation to Indochina, and we do not believe that the mere fact that the high representatives of the three nations physically reappear together at Geneva will serve as a substitute for a clear agreement on a joint position which includes agreement as to what will happen if that position is not accepted by the Communists. We fear that unless there is the reality of such a united front, the events at Geneva will expose differences under conditions which will only serve to accentuate them with consequent strain upon the relations between our two countries greater than if the US does not reappear at Geneva, in the person of General Smith or myself.

Beginning early last April the US worked intensively with the French Government and with that of Great Britain in an effort to create a common position of strength. This did not prove possible. The reasons were understandable, and derived from fundamental causes which still subsist and influence the possibility of achieving at the present time a genuine "united front."

During the talks of Prime Minister Churchill and Foreign Secretary Eden with President Eisenhower and me, an effort was made to find a common position which might be acceptable to the two of us, and we hoped, to the French Government. This was expressed in the seven point memorandum of which you are aware. I believe that this represented a constructive contribution. However, I do not yet feel that there is a united position in the sense that the three of us would be prepared to stand firmly on this as a minimum acceptable solution and to see the negotiations break off and the war resume if this position was not accepted by the Communist side. We doubt very much that the Communists will in fact accept this seven-point position unless they realize that the alternative is some common action upon which all have agreed. So far, there is no such alternative.

Under these circumstances, we greatly fear that the seven points which constitute a minimum as far as the US is concerned will constitute merely an optimum solution so far as your Government and perhaps the UK are concerned, and that an armistice might be concluded on terms substantially less favorable than those we could respect.

We gather that there is already considerable French thinking in terms of the acceptability of departures from certain of the seven points. For example:

Allowing Communists forces to remain in Northern Laos; accepting a Vietnam line of military demarcation considerably south of Donghoi; neutralizing and demilitarizing Laos, Cambodia, and Vietnam so far as to impair their capacity to maintain stable, non-Communists regimes; accepting elections so early and so ill-prepared and ill-supervised as to risk the loss of the entire area to Communism; accepting international supervision by a body which cannot be effective because it includes a Communist state which has veto power.

These are but illustrations of a whittling-away process, each stroke of which may in itself seem unessential, but which cumulatively could produce a result quite different from that envisaged by the seven points. Also, of course, there is the danger that the same unacceptable result might come about through the Communist habit of using words in a double sense and destroying the significance of good principles with stultifying implementations.

We do not for a moment question the right of the French Government to exercise its own judgment in all of these respects. Indeed, we recognize that the issues for France are so vital that the French Government has a duty to exercise its own judgment. I have from the beginning recognized the nation which has borne for so many years the burden of a cruel and costly war. However, my government equally has the duty not to endorse a solution which would seem to us to impair seriously certain principles which the US believes must, as far as it is concerned, be kept unimpaired, if our own struggle against Communism is to be successfully pursued. At the same time, we do not wish to put ourselves in the position where we would seem to be passing moral judgment upon French action or disassociating ourselves from the settlement at a moment and under circumstances which might be unnecessarily dramatic.

It is also to be considered that if our conduct creates a certain uncertainty in the minds of the Communists, this might strengthen your hand more than our presence at Geneva in a form which would expose probably to the world, and certainly to the Communists themselves, differences which the Communists would exploit to the discomfiture of all three of us.

Under all these circumstances, it seems to us that the interests of both of our countries are best served by continuing for the time being the present type of US representation at Geneva. This consists of able and responsible persons who are in close contact with the President and me.

If circumstances should alter so that it appeared that our common interests would be better served higher ranking officials became our representatives, then we would be alert to act accordingly.

It is because I am fully aware of the serious and solemn nature of the moment that I have gone into the matter at this considerable length. It is possible that by the first of the week, the Communist position will be sufficiently disclosed so that some of the answers to the foregoing queries can be foreseen. This might clarify in one sense or another the thinking of us all.

In this connection, let me emphasize that it is our ardent hope that circumstances might become such that consistently with the foregoing either General Bedell Smith or I can personally come to Geneva and stand beside you.

(371) <u>TELEGRAM FROM DILLON TO DULLES</u>, JULY 11, 1954

Source: *U.S. Vietnam Relations, Book 9*, pp. 631-632.

Mendes-France argued with Dillon that the U.S. decision not to be represent-
ed at the Conference at the Ministerial level would weaken the French bargain-
ing position and would give the impression that the U.S. was turning isolation-
ist. He challenged the suggestion in Dulles' letter that France was prepared
to accept disadvantageous terms, and offered Dulles a veto power over the
French position if he would return to Geneva.

I delivered Secretary's message Department telegram 127 to Mendes in Geneva
after lunch Sunday. At same time I gave him personal message contained in
first paragraph Department telegram 128. In view Eden's absence (SECTO 585),
I did not (repeat not) see him. Johnson will deliver message to Eden tomorrow, if Aldrich has not (repeat not) already done so.

Mendes was very touched by personal message in Department telegram 128
and twice asked me to be sure and thank Secretary on his behalf for this
thought.

Regarding Department telegram 127, Mendes expressed extreme disappointment
and gave concern at United States decesion not (repeat not) to be represented
at Ministerial level. He divided his remarks into two categories, first, the
effect of our decision on Conference itself, and second, the overall effect of
our decision on world affairs.

Regarding first category, Mendes stated that our absence made French bargaining position far weaker. He stated that if Secretary was present, France
would not (repeat not) accept anything at Conference that was unacceptable to
the United States. As he put it in his own words, presence of Secretary would
give United States in effect a veto power on decisions of Conference. He felt
it particularly important that we have someone at Geneva who could take strong
personal attention with Molotov, if and when necessary, and without having to
refer to Washington for instructions. Mendes also feels that United States
absence at Ministerial level will lead Communists to increase their pressure
and be more demanding in order to deepen the obvious rift between the Western
powers. He said France had not (repeat not) as yet departed from the Seven
Point United States-United Kingdom position and he did not (repeat not) make
any commitment to hold to these points during coming week, except for statement regarding United States veto power if Secretary present.

On the overall effect of our decision, Mendes pointed out that this will
be first time since the war that United States not (repeat not) represented at
equal level with other powers in an important conference. He said that he
felt certain that Europe would interpret United States absence as first step
in return to a policy of isolationism. This he felt, would have catastrophic effects not (repeat not) only in Far East, but also in Europe and
would be great cold war victory for Communism. According to Mendes, we would
in effect be saying "do your best, you have our sympathy, but result is no
(repeat no) real concern to us."

I tried to dissuade Mendes from this viewpoint, but without much success.
His statement regarding United States veto power if Secretary present, led me
to point out that there must also be an agreed alternative if Conference failed.
Mendes promptly replied that the only alternative to cease-fire at Geneva would
be internationalization of war with United States military forces coming promptly to assistance of French. This aspect of our talk being covered more fully
in separate telegram, being repeated to Saigon.

Finally, Mendes asked if there was anything he could do specifically to
create a situation that would make it possible to Secretary to come to Geneva.
He asked me to pass this question on to Washington. In this connection, he
specifically questioned sixth paragraph of Secretary's letter, and said he
knew of no (repeat no) French thinking along such lines, except possibly on

subject of international supervision. He wondered where United States had got the ideas expressed in this paragraph.

While I was talking with Mendes, Johnson talked with Chauvel and showed him a copy of Secretary's letter. Chauvel showed Johnson a cable from Bonnet which indicated that Bonnet may have given Secretary the impression that French were considering retreating from Seven-point program.

Chauvel and Johnson joined us at end of our talk, and Johnson and I suggested that if Mendes developed any concrete ideas which would help meet United States fears, it would be helpful if would put them into a reply to Secretary's letter. While Mendes was non-committal to a formal reply, I rather expect he will make one. In closing, Mendes said he would keep in close touch with Johnson. During talk, Mendes made it clear that while presence of Under Secretary at Geneva would be most helpful, he very much hoped that Secretary himself could come.

(372) REPORT BY DULLES TO THE NATIONAL SECURITY COUNCIL, JULY 15, 1954

Source: *U.S. Vietnam Relations, Book 9*, pp. 644-645.

Responding to Mendes-France's plea, Dulles flew to Paris to confer on the Geneva talks and the issue of U.S. representation. Dulles and Mendes-France negotiated a compromise under which Smith would return to Geneva with instructions agreed upon by the U.S. and France, but the U.S. still would not guarantee the settlement.

At the NSC meeting of 15 July, Secretary Dulles reported on his recent trip to Paris as follows:

1. He had been in practically continuous meetings with Mendes-France and Mr. Eden from the time of his arrival to his departure, sometimes with one or the other individually and sometimes with the two together. He had told Mendes that, in his opinion, most of France's troubles stem from a lack of French decision on EDC. Because of this, the Soviets were being successful in splitting France and Germany. Therefore, he put the greatest urgency on French action on EDC. Mendes said that it might not be possible now to get a constitutional majority of 314 votes in the Assemble without some face-saving formula. He hoped this could be done through minor amendments which would not require negotiation, but in any event, Mendes had promised Secretary Dulles action by the Assembly by early August. Mr. Dulles had pointed out that the U.S. public was getting a trifle short-tempered on the EDC topic and that if Mendes was not careful, the U.S. Congress might terminate aid to NATO which would be detrimental to the military effort of all Europe, especially France.

2. a. Regarding the dilemma of U.S. participation in the Geneva Conference, Secretary Dulles had pointed out that if the U.S. participates in the Conference and then finds itself unable to guarantee the results, a violent French public reaction against the U.S. would ensue. Similarly if the U.S. participates and so stiffens French will that France does not accept the Communists' best offer, then again, the U.S. would be blamed and a major strain placed upon U.S.-French relations. Thereforce, the U.S. was seeking to play an inconspicuous role.

b. The original VM proposal had been for a partition line along the 14th parallel; their second proposal along the 16th parallel. Both had been rejected and the French position was to hold out for the 18th parallel, along with the guaranteed independence of Laos and Cambodia.

c. The Secretary had worked up with the French a joint U.S.-French paper along the lines of the seven points on the U.S.-U.K. paper which had resulted from the Churchill-Eden talks. Mr. Dulles had said there would be no U.S. guarantee of the settlement, but rather a unilateral declaration that the U.S. would not attempt to change it by force. Mendes had provided Mr. Dulles with a letter of reply and acceptance of the U.S.-French position paper. Accordingly, Gen Smith was returning to Geneva with his instructions contained in these two papers.

3. Mr. Dulles said that the French Government put more emphasis on the granting of independence to the Associated States than had the Laniel Government. Mendes even agreed that French *functionaires* and eventually armed forces would have to leave the area. It was current French planning to hold Haiphong until French forces *and their equipment* could be evacuated but not to attempt to maintain Haiphong as a permanent enclave.

4. When asked if the UN would agree to the seven points, the Secretary said he was not sure but he could count on support from Laos and Cambodia. Mr. Allen Dulles felt the possibility of VN uprising against the French was a real one.

5. Mendes had assured Secretary Dulles that if the Geneva Conference was a failure, he would send two additional French divisions to Indochina, although they could not arrive before September, 1954.

(373) REPORT BY HO CHI MINH TO THE 6TH PLENUM OF THE PARTY CENTRAL COMMITTEE, JULY 15, 1954

Source: Ho Chi Minh, *Selected Writings,* pp. 172-173.

Even before the agreement was reached at Geneva, the Viet-nam Workers' Party changed its strategic line from concentrating on resisting the French to win final victory to compromise with the French in order to ward off U.S. direct intervention in the war. Ho's report indicated that the Party leadership was counting heavily on contradictions between the French and the Americans to bring about ratification of the country through elections. But he warned that the new struggle after a peace agreement would fall under enemy control.

The 6th Plenum of the Central Committee has been enlarged to include a number of high-ranking cadres and is to discuss the new situation and the new tasks.

On behalf of the Central Committee, I express my cordial regards to our fighters and cadres on all fronts, my encouragement to our compatriots in the free and the newly-liberated zones, and my sympathy to those living in areas still under enemy control.

On behalf of the Central Committee I thank the fraternal Parties and the peoples of the friendly countries for having assisted us in our war of resistance and struggle for peace, and peace-loving people all over the world for their support to our cause.

Now I shall report on the new situation.

1. THE NEW SITUATION

1. *World situation*

Owing to the all-sided development, consolidation and advance of the Soviet Union, China and the People's Democracies, the world movement for peace and democracy is growing ever stronger. Thanks to the skillful and wise diplomacy

of the Soviet Union, the imperialists, and above all the American imperialists,
have been compelled to attend the Berlin and the Geneva Conferences. The holding of these two conferences alone is in itself victory for our side and a
defeat for the imperialists.

The inner contradictions of the US-headed imperialist camp have steadily
deepened and widened. For instance:

Contradictions between Britain and the United States: conflict of interests
in the Mediterranean and in the Middle East and Near East. The United States
has pulled Pakistan, New Zealand and Australia away from the British and to its
own side. In the Far East, British policy towards China and Japan runs counter
to that of the United States, etc.

Contradictions between the United States and France: outwardly, the United
States is helping France, but this is done with the intention of putting pressure on it. It has done its utmost to force France into signing the Franco-
German treaty and that on the organization of a European army. But it would
be suicidal for France to do so. In Indochina, these two countries seemed united in coping with our resistance, but in fact the United States wants to have
the puppets well in hand in order to oust the French, and has already put Ngo
Dinh Diem - its zealous valet - at the head of a puppet government.

The American policy of a treaty on a "European Army" has sown discord
among and within the Western European countries. The people of these countries
oppose their pro-American governments, and contradictions crop up between the
pro-American capitalists and the others. In Asia, the United States wants to
set up S.E.A.T.O. with a view to using Asians to fight Asians. However, this
extremely reactionary policy has met with repeated failures. The Americans
practise a "policy of force" and brandish their A and H bombs to threaten the
other countries. But the world peace movement opposing their policy of violence and their A and H bombs becomes stronger day by day. Even the Pope has
been forced to oppose the use of such weapons. Thus the peace movement has
drawn support from the vast majority of the people in the world, from many
members of the bourgeoisie in various countries, and from the Pope himself.

Faced with the Geneva Conference and our victory at Dien Bien Phu, the
United States plotted to issue a "joint declaration" with France, Britain and
a number of other countries to intimidate China, charging it with intervention
in the Indochina war. But due to opposition from Britain and reluctance from
the other countries, the move failed. Then the Americans proposed "joint
action" to save France at Dien Bien Phu but Britain and the other countries
again disagreed, and this scheme also failed. The Americans have used every
means to sabotage the Geneva Conference. The US Secretary of State attended
the Conference for only a few days then left, but the Conference has continued
none the less and has led to some results.

For all their setbacks, the Americans are still obdurate and are speeding
up the formation of S.E.A.T.O. Their failure means success for our camp.
US imperialism is the main enemy of world peace, consequently we must concentrate our forces against it.

2. *Home situation*

The Vietnamese, Cambodian and Lao peoples are united and their resistance
grows ever more vigorous. Our guerilla forces in South, Central and North Viet
Nam, not only have stood firm but have grown ever stronger. From the Border
Campaign to the Hoa Binh, Tay Bac and other campaigns, our regular forces have
recorded repeated successes. These victories plus the major one at Dien Bien
Phu have brought about an important change in the situation. The fiasco of
the Navarre plan has led to the collapse of the Laniel-Bidault cabinet and
the shrinking of French-occupied zones.

We owe our successes to the correct policy of our Party and Government,
the heroism of our armed forces and people, and the support of the fraternal

countries and the world's people. Our successes also belong to the world
movement for peace and democracy.

Besides military successes, initial ones have also been scored on the anti-
feudal front. The former have had a good effect on the mobilization of the
masses to implement our land policy and the latter, on our struggle against
imperialism. Our successes inspire our people and the peoples of the world
and reinforce our diplomatic position at Geneva; they have compelled our enemy
to enter into talks with us. Compared with what Bollaert put forward in 1947,
France's attitude at present has noticeably changed. Thus, since the start
of the resistance, our posture has grown stronger and the enemy's weaker.
But we should bear in mind that this should be understood in a relative, not
absolute, sense. We must guard against subjectiveness and not underrate our
enemy. Our successes have awakened the American imperialists. After the Dien
Bien Phu campaign, the latter's intentions and plan for intervention have also
undergone changes aimed at protracting and internationalizing the Indochina
war, sabotaging the Geneva Conference, and ousting the French by every means,
in order to occupy Viet Nam, Cambodia and Laos, enslave the peoples of these
countries and create further tension in the world.

Therefore, the *US imperialists* not only are the enemy of the world's people
but are becoming the *main and direct enemy of the Vietnamese, Cambodian and
Lao peoples*.

These changes in the world and domestic situation have led to the Geneva
Conference. This Conference has further exacerbated the contradictions between
the imperialist countries, with France willing to negotiate, Britain wavering,
and the United States bent on sabotaging the talks. The Americans have grown
ever more isolated.

Viet Nam, China and the Soviet Union are closely united. Owing to contradictions among the imperialists, to our own efforts and to those of our camp,
we have managed to secure a few fairly important agreements. The French Government being now in the hands of those who stand for peace, there are better
chances for an end to the Indochina war.

During the recess of the Geneva Conference, the chief delegates have returned home, leaving things in the hands of their deputies. Availing himself
of this occasion, Comrade Chou En-lai, Prime Minister of the People's Republic
of China, has visited India and Burma. Comrade Chou and the prime ministers
of India and Burma have issued a joint peace declaration. Though briefly
worded, the five principles stated in the declaration are very clearly set
forth and most judicious, and are warmly approved of by the peoples of the
world and particularly of Asia; at the same time they frustrate the US imperialists' scheme of sabotaging solidarity among the Asian nations.

These five principles are:
1. Mutual respect of sovereignty and territorial integrity.
2. Non-aggression.
3. Non-interference in each other's internal affairs.
4. Equality and friendship in mutual relations.
5. Peaceful coexistence.

My meeting with Comrade Chou has also been fruitful. The friendly meetings
between Comrade Chou En-lai and the representatives of India, Burma and Viet
Nam have tightened solidarity among the Asian nations. This is a success for
our camp.

The present situation in the world, in Asia and at home holds our prospects
of peace for our country. However, the US imperialists are bent on sabotage;
in France there remain bellicose groups; the pro-American puppets also strive
to wreck the peace; and so the war may still go on.

That is the characteristic feature of the new situation in our country.

II. NEW TASKS

The new situation has set new tasks, new guidelines and new tactics. Over nearly nine years of resistance, under the leadership of our Party and Government, our people and army have overcome difficulties, fought heroically, and won glorious victories. Our forces have made headway in all respects. Thanks to the correct policy of our Party and Government, we have recorded good achievements.

At present the situation has changed; so have our tasks and consequently so should our policy and slogans. Up to now we have concentrated our efforts on wiping out the forces of the French imperialist aggressors. But now the French are having talks with us while the American imperialists are becoming our main and direct enemy; so our spearhead must be directed at the latter. Until peace is restored, we shall keep fighting the French; but the brunt of our attack and that of the world's peoples should be focused on the United States. US policy is to expand and internationalize the Indochina war. Ours is to struggle for peace and oppose the US war policy. For some nine years now, our Party has made clear its programme: Complete independence for Viet Nam, Cambodia and Laos, which must be freed from the French yoke; to refuse to recognize the French Union, drive out all French troops from Indochina, destroy the puppet administrations and armed forces, confiscate all properties of the imperialists and the traitors, launch a drive for the reduction of land rents and interest rates as a step towards agrarian reform, bring democracy to the whole nation, and carry our war of resistance through to final victory. This programme has won many successes. It is a correct one.

However, in the new situation we cannot maintain the old programme. Our previous motto was "Resistance to the end". At present, we must put forward a new one: "Peace, Unity, Independence, Democracy". We must take firm hold of the banner of peace to oppose the US imperialists' policy of direct interference in, and prolongation and expansion of, the war in Indochina. Our policy must change in consequence: formerly we confiscated the French imperialists' properties; now, as negotiations are going on, we may, in accordance with the principle of equality and mutual benefit, allow French economic and cultural interests to be preserved in Indochina. Negotiations entail reasonable mutual concessions. Formerly we said we would drive out and wipe out all French aggressive forces; now, in the talks held, we have demanded and the French have accepted, that a date be set for the withdrawal of their troops. In the past, our aim was to wipe out the puppet administration and army with a view to national reunification; now we practise a policy of leniency and seek reunification of the country through nation-wide elections.

Peace calls for an end to the war; and to end the war one must agree on a cease-fire. A cease-fire requires regrouping zones, that is, enemy troops should be regrouped in a zone with a view to their gradual withdrawal, and ours in another. We must secure a vast area where we would have ample means for building, consolidating and developing our forces so as to exert influence over other regions and thereby advance towards reunification. The setting up of regrouping zones does not mean partition of the country; it is a temporary measure leading to reunification. Owing to the delimitation and exchange of zones, some previously free areas will be temporarily occupied by the enemy; their inhabitants will be dissatisfied; some people might fall prey to discouragement and to enemy deception. We should make it clear to our compatriots that the trials they are going to endure for the sake of the interests of the whole country, for the sake of our long-range interests, will be a cause for glory and will earn them the gratitude of the whole nation. We should keep everyone free from pessimism and negativism and urge all to continue a vigorous struggle for the complete withdrawal of French forces and for independence.

To set up regrouping zones as a step towards peace, to hold nationwide elections to achieve national reunification, such is our policy. The aims of our war of resistance and independence, unity, democracy and peace. The very restoration of peace is aimed at serving the cause of reunification, independence and democracy. The new situation requires a new policy for securing new successes.

At any juncture, peace or war, we must firmly hold the initiative, show foresight and be in full readiness.

To secure peace is not an easy task; it is a long, hard and complex struggle; with advantageous conditions but also with difficulties. The advantageous conditions: the friendly countries support us, so do the world's people; our people are full of spirit and confidence in our Party and Government, under whose wise leadership they will certainly unite and struggle in peace as in war. The difficulties: the United States is trying its hardest to sabotage the restoration of peace in Indochina, the partisans of peace in France have not completely freed themselves from American influence.

The new situation is not only a difficult but also a complex one. Here are some instances: we should apply different policies to the old free areas and the newly-liberated areas; to our own free zone and to the zone temporarily reserved for regrouped enemy troops; in the past we only worked in the countryside, at present we must have a policy for cities. The present policy with regard to France should be different from the past. Policies are not the same with respect to the pro-American traitors and the pro-French traitors. In the past we only had to care about home affairs and relations with friendly countries; now we have extended our foreign relations to other countries.

We should make a distinction between immediate and future interests, between local interests and over-all interests.

The situation is undergoing great changes; furthermore difficulties and complications have cropped up; as a result, changes are also happening in the minds of the people and cadres. Failing good preparations and timely leadership, confusion might be thrown into thought and action.

The following ideological errors may be committed: *Leftist deviation*. Some people, intoxicated with our repeated victories, want to fight on at all costs, to a finish; they see only the trees, not the whole forest; with their attention focused on the withdrawal of the French they fail to detect their schemes; they see the French but not the Americans; they are partial to military action and make light of diplomacy. They are unaware that we are struggling in international conferences as well as on the battlefields in order to attain our goal. They will oppose the new slogans, which they deem to be rightist manifestations and to imply too many concessions. They set forth excessive conditions unacceptable to the enemy. They want quick results, unaware that the struggle for peace is a hard and complex one. Leftist deviation will cause one to be isolated, alienated from one's own people and those of the world, and suffer setbacks. *Rightist deviation* will lead to pessimism, inaction and unprincipled concessions. It causes one to lack confidence in the people's strength and to blunt their combative spirit; to lose the power to endure hardships and to aspire only to a quiet and easy life.

Leftist and rightist tendencies are both wrong. They will be exploited by the enemy; they will benefit them and harm us.

TASKS AND WORK

The new situation has set us three new responsibilities:

1. To secure and consolidate peace; to achieve unity, independence, and democracy for the whole country.

2. To strengthen the people's armed forces and build up a mighty people's army capable of meeting the requirements of the new situation.

3. To keep implementing the slogan: land to the tiller. To strive to restore production and to prepare for national reconstruction.

These three responsibilities entail ten tasks:

1. To create unity of mind in the whole Party and among the entire people as regards the new situation and the new tasks.

2. To strengthen leadership in diplomatic struggle.

3. To strengthen the people's army.

4. To take over the newly-liberated zones; especial attention to be paid to the taking over and management of the cities.

5. To give a new orientation to work in the zone temporarily reserved for regrouped enemy forces.

6. To keep consolidating the former free zones.

7. To mobilize the masses vigorously for land reform.

8. To improve economic and financial work and prepare conditions for the reconstruction of the country.

9. To assist the Pathet Lao and Khmer forces.

10. To continue the work of reorganization and ideological rectification of the Party in the newly-liberated areas.

These 10 tasks are under the leadership of the Central Committee. Each locality and each branch will not necessarily have to carry out all ten but each will be assigned a certain number of tasks.

Of the above ten tasks, ideological leadership is the most important. For both members and non-members of the Party, only a clear grasp of the new situation and the new tasks can bring about unity of mind, which will lead to unity of action. If all of us, both inside and outside the Party and at all levels, are at one in thought and action, we will successfully carry out our tasks, however difficult and complex.

At present, the US imperialists are the main enemy of the world's people and the main and direct enemy of the Indochinese people and so all our actions must be directed against them. Any person or country that is not pro-American can (even temporarily) join us in a united front. Our unalterable goal is peace, independence, unity and democracy. We must unswervingly stick to principles but show flexibility in tactics. All our activities should be inter-related and well co-ordinated, each part being integrated into the whole. Each task should be done in accordance with the concrete situation in each locality at a given moment.

Thanks to the correct leadership of our Party and Government, the unity and efforts of all our cadres and people, the sympathy and support of the people of the friendly countries and peace-loving people all over the world we will surely fulfill the above three responsibilities and ten tasks.

(374) TELEGRAM FROM ALEXIS JOHNSON, U.S. DELEGATION TO THE GENEVA CONFERENCE, TO DULLES, JULY 16, 1954

Source: *U.S.-Vietnam Relations, Book 9,* pp. 646-647.

Molotov offered Mendes-France a compromise on the issue of setting a date for elections to reunify Viet-nam by proposing that the agreement specify the date by which the two Vietnamese governments would have agreed on the election date, but Mendes-France rejected it.

Saw Chauvel this afternoon. He told me that Mendes-France and Molotov had dinner last night, and Soviets had launched into substantive discussion even before cocktails were served and continued throughout dinner, and Mendes-France and Molotov had discussion following dinner with only interpreters present which lasted more than 3 hours until almost 1:00 a.m. Discussion covering whole range of outstanding questions at least once; according to

Chauvel some of them "twenty times". Chauvel said Mendes had stuck firmly to French positions and with very minor exceptions of elections mentioned below, Molotov had, while being very pleasant, not (repeat not) budged an inch. On elections Molotov finally made suggestion that conference agree on date by which two governments of Vietnam would have decided date for elections. Mendes rejected this. Chauvel's assessment was that Communists expected to find Mendes "soft", are somewhat confused at his firmness, and are still testing him.

There have been no (repeat no) other major developments. I called Chauvel's particular attention to paragraph 3 of position paper on Indochina agreed at Paris and noted that French were still using term "guaranteeing powers" in draft armistice, and asked how he perceived the situation in this regard. He said that he conceived guarantee to be more than that embodied in French draft of conference declaration (SECTO 597). I pointed out that position paper made it clear that US will express its position unilaterally or in association only with non-Communist states, and was not quite sure how French concept of conference declaration fitted therewith. I said I had particularly instructed Bonsal reserve our position on last paragraph of French draft providing for consultation among conference powers on reports of violations by supervisory commission. Although I had no (repeat no) instructions on subject, I did not (repeat not) believe US would be willing assume continuing obligation consult with all conference powers including Communist China and Viet Minh. Chauvel said that in light of paragraph 3 of position paper, French draft provided only for conference [illegible] armistice agreement.

Chauvel said French were concerned over reports continued contacts between Fran Van Do and Dong. They did not know exactly what was happening, they know very little about Do, but they had impression he was unsophisticated and might be "taken into camp" by Dong. They felt after zones between defined and two governments each clearly responsible for own territories, such contacts would probably be desirable and necessary, but in present situation might be dangerous and could even result in surprise more bringing about something in nature of coalition government. Chauvel said De Jean was going to see Bao Dai to determine what Bao Dai knew about the matter and whether he had approved.

In reply to my question on what French conceived to be major outstanding issue, Chauvel listed: (1) military demarcation line in Vietnam, (2) regrouping in Vietnam, particularly in delta area, where Chauvel said Viet Minh would be required to move out two divisions from areas that they now occupied so as permit separation from French-Vietnamese forces. In Laos he said major question retention small number French troops there (consideration was being given to "changing their flag" from French to Laos), and also political questions in Laos. He said there were no major issues on Cambodia.

Chauvel also mentioned international control and asked whether I had any new instructions on subject. I said I had not and subject had not been discussed at Paris in any detail.

UK informed me today that meeting was proposed this afternoon between Mendes, Eden and Molotov to go over present stage of work of conference and make catalogue of work to be done. They asked whether I wished to be present, pointing out if US were present Soviets would probably insist on presence of Chinese, thus turning meeting into "five power affair". I replied that I had no objection to their going ahead on three-power basis.

(375) <u>TELEGRAM FROM SMITH TO DULLES</u>, JULY 17, 1954

Source: *U.S.-Vietnam Relations, Book 9*, pp. 648-650.

Mendes-France, Eden and Molotov were unable to make any progress on the key issues of setting a date for Vietnamese elections and the demarcation line

*for the zones of administration in Viet-nam. Mendes-France finally suggested
that the two issues would be linked, with each side making a concession on one
of them. Although there was no immediate response, it was apparently on this
basis that the D.R.V. was induced to make a further concession on the partition
line in return for setting a specific date for the elections.*

Following account of Mendes-France-Eden-Molotov meeting last night is based
on report of this meeting to Foreign Office made available to Johnson by Caccia.
This telegram expands upon and supersedes preliminary account transmitted in
first three paragraphs SECTO 630 (repeated information Paris 76, Saigon 48).

At Eden's suggestion, French enumerated documents before conference:

(A) Armistice agreements to be signed by local commanders-in-chief.
French have prepared drafts for Vietnam and Laos and Cambodians draft for Cambodia. Viet Minh delegation preparing counter draft for Vietnam.

(B) Control arrangements. French have circulated papers for Vietnam,
Laos, and Cambodia.

(C) Political arrangements. After having seen military documents, certain
delegations might make unilateral statements. For example, Laos and Cambodia
are preparing statements on their willingness to limit their armed forces.
Conference as whole would then agree upon common statement taking note of military agreements and unilateral declarations. French have circulated draft of
such statement. Soviets have prepared counter draft and French second redraft.

French explained that if conference did not (repeat not) have time to
agree on all details of armistice, it might approve only parts providing for
cessation of hostilities and first stage of regroupment. Remaining aspects of
agreements could be covered by statement of general principles for guidance of
experts who would work out details after conference had dispersed.

It was agreed that British, French, and Soviet experts would meet July 17
to consider various drafts.

At Eden's suggestion, Mendes-France summarized main outstanding problems
as (A) demarcation line for Vietnam; (B) elections, and (C) control arrangements. Concerning demarcation line, he said French had proposed line near
18th parallel whereas Viet Minh proposed 16th parallel. On elections in Viet-
nam, he said question was whether to fix firm date now (repeat now) (Soviets
had proposed June 1955) or whether, as French proposed, to settle now (repeat
now) only manner in which date would be set. Elections in Laos and Cambodia
already provided for in constitutions for August and September 1955, respectively. On control, he said main questions were: Whether there should be
one commission or three, composition, voting, execution of commissions' recommendations, and freedom of movement for inspection teams.

Molotov added to outstanding issues: (D) time required for regrouping
(French have proposed 380 days and Soviets 6 months); and (E) prevention of
importation of new arms and military personnel subject to certain exceptions
for Laos and Cambodia, prohibition of foreign military bases, and prohibition
of military alliances by three states.

Eden added (F) question of regroupment areas for resistance forces in
Laos.

Discussion then turned to substantive issues:

(A) Elections in Vietnam. Molotov said conference should fix date for
elections. He conceded more flexible formula might be found than firm date
of June 1955 previously proposed by Soviets and suggested agreement merely
that elections be held during 1955 with precise date to be fixed by Vietnamese and Viet Minh authorities.

Mendes-France argued that it would be imprudent to fix date as early as
the end of 1955. He suggested two ways of providing necessary flexibility in
arrangements: Date for elections might be fixed after completion of regroup-

ing; or exact date might be fixed now (repeat now) and international control commission be given authority to advance date if necessary.

Eden supported Mendes-France on need for flexibility and suggested that two parts of Vietnam fix date after completion of regrouping. Mendes-France agreed to consider this suggestion, but Molotov continued to urge elections during 1955.

(B) Demarcation line. Molotov argued that in moving from 13th to 16th parallel, Viet Minh had made substantial concession which called for proper response from French. Mendes-France disagreed, arguing that Viet Minh would be giving up much less in Annam than they would be getting in Tonkin. He said that Pham Van Dong had admitted that line on 16th parallel would require special arrangements for Tourane, Bue, on route No. 9 leading into Laos. Mendes-France stated that necessity for such special arrangements showed how unnatural demarcation line at 16th parallel would be. He said that there was no (repeat no) chance of persuading French Government to accept line which excluded either Hue or route No. 9. Eden supported Mendes-France.

Molotov suggested that discussion move to question of control arrangements. Mendes-France replied might be better to postpone such discussion. He observed that questions of elections and demarcation line had been discussed together and might be linked in sense that conceivably one party might yield on one question and another party on other.

(376) TELEGRAM FROM SMITH TO DULLES, JULY 18, 1954

Source: *U.S.-Vietnam Relations, Book 9*, p. 662.

Two representatives of the State of Viet-nam informed the U.S. delegation confidentially that they were rejecting the bases of the settlement already agreed to in principle by the French and the Communist delegations only for public purposes, knowing that it was impractical. They said that after their own proposal had been rejected by the Communist side, they would accept the settlement which was being negotiated.

At recess after today's meeting Tran Van Do and Tran Van Chuong immediately approached Johnson stating they wished US clearly understand reasons they felt compelled make their statement at today's meeting (SECTO 654) and why they were asking for a plenary session. They said they desired at such a plenary session put forward position contained their note to French (SECTO 633) and asked Johnson's opinion on position. Johnson replied that did not feel it was practicable proposal, to which they responded they fully realized that it was not practicable and would be rejected by other side, but they felt they must make moral position their government clear to world and to Vietnamese people. If other side rejected, it, position of their government would have been improved. Upon rejection by other side they would be prepeared accept settlement along lines now being discussed.

Johnson pointed out that time was short and it was late for such proposal to which they replied that Mendes could of course ask for and obtain additional time from French Assembly. Johnson expressed strong doubt and urged they speak directly with French. After repeated strong urgings they finally approached Mendes, who listened sympathetically and at length. He suggested and they promised to consider formulation their proposal in writing and circulation to other delegations. He categorically stated he could not even if he so desired ask Assembly for any extension time he has given self.

Johnson told Mendes he was concerned over reaction to Vietnamese statement and reminded Mendes of US position on Vietnamese concurrence with any agreement. Mendes stated he was very conscious of [*officially deleted*] and was asking De Jean immediately go to Cannes to see Bao Dai.

Chauvel said that from De Jean's previous talk with Bao Dai it appeared Bao Dai had no knowledge of Do's conversations with Dong and in general had given delegation here free hand.

(377) PROPOSAL BY THE DELEGATION OF THE STATE OF VIET-NAM TO THE GENEVA CONFERENCE, JULY 19, 1954

Source: *U.S.-Vietnam Relations, Book 9*, pp. 669-670.

The proposal of the delegation of the Diem government rejected partition and an international commission to inspect the ceasefire and elections, demanding United Nations control over the entire process and the postponement of elections until security had been "truly restored."

French, Soviet, and Viet Minh drafts all admit the principles of a partition of Vietnam in two zones, all of North Vietnam being abandoned to the Viet Minh.

Although this partition is only provisional in theory, it would not fail to produce in Vietnam the same effects as in Germany, Austria, and Korea.

It would not bring the peace which is sought for, deeply wounding the national sentiment of the Vietnamese people, it would provoke trouble throughout the country, trouble which would not fail to threaten a peace so dearly acquired.

Before discussing the conditions of a *de facto* partition with disastrous consequences for the people of Vietnam and for the peace of the world, the delegation of the state of Vietnam renews its proposal for a cease-fire without a demarcation line, without partition, even provisionally.

The Vietnamese delegation therefore proposes:

1. A cease-fire on present positions.
2. Regroupment of troops in two zones which would be as small as possible.
3. Disarmament of irregular troops.
4. After a period to be fixed, disarmament of Viet Minh troops and simultaneous withdrawal of foreign troops.
5. Control by the United Nations:
A. Of the cease-fire
B. Of the regroupment
C. Of the disarmament and the withdrawal
D. Of the administration of the entire country
E. Of the general elections, when the United Nations believes that order and security will have been everywhere truly restored.

This proposal made on the formal instructions of His Majesty Bao Dai, and of President Ngo Dinh Diem, shows that the chief of state of Vietnam once more places the independence and the unity of his country above any other consideration, and that the national government of Vietnam would prefer this provisional UN control over a truly independent and United Vietnam to its maintenance in power in a country dismembered and condemned to slavery.

Vietnamese delegation renews its request that a conference session be devoted to the study of its proposal for a cease-fire without partition.

In adding this proposal to those of other members of the conference, the delegation of the state of Vietnam means to bring a positive contribution to the search for a real and durable peace which conforms to the aspirations of the Vietnamese people.

(378) <u>AGREEMENT ON THE CESSATION OF HOSTILITIES IN VIET-NAM</u>, JULY 20, 1954

Source: Great Britain, Parliament, Papers by Command, *Further Documents Relating to the Discussion of Indo-China at the Geneva Conference June 16-July 21, 1954* (London: Her Majesty's Stationery Office. Cmd. 9239, 1954, reprinted 1965), pp. 27-38.

CHAPTER I

PROVISIONAL MILITARY DEMARCATION LINE AND
DEMILITARISED ZONE

Article 1

A provisional military demarcation line shall be fixed, on either side of which the forces of the two parties shall be regrouped after their withdrawal, the forces of the People's Army of Viet Nam to the north of the line and the forces of the French Union to the south.

The provisional military demarcation line is fixed as shown on the map attached (see Map No. 1).[1]

It is also agreed that a demilitarised zone shall be established on either side of the demarcation line, to a width of not more than 5 kms. from it, to act as a buffer zone and avoid any incidents which might result in the resumption of hostilities.

Article 2

The period within which the movement of all forces of either party into its regrouping zone on either side of the provisional military demarcation line shall be completed shall not exceed three hundred (300) days from the date of the present Agreement's entry into force.

Article 3

When the provisional military demarcation line coincides with a waterway, the waters of such waterway shall be open to civil navigation by both parties wherever one bank is controlled by one party and the other bank by the other party. The Joint Commission shall establish rules of navigation for the stretch of waterway in question. The merchant shipping and other civilian craft of each party shall have unrestricted access to the land under its military control.

Article 4

The provisional military demarcation line between the two final regrouping zones is extended into the territorial waters by a line perpendicular to the general line of the coast.

All coastal islands north of this boundary shall be evacuated by the armed forces of the French Union, and all islands south of it shall be evacuated by the forces of the People's Army of Viet Nam.

Article 5

To avoid any incidents which might result in the resumption of hostilities, all military forces, supplies and equipment shall be withdrawn from the demilitarised zone within twenty-five (25) days of the present Agreement's entry into force.

Article 6

No person, military or civilian, shall be permitted to cross the provisional military demarcation line unless specifically authorised to do so by the Joint Commission.

Article 7

No person, military or civilian, shall be permitted to enter the demilitarised zone except persons concerned with the conduct of civil administration and relief and persons specifically authorised to enter by the Joint Commission.

Article 8

Civil administration and relief in the demilitarised zone on either side of the provisional military demarcation line shall be the responsibility of the Commanders-in-Chief of the two parties in their respective zones. The number of persons, military or civilian, from each side who are permitted to enter the demilitarised zone for the conduct of civil administration and relief shall be determined by the respective Commanders, but in no case shall the total number authorised by either side exceed at any one time a figure to be determined by the Trung Gia Military Commission[2] or by the Joint Commission. The number of civil police and the arms to be carried by them shall be determined by the Joint Commission. No one else shall carry arms unless specifically authorised to do so by the Joint Commission.

Article 9

Nothing contained in this chapter shall be construed as limiting the complete freedom of movement, into, out of or within the demilitarised zone, of the Joint Commission, its joint groups, the International Commission to be set up as indicated below, its inspection teams and any other persons, supplies or equipment specifically authorised to enter the demilitarised zone by the Joint Commission. Freedom of movement shall be permitted across the territory under the military control of either side over any road or waterway which has to be taken between points within the demilitarised zone when such points are not connected by roads or waterways lying completely within the demilitarised zone.

CHAPTER II

PRINCIPLES AND PROCEDURE GOVERNING IMPLEMENTATION
OF THE PRESENT AGREEMENT

Article 10

The Commanders of the Forces on each side, on the one side the Commander-in-Chief of the French Union forces in Indo-China and on the other side the Commander-in-Chief of the People's Army of Viet Nam, shall order and enforce the complete cessation of all hostilities in Viet Nam by all armed forces under their control, including all units and personnel of the ground, naval and air forces.

Article 11

In accordance with the principle of a simultaneous cease-fire throughout Indo-China, the cessation of hostilities shall be simultaneous throughout all parts of Viet Nam, in all areas of hostilities and for all the forces of the two parties.

Taking into account the time effectively required to transmit the cease-fire order down to the lowest echelons of the combatant forces on both sides, the two parties are agreed that the cease-fire shall take effect completely and simultaneously for the different sectors of the country as follows:

Northern Viet Nam at 8:00 A.M. (local time) on July 27, 1954.
Central Viet Nam at 8:00 A.M. (local time) on August 1, 1954.
Southern Viet Nam at 8:00 A.M. (local time) on August 11, 1954.

It is agreed that Peking mean time shall be taken as local time.

From such time as the cease-fire becomes effective in Northern Viet Nam, both parties undertake not to engage in any large-scale offensive action in any part of the Indo-Chinese theatre of operations and not to commit the air forces based on Northern Viet Nam outside that sector. The two parties also undertake to inform each other of their plans for movement from one regrouping zone to another within twenty-five (25) days of the present Agreement's entry into force.

Article 12

All the operations and movements entailed in the cessation of hostilities and regrouping must proceed in a safe and orderly fashion:

(*a*) Within a certain number of days after the cease-fire Agreement shall become effective, the number to be determined on the spot by the Trung Gia Military Commission, each party shall be responsible for removing and neutralising mines (including river- and sea-mines), booby traps, explosives and any other dangerous substances placed by it. In the event of its being impossible to complete the work of removal and neutralisation in time, the party concerned shall mark the spot by placing visible signs there. All demolitions, mine fields, wire entaglements and other hazards to the free movement of the personnel of the Joint Commission and its joint groups, known to be present after the withdrawal of the military forces, shall be reported to the Joint Commission by the Commanders of the opposing forces;

(*b*) From the time of the cease-fire until regrouping is completed on either side of the demarcation line:
    (1) The forces of either party shall be provisionally withdrawn from the provisional assembly areas assigned to the other party.
    (2) When one party's forces withdraw by a route (road, rail, waterway, sea route) which passes through the territory of the other party (see Article 24), the latter party's forces must provisionally withdraw three kilometres on each side of such route, but in such a manner as to avoid interfering with the movements of the civil population.

Article 13

From the time of the cease-fire until the completion of the movements from one regrouping zone into the other, civil and military transport aircraft shall follow air-corridors between the provisional assembly areas assigned to the French Union forces north of the demarcation line on the one hand and the Laotian frontier and the regrouping zone assigned to the French Union forces on the other hand.
The position of the air-corridors, their width, the safety route for single-engined military aircraft transferred to the south and the search and rescue procedure for aircraft in distress shall be determined on the spot by the Trung Gia Military Commission.

Article 14

Political and administrative measures in the two regrouping zones, on either side of the provisional military demarcation line:

(*a*) Pending the general elections which will bring about the unification of Viet Nam, the conduct of civil administration in each regrouping zone shall be in the hands of the party whose forces are to be regrouped there in virtue of the present Agreement.
(*b*) Any territory controlled by one party which is transferred to the other party by the regrouping plan shall continue to be administered by the former party until such date as all the troops who are to be transferred have completely left that territory so as to free the zone assigned to the party in question. From then on, such territory shall be regarded as transferred

to the other party, who shall assume responsibility for it.

Steps shall be taken to ensure that there is no break in the transfer of responsibilities. For this purpose, adequate notice shall be given by the withdrawing party to the other party, which shall make the necessary arrangements, in particular by sending administrative and police detachments to prepare for the assumption of administrative responsibility. The length of such notice shall be determined by the Trung Gia Military Commission. The transfer shall be effected in successive stages for the various territorial sectors.

The transfer of the civil administration of Hanoi and Haiphong to the authorities of the Democratic Republic of Viet Nam shall be completed within the respective time-limits laid down in Article 15 for military movements.

(*c*) Each party undertakes to refrain from any reprisals or discrimination against persons or organisations on account of their activities during the hostilities and to guarantee their democratic rights.

(*d*) From the date of entry into force of the present Agreement until the movement of troops is completed, any civilians residing in a district controlled by one party who wish to go and live in the zone assigned to the other party shall be permitted and helped to do so by the authorities in that district.

Article 15

The disengagement of the combatants, and the withdrawals and transfers of military forces, equipment and supplies shall take place in accordance with the following principles:

(*a*) The withdrawals and transfers of the military forces, equipment and supplies of the two parties shall be completed within three hundred (300) days, as laid down in Article 2 of the present Agreement:

(*b*) Within either territory successive withdrawals shall be made by sectors, portions of sectors or provinces. Transfers from one regrouping zone to another shall be made in successive monthly instalments proportionate to the number of troops to be transferred;

(*c*) The two parties shall undertake to carry out all troop withdrawals and transfers in accordance with the aims of the present Agreement, shall permit no hostile act and shall take no step whatsoever which might hamper such withdrawals and transfers. They shall assist one another as far as this is possible;

(*d*) The two parties shall permit no destruction or sabotage of any public property and no injury to the life and property of the civil population. They shall permit no interference in local civil administration;

(*e*) The Joint Commission and the International Commission shall ensure that steps are taken to safeguard the forces in the course of withdrawal and transfer;

(*f*) The Trung Gia Military Commission, and later the Joint Commission shall determine by common agreement the exact procedure for the disengagement of the combatants and for troop withdrawals and transfers, on the basis of the principles mentioned above and within the framework laid down below:

1. The disengagement of the combatants, including the concentration of the armed forces of all kinds and also each party's movements into the provisional assembly areas assigned to it and the other party's provisional withdrawal from it, shall be completed within a period not exceeding fifteen (15) days after the date when the cease-fire becomes effective.

The general delineation of the provisional assembly areas is set out in the maps[3] annexed to the present Agreement.

In order to avoid any incidents, no troops shall be stationed less than 1,500 metres from the lines delimiting the provisional assembly areas.

During the period until the transfers are concluded, all the coastal islands west of the following lines shall be included in the Haiphong perimeter:

meridian of the southern point of Kebao Island, northern coast of Ile Rousse (excluding the island), extended as far as the meridian of Campha-Mines, meridian of Campha-mines.

2. The withdrawals and transfers shall be effected in the following order and within the following periods (from the date of the entry into force of the present Agreement):

Forces of the French Union

Hanoi perimeter	80 days
Haiduong perimeter	100 days
Haiphong perimeter	300 days

Forces of the People's Army of Viet Nam

Ham Tan and Xuyenmoc provisional assembly area	80 days
Central Viet Nam provisional assembly area - first instalment	80 days
Plaine des Joncs provisional assembly area	100 days
Central Viet Nam provisional assembly area - second instalment	100 days
Pointe Camau provisional assembly area	200 days
Central Viet Nam provisional assembly area - last instalment	300 days

CHAPTER III

BAN ON THE INTRODUCTION OF FRESH TROOPS, MILITARY PERSONNEL, ARMS AND MUNITIONS. MILITARY BASES

Article 16

With effect from the date of entry into force of the present Agreement, the introduction into Viet Nam of any troop reinforcements and additional military personnel is prohibited.

It is understood, however, that the rotation of units and groups of personnel, the arrival in Viet Nam of individual personnel on a temporary basis and the return to Viet Nam of the individual personnel after short periods of leave or temporary duty outside Viet Nam shall be permitted under the conditions laid down below:

(*a*) Rotation of units (defined in paragraph (c) of this Article) and groups of personnel shall not be permitted for French Union troops stationed north of the provisional military demarcation line lain down in Article 1 of the present Agreement during the withdrawal period provided for in Article 2.

However, under the heading of individual personnel not more that fifty (50) men, including officers, shall during any one month be permitted to enter that part of the country north of the provisional military demarcation line on a temporary basis or to return there after short periods of leave or temporary duty outside Viet Nam.

(*b*) "Rotation" is defined as the replacement of units or groups of personnel by other units of the same echelon or by personnel who are arriving in Viet Nam territory to do their overseas service there;

(*c*) The units rotated shall never be larger than a battalion - or the corresponding echelon for air and naval forces;

(*d*) Rotation shall be conducted on a man-for-man basis, provided however, that in any one quarter neither party shall introduce more than fifteen thousand five hundred (15,500) members of its armed forces into Viet Nam under the rotation policy.

(*e*) Rotation units (defined in paragraph (c) of this Article) and groups of personnel, and the individual personnel mentioned in this Article, shall enter and leave Viet Nam only through the entry points enumerated in Article 20 below;

(*f*) Each party shall notify the Joint Commission and the International Commission at least two days in advance of any arrivals or departures of units groups of personnel and individual personnel in or from Viet Nam. Reports on the arrivals or departures of units, groups of personnel and individual personnel in or from Viet Nam shall be submitted daily to the Joint Commission and the International Commission.

All the above-mentioned notifications and reports shall indicate the places and dates of arrival or departure and the number of persons arriving or departing;

(*g*) The International Commission, through its Inspection Teams, shall supervise and inspect the rotation of units and groups of personnel and the arrival and departure of individual personnel as authorised above, at the points of entry enumerated in Article 20 below.

Article 17

(*a*) With effect from the date of entry into force of the present Agreement, the introduction into Viet Nam of any reinforcements in the form of all types of arms, munitions and other war material, such as combat aircraft, naval craft, pieces of ordnance, jet engines and jet weapons and armoured vehicles is prohibited.

(*b*) It is understood, however, that war material, arms and munitions which have been destroyed, damaged, worn out or used up after the cessation of hostilities may be replaced on the basis of piece-for piece of the same type and with similar characteristics. Such replacement of war material, arms and ammunitions shall not be permitted for French Union troops stationed north of the provisional military demarcation line laid down in Article 1 of the present Agreement, during the withdrawal period provided for in Article 2.

Naval craft may perform transport operations between the regrouping zones.

(*c*) The war material, arms and munitions for replacement purposes provided for in paragraph (b) of this Article, shall be introduced into Viet Nam only through the points of entry enumerated in Article 20 below. War material, arms, and munitions to be replaced shall be shipped from Viet Nam only through the points of entry enumerated in Article 20 below.

(*d*) Apart from the replacements permitted within the limits laid down in paragraph (b) of this Article, the introduction of war material, arms and munitions of all types in the form of unassembled parts for subsequent assembly is prohibited.

(*e*) Each party shall notify the Joint Commission and the International Commission at least two days in advance of any arrivals or departures which may take place of war material, arms and munitions of all types.

In order to justify the requests for the introduction into Viet Nam of arms, munitions and other war material (as defined in paragraph (a) of this Article) for replacement purposes, a report concerning each incoming shipment shall be submitted to the Joint Commission and the International Commission. Such reports shall indicate the use made of the items so replaced.

(*f*) The International Commission, through its Inspection Teams, shall supervise and inspect the replacements permitted in the circumstances laid down in this Article, at the points of entry enumerated in Article 20 below.

Article 18

With effect from the date of entry into force of the present Agreement, the establishment of new military bases is prohibited throughout Viet Nam territory.

Article 19

With effect from the date of entry into force of the present Agreement, no military base under the control of a foreign State may be established in the regrouping zone of either party; the two parties shall ensure that the zones assigned to them do not adhere to any military alliance and are not used for the resumption of hostilities or to further an aggressive policy.

Article 20

The points of entry into Viet Nam for rotation personnel and replacements of material are fixed as follows:

Zone to the north of the provisional military demarcation line: Laokay, Langson, Tien-Yen, Haiphong, Vinh, Dong-Hoi, Muong-Sen;

Zone to the south of the provisional military demarcation line: Tourane, Quinhon, Nhatrang, Bangoi, Saigon, Cap St. Jacques, Tanchau.

CHAPTER IV

PRISONERS OF WAR AND CIVILIAN INTERNEES

Article 21

The liberation and repatriation of all prisoners of war and civilian internees detained by each of the two parties at the coming into force of the present Agreement shall be carried out under the following conditions:

(*a*) All prisoners of war and civilian internees of Viet Nam, French and other nationalities captured since the beginning of hostilities in Viet Nam during military operations or in any other circumstances of war and in any part of the territory of Viet Nam shall be liberated within a period of thirty (30) days after the date when the cease-fire becomes effective in each theater

(*b*) The term "civilian internees" is understood to mean all persons who, having in any way contributed to the political and armed struggle between the two parties, have been arrested for that reason and have been kept in detention by either party during the period of hostilities.

(*c*) All prisoners of war and civilian internees held by either party shall be surrendered to the appropriate authorities of the other party, who shall give them all possible assistance in proceeding to their country of origin, place of habitual residence or the zone of their choice.

CHAPTER V

MISCELLANEOUS

Article 22

The Commanders of the Forces of the two parties shall ensure that persons under their respective commands who violate any of the provisions of the present Agreement are suitably punished.

Article 23

In cases in which the place of burial is known and the existence of graves has been established, the Commander of the Forces of either party shall, within a specific period after the entry into force of the Armistice Agreement, permit the graves service personnel of the other party to enter the part of Viet Nam territory under their military control for the purpose of finding and removing the bodies of deceased military personnel of that party, including the bodies of deceased prisoners of war. The Joint Commission shall determine the procedures and the time limit for the performance of this task. The Commanders of the Forces of the two parties shall communicate to each other all information in their possession as to the place of burial of military personnel of the other party.

Article 24

The present Agreement shall apply to all the armed forces of either party. The armed forces of each party shall respect the demilitarised zone and the territory under the military control of the other party, and shall commit no act and undertake no operation against the other party and shall not engage in blockade of any kind in Viet Nam.

For the purposes of the present Article, the word "territory" includes territorial waters and air space.

Article 25

The Commanders of the Forces of the two parties shall afford full protection and all possible assistance and co-operation to the Joint Commission and its joint groups and to the International Commission and its inspection teams in the performance of the functions and tasks assigned to them by the present Agreement.

Article 26

The costs involved in the operations of the Joint Commission and joint groups and of the International Commission and its Inspection Teams shall be shared equally between the two parties.

Article 27

The signatories of the present Agreement and their successors in their functions shall be responsible for ensuring the observance and enforcement of the terms and provisions thereof. The Commanders of the Forces of the two parties shall, within their respective commands, take all steps and make all arrangements necessary to ensure full compliance with all the provisions of the present Agreement by all elements and military personnel under their command.

The procedures laid down in the present Agreement shall, whenever necessary, be studied by the Commanders of the two parties and, if necessary, defined more specifically by the Joint Commission.

CHAPTER VI

JOINT COMMISSION AND INTERNATIONAL COMMISSION
FOR SUPERVISION AND CONTROL IN VIET NAM

Article 28

Responsibility for the execution of the agreement on the cessation of hostilities shall rest with the parties.

Article 29

An International Commission shall ensure the control and supervision of this execution.

Article 30

In order to facilitate, under the conditions shown below, the execution of provisions concerning joint actions by the two parties, a Joint Commission shall be set up in Viet Nam.

Article 31

The Joint Commission shall be composed of an equal number of representatives of the Commanders of the two parties.

Article 32

The Presidents of the delegations to the Joint Commission shall hold the rank of General.

The Joint Commission shall set up joint groups, the number of which shall be determined by mutual agreement between the parties. The Joint groups shall be composed of an equal number of officers from both parties. Their location on the demarcation line between the regrouping zones shall be determined by the parties whilst taking into account the powers of the Joint Commission.

Article 33

The Joint Commission shall ensure the execution of the following provisions of the Agreement on the cessation of hostilities:

(*a*) A simultaneous and general cease-fire in Viet Nam for all regular and irregular armed forces of the two parties.

(*b*) A regroupment of the armed forces of the two parties.

(*c*) Observance of the demarcation lines between the regrouping zones and of the demilitarised sectors.

Within the limits of its competence it shall help the parties to execute the said provisions, shall ensure liaison between them for the purpose of preparing and carrying out plans for the application of these provisions, and shall endeavour to solve such disputed questions as may arise between the parties in the course of executing these provisions.

Article 34

An International Commission shall be set up for the control and supervision over the application of the provisions of the agreement on the cessation of hostilities in Viet Nam. It shall be composed of representatives of the following States: Canada, India and Poland.

It shall be presided over by the Representative of India.

Article 35

The International Commission shall set up fixed and mobile inspection teams, composed of an equal number of officers appointed by each of the above-mentioned States. The mixed [*fixed*] teams shall be located at the following points: Laokay, Langson, Tien-Yen, Haiphong, Vinh, Dong-Hoi, Muong-Sen, Tourante, Quinhon, Nhatrang, Bangoi, Saigon, Cap St. Jacques, Tranchau. These points of location may, at a later date, be altered at the request of the Joint Commission, or of one of the parties, or of the International Commission itself, by agreement between the International Commission and the command of the party concerned. The zones of action of the mobile teams shall be the regions bordering the land and sea frontiers of Viet Nam, the demarcation lines between the regrouping zones and the demilitarised zones. Within the limits of these zones they shall have the right to move freely and shall receive from the local civil and military authorities all facilities they may require for the fulfilment of their tasks (provision of personnel, placing at their disposal documents needed for supervision, summoning witnesses necessary for holding enquiries, ensuring the security and freedom of movement of the inspection teams, &c....). They shall have at their disposal such modern means of transport, observation and communication as they may require. Beyond the zones of action as defined above, the mobile teams may, by agreement with the command of the party concerned, carry out other movements within the limits of the tasks given them by the present agreement.

Article 36

The International Commission shall be responsible for supervising the proper execution by the parties of the provisions of the agreement. For this purpose it shall fulfil the tasks of control, observation, inspection and investigation connected with the application of the provisions of the agreement on the cessation of hostilities, and it shall in particular:

(a) Control the movement of the armed forces of the two parties, effected within the framework of the regroupment plan.

(b) Supervise the demarcation lines between the regrouping areas, and also the demilitarised zones.

(c) Control the operations of releasing prisoners of war and civilian internees.

(d) Supervise at ports and airfields as well as along all frontiers of Viet Nam the execution of the provisions of the agreement on the cessation of hostilities, regulating the introduction into the country of armed forces, military personnel and of all kinds of arms, munitions and war material.

Article 37

The International Commission shall, through the medium of the inspection teams mentioned above, and as soon as possible either on its own initiative, or at the request of the Joint Commission, or of one of the parties, undertake the necessary investigations both documentary and on the ground.

Article 38

The inspection teams shall submit to the International Commission the results of their supervision, their investigation and their observations, furthermore they shall draw up such special reports as they may consider necessary or as may be requested from them by the Commission. In the case of a disagreement within the teams, the conclusions of each member shall be submitted to the Commission.

Article 39

If any one inspection team is unable to settle an incident or considers that there is a violation or a threat of a serious violation, the International Commission shall be informed; the latter shall study the reports and the conclusions of the inspection teams and shall inform the parties of the measures which should be taken for the settlement of the incident, ending of the violation or removal of the threat of violation.

Article 40

When the Joint Commission is unable to reach an agreement on the interpretation to be given to some provision or on the appraisal of a fact, the International Commission shall be informed of the disputed question. Its recommendations shall be sent directly to the parties and shall be notified to the Joint Commission.

Article 41

The recommendations of the International Commission shall be adopted by majority vote, subject to the provisions contained in Article 42. If the votes are divided, the chairman's vote shall be decisive.

The International Commission may formulate recommendations concerning amendments and additions which should be made to the provisions of the agreement on the cessation of hostilities in Viet Nam, in order to ensure a more effective execution of that agreement. These recommendations shall be adopted unanimously.

Article 42

When dealing with questions concerning violations, or threats of violations, which might lead to a resumption of hostilities, namely: (*a*) Refusal by the armed forces of one party to effect the movements provided for in the regrouping plan; (*b*) Violation by the armed forces of one of the parties of the regrouping zones, territorial waters, or air space of the other party; the decisions of the International Commission must be unanimous.

Article 43

If one of the parties refuses to put into effect a recommendation of the International Commission, the parties concerned or the Commission itself shall inform the members of the Geneva Conference.

If the International Commission does not reach unanimity in the cases provided for in Article 42, it shall submit a majority report and one or more minority reports to the members of the Conference.

The International Commission shall inform the members of the Conference in all cases where its activity is being hindered.

Article 44

The International Commission shall be set up at the time of the cessation of hostilities in Indo-China in order that it should be able to fulfil the tasks provided for in Article 36.

Article 45

The International Commission for Supervision and Control in Viet Nam shall act in close co-operation with the International Commissions for Supervision and Control in Cambodia and Laos.

The Secretaries-General of these three Commissions shall be responsible for co-ordinating their work and for relations between them.

Article 46

The International Commission for Supervision and Control in Viet Nam may, after consultation with the International Commissions for Supervision and Control in Cambodia and Laos, and having regard to the development of the situation in Cambodia and Laos, progressively reduce its activities. Such a decision must be adopted unanimously.

Article 47

All the provisions of the present Agreement, save the second subparagraph of Article 11, shall enter into force at 2400 hours (Geneva time) on July 22, 1954.

Done in Geneva at 2400 hours on the 20th of July, 1954, in French and in Vietnamese, both texts being equally authentic.

For the Commander-in-Chief of the French Union Forces in Indo-China:

DELTIEL
Brigadier-General

For the Commander-in-Chief of the People's Army of Viet Nam
TA-QUANG-BUU
Vice-Minister of National Defence of
the Democratic Republic of Viet Nam

[The Annex, specifically delineating the provisional military demarcation line and demilitarised zone and the provisional assembly areas, is omitted.]

[1]Footnote in the original: "Map not printed - See Annex for details," The Annex is not printed in this collection; it may be found in Great Britain, Parliament, Papers by Command, *Further Documents Relating to the Discussion of Indo-China at the Geneva Conference, July 16 - July 21, 1954* (London: Her Majesty's Stationery Office, Cmd. 9239. 1954, reprinted 1965), pp. 39-40.

[2]The Trung Gia Military Commission was the form agreed upon by the Geneva Conference to handle the "on the ground" details of conclusion and implementation of the cease-fire in Viet-Nam. Meeting at Trung Gia in Tonkin, it consisted of representatives of the French and Viet Minh high commands; representatives of the State of Viet-Nam were present only as observers.

[3]Footnote in the original: "Map not printed - See Annex for details." See note 1.

(379) DECLARATIONS BY THE ROYAL GOVERNMENT OF LAOS, JULY 21, 1954

Source: *Documents Relating to British Involvement in the Indochina Conflict,* pp. 78-79.

As part of the compromise on which the settlement was based, the Laotian government issued two declarations, one binding itself to remain outside any military alliance, and the other pledging to reintegrate those who opposed the government during the war. The latter declaration did not specify how the integration was to take place, leaving that to the Royal Government and the Pathet Lao to negotiate.

(Reference: Article 3 of the Final Declaration)

The Royal Government of Laos.

In the desire to ensure harmony and agreement among the peoples of the Kingdom,

Declares itself resolved to take the necessary measures to integrate all citizens, without discrimination, into the national community and to guarantee them the enjoyment of the rights and freedoms for which the Constitution of the Kingdom provides;

Affirms that all Laotian citizens may freely participate as electors of candidates in general elections by secret ballot;

Announces, furthermore, that it will promulgate measures to provide for special representation in the Royal Administration of the provinces of Phang Saly and Sam Neua during the interval between the cessation of hostilities and the the general elections of the interests of Laotian nationals who did not support the Royal forces during hostilities.

(References: Articles 4 and 5 of the Final Declaration)

The Royal Government of Laos is resolved never to pursue a policy of aggression and will never permit the territory of Laos to be used in furtherance of such a policy.

The Royal Government of Laos will never join in any agreement with other States if this agreement includes the obligation for the Royal Government of Laos to participate in a military alliance not in conformity with the principles of the Charter of the United Nations or with the principles of the agreement on the cessation of hostilities or, unless its security is threatened, the obligation to establish bases on Laotian territory for military forces of foreign powers.

The Royal Government of Laos is resolved to settle its international disputes by peaceful means so that international peace and security and justice are not endangered.

During the period between the cessation of hostilities in Viet-Nam and the final settlement of that country's political problems, the Royal Government of Laos will not request foreign aid, whether in war material, in personnel or in instructors, except for the purpose of its effective territorial defence and to the extent defined by the agreement on the cessation of hostilities.

(380) FINAL DECLARATION OF THE GENEVA CONFERNECE OF THE PROBLEM OF RESTORING PEACE IN INDOCHINA, JULY 1954

Source: Democratic Republic of Viet-nam Ministry of Foreign Affairs, Press and Information Department, *Documents Related to the Implementation of the Geneva Agreements Concerning Viet-nam* (Hanoi: 1956), pp. 181-183.

1. - The Conference takes note of the Agreements ending hostilities in Cambodia, Laos, and Viet-Nam and organizing international control and the supervision of the execution of the provisions of these agreements.

2. - The Conference expresses satisfaction at the ending of hostilities in Cambodia, Laos and Viet-Nam; the Conference expresses its conviction that the execution of the provisions set out in the present Declaration and in the Agreements on the cessation of hostilities will permit Cambodia, Laos and Viet-Nam henceforth to play their part, in full independence and sovereignty, in the peaceful community of nations.

3. - The Conference takes note of the declarations made by the Governments of Cambodia and of Laos of their intention to adopt measures permitting all citizens to take their place in the national community, in particular by participating in the next general elections, which, in conformity with the constitution of each of these countries, shall take place in the course of the year 1955, by secret ballot and in conditions of respect for fundamental freedoms.

4. - The Conference takes note of the clauses in the Agreement on the cessation of hostilities in Viet-Nam prohibiting the introduction into Viet-Nam of foreign troops and military personnel as well as all kinds of arms and munitions. The Conference also takes note of the declarations made by the Governments of Cambodia and Laos of their resolution not to request foreign aid, whether in war material, in personnel or in instructors except for the purpose of the effective defence of their territory and, in the case of Laos, to the extent defined by the Agreements on the cessation of hostilities in Laos.

5. - The Conference takes note of the clauses in the Agreement on the cessation of hostilities in Viet-nam to the effect that no military base under the control of a foreign State may be established in the regrouping zones of the two parties, the latter having the obligation to see that the zones allotted to them shall not constitute part of any military alliance and shall not be utilized for the resumption of hostilities or in the service of an aggressive policy. The Conference also takes note of the declarations of the Governments of Cambodia and Laos to the effect that they will not join in any agreement with other States if this agreement includes the obligation to participate in a military alliance not in conformity with the principles of the Charter of the United Nations or, in the case of Laos, with the principles of the Agreement on the cessation of hostilities in Laos or, so long as their accurity is not threatened, the obligation to establish bases on Cambodian or Laotian territory for the military forces of foreign powers.

6. - The Conference recognizes that the essential purpose of the Agreement relating to Viet-nam is to settle military questions with a view to ending hostilities and that the military demarcation line is provisional and should not in any way be interpreted as constituting a political or territorial bound-

ary. The Conference expresses its conviction that the execution of the provisions set out in the present Declaration and in the Agreement on the cessation of hostilities creates the necessary basis for the achievement in the near future of a political settlement in Viet-nam.

7. - The Conference declares that, so far as Viet-nam is concerned, the settlement of political problems, effected on the basis of respect for principles of independence, unity and territorial integrity, shall permit the Vietnamese people to enjoy the fundamental freedoms, guaranteed by democratic institutions established as a result of free general elections by secret ballot. In order to ensure that sufficient progress in the restoration of peace has been made and that all the necessary conditions obtain for free expression of the national will, general elections shall be held in July 1956, under the supervision of an international commission composed of representatives of the Member States of the International Supervisory Commission, referred to in the Agreement on the cessation of hostilities. Consultations will be held on this subject between the competent representative authorities of the two zones from 20 July 1955 onwards.

8. - The provisions of the Agreements on the cessation of hostilities intended to ensure the protection of individuals and of property must be most strictly applied and must, in particular, allow everyone in Viet-nam to decide freely in which zone he wishes to live.

9. - The competent representative authorities of the Northern and Southern zones of Viet-nam, as well as the authorities of Laos and Cambodia, must not permit any individual or collective reprisals against persons who have collaborated in any way with one of the parties during the war, or against members of such persons' families.

10. - The Conference takes note of the declaration of the Government of the French Republic to the effect that it is ready to withdraw its troops from the territory of Cambodia, Laos and Viet-nam, at the request of the governments concerned and within periods which shall be fixed by agreement between the parties except in the cases where, by agreement between the two parties, a certain number of French troops shall remain at specified points and for a specified time.

11. - The Conference takes note of the declaration of the French Government to the effect that for the settlement of all the problems connected with the re-establishment and consolidation of peace in Cambodia, Laos and Viet-nam, the French Government will proceed from the principle of respect for the independence and sovereignty, unity and territorial integrity of Cambodia, Laos and Viet-nam.

12. - In their relations with Cambodia, Laos and Viet-nam, each member of the Geneva Conference undertakes to respect the sovereignty, the independence, the unity and the territorial integrity of the above-mentioned States, and to refrain from any interference in their internal affairs.

13. - The members of the Conference agree to consult one another on any question which may be referred to them by the International Supervisory Commission, in order to study such measures as may prove necessary to ensure that the Agreements on the cessation of hostilities in Cambodia, Laos and Viet-nam are respected.

(381) DECLARATION BY SMITH, REPRESENTING THE U.S. DELEGATION TO THE GENEVA CONFERENCE, JULY 21, 1954

Source: *Documents relating to British involvement in the Indochina Conflict*, p. 86.

The official U.S. response to the political provisions of the final declaration was to make explicit reservations to the provision for elections by

July 1956. Smith said that only United Nations supervision of elections would be acceptable to the U.S.

The Government of the United States being resolved to devote its efforts to the strengthening of peace in accordance with the principles and purposes of the United Nations.

Takes note of the Agreements concluded at Geneva on July 20 and 21, 1954 between the (*a*) Franco-Laotian Command and the Command of the People's Army of Viet-Nam; (*b*) The Royal Khmer Army Command and the Command of the People's Army of Viet-Nam; (*c*) Franco-Viet-Namese Command and the Command of the People's Army of Viet-Nam, and of paragraphs 1 to 12 inclusive of the Declaration presented to the Geneva Conference on July 21, 1954.

Declares with regard to the aforesaid Agreements and paragraphs (i) it will refrain from the threat or the use of force to disturb them, in accordance with Article 2 (4) of the Charter of the United Nations dealing with the obligation of Members to refrain in their international relations from the threat or use of force; and (ii) it would view any renewal of the aggression in violation of the aforesaid agreements with grave concern and as seriously threatening international peace and security.

In connection with this statement in the Declaration concerning free elections in Viet-Nam, my Government wishes to make clear its position which it has expressed in a Declaration made in Washington on June 29, 1954, as follows:

"In the case of nations now divided against their will, we shall continue to seek to achieve unity through free elections, supervised by the United Nations to ensure that they are conducted fairly."

With respect to the statement made by the Representative of the State of Viet-Nam, the United States reiterates its traditional position that peoples are entitled to determine their own future and that it will not join in any arrangement which would hinder this. Nothing in its declaration just made is intended to or does indicate any departure from this traditional position.

We share the hope that the agreement will permit Cambodia, Laos and Viet-Nam to play their part in full independence and sovereignty, in the peaceful community of nations, and will enable the peoples of that area to determine their own future.

(382) STATEMENT BY PREMIER NGO DINH DIEM ON THE GENEVA AGREEMENTS, JULY 22, 1954

Source: Republic of Vietnam, Ministry of Information, *The Problem of Reunification of Viet-Nam* (Saigon: 1958), p. 29.

Ngo Dinh Diem, who was named Premier of the State of Viet-nam on June 16 and took office in the second week in July, reiterated his government's refusal to sign the Geneva Agreements but gave no indication of how he would deal diplomatically with the question of reunification of the country.

Dear Compatriots,

You know the facts: a cease-fire concluded at Geneva without the concurrence of the Vietnamese delegation has surrendered to the Communists all the northern and more than four provinces of the central part of our country.

The national Government, constituted less than two weeks ago, in spite of its profound attachment to peace, has lodged the most solemn protest against that injustice. Our delegation at Geneva has not signed that agreement, for we cannot recognise the seizure by Soviet China [*sic*] - through its satellite the Vietminh - of over half of our national territory. We can neither concur in the enslavement of millions of compatriots faithful to the nationalists ideal, nor to the complete destitution of those who, thanks to our efforts, will have succeeded in joining the zone left to us.

Brutally placed before an accomplished fact, Vietnam cannot resort to violence, for that would be moving toward a catastrope and destroying all hope [of] remaking one day a free Vietnam from the South to the North.

In spite of our grief, in spite of our indignation, let us keep our self-control and remain united in order to give our brother refugees help and comfort and begin at once the peaceful and difficult struggle which will eventually free our country from all foreign intervention, whatever it may be, and from all oppression.

(383) <u>DECLARATION BY TRAN VAN DO AT THE GENEVA CONFERENCE</u>, JULY 21, 1954

Source: *Documents relating to British involvement in the Indochina conflict*, p. 87.

As regards the Final Declaration of the Conference, the Viet-Namese Delegation requests the Conference to incorporate in this Declaration after Article 10 the following text:

"The Conference takes note of the Declaration of the Government of the State of Viet-Nam undertaking:

to make and support every effort to re-establish a real and lasting peace in Viet-Nam;
not to use force to resist procedures for carrying the cease-fire into effect, in spite of the objections and reservations that the State of Viet-Nam has expressed."

(384) <u>NIE 63-5-54 ON THE POST-GENEVA OUTLOOK IN INDOCHINA</u>, AUGUST 3, 1954

Source: *U.S.-Vietnam Relations, Book 9*, pp. 692-698.

The intelligence community predicted in its first assessment after the Geneva Agreements that the D.R.V. would probably increase its attractiveness to the Vietnamese population, and would "almost certainly win" the scheduled elections if it did not "prejudice its political prospects." The intelligence estimate also noted the difficulty which the Diem regime would have in dealing with Viet Minh cadres in the South, because of armistice provisions guaranteeing them against reprisals.

THE PROBLEM

To assess the probable outlook in Indochina in the light of the agreements reached at the Geneva Conference.

CONCLUSIONS

1. The signing of the agreements at Geneva has accorded international recognition to Communist military and political power in Indochina and has given that power a defined geographic base.

2. We believe that the Communists will not give up their objective of securing control of all Indochina but will, without violating the armistice to the extent of launching an armed invasion to the south or west, pursue their objective by political, psychological, and paramilitary means.

3. We believe the Communists will consolidate control over North Vietnam with little difficulty. Present indications are that the Viet Minh will pursue a moderate political program, which together with its strong military pos-

ture, will be calculated to make that regime appeal to the nationalist feelings of the Vietnamese population generally. It is possible, however, that the Viet Minh may find it desirable or necessary to adopt a strongly repressive domestic program which would diminish its appeal in South Vietnam. In any event, from its new territorial base, the Viet Minh will intensify Communist activities throughout Indochina.

4. Although it is possible that the French and Vietnamese, even with firm support from the US and other powers, may be able to establish a strong regime in South Vietnam, we believe that the chances for this development are poor and, moreover, that the situation is more likely to continue to deteriorate progressively over the next year. It is even possible that, at some time during the next two years, the South Vietnam Government could be taken over by elements that would seek unification with the North even at the expense of Communist domination. If the scheduled national elections are held in July 1956, and if the Viet Minh does not prejudice its political prospects the Viet Minh will almost certainly win.

5. The ability of the Laotian Government to retain control in Laos will depend upon developments in South Vietnam and upon the receipt of French military and other assistance. Even with such assistance, however, Laos will be faced by a growing Communist threat which might result in the overthrow of the present government through subversion or elections, and in any case would be greatly intensified if all Vietnam were to fall under Communist control.

6. We believe that if adequate outside assistance is made available, the Cambodian Government will probably increase its effectiveness and the effectiveness of its internal security forces and will be able to suppress Communist guerrilla activity and to counter Communist political activity. The situation in Cambodia would probably deteriorate, however, if a Communist government should emerge in Laos or South Vietnam.

DISCUSSION

I. THE CURRENT SITUATION

General

7. The signing of the agreements at Geneva has ended large-scale warfare in Indochina and has affirmed the independence of Laos and Cambodia. It has, on the other hand, accorded international recognition to Communist military and political power in Indochina and has given that power a defined geographic base. Finally, the agreements have dealt a blow to the prestige of the Western Powers and particularly of France.

North Vietnam

8. The Viet Minh has emerged from Geneva with international recognition and with greatly enhanced power and prestige in Indochina. The Viet Minh leaders, while admitting that their ultimate objectives may have been temporarily compromised "for the sake of peace," are acclaiming the agreements as denoting a major victory and ensuring the eventual reunification of all Vietnam under Communist aegis. Ho Chi-Minh is generally regarded as the man who liberated Tonkin from 70 years of French rule. The Viet Minh has initiated a program to absorb presently French-controlled areas in the Tonkin Delta.

South Vietnam

9. In South Vietnam, the agreements and the fact of the imposed partition have engendered an atmosphere of frustration and disillusionment, which has been compounded by widespread uncertainty as to French and US intentions. The present political leadership appears to retain the passive support of the more important nationalist organizations and individuals. However, the govern-

ment's already weak administrative base has been further dislocated, and it has only uncertain assurances of continued outside military and financial support. Mutual jealousies and a lack of a single policy continue to divide Vietnamese politicians. Moreover, certain pro-French elements are seeking the overthrow of the Diem government with the apparent support of French colonial interests anxious to retain their control.

10. The North Vietnam population is somewhat greater than the South Vietnam population and, in any event, the loss of the Tonkin Delta has deprived South Vietnam of the most energetic and nationalist segment of the population. Although South Vietnam has the capability for agricultural self-sufficiency, the principal industrial establishments and fuel and mineral resources are located in North Vietnam.

11. Provided that the terms of the cease-fire agreement are observed, the combined French-Vietnamese forces in South Vietnam now have the capability of maintaining internal security.

Laos

12. The relatively stable internal situation in Laos, which in the past has depended upon French support, remains essentially unchanged. The Laotian Army is poorly armed and trained and, without the support of French forces and advisers, does not have the capability to maintain internal security. Moreover, "Pathet Lao" Communists continue to have *de facto* control of two northern provinces adjoining the Communist-controlled areas of Northern Vietnam. Furthermore, the Geneva agreements give members of the "Pathet Lao" movement freedom of political action throughout Laos.

Cambodia

13. The internal Cambodian situation, except for sharp political rivalries among leading Cambodians, is at present relatively stable. Non-Communist dissidence appears to have abated and the principal dissident leader, Son Ngoc Thanh, no longer poses any real threat to the government. The King retains widespread popular support for having obtained a large degree of effective independence from the French and for having safeguarded Cambodia's integrity at Geneva. Although the Communists are permitted freedom of political action in in Cambodia, they have only a minimum appeal. The Cambodian forces, although somewhat weakened by the withdrawal of French forces, have the capability of dealing with current Communist subversive action.

II. OUTLOOK IN INDOCHINA

General Considerations

14. The Geneva agreements, although precise and detailed concerning the time and place of troops redeployments and related matters, are imprecise about matters pertaining to future military aid and training. Moreover, the agreements are vague with respect to political matters. Details on the implementation of national elections are left for the interested parties to determine. Except for such influence as may be exerted by the presence of supervisory teams from India, Canada, and Poland, there is no provision for forcing the parties concerned to implement or adhere to the agreements.

15. The course of future developments will be determined less by the Geneva agreements than by the relative capabilities and actions of the Communist and non-Communist entities in Indochina, and of interested outside powers.

16. *Communist policy.* Communist willingness to reach agreement for an armistice in Indochina, at a time when prolongation of the conflict could have produced a steadily deteriorating situation in Indochina, was probably derived in substantial part from the Communist estimate that: (a) an effort to win a total military victory in Indochina might precipitate US military intervention,

and (b) the objective of gaining political control over all Indochina could be achieved as a result of the armistice agreement. The Communists also apparently believed that an attitude of "reasonableness" and the acceptance of an armistice in Indochina would contribute to the realization of their objective to undermine western efforts to develop an effective military coalition. They probably consider, therefore, that a deliberate resumption of large-scale military operations from their zone in the north would negate the political and psychological advantages the Communists have gained by negotiating a settlement and could involve grave risk of expanded war.

17. In the light of these considerations, we believe that the broad outlines of Communist policy in Indochina will be to: (a) refrain from deliberately taking major military action to break the armistice agreement while seeking to gain every advantage in the implementation of the agreements; (b) consolidate the Communist political, military, and economic position in North Vietnam; (c) conduct intensive political warfare against non-Communist Indochinese governments and people; (d) work for the ultimate removal of all Western influence, particularly French and US, from Indochina; and (e) emphasize and exploit issues in Indochina which will create and intensify divisions among non-Communist countries. In sum, we believe that the Communists will not give up their objective of securing control of all Indochina but will, without violating the armistice to the extent of launching an armed invasion to the south or west, pursue their objective by political, psychological, and paramilitary means.

18. *French policy.* It is impossible at this time to predict even the broad outlines of French policy in Indochina. The following appear to be the main alternatives:

a. Grant of complete political independence to the Indochina states, accompanied by an attempt to organize strong political regimes in those states. We believe that the French might be persuaded to adopt this policy by strong US-UK pressure, together with economic and military assistance to France and a guarantee of the defense of the free areas of Indochina against further Communist military attack.

b. Continuation of French Union ties with the non-Communist Indochinese states, with indirect French political controls and French economic domination. We believe that French policy may proceed along these lines if the French estimate that: (1) the Communists will follow a conciliatory policy in Indochina; (2) the non-Communist leadership will offer very little difficulty; and (3) the US and UK will not exert pressure toward a grant of full independence to the Indochinese states.

c. Some form of agreement with the Viet Minh providing for expediting elections and achieving a unification of Vietnam. The French might be inclined to follow this line if the Viet Minh held out promises of the maintenance of French economic and cultural interests, and of the continuance of some form of association of the unified Vietnamese state with France.

d. Withdrawal of all French military, administrative, and economic support from Indochina. We believe that this would occur only in the event of a hopeless deterioration of political, military, and economic conditions in the area.

19. *International policies.* The political survival of the Indochinese states is endangered not only by the threat of external Communist attack and internal Communist subversion, but also by their own inherent inexperience, immaturity, and weakness. We believe that without outside support the Indochinese states cannot become strong enough to withstand Communist pressures. The course of developments in Indochina will be largely influenced by the attitudes and policies of other powers. In general, we believe that in the absence of firm support from the US, the non-Communist states of Indochina cannot long remain non-Communist. If they are given opportunity, guidance, and material help in building national states, they may be able to attain viability. We

believe that the energy and resourcefulness necessary for this achievement will not arise spontaneously among the non-Communist Indochinese but will have to be sponsored and nurtured from without.

Outlook in Vietnam

20. *Outlook in North Vietnam.* Communist activities in North Vietnam will be concentrated upon consolidation of Communist control, with their efforts in this respect probably appearing moderate at the outset. The Viet Minh will probably emphasize social and economic reforms and the participation of all political, economic, and religious groups in state activity. At the same time, Viet Minh cadres will establish themselves throughout the Delta, will begin the process of neutralizing all effective opposition groups, will undertake the usual Communist program of popular indoctrination, and will prepare for the election scheduled in July 1956. We believe the Communists will be able to achieve the consolidation of North Vietnam with little difficulty.

21. We believe that the Viet Minh will continue to develop their armed forces. Although the armistice provisions forbid the Viet Minh from increasing their supply of arms, we believe they will covertly strengthen and possibly expand their armed forces with Chinese Communist aid. Viet Minh forces will almost certainly continue to receive training in China.

22. Thus established firmly in North Vietnam, the Viet Minh regime will probably retain and may increase its symbolic attraction as the base of Vietnamese national independence. Its methods of consolidating control will probably continue for some time to be moderate, and, its internal program together with its military power, will be calculated to make the regime attractive to the remaining peoples of Indochina. It is possible however, that the Viet Minh may find it desirable or necessary to adopt a strongly repressive domestic program which would prejudice its psychological appeal and political prospects. Barring such repressive Viet Minh policies, the unification issue will continue to be exploited to Communist advantage throughout Vietnam. Meanwhile, the Viet Minh regime will continue to strengthen the Communist underground apparatus in South Vietnam, Laos, and Cambodia, aware that significant Communist gains in any one of these countries will strengthen the Communist movement in the others. It will seek to develop strong overt Communist political groups where possible and will generally use all available means towards the eventual unification of the country under Communist control.

23. *Outlook in South Vietnam.* We believe that the Viet Minh will seek to retain sizeable military and political assets in South Vietnam. Although the agreements provide for the removal to the north of all Viet Minh forces, many of the regular and irregular Viet Minh soldiers now in the south are natives of the area, and large numbers of them will probably cache their arms and remain in South Vietnam. In addition, Viet Minh administrative cadres have been in firm control of several large areas in central and south Vietnam for several years. These cadres will probably remain in place. French and Vietnamese efforts to deal with "stay-behind" military and administrative units and personnel will be greatly hampered by armistice provisions guaranteeing the security of pre-armistice dissidents from reprisals.

24. The severe problem of establishing and maintaining security in South Vietnam will probably be increased by certain provisions of the Geneva agreements which prohibit the import of arms and military equipment, except as replacements, and the introduction of additional foreign military personnel, the establishment of new military bases, and military alliances. These provisions limit the development of a Vietnamese national army to such numbers as may be equipped by stocks evacuated from Tonkin, plus stocks now held in Saigon. However, in the last analysis, Vietnamese security will be determined by the degree of French protection and assistance in the development of a national army, the energy with which the Vietnamese themselves attack the problem, and

by the will of the non-Communist powers to provide South Vietnam with effective guarantees.

25.   In addition to the activities of stay-behind military and administrative groups, the Viet Minh will make a major effort to discredit any South Vietnam administration, and to exacerbate French-Vietnamese relations, and appeal to the feeling for national unification which will almost certainly continue strong among the South Vietnamese population. The Communist goal will be to cause the collapse of any non-Communist efforts to stabilize the situation in South Vietnam, and thus to leave North Vietnam the only visible foundation on which to re-establish Vietnamese unity. French and anti-Communist Vietnamese efforts to counter the Viet Minh unity appeal and Communist subversive activities will be complicated at the outset by the strong resentment of Vietnamese nationalists over the partitioning of Vietnam and the abandoning of Tonkin to Communist control. It may be difficult to convince many Vietnamese troops, political leaders, and administrative personnel in Tonkin to go south, let alone to assist actively in the development of an effective administration in South Vietnam.

26.   Developments in South Vietnam will also depend in parge part on French courses of action. Prospects for stability in South Vietnam would be considerably enhanced if the French acted swiftly to insure Vietnam full independence and to encourage strong nationalist leadership. If this were done, anti-French nationalist activity might be lessened. With French military and economic assistance - backed by US aid - the Vietnamese could proceed to develop gradually an effective security force, local government organization, and a long-range program for economic and social reform. Nevertheless, it will be very difficult for the French to furnish the degree of assistance which will be required without at the same time reviving anti-French feeling to the point of endangering the whole effort.

27.   On the basis of the evidence we have at this early date, however, we believe that a favorable development of the situation in South Vietnam is unlikely. Unless Mendes-Frances is able to overcome the force of French traditional interests and emotions which have in the past governed the implementation of policy in Indochina, we do not believe there will be the dramatic transformation in French policy necessary to win the active loyalty and support of the local population for a South Vietnam Government. At the present time, it appears more likely that the situation will deteriorate in South Vietnam and that the withdrawal from Tonkin will involve recriminations, distrust, and possibly violence. There will be delays in the development of effective administration in the south; the French military will probably be forced to retain a large measure of control for reasons of "security"; and efforts by French colonial interests to develop a puppet Cochin-China state will persist. It is even possible that at some point during the next two years the South Vietnam Government could be taken over by elements that would seek unification with the Viet Minh in the North even at the expense of Communist domination. Even "If the scheduled national elections are held in July 1956, and if the Viet Minh does not prejudice its political prospects, the Viet Minh will almost certainly win."

28.   In the interim, Viet Minh propaganda will find ample opportunities to influence Vietnamese attitudes. Within a year, Viet Minh stay-behind units will probably be active politically, and possibly involved in open guerrilla fighting. In these circumstances, the French will probably be able to maintain their "presence" in South Vietnam through mid-1956, but their influence will probably become increasingly restricted to major cities and the perimeters of military installations and bases. The French might be willing to resolve this situation by an arrangement with the Communists which seemed to offer a chance of saving some remnant of the French economic and cultural position in Vietnam. Such an arrangement might include an agreement to hold

early elections, even with the virtual certainty of Viet Minh victory. Only if such an arrangement proved impossible, and the situation deteriorated to the point of hopelessness, would the French withdraw completely from the country.

Outlook in Laos

29. Providing the French maintain the 5,000 troops in Laos which the Geneva agreements permit them, and continue to develop the Laotian forces, the Royal Laotian Government should be able to improve its security forces and, excluding the two northern provinces, to deal with isolated, small-scale Communist guerrilla actions. Also, providing the Laotians continue to receive French and US technical and financial assistance, they probably will be able to maintain an adequate government administration. There is nothing in the Geneva agreements to prevent Laos from becoming a member of a defense arrangement so long as no foreign troops other than specified French personnel are based in Laos.

30. However, if the French for any reason decide not to maintain their troops nor to continue military training in Laos, it will be impossible for the non-Communist powers to provide effective aid to the Laotians without breaching the Geneva agreement. At the same time, Laos will be faced with a growing communist threat, and the freedom of political action permitted members of the Pathet Lao movement, strengthened by support from the Viet Minh, may result in the overthrow of the present government through subversion or elections. Finally, further successes for the Viet Minh in Vietnam will have an immediate adverse effect on the situation in Laos.

Outlook in Cambodia

31. We believe that the Communists, in withdrawing organized units from Cambodia, will leave behind organizers, guerrilla leaders, and weapons. Initially, the Communists will probably minimize guerrilla action in order to concentrate on building their political potential in Cambodia.

32. Providing the withdrawal of the Communists is substantially in accord with the agreement, the development of stability in Cambodia during the next year or so will depend largely on two interrelated factors: (a) the ability of the Cambodians to develop effective government and internal security forces; and (b) the ability of the Cambodians to obtain external technical and financial assistance. There is no prohibition in the Geneva agreement against Cambodia's obtaining outside assistance to develop its defense forces or on joining a defensive alliance, providing the latter is in consonance with the UN Charter and that no foreign troops are based in Cambodia in the absence of a threat to Cambodian security. If adequate outside assistance is made available, the Cambodians will probably increase the effectiveness both of their government and their internal security forces, and will be able to suppress Communist guerrilla activity and to counter Communist political activity. The efforts of the Cambodians to strengthen their position would probably be more energetic if their independence were guaranteed by some regional defense arrangement. The situation in Cambodia would deteriorate gravely, however, if a Communist government should emerge in Laos or South Vietnam.

(385) APPEAL BY THE VIETNAM WORKER'S PARTY CENTRAL EXECUTIVE COMMITTEE, AUGUST 5, 1954

Source: Viet-nam News Agency in English Morse to Southeast Asia, August 5, 1954, translated in Foreign Broadcast Information Service, August 9, 1954, pp. CCC1-4.

The Party Central Committee explained the Geneva Agreement as ending the phase of armed struggle and inaugurating the phase of political struggle, which it said would be "long and hard," an indication that the elections called for in the Final Declaration were not being taken for granted.

Dear Compatriots: To the fighters of the heroic Vietnamese People's Army; to cadres and personnel members in various branches of activity; to all Party Members:

For the sake of peace and unity, independence and democracy for our Fatherland, our compatriots, fighters, and cadres have been heroically fighting during the past 9 years, and have scored brilliant victories. Through these years of struggle our people's force has steadily grown up. Our war of resistance has enjoyed the warm approval and support of peace-loving peoples all over the world.

The successive victories we have won during the patriotic war, especially the victory during the last winter-spring campaign, have obliged the French colonialists to recognize that they can no longer use violence to put again their yoke of domination on Vietnam, as well as Laos and Cambodia. For this reason the French Government had to open negotiations with our Government to bring about an armistice in Indochina.

Due to the brilliant exploits of our Army and people at Dien Bien Phu; due to the struggle of our compatriots living behind the French lines to urge the cessation of the aggressive war in Indochina; due to the persistent struggle of the delegation of the Vietnam Democratic Republic and those of the USSR and the Chinese People's Republic; due to the support of the French people and peace lovers of the world, the agreements on the cessation of hostilities in Vietnam, Laos, and Cambodia were concluded at the Geneva Conference on July 21, 1954.

Gunshots are being silenced in Indochina. Peace is being restored in this peninsula on the following basis:

The French Government respects the independence, sovereignty, unity, and territorial integrity of Vietnam, Laos, and Cambodia; in a given period of time, national unification of each state of Indochina will be realized through free general elections; no military base belonging to a foreign country shall be established in Indochina; Vietnam and France will establish economic and cultural relations on the basis of equality and mutual interests, and so forth.

The signing of the above-mentioned armistice is a tremendous success for our people and Army, who closely united and singlemindedly have valiantly struggled under the leadership of President Ho Chi Minh and the Party.

This is an outcome of the 9 years of resistance of our compatriots throughout the country, from the north to the south, in the free zones as well as in the French-controlled areas; of the whole Army, including regular people's forces, local troops and militiamen, and guerrillas; of cadres and personnel members in various branches of activity of the Army, People's Government, and Party. We cordially congratulate all compatriots, fighters, and cadres, and pay homage to the martyrs who have sacrificed themselves for the sake of national liberation.

Our victory is also a victory for peace-loving peoples in all the world and peoples in fraternal countries who have been fighting for the reduction of international tension. This is a victory for the French people, who, with the French Communist Party in the vanguard, have for many years struggled against the dirty war unleashed by the French colonialists.

On this occasion our compatriots should manifest their gratitude to the brotherly peoples, first and foremost to the peoples of the Soviet Union and China, to the French people, the peoples of Southeast Asia, and peace-loving peoples in the world who have actively supported the patriotic war of the peoples of Vietnam, Laos, and Cambodia.

Our Victory is a defeat of the colonialist aggressors, who plot to subjugate the Indochina peoples; a defeat of the imperialists now contriving to turn Indochina into an American colony and strategic base; a defeat of the U.S. imperialists and French warmongers and lackeys who unscrupulously sell out the country to alien invaders to get some dregs and remains.

(The following portion was transmitted on Aug. 6 at 0515 GMT--Ed.)

This victory proves that neither perfidious plot nor power in the world may vanquish a nation that is united and resolved to break off the shackles of slavery and to defeat foreign aggressors.

This victory also proves that the forces of peace in the world have been growing with every passing day and may hold back the bloody hands of the imperialist warmongers, quench the flame of war in a given place, safeguard world peace, and relieve international tension.

This victory has, moreover, stimulated the people in the countries now struggling for national independence and the right to live free and in peace. It has opened new prospects for the settlement of other international disputes through negotiations. It explains why this victory has enhanced the confidence of our people in their own strength and in the bright future of the Nation; at the same time, it has given new impetus to people in the world and heightened their confidence in the movement to safeguard peace. Today peace is being restored under fair and reasonable conditions which conform to the current situation in Vietnam, Laos, and Cambodia. But our people still have to struggle and urge the other side faithfully to implement the terms already agreed upon and to continue to negotiate with us so as to settle the remaining issues.

Compatriots throughout the country, fighters and cadres, everyone should strictly abide by the orders of the Government within the framework of his responsibility and scrupulously carry out the terms which the delegation of our Government has signed at the Geneva Conference. The armistice agreement has stipulated the zonal readjustment; our armed forces will pull back from southern Vietnam and regroup in the north while the French Union Forces will withdraw from the north and temporarily garrison in the south. The intricate situation of the Vietnam battlefront has required such a measure to facilitate the restoration and consolidation of peace. But we will struggle and resolutely carry out free general elections throughout the country to realize national unification. Our compatriots should not be deceived by the lying propaganda of the American imperialists and the French warmongers and should not think that the zonal readjustment implies a "division of the country."

At present the armistice is being materialized. The patriotic struggle of our people has entered a new phase. The phase of armed struggle is now being replaced by the phase of political struggle. However, like the armed fighting, the political struggle will certainly be long and hard before reaching complete victory. The present tasks of our entire people and Party are still very heavy. We must endeavor to struggle to consolidate peace, realize unification, and achieve independence and democracy throughout the country.

To this end we must further strengthen our people's Army and turn it into an unshakeable bulwark for peace and national defense.

We must push forward the peasant mass mobilization and carry out agrarian reform because this is a necessary condition to replenish our people's forces, stabilize our rear areas, and perfect the basic organizations of our Party, Government and National United Front. Moreover, we must secure the ties of friendship between our people and the peoples of Laos and Cambodia, with the peoples of the Soviet Union and China. We must unite still more closely with the French people and maintain close relations with the peace movement in Southeast Asia and the world. These are firm guarantees for the consolidation of peace in Indochina.

Neither should we forget that the American imperialists, the French warmongers, and their lackeys are seeking every possible means to sabotage the armistice and obstruct the consolidation of peace in Indochina. A handful of greedy and reluctant colonialists still plot to violate the armistice agreement and do not want to settle political issues relating to Vietnam. Our whole People's Army and Party should keep their vigilance high, continuously raise their struggling spirit, overcome objectivism, indetermination of the opponent's strength.

defeatism, complacency, and pride.

Comrade Party members! At present singlemindedness and unity in the whole Party are more necessary than ever. Only with unity in thought shall there be unity in action and shall the whole Party be united as one man or be able to fulfill the new policy and push forward the new tasks. Only with inner Party unity can the whole Party succeed in uniting the working class and the entire people to implement the new tasks set by President Ho Chi Minh, our Party, and Government.

The whole people, the Army and the Party must close their ranks more tightly around President Ho Chi Minh, the Party's Central Executive Committee, and the Government of the Vietnam Democratic Republic, and must devote their heroic fighting spirit - steeled and tempered in the patriotic war to the struggle to the end in order to realize a peaceful, unified, independent, and democratic Vietnam.

Under the glorious banner of President Ho Chi Minh, our people wil fulfill the great task entrusted to us by the new historical situation and will certainly reach the above-mentioned goal. July 25, 1954. The Central Executive Committee of the Vietnam Lao Dong Party.

(386) NSC 5492/2 "REVIEW OF U.S. POLICY IN THE FAR EAST," AUGUST 20, 1954

Source: *U.S. Vietnam Relations, Book 10,* pp. 731-733, 726-737.

The NSC viewed the results of the Geneva settlement as a loss in prestige for the U.S. and as giving the Communists an "advance salient" for pressures against non-Communist states in Southeast Asia. The first post-Geneva statement of policy called for negotiating a Southeast Asia collective security treaty and urged "covert operations on a large and effective scale" to maintain non-Communist governments in Indochina and make Communist control of North Vietnam more difficult.

PREFACE

Consequences of the Geneva Conference

Communist successes in Indochina, culminating in the agreement reached at the Geneva Conference, have produced the following significant consequences which jeopardize the security interests of the U.S. in the Far East and increase Communist strength there:

a. Regardless of the fate of South Vietnam, Laos and Cambodia, the Communists have secured possession of an advance salient in Vietnam from which military and non-military pressures can be mounted against adjacent and more remote non-Communist areas.

b. The loss of prestige in Asia suffered by the U.S. as a backer of the French and the Bao Dai Government will raise further doubts in Asia concerning U.S. leadership and the ability of the U.S. to check the further expansion of Communism in Asia. Furthermore, U.S. prestige will inescapably be associated with subsequent developments in Southeast Asia.

c. By adopting an appearance of moderation at Geneva and taking credit for the cessation of hostilities in Indochina, the Communists will be in a better position to exploit their political strategy of imputing to the United States motives of extremism, belligerency, and opposition to coexistence seeking thereby to alienate the U.S. from its allies. The Communists thus have a basis for sharply accentuating their "peace propaganda" and "peace program" in Asia in an attempt to allay fears of Communist expansionist policy and to establish closer relations with the nations of free Asia.

d. The Communists have increased their military and political prestige in Asia and their capacity for expanding Communist influence by exploiting political and economic weakness and instability in the countries of free Asia without resort to armed attack.

e. The loss of Southeast Asia would imperil retention of Japan as a key element in the off-shore island chain.

COURSES OF ACTION

I. COMMUNIST CHINA

1. Reduce the power of Communist China in Asia even at the risk of, but without deliberately provoking, war:

a. (1) React with force, if necessary and advantageous, to expansion and subversion recognizable as such, supported and supplied by Communist China.

(2) React with immediate, positive, armed force against any belligerent move by Communist China.

b. Increase efforts to develop the political economic and military strength of non-Communist Asian countries, including the progressive development of the military strength of Japan to the point where she can provide for her own national defense and, in time, contribute to the collective defense of the Far East.

c. Maintain political and economic pressures against Communist China, including the existing embargo and support for Chinese Nationalist harassing actions.

d. Support for the Chinese National Government on Formosa as the Government of China and the representative of China in all UN agencies.

e. Create internal division in the Chinese Communist regime and impair Sino-Soviet relations by all feasible overt and covert means.

IV. SOUTHEAST ASIA

7. General. The U.S. must protect its position and restore its prestige in the Far East by a new initiative in Southeast Asia, where the situation must be stabilized as soon as possible to prevent further losses to Communism through (1) creeping expansion and subversion, or (2) overt aggression.

8. Security Treaty. Negotiate a Southeast Asia security treaty with the UK, Australia, New Zealand, France, the Philippines, Thailand and, as appropriate, other free South and Southeast Asian countries willing to participate, which would:

a. Commit each member to treat an armed attack on the agreed area (including Laos, Cambodia and South Vietnam) as dangerous to its own peace, safety and vital interests, and to act promptly to meet the common danger in accordance with its own constitutional processes.

b. Provide so far as possible a legal basis to the President to order attack on Communist China in the event it commits such armed aggression which endangers the peace, safety and vital interests of the United States.

c. Ensure that, in such event, other nations would be obligated in accordance with the treaty to support such U.S. action.

d. Not limit U.S. freedom to use nuclear weapons, or involve a U.S. commitment for local defense or for stationing U.S. forces in Southeast Asia.

The U.S. would continue to provide a limited military assistance and training missions, wherever possible, to the states of Southeast Asia in order to bolster their will to fight, to stabilize legal governments, and to assist them in controlling subversion.

9. Action in the Event of Local Subversion. If requested by a legitimate local government which requires assistance to defeat local Communist subversion or rebellion not constituting armed attack, the U.S. should view such a situa-

tion so gravely that, in addition to giving all possible covert and overt support within Executive Branch authority, the President should at once consider requesting Congressional authority to take appropriate action, which might if necessary and feasible include the use of U.S. military forces either locally or against the external source of such subversion or rebellion (including) Comunist China if determined to be the source).

10. Indochina: Political and Covert Action.

<u>a</u>. Make every possible effort, not openly inconsistent with the U.S. position as to the armistice to maintain and support friendly non-Communist governments in Cambodia and Laos, to maintain a friendly non-Communist South Vietnam, and to prevent a Communist victory through all-Vietnam elections.

<u>b</u>. Urge that the French promptly recognize and deal with Cambodia, Laos and free Vietnam as independent sovereign nations.

<u>c</u>. Strengthen U.S. representation and deal directly, wherever advantageous to the U.S., with the governments of Cambodia, Laos, and free Vietnam.

<u>d</u>. Working through the French only insofar as necessary, assist Cambodia, Laos and free Vietnam to maintain (1) military forces necessary for internal security and (2) economic conditions conducive to the maintenance and strength of non-Communist regimes and comparing favorably with those in adjacent Communist areas.

<u>e</u>. Aid emigration from North Vietnam and resettlement of peoples unwilling to remain under Communist rule.

<u>f</u>. Exploit available means to prevent North Vietnam from becoming permanently incorporated in the Soviet bloc, using as feasible and desirable consular relations and non-strategic trade.

<u>h</u>. Conduct covert operations on a large and effective scale in support of the foregoing policies.

(387) APPEAL BY HO CHI MINH ON THE OCCASION OF THE CELEBRATION OF THE AUGUST REVOLUTION AND NATIONAL DAY, SEPTEMBER 2, 1954.

Source: *Selected Works, Vol IV,* pp. 25-31.

Discussing the new tasks of the country after the Geneva Agreement, Ho called on his compatriots in the South to launch a political struggle for democratic rights, in anticipation of the general elections scheduled for July 1956. He emphasized Viet-nam's desire to establish good relations with France and its insistance that France "fully guarantee" the political provisions of the final declaration, in a situation in which both the U.S. and the Diem government were clearly hostile to them.

Compatriots, armymen and cadres all over the country and Vietnamese residents abroad,

On the occasion of the 9th anniversary of the August Revolution and the National Day, on behalf of the Government, I solemnly send you our cordial greetings.

During eighty years, the feudal kings and princes sold out our Fatherland and people to the French colonialists. In the course of this gloomy period, our ancestors and then our generation unremittingly struggled to regain freedom and national independence.

The great victory of the Soviet Union over the German fascists and Japanese militarists in the Second World War contributed to the success of our August Revolution.

What was the aim of the August Revolution?

It was to restore peace, national unity, independence and democracy to our country and people.

The August Revolution being achieved, independence was declared on September the Second. The Democratic Republic of Veit Nam was born. General elections were held and our people throughout the country elected a National Assembly, which ratified the Constitution and chose the central government. Local administrations, from village to province, were entirely appointed by the people. Since that time, national unity, independence and democracy have begun to materialize in our country.

Our people and government long for peace to construct our country and build a free and happy life.

But soon the bellicose French colonialists unleashed a new war in an attempt to invade our country and to enslave our people once more.

In face of this danger, our people, army, cadres and government, closely united, resolutely waged a war of resistance which lasted nearly nine years and won many great victories.

The aim of our Resistance was to preserve and develop the achievements secured by the August Revolution, that is to say, independence and democracy.

Thanks to the valiant struggle waged by our army and people, supported by the peoples of brother countries, the French people and peace-loving people of the world, we have won the day at the Geneva Conference.

The French Government has recognized the following points, approved by member countries of the Geneva Conference.

- Peace shall be restored in Indo-China, on the basis of France respecting the independence, sovereignty, national unity and territorial integrity of Viet Nam, Cambodia and Laos.

- The peoples of Viet Nam, Cambodia and Laos shall hold free elections to reunify their country.

- France shall withdraw its army from Indo-China.

We have signed an armistice with France, peace is being restored in Viet Nam and all over Indo-China.

This great victory was made possible by the ardent patriotism, monolithic solidarity, fighting spirit and sacrifice of our army and people from North to South, from the temporarily enemy-controlled zone to the free zones.

This victory was the outcome of the August Revolution, of the Independence Day of September the Second and of the heroic Resistance waged during the past eight to nine years.

This is a victory of the people of Viet Nam, Cambodia and Laos, a victory of the French people and the peace-loving people of the world.

***

This new victory changes the situation of our country which shifts from a state of war to a state of peace. In order to secure all-out and lasting peace, we must fight with might and main.

This situation sets new tasks for our people, army, cadres and government. At present our common tasks are: correct implementation of the Armistice Agreement, the struggle to maintain and consolidate peace, to achieve national reunification, independence and democracy all over the country.

To achieve national reunification and democracy throughout the country, we must first of all, preserve and strengthen peace.

To preserve and strengthen peace, it is necessary for both the Vietnamese and French sides to be sincere. On this occasion, I solemnly declare once again that:

We are resolved to respect and implement the Armistice Agreement entered into with France. We shall protect French economic and cultural interests in Viet Nam. We are ready to resume negotiations with the French government and to re-establish good relations with France on the basis of equality and mutual benefit.

At the same time we trust the French government will also respect and implement the Armistice Agreement and fully guarantee the execution of the points mentioned in the declaration of the Geneva Conference and in the statement made by the French government.

Maintenance and consolidation of peace require close solidarity on our part - solidarity among the entire people from North to South as in one family; solidarity with the peoples of Cambodia and Laos; solidarity with the Asian people, with the French people, and the peace-loving people of the world, in particular the Chinese and Soviet peoples.

We must unite in a monolithic bloc against the maneuvers of peace wreckers, the U.S. imperialists, the war thirsty French clique and their henchmen.

Our people from North to South must fight for the organization of free general elections to reunify the whole country.

Independence and democracy will be achieved throughout the country if peace is maintained and consolidated and the whole country reunified.

***

The new development of the situation imposes upon us the following urgent tasks:

To strengthen the people's army which is the leading force to defend the Fatherland and maintain peace.

To continue to put into practice the motto "land to the tillers" to liberate the peasantry, the overwhelming majority of our people.

In the former free zones, the work of consolidation to be carried on in every field: improvement of the people's livelihood, development of the valiant tradition of our people.

To enhance solidarity among the various nationalities in the country and gradually introduce autonomy into minority regions.

In newly liberated rural and urban areas, to first and foremost restore order and stabilize the people's living conditions, protect the lives and property of our compatriots as well as of foreign residents, including the Frenchmen.

To guarantee freedom of conscience. To employ and treat well the employees and officials who formerly worked with the opposite side and who now wish to serve the country and the people.

To re-habilitate commerce, education, etc.

In the political field, to consolidate the people's power in former free zones and in newly liberated areas, develop and strengthen the patriotic organizations, raise the political and moral level of our people, unite our efforts to defend peace and achieve national unity, independence and democracy throughout the country.

In the economic field, to accelerate the emulation movement in production and implement the policy of paying attention to public as well as private interests, of benefiting both employers and employees. Town and countryside will help each other. Free circulation of commodities within and without the country will be guaranteed so as to rehabilitate and expand production to contribute to economic prosperity and to improve the people's livelihood.

In the cultural field, to wipe out illiteracy, train cadres to serve national construction, protect our people's health and promote our good traditions.

In the regions where the French troops are temporarily stationed, our people will have to lead the political struggle to secure such democratic rights as freedom of organization, freedom of opinion, etc., to prepare free general elections for national reunification.

Our compatriots residing abroad must love one another and help each other. They must constantly support the Fatherland and strengthen the friendship between our people and those of the countries in which they live.

As far as the patriots are concerned, whatever classes they may belong to and even if they had formerly collaborated with the other side, we are ready to unite with them to defend and strengthen peace and achieve national unity, independence and democracy all over the country.

We have carried the day, but peace is not definitely consolidated, unity, independence and democracy are not yet achieved throughout the country. Therefore it is necessary for us to wage a long and hard struggle to reach that goal. Meanwhile we must always be vigilant to thwart the manoeuvres which are likely to sabotage our common work.

Our tasks are many and difficult indeed, but we disposed of a powerful force, we are closely united, and resolved to fight. The progressive people in the world support us. Victory will certainly be ours.

***

On behalf of the people and government of the Democratic Republic of Viet Nam, I take this opportunity of thanking the peoples and governments of brother countries, the French people's organizations, the peace and democratic organizations of the world, and the progressive personalities in the countries which had supported us during our Resistance and shared our joy when peace was restored. This internationalism is invaluable. It encouraged us through the trying days of our Resistance. It will help us to build a lasting peace.

The evergrowing movement of peace and democracy in the world was conducive to our victory. And this will be a worthy contribution to the defence of peace in Asia and in the world.

Compatriots, armymen, cadres and Vietnamese residents abroad! March enthusiastically forward!

Long live a peaceful, unified, independent and democratic Viet Nam!

The peaceable and democratic forces in the world will win!

(388) SPECIAL NATIONAL INTELLIGENCE ESTIMATE NUMBER 63-6-54, SEPTEMBER 15, 1954

Source: *U.S.-Vietnam Relations, Book 10*, pp. 751-752.

The intelligence community's estimate of the trends in South Viet-nam concluded that the prospects of a Communist takeover in the South by means other than an invasion from the North had been "enhanced." One factor in that estimate was the lack of any clear policy toward the South on the part of the French government which was then considering how it could best preserve its long-term interests in Viet-nam.

CURRENT TRENDS IN SOUTH VIETNAM

Estimate

1. Since assuming office Premier Diem has been confronted with the usual problems of inefficiency, disunity, and corruption in Vietnamese politics and with the extraordinary problems of a mass evacuation of the Northern population and the hostility of many French officials. Despite his qualities of honesty and zeal, he has not yet demonstrated the necessary ability to deal with practical problems of politics and administration. Lacking an organized political machine and finding control of the Army in the hands of an uncooperative chief of staff, Diem's freedom of action has been severely circumscribed.

2. The French Government appears to have no definite policy toward South Vietnam. While the French Government has not openly opposed the Diem Government, France has failed to support Diem and there is no evidence that the French are prepared to carry out a policy based on unreserved support for

Vietnamese independence and nationalism. Accordingly, close cooperation between the French and Vietnamese governments, essential for the survival of South Vietnam, has been lacking and French motives have become more suspect.

3. Although little real progress has been made under Diem's administration in dealing with pressing political, military, and social problems, he still retains considerable unorganized popular support, particularly among Catholic elements of South Vietnam. He has also made some progress in reaching agreement with the powerful Cochin China sects.

4. At the moment the Diem Government is threatened by the insubordination of General Hinh, the politically ambitious Chief of Staff whom Diem has discharged. It does not now appear that the present struggle between Diem and Hinh will degenerate into civil strife. In fact Diem now appears to be making some headway in his efforts to control or exile Hinh, either of which would enhance his prestige and remove an obstacle to the strengthening of his government.

5. Bao Dai has remained in France and apparently is refraining from direct participation in political affairs in South Vietnam. His prestige among Vietnamese nationalists has been considerably lessened by his apathy toward the fate of his country. We believe that if Bao Dai were now to return to Vietnam, he would almost certainly become a center of political intrigue and would further complicate an already complex and confused situation and weaken rather than strengthen the ability of South Vietnam to achieve political stability.

6. Trends in South Vietnam since the end of the Geneva Conference have enhanced the prospects of an eventual extension of Communist control over the area by means short of large-scale military attacks. Although Diem's government will probably survive the present crisis of Hinh's insubordination, and may achieve greater strength and popular support, it will continue to be threatened by Vietminh activity, and hampered by French indecision. Diem appears to be the only figure now on the political scene behind whom genuine nationalist support can be mobilized. However, his ability to create a government that could reverse the current trend in South Vietnam depends at a minimum on an early and convincing demonstration by the French of their wholehearted support.

(389) SOUTHEAST ASIA COLLECTIVE DEFENSE TREATY, SEPTEMBER 8, 1954

Source: *Southeast Asia Treaty Organization*, Department of State Publication 6305 (Washington: U.S. Government Printing Office, 1956).

The original purpose of a Southeast Asia collective defense agreement had been to provide a protective shield around Cambodia, Laos and South Viet-nam. None of the non-Communist states of Indochina joined the pact, but a protocol to the Manila Pact designated Cambodia, Laos and South Viet-nam as part of the "treaty area" mentioned in the treaty, so that the members would be committed to acting on any threat to those governments.

The Parties to this Treaty,
Recognizing the sovereign equality of all the Parties,
Reiterating their faith in the purposes and principles set forth in the Charter of the United Nations and their desire to live in peace with all peoples and all governments,
Reaffirming that, in accordance with the Charter of the United Nations, they uphold the principle of equal rights and self-determinination of peoples, and declaring that they will earnestly strive by every peaceful means to promote self-government and to secure the independence of all countries whose peoples desire it and are able to undertake its responsibilities,
Desiring to strengthen the fabric of peace and freedom and to uphold the principles of democracy, individual liberty and the rule of law, and to promote

the economic well-being and development of all peoples in the treaty area,

Intending to declare publicly and formally their sense of unity, so that any potential aggressor will appreciate that the Parties stand together in the area, and

Desiring further to coordinate their efforts for collective defense for the preservation of peace and security,

Therefore agree as follows:

Article I

The Parties undertake, as set forth in the Charter of the United Nations, to settle any international disputes in which they may be involved by peaceful means in such a manner that international peace and security and justice are not endangered, and to refrain in their international relations from the threat or use of force in any manner inconsistent with the purposes of the United Nations.

Article II

In order more effectively to achieve the objectives of this Treaty, the Parties, separately and jointly, by means of continuous and effective self-help and mutual aid will maintain and develop their individual and collective capacity to resist armed attack and to prevent and counter subversive activities directed from without against their territorial integrity and political stability.

Article III

The Parties undertake to strengthen their free institutions and to cooperate with one another in the further development of economic measures, including technical assistance, designed both to promote economic progress and social well-being and to further the individual and collective efforts of governments toward these ends.

Article IV

1. Each Party recognizes that aggression by means of armed attack in the treaty area against any of the Parties or against any State or territory which the Parties by unanimous agreement may hereafter designate, would endanger its own peace and safety, and agrees that it will in that event act to meet the common danger in accordance with its constitutional processes. Measures taken under this paragraph shall be immediately reported to the Security Council of the United Nations.

2. If, in the opinion of any of the Parties, the inviolability or the integrity of the territory or the sovereignty or political independence of any Party in the treaty area or of any other State or territory to which the provisions of paragraph 1 of this Article from time to time apply is threatened in any way other than by armed attack or is affected or threatened by any fact or situation which might endanger the peace of the area, the Parties shall consult immediately in order to agree on the measures which should be taken for the common defense.

3. It is understood that no action on the territory of any State designated by unanimous agreement under paragraph 1 of this Article or on any territory so designated shall be taken except at the invitation or with the consent of the government concerned.

Article V

The Parties hereby establish a Council, on which each of them shall be represented, to consider matters concerning the implementation of this Treaty. The Council shall provide for consultation with regard to military and any other planning as the situation obtaining in the treaty area may from time to time require. The Council shall be so organized as to be able to meet at any time.

Article VI

This Treaty does not affect and shall not be interpreted as affecting in any way the rights and obligations of any of the Parties under the Charter of the United Nations or the responsibility of the United Nations for the maintenance of international peace and security. Each Party declares that none of the international engagements now in force between it and any other of the Parties or any third party is in conflict with the provisions of this Treaty, and undertakes not to enter into any international engagement in conflict with this Treaty.

Article VII

Any other State in a position to further the objectives of this Treaty and to contribute to the Security of the area may, by unanimous agreement of the Parties, be invited to accede to this Treaty. Any State so invited may become a Party to the Treaty by depositing its instrument of accession with the Government of the Republic of the Philippines. The Government of the Republic of the Philippines shall inform each of the Parties of the deposit of each instrument of accession.

Article VIII

As used in this Treaty, the "treaty area" in the general area of Southeast Asia, including also the entire territories of the Asian Parties, and the general area of the Southwest Pacific not including the Pacific area north of 21 degrees 30 minutes north latitude. The Parties may, by unanimous agreement, amend this Article to include within the treaty area the territory of any State acceding to this Treaty in accordance with Article VII or otherwise to change the treaty area.

Article IX

1. This Treaty shall be deposited in the archives of the Government of the Republic of the Philippines. Duly certified copies thereof shall be transmitted by that government to the other signatories.

2. The Treaty shall be ratified and its provisions carried out by the Parties in accordance with their respective constitutional processes. The instruments of ratification shall be deposited as soon as possible with the Government of the Republic of the Philippines, which shall notify all of the other signatories of such deposit.

3. The Treaty shall enter into force between the States which have ratified it as soon as the instruments of ratification of a majority of the signatories shall have been deposited, and shall come into effect with respect to each other State on the date of the deposit of its instrument of ratification.

Article X

This Treaty shall remain in force indefinitely, but any Party may cease to be a Party one year after its notice of denunciation has been given to the Government of the Republic of the Philippines, which shall inform the governments of the other Parties of the deposit of each notice of denunciation.

Article XI

The English text of this Treaty is binding on the Parties, but when the Parties have agreed to the French text thereof and have so notified the Government of the Republic of the Philippines, the French text shall be equally authentic and binding on the Parties.

Understanding of the United States of America

The United States of America in executing the present Treaty does so with the understanding that its recognition of the effect of aggression and armed attack and its agreement with reference thereto in Article IV, paragraph 1, apply only to communist aggression but affirms that in the event of other aggression or armed attack it will consult under the provisions of Article IV, paragraph 2.

In witness whereof, the undersigned Plenipotentiaries have signed this Treaty.

Done at Manila, this eighth day of September, 1954.

Protocol to the Southeast Asia
Collective Defense Treaty

Designation of states and territory as to which provisions of Article IV and Article III are to be applicable:

The Parties to the Southeast Asia Collective Defense Treaty unanimously designate for the purposes of Article IV of the Treaty the States of Cambodia and Laos and the free territory under the jurisdiction of the State of Vietnam.

The Parties further agree that the above mentioned states and territory shall be eligible in respect of the economic measures contemplated by Article III.

This Protocol shall enter into force simultaneously with the coming into force of the Treaty.

In witness whereof, the undersigned Plenipotentiaries have signed this Protocol to the Southeast Asia Collective Defense Treaty.

Done at Manila, this eighth day of September, 1954.

(390) 8-POINT POLICY OF THE D.R.V. REGARDING NEWLY-LIBERATED AREAS, SEPTEMBER 17, 1954 [Excerpt]

Source: *Documents Related to the Implementation of the Geneva Agreements,* p. 39.

The D.R.V. made a special point of forbidding reprisals or discrimination against those who worked for the Bao Dai or French governments during the war. When the Hanoi government took over the administration of the North, the Council of Ministers approved a policy statement which included the following points.

5. - PERSONNEL WORKING IN THE BAO-DAI AND FRENCH ADMINISTRATIONS WILL BE GIVEN JOBS ACCORDING TO THEIR ABILITIES.

All the civil servants in the Bao-dai and French Administrations, including policemen and civil servants in charge of city sections will be employed according to their abilities, and will keep their former salaries.

Everyone is supposed to obey and execute the orders of the Government of the Democratic Republic of Viet-nam, to look after property, records of the administrative offices, until the Government representatives take them over. Those who deliberately sabotage and steal public property, contravene the orders of the Government of the Democratic Republic of Viet-nam will be severely punished.

6. - VIETNAMESE OFFICERS AND MEN OF THE FRENCH AND BAO-DAI ARMIES STAYING BEHIND IN THE NEWLY-LIBERATED AREAS WILL, AFTER REGISTRATION, BE GIVEN ASSIS-

TANCE TO RETURN TO THEIR NATIVE PLACES OR GIVEN JOBS ACCORDING TO THEIR ABILI-
TIES.

In order to ensure security in the city and to stabilize social order, all
officers and men of the French and Bao-dai armies who are staying behind in the
newly-liberated areas should register at the Military and Administrative Committees and surrender all their arms. Those who have registered will be assisted to the greatest possible extent to return to their home villages. Those
who want to work for the Government may apply for employment. Their applications will be considered and jobs will be given accordingly.....

***

8. - ENFORCEMENT OF DEMOCRATIC FREEDOMS, PROTECTION OF FREEDOM OF CON-
SCIENCE OF THE PEOPLE.

The Government of the Democratic Republic of Viet-nam guarantees democratic freedoms to all Vietnamese citizens.
The Government also guarantees freedom of conscience to believers of all
religions; no one is allowed to desecrate churches, temples, pagodas, sanctums
or to impair the security of priests.
All the Vietnamese citizens of the Democratic Republic of Viet-nam including
believers of all religions and priests should comply with the laws and regulations of the Government, should discharge their civic obligations.

(391) <u>TELEGRAM FROM SMITH TO HEATH AND ALDRICH</u>, SEPTEMBER 30, 1954

*At the request of the French, General Ely and French Minister of State for
the Associated States Guy La Chambre met with U.S. officials from September 27
through September 30, 1954. They reached accord on support for the Diem regime,
warning to Bao Dai that he must help strengthen Diem and coordination of strategy for reconciliation between Diem and his Chief of Staff and for bringing the
sects under control.*

Follows text of message which approved by US and French delegations for
transmittal to respective missions SAIGON.

QUOTE: In French-US discussions here, we and French have reached conclu-
sion we should support Diem in establishment and maintenance of strong anti-
Communist nationalist government. To this end France and US will both urge
all anti-Communist elements in Viet-Nam to cooperate fully with government of
Ngo Dinh Diem.
We recognize five key elements which, can provide a stable anti-Communist
nationalist government under Diem's leadership with chance of success: Bao
Dai, Hinh and national army and three sects.
As result our discusisons we giving consideration to action along following
lines and desire your comments:
The problems relating to Chief of State will require further consideration
when Government of Viet-Nam consolidated. Under present circumstances further
demarches should be made jointly or separately to Bao Dai emphasizing consequences in terms of US and French support of failure on his part to act in such
way to strengthen Diem Government. French and United States representatives
Saigon, who should be given broad delegation powers for this purpose, should
encourage Diem support our actions re Bao Dai with appropriate measures within
competence Vietnamese Government.
With respect to General Hinh, it essential that Chief Staff obey orders
given by civil authority. However, same time, it most difficult find replacement for him. Consequently, demarches should be made to General Hinh and

President Diem towards reconciliation. It would be emphasized that France and United States are firmly supporting President Diem and that once his position consolidated and only then extensive program designed to develop national army under General Hinh could be undertaken. There remains problem of who would be Minister of Defense over Hinh. In the future, relations with Hinh as Chief Staff, should be limited purely military matters in effort discourage him from entering into political affairs.

Sects play an essential role in their respective territories but have limited importance on national scale. Sects have maintained flexible positions with regard Diem, Viet Minh, Bao Dai, France and the United States. It of vital importance that France and the United States maintain carefully coordinated strategy towards sects. Sects should be informed of intent of United States and France with regard support for Diem. Diem might be advised attempt influence sects through his handling of integration of their forces into national army and through ability grant them administrative control over areas being evacuated by Viet Minh. The representatives in Vietnam of France and United States should be given broadest possible delegation of powers to determine coordinated positions these matters.

With specific regard to Binh Xuyen recognized that whatever their unsatisfactory and undesirable qualities may be, their position of power should not be underestimated particularly as they control police, are closely tied in with Bao Dai, and in past have been responsible for extensive terroristic activity in Saigon.

Therefore, our course of action should be to seek to isolate the Binh Xuyen particularly from Bao Dai and to minimize their power and influence through strengthening national army as counter. This can only be achieved progressively. At present time it seems necessary to associate them with the government, which might in long run be best method to be in position control them. UNQUOTE.

As noted third paragraph above, Saigon comments requested regarding specific means by which we could carry out courses action included above text.

French Delegation requests text above included within quotes be given Daridan with explanation this sent by US channels their request for his comments.

(392) LETTER FROM DULLES TO WILSON, OCTOBER 11, 1954

Source: *U.S.-Vietnam Relations, Book 9*, pp. 768-769.

Dulles tried to convince Wilson and the Joint Chiefs, who had expressed reservations about becoming involved in the training of native armies in Indochina, that a U.S. training program in Viet-nam would "substantially influence" the political and military stability of the country. He requested the Pentagon's views on the appropriate level of forces in Viet-nam, the amount the U.S. would spend to maintain them and a plan for training them.

With reference to the enclosures from the Joint Chiefs of Staff in your letter of September 28, there are several important political and policy aspects of both the manpower and cost estimates of force goals for the Associated States totalling about $536,400,000, and the Joint Chiefs of Staff reservations on the support and training of Vietnamese forces.

With respect to the magnitude of force levels and costs for Viet-Nam and Cambodia, I believe that United States policy should be based on NSC 5429/2, which envisages the maintenance in Indochina of forces necessary to assure the internal security of the area, and upon the arrangements concluded at Manila to deter aggression in Southeast Asia. The concepts underlying the Southeast Asia Collective Defense Treaty should make the maintenance of relatively large ground forces unnecessary in the Associated States, since the military establishment of a single state within such a collective security group need not be so large as would be required if that nation had to act alone to defend its security against external aggression. It seems to me that the mission of the Vietnamese National Armed Forces should be to provide internal security. The manpower and cost estimates in the JCS attachment would seem to be excessive in the above context.

From the political viewpoint some armed forces are necessary. If adequately trained and equipped they would give the people of free Viet-Nam some assurance of internal security and provide the Government of Free Viet-Nam with an increased sense of stability. This would produce definite political and psychological advantages and would help fulfill the objectives of NSC 5429/2. I would appreciate having your views as to the forces we should contemplate to carry out this policy as well as the amount of funds we should devote to this purpose.

With respect to the question of U.S. support and training for the Vietnamese forces there are two political aspects: purpose and timing. Effective execution of NSC policy on U.S. support for such forces can have a significant bearing on the political objective of creating a stable, capable anti-Communist government in Viet-Nam, and on assisting it in carrying out a vigorous internal program with Congressional approval. One effective way to strengthen the Vietnamese Government is to assist in the reorganizing and training of its armed forces, as I noted in my letter to you of August 18, 1954. This point was again referred to in the Acting Secretary's letter of September 7, 1954, to the Deputy Secretary of Defense. In addition to budgetary support, a direct means of helping to create and maintain political stability will be by appropriate participation of the U.S. MAAG in the planning, developing and training of Vietnamese security forces. The Department of State is aware of the risks, difficulties and impediments in any such program of U.S. training and assistance for Vietnamese forces. Nevertheless, within these difficulties and limitations, I feel there are many reasons to consider a vigorous, imaginative and effective program for planning, developing and training Vietnamese security forces both in Viet-Nam and perhaps even in nearby countries or in the United States itself. We could substantially influence the development of political, as well as military stability in free Viet-Nam if we had such a training project with Vietnamese forces. The provision of direct budgetary support to these forces would have far less impact if the United States eschews any participation in training these forces.

Then there is the question of timing regarding the degree of political stability which the Joint Chiefs of Staff raised in their memorandum of September 22, 1954, I believe that potential political developments now warrant your consideration of the necessary preliminary steps for working out an appropriate U.S. training function for Vietnamese security forces.

With respect to these considerations regarding force goals and training in Viet-Nam, we need to take some decisions promptly to enable us to respond to the Cambodian, Vietnamese, and French Governments concerning financial and other support for their forces in Indochina.

The President has signed a letter to the Prime Minister of Viet-Nam authorizing the American Ambassador to Viet-Nam to examine with him an intelligent program of direct American aid to assist Viet-Nam. A similar letter has already been delivered to the King of Cambodia. In the meantime the Vietnamese Government has submitted a note to this Government stating that it is considering increasing the Vietnamese army to a total force of 230,000 men in order to "guarantee the internal and external security of the country" and requesting United States assistance in this endeavor. The French Finance Minister in his recent talks in Washington expressed a desire for U.S. financial support for the French Expeditionary Corps in Indochina, which the French contemplate retaining at an average strength of about 150,000 men during 1955. The United

States representatives indicated that we would strive to give some indication to the French Government of our thinking on these matters by December 1, 1954. The plans of the French and the Vietnamese both seem to me to be beyond what the United States should consider feasible to support for maintaining the security of free Indochina at this time.

In view of the political considerations and the requirements of timing, it is imperative that the United States Government prepare a firm position on the size of the forces we consider a minimum level to assure the internal security of Indochina. This position will also have to include the amounts of money we will be prepared to make available for this purpose, and the steps we will be willing to take to assist in the training and formation of these forces. It seems to me that we cannot realistically enter into discussions with the other governments concerned until we have made this determination. I would therefore also appreciate your views on how best we should proceed in making this determination.

I am sending a copy of this letter to Governor Stassen.

(393) MEMORANDUM FROM THE JOINT CHIEFS OF STAFF TO WILSON, OCTOBER 19, 1954

Source: *U.S.-Vietnam Relations*, pp. 771-774.

The Joint Chiefs again rejected Dulles' arguments and recommended against a U.S. military training mission in Indochina, citing political instability in South Viet-nam as well as the limitations in the Geneva Agreement on foreign military personnel.

> Subject: Development and Training of Indigenous Forces
> in Indochina

1. This memorandum is in response to a memorandum by the Assistant Secretary of Defense (ISA), dated 14 October 1954, subject as above.

2. The Joint Chiefs of Staff have reconsidered the recommendations contained in their memorandums for you, dated 22 September 1954, on the subjects, "Retention and Development of forces in Indochina" and "U.S. Assumption of Training Responsibilities in Indochina" in the light of the most recent comments of the Secretary of State.

3. The justification for forces in excess of those necessary for internal security is as follows:

a. The Southeast Asia Collective Defense Treaty does not provide for specific military force commitments. It does provide for consultation and military planning and for action in accordance with the constitutional processes of each party in the case of armed attack against any party to the Treaty. It also provides for consultation among the parties in the case of a threat to the inviolability or integrity of the territory or to the sovereignty or political independence of any party to the Treaty. By a special protocol the parties to the Treaty unanimously made those terms applicable to Cambodia, Laos and Vietnam.

b. NSC 162/2 envisages reliance on indigenous ground forces to the maximum extent possible. Considerable numbers of Viet Minh guerrillas and sympathizers are known to be or suspected of being within the territory of free Vietnam and the government of Vietnam has announced an intention of requesting the phased withdrawal of the French forces by 1956. This would result in a complete military vacuum unless the Vietnamese are adequately prepared to take over progressively as the French withdraw.

4. The Joint Chiefs of Staff consider that the ultimate objective of the military forces of the Associated States should be:

VIETNAM - To attain and maintain internal security and to deter Viet Minh aggression by a limited defense of the Geneva Armistice demarcation line.

CAMBODIA - To maintain internal security and provide for a limited defense of the country.

LAOS - To maintain insofar as possible internal security. (It is recognized that LAOS does not have the capability to defend against overt aggression.)

5. The Vietnamese and Cambodian forces considered as the minimum required ultimately to carry out the above objectives are as contained in the memorandum for you by the Joint Chiefs of Staff, dated 22 September 1954, subject, "Retention and Development of Forces in Indochina." These forces should be developed in phased increments dependent upon continued resistance to Communist encroachment by the Governments of Vietnam and Cambodia consistent with:

    a. French willingness to accept U.S. training responsibility.
    b. Capability of the Associated States to develop effective and reliable forces.
    c. The ability of a limited U.S. MAAG to conduct training.
    d. The continued availability of MDAP funds without detriment to other programs.

The estimated cost of training and maintaining these forces is also contained in the same memorandum. Under the terms of the Geneva Armistice Agreement, the introduction of foreign military personnel into Laos is limited to specified numbers of French personnel. In view of this limitation and the resulting prohibition of establishment of a U.S. MAAG to supervise such MDAP aid as may be granted, no recommendations are made at this time as to force levels for Laos. However, Laos is capable of supporting armed forces of 12-15,000.

6. An examination of the estimated costs involved in creating and maintaining these forces will reveal that approximately $240 million for Vietnam and $54 million for Cambodia, is for pay and allowance of the indigenous personnel. This is computed at the prevailing national scales and may be reduced but only through negotiations with the respective governments to reduce pay and allowances. Slight savings in the first year maintenance costs may be possible also is sufficient quantities of spares and replacement equipment become available in Indochina. This can be determined only after completion of an inventory following the evacuation of the Tonkin Delta. Despite any major reduction that may be accomplished by these means, U.S. support to this area should not be allowed to impair the development of effective and reliable allied forces elsewhere.

7. With reference to the question of training Veitnamese forces the Joint Chiefs of Staff desire to point out that in addition to the current unstable political situation in Vietnam the terms of the Geneva Armistice Agreement have been interpreted to limit the strength of MAAG, Indochina to 342 military personnel. Even if all these military personnel were replaced by U.S. civilians to perform the normal functions of the MAAG and the military personnel were thereby released for training duties only, the number of U.S. military personnel would permit only limited participation in the over-all training program. Under these conditions, U.S. participation in training not only would probably have but limited beneficial effect but also would assure responsibility for any failure of the program. In light of the foregoing and from a military point of view, the Joint Chiefs of Staff consider that the United States should not participate in the training of Vietnamese forces in Indochina. However, if considered that political considerations are overwhelming, the Joint Chiefs of Staff would agree to the assignment of a training mission to MAAG, Saigon, with safeguards against French interference with the U.S. training effort.

(394) DECLARATION OF THE D.R.V. REGARDING THE SOUTHEAST ASIA TREATY ORGANIZA-
TION, OCTOBER 22, 1954

Source: *Documents Related to the Implementation of the Geneva Agreements,*
pp. 70-71.

*The formation of the Southeast Asia Treaty Organization in Manila in Oct-
ober 1954 brought charges by Hanoi that the organization's charter violated
the Geneva Agreements.*

Prior to , and during, the Geneva Conference, the U.S. interventionist
circles wanted to create an aggressive military bloc in South East Asia aiming
at preventing the Conference from reaching an agreement, and at prolonging and
extending the Indo-China war under their direction. But they have failed in
their attempt. The Geneva Conference has brought about agreements aiming at
re-establishing peace in Indochina on the basis of recognition of the national
rights of the Indochinese peoples.
    As they could not sabotage the signing of these Agreements the U.S. inter-
ventionist circles are finding the way to hinder the implementation of the
terms arrived at to create conditions for a deeper American intervention in
South East Asia and to turn the countries of this area into American military
bases and colonies. That is the political significance of the Manila Conference and the so-called South East Asia Defense Treaty.
    Everybody knows it is the U.S.A that has prepared the Manila Conference and
drawn up the draft treaty, whereas the countries of South East Asia such as
India, Indonesia, Burma and Ceylon did not only refuse to adhere to this treaty
but also denounced its aggressive aim. Paragraph 5 of the Final Declaration of
the Geneva Conference stipulates that the Two signatory parties in Viet-nam
have the obligation to see that the zones allotted to them shall not constitute
part of any military alliance and shall not be utilized for the resumption of
hostolities or in the service of an aggressive policy.
    The Governments of Cambodia and Laos have also made similar declarations.
Nevertheless, the Manila Treaty, and in particular the additional protocol to
this Treaty, have, in a unilateral manner and counter to the Geneva Agreements,
placed Laos, Cambodia and South Viet-nam in the sphere of implementation of the
so-called South East Asia Defence Treaty.
    This is a flagrant violation of the Geneva Agreements, an infringement upon
the independence and sovereignty of Viet-nam, Laos and Cambodia, a threat to
the security and peace of the peoples of South East Asia.

(395) LETTER FROM EISENHOWER TO PRESIDENT NGO DINH DIEM, OCTOBER 23, 1954

Source: *Department of State Bulletin,* November 15, 1954, pp. 735-36.

*Eisenhower in a letter made public by the U.S. offered economic and mili-
tary aid to the Government of Viet-nam, but cautiously posed conditions regarding "performance" and the undertaking of "needed reforms."*

Dear Mr. President: I have been following with great interest the course
of developments in Viet-Nam, particularly since the conclusion of the conference at Geneva. The implications of the agreement concerning Viet-Nam have
caused grave concern regarding the future of a country temporarily divided by
an artificial military grouping, weakened by a long and exhausting war and faced
with enemies without and by their subversive collaborators within.
    Your recent requests for aid to assist in the formidable project of the
movement of several hundred thousand loyal Vietnamese citizens away from areas
which are passing under a *de facto* rule and political ideology which they ab-
hor, are being fulfilled. I am glad that the United States is able to assist
in this humanitarian effort.

We have been exploring ways and means to permit our aid to Viet-Nam to be more effective and to make a greater contribution to the welfare and stability of the government of Viet-Nam. I am, accordingly, instructing the American Ambassador to Viet-Nam to examine with you in your capacity as Chief of Government, how an intelligent program of American aid given directly to your Government can serve to assist Viet-Nam in its present hour of trial, provided that your Government is prepared to give assurances as to the standards of performance it would be able to maintain in the event such aid were supplied.

The purpose of this offer is to assist the Government of Viet-Nam in developing and maintaining a strong, viable state, capable of resisting attempted subversion or aggression through military means. The Government of the United States expects that this aid will be met by performance on the part of the Government of Viet-Nam in undertaking needed reforms. It hopes that such aid, combined with your own continuing efforts, will contribute effectively toward an independent Viet-Nam endowed with a strong government. Such a government would, I hope, be so responsive to the nationalist aspirations of its people, so enlightened in purpose and effective in performance, that it will be respected both at home and abroad and discourage any who might wish to impose a foreign ideology on your free people.

        Sincerely,

                Dwight D. Eisenhower

With reference to the President's remarks concerning the provision of American aid directly to the Vietnamese Government, the decision was announced in a joint communique issued at Washington on September 29 at the end of the U.S. - French talks on Indochina that the channel for French and for United States economic aid, financial support, and other assistance to Cambodia, Laos, and Viet-Nam would direct to each state. It was also announced that the United States representatives would begin discussion soon with the respective governments of the three states regarding direct aid.

United States economic assistance to Viet-Nam, as well as to Cambodia and Laos, has been provided directly to these states for some time.

United States financial assistance for the support of the armed forces of Veit-Nam, Cambodia, and Laos, however, has until now been provided through the French Government. As soon as arrangement can be made, financial support for the Vietnamese National Army will be provided directly to the Government of Viet-Nam, as will be done in the case of Cambodia and Laos.

The decision to provide assistance through direct channels conforms with the sense of Congress as expressed in the Mutual Security Act of 1954, which provides that, as far as possible, assistance furnished to Cambodia, Laos, and Viet-Nam should be direct. It also conforms with the previously expressed wishes of the Vietnamese Government, which signified its full accord with the decision.

Relative to the President's reference to United States assistance in the movement of Vietnamese citizens from areas passing under Communist military control, the number so far evacuated, largely through assistance provided to the Vietnamese Government by the United States and France, now comes to over 400,000. Of these, approximately 140,000 have been evacuated by the U.S. Navy. The United States is also assisting the Government of Viet-Nam in the resettlement of refugees.

(396) APPEAL BY FORMER CHAIRMAN OF THE RESISTANCE ADMINISTRATIVE COMMITTEE OF NAM BO PHAM VAN BACH TO PEOPLE IN THE SOUTH, NOVEMBER 4, 1954

Source: *Voice of Vietnam*, in Vietnamese to Southeast Asia, November 4, 1954. Translated in FBIS, November 8, 1954, pp. CCC7-10.

Some 100,000 Party and resistance cadres and People's Army troops regrouped under the terms of the Geneva Agreement to North Viet-nam, leaving behind families and friends. These southerners constituted one of the most important links between the D.R.V. and those in the South who had supported the resistance. Concerned about maintaining the confidence of the southerners in the leadership of the Workers' Party, Hanoi used the former Chairman of the Resistance Committee in the South, Pham Van Bach, to reassure them and to explain the new line of political struggle. Bach's appeal urged them to unite with anyone who would support the Geneva elections for reunification, regardless of their past political standpoint.

To all the compatriots, combatants, and cadres throughout Nambo: Applying the orders of President Ho and the Government in conformity with the armistice accords, up to this day, an important part of our troops and cadres of the south have been regrouped and have arrived in the north. Having come with the combatant and cadre comrades during the first trip, I want to inform you of the welcome reserved for the combatants and cadres of the south.

It is certain that all strata of the Lao people acclaim this lofty attitude. The Vietnamese people also hail it. Moreover, the Lao people hope that the Government of the Kingdom of Laos will clearly realize its responsibility toward the Lao Nation, to the cause of peace, the independence and democracy of the country so as to carry our correctly Provision No. 15 in the Laos armistice agreement, which provides that each side undertake no retaliatory steps or show discrimination against any person or organization that cooperated with the other side during the war and to guarantee their democratic liberation.

The Lao people also hope that the Royal Government and the French Union forces in Laos will take the necessary measures to prevent the renewal of acts of violation of the armistice agreement, such as dropping armed bandits in the regrouping areas of Phong Saly and Sam Neua to plunder the people. There are examples such as the cause of Bun Nua, Phong Saly Province, and the reprisals and massacre directed against Lao civilians as in the case of Sop Say at the border of Sam Neua and Vientiane province last Oct. 19.

The Vietnamese people heartily wish that the cooperation between the Royal Government of Laos and the Pathet Lao resistance forces will bring about good results.

PHAM VAN BACH APPEALS TO NAMBO POPULACE

After meeting President Ho to report his activities, Mr. Pham Van Bach has sent an appeal to the compatriots in the south. Here is this appeal:

"To all the compatriots, combatants and cadres throughout Nambo: Applying the orders of President Ho and the Government in conformity with the armistice accords, up to this day, an important part of our troops and cadres of the south have been regrouped and have arrived in the north. Having come with the combatant and cadre comrades during the first trip, I want to inform you of the welcome reserved for the combatants and cadres of the south.

"...particular points of the common situation on the north, and then, of the mission of the political struggle of our compatriots of the south in the present new phase. The reception of our combatants and cadres has been minutely prepared by the Government and compatriots of the north. Upon their landing the comrades have their board and lodging. For more than a month, every time there is an arrival, the representatives of the Central Government, of the people's groups, workers, compatriots of the region and the combatants of the north come to the quay to warmly welcome our combatants and cadres.

"The comrades are happy to hear the letters of salutation from President Ho, Mr. Ton Duc Thang, chairman of the Standing Committee of the National Assembly of Vietnam, Generalissimo Vo Nguyen Giap, from the Central Committee of Lien Viet, from the central committees of the various workers' and peasants' groups.

"It is hard to describe the enthusiastic welcome of the war godmothers and of the comrades of the youth and children, of the various meetings... to tell you again of the sincere words of the compatriots of the north which have moved our combatants, cadres, and their families. The sympathy of the compatriots of the north has keenly impressed our compatriots and cadres who have immediately written letters to President Ho to wish him good health, to report their activities and to promise to strive to accomplish the missions which President Ho, the Party, the Government, and the High Command have entrusted to them.

"In particular, a delegation of the cadres, combatants, and personalities has been introduced to President Ho. I have had the honor to be part of it. We have been very happy to see the Uncle in good health. His affectionate welcome and his joviality have shown us his immense love and his constant solicitude with respect to the combatants and compatriots of the south. We have solemenly transmitted to him the wishes of the compatriots and their promises to struggle for the unification of the country. Uncle Ho has...in 2 years, it would come to the south with the combatants and cadres of the south.

"For several days the Uncle, the Central Government, the Party, the Standing Committee of the National Assembly, and the Central Lien Viet Committee have warmly acclaimed the delegation of the military, political, and administrative organizations of (Cau Xay?), Nambo. That is a great honor for all the compatriots, combatants, and cadres of Nambo, the most distant children of the Fatherland, who have heroically and painfully resisted, contributing an important part to the great victories which our people and Government have won at Geneva.

"Such receptions have permitted our combatants and cadres to be more imbued with the words of 'Old Father.' The combatants and cadres of the south coming to the north have expressed to President Ho, the Central Executive Committee of the Party, and the Government the sentiments of confidence and respect which animate the population of the south toward them.

"Since our arrival here being near President Ho and the leading organizations of the heroic Vietnamese People's Army which has courageously fought on every battlefield and at Dien Bien Phu, having learned the agrarian reform work and attended the ceremonies of the transfer of the capital, we have more confidence in the future of the great struggle of our people to realize unity, the primordial condition to consolidate peace and to perfect independence and democracy throughout the country. Most noteworthy in the north is the profound spirit of union of our compatriots of all people's classes, in the countryside as well as in the cities. There is no distinction of religions, political parties, tendencies...and the Central Government.

"The persons who have...now enjoy democratic freedoms. The functionaries who, in the old days, worked in the French and Bao Dai administrations, have been reemployed in ours. Our Government has moreover ordered that the properties of the persons brought to the south by force or by belief be preserved. All the maneuvers of lying propaganda of the Ngo Dinh Diem clique have failed, and can only make the people detest them. The people more and more clearly see the acts of the armistice sabotaged...

"Dear compatriots and cadres, in order to safeguard and reinforce peace, to realize national unity and perfect independence, the compatriots of the south must strive to accomplish the tasks fixed by President Ho and the Central Committee of the Party. Those tasks consist of struggling for the realization of the democratic freedoms such as freedom of meeting,...opinion, moving, and so forth, and organizing free general elections in order to realize national unity.

"We must unite more closely with all the compatriots regardless of their political parties or political tendencies, even with the compatriots who have cooperated with the adversary camp and who now want to...approve peace, national unity, and independence. We must also unite with the peoples of

Khmerland and PathetLao, with the French and with all the peace-loving peoples
of the world in order to form a powerful bloc against the machinations of aggression of the American imperialists, the French colonialists, and their lackeys who want to sabotage the armistice in Indochina.

"The troops and cadres of the south transferred to the north promise to the
compatriots of Nambo to contribute with all their forces to the work of consolidation of the north, to the strengthening of the People's Army, the principal
force for the defense of the Fatherland, and for the safeguard of peace; to
eagerly participate in the national reconstruction and to actively struggle for
the connection of the south to our dear Fatherland.

"May the compatriots of Nambo be calm and firmly struggle to be faithful to
our traditional heroism. They must always remind the recommendations of Uncle
Ho who has announced a long-term struggle.

"The more we will meet difficulties, the more our forces will become powerful. We have proved that we know how to unite ourselves and how to be firm.
The progressive peoples of the world bring us their support.

"President Ho, the Central Committee of the Party, and the Government, as
well as the compatriots of the north, closely follow the painful struggle of
the compatriots of the south. No force will succeed in shaking the spirit of
insubordination of the population of Nambo and the will of union of the population of Vietnam.

"Long live pacific, unified, independent, and democratic Vietnam! Long
live President Ho!"

(397) TELEGRAM FROM SPECIAL REPRESENTATIVE GENERAL LAWTON COLLINS TO DULLES,
DECEMBER 13, 1954. [Extract]

Source: *U.S. Vietnam Relations, Book 9,* pp. 811-813.

*On November 3, former Army Chief of Staff General Lawton Collins was named
Special Representative in Saigon in charge of coordinating U.S. aid programs to
the Diem Government. Among the problems he faced in his first weeks in Saigon
were obtaining official French approval of a U.S. military training program
and maneuvering to get the U.S. choice named as Minister of Defense. Collins
reported his rebuff of French efforts to get the U.S. to agree that France had
"responsibilities under the Geneva accords."*

Recent developments current situation follow:

1. Relations with French:

(A) Earlier this week Ely was on verge of signing minute of understanding
on organization and training of Vietnamese armed forces. Now French have come
up with new amendments requiring US respect Ely's responsibilities "under Geneva accords" and including long new "protocol" with several references to Geneva. Whether these new proposals come from Ely's legal staff or Paris I do
not (repeat not) know, but inclined believe latter since Ely agreed to resolve
few remaining minor points directly with me and since he has said several times
that Paris political circles would have to be satisfied. I intend refuse accept any reference to Geneva accord or make any further concessions reference
O'Daniel's full responsibility for training under Ely's broad direction.

(B) Interview with Sainteny, to which Ely and his officers continue to
refer with chagrin, appears reinforce view that our relations with French in
Indochina may remain less clear-cut than Ely wishes and has given me to believe
they are *(Officially Deleted).*

2. Latest developments re Quat:

(A) Since Luyen's return from Paris, his open opposition to Quat has
undermined Diem's decision to appoint Quat Minister of Defense. On 11 December

Diem informed Fishel as follows: six of seven cabinet members consulted by Diem have voiced strong opposition to Quat. Generals Phuong (Cao Dai) and Soai (Hoa Hao) have declared they will withdraw from government and threaten open rebellion if Quat appointed. Because of location Hoa Hao territory, Diem purports to fear General Soai might cut off rice supply of Saigon-Cholon, block road and waterway traffic through coastal areas and to Saigon, make war in Hoa Hao areas against national army which in present condition could not (repeat not) handle situation. Diem fears also comparable action might be taken by Bao Dai forces, including possible moves against government in Saigon and vicinity.

(B) Diem told Fishel that he had informed Phuong and Soai that Americans wanted Quat as Defense Minister. The Generals replied, "a responsible American should speak for the Americans". Hence Diem asked Fishel to transmit these "facts" to me, saying if I or "some other person" can convince Phuong and Soai not (repeat not) oppose actively the appointment, Diem will appoint Quat at once. (A neat passing of the buck, we must admit). If sect leaders persist in their opposition, Diem says he would be inclined raise present Deputy Minh to Defense Minister and give him full authority and responsibility over armed forces.

(C) I am quite convinced that Diem and brothers Luyen and Nhu are afraid to turn over control of armed forces to Quat or any other strong man. They may also fear Quat as potential successor to Diem and hence are doing everything they can to keep him out of any post in government. With General Hinh fired and General Vy replaced as Chief of Staff by spineless General Ky, Diem has fairly effectively seized control of army. I doubt Diem would delegate real authority to Minh, but would retain meddling hand on details to detriment O'Daniel's training mission and effective development of armed forces.

(D) Through Colonel Lansdale's group and CAS, I am canvassing attitude of sect leaders and genuineness of their alleged threats. Depending on Lansdale's findings, I will consider (1) proposing to Ely a direct US-French approach to General Soai, who Quat has said will bow to French pressure; (2) having Lansdale suggest to Soai that with Quat in defense all rice for armed forces would be purchased from Hoa Hao (this was hint dropped some time ago by Quat as means of buying off Hoa Hao); (3) sending emissaries to Soai, Huong and Cao Dai Pope (Pham Cong Tan) making clear that any rebellion would lead to withdrawal all American aid and inevitable victory for Ho Chi Minh who would certainly not (repeat not) tolerate private empires of Hoa Hao or Cao Dai.

(E) I realize disadvantages of forcing Diem to accept "American choice" of Quat. However acceptance of status Quo, with Minh elevated to Defense Ministry and sects reinforced in veto power over government, is simply postponing evil day of reckoning as to when, if ever, Diem will assert type of leadership that can unify this country and give it chance of competing with hard, effective, unified control of Ho Chi Minh. Such a delaying action would appear to be justified only if we are preparing way for alternatives, as indicated in part II.

(398) <u>TELEGRAM FROM DILLON TO STATE DEPARTMENT</u>, DECEMBER 19, 1954

Source: *U.S.-Vietnam Relations, Book 9*, pp. 826-829.

In discussions among Dulles, Eden and Mendes-France, the French Premier insisted that the time had come to prepare an alternative to Diem. Dulles demurred on the ground that no alternative had yet been suggested, intimating that the U.S. and France continue to back Diem while putting more pressure on him. Both Eden and Mendes-France agreed that the Vietnamese monarchy could still be useful in preparing a possible political alternative.

Tripartite discussions on Indochina took place this afternoon at Matignon.

Dulles opened conversations by greeting Ely and citing appreciation of cooperation he had shown U.S. authorities in Vietnam. Ely gave report current situation at Mendes' suggestion. He said first point to be cleared up after Collins arrived was settlement Government-National Army conflict. Accomplished by means Bao Dai's recall Hinh, second was to try prepare program for Diem government. This done but question now how to get Diem accept formula. Theirs was how strengthen Diem. Ely and Collins tried introduce Quat who is better politician and administrator than Diem into government but sects and Diem balked. He said only suggestion ever accepted by Diem was appointment Minh as Minister Defense.

Mendes interrupted to make two points. First that Collins and Ely thought that Ministries of Interior and National Defense should be combined. Both offices are concerned with internal affairs and it is unnecessary separate them at this time. Diem had refused this suggestion too. Second point was that working groups had been established in Saigon to suggest reforms to government - both administrative and agrarian. Not a single reform suggested accepted by Diem. Mendes described Diem's approach as wholly negative. French government now considered that as a result of today's talks strong approach would have to be made to Diem. Suggestions should be precise and energetic. There was no time left to allow for anything less. Mendes wished reaffirm his past agreement with Secretary's thesis that we must do our maximum to permit Diem government to succeed. Now he wished add that he was no longer sure that even maximum would help. He said we must now have alternate formula in mind. Without varying from our stated purpose of supporting Diem government as long as it exists we must now prepare in our minds for alternative.

Secretary replied that he recognized task in South Vietnam was difficult one. Difficult because it required that government be built of indigenous peoples with little or no experience. Moreover, they had to build in time of great stress following military defeat, temporary partition and while there was great influx of refugees from North. Secretary regarded basic factors as favorable. People were opposed to communism and had great natural resources. They had exportable surplus. They received greater aid from abroad than North. Beginning of joint Franco-U.S. task difficult, but situation was much improved now that there was full cooperation between French and American authorities. Problem must not be approached in spirit of defeatism. Only serious problem we have not yet solved is that of indigenous leadership. We cannot expect it to be solved ideally because there is no tradition among indigenous people for self-government. We must get along with something less good than best.

Secretary continued to say that he had no RPT no personal judgement of personalities involved, but our indications were that Diem was best man available in spite of failings. We visualized cabinet with broad appeal and authority. This vision has not been realized. Diem appears to be man constitutionally incapable of making decisions. US not RPT not committed to Diem in any irrevocable sense. We have accepted him because we knew of no one better. Developments have confirmed our fears as to his limitations but no substitute for him has yet been proposed. Those suggested in past varied from month to month. Now it is claimed that only Bao Dai can save situation. If that is case, then we must indeed be desperate. Secretary's view we should continue back Diem but exert more pressure on him to make changes we consider necessary. Secretary finished by asking whether Ely had, with Collins, already applied maximum pressures to Diem.

Ely replied they had and that both were now virtually convinced that it was hopeless to expect anything of Diem. Nevertheless they continued pressures. Secretary asked whether Diem had yet been confronted with ultimatum that unless such and such were done by certain date our support would be withdrawn. Ely said he had not RPT not. He characterized Diem as extremely pig-headed man who became more so under pressure. Secretary asked if this meant that ultimatum would make him more stubborn and Ely replied it would.

Mendes then pursued subject with Ely who stated that he felt that to exert too much pressure on Diem was not RPT not in keeping with the new independent status of Vietnam and that in any case such pressure should not RPT not be exerted jointly but separately by himself and Collins. Moreover, he described Diem as having tendency play one man against other in typical Asiatic style and that this was to be avoided. He commented on Diem's own difficulties, especially those he had had in reconciling sects. Principal question was to decide now whether Diem was really man capable of national union. He and Collins must decide that question.

Secretary stated that he was opposed to issuance ultimatum until we knew what we would do if it were rejected. At the moment we have nothing else to offer, he commented. Mendes recommended that we approach Bao Dai because of his legal powers and usefulness and fact that presumably would have to appoint any successor to Diem. He had proven in Hinh case that he could be useful and Mendes felt that Bao Dai could again serve purpose. He could be used to put alternate plan into effect if ultimatum to Diem failed. Secretary commented that he realized that we must be prepared to use Bao Dai but felt that we must go to him prepared with our own ideas and not RPT not simply to accept his. Mendes agreed but commented that Bao Dai's personal position had weaked recently. In spite of this fact, he still represented legality and could serve in future if "legality" had to be provided to any step we would wish to take.

Mendes then spoke of a plan French have been considering. First phase was to ask Bao Dai to place on spot in Vietnam a representative who would exercise Bao Dai's authority. He would be "delegate" or viceroy. He would have full authority to use Bao Dai's powers. Usefulness would persist even if Diem should succeed for he could act as supreme arbitrator to settle squabbles.

Mendes said that French were now prepared talk to Bao Dai along these lines and urge him establish viceroy without delay.

French also proposed approach Bao Dai with view reinforcing present govt and preparing legal grounds for new one if it should be found necessary.

Eden intervened to state that in his opinion it would be mistake for Bao Dai to go back now but British recognized advantage of Vietnamese royal tradition and agreed that "royal commission" of some sort should be set up and might prove be best way out.

He inquired about personality and usefulness of Empress and Mendes replied that she was exemplary person who could prove very useful in Vietnam.

1955

(399) DECLARATION OF THE D.R.V., ON NORMAL RELATIONS BETWEEN NORTHERN AND
SOUTHERN ZONES, February 4, 1955

Source: *Documents Related to the Implementation of the Geneva Agreements,*
pp. 33-35.

*At a time when it was increasingly clear that Diem would not enter into
discussions with the D.R.V. on elections, Hanoi made a major political-
diplomatic move aimed at exploiting nationalist sentiments in the South: it
announced its willingness to enter into economic, cultural and social exchanges
between the two zones. It presented such North-South relations as creating
the basis for the "political settlement" provided in the Geneva Conference's
Final Declaration. The Diem government did not respond to the initiative.*

Following the appeal made by President Ho-Chi-Minh on New Year's Day, the
Council of Ministers of the Democratic Republic of Viet-nam has, in its session
early in February 1955, considered the question of restoring normal relations
between North and South Viet-nam on either side of the provisional military
demarcation line. The Council holds that:

1 - Viet-nam is a unified country from the North to the South. The political, economic, cultural, social and sentimental relations and the solidarity of
the Vietnamese people are indivisible. During the eight to nine years of the
patriotic war, the Vietnamese people from the North to the South have heroically fought to restore peace and struggled together to build up the Fatherland.
That is why, after the implementation of the armistice and pending the general
elections to bring about the reunification of the country, the re-establishment
of normal relations between the Northern and Southern zones fully conforms to
the earnest aspiration of the various strata of the population in the two zones
and is indispensable for the restoration of a normal and prosperous life of the
Vietnamese people throughout the country;
2 - The restoration of normal relations between the two zones is in complete conformity with the spirit of the Geneva Armistice Agreement.

The first sentence of the Agreement on the cessation of hostilities in Viet-
nam stipulates that the demarcation line, on either side of which the forces of
the two parties shall be regrouped after their withdrawal, is only provisional.
The Final Declaration of the Geneva Conference clearly mentioned that:

> *"The military demarcation line should not in any way be interpreted
> as constituting a political or territorial boundary".*

The restoration of relations between the two zones does not infringe upon
the the administrative control of each side. On the contrary, it will provide
the authorities of both sides with good opportunity for mutual understanding,

thereby creating *"the necessary basis for the achievement of a political settlement in Viet-nam"*, as stipulated in the Final Declaration of the Geneva Conference.

Due to the above-mentioned reasons, the Government of the Democratic Republic of Viet-nam declares that:

1 - Responding to the earnest desire of the Vietnamese people and in conformity with the spirit of the Geneva Armistice Agreement, the Government of the Democratic Republic of Viet-nam is disposed to grant all facilities to the people in the Northern and Southern zones on either side of the provisional military demarcation line in sending mail, moving, carrying out business or enterprises from one zone to the other, and in exchanging cultural, artistic, scientific, technical, sporting and other activities. The Government of the Democratic Republic of Viet-nam fully encourages and helps the population in the two zones in all economic, cultural and social exchanges advantageous for the restoration of normal life of the people,

2 - The Government of the Democratic Republic of Viet-nam hopes that the authorities in South Viet-nam will agree to the restoration of normal relations between the Northern and Southern zones with a view to bringing about solutions favourable for the entire people.

(400) MEMORANDUM BY THE JOINT CHIEFS OF STAFF FOR WILSON, February 11, 1955

Source: Document declassified by the Joint Chiefs of Staff, November 10, 1976.

The Joint Chiefs presented their concept of how the U.S. would carry out armed intervention under the Manila Pact as one of retaliatory attacks against the "aggressor country," including the use of atomic weapons if it would quickly halt the aggression and was considered as being in U.S. security interests.

1. This is in response to a memorandum by the Deputy Secretary of Defense, dated 6 January 1955, subject as above, in which it was requested that the Joint Chiefs of Staff recommend a concept and broad outline plans for the application of U.S. military power under the Manila Pact with a primary objective being the deterrence of " . . . overt aggression by China or other Communist nations."

2. There are three basic forms in which aggression in Southeast Asia can occur:

    a. Overt armed attack from outside of the area.
    b. Overt armed attack from within the area of each of the sovereign states.
    c. Aggression other than armed, i.e., political warfare, or subversion.

3. The Joint Chiefs of Staff consider that their views previously expressed in a memorandum for the Secretary of Defense, dated 8 October 1954, subject: "Military Consultation Under the Southeast Asia Collective Defense Treaty," in which the Joint Chiefs of Staff stated that "U.S. commitments to Formosa, Japan and Korea, which nations have been excluded from the treaty, make it imperative that the United States not be restricted by force commitments in the subject treaty area" remain valid.

4. In order to retain this freedom of action it is considered that the United States should not enter into combined military planning for the defense of the treaty area with the other Manila Pact powers nor should details of United States unilateral plans for military action in the event of Communist aggression in Southeast Asia be disclosed to the other powers.

5. Based on the above considerations, the Joint Chiefs of Staff recommend the following as a concept and broad outline plan for the application of U.S. military power under the Manila Pact:

    a. Continued development of combat effective indigenous forces, with their structure and training mutually coordinated to develop local leadership and prestige, and with improved capabilities to create a cohesive fighting force through integration of their operations with adjacent indigenous forces and with support by operations of forces of other Manila Pact members.

    b. Readiness to retaliate promptly with attacks by the most effective combination of U.S. armed forces against the military power of the aggressor.

    c. Encouragement of other Manila Pact countries to maintain forces in readiness to counter aggression.

    d. Discussion, in general terms, of unilateral military plans by the Military Representatives to the Council to the extent necessary to insure maximum participation and cooperation by other member nations but not to the extent that U.S. strategic plans or the availability of U.S. forces for implementing such plans might be revealed.

    e. Periodic visits by U.S. forces into the area as demonstrations of intent, and for joint and combined training exercises.

    f. Availability of appropriate mechanism for the employment of U.S. forces in support of friendly indigenous forces in the general area.

6. The concept of prompt retaliatory attacks does not envisage attacks on targets within the aggressor country other than on military targets involved in the direct support of the aggressor action. If authorized, atomic weapons would be used, even in a local situation, if such use will bring the aggression to a swift and positive cessation, and if, on a balance of political and military consideration, such use will best advance U.S. security interests. Under the alternative assumption that authority to use atomic weapons cannot be assured, the above concept would not require change, but this assumption would not permit the most effective employment of the U.S. armed forces, and consequently might require greater forces than the U.S. would be justified in providing from the over-all point of view.

7. In the event general war should develop, U.S. forces will be deployed as indicated in emergency war plans, and with the principal effort devoted to strategic areas considered more vital than Southeast Asia. However, should an aggression result in a prolonged localized conflict of limited objectives, additional U.S. forces could be deployed to the area if required. The application of this additional U.S. military power, in conjunction with the military power of other member nations of the Manila Pact, would involve the movement, deployment, and support of U.S. forces not within presently approved force levels, and the mobilization of the defense effort of the Manila Pact nations. In order for the United States to support this additional effort, the military budget and personnel ceilings would require considerable increases.

8. The above considerations are based on currently planned U.S. military capabilities and on the assumption that the United States will not enter into specific agreements with other Manila Pact countries in regard to commitment or earmarking of U.S. forces for employment in the Southeast Asia area or Western Pacific. Such a position will permit the United States, in the event of further Communist aggression in Southeast Asia, freedom of action in determining the type of U.S. forces to be employed and the method of their employment, and can be so implemented as to retain the support of member nations of the Manila Pact and other friendly or netural countries in the general area. It must be fully understood that the United States cannot guarantee the territorial in-

tegrity of any member nation, but at most can help secure the independence of those countries whose peoples desire it and who are willing to undertake the responsibilities of self-government.

9. The Joint Chiefs of Staff consider that success in implementing the above concept will be dependent on the resolution with which future U.S. decisions concerning the Manila Pact are made and carried out. However, frequent pronouncements by high government officials to insure better public understanding of our objectives and necessary courses of action will materially assist in obtaining success.

(401) SPEECH BY HO CHI MINH TO THE 7TH ENLARGED PLENUM OF THE VIET-NAM WORKERS' PARTY CENTRAL COMMITTEE, March 12, 1955

Source: Ho Chi Minh, *Selected Work's, Vol. IV*, pp. 68-71.

The Central Committee's Enlarged Plenum in March 1955, was devoted largely to the completion of the land reform program, the struggle against "counter-revolutionaries" and the rehabilitation of the war-torn economy. Ho's remarks, which concluded the Conference, sounded a pessimistic note on the world situation and the situation in Indochina. Hanoi appears to have decided that its earlier hopes for negotiations on the Geneva elections were unrealistic.

Although not carefully prepared, this session of the Central Committee has recorded good results thanks to the efforts of you all.

Clear appreciation of the situation. In international affairs, since the beginning of our Resistance, the camp of peace, democracy and Socialism has been growing in size and strength. The Soviet Union and the other socialist countries in East Europe are becoming stronger and stronger. The Chinese revolution has been brought to a successful end. Viet Nam and Korea victoriously resisted the invaders. Composed of twelve countries embracing more than 900 million people, our camp is, geographically speaking, a bloc running from Europe to Asia and, politically, it is sealed in monolithic solidarity.

Furthermore, there are 500 million Indian, Indonesian and Burmese peoples who have cast off their colonial status and support peace.

Not including the people of capitalist countries who also love peace, these 1,400 million people, or more than half the people of the world, stand for peace and are resolved to struggle against war. This is a gigantic force.

But the imperialist camp headed by the U.S. is also very active. As early as 1948, the imperialists set up the N.A.T.O. bloc. After the Geneva Conference, they signed the Paris treaty, created the S.E.A.T.O. and staged the U.S.-Chian Kai-shek pact, etc. In a word, they are preparing for war: the international situation is therefore more tense than after the Geneva Conference.

Internal situation. Our resistance and the Geneva Conference ended victoriously. Quite a large territory has been liberated. Our country, together with the great family of new democracy and socialism, forms an inseparable bloc. We therefore enjoy favourable conditions to defend peace and achieve national reunification.

However our country is temporarily divided into two parts. The North is not yet consolidated. The South is in a precarious situation. The U.S. imperialists and their henchmen seek every means to torpedo the Geneva Agreement. They engineer the evacuation of northern people to the South. Famine prevails. Cambodia and Laos are in difficulties. The international situation is tense. These are our handicaps.

Nevertheless these difficulties, though great and many, are temporary ones. The determination of all our Party and people will overcome them.

Favourable conditions are our fundamental advantages. We must endeavour to develop them.

The successes of the session. A careful review was made of the leadership of the Central Committee pointing out the mistakes so as to correct them. Only the Party of the working class, the genuinely revolutionary Party, is able to detect mistakes amidst its victories. The session has clearly pointed out effective methods for perfecting leadership, such as:

"Leadership must be closer to reality."

"Leadership must be collective, democratic, unified and centralized."

The ideological level and organizational ability of all Party members must be raised so as to respond to the new tasks. Leadership in organization must be improved.

Criticism and self-criticism must continuously be made, especially criticism of the higher level by the lower levels.

Thanks to the Party's correct policy and directives, we have recorded fair results. If we are determined to carry out the above-mentioned points, the results will be greater.

Today, as never before, solidarity within the Party is important, especially between responsible cadres.

As this session has shown, there is enlargement of inner-party democracy and general use of criticism and self-criticism. After this session, the Central Committee has come to a closer understanding; it is more united, and firmly guarantees the unity and solidarity of the whole Party.

Under the leadership of the Central Committee, in the light of the Party's principles and policies, all the Party members and the cadres - whether old or new, and wherever they are: in the North or in the South, in the Army or in any branches or regions, in the towns or in the countryside - should unite closely and raise their political consciousness. They should exercise community of ideas and actions and be determined to carry through their tasks.

Our Party is firm and united, our people are united and enthusiastic; our army is powerful; our policies are correct; basically we enjoy favourable conditions, we have a firm determination and we enjoy the assistance of the Parties of brother countries. Therefore, though great difficulties and obstacles still lie ahead, we shall certainly be victorious in our task of consolidating peace, achieving reunification and completing independence and democracy throughout our beloved Viet Nam, and thereby make a worthwhile contribution to the defence of world peace.

(402) TELEGRAM FROM DULLES TO THE EMBASSY IN SAIGON, April 6, 1955

Source: *U.S.-Vietnam Relations, Book 10,* pp. 892-893.

In the only document which reveals his private thinking on the subject of the Geneva elections in Viet-nam after the accords, Dulles instructed the Embassy that the general U.S. approach would be to insist on agreement on "safeguards" for free elections as a precondition to discussion of any other issues connected with the elections. He indicated that the "safeguards" to be demanded would be such that the Communists would be expected to reject them. The Saigon Embassy was instructed to sound out Diem to see if he went along with the approach.

FYI. We have been working on problem of elections in Viet-Nam, in great detail over last several weeks. NSC has asked Department submit policy for consideration by mid-April and we sure that elections will be discussed during proposed U.S.-French talks Washington April 20. The British have offered give use their views on elections prior these talks.

We feel best solution is for us be in position inform French British our views prior talks and believe it best we can put such forward as support of policy of Free Viet-Nam rather than as unilateral U.S. recommendations.

Our proposal is based on Eden's plan put forward at Berlin- Conference for all German elections and has already been approved by France for use Germany and rejected by the Communists. The basic principle is that Free Viet-Nam will insist to the Viet Minh that unless agreement is first reached by the latter's acceptance of the safeguards spelled out, that no repeat no further discussions are possible regarding the type of elections, the issues to be voted on or any other factors.

After we have Diem's general acceptance we can proceed inform UK and France of this plan which we think only formula which ensures both satisfactory response to Geneva Agreement and at same time plan which is unassailable in intent but probably unacceptable to Communists because of provisions for strict compliance to ensure genuinely free elections. END FYI.

You should speak to Diem privately regarding elections, without showing him formula outlined next telegram. We are not now attempting secure his approval as such to our position but to assure he understands our viewpoint and accepts it to degree we can proceed with French British on broad assumption Free Viet-Nam's position similar our own.

Believe best way accomplish this is to remind him of his foreign ministers conversations with Secretary on this subject and to continue that in specific cases of elections in Korea and Germany Free World has stood firm on issue of guarantees of genuine free elections, supervised by body having authority guarantee elements free elections PAREN outlined last paragraph following telegram UNPAREN. In each case Communists have refused accept these safeguards which we think basic and fundamental. We believe unless such guarantees previously agreed upon would be dangerous for Free Viet-Nam be drawn into further discussions of other issues of election. Ask Diem if we can assume our thinking is alike on this point.

Since time exceedingly important, hope we can have affirmative answer soonest.

(403) LETTER FROM GENERAL COLLINS TO DULLES, April 7, 1955

Source: Document Declassified by the State Department, December 12, 1975

After five months in Saigon, Collins had come to the firm conclusion that Diem was a liability rather than an asset to U.S. policy in Viet-nam. In his personal assessment for Dulles, he recommended that the U.S. replace Diem with the government's representative at Geneva, Tran Van Do, or the U.S. choice for Minister of Defense, Dr. Phan Huy Quat.

Even before receiving your kind letter (DEPTEL 4330) I had been considering writing you personally as to my estimate of President Diem's chances of successfully remaining as President of Viet Nam. I have just filed a despatch (EMBTEL 4382) giving General Ely's final views on this point. You and the President are entitled to my judgement in light of this and other recent events.

As you know, I have been doing everything within my power to assist Diem in accordance with my original directive from the President and subsequent instructions from you and the department. In various messages, and in my January report, I have indicated my growing doubts as to Diem's capacity for leadership under the difficult and complex conditions existing in Viet Nam.

I must say now that my judgment is that Diem does not have the capacity to achieve the necessary unity of purpose and action from his people which is essential to prevent this country from falling under communist control. I say this with great regret, but with firm conviction.

During the five months that I have been here I have come to admire Diem greatly in many ways. He has valuable spiritual qualities, is incorruptible, is a devoted nationalist, has great tenacity. However, these very qualities, linked with his lack of practical political sense, his inability to compromise, his inherent incapacity to get along with other able men, and his tendency to be suspicious of the motives of any one who disagrees with him, make him practically incapable of holding this government together. As I have often pointed out, he pays more attention to the advice of his brothers Luyen and Nhu than he does to General Ely or me. He has consistently failed to decentralize responsibility to his ministers, or to consult with them in advance of reaching important decisions. This has resulted in the resignation of the few able men in his cabinet who were not repeat not "yes men."

I agree with the appraisal of General Ely and of men like Dr. Quat, Do and Minh, that Diem will not succeed in getting any new men of ability to join even a reorganized government. Damaging as the above facts are, perhaps even more serious is the President's apparent incapacity for creative thinking and planning. At no time since I have been here has he offered to me a single constructive thought of his own volition. All of the progressive programs which we have attributed to him have in fact been developed through the cooperative efforts of General Ely and me, and our staffs. I am still not sure whether Diem really grasps the full significance of these programs, or the great difficulties of implementing them.

Instead of sticking to the clear but difficult road leading to the conversion of these paper plans into accomplished facts, Diem has been ever ready like Don Quixote to dash off on side excursions to tilt with windmills. And while bent on these excursions, whether they be to displace officers of the army whom he regarded as loyal to General Hinh, to take action against Soai or Ba Cut, or to relieve a police chief, he loses all sense of direction toward the essential goals, and it is almost impossible to bring him back to the high road. We have had many such tiltings.

In summary, despite his several fine qualities, it is my considered judgment that the man lacks the personal qualities of leadership and the executive ability successfully to head a government that must compete with the unity of purpose and efficiency of the Viet Minh under Ho Chi Minh.

In saying this I hasten to add that I do not believe that Diem is indispensable for the accomplishment of our purposes in Viet Nam, that is, to save the country from communism. Programs which General Ely and I have developed are, I believe, sound and susceptible of accomplishment. But our successors here must have a president and a cabinet to work with, which to some degree will talk our language and will stick steadfastly to the implementation of these programs.

I believe that Tran Van Do or Dr. Quat could form and successfully head such a government.

If our government should accept such a change, I would urge that we stipulate as a prior condition the removal, by President Diem with the complete support of Bao Dai, of the control of the national police and surete from the Binh Xuyen. You may feel that if this is done, Diem should be given further time to see whether he can broaden his government and speed up progress. I believe it would be better not to wait. By having saved a certain amount of face for Diem by the transfer of police powers from the Binh Xuyen we should then accede to the appointment of Do or Quat as president of the country.

I feel it better not further to lengthen this letter by outlining the successive steps which I would recommend be followed in order to constitute a new government and settle the short and long term problems of the sects. I shall be prepared to submit such recommendations promptly, if you so desire.

I fully appreciate gravity of the recommendations I have made above. I need not tell you with what a heavy heart I file this message. However, it is by no means with a feeling of defeat for our objective here. I still feel that under proper native leadership, which can be had, the programs which we have initiated can still be made effective and can save Viet Nam from communism.

(404) <u>TELEGRAM FROM DULLES TO COLLINS</u>, April 9, 1955

Source: *U.S.-Vietnam Relations, Book 10*, pp. 907-909.

Dulles told Collins he and Eisenhower were inclined to continue supporting Diem because they saw no better alternative, and because replacing him under existing circumstances would mean that U.S. influence, which had kept Diem in power, would be replaced by French influence in South Vietnam.

Have this morning discussed situation with highest authority. We are disposed to back whatever your final decision is but before you actually finalize we want to be sure you have weighed all of the factors which concern us here.

We feel that what has happened does not reveal anything new about Diem but rather a basic and dangerous misunderstanding as between France and the U.S.

We have always known the qualities which Diem possesses and those which he lacks. Nevertheless our two countries agreed to support him in default of anyone possessing better qualifications. The only alternatives now suggested are the same persons who were regarded as unacceptable substitutes some months ago.

What has happened is that whereas the United States has been proceeding on the assumption that Diem would be backed as against any who might challenge him assuming that he had the capability, apparently the French have given their support only on the assumption that the Binh Suyen would also be supported on an autonomous authority and that when they challenged Diem he would not be allowed to use force to assert his authority over it.

We can appreciate the reluctance of the French to see force used but if it cannot be used then what is the point of our supporting at great cost the national army which I thought it had been agreed was primarily to be an army for domestic security rather than an army to fight external aggression.

U.S. recognizes the Cao Dai and even the Hoa Hao are genuine sects with cultural religious and political roots which cannot be forcibly torn up without grave consequences which should be avoided but we do not believe that any central government can exist as more than a figurehead if it does not have control over the national police and if this control is farmed out to a gang which exploits its privileges to protect vice on a vastly profitable scale and which exists by virtue of the backing of the self-exiled Bao Dai and the French.

We cannot see that replacement of Diem by any persons you mentioned will of itself correct this situation and indeed we have had the impression that Quat was less acceptable to the sects than is Diem.

There are two other factors to be borne in mind.

One is that it is widely known that Diem has so far existed by reason of U.S. support despite French reluctance. If, however, when the showdown comes the French view prevails then that will gravely weaken our influence for the future both in Vietnam and elsewhere. Removal of Diem under these circumstances may well be interpreted in Vietnam and Asia as example of U.S. paying lip service to nationalist cause and then forsaking true nationalist leader when QUOTE colonial interests UNQUOTE put enough pressure on us. The French constantly assert that the U.S. has a primary responsibility in this part of the world but it is difficult to have responsibility without authority. In essence, will not the ouster of Diem on the present conditions mean that from now on we will be merely paying the bill and the French will be calling the tune. Any successor of Diem will clearly know where the real authority lies.

The second factor is that there will be very strong opposition in the Congress to supporting the situation in Indochina generally and Vietnam in particular if Diem is replaced under existing circumstances. We do not say that this opposition may not in the last instance be overcome, particularly if you personally can make a case before the Congressional committees but Mansfield who is looked upon with great respect by his colleagues with reference to this matter, is adamantly opposed to abandonment of Diem under present conditions. I wonder whether there is not some intermediate solution between the present extremes now discussed and that Diem can be allowed to regain his damaged prestige by an assertion of authority over the Binh Suyen and at the same time other elements be brought into the government under conditions which will assure a real delegation of authority.

I feel that as with most Orientals Diem must be highly suspciious of what is going on about him and that this suspicion exaggerates his natural disposition to be secretive and untrustful. If he ever really felt that the French and ourselves were solidly behind him might he not really broaden his government? We must I think have some sympathy for his predicament as he is constantly called QUOTE the Diem experiment UNQUOTE.

In conclusion I want to reaffirm the very great confidence which we all have in you and in your judgment. You have done and are doing a wonderful job in the face of tremendous difficulties.

Your 4448 has just arrived in Department but is not yet decoded. We will comment on it in subsequent telegram.

(405) NSC 5519, DRAFT STATEMENT AND NSC STAFF STUDY ON U.S. POLICY ON ALL-VIETNAM ELECTIONS, May 17, 1955

Source: Document declassified by the National Security Council, May 11, 1977.

In an analysis and draft policy statement, the N.S.C. staff observed that the Communists would have the advantage in the elections to be held in 1956, but urged that the Diem government be encouraged to agree to preliminary consultations. Primary considerations in this position were the belief that rejecting elections would be extremely unpopular in South Vietnam, the fear that it would conflict with U.S. policy elsewhere in the world, as well as with French-British commitment to the elections.

GENERAL CONSIDERATIONS

1. It is U.S. policy to maintain a friendly non-Communist Free Vietnam; to assist Free Vietnam to maintain (a) military forces necessary for internal security, and (b) economic conditions conducive to the maintenance of the strength of the non-Communist regime; and to prevent a Communist victory through all-Vietnam elections.

2. Free Vietnamese strength is essential to any effective approach to the election problem. If Free Vietnam is to cope adequately with national elections it will have to be strong enough to deter or defeat Vietminh insurrections in its territory, to impose and sustain order in its territory, and to win a free election limited to its own zone and held under its own auspices and control. Otherwise, the Vietminh can take over through internal insurrections or the Government of Free Vietnam will be so weak that it will find it difficult even to give lip service to the idea of national unification through elections, or to insist on adequate conditions for free elections.

3. U.S. policy toward all-Vietnam elections should be predicated on the assumption that there is a possibility of assisting Free Vietnam to achieve the degree of strength described above. If it becomes clear that Free Vietnam cannot achieve such strength, U.S. policy toward Free Vietnam should be reviewed.

4. U.S. policy must also protect against a Communist take-over of Free Vietnam, even if the Communists were able to win elections under safeguards in North Vietnam. On the other hand, U.S. policy should be prepared to take advantage of the unlikely possibility that North Vietnam might be freed through elections.

COURSES OF ACTION

5. Continue to encourage the Government of Free Vietnam to proceed with the consultations about elections called for in July 1955 by the Geneva Agreements.

6. Provide the Government of Free Vietnam with information and advice about Communist positions and tactics with regard to elections elsewhere, e.g., Greece, Germany, Austria and Korea.

7. Assist the Government of Free Vietnam to make it clear that any failure to secure free elections is the fault of the Communists.

8. Encourage the Government of Free Vietnam:

a. To lay stress on the necessity of compliance with the stipulation of the Geneva Agreements that "all the necessary conditions obtain for free experession of the national will" before all-Vietnam elections can take place. For this purpose the Govenment of Free Vietnam should insist in the first instance on adequate guarantees of freedom of elections* and adequate supervisory powers in a Supervisory Commission.

b. To adopt positions with respect to the objectives and details of elections which: (1) will avoid terms which would be likely to result in a Communist take-over of Free Vietnam; and (2) to the degree feasible, will maintain a position generally consistent with that adopted by the Free World in other areas such as Korea and Germany.

9. Seek British and French support for the foregoing courses of action.

10. If pursuit of the above policy should result in a renewal of hostilities by the Communists, the U.S., in the light of the general circumstances then prevailing, should be prepared to oppose any Communist attack with U.S. armed forces, if necessary and feasible - consulting the Congress in advance if the emergency permits - preferably in concert with the Manila Pact allies of the U.S., but if necessary alone.

*For examples of such guarantees, see para. 8 of the attached Staff Study.

THE PROBLEM

Terms of the Geneva Agreements

1. The Geneva Agreements make only two specific references to elections in Vietnam:

a. Article 7 of the Conference Declaration states:

" . . . so far as Vietnam is concerned, the settlement of political problems, effected on the basis of respect for the principles of independence, unity and territorial integrity, shall permit the Vietnamese people to enjoy the fundamental freedoms, guaranteed by democratic institutions established as a result of free general elections by secret ballot."

and "In order to ensure that sufficient progress in the restoration of peace has been made, and that all the necessary conditions obtain for free expression of the national will, general elections shall be held in July 1956, under the supervision of an international commission composed of representatives of the Member States of the International Supervisory Commission, referred to in the agreement on the cessation of hostilities. Consultations will be held on this subject between the competent representative authorities of the two zones from 20 July 1955 onwards."

<u>b</u>. Article 14(a) of the Agreement on the Cessation of Hostilities in Vietnam states:

"Pending the general elections which will bring about the unification of Vietnam, the conduct of civil administration in each regrouping zone shall be in the hands of the party whose forces are to be regrouped there in virtue of the present Agreement."

2. The provisions of the Geneva Agreements on elections in Vietnam are thus specific in only three respects:

a. <u>Character</u> ("free expression of the national will").
<u>b</u>. <u>Supervision</u> (by representatives of the Member States - India, Canada, Poland - of the International Supervisory Commission).
c. <u>Timing</u> (preliminary consultations between competent representative authorities of the two zones are to begin on July 20, 1955; general elections are to be held in July 1956).

On all other aspects of the elections the Geneva Agreements are generally ambiguous. They do not specify the type of election which should be held, the procedures which should govern the elections, or the purposes of the elections except for a single statement that they "will bring about the unification of Vietnam." All those matters are left to the consultations between the representatives of the two zones "from 20 July 1955 onwards."

Legal Obligations Under the Geneva Agreements

3. <u>a</u>. The UK, France and the Vietminh signed the Geneva Agreements without comment on the election provision and are therefore presumably bound by them.
<u>b</u>. Free Vietnam specifically reserved its position with regard to elections in the following statement made to the Final Plenary Session of the Indochina Phase of the Geneva Conference on July 21, 1954:

"It [the Delegation of the State of Vietnam] also solemnly protests against the fact that the French High Command was pleased to take the right without a preliminary agreement of the Delegation of the State of Vietnam to set the date of future elections, whereas we deal here with a provision of an obviously political character. Consequently, the Government of the State of Vietnam requests that this Conference note that it does protest solemnly against the way in which the Armistice has been concluded and against the conditions of this Armistice which have not taken into account the deep aspirations of the Vietnamese people.
"And the Government of the State of Vietnam wishes the Conference to take note of the fact that it reserves its full freedom of action in order to safeguard the sacred right of the Vietnamese people to its territorial unity, national independence, and freedom."

Accordingly, Free Vietnam is not legally bound by provisions with respect to elections in the Geneva Agreements.
<u>c</u>. The United States is not a party to the Geneva Agreements. In the Final Plenary Session the United States (1) took note of the Armistice Agreements and paragraphs 1-12 of the Declaration; (2) declared that the

United States "will refrain from the threat or the use of force to disturb them" and "would view any renewal of the aggression in violation of the aforesaid agreements with grave concern and as seriously threatening international peace and security"; (3) stated with respect to elections that "in the case of nations now divided against their will, we shall continue to seek to achieve unity through free elections, supervised by the United Nations to insure that they are conducted fairly"; (4) noted the reservation of Free Vietnam and reiterated the traditional U.S. position "that peoples are entitled to determine their own future and that [the United States] will not join in an arrangement which will hinder this." The U.S. representatives stated that "nothing in the Declarations made by it [1, 2 and 3 above] is intended to or does indicate any departure from this traditional position."

Difficulties Involved in Elections

4. The Communists would hold certain advantages in all Vietnam elections, particularly if such elections were not held under conditions of complete freedom and rigorous supervision: (a) Communist popular appeal derived from long identification with the struggle for independence; (b) the greater organizational capacity of the Communists to influence elections through propaganda, control, and coercion; (c) the continuing difficulties of the Free Vietnam Government in consolidating its political control in its own zone and moving ahead with programs of popular appeal.

Problems Involved in Avoiding the Elections

5. Despite these Communist advantages, there are a number of factors which have led the U.S. to encourage Free Vietnam to agree to the preliminary consultations stipulated in the Geneva Agreements in order to determine whether the conditions of free elections and international supervision can be met.

a. Free Vietnam has already suffered in its contest with the Communists from the fact that the Communists have been able, largely because of the French position in Vietnam, to pre-empt for themselves identification with the slogan of national independence. Actions by Free Vietnam which were clearly directed towards avoiding elections would be seized on by the Communists to demonstrate that Free Vietnam was opposed to unification. To allow the Communists to pose as the sole champions of national unification would greatly increase the problems of Free Vietnam in securing popular support.

b. The over-all United States position in the world would be harmed by U.S. identification with a policy which appeared to be directed towards avoidance of elections. World public opinion, and for that matter domestic U.S. opinion, would have difficulty in understanding why the U.S. should oppose in Vietnam the democratic procedures which the U.S. has advocated for Korea, Austria and Germany.

c. It is clear that both the French and the British believe themselves committed as signatories of the Geneva Agreements to a program of encouraging the holding of elections. In addition, the French fear that failure to hold elections would provoke a resumption of hostilities by the Vietminh in which France would be directly and involuntarily involved due to the probable presence of at least large numbers of the French Expeditionary Corps through 1955 and the first half of 1956.

Relationship of Free Vietnamese Strength to the Election Question

6. The question of Free Vietnamese strength is central to the election problem. The Government of Free Vietnam will have not only to maintain itself as an anti-Communist entity but also to develop considerably more unity and strength than it now appears able to command. U.S. policy with respect to

elections is therefore dependent upon the success, in the interim before elections, of U.S. efforts to assist Free Vietnam to establish and maintain a position of strength which alone would permit U.S. advice on the holding of elections to be of utility.

a. Free Vietnam will have to be strong enough to deter or defeat Vietminh insurrections in its territory. If Free Vietnam were militarily and politically so weak that it could not successfully counter internal Vietminh insurrections in its territory, the question of national elections would be largely academic.

b. Free Vietnam will have to be strong enough to impose and sustain order in its own territory. If developments in Free Vietnam were to lead to civil war or a collapse of administration that Vietminh would probably be in a position to take over Free Vietnam without either major military activity or elections. Elections and consultations for elections would in that case probably only be a species of formality to register effectiveness of Vietminh control.

c. Free Vietnam will have to be strong enough politically to win a free election limited to its own zone and held under its own auspices and control. If the Government of Free Vietnam is too weak to do this, it would find it difficult even to give lip service to the idea of national unification through elections, or to insist on adequate conditions for free elections.

Free Vietnam Position in Election Negotiations

7. It will be advantageous to the U.S. if Free Vietnam, in negotiating on elections with the Communists, adopts a position which: (a) will avoid terms which would be likely to result in a Communist takeover of Free Vietnam; (b) will, to the degree feasible, maintain a position generally consistent with that adopted by the Free World in other areas such as Korea and Germany.

8. In negotiating for conditions of genuine freedom for the holding of elections, Free Vietnam can serve both these objectives by insisting on provisions such as those already supported by the Western Powers at Berlin: Agreement on safeguards to assure conditions of genuine freedom before, after, and during elections; full powers for any Supervisory Commission to act to ensure free elections and to guarantee against prior coercion or subsequent reprisal; adequate guarantees for, among other things, freedom of movement, freedom of presentation of candidates, immunity of candidates, freedom from arbitrary arrest or victimization, freedom of association and political meetings, freedom of expression for all, freedom of press, radio, and free circulation of newspapers, secrecy of vote, security of polling stations and ballot boxes. The Communists would find it most difficult to accept such conditions or to allow their implementation if accepted. Accordingly, it would be useful for the Free Vietnamese to center their position on securing agreement to conditions for free elections prior to discussion of the forms and objectives of the elections.

9. If the negotiations extend to the subjects of the forms and objectives of elections it will be more difficult for Free Vietnam to adopt positions which clearly protect the interests of Free Vietnam and at the same time are completely consistent with Free World positions on Germany or Korea. Free Vietnam is probably slightly less populous than North Vietnam (although there has been a substantial refugee movement to the Southand there are no firm population statistics), so that representation proportionate to population which we have insisted on in other areas, would be less advantageous in Vietnam than would be equal representation from the two zones. Limitation of the functions of any elected body solely to drafting of a constitution would be clearly de-

sirable in the case of Vietnam, while in other areas we are considering bodies which may have additional functions. It would be advantageous for the Free Vietnam Government to reserve the power to accept or reject any constitution that might be agreed upon in an elected constituent assembly. Such a position is probably not desirable in the other areas. In general, however, it should be possible to devise positions with regard to the details and objectives of elections which would safeguard the non-Communist position of Free Vietnam without violating important principles on which the U.S. is standing elsewhere. Insistence on limiting the powers of any elected body to drafting a constitution, or insisting on a census prior to agreeing to number of representatives, would not, for example, weaken the U.S. position with respect to either German or Korean elections.

Implications of U.S. Support for Free Vietnam Position in Elections

10. If the Free Vietnamese Government achieves that degree of unity and strength which will enable it to insist on conditions of genuine freedom for elections and on electoral details and objectives which will preserve a non-Communist Free Vietnam, there is always the possibility that at some point the Vietminh will break off negotiations and reopen hostilities. Such a course of action is not a foregone conclusion. Much may depend on the reports of the International Supervisory Commission; and the attitudes of Peiping and Moscow may be decisive. But if the Vietminh do renew hostilities, the Manila Pact signatories will face a test of their obligations. In these circumstances should the U.S. fail to react forcefully it will depreciate the value of the Manila Pact, encourage the Communists to further aggression, discourage U.S. allies in the Far East, and jeopardize the achievement of U.S. objectives in that area.

11. If present British and French policy persists, the U.S. may well find that, initially at least, forceful U.S. action to counter Vietminh renewal of hostilities may lack the support of the British and the French, and that Australia and New Zealand may be placed in the difficult position of choosing between their Commonwealth ties and their U.S. alliance. On the other hand, the possibility of obtaining international support for resistance to further Vietminh aggression would seem more promising on the grounds of a Vietminh repudiation of the Geneva Agreements and resort to force in an unwillingness to accept conditions guaranteeing the freedom of elections, than on any other basis now apparent. The possibility of such support would, of course, be materially increased by clear and appropriate findings on the part of the International Supervisory Commission.

(406) <u>ACCOUNT OF DISCUSSION AT A VIET-NAM WORKERS' PARTY CADRE CONFERENCE</u>, June 7, 1955 (Extract)

Source: *Nhan Dan,* June 7, 1955.

At a Cadre Conference following the 7th Enlarged Plenum of the Central Committee, both the world situation and the problem of reunification were discussed frankly, and the Central Committee admitted previously having over estimated the "contradictions" on the anti-Communist side.

With regard to the situation in the country, the conference clearly recognized that the U.S. imperialists, French colonialists and U.S.-French lackeys while having deep contradictions with each other regarding interests and positions are fundamentally agreed in opposing the independence and unity of our people and opposing communism. The Conference recognized the mistake previous to this of only seeing the contradictions between the U.S., France and between them and their lackeys, and not seeing the points of agreement among them. Be-cuase of this, there was a lack of vigilance against their schemes. The U.S. is directly intervening more and more deeply in Vietnam. They agreed with the French colonialist faction to opposing the agreement and used Ngo Dinh Diem to try to destroy the results of the Geneva Conference, sabotage the unity of our country and prepare to provoke war again in Indochina.

The concrete enemy immediately confronting us is American imperialism, the anti-agreement French colonialists and Ngo Dinh Diem. American imperialism is the ringleader and most dangerous enemy. Thus on the ideological plane, the comrades affirmed the protracted, difficult and complex character of our struggle for peace, unification, independence and democracy at present.

(407) AIDE MEMOIRE FROM THE GOVERNMENT OF INDIA TO THE CO-CHAIRMAN OF THE GENEVA CONFERENCE, June 14, 1955

Source: *Documents Relating to British Involvement in the Indo-China Conflict, 1954-1965*, pp. 103-105.

Noting that there would apparently be no consultations on the elections without some initiative from outside, the Indian government, as the Chair of the International Control Commission, proposed that the delegates of the Commission convene a conference of the two Vietnamese parties, assist the drawing up of an agenda, and assist in the election of a third-party Chairman to preside over the consultations before withdrawing. Nothing ever became of the proposal. The British and Soviet responses have never been published, even though the Indian proposal was published in a British compilation of documents on its own involvement in Indochina.

The military phase of the implementation of the Geneva Agreement on the Cessation of Hostilities in Viet-Nam having been concluded, it remains now to give attention to the question of general elections which will bring about the unification of Viet-Nam.

2. Paragraph 7 of the Final Declaration of the Geneva Conference mentions that "so far as Viet-Nam is concerned, the settlement of political problems, effected on the basis of respect for the principles of independence, unity and territorial integrity shall permit the Viet-Namese people to enjoy the funda-mental freedoms, guaranteed by democratic institutions established as a result of free general elections by secret ballot". According to the time schedule fixed in this paragraph consultations are to be held from July, 1955, onwards between the competent representative authorities of the two zones on the sub-ject of holding general elections in July, 1956.

3. Under Article 14(a) of the Geneva Agreement on the Cessation of Hostil-ities in Viet-Nam, "pending the general elections which will bring about the unification of Viet-Nam, the conduct of civil administration in each regrouping zone shall be in the hands of the party whose forces are to be regrouped there in virtue of the present Agreement". Accordingly, the civil administration in North Viet-Nam was, pending the general elections, to be with the Democratic Republic of Viet-Nam and in South Viet-Nam with the French Union. Subsequently, however, the French Union transferred their sovereign authority in the southern zone to the State of Viet-Nam. The representative authorities of the two zones between whom consultations are to be held are, therefore, the Democratic Repub-lic of Viet-Nam which is responsibile for civil administration in North Viet-Nam and, in virtue of Article 27, the State of Viet-Nam which has taken over the civil administration in South Viet-Nam from the French authorities.

4. The date on which these consultations are to commence (20th July, 1955) is not far off, and if paragraph 7 of the Final Declaration of the Geneva Powers is to be implemented, expeditious steps have to be taken to ensure that such consultations do take place on and from the appointed date. The implementation of paragraph 7 of the Declaration must be a matter of vital interest to those who subscribed to the Final Declaration at Geneva. It is also of interest to Canada, Poland and India who as supervisory countries on the International Commission are associated with the implemention of the Geneva Agreement, particularly as non-implementation of paragraph 7 of the Geneva Declaration involves the risk of reversion to a state of war between the parties through breakdown of the main structure of the Geneva settlement.

5. Having regard to the relations between the parties and the circumstances prevailing in Viet-Nam, it appears to the Government of India that consultations may not take place without some initiative being taken by the two Co-Chairmen. The Government of India, therefore, feel that the Co-Chairmen should request the authorities in charge of the Democratic Republic of Viet-Nam and the State of Viet-Nam to start consultations. To facilitate such consultations they may further offer the parties the services of the three Delegates on the International Supervisory Commission in Viet-Nam. The Delegates will act not as members of the Commission but as individuals representing their respective Governments and their task will be to assist the parties:

(i) to convene a conference of competent representative authorities of the two sides for inter-zonal consultations and to assist in the preparation and approval of the agenda; and

(ii) to elect a Chairman either from among themselves or from outside to preside over the deliberations of the consultative conference.

The Delegates from the Supervisory Commission will withdraw from the conference after the agenda has been settled and a Chairman has been chosen to preside over the deliberations.

6. The Chairman agreed upon by the parties will act both as conciliator and as technical expert on the essentials of a free general election by secret ballot and will assist the parties to come to agreed conclusions as regards the principles and procedure which would ensure free and fair general elections by secret ballot. The agreed modalities of the elections can thereafter be worked out and adopted by the authorities in each of the two zones as the law in force for the time being to regulate the elections. Thereafter, the Electoral Commission, envisaged in paragraph 7 of the Geneva Declaration, will be set up to supervise the elections in accordance with the agreed principles and procedure.

7. The Government of India would request the two Co-Chairmen to address the authorities in charge of the Democratic Republic of Viet-Nam and the State of Viet-Nam on the lines indicated in paragraphs 5 and 6 above. They are informing the Governments of Canada and Poland that they are making this request with an expression of their hope that the Governments of Canada and Poland would agree with the procedure outlined herein.

(408) NEWS CONFERENCE STATEMENT BY DULLES, June 28, 1955

Source: Department of State *Bulletin*, July 11, 1955, 1955, p. 50.

The only public statement by Dulles on elections prior to the July 20 date for the beginning of consultations was consistent with the position outlined in April and May in agreeing in principle to elections, provided there were sufficient safeguards. But it did not specifically address the question of beginning the consultations, suggesting that the U.S. was already aware of Diem's refusal to go ahead with them and was positioning itself to support that policy later.

At his news conference on June 28, Secretary Dulles was asked the position of the United States with respect to elections in Viet-Nam. The Secretary replied:

Neither the United States Government nor the Government of Viet-Nam is, of course a party to the Geneva armistice agreements. We did not sign them, and the Government of Viet-Nam did not sign them and, indeed, protested against them. On the other hand, the United States believes, broadly speaking, in the unification of countries which have a historic unity, where the people are akin. We also believe that, if there are conditions of really free elections, there is no serious risk that the Communists would win.

The Communists have never yet won any free election. I don't think they ever will. Therefore, we are not afraid at all of elections, provided they are held under conditions of genuine freedom which the Geneva armistice agreement calls for. If those conditions can be provided we would be in favor of elections, because we believe that they would bring about the unificiation of the country under free government auspices.

(409) JOINT COMMUNIQUE ISSUED BY THE GOVERNMENTS OF THE PEOPLE'S REPUBLIC OF CHINA AND THE DEMOCRATIC REPUBLIC OF VIET-NAM, PEKING, July 7, 1955 (Extract)

Source: *People's China, No. 15 (August 1, 1955), Supplement,* pp. 2-4.

The first foreign diplomatic trip by Ho Chi Minh as President of the D.R.V. took him first to China, where he conferred from June 27 to July 7 with Chairman Mao-Tse-tung, and other officials. The Joint Communique contained a strong attack on U.S. policy for the establishment of SEATO, and obstructing the consultations on general elections, and equipping and training the South Vietnamese troops. It also called obliquely on France to guarantee the implementation of the political provisions of the settlement.

During the visit to China of the Delegation of the Government of the Democratic Republic of Viet-Nam headed by President Ho Chi Minh, talks were held in Peking from June 27 to July 7 between a delegation of the Government of the People's Republic of China and the Delegation of the Government of the Democratic Republic of Viet-Nam on the basis of principles laid down in the course of consultation by Chairman Mao Tse-tung of the People's Republic of China and President Ho Chi Minh of the Democratic Republic of Viet-Nam.

[Two paragraphs listing the members of the delegations are omitted. The Chinese delegation was headed by Chou En-lai and included Vice Premiers Chen Yun and Teng Hsiao-ping. The DRV delegation included Truong Chinh, Le Van Hien, Phan Anh, Nguyen Van Huyen, Nghiem Xuan Yem, Ung Van Khiem, Nguyen Duy Trinh, Pham Ngoc Thach, and Hoang Van Hoan.]

In the course of the talks, the two parties discussed matters of common interest to the People's Republic of China and the Democratic Republic of Viet-Nam and questions of major significance in the present international situation.

The two parties note with satisfaction that the regrouping and transfer of military forces as provided for in the Geneva agreements have been completed, and that the International Commissions for supervision and control in the three Indo-China states, composed of representatives of India, Poland and Canada and with the Indian representatives as chairmen, have made important contributions in supervising and controlling the implementation of the Geneva agreement. The two parties express the hope that the International Commissions for supervision and control will continue to play an active role in ensuring the thorough implementation of the Geneva agreements.

However, the two parties are aware that the implementation of the Geneva agreements has been obstructed and sabotaged and is threatened with new sabotage. Shortly after the Geneva Conference, the United States Government violated the Geneva agreements by including South Viet-Nam, Cambodia and Laos in the so-called designated area "protected" by the Manila Treaty and by stepping up the equipping and training of troops in South Viet-Nam in order to convert the southern part of Viet-Nam into a colony and war base of the United States. At present, the United States is actively obstructing the holding of consultations for the general elections in Viet-Nam in an attempt to sabotage the cause of consolidating the peace and achieving the unification of Viet-Nam. The United States, again in violation of the Geneva agreements, signed a Military Assistance Agreement with Cambodia and is further attempting to conclude a similar agreement with Laos so as to destroy the neutrality of Cambodia and Laos and jeopardize peace in Indo-China. The two parties to the talks are in agreement that these and similar violations of the Geneva Agreement must be stopped and that the Geneva agreements must be carried through.

In accordance with the agreement reached in Geneva on the peaceful unification of Viet-Nam through general elections, consultations shall be held on the subject of general elections between the competent authorities of the two zones in Viet-Nam from July 20, 1955 so that free general elections may be held in July 1956 under the supervision of the International Commission composed of the representatives of India, Poland and Canada to bring about the unification of Viet-Nam. The Government of the Democratic Republic of Viet-Nam is determined to continue to carry out the Geneva agreements faithfully and has already declared it readiness to hold consultations with the competent authorities of South Viet-Nam on matters concerning the general elections. The two parties to the talks are of the common opinion that the countries which participated in the Geneva Conference have the responsibility for guaranteeing the implementation of the Geneva agreements. The two parties fully endorse the appeal and exhortation made by the Chairman of the Council of Ministers of the Soviet Union and the Prime Minister of India in their Joint Declaration on June 22, 1955, namely, that all governments concerned with the carrying out of the Geneva agreements should do their utmost to discharge their obligations so that the purposes of the agreements may be completely achieved; and that where elections are to be held as a preliminary to a political settlements, the efforts of the governments. The two parties are deeply convinced that the efforts of the Vietnamese people to achieve the unification of their country through consultations between the northern and the southern zones and through free general elections will certainly enjoy the full support of all countries and peoples who love peace and uphold the Geneva agreements.

(410) BROADCAST DECLARATION BY PRESIDENT DIEM ON THE GENEVA AGREEMENT AND FREE ELECTIONS, July 16, 1955

Source: *The Problem of Reunification of Viet-Nam*, pp. 30-31.

In his only declaration on the subject of the consultations on elections which were to have begun on July 20, 1955, Diem made it clear that he rejected any talks on the subject. He demanded as an apparent condition for any talks that the D.R.V. put the "interests of the national community above those of communism," a phrase which could be interpreted as a demand that the D.R.V. give up its form of government and economic system entirely.

Countrymen,

The National Government, time and again has emphasized the price it has paid for the defence of the unity of the country, and of true democracy.

We are not bound in any way be these agreements, signed against the will of the Vietnamese people.

Our policy is a policy for peace. But nothing will lead us astray of our goal, the unity of our country, a unity in freedom and not in slavery. Serving the cause of our nation, more than ever we will struggle for the reunification of our homeland.

We do not reject the principle of free elections as peaceful and democratic means to achieve the unity. However, if elections constitute one of the bases of true democracy, they will be meaningful only at the condition that they are absolutely free.

Now, faced with a regime of oppression as practiced by the Vietminh, we remain skeptical concerning the possibility of fulfilling the conditions of free elections in the North.

We shall not miss any opportunity which would permit the unification of our homeland in freedom, but it is out of the question for us to consider any proposal from the Vietminh, if proof is not given us that they put the superior interests of the national community above those of communism; if they do not give up terrorism and totalitarian methods; if they do not cease violating their obligations, as they have done by preventing our countrymen of the North from going South, by attacking recently still another, together with the communist Pathet Lao, the friendly State of Laos.

The mission falls to us nationalists, to accomplish the reunification of our country, in conditions that are most democratic and most effective, to guarantee our independence.

The Free World is with us, of this we are certain.

I am confident that I am a faithful interpreter of our state of mind, then I affirm solemnly our will to resist communism.

To those who live above the 17th parallel, I ask to have confidence. With the agreement and the backing of the Free World, the National Government will bring you Independence in freedom.

(411) JOINT COMMUNIQUE ISSUED BY THE GOVERNMENTS OF THE SOVIET UNION AND THE D.R.V., MOSCOW, July 18, 1955

Source: *Moscow, Soviet Home Service*, July 18, 1955. Translated by the Foreign Broadcast Information Service, July 19, 1955, pp. CC1-CC4.

After talks with Soviet Premier Nikita Khrushchev and other Soviet leaders, Ho obtained Soviet agreement on the necessity for "signatories" to the agreement to "take necessary measures to realize them." But there was no accusation against the U.S. for obstructing the consultations on elections, as there had been in the Chinese-Vietnamese communique. And the criticism of SEATO was both milder in wording and further down in the communique than in its Chinese-Vietnamese counterpart - these were indications that the Soviets were refusing to take as strong a position on the issue as the Vietnamese desired.

The USSR and the DRV Governments unanimously confirmed their readiness to seek unswervingly a strict implementation of the Geneva Agreements on Indochina. Both Governments attach special importance to the fulfillment of the conditions of the Geneva Agreements regarding Vietnam, proceeding from the precept that peace in Indochina can be consolidated only after the unification of Vietnam on the basis of the respect for its sovereignty, independence, unity, and territorial integrity - as laid down in the Geneva Agreements.

Both Governments noted with satsifaction stated the successful completion of the regrouping of troops envisaged by the Geneva Agreements, and the realization of other military conditions of the Geneva Agreements regarding Vietnam, which have been achieved as a result of the joint effort of the states in question.

They recognized that the success in fulfilling the Geneva Agreements is a considerable contribution to the cause of consolidation of peace and security in Indochina and the whole world.

They noted the fruitful work of the International Supervision and Control Committees for Vietnam, Laos, and Cambodia consisting of representatives of India, Poland, and Canada and headed by a representative of India. They expressed the hope that these committees will successfully complete their mission in the work of achieving a political settlement according to the Geneva Agreements.

Both Governments unanimously emphasized the importance of conducting consultations, within the time limit provided for in the Geneva Agreements between competent representatives of the Democratic Republic of Vietnam and South Vietnam on questions connected with the preparations for the general elections in July 1956 for the purpose of uniting Vietnam.

The Governments of the Soviet Union and the Democratic Republic of Vietnam think that the states signatories of the Geneva Agreements as well as all states which have a place in the carrying out of the Geneva Agreements should take the necessary measures to realize them. Both Governments have noted with satisfaction the great and positive significance of the Afro-Asian Conference at Bandung, where an especially fruitful role was played by the Chinese People's Republic and the Republic of India. This conference was a graphic example of successful cooperation in the interests of peace between countries with different political, social, and economic systems.

In the course of the negotiations it was stated that in their relations both Governments followed the principles of mutual regard for sovereignty and territorial integrity, nonaggression and noninterference in internal affairs, equality and mutual benefit, and peaceful coexistence. It was also noted with satisfaction that the above principles were being more and more widely accepted and applied by various states as a basis of extensive and fruitful international collaboration. Both Governments believe that friendly relations between the DRV and other Asian countries based on these principles will contribute to the establishment and widening of the zone of peace in Southeast Asia, and thus to the cause of consolidating peace throughout the world.

The Governments of the USSR and the DRV are determined in their condemnation of attempts to include South Vietnam, Laos, and Cambodia in the sphere of operations of the aggressive military bloc in Southeast Asia - SEATO - which is contrary to the Geneva Agreements. They also draw attention to the incompatibility with the Geneva Agreement of these attempts on the part of some foreign powers to interfere in internal affairs of South Vietnam, Cambodia, and Laos, and of attempts to enforce on these countries agreements of a military nature. Both governments believe that the settlement of international political problems is at present entirely dependent on the readiness of interested states to achieve agreement among them on the basis of regard for the just interests of either side.

The Governments of the Soviet Union and the DRV noted with satisfaction the growing activity of peoples aimed at the safeguarding of peace which has already led to certain relaxation of tension in international relations. This has found expression specifically in the fact of the convocation of the conference of the heads of the Government of the Four Powers.

Both Governments expressed the hope that the great powers will continue their efforts for the regulation of controversial questions by means of negotiations, which undoubtedly will foster the establishment of an atmosphere of mutual trust and the strengthening of universal peace.

(412)   NIE 63-1-55, "PROBABLE DEVELOPEMENTS IN NORTH VIETNAM TO JULY 1956," July 19, 1955 (Extract)

Source: *U.S.-Vietnam Relations, Book 10*, pp. 994-996.

The intelligence community guessed that Vietnamese Communists would be willing to accept "neutral" supervision of all-Vietnamese elections, though not "complex and elaborate safeguards and guarantees," but did not rule out reactivation of guerrilla activities in the South should the Diem government refuse to agree on an election plan or consolidate its strength.

THE PROBLEM

To analyze the present strengths and weaknesses of North Vietnam and to estimate probable future developments and trends to July 1956.

CONCLUSIONS

1. The immediate concern of the "Democratic Republic of Vietnam" (DRV) is to consolidate its control in the area north of the 17th Parallel and to gain control of South Vietnam.   *(Para. 14)*

2. We believe that the DRV will experience no great difficulty in maintaining effective control of North Vietnam during the period of this estimate and will probably retain a considerable measure of prestige and general acceptance. However, passive resistance and discontent resulting from harsh control measures and poor economic conditions may increase toward the end of the period. If the situation in the South does not deteriorate, the nationalist appeal of Ho Chi Minh and the DRV will probably be reduced throughout Vietnam.   *(Para. 23)*

3. The DRV is confronted by serious economic problems of which the current rice shortage is the most critical.   Its present export potential falls far short of providing sufficient funds to pay for necessary imports.   However, the Sino-Soviet Bloc will almost certainly provide sufficient economic and technical assistance to meet minimum requirements for stability and control.   With such assistance the DRV will probably make gradual progress in gaining control of the economy and in rehabilitating transportation, irrigation, and industrial facilities.   *(Paras. 24-30)*

4. Since the Geneva Conference, the strength of the DRV regular army has been increased substantially by drawing on regional forces to form new units and by the receipt of new and heavier military equipment from Communist China.   DRV forces are capable of defeating all military forces, including the French, now located in South Vietnam, Laos, and Cambodia.   *(Paras. 31-35)*

5. The present DRV tactic with respect to South Vietnam is to pose as the champion of Vietnamese independence and unification, and as the defender of the provisions of the Geneva Agreement.[1]   The DRV probably still believes that it could emerge from free nationwide elections with control of all Vietnam.   It will attempt to appear reasonable in any negotiations concerning procedures for elections.   While the Communists almost certainly would not agree to complex and eleborate safeguards and guarantees, they probably would agree to some form of "neutral" (but not UN) supervision.   They would probably estimate that such election controls would work to their advantage in the South and, as manipulated, would not adversely affect their position in the North.   *(Paras. 44-45)*

6.   In the meantime, the DRV will continue its efforts, through subversion, intimidation, and propaganda, to weaken the Diem government, and to bring to power in the South men prepared to accept a coalition with the DRV.   (*Para. 46*)

7.   The Communists in their propaganda have revealed sensitivity to the implcation of the Manila Pact which incorporated Vietnam, Cambodia, and Laos in its area of protection.   We believe that concern for Western, and particularly US reactions, together with general considerations arising from over-all Bloc policy, will prevent the DRV from openly invading the South during the period of this estimate.   Similarly, the resumption of widespread guerrilla activities appears unlikely prior to the election deadline, unless the DRV should come to the conclusion that South Vietnam can be won only by force.   Such a conclusion would become more likely should the Diem government persist in refusing to enter the election discussions, should election discussions not proceed favorably for the DRV, or should the Diem government succeed, with US assistance, in consolidating its strength to the point of becoming a nationalist alternative to the Ho regime.   Moreover, if during the period of this estimate little progress is made towards relaxing tension, Peiping and Moscow might permit the DRV greater freedom of action.   Should the DRV decide to use force short of open invasion, it would probably attempt to undermine the Saigon government by initiating a campaign of sabotage and terror, seeking to formation of a new government more amenable to demands for a national coalition.   These tactics are likely to include the activation of DRV guerrilla units now in South Vietnam and their reinforcement by the infiltration in small units of regulars from the North.   (*Para. 47*)

8.   The DRV will probably refrain from launching an attack with its own forces to seize Laos during the period of this estimate.[2]   It will probably continue efforts to convince the Royal Laotian government of the propriety of the DRV attitude toward Laos, while covertly strengthening the rebel Pathet Lao movement.   The DRV would probably infiltrate armed units into Laos to assist the Pathet Lao if Royal government military action should seriously threaten the Pathet Lao position in the northern provinces.   (*Paras. 48-49*)

9.   The Communists now have few assets in Cambodia and will probably be unable to develop a significant internal threat in that country until their position is greatly strengthened in Laos or South Vietnam.   In the meantime, the DRV will probably continue its efforts to promote friendly relations and to secure Cambodian neutrality.   (*Para. 50*)

10. We believe the DRV will be willing to continue political and economic contact with the French.   However, it most certainly will be unwilling to make an agreement which in fact would permit the French to retain an economic and cultural position in North Vietnam.   (*Paras. 51-56*)

[1]For an estimate of probable developments in South Vietnam, see NIE 63.1-3-55, "Probable Developments in South Vietnam Through July 1956," to be published in August 1955.

[2]For an estimate of probable developments in Laos, see NIE 63.3-55, "Probable Developments in Laos Through July 1956," to be published in July 1955.

(413) MESSAGE FROM THE PRESIDENT AND PRIME MINISTER OF THE DEMOCRATIC REPUBLIC OF VIET-NAM TO THE CHIEF OF STATE AND PRIME MINISTER OF THE STATE OF VIET-NAM, July 19, 1955

Source: *Documents Related to the Implementation of the Geneva Agreement,* pp. 41-44.

One day before the date for the beginning of consultations on elections under the Geneva Agreement, the D.R.V., in a letter signed by Deputy Premier Pham Van Dong, proposed that the South Vietnamese government nominate its representative for those consultations. But the deadline passed without any response from Saigon.

Messieurs,

After so many years of war, the Geneva Agreements have brought back peace to the Indochinese countries, on the basis of respect for the independence, sovereignty, unity and territorial integrity of the three countries: Viet-nam, Cambodia and Laos.

As far as Viet-nam is concerned, the Geneva Agreements have provided for the cessation of hostilities, the political settlement, the consolidation of peace, the achievement of the unity of Viet-nam by means of free general elections.

Paragraph 7 of the Final Declaration of the Geneva Conference very clearly stipulates that:

> *"General elections shall be held in July 1956, under the supervision of an international commission composed of the representatives of the Member States of the International Supervisory Commission referred to in the Agreement on the cessation of hostilities. Consultations will be held on this subject between the competent representative authorities of the two zones for 20 July 1955 onwards".*

Article 14 (a) of the Agreement on the cessation of hostilities in Viet-nam also stipulates that: *"Pending the general elections which will bring about the reunification of Viet-nam, the conduct of civil administration in each regrouping zone shall be in the hands of the party whose forces are to be regrouped there in virtue of the present Agreement."*

Thus the Agreement on the cessation of hostilities in Viet-nam and the Final Declaration of the Geneva Conference have clearly defined the principle of achieving the reunification of Viet-nam by means of free general elections, fixed the date for the holding of the consultative conference and the date of the general elections, and laid down in a concrete manner the responsibility of each party in this matter.

Up to now, in the cease-fire, the withdrawals and transfers of the military forces, as well as in other questions, the Government of the Democratic Republic of Viet-nam has loyally implemented the Geneva Agreements.

At present the military forces of the two parties have been regrouped in the two zones North and South, thus creating *"the necessary basis for the achievement in the near future of a political settlement in Viet-nam."*

The Government of the Democratic Republic of Viet-nam will continue to fully implement the Geneva Agreements and is of the opinion that the Governments concerned must make efforts to ensure the respect of the Geneva Agreements, the achievement of the unity of Viet-nam, the consolidation of peace in Indo-China. That is why, on June 6, 19 55, the Government of the Democratic Republic of Viet-nam declared its readiness to hold the consultative conference with the competent representative authorities of the South for the preparation for general elections and achievement of the unity of our country. Following this, the Delegation of the Viet-nam People's Army to the Central Joint Commission has raised with the representatives of the French Union Forces the problem of preparing for the meeting of the competent representative authorities of the two zones.

The holding on schedule of the consultative conference by the competent authorities of the North and the South is of great importance, and has a bearing not only on the prospect of the unity of our country but also on the loyal implementation of the Geneva Agreements, and the consolidation of peace in Indo-China and in the world.

Following the June 6, 1955 declaration by the Government of the Democratic Republic of Viet-nam, Sai-gon Radio on July 16, 1955, made known the "position of the Government of the State of Viet-nam on the problem of general elections for the unification of the national territory". The statement mentioned general elections and reunification but did not touch upon a very important and most realistic issue, that of the meeting of the competent representative authorities of the two zones, of the holding of the consultative conference on the question of general elections and reunification, as provided for by the Geneva Agreements. Moreover there were in the statement things which are untrue and which would not help to create a favourable climate for the convening of the consultative conference.

Our compatriots from the South to the North, irrespective of classes, creeds and political affiliations have deeply at heart the reunification of the country, and are looking forward to the early convening of the consultative conference and to its good outcome. All the countries responsible for the guarantee of the implementation of the Geneva Agreements and in general all the peace-loving countries in the world are anxious to see that the consultative conference will be held and yield good results and that the reunification of our country will be achieved.

The Government of the Democratic Republic of Viet-nam proposes that you appoint your representatives and that they and ours hold the consultative conference from July 20, 1955 onwards, as provided for by the Geneva Agreements, at a place agreeable to both sides, on the Vietnamese territory, in order to discuss the problem of reunification of our country by means of free general elections all over Viet-nam.

Chou En-lai's speech at - 584
communique of - 599
decision on cessation of hostili-
ties in Vietnam - 642-52
Dong's speech at - 564
DRV's proposal at - 566
effect on Indochina of - 659
Laniel on - 495
military implications of U.S.
negotiations on Indochina
at - 502
Molotov's speech at - 562, 575
Sanikone's speech at - 563
Sary's speech at - 561
Smith's speech at - 563, 579, 609
state of Vietnamese proposal - 641
U.S. on Geneva accords and
proposed elections - 698
U.S. on peace settlement at - 501
U.S. position on - 509

Griffin Mission

report on economic assistance -
253
report on political and economic
significance of Indochina -
253-59

India

Aide-memoire to the Geneva
Conference from - 703

Indochina

abdication of Bao Dai - 62
characteristics of revolution
in - 8
CIA estimate of developments
in - 364-66, 397-400
communist aggression in - 409
communist implications in - 511
communism in - 249-53
discussion of U.S. military
interest in - 515-28
economic situation of - 52,68
economy of - 3
escalation of U.S. involvement
in - 448, 451
effect of Geneva Accords on -
659
Foreign Relations Committee
on - 265
French control of - 78-79
French policy on - 147-50, 151-155
French national assembly resolution on - 481

Geneva Agreement - 642-52
Geneva Conference on - 654
Giap on French intentions
in - 66-71
Giap's plea to allies on - 67-71
implications of loss to communists
of - 457
independence for - 25
instructions of Central Committee
of ICCP - 17
JCS on - 249-53, 305-7
National Liberation Revolution
in - 4,7
NIE-5-54 on post Geneva outlook
in - 657-62
political and economic problems
of - 254-59
problems of an armistice - 598
prospects for coalition government in - 498
prospects for loss of - 516
recognition of DRV, Laos, and
Cambodia - 228, 230
resistance effort of - 53-4
Rusk on need for U.S. success
in - 324-28
security against communism
of - 392-5
situation in - 3
special committee on - 501
trusteeship for - 11, 13, 26, 40
U.S. French supplemental aid
agreement for - 475
U.S. military aid for France
in - 225, 239-41
U.S. policy on - 23, 26, 40-41,
42-46, 178-81, 203, 207, 273-76,
283-4, 299-303, 349-50, 352-
357, 528-34, 552-6
U.S. affirmation of French
sovereignty over - 139

Indochinese Communist Party

foreign policy of - 59
Ho's offer to dissolve - 89
organization of - 8
policy of - 2, 58
proposal of - 7
resolution of 57-9

Japan

Ho on - 1, 3
ICCP on Japanese attack on
France - 17-22

PUBLIC FIGURE INDEX